THE OXFORD HANDBOOK OF

THE CANADIAN CONSTITUTION

THE OXFORD HANDBOOK OF

THE CANADIAN CONSTITUTION

Edited by

PETER OLIVER

PATRICK MACKLEM

and

NATHALIE DES ROSIERS

OXFORD

UNIVERSITY PRESS

OXFORD
UNIVERSITY PRESS

Oxford University Press is a department of the University of Oxford. It furthers the University's objective of excellence in research, scholarship, and education by publishing worldwide. Oxford is a registered trademark of Oxford University Press in the UK and certain other countries.

Published in the United States of America by Oxford University Press
198 Madison Avenue, New York, NY 10016, United States of America.

Library of Congress Cataloging-in-Publication Data
Names: Oliver, Peter C. (Peter Crawford), 1960- editor. | Macklem, Patrick, 1959- editor. |
    Des Rosiers, Nathalie, 1959- editor.
Title: The Oxford handbook of the Canadian Constitution / Edited by Peter Oliver, Patrick Macklem
    and Nathalie Des Rosiers.
Other titles: Handbook of the Canadian Constitution
Description: New York : Oxford University Press, 2017. | Includes bibliographical references and index.
Identifiers: LCCN 2017006320 | ISBN 9780190664817 ((hardback) : alk. paper)
Subjects: LCSH: Constitutional law—Canada. | Constitutional history—Canada.
Classification: LCC KE4219 .O94 2017 | DDC 342.71—dc23
LC record available at https://lccn.loc.gov/2017006320

1 3 5 7 9 8 6 4 2

Printed by Sheridan Books, Inc., United States of America

Note to Readers
This publication is designed to provide accurate and authoritative information in regard to the subject matter covered. It is based upon sources believed to be accurate and reliable and is intended to be current as of the time it was written. It is sold with the understanding that the publisher is not engaged in rendering legal, accounting, or other professional services. If legal advice or other expert assistance is required, the services of a competent professional person should be sought. Also, to confirm that the information has not been affected or changed by recent developments, traditional legal research techniques should be used, including checking primary sources where appropriate.

*(Based on the Declaration of Principles jointly adopted by a Committee of the
American Bar Association and a Committee of Publishers and Associations.)*

**You may order this or any other Oxford University Press publication
by visiting the Oxford University Press website at www.oup.com.**

CONTENTS

PART III   INDIGENOUS PEOPLES AND THE CANADIAN CONSTITUTION

PART IV FEDERALISM

A. Federalism in Canada

B. Federalism in Context

Contributors

Ravi Amarnath, Litigation Associate, Blake, Cassels & Graydon LLP

Anita Anand, J.R. Kimber Chair in Investor Protection and Corporate Governance, University of Toronto

Beverley Baines, Professor, Faculty of Law, Queen's University

Stéphane Beaulac, Full Professor, Faculty of Law, Université de Montréal, and Flaherty Visiting Professor, University College Cork (2016–17).

Benjamin L. Berger, Professor and Associate Dean (Students), Osgoode Hall Law School, York University

John Borrows, Canada Research Chair in Indigenous Law, University of Victoria Law School

Eugénie Brouillet, Dean and Full Professor, Faculty of Law, Université Laval

Jamie Cameron, Professor, Osgoode Hall Law School, York University

Linda Cardinal, Professor of Politics and Holder of the University of Ottawa Research Chair in Francophone Studies and Public Policy

Mark Carter, Professor, College of Law, University of Saskatchewan

Larry Chartrand, Full Professor, Faculty of Law, University of Ottawa

Sujit Choudhry, I. Michael Heyman Professor of Law, University of California, Berkeley

Hugo Cyr, Dean and Professor of Public Law and Legal Theory, Université du Québec à Montréal

Yasmin Dawood, Canada Research Chair in Democracy, Constitutionalism, and Electoral Law, and Associate Professor of Law and Political Science, University of Toronto

Nathalie Des Rosiers, Full Professor, Common Law Section, Faculty of Law, University of Ottawa

Adam Dodek, Full Professor, Faculty of Law, University of Ottawa

Timothy Endicott, Professor of Legal Philosophy, University of Oxford

Marcella Firmini, Assistant Professor, Department of Political Science, Dalhousie University

Colleen M. Flood, Inaugural Director of the University of Ottawa, Centre for Health Law, Policy and Ethics, Professor and University of Ottawa Research Chair in Health Law & Policy

Craig Forcese, Full Professor, Faculty of Law, University of Ottawa

Pierre Foucher, Professor of Law, University of Ottawa and Director of the Research Center on French-Canadian Civilization

Jean-François Gaudreault-DesBiens, Dean of Law and Canada Research Chair in North American and Comparative Juridical and Cultural Identities, Faculty of Law, Université de Montréal

Sébastien Grammond, Professor, Civil Law Section, University of Ottawa; Counsel, Dentons Canada LLP

Joanna Harrington, Professor of Law, Faculty of Law, University of Alberta

Janet L. Hiebert, Professor, Department of Political Studies, Queen's University

Peter W. Hogg, Professor Emeritus, Osgoode Hall Law School, York University; Scholar in Residence, Blake, Cassels & Graydon LLP

Allan Hutchinson, Distinguished Research Professor, Osgoode Hall Law School, York University

Martha Jackman, Full Professor, Faculty of Law, University of Ottawa

Hoi L. Kong, Associate Professor, Faculty of Law, McGill University

William Lahey, Professor, Schulich School of Law, Dalhousie University; President, University of King's College

Sonia Lawrence, Associate Professor, Osgoode Hall Law School, York University

Robert Leckey, Dean and Samuel Gale Professor, Faculty of Law, McGill University

Jean Leclair, Professor, Faculty of Law, Université de Montréal

John Lovell, Constitutional Solicitor, Ministry of Justice, Victoria, British Columbia

Patrick Macklem, William C. Graham Professor of Law, University of Toronto

Carissima Mathen, Associate Professor, Faculty of Law, University of Ottawa

Armand de Mestral, Emeritus Professor, Jean Monnet Professor of Law, McGill University

Michel Morin, Full Professor, Faculty of Law, Université de Montréal

Dwight Newman, Professor and Canada Research Chair in Indigenous Rights in Constitutional and International Law, College of Law, University of Saskatchewan

Warren J. Newman, Senior General Counsel, Constitutional, Administrative and International Law Section, Department of Justice of Canada

Peter Oliver, Full Professor and Vice Dean Research, Faculty of Law, University of Ottawa

Charles-Maxime Panaccio, Associate Professor, Civil Law Section, Faculty of Law, University of Ottawa

Benoît Pelletier, Full Professor, Faculty of Law, University of Ottawa

Johanne Poirier, Professor and Holder of the Peter MacKell Chair in Federalism, Faculty of Law, McGill University

Bruce Porter, Director, Social Rights Advocacy Centre

Kent Roach, Professor & Prichard Wilson Chair in Law and Public Policy, Faculty of Law, University of Toronto

Carol Rogerson, Professor of Law, Faculty of Law, University of Toronto

Ruth Rubio-Marin, Professor of Constitutional Law, University of Seville

Bruce Ryder, Associate Professor, Osgoode Hall Law School, York University

David Schneiderman, Professor, Faculty of Law, University of Toronto

Dayna Nadine Scott, Associate Professor, Osgoode Hall Law School and the Faculty of Environmental Studies, York University

Jennifer Smith, Professor Emeritus, Dalhousie University

Lorne Sossin, Dean and Professor, Osgoode Hall Law School, York University

Don Stuart, Professor, Faculty of Law, Queen's University

Bryan Thomas, Adjunct Professor and Senior Research Associate, University of Ottawa Centre for Health Law, Policy and Ethics

Lori Turnbull, Associate Professor, Department of Political Science, Dalhousie University

Robert Vipond, Professor, Department of Political Science, University of Toronto

Mark D. Walters, F.R. Scott Chair in Public and Constitutional Law, Faculty of Law, McGill University

Luanne A. Walton, General Counsel, Constitutional, Administrative and International Law Section, Justice Canada

W. J. Waluchow, Professor and Senator William McMaster Chair in Constitutional Studies, McMaster University

Rosemary Cairns Way, Full Professor, Faculty of Law, University of Ottawa

Jeremy Webber, Dean and Professor of Law, University of Victoria

Margot Young, Professor, Allard School of Law, University of British Columbia

CHAPTER 1

....

INTRODUCTION

....

PETER OLIVER, PATRICK MACKLEM & NATHALIE DES ROSIERS

We are delighted to publish the *Oxford Handbook of the Canadian Constitution* as part of the successful Oxford Handbook series. The Handbooks on national constitutions span each country's history, law, and politics. They gather together leading constitutional scholars to give overviews of the core debates and critical literature on major topics in constitutionalism. Accordingly, the Handbooks are valuable reference works in the area of comparative constitutional law; they are also a first-class resource for students of the constitution in the country under study. Oxford University Press already has other Handbooks on constitutional law published or in development, including studies of the United States, Indian, South African, and Australian constitutions. Each of these countries has a rich constitutional history, case-law, and theoretical literature. We hope that readers will agree that the *Handbook of the Canadian Constitution* is an appropriate addition to this fine collection.

1. Distinctive Features of the Canadian Constitution

....

This *Handbook* is first and foremost an authoritative first stop for Canadians and non-Canadians seeking a clear, concise, and critical account of Canadian constitutional law. We will describe in the next section the considerable extent to which the Canadian Constitution has become a focus for comparative constitutional law. Here, we set out what makes the Canadian Constitution distinctive.

The Canadian Constitution is in important ways a constitution in the tradition of the British Commonwealth. The preamble of the *Constitution Act, 1867* sets this out in a phrase that has been cited by the Supreme Court of Canada on many occasions: 'a Constitution similar in Principle to that of the United Kingdom'. This phrase signalled that many of the most important features of the unwritten British Constitution would persist in the partly written, partly unwritten Canadian Constitution. Those features include the monarchical system as well as the many constitutional conventions which ensure that such a system conforms with contemporary democratic ideals.[1] They also include the rules regarding the internal workings of Parliament, which we refer to as parliamentary privilege.[2] In 1867, the preamble would have also communicated the sovereignty of legislative enactments, though more recently the Supreme Court of Canada has used that same preamble as a textual foothold for principles which both justify (e.g., democracy) and temper (e.g., the rule of law, the separation of powers, protection of minorities, judicial independence) that sovereignty.[3]

The British constitutional connection is undoubtedly important, and it provides many natural opportunities for comparison with other countries whose constitutions share (to varying degrees) this heritage: Australia, India, Ireland, New Zealand, South Africa, the United States, and many more. However, the British connection must not be over-emphasized, otherwise some of the most distinctive features of the Canadian Constitution will be over-looked: the importance of Indigenous legal systems, the long-standing presence of a French-speaking population and French civil law, the more recent phenomenon of multiculturalism, and the new features that appear in the *Constitution Act, 1982*, most notably the *Charter of Rights and Freedoms*, section 35 regarding Aboriginal and treaty rights, and Part V regarding the procedures for constitutional amendment.

The Canadian Constitution had its beginnings in a context already characterized by the widespread presence of Indigenous peoples and Indigenous law. The coexistence of Canadian and Indigenous law, and the extent to which the former recognizes and affirms the latter, are important topics discussed in this volume. Significantly, the Canadian Constitution explicitly recognizes and affirms Aboriginal and treaty rights, protecting Indigenous cultural and territorial interests in the form of constitutional rights, and enabling treaties to serve as constitutional instruments that mediate relationships between Indigenous peoples and the Canadian legal order.[4]

The first European settlement in what is now Canada occurred over 400 years ago. The French language and culture, including a civil law legal system, thereby became permanent features of the Canadian legal and constitutional landscape. At the end of the Seven Years War, with the Treaty of Paris of 1763, the area that is now embraced by the province of Quebec fell under British control, at least in so far as European nations were

---

[1] For example, the Executive is based in the Queen and Governor General according to the *Constitution Act, 1867* (see Part III). The Prime Minister is not mentioned (see, however, *Constitution Act, 1982*, ss 35.1 and 49).

[2] See *Constitution Act, 1867*, s. 18 regarding Parliament, and *New Brunswick Broadcasting* [1993] 1 SCR 319 regarding provincial legislatures.

[3] See, e.g., the *Secession Reference* [1998] 2 SCR 217, *Reference re Provincial Judges* [1997] 3 SCR 3, *British Columbia v Imperial Tobacco* [2005] 2 SCR 473.

[4] See s. 35(1) of the *Constitution Act, 1982*: 'The existing aboriginal and treaty rights of the aboriginal peoples of Canada are hereby recognized and affirmed'.

concerned. The Royal Proclamation of 1763 declared that British public and private law would govern this territory. However, just as Indigenous legal systems persisted with the arrival of the French (along with Indigenous territorial interests explicitly affirmed by the Royal Proclamation), so French legal practices continued even after the imposition of British law. And when the American colonies threatened to revolt, and the allegiance of French settlers needed to be secured, protection for the French settlers' (private) law and religion was granted in more formal constitutional terms.[5]

Canada's constitutional beginnings thus also involved a series of political compacts between two European cultures, one predominantly French-speaking, Catholic, and governed by civil law; the other English speaking, more heterogeneous in terms of religion, and governed by common law. The mutual accommodation of French-speaking and English-speaking Canadians, and the creation of a majority-French-speaking polity (Quebec) is an important part of the Canadian constitutional story.

It is important not to forget, however, that at certain points in Canadian history, governments were intent not on mutual accommodation but on assimilation. In terms of French-English relations, this occurred most notably at the time of the Acadian deportation in the eighteenth century and in the wake of the Durham Report of 1840. In terms of settler-Indigenous relations this occurred in the form of policies such as the Residential School Program designed to 'kill the Indian in the child'.[6]

The main way in which the mutual accommodation of French-speaking and English-speaking Canadians is manifested is in the choice of federalism for Canada's constitutional arrangements. It is a well-known fact that some of the strongest political voices in the years leading up to Confederation were in favour of a unitary form of government, in part in an attempt to avoid the divisions that were at that moment tearing the United States of America apart. However, some of the same pro-unitary voices took stock of political reality and realized that without federalism there would be no union. So the 1867 Constitution set out a federal division of powers and created one of the four founding provinces, Quebec, with for the first time a French-speaking majority and its own legislature. That legislature, like the federal Parliament, would have to abide by rules which required that English and French be the languages of debate and of government publications, but both levels of government had significant powers of self-government.

No two federal systems are alike, so it will be important to look closely at the initial unitary tilt in Canadian federal arrangements, as well as the pro-province tilt of much of the early interpretation of those arrangements. This story emerges in many of the chapters included in the Part on Federalism.

Canada is also a country of immigration. In the late nineteenth, twentieth, and early twenty-first centuries, many new Canadians joined the Indigenous peoples and the founding European communities. It is often said that Canada differs from the United

---

[5] *Quebec Act 1774* (Imp.).

[6] For an exhaustive examination of this program, see Truth and Reconciliation Commission, *Honouring the Truth, Reconciling for the Future: Summary of the Final Report of the Truth and Reconciliation Commission of Canada* (Truth and Reconciliation Commission of Canada, 2015).

States of America in creating a cultural mosaic rather than a melting pot. A country founded on the recognition of at least two cultures was already committed to maintaining difference. However, debates regarding the legal protection of difference can play out differently depending on whether the context in question is majority or minority, culturally secure or culturally threatened. Questions of multiculturalism (or interculturalism as they are often referred to in Quebec) and questions of the protection of minority rights therefore run alongside the legal treatment of Indigenous and founding peoples.

The first century of the Canadian Constitution was a period of discovering answers to some of the fundamental questions presented by the *Constitution Act, 1867*, notably the meaning of the various federal and provincial powers and the doctrines that would be used to resolve federalism disputes. It was often through the frame of federalism that questions regarding the rights and freedoms of Canadians were worked out during this period.

That first century was also a period of transition to full nationhood. In constitutional terms this prompts us to note the significance of, for example: the Statute of Westminster, 1931, specifying Canada's legislative independence; the end of appeals to the Privy Council in 1949; the expansion of Canada's role in international affairs; the search for a domestic amending formula; and the (sometimes implied, indirect, or failed) protection of rights and freedoms. Many of these elements allow us to chart the early Canadian variations on otherwise familiar constitutional themes.

We will see, however, that variations became sea-changes when the *Constitution Act, 1982* set out a new Canadian amending formula, a new *Charter of Rights and Freedoms* and constitutional protections for Aboriginal and treaty rights. Many of the most important Supreme Court of Canada cases of the past 35 or so years deal with those three important subject matters. Several chapters in this volume look closely at this case-law.

In commissioning the best commentators to write about the Canadian Constitution, we asked that each dwell briefly, if appropriate, on theoretical and methodological issues regarding their assigned subject matter. After all, how we (commentators, courts, critics) approach a given subject matter determines to a considerable degree where we come out. The final Part of this volume expands on this topic. Here we asked experts to identify and describe some of the most important currents in constitutional theory. Readers of the *Oxford Handbook of the Canadian Constitution* will thereby gain a basic understanding of both the fundamentals of Canadian constitutional law and some of the most important fault-lines of Canadian constitutional debate.

Canada has a relatively small population, when compared, for example, to India or the United States. And, in Northrup Frye's words, 'Canada has always been a cool climate for heroes'.[7] However, constitutional matters loom large in Canada, and we anticipate that there will be considerable local interest in what this *Handbook* has to say. The country's 150th anniversary strikes us as a particularly important opportunity to publish a comprehensive study. Furthermore, as the next section suggests, there is every reason

---

[7] Northrup Frye, *Divisions on a Ground: Essays on Canadian Culture* (Anansi Press, 1982), at 85.

to believe that a *Handbook* on the Canadian Constitution will attract interest from many readers outside Canada.

2. INTEREST IN THE CANADIAN CONSTITUTION

The Canadian Constitution is a long-standing subject of comparative law interest.[8] As one of the first and most elaborate constitutions of a colony of the former British Empire (later Commonwealth), the *Constitution Act, 1867* was a natural reference point for other countries. However, it was only with the patriation and fleshing out of the Canadian Constitution in 1982, most notably the adoption of the *Canadian Charter of Rights and Freedoms*, that the Canadian Constitution (including the *Constitution Act, 1867* and the *Constitution Act, 1982*) became a subject of notable comparative relevance and interest. Recent writing confirms the influence of the Canadian Constitution, both in terms of the number of countries affected and of its relative importance in comparison with the long-standing status of the U.S. Constitution as a global constitutional reference point.

First, in terms of countries which have looked to the Canadian Constitution for inspiration, frequently cited examples[9] include New Zealand,[10] South Africa,[11] Israel,[12] and Hong Kong.[13] In New Zealand, Canadian decisions have been cited more than those of any other country in rights litigation.[14] To this we should add the numerous members of

---

[8]   Thanks are due to Marie-France Chartier for research assistance in the prepartion of this section of the Introduction.

[9]   See S. Choudhry, 'Globalization in Search of Justification: Toward a Theory of Comparative Constitutional Interpretation' (1999) 74 Indiana LJ 819: 'One prominent model has been the American Constitution, in particular its Bill of Rights; however the *Canadian Charter of Rights and Freedoms* has, in recent years, become a leading alternative, and has influenced the drafting of the South African Bill of Rights, the Israeli Basic Law, the New Zealand Bill of Rights, and the Hong Kong Bill of Rights'.

[10]   James Allan et al. 'The Citation of Overseas Authority in Rights Litigation in New Zealand: How Much Bark? How Much Bite?' (2007) 11 Otago L Rev 433 at 437: 'Appendix D sets out the data . . . , and the results here come as no surprise. In terms of raw numbers, the decisions of Canadian courts are cited by New Zealand judges far more than those from any other jurisdiction.' See also Adam Liptak, 'U.S. Court Is Now Guiding Fewer Nations' (2008) *New York Times*, 18 September 2008: 'In New Zealand . . . Canadian decisions were cited far more often than those of any other nation from 1990 to 2006 in civil rights cases . . .'.

[11]   See A. Dodek, 'Canada as Constitutional Exporter: The Rise of the "Canadian Model" of Constitutionalism' (2007) 36 Sup Ct L Rev 309. See Choudhry, above (n 9).

[12]   See L. Weinrib, 'The Canadian Charter as a Model for Israel's Basic Laws' (1993) 4 Const Forum 85: 'Although there are vast contrasts in the constitutional arrangements, history, economic substructure, demographics, security and political cultures of Canada and Israel, these countries share a common approach to rights protection. Israel has continually looked to Canada's Charter experience to inform its own stance.' See also Choudhry, above (n 9).

[13]   See Choudhry, ibid.

[14]   Allan et al., above (n 10).

the Council of Europe: the *Canadian Charter of Rights and Freedoms* was modelled in part on the European Convention on Human Rights, and the influence has subsequently proved reciprocal, notably in the United Kingdom where the effect of the European Convention was structured by means of the *Human Rights Act 1998*, the latter having been clearly influenced by the Canadian *Charter*.[15] Together with the German Federal Constitutional Court and the European Court of Human Rights, the Supreme Court of Canada is one of the 'three most frequently cited courts in the world'.[16]

Second, the comparative law importance of the Canadian Constitution is often stated in relative terms. The U.S. Constitution has been the global point of comparison where constitutions are concerned, and this influence will no doubt continue; but commentators regularly note that the Canadian Constitution has recently stolen a march on its cross-border counterpart.[17] Numerous explanations have been proposed for this change in influence, including: 'the relative ages of the constitutions; the U.S. Supreme Court's recent conservatism; the Canadian Supreme Court's role in developing the doctrine of proportionality; the U.S. Supreme Court's interest in originalism; differing structures of constitutional review and judicial supremacy; ... the two courts relative openness to transnational influences';[18] 'the Canadian Charter ... both more expansive and absolute'[19] and 'in sync with global constitutionalism'[20]; 'the most powerful metaphorical counter to originalism: "the living tree" metaphor'[21]; and 'the simple fact that [it is] *not* American'.[22] What matters is not the relative status of the American and Canadian

---

[15] Constitution Unit, *The Impact of the Human Rights Act: Lessons from Canada and New Zealand* (Constitution Unit, 1999).

[16] Ran Hirschl, *Comparative Matters: The Renaissance of Comparative Constitutional Law* (Oxford University Press, 2014), at 27.

[17] See M. Tushnet, 'The Charter's Influence around the World' (2013) 50 Osgoode Hall LJ 527. Tushnet asserts that '[o]ver the past decades, the influence of the United States Constitution and Supreme Court around the world has waned while that of the Canadian Charter and Supreme Court has increased'. See also David S. Law & Mila Versteeg, 'The Declining Influence of the United States Constitution' (2012) 87 NYU L Rev 762 at 810, 820–821: 'The Canadian Constitution has often been described as more consistent with, and more influential upon, prevailing global standards and practices than the U.S. Constitution. . . . [T]he most plausible inference to be drawn from our empirical findings is that Canada is, at least to some degree, a constitutional trendsetter among common law countries'; see also 'We the People' Loses Appeal with People around the World' *New York Times*, 6 February 2012, quoting Aharon Barak, the former president of the Supreme Court of Israel: ' "Canadian law", he wrote, "serves as a source of inspiration for many countries around the world" '. [A] new study also suggests that the Canadian Charter of Rights and Freedoms, adopted in 1982, may now be more influential than its American counterpart.'; see also Liptak, above (n 10): 'Many legal scholars singled out the Canadian Supreme Court and the Constitutional Court of South Africa as increasingly influential.'

[18] See Tushnet, *ibid.*

[19] *New York Times*, above (n 17).

[20] Law & Versteeg, above (n 17): 'Initial analysis of data reveals that the Canadian Constitution, unlike the U.S. Constitution, is increasingly in sync with global constitutionalism'.

[21] Tushnet, above (n 17), 540.

[22] ' "In part, their influence [i.e. the Supreme Court of Canada and the Constitutional Court of South Africa] may spring from the simple fact that they are not American", Dean Slaughter wrote in a 2005 essay, "which renders their reasoning more politically palatable to domestic audiences in an era of

or other constitutions, but rather the clear evidence that the Canadian Constitution is highly relevant to contemporary constitutional debates around the globe.

Accordingly, we very much hope that the *Oxford Handbook of the Canadian Constitution* will attract considerable interest from constitutional lawyers, scholars, and students outside Canada. We also subscribe to Canadian law professor Adam Dodek's conclusion that 'Canadian constitutional influence is only likely to continue if Canadian jurists and scholars take a greater interest in constitutional developments abroad, particularly in those countries that have looked to the Canadian constitutional model for guidance'.[23] Accordingly, we hope that the publication of the *Oxford Handbook of the Canadian Constitution* will stir an interest in comparative constitutional law in Canadian jurists.

* * *

In closing this Introduction, we would like to record our profound regret that Roderick A. Macdonald, one of the most loved and admired Canadian constitutional lawyers of his generation, was not able to participate in this *Handbook*. Both he and we had hoped that he would be able to act as an Editor, and no doubt he would have contributed a new, original, and wonderful chapter. We all miss him greatly, even as we continue to admire and value his remarkable legacy.

In one of his later articles,[24] Rod Macdonald (and his co-author) referred to Canada's first and second National Policies (railways and immigration followed by health care and other social provision) and encouraged us to think about a third National Policy. The main point of this article was that we should work out what it is that we want to do collectively before obsessing about the constitutional machinery that needs to be in place.

The chapters of this Handbook do not identify a new National Policy. If they do nothing else, they reveal both the great challenge and the great potential in doing so. However, it is hoped that Canadian readers will find themselves better equipped, and that foreign readers will better understand the types of questions for which Canadians are seeking answers in 2017 and beyond. These include at the very least: decolonization and reconciliation with Indigenous peoples; maintaining a federation and a democracy that works for all its communities and inhabitants; and protecting rights and freedoms in the face of global security, environmental, and other threats.

It has been 150 years since Confederation, and Canadians enjoy advantages that are the envy of many. We are very pleased to see this *Handbook* come together as part of the celebration of Canada's first century and a half as a federation. We would like to thank the dedicated team at OUP and the wonderful contributors who make this

---

extraordinary U.S. military, political, economic and cultural power and accompanying resentments." '
Liptak, above (n 10).

[23] Dodek, above (n 11) 309.

[24] R. Macdonald & R. Wolfe, 'Canada's Third National Policy: The Epiphenomenal or the Real Constitution?' (2009) 49 UTLJ 469–523.

possible,[25] and we commend the *Oxford Handbook of the Canadian Constitution* to readers from across Canada and around the globe.

Ottawa and Toronto
17 January 2017

SELECT BIBLIOGRAPHY

Secondary Sources

Allan, J. *et al.* 'The Citation of Overseas Authority in Rights Litigation in New Zealand: How Much Bark? How Much Bite?' (2007) 11 Otago L Rev 433.

Choudhry, S. 'Globalization in Search of Justification: Toward a Theory of Comparative Constitutional Interpretation' (1999) 74 Indiana LJ 819.

Constitution Unit, *The Impact of the Human Rights Act: Lessons from Canada and New Zealand* (Constitution Unit, 1999).

Dodek, A. 'Canada as Constitutional Exporter: The Rise of the "Canadian Model" of Constitutionalism' (2007) 36 Sup Ct L Rev 309.

Frye, N. *Divisions on a Ground: Essays on Canadian Culture* (Anansi Press, 1982)

Hirschl, R. *Comparative Matters: The Renaissance of Comparative Constitutional Law* (Oxford University Press, 2014).

Macdonald R. & R. Wolfe, 'Canada's Third National Policy: The Epiphenomenal or the Real Constitution?' (2009) 49 UTLJ 469–523.

Truth and Reconciliation Commission, *Honouring the Truth, Reconciling for the Future: Summary of the Final Report of the Truth and Reconciliation Commission of Canada* (Truth and Reconciliation Commission of Canada, 2015).

Tushnet, M. 'The Charter's Influence around the World' (2013) 50 Osgoode Hall LJ 527.

Weinrib, L. 'The Canadian Charter as a Model for Israel's Basic Laws' (1993) 4 Const Forum 85.

Legislation

Canada Act 1982
Constitution Act, 1867
Constitution Act, 1982
Quebec Act 1774
Royal Proclamation of 1763
Statute of Westminster 1931

Case Law

British Columbia v Imperial Tobacco [2005] 2 SCR 473.
New Brunswick Broadcasting [1993] 1 SCR 319.
Reference re Provincial Judges [1997] 3 SCR 3.
Secession Reference [1998] 2 SCR 217.

---

[25] The Editors would also like to thank two University of Ottawa *Programme de droit canadien* students, Marie-France Chartier and Allison Lowenger, for their excellent work in the preparation of this *Handbook*. Marie-France Chartier provided research assistance in the early stages of this project, while Allison Lowenger prepared the Index and reviewed the Table of Cases.

PART I

CONSTITUTIONAL HISTORY

A. Indigenous Legal Systems and Governance

CHAPTER 2

....

INDIGENOUS
CONSTITUTIONALISM

Pre-existing Legal Genealogies in Canada

....

JOHN BORROWS*

1. INTRODUCTION

....

THE territory we now call Canada has a rich, varied, and ancient legal history.[1] Prior to European arrival Indigenous peoples regulated their affairs and addressed their disputes by reference to a vast array of laws, practices, customs, and traditions.[2] Although (like every human society) they did not always abide by their highest values they nevertheless had recognizable sources of authority which guided their governance and collective decision-making. Indigenous peoples "constituted" their societies in different ways—through, inter alia, Confederacies, House-structures, Leagues, Chieftainships, Tribes, Bands, and extended kin-based groupings. These structures facilitated world views which enhanced relationships of peace, friendship, and respect. At the same time, they were not always successful in cultivating goodwill. War, conflict, and social disorder were painful and periodic facts of life, as is the case with all peoples. Indigenous constitutional law prior to European arrival was complex. It produced tremendous innovations in human care and sustainable land use while struggling to deal with humanity's inevitable limitations.

Like all legal systems, Indigenous constitutional structures were entangled with their broader life ways.[3] Furthermore, these structures were fluid and changed through time.

---

* John Borrows, Canada Research Chair in Indigenous Law, University of Victoria Law School.
[1] Canada, Royal Commission on Aboriginal Peoples, *Partners in Confederation: Aboriginal Peoples, Self-Government and the Constitution* (Supply and Services, 1993).
[2] *R. v Van der Peet*, [1996] 2 SCR 507 [40], [44–47].
[3] Françoise Dussart and Sylvie Poirier (eds), *Entangled Territorialities: Negotiating Indigenous Lands in Australia and Canada* (University of Toronto Press, 2017) (forthcoming).

They shifted, transformed, or retrenched in accordance with the ebb and flow of political, economic, and social considerations at play across the continent. Long and complicated legal genealogies preceded European arrival in North America.[4] Indigenous constitutional arrangements continued to develop after Europeans contact too. In fact, Indigenous legal orders renew themselves even in the present day. All living traditions must adapt and change in order to stay relevant amidst changing circumstances. The presence of law is a necessary but not sufficient condition for securing any society's health, stability, and vitality. Law must always be seen in its broader light to understand it can never be an autonomous source of power.[5] This is as true in a historical context as it is in the present day. Law draws upon wider social networks even as it simultaneously constitutes those relationships.[6]

This chapter introduces the fact of historic Indigenous constitutionalism in the place we now call Canada.[7] Indigenous constitutionalism has provided the standards through which social change is managed or resisted within Indigenous societies. There are approximately as many Indigenous peoples in Canada today as there were when Jacques Cartier arrived on Indigenous shores in 1534.[8] They are comprised of over 11 different language families, which include 50 different languages. This linguistic diversity signals the wider legal, economic, social, political, and spiritual diversity among Indigenous Peoples of northern North America.[9] The variation in Indigenous constitutional traditions is what one would expect when societies distinctly develop in diverse ecological spaces over vast epochs of time.

For instance, the Inuit people of the Canadian arctic have very different constitutional traditions than the Nuu-chah-nulth people on the Pacific-ocean's coast. Likewise, the Mikmaq people of Atlantic Canada legally orient themselves in ways which are profoundly dissimilar from the Athapaskan-speaking peoples in the McKenzie delta. Furthermore, the Cree of the Hudson Bay lowlands, boreal forests, and Canadian prairies have diverse legal ideas within their linguistic family which are vastly different from

---

[4] This broader phenomenon was traced in a specific context in J. Borrows, "A Genealogy of Law: Inherent Sovereignty and First Nations Self-Government" (1992) 30 *Osgoode Hall Law Journal* 291.

[5] Roderick Macdonald, "Critical Legal Pluralism as a Construction of Normativity and the Emergence of Law" in Andrée Lajoie *et al.* (eds), *Théories et émergence du droit: pluralisme, surdétermination et effectivité* (Thémis, 1998) 9 ("Explicitly made legal rules . . . are not the only vehicles of normativity, but compete with a variety of indigenous and customary rules, practices and purely implicit interactional expectancies". Ibid., 15). See also R. Macdonald, *Lessons of Everyday Law* (McGill-Queen's University Press, 2002).

[6] This point is made more generally in Jeremy Webber, *The Constitution of Canada: A Contextual Analysis* (Hart Publishing, 2015).

[7] Earlier work of mine addressing this subject is found in John Borrows, *Canada's Indigenous Constitution* (University of Toronto Press, 2010). Some of the information in the following paragraphs is drawn from this work.

[8] Canada, *Report of the Royal Commission on Aboriginal Peoples: Looking Forward and Looking Back*, Vol. 1 (Supply and Services Canada, 1996) at 13.

[9] For more information about the diversity and history of Indigenous peoples in what is now Canada see Olive P. Dickason, *Canada's First Nations: A History of Founding Peoples from Earliest Times*

non-Cree groups. Their historic constitutional practices would have been inaccessible and generally meaningless to Gitksan, Tsilhqot'in, Haida, Salish, Tsimshian, Scwepmec, Kwakwakwa'ak, Ktunaxa, Tahltan, and other First Nations in the area now called British Columbia (in Canada's far west) in the time before Europeans arrived in northern North America. Moreover, all these traditions are also quite distinct when measured against European and colonially derived constitutional law.

Historic constitutionalism in what is now Canada should be judged in its own light and judged on its own terms.[10] The mere fact of Indigenous difference should not prevent us from recognizing and affirming our country's pre-European constitutional roots.[11]

Aboriginal peoples in section 35(2) of the *Constitution Act 1982* are described as the Inuit, Métis, and Indian Peoples of Canada.[12] A few historic examples of Indigenous constitutionalism will be this chapter's remaining focus in order to place Canadian constitutional law in a broader light. We will briefly consider constitutional traditions from varied perspectives including the Inuit, Métis, Mikmaq, Haudenosaunee, Anishinaabe, Cree, and BC First Nations generally, including the Secwepmec and Gitksan nations.

2. INUIT: ARCTIC LAW

The Inuit people of the circumpolar world have long occupied territories characterized by extreme cold and harsh climatic conditions. The arctic land and sea is covered by ice and snow for three-quarters of the year. Long dark winters where the sun barely shows itself are broken by summer seasons with 24 hours of daylight. The territory is largely treeless, and lakes, rivers, and streams are largely inaccessible when the land is snow-bound. In this environment Inuit constitutionalism rested on social and political forces which compelled the diffusion of legal order across wide spaces.[13] Animals, fish, and plant life were not easily detected and harvested. Thus extended families were obliged

---

(McClelland & Stewart, 1992); Arthur Ray, *I Have Lived Here since the World Began: An Illustrated History of Canada's Native Peoples* (Lester Publishing, 1996); J.R. Miller, *Skyscrapers Hide the Heavens: A History of Indian-White Relations in Canada* (University of Toronto Press, 2000).

[10] *Amodu Tijani v Secretary, Southern Nigeria*, [1921] 2 A.C. 399 at 402–404 (JCPC).

[11] Patrick Macklem, *Indigenous Difference and the Constitution of Canada* (University of Toronto Press, 2001).

[12] "Aboriginal" in Canadian law includes Indian, Inuit, and Métis people: see s. 35(2) of the *Constitution Act, 1982* (Canada), enacted as Schedule B to the *Canada Act, 1982* (U.K.) 1982, c. 11.

[13] Susan Inuaraq, "Traditional Justice among the Inuit", in Anne-Victoire Charrin, Jean-Michel Lacroix, and Michèle Therrien (eds), *Peoples des Grands Nords Traditions et Transitions* (Sorbonne Press, 1995) 255.

to spread out across the landscape to make a living.[14] The placement of constitutional regulation and decision-making in small kin-based harvesting groups was an identifiable feature of this system.[15]

Inuit constitutional law was based on concepts that gave primacy to the sacred nature of breath in a life-and-death environment. Sila (the world's breath) was regarded as a life-force which ordered and unified existence in the arctic and thus was constitutional in a broad legal sense.[16] It gave structure to governance, life-regulation, and decision-making. Agency could be exercised by both the broader environment and humans within these structures.[17] Attentiveness to non-human agency bestowed upon Inuit legal order a distinct set of societal rules and procedures.[18] This gave special place to forces such as the weather, the decisions of animals, or the role of incorporeal living in legal affairs.[19]

Much of historic Inuit constitutionalism chronicles the self-governing obligations humans have to one another and these forces at different seasons of the year.[20] Inuit laws would be recited at feasts or during "the prolonged period of enforced relative idleness during the dark period."[21] The failure to abide by these rules and precepts were not just private matters but affected entire communities.[22] In this sense they had a public law-like dimension (though the "public" of contemporary Canadian constitutional law must be distinguished from the "public" of Inuit society, which was dispersed across communities remote from one another and the broader world).[23] It was directed towards sustaining communities' broader social and political order through the prevention of starvation and the facilitation of social peace.[24] Inuit constitutionalism aimed at these purposes is still an important force in northern Canada today.[25]

---

[14] Mariano Aupilaarjuk, Marie Tulimaaq, Emile Imaruittuq, Lucassie Nutaraaluk, Akisu Joamie in Jarich Oosten, Frédéric Laugrand, and Wim Rasing (eds), *Interviewing Inuit Elders, Volume 2: Perspectives on Traditional Law* (Nunavut Arctic College, 1999) at 2.

[15] For a discussion of Inuit traditional law see, generally, Mariano Aupilaarjuk, Marie Tulimaaq, Emile Imaruittuq, Lucassie Nutaraaluk, and Akisu Joamie in Jarich Oosten, Frédéric Laugrand, and Wim Rasing (eds), *Interviewing Inuit Elders, Volume 2: Perspectives on Traditional Law*, (Nunavut Arctic College, 1999).

[16] Daniel Merkur, "Breath-Soul and Wind Owner: The Many and the One in Inuit Religion" (1983) 7 *American Indian Quarterly* 23.

[17] Thomas Stone, "Making Law for the Spirits: Angakkuit, Revelation and Rulemaking in the Canadian Arctic" (2010) 57 *Numen* 127 at 131.

[18] Ibid. at 130.

[19] Natalia Loukacheva, "Indigenous Inuit Law, 'Western' Law and Northern Issues" (2012) 3 *Arctic Review on Law and Politics* 200 at 203.

[20] David Damas, *Arctic Migrants/Arctic Villagers: The Transformation of Inuit Settlement in the Central Arctic* (McGill-Queens University Press, 2002) 7–17.

[21] Franz Boas [1888] *The Central Eskimo* (University of Nebraska Press, 1964).

[22] Stone, above (n 17) at 130.

[23] Ibid. at 148–150.

[24] E. Adamson, Hoebel, "Law-Ways of the Primitive Eskimos," (1940–1941) 31 *Journal of the American Institute of Criminal Law and Criminology* 663–883 at 669.

[25] For example *Inuit Qaujimajatuqangit* plays an important part in Nunavut's legislative principles. This concept advances the idea "as a living technology for rationalizing thought and action, organizing

3. MÉTIS LAW: THE RED RIVER EXAMPLE

Métis people also lived by constitutional forms in their societies.[26] Métis people are found in many places across Canada where distinct Indigenous societies developed prior to "the time when Europeans effectively established political and legal control in a particular area."[27] "Being Métis . . . can mean different things in different contexts: one context may speak to an individual's inner sense of personal identity; another may refer to membership in a particular Métis community; a third may signal entitlement to Métis rights as recognized by section 35 of the *Constitution Act, 1982*."[28]

The Métis of the Red River Valley at the south-eastern edge of Canada's prairies developed a distinctive constitutional order in the early 1800s. A unique language, culture, economy, and world-view was established which was separate from both First Nation and European people who were the Métis' ancestors. During the time of their Nation's growth agricultural activity was intensified in the Red River Valley, and a buffalo hunt developed which operated in accordance with Métis ideas and practices. "The buffalo hunt involved hundreds of men, women, and children, together with their Red River carts, horses and tools for processing and preserving the meat and hides."[29] Laws of the Buffalo Hunt were codified and included provisions such as:

A. No buffalo to be run on the Sabbath-Day.
B. No party to fork off, lag behind, or go before, without permission.
C. No person or party to run buffalo before the general order.
D. Every captain with his men, in turn, to patrol the camp, and keep guard.
E. For the first trespass against these laws, the offender to have his saddle and bridle cut up.
F. For the second offence, the coat to be taken off the offender's back, and be cut up.

---

tasks, resources, family and society into a coherent whole", Jaypetee Arnakak, "Commentary: What Is Inuit Qaujimajatuqangit?", *Nunatsiaq News*, 25 August 2000. In 2008, the Nunavut Legislative Assembly passed four Acts that develop Inuit law in a democratic setting, see: the *Midwifery Profession Act*, S.Nu 2008, c 18; the *Education Act*, S.Nu 2008, c 15; the *Official Languages Act*, S.Nu 2008, c 10; and the *Inuit Language Protection Act*, S.Nu 2008, c 17. Each of these four Acts expresses Inuit aspirations in a way that combines historic and contemporary legal perspectives. These Acts build upon innovative expressions of Inuit tradition in explicit ways.

[26] For a general discussion of Métis forms of legal organization see Kerry Sloan, *The Community Conundrum: Métis Critical Perspectives on the Application of R v Powley in British Columbia*, PhD dissertation, University of Victoria, Faculty of Law, 2016 [unpublished].

[27] The legal test describing effective European control on different parts of Canadian territory is found in *R. v Powley* [2003] 2 S.C.R. 207 [36–40].

[28] Canada, Royal Commission on Aboriginal Peoples, *Report of the Royal Commission on Aboriginal Peoples: Perspectives and Realities, Vol. 4* (Ministry of Supply and Services, 1996) ("Métis Perspectives") at 199.

[29] Borrows, above (n 7) at 87.

G. For the third offence, the offender to be flogged.

H. Any person convicted of theft, even to the value of a sinew, to be brought to the middle of the camp, and the crier to call out his or her name three times, adding the word "Thief", at each time.[30]

The Law of the Hunt was a constitutional expression of public principles which assisted Métis in governing their main socio-economic activity. By "1869, the Red River Settlement was a vibrant community, with a free enterprise system and established judicial and civic institutions, centred on the retail stores, hotels, trading undertakings and saloons of what is now downtown Winnipeg."[31] In fact, "[t]he Métis were the dominant demographic group in the Settlement, comprising around 85 percent of the population, and held leadership positions in business, church and government." When Canada intruded into this area to create its first province after Confederation, the Métis organized themselves into a Provisional Government. They at first strenuously resisted and later ushered the territory's entry into Confederation as Manitoba.[32]

As a result, Métis constitutionalism was an important factor in bringing Canada into existence in this area. The Supreme Court of Canada wrote in the case of *Daniels v Canada*: "The Métis Nation was . . . crucial in ushering western and northern Canada into Confederation and in increasing the wealth of the Canadian nation by opening up the prairies to agriculture and settlement. These developments could not have occurred without Métis intercession and legal presence."[33] As such Métis political and legal organization had a direct impact on the construction of wider constitutional law structures in an important formative moment in the country's history.

4. MIKMAQ CONSTITUTIONALISM

Mikmaq people live on Canada's east coast in what is now Newfoundland, Nova Scotia, New Brunswick, Prince Edward Island, and Quebec.[34] The Mikmaq were a maritime power on the north-eastern edge of the continent long before Canada was formed. They occupied broad stretches of territory in the area and welcomed or repelled fishermen

[30] Alexander Ross, *The Red River Settlement: Its Rise, Progress, and Present State* (Ross and Haines, 1957) at 249–250.
[31] *Manitoba Métis Federation Inc. v Canada (Attorney General)* [2013] 1 S.C.R. 623 [23].
[32] Ibid. [24–31].
[33] *Daniels v Canada (Indian Affairs and Northern Development)*, 2016 SCC 12 [25] citing Borrows, above (n 7) at 87–88.
[34] Charles A. Martijn, "Early Mikmaq Presence in Southern Newfoundland: An Ethnohistorical Perspective, c.1500–1763" (2003) 19, *The New Early Modern Newfoundland* at https://journals.lib.unb.ca/index.php/NFLDS/article/viewArticle/141/238; Trudy Sable and Bernie Francis, *The Language of This Land* (Cape Breton University Press, 2012) 17–25.

from Europe for perhaps a thousand years before the country came into existence. Mikmaq people generally regarded their constitutional order as springing from their relationship with the earth—which is a living being in their language.[35] The presence of a legal "langscape" drawn from the living earth helped to unify Mikmaq people across their territories. It encouraged an earth-centred constitutionalism. As Professor Sakej Henderson observed: "Out of the sounds of life forces in the ecology . . . [a] cognitive rec-ognition and acceptance of the interrelations of the shared space inform their languages, thus creating a shared worldview, a cognitive solidarity, and a tradition of responsible action."[36] The Mikmaq law of responsible action encouraged mutual regard and respect, making land and ecological language a bedrock of Mikmaq constitutional law.[37]

The word which described (and describes) Mikmaq laws for caring the earth is *netukulimk*.[38] *Netukulimk* are sets of customary legal practices focused on Mikmaq obligations related to land and resource use. Non-human forms participate in these con-stituting governance relationships. Detailed rules and processes guided their behavior and were aimed at fostering sustainability under this rubric. The performance of these duties was and is "interpreted as an expression of Mi'kmaq law ways" and provided a management structure for working with Mikmaq law across communities.[39]

Although Canadian courts have not accepted this view,[40] Mikmaq people believe they have long exercised this jurisdictional authority through a Grand Council structure or *Santé Mawíomi*.[41] The Mikmaq confederacy, or *Awitkatultik*, divided their territory across the Maritimes into seven districts, or *sakamowati*. Their names were: *Kespukwitk, Sipekne'katik, Eskikewa'kik, Unama'kik, Epekwitk Aqq Piktuk,*

[35] Sakej Henderson, "Ayukpachi: Empowering Aboriginal Thought", in Marie Batiste, *Reclaiming Indigenous Voice and Vision* (University of British Columbia Press, 2000) at 264.
[36] Sakej Henderson, "Mikmaw Tenure in Atlantic Canada" (1995) 18 *Dalhousie Law Journal* 196 at 220–221.
[37] Sakej Henderson, "First Nations' Legal Inheritances: The Mikmaq Model" (1995) 23 *Manitoba Law Journal* at 12.
[38] Kerry Prosper, Jane McMillan, Anthony Davis, and Morgan Moffitt, "Returning to Netukulimk: Mi'kmaq Cultural and Spiritual Connections with Resource Stewardship and Self-Governance" (2011) 2(4) *The International Indigenous Policy Journal* 1–17.
[39] Ibid.
[40] *R. v Marshall* (2001), 191 N.S.R. (2d) 323; [2001] 2 C.N.L.R. 256 [65]: "I was not persuaded by him that the Grand Council or the seven districts were ancient Mi'kmaq traditions. The written record proves otherwise."
[41] Ibid. For further discussion of the *Santé Mawíomi* see Canada, *Royal Commission on Aboriginal Peoples, Report of the Royal Commission on Aboriginal Peoples, Looking Forward, Looking Back, Vol. 1* (Supply and Services, 1996) at chapter 4:

The Mawíomi, which continues into the present time, recognizes one or more *kep'tinaq* (captains; singular: *kep'tin*) to show the people the good path, to help them with gifts of knowledge and goods, and to sit with the whole Mawíomi as the government of all the Mi'kmaq. From among themselves, the kep'tinaq recognize a *jisaqamow* (grand chief) and *jikeptin* (grand captain), both to guide them and one to speak for them. From others of good spirit they choose advisers and speakers, including the *putu's*, and the leader of the warriors, or *smaknis*.

Siknikt, and *Kespek*.[42] This council structure was a mechanism for encouraging delib-eration and building consensus in matters that affected the entire nation.[43] The Grand Council operated under the direction of the *Sakamaw* (Grand Chief) and *Kji-Keptin* (Grand Captain) and dealt with important issues throughout Mi'kma'ki. Earlier European observers who witnessed Mikmaq councils were not impressed with their non-hierarchical form. Indeed, they had difficulty attributing governmental powers to Mikmaq people. For example, Jesuit missionary Father Baird wrote:

> In these assemblies so general, they resolve upon peace, truce, war, or nothing at all, as often happens in the councils where there are several chiefs, without order and subordination, whence they frequently depart more confused and disunited than when they came. [Translation][44]

It was hard for some Europeans to believe Indigenous peoples exercised law and gov-ernance powers.[45] These Europeans were biased and partial in their descriptions.[46] Indigenous peoples were considered to be primitive.[47] As Indigenous governance struc-tures did not have kings, parliaments, or written laws they were not regarded as hav-ing anything like a constitution.[48] Of course British constitutionalism was unwritten.[49] Furthermore, European societies were in an almost constant of war despite hierarchi-cal structures.[50] But this did not lead church writers to conclude Western nations were

---

[42]   Daniel Paul, *We Were Not Savages, First Nations History* (Fernwood, 2006) at http://www.danielnpaul.com/Mi'kmaqCulture.html.

[43]   See Canada, Royal Commission on Aboriginal Peoples, above (n 41). At the annual meeting, the *kep'tinaq* and *Mawíomi* saw that each family had sufficient planting grounds for the summer, fishing stations for spring and autumn, and hunting range for winter. Once assigned and managed for seven generations, these properties were inviolable. If disputes arose, they were arbitrated by the *kep'tinaq* individually or in council.

[44]   *R. v Marshall* (2001), 191 N.S.R. (2d) 323; [2001] 2 C.N.L.R. 256 [45].

[45]   For the challenges Europeans encountered in recognizing Indigenous governance and law rights see, generally, R.A. Williams Jr., *The American Indian in Western Legal Thought: The Discourses of Conquest* (Oxford University Press, 1990); Robert J. Miller, Jacinta Ruru, Larissa Berendht, and Tracey Lindberg, *Discovering Indigenous Lands: The Doctrine of Discovery in the English Colonies* (Oxford University Press, 2010).

[46]   James Thomas Baker, *Religion in America Vol 1* (Thomson Wadsworth, 2005) at 19; James Ronda, "We Are Well as We Are": An Indian Critique of Seventeenth-Century Christian Missions (1977) 34 *William and Mary Quarterly* 66–82. For further information on the Jesuit Relations see Allen Greer, *The Jesuit Relations: Natives and Missionaries in Seventeenth-Century North America* (Bedford Books, 2000).

[47]   J.E. Cote, "The Reception of English Law" (1977) XV *Alberta Law Review* 29 at 38.

[48]   John Austin, *The Province of Jurisprudence Determined*, 2nd ed., Vol. I., W. Rumble (ed.), (Cambridge University Press, 1995) (first published 1832) at 176.

[49]   John H. Baker, *An Introduction to English Legal History*, 2nd ed. (Butterworths, 1979); Frederic W. Maitland & Francis C. Montague, *A Sketch of English Legal History* (G.P. Putnam and Sons, 1915) at 1–130.

[50]   For a discussion of law being present across nations despite European disorder at the time of contact with Indigenous peoples in North America see Laurie Benton and Richard Ross (eds), *Legal Pluralism and Empires, 1500–1850* (New York University Press, 2013); Laurie Benton, *A Search for*

without law, unlike their views of Indigenous peoples. For example, when describing Mikmaq councils Jesuit writers observed:

> There can be no more polity than there is commonwealth since polity is nothing more than the regulation of government of the Commonwealth. Now these savages not having a great commonwealth, either in number of people, since they are few, nor in wealth, since they are poor, only living from hand to mouth, nor ties or bonds of union, since they are scattered and wandering, cannot have great polity. Yet they cannot do without it since they are men and brethren. [Translation][51]

Although European writers acknowledged the council processes within Mikmaq territory in making these observations (stating "they cannot do without it"), their bias regarding the "low" state of Indigenous political organization must be revised.[52] Their views were ethnocentric. They certainly do not explain Mikmaq law from an Indigenous perspective at the time they were recorded.

In fact, the Mikmaq likewise regarded the French as having a lower level of social organization in this same period; they were likewise ethnocentric and biased in their views of Europeans. They regarded the French as living a lower form of life. This is evidenced in a leading Mikmaq Indian's observations of French life:

> Thou sayest of us also that we are the most miserable and most unhappy of all men, living without religion, without manners, without honour, without social order, and, in a word, without any rules, like the beasts in our woods and our forests, lacking bread, wine, and a thousand other comforts which thou hast in superfluity in Europe. Well, my brother, if thou dost not yet know the real feelings which our Indians have towards thy country and towards all thy nation, it is proper that I inform thee at once. I beg thee now to believe that, all miserable as we seem in thine eyes, we consider ourselves nevertheless much happier than thou in this, that we are very content with the little that we have; and believe also once for all, I pray, that thou deceivest thyself greatly if thou thinkest to persuade us that thy country is better than ours. For if France, as thou sayest, is a little terrestrial paradise, art thou sensible to leave it? . . . We believe, further, that you are also incomparably poorer than we, and that you are only simple journeymen, valets, servants, and slaves, all masters and grand captains though you may appear, seeing that you glory in our old rags and in our miserable suits of beaver which can no longer be of use to us, and that you find among us, in the fishery for cod which you make in these parts, the wherewithal to comfort your misery and the poverty which oppresses you.[53]

Sovereignty: Law and Geography in European Empires, 1400–1900 (Cambridge University Press, 2010); Laurie Benton, *Law and Colonial Cultures: Legal Regimes in World History, 1400–1900* (Cambridge University Press, 2002).

[51] *R. v Marshall* (2001), 191 N.S.R. (2d) 323; [2001] 2 C.N.L.R. 256 [46].

[52] *Amodu Tijani v Secretary, Southern Nigeria* [1921] 2 A.C. 399 at 402–404 (JCPC).

[53] William F. Ganong (trans. and ed.), *New Relation of Gaspesia, with the Customs and Religion of the Gaspesian Indians, by Chrestien LeClerq* (Champlain Society, 1910) at 103–106.

What is clear in these exchanges is that understanding pre-contact Indigenous constitutionalism from contemporaneous sources is exceedingly problematic. Both European and Indigenous views of one another's legal structures must be interrogated. Subsequent recollections and reconstructions must also be open to question.[54] Although written and oral traditions can give us insight they can also misrepresent the field in troubling ways.[55]

The implications of these observations for understanding pre-contact Indigenous constitutionalism prior to European arrival are significant. Calibrating constitutional law to align with questionable pre- and post-contact distinctions problematically freezes Canadian constitutionalism.[56] It synchronizes contemporary forms with historic colonial biases and replicates them in the present day.[57] Originalism in Canadian constitutional law—which pins rights to contact or Crown sovereign assertions—is deeply problematic.[58] Although the genealogy of law includes Indigenous and European-derived sources, when it comes to Indigenous issues Canada's constitution would be much stronger if it focused on contemporary expressions of Indigenous law bolstered by instruments such as the United Nations Declaration of Indigenous Peoples which characterizes Indigenous rights in contemporary terms.[59]

Although it is important to understand Indigenous constitutional roots, Indigenous "law" should not be equated with Indigenous "history" in understanding the country's constitution. Aside from the dangers of reproducing bias from colonial eras, treating Indigenous law as history obscures the fluidity, mobility, and contingencies of Indigenous peoples' past and present social organization. Law and history have different disciplinary criteria.[60] Historians search for evidence of past events relatively

---

[54] John Borrows, Challenging Historical Frameworks: Aboriginal Rights, The Trickster, and Originalism (2017) 98 *Canadian Historical Review* 114.

[55] John Borrows, "Listening for a Change: The Courts and Oral Tradition" (2001) 39 *Osgoode Hall Law Journal* 1.

[56] Bradford W. Morse, "Permafrost Rights: Aboriginal Self-Government and the Supreme Court in R. v. Pamajewon" (1997) 42 *McGill Law Journal*. 1011; John Borrows, "Frozen Rights in Canada: Constitutional Interpretation and the Trickster" (1997) 22 *American Indian Law Review* 37; Russell Barsh and Sakej Henderson, "The Supreme Court's Vanderpeet Trilogy: Native Imperialism and Ropes of Sand" (1997) 42 *McGill Law Journal* 993.

[57] Discussion of the replication of colonial ideas in present jurisprudence is found in John Borrows, "The Durability of Terra Nullius: Tsilhqot'in v. the Queen" (2015) 48 *University of British Columbia Law Review* 701; John Borrows, "Sovereignty's Alchemy: An Analysis of Delgamuukw v. British Columbia" (1999) 37 *Osgoode Hall Law Journal* 537.

[58] John Borrows, "(Ab)Originalism and Canada's Constitution" (2012) 58 *Supreme Court Law Review* 2nd ed. 351.

[59] The United Nations Declaration on the Rights of Indigenous Peoples was enacted by the United Nations in 2007, United Nations Declaration on the Rights of Indigenous Peoples, UNGA Res 61/295 (13 September 2007) [UNDRIP].

[60] However, it is important to note the challenge in creating too sharp a distinction between the disciplines of history and law, see Alan Carr, *What Is History?* (2nd ed.) (Penguin Books, 1987) at 30: History "is a continuous process of interaction between the historian and his facts, an unending dialogue between the past and the present."

uncontaminated by the interpretations which flow from the passage of time.[61] Lawyers seek to explicitly interpret the past in light of the present.[62] Although it is important to generally understand that Canada's constitution has strong Indigenous genealogies, the separation of history from law would also help us see Indigenous constitutionalism in a contemporary light.[63]

5. Haudenosaunee Constitutionalism

The northern and southern shores of what came to be called Lakes Ontario and Erie were occupied by Algonkian- and Iroquoian-speaking peoples prior to European contact. The Iroquoian-speaking people were organized into confederacies. The Wendat or Huron Confederacy lived north of Lake Ontario around Lake Simcoe and eastern Georgian Bay. Their confederacy was divided into four clans: Attignawantan, Arendarhonon, Attigneenongnahac, and Tahontaenrat.[64] In the early 1600s they lived in 18 to 25 villages and numbered some 18,000 to 40,000 inhabitants. Over two hundred miles of roads connected their villages, and they had sophisticated relationships of war and peace with their neighbours.[65] This is in the area which is now framed by the cities of Orillia, Barrie, and Collingwood. After a period of intense conflict, the Wendat were removed to various locations in Oklahoma, Quebec, and the Ohio River valley, as well as being taken into Anishinaabe and Haudenosaunee families by marriage, adoption, and other forms.[66]

---

[61] The challenge of understanding history without reference to a historian's own social positioning is discussed in Daniel Woolf, *The Social Circulation of the Past* (Oxford University Press, 2003).

[62] For further discussion, see Helen Irving, "Outsourcing the Law: History and the Disciplinary Limits of Constitutional Reasoning" (2015) 84 *Fordham Law Review* 957 at 958: "History and judging operate in different fields; they belong to different disciplines. Historians and judges are not just people with different titles; they are people with different jobs."

[63] *R. v Pamajewon* [1996] 2 S.C.R. 821; *Lax Kw'alaams Indian Band v Canada (Attorney General)*, 2011 SCC 56 [46]. The courts should not demand historic proof of Aboriginal governance and other practices prior to the arrival of Europeans to recognize and affirm their contemporary necessity.

[64] Bruce G. Trigger, *The Children of Aataentsic: A History of the Huron People to 1600* (McGill-Queen's Press, 1976) at 30.

[65] Wendat residency has been studied in the following sources: Conrad Heidenreich, "Mapping the Location of Native Groups, 1600–1760" (1981) *Journal of the Historical Atlas of Canada* 6–13; Conrad Heidenreich, "Maps Relating to the First Half of the 17th Century and Their Use in Determining the Location of Jesuit Missions in Huronia" (1966) 3 *The Cartographer* 103–126; Conrad Heidenreich, "Mapping the Great Lakes: The Period of Exploration, 1603–1700" (1980) 17 *Cartographica* 32–63; Conrad E. Heidenreich, "Mapping the Great Lakes: The Period of Imperial Rivalries" (1981) 18 *Cartographica* 74–108; G. Malcolm Lewis, "Changing National Perspectives and the Mapping of the Great Lakes Between 1755 and 1795" (1980) 17 *Cartographica* 1–31; Conrad Heidenreich, "An Analysis of the 17th Century Map 'Nouvelle France'" (1988) 25 *Cartographica* 67–111.

[66] For a description of Wendat history from a Wendat perspective see Georges Sioui, *Huron-Wendat. The Heritage of the Circle* (University of British Columbia Press, 1999).

The Haudenosaunee Confederacy of the lower Great Lakes were also an Iroquoian-speaking people. They also have a legal history which pre-dates Canada.[67] The Confederacy was initially composed of five nations: Mohawk, Oneida, Onondaga, Cayuga, and Seneca.[68] They were later joined by a sixth nation, the Tuscarora, after this nation was forced out of its more southerly homelands.[69] The Six Nations lived on the northern shores of Lakes Ontario and Erie and into the St. Lawrence Valley, and they had their largest settlements below Lake Ontario in what is now New York State.

The Confederacy's formation is contested by academics and the Keepers of the tradition,[70] with the Keepers saying it is at least a thousand years old and some scholars saying it has a post-contact genesis.[71] The Confederacy had at its heart the *Kaianerekowa* or Great Law of Peace.[72] Its focused on peace, power, and righteousness as central constitutional principles to advance collective and individual well-being.[73] The Great Law takes seven days to recite in its oral form, and this is done at least annually as has occurred for generations. The Great Law brought nations and clans together in council, with elaborate procedures for deliberating and deciding on contentious issues.[74] Unanimity in council decisions was (and is) a necessary part of this structure whereas each party to the deliberations retains its independence within the Great Law's centralized decision-making structure.[75] Gender also plays a significant role in the Great Law, as women have the power to select and remove chiefs in this largely matriarchal constitutional order.[76]

Furthermore, the Haudenosaunee had an elaborate diplomatic tradition within the constitutional spheres.[77] This brought them into treaty relationships with other Indigenous and non-Indigenous nations prior to Canada's formation.[78] Haudenosaunee constitutional forms and aspirations had a significant influence on the country's own

[67] A leading text of Haudenosaunee political order is William Fenton, *The Great Law and the Longhouse* (University of Oklahoma Press, 1998).

[68] Bruce Elliott Johansen and Barbara Alice Mann (eds), *Encyclopedia of the Haudenosaunee (Iroquois Confederacy)* (Greenwood Press, 2000) at 265.

[69] More information about the Tuscarora, including their migration from around what is now North Carolina, can be found in Anthony Wallace, *Tuscarora: A History* (State University of New York Press, 2012).

[70] Ibid.

[71] A critique of the time-depth of the Haudenosaunee Confederacy's historical origins is found in William Starna, "Retrospecting the Origins of the League of the Iroquois" (2008) 152 *Proceedings of the American Philosophical Society* 279.

[72] Francis Jennings, *The Ambiguous Iroquois Empire* (W.W. Norton and Company, 1990).

[73] Taiaiake Alfred, *Peace, Power, Righteousness: An Indigenous Manifesto* (Oxford University Press, 1999).

[74] John Hurley, *Children or Brethren: Aboriginal Rights in Colonial Iroquoia* (Native Law Centre, 1985) at 40.

[75] Henry Lewis Morgan, *League of the Ho-De-No-Sau-Nee or Iroquois* (Sage, 1851) at 77.

[76] Robert A. Williams Jr., "Gendered Checks and Balances: Understanding the Legacy of White Patriarchy in an American Indian Cultural Context" (1990) 24 *Georgia Law Review* 1019.

[77] William Fenton, "Structure, Continuity and Change in the Process of Iroquois Treaty Making" in Francis Jennings et al., *The History and Culture of Iroquois Diplomacy* (Syracuse University Press, 1985).

[78] The Haudenosaunee could invite others into their Confederacy and Great Law; see William Fenton, *The Great Law and the Longhouse: A Political History of the Iroquois Confederacy* (University of Oklahoma Press, 1998) at 73.

treaty relationships through time and at the state's formation.[79] As I wrote elsewhere about the Haudenosaunee treaty tradition:

> One of the most prominent accords relates to the Gus Wen Tah, or Two Row Wampum. The fundamental principles of the Two Row Wampum became the basis for the agreements made between the Haudenosaunee and the Dutch in 1645, with the French in 1701, and with the English in 1763–64. The belt consists of two rows of purple wampum beads on a white background. Three rows of white beads symbolizing peace, friendship, and respect separate the two purple rows. The two purple rows symbolize two paths or two vessels travelling down the same river. One row symbolizes Haudenosaunee people with their law and customs, while the other row symbolizes European laws and customs. As nations move together side by side on the river of life, they are to avoid overlapping or interfering with one another. These legal precepts are said to be embedded in subsequent agreements. Another symbol related to the Gus Wen Tah that communicates Haudenosaunee independence is the Silver Covenant Chain. It is to be pure, strong and untarnished, and bind nations together without causing them to lose their individual characteristics or their independence. Those holding the Covenant Chain are responsible for keeping their relationships bright and preventing them from breaking.[80]

Thus, although the internal organization of the Confederacy is impressive, what is important for constitutional purposes is that the confederacy played a significant role in Canada's constitutional development. They helped set the stage for subsequent treaty relationships between Indigenous peoples and the Crown. They were a key ally of the British during the United States struggle for independence against Great Britain in the 1770s and 1780s.[81] After the war British officials invited the Haudenosaunee to resettle on the Grand River near what is now Brantford Ontario.[82] This required treaties with the Anishinaabe of the region to ensure peaceful relationships.[83]

Governor Simcoe who presided over this scheme envisioned the Haudenosaunee as a buffer state between British North America and the newly formed United States of America.[84] Thus, constitutionally, the Haudenosaunee were regarded as separate peoples from the developing nation of Canada which would itself grow and be named

---

[79] John Borrows, "Wampum at Niagara: The Royal Proclamation, Canadian Legal History, and Self-Government" in Michael Asch (ed.), *Aboriginal and Treaty Rights in Canada: Essays on Law, Equity, and Respect for Difference* (University of British Columbia Press, 1997).

[80] Borrows, above (n 7) at 75–76.

[81] Barbara Graymont, *The Iroquois in the American Revolution* (Syracuse University Press, 1972); Max Mintz, *Seeds of Empire: The American Revolutionary Conquest of the Iroquois* (New York University Press, 1999).

[82] James Paxton, *Joseph Brant and His World: 18th Century Mohawk Warrior and Statesman* (Lorimer, 2008) at 47–76.

[83] Timothy Shannon, "Iroquoia" in Frederick Hoxie (ed.), *The Oxford Handbook of American Indian History* (Oxford University Press, 2016) 199 at 211.

[84] Sidney Harring, *White Man's Law: Native People in Nineteenth Century Jurisprudence* (University of Toronto Press, 1998 at 314.

a Dominion some 80 years later—in 1867. Unfortunately, from a Haudenosaunee per-spective, British North Americans (later Canadians) failed to keep their promises to treat them as nations and allies.[85] Their efforts at the League of Nations in the 1920s,[86] along with the forcible removal of their traditional government from their Longhouse, signals the failure of the British and Canadian governments to honour their founda-tional governing relationships with the Haudenosaunee, from their perspective.[87] This demonstrates that a significant strand of Canada's constitutional genealogy has been periodically marked by its failure to acknowledge the Indigenous pluralism that under-lies the nation state in many complex ways.[88]

6. Anishinaabe Constitutionalism

Like the Haudenosaunee the Anishinaabe also had a strong Great Lakes presence and a vibrant constitutionalism. Their territory was likewise north of Lakes Ontario and Erie; it also extended across the other Great Lakes into the southern woodlands and prairies of Canada's west. The Anishinaabe constitutional tradition is embodied in the word *chi-inaakonigewin*, which means the great guided way of decision-making.[89] This is a verb in Anishinaabemowin (the Ojibwe language) indicating that constitutionalism in this tradition was/is focused on action-oriented relationships in this governance structure. Historically, the Anishinaabe were organized as clans in loose confederacies,[90] more recently called the Council of the Three Fires in the eastern parts of their homelands.[91]

---

[85] The historic roots of the contemporary Haudenosaunee struggle to have their alliance status recognized in Canadian constitutional law is chronicled in Laura Devries, *Conflict in Caledonia: Aboriginal Land Rights and the Rule of Law* (University of Toronto Press, 2011) at 81–109, 130–159.

[86] "The Last Speech of DeskaHeh" (25 March 1925) in John Borrows and Len Rotman, *Aboriginal Legal Issues: Cases, Materials and Commentary* (3rd ed.) (Butterworth's, 2007) at 45.

[87] Haudenosaunee and Canadian perspectives of Six Nations governance are explored in *Logan v Styres* (1959), 20 D.L.R. (2d) 416 (Ontario H.C.) (upholding forcible eviction of traditional Haudenosaunee government).

[88] For a fuller treatment of how Canadian law has dealt with Indigenous legal pluralism see Patrick Macklem, "Indigenous Peoples and the Ethos of Legal Pluralism in Canada" in Patrick Macklem and Douglas Sanderson (eds), *Section 35 @ 25* (University of Toronto Press, 2016) at 17; Michael Asch and Patrick Macklem. "Aboriginal Rights and Canadian Sovereignty: An Essay on *R. v. Sparrow*" (1991) 29 *Alberta Law Journal* 498; Patrick Macklem, *Indigenous Difference and the Constitution of Canada* (University of Toronto Press, 2001).

[89] A contemporary example of chi-inaakonigewin is found in Ngo Dwe Waangizid Anishinaabe, Preamble to the Anishinaabe Chi-Naaknigewin- as adopted by the Grand Council of the Anishinabek Nation in June 2011 (describing the background of the Anishinaabek constitution's creation), http://www.anishinabek.ca/roj/download/NDWABrochureMarch2012.pdf.

[90] *See* Lisa Brooks, The Constitution of the White Earth Nation: A New Innovation in a Longstanding Indigenous Literary Tradition, 23 *Studies in American Indian Literatures* 48, 62 (Winter 2011) (discussing totemic associations in the political context).

[91] *See* Diamond Jenness, *The Indians of Canada* (Queen's Printer 1967) at 277.

As families and clans lay at the heart of traditional Anishinaabe constitutionalism the constitutional order was diverse as it encouraged diffusion and local place-based decision-making.

Historically, Anishinaabe people did not generally permit leaders to consolidate power within their legal tradition.[92] Leadership was decentralized and most often associated with a situation and not a particular person.[93] As authority was transient and moved from person to person as circumstances required, this encouraged a constitutionalism which enhanced individual agency and decision-making power.[94] For example, the Anishinaabe word for Chief is *Ogimaa*, which means one who counts their followers.[95] Followers could often only be counted on for the duration of a particular task assigned to any given leader.[96] Mary Black Rogers recorded the Anishinaabe understanding of leadership in these words:

> An Ojibwe root, debinimaa, has been variously translated as "boss", "master", "the one in charge", or "the one in control". But the favoured translation of a sensitive bilingual was "those who I am responsible for". The idea of bossing is generally rejected, as is the idea of competition, yet both must occur at times. It can be seen that the area of social control, of leadership and political structure, of the various cooperating social units necessary to kinship organization and subsistence activities—all these units must be balanced somehow to accord with the rules of the system about power.[97]

[92] Richard White, *The Middle Ground: Indians, Empires, and Republics in the Great Lakes Region, 1650–1815* (Cambridge University Press, 1991) at 37–40. However, Anishinaabe leadership values changed through time; see Anton Truer, *The Assassination of Hole in the Day* (Borealis Books, 2011) at 9–34.

[93] For the application of this concept to war and diplomacy see Rebecca Kugel, *To Be the Main Leaders of Our People: A History of Minnesota Ojibwe Politics, 1825–1898* (Michigan State University Press, 1998).

[94] Theresa Schenck, *The Voice of the Crane Echoes Afar* (Garland, 1997); *My First Years in the Fur Trade: The Journals of 1802–1804* (McGill-Queen's, 2002) (co-edited with Laura Peers) at 71, citing Morton Fried, *The Evolution of Political Society: An Essay in Political Anthropology* (Random House, 1967) at 83.

[95] Basil Johnston, an Elder from Cape Croker who taught about the Anishinaabe language, in oral communication to me said: ogimaa is related to the word *agindaussoowin*, which means to count. He told me that a leader counts his or her followers because he knows who they are. He said there could be different kinds of people who count followers in leadership terms. A band leader could be an *ogimaa* to his orchestra, as that person could count his or her follower; likewise an effective teacher could be an *ogimaa* for those who followed. However, see an alternative meaning published by Anton Truer, who writes:

> The Ojibwe word for leadership—ogimaawiwin—literally means "to be esteemed" or "to be held to high principle". It comes from the morpheme ogi, meaning high, found in other Ojibwe words such as ogichidaa (warrior), ogidakamig (on top of the earth) and ogidaaki (hilltop).

Truer, above (n 92) at 14.

[96] Janet Elizabeth Chute, *The Legacy of Shingwaukonse: A Century of Native Leadership* (University of Toronto Press, 1998) at 13–14.

[97] Mary Black, "Ojibwa Power Belief System," in Raymond D. Fogelson and Richard N. Adams (eds), *The Anthropology of Power* (Academic Press, 1977) at 147.

The balance of power in Anishinaabe leadership practices demonstrates an attentiveness to individual autonomy and decentralized power in this constitutional tradition.

Like the Haudenosaunee, Mikmaq and other eastern First Nations, the Anishinanaabe likewise influenced the development of Canada's now constitutionalized treaty order (protected within section 35(1) of the *Constitution Act 1982*[98]). This impact is perhaps best illustrated in the Treaty of Niagara of 1764. The Treaty of Niagara gathered over 2,000 Indigenous individuals from 22 different First Nations at the dawn of Britain's constitutional development in central Canada.[99] On the heels of the Royal Proclamation of 1763, the Treaty of Niagara was an event designed to facilitate peace, order, and friendship among Indigenous peoples and the Crown. Thus it provided a foundation for government on this land. The two-month meeting at Niagara came after the Seven Years War which saw the English defeat the French in North America, but not the Indigenous peoples.[100] After Indigenous leaders continued to defeat the British, the former issued ultimatums and invitations,[101] and the Crown decided to issue a Proclamation.[102] This document reserved Indian land from settlement, placed authority for treaties in non-colonial (i.e. Imperial) government, and outlined a public process for treaty relationships.[103] The Treaty of Niagara affirmed these principles through protocols, principles, and processes which were rooted in Anishinaabe, Haudenosaunee, and other Indigenous legal traditions.

The Treaty of Niagara promised First Nations that the Crown would recognize Indigenous governance,[104] free trade, open migration, respect for Indigenous land holdings, criminal justice protection, military assistance,[105] respect for hunting and

---

[98] *Constitution Act, 1982*, Schedule B to the *Canada Act, 1982*, (U.K.) 1982 c. 11.

[99] William G. Godfrey, *Pursuit of Profit and Preferment in Colonial North America: John Bradstreet's Quest* (Wilfred Laurier Press, 1982) at 197; William Warren, an Ojibwe historian, records "twenty-two different tribes were represented" at the council at Niagara. William Warren, *History of the Ojibway of Lake Superior* (Minnesota Historical Society, 1885; reprinted Ross & Haines, 1970) at 219.

[100] Colin Calloway, *The Scratch of a Pen: 1763 and the Transformation of North American* (Penguin, 2006) at 60–65.

[101] For example, B.B. Thatcher, *Indian Biography*, vol. II (Werner, 1841) at 76–77.

[102] Alexander Henry, *Travels and Adventures in Canada and the Indian Territories between the Years 1760–1776* (Morang, 1901) at 157–174.

[103] Brian Slattery, "First Nations and the Constitution" (1992), 71 *Canadian Bar Review* 261 at 290:

> Three basic principles underlie the Proclamation's detailed provisions. First, First Nations are to be protected in their lands by the Crown. Second, legitimate settlement may take place in areas designated from time to time by the Crown. Third, before an area can be settled, any native land rights must be ceded voluntarily to the Crown.

[104] See Paul Williams, *The Chain* (LL.M. Thesis, York University, 1982) [unpublished] at 83, quoting Sir William Johnson.

[105] Johnson promised that the agreement at Niagara would be a "Treaty of Offensive and Defensive Alliance" that would include promises to "assure them of a Free Fair & open trade, at the principal Posts, & a free intercourse & passage into our Country, That we will make no Settlements or Encroachments contrary to Treaty, or without their permission." "That we will bring to justice any persons who commit Robberys or Murders on them & that we will protect & aid them against their and our Enemys & duly observe our engagements with them." C. Flick (ed.), *The Papers of Sir William Johnson*, Vol. 4 (The University of the State of New York, 1925) at 328.

fishing rights, and the development of peace and friendship.[106] The principles of this treaty served as a template for many subsequent treaties in areas to the west. The Ontario Court of Appeal framed the constitutional significance of the arrangement in this way:

> The meeting at Niagara and the Treaty of Niagara were watershed events in Crown-First Nations relations. The Treaty established friendly relations with many First Nations who had supported the French in the previous war. It also gave treaty recognition to the nation-to-nation relationship between the First Nations and the British Crown, Indian rights in their lands and the process to be followed when Indian lands were surrendered.[107]

These promises have not always been adequately recognized and affirmed. In that regard, as with the other examples provided in this chapter, Canada's constitutional order has been diminished. Nevertheless, the Treaty of Niagara's development during the first moments of British constitutional law in central Canada points to principles that puts deliberation, persuasion, and consent at the heart of our constitutional aspirations. This genealogical root is part of Canada's living tree, and it should be more fully nurtured in future developments between the Crown and First Nations.

7. CREE CONSTITUTIONALISM

Cree people live in the James Bay watershed, the northern boreal forests and prairies of Canada. Like the Mikmaq and Anishinaabe, they are an Algonkian-speaking people whose constitutional traditions are also strongly influenced by their language and ecosystems.[108] Cree law-keepers are called *Onisinweuk* and Cree law embodies foundational principles related to *wahkohtowin, miyo-wicehtowin, pastahowin, ohcinewin,* and *kwayaskitotamowin.*[109] *Wahkohtowin* in particular has strong constitutional connotations and is

[106] Cptn. T.G. Anderson, "Report on the Affairs of the Indians of Canada, Section III", Appendix No. 95 in App. T of the *Journals of the Legislative Assembly of Canada*, Vol. 6.
[107] *Chippewas of Sarnia Band v Canada (Attorney General)*, 51 OR (3d) 641, [2000] OJ No 4804, [56].
[108] Fikret Berkes, *Sacred Ecology: Traditional Ecological Knowledge and Resource Management* (Taylor & Francis, 1999).
[109] The meaning of these words is as follows:

- *Wahkohtowin*—laws governing all relations.
- *Miyo-wicehtowin*—having or possessing just relations as in the way Cree will conduct their lives individually or collectively.
- *Pastahowin*—a transgression of spiritual or natural law, sin, use of bad medicine or evil doings all of which will be responded to by the Creator.
- *Ohcinewin*—part of the concept of *pastahowin*, to suffer in retribution for an action against creation.
- *Kwayaskitotamowin*—doing things in a right way, treating creation in a good way, a just or legal dealing.

considered to be the principal law governing all relations.[110] This law is based on relationships found in the natural world,[111] and thus draws on environmental observations and analogies to bring them into the human sphere.[112]

Cree constitutionalism, like other systems described herein, also had a role in Canada's broader constitutional development. Treaties signed between the Cree and the Crown, like the Treaty of Niagara and Mikmaq treaties, allowed Canada to expand with some measure of participation by Indigenous peoples.[113] Although strong critiques exist about Canada's treaty formations,[114] at least some Crown representatives intended to act with the highest honour and create Canada by reference to Indigenous views and interests.[115]

In this light, when seen from an Indigenous perspective, it is possible to regard treaties between Aboriginal peoples and the Crown as foundational agreements in Canada.[116] They underlie Canada's political order because they allowed for the peaceful settlement and development of large portions of the country, while at the same time promising certainty for Aboriginal peoples' possession of lands and in pursuit of their livelihoods.[117] They are also important because they implement Indigenous law in Canada by grounding Aboriginal peoples' deepest obligations to the Creator and others in a framework of reciprocity and mutual exchange. This is a vital part of Canada's constitutional genealogy.

---

[110] Kathleen O'Reilly-Scanlon, Kristine Crowe, and Angelina Weenie "Pathways to Understanding: Wahkohtowin as a Research Methodology" (2004) 39 *McGill Journal of Education* 1 at 29.

[111] Robert Brighton, *Grateful Prey: Rock Cree Human-Animal Relations* (University of California Press, 1993).

[112] Elder Dolly Neapetung, in H. Cardinal and W. Hildebrandt, *Treaty Elders of Saskatchewan* (University of Calgary Press, 2000) at 6.

[113] Arthur Ray, J.R. Miller, and Frank Tough, *Bounty and Benevolence: A History of Saskatchewan Treaties* (McGill-Queen's Press, 2000).

[114] In *Paulette v Register of Titles (No.2)*, the Court held:

> it was almost unbelievable that the Government party could have ever returned from their efforts [to sign a treaty] with any impression but that they had given an assurance in perpetuity to the Indians in their territories that their traditional use of land was not affected.

(1973) 42 D.L.R. (3d) 8 (N.W.T.S.C.); rev'd on other grounds 63 D.L.R. (3d) 1 (N.W.T.C.A.); aff'd on other grounds 72 D.L.R. (3d) 161 (S.C.C.).

[115] Michael Asch, *On Being Here to Stay: Treaty and Aboriginal Rights in Canada* (University of Toronto Press, 2014).

[116] When Alexander Morris proposed Treaty 6 he said:

> What I trust and hope we will do is not for today or tomorrow only; what I promise and what I believe and hope you will take, is to last as long as that sun shines and yonder river flows,

Alexander Morris, *The Treaties of Canada with the Indians of Manitoba and the North-West Territories, Including the Negotiations on Which They Were Based, and Other Information Relating Thereto* (Fifth House Publishers, 1991) at 202.

[117] This is generally one of the thesis points underlying the book: J.R. Miller, *Compact, Contract, Covenant: Aboriginal Treaty-Making in Canada* (University of Toronto Press, 2009).

In coming to this view the written words of a treaty document alone cannot be relied upon to provide the whole picture.[118] The written sources are often biased, being written in English, not the Aboriginal language of the negotiation.[119] Furthermore, the treaties use technical legal words and their transcription was usually in the hands of non-Aboriginal parties. The limitations of the written word mean that Elders' oral traditions and perspectives must be taken into account to determine the meaning of the treaties. For example, each of the numbered treaties entered into by the Cree contains a "peace and order clause." In the Cree language this promise is understood by the word *miyo-wicehtowin*. It asks, directs, admonishes, or requires people to conduct themselves in a manner such that they create positive and good relations in all their experiences. Similarly, *pastahowin*: "Crossing the line" was another important teaching relating to peace, order, and justice in Saskatchewan treaties. It means that certain things cannot be done without experiencing bad consequences. Finally, *wahkohtowin* is an important part of the meaning of the peace and order clauses because it conveys the idea that laws and duties must be followed in order to have good relationships.

Further, as part of our constitutional genealogy we should understand that First Nations peoples are not the only treaty beneficiaries. Non-Indigenous peoples also have treaty rights. Both groups are recipients of the promises made in the negotiation process. The mutuality of Indigenous and non-Indigenous peoples as beneficiaries of the treaties is overlooked because it is most often Indigenous peoples striving to assert their rights. Yet there are a number of potential inheritors of treaty rights beyond Indigenous nations, bands, and First Nation individuals. The British and Canadian Crown certainly received many benefits from the treaties. Their citizens were able to peacefully settle and develop the prairies. Non-Indigenous Canadians trace many of their rights to do certain things in this country to the consent that was granted to the Crown by Indigenous peoples in the treaty process.

The Office of the Treaty Commission in Saskatchewan recognized this gap in understanding and highlighted the mutuality of the treaty relationship in the following terms:

> The people of Saskatchewan can benefit from learning more about the historical events associated with the making of the treaties as they reveal the mutual benefits and responsibilities of the parties. There is ample evidence that many people are misinformed about the history of the Canada-Treaty First Nations relations, and about the consequent experiences of Treaty First Nations communities and individuals. Until recently, the perspective of many Canadians has been to view treaties as remnants of antiquity, with little relevance to the present. Treaties were seen as frozen in time, part of Canada's ancient history. Some no doubt still hold this view of treaties

---

[118] For a general discussion of how courts deal with this issue see Leonard Rotman, "Taking Aim at the Canons of Treaty Interpretation in Canadian Aboriginal Rights Jurisprudence" (1997) 46 *University of New Brunswick Law Journal* 1.

[119] Doctrines developed to address this problem are found in *R. v Horseman* [1990] 1 S.C.R. 901 at 907; *R. v Badger* [1996] 1 S.C.R. 771 [4] [41]; *R. v Sundown*, [1999] 1 S.C.R. 393 [25]; *R. v Marshall* [1999] 3 S.C.R. 456 [43]; *R. v. Bernard* [2005] 2 S.C.R. 220 [25].

as primarily "real estate transactions" modeled on business contracts and British common law. *Non-Aboriginal Canadians forgot that they, too, gained rights through treaty–rights to the rich lands and resources from which they have benefited greatly. They also forgot about the partnership formed at the time of treaty-making. The benefits of the treaties were to be mutual, assisting both parties.*[120]

8. FIRST NATIONS CONSTITUTIONALISM IN BRITISH COLUMBIA

When we move into the province now called British Columbia constitutional genealogies are muted or absent insofar as they positively influenced the development of Canada's constitution.[121] This is the case despite the fact that British Columbia has the richest diversity of First Nations in the country. Six of the eleven language families are found in the area. Economic and social relations were also very complex. The presence of salmon in most of the territory was a unique source of life. People could often fill their entire community's yearly need for protein in a single run. Salmon also attracted other food sources, such as bears and smaller mammals, which would further feed the people through the year. Furthermore, salmon carcasses which escaped predation nourished the surrounding land. Vegetation grew more abundantly when these bodies fertilized the forest floor, plateau, and alpine regions. Rain is also abundant in the coastal regions of the province. This further added to the bounty Indigenous peoples enjoyed prior to European arrival which fed their social and legal systems.

Within British Columbia, First Nations dot the land, with names such as the Coast Salish, Kwakwaka'wakw, Nuu-chah-nuulth, Haisla, Gitksan, Wet'suwet'en, Tsimshian, Nisga'a, Haida, Tsilhqot'in, St'at'imc, Secwepmec, Ktunaxa, Kootney, Syilx, Nlaka'pamux, Cree, Ojibwe, and Dunne-Za.[122] Each had/has its own unwritten constitutional traditions. This allowed their governments to function in ways which enriched their families and managed their environments. In making this observation we must remind ourselves that Indigenous constitutionalism in British Columbia was also imperfect, as is the case with all legal traditions. War, internal conflict, and other human flaws contributed to their challenges. This is evidenced in the abundant stories of social dislocation among First Nations.[123] Indigenous peoples' constitutional law flows not

---

[120] Treaty Commission of Saskatchewan, *Statement of Treaty Issues: Treaties as a Bridge to the Future* (Office of the Treaty Commissioner, 1998) at 74. [emphasis added]

[121] A good general history of British Columbia which discusses Indigenous issues in detail is Jean Barman, *The West beyond the West: A History of British Columbia* (University of Toronto Press, 1996).

[122] More information about First Nations in British Columbia is found in Robin Fisher, *Contact and Conflict: Indian-European Relations in British Columbia, 1774–1890* (University of British Columbia Press, 1992).

[123] The role of conflict as a source of Indigenous law is developed more fully in Emily Snyder, Val Napoleon, and John Borrows, "Gender and Violence: Drawing on Indigenous Legal Resources" (2014) 47 *University of British Columbia Law Review* 593.

only from agreement, harmony, and consensus, but also from conflict and the need to address this conflict through governmental and management structures at foundational levels.[124]

Unfortunately, when we examine the influence of Indigenous constitutionalism in British Columbia we find fewer inter-societal legal arrangements which allowed Indigenous forms to impact non-native constitutionalism. Except for the Douglas Treaties on small portions of Vancouver Island,[125] pre-Confederation legal arrangements between the parties are almost completely absent.[126] Moreover, soon after Confederation, British Columbia took active steps to explicitly deny Indigenous land and governance rights.[127] Joseph Truth, land commissioner and the first Lieutenant-Governor of British Columbia, led and illustrated this movement.[128] He spoke in the following way:

> The title of Indians in the fee of the public lands, or any portion thereof, is distinctly denied. In no case has any special agreement been made with any of the tribes of the Mainland for the extinction of their claims of possession; but these claims have been held to have been fully satisfied by securing to each tribe, as the progress of settlement of the country seemed to require, the use of sufficient tracts of land for their wants of agriculture and pastoral purposes.[129]

The denial of Indigenous land rights and the resettlement of British Columbia by non-native people had a severely negative impact on Indigenous social and spatial organization in the province.[130] At the same time, we should be clear that Indigenous constitutionalism was a vital force in helping First Nations critique and resist colonial conceits. In this regard it is part of the constitutional genealogy of Canada through its agonistic engagement with the nation-state.[131] To round out this chapter two brief examples of Indigenous constitutionalism in British Columbia will be canvassed. This is done to illustrate the active nature of Indigenous constitutionalism in Indigenous communities despite their negative reception by the province and country more generally.

---

[124] An excellent illustration of these points is found in Val Napoleon and Hadley Friedland, "Indigenous Legal Traditions: Roots to Renaissance", in Markus D. Dubber and Tatjana Hörnle, *The Oxford Handbook of Criminal Law* (Oxford University Press, 2014).

[125] Wilson Duff, "The Fort Victoria Treaties" (1969) 3 *British Columbia Studies* 3 at 53–54.

[126] See, generally, Robert E. Cail, *Land, Man and Law* (University of British Columbia Press, 1974).

[127] Robin Fisher, "Joseph Trutch and Indian Land Policy" (1971–1972) 12 *British Columbia Studies* 3.

[128] See generally, Paul Tennant, *Aboriginal Peoples and Politics: Indian Land Question in British Columbia, 1849–1989* (University of British Columbia Press, 1990).

[129] British Columbia, Ministry of Aboriginal Affairs, "Report on Indian Reserves" in *Papers Connected with the Indian Land Question, 1850–1875* (Victoria, 1875) 11.

[130] Cole Harris, *The Resettlement of British Columbia: Essays on Colonialism and Geographical Change* (Vancouver: University of British Columbia Press, 1997); Cole Harris, *Making Native Space: Colonialism Resistance, and Reserves in British Columbia* (University of British Columbia Press, 2002.

[131] For a discussion of the agonistic nature of Canadian constitutional law see Jeremy Webber, above (n 6).

9. SECWEPEMC CONSTITUTIONALISM

The Secwepemc people of the interior plateau of British Columbia currently live in 17 Indian Bands: *Stẃecemʼc/Xgatʼtam* (Canoe Creek/Dog Creek Indian Band), *Tsqescen* (Canim Lake Indian Band), *Xatsull First Nation* (Deep Creek/Soda Creek Indian Band), and *Tʼexelc* (Williams Lake Indian Band), *Esketemc First Nation* (Alkali Lake Indian Band); *Sexqeltqín* (Adams Lake Indian Band), *Stʼuxwtéws* (Bonaparte Indian Band), *Llenllenéyʼten* (High Bar Indian Band), *Tkʼemlúps* (Kamloops Indian Band), *Qw7ewt* (Little Shuswap Indian Band), *Skʼatsin*, (Neskonlith Indian Band), *Simpcw*, North Thompson, *Tskʼwéylecw* (Pavilion Indian Band), *Kepésqʼt* (Shuswap Indian Band), *Skíitsestn* (Skeetchestn Indian Band), *Splatsín* (Spallumcheen Indian Band), and *Stilʼw/ Pelltʼíqt* (Whispering Pines Indian Band/Clinton). Their traditional territory consists of some 5,500,000 hectares of land extending north to Quesnel, southwest to Salmon Arm, west to Alexis Creek, and east to Wells Grey Park.

Like many Indigenous constitutional regimes which start with origin stories,[132] Secwepemc creation stories contain principles which emphasize governmental obligations in both the human and natural worlds.[133] The close relationship between humankind and the broader natural world generated principles for humans and animals to facilitate self-governance.[134] The Creator, the Trickster, and the Old One in their stories all offer words and examples about how (or how not) to organize communities. Secwepemc scholar Ron Ignace discussed this historic idea in contemporary form as follows:

> The ancient history of Secwépemcúlʼecw gave us the laws, what we call "yirí7 re stsqʼʼeyʼs-kucw," that defined us as Secwépemc, and that gave us what I call "equipment for living"

---

[132] The role of non-human forces is found in many Indigenous legal traditions; see generally K. Llewellyn and E.A. Hoebel, "The Cheyene Way: Conflict and Case Law in *Primitive Jurisprudence* (Norman: University of Oklahoma Press, 1941); See E. Adamson Hoebel, *The Law of Primitive Man* (Atheneum, 1974); Karl N. Llewellyn and E. Adamson Hoebel, *The Cheyenne Way: Conflict and Case Law in Primitive Jurisprudence* (University of Oklahoma Press, 1941); Max Gluckman, *Politics, Law and Ritual in Primitive Society* (Aldine Publishing, 1965); Rennard Strickland, *Fire and the Spirits: Cherokee Law from Clan to Court* (University of Oklahoma Press, 1982); Antonio Mills, *Eagle Down Is Our Law: Witsuwitʼen Law, Feasts and Land Claims* (University of British Columbia Press, 1994).

[133] James Alexander Teir, *Part VII—The Shuswap, The Jesup North Pacific Expedition: Memoir of the American Museum of Natural History*, Franz Boas (ed), Vol. 2 (AMS Press, 1975 at 595–597.

[134] Ibid. at 597:

> He also regulated the winds, telling them the proper directions from which to blow, and when to be calm. He introduced trout into many of the streams and lakes, and ordered salmon to ascend new rivers. He made many new kinds of trees, bushes, and plants to grow in places where they were required. He introduced certain kinds of animals, such as the deer, elk, bear, and hare, and told them to multiply. Before that, they had lived all together in their own worlds, underneath the ground. He told the people to be respectful to them, use them properly, and not make them angry. At that time the people were all poor and foolish, and he taught them what kinds of

as a people: What is traditionally marked on the land through our own history and existence on the land is mirrored in our ways of dealing with things by giving counsel to one
another when issues arise that need to be dealt with and solved. "Yirí7 re stsq"eý's kucw,"
thus requires the tkw"enemíple7ten, the ongoing advisors, to implement the ways that
were set forth by our ancestors.[135]

Secwepemc constitutional law thus had/has its adherents focus on the resources for reasoning found in the stories which could be identified when people counselled together. It could
be applied through reasoning by analogy or creating distinctions between past stories and
present circumstances. These stories are recorded in rock landforms throughout the territory, in 'transformer' sites and pictoglyphs. Reading the land and stories at origin story locations helped/helps Secwepemc people identify the sources and limits of their jurisdiction
within their territories.[136] Hereditary chiefs and sub-chiefs were/are responsible for asserting and bringing this jurisdiction to life in the face of challenge and conflict.[137] Kinship also
played an important role in governance, encouraging respect for land and resource use
throughout the territory.[138]

    The metes and bounds of Secwepemc sovereignty found in the stories as expressed
by the Chiefs was used to defend their lands and governments from intrusion. As noted
in the last section, First Nations constitutionalism in the province was a source of resistance. A Secwepemc petition to Sir Wilfrid Laurier in 1910 makes this point: "When
[the first whites] first came amongst us there were only Indians here. They found the
people of each tribe supreme in their own territory, and having tribal boundaries known
and recognized by all.[139] The Secwepemc people were contesting their treatment at the
hands of colonial governments by drawing on their own legal traditions. Secwepemc
constitutionalism in this instance intruded in Canadian political life only to be ignored
by subsequent commissions, inquiries, and other national developments.[140] This reinforces the point made earlier concerning British Columbia's development and its denial

animals, fishes, and roots to eat. He also taught them many methods of catching, procuring, and
preserving the food, and how to make certain tools and weapons. He introduced sweat-bathing
and smoking, and taught the people how to make baskets, snowshoes, and canoes. He transformed the remaining bad people into animals, birds, fishes, and rocks. Where he found too
many people in one place, he told them to move, and live in other places.

[135] Ron Ignace, *Our Oral Histories Are Our Iron Posts: Secwepemc Stories and Historical Consciousness*,
PhD dissertation, SFU Vancouver, 2008 [unpublished] at http://shuswapnation.org/wordpress/wp-
content/uploads/2016/01/Ron-Ignace-PhD-Thesis.pdf at 4–5.

[136] The use of toponyms at significant sites aided this process. Ibid. at 172–180.

[137] Teir, above (n 133) at 569.

[138] Ignace, above (n 135) at 185.

[139] Memorial to Sir Wilfrid Laurier, Premier of the Dominion of Canada, From the Chiefs of
the Shuswap, Okanagan and Couteau Tribes of British Columbia, presented at Kamloops, B.C. 25
August 1910.

[140] See the work of the McKenna McBride Commission: British Columbia, *Report of the Royal
Commission on Indian Affairs for the Province of British Columbia* (1916) at http://www.ubcic.bc.ca/
Resources/final_report.htm#axzz4KF1C4tlr.

of Indigenous governance in Canada's unfolding constitutional processes. Nevertheless, Secwepemc traditions of governance survive in many forms throughout the territory. They await further future reference as source of authority not only for authority for Secwepmec governance but also for how Canadian constitutional relationships develop in the territory more generally.

10. GITKSAN CONSTITUTIONALISM

The north-west coast of British Columbia is home to Indigenous groups that organize their constitutional structures in ways more hierarchical than other groups discussed in this chapter. The Haida, Tsimshian. Nisga'a, Tahltan, Wet'suwet'en, Dakelh, and others in the region have elaborate House and Clan structures which direct their governmental affairs. These constitutional traditions surfaced in the recent case of *Delgamuukw v British Columbia* which revolved around the issue of whether the Gitksan and Wet'suwet'en people had jurisdiction and/or self-government in their territories in north-western British Columbia.[141] Although this issue was ultimately sent back to trial for determination the case has not been re-litigated to test the continuing existence of Indigenous governance to this point.

Despite the lack of attention to this constitutional tradition the Gitksan had/have a nuanced, strong, and sophisticated governance structure.[142] The basic structure of Gitksan political, social, and legal organization is the House. A House is a matrilineal kinship group that creates rights to access land and resources and participate in varying ways in group decisions. Houses belong to four larger clans: the *ganeda* (frog), *gisgahast* (fireweed), *lax gibuu* (wolf), and *lax skiik* (eagle). Within each House a head chief (*simoogit*) and wing chiefs (*hla ga kaaxhl simoogit*) work to keep peace and order amongst the group through *adaawk* and *antamahlaswx*, which contain stories about how to manage relations across the group.[143] The Gitksan use their crests and feasts to formalize the implications of these stories in each generation. As the Supreme Court of Canada reported in the *Delgamuukw* decision:

> The most significant evidence of spiritual connection between the Houses and their territory is a feast hall. This is where the Gitksan and Wet'suwet'en peoples tell and retell their stories and identify their territories to remind themselves of the sacred connection that they have with their lands. The feast has a ceremonial purpose, but is also used for making important decisions.[144]

---

[141] *Delgamuukw v British Columbia* [1997] 3 S.C.R. 1010 [170–171].

[142] For a general discussion of Gitksan law see Antonia Mills (ed.), *Hang Onto These Words: Johnny David's Delgamuukw Evidence* (University of Toronto Press, 2005).

[143] Val Napoleon, *Ayook: Gitksan Legal Order, Law and Legal Theory*, PhD Dissertation, University of Victoria Faculty of Law, 2009 at http://dspace.library.uvic.ca:8080/bitstream/handle/1828/1392/napoleon%20dissertation%20April%2026-09.pdf?sequence=1 at 7.

[144] *Delgamuukw v. British Columbia*, [1997] 3 S.C.R. 1010 [14].

Gitksan constitutionalism through the feasting structures deals with questions of "marriage, shaming (to control harmful and injurious behaviour), cleansing (to restore spirits after serious injury), restitution, birth, graduation (to celebrate achievements), naming, reinstatement (for Gitksan people who disobeyed the laws), coming of age, "smoke" (for obligations related to organizing settlement feasts), grave-stone placing, settlement (repayment of obligations arising from a death), divorce, and pole raising."[145] Gitksan constitutionalism decentralizes political power through reciprocal kinship relationships which are maintained through frequent negotiation.[146]

When Europeans arrived in Gitksan territory the power of Gitksan law structured the interactions. William Brown was the first European to live among the Gitksan in 1822. He was a Hudson's Bay Company trader who set up residence on Lake Babine in 1822. He described Gitksan people as "men of property" and "possessors of lands"[147] who regulated access to their territory through a "structure of nobles or chiefs, commoners, kinship arrangements of some kind and priority relating to the trapping of beaver in the vicinity of the villages".[148] Writing in his journal in 1823, Brown observed that the Chiefs "have certain tracts of country, which they claim an exclusive right to and will not allow any other person to hunt upon them".[149] Following this early period of contact there were sporadic interactions between Gitksan and European people. Unfortunately, "[t]he 1870–80's were turbulent times in the territory with some difficulty and much hard feeling. Specific incidents, such as the accidental burning of Kitsegeucla in 1872, Youman's murder in 1884, the killing of Kitwankool Jim (sometimes called the Skeena uprising) in 1888, and other incidents are examples of strained relations between the old and the new cultures."[150] Following this period Gitksan and Canadian constitutional law had different rules regarding governance in the territory.

Although British Columbia and Canada regard themselves as possessing overarching jurisdiction power in the area, the Gitksan people continue to believe their authority is the legitimate power in the territory. At some point in the future this issue will be tested again in the courts or addressed through negotiation. Until this occurs the Gitksan will continue to question Canada and British Columbia's constitutional claims in their ancient territories.[151]

---

[145] Napoleon, above (n 143) at 8–9.

[146] For detail concerning feasts see Marjorie M. Halpin and Margaret Seguin Anderson (eds), *Potlatch at Gitsegukla: William Beynon's 1945 Field Notebooks* (University of British Columbia Press, 2000).

[147] Arthur Ray, "Fur Trade History and the Gitksan and Wet'suwet'en Comprehensive Claim: Men of Property and the Exercise of Title" in Kerry Abel and Jean Friesen (eds), *Aboriginal Resource Use in Canada: Historical and Legal Aspects* (University of Manitoba Press, 1990) 301–315.

[148] *Delgamuukw* at 281 (B.C.S.C.).

[149] Arthur Ray, Trial document Ex. 964-5, p. 1(87).

[150] *Delgamuukw v British Columbia*, 79 DLR (4th) 185; [1991] 3 WWR 97; [1991] BCJ No 525 (QL); [1991] 5 CNLR 5.

[151] John Borrows, "Sovereignty's Alchemy: An Analysis of *Delgamuukw v. British Columbia*, (1999) 37 *Osgoode Hall Law Journal* 537.

11. CONCLUSION

Canada's constitutional development was influenced by Indigenous constitutionalism to differing degrees across the country. Even the failure to recognize Indigenous constitutional orders influenced Canada's constitutional development. The country lost the benefit of struggling with this kind of diversity in earlier periods and the state had to develop discriminatory policies which transferred the Indigenous estate to people who arrived from other parts of the world. The active suppression and selective recognition of Indigenous constitutionalism by Parliament and the judiciary confirms the Supreme Court of Canada's observation: "there can be no doubt that over the years the rights of the Indians were often honoured in the breach".[152]

Despite their ambiguous treatment by Canadian courts Indigenous peoples' constitutional orders were a vital part of the land for thousands of years prior to European arrival. These traditions continue to exist and they give structure (both positive and negative) to Canada's broader constitutional tradition. This chapter has gestured towards the diverse constitutional pluralism that existed before Europeans arrived in North America, and which continues to underlie our country's political and legal experience. It has shown how Canada's constitutional genealogy cannot be recounted without accounting for Indigenous constitutionalism across the land.

BIBLIOGRAPHY

Alfred T, *Peace, Power, Righteousness: An Indigenous Manifesto* (Oxford University Press, 1999)

Anderson TG, 'Report on the Affairs of the Indians of Canada, Section III' Appendix No. 95 in App. T of the *Journals of the Legislative Assembly of Canada*, Vol. 6

Arnakak J, 'Commentary: What is Inuit Qaujimajatuqangit?' *Nunatsiaq News* (Iqaluit, 25 August 2000)

Asch M and Macklem P, 'Aboriginal Rights and Canadian Sovereignty: An Essay on *R. v. Sparrow*' (1991) 29 *Alberta Law Journal* 498

Asch M, *On Being Here to Stay: Treaty and Aboriginal Rights in Canada* (University of Toronto Press, 2014)

Aupilaarjuk M, and others, *Interviewing Inuit Elders, Volume 2: Perspectives on Traditional Law* (Oosten J, Laugrand F, and Rasing W eds, Nunavut Arctic College, 1999) 2

Austin A, *The Province of Jurisprudence Determined* (first published 1832, Rumble W ed, 2nd edn, Cambridge University Press, 1995) 176

Baker JH, *An Introduction to English Legal History* (2nd edn, Butterworths, 1979)

Baker JT, *Religion in America Vol 1* (Thomson Wadsworth, 2005) 19

Barman J, *The West Beyond the West: A History of British Columbia* (University of Toronto Press, 1996)

---

[152] *R. v Sparrow* [1990] 1 SCR 1075.

Barsh R and Henderson S, 'The Supreme Court's Vanderpeet Trilogy: Native Imperialism and Ropes of Sand' (1997) 42 *McGill Law Journal* 993

Benton L, *Law and Colonial Cultures: Legal Regimes in World History, 1400-1900* (Cambridge University Press, 2002)

_____ *A Search for Sovereignty: Law and Geography in European Empires, 1400-1900* (Cambridge University Press, 2010)

_____ and Ross R eds, *Legal Pluralism and Empires, 1500-1850* (New York University Press, 2013)

Berkes F, *Sacred Ecology: Traditional Ecological Knowledge and Resource Management* (Taylor & Francis, 1999)

Black M, 'Ojibwa Power Belief System' in Fogelson and Adams eds, *The Anthropology of Power* (Academic Press, 1977) 147

Boas F, [1888] *The Central Eskimo* (University of Nebraska Press, 1964)

Borrows J, 'A Genealogy of Law: Inherent Sovereignty and First Nations Self-Government' (1992) 30 *Osgoode Hall Law Journal* 291

_____ 'Frozen Rights in Canada: Constitutional Interpretation and the Trickster' (1997) 22 *American Indian Law Review* 37

_____ 'Wampum at Niagara: The Royal Proclamation, Canadian Legal History, and Self-Government' in Michael Asch ed, *Aboriginal and Treaty Rights in Canada: Essays on Law, Equity, and Respect for Difference* (UBC Press, 1997)

_____ 'Sovereignty's Alchemy: An Analysis of Delgamuukw v. British Columbia' (1999) 37 *Osgoode Hall Law Journal* 537

_____ 'Listening for a Change: The Courts and Oral Tradition' (2001) 39 *Osgoode Hall Law Journal* 1

_____ *Canada's Indigenous Constitution* (University of Toronto Press, 2010)

_____'(Ab)Originalism and Canada's Constitution' (2012) 58 *Supreme Court Law Review* 2nd. 351.

_____ 'The Durability of Terra Nullius: Tsilhqot'in v. the Queen' (2015) 48 *University of British Columbia Law Review* 701

_____ 'Challenging Historical Frameworks: Aboriginal Rights, Agency and Originalism' (2016) *Canadian Historical Review* (forthcoming)

Brighton R, *Grateful Prey: Rock Cree Human-Animal Relations* (University of California Press, 1993)

Brooks L, 'The Constitution of the White Earth Nation: A New Innovation in a Longstanding Indigenous Literary Tradition' (2011) 23 *Studies in American Indian Literatures* 48, 62

Cail RE, *Land, Man and Law,* (UBC Press, 1974)

Calloway C, *The Scratch of a Pen: 1763 and the Transformation of North American* (Penguin, 2006) 60-65

Cardinal H and Hildebrandt W, *Treaty Elders of Saskatchewan: Our Dream is That One Day Our People Will One Day Be Clearly Recognized as Nations* (University of Calgary Press 2000) 6

Carr A, *What is History?* (2nd edn, Penguin Books, 1987)

Chute JE, *The Legacy of Shingwaukonse: A Century of Native Leadership* (University of Toronto Press, 1998) 13-14

Cote E, 'The Reception of English Law' (1977) XV *Alberta Law Review* 29, 38

Damas D, *Arctic Migrants/Arctic Villagers: The Transformation of Inuit Settlement in the Central Arctic* (McGill-Queens University Press, 2002) 7-17

Devries L, *Conflict in Caledonia: Aboriginal Land Rights and the Rule of Law* (University of Toronto Press, 2011) 81-109, 130-159

Dickason OP, *Canada's First Nations: A History of Founding Peoples From Earliest Times* (McClelland & Stewart, 1992)

Duff W, 'The Fort Victoria Treaties' (1969) 3 *BC Studies* 3, 53-54

Dussart F and Poirier S eds, *Entangled Territorialities: Negotiating Indigenous Lands in Australia and Canada* (University of Toronto Press, 2017) (forthcoming)

Fenton W, 'Structure, Continuity and Change in the Process of Iroquois Treaty Making' in Francis Jennings and others, *The History and Culture of Iroquois Diplomacy* (Syracuse University Press, 1985)

_____ *The Great Law and the Longhouse: A Political History of the Iroquois Confederacy* (University of Oklahoma Press, 1998)

Fisher R, 'Joseph Trutch and Indian Land Policy' (1971-1972) 12 *B.C Studies* 3

_____ *Contact and conflict: Indian-European relations in British Columbia, 1774-1890* (UBC Press, 1992)

Flick C (ed), *The Papers of Sir William Johnson*, Vol. 4 (The University of the State of New York, 1925) 328

Ganong WF (tr and ed), *New Relation of Gaspesia, with the Customs and Religion of the Gaspesian Indians, by Chrestien LeClerq* (Champlain Society, 1910) 103-06

Gluckman M, *Politics, Law and Ritual in Primitive Society* (Aldine Publishing, 1965)

Godfrey WG, *Pursuit of Profit and Preferment in Colonial North America: John Bradstreet's Quest* (Wilfred Laurier Press, 1982) 197

Graymont B, *The Iroquois in the American Revolution* (Syracuse University Press, 1972)

Greer A, *The Jesuit Relations: Natives and Missionaries in Seventeenth-Century North America*, (Bedford Books, 2000)

Halpin MM and Anderson MS (eds), *Potlatch at Gitsegukla: William Beynon's 1945 Field Notebooks* (UBC Press, 2000)

Harring S, *White Man's Law: Native People in Nineteenth Century Jurisprudence* (University of Toronto Press, 1998) 314

Harris C, *The Resettlement of British Columbia: Essays on Colonialism and Geographical Change* (UBC Press, 1997)

_____ *Making Native Space: Colonialism Resistance, and Reserves in British Columbia* (UBC Press, 2002

Heidenreich C, 'Maps Relating to the First Half of the 17th Century and Their Use in Determining the Location of Jesuit Missions in Huronia' (1966) *The Cartographer*, 103-126

_____ 'Mapping the Location of Native Groups, 1600-1760' (1981) *Journal of the Historical Atlas of Canada*, 6-13

_____ 'Mapping the Great Lakes: The Period of Exploration, 1603-1700' (1980) 17 *Cartographica* 32-63

_____ 'Mapping the Great Lakes: The Period of Imperial Rivalries' (1981) 18 *Cartographica* 74-108

_____ 'An Analysis of the 17th Century Map "Nouvelle France"' (1988) 25 *Cartographica* 67-111

Henry A, *Travels and Adventures in Canada and the Indian Territories between the years 1760-1776* (Morang, 1901) 157-174

Hoebel EA, 'Law-ways of the Primitive Eskimos' (1940-1941) 31 *Journal of the American Institute of Criminal Law and Criminology*, 663–883, 669

_____ *The Law of Primitive Man* (Atheneum, 1974)

Hurley J, *Children or Brethren: Aboriginal Rights in Colonial Iroquoia* (Saskatoon, Native Law Centre, 1985)

Ignace R, 'Our Oral Histories are Our Iron Posts: Secwepemc Stories and Historical Consciousness' (Ph.D. dissertation, Simon Fraser University 2008) [unpublished] <http://shuswapnation.org/wordpress/wp-content/uploads/2016/01/Ron-Ignace-PhD-Thesis.pdf>, 4-5

Inuaraq S, 'Traditional Justice among the Inuit' in Charrin A, Lacroix J, and Therrien M eds, *Peoples des Grands Nords Traditions et Transitions* (Sorbonne Press, 1995) 255

Irving H, 'Outsourcing the Law: History and the Disciplinary Limits of Constitutional Reasoning' (2015) 84 *Fordham Law Review* 957, 958

Jenness D, *The Indians of Canada* (Ottawa, Queen's Printer 1967)

Jennings F, *The Ambiguous Iroquois Empire* (W.W. Norton and Company, 1990)

Johansen BE and Mann BA eds, *Encyclopedia of the Haudenosaunee (Iroquois Confederacy)* Greenwood Press, 2000), 265

Kugel R, *To Be the Main Leaders of Our People: A History of Minnesota Ojibwe Politics, 1825-1898* (Michigan State University Press, 1998)

Lewis GM, 'Changing National Perspectives and the Mapping of the Great Lakes Between 1755 and 1795' (1980) 17 *Cartographica*, 1-31

Llewellyn K and Hoebel EA, 'The Cheyene Way: Conflict and Case Law in *Primitive Jurisprudence*' (University of Oklahoma Press, 1941)

Loukacheva N, 'Indigenous Inuit Law, "Western" Law and Northern Issues' (2012) 3 *Arctic Review on Law and Politics* 200, 203

Macklem P, *Indigenous Difference and the Constitution of Canada* (University of Toronto Press, 2001)

_____ 'Indigenous Peoples and the Ethos of Legal Pluralism in Canada' in Macklem P and Sanderson D eds, *From Recognition to Reconciliation* (University of Toronto Press, 2016)

Maitland FW and Montague FC, *A Sketch of English Legal History* (G.P. Putnam and Sons, 1915) 1-130

Martijn CA, 'Early Mikmaq Presence in Southern Newfoundland: An Ethnohistorical Perspective, c.1500-1763' (2003) 19, *The New Early Modern Newfoundland* <https://journals.lib.unb.ca/index.php/NFLDS/article/viewArticle/141/238>

Macdonald R, 'Critical Legal Pluralism as a Construction of Normativity and the Emergence of Law' in Lajoie A and others eds., *Théories et émergence du droit: pluralisme, surdétermination et effectivité* (Thémis, 1998) 9

_____ *Lessons of Everyday Law* (McGill-Queen's University Press, 2002)

McKenna McBride Commission, Report of the Royal Commission on Indian Affairs for the Province of British Columbia, <http://www.ubcic.bc.ca/Resources/final_report.htm#axzz4KF1C4tlr>

Merkur D, 'Breath-Soul and Wind Owner: The Many and the One in Inuit Religion' (1983) 7 *American Indian Quarterly* 23

Miller JR, *Compact, Contract, Covenant: Aboriginal Treaty-Making in Canada* (University of Toronto Press, 2009)

_____ *Skyscrapers Hide the Heavens: A History of Indian-white Relations in Canada* (University of Toronto Press, 2000).

Miller RJ and others, *Discovering Indigenous Lands: The Doctrine of Discovery in the English Colonies* (Oxford University Press, 2010)

Mills A, *Eagle Down is Our Law: Witsuwit'en Law, Feasts and Land Claims* (UBC Press, 1994)

Mills A, ed. *Hang Onto These Words: Johnny David's Delgamuukw Evidence* (University of Toronto Press, 2005)

Ministry of Aboriginal Affairs, 'Report on Indian Reserves' in *Papers Connected with the Indian Land Question, 1850-1875* (Victoria, 1875) 11

Mintz Max, *Seeds of Empire: The American Revolutionary Conquest of the Iroquois* (NYU Press, 1999)

Morgan HL, *League of the Ho-De-No-Sau-Nee or Iroquois* (Sage, 1851)

Morris A, *The Treaties of Canada with the Indians of Manitoba and the North-West Territories, Including the Negotiations on Which They were Based, and other Information Relating Thereto*, (Saskatoon, Fifth House Publishers, 1991) 202

Morse BW, 'Permafrost Rights: Aboriginal Self-Government and the Supreme Court in R. v. Pamajewon' (1997) 42 *McGill Law Journal* 1011

Napoleon V and Friedland H, 'Indigenous Legal Traditions: Roots to Renaissance', in Dubber MD, and Hörnle T, *The Oxford Handbook of Criminal Law* (Oxford University Press, 2014)

Napoleon V, 'Ayook: Gitksan Legal Order, Law and Legal Theory' (Ph.D. Dissertation, University of Victoria Faculty of Law, 2009) <http://dspace.library.uvic.ca:8080/bitstream/handle/1828/1392/napoleon%20dissertation%20April%2026-09.pdf?sequence=1>

O'Reilly-Scanlon K, Crowe K and Weenie A, 'Pathways to Understanding: Wahkohtowin as a research methodology' (2004) 39 *McGill Journal of Education*, 1, 29

Paul D, *We Were Not Savages*, First Nations History <http://www.danielnpaul.com/Mi'kmaqCulture.html>

Paxton J, *Joseph Brant and His World: 18th Century Mohawk Warrior and Statesman* (Lorimer, 2008) 47-76

Prosper K and others, 'Returning to Netukulimk: Mi'kmaq Cultural and Spiritual Connections with Resource Stewardship and Self-Governance' (2011) 2(4) *The International Indigenous Policy Journal*

Ray A, 'Fur Trade History and the Gitksan and Wet'suwet'en Comprehensive Claim: Men of Property and the Exercise of Title' in Abel K and Friesen J eds, *Aboriginal Resource Use in Canada: Historical and Legal Aspects* (University of Manitoba Press, 1990) 301-15

_____ *I Have Lived Here Since the World Began: An Illustrated History of Canada's Native Peoples* (Lester Publishing, 1996)

_____ Miller JR and Tough F, *Bounty and Benevolence: A History of Saskatchewan Treaties* (McGill-Queen's Press, 2000)

_____ Trial document Ex. 964-5, 1(87)

Ronda J, 'We Are Well As We Are': An Indian Critique of Seventeenth-Century Christian Missions, (1977) 34 *William and Mary Quarterly* 66-82

Ross A, *The Red River Settlement: Its Rise, Progress, and Present State* (Ross and Haines, 1957) 249–50

Rotman L, 'Taking Aim at the Canons of Treaty Interpretation in Canadian Aboriginal Rights Jurisprudence' (1997) 46 *University of New Brunswick Law Journal* 1

Royal Commission on Aboriginal Peoples, *Partners in Confederation: Aboriginal Peoples, Self-Government and the Constitution* (Ottawa: Ministry of Supply and Services Canada, 1993)

Royal Commission on Aboriginal Peoples, *Report of the Royal Commission on Aboriginal Peoples, Looking Forward, Looking Back, Vol. 1* (Ottawa: Ministry of Supply and Services, 1996)

Royal Commission on Aboriginal Peoples, *Report of the Royal Commission on Aboriginal Peoples: Perspectives and Realities, Vol. 4* (Ottawa: Ministry of Supply and Services, 1996) 'Métis Perspectives' 199

Sable T and Francis B, *The Language of this Land* (Cape Breton University Press, 2012) 17-25

Sakej Henderson, 'First Nations' Legal Inheritances: The Mikmaq Model' (1995) 23 *Manitoba Law Journal* 12

_____ 'Ayukpachi: Empowering Aboriginal Thought' in Marie Batiste, Reclaiming Indigenous Voice and Vision (UBC Press, 2000) 264

_____ 'Mikmaw Tenure in Atlantic Canada' (1995) 18 *Dalhousie Law Journal* 196, 220-221

Schenck T, *The Voice of the Crane Echoes Afar* (Routledge, 1997)

_____ and Peers L eds, *My First Years in the Fur Trade* (McGill-Queen's University Press, 2002) 71

Fried M, *The Evolution of Political Society: An Essay in Political Anthropology* (Random House, 1967) 83

Shannon T, 'Iroquoia' in Hoxie F ed, *The Oxford Handbook of American Indian History* (Oxford University Press, 2016) 199, 211

Sioui G, *Huron-Wendat. The Heritage of the Circle* (UBC Press, 1999)

Slattery B, 'First Nations and the Constitution' (1992) 71 Canadian Bar Review 261

Sloan K, *The Community Conundrum: Metis Critical Perspectives on the Application of R v Powley in British Columbia* (Ph.D. dissertation, University of Victoria, Faculty of Law, 2016 [unpublished])

Snyder E, Napoleon V, Borrows J, 'Gender and Violence: Drawing on Indigenous Legal Resources' (2014) 47 *University of British Columbia Law Review* 593

Starna W, 'Retrospecting the Origins of the League of the Iroquois' (2008) 152 *Proceedings of the American Philosophical Society* 279

Statement of Treaty Issues: Treaties as a Bridge to the Future (Saskatoon, Office of the Treaty Commissioner, 1998) 74

Stone T, 'Making Law for the Spirits: Angakkuit, Revelation and Rulemaking in the Canadian Arctic' (2010) 57 *Numen* 127, 131

Strickland R, *Fire and the Spirits: Cherokee Law from Clan to Court* (University of Oklahoma Press, 1982)

Teir JA, *Part VII—The Shuswap, The Jesup North Pacific Expedition: Memoir of the American Museum of Natural History,* (Franz Boas ed, Vol. 2, AMS Press, 1975)

Tennant P, *Aboriginal Peoples and Politics: Indian Land Question in British Columbia, 1849-1989* (UBC Press, 1990)

Thatcher BB, *Indian Biography* (Vol. 2, Werner, 1841) 76-77

Trigger BG, *The Children of Aataentsic: A History of the Huron People to 1600* (McGill-Queen's Press, 1976) 30

Truer A, *The Assassination of Hole in the Day* (Borealis Books, 2011) 9-34

Wallace A, *Tuscarora: A History* (SUNY Press, 2012)

Warren W, *History of the Ojibway of Lake Superior* (Minnesota Historical Society, 1885; reprinted Minneapolis: Ross & Haines, 1970) 219

Webber J, *The Constitution of Canada A Contextual Analysis* (Hart Publishing, 2015)

White R, *The Middle Ground: Indians, Empires, and Republics in the Great Lakes Region, 1650-1815* (Cambridge University Press, 1991) 37-40

Williams P, *The Chain* (LL.M. Thesis [unpublished], York University, 1982) 83

Williams Jr. RA, 'Gendered Checks and Balances: Understanding the Legacy of White Patriarchy in an American Indian Cultural Context' (1990) 24:4 *Georgia Law Review* 1019

_____ *The American Indian in Western Legal Thought: The Discourses of Conquest* (Oxford University Press, 1990)

Woolf D, *The Social Circulation of the Past,* (Oxford University Press, 2003)

B. French-Canadians and the Constitution

CHAPTER 3

....

CONSTITUTIONAL DEBATES
IN FRENCH CANADA,
1764–1774

....

MICHEL MORIN*

Are the Canadian inhabitants desirous of having assemblies in the province?—Certainly not

Governor Guy Carleton, 1774[1]

1. INTRODUCTION

....

IN 1760, at least 60,000 persons inhabited the territory called "New France," concentrated
in the St. Lawrence Valley ("Canada" properly said). These Catholics of French descent
(with very few exceptions) were surrounded by Aboriginal peoples, who were generally
considered allies rather than subjects of the King.[2] On 8 September, the Capitulation of
Montreal marked the beginning of a period of debates concerning the legal regime applicable to the new colony. At first, the integration of francophone and Catholic inhabitants

* Michel Morin, Full Professor, Faculty of Law, University of Montreal. Research for this chapter was
made possible by a grant of the Marcel-Faribault fund of the University of Montreal. The author wishes to
express his gratitude to Mr. Mathieu Vaugeois and Mrs. Stéphanie-Alexandra LoVasco, LLM candidates
of the Faculty of Law, University of Montreal, for their research assistance, as well as to his colleague Jean
Leclair and to Dr Hannah Weiss Muller for their thoughtful comments on a previous version. As always,
he is entirely responsible for any error or omission. This chapter is a slightly modified version of "The
Discovery and Assimilation of British Constitutional Law Principles in Quebec, 1764–1774" (2013) 36(2)
Dalhousie Law Journal 581–616.
  [1] Henry Cavendish, *Debates of the House of Commons in the Year 1774 on the Bill for Making a More
Effectual Provision for the Government of the Province of Quebec* (SR Publishers, Johnson Reprint, 1966) at 105.
  [2] See among others Luc Huppé, "L'établissement de la souveraineté européenne au Canada" (2009) 50
Cahiers de Droit 153; Michel Morin, "Des nations libres sans territoire? Les Autochtones et la colonisation
de l'Amérique française du XVIe au XVIIIe siècle" (2010) 12 *Journal of the History of International Law* 1.

in the British Empire—the so-called "new subjects"—did not seem to be problematic. Both in Great Britain and in the colonies, most people felt that major public offices must be reserved for Anglicans and that all colonists should enjoy such rights as trial by jury, habeas corpus, representative institutions, and freedom of speech.[3] British constitutional rights were also conceived as the antithesis of the subjection allegedly imposed by French kings.[4]

Many Americans believed as well that an Imperial Constitution founded on usage and custom curtailed the powers of the British Parliament, although this implicit limit remained highly controversial.[5] Non-Christians were generally considered incapable of enjoying political rights. As for Catholics, their status varied.[6] In Ireland and in Nova Scotia, they were subject to the discriminatory laws of Great Britain, but where the British represented a small fraction of the population, such as in Minorca or Gibraltar, they held important public functions and retained their own legal system, including the Criminal Law.[7]

In 1763, the *Royal Proclamation* created the Province of Quebec.[8] Anxious to encourage its "speedy settling," the King declared that "so soon as the state and circumstances" would "admit," the Governor and his Council would summon an assembly, following

[3] See, notably, Elizabeth Mancke, "Colonial and Imperial Contexts" in Philip Girard, Jim Phillips and Barry Cahill (eds) *The Supreme Court of Nova Scotia, 1754–2004: From Imperial Bastion to Provincial Oracle* (University of Toronto Press, 2004) 30 at 31; Peter James Marshall, *The Making and Unmaking of Empires: Britain, India, and America c. 1750–1783* (Oxford University Press, 2005) at 160.

[4] See Karl David Milobar, *The Constitutional Development of Quebec from the Time of the French Regime to the Canada Act of 1791* (PhD Thesis, University of London, 1990) [unpublished] at 23–28 [hereinafter Milobar, Thesis]; and Karl David Milobar, "The Origins of British-Quebec Merchant Ideology: New France, the British Atlantic and the Constitutional Periphery, 1720–1770" (1996) 24:3 *Journal of Imperial and Constitutional History* 264–390.

[5] See Jack P. Greene, *The Constitutional Origins of the American Revolution* (Cambridge University Press, 2010) at 50–55; Jack P. Greene, "1759: The Perils of Success" in Philip Buckner & John G. Reid (eds), *Revisiting 1759: The Conquest of Canada in Historical Perspective* (University of Toronto Press, 2012) at 95; see also Daniel J. Hulsebosch, *Constituting Empire: New York and the Transformation of Constitutionalism in the Atlantic World* (University of North Carolina Press, 2005).

[6] Marshall, above (n 3) at 193–195 & 201–02.

[7] Peter Marshall, "The Incorporation of Quebec in the British Empire" in Virginia Bever Platt & David Curtis Skaggs, *Of Mother Country and Plantations: Proceedings of the Twenty-Seventh Conference in Early American History* (Bowling Green State University Press, 1971) at 43–63; Thomas Garden Barnes, "'The Dayly Cry for Justice': The Juridical Failure of the Annapolis Royal Regime, 1713–1749" in Philip Girard & Jim Phillips (eds), *Essays in the History of Canadian Law, Nova Scotia*, vol 3 (University of Toronto Press for the Osgoode Society, 1990) at 10; Jacques Vanderlinden, "À propos de l'introduction de la common law en Nouvelle-Écosse (1710–1749)" (2008) 10 *Revue de la common law en français* 81; John G. Reid & Elizabeth Mancke, "From Global Processes to Continental Strategies: The Emergence of British North America to 1783" in Philip Buckner (ed), *Canada and the British Empire* (Oxford University Press, 2008) at 22; Hannah Weiss Muller, *An Empire of Subjects: Unities and Disunities in the British Empire, 1760–1790* (PhD Thesis, Princeton University, 2010); Stephen Conway, "The Consequences of the Conquest: Quebec and British Politics, 1760–1774" in Buckner & Reid, above (n 5) at 141; Heather Welland, "Commercial Interests and Political Allegiance: The Origins of the Quebec Act," in Buckner & Reid, above (n 5) at 166; Barry M. Moody, "Delivered from All Your Distresses: The Fall of Quebec and the Remaking of Nova Scotia" in Buckner & Reid, above (n 5) at 218.

[8] Adam Shortt & Arthur Doughty (eds), *Documents Relating to the Constitutional History of Canada, 1759–1791*, 2d ed, Part I (King's Printer, 1918) at 7 (Capitulation of 1760), 97 (Treaty of Paris of 1763) & 163 (Royal Proclamation) [hereinafter *CD I*].

the practice of other colonies in British America. Local legislation should strive to be "as near as may be agreeable to the Laws of England." In "the mean Time," all inhabitants of the new province were promised "the Benefit" of these laws, while Courts constituted by the Council were to determine "all Causes, as well Criminal as Civil, according to Law and Equity, and as near as may be agreeable to the Laws of England." As it happened, an assembly was never summoned. Confronted with a population composed of roughly 95 percent French-speaking Catholics, the Governors refused to call elections in which only Protestant subjects would be eligible, as only British-born or "old" subjects would qualify, as well as a handful of Protestants living in New France prior to 1760.[9] In large measure, the introduction of English law was also delayed in civil matters.[10]

Historians often assume that the inhabitants of New France had a distinct identity. Recent research, however, has shown that they considered themselves to be, first and foremost, French subjects, although Denys Delâge has provided much evidence supporting the opposite view.[11] Following the Conquest, they had to redefine their identity and call themselves "Canadians," at a time when the relationship between the British Empire and its colonies was in a state of flux.[12] Indeed, conquered peoples who requested reforms often relied deftly on their rights as British subjects. Meanwhile, colonial authorities tried to rally the elites until it was possible to impose effectively British institutions.[13]

When discussing such issues, it is important to eschew a deterministic vision of the Conquest of New France, which has often been considered the distant cause of the socio-economic retardation of Quebec in the 1960s. For some, this was due to the decimation of the francophone elite (the clergy, the nobility, the seigneurs, merchants, and the more successful professionals, such as notaries, surveyors, etc.); others blamed the prolonged

[9] The Commission of the Governor required him to ensure that all members of the Assembly swear the Test Acts in force in Great Britain, which no Catholic could do in conscience, Shortt & Doughty, *ibid* at 175.

[10] See text accompanying note 110 below.

[11] See Denys Delâge, "Les Premières Nations et la Guerre de la Conquête (1754–1765)", (2009) 63 *Les Cahiers des dix* 1; Denys Delâge, "La peur de 'passer pour des Sauvages'," (2011) 65 *Les Cahiers des dix* 1; those denying the existence of a distinct identity at this stage include Christophe Horguelin, "Le XVIIIe siècle des Canadiens: discours public et identité" in Philippe Joutard & Thomas Wien, *Mémoires de Nouvelle-France, De France en Nouvelle-France* (Presses Universitaires de Rennes, 2005) at 209; Louise Dechêne, *Le Peuple, l'État et la Guerre au Canada sous le Régime français* (Boréal, 2008) at 438; John A. Dickinson, "L'héritage laissé par la France au Canada en 1763" in Serge Joyal & Paul-André Linteau (eds), *France-Canada-Québec 400 ans de relations d'exceptions* (Presses de l'Université de Montréal, 2008) at 39; Colin M. Coates, "French Canadians' Ambivalence to the British Empire" in Philip Buckner (ed), *Canada and the British Empire* (Oxford University Press, 2008) at 181.

[12] Nancy Christie, "Introduction: Theorizing a Colonial Past," in Nancy Christie (ed), *Transatlantic Subjects: Ideas, Institutions and Identities in Post-Revolutionary British North America* (McGill-Queen's University Press, 2008) at 3 *et seq.*

[13] See Marshall, above (n 3); Muller, above (n 7); some groups or individuals can adhere more quickly to the institutions of the conquering nation or use them selectively: Laura Benton, *Law and Colonial Cultures: Legal Regimes in World History, 1400–1900* (Cambridge University Press, 2002).

survival of ancien régime structures.[14] In general, the idea that francophone persons had little interest for a representative assembly at this early stage seems plausible, as nothing similar existed in France or in New France.[15] Furthermore, the vast majority of the population derived their subsistence from agriculture and had little or no education. Louise Dechêne has also observed that there were no urban riots in the colony, contrary to what occurred in France.[16] A similar indifference might be expected towards the cherished rights of British subjects, which had to be found in a constitution that was mostly unwritten. According to British administrators, Canadians were indifferent to these privileges, a statement that has seldom been questioned in the historiography.[17]

For instance, in 1774, Governor Carleton, Francis Maseres (a former Attorney General of Quebec), and Chief Justice William Hey stated before a House of Commons Committee that most or all Canadians had no interest in an Assembly but were quite satisfied with the introduction of English Criminal Law.[18] Therefore, in 1774, the *Quebec Act* reinstated the rules relating to property and civil rights that were applicable in New France, but retained English Criminal Law. The King could now appoint the members

---

[14] See, generally, Charles-Philippe Courtois (ed), *La Conquête, une anthologie* (Typo, 2009); and the papers by Michel Bock, Brian Young, Nicole Neatby & Jocelyn Létourneau in Philip Buckner & John G. Reid (eds), *Remembering 1759: The Conquest of Canada in Historical Memory* (University of Toronto Press, 2012).

[15] Christian Blais, "La représentation en Nouvelle-France," (2009) 18:1 *Bulletin d'histoire politique* 51–75; Gustave Lanctôt, *L'administration de la Nouvelle-France* (Honoré Champion, 1929).

[16] Dechêne, above (n 11) at 268–269.

[17] See among others Henry Brun, *La formation des institutions parlementaires québécoises, 1791–1838* (Presses de l'Université Laval, 1970) at 10; Marcel Trudel, *La Révolution américaine, Pourquoi la France refuse le Canada* (Boréal Express, 1976) at 68; Philip Lawson, *The Imperial Challenge: Quebec and Britain in the American Revolution* (McGill-Queen's University Press, 1989) at 75–76 & 111; Milobar Thesis, above (n 4) at 107 & 159; Jacques-Yvan Morin & José Woehrling, *Les constitutions du Canada et du Québec—du Régime français à nos jours* (Les Éditions Thémis, 1992) at 43 & 49; Denis Vaugeois, *Québec 1792: Les acteurs, les institutions et les frontières* (Fides, 1992) at 32–38; Jean-Paul De Lagrave, *L'époque de Voltaire au Canada* (L'Étincelle, 1994) at 71–73; Yvan Lamonde, *Histoire sociale des idées au Québec, 1760–1896* (Fides, 2000) at 70–71; Michael Dorland & Maurice Charland, *Law, Rhetoric and Irony in the Formation of Canadian Civil Culture* (University of Toronto Press, 2002) at 98 & 127–133; Michel Ducharme, *The Idea of Liberty in Canada during the Age of Atlantic Revolutions, 1776–1838* (McGill-Queen's University Press, 2014); Muller, above (n 7) at 107 & 118–119. A notable exception is the unpublished dissertation of Pierre Tousignant: *La genèse et l'avènement de l'Acte constitutionnel de 1791* (PhD Thesis, Université de Montréal, 1971) for instance at 23–40; Hilda Neatby also systematically relates the initiatives of a political nature taken by francophone subjects in *Quebec, The Revolutionary Age, 1760–1791* (McClelland & Stewart, 1966) notably at 127–133.

[18] Cavendish, above (n 1) at 105–106 (Carleton), 124–125 (Maseres) & 160 (Hey). There were very few criticisms of the English criminal law, but almost no evidence that it was universally admired in the colony: see André Morel, "La réception du droit criminel anglais au Québec (1760–1892)" (1978) 13 *Revue juridique Thémis* 449. Statistics on convictions and executions were quite similar prior to and after the Conquest. Before the King's Bench, anglophone plaintiffs or victims were also over-represented; francophone accused were systematically tried by mixed juries, which was not the case for anglophones. Finally, seigneurs despised trial by jury: Douglas Hay, "The Meanings of the Criminal Law in Quebec, 1764–1774" in Louis A. Knafla (ed), *Crime and Criminal Justice in Europe and Canada* (Wilfrid Laurier University Press, 1981) at 77. These differences are much less pronounced before justices of the peace, which try misdemeanours: see Donald Fyson, *Magistrates, Police and People: Everyday Criminal Justice in Quebec and Lower Canada, 1764–1837* (University of Toronto Press for The Osgoode Society, 2006).

of the Legislative Council, with no power of taxation, except for local works; ordinances touching on religion or providing for a sentence of imprisonment exceeding three months had to be approved by the King.[19]

Prior to the adoption of this legislation, how could members of the francophone elite familiarize themselves with the fundamental rules of British Law and use them to their advantage? What information was available to them? In Quebec, there seems to exist few manuscripts allowing us to answer these questions. In any case, they would represent only the views of a small number of literate persons.[20] From 1764 to 1774, however, the bilingual *Quebec Gazette/La Gazette de Québec* (hereinafter the "*Gazette*") contained a lot of information on these issues; it could be supplemented with other sources, such as books and foreign or colonial periodicals.[21] During this period, the ideas of the Enlightenment are generally thought to have been absent from Quebec.[22] But the *Gazette* kept its readers informed of current developments in France, where this new way of thinking was steadily gaining ground and sparked off many political controversies. It also opened a window on the British "Atlantic world" and on debates concerning the rights of British subjects in England and the Empire. The premises of a public sphere were therefore present, although there was as yet no mass movement claiming to represent public opinion in an overt attempt to influence governmental decisions.[23]

Though there is no conclusive evidence about this, we assume that the ideas disseminated in the press or other publications found their way in the political discourse of "Canadians". For them, the religious issue—the possibility for Catholics to hold positions of trust in the colonial government—was no doubt dominant, but they were interested in their new constitutional rights.[24] To reflect the variety of issues that were being discussed between 1764 and 1774, the chapter will be divided into two sections. First, we will examine the reports published in the *Gazette* concerning constitutional debates occurring in France, England, and the British Colonies, in order to ascertain what a

---

[19] *An Act for making more effectual Provision for the Government of the Province of Quebec in North America*, 1774 (UK), 14 Geo III, c 83 [hereinafter *Quebec Act*]; there is a vast literature on this Act; see, for instance, Philip Lawson, *The Imperial Challenge, Quebec and Britain in the American Revolution* (McGill-Queen's University Press, 1989); Hilda Neatby, *The Quebec Act: Protest and Policy* (Prentice-Hall of Canada, 1972); Karen Stanbridge, "Quebec and the Irish Catholic Relief Act of 1778: An Institutional Approach" (2003) 16:3 *Journal of Historical Sociology* 375; Michel Morin, "Les débats concernant le droit français et le droit anglais antérieurement à l'adoption de l'*Acte de Québec* de 1774" (2014) 44 *Revue de droit de l'Université de Sherbrooke* 259–306.

[20] It is estimated that only 4 percent of the population could read: Maurice Lemire (ed), *La vie littéraire au Québec Tome 1 (1764–1805): La voix française des nouveaux sujets britanniques*, vol I (Presses de l'Université Laval, 1991) at 82.

[21] *Quebec Gazette/La Gazette de Québec*, printed by Brown & Gilmore (1764–1850), Ottawa, National Archibes of Canada (NLC reels N-25-N38). All subsequent references to the *Gazette* are from this source.

[22] See for instance Lagrave, above (n 17) at 71–73; Lamonde, above (n 17) at 70–71; and Ducharme, above (n 17).

[23] David Zaret, *Origins of Democratic Culture, Printing, Petitions and the Public Sphere in Early-Modern England* (Princeton University Press, 2000) at 14–15.

[24] For the religious debates see Neatby, above (n 19).

francophone reader could learn about Imperial Constitutional Law (Section 2).[25] Next, we will try to document the reception and acceptance of these principles in the political and legal discourse of the time, as well as the strategies chosen by members of the francophone elite to preserve some fundamental aspects of their identity and culture (Section 3). [26]

2. Constitutional Debates in France, Great-Britain, and the British Empire, 1764–1774

Prior to the Conquest there was no printing, nor a tradition of large-scale petitioning for political grievances in New France. Starting in 1764, the *Gazette* (which was founded by a relative of Benjamin Franklin) published governmental documents, news reports (lifted mostly from British and colonial newspapers, perhaps with some taken directly from French Gazettes), letters to the editor, and commercial or personal advertisements, which occasionally contained political opinions. There were 148 subscribers out of approximately 70,000 inhabitants, though at the time, one copy was normally used by multiple readers.[27] Curates in parishes were required to read aloud recently adopted colonial ordinances after mass.[28] One would expect justices of the peace and legal professionals to have been subscribers as well. Thus, the information contained in the *Gazette* did circulate in the countryside, like secular books.[29] Another important

[25] This is an abridged version of Michel Morin, "La découverte du droit constitutionnel dans une colonie francophone: la Gazette de Québec, 1764–1774" (2013) 47:2 *Revue juridique Thémis* 319 [hereinafter Morin, "Découverte"].

[26] This is a condensed version of Michel Morin, "Les revendications des nouveaux sujets, francophones et catholiques, de la Province de Québec, 1764–1774" in Blaine Baker & Donald Fyson (eds), *Essays in the History of Canadian Law: Quebec and the Canadas* (Osgoode Society for Canadian Legal History and University of Toronto Press, 2013) at 131 [hereinafter Morin, "Revendications"].

[27] Lemire, above (n 20) at 212–215 & 227–231. In France, around 1760, about 12 000 copies of the official *Gazette de France* were printed each week; 3,000 copies of various Gazettes were sold, each circulating in many hands: Gilles Feyel, *L'Annonce et la Nouvelle, La presse d'information en France sous l'Ancien Régime (1630–1788)* (Voltaire Foundation, 2000) at 531–545; Jack R. Censer, *The French Press in the Age of Enlightenment* (Routledge, 1994) at 11–12 & 184. In England, about 20,000 copies of newspapers were printed daily, with a number of readers or listeners 5 to 10 times higher. Foreign newspaper reports were liberally used after being translated: Hannah Barker, *Newspapers, Politics and English Society, 1695–1855: Themes in British Social History* (Longman, 2000) at 46, 63, 105. Overall, very rough calculations show that the availability of copies was proportionally higher in Quebec than in Europe.

[28] *Quebec Gazette* (21 February 1765).

[29] Most books in rural areas belonged to the clergy, but some seigneurs or jurists also possessed secular works: Gilles Proulx, *Loisirs québécois: des livres et des cabarets, 1690–1760* (Service canadien des parcs, 1987) at 44–45.

feature of the *Gazette* was its bilingual character: each text (or almost) appeared in both languages.

The *Gazette* was similar to many British North-American papers. It was privately-run and was primarily a newspaper, with a pronounced interest in international and colonial issues and a section containing private advertisements.[30] In 1760, there were 42 printers in the British colonies; a few cities had 5 or more.[31] Personal relationships and business networks among colonial printers greatly facilitated the circulation of news reports.[32] According to Michael Warner, during the 1720s a public discourse appeared in the press. It assumed the presence of a community whose readers could oversee the decisions of public authorities.[33] In the mid-eighteenth century, in all major cities, local issues were also debated. As for the *Gazette*, it also served as the official vehicle for the publication of governmental documents such as ordinances, proclamations, Imperial statutes, etc. This could represent an important source of income; therefore, its editors could not totally alienate the Government.

Notwithstanding the need to maintain a good relationship with colonial admin-istrators, the editors of the *Gazette* made a large place for new ideas and criticism. In this regard, their paper was quite similar to the *Halifax Gazette*, which did not shy away from publishing controversial reports about events occurring in England or the colonies generally. On the other hand, the editor either suppressed infor-mation or comments on local matters that seemed controversial, or asked for the approval of the Provincial Secretary, unless he was reprinting a piece first published in London.[34]

To understand the importance of the information relayed by the *Gazette*, this sec-tion will recall the main political and constitutional issues discussed at the time. It will focus first on the challenges posed to royal authority in France (Subsection A). Next, the consolidation of constitutional rights in Great Britain will be examined (Subsection B). Finally, the claims of the American colonies to a greater autonomy will be discussed (Subsection C). Although these events are well known, the avail-ability of translated versions of news reports published in English outside of Quebec is not.[35]

---

[30] Patricia Lockhart Fleming, Gilles Gallichan & Yvan Lamonde (eds), *History of the Book in Canada. Beginnings to 1840*, vol 1 (University of Toronto Press, 2004) at 63–64, 72–75.

[31] Michael Warner, *Letters of the Republic: Publication and the Public Sphere in Eighteenth-Century America* (Harvard University Press, 1990) at 23.

[32] *Ibid* at 68.

[33] *Ibid* at 29–41.

[34] Dean Jobb, " 'The First That Was Ever Publish'd in the Province': John Bushell's *Halifax Gazette*, 1752–1761" (2008) 11 Journal of the Royal Nova Scotia Historical Society 1.

[35] One exception would be Pierre Tousignant's dissertation, see Tousignant, above (n 17) but he focuses on events occurring in Quebec.

A. The Contestation of Royal Authority in France

Beginning in 1764, readers of the *Gazette* could easily follow the burning controversies taking place in their former mother country, in which an absolutist conception of monarchy was being forcefully challenged. The ideal of a constitutional order superior to the King, with some immutable aspects restraining his powers, was asserted vigorously, but did not prevail. Nonetheless, during the second half of the eighteenth century, there was a call to reform French laws and institutions, using arguments based on reason and natural law. Montesquieus's *The Spirit of the Laws* appeared in 1748, whereas Rousseau's *Social Contract* was published in 1762.[36] Philosophers began criticizing the administration of justice.[37] Thus, Voltaire launched into a crusade to rehabilitate a Protestant who was unfairly sentenced to death and Beccaria criticizedthe immoderate use of the death penalty.[38] These authors were not widely known in Quebec, but a few high-ranking officials or jurists owned many of their books.[39]

In these days, the French king could order his subjects imprisoned by a simple administrative document, the lettre de cachet (sealed letter), in marked contrast to the protection of individual freedom afforded by the writ of habeas corpus. He could make laws or impose taxes of his own free will. The French *parlements* (which were actually courts of appeal) could delay the registration of an ordinance before them, an essential formality for the coming into force of royal legislation.[40] In this way, judges hoped to convince the king to modify the text or to abandon it, often publishing their "remonstrances."[41] Some

[36] Charles Louis de Secondat Monstesquieu, *De l'esprit des lois* (Barillot & fils, 1748); Jean-Jacques Rousseau, *Du contract social* (Marc Michel Rey, 1762).

[37] Élizabeth Badinter, *Les passions intellectuelles, III: Volonté de pouvoir (1762–1778)* (Fayard, Références le Livre de Poche, 2007) at 128–141 [hereinafter Badinter, *Volonté de pouvoir*].

[38] On the Calas affair, see for instance Élizabeth Badinter, *Les passions intellectuelles, II. Exigences de dignité (1751–1762)* (Fayard, Références le Livre de Poche, 2002) at 490–491 [hereinafter Badinter, *Exigences de dignité*]; Cesare Beccaria, *Traité des délits et des peines* (Lausanne: np, 1766) or (Philadelphia: np, 1766). The *Gazette* mentions the execution of the Chevalier de la Barre and the burning of the *Dictionnaire philosphique*, see *Quebec Gazette* (27 October 1766 & 16 February 1767). Other references are more superficial, see *Quebec Gazette* (25 April 1765); "Epitre de Monsieur Voltaire à Monsieur le Cardinal Querini [. . .]" (23 March 1767); (29 November 1767); "Ode par M. De Voltaire, à un Marchand de Bretagne, qui avoit nommé un de ses vaisseaux de son nom" (9 February 1769); (3 January 1771); "Lettre de Monsieur de Voltaire au Roi de Prusse" (4 July 1771); (28 November 1771). See also, Marcel Trudel, *Le siècle de Voltaire au Canada, de 1760 à 1850*, vol I (Les Publications de l'Université Laval, 1945) at 30, 39, 58–64.

[39] Mario Robert, "Le livre et la lecture dans la noblesse canadienne 1670–1764" (2002) 56:1 *Revue d'histoire de l'Amérique française* 3 at para 30; Nathalie Battershill, *Les bibliothèques privées sur l'île de Montréal, 1765–1790* (MA thesis, Université de Montréal, 1993) at 49–50 [unpublished]; Proulx, above (n 29) at 92 (Montaigne), 95 (Voltaire), 120 (Locke & Montesquieu); Lemire, above (n 20) at 90 (Montesquieu, Buffon, Rousseau, Voltaire).

[40] This was often the case for fiscal edicts; see *Quebec Gazette* (4 June 1767; 29 September 1768; 14 June 1770; 31 January 1771; 4 June 1772; 5 November 1772).

[41] See Jean-Louis Harouel et al., *Histoire des institutions de l'époque franque à la Révolution*, 6th ed (Presses Universitaires de France, 1994); John A Carey, *Judicial Reform in France before the Revolution of 1789* (Harvard University Press, 1981) at 9–10; Julian Swann, *Politics and the Parlement of Paris under Louis XV 1754–1774* (Cambridge University Press, 1995).

of these found their way to New France, as can be seen from the library of Guillaume Verrier, the Attorney General for the French king from 1728 to 1758 and the first person to teach law in the colony.[42] Though local judges never indulged in such political activity, we may suppose that jurists formed by Verrier knew about challenges to royal authority occurring in France.

In November 1763, after a royal edict seemed to invite suggestions for fiscal reforms, a flood of criticism was directed at the government. This was followed by an outright prohibition (in March 1764) to print anything relating to such issues, a fact which was noted in the *Gazette*.[43] Readers were also reminded that the Parliament of Paris or the King's Council ordered books to be burned.[44] Nowadays, we know that the director of the censorship bureau, Malesherbes, deliberately protected philosophers and turned a blind eye to their activities, partly to shield printers from foreign competition.[45] Be that as it may, officially, freedom of the press was not recognized in France.

The famous case of La Chalotais, Attorney General for the *parlement* of Brittany is illustrative of the challenges to royal authority reported in the *Gazette*. He was exiled in another part of the kingdom for having criticized the commander-in-chief of his province. Members of this *parlement* then resigned to protest this decision, and some fiscal measures, but the king replaced them all. Other *parlements* rallied in support, arguing that they were emanations or classes derived from the first general court of the kingdom and, as such, depositaries of the rights of the nation.[46] In 1766, the king declared bluntly that he alone held "the legislative power, without dependency or sharing" and that the "Rights or Interests of the Nation, which some dare to make a separate body from the monarch" were "necessarily united into his hands."[47] Soon after, in the *Gazette*, a "Champion Of the Rights of Nature" complained that the coronation

[42]   See Claude Vachon, "Louis-Guillaume, Verrier," online: *Dictionnary of Canadian Biography* http://www.biographi.ca (last accessed: 28-03-2017); Edouard-Fabre Surveyer, "Louis-Guillaume Verrier (1690–1758)" (1952) 6:2 *Revue d'histoire de l'Amérique française* 159–176; and, *Inventaire des biens de feu Me Guillaume Verrier, Conseiller du Roy son Procureur Général au Conseil Supérieur de Québec* (5 octobre 1755), Québec, Archives du Séminaire de Québec, Centre d'histoire de l'Amérique française (Polygraphie 15, no 81, fos. 33, 48–51).

[43]   Arnaud Decroix, *Question fiscale et réforme financière en France (1749–1789). Logique de la transparence et recherche de la confiance publique* (Presses Universitaires d'Aix-Marseille, 2006) at 227–304; *Quebec Gazette* (23 August 1764).

[44]   "Une réponse à l'auteur de l'Anti-financier," *Quebec Gazette* (27 September 1764); *Quebec Gazette* (19 July 1764, religious controversy; 4 April 1765); Élizabeth Badinter, *Les passions intellectuelles, I. Désirs de gloire (1735–1751)* (Paris: Références le Livre de Poche, Fayard, 1999) at 78–83, 345, 416 & 499; Badinter, *Exigences de dignité*, above (n 38), at 456, 538, 551–552; Badinter, *Volonté de pouvoir*, above (n 31) at 217–218; Swann, above (n 41) at 24.

[45]   See Raymond Birn, *La censure royale des livres dans la France des Lumières* (Odile Jacob, 2007) at 70–88.

[46]   See Harouel, above (n 41) at 531–533, 499–500; Swann, above (n 41) at 251 *et seq*; *Quebec Gazette* (19 June 1766; 14 May 1767; 21 May 1767; 28 May 1767; 15 October 1767; 30 August 1770; 13 December 1770; 20 December 1770).

[47]   See the excerpt in Daniel Teyssiere, "Un modèle autoritaire: le discours de la 'flagellation'" (1995) 43 *Mots* 118 at 126–127; [translated by author].

oath was understood as authorizing the "enslaving" of the people and as requiring a "blind Obedience" to ministers who acted as "Instruments for plaguing and oppressing Mankind."[48] This was an "Insult offered to common Sense."

In 1770, the conflict entered a new phase, which was also well covered by the *Gazette*. The king forbade references to the theory of classes or the cessation of the *parlements*' activities. Nonetheless, the *parlement* of Paris did just that, asserting that the letter and spirit of the constitution of France had been violated in an attempt to change the form of government.[49] For their pains, the king exiled them to barely inhabited villages and subsequently confiscated their offices; other *parlements* suffered the same fate.[50] As he explained to the *parlement* of Bordeaux, "obedience is a duty imposed by all the laws," for he was the "sole legislator in this Kingdom, independent and undivided" who alone had "the right of putting the antient laws in execution, of interpreting them, of abolishing them, and of making new ones" if necessary for "the good of the State."[51]

The *Gazette* also published a letter addressed to the princes of royal blood who challenged this conception of royal authority. For the authors, "the Constitution of the Government and the Rights of the People are attacked" and "the Laws, Forms and Parliaments, established for securing the Honor, the Lives and Fortunes of the Citizens, are destroyed."[52] In these circumstances, the "Nobility would immediately have the Privilege of assembling themselves." Though the "Nation" did not think of meeting while the Parliaments existed, it did not "forfeit its Right" to do so. However, the authors hoped that the king would soon restore "the Constitution with which the Nation was satisfied." The famous remonstrances of Malesherbes are to the same effect.[53] The convocation of the General Estates and the French Revolution are lurking here.

Another letter addressed to the sovereign appeared in the *Gazette*:

> It is not then the Sovereign: It is the law, Sire, that ought to reign over the people. You are only its minister and first depositary—it is the law that ought to regulate the exercise of authority; and it is by the law that this authority is no longer a yoke to the subjects, but a rule that guides them; a help that protects them; a paternal watchfulness, that secures their submission, only because it secures their love.[54]

In 1771, the *Gazette* reported that there were riots in France and talks of refusing to pay taxes; numerous persons were imprisoned, some for having printed criticism of the

---

[48] "To the Printers," *Quebec Gazette* (26 June 1766).

[49] *Quebec Gazette* (3 January 1771; 31 January 1771; 21 March 1771; 2 May 1771); see also Badinter, *Volonté de pouvoir*, above (n 37) at 236–237.

[50] *Quebec Gazette* (23 May 1771, supp.; 30 May 1771; 13 June 1771; 25 July 1771; 10 October 1771; 2 January 1772; 23 January 1772; 13 February 1772). Some magistrates died in exile: Swann, above (n 41) at 299 & 302.

[51] *Quebec Gazette* (21 March 1771).

[52] "From the AMSTERDAM GAZETTE, Paris, March 18," *Quebec* Gazette (19 September 1771); Swann, above (n 41) at 358.

[53] Badinter, *Volonté de pouvoir*, above (n 37) at 248–251; Swann, above (n 41) at 358.

[54] *Quebec Gazette* (26 September 1771).

king. According to a London article, ministers apprehended a civil war.[55] The author exclaimed, in relation to the English people: "Happy then that Nation, whose liberties are preserved sacred and inviolable."[56] Though French philosophers were divided at the time, in October, everything seemed quiet. One observer opined that the reform was taking root, as the former courts were abolished because of their injustice and venality.[57] Indeed, the new ones functioned relatively well, until Louis the XVI recalled the *parlements* in 1774.[58]

The *Gazette* thus offered a striking image of the unremitting grip of the absolute monarchy in France. As for former *Canadiens* who decided to remain in Quebec, the French Crown finally paid only 25 percent of the face value of "card money," the currency used in New France.[59] Many military officers, generally nobles, found no employment in the French army and returned to Quebec.[60] In these conditions, the privileges inhering to British subjects may have seemed quite advantageous to readers of the *Gazette*.[61]

B. The Consolidation of Constitutional Rights in Great Britain

In the early years of the reign of King George III (1760–1820), the *Gazette* related the stringent criticism of the government and controversial litigation, such as prosecutions against printers for seditious libel or against government officials for acting unlawfully. By doing this, it allowed francophone readers to better understand their new rights as British subjects. This was especially true of the tribulations of John Wilkes, a Francophile Member of Parliament who briefly considered becoming "Governor of Canada" but

---

[55] *Quebec Gazette* (12 September 1771; 19 September 1771; 2 January 1772); see also, concerning a pretended crisis in Britanny, *ibid* (26 September 1771). According to Badinter, *Volonté de pouvoir*, it seemed as though Paris was ready to explode at the time, above (n 37) at 252; see also George Rudé, *The Crowd in History, A Study of Popular Disturbances in France and England, 1730–1848* (New York & London: John Wiley & Sons, 1964) at 50.

[56] *Quebec Gazette* (12 September 1771; see also 26 December 1771).

[57] *Quebec Gazette* (27 February 1772); Badinter, *Volonté de pouvoir*, above (n 37) 254–262; Swann, above (n 41) at 360.

[58] Harouel, above (n 41) at 533–536 fn 501–503; Carey, above (n 41) at 93–99; *Quebec Gazette* (11 October 1770; 13 June 1771).

[59] See *Quebec Gazette* (18 October 1764; 1 November 1764; 22 November 1764; 29 November 1764; 30 May 1765; 24 October 1771; 30 January 1772; 4 June 1772; 13 August 1772).

[60] Robert Larin & Yves Drolet, "Les listes de Carleton et de Haldimand. États de la noblesse canadienne en 1768 et en 1778" (2008) 41:82 Social History 563.

[61] France was absolutely not interested in regaining its former colony: Françoise Le Jeune, "La France et le Canada du milieu du XVIIIe siècle au milieu du XIXe siècle: Cession ou Conquête?" in Serge Joyal & Paul-André Linteau (eds) *France-Canada-Québec 400 ans de relations d'exceptions* (Presses de l'Université de Montréal, 2008) 57; François-Joseph Ruggiu, "Falling into Oblivion? Canada and the French Monarchy" in Buckner & Reid, above (n 5) 69.

eventually decided to lead the opposition.[62] Arrested in 1763 for publishing a vitriolic pamphlet against the king, he was released following a habeas corpus petition.[63] He was also awarded punitive damages by a jury after an illegal search of his house.[64] This highlighted to Quebec readers the power of juries, except in contempt of court proceedings.[65] For instance, a London letter complained of "arbitrary Ministers" who opposed freedom of the press, which acted as "a Check upon their tyranny."[66] Without trial by jury, this "Great and solemn Privilege of Englishmen" inherited from "virtuous and spirited Ancestors," England's liberties, and the "blessings which it boasts above other Nations," would be lost. The people would become the "Slaves of a Minister." Another author added: "Can our Liberties be secure, when that great and essential one of the PRESS is daily attacked, and PRINTERS and Book-sellers are so terrified by uncommon Rigour, that they will neither print nor publish? Can our Liberties be secure, if that highest and most valuable of all our Liberties, a JURY, be taken from us?"[67]

After fleeing to France, Wilkes returned in 1768 and was sentenced to two years in jail and a £1,000 fine.[68] He was elected three times to the House of Commons, but expelled thereafter; the third time, his closest opponent was declared elected. All these events were immensely controversial and well publicized in England, in America, and in the *Gazette*. Celebrations were organized in his honour, and his image was widely reproduced, though not in Quebec.[69] In 1769, he created the *Society for the Defence of the Bill of Rights*, with the aim of reforming the electoral system.[70] Petitions requested that he be seated in the Commons, with more than sixty thousand signatures collected in England,

---

[62] See the excellent biography by Arthur H. Cash, *John Wilkes, The Scandalous Father of Civil Liberty* (Yale University Press, 2006) at 58 & 90. For a much fuller discussion, see Morin, "Découverte," above (n 25).

[63] See Ann Lyon, *Constitutional History of the United Kingdom* (Cavendish, 2003) at 291–292; *R v Wilkes* (1763) 2 Wils 151; and the later account by Wilkes, *Quebec Gazette* (3 September 1767; 10 September 1767).

[64] *Wilkes v Wood* (1763), 3 Lofft 1 98 ER 489 (C Pls); for a summary by Wilkes, see *Quebec Gazette* (3 September 1767; 10 September 1767); in 1769 Wilkes also obtained £4,000 against the Secretary of State: *Quebec Gazette* (15 March 1770); Cash, above (n 62) at 160 and John Brewer, "The Wilkites and the Law, 1763–74: A Study of Radical Notions of Governance" in John Brewer & John Styles (eds), *An Ungovernable People: the English and Their Law in the Seventeenth and Eighteenth Centuries* (Hutchinson, 1980) 128–171 at 143.

[65] Douglas Hay, "Contempt by Scandalizing the Court: A Political History of the First Hundred Years" (1987) 25 Osgoode Hall Law Journal 431–484; see also the proceedings against Mr. Bingley for publishing another issue of the North Briton, *Quebec Gazette* (13 October 1768).

[66] "London, *April 19*," *Quebec Gazette* (25 July 1765).

[67] *Ibid.*

[68] Cash, above (n 61) at 163–164; *Quebec Gazette* (14 February 1765; 21 February 1765; 2 May 1765; 30 May 1765). The *Gazette* did not explain why Wilkes has been forced to flee.

[69] Cash, above (n 61) at 245–256; see *Quebec Gazette* (9 April 1767; 27 August 1767; 31 March 1768; 25 August 1768; 1 September 1768; 22 September 1768; 1 December 1768; 9 February 1769; 21 September 1769; 19 July 1770; 26 July 1770; 2 August 1770; 6 September 1770; see also 6 June 1771).

[70] For an overview of the English electoral system, see Ann Lyon, *Constitutional History of the United Kingdom* (Cavendish, 2003); on the *Society for the Defence of the Bill of Rights*, see *Quebec Gazette* (8 June 1769; 15 December 1774).

which represented one-quarter of the electorate. In 1770 and in 1773, because his election had not been recognized, the mayor and the aldermen of the City of London questioned the legitimacy of Parliament. [71] In 1771, after becoming an alderman himself, he secured the acquittal of printers prosecuted in the municipal court for publishing parliamentary debates.[72] After his election as Mayor of London, in 1774, he was no longer a symbol of opposition to the King or the Government.[73]

In 1767, another parliamentary debate concerned a proposal to grant immunity to officers who had relied on an illegal proclamation. The *Gazette* published the speech of Lord Mansfield, for whom the British Constitution established "a Government by Law" in which "no Person, or Set of Men" and "no Power or Authority" were "superior to the Law." In "no Case whatever can any Necessity be set up, or pleaded to extend the King's Prerogative."[74] It can be seen, therefore, that the *Gazette* allowed its readers to discover many important constitutional principles relating to freedom of the press, the electoral system, and protection against arbitrary detention or abusive search and seizures, as well as the crucial role played by the jury. A similar phenomenon could be observed for the American colonies to the south, as we shall see.

C. The Quest for Constitutional Autonomy in the British Colonies

Many themes discussed above resurfaced in various debates occurring in the colonies of British North America that were reported in the *Gazette*. For the imposition of taxes by the British Parliament sparked off a prolonged controversy over the extent of its powers. This resulted in systematic protests and an open confrontation between Great Britain and its colonies.

In 1765, the *Stamp Act* required the stamping—for a fee—of various colonial documents, including judicial proceedings.[75] This provoked an intense controversy and forced many papers out of business, including the *Gazette*, from 10 October 1765 to 27 May 1766.[76] British products were boycotted, riots erupted, and customs officers' houses

---

[71] *Quebec Gazette* (14 June 1770; 28 June 1770; 3 June 1773).

[72] Cash, above (n 61) at 277–285; Brewer, above (n 64) at 140–141; as the sheriff of the City of London, Wilkes made reforms favourable to prisoners and debtors (Cash, *ibid* at 293; Brewer, *ibid* at 166); he also set free a Black man who was supposedly a slave, as this could not be recognized in England (Brewer, *ibid* at 307); on the publication of parliamentary debates, see *Quebec Gazette* (23 May 1771; 13 June 1771; 20 June 1771; 18 July 1771; 1 August 1771). The Society for the Bill of Rights paid £100 to three printers who were accused in 1771: *Quebec Gazette* (1 August 1771).

[73] Brewer, above (n 64) at 348.

[74] *Quebec Gazette* (14 May 1767).

[75] On the contents of the Act and its receiving royal assent, see *Quebec Gazette* (9 May 1765 & 30 May 1765); see also the inflamed speech of Colonel Barré in the Commons, who defended the rights of the colonies, 25 July 1765, like another member, 1 August 1765.

[76] A MERCHANT, "To the Printer of the PUBLIC LEDGER," *Quebec Gazette* (15 August 1765); and *Quebec Gazette* (10 October 1765).

were ransacked or burnt. In New York, lawyers stopped acting before the courts.[77] Some even feared that violence would spread to England and Ireland.[78] In London, delegates from the colonies famously complained of "Taxation without Representation." In 1766, this legislation was repealed, but a concomitant act solemnly declared the power of Parliament over the colonies to be unlimited.[79] In the *Gazette*, William Pitt could be seen to oppose the *Stamp Act*, whereas Benjamin Franklin defended the position of the colonies.[80]

In Montreal, the tax was dutifully paid, but local merchants knew all about "the proceedings of the Sons of Liberty and their Intention to oppose the Stamp Act"; for their part, Canadians expressed "an uneasiness at paying a Tax from which the other provinces are at present exempt" as a result of public protests.[81] Following the repeal, British merchants who supported the colonies reproached their New York counterparts for the violence that occurred there.[82] They sent the same letter to Quebec merchants.[83] An anonymous writer claimed that the latter were outraged by this accusation, as the province, which lived under a "military" government, had remained peaceful.[84] A reader replied that this has nothing to do with the form of government in the province.[85]

A few weeks later, Lieutenant-Governor Carleton, who replaced Governor Murray, was presented with a laudatory address by the "Merchants" and "Inhabitants" of the City of Quebec. They emphasized their "hearty and untainted Loyalty" to their sovereign and their "most profound Reverence to the Legislative Authority of the British Parliament," as illustrated by the "immediate and universal Obedience to the Stamp-Act" in the province.[86] Of the 68 signatories, 39 or 56 percent have English-sounding names, whereas 30 or 44 percent seem to have francophone ones, including a handful of Protestants born in Great Britain of French descent.

---

[77]   Jack P. Greene, "Law and the Origins of the American Revolution" in Michael Grossberg & Christopher Tomlins (eds), *The Cambridge History of Law in America*, vol 1 (Cambridge University Press, 2008) 447–480 at 469; Hulsebosch, above (n 5) at 139.

[78]   Marshall, above (n 3) at 175.

[79]   *AN ACT for the better securing the dependency of his Majesty's dominions in America upon the crown and parliament of Great Britain*, 1766 (GB), 6 Geo III, c 12; *Quebec Gazette* (5 June 1766). The festivities following the repeal of the *Stamp Act* were also described by the Gazette: *Quebec Gazette* (26 May 1766; 14 July 1766, suppl; 13 October 1766; see also 4 August 1766).

[80]   *Quebec Gazette* (29 May 1766; a debate ensued: 5 June 1766); "The EXAMINATION of Doctor BENJAMIN FRANKLIN, before an August Assembly, relating to the Repeal of the Stamp-Act, &c." *Quebec Gazette* (1 December 1766); *Quebec Gazette* (8 December 1766; 15 December 1766; 22 December 1766; 29 December 1766; 5 January 1767); see also "The Lords Protest against the Repeal of the American Stamp-Act," *Quebec Gazette* (21 July 1766, suppl; 28 July 1766, suppl).

[81]   *Register of the Legislative Council of the Province of Quebec*, Library and Archives Canada [hereinafter "LAC"] (RG1, E1, vol 2, fo 123v).

[82]   *Quebec Gazette* (29 May 1766).

[83]   *Quebec Gazette* (21 July 1766).

[84]   "Copy of a Letter from the Merchants of Canada, in Answer to One Received from a Committee of Merchants in London," *Quebec Gazette* (28 July 1766).

[85]   ANONYMOUS, "To the Printers," *Quebec Gazette* (25 August 1766).

[86]   *Quebec Gazette* (29 September 1766).

Simultaneously, an address from other merchants complained of the decline in business. They hoped that "the Clogs of Commerce" would be removed. If a "good and wise Administration" ensured this, the Lieutenant-Governor's administration would be "happy and agreeable."[87] Of the 46 signatories, 29 or 63 percent seem to be anglophones, and 17 or 37 percent seem to be francophone names. This very qualified endorsement indicates a negative opinion of Governor Murray's administration and, implicitly, of the *Stamp Act*.[88] The proportion of francophone individuals who took a critical stance (37 percent) does not vary significantly from those who offered unwavering support (44 percent) in the first address.[89]

In 1767, the British Parliament imposed new taxes on products imported by the colonies and provided for the payment of Governors and judges salaries out of this additional income, thus depriving colonial assemblies of an important leverage against the Executive.[90] Even a cursory reading of the *Gazette* revealed the blatant conflict between the position of colonies and of the metropolis. Representatives from Massachusetts asserted the "most sacred Right, of being taxed only by Representatives of their own Free Election," as they had an "equitable Claim to the full Enjoyment of the fundamental Rules of the British Constitution."[91] They were supported by many other colonies.[92] The King and Parliament insisted on a proper constitutional subordination.[93] One London observer emphatically agreed: "to deny the Right of the Mother Country to tax" her colonies "is to deny her Sovereignty [. . .] and in Place of Sons and Provinces of their Mother Country, to become Aliens, and to form themselves into a Mother Country, and an independent Nation."[94] In New York, in 1767, a British statute even forbade the Governor to assent to legislation until the Assembly provided the supplies needed by the military.[95] In this volatile context, relations between representatives of the Crown and colonial representatives were tense everywhere.[96]

---

[87] *Ibid.*

[88] Alfred Leroy Burt, *The Old Province of Quebec* (Ryerson Press-University of Minnesota Press, 1933) at 136.

[89] Burt estimates that the proportion of Canadian signatories is the same for both addresses, *ibid.*

[90] That same year another act provided for the nomination of customs commissioners charged with collecting the new duties: *Quebec Gazette* (26 November 1767).

[91] *Quebec Gazette* (12 May 1768; 19 May 1768).

[92] *Quebec Gazette* (18 August 1768, Maryland and New Jersey; 23 February 1769, South Carolina, representatives from Georgia take no position; 23 March 1769 & 30 March 1769, Pennsylvania).

[93] *Quebec Gazette* (9 June 1768; 28 July 1768; 16 February 1769; 2 March 1769).

[94] "LONDON, November 20. EXTRACT from the Constitutional Right of the LEGISLATURE OF GREAT BRITAIN TO TAX THE colonies," *Quebec Gazette* (30 March 1769). The author nonetheless supports the admission of representatives from the colonies in the House of Commons, see *Quebec Gazette* (27 April 1769).

[95] Hulsebosch, above (n 5) at 126; see *Quebec Gazette* (16 February 1769).

[96] The *Gazette* regularly published speeches of the King or of Governors as well as addresses of the Commons or of colonial representatives, especially if they criticized the policy of the Crown: see, among others, 16 May 1765, 21 February 1771, 22 August 1771 (House of Lords and House of Commons); 2 April 1767, 24 April 1767, 21 April 1768, 22 December 1768 (Massachusetts); 2 July 1767, 7 May 1767, 17 September 1767, 24 September 1767 (West Florida); 3 September 1767 (New York); see also 22 October 1767, 24 March 1768, 7 April 1768, 19 May 1768, 21 May 1772 (Ireland); 20 January 1774 (Prince Edward Island). For the

In North Carolina, a rebellion even occurred in 1771 because of the high fees of public officials, a frequent subject of complaints in Quebec.[97] In 1773, Benjamin Franklin predicted the independence of the colonies.[98] The grant to the East India Company of a monopoly on the importation of tea reignited the conflict.[99] Following the Boston Tea Party, the Intolerable Acts of 1774 were adopted.[100] The colonies protested immediately against the laws concerning Massachusetts.[101] The adoption of the *Quebec Act* also raised a storm.[102]

The fundamental individual rights of colonists were also debated in the *Gazette*. In 1765, a bill before the British Parliament would have allowed the billeting of soldiers in private houses, though the final version provided that they would be lodged in vacant buildings, at the expense of colonial governments.[103] The *Gazette* reproduced a horrified comment concerning the initial bill: would no one "oppose a Measure . . . destructive of the Happiness every English Man" which he has the "Right to Enjoy in his own House?" Indeed, the "Laws of England call every Man's House, *his Castle*, but surely they never meant it should be garrisoned by hireling Soldiers!" A "Measure so contrary to the very *Being* of Liberty" must make "every Englishman . . . shudder at the Thoughts of so unconstitutional a Design," because "Arguments, of one Sort or other, will not be wanting to impose the same on the *Mother Country*, whenever in future any weak, wicked, or arbitrary Minister shall please to attempt it."[104]

summoning of the house of representatives outside the colonial capital, see Greene, above (n 77) at 468; *Quebec Gazette* (19 July 1770; 2 August 1770; 9 August 1770 & 14 July 1774); for debates on public expenditures, see *Quebec Gazette* (1 August 1765); on the right to address public resolutions, see *Quebec Gazette* (18 August 1766).

[97] *Quebec Gazette* (4 July 1771; 11 July 1771; 8 August 1771; 28 November 1771; 5 December 1771).

[98] *Quebec Gazette* (3 March 1774; 10 March 1774); the authorship was not known at the time.

[99] For the prior repeal of most taxes on colonial imports, see *Quebec Gazette* (28 June 1770).

[100] For the closing of Boston Harbour, see *Quebec Gazette* (9 June 1774); for the designation of public officers by the Crown instead of the Massachusetts Legislature, see *Quebec Gazette* (23 June 1774; 21 July 1774; 15 September 1774); for the trial of royal officers in other colonies or in England, see *Quebec Gazette* (7 July 1774; 8 September 1774); the Act granting the right to requisition unoccupied buildings to lodge the army is not reproduced.

[101] *Quebec Gazette* (30 June 1774, Virginia and creation of a General Congress; see also 23 June 1774, Maryland; 28 July 1774; 29 September 1774, refusal of jurors to be sworn in Massachusetts; 17 November 1774, protests of the representatives of Massachusetts; 9 February 1775, speech of the Governor who admitted there was no quorum at the opening of the session in New York; 23 February 1775, address of the Council of New York; 16 March 1775, South Carolina Congress and Quakers from Pennsylvania and New Jersey were opposed to the use of force; 30 March 1775, the Governor of Georgia deplored the troubles in other colonies; 6 April 1775, cautious answer of the Assembly). In February, the Commons declared the inhabitants of Massachusetts to be in a state of rebellion, *Quebec Gazette* (4 May 1775), whereas merchants trading in America still sought a compromise: *Quebec Gazette* (11 May 1775).

[102] The discussion of the first bill in the House of Lords was mentioned in the *Quebec Gazette* on 28 July 1774; a summary of the bill was published on 18 August 1774, as well as an overview of the debates in the Commons (25 August 1774 & 8 September 1774) and of those concerning the act imposing dues on alcohol in Quebec (1 September 1774). Another version of the *Quebec Act* appeared on 8 September 1774. The brief comment made by the King was published on 15 September 1774; the official text appeared on 8 December 1774.

[103] Marshall, above (n 3) at 283.

[104] *Quebec Gazette* (1 August 1765).

Problems concerning the administration of justice in the colonies were also debated in the *Gazette*. For instance, in cases pitting the interests of the Imperial Government against those of the colony, jurors would often refuse to indict a suspect or to convict an accused.[105] Courts sitting without a jury were regularly criticized in the colonies.[106] When personal liberty was at stake, however, English courts were willing to intervene. Thus in 1773, a merchant from the Island of Minorca was sent to jail and banished by the British governor without any kind of trial. He sued his persecutor in London and was awarded £3,000 in damages by a jury.[107]

* * *

By translating news and comments concerning political and constitutional crises occurring in France, in Great Britain, and in the American colonies, the *Quebec Gazette* allowed its readers to understand the important developments that occurred in all these jurisdictions between 1764 and 1774.[108] The idea that the French monarch was bound to respect a constitution and the law contradicted orthodox thinking. The suppression of parliaments ignited a crisis, which was easily resolved with the creation of new courts. In the end, the doctrine of the absolute power of the king carried the day.

In Great Britain, the attacks of government officials against pamphleteers and printers were successfully challenged. Involved in numerous judicial proceedings, John Wilkes became a symbol of the right of the electorate to choose even vitriolic critics as their representatives. All these events gave rise to a summary discussion of legal principles. This overview certainly allowed readers of the *Gazette* to appreciate the many differences between the French and British legal systems. Freedom of the press or abusive search and seizures were not live issues in Quebec, however; only the quartering of troops created serious problems.[109]

During this period, the American colonies were challenging the power of the British Parliament to impose taxes within their borders or to legislate in their stead. Numerous conflicts between elected representatives and Governors were discussed in the *Gazette*. Constitutional and natural law principles were asserted on both sides of these debates. The role of juries in thwarting the will of Imperial authorities could also be observed.

---

[105] Greene, above (n 77) at 469–474; Hulsebosch, above (n 5) at 48 & 120–122; James A. Henretta, "Magistrates, Common Law Lawyers, Legislators: The Three Legal Systems of British America" in Grossberg & Tomlins, above (n 77) 555 at 581. On the role of jurors regarding facts and legal issues, see "To the Printers," *Quebec Gazette* (1 November 1770). See also the acquittal of the commander accused of having fired on a crowd near Boston: *Quebec Gazette* (23 August 1770; 13 December 1770); and a similar case from Boston, *Quebec Gazette* (24 January 1771).

[106] Henretta, above (n 105) at 566; Hulsebosch, above (n 5) at 60, 92 & 120–121; *Quebec Gazette* (15 August 1765; 28 July 1768; 19 January 1769; 11 February 1773).

[107] *Quebec Gazette* (3 January 1774) summarizing *Fabrigas v Mostyn*, 1 Cowp 161; 20 State Tr 81, 226; 98 ER 1021 (BR).

[108] French Canadians would continue to pay close attention to events occurring abroad and reflect on their implication for them: see Lamonde, above (n 17).

[109] Neatby, above (n 19) at 42–43.

Again, taxation by Imperial legislation was not a pressing issue in a colony where no local taxes could be imposed, in the absence of an elected assembly.[110] No riots or massive demonstrations occurred in Quebec, contrary to what happened south of the province. To what extent, then, did members of the francophone elite master the principles debated in the British and colonial press? Can we speak of a public sphere in which public opinion was expressed? Why did Quebec refrain from openly supporting the rebellious colonies? We will attempt to provide some partial answers to these questions in Section 3.

3. The Assimilation of British Constitutional Principles in Quebec

To understand the debates concerning the rights of British subjects in Quebec, it is necessary to examine the problems associated with the courts of that province. In the aftermath of the Conquest, a military regime was put in place.[111] This justice exacerbated the conflicts between soldiers and newly arrived British merchants, who were often obligated to receive officers in their own houses. For instance, after two relatively minor altercations in Montreal, a military court imposed a fine or a period of imprisonment on civilians—it also ordered them to make apologies.[112]

A new system was established in 1764. If the amount at issue exceeded 10 pounds, the plaintiff could choose between the Court of King's Bench, in which the "Laws of England" applied, or the Court of Common Pleas, which had to rely on "Equity" and, as far as possible, the Laws of England.[113] Equity was synonymous with fairness, because the

---

[110] For the legal arguments, see Michel Morin, "Les changements de régimes juridiques consécutifs à la Conquête de 1760" (1997) 57 R du B 689–700 [hereinafter Morin, "Conquête"].

[111] During the military Regime, which ended on 10 August 1764, military courts are said to have applied the private law of New France: Jose Igartua, *The Merchants and Negociants of Montreal: A Study in Socio-economic History* (PhD Thesis, East Lansing College of Social Science Michigan State University, 1974) at 174–199 [unpublished]; Marcel Trudel, *Histoire de la Nouvelle-France, X, Le régime militaire et la disparition de la Nouvelle-France, 1759–1774* (Fides, 1999) at 137–184; Douglas Hay, "Civilians Tried in Military Courts: Quebec, 1759–1764" in Frank Murray Greenwood & Barry Wright, *Canadian State Trials: Law, Politics, and Security Measures, 1608–1837* (University of Toronto Press, 1996) at 114–128 [hereinafter Hay, "Military Courts"]; Morin, "Conquête," above (n 110); Donald Fyson, "Judicial Auxiliaries across Legal Regimes: From New France to Lower Canada" in Claire Dolan (ed), *Entre justice et justiciables: les auxiliaires de la justice du Moyen Âge au XXe siècle* (Presses de l'Université Laval, 2005) at 383; Arnaud Decroix, David Gilles & Michel Morin, *Les tribunaux et l'arbitrage en Nouvelle-France et au Québec de 1740 à 1784* (Les Éditions Thémis, 2012) at 394–397.

[112] Hay, above (n 111) at 122.

[113] *Ordinance Establishing Civil Courts, CD I*, above (n 8) at 205. If the value of the controversy did not exceed 5 pounds, a single justice of the peace would hear the case; below 10 pounds, two justices were competent; for 10 pounds and above but below 30, three justices of the peace would hear the case during the Quarter-Sessions, with a right of appeal to the King's Bench. This jurisdiction was abolished in 1770 (*An Ordinance for the More Effectual Administration of Justice, and for Regulating the Courts of Law in This Province, ibid* at 401; see also Fyson, above (n 18)).

Council acted as a separate Court of Chancery. Criminal cases were heard in the King's Bench or Sessions of the Peace. If the cause of action occurred prior to 1 October 1764, "French Laws and Customs" applied between former French subjects.[114] Nevertheless, according to contemporary reports, in practice, for substantive issues French Laws were regularly resorted to under the guise of "Equity."[115] Initially, natives of the province were allowed to sit on all juries, but "Canadian" lawyers could appear only before the Common Pleas. A 1766 ordinance decreed, however, that the composition of civil juries must reflect the origin of the parties; if it differed from the latter, six Canadians and six "old subjects" had to be selected. Canadians lawyers were also allowed to practice in every court.[116] Contrary to what has long been assumed, there was no boycott of the courts or a widespread recourse to arbitration in family matters.[117] Donald Fyson also emphasizes that in most cases francophone litigants had access to bilingual judges and that anglophones easily adjusted to French rules and institutions, such as notarial acts.[118] The 1764 ordinance on the administration of justice also provided for the election of bailiffs in each parish; Canadians were enthusiastic participants in this novel political activity.[119]

The small civilian anglophone community was composed mainly of merchants, whose relations with the military were often strained. They expected to enjoy the rights recognized in other colonies. They criticized the accommodations just discussed and demanded an Assembly, especially in the famous presentment of 1764, in which they implied that Catholics could not sit on juries; later, they explained they were talking of litigation in which all the parties were Protestants.[120] This document generated a heated controversy in which francophones started taking sides, with a few of them supporting

[114] *Ordinance Establishing Civil Courts, CD I*, above (n 8) at 205; for lands and immovable rights of inheritance, French laws remained applicable until 10 August 1765: *Ordinance of November 6th, 1764, ibid* at 229.

[115] Seaman M. Scott, *Chapters in the History of the Law of Quebec, 1764-1775* (University of Michigan, 1933); Neatby, above (n 19).

[116] *An ORDINANCE, To alter and amend an Ordinance of His Excellency the Governor and His Majesty's Council of this Province, passed the Seventeenth of September 1764, CD I*, above (n 8) at 249.

[117] Donald Fyson, "Judicial Auxiliaries across Legal Regimes: From New France to Lower Canada" in Dolan, above (n 111) at 383–403; Donald Fyson, "The Conquered and the Conqueror: The Mutual Adaptation of the Canadiens and the British in Quebec, 1759–1775" in Buckner & Reid, above (n 5), 190 [hereinafter Fyson, "Conqueror"]; Decroix et al., above (n 111) (with a full bibliography).

[118] Fyson, "Conqueror," above (n 117); Donald Fyson, "De la common law à la Coutume de Paris: les nouveaux habitants britanniques du Québec et le droit civil français 1764–1775" in Florent Garnier & Jacqueline Vendrand-Voyer (eds) *La coutume dans tous ses états* (La Mémoire du Droit, 2013) at 157–172.

[119] Donald Fyson, "Les dynamiques politiques locales et la justice au Québec entre la Conquête et les Rébellions" (2007) 16:1 Bulletin d'histoire politique 337–346; Donald Fyson, "The Canadiens and British Institutions of Local Governance in Quebec, from the Conquest to the Rebellions" in *Transatlantic Subjects: Ideas, Institutions and Identities in Post-Revolutionary British North America* (McGill-Queen's University Press, 2008) at 45–82.

[120] See, for instance, Presentments of the Grand Jury of Quebec, 16 October 1764, *CD I*, above (n 8) at 212; Petition for a General Assembly, *ibid* at 401; Petition to the King for an Assembly, 31 December 1773, *ibid* at 485; Heather Welland, "Commercial Interest and Political Allegiance: The Origins of the Quebec Act" in Buckner & Reid, above (n 5) 166.

the grand jurors.[121] Similarly, in a 1766 petition addressed to the King from Quebec City, 20 anglophones recalled that, with the ending of an "oppressive" military government, they expected to "enjoy the Blessings of British Liberty," including an Assembly composed of Protestants.[122] They complained of "Ordinances Vexatious, Oppressive, unconstitutional, injurious to civil Liberty and the Protestant cause" and of the Governor's rude or divisive behaviour, such as encouraging the new subjects "to apply for Judges of their Own National Language!"

In the following years, anglophone juries denied the validity of taxes carried over from the French regime.[123] They acquitted members of the military accused of savagely assaulting a justice of the peace.[124] Thus, the old subjects openly opposed the government, which would have been unthinkable in New France.[125] For their part, members of the francophone elites—seigneurs and legal professionals—wanted an end to religious discrimination, so that they could be appointed to the executive council, the courts, or other public positions. They asked that French Laws be reinstated and complained regularly of the high cost of judicial proceedings, as well as the numerous cases of imprisonment for debt.[126]

In this heated context, some "new" British subjects wrote to the *Gazette*, sometimes with a tone that was quite critical. In 1766, the editors insisted that no system of prior examination existed or would be accepted, though they were secretly forced to do just that four years later.[127] Indeed, we will see that while he governed the colony, Guy Carleton prevented the discussion of controversial issues in the *Gazette* or in petitions.

---

[121] Michel Morin, "Les premières controverses concernant la justice au Québec sous le régime de la Proclamation royale de 1763" in P. Bastien et al. (eds), *Justices et Espaces Publics en Occident* (Presses Universitaire du Québec, 2014), 147 [hereinafter Morin, "Controverses"]; Fyson, "Conqueror," above (n 117); *At the First Court of Quarter-Sessions of the Peace, Held at Quebec in October, 1764*, (sl: sd)(microfiche CHIM 41562) at 11, online: http://www.archive.org/details/cihm_41562 (last accessed: 29-03-2017).

[122] *Petition of the Quebec Traders, CD I*, above (n 8) at 232.

[123] Francis Maseres, *A Collection of Several Commissions, and Other Public Instruments, Proceeding from His Majesty's Royal Authority, and Other Papers, Relating to the State of the Province of Quebec in North America, since the Conquest of It by the Bristish Arms in 1760* (SR Publishers Ltd, 1966); see also the works of Milobar, above (n 4).

[124] Morin, "Controverses," above (n 121); Alfred Leroy Burt, "The Mystery of Walker's Ear" (1922) 3:2 Canadian Historical Review 233–255. The report of the third trial discusses some legal issues: ANONYMOUS, *The Trial of Daniel Disney, Esq.: Captain of a company in His Majesty's 44th Regiment of Foot, and town major of the garrison of Montreal, at the session of the Supreme-Court of Judicature, holden at Montreal, on Saturday the 28th day of February, 1767, before the Honourable William Hey, Esq., chief-justice of the province of Quebec . . . in that case made and provided* (Brown and Gilmore, 1767) at 15–16.

[125] See Morin, "Controverses", above (n 121).

[126] See *Address of the French Citizens to the King regarding the Legal System, Jan. 7, 1765*, French text, *CD I*, above (n 8) at 223; *Petitions of Seigneurs of Montreal to the King, Feb. 3, 1767*, French Text, *ibid* at 270; *Petition for the Restoration of French Law and Custom*, French Text, *ibid* at 419; *Petition of French Subjects to the King, Dec. 1773, ibid* at 504.

[127] *Quebec Gazette* (29 May 1766); Tousignant, above (n 17) at 39. Many articles discussed in this section were also examined by Professor Tousignant in his dissertation.

Nonetheless, some comments on the new legal regime did appear (Subsection A).[128] In this fluid context, merchants, seigneurs, and legal professionals positioned themselves in the tortuous process that would lead to the adoption of the *Quebec Act*. Actual petitions or projected ones, as well as private correspondence, show them invoking the rights of British subjects. By 1773, many of the new subjects were almost ready to demand the right to elect their own representatives, but they were convinced to remain silent in order to achieve religious equality (Subsection B).

A. Discovering British Constitutional Law in the *Gazette*

Some readers of the *Gazette* initially expressed some uneasiness about public debates concerning political issues. Thus, a "Canadian Citizen" was surprised by the "bitter Complaints" and the "Alarms" about English liberties. He wanted to understand the "Rights, Privileges and Liberties" of British subjects, but could only form conjectures in this regard. He wondered whether "requiring that we should support the Army, that we should be taxed, that our Trade should be confined, or that Printers should be discommoded" amounted to "a Violation of English Liberty." For him, it was natural for those who governed to decide what was in the common interest; he did not care to give his opinion on every issue "under Pretext of Liberty." But he expected to be told that he was still under the influence of despotism![129]

A reader answered him that "tho' the Law of Nature, not only permits, but also prompts us to those evil Action to which we are naturally inclined, the English Laws certainly forbid us from indulging this Bent"; he believed that the "wise" ordinances recently made will encourage people to behave well.[130] Confronted with a multiplicity of opinions, a new subject did not know what to think about the power to levy taxes in the colonies.[131] He attempted to gain a better understanding of the British Constitution by reading the Magna Carta, without much success.[132] Following some advice, he read the second part of the *Institutes of the Laws of England* by Coke and exclaimed: "all my Labour has been in vain." He added: "If you will have me to speak sincerely, I believe you

---

[128] But see, on bankruptcy laws, *Quebec Gazette* (10 December 1767; 10 December 1767; 24 December 1767; 31 December 1767; 31 December 1767; 7 January 1768; 14 January 1768); on the role of juries regarding questions of fact, *Quebec Gazette* (1 November 1770); on the benefit of clergy, *Quebec Gazette* (28 March 1765).

[129] CIVIS CANADIENSIS, "To the Printers," *Quebec Gazette* (3 October 1765).

[130] CIVIS BONUS USQUE AD MORTEM, "To the Printers. An Answer to a Letter from a CANADIAN CITIZEN, addressed to the Printers of the Quebec-Gazette," *Quebec Gazette* (10 October 1765).

[131] "Copy of a Letter from Quebec, dated the 7th of August, 1766, to a Friend at Montreal," *Quebec Gazette* (18 August 1766).

[132] "Copy of a Letter from Quebec, dated the 15th of August, 1766, to a Friend at Montreal," *Quebec Gazette* (25 August 1766).

meant to joke with me . . . for you have made me to pore three whole Days, and as many Nights, over a Quarto, written in three different Languages, almost unintelligible."[133]

At the time, Blackstone's *Commentaries on the Laws of England* was the most accessible work on these issues.[134] In 1767, the *Gazette* published an opinion written by three Parisian lawyers, which concerned the right to be compensated for the public taking of oak wood located on seigneuries. In such a case, the wording of the initial grant was determinative. The authors relied on the "excellent work of Mister Blackstone," who distinguished between colonies "founded by Englishmen . . . first occupying the land; these were from the moment of their creation subject to the Laws of England," and "conquered or ceded countries." In the latter case, "the King may, in truth, reform and change their laws, but until he has done so, the ancient laws subsist." They concluded that the obligation to compensate some seigneurs for the taking of oaks had been transmitted to the new sovereign.[135]

In 1765, the *Gazette* reprinted a paper taken from the North Briton.[136] Its author explained that the House of Commons was "a third Part of the Legislative Power" and that the three Estates of the Kingdom acted "as Checks and Counterpoises to one another, for the better securing of our Liberty." For the Commons, taxation under pretence of the prerogative had always been considered incompatible with the Constitution. This was recognized by the *Bill of Rights* of 1689. Hence British subjects had the right to "tax themselves," although they delegated this right to their representatives. Without this privilege, their liberty and property would be at risk. Nevertheless, the King had imposed taxes in the French colonies conquered during the last war. But he could not do so, because its inhabitants were now entitled to the privileges of a British government. Indeed, the Court of King's Bench would annul this measure in the celebrated case of *Campbell v Hall*, albeit for different reasons.[137] In a similar vein, Francis Maseres devoted a few interesting pages, written in French, to the history of habeas corpus and of the English Parliament.[138]

---

[133] "Copy of a Letter from Quebec, dated the 20th of August, 1766, to a Friend at Montreal," *Quebec Gazette* (1 September 1766).

[134] William Blackstone, *Commentaries on the Laws of England*, vol 4 (Clarendon Press, 1765–1769). The first French translation is by Auguste-Pierre Damiens De Gomicourt, *Commentaires sur les loix angloises de M. Blackstone*, 4 vols (Chez J de L Boubers, imprimeur-libraire, 1774–1776).

[135] Élie De Beaumont, Rouhette & Target, "Consultations rendues par trois des plus célèbres Avocats de Paris, au sujet des droits et propriétés des Seigneurs du Canada," *Quebec Gazette* (3 September 1767). No English version appeared in the Gazette; the author has translated the quoted excerpts.

[136] "North Briton, No. 135," *Quebec Gazette* (1 September 1766).

[137] First mentioned in *Quebec Gazette* (9 March 1775); a short but correct summary appeared in the edition of 16 March 1775; *Campbell v Hall*, 1 Cowp 204, 98 ER 1048 (BR); *CD I*, above (n 8) at 522.

[138] *Mémoire à la défense d'un Plan d'Acte de Parlement pour l'Établissement des Loix de la Province de Québec, dressé par Mr. François Masères, Avocat Anglois, cy-devant Procureur- général de sa Majesté le Roi de la Grande Bretagne en la ditte Province, contre les Objections de M. François Joseph Cugnet, Gentilhomme Canadien, Secrétaire du Gouverneur et Conseil de la ditte Province pour la Langue Françoise* (Edmund Allen, 1773) at 24–26 (habeas corpus) & at 65–80 (Parliament).

Another example of the new-found freedom of expression in Quebec concerned economic policy. One author asked for increased spending through the sending of additional soldiers and the undertaking of public works.[139] From Kamouraska, "Misopigros" wrote back that this was asking England to act like France "before the Conquest of this Country, viz. That she should drain her own subjects in Europe, to entertain here, like Lords, a Handful of idle People."[140] He added that under the new regime, there was "no more an Intendant to coin Money, nor so many Placemen to disperse it everywhere liberally and by Caprice; and the English Government is rigid enough to expect that every Individual should live on his own Substance, or by the Trade he professes, without suffering one Part of its Subjects to be pillaged to feed the other in Laziness and Abundance." Obviously this opinion, which is generally in accord with what we know of the French regime, was not necessarily shared by all. One cannot be assured that the opposite position—that is, a ferocious criticism of the new regime—would have been published in the *Gazette*. Be that as it may, some new British subjects were not shy about expressing their opinion forcefully.

B. Invoking the Rights of British Subjects

Canadians soon found themselves petitioning the King, another fundamental right of the British Constitution which had been exercised on a large scale with the advent of printing. After 1642, a public sphere appeared in the kingdom, with some illiterate persons taking part in discussions.[141] The number of signatories could vary between 3,000 and 20,000.[142] After 1661, a petition with more than 20 signatures had to be approved either by justices of the peace, grand jurors, or the mayor and council of the City of London; furthermore, a delegation presenting the document could not exceed 10 persons.[143] A century later, a petition received on the throne was made public; if presented during the royal levee, it remained confidential.[144] The number of signatures could reach 50,000 or 60,000 (in 1769, 1775, and 1784).[145] This represented roughly 1 percent of the total population of England.[146]

It was only in 1784 that printed petitions appeared in Quebec, with 2,291 signatures asking for an elected Assembly and 2,400 opposing it; this represented approximately

---

[139] XP, "To the Printers," *Quebec Gazette* (17 December 1767).

[140] "To the Printers of the Quebec-Gazette," *Quebec Gazette* (28 January 1768).

[141] Zaret, above (n 23) at 14–19, 85–87, 91, 226, 248, 253 & 261.

[142] *Ibid* at 222–224, 235 & 269.

[143] *An Act against Tumults and Disorders upon pretence of preparing or presenting publick Peticions or other Addresses to His Majesty or the Parliament*, 1661 (UK), 13 Car II, c 5, s 1.

[144] James E Bradley, *Popular Politics and the American Revolution in England, Petitions, the Crown, and Public Opinion* (Mercer University Press, 1986) at 5, 41 & 48.

[145] *Ibid* at 136–140.

[146] The English population is estimated at 5,742,415 in 1751: Edward A. Wrigley & Roger S. Schofield, *The Population History of England 1541–1871: A Reconstruction* (Edward Arnold, 1981) at 529.

2 percent of the population.[147] But from 1764 to 1774, "petitions" to the Council generally requested personal favours.[148] Some were signed by francophone and anglophone merchants alike.[149] For political issues, the procedure followed in 1773 seems typical. First, in Quebec and Montreal, committees discussed the document, then circulated it for signatures and engrossed it on parchment. If the Governor allowed its presentation to the Council, a delegation attended in person; it was then sent to London.[150] In these years, francophone signatories did not exceed 0.1 percent of the total population; the figure should be doubled for anglophones.[151] Petitions were not printed—a fact which is often overlooked—and the *Gazette* quickly avoided publishing controversial comments on local affairs. Hence the province did not have, as yet, a true public sphere.[152]

In 1773, Lieutenant-Governor Cramahé regretted having authorized the publication in the *Gazette* of a brief exchange in the House of Commons concerning Quebec's legal system. He declared privately that the inhabitants of the province did not need information "about what was happening in London concerning them"; rather, they must "wait respectfully for the arrangements" made by the Court, confiding entirely in Governor Carleton, who was in London at the time, for this purpose.[153] Freedom of the press was far from unlimited in the colony, as we can see.

---

[147] See Tousignant, above (n 17) at 311 & 322; Marie Tremaine, *A Bibliography of Canadian Imprints 1751–1800* (University of Toronto Press, 1999) at 201, 305 & 337; Patricia Lockhart Fleming & Sandra Alston, *Early Canadian Printing: A Supplement to Marie Tremaine's 'A Bibliography of Canadian Imprints'* (University of Toronto Press, 1999) at 161–162 & 222. The petitions of 1773 which preceded the adoption of the *Quebec Act* were published shortly thereafter by Francis Maseres: *An Account of the Proceedings of the British, And other Protestants Inhabitants, of the Province of Quebeck, in North-America, in order to obtain An House of Assembly in that Province* (B White, 1775) at 35 [hereinafter Maseres, "Account"].

[148] Fyson, "Conqueror," above (n 117) at 204; a simple perusal of the Council's registers allows us to draw this conclusion: see *Register of the Legislative Council of the Province of Quebec*, LAC (RG1, E1, vol 1).

[149] See for instance (30 March 1766) LAC (RG4 A1, vol 15, at 5732 MFILM C-2998).

[150] "Délibération d'un groupe de onze marchands anglais—6 décembre 1773," Québec, Bibliothèques et archives nationales du Québec (P1000, S3, D1741) online: http://pistard.banq.qc.ca (last accessed : 29-03-2017).

[151] There were 65 francophone signatories for the 1773 petition and 151 for its counterpart (*Petition to the King for an Assembly, Dec. 31, 1773*, CD I, above (n 8) at 485; *Petition of French Subjects to the King, Dec. 1773, ibid* at 504); the total population of the small Province of Quebec, as defined in 1763, was roughly between 70,000 and 80,000 people. For the importance of petitions in later days, see Steven Watt, "Pétition et démocratie. Le cas du Bas-Canada et du Maine, 1820–1840" (2006) 14:2 Bulletin d'histoire politique 51–62; Steven Watt, *"Duty Bound and Ever Praying": Collective Petitioning to Governors and Legislatures in Selected Regions of Lower Canada and Maine, 1820–1838* (PhD Thesis, Université du Québec à Montréal, 2006); Mathieu Fraser, "'La pratique pétitionnaire' à la Chambre d'assemblée du Bas-Canada, 1792–1795: origines et usages" (2008) online: http://www.fondationbonenfant.qc.ca/stages/essais/2008/2008Fraser.pdf (last accessed: 29-03-2017; J. O'Connor, "Review Essay: Politics, Indoors and Out" (2002) 69 Social History 235.

[152] Dorland & Charland, above (n 17) at 98.

[153] Marine Leland, "François-Joseph Cugnet 1720–1789—XI" (1963) 18 Revue de l'Université Laval 339 at 358–360, Appendice H. The excerpts quoted in the text have been translated by the author; for more information on this episode, see Michel Morin, "William Blackstone's and the Birth of Quebec's Bi-juridical and Bilingual Legal Culture, 1765–1867" in Wilfrid Prest (ed), *Re-interpreting Blackstone's*

Initially, francophone persons solicited the permission to meet and discuss their grievances, as requested by British legislation.[154] In 1766, the Council agreed, but two of its members had to attend the meeting, with the power to dissolve it.[155] Soon after, the Secretary of State declared that the new subjects could communicate freely their requests to the King.[156] Guy Carleton, however, dissuaded old subjects from petitioning for an Assembly, unless they could suggest a scheme advantageous for the whole province.[157] He did not take public dissent well. Thus, he dismissed two members of the Council, who had signed a petition criticizing the decision of Chief Justice Hey to deny bail to some accused.[158] Carleton believed that there had been an abuse of "addresses of every kind" in the province; he had ". . . taken a fixed resolution . . . to be recalled" as soon as a petition was sent to London against his will.[159]

In 1766, prior to Carleton's arrival, the Council had authorized 20 seigneurs of the Montreal area to prepare representations to the British government under the surveillance of a councillor and local magistrates.[160] Previously, military commanders had intimated that an assembly of Catholics would be illegal. On the day announced, some old and new subjects attempted to block the meeting; they dispersed only under the threat of forceful expulsion.[161] The seigneurs then wrote an address thanking the King for his kindness, asking for the continuation of the free exercise of their religion and that Catholics be allowed to serve their (new) country. They also requested the reinstatement of their former customs and usages "in the most advantageous manner."[162]

The following day, their opponents lodged two formal protests before the Council. One, written in English, was signed by 15 old subjects. The first three paragraphs complained that seigneurs, who pretended to act as agents of their tenants, had previously sworn an oath to the French king. They could not, therefore, be "Representatives . . . under the British Constitution" or "guardians of the Liberty of a free people." Supposedly, some were paid by the French king and had not sworn the British oath of allegiance; others had circulated a letter and assembled without the consent of the authorities.[163]

The rest of the protest was translated and signed by 32 new subjects. Both documents underlined that not every seigneur was summoned to the Montreal meeting. The

Commentaries: The Evolution and Influence of a Seminal Text in National and International Context (Hart, 2014) at 105–124.

[154] See above (n 143).

[155] 25 April 1765, 2 January 1766 & petition of the seigneurs, 27 March 1766, LAC (RG1, E1, vol 1, fo 235; RG1 E1, vol 2, fo 112 & RG1 E1, vol 2, 120).

[156] 27 March 27 1766, LAC (RG1, E1, vol 2, fo 120).

[157] *Carleton to Shelburne, CD I*, above (n 8) at 294.

[158] Neatby, above (n 19) at 89–93; *New York Gazette* (18 February 1767, no 410), Archives du Séminaire de Québec (Fonds George-Barthélémy Faribault (P29), pièce no 267).

[159] William Hey to Fowler Walker (16 February 1767), LAC (Hardwicke Papers, Add Mss 3595 [transcription], fo 102).

[160] *Register of the Legislative Council of the Province of Quebec*, LAC (RG1, E1, vol 2, fo 120).

[161] *Ibid* at fo 123v–125.

[162] "Resolutions No. 9 in the Report," *ibid* at fo 128–129.

[163] "Protest No.10 in the Report," *ibid* at fo 129–132.

signatories strenuously denied that the persons assembled there represented the public, as they were acting in "a private concealed Manner," to the "intire exclusion" of the "Ancient British Subjects in general" and of "the Mercantile part of His Majestys new Subjects." This division between the latter and "the noblesse" would soon infuse "a Spirit of Discontent." Furthermore, the new subjects were led to believe that only the Governor could protect their religion and their participation in the administration of justice. The old subjects also demanded to have "a share in the Choice of their representatives."[164] This little known document reveals the existence of a contest between different people claiming to speak for the new subjects.

In 1766, a very different address was signed by 21 francophone seigneurs of Quebec, "as well in their own names as in those of all the inhabitants, their tenants."[165] They deplored the recall of Governor Murray and the "Cabal, trouble and confusion" they had witnessed, as well as some "infamous libels." Having been taught to respect their superiors and obey the sovereign, they complied with the orders of civil officers whose high salaries "astonished" them. Meanwhile, old subjects sought to "oppress" the new ones, even to render them their "slaves," and to seize their property. In such cases, Murray acted as their "protector" and "father."

For them, followers of the army and clerks or agents of London merchants were "contemptible" because of their "want of education." Some Canadians who had rallied to their cause did not understand what they signed. The rest were people "without birth, without education and without scruple, disbanded soldiers from the French army, barbers, servants, even children" and shopkeepers who had "made themselves the slaves of their creditors, even Jews, who . . . exalt themselves above the King's new subjects." However wise were English laws, of what use would be British liberty if it was "granted only to the old subjects?" Hence, they insisted on a traditional, elitist, and racist vision of government and authority, which protected their rights and privileges, while dismissing with contempt the criticism of British-born subjects and Canadians.

Another example of a francophone relying on the rights of British subjects is found in an attempt to thwart the homologation of an arbitral award. This petition to the Council was based on the "precision of the ordinance" adopted in 1764 and "the right held by a subject of His Majesty to have a jury hear his case."[166] In reply, the judges explained that the litigation was sent to arbitrators before the request for a jury trial; the petition was therefore dismissed.[167]

[164] *Register of the Legislative council of the Province of Quebec*, LAC (RG1, E1, vol 2, fo 130–132).

[165] Douglas Brymner (ed), *Report on Canadian Archives, 1888* (A Sénécal, 1889) at 19 [translated by author].

[166] Petition of Guillaime LeRoy to the Council (untitled), 1767, LAC (RG4, B17, vol 2, file 1a) [translated by the author]: "Cette ditte Cour arefusé aux instances du suppliant deluy accorder uncorp dejuré parluy reclamé malgrés la précision de l'ordonnance susmentionné, Et qu'il a différente fois cité a cette dite Cour, Et malgrés en outre Ledroit qu'a unsujet deSaMajesté d'avoir dans sacause un corp de juré, rien de tout cela napüe operer enfaveur duSuppliant."

[167] *Register of the Legislative council of the Province of Quebec* (4 May 1767), LAC (RG1, E1, vol 3, fo 234–235).

The use made by François-Joseph Cugnet of the principles of British constitutional law is also interesting. Born in a prestigious seigneurial family and trained in the law, he became, in 1766, the official translator of the Government and was asked to draft an overview of the rules in force during the French regime, which would lead to numerous publications.[168] In 1771 or in 1772, he criticized strongly one of the many draft bills printed privately by Maseres in London, whose object was to reform the rules of inheritance in Quebec.[169] Maseres answered in French, producing a 159-page memoir that was published in 1773 and circulated in Quebec.[170] This is the only information we have on the contents of Cugnet's initial criticism.

For Cugnet, the Royal Proclamation did not introduce English laws to their full extent. Furthermore, the King's private instructions, sent in 1764, could not delegate to the Council a power to legislate; only the Governor's commission could achieve this purpose. It followed that the 1764 ordinance introducing English law was void.[171] For him, if the British government were to adopt Maseres's proposals, "it would be harsher than the Turkish Government!"[172] Similarly, asserting that the laws of New France were entirely repealed in 1763 disregarded the King's righteous intent and portrayed him as a harsh and barbarous conqueror.[173] Overall, Cugnet believed the Proclamation had introduced English criminal law and habeas corpus, but left intact the French laws governing successions (including matrimonial regimes) and property (which were guaranteed by article 37 of the Capitulation of Montreal).

This reasoning is strikingly similar to the 1766 opinion of the English law officers summarized by Maseres.[174] Lord Hillsborough, a member of the Cabinet in 1763, also wrote in 1768 that "whatever the legal sense" of the Proclamation, he never intended "to overturn the Laws and Customs of Canada, with regard to Property"; instead, these were to be applied by local courts following English procedural rules, as was the case in many "parts of England, where Gavel-king Bourough-English and several other particular customs prevail."[175]

---

[168] See *Quebec Gazette* (24 February 1768); see Sylvio Normand, "François-Joseph Cugnet et la reconstitution du droit de la Nouvelle-France" (2002) 1 Cahiers aixois d'histoire des droits de l'outre-mer français 127.

[169] *A Draught of an act of Parliament for settling the laws of the Province of Quebec*, (London, UK: available only in the British Library, Adams and Bonswick Pamphlets, 1771, at 177).

[170] See above (n 138). Following Cugnet's criticism, Maseres revised his draft bill: *A Draught of an act of Parliament for settling the laws of the Province of Quebec*, (London, UK: available only in the British Library, Adams and Bonswick Pamphlets, 1772, at 188) [hereinafter *Draught, 1772*].

[171] *Ibid* at 2–3. Maseres had made the same point in his writings: Francis Maseres, "Considerations on the Expediency of Procuring an Act of Parliament for the Settlement of the Province of Quebec," reprinted in Francis Maseres, *Occasional Essays on Various Subjects, Chiefly Political and Historical* (Robert Wilks, 1809) at 333; Maseres, above (n 123).

[172] *Draught, 1772*, above (n 170) at 9.

[173] *Ibid* at 17.

[174] "Report of the Attorney and Solicitor General regarding the Civil Government of Quebec," *CD I*, above (n 8) at 251; Maseres, above (n 123) at 17–18.

[175] *Hillsborough to Carleton, CD I*, above (n 8) at 297.

Cugnet's positions was similar to ideas found in previous petitions, but he added an important element: he did not object to English criminal law or public law. Following the Law Officers of the Crown, he argued that the Royal Proclamation introduced the public and criminal law of England, but not the laws governing immovable property, successions, or matrimonial regimes. Although not mentioned in the text, this distinction flowed from the promise made in the Capitulation of 1760 to respect both seigneurial and commoner's property rights, whether movable or immovable. In a letter to William Blackstone which was later sent to the government, Cugnet also argued that testamentary freedom was a necessary part of British liberties that enjoyed the support of his countrymen.[176] This would represent a substantial derogation from the rules of the (written) Custom of Paris, which were in force in New France since 1664 and which reserved a share of the estate to all descendants.[177]

In 1773, at the urging of Cugnet, a draft petition was prepared by a group of francophone merchants and lawyers.[178] This document, whose legal contents does not seem to have been studied before, claimed that Canadians were entitled to "... the enjoyment of those parts of the constitution of the British government, which tend to secure their personal liberty, their rights, and possessions." They demanded "an assembly of the people ... consisting indifferently of Canadian and English members," for this was "one of the most essential branches of the said British constitution." They added that the choice of the legal system "ought to be left to the inhabitants of the province themselves," who must be "the best judges, (as they are evidently the most natural ones,) of their own interests and wants," just like in other colonies. This petition was shelved, however, because anglophones wanted the British government to decide freely if Catholics should be eligible in the new assembly.[179] But in 1774,

---

[176] For a detailed analysis, see Morin, "Revendications," above (n 25), Part II D or above (n 153).

[177] Essentially, after the debts of a deceased parent had been paid, each descendant who had renounced the estate was entitled to his or her share of the *reserve des quatre-quints*, namely four-fifths of a parent's particular property, called *propres*. This consisted in immovables inherited from the deceased parent's ascendants, as well as those given or bequeathed by them (art CCXCV of the *Custom of Paris*, in T.K. Ramsay, *Notes diverses sur la Coutume de Paris* (La Minerve, 1863)). In general, the share of each child was equal (art CCCII), except for fiefs, in which case the eldest son was entitled to the manor (art XIII) and to either two-thirds, if he had only one sibling, or half of the fief, if he had more (arts XV–XVI). Descendants were also entitled to half their share of the net value of the estate, augmented by the value of all bequeaths and gifts made during the life of the deceased (art CCXCVIII). In both cases, such liberalities could be annulled or reduced to insure payment of the *quatre-quints* or of the *légitime*. Finally, the wife was entitled to the usufruct of half the *propres* of her husband, with a somewhat different definition for this category of property and the possibility of renouncing or changing the amount and extent of the dower in the marriage contract. Upon her death, ownership of these *propres* was transferred to the children of the marriage who were not heirs; therefore, they were not required to pay any of their deceased father's debts (arts CCXLVII–CCLXIV).

[178] Francis Maseres, *Additional Papers concerning the Province of Quebeck: Being an Appendix to the Book Entitled, "An Account of the Proceedings of the British and Other Protestant Inhabitants of the Province of Quebeck in North America, ..."* (London: sold by W White, 1776) at 35 [hereinafter Maseres, "Additional Papers"]. For a detailed analysis, see Morin, "Revendications," above (n 25), Part II E.

[179] See Morin, *ibid*, part II D or above (n 153).

Michel-Chartier de Lotbinière, a seigneur, expressed similar ideas before the House of Commons.[180]

Meanwhile, in a repeat of the events of 1766, a group of seigneurs and jurists, mostly from Montreal, drafted their own petition. They asked for the reinstatement of the laws of New France and for the end of religious discrimination.[181] They also emphasized that the colony was too poor to pay for the cost of the colonial government and could not support a representative legislature endowed with a power of taxation.[182]

Though they were initially puzzled by the rights recognized to British subjects, literate individuals in Quebec mastered these concepts relatively easily. The information available in the *Gazette* obviously made their task easier and drew their attention to some legal literature. In 1773, a representative assembly did not rally the support of those claiming to speak in their name. Some wanted to enjoy this part of the British Constitution, but their views did not carry the day. Meanwhile, a small group of seigneurs and lawyers were content to demand religious equality and the reinstatement of the laws of New France, two issues about which there seems to have been a broad consensus. Considering the hostility against Catholics all over the Empire, an assembly in which they would have been eligible did not seem to be a realistic prospect in 1773.[183] Those of them who resided in Quebec were assumed to be more deferent than Protestant ones and less in need of representative institutions. Whether this vision was shared widely in the colony is unknown, but the image of an ignorant people with no appetite whatsoever for democratic institutions clearly needs to be revised.

4. CONCLUSION

From 1764 to 1774, the bilingual *Gazette* discussed important political issues occurring in France, Great Britain, and its colonies. It provided a substantial amount of information on principles of constitutional law, such as the right to elect lawmakers, freedom of the press, trial by jury, and habeas corpus. Some Canadians were puzzled by the controversies in the neighbouring colonies surrounding the rights of British subjects; they were directed to the legal literature of England. With the arrival of Guy Carleton, the *Gazette* avoided discussing controversial local issues. During this decade, petitions sent to London were not published. They were prepared by a handful of persons and signed by an extremely small percentage of the population. In these conditions a true public sphere in which political issues could have been debated had yet to emerge.

---

[180] "Examination of Chartier de Lotbinière before the House of Commons" in Cavendish, above (n 1) at 162.

[181] *Petition of French Subjects to the King, Dec. 1773*, CD I, above (n 8) at 504.

[182] *Ibid.*

[183] For a detailed analysis, see Morin, "Revendications," above (n 25), Part II B.

By 1773, a few francophone Canadians had mastered the main concepts of British constitutional law. They claimed for themselves the rights of British subjects, a fact seldom mentioned in the historiography. For them, this included respect of seigneurial or property rights and, by extension, testamentary freedom. It is not clear if these ideas had been internalized by other people, especially merchants. But Governor Carleton was able to discourage Canadians from pressing for an assembly, giving the false impression that almost no one was interested in such a body. Those who disagreed said nothing, for they could not support an anglophone petition which did not recognize religious equality.

When American soldiers invaded Quebec in 1775, they met with little resistance and received some active support, although they failed to capture Quebec City and retreated in 1776. Some farmers refused to follow the orders given by their seigneurs to take arms for the defence of the province—one of them was forcefully expelled from a village.[184] Both colonial administrators and local elites had fallen prey to the myth of peasant apathy, which they had created in large measure. Letters sent by the American Congress also had circulated widely.[185] On 26 October 1774, this body promised that if the Quebec population joined force with them, they would enjoy the benefit of an elected assembly, trial by jury in civil matters, habeas corpus, and moderate quit-rents—an implicit attack on the seigneurial regime.[186] These first three rights had been suppressed by the *Quebec Act*, which was consistently criticized for that reason. Congress also emphasized that "the Crown and its Ministers" now enjoyed absolute power in the Province, like "the despots of Asia or Africa."[187] Meanwhile, the arrogance and insolence of the nobility was deeply resented, although no formal protest was made, in order to avoid jeopardizing the rights granted to Catholics.[188]

On 8 January 1776, Christophe Pélissier, who supported the invaders, wrote a letter to the President of the Continental Congress.[189] This hitherto unknown document lucidly summarizes the events of the previous decade. For him, the British government attempted to persuade Canadians that the *Quebec Act* was for their own good and that

---

[184] Maseres, "Additional Papers," above (n 178) at 105–106; Neatby, above (n 19) at 144–146.

[185] See Pierre Monette, *Rendez-vous manqué avec la révolution américaine* (Québec-Amérique, 2007) at 94.

[186] "To the Inhabitants of the Province of Quebec" in *Journals of the Continental Congress, 1774*, vol 1 (Government Printing Office, 1904) at 105, online: http://www.memory.loc.gov/ammem/amlaw/lwjc. html (last accessed: 29-03-2017).

[187] *Ibid* at 111.

[188] Maseres, "Additional Papers," above (n 178) at 131–135, 138–140; Maseres "Account," above (n 147) at 96–97, 105–106.

[189] "Translation of M. Pelissier's Letter," Peter Force (ed) *American Archives: Consisting of a collection of authentick records, state papers, debates, and letters and other notices of publick affairs, the whole forming a documentary history of the origin and progress of the North American colonies; of the causes and accomplishment of the American revolution; and of the Constitution of government for the United States, to the final ratification thereof* (M St Clair Clarke and Peter Force, nd) ser 4, vol 4 at 596, online: https://ia902706.us.archive.org/15/items/americanarchive04forcuoft/americanarchive04forcuoft.pdf (last accessed: 28-03-2017).

they should show their "everlasting gratitude" to the Crown. This was "the height of con-tempt" and a mistaken assumption.[190] For after the first Governor of the province was unable to "re-establish the Government on the same footing it had been under France," his successor, General Carleton, sought to persuade Canadians that "their ancient laws would be most suitable and convenient for them." But "those who knew the difference between liberty and despotism" opposed this plan. So he only communicated with "some *Canadian* officers and the clergy." Those "courtiers," hoping to "domineer over the people" again, served him well and "addressed a petition to the King, in the name of all the inhabitants of the Province of *Quebeck,* to have the wise *British* Constitution withdrawn; which, In effect, was asking chains for their fellow-citizens." He concluded:

> It ought not to be supposed that the *Canadians,* in general, were so base. Some flat-terers, and some ignorant people, bigoted to ancient customs, signed this shamful [sic] petition, without being authorized by any but themselves, to the number of sixty-five only.
>
> It was upon this bespoken petition that the Ministry, who had their views in obtaining it, seized with eagerness the opportunity of establishing arbitrary power in this country, by the *Quebeck* Act.

Thus, the favourable reception given the Americans invaders can be explained, at least in part, by the previous dissemination of British Constitutional Law principles. The fail-ure of the invasion and the imposition of martial law put an end to such discussions until the end of the American War of Independence. A new period of debates followed, which culminated with the creation of an elected assembly by the *Constitutional Act,* 1791.[191] By that time, though most seigneurs and many farmers still opposed this reform, the constitutional stage has been set. Trial by jury in civil matters and habeas corpus were put in place or restored between 1784 and 1792. The ideas that were sown between 1764 and 1774 thus came to fruition. The right to challenge governmental decisions and to obtain reforms by peaceful means was now taken for granted, consummating the sep-aration from France. Although the ancien régime mentality would continue to strive in Quebec, the identity of the francophone elite had been indelibly marked by the ideals of representative institutions, for which Great Britain and its colonies were so famous in the Western world at the time.

SELECT BIBLIOGRAPHY

Brun, Henri, *La formation des institutions parlementaires québécoises, 1791–1838* (Presses de l'Université Laval, 1970)

Buckner, Philip & John G Reid, eds, *Revisiting 1759: The Conquest of Canada in Historical Perspective* (University of Toronto Press, 2012)

---

[190] *Ibid* at 602.
[191] See generally above (n 17).

Coupland, Reginald, *The Quebec Act* (Clarendon Press: 1925)

Dorland, Michael & Maurice Charland, *Law, Rhetoric and Irony in the Formation of Canadian Civil Culture* (University of Toronto Press, 2002)

Ducharme, Michel, *The Idea of Liberty in Canada during the Age of Atlantic Revolutions, 1776–1838*, trans. Peter Feldstein (McGill-Queen's Studies in the History of Ideas, no. 62.) (McGill-Queen's University Press, 2014) 279

Fecteau, Jean-Marie and Douglas Hay, "'Government by Will and Pleasure instead of Law': Military Justice and the Legal System of Quebec, 1775–1783" in F. Murray Greenwood & Barry Wright, *Canadian State Trials, Vol. I: Law, Politics, and Security Measures, 1608–1837* (Toronto, Osgoode Society, 1996) 129–171

Fyson, Donald, *Magistrates, Police and People: Everyday Criminal Justice in Quebec and Lower Canada, 1764–1837* (University of Toronto Press for The Osgoode Society, 2006)

Fyson, Donald, "Les Canadiens et le Serment du Test", in Sophie Imbeault, Denys Vaugeois, and Laurent Veyssière (eds), *1763 Le traité de Paris bouleverse l'Amérique* (Septentrion, 2013) 272

Halliday, Paul D., *Habeas Corpus, from England to Empire* (Belknap Press, 2010)

Hay, Douglas, "The Meanings of the Criminal Law in Quebec, 1764–1774" in Louis A Knafla (ed), *Crime and Criminal Justice in Europe and Canada* (Wilfrid Laurier University Press, 1981) 77

Hay, Douglas, "Civilians Tried in Military Courts: Quebec, 1759–1764", in F.M. Greenwood and B. Wright (eds), *Canadian State Trials. Law, Politics, and Security Measures, 1608–1837* (University of Toronto Press, 1996) 114–128

Kennedy, William Paul McLure, *The Constitution of Canada 1534-1937*, 2nd ed., (Russel & Russel), 1938

Kennedy, William Paul McLure & Lancôt, Gustave, *Reports on the Laws of Quebec (1767-1770)*, (King's Printer) 1931.

Kolish, Evelyn, *Nationalismes et conflits de droits: le débat du droit privé au Québec, 1760–1840* (Ville LaSalle, Hurtubise, 1994)

Lamonde, Yvan, *Histoire sociale des idées au Québec, 1760–1896* (Fides, 2000)

Lawson, Philip, *The Imperial Challenge: Quebec and Britain in the American Revolution* (McGill-Queen's University Press, 1989)

Marshall, Peter, "The Incorporation of Quebec in the British Empire", in Virginia Bever Platt and David Curtis Skaggs (eds), *Of Mother Country and Plantations: Proceedings of the Twenty-Seventh Conference in Early American History*, (Bowling Green State University Press, 1971) 43–63

Milobar, Karl David, *The Constitutional Development of Quebec from the Time of the French Regime to the Canada Act of 1791* (PhD Thesis, University of London, 1990)

Milobar, Karl David, "Quebec Reform, the British Constitution and the Atlantic Empire, 1774–1775" in Philip Lawson (ed), *Parliamentary History: Parliament and the Atlantic Empire* (Edinburgh University Press, 1995) 65–88

Milobar, Karl David, "The Origins of British-Quebec Merchant Ideology: New France, the British Atlantic and the Constitutional Periphery, 1720–1770" (1996) 24:3 Journal of Imperial and Constitutional History 264–390

Morel, André, "La réception du droit criminel anglais au Québec (1760–1892)" (1978) 13 Revue juridique Thémis 449

Morin, Jacques-Yvan and José Woehrling, *Les constitutions du Canada et du Québec—du Régime français à nos jours* (Les Éditions Thémis, 1992) 43 & 49

Morin, Michel, "Les débats concernant le droit français et le droit anglais antérieurement à l'adoption de l'*Acte de Québec* de 1774" (2014) 44 *Revue de Droit l'Université. Sherbrooke* 259–306

Morin, Michel, "William Blackstone's and the Birth of Quebec's Bi-juridical and Bilingual Legal Culture, 1765–1867" in Wilfrid Prest (ed) *Re-interpreting Blackstone's Commentaries: The Evolution and Influence of a Seminal Text in National and International Context* (Hart, 2014) 105–124

Morin, Michel, "L'élection des membres de la Chambre Haute du Canada-Uni, 1856–1867", (1994) 35 *Cahiers de Droit* 23–50

Muller, Hannah Weiss, *An Empire of Subjects: Unities and Disunities in the British Empire, 1760–1790* (PhD Thesis, Princeton University, 2010)

Muller, Hannah Weiss, "Bonds of Belonging: Subjecthood and the British Empire", (2014) 53(1) *Journal of British Studies* 29–58

Neatby, Hilda, *Quebec, The Revolutionary Age, 1760–1791* (McClelland & Stewart, 1966)

Norman, Sylvio, "An Introduction to Quebec Civil Law", in Aline Grenon and Louise Bélanger-Hardy (eds), *Elements of Quebec Civil Law: A Comparison with the Common Law of Canada* (Thomson-Carswell, 2008) 25–97

Shortt, Adam & A.G. Doughty, eds, *Documents Relating to the Constitutional History of Canada, 1759–1791*, 2 vols., (J. de L. Tache, 1918).

Scott, Seaman Morley, *Chapters in the History of the Law of Quebec 1764–1775* (PhD dissertation, University of Michigan, 1933)

Stanbridge, Karen, "Quebec and the Irish Catholic Relief Act of 1778: An Institutional Approach", 2003 16 (3) *Journal of Historical Sociology* 375–404

Tousignant, Pierre, *La genèse et l'avènement de l'Acte constitutionnel de 1791* (PhD Thesis, Université de Montréal, 1971)

Toussignant, Pierre, "L'incorporation de la province de Québec dans l'Empire britannique, 1763–1791—Ire partie de la Proclamation royale du Canada à l'Acte de Québec" in George Brown, Marcel Trudel, and André Vachon (eds.), *Dictionnaire biographique du Canada*, vol. IV (Sainte-Foy/Toronto, Presses de l'Université Laval/University of Toronto Press, 1980) xxxiv

Vaugeois, Denis, *Québec 1792: Les acteurs, les institutions et les frontières* (Fides, 1992)

C. 1867: Confederation

CHAPTER 4

....

1867: CONFEDERATION

....

ROBERT VIPOND*

1. INTRODUCTION

....

ACCORDING to data from a long-term research initiative on the origins and characteristics of written constitutions, the average life expectancy of a national constitution
is approximately 19 years.[1] At 150 years and counting, Canada's *Constitution Act, 1867*
(originally known as the *British North America Act*) is an impressive outlier. Where
many other national constitutions have failed, expired, or been replaced, the Canadian
Constitution has endured—amended and renamed to be sure, but endured all the
same. What accounts for its longevity? This chapter addresses this question from three
intersecting perspectives. The first surveys the environment in which the *Constitution
Act, 1867* was produced, in an attempt to identify the most important factors that influenced its creation. The second explores the possibility that this constitutional longevity
may reflect crucial design decisions made by the architects responsible for drafting the
Constitution Act, 1867, the group conventionally known as the Fathers of Confederation.
More specifically, it suggests that key to understanding the endurance of the Canadian
Constitution is the extent to which it embodies "constitutional ambivalence." The third
part examines the counterfactual possibility that when the Fathers ignored these elements of successful design, the structure they generated became vulnerable to protracted constitutional conflict and instability.

In constitution-making, timing is important.[2] In the Canadian context, then, it is
important to understand why the political movement that culminated in Confederation
occurred when it did, in the mid-1860s. After all, some form of political, indeed federal, union of the British North American colonies (or provinces) had been discussed

---

* Professor Department of Political Science, University of Toronto.
[1] Zachary Elkins, Tom Ginsburg, and James Melton, *The Endurance of National Constitutions*
(Cambridge 2009) Introduction.
[2] Ibid., ch 6.

seriously in the 1850s in both Canada (the current provinces of Ontario and Quebec) and the Maritimes (New Brunswick, Nova Scotia, and Prince Edward Island), and had been floated frequently before that.[3] Yet those earlier discussions came to nothing whereas the discussions in the mid-1860s ultimately produced a constitutional agreement to create a federal union, or Confederation, in British North America. What was the difference? The simple answer is that a variety of forces—some structural, others more contingent—came together to convince political elites in most of the British North American provinces that some form of dramatic constitutional change was either necessary or desirable, and that the conditions of the mid-1860s made action either urgent or propitious. It has become something of a mug's game among historians to determine the relative weight of each factor in the Confederation calculus, and to analyze the complex configuration of "pro" and "anti" forces in each of the affected colonies. It is perhaps sufficient, and more helpful for our purposes here, to say that it is the confluence of factors rather than any single cause that ultimately drove the Confederation debate forward and produced its stiffest resistance.

What were the most important of these factors? Among the structural changes that commanded attention, none was more important than the transformation of a staple-based into an industrial economy. As Donald Creighton put it in an important study for the Rowell-Sirois Commission in 1938:

> In Great Britain, and to a lesser extent in the United States, the twenty years which preceded Canadian Confederation formed a stage of importance in the great transition from commercialism to industrial capitalism. The revolution in technology, which had begun far back in the 18th century, continued without interruption; iron and coal provided at once the physical expression from human inventions and the power to drive them; and mechanized land and water transport carried the productions of large-scale industry to the four corners of the globe. The shift from wood to iron, from water-power to steam, from canals to railways and from sailing-ships to steamboats became virtually an accomplished fact.[4]

These technological developments affected British North America as well. As Creighton noted, the growth of railways in the province of Canada—from 60 miles of track in 1850 to more than two thousand by 1860—conveys a sense of the rapid pace of change.[5] The new industrial economy presented enormous opportunities for the accumulation of wealth, and the evidence suggests that across the British North American provinces "there was a growing desire to participate in [it]."[6] The challenge facing the British North

---

[3] See, for instance, G.P. Browne, *Documents on the Confederation of British North America* (McClelland and Stewart 1969); Phillip Buckner, "The Maritimes and Confederation: A Reassessment" (1990) 71 CHR 1; and J.M.S. Careless, *Canada: A Story of Challenge* (Macmillan 1963).

[4] D.G. Creighton, *British North America at Confederation: A Study Prepared for the Royal Commission on Dominion Provincial Relations* (Queen's Printer, 1938, reprinted 1963) 7.

[5] Ibid., 15.

[6] Buckner, *Maritimes and Confederation*, above (n 3) 12.

Americans, however, was to find a way to sustain "the tremendous and expensive adjustments involved."[7] The inability of individual colonies to raise large amounts of capital, build infrastructure, create a coordinated transportation network for manufactured goods (including secure rail access to ocean ports), and provide security against economic shocks over which they had little control all stood in the way of full participation in the new international economy. As a response to all of these challenges, the creation of a national economy, led by a strong central government, rose to the top of the dance card of potential remedies.

The combination of opportunity and challenge was particularly striking with respect to western expansion. Until the mid-1850s, the North West (controlled by the Hudson's Bay Company under royal charter) was viewed by most members of the Canadian political and economic elite as "a barren tract, forever destined by its soil and climate to remain a wilderness" and, therefore, "of limited use" beyond its traditional role in the fur trade.[8] This view changed dramatically in the latter half of the 1850s after a series of blue-ribbon geological surveys[9] concluded that, in fact, the prairie west was eminently suitable for agriculture and settlement. And although it took slightly longer for politicians to grasp the importance of these findings, by the time of the Confederation debates in the mid-1860s western expansion had become a key argument for union. "As George Brown pointed out, (the North West) involved an area 'greater in extent than the whole soil of Russia,' and that vast resource would be 'opened up to civilization under the auspices of the British American Confederation.' "[10] Aided by European emigration, the prairie west would become "the seat of an industrious, prosperous and powerful people"[11] and provide linkage to other British colonies on the Pacific coast. But to do that would require a massive investment of both economic and political capital, neither of which was available in sufficient quantities in any single province.

Although the economic transformation created by industrialization affected all of the British North American colonies, the province of Canada faced an additional structural constraint of its own in the 1860s, namely institutional deadlock. As a result of the Act of Union of 1840, the communities of Canada East (Quebec) and Canada West (Ontario) had been united politically through a single legislative assembly. The two communities themselves, however, were quite different in composition: Canada East was largely French-speaking and Catholic; Canada West was overwhelmingly English-speaking and largely Protestant. To accommodate this linguistic and religious dualism a number of norms were developed to govern political life. Each community had equal representation in the legislative assembly (a principle that initially favoured Canada West because it had the smaller population). Political and administrative positions, including political

---

[7] Creighton, above (n 4) 11.

[8] Doug Owram, *Promise of Eden: The Canadian Expansionist Movement and the Idea of the West, 1856–1900* (University of Toronto Press, 1980) 59.

[9] Ibid., ch 3.

[10] Ibid., 73.

[11] George Brown, cited in Owram, ibid., 76.

leadership, were apportioned on the basis of equality. A proto-federal system emerged, in which decision-making was decentralized so as to permit each section to have legislative autonomy and control over matters that affected only the local population, although which subjects were truly local and which not remained controversial. This sort of ambiguity was crucially important because on matters that pertained to the province as a whole the principle of "double majority" prevailed; legislation, by this rule, could only succeed if it was supported by a majority of representatives from each of the sections. All of these provisions produced collective action and coordination problems. The result was that the province of Canada was beset by "an almost chronic state of sectional rivalries" characterized by "small, precarious majorities in parliament, short-lived governments, frequent elections, and a permanent condition of governmental instability."[12]

Dysfunctional though it was, this political dualism might have endured had it not been accompanied by a dramatic demographic shift between the two Canadas. When the Act of Union was promulgated in 1840, the population of Canada East exceeded that of Canada West. By 1851, Canada West had caught up, and by 1861 the population gap between Canada West and Canada East had widened significantly, propelled by large-scale immigration from the British Isles.[13] This population imbalance emboldened leading anglophone politicians to argue relentlessly (and opportunistically) that legislative representation should be apportioned on the basis of population ("rep by pop") rather than according to a principle of sectional equality. The likelihood that expansion to the prairie west would provide the basis for even greater Anglo-Protestant dominance reinforced the view in Canada West that the current constitutional arrangement could not hold. Most francophone politicians in Canada East resigned themselves to the inevitability of representational change, which produced a powerful incentive to find some better, more lasting form of protection for their social, cultural, linguistic, and legal distinctiveness. The best alternative on offer was some sort of federal arrangement that would provide for a general government apportioned roughly on the basis of population to govern on matters of general concern while leaving "perfect freedom and authority for the provinces to run their own internal affairs."[14]

The political deadlock in Canada was largely home-grown or endogenous, but there were other external or exogenous structural changes that underscored the seismic changes associated with the 1860s. The most notable in this regard were the changing geo-political calculations that followed from the American Civil War. The *Trent* affair of 1861, in which American officials boarded a British vessel to intercept Confederate recruiters on their way to London, is a case in point. The episode was important at the time because it almost led to war, but in retrospect its real importance lies in the way

---

[12] Donald Creighton, "The 1860s," in J.M.S. Careless and R. Craig Brown (eds), *The Canadians* (MacMillan, 1967) 8.

[13] A.I. Silver, *The French-Canadian Idea of Confederation 1864–1900* (University of Toronto Press, 1982) Introduction.

[14] Ibid., 37. See also Yvan Lamonde, *The Social History of Ideas in Quebec, 1760–1896* (Phyllis Aronoff tr, McGill-Queen's Press, 2013) ch 10 & 12.

it exposed the basic dilemma of mid-nineteenth-century British imperialism. On the one hand, Britain remained committed to defending its colonies, but wanted or needed to reduce its military expenditures. On the other, the Civil War demonstrated clearly that the United States possessed both growing military capacity and distinctly different national interests. The large question was what would happen, after the Civil War ended, to prevent British North America's "absorption into the vortex of American confederation"[15] by military means. The only satisfactory solution was through collective security. "In order to secure the help of (England's) power in our defence, we must help ourselves. We could not do this satisfactorily or efficiently unless we had a Confederation. When all united, the enemy would know that if he attacked any part of these Provinces—Prince Edward Island or Canada—he would have to encounter the combined strength of the empire."[16] Or as Thomas D'Arcy McGee, another leading member of the Confederation coalition, put it pithily: "Let us remember this, that when the three cries among our next neighbours are money, taxation, blood, it is time for us to provide for our own security."[17]

Nor was this structural geo-political change entirely abstract. A series of more contingent provocations galvanized sentiment in favour of union. The abrogation, in 1866, of the Reciprocity Treaty which had lubricated cross-border trade for more than a decade, was one sign of what Donald Creighton called America's political truculence and economic aggressiveness.[18] Various semi-official initiatives, including the introduction of a bill in the House of Representatives to annex Canada and an American warning that it did not consider itself bound to the agreement that had effectively de-militarized the Great Lakes after the War of 1812, were equally provocative (if improbable). And various border skirmishes, the most famous of which involved a group of Irish nationalists (Fenians), freshly energized by the end of the Civil War, added fuel to the fire at crucial moments in the run-up to Confederation. The desultory Fenian "raids" posed no serious threat to New Brunswick, but they became a lightning rod for those who argued that political union was necessary to ensure territorial integrity against a military power wanting to punish Britain for its support of the South. Eighty years ago, Chester Martin quipped that "it might almost be claimed that the Civil War which saved the American union created the Canadian."[19] This observation still has the ring of truth about it.

Yet if these structural conditions—economic, institutional, and geo-political— provided an inviting environment for constitutional change, the push for Confederation itself required a combination of *virtu* and *fortuna* as well. One crucial trigger was the

---

[15] Canada, Legislative Assembly, *Parliamentary Debates on the Subject of the Confederation of the British North American Provinces* (Hunter, Rose and Company, 1865) 55 (G.-E. Cartier). [hereinafter *Confederation Debates*].

[16] Ibid., 55.

[17] Ibid., 131.

[18] Creighton, *British North America at Confederation*, above (n 4) 10.

[19] Chester Martin, "The British Policy in Canadian Confederation" (1932) 13 CHR 5. See also Phillip Buckner, "L'élaboration de la constitution canadienne au sein du monde britannique," in Eugénie Brouillet, Alain-G. Gagnon, and Guy Laforest (eds), *La Conférence de Quebec de 1864: 150 ans plus tard* (Presses de l'Université Laval, 2016) 71.

formation, in June 1864, of the "Great Coalition" in Canada that brought together George Brown (leader of the Liberals/Grits in Canada West), John A. Macdonald (leader of the Conservatives in Canada West), and George-Étienne Cartier (leader of the Conservatives or *Bleus* in Canada East). The creation of this tri-party coalition (missing only the Liberals or *Rouges* of Canada East) was crucial because it broke the bitter and intractable partisan conflict that had characterized Canadian politics since the Act of Union.

Although their calculations varied, each of the three party leaders was willing to take a significant political risk in joining the Coalition.[20] What brought, and ultimately held, them together was support for some form of federal union. But which form? One possibility was to officially or formally federalize the two Canadas, East and West, by revising the Act of Union into a more coherent, workable, and formal constitution. A more ambitious possibility was to construct a broader union within British North America that included the Maritime provinces and perhaps even the more distant Newfoundland as well. Prodded by the activist Lieutenant Governor of New Brunswick, Arthur Gordon, the governments of Nova Scotia, New Brunswick, and Prince Edward Island had decided, independently, to meet in September 1864 to discuss the possibility of a maritime union. In the event, the Canadian and Maritime delegates met together in Charlottetown, and reached an agreement in principle about the desirability of a British North American union. The same group (now with the addition of Newfoundland) reconvened in Quebec City in October 1864 to design a constitution in greater detail. The 72 Quebec Resolutions (as the draft constitution produced at Quebec was known) were then sent back to each of the provinces for approval (or rejection), and thereafter on to London. Revisions, refinements, and additions—some of them quite significant—were made in London over the course of 1866, both by the Canadian representatives and the British drafters. Introduced, debated, and passed by the Imperial Parliament in the early months of 1867, the *British North America Act* was given royal assent at the end of March, and came into effect on 1 July 1867.

2. CONSTITUTIONAL AMBIVALENCE

What were the distinctive constitutional design choices embodied first in the Quebec Resolutions (1864), then the *Constitution Act, 1867*? Let us consider three pillars of the original Canadian constitutional design—federalism, democracy, and minority rights.

Clearly, the creation of a specifically federal union was central to the Confederation project. The Preamble to the *Constitution Act, 1867* is explicit about the motivation that

---

[20] The story of the formation of the Great Coalition is well told in Christopher Moore, *1867: How the Fathers Made a Deal* (McClelland and Stewart, 1997).

led to the Act's creation. It begins: "Whereas the Provinces of Canada, Nova Scotia and New Brunswick have expressed their Desire to be *federally united* . . . ."[21] Yet just as clearly, the genus of federalism includes a wide variety of species. If one takes as a pared-down working definition of federalism the division of legislative authority between a central government and some number of regional governments, the possibilities for variation in constitutional design are immense, ranging by example along a continuum from highly centralized to highly decentralized. What was distinctive about the federal design created by the delegates in Quebec in 1864 and embodied in the *Constitution Act, 1867*?

A significant number of the Confederation architects favoured a federation that endowed the national government with a full quiver of governmental powers adequate to the task of building and defending a prosperous trans-continental nation-state. This view followed logically and directly from the economic and geopolitical imperatives summarized above. As Donald Creighton, Macdonald's biographer, put it in his study for the Rowell-Sirois Commission: "(T)he chief economic objective of the Dominion was the commercial integration of the country on a continental scale; and, as the authority which was obviously designed to assume the role of leadership in material development, the federal government was naturally accepted as the regulator of the business affairs of the new, commercial federation."[22]

But strength at the centre was also a matter of sound constitutional design. John A. Macdonald articulated this argument explicitly in the course of a major speech during the debate on the Quebec Resolutions held in the Canadian legislative assembly in February–March 1865. The confederation plan had been developed in the long shadows of the American Civil War, and Macdonald maintained that he and the other architects had been keen to avoid the design flaws that, in their view, had led to the War:

> Ever since the union was formed the difficulty of what is called "State Rights" has existed, and this had much to do in bringing on the present unhappy war in the United States. They commenced, in fact, at the wrong end. They declared by their Constitution that each state was a sovereignty in itself, and that all powers incident to a sovereignty belonged to each state, except those powers which, by the Constitution, were conferred upon the General Government and Congress. Here we have adopted a different system. We have strengthened the General Government. We have given the General Legislature all the great subjects of legislation. We have conferred on them, not only specifically and in detail, all the powers which are incident to sovereignty, but we have expressly declared that all subjects of general interest not distinctly and exclusively conferred upon the local governments and legislatures, shall be conferred upon the General Government and Legislature. We have thus avoided that great source of the disruption of the United States.

---

[21] *Constitution Act, 1867*, Preamble [emphasis added].
[22] Creighton, *British North America at Confederation*, above (n 4) 51.

Having learned from these American errors, Macdonald maintained that the Canadian plan combined "all the advantages of a legislative union under one administration, with, at the same time, the guarantees for local institutions and local laws."[23]

There is, indeed, considerable evidence to substantiate Creighton's claim that the federal government was expected to provide leadership in the "business affairs of the new, commercial federation" and Macdonald's that the federal (or national) government had been assigned "all the great subjects of legislation" at Quebec. The list of federal powers in the Quebec Resolutions, carried over to Section 91 of the *Constitution Act, 1867*, is impressive. It includes broad power to make laws with respect to "the regulation of trade and commerce" (not just inter-provincial trade), "banking, incorporation of banks, and the issue of paper money" (that is, control of monetary policy), raising money by any mode of taxation (that is, control of fiscal policy and with it, on one view, the controversial power to spend money on matters that fall within provincial jurisdiction), defence (in response to the perceived need to provide collective security), and the criminal law (thus establishing national standards of justice and the power to appoint judges even in provincial superior courts).[24] All of these were examples of the general authority, to cite the formulation used in the Quebec Resolutions, "to make laws for the peace, welfare, and good government" of the country.[25]

Macdonald's criticism of the U.S. Constitution notwithstanding, the delegates to the Quebec Conference also took care to include what, in American constitutionalism, is called a supremacy clause—a rule to deal with cases in which federal and state legislation collide. The version in the Quebec Resolutions reads: "In regard to all subjects over which jurisdiction belongs to both the General and Local Legislatures, the laws of the General Parliament shall control and supersede those made by the Local Legislature, and the latter shall be void so far as they are repugnant to, or inconsistent with, the former."[26] The basic rule, in other words, is that in the event that two laws—one federal and one provincial—collide, the federal claim prevails. Consigned to the category of "miscellaneous" provisions passed at Quebec, this supremacy clause supplied a general line of "defence" to accompany the federal government's "offence"—the capacious list of subjects on which it had exclusive jurisdiction.

As if there were not enough, the Quebec Resolutions also provided the federal government with two open-ended constitutional instruments that could be used to de-rail or veto unwelcome provincial legislation. The power of reservation permitted a provincial Lieutenant-Governor to withhold royal assent from provincial bills so as to prevent them from having the force of law. Disallowance effectively permitted the federal

---

[23] *Confederation Debates* above (n 15) 33 (Macdonald).

[24] Compare Quebec Resolutions (#29) in Browne (ed), *Documents* above (n 3) with *Constitution Act, 1867* (section 91).

[25] The phrase "peace, welfare, and good government" (Quebec Resolutions in Browne (ed), *Documents,* above (n 3)) was changed to "peace, order and good government" in the *Constitution Act, 1867.* Both phrases were commonly used in imperial statutes at the time.

[26] See Quebec Resolutions in Browne (ed), *Documents,* above (n 3) (#45).

government to veto any piece of provincial legislation within a year of enactment. These veto powers did not appear out of thin air. They were miniature versions of the same veto powers that the Imperial Government could exercise over its colonial governments. As Macdonald put it in the Confederation Debates: "The General Government assumes towards the local governments precisely the same position as the Imperial Government holds with respect to each of the colonies now." One level is superior, the other "subordinate."[27]

On the basis of this sort of evidence—broad legislative powers, supremacy in the case of jurisdictional conflict, and unlimited federal veto powers—many commentators have concluded that the Confederation settlement tilted strongly towards a form of high centralism. Indeed, in the oft-quoted formulation of K.C. Wheare, Canada is really not a federal state at all; it is, at best, "quasi-federal."[28] If additional evidence were needed to clinch this characterization, it is supplied by the vigorous opposition voiced by those actors, both in Canada and the Maritimes, who rejected the Quebec plan on the grounds that it would undermine and overwhelm local legislatures.[29]

In fact, however, this interpretation overstates the centralism built into the *Constitution Act, 1867* in at least three ways. First, it is true that the constitutional division of powers assigned the lion's share of legislative powers to the federal government, and it is certainly true as well that Ottawa had broad authority and capacity to mould fiscal and monetary policy. Yet this does not mean that provincial governments would be little more than glorified municipalities. After all, the provinces were assigned responsibility for such matters as education (which was, already by the 1860s, a significant policy field),[30] property and civil rights (defended by supporters of Confederation as the basis for protecting cultural diversity, especially the civil law tradition in Quebec),[31] the management and sale of public lands (the principal source of revenue for provincial governments at the time),[32] and hospitals (which, though less important in the 1860s, soon evolved into broader responsibility for healthcare). Beyond this, the provinces shared responsibility for agriculture and immigration (which provided leverage in two policy areas central to the nation-building objectives of the Confederation plan). Taken

[27] *Confederation Debates,* above (n 15) 42. The powers of reservation and disallowance are set out in the Quebec Resolutions in Browne (ed), *Documents,* above (n 3) #50 and #51, and in the *Constitution Act, 1867* in sections 56 and 90.

[28] K.C. Wheare, *Federal Government* (4th ed, Oxford University Press, 1963).

[29] See, for example, Silver, *French-Canadian Idea of Confederation,* above (n 13) ch 2; Buckner, "The Maritimes and Confederation," above (n 3); and Robert C. Vipond, "1787 and 1867: The Federal Principle and Canadian Confederation Reconsidered" (1989) 22 CJPS 9–12. See also Éric Bédard, "Éviter ce 'gouffre d'inique liberté'. Le fédéralisme centralisateur de Joseph-Edouard Cauchon," in Brouillet, Gagnon, and Laforest (eds), *La Conférence de Québec de 1864,* above (n 19) 109.

[30] Paul Axelrod, *The Promise of Schooling: Education in Canada, 1800–1914* (University of Toronto Press, 1997).

[31] Eugénie Brouillet, *La Négation de la Nation* (Septentrion, 2005).

[32] H.V. Nelles, *The Politics of Development: Forests, Mines, and Hydro-electric Power in Ontario, 1849–1941* (Macmillan, 1974).

together, these legislative powers provided provincial governments with ample constitutional arguments to claim significant legislative space for themselves after 1867.

Second, the image of a federal constitutional order in which the national government
is superior and the provincial governments subordinate is an unhelpful caricature. For
reasons that are obscure, the supremacy clause (which was one potential tool of federal domination embedded in the Quebec Resolutions) was removed from the constitutional plan during the drafting process in London.[33] For reasons that are equally
opaque, what appeared in the *Constitution Act, 1867* instead was a clear statement that,
within their respective jurisdictional spheres, both Ottawa and the provinces enjoyed
"exclusive" legislative authority.[34] Whether the constitutional drafters understood the
full implications of this statement is unclear. What is clear is that those actors who, post-
1867, began to agitate for provincial autonomy or provincial rights seized on this formulation to challenge the idea that the Canadian constitutional order was a hierarchical
arrangement in which the federal government was superior and the provinces subordinate. In their view, the assignment of "exclusive" legislative authority to the provinces
demonstrated a commitment to the federal principle, according to which the two levels
of government are constitutionally "co-equal" or coordinate, each enjoying autonomy
or sovereignty to legislate on those matters assigned to it.[35]

To be sure, this interpretation of co-equal sovereignty was difficult to square with the
existence of the veto powers of disallowance and reservation, which apparently permitted precisely the sort of interference that the provincial autonomists claimed was inconsistent with the federal principle. This explains, third, why the provincial autonomists
devoted significant political and intellectual resources to disabling the veto powers in
the years after 1867. In fact, the Imperial analogy Macdonald used to describe the federal
veto powers was rather hollow from the outset because, by the 1860s, London had largely
abandoned their use. Everyone understood that the Imperial vetoes were an affront to
colonial self-government, which is exactly the argument the provincial autonomists
deployed effectively to undercut the federal government's use of disallowance and reservation post-1867. Besides, successive federal governments quickly learned that they
did not necessarily want to be dragged into thorny local disputes—concerning minority education rights, for example—by striking down contentious provincial legislation.
The result is that, reasonably soon after Confederation, both reservation and disallowance became tainted. Reservation was used on a regular basis only for about a decade;
disallowance was deployed with some frequency as a jurisdictional veto until about
1890, then quickly abandoned. Although both veto powers remain on the constitutional

---

[33] The basic principle underlying the supremacy clause resurfaced in a weaker and more limited form
in the context of the subjects of immigration and agriculture, two policy areas over which federal and
provincial governments share responsibility. See *Constitution Act, 1867*, s. 95.

[34] *Constitution Act, 1867*, s. 91 and s. 92. The addition of the word "exclusive" appeared only in the final
drafts of the Act, suggesting that it was included as a matter of legal form rather than as a political claim.
Whatever its origins, its inclusion had a profound effect on subsequent debate in Canada.

[35] See Vipond, *1787 and 1867*, above (n 29).

books, it is now almost unimaginable that they would be used as a constitutional remedy, especially when judicial review is available as an alternative.[36]

What does this characterization of the constitutional origins of Canadian federalism have to do with constitutional longevity? In her sweeping account of the history and dynamics of Canadian public policy, Carolyn Tuohy has argued that what distinguishes the Canadian policy process is "its quintessential ambivalence," which she defines as a system that "legitimizes competing principles" and that allows "principles to co-exist in a context of constitutional and institutional ambiguity." The basic principles may pull "in competing directions," but their common legitimacy means that it is difficult to embrace some and utterly reject others; however awkward the fit, the dyads of state and market, national and regional, individual and collective remain in dynamic tension with each other.[37]

Building on Tuohy's insight, I want to suggest that competing but co-existing principles—what we might term "ambivalence"—was embedded in the constitutional design of Canadian federalism from the outset. Rather than endorsing one (and only one) authoritative view of federalism, the Confederation settlement embodied two quite different visions. Competitive and contested, these different visions of federalism nevertheless had the effect of producing the constitutional flexibility necessary to adjust to significant political, social, and economic change. Because both centralized and decentralized conceptions of federalism were constitutionally embedded, it was possible to change policy direction without necessarily engaging basic questions of constitutional legitimacy or creating the need to destroy the constitutional structure (though we have come close). Moreover, the fact that competing principles were equally legitimate meant that there was also a limit on the extent of change that could be accommodated. Change, even quite massive change, could occur to Canada's federal system, but none of it required (or allowed) gutting the constitutional structure. Far from being a pathological element in Canadian constitutionalism, ambivalence by this interpretation is actually a salutary design feature. By permitting a significant amount of constitutional flexibility in response to political and social change, it has contributed significantly to the longevity of Canada's constitution.[38]

Nor are the federal features of the Canadian constitutional order unique in their tolerance of constitutional ambivalence. In the *Secession Reference Case* (1998),[39] the Supreme Court of Canada identified the principle of democracy as one of the four pillars of Canadian constitutionalism. In its words, "the principle of democracy has always

[36] See Robert C. Vipond, *Liberty and Community: Canadian Federalism and the Failure of the Constitution* (SUNY, 1991) for an elaboration of this argument.

[37] Carolyn J. Tuohy, *Policy and Politics in Canada: Institutionalized Ambivalence* (Temple, 1992) 4–5.

[38] This interpretation runs parallel to, and generally supports, the argument of Elkins, Ginsburg, and Melton in *The Endurance of National Constitutions* above (n 1) who also emphasize the connection between flexibility and constitutional endurance. However, my emphasis on the way this flexibility is achieved through ambivalence is somewhat different. See Elkins, Ginsburg, and Melton, *Endurance of National Constitutions* above (n 1) 81–83.

[39] *Reference Re Secession of Quebec* [1998] 2 S.C.R. 217.

informed the design of our constitutional structure, and continues to act as an essential interpretive consideration to this day." Democracy was (and remains) a "baseline" from which "the framers of our Constitution" operated. "It is perhaps for this reason," the Court speculates, "that the principle was not explicitly identified in the text of the *Constitution Act, 1867* itself. To have done so might have appeared redundant, even silly to the framers"—although this seems a curious reason not to enunciate fundamental principles.[40]

An alternative interpretation to the one proffered by the Court is that the framers of the Constitution did not identify democracy explicitly as a principle because they were, as a group, deeply ambivalent about it. The Fathers clearly and unequivocally embraced the idea of responsible self-government: the fundamental institutional principle that the Executive should be drawn from, and accountable to, the legislature. That is one meaning of the terse and deeply encoded statement in the preamble to the *Constitution Act, 1867* that Canada would have "a constitution similar in principle to that of the United Kingdom." As the framers understood it, responsible self-government entailed two commitments. The first is that the House of Commons had to be sufficiently democratic to establish its legitimacy as the "popular" branch; this is one reason the principle of "representation by population" fit so neatly as part of the Confederation plan. The second commitment is that Parliament, as the central institution of governance, had to be carefully constructed so as to create a fine balance between the many and varied social interests, classes, regions, and communities that comprised British North American society. Parliament was sovereign precisely because it was the one place in which all social actors or "estates" were represented. The dilemma is that these requirements, electoral and institutional, pulled in different directions. The lower house had to represent the people as a whole, but it couldn't be too democratic for fear that American-style "universal democracy"[41] and "mob rule"[42] would undermine the institutional balance of interests preserved by Parliament.

Macdonald articulated this ambivalence explicitly in the Canadian legislative assembly: "In settling the constitution of the lower house, that which peculiarly represents the people, it was agreed that the principle of representation based on population should be adopted, and the mode of applying that principle is fully developed in these resolutions." Such is the logic, derived from a principle of equality, that sustains standard liberal accounts of representation. But he proceeded, in the very next breath, to reassure his fellow parliamentarians that, when he spoke of "representation by population, the house will of course understand that universal suffrage is not in any way sanctioned, or admitted by these resolutions, as the basis on which the constitution of the popular branch should rest."[43] Take democracy (or equality) too far, in other words, and the "calm and

---

[40] *Reference Re Secession of Quebec* [1998] 2 S.C.R. 217, [62].
[41] *Confederation Debates* above (n 15) 143 (McGee).
[42] *Confederation Debates* above (n 15) 59 (Cartier).
[43] *Confederation Debates* above (n 15) 35 (Macdonald).

deliberate judgments of the people, as expressed through their representatives" threatens to degenerate into "a mere form and cover to tyranny."[44]

No national institution better illustrates this democratic ambivalence than the Senate, the upper house created in imitation of the British House of Lords. The Senate's remit was defined in several different ways in the debates surrounding the Confederation proposal. One purpose was to apply "sober second thought"[45] to ill-considered or impetuous legislation passed by the House of Commons. A second was to provide a more substantial voice for regional interests otherwise overwhelmed by population-based representation in the House of Commons.[46] A third, underscored by a sizeable property qualification, was "to represent the principle of property. The rights of the minority must be protected," Macdonald argued at Quebec, "and the rich are always fewer in number than the poor."[47] These functions, but especially the last, led the architects to make the Senate an appointed rather than an elected body—even (or especially) if that characteristic reduced its leverage over the House. As Macdonald described the parliamentary order: "(The Senate) must be an independent house, having a free action of its own, for it is only valuable as being a regulating body, calmly considering the legislation initiated by the popular branch and preventing any hasty or ill-considered legislation which may come from that body, but it will never set itself in opposition against the deliberate and well understood wishes of the people."[48] As an appointed body, the Senate was simultaneously enabled *and* constrained. Which is to say that the Senate was deliberately designed to allow competing principles—democratic and anti-democratic—to co-exist over the long term. And, indeed, despite many attempts either to reform or abolish it, the Senate remains largely intact—sustained by the ambivalence with which it was designed.

The imperative to protect minority (often called group) rights, the third constitutional pillar, was one of the main drivers that produced Confederation, especially in the province of Canada where 25 years of acrimony between French and English, Catholic and Protestant, majority and minority had convinced most members of the political elite that the status quo was unsustainable. Considering the extent to which the issue preoccupied pre-Confederation Canadian politics, the provisions for protecting minority rights, first in the Quebec Resolutions, then in the *Constitution Act, 1867* were actually quite modest. The use of either French or English was guaranteed in Parliament whereas the use of English was protected in the Quebec Assembly.[49] French could be used in federal courts just as the English minority in Quebec could use English to plead cases in that province.[50] And the Resolutions promised reciprocal rights to Ontario Catholics

[44] *Confederation Debates* above (n 15) 1004 (Macdonald).
[45] *Confederation Debates* above (n 15) 35 (Macdonald).
[46] Macdonald summarizes the case for extended regional representation in the Senate in his main speech during the Confederation Debates. See *Confederation Debates* above (n 15) 35–38.
[47] Browne, *Documents* above (n 3) 98.
[48] *Confederation Debates* above (n 15) 36 (Macdonald).
[49] *Quebec Resolutions* in Browne (ed) *Documents,* above (n 3) (#46); *Constitution Act, 1867* s. 133.
[50] *Quebec Resolutions* in Browne (ed) *Documents,* above (n 3) (#46); *Constitution Act, 1867* s. 133.

and Quebec Protestants with respect to denominational schools.[51] But it is striking that no Acadian (the French, Catholic minority in New Brunswick) was present at the Quebec Conference to press the case for minority religious and linguistic rights in the Maritimes, and although the possibility of western expansion was clearly on the minds of some of the most prominent Fathers, the idea of a truly national dualism received little air time at Quebec.[52]

One explanation for the modest scope of these provisions is that most French Canadians, concentrated in Quebec, did not identify strongly with their co-linguists and co-religionists in the rest of the country, because they believed that the best hope for French, Catholic Canada rested with the survival of Quebec.[53] As a consequence, they reasoned that robust provincial autonomy overseen by a legislature in which francophones were a majority was the most efficient way to protect their position and their rights as a minority within the new Canada. But this move—protecting a minority by transforming it into a majority—introduced an element of ambivalence into the Canadian understanding of rights because it complicated the conventional understanding of rights as vulnerable to, and threatened by, democratic majorities. The architects of 1867 were certainly familiar with and embraced the importance of protecting individual rights. Most of them assumed the existence of certain individual rights and civil liberties protected by the British constitution and the common law, such as the right to a jury trial in serious criminal matters, access to the writ of habeas corpus to test the validity of imprisonment, and the right to hold and enjoy property. These rights had been elaborated over the centuries, and although subject to some limitation by legislatures had a relatively well-defined content. But they also understood, thanks in part to their experience in dealing with questions of language and religion, that legislatures (as in the case of Quebec) could protect rights (both individual and collective) as well as violate them. Thus, rights pulled in both directions—both towards and away from legislatures.[54] In a word, the goal was to redeem "constitutional liberty"[55]—a versatile (and I would add, ambivalent) ideal that placed the onus for striking the balance between majority and minority and between public good and private rights on the institutions and structures

---

[51] *Quebec Resolutions* in Browne (ed) *Documents*, above (n 3) (#43.6); *Constitution Act, 1867* s. 93.2.

[52] See Gaétan Migneault, "Le Canada français et la Confédération: les Acadiens du Nouveau-Brunswick," in Jean-François Caron and Marcel Martel (eds), *Le Canada français et la Confédération* (Presses de l'Université Laval, 2016). In London, constitutional protection of minority school rights was extended to apply in all provinces to denominational schools established in law after as well as before union. See *Constitution Act, 1867*, s. 93:1, 3.

[53] Silver, *French-Canadian Idea of Confederation* above (n 13) chs 2 & 3.

[54] This paragraph draws on David R. Cameron, Jacqueline D. Krikorian, and Robert C. Vipond, "Revisiting the 1865 Canadian Debates on Confederation: Rights and the Constitution," *Canada Watch* (York University, Spring 2016) 13. The larger idea of rights protection is developed in Richard Risk and Robert C. Vipond, "Rights Talk in Canada in the Late Nineteenth Century: 'The Good Sense and Right Feeling of the People'" (1996) 14 Law and History Review 1.

[55] For numerous examples showing how the term *constitutional liberty* was used in the debates over Confederation, see Janet Ajzenstat, Paul Romney, Ian Gentles, and William D. Gairdner (eds), *Canada's Founding Debates* (Stoddart, 1999) Part One.

of government as a whole; and that made rights protection more about creating "dialogue" among institutions than on erecting bright-line boundaries between them.

3. DESIGN FAILURES: SOVEREIGNTY AND INDIGENOUS PEOPLES

I have argued that constitutional ambivalence—competing principles co-existing in the same constitutional structure—helps to explain the longevity of Canada's constitution. But is the converse true as well? If constitutional ambivalence was absent in 1867, did this absence de-stabilize the constitution in any significant way? To answer this question, let us turn to two final architectural features—the locus of sovereignty and the place of Indigenous peoples.

Constitution-making raises questions of sovereignty—both legal and political— because it both allocates coercive governmental power in authoritative ways and because it requires some agreement about who may legitimately make (and remake) such authoritative decisions. In other words, sovereignty is both constituted (it defines what the rules are and how they will be enforced) and constituent (it defines who gets to make the rules). The debates surrounding Confederation had lots to say about what was *constituted* by the Quebec Resolutions and the *Constitution Act, 1867*. I have already summarized some of these debates, grouped together under the themes of federalism, democracy, and rights. About sovereignty in the *constituent* sense, however, about who may make (or re-make, or unmake) the constitution, there was much less discussion. One strategy was simply to avoid engaging the question of where the legitimate authority to make and amend the fundamental law is lodged. Some Confederationists argued that it was actually unnecessary to talk about the source of constitutional power because the constituent power in this sense rested with the Queen in the Imperial Parliament. As one Canadian legislator put it: "We have not the power to (make constitutional changes for British North America). We merely propose to address Her Majesty on the subject. The imperial parliament alone has that power."[56]

But this argument was transparently disingenuous. It was clear that the British authorities were not going to act on a constitutional proposal without a clear mandate from the colonies themselves. Indeed, the Quebec Resolutions contained clear instructions to the effect that "the sanction of the imperial *and* local parliaments shall be sought for the union of the provinces, on the principles adopted by the conference."[57] The point is that everyone involved in the Confederation initiative agreed that some form of local consent was necessary for the initiative to be considered legitimate. The only real question, therefore, was *how* this local sanction would be obtained and registered. In the

---

[56] *Confederation Debates,* above (n 15) 219 (Christie).
[57] *Quebec Resolutions* in Browne (ed) *Documents,* above (n 3) (#70) [emphasis added].

event, a lively (if often desultory) debate rippled across British North America between those who thought legislative ratification in each province was sufficient to meet the requirement of consent and those who believed that some more direct, focused, and extra-legislative ratification was required in each province—whether in the form of a general election, a referendum, or a special convention.[58] This discussion became, in effect, a proxy for a debate about the relative virtues of parliamentary as opposed to popular sovereignty.[59] At one extreme were those, like the prominent *Bleu* (or Conservative) legislator Joseph Cauchon, who objected strenuously to the "democratic-republican" idea that would "deny one of the most essential and fundamental principles of the British Constitution—that is to say, that parliament may change the constitution without special appeals to the electoral body, and without recourse to popular conventions."[60] At the other extreme were those, like the Canadian legislator James O'Halloran, who put the case for extra-legislative consent this way: "When we assume the power to deal with this question, to change the whole system of government, to effect a revolution, peaceful though it be, without reference to the will of the people of this country, we arrogate to ourselves a right never conferred upon us, and our act is a usurpation."[61] And, in fact, the processes by which the Quebec Resolutions were ratified (or in the case of Prince Edward Island and Newfoundland, rejected) were similarly varied (although it should be noted that none of the provinces, unlike the American states in 1787, created special, extra-legislative conventions to consider the resolutions).

Yet for all their variety, these debates did not really get to the heart of constituent sovereignty. As much as participants talked about *how* the people should register their consent, no one seems to have thought to ask just *who* the people are. These are different questions. The first, "how" question seized the attention of those involved in making the constitution because it had an immediate, "next steps" quality about it. The second, "who" question was less immediate (though no less important) because it concerned remaking (or amending) the constitution in the future. By whom may the constitution be changed? All of the people of all of the provinces? Most of the people of most of the provinces? Most of the provinces but always Quebec? Most of the provinces with or without Quebec? A national majority? Neither the Quebec Resolutions nor the *Constitution Act, 1867* contained rules that govern the amending process. And neither provided clear principles of constituent sovereignty that could be used to create rules in the absence of an explicit amending formula.

The absence of such principles did not stop political actors post-Confederation from conjuring them. If the provinces had negotiated the terms of union in the first instance,

---

[58] See Ajzenstat, Romney, Gentles and Gairdner, *Canada's Founding Debates* above (n 55) Part Five for a good sample of opinion drawn from across British North America.

[59] This debate has been reproduced in recent scholarship about Confederation. Contrast Janet Ajzenstat, *The Canadian Founding: John Locke and Parliament* (MQUP, 2007) ch 2 with Peter H. Russell, *Constitutional Odyssey* (2nd ed, University of Toronto Press, 2004) ch 3.

[60] *Confederation Debates*, above (n 15) 579 (Cauchon).

[61] *Confederation Debates*, above (n 15) 792 (O'Halloran).

perhaps they (and only they) should have the power to change the terms thereafter; this is the nub of what came to be known as the compact theory.[62] Alternatively, perhaps the union represents less a compact among provinces than a pact between French and English, the country's founding *deux nations*, both of which would have to agree on significant constitutional changes to the pact.[63] Or perhaps instead of focusing on who created the union, one should take one's bearings from what was created by the union. This was the tack taken in the *Patriation Reference* case of 1981, in which the Supreme Court of Canada divined a norm governing amendment from the existence of the federal principle.[64] Although this decision cleared the way, in 1982, for a constitutional renovation that includes a multi-dimensional and complex amending formula, Quebec's unwillingness to ratify the *Constitution Act, 1982* remains a scar on the Canadian body politic. The point is simply this: the architects of 1867 found a way to inter-weave the principles of federalism, democracy, and the protection of minorities in a way that created enduring but ultimately workable constitutional ambivalence. Their record with respect to the question of political sovereignty is much less positive. Not only did they not marry competing principles of sovereignty in a way that produced co-existence, the more serious criticism is that they neglected to pose the question of constituent sovereignty at all, with damaging results.

The other signal design failure concerns the place of Indigenous peoples. For ambivalence to work as a constitutional design principle, the actors responsible for the design decisions have to recognize and acknowledge the legitimacy of the competing principles involved. If one set of constitutional principles is not included in the discussion, or if there is a wide gulf in perceived legitimacy between potentially competing principles, then constitutional unilateralism, rather than ambivalence, will result. In fact, this sort of unilateralism describes the constitutional approach adopted with respect to Indigenous peoples in the period leading to Confederation. As John Borrows and others have shown, there were deep traditions of Indigenous constitutionalism from which the Fathers of Confederation could have drawn or against which they could have measured their own constitutional commitments.[65] But none of this occurred, in part because there were no Indigenous representatives at any of the pre-Confederation meetings.[66] Indeed, in many ways Indigenous peoples were something of an after-thought in the grand scheme of constitutional things. On the one hand, the subject line "Indians, and lands reserved for the Indians" was not on the original jurisdictional list prepared in advance of the Quebec Conference by the Canadian delegation; it was added by

[62] See Norman McL. Rogers, "The Genesis of Provincial Rights" (1933) 14 CHR 9 and Ramsay Cook, *Provincial Autonomy, Minority Rights and the Compact Theory: 1867–1921* (Queen's Printer, 1969).

[63] See Cook, *Provincial Autonomy* above (n 62) ch 5 and Richard Arès, *Dossier sur le pacte fédératif de 1867* (Bellarmin, 1967).

[64] See Robert C. Vipond, "Whatever Became of the Compact Theory? Meech Lake and the New Politics of Constitutional Amendment in Canada" (1989) 96 *Queen's Quarterly* 793.

[65] John Borrows, *Canada's Indigenous Constitution* (University of Toronto Press, 2010).

[66] This point supports the argument advanced by Elkins, Ginsburg, and Melton that inclusion, participation in the formation of a constitution, helps to generate allegiance to a constitution and so is an important factor in explaining constitutional durability. See Elkins, Ginsburg, and Melton, above (n 1) 78–81.

Macdonald, apparently between daily sessions.[67] On the other, the place of Indigenous peoples in the constitutional order elicited almost no discussion or debate whatsoever. Indeed, over the course of the three-week debate about the Confederation plan held in the Canadian legislative assembly, the representatives referred as frequently to the State of Indiana as they did to Indians.[68] In short Indigenous peoples were subjects (rather than equal citizens), and additional subjects of legislative authority (rather than essential sources of constitutional meaning). One hundred and fifty years later, this legacy remains arguably the most serious blot on the Canadian constitutional project.

4. Conclusion

At one of the first sessions of the Quebec Conference, John A. Macdonald explained to the delegates that one of the virtues of the schematic plan before them was its elasticity. "(Our constitution) should be a mere skeleton and framework that would not bind us down. We have now all the elasticity which has kept England together."[69] Macdonald was right, though for the wrong reasons. The Canadian Constitution *has* been remarkably elastic, in ways that have allowed it to adapt to, and hence endure, significant social, political, and economic change. The source of this elasticity, however, is not so much its skeletal design (as Macdonald suggested) as the ambivalence that lies at its core. For Macdonald the "less is more" nature of the Quebec plan meant that future leaders would have relative autonomy to act in ways they thought best; because it was so skeletal, it would not "bind us down" to any fixed and immovable principles. But in fact Canadians have been "bound" by their constitution—for some 150 (often contentious) years. Far from being principle shy, the Confederation plan embedded and legitimized a series of competing principles which, taken together, created a system of what I have called constitutionalized ambivalence. The Canadian constitutional architects did not supply, nor did they intend to supply, a toolkit to resolve the tensions among these competing principles. What they did do was structure constitutional politics in ways that locked in the co-existence of these competing, but also mutually entangling, principles. The echoes of these design decisions remain with us, some of which reverberate on the pages of this *Handbook*. That is why 1867 matters for anyone who wants to understand the Canadian Constitution.

---

[67] The Canadian delegation arrived at the Quebec Conference with a draft constitution, which became the basis of the Quebec Resolutions. The first draft contained no reference to Indigenous peoples whatsoever. The second draft, the original of which shows various annotations in Macdonald's handwriting, does. Compare Browne, *Documents*, above (n 3) 81 (October 24) and 85 (October 25). The various drafts, showing changes, are preserved in the National Archives of Canada. The first draft is simply entitled "Resolutions" MG 26, vol 53, Series A1 (a), 21313–21317. The second version (with Macdonald's annotations) bears the same title. It can be found at MG 26, vol 53, Series A1 (a), 18142–18155.

[68] Cameron, Krikorian, and Vipond, "Revisiting the 1865 Canadian Debates," above (n 54) 14.

[69] Browne, *Documents*, above (n 3) 98.

BIBLIOGRAPHY

Ajzenstat, Janet. *The Canadian Founding: John Locke and Parliament.* Montreal and Kingston: MCQUP, 2007.

Ajzenstat, Janet, Paul Romney, Ian Gentles, and William D. Gairdner, eds. *Canada's Founding Debates.* Toronto: Stoddart, 1999.

Borrows, John. *Canada's Indigenous Constitution.* Toronto: UTP, 2010.

Brouillet, Eugénie. *La Négation de la Nation.* Montreal: Septentrion, 2005.

Brouillet, Eugénie, Alain-G. Gagnon, and Guy Laforest, eds. *La Conférence de Québec de 1864: 150 Ans Plus Tard.* Québec: Presses de l'Université Laval, 2016.

Browne, G.P. *Documents on the Confederation of British North America.* Toronto: McClelland and Stewart, 1969.

Buckner, Phillip. "The Maritimes and Confederation: A Reassessment." *Canadian Historical Review* 71 (1990): 1.

Canada, Legislative Assembly. *Parliamentary Debates on the Subject of the Confederation of the British North American Provinces.* Quebec: Hunter, Rose and Co., 1865.

Cook, Ramsay. *Canada and the French-Canadian Question.* Toronto: Macmillan, 1966.

Creighton, Donald. *British North America at Confederation: A Study Prepared for the Royal Commission on Dominion Provincial Relations.* Ottawa: Queen's Printer, 1938 (reprinted 1963).

Creighton, Donald. *The Road to Confederation: The Emergence of Canada, 1863–1867.* Toronto: Macmillan, 1964.

Dumont, Fernand. *Genèse de la société québécoise.* Montreal: Boréal, 1996.

Elkins, Zachary, Tom Ginsburg, and James Melton. *The Endurance of National Constitutions.* Cambridge: CUP 2009.

Lamonde, Yvan. *The Social History of Ideas in Quebec, 1760–1896.* Trans. Phyllis Aronoff and Howard Scott. Montreal and Kingston: MCQUP, 2013.

Martin, Chester. "The British Policy in Canadian Confederation." *Canadian Historical Review* 13 (1932): 5.

Martin, Ged. *Britain and the Origins of the Canadian Confederation.* Basingstoke: Macmillan, 1995.

Moore, Christopher. *1867: How the Fathers Made a Deal.* Toronto: McClelland and Stewart, 1997.

Morton, W.L. *The Critical Years: The Union of British North America, 1857–1873.* Toronto: McClelland and Stewart, 1964.

Romney, Paul. *Getting It Wrong: How Canadians Forgot Their Past and Imperilled Confederation.* Toronto: UTP, 1999.

Russell, Peter H. *Constitutional Odyssey.* 2nd ed. Toronto: UTP, 2004.

Ryerson, Stanley B. *Unequal Union: Confederation and the Roots of Conflict in the Canadas, 1815–1873.* Toronto: Progress Books, 1973.

Silver, A.I. *The French-Canadian Idea of Confederation, 1864–1900.* Toronto: UTP, 1982.

Supreme Court of Canada, *Reference Re Secession of Quebec* (1998) 2 S.C.R.

Tuohy, Carolyn J. *Policy and Politics in Canada: Institutionalized Ambivalence.* Philadelphia: Temple, 1992.

Vipond, Robert C. *Liberty and Community: Canadian Federalism and the Failure of the Constitution.* Albany: SUNY, 1991.

Waite, P.B. *The Life and Times of Confederation; Politics, Newspapers, and the Union of British North America, 1864–1867.* Toronto: UTP, 1962.

D. The British Constitutional Tradition

CHAPTER 5

THE BRITISH LEGAL TRADITION IN CANADIAN CONSTITUTIONAL LAW

MARK D. WALTERS*

1. INTRODUCTION

THE *British North America Act, 1867* is one of Canada's foundational constitutional texts.[1] Although enacted as a statute by the United Kingdom Parliament, the 'BNA Act' was based upon resolutions negotiated at Quebec by delegates from colonies intent upon forming a federation within the British Empire.[2] The federation would quickly expand and the empire would eventually dissolve, and Canada would in time emerge as a sovereign state. However, these developments involved few formal constitutional changes. The BNA Act, now called the *Constitution Act, 1867*, is still in force at the centre of Canada's constitution.[3] It therefore remains important today that the framers of the Act resolved at Quebec that the federal government would be based upon 'the model' and 'administered according to the well-understood principles' of the 'British Constitution'.[4] The Act is a sparse document, and the well-understood principles of the British constitution were left undefined. However, the preamble to the Act states that it is the 'Desire' of the provinces to unite federally into 'One Dominion . . . with a Constitution similar in Principle to that of the United Kingdom'.

---

* F.R. Scott Chair in Public and Constitutional Law, Faculty of Law, McGill University.

[1] *British North America Act 1867*, 30 & 31 Vict c 3 (UK) [hereinafter BNA Act or the 1867 Act].

[2] For more regarding the lead up to Confederation, see the chapter by Vipond in this *Handbook*.

[3] See the Schedule to the *Constitution Act 1982*, which is itself a Schedule to the *Canada Act 1982* (UK) c 11.

[4] Quebec Resolutions, 10 October 1864, in WPM Kennedy (ed), *Statutes, Treaties and Documents of the Canadian Constitution, 1713–1929* (Oxford University Press, 1930), 541–547.

The British constitution is thus stamped on the face of Canada's principal constitutional text. But to what affect? During arguments made in 1888 before the Judicial Committee of the Privy Council in London, the final court of appeal for the empire, Edward Blake stated that although the BNA Act is 'little more than a skeleton', 'a single line' within its preamble 'imports into the system that mighty and complex and somewhat indefinite aggregate called the British Constitution'.[5] Blake's statement is not wholly inaccurate, but it is misleading in two ways. First, it would be wrong to suggest that the 'aggregate' or whole British constitution is adopted in Canada. The similarity in constitutions is one of 'principle' only. Indeed, even this claim was regarded with scepticism at the time. In his leading book on the British Constitution, A.V. Dicey insisted that the similar-in-principle recital in the Act was a piece of 'official mendacity'.[6] 'If preambles were intended to express the truth,' wrote Dicey, 'for the word "*Kingdom*" ought to have been substituted "*States*".'[7] Dicey's equation of the Canadian Constitution with the United States Constitution rather than the United Kingdom Constitution is problematic, but he was right to approach claims about the Britishness of the Canadian Constitution with caution. Second, Blake's suggestion that the preamble 'imports' the British Constitution into the system established by the BNA Act is incomplete. Although it imports or copies certain British institutions, the Act itself was imported into, or enacted within, a larger legal context informed by British constitutional principles and also by other factors unique to Canadian history and experience. Indeed, the case in which Blake made his statement implicated British, French, and Aboriginal legal realities in Canada.[8]

In this chapter, I examine these points about the similarities and differences between the Canadian and British Constitutions mainly from a historical perspective. The story of Canada's constitutional development is a long one, and my analysis will necessarily be thematic and selective rather than chronological and comprehensive in nature. I will begin by examining institutions and institutional structure, and then turn to the question of underlying normative value, or what Dicey called the 'spirit' of the constitution. My objective will be to show that by the mid-point of the twentieth century, the point at which appeals to the Judicial Committee of the Privy Council, the last meaningful exercise of British power over Canada, ended, a distinctively *Canadian* approach to British constitutional principles had begun to emerge.

---

[5] *The Ontario Lands Case: Argument of Mr. Blake, Q.C. before the Privy Council* (Press of the Budget, 1888), 6. Blake was an influential lawyer who served as Premier of Ontario and later Attorney General of Canada.

[6] A.V. Dicey, *Lectures Introductory to the Study of the Law of the Constitution* (Macmillan, 1885), 152–153.

[7] Ibid.

[8] *St Catherine's Milling and Lumber Co v R* (1889) 14 App Cas 46 (PC).

2. SIMILARITY IN INSTITUTIONAL STRUCTURE

Canadian legal scholars of the late nineteenth-century bristled with indignation at Dicey's claim that Canada's constitution was similar to the American rather than the British Constitution.[9] True, Canada was like the United States and unlike the United Kingdom in that it had a federal rather than a unitary constitution. However, as J.G. Bourinot argued, Dicey had overlooked the fact that Canadian institutions were otherwise 'copies, exact copies in some respects', of those found within the Westminster parliamentary system.[10] The principal institutions within that system—an *executive* consisting of the Crown advised by a Privy Council; a *legislature* consisting of the Crown together with two houses of Parliament, the hereditary House of Lords and the elected House of Commons; and a *judiciary* centred upon the Queen's Bench and other superior common law courts then located at Westminster Hall—served as the model for Canadian institutions.

The 1867 Act provides that the 'Executive Government' over Canada is 'vested in the Queen', that a 'Governor General' may carry on government 'in the Name of the Queen', that there shall be a 'Queen's Privy Council for Canada' to 'aid and advise' in the government, and that there shall be a 'Parliament for Canada' consisting of 'the Queen, an Upper House styled the Senate, and the House of Commons'.[11] The labels used (with the exception of 'Senate') copy British not American terms. Indeed, the Queen is not a copy at all: the 'Queen' in the 1867 Act *is* Victoria and her heirs and successors the 'Kings and Queens of the United Kingdom'.[12] One consequence of the emergence of Canada as an independent state, however, is that the office of 'Queen' under the 1867 Act is now legally separate from the office that its occupants hold as British monarchs.[13] Furthermore, the Queen has authorized the Governor General to exercise, upon the advice of the Canadian privy council, all of her powers in relation to Canada.[14]

As for the provinces, the terms employed by the 1867 Act—each province has an executive consisting of a 'lieutenant governor' advised by an 'executive council' and

---

[9] J.G. Bourinot, 'The Federal Constitution of Canada' (1890) 2 Jur Rev 131; WHP Clement, *The Law of the Canadian Constitution* (Carswell, 1892), 3–25; AHF Lefroy, *The Law of Legislative Power in Canada* (Toronto Law Book, 1897–1898), xliii–xliv, xlv.

[10] Bourinot, ibid 136.

[11] BNA Act, ss 9, 10, 11, 17, 91.

[12] BNA Act, s 2. See Mark D. Walters, 'Succession to the Throne and the Architecture of the Constitution of Canada' in Philippe Lagassé and Michel Bédard (eds), *The Crown and Parliament* (Éditions Yvon Blais, 2015), 263–292.

[13] *The Queen v Secretary of State for Foreign and Commonwealth Affairs, ex parte Indian Association of Alberta* [1982] QB 892 (CA), 913.

[14] Letters Patent Constituting the Office of Governor General of Canada, art II [1947] RSC 1985 appendix II no 31).

legislatures consisting (initially) of the Lieutenant-Governor, an appointed 'legislative council', and an elected 'legislative assembly'[15]—follow pre-Confederation terminology that was understood to imply the Westminster model. Indeed, W.H.P. Clement argued that Dicey's failure to acknowledge the existence of provincial constitutions modeled along British lines prior to 1867 and their continuity under the BNA Act was one reason among others to object to his 'official mendacity' argument.[16]

Claims by Britain to the territories that form what is now Canada did not lead immediately to British modes of governance. Under the *Royal Proclamation of 1763*, for example, extensive territories were left without British institutions, and relations with Aboriginal nations were conducted through treaty councils.[17] In the territories conquered from France and included within the province of Quebec by the *Quebec Act, 1774*, legislative power was in the hands of a Governor and appointed council, and although English law on 'criminal' matters was introduced the continuity of French-Canadian law on 'property and civil rights' was affirmed.[18] For Edmund Burke and other critics of the *Quebec Act*, this 'constitution' was based on 'the old law of France' not 'the laws of England' and so was one of 'despotic' power (the prospect of arbitrary detention by lettres de cachet was even raised) rather than the rule of law.[19]

Once circumstances permitted, however, British modes of governance were introduced. The first legislature resembling the Westminster Parliament in what is now Canada convened in October 1758 in the province of Nova Scotia—an integral part (it was said) of a constitution based on 'the general principles of British law and liberty considered the birthright of a free people'.[20] The most ambitious attempt to establish the British Constitution, complete with the monarchical, aristocratic, and democratic elements celebrated by Blackstone, is found in the legislatures contemplated for the provinces of Upper and Lower Canada established upon the division of Quebec by the *Constitutional Act, 1791*.[21] Legislative power was vested in the Crown, elected assemblies, and legislative councils the members of which were to be 'discreet and proper' persons appointed for life upon whom the Crown could confer titles that would make council membership 'hereditary'. The parliamentary debates on the 1791 Act took place in the shadow of the French Revolution and prompted Burke to issue an impassioned defence of the Whig idea of the constitution as an ancient ordering of royal, noble, and popular

---

[15] BNA Act, ss 58, 63, 69, 71, 88.

[16] Clement, above (n 9) 3–4.

[17] See the chapter in this *Handbook* by John Borrows.

[18] Quebec Act 1774, 14 Geo III c 83 (GB).

[19] Sir Henry Cavendish, *Debates of the House of Commons in the Year 1774, on the Bill for Making More Effectual Provision for the Government of the Province of Quebec* (J. Wright, 1839), 213; also 20–21, 48–49, 89, 134–136, 196, 214–215.

[20] Beamish Murdoch, *Epitome of the Laws of Nova-Scotia* (Joseph Howe, 1832), I, 30.

[21] *Constitutional Act, 1791* 31 Geo III c 31 (GB). For Blackstone's eulogy for the mixed constitution see: Sir William Blackstone, *Commentaries on the Laws of England* (Clarendon Press, 1765–1769), I, 48–52.

sentiment.[22] The provincial constitutions for Canada were to be 'a perfect Image and Transcript' of this constitutional ideal.[23]

In fact, no hereditary titles would be conferred upon members of upper legislative chambers. The old Whig constitution was the product of social conditions that could not be reproduced in Canada. Members of upper legislative chambers would align politically with Governors, and no independent landed gentry would emerge capable of mediating between Crown prerogative and democratic sentiment.[24] Upon Confederation, one province, Ontario, would opt for a legislature with a single elected chamber, and the other provinces would later follow suit. The only bicameral legislature left today in Canada is the federal Parliament. Its upper chamber was modeled only loosely on the House of Lords, the Governor General appointing its members for life (now until age 75), and an American influence *was* explicitly acknowledged by the framers of the constitution in relation to the provision for an equal number of Senators from regional divisions in the country.[25]

Although not perfect transcripts of Parliament, local legislatures in Canada were assumed to be like Parliament. It was held that because provinces had 'a constitution similar to that of England', provincial legislative chambers enjoyed the privilege of controlling their internal proceedings free from executive or judicial interference just as, by custom and the *Bill of Rights, 1689*, the houses of Parliament in England did[26]—or at least they enjoyed those parliamentary privileges essential for their proper functioning.[27] Today, the principles associated with parliamentary privilege as affirmed by the *Bill of Rights, 1689* are regarded as forming part of the unwritten constitutional law of Canada by virtue of the preamble's similar-in-principle recital.[28]

Acknowledging that the 1867 Act builds upon rather than breaks from previous legal realities assists in the interpretation of the provisions on the judiciary. Provinces are given the authority to constitute courts, but judges of 'superior' courts in the provinces are to be appointed by the Governor General, that is, the federal government, and these judges hold office during good behaviour and may not be removed except upon addresses by both houses of the federal Parliament.[29] To understand what a 'superior' court is within the meaning of the Act, it helps to know that the provision on removal is copied directly from provisions in the *Act of Settlement, 1701* protecting

---

[22] [Edmund Burke], *An Appeal from the New to the Old Whigs, in consequence of some late discussions in Parliament, relative to the Reflections on the French Revolution* (3rd edn, J Dodsley, 1791).

[23] J.G. Simcoe, Lt Gov UC, to Lord Portland, 30 October 1795 in EA Cruikshank (ed), *The Correspondence of Lieut. Governor John Graves Simcoe* (Ontario Historical Society, 1923), IV, 115–117.

[24] Paul Romney, 'From Constitutionalism to Legalism: Trial by Jury, Responsible Government, and the Rule of Law in the Canadian Political Culture' (1989) 7 Law & Hist Rev 121, 153.

[25] BNA Act, ss 21–29. *Parliamentary Debates on the Subject of the Confederation of the British North American Colonies* (Hunter, Rose, 1865), 37–38 (John A. Macdonald).

[26] *In the Case of Daniel Tracey* (1832) Stuart's Rep 478 (LCKB), 513–514, 516. See also *M'Nab v Bidwell and Baldwin* (1830), Draper 144 (UCKB).

[27] *Kielley v Carson* (1842) 4 Moore 63 (PC).

[28] *New Brunswick Co v Nova Scotia (Speaker of the House of Assembly)* [1993] 1 SCR 319.

[29] BNA Act, ss 92(14), 96, 99.

the independence of superior court judges in England.[30] It also helps to consider the courts actually existing in Canada in 1867, the continuity of which was provided for by the BNA Act.[31] For example, the 'Court of Queen's Bench for Upper Canada' possessed 'all such powers and authorities as by the law of England are incident to a Superior Court of Civil and Criminal jurisdiction' and 'all the rights, incidents and privileges' enjoyed by 'any of Her Majesty's Superior Courts of Common Law at Westminster, in England'.[32] Here was one clear attempt to create an 'exact copy'. It should be noted, however, that the protections for judicial independence found in the *Act of Settlement* were not considered to apply automatically in pre-Confederation Canada; instead, similar provisions were introduced gradually through local legislation, starting with Upper Canada in 1834.[33] Today, the principle of judicial independence, as evidenced in part by the *Act of Settlement*, is regarded as forming part of Canada's unwritten constitutional law by virtue of the preamble's similar-in-principle recital.[34]

Reference to the conception of 'superior' court that developed within the common law tradition is important to the interpretation of the judiciary provisions of the 1867 Act. This is true of other institutions as well. For example, what powers does the 'Queen' have by virtue of being the 'Executive Authority' over Canada? She has those prerogative powers inherent in the Crown recognized '[b]y the law of the constitution, or in other words, by the common law of England'.[35] It is this necessity of reading the 1867 Act together with 'a great body of unwritten law'—the common law—that was, Bourinot argued, another reason to reject Dicey's claim that Canada's constitution was more American than British.[36]

Canada's constitutional texts must also be read in light of unwritten constitutional customs or 'conventions'. Perhaps the most important constitutional convention to emerge within the British parliamentary tradition is that the Crown may only exercise legal power on the advice of privy councilors who hold ministerial office and are responsible to and have the on-going confidence or support of the elected members of Parliament. The principal constitutional question in pre-Confederation Canada was whether Governors, as Crown representatives, were to exercise power on the advice of ministers responsible to the imperial Parliament in London or executive council members responsible to local assemblies—whether, in other words, there was to be genuine local self-government or not. The conflict produced by this question, exacerbated by national and linguistic divisions, erupted in rebellions in 1837–1838. The solution,

---

[30]   Act of Settlement, 1701, 12 & 13 Will III, c 2 (Eng), s 3.

[31]   BNA Act, s 129.

[32]   An Act respecting the Superior Courts of Civil and Criminal Jurisdiction, 1859, 22 Vict c 10 (Can), ss 1, 3.

[33]   An Act to Render the Judges of the Court of King's Bench in this Province Independent of the Crown, 1834, 4 Will IV c 2 (UC). WR Lederman, 'The Independence of the Judiciary' (1956) 34 Can Bar Rev 769, 1139.

[34]   *Reference re Remuneration of Judges of the Provincial Court of Prince Edward Island* [1997] 3 SCR 3.

[35]   *Canada (Attorney General) v Ontario (Attorney General)* (1894) 23 SCR 458, 468.

[36]   Bourinot, above (n 9) 136.

Governor General Lord Durham stated, required 'no invention of a new constitutional theory', only the resolve 'to follow out consistently the principles of the British constitution' within the colonies.[37] It required, as the Nova Scotian politician Joseph Howe explained, the adoption within each province of 'the principle of responsible government', 'the corner-stone of the British Constitution'.[38] These recommendations would be implemented through instructions to Governors, and the colonial minister in Britain was able to state in 1852 that a system of 'responsible government' 'copied from our own' had been established in British North America.[39] When the framers of the BNA Act referred to 'the well-understood principles of the British Constitution', it was mainly this system that they had in mind.[40] In fact, the Act says nothing explicitly about responsible government. However, as A.H.F. Lefroy observed in his critique of Dicey's 'official mendacity' claim, the Act does not prohibit members of the Canadian Privy Council or provincial executive councils from being members of the federal Parliament or provincial legislatures respectively, 'and so [was] preserved the British system of responsible government'.[41] In other words, no legal obstacle inhibits the constitutional convention, central to Canadian constitutional government to this day but impossible in the United States, by which executive power is exercised by a prime minister and cabinet ministers drawn from and responsible to the elected members of the legislature. Dicey later acknowledged this point, but merely changed his description of the preamble's similar-in-principle recital from 'official mendacity' to 'diplomatic inaccuracy'.[42] It bears emphasizing that the rules governing responsible government, which are essential to the functioning of parliamentary democracy in Canada, are still considered to be, as they are in Britain, conventional rather than legal in character.[43]

The American influence in Dicey's view was partly found in the fact that the 1867 Act establishes a federal rather than unitary constitution. Section 91 provides that the federal Parliament has authority to make laws for 'the Peace, Order, and good Government of Canada' in relation to all matters not assigned exclusively to the provinces. Canadian critics of Dicey were quick to point out, however, that this scheme does *not* follow the American example, for it leaves residual legislative power in federal hands whereas in the United States it is left with the individual states. J.H. Gray, one of the framers of the Quebec resolutions, stated that the Act was premised upon 'the theory of the British constitution' according to which power flows down from the Imperial Parliament to subordinate entities, in contrast to the United States where 'power springs from the

---

[37] Sir Reginald Coupland (ed), *The Durham Report* [1839] (Clarendon Press, 1945), 141.
[38] Joseph Howe to Lord John Russell, 18 September 1839, in Kennedy above (n 4) 384–390, at 384, 387.
[39] Earl Grey, *The Colonial Policy of Lord John Russell's Administration* (Richard Bentley, 1853), 202, 269.
[40] *Debates on Confederation*, above (n 25) 387 (HL Langevin).
[41] Lefroy, above (n 9) lxiii.
[42] A.V. Dicey, *An Introduction to the Study of the Law of the Constitution* (4th edn, Macmillan, 1893), 156.
[43] *Re Resolution to Amend the Constitution* [1981] 1 SCR 753, 876–884.

people'.[44] On this view, the Canadian approach emphasises central power and unity. This argument is reinforced by other provisions within the Act, in particular the allocation to the Governor General, that is, the federal government, of the power to appoint provincial Lieutenant-Governors, to appoint provincial superior court judges, and to disallow provincial statutes within two years of enactment.[45] Indeed, leading framers of the BNA Act, as well as the first judges to interpret the Act, thought that it established the federal government as a quasi-imperial authority with the provinces being subordinate entities equivalent to municipal councils, the provincial Lieutenant-Governors being officers of the federal government rather than Crown representatives.[46]

This view of the Constitution did not last. The Judicial Committee of the Privy Council held that provinces are not subordinate but are coordinate and equal to the federal government enjoying independence and autonomy within the spheres of power allocated to them.[47] In reaching this conclusion, however, judges were influenced by British rather than American principles. The 'analogy of the British Constitution ... on which the entire scheme is founded', stated Viscount Haldane, means that provincial Lieutenant-Governors, although appointed by the Governor General, represent the Crown directly as a component of provincial legislatures, and the act by a Lieutenant-Governor of assenting to bills passed by a provincial assembly is therefore 'in contemplation of law' an act of the Crown not the federal government.[48] Judges thus assumed that full-scale Westminster parliamentary systems were to operate at *both* federal and provincial levels. In a counterintuitive way, then, judicial commitment to British constitutional structures reinforced a strong version of federalism in Canada.

The judges on the Empire's high court were also concerned that unless provincial powers, especially the power over 'property and civil rights' allocated to the provinces by section 92(13) of the 1867 Act, were judicially protected from federal intrusion, the continued survival of Quebec's distinctive legal system would be threatened.[49] This was another reason for a strong interpretation of federalism by the courts, and, again, it was arguably informed by British legal principles. The Judicial Committee recalled that the phrase 'property and civil rights' had been employed in the *Quebec Act* when the continuity of French-Canadian law had been affirmed in Quebec in 1774. The *Quebec Act*, in turn, affirmed the general common law presumption that local laws in

---

[44] J.H. Gray, *Confederation; or, the Political and Parliamentary History of Canada* (Copp Clark, 1872), 56. Gray wrote before Dicey made his comment, but the basic point he makes was adopted by critics of Dicey: Lefroy, above (n 9), xlvi, lxvi.

[45] BNA Act, ss 58, 96, 90.

[46] *Debates on Confederation* above (n 25) 42 (John A Macdonald); *Lenoir v Ritchie* (1879), 3 SCR 575, 622–625, 632–635.

[47] *Hodge v The Queen* (1883) 9 App Cas 117 (PC); *Liquidators of Maritime Bank v Receiver-General of New Brunswick* [1892] AC 437 (PC).

[48] *In re Initiative and Referendum Act* [1919] AC 935 (PC), 943.

[49] *Citizens Ins Co v Parsons* (1881) 7 App Cas 96 (PC), 113.

lands newly acquired by the Crown continued in force until explicitly repealed or modi-fied.[50] There was thus a connection between federalism in Canada and the older idea of legal pluralism within the Empire. Indeed, Clement argued that Dicey, in claiming that Canada's constitution was more American than British because of its federal character, overlooked 'the presence of the federal principle in the British constitution'.[51] The 'fed-eral idea' of 'reconcil[ing] national unity with the right of local self-government' was, Clement said, part of British Imperial constitutional law long before American federal-ism was established.[52]

That judges in Britain were in a position to dictate how the Canadian Constitution was to be interpreted is a reminder, if one were needed, of the fact that the Dominion of Canada began its life as a British colony. Canadian institutions were subject to a variety of Imperial controls, most of which had fallen into disuse by the late nineteenth-century. The *Statute of Westminster, 1931* would confirm legally what was already true politically, that the British Parliament was no longer sovereign over Canada and other dominions. One exception to the atrophy of Imperial authority, however, was the Judicial Committee of the Privy Council, which continued hearing appeals from Canadian courts even after a Supreme Court of Canada was established in 1875. Not only were its decisions binding on Canadian courts, but the Judicial Committee held that in cases involving English law judicial interpretation was to be 'as nearly as possible the same' throughout the Empire, and so the decisions of domestic appellate courts within the United Kingdom were also binding in Canada.[53] The effect of this view on Canadian public law cannot be over-stated.[54] Not only were significant parts of Canadian constitutional law based on the common law, but Canadian law and English law on constitutional matters were, at least until the abolition of appeals to the Judicial Committee from Canadian courts in 1949, supposed to remain perfectly aligned.

3. SIMILARITY IN CONSTITUTIONAL SPIRIT?

It is one thing to borrow institutional forms from another country; it is another to adopt the same normative values or attitudes that shape the behaviour of institutional actors. For his part, Dicey thought that attempts by other countries to emulate the British Constitution had often failed because the countries in question were unable to embrace

---

[50] Charles Yorke (Att Gen) and William de Grey (Sol Gen) to Lords of Trade, 14 April 1766, in Adam Shortt and Arthur G Doughty (eds), *Documents Relating to the Constitutional History of Canada, 1759–1791* (SE Dawson, 1907), I, 255–256; Cavendish (n 19) 29 (Att Gen Edward Thurlow).

[51] Clement above (n 9) 10.

[52] Ibid 5, 8–9.

[53] *Trimble v Hill* (1879) 5 App Cas 342 (PC), 345.

[54] Bora Laskin, *The British Tradition in Canadian Law* (Stevens & Sons, 1969).

'the spirit of English constitutionalism'.[55] Canadian institutions may have been copies of British institutions, but did they embrace the same constitutional 'spirit'?

In answering this question, I will consider two cases from early twentieth-century Canada. In the first, *Florence Mining Co. v Cobalt Lake Mining Co.*, a company that had staked claims to mining rights in a certain lakebed in Ontario sued a company that had later purchased the lakebed from the Crown, arguing that its rights had priority. After the action was commenced, however, the provincial legislature intervened with a statute confirming the second company's title free from all competing claims.[56] The second case arose after Ontario established a hydro-electricity commission to supply energy to municipalities through a contract to be approved by electors. In the second case, *Smith v City of London*, the validity of changes to the contract made without elector approval was challenged in court, and, again, the legislature intervened, amending the relevant statute to provide that the validity of the contract 'shall not be called in question ... in any court' and that every action pending that sought to attack the validity of the contract or any municipal bylaw authorizing it 'or calling into question the jurisdiction' of the commission or any municipality was 'forever stayed'.[57] The cases were something of a *cause célèbre* at the time. In leading a campaign against the legislature's interventions, Goldwin Smith, the British historian and journalist who then lived in Toronto, sought the assistance of his friend—Dicey. Smith thought that similar legislation in England would have been denounced as contrary to the Magna Carta, and he was surprised that there had been no such outcry in Canada.[58] Before judgments in the cases were rendered, Smith asked Dicey to provide a legal opinion on the validity of the two statutes. Any thoughts he might express as to their inconsistency with 'the spirit of English constitutional law' would, Smith said, have 'wide influence here'.[59] Before looking at Dicey's opinion, it is worth pausing to consider what this 'spirit' was and whether there had been evidence of it within Canada.

In his earlier work, Dicey had argued that unlike continental constitutions based on the civilian legal tradition, which he said were animated by an 'administrative' spirit, the British Constitution was animated by 'the spirit of legality'.[60] The spirit of legality implied, first, the 'rule of law', the idea that rights and liberties could not be denied arbitrarily but only through ordinary laws administered by ordinary courts, as well as the idea of 'equality before the law', or that public officials were subject to the same laws and courts as citizens and could be sued when they infringed rights or liberties without statutory authority—though it should be added that Dicey also acknowledged that

---

[55] A.V. Dicey, 'Will Parliamentary Government Be Permanent?' (1902) 7 Working Men's College J 380, 383.

[56] *Florence Mining Co v Cobalt Lake Mining Co* (1908) 12 OWR 297 (HC).

[57] Hydro Electric Power Commission Act, 1909, 9 Edw VII, c 9 (Ont), ss 4, 8; *Smith v London (City of)* (1909) 13 OWR 1148 (HC).

[58] Goldwin Smith to AV Dicey, 3 April 1909, Goldwin Smith Papers, Rare and Manuscript Collections (no. 14-17-134), Carl A Kroch Library, Cornell University, reel 20.

[59] Smith to Dicey, 11 May 1909, ibid.

[60] Dicey, above (n 6) 277.

officials were supervised by the superior common law courts through the prerogative writs, emphasizing in particular protections of liberty provided by the writ of habeas corpus.[61] The spirit of legality implied, second, 'parliamentary sovereignty', the idea that ultimate sovereign power in the state vested in the legislature not the executive. One feature of parliamentary sovereignty was the assumption that parliamentary power was legally unlimited, and Acts of Parliament could not be set aside by either the executive or courts. For Dicey, however, the spirit of legality was ensured because the rule of law and parliamentary sovereignty were mutually reinforcing ideas. Unlike an executive sovereign who can rule through 'decrees', a parliamentary sovereign must act through 'formal and deliberate legislation'.[62] This is 'no mere matter of form'.[63] If Parliament must act through laws rather than decrees it cannot easily 'interfere in the details of administration' or 'with the regular course of law'.[64] Its acts are ordinary laws that must be interpreted and applied in individual cases by judges who will invariably read statutory language, and especially any delegation of power to public officials, consistently with 'the general spirit of the common law'.[65] Things might have been different. Drawing upon civilian ideas, Crown lawyers had argued in the early seventeenth century that there was a 'law of state' permitting the executive to act above ordinary law to protect public welfare in cases of necessity, a law administered, if at all, by prerogative tribunals rather than regular courts. This kind of reasoning was accepted in France where a sharp substantive and institutional separation between public and other law emerged—a reflection, Dicey thought, of administrative rather than legalistic constitutionalism.[66] However, the argument was rejected in England in the seventeenth century. As Lord Camden would state in *Entick v Carrington*, 'the common law does not understand that kind of reasoning'.[67] The British Constitution would be, in effect, a common law constitution based upon 'the due supremacy of the ordinary law of the land'.[68]

It is not hard to find evidence of this constitutional spirit in Canada. First, something like the principle of parliamentary sovereignty was acknowledged—albeit in a modified form. As the Chief Justice of New Brunswick explained in 1838, the local legislature is 'subordinate' to the Imperial Parliament but otherwise has 'the same power to make laws binding within the province that the Imperial Parliament has in the United Kingdom', and, moreover, it is 'a thing unheard of under British institutions for a judicial tribunal to question the validity and binding force of any such law when duly enacted'—unless, he added, the statute is 'repugnan[t]' to an Imperial statute extending to the colony.[69]

---

[61] Ibid 181, 182.

[62] Ibid 333.

[63] Ibid.

[64] Ibid 335–336.

[65] Ibid 339–340.

[66] Mark D. Walters, 'Public Law and Ordinary Legal Method: Revisiting Dicey's Approach to *Droit Administratif*' (2016) 66 UTLJ 53.

[67] *Entick* v *Carrington* (1765) 19 St Tr 1029 (KB), 1073.

[68] Dicey, above (n 6) 181, 182.

[69] *Regina v Kerr* (1838) 2 NBR 553 (SC), 555, 557.

A modified theory of parliamentary sovereignty along these lines would become the dominant theory in Canada after Confederation: it was held that federal and provincial legislatures have powers as plenary in nature as those of the UK Parliament so long as they operate within the areas allocated to them by the 1867 Act.[70] We leave to the side for now the question of whether a legislature can really be sovereign and limited at the same time.

Second, once English law and courts based on English models were established in pre-Confederation Canada, proceedings that Dicey associated with the rule of law quickly appear. In Upper Canada, where these conditions obtained in the early 1790s[71], we thus find courts entertaining actions against public officials for neglect or abuse of powers and issuing prerogative writs like certiorari and mandamus to supervise public authorities.[72] What is perhaps more interesting is that we find the same pattern emerging in Lower Canada/Quebec where the powers of courts were not defined by explicit reference to those of English courts, and where French-Canadian law governed property and civil rights.[73] Judges in Lower Canada held that if '[i]n England' the superior courts 'superintended' inferior jurisdictions by issuing prerogative writs of prohibition or certiorari, then courts having 'ordinary jurisdiction' in the province had the same power.[74] Actions against public officials for neglect or abuse of power were also entertained by the ordinary courts in Lower Canada, an impossibility within the French civilian tradition.[75] The view emerged that those parts of French-Canadian law that formed 'part of the public law' were 'superseded'[76] and questions of 'constitutional law' were regulated by 'the political law of England'.[77] The fears of opponents of the *Quebec Act* proved unfounded. The affirmation of the 'ancient laws of Canada' in property and civil rights did not, as one judge said, 'give up the Canadians to the rule of *Lettres de Cachet* and arbitrary imprisonment'.[78] During the rebellions of 1837–1838, judges in Lower

---

[70] *Hodge v The Queen* (1883) 9 App Cas 117 (PC), 132.

[71] An Act to introduce the English law 1792 32 Geo III c 1 (UC). An act to establish a superior court of civil and criminal jurisdiction, 1794, 34 Geo III c 2 (UC) established a court of King's Bench with all such powers 'as by the law of England are incident to a superior court'.

[72] *Phillips v Redpath and McKay* (1830) Draper 68 (UCKB); *The King v Harris* (1823) 1 Taylor 10 (UCKB), 16; *The King v The Justices of the District of Niagara* (1826) Taylor 394 (UCKB), 398; *The King v The Justices of Newcastle* (1830) Draper 114 (UCKB), 115–116; *In re Sheriff of Newcastle* (1831) Draper 503 (UCKB).

[73] The affirmation of French-Canadian law by the Quebec Act, 1774 remained in force in Lower Canada. An Act for amending the Judicature, 1793, 34 Geo III c 6 (LC), s 2 established courts of 'King's Bench' with 'original jurisdiction' in 'all causes as well civil as criminal'.

[74] *Hamilton v Fraser* (1811) Stuart's Rep 21.

[75] *Scott v Lindsay* (1811) Stuart's Rep 68; *McClure v Shepherd* (1813) Stuart's Rep 75; *Price v. Perceval* (1824) Stuart's Rep 179; *Patersons and Weir v Perceval* (1828) Stuart's Rep 271.

[76] *Baldwin v Gibbon and McCallum* (1813) Stuart's Rep 72, 74.

[77] *Donegani v Donegani* (1831) Stuart's Rep 460, 463 (counsel); *Donegani v Donegani* (1835) 3 Knapp 63 (PC), 85.

[78] *Re Celestin Houde*, 3 December 1838 (LCQB) in *Judicial Decisions on the Writ of Habeas Corpus ad Subjiciendum, and on the Provincial Ordinance 2d Victoria, Chap. 4* (Three Rivers 1839), 6. See also *Hay v Haldimand* (Eng KB 1787) reported in *The British Register* III (July–Sept 1787), 294–295 (Governor of Quebec liable in trespass for imprisoning suspected revolutionary without trial).

Canada rejected arguments that the executive could, without statutory authorization, 'silence the laws' and detain rebels without trial on the basis that the 'weal of the state' was the 'supreme law'.[79] In Canada, as in England, the common law did not understand that kind of reasoning. Of course, these propositions do not, in themselves, confirm a flourishing spirit of legality.[80] Government responses to emergencies in Canada were often heavy-handed.[81] However, it was assumed then, as it is now, that measures adopted by the executive to secure public welfare must be authorized or indemnified by statutes enacted by the legislature.

Third, we find examples of the distinctive interpretive attitude that Dicey thought secured the reconciliation of legislative sovereignty and the rule of law. The case of *Phillips v Redpath* is exemplary in this respect.[82] In this case, officials supervising the building of the Rideau Canal in Upper Canada were sued in trespass after they demolished a house, the plaintiff claiming that the defendants had acted to prevent the opening of a tavern by a 'Yankee', and the defendants offering no explanation but relying solely upon a provincial statute authorizing officials to appropriate land if needed for the canal.[83] The justices found for the plaintiff. Justice James Macaulay concluded that although officials were responsible politically for how they exercised their 'discretion' under the statute, they were 'liable to be proceeded against in the courts' when by 'exceeding the powers conferred' they 'tortiously' invaded property rights.[84] Chief Justice John Beverley Robinson agreed: when the legislature gives 'large and liberal powers' to officials, it is 'inherent in the constitution' that the courts may correct the 'abuse' of those powers, and it is insufficient merely to show that the defendant is 'a public officer'.[85] 'It is not their public character alone,' he wrote, 'but their conduct in that character, which constitutes their protection, and that conduct therefore must be shewn by them to be legal.'[86] Of course, judges could not second-guess the wisdom of each decision; however, where an official invoked the statute under 'pretence merely' and was 'actuated by a different and therefore an unjustifiable object', or when it was 'manifest and obvious that not a sound but an arbitrary discretion had prevailed', judicial intervention was warranted.[87] To exercise powers conferred to build a canal in order to further an unrelated object based upon animosity toward a group or activity was not legal.[88] 'It

[79] *Celestin Houde* (n 78) 10–11; also *Re Joseph Guillaume Barthe*, 7 January 1839 (LCQB) in *Judicial Decisions* (n 78) 20.

[80] The province was under constant threat and its judges were sometimes 'Baconian' in attitude: F. Murray Greenwood, *Legacies of Fear: Law and Politics in Quebec in the Era of the French Revolution* (Osgoode Society/University of Toronto Press, 1993), 27–32.

[81] See in general Barry Wright and Susan Binnie (eds), *Canadian State Trials, Volume III: Political Trials and Security Measures, 1840–1914* (Osgoode Society/University of Toronto Press, 2009).

[82] *Phillips v Redpath and McKay* (1830) Draper 68 (UCKB).

[83] Ibid 79.

[84] Ibid 83.

[85] Ibid 72, 75.

[86] Ibid 75.

[87] Ibid 84–85.

[88] Ibid 78–79.

is unnecessary to remark,' Macaulay J. observed, that 'the laws we enjoy extend equal protection to all'.[89] The rule of law may not always have flourished in a practical sense in pre-Confederation Canada.[90] However, *Phillips v Redpath* aligns with Dicey's sense of how the spirit of legality should flourish. Indeed, the case resembles in many respects the celebrated decision in *Roncarelli v Duplessis*, the leading case on statutory powers and the rule of law in Canada today in which Dicey's theory of constitutionalism was expressly invoked.[91]

There is considerable evidence, then, that Dicey's spirit of legality existed in Canada from an early stage. Of course, Dicey's account of constitutionalism was a product of a distinctive history in which the threat to liberties came from arbitrary royal or executive power and the solution lay in the alliance of common law reason with parliamentary authority. If we return to the statutes in the *Cobalt* and *Smith* cases, however, it is clear that they reveal a different kind of problem: here parliamentary authority was wielded not through general laws open to judicial interpretation but through what were, in substance if not form, individuated decrees immune from judicial interpretation. The common law-parliamentary alliance necessary for the Diceyan spirit of legality had, in effect, broken down. The Ontario statutes thus reveal a weakness in Dicey's theory of constitutionalism: if parliamentary authority is exercised through decrees rather than laws it cannot be reconciled with the rule of law, and the spirit of legality dissipates.

Dicey seemed to have grasped this point. In his opinion on the statutes, which Goldwin Smith quickly published, he concluded that there were no restrictions in the BNA Act preventing a province from exercising its legislative authority over property and civil rights in a 'palpably unjust' way.[92] But were the specific statutes at issue in *Cobalt* and *Smith* valid? Here Dicey expressed 'some hesitation' and suggested that because the statutes were 'so strange and manifestly unjust' it was 'at least possible the court . . . might be inclined to hold them invalid'.[93] Dicey did not elaborate. However, later in his opinion he mused that perhaps a statute taking property from 'designated individuals' 'might be held invalid as not being a law at all, i.e., as lacking that generality which some writers ascribe to a law (see e.g., Pollock, First Book of Jurisprudence, p. 35)'.[94] The passage from Frederick Pollock's book that Dicey cited may suggest what he had in mind. Here, Pollock argued that certain basic forms must be honoured if law and a system of justice administered according to law are to exist, including 'generality' (the law cannot be a rule made 'merely for the individual'), 'equality' ('the rule must have the like application to all persons and facts coming within it'), and 'certainty' (the rule must

[89] Ibid 87.

[90] Romney, above (n 24); G. Blaine Baker 'So Elegant a Web: Providential Order and the Rule of Law in Early Nineteenth-Century Upper Canada' (1988) 38 UTLJ 184.

[91] *Roncarelli v Duplessis* [1959] SCR 121; Mark D. Walters, 'Legality as Reason: Dicey, Rand and the Rule of Law' (2010) 55 McGill LJ 563.

[92] A.V. Dicey, 'Unjust and Impolitic Provincial Legislation and Its Disallowance by the Governor-General' (1909) 45 Can LJ 457, 459–460.

[93] Ibid 461.

[94] Ibid 462.

be known, defined and recorded in advance).[95] In other words, to succeed in making a *law*, certain values associated with the rule of law must be respected, which the Ontario legislature had failed to do. It is worth remembering that federal and provincial legislatures in Canada are authorized by the 1867 Act not to do anything they want, but only to make '*Laws*'.[96]

Judgments in the two cases were rendered and the impugned statues upheld. Justice W.R. Riddell presided over both cases and his reasons represent a tour de force on parliamentary sovereignty: within the powers allocated to them provincial legislatures are sovereign and supreme just as Coke, Blackstone, and Dicey said the British Parliament was.[97] 'All these powers are possessed in fact by our kinsmen across the seas,' Riddell wrote, 'and for myself I can see no reason why our rights in Ontario in local matters should be any less than the rights of those in the British Isles'.[98] Writing extra-judicially, Riddell was critical of Goldwin Smith's position, and he insisted that Canadian legislatures were not, as American legislatures were, 'cribb'd, cabined and confined' by the constitution; '[w]e will not', he insisted, 'submit to have our great public works delayed by cranks or the litigious'.[99] Riddell's views were consistent with other jurists of the day who celebrated the unfettered sovereignty of Canadian legislatures. '[If] Canadians are to enjoy a political life as inspiring, as vivid, and as free, as that of the people of the United Kingdom,' Lefroy wrote, 'no other theory of legislative power in Canada could suffice'.[100]

Two routes were taken in response to the judgments: one political, the other legal. Before a committee of the federal cabinet, counsel argued that the statute at issue in the *Smith* case be disallowed by the Governor General. Emphasis was placed upon the 'doubt' that Dicey had expressed about its legal validity.[101] It was argued that if the legislature can 'declare away the power of the courts in one Act' then it could to so 'in every Act' and the judiciary would then become a 'nullity'.[102] It was not claimed that the statute was '*ultra vires*' in the sense that it infringed 'any particular rule or section of the British North America Act upon which we can lay our hands'; rather, the point was that the BNA Act 'is not a complete category' of constitutional rights and that legislative power was confined by, in addition to its written terms, 'the spirit and purport of the Act', including the principle, prized within the classic texts of English constitutionalism,

---

[95] Frederick Pollock, *A First Book of Jurisprudence for Students of the Common Law* (Macmillan, 1896), 35, 36–37, 39–40.

[96] BNA Act, ss. 91, 92 (emphasis added).

[97] *Cobalt*, above (n 56); *Smith*, above (n 57).

[98] *Smith*, above (n 57) [30].

[99] W.R. Riddell, *The Constitution of Canada in Its History and Practical Working* (Yale University Press, 1917), 90, 99, 148–149.

[100] A.H.F. Lefroy, *Canada's Federal System, Being a Treatise on Canadian Constitutional Law under the British North America Act* (Carswell, 1913), 66–67.

[101] F.H. Chrysler, *A Question of Disallowance: Argument before the Privy Council on the Petitions for the Vetoing of the Power Legislation of Ontario* (Ottawa, 1909), 39.

[102] Ibid 44.

of 'free access to the courts of law for the redress of grievances'.[103] The request for disallowance was refused.

The *Cobalt* case was appealed. Before the Judicial Committee of the Privy Council, counsel submitted that by virtue of the similar-in-principle recital in the BNA Act's preamble, 'the fundamental principles of British jurisprudence' became 'embodied as part of the Canadian constitution' and binding on Canadian legislatures.[104] One strand of argument developed in this respect, seemingly inspired by the point in Dicey's opinion about the need for generality in law, was that the impugned act was not 'Legislative' but rather embraced 'arbitrary decrees'.[105] It was argued that there must be a 'general permanent law for Courts to administer or men to live under', otherwise the administration of justice would be 'an empty form, an idle ceremony'.[106] Counsel concluded:

> The Judges to be appointed by the Federal authorities were . . . not intended to sit to execute such arbitrary judgments of the Legislature but to administer justice according to law. The authority given to the Legislature is a power to make laws. The very nature of this power implies the element of generality.[107]

The appeal was unsuccessful.[108] Dicey thought that the ruling was 'disheartening'[109] and he intended to issue, through Goldwin Smith, a sort of call to arms to Canadians: 'Whether the government of Canada is to mean the rule of strict law & of justice, or of party spirit & of injustice now depends, & depends wholly upon the will of the Canadian citizen.'[110] However, Smith would soon die and Dicey's statement was never published.

It might seem surprising that Dicey, known as the defender of parliamentary sovereignty, would find the results in *Cobalt* and *Smith* disheartening. However, his position in this respect is consistent with his claim that Canada's constitution was more American than British in nature. He meant no disrespect in saying this. Indeed, he thought that American institutions were 'in their spirit' essentially a 'gigantic development' of English political and legal ideas.[111] However, he also insisted that the theoretical character of legislative authority in Britain was fundamentally different from legislative authority in either the United States or Canada. Dicey argued that American legislatures and legislatures in British dominions such as Canada were essentially the same

[103] Ibid 54.
[104] *In the Privy Council. On Appeal from the Court of Appeal for Ontario. Between The Florence Mining Company, Limited and The Cobalt Lake Mining Company, Limited. Appellants' Case. Respondents' Case. Record of Proceeding* (London, 1910), 18.
[105] Ibid.
[106] Ibid.
[107] Ibid 19.
[108] *Florence Mining Co v Cobalt Lake Mining Co* [1911] 2 AC 412 (PC).
[109] Dicey to Smith, 19 April 1910 above (n 58) reel 21.
[110] 'Memorandum on the Judgment of the Privy Council' enclosed in Dicey to Smith, ibid.
[111] Dicey, above (n 6) 129.

as municipalities and railway corporations with bylaw-making powers: they were not sovereign but subordinate entities exercising powers under a legal instrument, and any law made beyond those powers could be found by judges to be ultra vires and void. Indeed, Dicey insisted that the 'American system' of judicial review of legislation was 'in principle borrowed from the common law of England' which contemplated judicial rulings on legislative validity 'whether the law making authority be the Parl[iamen]t of the Canadian Dominion or the Corporation of Oxford.'[112]

If this were so, Dicey's critics claimed, then Canadian statutes could, like municipal bylaws, be judicially ruled invalid on the basis not just of the express terms of the governing statute but also if unreasonable.[113] Or, more to the point, they could, like statutes in the United States, be judicially reviewed on the basis not just of written constitutional provisions but also 'implied' restrictions arising from 'the general spirit of the Constitution' including those principles relating to the nature of law that are 'essential' to the concept of a 'free' government.[114] In other words, if the Canadian constitution were treated like ordinary law then the powers it conferred would always be shaped and moulded by the 'general spirit of the common law' or the 'spirit of legality'. The 'hesitation' that he expressed in his opinion on the *Cobalt* and *Smith* cases is the closest that Dicey came to conceding that these were indeed the implications of his argument. However, this expression of hesitation seems to have been enough to inspire counsel in the two cases to develop in considerable detail the argument for implied limitations on legislative power based upon principles of legality.

What should also have been apparent to Dicey from his consideration of the Ontario cases was that the same threat to constitutional values existed in Britain itself: unless parliamentary authority in Britain was also limited implicitly by the demands of legality, unless Parliament was legally required to act through laws rather than decrees, his argument on the reconciliation of parliamentary sovereignty and the rule of law would collapse. However, Dicey never pursued this line of thought. Indeed, it would be many years before the argument was forcefully and elegantly made that legislative power in *all* common law jurisdictions, whether having written and entrenched constitutional instruments or not, is essentially the same and must always be exercised consistently with the implicit demands of legality.[115]

---

[112] A.V. Dicey, 'Division of Constitutions' [1900] in J.W.F. Allison (ed), *Comparative Constitutionalism: Oxford Edition of Dicey Volume II* (Oxford University Press, 2013), 237.

[113] Henry Jenkyns, 'Remarks on Certain Points in Mr. Dicey's Law of the Constitution' (1887) 3 LQR 204, 205–206.

[114] Lefroy, *Legislative Power in Canada*, above (n 9) lii, citing *Loan Assoc'n v. Topeka*, 87 U.S. 655 (1874). On this case and the American approach to implied constitutional limits on legislative power in general, see Mark D. Walters, 'Written Constitutions and Unwritten Constitutionalism' in Grant Huscroft (ed), *Expounding the Constitution: Essays in Constitutional Theory* (Cambridge University Press, 2008), 245–276.

[115] T.R.S. Allan, *Constitutional Justice: A Liberal Theory of the Rule of Law* (Oxford University Press, 2001).

In Canada, the general line of argument developed by counsel in the *Cobalt* and *Smith* cases based upon the preamble's similar-in-principle recital, the rule of law, access to independent superior courts, and the Constitution's implicit spirit, purport, or struc-ture, would, in time, be accepted by the country's judges. In 1949—the year that appeals to the Judicial Committee of the Privy Council were finally abolished—a judge held a federal statutory provision invalid based upon principles of legality and judicial inde-pendence derived from the common law tradition.[116] The Supreme Court of Canada would gradually accept this general style of constitutional reasoning and the similar-in-principle recital in the preamble to the 1867 Act would play a central part in this evolving constitutional narrative[117]—even if, on occasion, the full implications of the reasoning were not always been appreciated.[118]

It is fair to say that Canada's constitution is still today similar in principle to the British Constitution. However, it can be argued that it is similar only to that version of the British Constitution that sees parliamentary sovereignty and the rule of law as comple-mentary not opposing ideals, and thus insists that legislative power manifest itself only through genuine laws and not decrees. We might even say that this is a Canadian contri-bution to the idea of constitutionalism. If so, then perhaps the question now is whether in Britain there is a willingness to see its constitution as similar in principle to Canada's.

BIBLIOGRAPHY

Secondary sources

Baker GB, 'So Elegant a Web: Providential Order and the Rule of Law in Early Nineteenth-Century Upper Canada' (1988) 38 UTLJ 184

Bourinot JG, 'The Federal Constitution of Canada' (1890) 2 Jur Rev 131

Cavendish H, *Debates of the House of Commons in the Year 1774, on the Bill for Making More Effectual Provision for the Government of the Province of Quebec* (J. Wright 1839)

Clement WHP, *The Law of the Canadian Constitution* (Carswell 1892)

Coupland R (ed), *The Durham Report* (Clarendon Press 1945)

Dicey AV, *Lectures Introductory to the Study of the Law of the Constitution* (Macmillan 1885)

———. 'Unjust and Impolitic Provincial Legislation and Its Disallowance by the Governor-General' (1909) 45 Can LJ 457

Gray JH, *Confederation; or, the Political and Parliamentary History of Canada* (Copp, Clark 1872)

Grey (Earl), *The Colonial Policy of Lord John Russell's Administration* (Richard Bentley 1853)

---

[116] *R v Hess (No 2)* [1949] 4 DLR 199 (BCCA), 205–206, 208–209 (O'Halloran JA in chambers).

[117] *Reference re Alberta Statutes* [1938] SCR 100, 133 (Duff J with Davies J concurring), 145–146 (Cannon J); *Saumur v Quebec* [1953] 2 SCR 299 (Rand and Kellock JJ); *Switzman v Elbling and A-G Que* [1957] SCR 285 (Rand, Kellock and Abbott JJ); *Reference re Remuneration of Judges of the Provincial Court of Prince Edward Island* [1997] 3 SCR 3 (Lamer CJC for the majority); *Trial Lawyers Association of British Columbia v British Columbia (Attorney General)* [2014] 3 SCR 31; *Reference re Senate Reform* [2014] 1 SCR 704; *Reference re Supreme Court Act, ss 5 and 6* [2014] 1 S.C.R. 433.

[118] *British Columbia v Imperial Tobacco Canada Ltd* [2005] 2 S.C.R. 473.

Greenwood FM, *Legacies of Fear: Law and Politics in Quebec in the Era of the French Revolution* (Osgoode Society/University of Toronto Press 1993)

Kennedy WPM (ed), *Statutes, Treaties and Documents of the Canadian Constitution, 1713–1929* (Oxford University Press 1930)

Laskin B, *The British Tradition in Canadian Law* (Stevens & Sons 1969)

Lederman, WR 'The Independence of the Judiciary' (1956) 34 Can Bar Rev 769 (pt I), 1139 (pt II).

Lefroy AHF, *Canada's Federal System, Being a Treatise on Canadian Constitutional Law under the British North America Act* (Carswell 1913)

_____. *The Law of Legislative Power in Canada* (Toronto Law Book 1897–1898)

Murdoch B, *Epitome of the Laws of Nova-Scotia* (Joseph Howe 1832)

Riddell WR, *The Constitution of Canada in Its History and Practical Working* (Yale University Press 1917)

Romney P, 'From Constitutionalism to Legalism: Trial by Jury, Responsible Government, and the Rule of Law in the Canadian Political Culture' (1989) 7 Law & Hist Rev 121

Shortt A and Doughty AG (eds), *Documents Relating to the Constitutional History of Canada, 1759–1791* (SE Dawson 1907)

Walters MD, 'Succession to the Throne and the Architecture of the Constitution of Canada' in Philippe Lagassé and Michel Bédard (eds), *The Crown and Parliament* (Éditions Yvon Blais 2015)

_____. 'Written Constitutions and Unwritten Constitutionalism' in Grant Huscroft (ed), *Expounding the Constitution: Essays in Constitutional Theory* (Cambridge University Press 2008), 245–276

Wright B and Binnie S (eds), *Canadian State Trials, Volume III: Political Trials and Security Measures, 1840–1914* (Osgoode Society/University of Toronto Press 2009)

Cases

Baldwin v Gibbon and McCallum (1813) Stuart's Rep 72

British Columbia v Imperial Tobacco Canada Ltd [2005] 2 S.C.R. 473

Canada (Attorney General) v Ontario (Attorney General) (1894) 23 SCR 458

Citizens Ins Co v Parsons (1881) 7 App Cas 96 (PC)

Donegani v Donegani (1831) Stuart's Rep 460; aff'd (1835) 3 Knapp 63 (PC)

Entick v Carrington (1765) 19 St Tr 1029 (KB), 1073

Florence Mining Co v Cobalt Lake Mining Co (1908) 12 OWR 297 (HC); aff'd [1911] 2 AC 412 (PC)

Hamilton v Fraser (1811) Stuart's Rep 21

Hodge v The Queen (1883) 9 App Cas 117 (PC)

In the Case of Daniel Tracey (1832) Stuart's Rep 478 (LCKB)

In re Initiative and Referendum Act [1919] AC 935 (PC)

Kielley v Carson (1842) 4 Moore 63 (PC)

Lenoir v Ritchie (1879), 3 SCR 575

Liquidators of Maritime Bank v Receiver-General of New Brunswick [1892] AC 437 (PC)

New Brunswick Co v Nova Scotia (Speaker of the House of Assembly) [1993] 1 SCR 319

M'Nab v Bidwell and Baldwin (1830), Draper 144 (UCKB)

Phillips v Redpath and McKay (1830) Draper 68 (UCKB)

Reference re Alberta Statutes [1938] SCR 100

Reference re Remuneration of Judges of the Provincial Court of Prince Edward Island [1997] 3 SCR 3

Re Resolution to Amend the Constitution [1981] 1 SCR 753

Reference re Senate Reform [2014] 1 SCR 704

Reference re Supreme Court Act, ss 5 and 6 [2014] 1 S.C.R. 433

R v Hess (No 2) [1949] 4 DLR 199 (BCCA)

Regina v Kerr (1838) 2 NBR 553 (SC)

Saumur v Quebec [1953] 2 SCR 299

Smith v London (City of) (1909) 13 OWR 1148 (HC)

St Catherine's Milling and Lumber Co v R (1889) 14 App Cas 46 (PC)

Switzman v Elbling and A-G Que [1957] SCR 285

The Queen v Secretary of State for Foreign and Commonwealth Affairs, ex parte Indian Association of Alberta [1982] QB 892 (CA)

Trial Lawyers Association of British Columbia v British Columbia (Attorney General) [2014] 3 SCR 31

Trimble v Hill (1879) 5 App Cas 342 (PC)

PART II

INSTITUTIONS AND CONSTITUTIONAL CHANGE

A. The Crown and the Executive

CHAPTER 6

....

THE CROWN IN CANADA

....

MARCELLA FIRMINI* & JENNIFER SMITH**

1. INTRODUCTION

....

STUDENTS of Canadian government are convinced that the monarch is merely a figurehead in the Canadian system of government. One can hardly blame them for this point of view, as it is after all the prevailing one. As a result, constitutional commentators must return to first principles, or at least to 1 July 1867, the date of Confederation, to explain the logical consequences that flow from the fact that Canada is a constitutional monarchy.

Her Majesty Queen Elizabeth II is the Queen of *Canada*[1] thus bearing the *Canadian* Crown. She is the head of state and all executive authority is vested in her; all those seeking to acquire Canadian citizenship, in fact, swear an oath to her.[2] She is not just a figurehead. Rather, she is *also* a figurehead—the symbol and the physical representation of the Crown.

The Crown has three functions. The first is *institutional* (or constitutional) being the 'principle' around which governing in Canada is organized.[3] The second is the *symbolic* representation of Canadian unity. The third is the *ceremonial* role fulfilled by the Queen and her representatives in Canada, namely, the Governor General and the Lieutenant-Governors. In the eyes of the public, the institutional function is often obscured by the

---

  * PhD, Assistant Professor, Department of Political Science, Dalhousie University.
 ** PhD, Professor Emeritus, Dalhousie University.
  [1] The Canadian Crown is distinct and independent from the British Crown since the passing of the *Statute of Westminster* (1931) which will be discussed later in this chapter. Queen Elizabeth II officially became *Queen of Canada* with the *Royal Style and Titles Act, 1953*.
  [2] Philippe Lagassé. 'Citizenship and the Hollowed Canadian Crown'. *Policy Options*, accessed 1 May 2016. http://policyoptions.irpp.org/2015/03/02/citizenship-and-the-hollowed-canadian-crown/ (para 4–5). Retrieved 11 January 2017.
  [3] David E. Smith. *The Invisible Crown: The First Principle of Canadian Government* (University of Toronto Press, 1995: 5 & 11).

symbolic and ceremonial functions, the result being confusion. Some think the Crown is constitutionally powerless and merely a relic of tradition, while others overestimate the power it retains to influence the conduct of political life. Only in distinguishing the institutional function from the symbolic and ceremonial ones is it possible to appreciate the role of the Crown in the Canadian system of government.

In the next section of the chapter there is a brief account of the symbolic and ceremonial functions of the Crown. The following and longest section deals with the institutional functions. It begins with a historical account of the institutional development of the Crown in Canada, in particular, the changes that coincide with the country's progress from colony to nation. There follows an assessment of the statutory and prerogative powers of the Crown. In the conclusion, we address the issues facing the Crown in Canada today.

2. SYMBOLIC AND CEREMONIAL FUNCTIONS

At Confederation the Crown and federal Parliament were to serve as symbols of Canadian unity[4] and identity[5] respectively. The Fathers of Confederation sought to rally a very diverse population *not* under a cultural umbrella, but under a political and institutional one.[6] They foresaw, or at least hoped for, a time when Canadians would share a *political identity* based on salient *political values* expressed through Parliament.[7] Meanwhile the constitutional monarch, a politically neutral figure staying above the fray of day-to-day politicking, was to remain a symbol of the country itself, in essence, a symbol of national unity. Arguably, today these unifying and nationalizing functions are served more by the Canadian Charter of Rights and Freedoms[8] than the Crown. Still,

---

[4] 'Here sit the representatives of the British population claiming justice—only justice; and here sit the representatives of the French population, discussing in the French tongue whether we shall have it. One hundred years have passed away since the conquest of Quebec, but here sit the children of the victor and of the vanquished, all avowing hearty attachment to the British crown—all earnestly debating how we shall best extend the blessings of British institutions—how a great people may be established on this continent in close and hearty connection with Great Britain'. George Brown, Legislative Assembly, 8 February 1865 (in J. Ajzenstat, P. Romney, I. Gentles & W.D. Gardner, *Canada's Founding Debates* (Stoddard, 1999: 15).

[5] 'We thereby strengthen the central parliament and make the Confederation one people and one government, instead of five peoples and five governments, with merely a point of authority connecting us to a limited and insufficient extent'. Sir John A. Macdonald, Legislative Assembly, 6 February 1865 (in Ajzenstat, ibid, 284).

[6] Janet Ajzenstat. *The Canadian Founding: John Locke and Parliament* (McGill-Queen's University Press, 2007), 11 & 81.

[7] Ibid, 81.

[8] Benjamin Shingler. 'Charter and Universal Health Care Top Canadian Unity Poll'. *Global News*. http://globalnews.ca/news/1424367/charter-universal-health-care-top-canadian-unity-poll/. Retrieved 16 February 2016.

affection for the current monarch remains strong despite declining sympathy for the institution of monarchy itself,[9] and she continues to fulfill the symbolic function.

As for the ceremonial functions, these are quite numerous: honours are granted in the name of the Crown in recognition of service to the country and other significant literary, academic, and artistic accomplishments and contributions to its well-being.[10] Some notable examples include the Order of Canada[11] and the Victoria Cross.[12] Finally, the Crown is an inescapable part of traditional political ceremonies, like the Speech from the Throne that is read by the Governor General at the opening of a new Parliament.

3. INSTITUTIONAL FUNCTION

Although the symbolic and ceremonial roles of the Crown are deeply significant, there can be no doubt that the institutional function of the Crown is the most important—albeit the least visible—and it affects every aspect of governing in Canada. In fact, the executive power is composed of the Crown (formal Executive), the Prime Minister and Cabinet (the political Executive), and the bureaucracy (the permanent Executive). In the words of David E. Smith, the Crown is the 'organizing principle of Canadian government'.[13] Its presence touches every other governmental institution. Importantly, it remains a (contested) bulwark against abuses of power—a function that becomes all the more important in an era in which notions of the concentration of power in the hands of prime ministers and their cabinets are widespread. So how did it get here?

A. The Crown(s) in Canada

(i) European Crowns Vie for Control of North America

England's King Henry VII, by way of the Italian navigator John Cabot, was the first European to claim land on Canada's east coast in 1497 even though no significant,

---

[9] Karen Pauls. 'Royal Family Support by Canadians Waning'. *Canadian Broadcasting Corporation (CBC)*. http://www.cbc.ca/news/canada/manitoba/royal-family-support-by-canadians-waning-poll-indicates-1.3072469. Retrieved 16 February 2016.

[10] A full list can be found at https://www.gg.ca/document.aspx?id=5&lan=eng. Retrieved 2 January 2017.

[11] One can become Companion of the Order (for national or international service and accomplishments), Officer of the Order (for national service and accomplishments), and Member of the Order (for local, regional, or field-specific service and accomplishments). Full descriptions can be found at https://www.gg.ca/document.aspx?id=14940&lan=eng. Retrieved 2 January 2017.

[12] The Victoria Cross honours qualities of bravery and duty. See C. McCreery, 'The Crown and Honours: Getting It Right' in Jennifer Smith & D. Michael Jackson (eds.) *The Evolving Canadian Crown* (McGill-Queen's University Press, 2012), pp. 139–154.

[13] Smith, above (n 3) 5 & 11.

long-lasting settlements or colonies were established at that time. The presence of the French Crown in Canada can be traced back to 1534 when Jacques Cartier erected a Christian cross on the Gaspé for King François I. Here, too, initial attempts to create a colony failed miserably, but in the 1600s, France claimed and settled a vast tract of land, naming it—perhaps unimaginatively—New France. By 1670, England had also established a solid presence on an immense swathe of territory to the north and west of New France, naming it Rupert's Land.

In the end, the Seven Years' War (1756–1763) resolved this European rivalry over empire. Engulfing almost all of Europe as well, the war ended with Great Britain's victory over France. King Louis XV was the last French king to rule over, and in, Canada, bringing to an end the 229-year presence of the French Crown (1534–1763). From a British perspective, the *Royal Proclamation* signed in 1763, among other things, placed Indigenous nations under the protection of the British Crown, in particular from land speculators and their dubious dealings. This protection was secured by stipulating that Indigenous lands could only be 'alienated' to the Crown, which would then proceed to negotiate sales in the best interest of the Indigenous nations. These provisions created a fiduciary responsibility of the Crown for Indigenous nations which continues today. The *Royal Proclamation* is, in fact, the seminal document which influenced—and continues to influence—Crown-Indigenous relationships. References to Indigenous peoples in founding (and foundational) documents of Canada highlight the significance of their enduring and distinctive bond with the Canadian Crown (as state and as symbol). In legal terms, it is a sui generis relationship which predates Confederation.[14]

Following the American War of Independence (1775–1783) those who remained loyal to the British Crown were dubbed 'United Empire Loyalists' and they relocated to Canada, settling in central Canada, New Brunswick, and Nova Scotia. This English-speaking group and the pre-established French-speaking populations in those areas soon found themselves at odds with each other, and the attempt to alleviate tensions led to the *Constitutional Act* of 1791 which created Upper and Lower Canada (currently portions of the provinces of Ontario and Québec respectively). This institutional remedy did not produce the desired effects; eventually, the strained relationship devolved into full-on rebellion (1837–1838). The British government sent Lord Durham to the Canadas to inquire into the causes of the uprisings. His observations are famously (or infamously) detailed in the *Report on the Affairs of British North America*. One of Durham's recommendations, the reunion of the Canadas, was accomplished in the *Act of Union*, 1840, which established the *Province of Canada*. Another was the adoption of responsible government in the colonies, which took longer to establish. Responsible government is the constitutional convention whereby, in modern terms, the Executive, meaning the

---

[14] The *Constitution Act, 1867* in section 91 (24) assigns jurisdiction to the federal government for 'Indians and lands reserved for Indians'. Jurisdiction over 'status Indians' and protection of their reserve lands continues under the *Indian Act* (1876) while section 35 of the *Constitution Act, 1982* reaffirms Indigenous rights. The *Charter of Rights and Freedoms* (section 25) guarantees that Aboriginal rights will not be diminished by its enforcement and, significantly, makes mention of the *Royal Proclamation 1763*.

Prime Minister and Cabinet, must have the confidence—the support—of the House of Commons in order to retain the right to govern. This convention remains the corner-stone of Westminster-style parliamentary democracy.

It is worth noting that in recommending responsible government, Durham was rather ahead of his time, as the practice of it in the British system was barely under-way. Responsible government is a system that evolved in a country famous for its evolu-tionary institutional developments. The key was the slow if inexorable transition from a government model that featured the monarch governing with the advice of individual ministers, and getting support from Parliament when required, to a government model that featured a cabinet of ministers headed by a first or prime minister that governs in the name of the monarch, but with the support of Parliament.

In the British colonies, Nova Scotia was the first to achieve responsible government (1848) followed in relatively short order by the other Maritime colonies, and then the Province of Canada. By the time of Confederation in 1867, the colonies had had several years' experience with the system. 1 July 1867 marks the birth of modern Canada—one very large colony of the British Empire. It also marks the Canadian journey from colony to independent country—from 1867 to the Imperial Conference of 1926 and the *Statute of Westminster* of 1931, and finally, full independence achieved by the repatriation of the constitution in 1982.

B. British Crown: From Colony to Independence

In the *British North America Act, 1867* (now called the *Constitution Act, 1867*), the Fathers of Confederation established a constitution 'similar in principle' to that of the United Kingdom. However, use of the term 'similar' should not lead readers to believe that the founding document is little more than a written compendium of British principles. For one thing, in fact crucially, the Fathers adopted the federal principle while retain-ing the monarchy. This untested experiment, novel at the time[15], effectively combined two contradictory principles: the first—monarchy—concentrates power, whereas the second—federalism—disperses it.[16] The Crown was further adapted to fit the exigen-cies of federalism via the creation of a 'compound monarchy'[17], that is, the establishment of Lieutenant-Governors to represent the Crown in the provinces. On this model, the Crown remained indivisible as its federal and provincial representatives, the Governor General and Lieutenant-Governors, operate concomitantly.

Despite Confederation, the stubborn persistence of a colonial ethos was evidenced by some provisions in the Constitution which strongly contradicted the federal principle of divided legislative jurisdiction and the valued ideals of unity in diversity and local self-government. In fact, Canada's colonial status at Confederation was marked in a number

---

[15] Smith, above (n 3) 156.
[16] Ibid, 8.
[17] Ibid, 11 & 156–173.

of ways that bore on the office of the Governor General who, importantly, was regarded not only as the Queen's representative in Canada, but the representative of the British government as well. In the latter capacity, he was the recipient of instructions from that government on various and sundry matters.

The clauses in the *Constitution Act, 1867* that bear on the role of the Governor General in the law-making process illustrate the colonial point. For example, sections 55–57 on the powers of reservation and disallowance specify that the Governor General, acting in the Queen's name, either assents to a bill passed by both houses of Parliament, withholds assent, or reserves the bill for the Queen's consideration. If he assents to the bill, the Queen on the advice of her British counsellors can *disallow* it within two years of its passage. She has the same period of time to decide upon bills that the Governor General *reserves*[18] for her consideration. Section 90 applies the same template in relation to the Lieutenant-Governors, except that they must refer provincial bills to the Governor General for decision, not the British monarch, and the time line for decision is shortened to one year. The use of the power to veto bills or reserve them for consideration by a higher authority, rather robust in the early years of Confederation, diminished sharply as the years passed.[19] Today these are considered constitutional anachronisms and have long since fallen into disuse. Nonetheless, their inclusion in the Constitution illustrates the colonial status of Canada at Confederation.

This status was reflected as well in *constitutional conventions* bearing on the Governor General. One example is the appointment of the Governor General, a subject not mentioned in the *Constitution Act, 1867*. According to practice followed at that time, and consistent with the office's role as representative of the British government, the Governor General was appointed by the Queen on the advice of the British Colonial Secretary, which carried with it the approval of the British Prime Minister. This was how Governors were appointed to the colonies before Confederation, and the practice was simply carried over to Canada when it was established. With the passage of time, the ongoing changes made in the appointment of the Governor General tracked Canada's progress toward autonomous status within the Commonwealth.

By the latter part of the nineteenth century, the British system of appointment by the sovereign on the advice of the British government was modified by the practice of consulting with the Canadian government before the appointment was made. However, after the Imperial Conference of 1926 had severed the connection between the British government and the Governor General, the old method was no longer an appropriate one. Instead, the appointment is made by the sovereign on the advice of the Canadian

---

[18] Disallowance has been used a total of 112 times; the last time was in 1943 to disallow a statute in Alberta prohibiting the sale of land to Hutterites. The powers of reservation were exercised 70 times with the last time being in Saskatchewan in 1961 in relation to mining contracts. The bill in question ultimately received Royal Assent.

[19] Andrew Heard, *Canadian Constitutional Conventions: The Marriage of Law & Politics*, 2nd ed. (Oxford University Press (Canada), 2014), 71.

Prime Minister.[20] Initially the Prime Minister made his recommendation from a list of British candidates. However, since 1952, which saw the appointment of Vincent Massey to the post, only Canadians have been recommended to the sovereign for the position.

Yet another mark of colonialism involved the relationship between the Governor General and the British government in relation to the governance of Canada. On the domestic front, and from the beginning, the Canadian Cabinet was wary of efforts by the British government to continue issuing instructions to Governors General, the execution of which would influence the course of the country's internal affairs. In 1878 Edward Blake, Minister of Justice in the Liberal government of Prime Minister Alexander Mackenzie, successfully resisted the British proposal to authorize the Governor General to preside at Cabinet meetings (this had not happened for years), and on occasion not only to override Cabinet decisions but to act without consulting the Cabinet (presumably when Imperial interests were at stake). Although part of the British Empire, Canada, said Blake, should not be treated like a small, young colony but a large, self-governing country.[21] In his review of these matters, R. MacGregor Dawson concluded that by 1914 Canada was to all intents and purposes autonomous in relation to its own internal affairs and the Governor General was no longer an active political figure in domestic political life.[22]

Canadian autonomy in relation to external affairs was much slower to develop. From the standpoint of the Governor General, again the key point in the shift to autonomy in this field was the status of the office as representative of the British government as well as the Crown. So long as the British government retained control of Imperial policies that implicated and affected the colonies—such as trade, treaty-making, and the declaration of war—the office was understood to combine both functions. Once the country effectively became an autonomous actor in the world, the achievement was reflected in the status of the Governor General as representative of the Crown only, not the British government. These developments emerged at the Imperial Conference of 1926, which issued a formal statement of the equality of the United Kingdom and the Dominions (including Canada) within the British Commonwealth. Moreover, the conference declared that as a consequence of this equal status, the Governors General of the Dominions were representatives of the Crown and held essentially the same position vis-à-vis their governments as the King to the British government. They were no longer the representative or agent of the British government. These declarations along with additional provisos bearing on the autonomy of the Dominions took formal shape later in the terms of the *Statute of Westminster* which was enacted by the British Parliament in 1931.[23]

---

[20] Robert MacGregor Dawson, *The Government of Canada,* 3rd ed. revised (University of Toronto Press, 1954), 174.
[21] Ibid, 53.
[22] Ibid, 58.
[23] Ibid, 60, 166–173.

Finally, there is the history of the Letters Patent,[24] which also reflects Canada's track from colony to independent nation. Under British colonial practice, Governors of colonies routinely were issued Commissions appointing them to the office, Letters Patent that defined the office and Royal Instructions that regulated specified matters such as oaths of office or the quorum needed for meetings of the Cabinet. As amended over the years, the Letters Patent broadened the space within which the Governor General could act as the sovereign's personal representative and, importantly, exercise the royal prerogative on his own. For example, in 1905 the Letters Patent were amended to vest in the Governor General the position of commander-in-chief for Canada, one previously held by the senior officer commanding British military forces in the country.

In 1931 the Letters Patent, following the spirit of the Imperial Conference of 1926 mentioned above, executed the transformation of the office of Governor General from agent of the British government and personal representative of the sovereign to the latter role alone. Notably, the Letters Patent 1947 authorized the Governor General to exercise on advice of the Canadian Cabinet all of the sovereign's powers and authority for Canada. But this did not include the royal prerogatives then exercised by the sovereign, who received submissions for approval from Canada for the authorization of declarations of war, the signing of treaties, the appointment of Canadian ambassadors and ministers to foreign countries, and the granting of honours and the appointment of the Governor General, to name a few. These and other prerogatives were delegated to the Governor General in later years. Significantly, in 1977 the delegations covered important matters of foreign affairs, such as the authorization of the declaration of war and treaties of peace, the signing of treaties and of letters of credence, and recall of Canadian ambassadors abroad. It should be stressed that the sovereign retains the prerogative to appoint the Governor General.

Readers will notice that in tracing the country's evolution from colony to independence from the standpoint of the office of Governor General, we make mention of several powers which are formally in the hands of the Crown. A detailed explanation of them is now in order.

4. THE POWERS OF THE CROWN: STATUTORY, PREROGATIVE, AND RESERVE

The *Constitution Act, 1867* suggests that the constitutional reach of the Crown is extensive and substantial. The powers at its disposition are *statutory, prerogative*, and *reserve* powers. In keeping with Canada's standing as a parliamentary democracy, however, constitutional conventions require that these powers be exercised *almost* exclusively on the advice of the Prime Minister and Cabinet (the active Executive). The operative word here is 'almost'. As explained below, some powers remain in the hands of the Governor General.

[24] McCreery, above (n 12) 34–37.

A. Statutory Powers

Let us begin with the statutory powers of the Governor General found in the written constitution. The strongest note is struck in section 9 of the *Constitution Act, 1867* which states: 'The Executive Government and Authority of and over Canada is hereby declared to continue and be vested in the Queen'. This means that the authority of the Executive to govern and carry out its activities flows exclusively from the Crown. In addition, a formidable array of specific powers is assigned to the Governor General throughout the Constitution, such as section 24, the power to appoint persons to the senate of Canada, or section 96, the power to appoint judges to federal courts. By convention, of course, the Governor General exercises these powers only on the advice of the Prime Minister and Cabinet, the obvious political beneficiaries of the arrangement. Noteworthy as well is section 15, which states that the commander-in-chief of the armed forces is the Queen. This is why Canadians see the Governor General, who represents her in this capacity, in military uniform on such occasions as the Remembrance Day service in Ottawa.

B. Prerogative Powers

In addition to statutory powers, the Crown also has prerogative powers which derive from common law and are largely undefined in scope, remain unwritten, and are exercised on advice of the Prime Minister. Among them are the appointment and dismissal of prime (first) ministers and summoning, proroguing, and dissolving Parliament (or provincial legislatures in the case of the Lieutenant-Governors). Again, according to convention, the prerogative powers of the Governor General, like the statutory powers, are exercised by him on the advice of the Prime Minister. Clearly, the conventions that govern the actions of the Governor General are an extremely important part of the Canadian parliamentary system. It is worth pausing here to expand on what has been said before and to consider the provenance of constitutional conventions.

In defining the phrase 'constitutional convention,' scholars often refer to an established practice that is considered binding upon the relevant political actors. However, it is not a practice that is enforced by the courts; instead, if it is enforced at all, it is through political pressure, and, ultimately by the people through public opinion or in an election. Sir Ivor Jennings added the idea that there must be a reason for the conventional rule. Thus, the reason for the conventions that circumscribe the powers of the Governor General is usually the democratic principle. Andrew Heard captures this point in his definition of the concept, which is cited here in full:

> Conventions, at heart, are obligation upon political actors to act in a way other than what the formal law prescribes or allows. These obligations rise directly from the constitutional principles that underlie the political system, and they give final form to the constitution as a living expression of a society's dominant values. The job of judges is to define and enforce the legal rules at stake in disputes that come before

them. But some of those laws are incomplete and utterly archaic. As a result, political actors must obey other rules of the constitution in order for our political system to function in ways that are considered legitimate by the attentive public.[25]

The conventions that circumscribe the legal powers of the formal Executive accomplish the task by requiring that the holders of the office exercise these powers only on the advice of the Prime Minister or in some instances the Prime Minister and Cabinet. Generally speaking, they ensure procedural smooth sailing. Year after year, decade after decade, government proceeds apace with no need for the Governor General and the Lieutenant-Governors of the provinces to exercise any of the legal powers available to them on their own initiative. For example, although the first duty of these officers is to see that there is a Prime Minister and Cabinet in place, the voters almost always make the decision a foregone conclusion. Again, because Prime Ministers and Premiers who cannot command majority support in the elected legislature generally follow convention and advise that an election be held or resign to make way for a rival team to try to gain a viable majority, whichever course of action is appropriate in the circumstances, the Governors and Lieutenant-Governors need not exercise the undoubted legal power of their offices to dismiss their first ministers. Or again, long gone are the days in which they exercised their legal power to refuse royal assent to bills duly passed by the legislature. And until recently at least, they evinced no hesitation in following the advice of the Prime Minister and Premiers to prorogue the legislature. As a result, Canadians, including the students mentioned in our introduction, can be forgiven for imagining that the representatives of the Crown retain no legal powers at all, and that the functions discharged are symbolic ones only. Mostly they see these personages at important ceremonies or reading the Speech from the Throne—a document that is drafted by the government and outlines its legislative intentions for the upcoming parliamentary session.

C. Reserve Powers

And yet, there are the (exceedingly) rare occasions when circumstances combine to produce a constitutional crisis, or near crisis, in the parliamentary system. Naturally, these are the ones of most interest to students of government because they reveal the stark reality that the parliamentary system is not always on auto-pilot from the procedural standpoint. Instead, in times of constitutional crises there is controversy about the basic rules of the system itself. In the end, a decision must be made, and it falls to the Governor General or the Lieutenant-Governor to make it. The power to make such decisions is referred to as the reserve power.

The prerogative powers include the reserve power which, as the word implies, is exercisable by the Crown at its own discretion. In other words, the reserve power is the

---

[25] Heard, above (n 18), 5–6.

right of the Crown's representative to reject the advice of the government. The rationale for the maintenance of the reserve power in the hands of the Governors General (and Lieutenant-Governors) is their role in protecting the practice of responsible government from the predations of political actors who would not scruple to bend the system to their own advantage. Of course, the scrutiny of Her Majesty's Loyal Opposition, other political parties, the media, and public opinion, to name a few, make their intervention in this respect unnecessary—almost.

(i) Reserve Power Controversies

At the federal level of government, there have been only two occasions of serious controversy about the reserve powers of the Governor General, one about dissolution and the other prorogation. It is instructive to take a close look at both for the following reasons. First, they demonstrate the complexity of the political context out of which such controversies emerge. There is no basis for easy judgments, except those of the partisan variety. Secondly, they demonstrate the depth and passion of the partisan divide between the political actors who confront one another over the issues. Each side is utterly convinced of the rightness of its position and prepared to act on that basis. Thirdly, they show that such crises are zero-sum games. There are winners and there are losers. There is no brokered or in-between position of the sort that might be reached, say, in a trade agreement. In these fights over who governs, the Governor General is in an awkward position indeed. It is too facile to suggest that the office is like an umpire or referee of constitutional crises because the crises are not occasions of rule-following. On the contrary, the rules themselves are at issue among opponents whose partisanship ensures that they will take anything but an objective approach to the problem.

Let us begin with the so-called King-Byng affair, the roots of which were nourished in the general election of 1921, which produced the first real third party in Canadian politics, namely, the largely Western-based Progressive Party comprised of former Liberals determined to press a low-tariff agenda on the government and a more radical Albertan group intent on replacing altogether the system of political parties in the House of Commons with representatives of group interests who would openly bargain with one another on public policy choices. Out of a total of 235 seats, the Progressives claimed 64, or roughly 27 percent, nearly depriving Prime Minister Mackenzie King of a Liberal majority government. In the next general election in October 1925, the combination of a resurgent Conservative Party and a much weaker, but still significant Progressive presence did the trick. The Liberals were reduced to 99 of 245 seats. King even lost his own seat in Ontario.

Arrayed against the Liberals were 116 Conservatives, more than double their 50 seats in the 1921 outing; 24 Progressives; 4 Independents; and 2 Labour.[26] The Conservatives were led by Arthur Meighen, who had taken over leadership of the party in 1920—a year after King won the leadership of the Liberal Party. It is worth noting that the two rivals,

---

[26] J. Murray Beck, *Pendulum of Power* (Prentice-Hall, 1968), 174–175.

as unalike as could be imagined, detested one another. Following accepted constitutional convention, King decided to stay on in office and let the House of Commons determine his fate, as was his undoubted right to do so. He spent the weeks before the House opened shoring up support from the Progressives by incorporating some of their demands in the government's legislative programme and on occasion by including them in Cabinet committee meetings. The protectionist Meighen could hardly win at this game. And for several months he was unable to topple King's government on a vote of no confidence.

King might have managed to stay in office for a good amount of time if it had not been for a scandal in the Customs Department under investigation by a special commit-tee of the House. When the committee reported the malodorous evidence back to the House, the Conservatives moved to censure the entire Cabinet. King got an adjourn-ment of the House before it could vote on the censure motion, and then asked Governor General Byng to dissolve Parliament in preparation for a general election. Eight months had passed since the election the previous October. Byng refused his request, and King promptly resigned. Byng then asked Meighen to form a government, which he attempted to do—unsuccessfully. It lasted three days. As a result, Meighen sought and received a dissolution from Byng, and the general election was set for September. The election was a triumph for King, for whom the constitutional issue was the key talking point. Indeed, some say it was the main reason for the win.[27]

Was Byng wrong to refuse King's request for dissolution? As might be imagined, some say no and some say yes. The constitutional expert Eugene Forsey, warning against the prospect of a 'diet of dissolutions,' said that a Governor could refuse a dissolution requested too soon after the election, or before the legislature could meet to determine the government's fate, or in the event of the government's defeat as soon as the legis-lature has met.[28] But this case does not fall nicely within such parameters. They never do. King had met the House and had not been defeated for several months—in fact, his government was never defeated—and eight months is not a short time. The problem, of course, was an unforeseen one, namely, King's decision to resign office forthwith once his request for dissolution was turned down. By resigning office to avoid the censure vote, he left Byng in the lurch, that is, without a Prime Minister and Cabinet in place. Byng had no choice but to ask Meighen to form a government.

What was King's alternative course of action to resigning forthwith? Obviously, it was to offer his resignation to Byng, who might have refused that too, thereby putting pres-sure on King to carry on towards the dreaded vote of censure. If King had flounced off at that point, determined to escape the vote, the optics of the decision would have looked terrible. On the other hand, if Byng had accepted an offer of resignation from King, the resulting scenario involving Meighen likely would have played out as before, with this difference—Byng would have appeared in a stronger light. Why? Because an offer of resignation from King would have implied some responsibility for the messy state of his

---

[27] Ibid, 177–189.

[28] Eugene A. Forsey, *The Royal Power of Dissolution of Parliament in the British Commonwealth* (Oxford University Press, 1943), 262.

government. The resignation forthwith sent off quite a different message by suggesting instead that it was Byng who was following the wrong course of action.

What was Byng's alternative course of action to the refusal of the dissolution request? Obviously it was to accede to it, thereby triggering a fresh election. Certainly that would have been the easier option. Moreover, from a political standpoint, it would have deprived King of the constitutional issue that he used to good effect in the campaign. And it would have ensured the prominence of the hanging censure vote instead. In other words, there might have been a different election result. A zero-sum game indeed.

Despite the development of Canada's multi-party system, which really got underway in the election of 1935, and the ensuing occasions of minority government since then, nothing approaching the Byng-King affair has ever recurred. But it could. Meanwhile, seemingly out of nowhere there erupted the prorogation imbroglio of 2008. Prorogation is a procedure under which the current session of the legislature is suspended, with no carry over to the next session. In other words, the next session begins afresh. By contrast, under adjournment, the legislative session is halted for a specified period, after which it is simply resumed.

In the wake of the general election in January 2006, the Conservative Party under the leadership of Stephen Harper formed a minority government, winning 127 out of a total of 308 seats. Some two-and-a-half years later, Harper sought and received from Governor General Michaëlle Jean dissolution of Parliament, and set an election date for October 14. He urged Canadian voters to give him a stronger mandate to govern the country during a period now referred to as the 'global economic crisis'. They declined. The Conservatives won 143 seats, still short of a majority; the Liberals under their new leader, Stephane Dion, sank to 77 seats from the 103 held going into the election; the New Democratic Party (NDP) under leader Jack Layton moved from 29 to 37; and the Bloc Québécois under Gilles Duceppe slipped slightly from 51 to 49. Shortly after the election, Dion confirmed his lame-duck leadership status by announcing that the Liberals would choose a new leader to succeed him the following May.

In light of the worsening economic situation, the government talked about the need of parliamentarians to set aside the bitter partisan differences on display during the campaign and work together to secure the stability of the economy. In the Speech from the Throne it incorporated some of the ideas of the opposition parties set out in the campaign. As a result of these blandishments, the Liberals (although not the NDP or the Bloc) decided to support the Speech from the Throne, thereby enabling the government to meet this critical test of the confidence of the House of Commons. Fresh from the triumph, the government then turned roundly on its opponents in the upcoming 'economic and fiscal update' to be delivered in November.

Such documents are like a mid-term economic report card. This one contained several provocative proposals to draw the ire of the opposition, among them the elimination of the subsidies awarded to the political parties for each vote received in the election.[29]

---

[29] Michael Valpy, 'The "Crisis": A Narrative' in Peter H. Russell and Lorne Sossin (eds.) *Parliamentary Democracy in Crisis* (University of Toronto Press, 2009), 9–10.

Elimination of the subsidies—unpopular with the public—was a real blow to the opposition parties, none of which could match the Conservatives' prowess at fundraising from supporters. They were bound to feel the pinch in the next election. In the event, at the beginning of December the three opposition parties reached a formal agreement to establish a Liberal-led coalition government, supported by the Bloc, that would govern until June 2011. They notified the Governor General that they had no confidence in the Conservative government and were prepared to govern in its place.[30]

For its part, the government signaled its intention to pursue a prorogation gambit by convincing the Governor General to prorogue Parliament until January, thereby putting off the need to face a confidence vote that it would almost certainly lose.[31] The public war of words that ensued are instructive in demonstrating how partisans interpret the conventions of the Constitution to suit their purposes. On behalf of the coalition, Dion explained that under Canada's parliamentary system the government needs to be sustained by majority support in the House of Commons, without which it simply cannot govern. The Harper government could not claim such support. As the last election was hardly two months ago, and the coalition was prepared to govern, the Governor General should have refused any prorogation request, and called on the coalition to establish a new government. Dion's was the classic understanding of the conventions of the Westminster-style parliamentary system.

The Prime Minister essayed a different, indeed novel, understanding of the system by removing from it the centrality of the House of Commons in choosing to support— or not support—a government. He did so first by questioning the legitimacy of the very idea of a coalition government, and especially one supported by the Bloc, a party devoted to the cause of Quebec sovereignty. Second, and more important, he made the claim that Canadians needed to vote on whether they wanted a coalition government. In his interpretation, the opposition parties were foisting a coalition government on Canadians rather than offering to establish a viable government supported by a majority of elected members of the House.[32]

Whether Harper used these same arguments in his conversation with Governor General Jean cannot be known, as such meetings are private affairs. In the event, he advised prorogation and she accepted his advice. As a result, and from the standpoint of the zero-sum game, the Harper Conservatives were spectacular winners. By contrast, the prorogation crisis was a debacle for Dion. Michael Ignatieff, a Liberal leadership aspirant with the support of most of the party's MPs, demanded that the caucus be allowed to elect him interim leader, which decision would be reviewed at the convention in May. The party executive agreed, and Dion's leadership was finished immediately. When Parliament reopened in late January, the Liberals under Ignatieff supported the government's Speech from the Throne, while only the NDP and Bloc voted against it.

[30] Ibid, 11–13.
[31] Ibid, 13–16.
[32] Jennifer Smith, 'Parliamentary Democracy versus Faux Populist Democracy' in Russell and Sossin, above (n 28) 175–188.

The government remained in office, eventually calling an election for May 2011, at which outing it finally won the majority that had eluded it in 2006 and 2008.

5. The Crown and Canadian Federalism: Lieutenant-Governors

In the section on Canada's development from colony to independent nation as viewed from the standpoint of the Crown, reference was made to the notion of a 'compound monarchy'[33] that bridges the seeming inconsistency between the unity represented by the monarchical principle and the diversity represented by the federal principle. It has to be said that this notion is a rationalization after the fact. Why? Because the terms of the *Constitution Act, 1867* reveal a system of government, the key feature of which is a dominant central government. Put another way, the bare words of the Constitution are a little light on the federal principle.

The dominance of the federal government is mirrored in the way in which the Lieutenant-Governor is appointed, that is, by the Governor General on the advice of the Prime Minister. The Fathers of Confederation used this model to designate an executive hierarchy in which the Governor General was dominant over the Lieutenant-Governors just as the federal government was dominant over the provincial governments. Indeed, some have argued that the Lieutenant-Governors were intended to be agents of the federal government tasked with the duty to ensure that provincial legislative actions aligned with federal interests. As long as this scheme prevailed, there was no need for the notion of a compound monarchy. But would it prevail?

The answer is no. Instead, Canada evolved towards a robust federal system in which the provinces could pursue their own constitutionally-designated areas of jurisdiction, independent of Ottawa. Among the reasons, one of the most interesting is the effect of judicial rulings on the status of the Lieutenant-Governors, and through them the status of the provinces, rulings that were bound up with conceptions about the role of the Crown and the nature of prerogative power. In these rulings, the judiciary adapted the Crown, a unitary institution if ever there was one, to the binary nature of the federal system.

The view of the provincial governments as inferior to the central government was not only articulated by many in the Confederation debates. It was also the view of the Canadian and British governments in the years following Confederation. The central government, it was understood, commanded the broad, important areas of legislative jurisdiction whereas the provincial governments were local entities with jurisdiction over merely local matters. This same hierarchy was thought to be reflected on the executive side in the relationship between the Governor General and the Lieutenant-Governors. Under the Constitution, the Governor General rather than the Queen

---

[33] Smith, above (n 3) 11 & 156–173.

appoints the Lieutenant-Governors; the Queen is expressly declared to be part of the central government but not the provincial governments, and although the Governor General assents to legislation in the Queen's name, the Lieutenant-Governors were expected to do so in the name of the Governor General. Essentially they were held to be officers of the central government who could be expected to exert influence on the latter's behalf in provincial circles rather than being direct representatives of the Queen, and independent of such orders.

On the other hand, as Saywell points out, there were contrary indicators of a different status. Lieutenant-Governors made appointments in the Queen's name, and they were also empowered to exercise the prerogative powers to summon, prorogue, and dissolve the legislature.[34] The inconsistency between the architecture of the Constitution and the practice in the provinces sparked a legal battle that lasted 25 years between the provincial governments on the one hand, and Ottawa and the British authorities on the other. It covered contested incidents of prerogative power in the hands (or not) of the Lieutenant-Governors, such as the appointment of Queen's Counsel, the use of the pardoning power for provincial offenses, and the prerogative right of escheats and forfeitures. Led by Oliver Mowat, Liberal Premier of Ontario, the provincial governments fought in the courts to secure these prerogative rights and powers for the Lieutenant-Governor.

However arcane such matters might sound to modern ears, it must be understood that they were a proxy for much larger issues. A successful result in the courts would directly benefit the Premier and the Cabinet, the chief advisers of the Lieutenant-Governor. More important, it would enhance the status of the provinces as well, thereby affecting which interpretation of the governmental system established at Confederation would prevail: the centralist version according to which the provinces are subordinate to the central government, or the federal version (often referred to as the provincial-rights version) according to which the provinces are the equals of the central government in the sense of being independent actors within their own established spheres of jurisdiction. Mowat himself was an advocate of provincial rights who often tilted against his chief adversary, the centralist-leaning John A. Macdonald, Conservative Prime Minister of Canada. Theirs was a political rivalry that dominated the early years of Confederation. In the event, it was Mowat's view of the role of the provinces that triumphed in the famous *Maritime Bank* decision handed down in 1892 by the Judicial Committee of the Privy Council (JCPC).

At issue in the case was whether Maritime Bank's debt to New Brunswick was a debt of the Crown. If it was, then the province could claim payment before any other creditors. Writing for the JCPC, Lord Watson said that it was a debt of the Crown because the Lieutenant-Governor is the representative of the Queen for the purposes of the provincial government. The fact that the Governor General rather than the Queen appoints the Lieutenant-Governor does not, he said, undermine the point. 'The act of the Governor

---

[34] John T. Saywell, *The Office of Lieutenant-Governor* (University of Toronto Press, 1957), 8–11.

general and his Council in making the appointment is, he reasoned, 'within the meaning of the statute [then the British North America Act, 1867], the act of the Crown; and
a lieutenant governor, when appointed, is as much the representative of Her Majesty for
all purposes of provincial government as the governor general himself is for all purposes
of Dominion government'.[35]

Lord Watson clearly spelled out the inferences to be drawn from the idea that the
Lieutenant-Governor represents the Crown for the purposes of the provincial government. The provincial legislature of New Brunswick, he wrote, derives no authority from
Ottawa; it is not subordinate to Ottawa in the way that municipalities are subordinate
to the provinces because they are the creatures of the provinces under the terms of the
Constitution. Instead, he explained, New Brunswick 'possesses powers, not of administration merely, but of legislation, in the strictest sense of that word; and, within the limits
assigned by sect. 92 of the Act of 1867, these powers are exclusive and supreme'.[36] In other
words, so long as they remain within the spheres of jurisdiction assigned to them in the
Constitution, the provinces are independent, autonomous actors. In conceiving of the
Lieutenant-Governor as representative of the Crown for provincial purposes, the JCPC
in effect placed the judicial seal of approval on Mowat's theory of provincial rights. The
governmental system established at Confederation could no longer be viewed in hierarchical terms. Instead, it was a real federation.

On the whole, the Lieutenant-Governors have demonstrated a more lively appreciation of their constitutional powers than the Governor General. For example, no
Governor General has ever dismissed a Prime Minister; by contrast, Lieutenant-
Governors have dismissed provincial Premiers five times, the last in 1903.[37] And apparently discussions have materialised since then. In 1991, British Columbia Premier Bill
Vander Zalm (in office from 1986 to 1991) resigned immediately following an investigation that found him in a 'conflict of interest between his public duties and his private
interests'.[38] The Lieutenant-Governor at the time, David Lam, told a newspaper reporter
for the *South China News* that he contemplated using his powers to dismiss the Premier
had he not resigned of his own accord.[39] If nothing else, events such as these serve as a
reminder that the role of the Crown is not merely symbolic. It is an institutional safeguard of the country's parliamentary democracy. It is worth restating that the Crown is
the 'organizing principle of Canadian government'.[40]

[35] J.M. Beck, ed., *The Shaping of Canadian Federalism: Central Authority or Provincial Right* (Copp
Clark Publishing Company, 1971), 96.
[36] Ibid, 95.
[37] Ronald I. Cheffins. "The Royal Prerogative and the Office of Lieutenant Governor' (2000) 23
Canadian Parliamentary Review 17.
[38] Ibid.
[39] Ibid. Notably, Cheffins maintains that during this interview, Lam was simply explaining the powers
at the Lieutenant-Governor's disposition and that using them would have been theoretically legitimate.
[40] Smith, above (n 3) 11.

6. CONCLUSION

Thomas Paine opined that '[a]ll hereditary government is in its nature tyranny'.[41] Few Canadians are as captivated by the kind of revolutionary ardor that animated him. Nevertheless, it is legitimate to ask whether monarchies in the twenty-first century are anachronistic, and whether republicanism in Canada is conceivable. We conclude our chapter with a cursory discussion about possible obstacles to establishing a republic should Canadians ever consider that route. By 'republicanism', we simply mean a form of government without a monarch. We do not engage in lengthy analyses of republican *theoretical* paradigms.

A. A Republican Future for Canada?

Debates about the relevance of monarchy wax and wane in Canada but, in the wake of Queen Elizabeth II's ninetieth birthday, the institution's fate is suddenly pertinent once again. A recent Angus Reid Institute survey shows that Canadians maintain a strong sense of respect for the current monarch (close to 70 percent), but Prince Charles, her direct heir, does not enjoy that same level of esteem (a little over 20 percent), and neither does his son Prince William (close to 50 percent); the survey also shows that only 42 percent of Canadians are in favour of retaining the monarchy in the future.[42]

Monarchy has proven to be astonishingly resilient not necessarily thanks to Burkean attachments to tradition but because, once entrenched, replacing the monarch proves to be an arduous task. Why is this so? The transformation from constitutional monarchy to republic is not simply a matter of substituting a president for a Governor General, elected or appointed. Rather, when the prospect of a republic is considered, a flurry of frequent and recurring questions begins to emerge: What role would a Canadian president have? How would a president be elevated to office—election or appointment? How will other parliamentary institutions be affected by the transition? What would become of constitutional conventions? Would they have to be codified under a republic? And what of the reserve powers currently in the hands of the Crown? If these questions are not enough, in addition there are three dreaded words in Canadian politics: 'opening the constitution'. Memories of the repatriation struggles (1982), the failed *Meech Lake Accord* (1987), and the equally unsuccessful *Charlottetown Accord* (1992) live indelibly in the minds of Canadians, to say nothing of the politicians. Constitutional changes of great magnitude—such as abolishing the monarchy—would require the application of

---

[41] Thomas Paine. *Common Sense and Selected Works of Thomas Paine.* (Canterbury Classics/Baker & Taylor Publishing Group, 2014), 191.

[42] Nicole Thompson. 'Canadians Like the Queen but Her Heir Not So Much Survey Says'. *The Globe and Mail*, http://www.theglobeandmail.com/news/national/canadians-like-the-queen-but-her-heir-not-so-much-surveysays/article29658118/, accessed 25 April 2016.

the most stringent amending formula available: unanimous consent of Parliament and the provincial legislatures. Moreover, once the Constitution is 'opened', there is always the possibility of political opportunism in the form of the provinces, say, looking for concessions in return for their agreement. Speaking of the provinces, they themselves would have to contend with the disappearance of Lieutenant-Governors and the associated ramifications. This is particularly important because Canadian provinces do not even have upper chambers of 'sober second thought'. So, even with the protections granted by the Charter of Rights and Freedoms, powers to 'check' the Executive, in absence of the Crown, must be pondered carefully.

Consider also Indigenous peoples who might be justifiably circumspect about any changes to the role of the monarch. A constitutional change of this nature might arguably trigger a duty to consult, so Indigenous peoples would have to be part of the conversation. Treaties were signed with the Crown; thus Indigenous peoples will want to safeguard their relationship with it until they are satisfied with the new arrangements. None of this is to suggest that the transition from constitutional monarchy to republic is impossible—only that it is much more difficult than many suspect. Australia offers a cautionary tale.

The Honourable Justice Michael Kirby (High Court of Australia) isolated 'ten possible reasons' that the referendum held there to decide whether the country should move to a republican system failed the test of popular opinion.[43] Of particular interest is the following:

> The opinion polls indicate that 70% of Australians insist that if Australia is to move to a republic, the President should be directly elected. This is said to be in harmony with Australia's basic democratic traditions. Yet if such a change to the Constitution were made, the office would be fundamentally different from any in our present system.[44]

These are matters of great concern in a Canadian context as well. The (Australian) Republican Advisory Committee explored four possible avenues for replacing the Crown with a new head of state: one option was direct election by the people; three additional options examined methods for the head of state's *appointment*—prime ministerial, parliamentary, and by an electoral college.[45] With these options in mind, Canadians might call for the direct election of a head of state. Appointments could proceed as they do currently, but it is specious to suggest that, once the Constitution is 'opened', Canadians would settle for yet another appointed office.

So, if we set aside the need to determine term duration, and qualification and removal criteria, what would be the implications of directly-elected presidents in terms of

---

[43] Michael Kirby, 'The Australian Republican Referendum 1999—Ten Lessons'. Law and Justice Foundation, para 49, http://www.lawfoundation.net.au/ljf/app/&id=DF4206863AE3C52DCA2571A3008 2B3D5, accessed 26 April, 2016.

[44] Ibid, para 79.

[45] Ibid, para 28.

their status and powers vis-à-vis an already powerful head of government, the Prime Minister?[46] One logical suggestion is to codify presidential powers. This presents more problems because codification would impact the prerogative and reserve powers that are now the Crown's right. The whole point of *discretionary* power is to offer flexible means of preventing a strong executive from running roughshod over the Constitution and responsible government. If these powers are codified, even with the *Charter of Rights and Freedoms* in place, will their scope be broad enough to ensure that a Prime Minister bent on defiance can be restrained?

The monarchy, in many ways, is the only remaining trace of Canada's colonial attachments, and when the time is right, Canadians may well contemplate taking the last remaining step toward *true* independence. Let us recall the Fathers of Confederation had two reasons to keep monarchical ties: national identity and the assurance of a permanent (non-partisan) caretaker of responsible government. The first task has been largely accomplished by the passage of time and the establishment of the *Charter of Rights and Freedoms*. The second presents problems akin to wading through formidable labyrinths in the dark. But difficulty should not indicate impossibility.

The last time changes to the office of the Governor General were discussed seriously was in 1978. Pierre Elliott Trudeau's government proposed Bill C-60 which contained reforms to the Senate, the Supreme Court, and the role of Governors General. These proposals were heavily criticized and led to charges of Trudeau's supposed anti-monarchical sentiments. He stated: 'If I were an anti-monarchist, I should leave the post alone and let it become obsolescent, let the Governor-General do nothing but attend Boy Scout rallies.'[47] When the Crown comes to appear 'obsolescent' to a significant majority of Canadians, they can only hope that diligent students of Canadian government have found the answers to the questions about the transition to republicanism that we have posed.

BIBLIOGRAPHY

Books, Chapters, and Articles

Ajzenstat, Janet. *The Canadian Founding: John Locke and Parliament*. Montreal: McGill-Queen's University Press, 2007.

Ajzenstat, Janet, Paul Romney, Ian Gentles, William D. Gardner. *Canada's Founding Debates*. Toronto: Stoddard Publishing Company, 1999.

Beck, J. Murray. *Pendulum of Power* (Scarborough, Ontario: Prentice-Hall Canada Ltd., 1968.

---

[46] This particular conundrum appears consistently throughout the literature—both Canadian and Australian—when discussing the possible transition from constitutional monarchy to republicanism. It surfaced during the Australian experience as evidenced in Kirby's work (Ibid, para 78).

[47] Sarah Schmidt. 'Monarchists Get a Rival in New Republican Movement', *The National Post*, 11 April 2002, http://www.canadian-republic.ca/national_post_4_11_02.html, para 16.

———. *The Shaping of Canadian Federalism: Central Authority or Provincial Right* Toronto: Copp Clark Publishing Company, 1971.

Cheffins, Ronald, I. 'The Royal Prerogative and the Office of Lieutenant Governor'. *Canadian Parliamentary Review* 23 (Spring 2000): 14–19.

Dawson, R. MacGregor. *The Government of Canada*. Toronto: University of Toronto Press, 1954.

Governor General of Canada (n.d.). https://www.gg.ca/document.aspx?id=5lan=eng and https://www.gg.ca/document.aspx?id=14940&lan=eng accessed January 2, 2017.

Heard, Andrew. *Canadian Constitutional Conventions: The Marriage of Law & Politics, Second Edition*. Don Mills, Ontario: Oxford University Press, 2014.

Kirby, Michael, 'The Australian Republican Referendum 1999—Ten Lessons' (2000) Address at the University of Buckingham http://www.lawfoundation.net.au/ljf/app/&id=DF420686 3AE3C52DCA2571A30082B3D5 accessed 26 April 2016.

Lagassé, Philippe. 'Citizenship and the Hollowed Canadian Crown'. *Policy Options*, http://policyoptions.irpp.org/2015/03/02/citizenship-and-the-hollowed-canadian-crown/, accessed 1 May, 2016.

McCreery, Christopher. 'The Crown and Honours: Getting It Right'. In *The Evolving Canadian Crown*, edited by Jennifer Smith and D. Michael Jackson, pp. 139–154. Montreal: McGill-Queen's University Press, 2012.

Paine, Thomas. *Common Sense and Selected Works of Thomas Paine*. San Diego, California: Canterbury Classics/Baker & Taylor Publishing Group, 2014.

Pauls, Karen. 'Royal Family Support by Canadians Waning' (*Canadian Broadcasting Corporation*, 18 May 2015) http://www.cbc.ca/news/canada/manitoba/royal-family-support-by-canadians-waning-poll-indicates-1.3072469 accessed 16 February 2016.

Russell, Peter H. and Lorne Sossin, eds. *Parliamentary Democracy in Crisis*. Toronto: University of Toronto Press, 2009.

Schmidt, Sarah. 'Monarchists Get a Rival in New Republican Movement' (*The National Post*, 11 April 2002) http://www.canadian-republic.ca/national_post_4_11_02.html accessed 26 April 2016.

Shingler, Benjamin. 'Charter and Universal Health Care Top Canadian Unity Poll' (*Global News*, 30 June 2014) http://globalnews.ca/news/1424367/charter-universal-health-care-top-canadian-unity-poll/ accessed 16 February 2016.

Smith, David E. *The Invisible Crown: The First Principle of Canadian Government*. Toronto: University of Toronto Press, 1995.

Smith, Jennifer and D. Michael Jackson, eds., *The Evolving Canadian Crown*. Montreal & Kingston: McGill-Queen's University Press, 2012.

Thompson, Nicole. 'Canadians Like the Queen but Her Heir Not So Much Survey Says' (*The Globe and Mail*, 22 April 2016) http://www.theglobeandmail.com/news/national/canadians-like-the-queen-but-her-heir-not-so-much-surveysays/article29658118/ accessed 25 April 2016.

Legislative and Constitutional Texts

Canadian Charter of Rights and Freedoms, 1982. *Canadian Charter of Rights and Freedoms*, being Schedule B to the *Canada Act 1982* (UK), 1982.

Constitution Act, 1867, (U.K.), 1867.

Constitution Act, 1982, being Schedule B to the Canada Act 1982 (U.K.), 1982.

Royal Style and Titles Act (R.S.C., 1985, c. R-12).

United Kingdom Royal Titles Act 1953 s: Royal Titles Act 1953: An Act to provide for an alteration of the Royal Style and Titles. 1 & 2 Eliz. 2 c. 9 [26 March 1953].

Cases

*The Liquidators of the Maritime Bank of the Dominion of Canada v. The Receiver-General of the
Province of New Brunswick* [1892] A.C. 43.

CHAPTER 7

....

THE EXECUTIVE,
THE ROYAL PREROGATIVE,
AND THE CONSTITUTION

....

CRAIG FORCESE[*]

1. INTRODUCTION

....

In Canadian governance, the royal prerogative is the preserve of specialists, a reflection of its irrelevance to most Canadians most of the time. And yet, this source of legal authority dominates in a small number of areas that are at times supremely consequential.

This chapter situates the royal prerogative in relation to executive power in Canada, and examines its interface with the Constitution. I begin with the concept of parliamentary supremacy, a necessary starting point in understanding the scope of the contemporary royal prerogative. I then examine prerogative powers as a source of executive authority, and discuss how the prerogative may be displaced by the legislature. The chapter analyzes the content of the remaining prerogative powers, focusing on defence and foreign affairs. It concludes by addressing the role of courts in reviewing the exercise of the prerogative.[1]

[*] Full Professor, Faculty of Law, University of Ottawa.
[1] For an excellent, alternative treatment of these same topics, see Philippe Lagassé, "Parliamentary and Judicial Ambivalence toward Executive Prerogative Powers in Canada" (2012) 55 *Canadian Public Administration* 157.

2. THE STARTING POINT: PARLIAMENT'S JURISDICTIONAL SUPREMACY

Since the Glorious Revolution in the late seventeenth century, parliamentary supremacy means that Parliament is the source of all power.[2] As discussed by John Lovell in this *Handbook*, parliamentary supremacy is tempered in Canada by other limitations in the Constitution. These provisos combine to result in limited government, circumscribing the jurisdiction of both legislatures and the executive branch. Limited government is a product of the division of powers between the federal and provincial governments, constitutionally codified rights and freedoms, and certain rare, constitutionalized aspects of the separation of powers.

But so long as they observe these constraints, Parliament and its provincial counterparts are free to do as they wish, no matter how ill-founded or unwise. As the Supreme Court of Canada has put it, so long as it does not fundamentally alter or interfere with the constitutionalized relationship between the courts and the other branches of government, "[i]t is well within the power of the legislature to enact laws, even laws which some would consider draconian."[3]

This concept of parliamentary sovereignty informs the legal status of the executive branch of government. It means that legally "there is a *hierarchical* relationship between the executive and the legislature, whereby the executive must execute and implement the policies which have been enacted by the legislature in statutory form."[4] Put more simply, official actions undertaken by the executive branch usually must flow from "statutory authority clearly granted and properly exercised."[5] The word "usually" is a key qualifier because, in practice, the executive does have a handful of self-standing, autonomous powers: those granted by the Constitution and those formally labeled "prerogative powers."

3. CONSTITUTIONALIZED SOURCES OF EXECUTIVE POWER

Certain powers discussed in other chapters are reserved for the Executive in the *Constitution Act, 1867*—technically in the person of the Queen or the Governor General,

---

[2] Some of the material in this section is adapted, but substantially recrafted, from Craig Forcese & Aaron Freeman, *The Laws of Government: The Legal Foundations of Canadian Democracy* (2d edn, Irwin Law, 2010).

[3] *Babcock v Canada*, 2002 SCC 57 [57].

[4] *Re Remuneration of Judges* [1997] 3 SCR 3 [139] (emphasis added).

[5] *Babcock*, above (n 3) [20].

but practically in the person of the Prime Minister or in the committee of ministers known as the "Cabinet." Many of these constitutionalized executive powers are still considered royal prerogative powers in the United Kingdom.[6] Examples include royal assent and the prorogation or dissolution of Parliament.

Moreover, the exercise of these and other constitutionalized executive powers in Canada is influenced by unwritten constitutional "conventions". Constitutional conventions are not codified in legal text, and are "not based on judicial precedents but on precedents established by the institutions of government themselves."[7] As a result, their identity and precise parameters can occasionally be a source of contention, as discussed in this *Handbook* by Benoit Pelletier.

Even so, Canada depends on constitutional conventions to "ensure that the legal framework of the constitution will be operated in accordance with generally accepted principles."[8] In some notable respect, they are the lynchpin that connects the written word of Canada's constitution—a text that, at least in the case of the 1867 Act, often cannot be read literally—and the reality of democratic and responsible government in Canada.

4. Delegated Sources of Executive Power

Other than these limited constitutionalized powers, parliamentary supremacy means that the Executive is beholden to the legislature for *all* of its legal authority. This dependence is either direct—the legislature delegates power to the Executive through legislation—or indirect: parliamentary tolerance of the Executive's historic royal prerogative.

Legislative delegation of power through legislation is, by far, the most important source of executive branch power. For example, Parliament and the provincial legislatures do not themselves conduct policing, regulate food safety, impose tariffs, collect taxes, or otherwise perform any of the millions of things that we typically associate with "government." Through statutes, they do, however, empower the Executive to do these things.

---

[6] United Kingdom, House of Commons, Public Administration Select Committee, *Taming the Prerogative: Strengthening Ministerial Accountability to Parliament*, HC 422 (4 March 2004) 5. www.publications.parliament.uk/pa/cm200304/cmselect/cmpubadm/422/422.pdf (accessed 4 May 2016).

[7] *Reference re Resolution to Amend the Constitution* [1981] 1 SCR 753, 880.

[8] *Reference Re Objection by Quebec to a Resolution to Amend the Constitution*, [1982] 2 SCR 793, 803.

5. THE PREROGATIVE SOURCE
OF EXECUTIVE POWER

The much less significant (in terms of volume) source of Executive power is the residue of discretionary or arbitrary authority possessed by the Crown.[9] Known as the royal (or Crown) prerogative, this power is described as "the pre-eminence the Sovereign enjoys over and above all other persons. It comprehends all the special dignities, liberties, privileges, powers and royalties allowed by common law to the Crown of England, and all parts of the Commonwealth."[10] More succinctly, the royal prerogative means "the powers and privileges accorded by the common law to the Crown."[11]

A. The Trouble with Prerogative Powers

It should be apparent that the royal prerogative is a dangerous concept in a constitutional democracy built on a system in which the Executive is responsible to the legislature. If the prerogative were truly a significant source of Executive power, invulnerable to parliamentary intervention, it would invest the Executive with an entrenched autonomy closer to that possessed by the Executive in a republican system, such as that of the United States (but without the discipline of that country's written constitutional text).

These responsible government concerns have been remedied in two ways. First, as with most constitutionalized Executive powers, the monarch and his or her agent, the Governor General, do not usually exercise the royal prerogative personally.[12] The Prime Minister and ministers, as Privy Councillors and thus part of the "Crown," are permitted to exercise some of these powers. In other instances, where the Governor General does exercise the royal prerogative in his or her name, he or she almost always does so on the advice of the Prime Minister or Cabinet. The Governor General may retain discretion to refuse to follow this advice, but "in Canada that discretion has been exercised only in the most exceptional circumstances."[13] These conventions preserve responsible government.

Second, in a contest of authority, the royal prerogative is a very weak source of legal power. At least in principle, it may be easily supplanted by legislatures, legislating in the area. As the British Columbia Court of Appeal recently noted, "Crown prerogative is a

---

[9] See *Krieger v Law Society of Alberta* [2002] 3 SCR 372 [31]; *Reference re Effect of Exercise of Royal Prerogative of Mercy upon Deportation Proceedings,* [1933] SCR 269, 272–73.

[10] *Ontario v Mar-Dive Corp* (1996), 141 D.L.R. (4th) 577, 588 (On Gen Div).

[11] *Ross River Dena Council Band v Canada* [2002] 2 SCR 816 [54] citing P. Hogg *Constitutional Law of Canada* (5th ed, Carswell, 2007) (loose leaf) vol 1, 1–14.

[12] *Black v Canada* (2001) 54 OR (3d) 215 [31].

[13] *Ibid.*

common law power that has not been overtaken by subsequent legislation."[14] However, there is ambiguity as to what exactly is required for this displacement.

B. Displacing the Prerogative

As this chapter is finalized, the circumstances in which the prerogative is displaced is a matter of contention in the United Kingdom, in the "Brexit" litigation.[15] In Canada, some courts suggest that the royal prerogative has substantial stickiness, concluding that it "cannot be limited except by clear and express statutory language."[16] This position seems consistent with the federal *Interpretation Act*, section 17, which provides: "No enactment is binding on Her Majesty or affects Her Majesty or Her Majesty's rights or prerogatives in any manner, except as mentioned or referred to in the enactment."[17]

This position is also consistent with parliamentary procedure on the topic. The unwritten rules and customs of Canadian parliamentary procedure include the notion of "royal consent"—a concept different from the royal assent associated with converting a bill to a statute and the royal recommendation required for executive approval of money bills. The royal consent is required for any "legislation that affects the prerogatives, hereditary revenues, property or interests of the Crown requires Royal Consent, which in Canada originates with the Governor General in his or her capacity as representative of the Sovereign."[18] This consent may be given at any stage in the enactment of a bill—typically through a verbal statement by a minister—and "is always necessary in matters involving the prerogatives of the Crown."[19] The Speaker of the Senate of Canada ruled in 2011: "Royal Consent is part of that process of putting the prerogative power within the framework of statute law. It is an internal parliamentary procedure that acknowledges that a common law power of the Crown is coming within the scope of Parliament."[20]

In United Kingdom practice, the absence of royal consent invalidates the parliamentary proceedings in which a bill has been passed. Indeed, British authorities suggest that the Crown may withhold royal assent of a bill for which royal consent was required, but

---

[14] *Askin v Law Society of British Columbia* 2013 BCCA 233 [30].

[15] *R (Miller) v. Secretary of State for Exiting the European Union*, [2016] EWHC 2768 (Admin).

[16] *Mar-Dive Corp* above (n 10), 588.

[17] *Interpretation Act*, RSC 1985 c I-21 s 17.

[18] Parliament of Canada, *House of Commons Procedure and Practice* (2d ed, 2009) http://www.parl. gc.ca/procedure-book-livre/document.aspx?sbdid=da2ac62f-bb39-4e5f-9f7d-90ba3496d0a6&sbpidx=6 (accessed 4 May 2016).

[19] Alistair Fraser, W.F. Dawson, and John Holtby, *Beauchesne's Rules and Forms of the House of Commons of Canada* (6th ed, Carswell) 213 http://www.lop.parl.gc.ca/parlinfo/compilations/HouseOfCommons/ legislation/CrownConsentDefinition.aspx?Definition=beau (accessed 4 May 2016).

[20] Honourable Noel A. Kinsella, 42nd Speaker of the Senate, *Speaker's Ruling: Bill C-232 and the Royal Consent* (11 March 2011) 4 http://sen.parl.gc.ca/nkinsella/PDF/Rulings/Ruling21mar11-e.pdf (accessed 4 May 2016).

has not been signified.[21] The Senate of Canada speaker has also implied that the absence of a royal consent may be lethal to a bill: "the lack of Royal Consent can ultimately block the passage of a bill."[22]

However, this rule has not been robustly applied in Canada. For one thing, royal consent as a prerequisite to displacement of a prerogative power seems a puzzling veto to impose on a sovereign parliament. For another, as the Senate Speaker observed, "Royal Consent has been invoked only about two dozen times over the course of almost 144 years and many, many bills."[23] Most of those bills were in the nineteenth century, and concerned Crown liens and railways. It seems difficult to imagine that there have not been more encroachments on prerogative powers than are accounted for in this parliamentary record since Canada's creation.

Finally, the courts have generally been indifferent (or unaware) of the royal consent requirement. It goes unmentioned in the case law. And more than that, many courts have been prepared to find a displacement of prerogative by *implication*—something that is very hard to reconcile with the idea of royal consent.

The precise scope of this displacement by implication is remarkably opaque in Canadian law. Some courts seem to require only that a statute occupy an area governed by prerogative. As one lower court has observed, "[w]here Parliament, or in the case of a province the legislature, has provided a regime of law to govern the affairs of citizens, the original prerogative of the Crown is excluded."[24] In these circumstances, "[t]he Crown may no longer act under the prerogative, but must act under and subject to the conditions imposed by the statute."[25] In the words of another lower court: "if the statute confers the power to do the same thing, the prerogative is displaced by necessary implication."[26]

Such a broad understanding of displacement by implication is difficult to square with section 17 of the *Interpretation Act*, reproduced above. On a plain reading, that provision suggests that express statutory language must preface displacement. That is not, however, the way things have turned out. The Supreme Court has endorsed the notion that less-than-express statutory language can displace the prerogative. Interpreting section 17's reference to "mentioned or referred to in the enactment" in *Alberta Government Telephones v. Canada (Canadian Radio-Television and Telecommunications Commission)*, a case that concerned whether a statute bound the Crown, the Supreme Court defined this *Interpretation Act* language broadly. It reaches not just "(1) expressly binding words ('Her Majesty is bound')" but also

> (2) a clear intention to bind which . . . "is manifest from the very terms of the statute", in other words, an intention revealed when provisions are read in the context

[21] Douglas Millar, *Erskine May: Parliamentary Practice* (LexisNexis, 24th ed 2011) 167 http://www.lop.parl.gc.ca/parlinfo/compilations/HouseOfCommons/legislation/CrownConsentDefinition.aspx?Definition=may (accessed 4 May 2016).

[22] Kinsella, above (n 20), 3.

[23] *Ibid* at 5.

[24] *Scarborough (City) v Ontario (Attorney-General)* (1997) 144 DLR (4th) 130, 135 (On Gen Div).

[25] *Black*, above (n 12) [27].

[26] *Delivery Drugs Ltd. (c.o.b. Gastown Pharmacy) v British Columbia (Deputy Minister of Health)*, 2007 BCCA 550 [59].

of other textual provisions . . . and, (3) an intention to bind where the purpose of the statute would be "wholly frustrated" if the government were not bound, or, in other words, if an absurdity (as opposed to simply an undesirable result) were produced. These three points should provide a guideline for when a statute has clearly conveyed an intention to bind the Crown.[27]

Lower courts have subsequently looked to this test, including in deciding whether a statute has displaced the prerogative either expressly or by necessary implication.[28]

Whether this test marks the outer limit of displacement by "necessary implication" appears, however, to be unsettled. The scope of displacement by "necessary implication" drove a split on the Supreme Court in *Ross River Dena Council Band v. Canada*. The dissent in that case was prepared to find implied displacement where Parliament provides "by statute for powers previously within the Prerogative being exercised subject to conditions and limitations contained in the statute."[29] This approach is consistent with that taken by the UK House of Lords in *A.G. v de Keyser's Royal Hotel Ltd*:

> Where . . . Parliament has intervened and has provided by statute for powers, previously within the prerogative, being exercised in a particular manner and subject to the limitations and provisions contained in the statute, they can only be so exercised. Otherwise, what use would there be in imposing limitations, if the Crown could at its pleasure disregard them and fall back on the prerogative?

The minority approach may also be reconciled with the Supreme Court's views in *Alberta Government Telephones v Canada*, noted above. There, the Court was prepared to find an intention to bind the Crown under section 17 of the *Interpretation Act* (and presumptively also displace the prerogative) where the "purpose of the statute would be 'wholly frustrated' if the government were not bound, or, in other words, if an absurdity (as opposed to simply an undesirable result) were produced." Such an absurdity would result if the Executive could ignore conditions and limitations on its prerogative, imposed by statute.

The majority in *Ross River Dena Council Band* was, however, seemingly prepared to go further than this "conditions and limitations" test, although without articulating its own threshold. In the words of Justice LeBel, writing for the majority: "as statute law expands and encroaches upon the purview of the royal prerogative, to that extent the royal prerogative contracts. However, this displacement occurs only to the extent that the statute does so explicitly or by necessary implication."[30]

---

[27] *Alberta Government Telephones v Canada (Canadian Radio-television and Telecommunications Commission)*, [1989] 2 S.C.R. 225, 281.

[28] *Canada (Minister of Citizenship and Immigration) v Kisluk*, (1999) 50 Imm. L.R. (2d) 1 [155].

[29] *Ross River Dena Council Band*, above (n 11) [4] [5].

[30] *Ibid* [54].

We are left, therefore, with uncertainty as to whether implied displacement of the prerogative by statute in Canada arises simply when the subject matter of the prerogative is occupied by legislation, or whether something more pointed is required of that legislation.

To further complicate matters, there are cases where courts have concluded that although Parliament has legislated in an area governed by prerogative, it has done so without covering the full scope of the prerogative.[31] The result is a partial displacement.

Whatever the precise means by which Parliament displaces the prerogative, courts have held that "legislation has severely curtailed the scope of the Crown prerogative."[32] As the Privy Council Office—effectively, the Prime Minister's governmental department—has noted, "[t]he history of parliamentary government has been a process of narrowing the exercise of the prerogative authority by subjecting it increasingly to the pre-eminence of the statutory authority, substituting the authority of the Crown in Parliament for the authority of the Crown alone."[33]

This progressive limitation of royal prerogative powers minimizes much of the concern that might be sparked by the executive branch de facto legislating in a fashion unanticipated by an Act of Parliament. Indeed, the Supreme Court would appear to have expressly ruled out that possibility: "There is no principle in this country, as there is not in Great Britain, that the Crown may legislate by proclamation or order in council to bind citizens where it so acts without the support of a statute of the Legislature."[34] (Although it should be noted that the Executive has sometimes codified its prerogatives in a form that has the shape and feel of a legislative instrument.[35])

6. The Content of the Royal Prerogative

A. Overview

It is not easy to enumerate the precise scope of the remaining, residual prerogative powers in Canadian law. As Robert MacGregor Dawson observed in his authoritative work on Canadian government, "the prerogative, finding its origin in the misty past and interpreted by the courts only as the occasion has arisen, is uncertain."[36]

---

[31] See *Kamal v Canada*, 2009 FCA 21 [22] [23].

[32] *Black*, above (n 12) [27].

[33] Canada, Privy Council Office, *Responsibility in the Constitution* (1993) http://www.pco.gc.ca/index.asp?lang=eng&page=information&sub=publications&doc=constitution/cho2-eng.htm (accessed 4 May 2016).

[34] *Reference re Anti-Inflation Act*, [1976] 2 SCR 373, p. 433.

[35] See, for example, *Canadian Passport Order* SI/81-86.

[36] Norman Ward (ed), *Dawson's the Government of Canada* (University of Toronto Press, 6th ed 1987) 178.

It is worth noting at the outset that although prerogatives may fall to each level of government, in parallel to the Canadian federal division of powers,[37] most remaining prerogatives are exercised at the federal level. For instance, the clearest residual prerogative is in the area of foreign affairs. There, the federal Executive has authority to make treaties and pursue Canada's foreign policy. The federal Executive also exercises prerogative powers over defence. These are obviously massively important subjects, and are dealt with in their own sections below.

An historic prerogative—grounded in the notion that the "King can do wrong"—is Crown immunity from lawsuit. That privilege has been surrendered by statute in instruments such as the *Crown Liability and Proceedings Act*.[38] But other prerogative powers continue in parallel with the modern statute. Thus, the authority to grant mercy to those convicted of crimes persists as a prerogative power, but one whose exercise is codified (at least in part) in the *Criminal Code*. As the Supreme Court of Canada has observed, "the provisions contained in Canadian statute law, including the Criminal Code, merely prescribe various ways to exercise that prerogative, without limiting its scope".[39]

The remaining chief prerogatives include the power to bestow honours (something shared at the federal and provincial levels), and to issue passports (a federal matter).[40] Both powers have been the subject of judicial review, as discussed further below. Another classic prerogative—the Governor General's appointment and dismissal of prime ministers—may have its origins in prerogative but is now more properly regarded in contemporary Canadian law as a constitutional convention. Other historical prerogative powers—such as the summoning of Parliament—are codified in the 1867 Act.[41]

This distinction between prerogative, constitutional conventions, and the Executive's powers codified in the written constitution may appear to some readers as one that produces little practical difference. Indeed, leading authorities in the area tend not to make such fine divisions.[42] A clear-eyed understanding of status is critical, however. For one thing, as Lagassé suggests, "when conventions develop around the exercise of Crown prerogatives, they can limit how government employs these powers. Although they do not affect the status of prerogatives in law, conventions can require that these powers be exercised in accordance with certain norms and procedures."[43]

---

[37] For a discussion of provincial prerogatives in the area of provincial jurisdiction, see the chapter by Hugo Cyr & Armand de Mestral in this *Handbook*.

[38] RSC, 1985, c. C-50.

[39] *Re Therrien*, [2001] 2 SCR 2 [113]. See also *Canada (Attorney General) v Hinse*, 2013 QCCA 1513.

[40] See Hogg, above (n 11), 1–16, 19–21.

[41] *Constitution Act, 1867*, s 38.

[42] See, for example, Robert Marleau and Camille Montpetit, *House of Commons Procedure and Practice* (Mc-Graw-Hill 1st ed, 2000) (describing the summoning of the House of Commons as a royal prerogative) http://www.parl.gc.ca/MarleauMontpetit/DocumentViewer.aspx?Sec=Ch08&Seq=7 (accessed 4 May 2016).

[43] Lagassé, above (n 1), at 168.

Even more critically, the distinction between a "plain" prerogative power and one buttressed with constitutional conventions (or entrenched in the written constitution) matters when contemplating how such rules could be changed. As noted, a prerogative power can be altered by regular statute. But powers constitutionalized in the written constitution or by constitutional convention would not necessarily be so easily amendable. Changes regarding the former (and possibly even the latter) could only be done in conformity with Canada's constitutional amendment formula.

Another area of imprecision concerns certain powers some authorities describe as the Prime Minister's "prerogative." An influential 1935 Order-in-Council[44] lists a number of appointment powers as "the special prerogative of the Prime Minister." The enumerated appointment powers are "appointment of: Privy Councillors; Cabinet Ministers; Lieutenant Governors; ... Provincial Administrators [an official who no longer exists]; Speaker of the Senate; Chief Justices of all Courts; Senators; Sub-Committees of Council; Treasury Board; Committee of Internal Economy, House of Commons; Deputy Heads of Departments; Librarians of Parliament; Crown Appointments in both Houses of Parliament; Governor General's Secretary's Staff; Recommendations in any Department."

Some courts have described the prime ministerial power to determine the identity of ministers as a "Crown prerogative."[45] But it is not at all clear that any of these prime ministerial appointment powers are truly themselves part of the "royal" prerogative. For one thing, appointment powers for some of these officials (such as senators) are assigned to the Governor General in the 1867 Act and, in the result, do not properly fall into the category of royal prerogative.[46] Further, these appointment powers may be best described, not as the residue of royal authority recognized by the common law, but as rules that determines *which* executive official may *instruct* the Governor General in the exercise of his or her prerogative or constitutional powers. Or put another way, these appointments powers are not formal examples of the Royal Prerogative, but rather the exercise of a prime ministerial personal prerogative, in the more colloquial, dictionary meaning of the term: "an inherent advantage or privilege."[47] That said, some of the personal prime ministerial prerogatives have themselves risen to the level of constitutional conventions. One that certainly has achieved this status is the role of the Prime Minister in instructing the Governor General on the timing of a Parliament's dissolution.[48] This prime ministerial privilege has not been displaced by statute, and probably could not be without further formality, possibly even constitutional amendment.[49]

[44] PC 3374 (25 Oct 1935).
[45] See, for example, *Guergis v Novak*, 2013 ONCA 449.
[46] Constitution Act, 1867, s. 24.
[47] Oxford Dictionary Online (accessed 14 December 2016): "prerogative".
[48] Canada, Library of Parliament, *Constitutional Conventions* (11 July 2006) http://www.lop.parl.gc.ca/content/lop/TeachersInstitute/ConstitutionalConventions.pdf (accessed 4 May 2016).
[49] This matter was discussed, although not definitively decided, in *Conacher v Canada (Prime Minister)*, 2010 FCA 131 [5].

B. The Royal Prerogative of Defence

A 2004 UK House of Commons study lists the prerogative powers in that country, and includes: "The deployment and use of the armed forces overseas, including involvement in armed conflict, or the declaration of war" and "[t]he use of the armed forces within the United Kingdom to maintain the peace in support of the police."[50] These are also apt descriptors of the royal prerogative of defence in Canadian law.

In Canada's division of powers, the federal Parliament has exclusive authority over defence.[51] Parliament has enacted the *National Defence Act* (NDA), which puts the Canadian Forces (now styled the Canadian Armed Forces, or CAF) on a statutory footing.[52] Constitutionally, command of this military vests in the Governor General.[53] However, in keeping with the constitutional conventions of responsible government, the Governor General does not decide when and where to deploy the CAF. In practice, this power is exercised by the federal Cabinet acting under the leadership of the Prime Minister.[54]

(i) Military Deployments

Ultimately, a decision to deploy the CAF to perform overseas military functions is made exclusively by the executive branch as an exercise of the royal prerogative. "The federal Cabinet," a 2006 Library of Parliament study concluded, "can, without parliamentary approval or consultation, commit Canadian Forces to action abroad, whether in the form of a specific current operation or future contingencies resulting from international treaty obligations."[55]

Although there have been occasional private members' bills that, if enacted, would create a parliamentary role in approving CAF international deployments,[56] there is no serious argument that Parliament has so far legislated to displace the royal prerogative of defence. That is, the Executive may choose to deploy the CAF abroad pursuant to the prerogative, and not statute law.

Certainly, Canadian statute law does foresee a parliamentary role in relation to some CAF functions. The dispatch of the CAF pursuant to an executive order under the *Emergencies Act* would be subject to scrutiny in Parliament, *per* that statute's system of

---

[50] UK, House of Commons, above (n 6), 6.
[51] *Constitution Act, 1867*, s 91(7).
[52] RSC, 1985, c. N-5 (NDA).
[53] *Constitution Act, 1867*, s. 15 (vesting the role of Commander in Chief in the Queen). By Letters Patent issued by George VI in 1947, C Gaz (1947) I.3104, vol. 81, the Governor General is empowered "to exercise all powers and authorities lawfully belonging to Us in respect of Canada."
[54] Canada, Library of Parliament, *International Deployment of Canadian Forces: Parliament's Role*, PRB 00-06E (18 May 2006) 1 http://www.lop.parl.gc.ca/content/lop/researchpublications/prb0006-e.htm (accessed 4 May 2016).
[55] *Ibid.* Some of the material in this section is adapted, but substantially recrafted, from Craig Forcese, *National Security Law: Canadian Practice in International Perspective* (Irwin Law, 2008).
[56] Library of Parliament, above (n 54), 7.

parliamentary review.[57] Further, the NDA does anticipate a parliamentary role when the CAF are placed on "active service." The Act requires that Parliament then be called back to session, if adjourned or prorogued, within 10 days.[58] Parliament will be in session, in other words, presumptively to scrutinize the active service order.

But although there are different views on the issue,[59] the active service provision has not been treated as a statutory rule regarding when the CAF may be deployed. Active service has no other implication than to affect some pension benefits, the application of the *Code of Service Discipline*, and provisions for release of personnel from the CAF.[60] Notably, the CAF have been in a standing state of active service for generations.[61]

Likewise, there is not even an obligation for deployments of the CAF to be preceded by a parliamentary debate. There is now a (non-binding) tradition of debating at least some aspects of deployments through a take-note debate in the House of Commons; that is, a debate on a motion asking the House to take note of an issue, but not requiring a vote and in no way binding on the government. It is conceivable that this practice will someday crystallize into a constitutional convention. That time has almost certainly not yet arrived, given the infrequency of these debates in practice and the extent to which remains a discretionary and uneven political practice rather than one undertaken with any sense of legal obligation.[62]

(ii) Aid of the Civil Power Deployments

The CAF's functions go well beyond international deployments. The CAF deployed during the 1970 October Crisis at the request of the Quebec Premier pursuant to the "aid of the civil power" provision of the NDA,[63] immediately prior to the ultimate invocation by the Pierre Trudeau government of the *War Measures Act* (the predecessor statute to the *Emergencies Act*). It deployed under the same aid-of-the-civil-power provisions during the 1990 Oka crisis. More recent amendments to the NDA establish powers for the federal government itself to order a domestic deployment of the CAF to assist civil authorities. Thus, the Governor-in-Council or the minister of national defence may authorize the Canadian Forces to perform any duty involving "public service."[64] This may include assistance to law enforcement.

---

[57] RSC, 1985, c.22 (4th Supp.).

[58] NDA, s 32.

[59] But see *Aleksic v Canada (Attorney General)* (2002), 215 DLR (4th) 720 [7] (On Gen Div), Wright J dissenting in the result (suggesting that the Executive may not use the royal prerogative to commit the CAF to active service because the active service provision displaces the common law prerogative). The majority did not come to a conclusion on this point. See *ibid.* [26].

[60] Library of Parliament, above (n 54), 2, n6.

[61] *Ibid* at 3.

[62] Library of Parliament, above (n 54).

[63] NDA, Part VI.

[64] NDA, s. 273.6.

These statutory authorities exist alongside analogous call-out powers found in two federal orders-in-council,[65] issued by the Governor-in-Council in the 1990s, pursuant to the royal prerogative. First, the *Canadian Forces Assistance to Provincial Police Forces Directions* (CFAPPFD) establishes a federal system of approving CAF assistance to provincial law enforcement agencies.[66]

Second, the CAF may provide law enforcement assistance to the Royal Canadian Mounted Police (RCMP) under the *Canadian Forces Armed Assistance Directions* (CFAAD).[67] The CFAAD is the means by which the Commissioner of the RCMP or the minister of public safety seeks the aid of the CAF's elite Special Forces and antiterrorism unit, JTF2.[68]

These developments have produced substantial duplication between the legal sources for CAF deployment. The statutory, NDA "public service" powers are obviously broad enough to encompass the more specific deployments anticipated in the CFAPPFD and the CFAAD. The latter two royal prerogative–based instruments predate the 1998 introduction of the NDA public service powers. The enactment of an NDA public service power encompassing a procedure for federally-authorized assistance to law enforcement may suggest that Parliament has now occupied that terrain. If displacement by implication because a statute has now occupied an area suffices, there is a real question as to whether the two orders-in-councils persist pursuant to an extant royal prerogative power.[69]

(iii) Other Defence-Related Prerogative Powers

Court cases suggest that the Canadian prerogative power over defence may also include such other things as authority to allow allied militaries to visit Canadian territory[70] and to test weapons systems in Canada. In *Operation Dismantle*, the Supreme Court of Canada seemed to accept without much discussion that Cabinet approval for the United States to test cruise missiles in Canada stemmed from a mix of prerogative powers in relation to defence and international relations.[71]

---

[65] A third, older OIC is the *Assistance to Federal Penitentiaries Order*, PC 1975-131, authorizing CAF assistance to suppress unrest at federal prisons.

[66] PC 1996-833.

[67] PC 1993-624.

[68] Colonel David E. Barr, Commander, Canadian Special Operations Forces Command CANSOFCOM, National Defence, Proceedings of the Standing Senate Committee on National Security and Defence, Issue 7, *Evidence* (20 Nov 2006) http://www.parl.gc.ca/Content/SEN/Committee/391/defe/07ev-e.htm?comm_id=76&Language=E&Parl=39&Ses=1 (accessed 4 May 2016).

[69] I have in the past raised doubts about this situation and have urged that the orders-in-council be treated as the procedures governing the application of the NDA public service provision, and not as self-standing legal authority. Craig Forcese, *National Security Law* (Irwin Law, 2007) 170. But see Philippe Lagassé, "The Crown's Power of Command-in-Chief: Interpretating Section 15 of Canada's Constitution Act, 1867" (2013) 18(2) *Review of Constitutional Studies* 189, for an argument that s. 15 of the *Constitution Act, 1867* creates robust constitutionalized executive powers to deploy the military that cannot be eroded by statute.

[70] *Vancouver Island Peace Society v Canada* [1994] 1 FC 102 (TD).

[71] *Operation Dismantle Inc. v Canada* [1985] 1 SCR 441 [50] (Wilson J).

In addition to these powers, the royal prerogative also extends to the power to grant or deny security clearances as a condition of appointments in the public service. This is a matter obviously related to defence, but which is in fact grounded legally in the historical powers of the monarch to appoint and manage the public service and now "in our times, a function of management controlled by the Crown".[72] Although statutes such as the *Public Service Employment Act* now govern most public service employment decisions, security clearances are still a matter of prerogative.

The prerogative has also been used to justify controlled access zones around certain Canadian military facilities.[73] But it seems much less likely that the prerogative would still reach such things as the imposition of martial law, or the requisition of ships, land, and chattels within Canada. These powers, although they may have existed historically, seem likely candidates for displacement by, initially the *War Measures Act* and now the much more comprehensive *Emergencies Act*.[74]

C. The Royal Prerogative over Foreign Affairs

The above-noted 2004 UK House of Commons study of prerogative powers also aptly summarizes the foreign affairs/international relations power: "The making and ratification of treaties" and "[t]he conduct of diplomacy, including the recognition of states, the relations (if any) between the United Kingdom and particular Governments, and the appointment of ambassadors and High Commissioners."[75]

In Canada, too, the conduct of foreign affairs is still a prerogative power. It has not been displaced by the statutory provisions charging the minister of foreign affairs with "conduct[ing] all diplomatic and consular relations on behalf of Canada" and "conduct[ing] and manag[ing] international negotiations as they relate to Canada."[76] Not least, these statutory provisions fail actually to articulate the precise content of the foreign relations power.

A potentially broad swath of government conduct continues to fall within the foreign affairs prerogative power. Treaty negotiation and then subsequent ratification and denunciation is entirely an exercise of royal prerogative by the federal executive.[77]

---

[72] *Thomson v Canada (Deputy Minister of Agriculture)*, 1992 1 SCR 385 [11].

[73] P.C. 2002-2190, S.I./2003-0002.

[74] For a dated discussion on these points, see Emergency Planning Canada, *The Scope of the Crown Prerogative as a Legal Basis for Government Measures to Deal with Various Classes of Foreign and Domestic Emergencies* (January 1983) 10–15.

[75] UK, House of Commons, above (n 6) at 6. For a magisterial treatment of the foreign relations power in Westminster democracies, see Campbell McLachlan, *Foreign Relations Law* (Cambridge University Press, 2014).

[76] *Department of Foreign Affairs, Trade and Development Act*, SC 2013, c 33, s 174, s 10. See *Khadr v Canada*, 2010 SCC 3 [35] (discussing a predecessor statute).

[77] *Hupacasath First Nation v Canada (Minister of Foreign Affairs)*, 2015 FCA 4; *Turp v. Canada (Justice)*, 2012 FC 893.

Although existing policy anticipates the tabling in Parliament of some treaties pending ratification,[78] this policy constitutes an exercise of discretion, not a mandatory legal requirement. (And of course, if treaties require further legislative implementation, this legislation must respect the constitutional division of powers.[79] In consequence, Canada follows a policy of consultation with the provinces where matters of provincial responsibility are implicated by a proposed treaty.)

More particular exercises of foreign relations are also within the prerogative's scope. Examples include expelling foreign diplomats,[80] and deciding what consular services or diplomatic protection Canada wishes to extend to Canadians[81] or foreigners[82] overseas.

For the provincial aspect of these matters, see the chapter in this *Handbook* by Cyr and de Mestral.

7. JUDICIAL REVIEW
OF PREROGATIVE POWERS

A key issue is whether exercises of prerogative power can be policed by the courts, a matter that has been a source of uncertainty. At core, judicial review of executive action is predicated on the principle that the Executive is a subordinate branch in a system built on parliamentary supremacy. To the extent the Executive immunizes its exercise of powers under the prerogative from judicial review, it removes courts as the enforcers of this relationship. In effect, the Executive then possesses a swath of inherently ambiguous powers whose limits would depend on Parliament itself legislating in the area. A very practical objection to Parliament as a check and balance stems from the reality of party discipline in Canada's Westminster system: generally, a majority of members of Parliament enjoy the same party affiliation as do ministers, and are conflicted in terms of supporting measures designed to oversee an assertive ministry.

Moreover, the check of parliamentary intervention may have been at least notionally acceptable prior to the advent of Canada's *Charter of Rights and Freedoms*. However, the idea of an executive equipped to determine the limits of its own prerogative powers, unencumbered by judicial review, is less satisfactory when that power potentially trenches on constitutionalized rights.

For these sorts of reasons, Canadian courts have regularly admonished that prerogative powers are not immunized from judicial review. The prerogative is a branch of judge-made common law "because decisions of courts determine both its existence and

---

[78] Global Affairs Canada, *Policy on Tabling of Treaties in Parliament*, http://www.treaty-accord.gc.ca/procedures.aspx?lang=eng (accessed 4 May 2016).

[79] *Canada (AG) v Ontario (AG)*, [1937] UKPC 6.

[80] *Copello v Canada (Minister of Foreign Affairs)*, 2001 FCT 1350.

[81] See such examples as *Khadr*, above (n 76); *Smith v. Canada*, 2009 FC 228.

[82] *Zeng v Canada (Attorney General)*.

its extent."[83] And so, "the courts clearly have the jurisdiction and the duty to determine whether a prerogative power asserted by the Crown does in fact exist."[84] Indeed, this fact is recognized in statute at the federal level. The *Federal Courts Act* anticipates that the Federal Court has judicial review authority over "any body, person or persons having, exercising or purporting to exercise jurisdiction or powers conferred . . . by or under an order made pursuant to a prerogative of the Crown."[85]

There are, however, circumstances where courts decline jurisdiction, applying the doctrine of non-justiciability. As described recently by the Federal Court of Appeal,

> In rare cases, . . . exercises of executive power are suffused with ideological, political, cultural, social, moral and historical concerns of a sort not at all amenable to the judicial process or suitable for judicial analysis. In those rare cases, assessing whether the executive has acted within a range of acceptability and defensibility is beyond the courts' ken or capability, taking courts beyond their proper role within the separation of powers.[86]

The most influential application of this doctrine to prerogative powers is the Ontario Court of Appeal's decision in *Black v Canada*.[87] This case concerned the discretionary granting of honours, and specifically advice given by the Canadian Prime Minister to the Queen about the conferral of an honour on a Canadian. The Court of Appeal concluded that the Prime Minister's conduct was non-justiciable, because "no Canadian citizen can have a legitimate expectation of receiving an honour" and no rights were at stake.[88] But in so concluding, the court also noted this outcome stemmed from the precise subject-matter of the prerogative, not the fact that the source of the power was the prerogative. It held "the exercise of the prerogative will be justiciable, or amenable to the judicial process, if its subject matter affects the rights or legitimate expectations of an individual. Where the rights or legitimate expectations of an individual are affected, the court is both competent and qualified to judicially review the exercise of the prerogative."[89]

This distinction partitions prerogative powers between those exercises of the power that fall into the category of high policy or discretionary honours (non-justiciable) and those that affect individual rights (justiciable). Matters of high policy include the executive decision to enter into a treaty or to declare war, or otherwise to direct the conduct of the Canadian Armed Forces.[90] Matters affecting individual rights include, for example,

---

[83] *Black*, above (n 12) [26]. *Scarborough (City)*, above (n 24), 134 (holding it would be inimical to principles of responsible government "if the court assumed that a residual royal prerogative prevails to validate any executive action for which legislative authorization is absent").

[84] *Khadr* above (n 76) [36].

[85] *Federal Courts Act*, RSC 1985, c F-7, s 2(1).

[86] *Hupacasath First Nation*, above (n 77) [66].

[87] *Black*, above (n 12).

[88] *Ibid* [61].

[89] *Ibid* [51].

[90] *Ibid* [50]. See also *Ganis v Canada (Minister of Justice)*, 2006 BCCA 543 [23]; *Turp v Chrétien*, [2003] JQ no 7019 (Qc SC); *Aleksic v Canada (Attorney General)* (2002), 215 DLR (4th) 720.

a decision concerning the issuance of passports,[91] the prerogative of mercy,[92] or efforts to seek commutation of a Canadian on death row in a foreign country.[93]

None of these latter cases involve "rights" in the true constitutional sense, and instead implicate matters that are better described as "strong individual interests." However, justiciable exercises of the prerogative also extend to those affecting truly constitutional rights. The most notable case involving the prerogative and constitutionalized rights is the Supreme Court of Canada's decision in *Canada (Prime Minister) v Khadr*.[94] In that matter, Canada's recalcitrance in advancing the interests of a Canadian detained by the United States at Guantanamo Bay was reviewable where, by reason of Canada's partial collaboration in interrogations, the Government had violated Omar Khadr's section 7 Charter rights.

A final category of justiciable exercises of the prerogative arises when other constitutional norms are at issue, such as federalism. And so the prerogative cannot be used to justify an exercise of governmental authority where, had that same authority been entrenched in statute, it would violate the constitutional division of powers. As the Supreme Court has put it: "all executive powers, whether they derive from statute, common law or prerogative, must be adapted to conform with constitutional imperatives."[95]

To say that an exercise of the prerogative is reviewable is not, however, to open the door to a full suite of judicial remedies, even where constitutional matters are at stake. This point was made most clearly by the Supreme Court of Canada in *Khadr*:

> The limited power of the courts to review exercises of the prerogative power for constitutionality reflects the fact that in a constitutional democracy, all government power must be exercised in accordance with the Constitution. This said, judicial review of the exercise of the prerogative power for constitutionality remains sensitive to the fact that the executive branch of government is responsible for decisions under this power, and that the executive is better placed to make such decisions within a range of constitutional options. The government must have flexibility in deciding how its duties under the power are to be discharged . . . . But it is for the courts to determine the legal and constitutional limits within which such decisions are to be taken. It follows that in the case of refusal by a government to abide by constitutional constraints, courts are empowered to make orders ensuring that the government's foreign affairs prerogative is exercised in accordance with the constitution.[96]

In that case, the Court simply issued a "declaration advising the government of its opinion on the records before it which, in turn, will provide the legal framework for the executive to exercise its functions and to consider what actions to take in respect of Khadr,

---

[91] *Kamal* above (n 31).
[92] *Black*, above (n 12) [55].
[93] *Smith* above (n 81).
[94] Above (n 81). See also *Operation Dismantle Inc.* above (n 71).
[95] *Air Canada v British Columbia (Attorney General)*, [1986] 2 SCR 539 [12].
[96] Above (n 81) [37].

in conformity with the Charter."[97] This mild rebuke provoked a very limited response from the Government. It simply sent a diplomatic note asking the United States not to use information provided by the Canadian government that stemmed from Canadian interrogations of Khadr at Guantanamo.

Khadr promptly judicially reviewed this (in)action. The Federal Court concluded that the diplomatic note did not, in fact, cure the Charter breach and that Canada was obliged to "advance a potential curative remedy as soon thereafter as is reasonably practicable and to continue advancing potential curative remedies until the breach has been cured or all such potential curative remedies have been exhausted."[98] This particular matter came to an end when Khadr subsequently entered a plea agreement with the United States, and was transferred to Canada.[99]

Read together, the *Khadr* decisions suggest a ready willingness on the part of courts to closely scrutinize the exercise of prerogative powers where Charter rights are at stake, subject to serious wariness in prescribing definitive remedies.

8. CONCLUSION

In sum, the royal prerogative persists in Canadian law as a source of executive authority in several special subject areas, some of which are matters of high policy and some of which may affect the interests and rights of individuals. Where exercises of the prerogative do affect interests and rights, and especially where Charter interests are in play, the prerogative has been treated no differently than any other exercise of executive power. Specifically, it has been subject to judicial review. Where, however, the prerogative implicates matters of high policy or discretionary bestowal of honours, courts have invoked the doctrine of justiciability in declining responsibility for examining executive branch conduct.

BIBLIOGAPHY

Secondary Sources

Canada, Privy Council Office, *Responsibility in the Constitution* (1993)
Forcese, C & Aaron Freeman, *The Laws of Government: The Legal Foundations of Canadian Democracy* (Irwin Law 2d edn 2010)
Lagassé, P., "Parliamentary and Judicial Ambivalence toward Executive Prerogative Powers in Canada," (2012) 55(2) *Canadian Public Administration* 157
Lordon, Paul (ed) *Crown Law* (Butterworths, 1991).

---

[97] *Ibid* [47].
[98] *Khadr v Canada (Prime Minister)*, 2010 FC 715 [96].
[99] *Khadr v Canada (Prime Minister)*, 2011 FCA 92.

United Kingdom, House of Commons, Public Administration Select Committee, *Taming the Prerogative: Strengthening Ministerial Accountability to Parliament*, HC 422 (4 Mar 2004)

Ward, N. (ed) *Dawson's The Government of Canada* (University of Toronto Press 6th ed. 1987)

Legislation

Interpretation Act, RSC 1985 c I-21 s 17

Cases

Alberta Government Telephones v Canada (Canadian Radio-Television and Telecommunications Commission), [1989] 2 S.C.R. 225

Black v Canada (2001) 54 OR (3d) 215

Khadr v Canada, 2010 SCC 3

Ross River Dena Council Band v Canada [2002] 2 SCR 816

B. The Parliamentary System

CHAPTER 8

....

POLITICAL INSTITUTIONS IN CANADA IN A NEW ERA

....

LORI TURNBULL[*]

1. INTRODUCTION

CANADA has a Westminster system of parliamentary government, in which the executive and legislative branches are fused together into a single Parliament. The Prime Minister and Cabinet make up the "active Executive" and the elected Members of Parliament (MPs) study, debate, amend, and vote on legislation in the House of Commons. For a bill to become law, it must pass through the House of Commons and the Senate in identical form. Though legislation can be introduced in either chamber, it is normally the case that bills are introduced by a Minister in the lower house.[1]

Responsible government is the set of constitutional conventions that make Canada's parliamentary system a democracy. In order to govern legitimately, a government needs the confidence of a majority of MPs in the House of Commons. Though there is no law that spells out exactly how to measure confidence, or whether and when it has been lost, practitioners and experts tend to agree that a Speech from the Throne and a budget bill are always treated as "confidence votes." Constitutional convention holds that, if a government were unable to secure the support of a majority of MPs on a confidence vote, it must either resign or seek the dissolution of the House, which would trigger a general election. However, as Don Desserud[2] and Andrew Heard[3] have argued, it is not always

---

[*] Associate Professor, Department of Political Science, Dalhousie University.
[1] It is important to note that although legislation can be initiated in either house, the Senate cannot introduce money bills.
[2] D. Desserud, *The Confidence Convention under the Canadian Parliamentary System* (Canadian Study of Parliament Group, 2007). Available at: http://cspg-gcep.ca/pdf/Parliamentary_Perspectives_7_2006-e.pdf.
[3] A. Heard, "Just What Is a Vote of Confidence? The Curious Case of May 10, 2005," (2007) 40:2 *Canadian Journal of Political Science* 395–416.

easy to determine whether confidence has been won or lost. Because the confidence convention is just that—a convention—it is binding in a political rather than a legal sense. In the end, it is the Prime Minister who makes a political determination as to whether the government holds the confidence of the House. Aucoin, Jarvis, and Turnbull[4] have argued that the lack of clarity around conventions, and their existence as political norms rather than enforceable legal rules, contributes to the excessive concentration of power in the hands of the Prime Minister. Simply put, the constitutional conventions that provide checks on the power of the Executive can be ignored easily, and so the Constitution becomes whatever the Prime Minister can get away with.

The theory of responsible government suggests that the balance of power rests with the legislative branch rather than the Executive. After all, the legislature has the right to defeat a government and replace it with another, at any time. However, in practice, power is heavily concentrated in the hands of the Prime Minister and a number of close advisors. The major reason for this reversal in the logic of responsible government is party discipline. Canadian politics is very much affected by party discipline, even in comparison to other Westminster systems. The expectation of complete solidarity among caucus members in political parties further consolidates the balance of power in favour of the political Executive because a Prime Minister is able to count on the support of every caucus member when there is a vote on government legislation. In majority government situations, a loss of confidence is virtually impossible.

Party leaders, and Prime Ministers especially, are able to command the allegiance of MPs through the implementation of a "carrot and stick" approach. Loyal MPs are rewarded with leadership positions within the party, including party whip and House leader, while rogues can be punished with uninspiring committee assignments, disappointing office space, or even expulsion from caucus. The Prime Minister has many, many "carrots" at his disposal, the most sought-after of which is Cabinet membership. The Prime Minister's power of appointment is perhaps the most important tool at his disposal to maintain discipline within his caucus and to affect the complexion of political institutions writ large. By virtue of the Prime Minister's exercise of the Crown's prerogative power to appoint, the Prime Minister appoints Senators, judges in provincial and federal courts, Supreme Court justices, Governors General and lieutenant governors, and, of course, Cabinet ministers.

The concentration-of-power phenomenon has been documented and explored by a number of academics, including Donald Savoie and Aucoin, Jarvis, and Turnbull. Westminster systems, by nature, tend to concentrate power in a strong Executive, which is then held to account by the legislative branch. Parliament, then, is not a lawmaking chamber but a confidence chamber; its primary function is to make and remake governments. This is in contrast to a congressional system such as the one in the United States, where the primary intent of the institutional design is to avoid the concentration

---

[4] P. Aucoin, M. Jarvis and L. Turnbull, *Democratizing the Constitution: Reforming Responsible Government* (Emond Montgomery Press, 2011).

of power and the corruption that could result. So, instead of fusing the executive and legislative branches as we do in Canada, the American Constitution clearly enumerates the specific responsibilities and powers of the legislative and executive branches so that neither one can overrule the other.

All of this to say is that, in parliamentary systems, the concentration of power is expected and even healthy—at least, to a certain degree. A strong Executive is able to govern efficiently and effectively and, when something goes wrong, the lines of account-ability and responsibility are clear. However, if power is accumulated in the executive branch to the point that *balance of power* between the executive and legislative branches is upset, the system does not operate as it should. Responsible government presupposes a strong Executive, but it requires a functional legislative branch as well.

The general election in October 2015 saw the Liberal Party of Canada form a major-ity government under the leadership of Justin Trudeau, the son of former prime minis-ter Pierre Elliott Trudeau. A significant element in the Liberals' campaign platform was democratic reform and, under this umbrella, they pledged to take a number of mea-sures designed to facilitate a more equitable balance of power between the executive and legislative branches. These proposals include: an empowered, gender-equal Cabinet; a new approach to the selection of committee chairs; limitations on the Prime Minister's ability to prorogue Parliament; more free votes and fewer omnibus bills in the House of Commons; and, a new approach to Senate and Supreme Court appointments.

The Liberal parliamentary reform agenda is safe politics, to a large extent, as many of their platform commitments can be described fairly as low-hanging fruit. For example, who can argue fervently against using secret ballots to elect committee chairs? The par-liamentary reform agenda makes political sense also because it resonates with calls for institutional reform that have echoed for decades. In this sense, the reform package is mainstream rather than revolutionary. However, the Trudeau government's approach to appointments stands alone in its capacity to cause a fundament shift away from the con-centration of power in the hands of the Prime Minister and his advisors. The Trudeau government has stepped away from the Prime Minister's power of appointment with respect to the Senate and the Supreme Court, giving much of the discretion over to inde-pendent advisory boards to make recommendations to the Prime Minister for appoint-ments on the basis of merit, objective qualifications, and the representation of Canada's diversity. The potential implications are enormous, not the least of which is that, to the extent that the Prime Minister now shares responsibility for appointments with inde-pendent advisory boards, the Prime Minister's box of "carrots and sticks" has signifi-cantly fewer "carrots."

This chapter explores the meaning and significance of the new Liberal government's parliamentary reform agenda, with particular attention to the new approach to appoint-ments. Each element of this agenda is described and assessed for its potential to facilitate a healthier balance of power between the executive and legislative branches. As stated above, the Trudeau government's approach to appointments stands to make the most significant change to the way our Westminster system of parliamentary government works. Although ceding some of the Prime Minister's control over appointments could help to bolster both the perception and reality of independence in our government institutions, it also comes at a cost with respect to executive accountability.

2. CAMPAIGN 2015: THE LIBERAL GOVERNMENT'S PARLIAMENTARY REFORM AGENDA

Prime Minister Stephen Harper's Conservative government held office for almost 10 years, from January 2006 till November 2015. Prime Minister Harper formed three governments: two minorities and one majority. During his tenure, he became known as a power-monger who was willing to resort to extreme measures in order to silence criticism and opposition. In a best-selling book, *Party of One: Stephen Harper and Canada's Radical Makeover,*[5] columnist Michael Harris cites the Harper government's muzzling of government scientists, agents of Parliament, and even Parliament itself, all in the name of message control and ultimate political survival. *Harperland: The Politics of Control*[6], a best-seller by columnist Lawrence Martin, offers relentless evidence to support Harper's control-freak reputation, including his decision to dismantle "sub-groups" within the Conservative Party—including youth wings—in order to ensure that there was no authority that could compete with his own.

Given Harper's vulnerability on the democracy file, it is little wonder that Trudeau's Liberals paid significant attention to parliamentary reform in its platform. In fact, many of its features can be understood as solutions to problems that appeared to either form or worsen under Harper's rule. In this chapter, I analyze the various components of the Trudeau government's parliamentary reform agenda and the degree to which they could contribute to a more equitable balance of power in Canada's Parliament.

A. A Gender-Equal Cabinet

At the swearing-in ceremony on 4 November 2015, Prime Minister Trudeau confirmed that his Cabinet would be made up of 15 men and 15 women, plus himself. Earlier that morning, Harper's last cabinet of 39 members resigned, only 12 of whom (31 percent) were women. Four of these 12 were Ministers of State, or junior Ministers, who are assigned specific responsibilities in support of senior Ministers and are paid less. In Prime Minister Trudeau's Cabinet there are no junior Ministers; all Ministers have the same rank.

---

[5] M. Harris, *Party of One: Stephen Harper and Canada's Radical Makeover* (Viking Canada, 2014).
[6] L. Martin, *Harperland: The Politics of Control* (Viking Canada, 2010).

In a press conference following the swearing-in ceremony, when asked why he appointed a gender-equal cabinet, Prime Minister Trudeau responded: "Because it's 2015. Canadians elected extraordinary Members of Parliament from across the country and I am glad to have been able to highlight a few of them in this cabinet here with me today."[7]

Gender equality in the Cabinet has never happened in Canada until now. It is significant in the sense that women are present in equal numbers in the *executive* branch, where power is concentrated. Women are still underrepresented in the House of Commons, where only 26 percent of Members of Parliament are women. By the United Nations' standards, Canada continues to underperform on this measure, as we do not meet the 30 percent threshold that "the UN suggests leads to a shift in policy and practice in government."[8] Systems that use proportional representation (PR) tend to perform better with respect to the inclusion of women in elected assemblies. So, if an electoral reform agenda were to lead to the adoption of a PR system, even a mixed one, the number of women in Parliament would likely increase as well.

Prime Minister Trudeau's cabinet is significantly smaller than Prime Minister Harper's last cabinet. At 31 members including the Prime Minister, it is the same size or smaller than every Cabinet appointed since 1980 by Prime Ministers Harper, Chretien, Martin, Mulroney, and former prime minister Trudeau. However, 31 members is a large Cabinet when compared to the United Kingdom, where legislation caps the size of the Cabinet at 25 members (in a House of 649 MPs compared to Canada's 338). Aucoin, Jarvis, and Turnbull have argued that although a large cabinet can be politically useful in that it has enough members to offer wide-ranging symbolic representation of Canada's diversity, it is not as useful for deliberation and decision. There are simply too many people around the table for decisions to be taken in earnest by a full Cabinet of over 30 people, and so the work of Cabinet committees is vitally important to Cabinet government.

Brent Rathgeber, former Conservative-turned-Independent MP from Edmonton, Alberta, tabled a private members' bill in 2015 aiming to cap Canada's Cabinet at 26 members.[9] He was inspired by the UK example. Because there are so few Cabinet positions, the likelihood of getting one is small, so MPs tend to focus more on their legislative work and devote less energy to cultivating positive relations with party leadership. It is possible that, if Canada were to work towards a smaller Cabinet size, a similar cultural effect could take hold. This would tip the balance of power towards a stronger, more independent legislative branch.

---

[7] A. Frisk, "'Because It's 2015': Trudea's Gender-Equal Cabinet Making Headlines around the World, Social Media," *Global News* (5 November 2015). Available at: www.globalnews.ca/news/2320795/because-its-2015-trudeaus-gender-equal-cabinet-makes-headlines-around-the-world-social-media/.

[8] E. Anderssen, "We Have a Record Number of Female MPs, but Hold the Applause." *The Globe and Mail* (20 October 2015). Available at: http://www.theglobeandmail.com/life/we-have-a-record-number-of-female-mps-but-hold-the-applause/article26887164/.

[9] A Raj, "Independent MP Seeks to Limit Size of Federal Cabinet," *Huffington Post* 2015. Available at: http://www.huffingtonpost.ca/news/brent-rathgeber-private-members-bill/.

B. Committee Reform

The Trudeau Liberals vowed that, if elected, they would take measures to enhance the power and independence of parliamentary committees. To this end, when Parliament resumed in 2015, parliamentary committee chairs were chosen by secret ballot so that voting MPs would be empowered to vote freely, rather than to rubber stamp the preference of the party leader, as was the norm previously. This change in approach to committee chair selection is consistent with trends in other Westminster countries such as the United Kingdom, where the entire House casts secret ballots to elect committee chairs. It is also in sync with a proposal from the Public Policy Forum, an Ottawa-based think tank, in a report entitled *Time for a Reboot: Nine Ways to Restore Trust in Canada's Public Institutions* released in the weeks following the 2015 election.[10]

The Trudeau government has determined that Ministers and parliamentary secretaries cannot be voting members on committees, and cannot vote if they are substituting for a voting member. This, combined with the new approach to electing committee chairs, is designed to bolster the independence of committees from the executive branch and from the government's agenda. Parliamentary committees are, to a large extent, the place where the legislative branch performs its essential functions, as it is in committee where proposed legislation and estimates are closely scrutinized, where witnesses are heard, and where amendments to legislation are crafted. Stronger committees mean a stronger legislative branch, with greater capacity to hold government to account.

It is too early to tell whether committees will be meaningfully transformed as a result of the Trudeau government's reforms. At the time of writing, which is just over a year after the October 2015 election, it is fair to say that party discipline is no less present in committees than it was before. Even though MPs are freer to vote their true preferences when it comes to selecting a chair, they seem to be no less bound to the party line. This is not surprising, as party whips continue to play a strong role, which includes ensuring that MPs are present at committee meetings and aware of their role in defending and advancing party positions. However, it is possible that the cultural and behavioural implications of the institutional reforms might take longer to appear.

C. Prorogation

Until December 2008, it seemed as though no one in Canada had ever heard the word "prorogation" before. But a prospective constitutional crisis brought it to the forefront of Canadian politics and governance. In November of that year, a newly-elected Conservative minority government under Prime Minister Stephen Harper delivered a

---

[10] Public Policy Forum, "Time for a Reboot: Nine Ways to Restore Trust in Canada's Public Institutions." Ottawa, Ontario (October 2015). Available at: http://www.ppforum.ca/sites/default/files/PPF_TimeForAReboot_ENG_v6.pdf.

fiscal update in the House of Commons. Among its contents was the proposal to end per-vote subsidies for political parties, which amounted to roughly $2 per vote in every year between general elections. Though the most popular parties stood to gain the most in absolute terms, the per-vote subsidy was an equalizer to the extent that it provided all parties that obtained at least 2 percent of the national vote with a guaranteed income each year, the effect of which could only be stabilizing.

The Conservatives' plan came as a shock to the other parties, as it was not part of the Conservative election platform that fall and the opposition parties had not been consulted on it. The opposition parties, together making up a majority in the House, indicated that they could not support the fiscal update and, given that it was comparable to a "mini-budget," it was interpreted as a confidence measure. It was merely weeks since the last general election. There would have been little appetite (or money) for a new election following the defeat of the government, so the Liberals and the New Democrats proposed that they form a coalition, with the Bloc Quebecois as a supporter. This proposal became public in the form of an open letter to the Governor General. However, in order for this proposed coalition government to become a reality, the Conservative government would have to be defeated first. Prior to the scheduled opposition day, on which the government was all but sure to be defeated, Prime Minister Harper requested that the Governor General prorogue Parliament, a measure that brings an end to the parliamentary session and its business.

Prime Minister Harper was widely criticized, by academics, journalists, politicians, and citizens, for his willingness to take extreme measures to avoid a confidence vote he knew his government was destined to lose. In 2009, he sought and obtained prorogation again, this time in coincidence with parliamentary inquiries into the Afghan detainee affair.[11] To be fair, Prime Minister Harper was not the first to use prorogation to quieten the House for political purposes. Prime Minister Chretien did as well, for example, in advance of the Auditor General's damning report on the sponsorship scandal in 2003. Less fuss was made at the time, perhaps because Prime Minister Chretien's government held a majority in the House and, though the report was damaging and embarrassing, confidence was not an issue. Prorogations do not happen very often (some Westminster systems do not use them at all), but Prime Ministers' willingness to resort to prorogation as a political tool has been a factor in upsetting the balance of power between the executive and the legislative branches. To be clear, the former can effectively shut the latter down for a period of time.

The Liberals campaigned on eliminating the government's ability to use prorogation to silence Parliament and avoid its scrutiny. The most commonly-suggested way to do this is to require a multi-party or even all-party agreement before Parliament is prorogued.[12] This would protect the legislative branch against a politically-motivated purging at the hands of the executive branch.

---

[11] R. Whitaker, "Prime Minister v. Parliament," *The Toronto Star* (18 December 2009). Available at: https://www.thestar.com/opinion/2009/12/18/prime_minister_vs_parliament.html.

[12] See Aucoin, Jarvis and Turnbull, above (n 4).

D. Free Votes and Omnibus Bills

As already mentioned, party discipline is strong in Canada. It is as though all votes are treated as confidence votes, and so deviation from the party line is a rarity. The Liberals campaigned on allowing more free votes in the House of Commons; specifically, the platform says that MPs should be free to vote as they wish on matters other than the following three: those that implement the Liberal Party platform, confidence votes, and, matters addressing the Charter of Rights.

Free votes are a tricky issue. On the one hand, they are appealing to the extent that they release MPs from the strict expectation of party solidarity and allow them to vote either according to their own judgment or conscience (the trustee model) or in a way that takes into consideration the wishes of constituents (the delegate model). On the other hand though, we know that voters take party into account when they cast their ballots. By voting for the Liberal candidate, there is an expectation that, if elected, this individual would support the platform that she campaigned on. In this sense, the three restrictions mentioned above make sense. And, the public expects solidarity from caucus members; there is not likely to be much in the way of a public outcry if no free votes come up during a parliamentary session.

Trudeau's Liberals are not the first to campaign on more free votes in the House; Paul Martin did too in his campaign for the Liberal leadership. He was looking for a way to connect with veteran MPs who were not Cabinet members but were looking for a more meaningful role to play as legislators. Martin proposed the British three-line whip approach, which would free backbenchers from the party line on votes that were considered less important to the government's mandate and survival. Martin's "democratic deficit" reform package got media and academic attention when he introduced it, but in general it failed to materialize once he became Prime Minister.[13]

The caveats specified in the Trudeau Liberal platform with respect to the use of free votes guarantee that a free vote would never lead to the defeat of the government; Liberal MPs are still expected to vote with the party on matters of confidence. And, the Liberals' pledge for more free votes affects the Liberal caucus alone; it would be up to other leaders to choose whether to follow suit. In light of these factors, the Liberals' willingness to tolerate more free votes might, in fact, do very little to change the current balance of power in the hands of the Executive.

The Liberal platform also pledges to change the Standing Orders to prevent the use of omnibus budget bills as a means of forcing legislation through the House of Commons quickly and without proper scrutiny. The Conservatives were accused of this when they introduced "monster omnibus budget bills" into the House of Commons. As argued in an editorial in *The Globe and Mail* in 2015, "(t)hey usurp Parliament's most important

---

[13]   P. Aucoin and L. Turnbull, "The Democratic Deficit: Paul Martin and Parliamentary Reform" (2003) 46 *Canadian Public Administration* 427–449.

role, that of oversight, by lumping a variety of matters into a single bill."[14] Further, because bills are studied by only one parliamentary committee, it means that no matter which committee is involved, it gets a huge, complex, unmanageable bill that incorporates a number of matters outside its normal expertise. To top it off, the fact that an omnibus budget bill is a confidence measure means that the Executive is essentially bullying Parliament by forcing them to pass it. To do otherwise would be to trigger an election, which would mean that the public would lose out on all of the goodies crammed into the bill.

The end of omnibus budget bills would be a good thing for Parliament and for the balance of power between the Executive and the legislature. They serve no purpose other than political advantage, and they come at the cost of Parliament's essential scrutiny function. Make no mistake, the Executive will always take ownership of the budget, and the role of MPs will always be to scrutinize and amend rather than to create. This is the proper division of labour in a Westminster system. But each role is essential, especially on budget bills—the most significant in the tenure of any government and the most vital to the implementation of the government's agenda and the delivery of public programs and services.

E. Senate Appointments

Canadians got a preview of Justin Trudeau's approach to appointments in January 2014, when he announced that Senators would no longer sit in the Liberal caucus. This came as a shock to the media, the public, and the Senators themselves, who were not given much in the way of advance notice of this change. At the time, Trudeau had been Liberal leader for less than a year. The party was in third place in the House of Commons and had the lowest number of seats it had ever held in Canadian history. The Liberals won a dismal 34 seats in the 2011 election. Trudeau had the daunting task of turning the party's fortunes around in time for the 2015 campaign. In this light, his decision to remove Senators from caucus was a way of breaking ranks with the Liberal Party of the past. His was a new party, one where only elected members could sit in caucus. In a way, this was Trudeau's first step in implementing a democratic reform agenda. Obviously, the implications of his decision stood to go beyond the Liberal Party itself and could affect the operation of the Senate as an institution. Once the former Liberal Senators were set free, they quickly decided to caucus together, which mitigated the initial institutional effects of Trudeau's decision. However, as the weeks and months went on, more Senators announced their decision to sit as true Independents. Slowly but surely, the ties

[14] Editorial, *The Globe and Mail* (12 May 2015). Available at: http://www.theglobeandmail.com/opinion/editorials/another-budget-another-contemptuous-tory-omnibus-bill/article24404300/. See also A. Dodek, "Battling the Omnibus Bills", *National Post* (29 August 2016). Available at: http://news.nationalpost.com/full-comment/adam-dodek-battling-the-omnibus-bills.

that bound the Senators to the House of Commons—and to the leaders who appointed them—were weakening.

As Prime Minister, Trudeau followed through on his promise to facilitate the appointment of Independent Senators which, in turn, could make the Senate a more independent institution. Historically, Prime Ministers have held closely their power to appoint members to the Senate. It has been a very useful tool to reward party loyalists and to ensure that the upper house has a critical mass of representatives from the Government so that bills get through in the form that they passed through the House. A hostile Senate could be a problem for a government, as it could slow down or thwart its agenda by introducing amendments, filibustering, or refusing to pass a bill altogether. In comparison, a Senate full of Independents is an unknown variable. Nevertheless, the Trudeau government has made good on its promise to establish an Independent Advisory Board for Senate Appointments. This five-member Board accepts applications from qualified Canadians when Senate positions become available. The Advisory Board assesses the applications and, on that basis, makes non-binding appointments to the Prime Minister based on merit.[15]

The recommendations have to be non-binding, as to do otherwise would require a constitutional amendment regarding the Crown's prerogative to appoint. Technically, according to the *Constitution Act, 1867*, it is the Governor General who appoints Senators on behalf of the Crown. However, the Prime Minister has always exercised discretion with respect to appointments and the Governor General's role is strictly ceremonial. A constitutional amendment would be very difficult to obtain and is unnecessary to achieving the desired outcome, so long as Prime Ministers respect the work of the Advisory Board.

The Liberal government's approach to appointing Senators follows a number of attempts to reform the Senate. By today's standards for democracy, it is difficult to justify the existence of an upper house full of political appointments. The impetus for reform is clear and the desire is widespread, but the practicalities have proven very difficult. As the Supreme Court of Canada ruled in 2014, the Conservatives' preference for fixed terms and provincial elections for Senators would require formal constitutional change and the consent of at least 7 of the 10 provinces representing at least 50 percent of the population.[16] There is no provincial consensus on Senate reform, which makes a constitutional amendment virtually impossible under the amending formula. The mere thought of reopening the constitutional debate sends shivers down the spines of most politicians and many Canadians as well. Aucoin, Jarvis, and Turnbull contend that the lack of political will to pursue constitutional reform impedes our growth and maturity as a democracy, as it prevents positive change from going forward. Upon drawing the conclusion that formal constitutional change is impossible but Senate reform is necessary, Prime Ministers Harper and Trudeau both pursued "informal constitutional change." Most

---

[15] Government of Canada, *Independent Advisory Board for Senate Appointments* (2016). Available at: https://www.canada.ca/en/campaign/independent-advisory-board-for-senate-appointments.html.

[16] 2014 SCC 32.

recently, Prime Minister Trudeau has introduced an appointments process that does not challenge the Crown's prerogative to appoint under the Constitution. Because the Advisory Board's recommendations are not binding on the Prime Minister, he retains his access to the Crown's prerogative power to appoint, and constitutional change is not required to implement the Liberal's platform promise on Senate reform.

To date, Prime Minister Trudeau has appointed 28 Senators under the new process including Senator Peter Harder, a former deputy minister and career public servant. Senator Harder serves as the Government's representative in the Senate, which means he works with the Government House Leader to ensure that legislation gets tabled in the Senate.[17] The changing role of the Government leader in the Senate has been a focal point of concern and speculation, as traditionally this individual was appointed to the Cabinet and was considered a key player in moving the Government's agenda through the Senate. This made political sense, as having a partisan operative in a leadership position in the Senate gave the Government assurance that its legislation will be treated favourably in the upper house. In the new independent Senate, where the idea is to appoint non-partisans and to operate independently from the House, what is the role of the Government's representative? How does this individual "oversee" a group of Independents? What does "representative" mean in this context?

Senator Harder has admitted that he anticipates challenges. With the new appointments, the number of Independent Senators has grown significantly, making the institution even more of a wild card. However, the lack of party and/or government affiliation in the Senate does not necessarily mean that it will become more wily or uncontrollable. It simply means that party caucuses will no longer be the primary organizational feature in the chamber. No doubt, factions will develop—perhaps around region, identity, language, or on a case-by-case basis according to the issue—as independence does not preclude cooperation and working together on a common cause.

We have had an opportunity to see how a less-partisan Senate interacts with government legislation. The Senate responded to the government's bill on doctor-assisted dying by proposing amendments. Among them was the suggestion that the bill be amended to include access to assisted dying for patients who are not terminally ill. The House agreed to most of the Senate's proposed amendments, including providing consultation on palliative care options, but did not accept the Senate amendment regarding access for patients who are not terminally ill. When the amended bill returned to the Senate, it deferred to the House's wishes and the bill passed.

The bill provided an opportunity for dialogue between the two chambers. The exchange that took place was constructive in the sense that the Senate did not shy away from its responsibility to provide "sober second thought." Indeed, many Canadians are onside with the Senate's concern with respect to limiting the application of the bill to terminally ill patients. By proposing the amendment, the Senate forced the House to

---

[17] H. Jackson, "Peter Harder, Trudeau's Senate representative, Seeks $800k Budget, Gets Half," *CBC News* (21 April 2016). Available at: www.cbc.ca/news/politics/peter-harder-senate-budget-1.3546501.

rethink its approach. But in the end, the Senate deferred to the will of the elected House of Commons. Independent Senator Andre Pratte described the situation as follows: "I am convinced the government is making a serious and cruel mistake by taking away the right to medically assisted dying from a group of patients, those who are not terminally ill yet suffering terribly. . . . But the government will answer to the people for that error."[18]

This quotation speaks to the appropriate balance of power between the House and the Senate. Though the latter can provide scrutiny and ask the government to reflect on its plans, it is ultimately the former that is accountable to the people. To the extent that a more independent Senate is more capable of providing a sincere sober, second thought, it will act as a more effective check on the executive branch than the Senate has ever been. Accountability in this context does not require that government legislation be defeated or changed substantially, but that it is scrutinized and debated in earnest, and that Senators are empowered to suggest amendments that they deem appropriate.

It is difficult to predict how future Senate appointees will interpret their role as Independents. After all, the Senate has historically been organized along party lines, though often with less partisan acrimony than what exists in the House of Commons. The Senate is not a confidence chamber, which means that strict party discipline has been less of an imperative. But the new Senate is charting a new course altogether and it remains to be seen how the upper chamber will perform its legislative review and regional representation functions. On a depressing note, nothing about the new appointments process prevents the occurrence of a scandal, or accusations of wrongdoing such as the ones against Senators Duffy, Brazeau, and Wallin that left the Senate in disgrace.

F. Supreme Court of Canada Appointments

The Prime Minister announced, in an opinion piece in *The Globe and Mail*, the government's new process for filling vacancies on the Supreme Court of Canada.[19] According to the new rules, any Canadian who is a qualified judge or lawyer, functionally bilingual, and "representative of the diversity of our great country" can apply. There is now an independent advisory board, chaired by former prime minister Kim Campbell, to review applications and make recommendations to the Prime Minister in the form of a short list of three to five candidates. Before the list is passed on to the Prime Minister, it is reviewed by provincial and territorial Attorneys General, the Chief Justice of

---

[18] L. Stone and S. Fine, "Senate Backs Down, Passes Assisted-Dying Legislation," *The Globe and Mail* (17 June 2016). Available at: http://www.theglobeandmail.com/news/politics/senate-passes-assisted-dying-legislation/article30507549/.

[19] J. Trudeau, "Why Canada Has a New Way to Choose Supreme Court Justicess," *The Globe and Mail* (2 August 2016). Available at: http://www.theglobeandmail.com/opinion/why-canada-has-a-new-way-to-choose-supreme-court-judges/article31220275/.

Canada, relevant Cabinet ministers, and opposition justice critics, and by a parliamentary committee as well. Applicants complete a questionnaire and the ultimate nominee faces questioning by MPs and Senators.[20] In December 2016, Justice Malcolm Rowe of Newfoundland was appointed to the Supreme Court of Canada via the new process. His appointment filled a vacancy created when Justice Thomas Cromwell of Nova Scotia retired.[21]

This is a rigorous process with much input and multiple check points. The previous appointment process involved input and review from provincial representatives, Cabinet ministers, and others, and since (and including) Justice Rothstein's appointment, some nominees have been subject to an "interview" of sorts in Parliament. So, the main differences between the old process and the new one are that individuals are to nominate themselves and an independent board will craft the short list. The Prime Minister's comments with respect to diversity indicate that the new advisory board will be looking to ensure that the Supreme Court's membership is reflective of Canada's rich diversity. Historically, the mandate of the Court to be representative has been a source of contention, as the bench has not always been balanced with respect to gender diversity and the inclusion of minorities, including of Aboriginal peoples.

The one element of Canada's diversity that is embedded in the composition of the Supreme Court is the representation of Quebec. By statute, three of the nine justices must come from Quebec. Apart from that, the convention has been to appoint three justices from Ontario, two from the West, and one from Atlantic Canada. Following the announcement of the new process, the Prime Minister's Office (PMO) confirmed that this process might cause a break with the tradition of regional representation described here. In fact, PMO went as far as to say that, when the retirement of Justice Cromwell created a vacancy, there was no guarantee that the spot would be filled by another Atlantic Canadian. In the end, Justice Rowe's appointment maintained the tradition of regional balance.

PMO might be said to have been picking an unnecessary fight with Atlantic Canada by departing from the convention to appoint a judge from the Atlantic region. Politically, it seemed a risky move and a snub to the region that elected Liberal candidates in every one of its 32 ridings. Provincial justice ministers from the region took to the airwaves to express their concern, so it might have been the case that the new appointments process would have caused a rift in federal-provincial relations if the nominee for this position had hailed from another region.

There is no clear consensus as to whether regional representation on the Court is necessary. As Robert Schertzer from the University of Toronto argues, there is little

[20] J.P. Tesker and C. Tunney, "Justin Trudeau Outlines Selection Process for New Supreme Court Justices," *CBC News* (2 August 2016). Available at: http://www.cbc.ca/news/politics/supreme-court-canada-justices-selection-1.3703779.

[21] CBC, "Justice Malcolm Rowe Is Welcomed to the Supreme Court of Canada," *CBC News* (2 December 2016). Available at: http://www.cbc.ca/news/politics/malcolm-rowe-supreme-court-1.3879443.

evidence to suggest that the regional affiliation of justices affects their rulings. However, "the power and importance of symbolism should not be underestimated. The Supreme Court itself has been clear that regional representation on the bench is of utmost importance."[22] In a country such as Canada, where regional identity is the most relevant political cleavage, even symbolic regional representation in Canada's foremost political institutions confers legitimacy. However, Atlantic Canada is the country's smallest region, with a population of just over 2.3 million people. The total population of the four Western Canadian provinces is approximately 10.3 million by comparison, and Quebec and Ontario have populations of 8.2 million and 13.6 million respectively. Therefore, Atlantic Canada cannot make the claim that, based on the principle of representation by population, there must be a Supreme Court justice from Atlantic Canada at all times. The numbers simply do not warrant it. But regional representation in Canada has been by convention and has been deeply embedded in our political culture. It is not simply about numbers.

Even apart from the issue of Atlantic Canada's representation on the Court, the new process for Supreme Court justice appointments is much more high-risk, from a political perspective, than the other reforms discussed here, including the reform of the Senate appointments process. The difference is that the Senate has long been the subject of proposals for reform, especially on the subject of the appointment of Senators by the Prime Minister. This process left the Senate vulnerable to appointments that were entirely politically-motivated and, as mentioned previously, it is difficult to justify an upper house full of patronage appointees. Today's standards for democracy are attentive to fairness, merit, equality, and the representation of diversity, but political loyalty has all too often been the primary criterion for becoming a Senator. On this file, the broad consensus was that it was time for change.

Supreme Court appointments, on the other hand, were never the subject of such intense criticism. Even though there are expectations that the Court be more representative of Canada's diversity, the appointments process has always been based on merit and so not vulnerable to accusations of patronage. Perhaps the most controversial moment in the history of Supreme Court appointments was the failed nomination of Justice Marc Nadon. His name was put forward by Prime Minister Stephen Harper, but the appointment was vetoed by the Supreme Court itself after Prime Minister Harper referred the question to the Court. The Court ruled that the appointment could not go ahead because Justice Nadon did not meet the statutory criteria set out in the *Supreme Court Act*.

Canadians' trust in the Supreme Court as an institution has been consistently very high. Public opinion data have shown that Canadians trust the Supreme Court more

---

[22] R. Schertzer, "Reflecting Canada's Regions Confers Legitimacy on the Top Court, even if Doesn't Influence the Judges' Rulings," *Policy Options* (17 August 2016). Available at: http://policyoptions.irpp. org/magazines/august-2016/why-regional-representation-on-the-supreme-court-does-and-doesnt-matter/.

than any other institution, including Parliament.[23] In contrast, the public's attitude toward the Senate is particularly hostile, especially following criminal charges against Senators Duffy and Brazeau and an investigation into Senator Wallin. The was no discernible public pressure to reform the Supreme Court appointments process, and there seems to have been no major problem to solve, and so the new process reflects a desire on the part of the Trudeau government to adopt a new, government-wide approach to appointments that is based on self-nominations, scrutiny by independent boards, merit, and the representation of diversity.

3. Conclusion

Justin Trudeau's approach to appointments could inoculate him politically, in the event that an appointee lands in hot water in the future. Consider the case of Senator Mike Duffy. In 2015, he went to trial on 31 criminal charges that related to four overarching themes: whether he met the residency requirement to represent Prince Edward Island in the Senate, whether his process for administering contracts using Senate funds was appropriate, whether his travel claims and reimbursements were legitimate according to the Senate financial administration rules, and, whether he intended to accept a bribe from Nigel Wright, Chief of Staff to the Prime Minister. He has been acquitted on all 31 charges, and has since returned to his work in the Senate, but his acquittal is understood to be largely a result of lax rules in the Senate about both residency and Senators' use of public funds. His own reputation remains in tatters, and the damage has not stopped with Duffy. The Prime Minister who appointed him, Stephen Harper, was held to account for Duffy's appointment on the campaign trail in 2015. This was by no means the only—or even the primary—reason for the defeat of the Harper government, but the Prime Minister could not escape political accountability for his decision to appoint Duffy to the Senate. To the extent that the new appointments process dilutes the discretion of the Prime Minister, and relies on the objective review of candidates by independent advisory boards, the Prime Minister is relatively immune from political blowback if appointees become engulfed in controversy.

There are a number of proposals in the Liberal Party's 2015 platform that could be placed in the category of democratic reform, including pledges to review election spending, to revisit the measures implemented under the *Fair Elections Act*, and to study alternative electoral systems. However, I chose to focus here on those campaign promises that relate most directly to the relationship between the Executive and the legislature. It is possible that electoral reform, for example, could lead to a transformed relationship between the two branches of government but, without knowing which new system—if

---

[23] B.J. Siekierski, "Vast Majority of Canadians Trust Supreme Court, including Most Tories," *iPolitics* (2005). Available at: http://ipolitics.ca/2015/08/16/vast-majority-of-canadians-trust-supreme-court-including-most-tories/.

any—will be adopted, musings on the effects of electoral reform on Westminster governance would be premature speculation.

The concentration-of-power phenomenon has long been a concern of students and observers of Canadian politics. The Liberal platform on parliamentary reform speaks to this concern and is largely a step in the right direction toward achieving a healthier balance of power between the political executive and elected MPs. Though some proposals, such as an increase in free votes, are unlikely to affect this relationship to a great extent, the Trudeau government's new approach to appointments stands to make a significant change to the traditional powers of the Prime Minister of Canada. Time will tell whether these changes will last or whether a subsequent Prime Minister will abandon independent advisory boards and return to the old model in which the Prime Minister's discretion over appointments was paramount.

BIBLIOGRAPHY

Aucoin P., M. Jarvis and L. Turnbull, *Democratizing the Constitution: Reforming Responsible Government* (Emond Montgomery Press, 2011).

Aucoin P. and L. Turnbull, "The Democratic Deficit: Paul Martin and Parliamentary Reform," (2003) 46 *Canadian Public Administration* 427–449.

Desserud D., *The Confidence Convention under the Canadian Parliamentary System* (Canadian Study of Parliament Group, 2007). Available at: http://cspg-gcep.ca/pdf/Parliamentary_Perspectives_7_2006-e.pdf.

Government of Canada, *Independent Advisory Board for Senate Appointments* (2016). Available at: https://www.canada.ca/en/campaign/independent-advisory-board-for-senate-appointments.html.

Harris M., *Party of One: Stephen Harper and Canada's Radical Makeover* (Viking Canada, 2014).

Heard A., "Just What Is a Vote of Confidence? The Curious Case of May 10, 2005," Canadian Journal of Political Science 40:2 (2007) 395–416.

Martin L., *Harperland: The Politics of Control* (Viking Canada, 2010).

Public Policy Forum, "Time for a Reboot: Nine Ways to Restore Trust in Canada's Public Institutions." Ottawa, Ontario (October 2015). Available at: http://www.ppforum.ca/sites/default/files/PPF_TimeForAReboot_ENG_v6.pdf.

Savoie D., *Court Government and the Collapse of Accountability in Canada and the United Kingdom* (IPAC Series in Public Management and Governance, University of Toronto Press, 2008).

CHAPTER 9

....

PARLIAMENTARY SOVEREIGNTY IN CANADA

....

JOHN LOVELL*

1. INTRODUCTION—CANADA'S VERSION OF PARLIAMENTARY SOVEREIGNTY

....

PARLIAMENTARY sovereignty has long held sway in the United Kingdom as the central organizing principle of its constitution. As traditionally understood, it means that Parliament remains legally free at all times to make or change any legal rule that it wants. There is no recognized class of constitutional rules to set limits on what a statute can or cannot do. There is no known procedure for entrenching fundamental rights, or fundamental anything, beyond the reach of ordinary legislation. Adherents may feel beleaguered these days but the concept exerts a tenacious grip. Short of British judges overthrowing the 1688 Glorious Revolution in a burst of 'judicial self-confidence', the main bone of contention is whether and to what extent Parliament can itself alter this state of affairs if it wants to.[1]

In comparison, what space does parliamentary sovereignty command in the Canadian constitutional landscape? Political scientist Peter Russell once offered a short answer: 'No Canadian legislature or parliament has ever been sovereign and I hope none ever shall be'.[2] According to the yardsticks traditionally applied to the Mother Parliament at Westminster, Russell's answer is irrefutable. Courts have been invalidating federal and provincial legislation since Confederation in 1867. But it would be misleading to leave

---

* Constitutional solicitor, Ministry of Justice, Victoria, British Columbia. The views in this article are those of the author and are not to be attributed to the Ministry.

[1] Michael Gordon, "The UK's Fundamental Constitutional Principle: Why the UK Is Still Sovereign and Why It Still Matters" (2015) 26 *King's Law Journal* 229.

[2] Peter H. Russell, "Standing Up for Notwithstanding" (1991), 29 *Alberta Law Review* 293, 294.

the answer at that. There has always been, and there remains, an abiding belief among Canadian judges, legislators, and government officials that the doctrine of parliamentary sovereignty, the principle of parliamentary sovereignty, or *some* sort of parliamentary sovereignty has been implanted in this country. And so it has, after a fashion. A few illustrations make the point:

(a) In the *Canada Assistance Plan Reference*, the Supreme Court of Canada upholds a legal proposition by saying that 'to assert the contrary is to negate the sovereignty of Parliament'. The Court considers the principle powerful enough to flow upstream: 'A restraint on the Executive in the introduction of legislation is a fetter on the sovereignty of Parliament itself'.[3]

(b) A Manitoba judge decides a case on the basis that '[t]he doctrine of parliamentary sovereignty prevents a legislative body from binding future legislative bodies as to the substance of its future legislation'.[4]

(c) It is undisputed that the framers of the *Canadian Charter of Rights and Freedoms* inserted Section 33—the so-called Notwithstanding Clause that enables ordinary statutes to override many of the *Charter's* constitutional rights—in order to allay concerns over an undue erosion of parliamentary sovereignty. On the 25th anniversary of the *Charter* the Chief Justice of Canada extols Section 33 as 'an ultimate guarantee of parliamentary supremacy for those rights to which it applies'.[5]

When constitutional provisions are drawn up to safeguard parliamentary sovereignty and judges decide cases according to their best understanding of what the doctrine entails, something must be going on. The English version was expounded by Professor Dicey in a series of influential Oxford University lectures published in 1885. His text went through many editions and reprints, and a key passage is often quoted by Canadian judges:

> The principle of Parliamentary sovereignty means neither more nor less than this, namely, that Parliament thus defined has, under the English constitution, the right to make or unmake any law whatever; and, further, that no person or body is recognised by the law of England as having a right to override or set aside the legislation of Parliament.[6]

This chapter will trace the pedigree of the Canadian version of parliamentary sovereignty (CVPS). It will also visit the issue of whether a present Parliament can bind its successors, and the question of what bodies—in addition to courts—are recognized by

---

[3] *Reference re Canada Assistance Plan*, [1991] 2 SCR 525.

[4] *Progressive Conservative Party of Manitoba v Government of Manitoba*, 2014 MBQB 155.

[5] Rt Hon Beverley McLachlin, 'The *Charter* 25 Years Later: The Good, the Bad, and the Challenges' (2007) 45 *Osgoode Hall Law Journal* 365, 369. See as well the chapter by Janet Hiebert in this *Handbook*.

[6] A.V. Dicey, *Introduction to the Study of the Law of Constitution* (10th edn, Macmillan, 1964) 39–40, cited in *Page v Mulcair*, 2013 FC 402.

the law of Canada as having the right to decide that legislation enacted by Parliament or a provincial legislature is invalid.

2. Sovereign within Their Jurisdiction

A. More Diceyan than Dicey

Professor Russell's denial of parliamentary sovereignty in Canada is nothing new. Dicey himself thought the same thing. He devoted his Fourth Lecture to contrasting, as starkly as night and day, Britain's regime of parliamentary sovereignty with regimes based on federalism. Federalism, explained Dicey, sets out to fracture and disperse legislative sovereignty among co-ordinate bodies. The inevitable consequence is for institutional supremacy to shift from the legislative branch to the judiciary. Canada's foundational text (the *British North America Act, 1867,* an imperial statute now known as the *Constitution Act, 1867*), having borrowed from the American system, was misleading in its preamble to pretend to aspire to 'a Constitution similar in Principle to that of the United Kingdom'. As far as Dicey was concerned, Confederation had achieved nothing of the sort, not because Canada remained a British colony after 1867 but because of its federal character.

Canadian writers took energetic exception.[7] They observed that our constitutional provisions were fully intended to operate in accordance with conventions of responsible government derived from British experience. If the phenomenon of parliamentary sovereignty happened to form part and parcel of that same experience, so much the better. Canadians would take a double helping—one for each order of government. By the time Dicey published his lectures it was too late to persuade Canadians otherwise. In 1878 Ontario's Attorney General and Premier, Oliver Mowat, appeared at the first constitutional case to be heard by the new Supreme Court of Canada. He trumpeted on behalf of his province that '[w]here there is jurisdiction the will of the Legislature is omnipotent according to British theory, and knows no superior law in the sense in which the American Courts are accustomed to adjudicate upon constitutional questions'.[8]

By 1883 the Judicial Committee of the Privy Council had bought into CVPS with enthusiasm. It portrayed provincial legislative authority to be 'as plenary and as ample within the limits prescribed by sec. 92 as the Imperial Parliament in the plenitude of its power possessed and could bestow'.[9] Lefroy's text, *The Law of Legislative Power in Canada*, painstakingly refuted Dicey's comment about Canada. Lefroy stressed the exhaustiveness with which all matters within the ambit of the country's internal affairs

[7] R.C.B. Risk, 'Constitutional Scholarship in the Late Nineteenth Century: Making Federalism Work' (1996) 46 *University of Toronto Law Journal* 427, at 433.
[8] *Severn v The Queen* (1878) 2 SCR 70, 81.
[9] *Hodge v The Queen* (1883) 9 App Cas 117, 132.

were distributed between the Dominion Parliament and the provincial legislatures. Unlike the American arrangements, our distribution was unmarked by special reservations. Nor did our Constitution play one branch of government against another. The result left each legislative body, in Lefroy's words, supreme in its own domain.[10]

CVPS would manage to surmount another impediment. Under sections 55–57 of the *Constitution Act, 1867*, the UK government could instruct Canada's Governor General to withhold royal assent to a bill, and could also disallow recently enacted federal legislation. The same intrusive features were replicated internally by section 90, enabling the federal government to disallow provincial legislation that it did not care for. These formidable fetters on sovereignty remain on the books to this day, but the will to exercise them atrophied long ago. The best explanation is that in Westminster political culture it simply did not feel right to treat elected legislative bodies, which the theory of responsible government places at the apex of political authority, as other than sovereign within their spheres.

There is a long-forgotten cause célèbre—the Cobalt Lake Controversy—that bears retelling. In 1906 the Ontario government refused to allow the Florence Mining Company to record a spectacular mineral discovery under the bed of Cobalt Lake. The government maintained that the lakebed had been withdrawn from exploration months earlier, and that subsequent orders in council, which had imposed and then reversed a more extensive withdrawal, continued to leave the lakebed off-limits. But no sooner did the government refuse Florence than it turned around and sold the lakebed to another mining consortium for the princely sum of a million dollars. Florence challenged the rival's land patent in the courts. Rather than allowing the lawsuit to run its course, the legislature rushed through a statute (S.O. 1907, c.15,) to validate the land patent and to confirm the purchasers' rights, 'freed from all claims and demands of every nature whatsoever in respect of or arising from any discovery, location or staking'. All the way up to the Judicial Committee of the Privy Council Florence begged the courts to disregard the draconian statute and decide its case on the merits. To no avail. Justice Riddell of the Ontario High Court offered a memorably acerbic salute to legislative sovereignty, which the Supreme Court of Canada still likes to reiterate once in a while:

> In short, the legislature, within its jurisdiction, can do everything that is not naturally impossible, and is restrained by no rule, human or divine. If it be that the plaintiffs acquired any rights—which I am far from finding—the legislature has the power to take them away. The prohibition 'Thou shalt not steal' has no legal force upon the sovereign body, and there would be no necessity for compensation to be given—we have no such restriction upon the power of the legislature as is found in some states.[11]

Florence was not ready to give up. It went on to petition the federal government to disallow the provincial law. But Ottawa declined. The Minister of Justice acknowledged

---

[10] A.H.F. Lefroy, *The Law of Legislative Power in Canada* (Toronto Law Book, 1898), lxiii.

[11] *Florence Mining Co. v Cobalt Lake Mining Co.* (1908) 18 OLR 275, 279, aff'd (1909), 43 OLR 474 (CA), aff'd [1911] 2 AC 412. See also *Authorson v Canada (Attorney General)*, 2003 SCC 39 [53].

to the House of Commons that in previous decades the government would not have flinched from coming to the rescue, but its philosophy had evolved profoundly in recent years: 'Every provincial legislature, within the limits prescribed for it by the terms of the British North America Act, is and ought to be supreme. I believe that this is a principle of greater importance to the welfare of this Dominion as a whole than even the sacredness of private rights or of property ownership.'[12]

The high profile of the affair prompted the Toronto *Sun* to contact the world's pre-eminent authority on parliamentary sovereignty, Professor Dicey. The learned scholar obligingly responded to several questions.[13] Dicey opined that provincial legislative jurisdiction included the ability to deprive individuals of their property without compensation. He also considered that the legislature could validly stay a court action for the enforcement of acquired rights. On the other hand, he contended that the federal disallowance power should be treated as being available to cure injustices such as the Cobalt Lake affair whether the provincial legislature was acting within its jurisdiction or not.

The moral of the story is that Canadians had managed to take parliamentary sovereignty more seriously than Professor Dicey himself, which is no mean feat. Nowadays it would never occur to anyone oppressed by provincial legislation to petition the federal government for disallowance. The Supreme Court teaches instead that '[t]he Canadian federation rests on the organizing principle that the orders of government are coordinate and not subordinate one to the other.'[14] One of the incidental by-products of the immensely successful drive by provinces for coordinate status in Canadian constitutional culture has been that parliamentary sovereignty went along for the ride.

B. Did Everything Change in 1982?

There is a modern variant of Russell's short answer. It runs to the effect that parliamentary sovereignty used to exist in Canada, but it was replaced in 1982 by something much better—or, depending on one's perspective—by something not nearly as good:

> When the *Charter* was introduced, Canada went, in the words of former Chief Justice Brian Dickson, from a system of Parliamentary supremacy to constitutional supremacy ("Keynote Address", in *The Cambridge Lectures 1985* (1985), at pp. 3–4).[15]

Supporters of this diagnosis point to the open-textured rights provisions in Parts I (*Canadian Charter of Rights and Freedoms*) and II (*Rights of the Aboriginal Peoples of Canada*) of the *Constitution Act, 1982*, together with the supremacy clause in subsection

---

[12] Canada, Parliament, *House of Commons Debates*, 1 March 1909, p 1754.
[13] Reprinted (1909), 45 *Canada Law Journal* 457, under the caption 'Unjust and Impolitic Provincial Legislation and Its Disallowance by the Governor General. Opinion of Professor Dicey'.
[14] *Reference re Securities Act*, 2011 SCC 66 [71].
[15] *Vriend v Alberta*, [1998] 1 SCR 493, at [131].

52(1). It declares that 'The Constitution of Canada is the supreme law of Canada, and any law that is inconsistent with the provisions of the Constitution is, to the extent of the inconsistency, of no force or effect'. Pressures for social change that would previously have had to play out through the mobilization of legislative support are now channeled into litigation seeking the invalidation of statutes or their judicial modification by way of "reading in". Confronted with the prospect of a major augmentation in their institutional role, Canadian courts rose to the occasion. Once the *Charter* arrived, it did not take long for the Supreme Court to shed the image of quietism that had dogged its record under the 1960 *Canadian Bill of Rights,* a federal statute discussed further on. For instance, the Court ruled that the word 'detention', as a trigger for the right to counsel, deserved a markedly broader interpretation under the *Charter* than the Court had assigned to the same word a few years earlier in virtually the same context under the *Bill of Rights.*[16]

Nevertheless, early predictions that constitutional supremacy would obliterate CVPS have had to become more nuanced as the jurisprudence evolves and as constitutional remedies become increasingly sophisticated. The high-water mark of the impulse towards constitutional supremacism has arguably passed. It crested in the late 1990s with a pair of remarkable Supreme Court judgments—the 1997 *Provincial Judges Reference* and the 1998 *Secession Reference.* As mentioned, Canadians were accustomed from the start to the idea of invalidating legislation for inconsistency with constitutional provisions. As well, there had been the occasional judicial rumination about the inability of either Parliament or a provincial legislature to enact statutes that would substantially interfere with the operation of Canada's basic constitutional structure by suppressing the public discussion on which democratic institutions depend.[17] But these ruminations had seldom occupied centre stage. What the two judgments seemed to portend was the discomfiting (or, depending on one's perspective, the welcome) prospect of statutes being struck down for failing to measure up to an open-ended assortment of judicially discerned and applied unwritten constitutional principles, including judicial independence, federalism, the protection of minorities, democracy, constitutionalism, and the rule of law.[18]

In the heady aftermath of the two judgments,[19] litigants offered to add to the list of unwritten principles, or to propose additional facets of the Rule of Law by which to question legislative validity. To give one example, courts were invited to discern an implicit constitutional guarantee of reasonable autonomy to shelter local school boards from the threat of statutory elimination of their delegated powers to raise and spend

---

[16] *R. v Therens,* [1985] 1 SCR 613.

[17] *OPSEU v Ontario (Attorney General),* [1987] 2 SCR 2.

[18] *Reference re Remuneration of Judges of the Provincial Court of Prince Edward Island,* [1997] 3 SCR 3; *Reference re Secession of Quebec,* [1998] 2 SCR 217.

[19] For citations to the abundant academic commentary on the judgments and the role of unwritten principles, see V. Kazmierski, 'Draconian but Not Despotic: The "Unwritten" Limits of Parliamentary Sovereignty in Canada" (2010), 41 *Ottawa Law Review* 245, 248 (footnote 4), 250 (footnote 12).

revenues.[20] To give another, and although Canada has no counterpart to the American Constitution's Contracts Clause or to its Takings Clause (property rights have been left out of the *Charter*), Canadian judges were urged to look to the rule of law for all the constitutional authority they would need in order to get rid of a statute that unjustifiably repudiated a government's contractual obligations.[21]

But thanks in large measure to two timely intermediate appeal court decisions reviewed below, Canadian judges managed to find a way into the post-1982 landscape along a path they were accustomed to traveling.

C. Traveling along Two Paths

In a 1999 judgment the Saskatchewan Court of Appeal refuted the proposition, to which a trial judge had subscribed, that the Rule of Law could prevent a legislature from arbitrarily freeing a government from its legal obligations. In a passage Dicey would have admired, Justice Wakeling wrote that:

> The protection we treasure as a democratic country with the rule of law as 'a fundamental postulate' of our constitution is twofold. Protection is provided by our courts against arbitrary and unlawful actions by officials while protection against arbitrary legislation is provided by the democratic process of calling our legislators into regular periods of accountability through the ballot box. This concept of the rule of law is not in any way restricted by the Supreme Court's statement that nobody including governments is beyond the law. That statement is a reference to the law as it exists from time to time and does not create a restriction on Parliament's right to make laws, but is only a recognition that when they are made they are then applicable to all, including governments.[22]

The next year, the Federal Court of Appeal dismissed a challenge to a provision of the *Canada Evidence Act*. Section 39 of the *Act* protects Cabinet confidentiality by shielding an extensive catalogue of government documents from compulsory disclosure in judicial and administrative proceedings. In its single-minded pursuit of this concern, section 39 displaces the common law approach by eliminating the ability of judges to balance the public interest in disclosure against the public interest in maintaining secrecy. Nor do judges get to examine a certified document in order to ascertain for themselves that it falls within the statutory description. The litigants accused the legislation of violating the separation of powers, the rule of law, and the independence of the judiciary. But they identified no particular constitutional provision that it contravened. In forceful reasons, Justice Strayer confronted head-on the widely circulating perception that

---

[20] *Public School Boards' Assn. of Alberta v Alberta (Attorney General)*, [2000] 2 SCR 409.
[21] *Bacon v Saskatchewan Crop Insurance Corporation* (1990), 180 Sask R 20 (Sask CA).
[22] *Bacon*, ibid, at [30].

Canada's constitutional regime had been radically transformed in 1982. He pointed out that in declaring legislation to be of no force or effect to the extent of its inconsistency with the provisions of the Constitution, section 52 was doing no more than what section 2 of the *Colonial Laws Validity Act*, and section 7 of the *Statute of Westminster, 1931*, had been doing all along. 'Both before and after 1982 our system was and is one of parliamentary sovereignty exercisable within the limits of a written constitution.'[23]

The Supreme Court appeared to endorse that line of reasoning in 2005. In the *Imperial Tobacco* case, the Court rebuffed several rule of law arguments advanced by tobacco companies against a novel fiscal recovery scheme. The scheme applied uniquely to tobacco-related health care costs historically incurred by the government. The companies claimed that instead of establishing rules of general application, the legislation arbitrarily singled them out as targets, that it subjected them to a previously unknown form of civil liability on a retroactive basis, and that it required courts to follow special evidentiary and causation rules that tilted unfairly in favour of the claimant government. According to the Court, the existing jurisprudence that spoke of the rule of law as a constraint on government action had been thinking primarily about the executive and judicial branches. 'Actions of the legislative branch are constrained too, but only in the sense that they must comply with legislated requirements as to manner and form (i.e., the procedures by which legislation is to be enacted, amended and repealed).' The Court observed that some academic writings would like to take the rule of law proposition much further, but it detected no clear consensus among the writers. As far as this case was concerned, the bottom line was that '[t]he rule of law is not an invitation to trivialize or supplant the Constitution's written terms. Nor is it a tool by which to avoid legislative initiatives of which one is not in favour. On the contrary, it requires that courts give effect to the Constitution's text, and apply, by whatever its terms, legislation that conforms to that text.'[24]

Despite the definitive tone that permeates *Imperial Tobacco*, the Court has since taken pains to clear a second path for itself, along which it is prepared, if need be, to deploy unwritten principles as normative controls over legislation. In addition, there is an overt recognition that the Court's appreciation of the Constitution's internal architecture—its sense of 'the assumptions that underlie the text'—can exert strong effects upon its textual interpretations.[25] This is most apparent in cases that implicate its vision of judicial independence, or where it sees fit to repel measures that would impermissibly choke off access to the courts or otherwise impair the core of the judicial mission.

A few weeks after the Supreme Court released its decision in *Imperial Tobacco*, the British Columbia Court of Appeal heard the *Christie* case. At issue in *Christie* was a 7 percent provincial tax on the provision of legal services. The plaintiff claimed that the application of the tax to impoverished clients was unconstitutional because the rule of law entails the right to representation by counsel in legal proceedings. Justice Southin,

---

[23] *Singh v Canada (Attorney General)*, [2000] 2 FCR 185 (FCA).
[24] *British Columbia v Imperial Tobacco Canada Ltd.*, 2005 SCC 49.
[25] *Trial Lawyers Association of BC v British Columbia (Attorney General)*, 2014 SCC 59, [24]–[27].

dissenting, would have dismissed the claim. In her view the controlling issue should be framed as follows: 'Has this or any court in Canada the power to hold a statute, which falls within the enacting authority's legislative mandate under the *Constitution Acts*, s. 91 or s. 92, as the case may be, does not infringe upon any other section of the *Constitution Act* (e.g. s. 96), and is not in breach of the express terms of the *Canadian Charter of Rights and Freedoms*, to be of no force and effect?' It was clear to her that in light of *Imperial Tobacco* the answer had to be no.

On further appeal, the Supreme Court did indeed dismiss the claim, but it chose a very different path to that same result. It reasoned that general access to legal services was not *currently* a recognized aspect of the rule of law. But that did not end the matter because 'in *Imperial Tobacco*, this Court left open the possibility that the rule of law may include additional principles'. If the claim failed here it was because, 'on the material presented in the case', the Court was left unpersuaded of a universal constitutional entitlement to legal representation in legal proceedings. The absence of such an entitlement among the written provisions of the Constitution was not portrayed as fatal in itself.[26]

More recently, the Court struck down a scheme of escalating hearing fees for litigants engaged in multi-day civil trials in a provincial superior court.[27] This time, it found that a constitutional provision was being infringed. Section 96 of the *Constitution Act, 1867*, provides for the judges of provincial superior courts to be appointed by the Governor General, who acts on advice from the federal government. Despite its straightforward function, the provision boasts an elaborate interpretive history in which it has served as a brake on the exercise of legislative power. There were precedents invalidating provincial laws that sought to transfer, to provincially-appointed courts or tribunals, judicial powers and functions that belonged at Confederation exclusively to the superior courts. The section had also provided an antidote against provincial (and potentially, federal) privative clauses that tried to shelter statutory decision makers from jurisdictional review by superior courts. The Court drew on that history and concluded that by necessary implication section 96 required the Province to go back to the drawing board and build into its fee structure a broad discretionary power allowing a judge to dispense any litigant to whom, in the judge's opinion, the fees would represent an undue hardship. Significantly, the majority judgment did not stop there. It went on to explain how the connection between section 96 and access to justice is further supported by considerations relating to the rule of law. This signal lines up precisely with a qualification planted years earlier in another unwritten principles case: 'It is well within the power of the legislature to enact laws, even laws which some would consider draconian, as long as it does not fundamentally alter or interfere with the relationship between the courts and the other branches of government'.[28]

Finally, the relationship between CVPS and section 35 (aboriginal and treaty rights) of the *Constitution Act, 1982*, remains to be fully worked out. Rights claims tended at

---

[26] *British Columbia (Attorney General) v Christie*, 2007 SCC 21, rev'g 205 BCCA 631.

[27] *Trial Lawyers Association of BC v British Columbia (Attorney General)*, 2014 SCC 59.

[28] *Babcock v Canada (Attorney General)*, 2002 SCC 57 at [57].

first to be raised by way of defence to enforcement proceedings initiated under generally worded statutes regulating resource harvesting (fisheries legislation or hunting or forestry laws). A successful claim would not usually be accompanied by a declaration of statutory invalidity, but would instead resemble a constitutional exemption for a particular class of rights holders in relation to certain activities in certain places. This matches the highly particularistic nature that the case law attributes to section 35 rights. One interesting issue involves the emerging jurisprudence on 'the Crown's duty to consult'. The Supreme Court delineated the duty in order to protect asserted section 35 rights whose existence and scope have yet to be authoritatively adjudicated at the time when a government contemplates a course of conduct that could adversely affect the interests at stake. How, if at all, might this duty be judicially enforceable in the context of the legislative process? Will parliamentary sovereignty 'flow upstream' in this special context as well? That is to say, will ministers, whose discharge of the duty to consult would elicit judicial supervision in many other contexts, be exempted from judicial review when acting in a legislative capacity, thanks to the concept of parliamentary sovereignty? The Supreme Court has so far left the question open,[29] but it is an issue of recurring interest.[30]

To sum up, Canadian judges have two paths available in dealing with CVPS. The older path acknowledges legislative sovereignty within limits set by constitutional provisions. The other path may render statutory validity contingent on a broader range of cues. It tends most likely to be followed if and when the judicial role itself is seen to be at stake. The two paths might someday merge. CVPS, as an unwritten constitutional principle in its own right, could become absorbed into a mix of unwritten principles where it could serve as an internal counterweight. As a Federal Court judge wrote in 2013, 'while the parameters of the unwritten principles of the Constitution remain undefined, they must be balanced against the concept of Parliamentary sovereignty which is also a component of the rule of law'.[31]

3. THE RIGHT TO UNMAKE ANY LAW— STATUTORY ENTRENCHMENT

Imperial Tobacco's passing reference to 'manner and form' as a constraint on legislation raises an issue that resonates across many Commonwealth jurisdictions. Can statutes

---

[29]   *Rio Tinto Alcan Inc. v Carrier Sekani Tribal Council*, 2010 SCC 43, [44].

[30]   *Chief Steve Courtoreille and Mikisew Cree First Nation v Governor General in Council*, 2016 FCA 311; submissions on application for leave to appeal to the Supreme Court of Canada completed on March 20, 2017 (docket 37441).

[31]   *Tabingo v Canada (Citizenship and Immigration)*, 2013 FC 377, aff'd 2014 FCA 191, at [52]. See also *Babcock v Canada (Attorney General)*, 2002 SCC 57, at [54]–[57].

speak authoritatively to their own subsequent amendment or repeal? Dicey had quoted approvingly from a respected Canadian author, Alpheus Todd:

> It is certain that a Parliament cannot so bind its successors by the terms of any statute, as to limit the discretion of a future Parliament, and thereby disable the Legislature from entire freedom of action at any future time when it might be needful to invoke the interposition of Parliament to legislate for the public welfare.[32]

Todd's view was not original. Blackstone had written generations earlier that 'Acts of parliament derogatory from the power of subsequent parliaments bind not'. The hard-line version of *continuing* parliamentary sovereignty predicts that a future Parliament can simply ignore any pre-conditions or constraints that an earlier statute attempts to place in the way of amendment or repeal. When Parliament legislates inconsistently with an existing enactment, courts normally infer that it must have intended to 'implicitly repeal' it to the extent necessary to give effect to the intention embodied in the new statute. The idea is succinctly conveyed in a modern American judgment: 'Among the powers of a legislature that a prior legislature cannot abridge is, of course, the power to make its will known in whatever fashion it deems appropriate—including the repeal of pre-existing provisions by simply and clearly contradicting them.'[33]

But contemporary Commonwealth jurists now tend to accept a newer view that conceives of sovereignty as *self-embracing* to some significant degree. Like the older understanding, it concedes that one Parliament should be unable to place the *substance* of its policy choices beyond the reach of its successors, but it considers that nothing prevents Parliament from changing the *procedural* rules associated with the lawmaking process, rules that courts follow in order to recognize duly enacted legislation.[34] The 1932 *Trethowan* case from New South Wales provides a key example. A bicameral legislature enacted a statute establishing a referendum requirement as a pre-condition to statutory abolition of the upper chamber. The referendum requirement was *doubly entrenched* (that is to say, self-referencing); it decreed that it could not be removed without a referendum approving its removal. The legal effectiveness of the technique was upheld in the courts.[35] In 2005, the House of Lords accepted in *Jackson* that the UK Parliament could fashion an alternative primary lawmaking process, such that (1) statutes could validly be enacted by a procedure that did not require passage of a bill in the House of Lords, and (2) a statute enacted in that special manner could further modify the applicable rules. The situation was deemed not to be akin to that of a delegate or creature of statute that,

[32] A Todd, (1880), *Parliamentary Government in the British Colonies*, 192, cited in Dicey, *Introduction to the Study of the Law of the Constitution* (9th edn, Macmillan, 1948), 67–68.

[33] *Lockhart v. United States*, 546 U.S.142, 148 (2005). For the links between parliamentary sovereignty and the unmistakability doctrine, see *United States v. Winstar Corp.*, 518 U.S. 839, 871–880 (1996).

[34] Peter W. Hogg, *Constitutional Law of Canada,* loose-leaf vol 1, chapter 12.3 ('Self-imposed restraints on legislative power').

[35] *Attorney-General for New South Wales v Trethowan*, [1932] A.C. 526.

except for the clearest of language, must be denied the capacity to unilaterally expand the boundaries of its own jurisdiction.[36]

Canadian courts have also accepted the effectiveness of statutory manner and form requirements, but only in special contexts. In *Mercure*, the Supreme Court determined that statutes of the Province of Saskatchewan suffered from wholesale invalidity. For generations, the Province had failed to adhere to a statutory requirement to publish its laws in French as well as English. The Court acknowledged that the requirement was not constitutionally entrenched in the usual sense. It lay within reach of the legislature to alter or eliminate by statute. But the Court refused to regularize the existing discrepancy on the basis of the doctrine of implied repeal. If the legislature wanted to put an end to the requirement, it could do so, but a repealing statute would have to be enacted and published in both official languages.[37]

A successful challenge under the 1960 *Canadian Bill of Rights* has also been portrayed—at least, in a later judgment—as another manner and form case.[38] In addition, it has now become commonplace for Canadian courts to speak of the *quasi-constitutional* status of human rights (anti-discrimination) legislation. When ordinary statutes collide, there are rules of interpretation for allocating precedence. The more recent trumps the older, except that the more specific will survive the more general. But not so where a human rights statute is involved.

> Human rights legislation is of a special nature and declares public policy regarding matters of general concern. It is not constitutional in nature in the sense that it may not be altered, amended, or repealed by the Legislature. It is, however, of such nature that it may not be altered, amended, or repealed, nor may exceptions be created to its provisions, save by clear legislative pronouncement. To adopt and apply any theory of implied repeal by later statutory enactment to legislation of this kind would be to rob it of its special nature and give scant protection to the rights it proclaims.[39]

Writers who have tried to identify a basis on which the *Canadian Bill of Rights* could prevail over future inconsistent statutes have tended to fall back on manner and form theory.[40] And yet, a largely unnoticed comment by the government official who drafted

---

[36] *R. (Jackson) v Attorney General* [2005] UKHL 56. Baroness Hale, [163], identifies the potential significance of the judgment. If a sovereign Parliament can redefine itself 'downwards' (by eliminating the requirement for passage of a bill in the House of Lords), why can it not redefine itself 'upwards' (by imposing a procedural hurdle such as a special majority vote, or a referendum requirement, as a precondition to amending or repealing a given statute)?

[37] *R. v Mercure*, [1988] 1 SCR 234.

[38] *Reference re Canada Assistance Plan*, [1991] 2 SCR 525, described *R v Drybones*, [1970] SCR 282, as a manner and form case.

[39] *Winnipeg School Division No. 1 v Craton*, [1985] 2 SCR 150; *Canada (Attorney General) v Druken*, [1989] 2 FC. 24 (FCA); *Gwinner v Alberta (Human Resources and Employment)*, 2002 ABQB 685.

[40] B. Strayer, *The Canadian Constitution and the Courts* (3rd edn, Butterworths, 1988) 44; P.W. Hogg, *Constitutional Law of Canada* (looseleaf vol 2, 5th ed. Carswell, 2007) chapter 35.3(c), ('Effect on later statutes').

the *Bill* seems to question whether it is necessary to resort to full rigour and severity of manner and form logic. The *Canadian Bill of Rights* does not expressly provide that future inconsistent statutes are not genuine statutes, or that they lack the force of law. What it does provide is that: 'Every law of Canada shall, unless it is expressly declared by an Act of the Parliament of Canada that it shall operate notwithstanding the Canadian Bill of Rights, be so construed and applied as not to abrogate . . . any of the rights or freedoms herein recognized and declared. . .' It also confirms that the expression 'law of Canada' is meant to include legislation enacted after the *Bill* itself. Writing many years after its enactment, Elmer Driedger lamented the emphasis that had been placed on its status as an ordinary statute and the associated lack of credentials by which to invalidate, or as some have put it, to 'render inoperative', inconsistent legislation. He felt that this exaggerated concern over the fate of the other statute was misplaced. Courts regularly use interpretive rules to resolve inconsistencies among statutes. Such interpretive exercises do not culminate in a declaration that the losing statute is invalid or inoperative. It maintains its validity although it gives way to the more recent or to the more specific, as the case may be, in circumstances where both statutes cannot simultaneously have their way. Driedger wrote that 'in the event of an apparent conflict between the Bill and another statute, the courts must go through exactly the same process they have always gone through in dealing with a conflict between two statutes, but with the important difference that this time the Bill of Rights stands firm and it is the other statute that must give way.'[41] Such a rule of interpretation is admittedly more demanding than most. It establishes a presumption that can only be rebutted expressly and not by necessary implication. However, the *Canadian Bill of Rights* concedes to future Parliaments the ability to derogate—all that they must do in order to displace the presumption is to use the 'notwithstanding' formula. And the *Bill* refrains from any attempt at insulating itself from repeal or amendment—it did not try to doubly entrench itself. According to Driedger, it should not have been seen as a threat to CVPS, and there was no need to give it a stingy reading.

   Except in contexts imbued with a constitutional flavour such as those above, Canadian judges strive against finding that statutory provisions are intended to produce entrenching effects. The federal *Interpretation Act* reinforces their predisposition when it provides that 'Every Act shall be so construed as to reserve to Parliament the power of repealing or amending it'. The *Canada Assistance Plan Reference* remains the leading case, but there are others. In 1999, the Ontario *Taxpayer Protection Act* imposed a referendum requirement on the introduction of any new tax or tax increase. Over time, fiscally hungry governments discovered that they did not want to trouble taxpayers with a referendum, but neither did they want to be branded as irresponsible for repealing the statute. They devised a two-step manoeuvre to circumvent the problem. First came an amendment enacting a one-time exemption for the particular tax measure the

---

[41] E.A. Driedger, "Meaning and Effect of the Canadian Bill of Rights: A Draftsman's Viewpoint" (1977) 9 *Ottawa Law Review* 303, 309.

government had in mind. Once the exemption was in place, along came a second bill introducing the referendum-exempt tax measure. Canadian courts often counsel legislators not to attempt to do indirectly that which they cannot do directly. However, this two-step modus operandi encountered no difficulty when it was challenged in an Ontario court.[42] The Court gave the referendum requirement a narrow reading. The statute may have insisted that new taxes be preceded by a referendum, but for whatever reason it had omitted to say anything about new exemptions. Nor did a subsequent challenge to a similar statute fare any better in neighbouring Manitoba.[43]

There is yet another Canadian case which suggests that statutory provisions will attract a particularly hostile reading if they are seen as intending to place a veto over future amendments into the hands of any group other than the entire electorate. Section 47.1 of the former *Canadian Wheat Board Act* purported to require a favourable vote among affected grain producers before the government could introduce a bill that would add or subtract a particular grain (such as wheat, barley, oats, or canola) from a compulsory marketing scheme commonly known as the Single Desk. The Federal Court of Appeal held that a bill to dismantle the Single Desk in its entirety, unlike a bill to withdraw a particular grain, was not caught by the requirement. The Court suggested in obiter that had it found otherwise, it would have been inclined to treat section 47.1 as an ineffective attempt at substantive entrenchment rather than a bona fide manner and form criterion.[44]

It can occasionally happen that constitutional provisions have the effect of rendering statutes easier to enact than to repeal. For example, Parliament can enact a statute providing force of law to a self-government agreement that describes the lawmaking powers available to an indigenous community government. If the parties so intend, the agreement can benefit from constitutional protection as a treaty pursuant to section 35 of the *Constitution Act, 1982*. In such a case, Parliament's subsequent ability to modify, undo, or otherwise override the implementing legislation in the future would be contingent on being able to justify the rights-infringing effects to the satisfaction of the courts.[45] Another example involves the Supreme Court of Canada. It owes its existence and its composition to federal statutes enacted pursuant to section 101 of the *Constitution Act, 1867*. Section 101 authorizes Parliament to provide for the constitution, maintenance, and organization of a general court of appeal for Canada. But because the composition of the Court was included in 1982 among a list of matters in relation to which constitutional amendments require unanimity among all provinces as well as

---

[42] *Canadian Taxpayers Federation v Ontario (Minister of Finance)* (2004) 73 OR (3d) 621 (ON SC). The stakes would have been higher if the referendum requirement had been doubly entrenched.

[43] *Progressive Conservative Party of Manitoba v Government of Manitoba*, 2014 MBQB 155.

[44] *Canada (Attorney General) v Friends of the Canadian Wheat Board*, 2012 FCA 183, [82]–[87]. See also *Oberg v Canada (Attorney General)*, 2012 MBQB 64 at [9]–[24].

[45] *Sga'nism Sim'augit (Chief Mountain) v Canada (Attorney General)*, 2013 BCCA 49.

Ottawa, Parliament is no longer in a position to unilaterally amend its own statute in respect of the Court's composition.[46]

4. WHO CAN DECIDE THAT A STATUTE IS INVALID?

Dicey made it a point of pride to say there was no forum in which the validity of an English statute could be disputed. As we know, this never held true for Canada. What remains to ask is whether, in addition to courts, there are other official bodies that Canadian law acknowledges as competent to determine a statute's validity.

The prevailing view in the United States is that administrative agencies are in no position to entertain facial challenges to statutes. 'An agency is not authorized to consider or question the constitutionality of a legislative act; nor may it declare unconstitutional statutes which it was created to administer and enforce.'[47] In Canada it is a very different story.

The early *Charter* years saw the topic debated in law journals, and inconsistent judgments emerge among the lower courts. When a trilogy of cases reached the Supreme Court in the early 1990s, the Court opted in favour of administrative tribunals treating questions of constitutional invalidity basically like any other legal questions they might encounter and have to resolve in discharging their statutory functions. In the 1996 *Cooper* case, the Court seemed to harbour second thoughts about whether it was quite as simple as that. It is difficult to tell whether the majority wanted to fine-tune the trilogy or to back away from it. In any event, the majority reasons were flanked on either side by minority judgments pointing in diametrically opposite directions. Chief Justice Lamer, writing for himself alone, set out a position premised on an unusually strong vision—for Canada—of the separation of powers. He considered that the historic relationship between Parliament and the Executive would be stood on its head if Executive-branch tribunals could disregard statutes according to their own appreciation of what the Constitution called for. Only the judicial branch could make constitutional determinations of statutory invalidity. As far as he was concerned, Parliament could not authorize a different arrangement even if it wanted to. An entirely different vision animated the reasons of Justice McLachlin (as she then was), with whom Justice L'Heureux-Dubé agreed:

> The *Charter* is not some holy grail which only judicial initiates of the superior courts may touch. The *Charter* belongs to the people. All law and law-makers that touch the

[46] *Reference re Supreme Court Act, ss. 5 and 6*, 2014 SCC 21.
[47] *Richardson v Tennessee Bd. of Dentistry*, 913 S.W.2d 446 (Tenn. 1995). See also Marykay Foy, "The Authority of an Administrative Agency to Decide Constitutional Questions: *Richardson v. Tennesee Board of Dentistry*" (1997) 17 *Journal of the National Association of Administrative Law Judges* 173.

people must conform to it. Tribunals and commissions charged with deciding legal issues are no exception. Many more citizens have their rights determined by these tribunals than by the courts. If the *Charter* is to be meaningful to ordinary people, then it must find its expression in the decisions of these tribunals.[48]

In subsequent cases that vision would prevail. The Court agreed unanimously in 2003 in *Martin* that '[t]he question of constitutional validity inheres in every legislative enactment by virtue of s. 52(1) of the *Constitution Act, 1982*.'[49] Simply put, judges don't invalidate statutes, nor do tribunal members. The Constitution does.

The case law acknowledges that it is possible for legislation to curtail the ability of statutory tribunals to engage in constitutional adjudication. However, it would have to overcome a strong presumption to the contrary. In the last resort it is said to boil down to a matter of statutory intent. In its 2010 *Conway* judgment, the Court wrote that 'administrative tribunals with the power to decide questions of law, and from whom constitutional jurisdiction has not been clearly withdrawn, have the authority to resolve constitutional questions that are linked to matters properly before them'.[50]

But what if a matter could only be *properly before the tribunal* if the tribunal were to disregard a statutory provision designed to withhold that very matter from its mandate? Some provincial jurisdictions have adopted legislation identifying those tribunals that can determine constitutional challenges and those tribunals that cannot. The day may come when an applicant approaches an excluded tribunal and asserts that the statutory exclusion is unconstitutional and must be ignored. If this sounds far-fetched, consider *Cuddy Chicks*.[51] In *Cuddy Chicks*, provincial legislation had established a labour board to administer a collective bargaining regime. The board was endowed with jurisdiction 'to determine all questions of fact or law that arise in any matter before it'. The legislation also stipulated that the regime did not apply 'to a person employed in agriculture.' A group of agricultural workers sought certification as a bargaining unit, and urged the board to ignore the stipulation as an invalid infringement of their *Charter* rights. The Supreme Court ruled that the board could determine the constitutional challenge. If it decided that the statutory obstacle was invalid, the labour board could presumably go on to entertain the certification application. It requires an unusually strong interpretive presumption to conclude that a sovereign legislature which chose to explicitly subtract a particular industry from a collective bargaining regime would implicitly intend to see

---

[48] *Cooper v Canada (Human Rights Commission)*, [1996] 3 SCR 854, at [70].
[49] *Nova Scotia (Workers' Compensation Board) v Martin*, 2003 SCC 54.
[50] *R v Conway*, 2010 SCC 22, at [78] (emphasis added).
[51] *Cuddy Chicks Ltd. v Ontario (Labour Relations Board)*, [1991] 2 SCR 5. The Court upheld the ability of a statutory tribunal to question—and potentially to disregard—a statutory limit on the scope of the program which the tribunal administered, if the tribunal considered the limit to be unconstitutional.

that choice second-guessed by an entity that it brought into being for the more convenient administration of that regime.

In some post-*Martin* cases the lower courts have taken a more balanced approach. In *Ferri*,[52] the Federal Court held that where Parliament enacts a jurisdiction-limiting provision which places the situation of a would-be appellant beyond an appeal tribunal's jurisdiction, *Martin* does not require or authorize the tribunal to entertain constitutional attacks against the limit. A recent Alberta Court of Appeal decision, in the AUPE case displays a similar penchant.[53] A labour arbitration board had the statutory authority to adjudicate disputes under a collective agreement. The board was expressly endowed with the ability to determine constitutional issues. The relevant collective agreement purported not to apply to certain categories of employees, such as managers, who were prevented by a statutory provision from being included in a bargaining unit. The agreement required the employer to deduct and remit union dues from employees who were in the bargaining unit. The union filed a grievance with the board against the failure to collect dues from excluded employees, on the ground that the statutory provision which excluded them infringed the *Charter*. However, the Court confined the board's ability to entertain constitutional challenges within the four corners of its statutory mandate: 'the essential character of this dispute is not, either expressly or impliedly, about the interpretation, application, administration, or alleged violation of the Collective Agreement. The dispute is about the constitutionality of *PSERA*. Accordingly, the Board did not have jurisdiction to hear the grievance in the first place'.[54] In cases such as the pair mentioned here, the enduring influence of parliamentary sovereignty is quietly at work.

5. CONCLUSION

Comedian Yvon Deschamps once ironically confessed to a paradoxical aspiration: *un Québec libre dans un Canada uni*. The Canadian version of parliamentary sovereignty is not without its paradoxical elements. There is a strong presumption that Parliament intends any statutory actor that can decide questions of law can also decide whether statutory provisions are unconstitutional and should be ignored. But should this presumption apply even to the statutory limits that Parliament places on the actor's jurisdiction and powers? Another paradox lurks beneath the manner and form debate. If we start from the premise that Parliament is sovereign, does it follow more plausibly that Parliament should be able to command itself, or that it should not? If such paradoxes do

---

[52] *Ferri v Canada (Minister of Citizenship & Immigration)* 2005 FC 1580.
[53] *Alberta Union of Provincial Employees v Alberta*, 2014 ABCA 43.
[54] *Alberta Union of Provincial Employees v Alberta*, 2014 ABCA 43, at [25]–[26].

not unduly disturb Canadians, they can thank their long exposure to an implicit paradox within CVPS itself—that there can be plenty of room for parliamentary sovereignty in the Canadian Constitution, provided, of course, that it is exercised within the applicable limits.

BIBLIOGRAPHY

Secondary sources

Driedger, Elmer, 'Meaning and Effect of the Canadian Bill of Rights: A Draftsman's Viewpoint' (1977), 9 *Ottawa Law Review* 303

Elliott, Robin, 'Rethinking Manner and Form: From Parliamentary Sovereignty to Constitutional Values' (1991) 29 *Osgoode Hall Law Journal* 215

Gordon, Michael, 'The UK's Fundamental Constitutional Principle: Why the UK Is Still Sovereign and Why It Still Matters' (2015) 26 *King's Law Journal* 229

Hogg, Peter W. *Constitutional Law of Canada* (5th edition, loose-leaf, Carswell, 2016) chapter 12.3.

Kazmierski, Vincent, 'Draconian but Not Despotic: The "Unwritten" Limits of Parliamentary Sovereignty in Canada' (2010) 41 *Ottawa Law Review* 245

Lovell, John, 'Legislating against the Grain: Parliamentary Sovereignty and Extra-Parliamentary Vetoes' (2008) 24 *National Journal of Constitutional Law* 1

Oliver, Peter C., *The Constitution of Independence: The Development of Constitutional Theory in Australia, Canada, and New Zealand* (Oxford University Press, 2005)

Cases

Alberta Union of Provincial Employees v Alberta 2014 ABCA 43

Babcock v Canada (Attorney General) 2002 SCC 57

Bacon v Saskatchewan Crop Insurance Corporation (1990) 180 Sask R 20 (Sask CA)

British Columbia v Imperial Tobacco Canada Ltd 2005 SCC 49

British Columbia (Attorney General) v Christie 2007 SCC 21

Canada (Attorney General) v Friends of the Canadian Wheat Board 2012 FCA 183

Canadian Taxpayers Federation v Ontario (Minister of Finance) (2004) 73 OR (3d) 621 (ON SC)

Cuddy Chicks Ltd v Ontario (Labour Relations Board) [1991] 2 SCR 5

Ferri v Canada (Minister of Citizenship & Immigration) 2005 FC 1580

Greater Vancouver Regional District v British Columbia (Attorney General) 2011 BCCA 345

Hodge v The Queen (1883) 9 App Cas 117 (PC)

Mikisew Cree First Nation v Governor General in Council 2016 FCA 311

Nova Scotia (Workers' Compensation Board) v Martin [2003] 2 SCR 504

Progressive Conservative Party of Manitoba v Government of Manitoba, 2014 MBQB 155

Public School Boards' Association of Alberta v Alberta (Attorney General) [2000] 2 SCR 409

R v Conway 2010 SCC 22

R v Drybones [1970] SCR 282

R v Mercure [1988] 1 S.C.R. 234

Reference re Canada Assistance Plan [1991] 2 SCR 525

Reference re Remuneration of Judges of the Provincial Court of Prince Edward Island [1997] 3 SCR 3

Reference re Secession of Quebec [1998] 2 SCR 217

Sga'nism Sim'augit (Chief Mountain) v Canada (Attorney General) 2013 BCCA 49

Trial Lawyers Association of BC v British Columbia (Attorney General) 2014 SCC 59

Winnipeg School Division No. 1 v Craton [1985] 2 SCR 150

C. The Courts

CHAPTER 10

....

THE SUPREME COURT OF CANADA AND APPOINTMENT OF JUDGES IN CANADA

....

ADAM DODEK &
ROSEMARY CAIRNS WAY*

1. THE SUPREME COURT OF CANADA

....

A. General

THE Supreme Court of Canada is one of the most important institutions under the Canadian Constitution but paradoxically it is not expressly provided for in the text of the Constitution itself. This is because when Canada was created in 1867, the Fathers of Confederation assumed that appeals to the Judicial Committee of the Privy Council in London would continue. However, they also recognized that not all appeals could go to London and there was a need for a general appellate court in the new Dominion of Canada. Consequently, the *British North America Act, 1867* (renamed the *Constitution Act, 1867* in 1982) empowered the federal Parliament to create 'a general court of appeal for Canada'.[1]

In 1875, the Parliament of Canada, acting pursuant to this power, created the Supreme Court of Canada. The *Supreme Court Act*[2] sets out the composition, jurisdiction, and procedure of the Supreme Court.

---

* Faculty of Law, University of Ottawa.
[1] Constitution Act, 1867, s 101.
[2] RSC 1985, c S-46 [hereinafter Supreme Court Act].

B. Judges

The Supreme Court consists of nine judges: the Chief Justice who is the Chief Justice of Canada and eight 'puisne' judges (from the French for 'junior').[3] Under the *Supreme Court Act*, three of the nine judges must come from Quebec.[4] This is because of that province's distinctive civil law tradition; until 1759, Quebec was a French colony. As discussed in chapter 2, successive constitutions preserved the civil law system that had been in place in Quebec. At present, Quebec is Canada's second most populous province with approximately one quarter of the population. Ontario is by far Canada's largest province with approximately 38 percent of Canada's population. As a result, historically Ontario has also been allotted three seats on the Supreme Court. The remaining three seats are apportioned two to the western provinces (British Columbia, Alberta, Saskatchewan, and Manitoba) and one to the Atlantic provinces (New Brunswick, Nova Scotia, Prince Edward Island, Newfoundland and Labrador).[5]

Over time, other characteristics besides regionalism have become notable. For example, the appointment of the first judge not from either of the two so-called 'founding peoples' of Canada, that is not English or French (the Jewish Bora Laskin in 1970), the first 'ethnic' judge (the Ukrainian John Sopinka in 1988), notable immigrant communities (the Italian-Canadian Frank Iacobucci in 1991 and Greek-Canadian Andromache Karakatsanis in 2011), and the Franco-Ontarian Louise Charron in 2004.

As discussed in more detail later in this chapter, increasingly gender of judicial appointments has become a concern at all levels. The first female Supreme Court judge was appointed in 1982 (Bertha Wilson), coinciding with the enactment of the new *Canadian Charter of Rights and Freedoms*. Between 1982 and 2015, a total of nine women have served on the Supreme Court (Bertha Wilson, Claire L'Heureux-Dubé, Beverley McLachlin, Louise Arbour, Marie Deschamps, Rosalie Silverman Abella, Louise Charron, Andromache Karakatsanis, and Suzanne Côté), peaking between 2004–2011 when four of the nine justices were women, including Chief Justice Beverley McLachlin who became the first female Chief Justice in 2000. In a diverse country such as Canada, there are concerns that as of 2017, there has never been a visible minority or an Aboriginal justice appointed to the Supreme Court, and it may be time to break out of the rigid regionalism that has dominated appointments to the Court since its creation.[6]

In practice, over the past 50 years, almost every justice has been appointed from the highest courts of appeals in the provinces or from the Federal Court of Appeal. For the last 40 years, at least one of the nine sitting justices has been a lawyer appointed directly from practice. Many have had academic or government experience prior to being

---

[3] ibid s 4(1).

[4] ibid s 6.

[5] See Peter W. Hogg, *Constitutional Law of Canada* (5th ed, Carswell, 2007) § 8.3.

[6] Cf Adam Dodek, 'Justin Trudeau's Court: The Force Awakens?' *Policy Options* (5 April 2016), http://policyoptions.irpp.org/magazines/april-2016/justin-trudeaus-court-the-force-awakens/ (last accessed 20 April 2016).

appointed as a justice but none has been appointed to the Supreme Court directly from those positions in many decades.

Under the *Supreme Court Act*, justices hold office 'during good behaviour' and can only be removed by the Governor General on a joint address of the Senate and the House of Commons.[7] This has never happened in the Supreme Court's history. Justices must retire upon reaching the mandatory retirement age of 75.[8] Over the past 30 years, it has become common for Supreme Court justices to resign before mandatory retirement age and take up positions in law firms or academia.

The Supreme Court is located in Ottawa, Canada's capital. Ottawa is Canada's sixth largest city with a population of just over 900,000 for the 'National Capital Region' which consists of greater Ottawa, Ontario, and Gatineau, Quebec. All justices are required to live within 40 kilometres of the National Capital Region.[9] Because of the geographic distribution of Supreme Court seats, almost all potential Supreme Court of Canada justices must relocate to Ottawa.

C. Jurisdiction, Caseload, and Procedure

Until 1949, decisions of the Supreme Court of Canada could be appealed to the Judicial Committee of the Privy Council in London. That year marks the point where the Supreme Court truly became 'supreme' under the Canadian legal system.[10] In 1975, appeals as of right in civil cases were abolished, thus giving the Supreme Court control over most of its docket.[11] Under the *Supreme Court Act*, 'leave' or permission of the Court must be obtained in all cases where there is not an automatic right of appeal or original jurisdiction. Until 1988, there were oral hearings for all leave applications.[12] Since then, all leave applications are generally decided in writing without reasons by a panel of three justices. Every once in a while the Court will order an oral hearing on a leave application.

Approximately 80 percent of the Supreme Court's caseload is by leave and 20 percent as of right cases. Litigants have a right to appeal largely only in certain criminal cases.[13] The Court's original jurisdiction is extremely limited. The federal government has a completely unfettered right to direct a 'reference' to the Supreme Court asking it to provide an advisory opinion on any number of questions that the federal Cabinet submits to it.[14] All provincial governments have similar powers respecting their highest courts of

---

[7] Supreme Court Act, above (n 2) s 9(1).

[8] ibid s 9(2).

[9] ibid s 8.

[10] See Peter McCormick, *Supreme at Last: The Evolution of the Supreme Court of Canada* (Lorimer, 2000) 2; Bora Laskin, 'The Supreme Court of Canada: A Final Court of Appeal of and for Canadians' (1951) 29 *Canadian Bar Review* 1038.

[11] ibid at 82.

[12] See discussion in Henry S. Brown, *Supreme Court Practice* (Carswell, 2016) 113–116.

[13] ibid 5–6.

[14] Supreme Court Act, s 53. See chapter by Professor Carissima Mathen in this *Handbook*.

appeals. The *Supreme Court Act* grants an automatic right of appeal from provincial references to the Supreme Court.[15] The Canadian Senate or House of Commons can direct a reference on a 'private bill', a bill that only affects the interests of a private party and not of the public generally.[16] This jurisdiction has not been invoked in at least the past 50 years and is not likely to be in the foreseeable future.

In practice, many of the most important Canadian constitutional decisions have been references. Although in theory, such cases are not decisions but rather only expressions of the Court's 'opinion', in practice the Supreme Court and the courts below treat references as having the same binding or precedential effect as other decisions.[17] Often such references are regarded as having stronger precedential effect than ordinary decisions precisely because they squarely address important constitutional issues.

Between 2005 and 2015, the Supreme Court heard an average of 74 cases per year—an average of 14.7 appeals as of right and 59 appeals with leave annually.[18] During this period an average of 537 leave-to-appeal applications were filed each year, and leave was granted in approximately 10.7 percent of them.[19]

A minimum of five justices is necessary for a quorum to transact business.[20] Unlike in other high courts, there is no general formal or informal rule that all nine justices sit in all cases. The panel number and composition is set by the Chief Justice. The practice under Chief Justice McLachlin (2000–) has been for all nine justices to sit in the most important cases unless one is unavailable. In such cases, the Court will usually be composed of an odd number to avoid a tie vote (which sustains the decision below). However, during a nine-month period between October 2013 and June 2014 when the Court only had 8 justices, the Court regularly sat in panels of eight. In appeals as of right, the Court will usually sit with the minimum of five justices.

D. Constitutional Status of the Supreme Court

Until 2014, the constitutional status of the Supreme Court was uncertain despite its long-accepted standing as the arbiter of the Constitution. As discussed above, the Supreme Court was not included in the *British North America Act, 1867*. Throughout the 1970s, various constitutional reform plans proposed constitutionalizing the Supreme Court but these were not included in the constitutional patriation package of 1982. However, confusingly, the Supreme Court was mentioned in the provisions of the *Constitution Act, 1982* dealing with amendments to the Constitution: one provision provided that

---

[15] Supreme Court Act, s 36.
[16] Supreme Court Act, s 54.
[17] Hogg, above (n 5) § 8.6(d).
[18] Supreme Court of Canada, *Statistics 2005 to 2015* (2016) http://www.scc-csc.ca/case-dossier/stat/index-eng.aspx (last accessed 19 August 2016).
[19] ibid.
[20] Supreme Court Act, s 25.

amendments to the 'composition of the Supreme Court of Canada' could only be made by the unanimous approval of the Parliament of Canada and the legislative assemblies of all the provinces.[21] The other provision stated that 'subject to' that section, amendments to the Constitution of Canada 'in relation to . . . the Supreme Court of Canada' could only be made by the approval of the Parliament of Canada and the legislative assemblies of two-thirds of the provinces having at least 50 percent of the population of the provinces (the general procedure).[22]

The *Reference re Supreme Court Act, ss 5 and 6* (2014)[23] stated that the Supreme Court had become constitutionalized prior to 1982 though its 'historical evolution into an institution whose continued existence and functioning engaged the interests of both Parliament and the provinces'.[24] The Court stated that the *Constitution Act, 1982* confirmed the Court's constitutional status and 'reflected the understanding that the Court's essential features formed part of the Constitution of Canada'.[25]

The unanimous consent of Parliament and all provincial legislatures is required for constitutional amendments relating to the 'composition' of the Supreme Court. The Supreme Court stated that this refers to the composition and eligibility requirements for appointment to the Court codified in sections 4(1), 5, and 6 of the *Supreme Court Act*.[26] In addition, the continued existence of the Court is protected, 'since abolition would altogether remove the Court's composition'.[27]

The general amending procedure applies to the 'essential features' of the Supreme Court rather than to all of the provisions of the *Supreme Court Act*.[28] According to the Supreme Court the mention of the Supreme Court in the amendment provision of the *Constitution Act* 'is intended to ensure the proper functioning of the Supreme Court' and '[t]his requires the constitutional protection of the essential features of the Court, understood in light of the role that it had come to play in the Canadian constitutional structure by the time of patriation'.[29] To be specific, '[t]hese essential features include, at the very least, the Court's jurisdiction as the final general court of appeal for Canada, including in matters of constitutional interpretation and its independence'.[30]

The implication of the Court's decision is that Parliament may amend the *Supreme Court Act* and make changes to the Supreme Court without the necessity of a constitutional amendment where such changes do not either (1) relate to the composition of the Court, or (2) alter the essential features of the Supreme Court. Many provisions of the *Supreme Court Act* dealing with the Registrar and Other Officers;[31] Costs, amendments,

---

[21] Constitution Act 1982, s 41(d).
[22] Constitution Act 1982, s 42(d). See chapter by Benoit Pelletier in this *Handbook*.
[23] 2014 SCC 21.
[24] ibid [76].
[25] ibid.
[26] ibid [91].
[27] ibid.
[28] ibid [94].
[29] ibid.
[30] ibid.
[31] Supreme Court Act, ss 12–21.

interest and certificate of judgment;[32] Procedure in Appeals;[33] Entry of Causes;[34] Evidence;[35] and other General provisions[36] likely fall within this category.

An open question is the extent to which Parliament or the government could make changes to the appointment process. Section 4(2) of the *Supreme Court Act* provides that judges are appointed by the Governor in Council, that is, the Cabinet. This provision was left out of the Court's explanation of the contents of the composition of the Supreme Court, whereas section 4(1) was specifically cited.[37] It cannot be an oversight. It is not clear whether the Court's statements about the 'essential features' of the Court are meant simply to protect those features against infringement without a constitutional amendment or whether any change—either expanding or contracting these features—would necessitate a constitutional amendment.[38]

2. THE APPOINTMENT OF SUPREME COURT OF CANADA JUSTICES

The *Supreme Court Act* sets out minimal formal qualifications for appointment as a justice to the Supreme Court. As a general matter, four classes of jurists are eligible for appointment to the Supreme Court: (1) current judges of a superior court of a province, including courts of appeal; (2) former judges of such a court; (3) current barristers or advocates of at least 10 years standing at the bar of a province; and (4) former barristers or advocates of at least 10 years standing.[39] In effect, judges of any court—not just those explicitly mentioned in the *Supreme Court Act*—are generally eligible because appointment to such courts either requires at least 10 years' experience at the bar or in practice such members have at least that amount of experience. As a result, provincial court judges and judges of the Federal Court and the Federal Court of Appeal are generally eligible for appointment to the Supreme Court.[40] A number of justices have been appointed to the Supreme Court from the Federal Court of Appeal.[41]

However, the *Supreme Court Act* provides that '[a]t least three of the judges shall be appointed from among the judges of the Court of Appeal or of the Superior Court of the Province of Quebec or from among the advocate of at least 10 years standing at the

---

[32] ibid at ss 47–51.
[33] ibid at ss 56–78.
[34] ibid at s 79.
[35] ibid at ss 80–93.
[36] ibid at ss 94–100.
[37] ibid [91].
[38] See *Senate Reform Reference*, 2014 SCC 32.
[39] Supreme Court Act, s 25; *Reference re Supreme Court Act, ss 5 and 6*, 2014 SCC 21 at [13].
[40] See *Reference re Supreme Court Act* above (n 39), [13].
[41] Justice Gerald Le Dain (1984), Justice Frank Iacobucci (1991), and Justice Marshall Rothstein (2006).

bar of that Province'.[42] In the *Supreme Court Act Reference*, the Supreme Court stated that this section 'narrows the pool' from the four groups of people who are generally eligible for appointment to only two: (1) current members of the Court of Appeal or of the Superior Court of the Province of Quebec, and (2) current members of the bar of Quebec with at least 10 years' experience.[43] Thus, judges of the provincial court, the Federal Court, and the Federal Court of Appeal would not be eligible for appointment to the Supreme Court as one of the three justices from Quebec. Indeed, in the *Supreme Court Act Reference,* the Supreme Court invalidated the Prime Minister's appointment of Federal Court of Appeal Justice Marc Nadon to the Supreme Court.[44]

Formally, justices of the Supreme Court of Canada are appointed by the Governor General acting on the advice of the federal Cabinet.[45] The Prime Minister alone advises the Governor General who to appoint[46] and thus in practice, historically, the selection of Supreme Court justices has been wholly within the discretion of the Prime Minister. Different Prime Ministers may have relied on advice of their Ministers of Justice to varying degrees but the choice lay wholly within the Prime Minister's discretion.

In the late 1990s and early years of this century, this absolute discretion came under criticism as part of the 'democratic reform' movement of that age.[47] The quality of appointments was not questioned but rather the unbridled and opaque power of appointment vested in the hands of the Prime Minister with no parliamentary or public involvement.

Until 2004, the Government of Canada provided no information about the process that was undertaken in the selection of Supreme Court justices or the qualities that were sought for the high court bench. This changed in 2004 because of reforms to the so-called 'democratic deficit' during a minority Parliament. For the first time, a parliamentary committee studied the issue, and the Minister of Justice at the time, the Hon. Irwin Cotler, explained the process for appointments that had historically been undertaken. He explained that the first step in the process was the identification of prospective candidates from the region where the vacancy originated, as per convention (except for Quebec where it is a matter of law under the *Supreme Court Act*). The minister explained that the candidates were drawn from judges of the courts in the region, particularly the courts of appeal, as well as from senior members of the bar and leading academics in the region. Names may sometimes be identified first through previous consultations regarding other judicial appointments. The Minister of Justice explained that he consulted with a broad range of individuals and organizations including: the Chief of Justice of Canada and perhaps other members of the Supreme Court, the chief justices of the

---

[42] Supreme Court Act, RSC 1985, c S-26, s 5.
[43] *Supreme Court Reference* (n 38), [17].
[44] ibid [17].
[45] Supreme Court Act, s 4(2).
[46] Privy Council Minute 3374 (1935).
[47] See generally Adam M. Dodek, 'Reforming the Supreme Court Appointment Process, 2004–2014: A 10-Year Democratic Audit' (2014), 67 *Supreme Court Law Review* (2d Series) 111.

courts of the relevant region, the attorneys general of the relevant region, at least one senior member of the Canadian Bar Association, and at least one senior member of the law society of the relevant region. The minister stated that he might also consider input from other interested persons who wished to recommend a candidate for consideration, including academics and organizations. The minister stated that anyone was free to recommend candidates, and some choose to do so by writing to the Minister of Justice.[48]

According to the minister, the second step involved the assessment of the potential candidates based on the following criteria: professional capacity, personal characteristics, and diversity. Professional capacity includes: highest level of proficiency in the law, superior intellectual ability and analytical and writing skills, proven ability to listen and to maintain an open mind while hearing all sides of the argument, decisiveness and soundness of judgment, capacity to manage and share consistently heavy workload and in a collaborative context, capacity to manage stress and the pressures of the isolation of the judicial role, strong cooperative interpersonal skills, awareness of social context, bilingual capacity, and specific expertise required for the Supreme Court. The minister stated that such expertise could be identified by the Court itself or by others. Personal qualities include: impeccable personal and professional ethics, honesty, integrity and forthrightness; respect and regard for others, patience, courtesy, tact, humility, impartiality, and tolerance; personal sense of responsibility, common sense, punctuality, and reliability.[49] According to the minister, the diversity criterion 'concerns the extent to which the court's composition adequately reflects the diversity of Canadian society'.[50]

The minister stated he might also consider jurisprudential profiles prepared by the Department of Justice which are intended to provide information about 'the volume of cases written, areas of expertise, the outcome of appeals of the cases, and the degree to which they have been followed in the lower courts'.[51]

Minister Cotler explained that after the completion of the above assessments and consultations, he would discuss the candidates with the Prime Minister. He may have had previous exchanges with the Prime Minister. The minister indicated that he may return to consult with persons who he had previously consulted with. Although the Minister stated rather passively that '[a] a preferred candidate is then chosen',[52] it is clear that such choice is the Prime Minister's. Different Prime Ministers have deferred to the recommendations and the judgement of their Ministers of Justice to different extents. Formally, the Prime Minister recommends a candidate to the Cabinet and the appointment proceeds by way of an order in council appointment, as per the *Supreme Court Act*.

---

[48] Standing Committee on Justice, Human Rights, Public Safety and Emergency Preparedness, 37th Parl., 3rd Sess., March 30, 2004 (The Hon. Irwin Cotler), reproduced in Irwin Cotler, 'The Supreme Court Appointment Process: Chronology, Context and Reform' (2007) 58 *University of New Brunswick Law Journal* 131.

[49] ibid.

[50] ibid.

[51] ibid.

[52] ibid.

The years between 2004 and 2014 saw a decade of reforms which began under the Liberal government of Paul Martin (2004–2006) and continued under the Conservative Government of Stephen Harper (2006–2015).[53] The Government continued to create a long list of candidates which a committee or panel of Members of Parliament vetted in order to create a shortlist from which the Prime Minister chose a 'nominee'. The nominee would then appear before an ad hoc committee of parliamentarians for questioning on very short notice, generally 48–72 hours. Under such circumstances and given the Canadian tradition of deference to judges (all the nominees were sitting judges), the questioning was rather dull and public interest significantly dropped off after the first televised hearing. Between 2004 and 2013, five justices were appointed to the Supreme Court in this manner: Marshall Rothstein (2006), Michael Moldaver and Andromache Karakatsanis (2011), Richard Wagner (2012), and Marc Nadon (2013). The Conservative government abandoned this entire process after the Supreme Court invalidated its appointment of Justice Marc Nadon.[54]

In any event, the Conservative government dispensed with any semblance of process with its subsequent three appointments in 2014 (Clément Gascon and Suzanne Côté) and 2015 (Russell Brown). In 2015, the Liberal Party headed by Prime Minister Justin Trudeau came to power promising, among many other things, to 'ensure that the process of appointing Supreme Court Justices is transparent, inclusive, and accountable to Canadians'.[55] One challenge is how to institute more enduring reforms that are truly inclusive and cannot simply be dispensed with at the whim of the government of the day. Such reforms could be made by amending the process of appointment in the *Supreme Court Act* but after the Supreme Court's 2014 reference decision, the constitutionality of doing so by the federal government alone is highly questionable. It is more likely that amending the Supreme Court Act in this manner would require the consent of 7/10 provinces with more than 50 percent of the population (under the General Amending formula)[56] or unanimity of the provinces and the federal Parliament.[57] It is unlikely that the provinces would agree to any such change without significant provincial input in Supreme Court appointments and likely concessions by the federal government on other files.

In August 2016, the Liberal government announced a new process for appointing Supreme Court judges which was used to fill a pending vacancy from Atlantic Canada.[58] An independent non-partisan Advisory Board was tasked with identifying and evaluating candidates who must formally apply in order to be considered for appointment. The

[53] Dodek above (n 47).

[54] *Supreme Court Reference*, above (n 38).

[55] Liberal Party of Canada, *Real Change: A New Plan for a Strong Middle Class* (2015) 31, https://www.liberal.ca/files/2015/10/A-new-plan-for-a-strong-middle-class-BW-1.pdf (last accessed 20 April 2016).

[56] See Constitution Act, 1982, s 42(d).

[57] See Constitution Act, 1982, s 41(d).

[58] Canada, "Prime Minister Announces New Supreme Court of Canada Judicial Appointments Process" (2 August 2016), http://pm.gc.ca/eng/news/2016/08/02/prime-minister-announces-new-supreme-court-canada-judicial-appointments-process (last accessed 4 August 2016).

Advisory Board recommended three to five candidates for the Prime Minister's consideration. The Prime Minister was not bound by the recommendations of the Advisory Board in selecting a nominee. After the Prime Minister announced his choice of Justice Malcolm Rowe of the Newfoundland and Labrador Court of Appeal, the Minister of Justice and the Chair of the Advisory Board (former Primer Minister Kim Campbell) appeared before the House of Commons Standing Committee on Justice and Human Rights to explain both how and why the nominee was selected. The final step in the new process was a moderated question and answer session involving the nominee and parliamentarians that took place at the University of Ottawa in October 2016. It is expected that the Trudeau government will continue to use the same process to fill future vacancies on the Supreme Court.

3. The Appointment of Other Judges in Canada

A. Overview

Judges in Canada are appointed by the relevant executive branch, with authority divided between the provincial and federal governments. Each province and territory (except Nunavut)[59] has the authority to appoint judges to provincial trial courts. Appointment processes vary, but the essential model relies on an advisory committee to accept and evaluate applications, and make recommendations to the provincial attorney general.[60] The federal government is authorized by section 96 of the *Constitution Act, 1867* to appoint judges to the country's superior courts. Federal judicial appointments are made by the Governor in Council (the Cabinet) on the recommendation of the Minister of Justice. During the last few decades a growing body of scholarship on judicial appointments at all levels has emerged.[61] In Canada, two concerns dominate the discussion. The first is the continuing disconnect between the federal appointments process and a political culture which increasingly values transparency and accountability. The second is the ongoing underrepresentation on the federal bench of women, Aboriginal peoples, and

---

[59] Nunavut has Canada's only unified trial court with judges appointed by the federal government.

[60] For a review of provincial appointment processes see Peter McCormick, *Selecting Trial Court Judges: A Comparison of Contemporary Practices* (Commission of Inquiry into the Appointment Process for Judges in Quebec, 2010).

[61] For example: Richard Devlin, A. Wayne MacKay, and Natasha Kim, 'Reducing the Democratic Deficit: Representation, Diversity and the Canadian Judiciary, or Towards a Triple "P" Judiciary' (2000) 38 *Alberta Law Review* 734; Lorne Sossin, 'Judicial Appointment, Democratic Aspirations, and the Culture of Accountability' (2008) 58 *University of New Brunswick Law Journal* 11.

members of racialized communities.[62] This institutional lack of diversity raises legitimate concerns about the system's capacity to deliver impartial justice.

Space considerations prevent us from examining the range of provincial and territorial appointment models. The discussion that follows focuses on the federal process.

B. Federal Judicial Appointments

The current federal appointment process is heir to reforms initiated by the Progressive Conservative government in 1989. These reforms were a partial response to a Canadian Bar Association Report that identified a 'widespread dissatisfaction with the method of judicial selection,' related primarily to the 'extent of political patronage.'[63] The Report concluded that a patronage based system was incapable of ensuring high-quality appointments, and called for change. The centerpiece of the reform was the creation of judicial advisory committees (JACs) in each province and territory. The committees were charged with screening qualified applicants, and interested lawyers meeting the minimum qualification, 10 years of relevant experience evidenced by membership in a provincial law society,[64] were invited to apply. The original committees included five members, each appointed by the Minister of Justice from a list provided by the nominating authority,[65] for a three-year, once-renewable term; a representative from the provincial or territorial bar society, a representative of the provincial or territorial branch of the Canadian Bar Association, a nominee of the relevant Chief Justice, a nominee of the provincial or territorial attorney general, and a nominee of the federal Minister of Justice. Their job was to advise the Minister of Justice whether an applicant was 'qualified' or 'not qualified' for appointment.

A number of changes have been made since 1988. First, there are more committees, a reflection of the substantial workload in larger jurisdictions.[66] Second, the committees have expanded. In 1994, the number of federal nominees was increased to three—two laypersons, and one lawyer. In 2007, the government of Conservative Prime Minister Stephen Harper added an eighth member to the committee, a representative of the

---

[62] Sonia Lawrence, 'Reflections: On Judicial Diversity and Judicial Independence' in Adam Dodek and Lorne Sossin (eds), *Judicial Independence in Context* (Irwin Law, 2010) 193; Rosemary Cairns Way, 'Deliberate Disregard: Judicial Appointments under the Harper Government' (2014) *Supreme Court Law Review* (2d) 43; Sabrina Lyon and Lorne Sossin, "Data and Diversity in the Canadian Justice Community" (2014) 11 *Journal of Law & Equality* 85.

[63] Canadian Bar Association, *Federal Judicial Appointment Process* (October 2005) www.cba.org/CMSPages/GetFile.aspx?guid=81a459b1-0bd3-4c2c-a88f-12371fa80de2 (last accessed 20 April 2016).

[64] *Judges Act* RSC 1985, c. J-1.

[65] André Millar, 'The "New" Federal Judicial Appointments Process: The First Ten Years' (2000) 38 *Alberta Law Review* 616.

[66] Currently, there are 17 committees, with at least one in every province and territory. There are three committees in Ontario, two committees in Quebec, and a specialized committee for the Tax Court of Canada. Office of the Commissioner for Federal Judicial Affairs Canada (OCFJA), www.fja-cmf.gc.ca/home-accueil/index-eng.html (last accessed 20 April 2016).

relevant law enforcement community. At the same time, the judicial nominee was made non-voting. Finally, the categories of recommendation have been reorganized twice. In 1991, qualified and not qualified were replaced by recommended, highly recommended, and unable to recommend. In 2007, the highly recommended classification was eliminated.

Federal judicial appointments are administered by the Office of the Commissioner for Federal Judicial Affairs (OCFJA) which was established in 1978 to 'safeguard the independence of the judiciary'.[67] Information for potential judicial applicants and about the JACs is publicly available on the OCFJA website. Primary qualifications for judicial appointment are 'professional competence and overall merit,' but committees are encouraged to 'respect diversity and to give due consideration to all legal experience, including that outside a mainstream legal practice.'[68] Assessment criteria are organized in two categories— professional competence and experience, and personal qualities.[69] The committee's deliberations are confidential. The OCFJA releases an annual report tracking the work of the JACs. These reports include information about the number of applications received, number of applications recommended and not recommended, number of applications from sitting provincial or territorial judges,[70] and the number of appointments made to superior courts. In addition, the OCFJA regularly reports on the number of federally appointed judges in Canada, the number of supernumerary judges and vacancies on each superior court, and the number of women judges on each superior court.[71] No other demographic information about the applicant pool is collected or made public.

C. Democracy

Although the 1989 reforms were intended to increase transparency in a manner consistent with judicial independence, the extent of their success is debatable. First, the composition of the JACs is heavily influenced by the Minister of Justice. Second, the committees have the power to screen candidates, but they neither have nor were intended to have the capacity to seriously limit the executive discretion to appoint. Ten years after the adoption of the advisory committee model, one commentator remarked that:

> Undoubtedly, this system guards against the egregious situations where positions are offered to candidates who are completely unsuited. Unfortunately, this can still leave room for a significant amount of patronage, especially if there are close connections

---

[67] ibid.

[68] www.fja-cmf.gc.ca/appointments-nominations/process-regime-eng.html (last accessed 20 April 2016).

[69] The assessment criteria are listed at www.fja-cmf.gc.ca/appointments-nominations/assessment-evaluation-eng.html (last accessed 20 April 2016).

[70] Applications from sitting provincial and territorial judges are not assessed by the committees, but the files are submitted for 'comments' which are forwarded to the minister.

[71] www.fja-cmf.gc.ca/appointments-nominations/committees-comites/reports-rapports/index-eng.html (last accessed 20 April 2016).

between the political and legal elites of a particular jurisdiction. . . . Indeed, it is sometimes suggested that perhaps the executive likes the new system because it 'takes the heat off' by creating an intermediate body that still allows the executive to make patronage appointments, but locates responsibility for the nomination elsewhere.[72]

Third, recent reforms to the committee structure and process appear overtly ideologi-cal.[73] The elimination of the highly recommended category in 2007 was clearly intended to limit the JAC's power to meaningfully differentiate between candidates. This reduc-tion in advisory capacity widens executive discretion, making it more likely that factors unrelated to merit will play a role in appointment. In addition, Prime Minister Harper defended the decision to add a law enforcement perspective to the committee by link-ing government 'tough on crime' policy with judicial appointments, stating: 'We want to make sure our selection of judges is in correspondence with those [safer streets and communities] objectives.'[74]

This overt acknowledgement of the political dimensions of the process provoked a highly unusual public intervention by the Canadian Judicial Council (the Council), the judicial governance body composed of Chief and Associate Chief Justices from every superior court in the country.[75] The Council raised three distinct concerns relating to the perceived and actual independence of the JACs.[76] First, the Council was highly critical of the government's 'unilateral' failure to consult with the legal community. Second, the Council maintained that the removal of the highly recom-mended designation raised 'questions about whether the most qualified individuals will continue to be identified for appointment'. Third, the Council was highly criti-cal of the compositional changes, suggesting that it had always been understood that independent committees would "reflect the diversity of each jurisdiction'. The Council concluded that:

Because the majority of voting members are now appointed by the Minister, the advisory committees may neither be, nor be seen to be, fully independent of the gov-ernment. This puts in peril the concept of an independent body that advises the gov-ernment on who is best qualified to be a judge.

[72] Devlin et al., above (n 61) 786.

[73] Sean Fine, 'Stephen Harper's Courts' *Globe and Mail* (Toronto, 24 July 2015).

[74] Carissima Mathen, 'Choices and Controversy: Judicial Appointment in Canada' (2008) 58 *University of New Brunswick Law Journal* 52, 61.

[75] www.cjc-ccm.gc.ca/english/about_en.asp?selMenu=about_main_en.asp (last accessed 20 April 2016).

[76] Canadian Judicial Council, 'Judicial Appointments: Perspective from the Canadian Judicial Council' www.cjc-ccm.gc.ca/english/news_en.asp?selMenu=news_2007_0220_en.asp (last accessed 20 April 2016).

Committee deliberations on individual applicants are confidential, and no public justification for the ensuing political appointment is made. The 29 assessment criteria enumerated on the OFCJA website have been described as 'a laundry list into which every conceivable consideration was inserted'.[77] Their generality suggests that they are not intended to constrain either the committees' or the executive's exercise of discretion. Although the JACs are exhorted to consult broadly, and involve the community, confidentiality requirements make it impossible to ascertain how any of these procedural ideals are implemented. In the absence of information about who is applying, how the criteria are assessed, and what procedures the committee follows, it is difficult to know whether and how merit is evaluated, and if, in fact, it is the primary criterion of selection.

Almost 30 years after the reform, federal judicial appointments remain a virtually unfettered exercise of executive prerogative. The Minister of Justice is not bound by the recommendations of the JAC, and in practice, the government may engage in its own independent consultative process prior to making an appointment. Although it is true that no federal Minister of Justice has appointed a candidate not recommended by a JAC, this reflects no more than an unenforceable 'personal undertaking' of one Minister of Justice.[78] The fact that the JACs are not statutory bodies and that their structure and mandate are entirely vulnerable to political manipulation makes them structurally incapable of serving any accountability function beyond the identification of the unqualified.

There has been no evidence of a political desire for accountability. The annual reports suggest that approximately 40 percent of applicants are recommended. Each recommendation lasts for two years, with the result that the Cabinet has a substantial pool of potential appointees. Appointments are announced on the Department of Justice website by way of three or four brief, boiler-plate paragraphs. The new justice's most recent professional experience, education, and professional history are listed, along with a nod to professional activities, and community service. No other information about or public justification of the appointment is made.

---

[77] Sossin, above (n 61) 34. The assessment criteria provide an open-ended list of factors intended to furnish a basis for assessing the suitability of candidates for judicial appointment. Professional Competence & Experience: general proficiency in the law; intellectual ability; analytical skills; ability to listen; ability to maintain an open mind while hearing all sides of an argument; ability to make decisions; capacity to exercise sound judgement; reputation among professional peers and in the general community; area(s) of professional specialization, specialized experience, or special skills; ability to manage time and workload without supervision; capacity to handle heavy workload; capacity to handle stress and pressures of the isolation of the judicial role; interpersonal skills—with peers and the general public; awareness of racial and gender issues; bilingual ability. Personal Characteristics: sense of ethics, patience, courtesy, honesty, common sense, tact, integrity, humility, punctuality, fairness, reliability, tolerance, sense of responsibility, consideration for others.

[78] This commitment was made by Justice Minister Allan Rock in 1994.

D. Diversity

The last decades have seen the emergence of a remarkable consensus on the importance of a judicial appointments process which takes account of diversity.[79] In 2012, Chief Justice Beverley McLachlin publicly recognized the need for 'a bench that better mirrors the people it judges'.[80] In August 2013, the Canadian Bar Association (CBA) reiterated its long-standing call for increased diversity, pointing out that 'the low number of women and members of racialized and other minority groups appointed to the federal courts does not reflect the gender balance or diversity in the Canadian population'.[81] The urgent need for Aboriginal judges has been pointed out by the CBA and the Indigenous Bar Association,[82] and the fact that this need persists at a time when there is a judicially acknowledged crisis of criminal justice legitimacy for Aboriginal peoples[83] makes it especially urgent.

The calls for change have had little apparent impact on the federal appointments process. Canada's federal judiciary remains overwhelmingly white and male, at the same time as Canadian society grows increasingly diverse. The number of women on the federal bench has crept upwards at a glacial pace.[84] As of 30 April 2016, 35 percent of the federal bench was female. Even more troubling are the statistics on indigeneity and race. A five-year study of federal appointments, from 2009 to 2014, concluded that Aboriginal judges were being appointed to superior courts at a rate of barely more than 1 percent, while visible minority judges were appointed at a rate of half that.[85] These statistics are deeply troubling.[86] Almost 20 percent of Canadians are members of visible minority

---

[79] Language is important. We agree with Sonia Lawrence that 'representation more squarely confronts the ways in which a homogenous—or otherwise non-representative—bench threatens impartiality, by calling attention to the disparity between the judges and the judged'. Lawrence above (n 62) 207. Nevertheless, diversity seems to have become the word of choice, both nationally and internationally: see, for example, Elizabeth Handsley and Andrew Lynch, 'Facing Up to Diversity? Transparency and the Reform of Commonwealth Judicial Appointments 2008–2013' (2015) 37 *Sydney Law Review* 186; The Report of the Advisory Panel on Judicial Diversity, Judiciary of England and Wales, www.judiciary.gov.uk/Resources/JCO/Documents/Reports/advisory-panel-judicial-diversity-2010. pdf as well as the most recent annual report of the Judicial Diversity Taskforce www.gov.uk/.../judicial-diversity-taskforce-annual-report-2014 (last accessed 20 April 2016).

[80] 'Judging: The Challenges of Diversity'; Remarks of the Right Honourable Beverley McLachlin, P.C., Chief Justice of Canada, Judicial Studies Committee Inaugural Annual Lecture, Edinburgh, Scotland, June 2012 www.scotland-judiciary.org.uk/Upload/Documents/JSCInauguralLectureJune2012.pdf 17 (last accessed 20 April 2016).

[81] CBA Resolution 13-04-A Equality in Judicial Appointments 18 August 2013.

[82] CBA Resolution 05-01-A Recognition of Legal Pluralism in Judicial Appointments August 2005; James C. Hopkins and Albert C. Peeling, 'Aboriginal Judicial Appointments to the Supreme Court of Canada' April 2004, www.indigenousbar.ca/pdf/Aboriginal%20Appointment%20to%20the%20 Supreme%20Court%20Final.pdf (last accessed 20 April 2016).

[83] *R v Gladue*, [1999] 1 SCR 688; *R v Ipeelee* 2012 SCC 13, [2012] 1 SCR 433.

[84] Kirk Makin, 'Appointments of Female Judges Slump under Harper's Tories' *Globe and Mail* (Toronto, 11 November 2011).

[85] Way, above (n 62).

[86] Space does not permit reference to all the primary statistical sources. See Rosemary Cairns Way, *ibid*.

communities. In large urban centres such as Toronto and Vancouver, visible minorities account for almost 50 percent of the population. Aboriginal peoples make up 4 percent of the Canadian population. There is clear evidence that the demographics of the legal profession are changing, although the profession is not as diverse as the general popula- tion.[87] Nevertheless a substantial pool of exceptionally talented women, Aboriginal, and visible minority lawyers are qualified for appointment.

Why does diversity matter? Two primary arguments support the call for increased judicial diversity. The first is utilitarian. The argument is that the more diverse the bench, the better the quality of judgment. Increasing the range of perspectives and experiences on the bench increases the likelihood of judgment which is truly impartial, which does not unintentionally replicate the perspectives and values of a limited subset of human experience at a systemic level. In Canada, the 'Ethical Principles for Judges' reflect a commitment at the highest levels of the Canadian judiciary to understand and promote equality.[88] The Honourable Lynn Smith has argued that the Principles:

> [S]trongly endorse the concept that judges must be impartial in the sense that they must understand the community in which they live, and avoid the mistake of confus- ing their own singular experience with the universal experience of humankind. That duty rests on every individual judge . . . I think that there is a corresponding duty on the judiciary as an institution, and that the judiciary would be better able to carry out that duty if its composition more accurately reflected the composition of the com- munity as a whole.[89]

American scholar Sherralyn Ifill makes a similar argument for structural (or institu- tional) diversity that is achieved, in her view, when 'judicial decision-making includes a cross-section of perspectives and values from the community'.[90] In a diverse society,

---

[87]   Michael Ornstein, *Racialization and Gender of Lawyers in Ontario* (The Law Society of Upper Canada, 2010) at 3. The report concludes: 'The legal profession in Ontario is changing dramatically. The number of lawyers who are women, Aboriginal and members of a visible minority continues to grow, transforming the face of a profession that until the early 1970s was primarily White and male. . . . Leading the transformation is an extraordinary increase in the percentage and number of women lawyers. Accounting for just 5 percent of Ontario lawyers in 1971, growth in the number of women lawyers has continued unabated for 35 years. In 2006 women accounted for nearly 60 percent of the youngest lawyers and 38 percent of all lawyers in Ontario. . . . In the last decade, gains in the representation of women are attributable largely to increased numbers of racialized women. Racialized women account for no less than 16 percent of all lawyers under 30, compared to just 5 percent of lawyers 30 and older; racialized men account for 7 percent of lawyers under 30, compared to 6 percent of lawyers 30 and older. The percentage of Ontario lawyers who were Aboriginal was unchanged between 1981 and 2001, but increased from 0.6 to 1.0 percent between 2001 and 2006.'

[88]   Canadian Judicial Council, "Ethical Principles for Judges" www.cjc-ccm.gc.ca/cmslib/general/ news_pub_judicialconduct_Principles_en.pdf explain (last accessed 20 April 2016).

[89]   The Honourable Lynn Smith, 'Speaking Notes: Diversity on the Bench' 12 July 2013 (on-file with the author).

[90]   Sherrilyn A. Ifill, 'Racial Diversity on the Bench: Beyond Role Models and Public Confidence' (2000) 57 *Washington & Lee Law Review* 404, 411.

it is imperative that powerful institutions are structurally impartial. The utilitarian argument in favour of diversity rests on a claim about both the likelihood of improved decision-making and the public perception of improved decision-making. Justice, in other words, is more likely to be seen to be done by a diverse public when the institution dispensing justice reflects that diversity.

The second argument in favour of diversity is normative and egalitarian. The homogenous character of the judiciary is evidence of a process which disproportionately denies opportunities to indigenous peoples, racialized individuals, women, and other members of equality-seeking groups. This is not a claim about intention. Rather it is a claim that executive discretion formally cabined by an uncritical commitment to 'professional competence and overall merit' has the potential to reinforce an unrepresentative status quo, while invisibly offering covert resistance to change. The opacity of the current appointments process lends substance to this claim, as the only proof of how the process works is in the still remarkably homogenous character of the federal bench.

A standard response to this concern identifies the 'pool problem' as primarily to blame, suggesting that the lack of diversity in appointments is a simple reflection of the applicant pool. In this analysis, demographic shifts will eventually 'trickle-up' to the judiciary. Unfortunately, in the absence of demographic data, it is impossible to pinpoint precisely where the problem, if it is in fact acknowledged as a problem, exists. Do fewer visible minority, or Aboriginal, or women lawyers apply to be judges? Are their applications disproportionately screened out at the Committee stage? Or are they disproportionately passed over at the political stage? Without data it is impossible to understand the nature of the diversity deficit, and equally impossible to devise the kinds of sophisticated remedial responses that might catalyze change. Data collection alone is incapable of shifting the culture and practice of judicial appointment in Canada. Real change will require the federal government to acknowledge that the current model of executive appointment is inconsistent not only with norms of political transparency and accountability, but, more importantly, with constitutional guarantees of judicial independence, judicial impartiality, and non-discrimination.

E. Postscript

In April 2016, as the first draft of this chapter was being finalized, the government of Prime Minister Justin Trudeau announced a review of the federal appointment process that would be consistent with 'the government's objectives to achieve transparency, accountability and diversity in the appointments process'.[91] Six months later, in October 2016, a sweeping package of reforms was announced,[92] along with twenty-four new

---

[91] Sean Fine, 'Federally Appointed Courts Grow Restive' *Globe and Mail* (Toronto, 11 April 2016).

[92] See "Government of Canada announces judicial appointments and reforms the appointments process to increase openness and transparency" available on-line at http://news.gc.ca/web/article-en.do? nid=1140619

judicial appointments. The reforms are responsive to the precise concerns which have dominated the discourse on judicial appointments in Canada for more than 30 years,[93] and the group of appointees was historically diverse, including two indigenous jurists, one racialized person, and equal numbers of women and men.[94] All federal judicial appointments are now made pursuant to the new process.

The reforms "strengthen the role of Judicial Advisory Committees."[95] They reverse the 2006 changes by: 1) restoring the right of judicial members on the JACs to vote; 2) removing the representative of law enforcement; and 3) re-instating the highly recommended category. Federal government nominees on the Committees represent the 'general public' and are selected through a new, application-based process. The committee selection process remains in the hands of the Minister of Justice but the process is intended to achieve gender balance as well as reflecting 'the diversity of members of each jurisdiction, including Indigenous peoples, persons with disabilities and members of linguistic, ethnic and other minority communities, including those whose members' gender identity or sexual orientation differs from that of the majority.' Along with their assessment of professional competence and overall merit, Committee members are overtly charged with attempting to create a candidate pool which is similarly reflective of the jurisdiction. The criteria for appointment are largely unchanged, but candidates for judicial appointment are required to complete a significantly revamped questionnaire which includes an option to self-identify which is presumably intended to allow the government to fulfil its promise of collecting and publishing "statistics and demographic information on both applicants for and appointments to judicial office to measure whether Canada is meeting its diversity goals."

It is too early to judge the significance of these changes. Judicial appointment in Canada has always been and remains political in a manner consistent with Canadian political traditions. The JACs are still advisory in nature, with the Minister of Justice retaining discretion over each individual appointment. And, as the fact of these changes demonstrates, there is nothing that guarantees the new process will outlive the government which created it, just as there was no guarantee that the changes made in 2006 would outlast the government that implemented them. The most recent reforms have the potential to replace pure partisan politics with a politics more grounded in the democratic and constitutional norms of transparency, public participation, and impartiality. It remains to be seen whether the government can sustain the political will to live up to the public promise of these reforms, but there is certainly reason for cautious optimism.

---

[93] An overview of the new process is found at www.fja-cmf.gc.ca/appointments-nominations/index-eng.html.

[94] Details of each appointment are available at http://www.justice.gc.ca/eng/news-nouv/ja-nj.asp?action=tdetail&tid=4&year=2016

[95] http://news.gc.ca/web/article-en.do?nid=1140619

Bibliography

Books and Articles

Cotler, Irwin. "The Supreme Court Appointment Process: Chronology, Context and Reform" (2007) 58 University of New Brunswick Law Journal 131.

McCormick, Peter. *Supreme at Last: The Evolution of the Supreme Court of Canada*. Toronto, On.: Lorimer, 2000.

Office of the Commissioner for Federal Judicial Affairs Canada (OCFJA), www.fja-cmf.gc.ca/home-accueil/index-eng.html accessed 20 April 2016.

Sossin, Lorne. "Judicial Appointment, Democratic Aspirations, and the Culture of Accountability" (2008) 58 University of New Brunswick Law Journal 11.

Legislation

Supreme Court Act. RSC 1985, c S-46

Cases

Reference re Supreme Court Act, ss 5 and 6, 2014 SCC 21

CHAPTER 11

....

COURTS, ADMINISTRATIVE AGENCIES, AND THE CONSTITUTION

....

LORNE SOSSIN[*]

1. INTRODUCTION

....

THIS chapter sets out the constitutional foundation for courts and administrative agencies in Canada. The chapter is organized into three parts. In the first part, I examine the constitutional foundations for Canadian courts, including Canada's constitutional texts, unwritten constitutional principles, quasi-constitutional statutes, and the common law Constitution. In the second part, I set out the constitutional foundations for administrative agencies, particularly around the extent to which agencies can implement and are subject to the Constitution.[1] Finally, in the third part, I examine Canada's separation-of-powers doctrine in light of the constitutional backdrop of the courts and administrative agencies, including emerging dynamics flowing from Indigenous adjudication.

2. COURTS AND THE CONSTITUTION

....

The Canadian Constitution includes both written and unwritten components, and a series of other statutes and instruments that have been recognized as possessing quasi-constitutional status. Below I explore the (1) constitutional foundation for the courts in

  * Dean and Professor, Osgoode Hall Law School, York University. I wish to thank Jenna Meguid and Marleigh Dick for their excellent research assistance.
  [1] "Agencies" in this analysis encompasses the full range of executive entities established by statute including boards, commissions, adjudicative tribunals, and regulatory bodies.

Canada in the federalism and judicature provisions of the *Constitution Act, 1867*;[2] (2) the *Constitution Act, 1982*,[3] (3) unwritten constitutional principles of judicial independence, access to justice, and the rule of law; (4) quasi-constitutional statutes such as the *Supreme Court Act*;[4] and (5) the common law Constitution such as the inherent powers doctrine by which Superior Courts control their own procedure.

A. *Constitution Act, 1867*

The Canadian Constitution establishes the foundation for federally and provincially appointed provincial courts throughout the country. The judicature provisions in the *Constitution Act, 1867* provide that the Superior Courts of the provinces are to be appointed by the federal executive from among the bars of the province where the Superior Court is located (sections 96–99). The Canadian Parliament is empowered to establish a "General Court of Appeal for Canada", and section 101 of the *Constitution Act, 1867* establishes additional federal courts for the "better Administration of the Laws of Canada". Under this authority, Parliament established the Supreme Court of Canada (in 1875) and the Federal Court of Canada (which includes a trial level Federal Court, a Tax Court, a Court Martial Appeals Court, and a Federal Court of Appeal).

The *Constitution Act, 1867* also allocated legislative responsibility to the provincial governments over "The Administration of Justice in the Province, including the Constitution, Maintenance, and Organization of Provincial Courts, both of Civil and of Criminal Jurisdiction, and including Procedure in Civil Matters in those Courts".[5] Under this authority, every province in Canada has established both Superior (federally appointed) and Provincial (provincially appointed) courts. As a result of this constitutional scheme, courts in a given province will consist of Superior Courts (at the trial and appellate levels) which are established and maintained by the provinces and territories but whose judges are appointed by the federal Executive, and Provincial Courts (at the trial level) which are established and maintained by the provinces and whose judges are appointed by the provincial executive. Additionally, and with separate jurisdiction over federal laws, a Federal Court structure has been established. The Supreme Court of Canada serves as the final appellate court for all decisions arising both from the courts of the provinces and from the Federal Court structure.

---

[2] *Constitution Act, 1867* (UK), 30 & 31 Vict, c 3, reprinted in RSC 1985, App II, No 5 [hereinafter *Constitution Act, 1867*].
[3] *Canadian Charter of Rights and Freedoms*, s.24(1), Part I of the *Constitution Act, 1982*, being Schedule B to the *Canada Act 1982* (U.K.), 1982, c.11 [hereinafter *Charter*].
[4] *Supreme Court Act*, RSC 1985, c. S-26.
[5] *Constitution Act, 1867*, s. 92(14).

B. *Constitution Act, 1982*

The *Constitution Act, 1982* contains the *Charter of Rights and Freedoms*, which guarantees independent and impartial courts through section 11(d) of the *Charter*. Although this protection is specified for criminal trials, it has been interpreted as a general source of authority for the independence of all adjudication before the courts. The rationale of and justification for judicial independence is to ensure impartiality in adjudication.[6] It is the litigant, rather than the judge (individually) or the court (institutionally), who has the right to this impartiality.[7]

The content of this constitutional principle was set out in *Valente v R*,[8] and consists of three discrete but related forms of protection not enshrined in the written provisions of the *Constitution Act, 1982* or the *Charter*: security of tenure, financial independence, and administrative independence.

C. Unwritten Constitutional Principles

(i) *Judicial Independence*

Judicial independence has been recognized as an unwritten constitutional principle—it was implied, although not set out, in the recognition in the preamble to the *Constitution Act, 1867* that Canada was to have a Constitution "similar in principle" to the United Kingdom, which in turn, by 1867, had an established common law doctrine of judicial independence.

In *Reference re Remuneration of Judges of the Provincial Court of Prince Edward Island*,[9] the Supreme Court of Canada considered a number of provinces' attempts to curtail or cut the salaries of provincially appointed judges (federally-appointed judges' salaries are fixed by the federal government). As Lamer C.J. stated, referring to the requirement that the financial security of courts be free from political interference, this question has turned out to play a pivotal role in the constitutional character of the judicial branch of government:

> These different components of the institutional financial security of the courts in here, in my view, in a fundamental principle of the Canadian Constitution, the separation of powers. As I discussed above, the institutional independence of the courts is inextricably bound up with the separation of powers, because in order to guarantee that the courts can protect the Constitution, they must be protected by a set of objective guarantees against intrusions by the executive and legislative branches of government.[10]

---

[6] *R. v Lippé* [1991] 2 SCR 114 at p.140.
[7] 2002 SCC 13.
[8] [1985] 2 SCR 673 [hereinafter *Valente*].
[9] [1997] 3 SCR 3.
[10] *Ibid.* at 90.

Lamer C.J. held that the remuneration of provincial judges could not be subject to government-wide cuts because to do so would compromise the independence of the judiciary, contrary to the unwritten guarantee of judicial independence incorporated into Canada's Constitution through the preamble of the *Constitution Act, 1867*.[11]

(ii) Access to Justice

Access to justice also has been recognized as an unwritten constitutional principle protecting the right of citizens to access the adjudicative functions of courts. In *British Columbia Government Employees' Union v British Columbia (Attorney General)* (*BCGEU*),[12] Dickson C.J. outlined the rationale for recognizing the principles of "access to justice" and the "rule of law" as aspects of the Canadian Constitution entrenched, like judicial independence, both through the preamble to the *Constitution Act, 1867*, and implicitly through the *Charter*. He stated,

> So we see that the rule of law is the very foundation of the Charter. Let us turn then to s. 52(1) of the Constitution Act, 1982 which states that the Constitution of Canada is the supreme law of Canada and any law that is inconsistent with the provisions of the Constitution is, to the extent of the inconsistency, of no force or effect. . . . it would be inconceivable that Parliament and the provinces should describe in such detail the rights and freedoms guaranteed by the Charter and should not first protect that which alone makes it in fact possible to benefit from such guarantees, that is, access to a court. . . . Of what value are the rights and freedoms guaranteed by the Charter if a person is denied or delayed access to a court of competent jurisdiction in order to vindicate them? How can the courts independently maintain the rule of law and effectively discharge the duties imposed by the Charter if court access is hindered, impeded or denied? The Charter protections would become merely illusory, the entire Charter undermined.[13]

In that case, the Supreme Court of Canada upheld an injunction issued by a trial judge in British Columbia, on his own initiative, barring striking workers from picketing on the courthouse steps, as they were impeding public access to the courthouse. In short, the Court held that the rule of law forms the infrastructure of the Constitution and that the rule of law is contingent on access to justice, which in turn must presuppose access to courts. The Court in *BCGEU* made clear that interference "from whatever source" falls into the same category as an infringement of access.[14] Subsequently, the Court has affirmed that access to justice may also be found in the constitutional establishment of the courts (so that, for example, court fees which cannot be waived have been held to violate this principle).[15]

---

[11] *Ibid.* at 64–69.
[12] 1988, 2 S.C.R. 214 [hereinafter *BCGEU*].
[13] *Ibid.* [24].
[14] *Ibid.* [230].
[15] *Trial Lawyers Association of British Columbia v British Columbia (Attorney General)*, 2014 SCC 59.

(iii) The Rule of Law

The rule of law has been recognized as an unwritten constitutional principle (in addition to forming part of the preamble to and precursor ideas undergirding the *Charter of Rights and Freedoms*). Although the role of the rule of law in shaping the operation of the courts is widely invoked (whether or not based on a shared understanding of the concept), its application to administrative agencies remains to be fully determined, as discussed below.

In the *Secession Reference*, the Supreme Court of Canada described the importance of the unwritten constitutional rule of law doctrine in the following terms:

> The principles of constitutionalism and the rule of law lie at the root of our system of government. The rule of law, as observed in *Roncarelli v. Duplessis*, [1959] S.C.R. 121, at p. 142, is "a fundamental postulate of our constitutional structure". As we noted in the *Patriation Reference*, *supra*, at pp. 805–6, "[t]he 'rule of law' is a highly textured expression, importing many things which are beyond the need of these reasons to explore but conveying, for example, a sense of orderliness, of subjection to known legal rules and of executive accountability to legal authority". At its most basic level, the rule of law vouchsafes to the citizens and residents of the country a stable, predictable and ordered society in which to conduct their affairs. *It provides a shield for individuals from arbitrary state action.*[16] [emphasis added.]

Since *Roncarelli*[17] and the *Secession Reference*, the rule of law is most often invoked to justify implied boundaries to what otherwise appears to be unfettered executive discretion. For example, in *CUPE v Ministry of Labour*, the Supreme Court held that the Ontario Ministry of Labour acted in a patently unreasonable fashion, contrary to the rule of law, by appointing retired judges to serve as per-diem chairs of labour arbitration panels.[18]

Although the rule of law is often invoked as a constraint on unbounded executive authority, it has proven less capable of grounding positive obligations in relation to the administration of justice. In *Christie*,[19] for example, the Supreme Court clarified that the unwritten constitutional principle of the rule of law does not preclude legislation which limits access to counsel or to the retroactive effect of changes to a cause of action before the courts. As the Court noted in *Christie*,

> The issue, however, is whether general access to legal services in relation to court and tribunal proceedings dealing with rights and obligations is a fundamental aspect of the rule of law. In our view, it is not. Access to legal services is fundamentally important in any free and democratic society. In some cases, it has been found essential to due process and a fair trial. But a review of the constitutional text, the jurisprudence

---

[16] *Reference re Secession of Quebec*, 1998 2 SCR. 217, [70] [hereinafter *Secession Reference*].
[17] [1959] SCR 121.
[18] 2003 SCC 29.
[19] 2007 SCC 21.

and the history of the concept does not support the respondent's contention that there is a broad general right to legal counsel as an aspect of, or precondition to, the rule of law.[20]

Similarly, in *Imperial Tobacco*,[21] the Supreme Court of Canada held that the rule of law did not preclude a legislature from altering (even retroactively) a cause of action.

D. Quasi-constitutional Statutes

The idea of quasi-constitutional statutes has been developed in a range of areas by the courts as they signal that certain statutes, because of their subject-matter and influence on the Constitution, must be treated as prevailing over other statutes to the extent of inconsistency, and may even be subject to change only by adherence to one of the Constitution's amending formulae (as opposed to by a similar act of Parliament or a legislature that created the Act). The *Canadian Bill of Rights*,[22] a precursor to the *Charter of Rights* which continues to provide overlapping (for example, the right to impartial and independent adjudication) and in some cases distinct rights protections (due process in relation to the enjoyment of property), is an archetype of the quasi-constitutional statute, along with provincial human rights codes and the Quebec *Charter of Human Rights and Freedoms*.[23]

Another good example is the *Supreme Court Act*.[24] This Act of Parliament provides the legislative basis for implementing section 101 of the *Constitution Act, 1867*, which as noted above provides for a general court of appeal for all of Canada. The *Supreme Court Act* was enacted in 1875 and amended by further Parliamentary actions in the years that followed.

In *Reference ss. 5 and 6 of the Supreme Court Act* (the "Nadon Reference"),[25] which considered the eligibility of a Federal Court judge to fill one of the spots on the Supreme Court reserved for someone from Quebec, the Court noted that the *Supreme Court Act* is a quasi-constitutional Act, and further, that at least some kinds of amendments to the Act would have to accord with one of the constitutional amending formulae.[26] In this way, a hierarchy of quasi-constitutional statutes may be emerging, some of which will be simply given more effect than ordinary statutes, whereas others may, in effect, be treated as part of the Constitution itself, and therefore subject to one of the amending formulae.

---

[20]   *Ibid.* [23].
[21]   2005 SCC 49.
[22]   SC 1960, c.44.
[23]   CQLR c C-12. See also Vanessa Macdonnell, "A Theory of Quasi-Constitutional Legislation" (2015) 53 Osgoode Hall Law Journal 508.
[24]   Above (n 4).
[25]   2014 SCC 21 [hereinafter *Nadon Reference*].
[26]   *Ibid.* [19].

E. Inherent Powers and the Common Law Constitution

In addition to the constitutional texts, unwritten constitutional principles, and the quasi-constitutional statutes, an additional unwritten component of the Canadian Constitution relates exclusively to the inherent powers of Superior Courts. The "inherent powers" doctrine is typically understood as a uniquely American doctrine which provides courts with an inherent right to direct and control any aspect necessary to carry out the judicial function, from budgets to personnel, and rules. Felix Stumpf describes the doctrine in the following terms:

> The doctrine of inherent power runs essentially as follows: the courts are a constitutionally created branch of government whose continued effective functioning is indispensable; performance of that constitutional function is a responsibility committed to the courts; this responsibility implies the authority necessary to carry it out; therefore the courts have the authority to raise money to sustain their essential functions.[27]

The traditional view is that the inherent powers doctrine has no analogue in Canada.[28] Stumpf himself noted, "the doctrine is uniquely American; it has no counterpart in England, which has no written constitution or separation of powers."[29] In Canada, the doctrine of inherent powers has emerged as a residual category governing court practice and the conduct of proceedings. In *R. v Felderhof*,[30] the Ontario Court of Appeal confirmed the wide ambit of judicial authority over the courtroom, including the conduct of a trial. As Rosenberg J.A. observed:

> Whatever may have been the case in the past, it is no longer possible to view the trial judge as little more than a referee who must sit passively while counsel call the case in any fashion they please . . . It would undermine the administration of justice if a trial judge had no power to intervene at an appropriate time and, like this trial judge, after hearing submissions, make directions necessary to ensure that the trial proceeds in an orderly manner. I do not see this power as a limited one resting solely on the court's power to intervene to prevent an abuse of its process. *Rather, the power is founded on the court's inherent jurisdiction to control its own process.*[31]

Rosenberg J.A. proceeded to affirm that statutory courts, such as provincial offence or municipal courts, also have the implied power to control their own processes.[32] Of course,

---

[27] Felix F. Stumpf, *Inherent Powers of the Courts. Sword and Shield of the Judiciary*, (The National Judicial College, 1994), p. 3 (footnote omitted).

[28] P. Millar and C. Baar, *Judicial Administration in Canada* (IPAC/McGill-Queen's University Press, 1981), p. 45.

[29] Stumpf, above (n 27), p.6.

[30] 2003 O.J. No. 4819 (C.A.).

[31] *Ibid.* [40]. [emphasis added].

[32] Rosenberg J.A. relied on *R. v 974649 Ontario Inc.*, [2001] 3 S.C.R. 575, in which the Supreme Court confirmed the jurisdiction of the Provincial Offences Court of Ontario to grant remedies under s. 24(1) of the *Charter*.

a judge's inherent power to control process is not the same as the inherent powers doctrine in the American sense of the term, which relates to control over court budget as well as process. This does suggest, however, that there are (or, at least, may be) aspects of court procedures which lie outside the power of the Executive to unilaterally determine. As discussed in the next section, these constraints do not apply to the creation of administrative agencies.

3. Constitutional Foundations of Administrative Agencies

At first glance, the constitutional foundations of administrative agencies appear rooted exclusively in parliamentary supremacy. Unlike other common law jurisdictions (the United Kingdom, for example) in which adjudicative tribunals are characterized as part of the judiciary, in Canada, all administrative agencies, including adjudicative tribunals, are part of the executive branch of government.[33]

Administrative agencies are established by statute, and enjoy only those powers provided by the governing statute (which may be subject to amendment, or repeal of the agency itself, at any time). In this sense, administrative agencies do not constitute a "headless" fourth branch of government.[34] That said, such agencies also cannot be seen simply as creatures of the Executive—indeed, in many cases, agencies exercise oversight over the executive branch, up to and including the interpretation of the Constitution (and its enforcement). In Canada, therefore, to the extent the tension around a fourth branch of government has arisen, it has concerned the relationship between the Executive's political leadership (Cabinet and the Prime Minister or Premier) and arm's length or independent executive agencies. This issue has arisen in different ways in different contexts, including whether administrative agencies possess the jurisdiction to apply the *Charter of Rights* (or other constitutional provisions) to their own governing statutes, and whether parties before administrative agencies have a right to an independent and impartial hearing. Each of these areas is discussed below.

The Constitution applies to administrative agencies as it would to "government action" more broadly (for example, an aggrieved person may challenge the action of

---

[33] For discussion, see L. Sossin, "Reflections on the U.K. Tribunal Reform: A Canadian Perspective" (2011) 24 C.J.A.L.P. 17.

[34] For discussion, see Lisa Schultz Bressman, "Judicial Review of Agency Inaction: An Arbitrariness Approach" (2004) 79 N.Y.U. L. Rev. 1657 at 1677; see also Trevor W. Morrison, "Constitutional Avoidance in the Executive Branch" (2006) 106 Colum. L. Rev. 1189. For a Canadian perspective, see France Houle "Constructing the Fourth Branch of Government for Administrative Tribunals" (2007) 37 Supreme Court Law Review 1; and Lorne Sossin, "The Ambivalence of Administrative Justice in Canada: Does Canada Need a Fourth Branch?" in *Lamer: The Sacred Fire*, D. Jutras and A. Dodek (eds.) (2009) 46 Supreme Court Law Review 51.

agencies as a breach of their *Charter* rights). Although it is clear that administrative agencies are *subject to* the Constitution, the issue of whether they can *apply* the Constitution—including with respect to their own governing legislation—has been a more complicated one. The Supreme Court of Canada addressed this question in *Cooper v Canada (Human Rights Commission)*[35] which came on the heels of a trilogy of Supreme Court cases which established that tribunals did have such jurisdiction providing certain criteria were met (for example, that the tribunal had a statutory power to resolve general questions of law).[36]

The Canadian Human Rights Commission is an executive body, established to screen and investigate human rights complaints and determine which should be referred to a hearing before a human rights tribunal. Allowing the Commission to review its empowering legislation, and possibly to strike down portions of that legislation as unconstitutional, would effectively result in the executive branch being able to reverse the actions of the legislative branch. Writing for the majority on this issue, La Forest J. held that, although some executive boards, commissions, and tribunals could invalidate the legislation that created them (labour boards, for example), the Human Rights Commission did not have such jurisdiction. There was no provision in its empowering legislation which explicitly gave the Commission authority to determine questions of law, and nothing in the scheme of the Act which implied that the Commission had this power. Chief Justice Lamer wrote a concurring decision where he argued:

> The assumption by administrative tribunals of jurisdiction over the *Charter* does no less than to invert this hierarchical relationship. Instead of putting the intent of the legislature into effect, the case law of this Court enables tribunals to challenge the decisions of the democratically elected legislature "by the assertion of overriding constitutional norm" (Kuttner, supra, at p. 97). Instead of being subject to the laws of the legislature, the executive can defeat the laws of the legislature. On each occasion that this occurs, a tribunal has disrupted the proper constitutional relationship between it and the legislature. Indeed, I would go so far as to say that a tribunal has, in these circumstances, unconstitutionally usurped power which it did not have.[37]

Writing for the dissent in what has become an oft-cited passage, Justice McLachlin (as she then was) observed:

> In my view, every tribunal charged with the duty of deciding issues of law has the concomitant power to do so. The fact that the question of law concerns the effect of the *Charter* does not change the matter. The *Charter* is not some holy grail which only judicial initiates of the superior courts may touch. The *Charter* belongs to the

---

[35] *Cooper v Canada (Human Rights Commission; Bell v Canada (Canadian Human Rights Commission)*, [1996] 3 S.C.R. 854 [hereinafter *Cooper*].

[36] *Douglas/Kwantlen Faculty Assn. v Douglas College*, [1990] 3 S.C.R. 570; *Cuddy Chicks Ltd. v Ontario (Labour Relations Board)*, [1991] 2 S.C.R. 5; *Tétreault-Gadoury v Canada (Employment and Immigration Commission)*, [1991] 2 S.C.R. 22.

[37] *Cooper*, above (n 35) [23]–[25].

people. All law and law-makers that touch the people must conform to it. Tribunals and commissions charged with deciding legal issues are no exception. Many more citizens have their rights determined by these tribunals than by the courts. If the *Charter* is to be meaningful to ordinary people, then it must find its expression in the decisions of these tribunals. If Parliament makes it clear that a particular tribunal can decide facts and facts alone, so be it. But if Parliament confers on the tribunal the power to decide questions of law, that power must, in the absence of counter-indications, be taken to extend to the *Charter*, and to the question of whether the *Charter* renders portions of its enabling statute unconstitutional.[38]

The tension was resolved in two subsequent Supreme Court decisions in 2003, *Martin*[39] and *Paul*,[40] in which the dissenting justices from *Cooper* carried the day, setting out an expansive approach to the constitutional jurisdiction of agencies (and expressly overruling *Cooper*).

Subsequently, in *R. v Conway*[41] the Supreme Court of Canada addressed the issue of constitutional remedies where administrative agencies hear and decide constitutional disputes. The earlier case law had made clear that tribunals could not invalidate statutes (harkening back to Chief Justice Lamer's concern over inverting the hierarchy between the legislative and executive branches of government). Rather, a tribunal finding that government action or a legislative provision was inconsistent with the Constitution would result in a remedy that applied only to the actual dispute before the tribunal. Such a decision would not follow stare decisis, and cannot have implications in other court or agency settings (or even before the same agency in a later decision).

In *Conway*, the Court decided that the Ontario Review Board (ORB) is a "court of competent jurisdiction" to grant *Charter* remedies under section 24(1) of the *Canadian Charter of Rights and Freedoms,* which empowers a court or tribunal to issue a remedy that is "just and appropriate" in the circumstances. Remedies can range from damages to quashing a decision, from a constitutional exemption to an injunction.

More broadly, *Conway* set an important precedent in refining the relationship among the *Charter*, its remedies, and administrative tribunals.[42] Rather than limiting an inquiry to whether a court or tribunal has jurisdiction for granting a particular remedy, the question became whether a particular tribunal has jurisdiction to grant *Charter* remedies generally, and then whether it can grant the particular remedy sought.[43] The Court's decision that tribunals can access *Charter* remedies means that many tribunals now have authority to consider constitutional questions that fall within their statutory mandate, as long as those remedies are constrained to those which the legislature has otherwise empowered administrative agencies to give.

---

[38] *Ibid.* [70].
[39] *Nova Scotia (Workers' Compensation Board) v Martin*, [2003] 2 S.C.R. 504 [hereinafter *Martin*)].
[40] *Paul v British Columbia (Forest Appeals Commission)*, [2003] 2 S.C.R. 585 [hereinafter *Paul*].
[41] [2010] 1 S.C.R. 765.
[42] *Ibid* [1], [22].
[43] *Ibid* [22].

It is now clear that administrative agencies will play a significant role in developing Canada's Constitution in more diverse and heterogeneous settings than courts.[44] It remains open to Parliament or the legislatures, however, to add provisions specifically removing the constitutional jurisdiction from tribunals.[45] Finally, although administrative agencies have been recognized as having the authority (and legitimacy) to decide constitutional questions, the Supreme Court has also held that parties bringing such challenges do not have the same constitutional rights to an independent and impartial decision-maker as they would before the courts.[46]

Early administrative law case law, such as *Consolidated Bathurst*, often referred to "judicial independence" as applicable to administrative adjudicators as well as judicial ones.[47] In *Canadian Pacific Ltd. v Matsqui Indian Band*,[48] the Supreme Court articulated a vision of independence for administrative agencies (as distinct from courts) for the first time. *Matsqui* concerned a challenge to a tax assessment tribunal established by an Aboriginal band under delegated statutory authority. The Supreme Court of Canada held that the test for institutional independence of courts set out in *Valente*[49] applied, with added flexibility, to administrative tribunals. Lamer C.J. stated:

> ... Moreover, the principles for judicial independence outlined in Valente are applicable in the case of an administrative tribunal, where the tribunal is functioning as an adjudicative body settling disputes and determining the rights of parties. However, I recognize that a strict application of these principles is not always warranted.[50]

Lamer C.J. concluded that the *Valente* principles apply to administrative tribunals on the basis of natural justice principles, but that the test for institutional independence may be less strict than for courts:

> Therefore, while administrative tribunals are subject to the Valente principles, the test for institutional independence must be applied in light of the functions being

---

[44] This diversity has been enhanced further by the Court's recognition that, absent a *Charter of Rights* challenge, administrative agencies nonetheless had an obligation to consider "Charter Values" in the exercise of discretion in the application of public authority. See *Doré v Barreau du Québec*, 2012 SCC 12; and *Loyola High School v Quebec (Attorney General)*, 2015 SCC 12.

[45] See BC *Administrative Tribunals Act* SBC 2004, Ch. 45, s.44.

[46] For a broader discussion, see Lorne Sossin, "The Uneasy Relationship between Independence and Appointments in Canadian Administrative Law" in G. Huscroft and M. Taggart (eds.), *Inside and Outside Canadian Administrative Law: Essays in Honour of David Mullan* (University of Toronto Press, 2006) pp. 50–80; and Gerald Heckman and Lorne Sossin, "How Canadian Administrative Law Protections Measure Up to International Human Rights Standards" (2005) 50 McGill Law Journal 193–264.

[47] *IWA Local 2-69 v Consolidated Bathurst*, [1990] 1 S.C.R. 282, [75]–[79]. [hereinafter *Consolidated Bathurst*].

[48] [1995] 1 S.C.R. 3 [hereinafter *Matsqui*].

[49] Above (n 8).

[50] *Ibid.*, [75], [79]–[80].

performed by the particular tribunal at issue. The requisite level of institutional independence (i.e., security of tenure, financial security and administrative control) will depend on the nature of the tribunal, the interests at stake, and other indices of independence such as oaths of office.[51]

Lamer C.J. did not write for the majority in *Matsqui*, but his decision was subsequently adopted by a majority of the Court in *2747–3174 Québec Inc. v Quebec (Régie des permis d'alcool)*.[52] *Régie* concerned the independence applicable to a liquor regulator. The Court clarified and refined the assertion in *Matsqui* that administrative tribunals are subject to the *Valente* principles of institutional independence, but that the requisite level of institutional independence may be lower than for a court. The Court concluded that the "directors" (adjudicators) of the Régie had sufficient security of tenure because they could not be simply removed at pleasure (i.e., without cause). Gonthier J. explained:

> In my view, the directors' conditions of employment meet the minimum requirements of independence. These do not require that all administrative adjudicators, like judges of courts of law, hold office for life. Fixed-term appointments, which are common, are acceptable. However, the removal of adjudicators must not simply be at the pleasure of the executive.[53]

Thus, by *Régie*, the focus of the Court was on objective guarantees and viewing administrative justice through a judicial lens. The bright-line distinction between judicial and executive adjudicative roles, however, was reinforced by the Supreme Court of Canada several years later in *Ocean Port Hotel Ltd. v British Columbia (General Manager, Liquor Control and Licensing Branch)*.[54] In *Ocean Port*, the Court confirmed that the guarantee of institutional independence in adjudicative tribunal settings is not a constitutional right, but rather a common law protection, and as such, is vulnerable to the government overriding it through ordinary statutory language at any time for any reason.[55]

Ocean Port involved a challenge to the independence of the B.C. Liquor Appeal Board, which heard an appeal from a hotel charged with liquor-related infractions. Pursuant to its empowering legislation, the chair and members of the Liquor Appeal Board "[served] at the pleasure of the Lieutenant Governor in Council".[56] In practice, members were appointed for a one-year term and served on a part-time basis. All members other than the chair were paid on a per diem basis. The Court of Appeal concluded

---

[51] *Ibid.*, [83–85].

[52] (1996), 140 D.L.R. (4th) 577 (SCC) [hereinafter *Régie*].

[53] *Ibid.*, [67].

[54] 2001 SCC 52 [hereinafter *Ocean Port*].

[55] For a more detailed appraisal of *Ocean Port*, see P. Bryden, "Structural Independence of Administrative Tribunals in the Wake of *Ocean Port*" (2003) 16 C.J.A.L.P. 125; and L. Sossin, "Developments in Administrative Law: The 2001–2002 Term" (2002) 18 Supreme Court Law Review (2nd) 41–74.

[56] *Ocean Port* above (n 54) [3].

that members of the Board lacked the necessary guarantees of independence required of administrative decision-makers imposing penalties, and set aside the Board's decision.[57] However, the Supreme Court of Canada pointed out that even if the tribunal did not meet the common law natural justice requirements for institutional independence, this was not fatal to its ability to function because of the clear legislative intent underlying the tribunal's structure:

> It is well-established that, absent constitutional constraints, the degree of independence required of a particular government decision-maker or tribunal is determined by its enabling statute. It is the legislature or Parliament that determines the degree of independence required of tribunal members. The statute must be construed as a whole to determine the degree of independence the legislature intended.[58]

McLachlin C.J., writing for the Court, went on to assert that, confronted with silent or ambiguous legislation, courts generally infer that Parliament or the legislature intended for the tribunal's process to comport with principles of natural justice:

> In such circumstances, administrative tribunals may be bound by the requirement of an independent and impartial decision-maker, one of the fundamental principles of natural justice: Matsqui, supra (per Lamer C.J. and Sopinka J.); Régie, supra, at para. 39; Katz v. Vancouver Stock Exchange, [1996] 3 S.C.R. 405, 139 D.L.R. (4th) 575 . . .
>   However, like all principles of natural justice, the degree of independence required of tribunal members may be ousted by express statutory language or necessary implication. . . . Ultimately, it is Parliament or the legislature that determines the nature of a tribunal's relationship to the executive. It is not open to a court to apply a common law rule in the face of clear statutory direction. Courts engaged in judicial review of administrative decisions must defer to the legislature's intention in assessing the degree of independence required of the tribunal in question.[59]

In *Ocean Port*, the Court concluded that the provincial legislature "spoke directly to the nature of the appointments to the Liquor Appeal Board"; under its enabling legislation, the chair and members of the Board were expressly stated to "serve at the pleasure of the Lieutenant Governor in Council".[60] Thus, the boundaries of independence for administrative agencies are set out by the legislature (or the judicial interpretation of the legislation), not by the Constitution.[61]

---

[57] (1999), 68 B.C.L.R. (3d) 82 (C.A.).

[58] *Ocean Port* above (n 54) [20].

[59] *Ibid.*, [20–22] [emphasis added].

[60] *Ibid.*, [25].

[61] See, for example, *Ell v Alberta* 2003 SCC 35; and *Bell Canada v Canadian Telephone Employees Association* 2003 SCC 36. For the high water mark of applying independence to the administrative justice setting, see *McKenzie v B.C.* (2007) 61 B.C.L.R. (4th) 57 (B.C.S.C.), aff'd on other grounds in *McKenzie v B.C.* (2008) 71 B.C.L.R. (4th) 1 (in which the B.C.S.C. invalidated due to a breach of natural justice and

In *Ocean Port*, McLachlin C.J. characterized tribunals as spanning "the constitutional divide between the judiciary and the executive".[62] This very metaphor suggests a set of institutions which, functionally at least, operate within both the judicial and executive spheres (or, alternatively, which operate within neither sphere). While conceding that courts and tribunals may share similar functions, McLachlin C.J. stressed that it is the constitutional status of each that was at issue in this case. Of tribunals, she stated, "[w]hile they may possess adjudicative functions, they ultimately operate as part of the executive branch of government, under the mandate of the legislature".[63]

In light of the analysis above, the ambivalence of Canada's constitutional foundations for administrative agencies becomes clear. On the one hand, the Supreme Court of Canada has not recognized constraints on the creation, repeal, or restructuring of administrative agencies, and has confirmed that such bodies only possess the powers conferred on them by statutes (subject to constitutional constraints). On the other hand, the Court has recognized the common law right of institutional independence for those who come before agencies, and has affirmed the jurisdiction of most agencies to interpret and apply the Constitution. This ambivalence, or inherent tension, has come to distinguish Canada's distinct doctrine of separation of powers, to which we now turn.

4. SEPARATION OF POWERS

The discussion above reflects the approach to the separation of powers that characterizes Canada's constitution.[64] That approach features a significant adjudicative role for the executive branch through administrative agencies and a significant executive role for the judiciary through the reference power. The executive branch funds and appoints both judges and adjudicators on administrative agencies, boards, and commissions. As a result, drawing boundaries between the Executive and the judiciary, and, within the Executive, between the Cabinet (as the political leadership or the public service which owes a duty of loyalty to the government of the day) and the arm's length adjudicative and regulatory bodies within the executive branch of government, can be immensely complex.

The separation of powers remains a critical but poorly understood facet of Canada's legal and political system.[65] It is often characterized first by what it is not—an explicit

---

infringement of independence the mid-term termination of a residential tenancy adjudicator, while the B.C.C.A. held the appeal was moot, though it expressed doubt as to the correctness of the independence analysis.)

[62] *Ocean Port* above (n 54) [22].

[63] *Ibid*. [12].

[64] For a more detailed discussion of this issue, see the chapter by Warren Newman in this *Handbook*.

[65] This analysis builds on L. Sossin, "The Ambivalence of Executive Power in Canada" in Adam Tomkins and Paul Craig (eds.), *The Executive and Public Law: Power and Accountability in Comparative Perspective* (Oxford University Press, 2005), pp. 52–88.

and rigid set of checks and balances as in the American Constitution. It was not an animating feature of the *Constitution Act, 1867,* which instead focused more on the infrastructure of parliamentary democracy and to a lesser extent on the judiciary. In Canada, one has to look harder in constitutional texts to find a separation of powers doctrine at all, and even then it is apparent only by reading between the lines.

Indeed, the separation of powers, understood as the constitutional and functional distinctiveness of the legislative, executive, and judicial branches of government, has only recently received formal recognition as a feature of Canada's political and legal system.[66] The increasing prominence of the relationship between the branches of Canadian government raises a host of questions. What ought the separation of powers to accomplish in a parliamentary democracy such as Canada? Why has it taken so long for the separation of powers to surface as a constitutional dilemma in Canada?

In addressing these questions, it is important to keep in mind that the separation of powers is as much a normative as a functional exercise in dividing the labour of governmental authority—intended to preserve freedom or promote accountability through diffusing power. Diffusing power requires not just dividing government authority between different branches (and, in a federal jurisdiction such as Canada, also across levels of government) but also ensuring that no single branch is invested with sufficient power to dominate the others. For example, according authority to the judiciary to supervise legislative and executive activities to ensure they comply with the rule of law would not curb the potential for oppression if one or the other of those branches could appoint or dismiss judges at will. Thus, the *separation* of powers and the *balance* of powers emerge as two interdependent principles of liberty.[67]

In his concurring reasons in *Cooper,* discussed above, Lamer C.J. acknowledged the earlier caselaw of the Court, which had held the separation of powers need not be "strict" in the sense of prohibiting non-judicial tribunals from assuming some judicial powers or prohibiting judges from assuming some non-judicial powers (for example, by responding to executive advisory references).[68] However, he cautioned that "the absence of a strict separation of powers does not mean that Canadian constitutional law does not recognize and sustain some notion of the separation of powers."[69] He concluded that

---

[66] The first clear articulation of the separation of powers as a feature of Canada's legal and political system was made by Dickson C.J. in *Fraser v Public Service Staff Relations Board,* [1985] 2 S.C.R. 455, at pp. 469–470, where he observed that:

> There is in Canada a separation of powers among the three branches of government—the legislature, the executive and the judiciary. In broad terms, the role of the judiciary is, of course, to interpret and apply the law; the role of the legislature is to decide upon and enunciate policy; the role of the executive is to administer and implement that policy.

[67] B. Knight, "Introduction" in B. Knight (ed), *Separation of Powers in the American Political System* (George Mason University Press, 1989), p.11.

[68] *Cooper,* above (n 35). A similar point was made by the Supreme Court in *Reference re Secession of Quebec,* [1998] 2 S.C.R. 486 [15].

[69] *Cooper* above (n 35), at 871.

246 OXFORD HANDBOOK OF THE CANADIAN CONSTITUTION

although the separation of powers doctrine in Canada may not be "strict", it nonetheless required that some functions be exclusively reserved to particular bodies.[70]

On the basis of the requirement that the judiciary be free from interference in its constitutional decision-making, Lamer C.J. held in *Cooper* that only courts, and not executive bodies such as the Commission or a human rights tribunal, had jurisdiction to consider the constitutionality of legislation.[71] Lamer C.J.'s concurring reasoning in *Cooper* was endorsed by the majority in the *P.E.I. Reference*.

The *P.E.I. Reference* involved a challenge to proposed salary decisions by provincial governments affecting provincially appointed judges. Lamer C.J., writing for the majority, asserted that "the institutional independence of the judiciary reflects a deeper commitment to the separation of powers between and amongst the legislative, executive, and judicial organs of government: see *Cooper*, supra, at para. 13."[72] In this way, what began as a sole concurring judgment in *Cooper* was incorporated by reference into the majority of the Court's reasons in the *P.E.I. Reference*. Lamer C.J. characterized Canada's separation of powers in the *P.E.I. Reference* as nothing less than "the backbone of our constitutional system."[73]

In the *P.E.I. Reference*, Lamer C.J. asserted that not only must some functions be exclusively reserved to particular bodies but also that the relationship between the branches must have a particular character. To illustrate this point, he cited the hierarchical relationship between the Executive and the legislature, whereby the Executive must execute and implement the policies of the legislature.[74] He also referred to the depoliticized nature of the relationship between the courts and the Executive, and the need for objective structures such as independent remuneration commissions to reflect the requirements of judicial independence.

Judicial independence is one setting which has allowed the Court to elaborate on Canada's separation of powers. Another is the creation of administrative agencies themselves. What would stop a legislature from simply transferring jurisdiction from courts to tribunals or other agencies, and in this way, limiting or removing altogether the jurisdiction of the judiciary?

Since 1981, the leading case regarding the power of the legislative branch to confer jurisdiction to executive administrative agencies has been the *Reference Re Residential Tenancies Act*,[75] which concerned the establishment of a tribunal to hear disputes over residential tenancies. In his decision, Dickson J. (as he then was) formulated a three-part test to determine whether the power conferred to an administrative tribunal is constitutional (which turned on protecting (and defending) the inherent power of Superior Courts), which constituted a constitutional restraint on legislative action.

---

[70] *Ibid.* See also *Reference re Provincial Judges Remuneration*, [1997] 3 S.C.R. 3 at 90 [hereinafter *P.E.I. Reference*].

[71] *Cooper*, above (n 35), [13].

[72] *PEI Reference* above (n 70) [125].

[73] *Ibid.* [867].

[74] *Ibid.* [139]–[140].

[75] [1981] 1 SCR 714 [hereinafter *Residential Tenancies*].

The test for whether a given function would be considered within this exclusive judicial preserve was as follows:

1) A determination of "whether the power or jurisdiction conforms to the power or jurisdiction exercised by superior, district or county courts (a s. 96 court) at the time of Confederation."[76]

2) If yes, a determination of "whether the function in question is 'judicial' in its institutional setting" as opposed to policy making functions.[77]

3) If yes, a determination of the context in which the power is exercised—whether the "judicial powers" are merely ancillary to general administrative functions assigned to the tribunal or necessarily incidental to the achievement of a broader policy goal of the legislature rather than the "sole or central function of the tribunal."[78]

   a. If so, the conferring of judicial power is valid.

   b. If not, the tribunal is "said to be operating like a s. 96 court" and the grant of power is invalid.[79]

Based on this application of the framework, the Court held the legislation creating the Commission to be unconstitutional, as the whole of a s. 96 court's jurisdiction in a certain area had been transferred to the Commission.

This framework was revised in *Sobeys Stores Ltd. v Yoemans* by Wilson J. who stated that the characterization of the "powers" in part 1 of the test "should highlight the type of dispute rather than the type of remedy sought"[80] and must be applied narrowly. She treated this act of characterization as a preliminary step to stage 1 of the three-stage test from *Residential Tenancies*.[81] Wilson also clarified that the first stage in the *Residential Tenancies* test must refer to powers that were exclusive to section 96 courts at the time of confederation, not "shared," meaning powers that are "broadly co-extensive" with inferior provincially appointed courts.[82]

This framework has continued to be revised as new kinds of administrative agencies have been proposed.[83] For example, in *Council of Canadians v Canada (Attorney General)*, the Ontario Court of Appeal determined that tribunals established under chapter 11 of the North American Free Trade Agreement (NAFTA) that resolve claims by aggrieved foreign investors are constitutional. The court found that because NAFTA had only received parliamentary approval and had not been made part of Canada's domestic law, the *Constitution Act, 1867* did not apply. Further, even if it had, the tribunals' duty to

---

[76] *Ibid.* at 734.

[77] *Ibid.*

[78] *Ibid.* at 736.

[79] *Ibid.*

[80] *Sobeys Stores Ltd. v Yeomans*, [1989] 1 SCR 238, [21] [hereinafter *Sobeys Stores*].

[81] *MacMillan Bloedel Ltd. v Simpson* [1995] 4 SCR 725.

[82] *Sobeys Stores* (n 80) [31].

[83] See for example *Re Young Offenders Act (P.E.I.)*, [1991] 1 SCR 252, *McMillan Bloedel* above (n 79), and *Reference re Amendments to the Residential Tenancies Act* (N.S.), [1996] 1 S.C.R. 186.

decide whether a NAFTA party had breached the treaty was not analogous to a jurisdiction exercised by superior courts at the time of Confederation, nor did NAFTA preclude an investor from taking its claim to a domestic court, as NAFTA did not give tribunals exclusive jurisdiction to resolve such disputes. Therefore, on the basis of the *Residential Tenancies* test, the act did not overstep a "core function of superior courts." [84]

This line of caselaw represents the ways in which the separation of powers interacts with the Canadian Constitution to produce both the boundaries of the courts and the boundaries of the legislature in establishing administrative agencies.

(i) Indigenous Adjudication and the Constitution

An emerging issue in Canada's "living tree" approach to constitutional evolution[85] is the growing importance of Indigenous self-government as an instantiation of Aboriginal rights and Aboriginal title, and as a mechanism for broader goals of reconciliation. Self-governing First Nations will often have authority to establish their own dispute resolution bodies (whether as part of a treaty or as an unextinguished Aboriginal right protected under section 35 of the *Constitution Act, 1982*). These bodies may apply Indigenous legal norms (including Indigenous constitutional principles and practices)[86] or other forms of statutory authority (over land use or wildlife protection, for example). These bodies may have jurisdiction delegated by other statutes or created through a First Nation legislative authority.[87]

Interestingly, in *Matsqui*, discussed above, the majority concluded that the requisite independence and impartiality of the Indigenous tax assessment tribunal at issue should be viewed by the Court through the lens of Indigenous self-government. This principle was affirmed by La Forest J. in *Mitchell v Peguis Indian Band*,[88] also in the tax exemption rights context:

> it is clear that in the interpretation of any statutory enactment dealing with Indians, and particularly the Indian Act, it is appropriate to interpret in a broad manner provisions that are aimed at maintaining Indian rights, and to interpret narrowly provisions aimed at limiting or abrogating them.[89]

For Chief Justice Lamer, however, the rules of natural justice could not be viewed differently in light of the Indigenous context, and for the moment, that view from the minority in *Matsqui* has subsequently been adopted as the guiding framework for the independence of administrative agencies at common law.

---

[84] *Council of Canadians v Canada (Attorney General)* [2006] O.J. No. 4751, [53].

[85] See the chapter by W.J. Waluchow in this *Handbook*.

[86] John Borrows, *Canada's Indigenous Constitution* (University of Toronto Press, 2010).

[87] See Lorne Sossin, "Indigenous Self-Government and the Future of Administrative Law" (2012) 45 UBC L. Rev. 595–630.

[88] [1990] 2 S.C.R. 85.

[89] *Ibid.*, [143].

More recently, initiatives geared toward more meaningful participation of Indigenous communities in administrative agencies (such as the National Energy Board), co-management agencies (such as the Mackenzie Valley Environmental Impact Review Board), and agencies within the territorial framework of Nunavut and within self-governing Indigenous communities (such as the Nisga'a Administrative Tribunal) all suggest that new relationships between Canada's constitutional infrastructure and administrative agencies, which are aimed at (or a reflection of) reconciliation with Indigenous communities, may be in the midst of forming.[90]

5. CONCLUSION

Canada's constitutional context for courts and administrative agencies reflect a tension between formalism and functionalism. There is real constitutional significance as to whether an adjudicative body is located in the judiciary as opposed to an executive agency. Judicial independence and the constitutional protections which characterize the judicial branch of government apply only as a more flexible, common law set of guarantees in the executive context (which are subject to statutory override).[91] Indeed, litigants coming before a court enjoy guarantees and protections not afforded by an adjudicative administrative tribunal, even where the rights at issue and subject matter of the adjudication are identical. In other contexts, however, such as the rule of law constraints on executive appointments, these apply equally to appointments for courts and administrative agencies.

BIBLIOGRAPHY

Secondary sources

Borrows, John *Canada's Indigenous Constitution* (University of Toronto Press, 2010).
Ellis, Ron *Unjust by Design* (University of British Columbia Press, 2013).
Houle, France "Constructing the Fourth Branch of Government for Administrative Tribunals" (2007) 37 Supreme Court Law Review 1.
Sossin, Lorne "The Ambivalence of Executive Power in Canada" in Adam Tomkins and Paul Craig (eds.), *The Executive and Public Law: Power and Accountability in Comparative Perspective* (Oxford University Press, 2005), pp. 52–88.

Cases

Canadian Pacific Ltd. v Matsqui Indian Band [1995] 1 S.C.R. 3

---

[90] See Janna Promislow and Lorne Sossin, "In Search of Aboriginal Administrative Law" in C. Flood and L. Sossin, (eds), *Administrative Law in Context* 2nd ed. (Emond Montgomery, 2012).

[91] This differentiation has been subject to criticism: see Ron Ellis, *Unjust by Design* (UBC Press, 2013).

Cooper v Canada (Human Rights Commission; Bell v Canada (Canadian Human Rights Commission), [1996] 3 S.C.R. 854

Nova Scotia (Workers' Compensation Board) v Martin, [2003] 2 S.C.R. 504

Ocean Port Hotel Ltd. v British Columbia (General Manager, Liquor Control and Licensing Branch 2001 SCC 52

Reference Re Residential Tenancies Act, [1981] 1 SCR 714

Roncarelli v Duplessis, [1959] S.C.R. 121

D. Constitutional Amendment

CHAPTER 12

....

AMENDING THE CONSTITUTION OF CANADA

....

BENOÎT PELLETIER[*]

In the past, Canadian constitutional reform, which has varied through different periods, has always been a laborious process, marked by surprising successes and resounding failures. But since the patriation of the Canadian Constitution in 1982, the latter has proven to be particularly difficult to amend. The recent attempt by the former Harper government to reform the Senate without resorting to a complex amendment procedure showed that there exists in Canada a temptation among many decision makers to circumvent the formal constitutional amendment process in hopes of facilitating the achievement of their goals.

This chapter reviews the history of Canadian constitutional reform, beginning with the amendment procedure that obliged Canada to address the United Kingdom Parliament at Westminster in order to amend the most substantial parts of its Constitution prior to patriation. It also examines the post-patriation constitutional amendment method in the form of five formulae, three of which require various degrees of participation of the federal and provincial orders of government. It will then move on to analyse the political and legal frameworks, that is, the latest formalities which have further complicated the already strict requirements of modern constitutional amendment in Canada. Finally, it will point out the diverse phenomena that favour paraconstitutional adaptation of the Constitution. These "paraconstitutional" procedures, developed by political players and Canadian courts, provide an additional—and probably unnecessary—overlay on the formal constitutional amendment procedure.

* C.M., O.Q., FRSC, Ad. E., Doctor of Laws, Full Professor at the Faculty of Law of the University of Ottawa. The author wishes to thank Ms. Afton Maisonneuve, student at law, for her contribution to this text, as well as Mr. Warren J. Newman, for his comments. The author assumes full responsibility for the content of his text.

Today, it is clear that no major constitutional reform is possible in Canada without a very strong political will and public support. Nevertheless, the word "Constitution" has practically become taboo in this country. It evokes, in the eyes of a portion of the population, heated debates with unsuccessful outcomes. Thus, the reform of the Canadian Constitution is first and foremost dependent on the rehabilitation of the word "Constitution" itself.

1. Introduction

The question of constitutional reform in Canada is but one dimension in the complex subject of the renewal of the Canadian political system. This renewal process, whether constitutional or non-constitutional in nature, should not only take into account and reconcile the interests of the various federative partners but should also be based upon continuing discussions and dialogue.

Despite the fact that constitutional reform remains a fundamental means of changing federalism, or other features of the constitutional arrangements, one must be careful not to consider it as a universal remedy or a solution for all problems. Indeed, the settlement of constitutional issues can never be definitive. Every society is in a constant state of flux. As Ernest Renan said, a nation's existence is a daily plebiscite.[1] To think that constitutional reform will suffice to put an end to the tensions that are the very leaven of life in society is to have a limited understanding of democracy.

Bearing these few thoughts in mind, this chapter intends to examine constitutional renewal in Canada. Following a historical review that highlights the different steps undertaken in the search for a constitutional amending procedure, it will examine the legal and political frameworks in which constitutional reform is envisioned today, as well as the paraconstitutional adaptation processes that sometimes serve as an alternative to the formal amendment procedure of the Canadian Constitution.

Although it is important to avoid confusing "constitutional reform" with "constitutional amendment",[2] the fact remains that the amending formula has played an important role in the challenge that is Canada's constitutional reform. Indeed, from the very outset, one of the objectives of this renewal has been the establishment of a constitutional amendment procedure based in Canadian institutions.

---

[1] E. Renan, "What Is a Nation?", in G. Eley and R.G. Suny (eds), *Becoming National: A Reader* (Oxford University Press, 1996) 53.
[2] "Constitutional reform" refers to the content of the projects seeking to develop the constitutional framework or to encourage its adaptation to the changing realities and needs of society. "Constitutional amendment" concerns the process that the reform must follow.

2. History

A. Pre-patriation

The *Constitution Act, 1867*,[3] which created the Canadian federation, did not include any general provisions containing an amendment procedure that would have allowed the alteration of the Act's main elements. The constituent authority thus remained part of the Parliament of the United Kingdom, at Westminster. With Canada's progressive evolution towards the status of an independent state, a process which began during the time of World War I, the absence of an internal method permitting broad constitutional change was increasingly perceived as an anomaly that was irreconcilable with the idea of true Canadian sovereignty.

Beginning in 1927, the question of the adoption of a domestic constitutional amendment procedure became the subject of discussion between the federal government and the provinces. However, these negotiations did not produce an agreement; as a result, a statutory provision prolonging the constitutional power of the British Parliament with respect to amending Canada's Constitution was incorporated into the *Statute of Westminster, 1931*, which, notwithstanding the aforementioned provision, formally confirmed Canada's independence.[4]

The discussions continued and in 1936, the Standing Committee on Constitutional Matters, established within the context of the Federal-Provincial Conference of 1935, put forward a set of conditions to which constitutional amendments would be subjected. There was no immediate follow-up to this proposal; however, it did exert influence over subsequent debates, notably the white paper on constitutional amendments that was released in 1965,[5] which established a "lasting distinction between amendments affecting the federal government only, the provinces only, and the federal government and some or all of the provinces".[6]

The classification of various subjects of constitutional amendment corresponded to graduated consent requirements. The proposal of 1936 contained the premises of each constitutional amendment method known today, including one similar to the current "7/50 procedure"[7] and another that recognized the provincial right to opt out.[8]

---

[3] Originally, the *British North America Act, 1867* (UK), 30 & 31 Vict., c 3; RSC 1985, App II, no 5, renamed in 1982 the *Constitution Act, 1867*, in the wake of the patriation of the Canadian Constitution and the "Canadianization" of the ensuing constitutional laws. The *Constitution Act, 1867*, shall hereafter be referred to as the Act of 1867.

[4] *Statute of Westminster, 1931* (UK), 22 Geo 5, c 4; RSC 1985, App. II, no 27, at s 7(1).

[5] Hon Guy Favreau, *The Amendment of the Constitution of Canada* (Queen's Printer, 1965) appendix 3, 110.

[6] *Ibid*, 22.

[7] P. Gérin-Lajoie, *Constitutional Amendment in Canada* (University of Toronto Press, 1950) 301–312. Of note, the current 7/50 procedure must be accomplished via a resolution of the Senate (which only has a suspensive veto of 180 days) and the House of Commons, in addition to resolutions of the legislatures of at least two-thirds of the provinces with at least 50 percent of the population of all the provinces. The 7/50 procedure is discussed at the end of this sub-heading.

[8] See draft s 148, paragraph 1c) prepared on the basis of a revision of the Act of 1867 and reproduced in P. Gérin-Lajoie, *ibid*, at p. 303–304; Also see William Hodge, "Patriation of the Canadian

In 1949, an amendment made by the United Kingdom to the Act of 1867 conferred upon Parliament[9] the power to amend the constitutional provisions that exclusively concerned the internal management of federal institutions. Following this amendment, the federal government convened a conference in 1950[10] to discuss, with the provinces, a more general constitutional amendment procedure based on the proposals of 1935–1936. However, the deliberations of this conference were suspended indefinitely at the end of 1950.

Intergovernmental discussions resumed in the 1960s. The "Fulton formula" was developed within the context of the Conference of Attorneys General in 1960 and 1961.[11] This formula proposed a constitutional amendment procedure that favoured the unanimous consent rule in the case of major constitutional changes, specifically those concerning the powers of the provinces. In order to give the system a certain level of flexibility, this formula also provided for a course of action making delegation of legislative powers possible.

This proposal served as the basis for the "Fulton-Favreau formula", to which all of the first ministers agreed at a federal-provincial conference held in 1964.[12] The formula was ratified by nine legislatures. In Quebec, however, the government of Jean Lesage abstained from seeking ratification, due to concerns that it would become impossible to obtain passage of a more comprehensive constitutional reform that would better meet Quebec's objectives.

Another unfruitful attempt was made in the form of the Canadian Constitutional Charter of 1971, often referred to as the "Victoria Charter".[13] This charter recommended a general approach to constitutional amendment based on the consent of the two Houses of Parliament (where the Senate would have only a suspensive veto of 90 days) and of each major region within the federation. In order for this regional consent to be valid, not only did the majority of provinces have to give their approval, but that consensus also had to include:

a) each province representing or having represented in the past at least 25 percent of the population of Canada (hence Quebec and Ontario);
b) at least two Atlantic provinces;

Constitution: Comparative Federalism in a New Context" (1984–1985) 60 Wash. L. Rev 585. As for the current right of the Canadian provinces to opt out of some constitutional amendments, it will be discussed below, under the present sub-heading and also under the "Legal Framework" sub-heading.

[9] In the rest of this text, "Parliament" will signify the Parliament of Canada, whereas "legislatures" will designate the provincial legislative assemblies.

[10] Canada, Constitutional Conference of Federal and Provincial Governments, *Amending the Constitution* (Ottawa and Quebec, 1950) 128 p. JL 69 A3, A11).

[11] Canada, Conference of Attorneys General of Canada on Constitutional Amendment, *Canadian Annual Review for 1960* (Ottawa, 1960) 45–48.

[12] Canada, Federal-Provincial Conference, *Agreement on a Formula to Amend and Repatriate the Constitution* (Ottawa, 1964) (JL 69 A3 1964 October A1) 44.

[13] Canada, Canadian Constitutional Conference, *Agreement on a Charter Containing a Constitutional Amending Formula* (Victoria, June 14, 1971) (JL 69 A3 1971 June A1) 77 [hereinafter Victoria Charter].

c) at least two Western provinces representing a minimum of 50 percent of the combined population of this region.

On 20 June 1978, Prime Minister Pierre Elliott Trudeau tabled the *Constitutional Amendment Act, 1978*, better known as Bill C-60, in the House of Commons. This bill contained the constitutional amendments that the Canadian government had made public shortly before, in a White Paper entitled *A Time for Action: Toward the Renewal of the Canadian Federation*.[14] The Bill was referred to the Supreme Court of Canada with regards to the reform of the Senate. The Supreme Court ruled that Parliament could act unilaterally only for what concerns matters of exclusive federal jurisdiction.[15] Following that decision along with a negative reaction from certain provinces, Bill C-60 was not adopted.

The regional approach of the Victoria Charter was employed once again in 1979 in the Pepin-Robarts Report.[16] However, the procedure proposed in that report included a specific requirement pertaining to the ratification by referendum of constitutional amendments passed beforehand by the House of Commons and by a new institution, to be called the Council of the Federation. The Report also recommended allowing the delegation of legislative powers between the two orders of government.

In October 1980, the federal government published a draft resolution in which it proposed proceeding unilaterally with the patriation of the Canadian Constitution accompanied with substantial amendments. Essentially, the draft resolution embodied the Victoria Charter approach, based on regional consent. However, it added a process reserved solely for the federal government whereby the latter could, in the absence of consent of the legislatures, resort to a referendum process.

The provinces, with the exception of Ontario and New Brunswick, formed a common front to oppose the aforementioned proposal. In their interprovincial accord of 16 April 1981, the eight provinces in question recommended their alternative to the unilateral patriation of the Constitution referred to in the federal resolution. Under their scheme, patriation was to be done in conjunction with changes dealing with two subjects: the constitutional amendment procedure on the one hand, and the delegation of legislative powers between the two orders of government on the other.

The interprovincial accord ruled out the regional approach to constitutional amendment embodied in the Victoria Charter and returned to the general and residual procedure based on the 7/50 rule. It also dismissed the idea of resorting to a referendum in the event of a deadlock between the governments. It incorporated an important element in

---

[14] Prime Minister of Canada, Supply and Services Canada, *A Time for Action: Toward the Renewal of the Canadian Federation* (1978).

[15] *Reference re Authority of Parliament in relation to the Upper House* [1980] 1 SCR 54.

[16] Canada, Task Force on Canadian Unity, *A Future Together: Observations and Recommendations* (Supply and Services Canada, 1979) 103–104 and 130–131.

the 7/50 formula, namely the right to opt out with full financial compensation in the case of a transfer of a power to Parliament.

The issue of the constitutionality of the federal proposal of unilateral patriation was also submitted to the appellate courts of three provinces (Quebec, Newfoundland, and Manitoba) and, on appeal, was referred to the Supreme Court of Canada. In September 1981, the highest court in the country concluded that the federal proposal was constitutionally valid from a legal standpoint, but that a constitutional convention existed requiring a "substantial degree of provincial consent". In other words, the fact that the federal proposal at stake could have been achieved unilaterally or with the consent of only two provinces would not have satisfied the conditions put forward by the Court; it would have been legal but conventionally unconstitutional.[17]

Following this ruling, the federal-provincial negotiations resumed and the governments succeeded in reaching, on 5 November 1981, an agreement on the patriation of the Constitution, to which Quebec refused to give its consent. This agreement finally opted for the 7/50 procedure, as was the case in the interprovincial accord of 16 April 1981, but made changes including limiting financial compensation to a number of specifically-contemplated situations where the right to opt out could be exercised and leaving out the formula for the delegation of legislative powers. Regardless of Quebec's refusal to give its consent,[18] this agreement led to the patriation of the Constitution and to the entry into force of the *Constitution Act, 1982*[19] on 17 April 1982. In a further reference by the Quebec government, first to the Quebec Court of Appeal and then on appeal to the Supreme Court of Canada, both courts ruled that the patriation of the Constitution satisfied the conventional requirement of a substantial consensus of the provinces.[20]

The Act of 1982 contains, in its Part V, the constitutional amendment procedure. It is composed of five different categories, two of which are based on the passage of a law by a legislative assembly. They respectively cover:

- the exercise of the exclusive power that section 44 confers on Parliament with respect to the amendment of constitutional provisions concerning federal institutions (executive government of Canada, Senate, and House of Commons);
- the exclusive provincial power stipulated in section 45 regarding the amendment of the constitution of a province.

---

[17] *Re: Resolution to amend the Constitution* [1981] 1 SCR 753, at pp. 904–905. On this subject, see the chapter by Carissima Mathen in this *Handbook*.

[18] James Ross Hurley, *Amending Canada's Constitution* History, Processes, Problems, and Prospects (Supply and Services Canada, 1996) 297.

[19] *Constitution Act, 1982*, schedule B of the *Canada Act 1982* c11 (UK). The *Constitution Act, 1982* shall hereafter be referred to as the Act of 1982.

[20] *Re: Objection by Quebec to a Resolution to amend the Constitution* [1982] 2 SCR 793, 806; [1982] CA 33, 134 DLR (3d) 719 (QCA).

The three other procedures require a proclamation of the Governor General under the Great Seal of Canada, authorized by resolutions adopted by Parliament and some or all legislatures. They include:

- the unanimous consent procedure of section 41, which demands, in addition to federal consent,[21] that of all the provinces. This formula only applies to a limited number of questions, which are specified in the Act of 1982;[22]
- the procedure defined in section 43 of the Act of 1982, which deals with constitutional amendments that only concern one or more, but not all, provinces. It stipulates that such amendments must be authorized at the federal level[23] and by the province(s) affected;
- the "7/50" procedure, which has already been defined above.[24] It is detailed at sections 38 to 40 of the Act of 1982 and it constitutes the general and residual provision. It should only be used when none of the other complex formulae are applicable. It provides for a provincial right to opt out in case of amendments that derogate "from the legislative powers, the proprietary rights or any other rights or privileges of the legislature or government of a province". However, when the right to opt out is exercised, a right to financial compensation may apply albeit very limited in its range.[25] Section 42

---

[21] Of note, the Senate only has a suspensive veto of 180 days by virtue of s 47 of the Act of 1982.

[22] These questions are as follows:

- the office of the Queen, the Governor General and the Lieutenant Governor of a province;
- the right of a province to a number of members in the House of Commons not less than the number of Senators by which the province is entitled to be represented at the time the constitutional amendment formulae come into force;
- subject to s 43 of the Act of 1982, the use of the English or the French language;
- the composition of the Supreme Court of Canada;
- an amendment to Part V of the Act of 1982, namely the constitutional amendment procedure itself.

In Philippe Lagassé and Patrick Baud, "The Crown and Constitutional Amendment after the *Senate Reform* and *Supreme Court References*" in Emmett Macfarlane (ed), *Constitutional Amendment in Canada* (University of Toronto Press 2016) 263, the authors examined the question as to how to determine what aspects of the Crown fall under s 41 of the Act of 1982. They came to the following conclusion:

First, does the function or power in question include an exercise of discretion by the Queen, the governor general, or a lieutenant-governor? If so, then a unanimous constitutional amendment is required, as per paragraph 41(a). Second, does the function or power affect the Queen's status as head of state, including the principles that govern who holds the office of the Queen? If so, then unanimity is also needed to alter these principles. If, however, the answers to these first two questions is no, then a third question must be asked: do the functions or powers of the Crown affect provincial interests or the fundamental nature and role of the Crown as the executive power? If the answer is yes, then the general amending procedure applies. But if the answer is no, then the unilateral amending procedures apply.

[23] Above (n 21).

[24] Above (n 7).

[25] Section 40 of the Act of 1982 limits the right to reasonable compensation to cases where powers are transferred to Parliament "relating to education or other cultural matters".

also refers to the 7/50 procedure, to which it expressly links a number of questions,[26] but specifies that the right to opt out does not apply to these specific cases.

B. Post-patriation

The unsuccessful Meech Lake Accord ratification process,[27] attempted between 1987 and 1990, clearly demonstrated how demanding the requirements for constitutional amendment had become. In spite of this, a number of amendments have been made since 1982. Except for the first amendment which was adopted in 1983 by way of the 7/50 procedure, most were implemented bilaterally under section 43 of the Act of 1982, which involves only the federal level and each province directly concerned by the amendment. The following is a list of constitutional amendments made since 1982, including three textual amendments that were made under the legislative authority granted to Parliament by section 44 of the Act of 1982. However, it should be noted that statutory enactments of an organic character, which were made under section 44 but which did not alter the text of the Constitution, have been excluded.[28]

- The *Constitution Amendment Proclamation,1983*,[29] which incorporated into the Act of 1982 a series of provisions with respect to the Aboriginal peoples, including section 35.1;
- the *Constitution Act, 1985 (Representation)*,[30] which amended section 51(1) of the Act of 1867 to establish new rules for readjustments to the number of members of the House of Commons and the representation of the provinces;
- the *Constitution Amendment, 1987 (Newfoundland Act)*,[31] which sought to extend education rights to the Pentecostal Church in Newfoundland;

---

[26] It involves the following questions:

- the principle of proportionate representation of the provinces in the House of Commons prescribed by the Constitution of Canada;
- the powers of the Senate and the method of selecting Senators;
- the number of members by which a province is entitled to be represented in the Senate and the residence qualifications of Senators;
- the Supreme Court of Canada, subject to s 41(*d*), dealing with the composition of the Court;
- the extension of existing provinces into the territories;
- "notwithstanding any other law or practice," the establishment of new provinces.

[27] Canada, Federal-Provincial Conference of First Ministers on the Constitution, *1987 Constitutional Accord* (Ottawa, 3 June, 1987), Doc 800-025/006) [hereinafter Meech Lake Accord]. The Meech Lake Accord was a package of constitutional amendments designed to have Quebec give its consent to the 1982 patriation. With that in mind, this accord focused on six main subjects: recognition that Quebec constitutes a distinct society within Canada, appointments to the Senate, agreements on immigration and aliens, constitutional amendment, appointments to the Supreme Court of Canada, and limitation on federal spending power.

[28] Such as the *Royal Assent Act* (SC 2002 c 15).

[29] *Constitution Amendment Proclamation, 1983* RSC 1985 App II n° 46.

[30] *Representation Act, 1985* (SC 1986 c 8), at s 4.

[31] *Constitution Amendment, 1987 (Newfoundland Act)*.

- the *Constitution Amendment, 1993 (New Brunswick)*,[32] which recognized the equality of the two official language communities of New Brunswick;
- the *Constitution Amendment, 1994 (Prince Edward Island)*,[33] which allowed the Confederation Bridge to replace the constitutionally-guaranteed steamship ferry service provided by Canada;
- the *Constitution Amendment, 1997 (Newfoundland Act)*,[34] which allowed the province of Newfoundland to establish a new secular school system to replace the church-based education system;
- the *Constitution Amendment, 1997 (Quebec)*,[35] which intended to permit the establishment of English and French linguistic school boards in Quebec and make the school system non-denominational;
- the *Constitution Amendment, 1998 (Newfoundland Act)*,[36] which gave the legislature of Newfoundland exclusive authority to make laws in relation to education in the province, subject to the obligation of providing courses in religion that would not be specific to a religious denomination;
- the *Constitution Act, 1999 (Nunavut)*,[37] which provided Senate and House of Commons representation for Nunavut;
- the *Constitution Amendment, 2001 (Newfoundland and Labrador)*,[38] which changed the name of the province of Newfoundland to that of "Newfoundland and Labrador";[39]
- the *Fair Representation Act*,[40] which replaced section 51(1) of the Act of 1867 with a new formula for seat number and distribution in the House of Commons.

3. Legal and Political Frameworks

A. Legal Framework

Not surprisingly, the amendment procedure set forth in Part V of the Act of 1982 plays a central role at the legal level. Recall that it is comprised of five main categories, two of which

---

[32] *Constitution Amendment, 1993 (New Brunswick)*.
[33] *Constitution Amendment, 1994 (Prince Edward Island)*.
[34] *Constitution Amendment, 1997 (Newfoundland Act)*.
[35] *Constitution Amendment, 1997 (Quebec)*.
[36] *Constitution Amendment, 1998 (Newfoundland Act)*.
[37] *An Act to amend the Nunavut Act and the Constitution Act, 1867.*
[38] *Constitution Amendment, 2001 (Newfoundland and Labrador)*.
[39] See http://www.pco-bcp.gc.ca/aia/index.asp?lang=eng&page=canada&doc=constitution-eng.htm accessed 27 March 2017 for a list of constitutional amendments since 1982 which involved both orders of government in the approval process.
[40] SC 2011 c 26, s 2.

are fairly simple to apply because their respective scope is limited to only one order of government, and because they are based uniquely on the enactment of a law.[41]

Naturally, constitutional amendments with an entrenched, supralegislative status are not included in these unilateral powers. Rather, as seen before,[42] they fall within more complex procedures requiring resolutions from the two Houses of Parliament and from a number of legislatures that vary according to the method in question.[43] By their legal character, these resolutions are separate from and independent of the constitutional accords contemplating such amendments; these accords are more in the nature of political realities falling within the sphere of intergovernmental relations.

The amendment procedure of 1982 is complex. Its consent standards are demanding, and a number of its more technical aspects can further complicate the situation. This is the case, for example, regarding the ratification time limits applicable to the 7/50 procedure.[44] Moreover, whatever formula is required for a resolution of assent, according to section 46(2) of the Act of 1982, it can be revoked at any time before the issue of a proclamation.[45]

Finally, within the context of fundamental matters related to the renewal of Canadian federalism, there has been a trend, if one considers the Meech Lake Accord and the Charlottetown Accord,[46] to bring together in one single resolution several amendments falling under different modalities at the procedural level. Indeed, when a single resolution embodies various proposals that are subject to different levels of approval, the most demanding formula is applicable. This approach has resulted in an "increase" in the global requirements related to the process, particularly concerning the consents required and the application of ratification time limits.

[41] Section 44 for federal institutions and s 45 for provincial constitutions. More precisely, concerning s 45 of the Act of 1982, see Emmanuelle Richez, "The Possibilities and Limits of Provincial Constitution-Making Power: The Case of Quebec" in Emmett Macfarlane (ed), above (n 22), at p. 165. Richez recalls that this provision does not prevent provinces from adopting a new constitution, although this would not necessarily involve substantial constitutional changes.

[42] Under the "Pre-patriation" sub-heading.

[43] As discussed under the "Pre-patriation" sub-heading, s 41 provides for unanimous consent; s 43 for federal consent as well as consent from the province or provinces concerned (i.e., those to which the amendment applies); s 38 to 40 stipulate the 7/50 procedure, also known as the "general" or "residual" formula, and include the provincial right to opt out and limited financial compensation; s 42 applies the 7/50 formula to some specific categories, while excluding in those cases the provincial right to opt out and financial compensation. Also, recall that the Senate only has a suspensive veto of 180 days in this context by virtue of s 47 of the Act of 1982.

[44] Benoît Pelletier, *La modification constitutionnelle au Canada* (Carswell, 1996) 305–307.

[45] Which is what occurred with the Meech Lake Accord in April 1990.

[46] Canada, Federal-Provincial Conference of First Ministers on the Constitution, *Consensus Report on the Constitution* (Charlottetown, 28 August, 1992) [hereinafter Charlottetown Accord]. This accord was a follow-up to the Meech Lake Accord. However, in comparison, it did not aim to merely respond to the conditions of the government of Quebec to obtain the latter's political acceptance of the Act of 1982. Instead, it intended to respond to the demands of all Canadian provinces, the three territories, and indigenous peoples. In order to do that, it made an extensive and global proposition to reform the Constitution of Canada. In other words, the Charlottetown Accord went well above the six main subjects addressed by the Meech Lake Accord. For more on the different subjects covered by the Meech Lake Accord, see above (n 27).

Since the enactment of the Act of 1982, Part V has not been amended. No follow-up has been given to the attempts at reforming the procedure for amending the Constitution of Canada like those that were undertaken within the context of the Meech Lake and Charlottetown Accords. This is despite section 49 of the Act of 1982 which obliged the Prime Minister of Canada to convene, within 15 years after the coming into force of the amendment procedure, a constitutional conference in order to re-examine it. Following the federal-provincial conference held in Ottawa on 20 and 21 June 1996, the Prime Minister considered that he had met this obligation, even though no action to review the procedure was initiated.[47]

Since 1982, one legislative initiative should be highlighted: Parliament's enactment of *An Act respecting constitutional amendments.*[48] This piece of legislation was passed in the wake of the Quebec Referendum held on 30 October 1995, and adds supplementary conditions to the process for authorizing amendments within Parliament on the margin of the existing constitutional provisions. Under the Act, the proposal by a federal minister of a motion for a resolution to authorize an amendment subject to the 7/50 procedure is conditional upon obtaining the prior consent of a majority of provinces. Ultimately, the definition of the term "majority of provinces" results in the existence of five different regional vetoes.[49]

The scope of the Act mentioned above remains broad because the conditions which it sets out are related to the 7/50 procedure, and as such, whatever that procedure applies by virtue of section 42 (which defines specific subjects) or by virtue of section 38 (as a general and residual constitutional approach). However, in the latter case, the Act does not involve amendments that give rise to the exercise of a right to opt out by a province, pursuant to section 38(3) of the Act of 1982.

The objective of *An Act respecting constitutional amendments* is therefore to provide additional guarantees on the requirement of consent for certain constitutional amendments. One of the "regional vetoes" is specifically granted to Quebec, where it is considered that the 7/50 procedure does not in fact provide sufficient protection in some respects. However, the federal measure does not have constitutional status and does not resolve the problem of the restrictive scope of the financial compensation provided for in the case of the exercise of the provincial right to opt out defined in section 38 of the Act of 1982.

Although the federal Act contains a commitment with respect to the consent of Quebec, it also adds extra conditions which are likely to have an impact on matters related to constitutional renewal. The regional consent standard adopted in the Act

---

[47] Benoît Pelletier, "Ottawa doit respecter l'article 49 de la Loi constitutionnelle de 1982" *La Presse* (Montreal, 21 June 1996) B3; Benoît Pelletier, "L'échéance de 1997 doit être respectée" *Le Devoir* (Montreal, 14 June 1996) A9; Benoît Pelletier, "Ottawa doit respecter l'article 49 de la Loi constitutionnelle de 1982" *Le Soleil* (Quebec, 14 June 1996) B7. Also see John Whyte, " 'A constitutional conference . . . shall be convened . . . ': Living with Constitutional Promises", (1996) 8 *Constitutional Forum* 15.

[48] *An Act respecting constitutional amendments* SC 1996 c 1.

[49] Which include Quebec, Ontario, British Columbia, 50 percent of the population of the Prairie provinces, and 50 percent of the population of the Atlantic provinces.

is difficult to achieve. In practice, the consent of at least seven provinces representing about 93 percent of the population of Canada would be required to meet the threshold.[50] Interestingly, the conditions that it imposes are harder to meet than those of the regional framework stipulated in the Victoria Charter of 1971.

B. Political Framework

The parameters of constitutional renewal are not limited to the legal aspects. Constitutional reform exists in an environment where many vested political interests are omnipresent.

According to section 46(1) of the Act of 1982, the initiative of constitutional amendment lies with the political players. However, does the fact of sponsoring such an initiative—which may either be federal or provincial—impose on these players an obligation to negotiate? More specifically, could the obligation to negotiate identified by the Supreme Court of Canada in the *Reference re Secession of Quebec*[51] apply to a matter other than Quebec's accession to sovereignty? This question is a current subject of debate and there seems to be no consensus on the general or specific nature of such an obligation. That being said, an argument could be made that the constitutional obligation to negotiate only applies in the context of secession, especially considering the fact that the Court emphasized the link between the said constitutional obligation and the international recognition of a sovereign state. In any event, whether the obligation to negotiate exists or not in a context other than that of secession, it is clear that the exercise by one

---

[50] In order to achieve this number, a calculation was made pursuant to *An Act respecting constitutional amendments*, based on the Statistics Canada data table on population and dwelling counts, for Canada, provinces and territories, 2011 and 2006 censuses, available online at: https://www12.statcan.gc.ca/census-recensement/2011/dp-pd/hlt-fst/pd-pl/Table-Tableau.cfm?LANG=Eng&T=101&S=50&O=A.

[51] *Reference re: Secession of Quebec* [1998] 2 SCR 217 [hereinafter *Secession Reference*]. (See the chapter by Jean Leclair in this *Handbook* for more regarding the *Secession Reference*.) In the *Secession Reference*, the Supreme Court of Canada considered whether there is a right for Quebec to conduct a unilateral secession under Canadian constitutional law or international law. The Court held that such a right to unilateral secession does not exist. Instead, as the Court tells us, secession should be negotiated between Quebec and other Canadian authorities (the other provinces and the federal government). According to the Court, a clear expression of a majority of Quebeckers' desire to no longer be part of Canada would create a constitutional duty to negotiate for Quebec and the other federative partners. If these negotiations were to succeed, a formalization or endorsement of the secession of Quebec under the constitutional amending procedure in Part V of the Act of 1982 should follow. The Court did not however specify which method of constitutional amendment would apply in the matter. Would the applicable procedure be 7/50, or would it rather be unanimity? Or should a brand new unique procedure be created altogether? It is very possible that unanimous consent would apply in the event of Quebec secession. This conclusion is built upon the *Reference re Senate Reform* [2014] 1 SCR 704, 752, in which the Supreme Court concluded that abolishing the Senate would result in an amendment of Part V of the Act of 1982 itself, which requires the unanimous consent of Parliament and the provinces by virtue of s 41(e) of that act. One is entitled to ask: Why would it be different for the disappearance (secession) of a Canadian province?

of the partners within the federation of the right to begin a constitutional amendment initiative constitutes a very important gesture which should not remain unanswered.

In Canadian practice, it is the first ministers who reach the accords seeking to renew or adapt federalism. This reality is frequently expressed by the term "executive federalism". In such a system, the first ministers begin by making a commitment on behalf of their respective governments in an intergovernmental accord; thereafter, they seek legislative (or parliamentary) approval. Hence, the will of the political players becomes an essential factor in achieving constitutional reform. Nonetheless, it would seem that such a will is lacking at this moment, although the Quebec government is still searching for constitutional changes which would render the patriation of 1982 acceptable from its perspective[52] and, in turn, increase the political legitimacy of the agreement of November 1981.

Overall, the political context in which the constitutional amendment process is situated has proven to be just as complex as its legal framework, which further adds to the difficulty surrounding constitutional reform. The approach taken with the Charlottetown Accord clearly revealed a number of factors that contributed to this political complexity.[53]

The first factor worth mentioning in this respect is the increase in the number of players called upon to participate in constitutional talks. On the one hand, the territories were invited to take part in the negotiation process, which constituted a precedent. On the other hand, the negotiation of this agreement made it possible to confirm the principle of the participation of the Aboriginal peoples in constitutional discussions, as per section 35.1 of the Act of 1982. The approach taken by the Charlottetown Accord, which complied with this provision, allowed the Aboriginal peoples to play a significant role in the negotiations and led other players to actively seek their consent.

Public participation in the constitutional renewal initiative represents another complex political factor. The Charlottetown Accord created a precedent by giving rise to the holding of referendums seeking the population's approval of the Accord. It should be noted that in Alberta and British Columbia, the approval by the legislature of any constitutional amendment is conditional upon the prior holding of a referendum.[54]

Some have also put forward the idea that the first ministers should submit every constitutional agreement proposal for public discussion prior to its final conclusion. This is what Quebec did in May 1987, when it submitted the political accord reached in the preceding month at Meech Lake to a committee of the National Assembly for examination. The outcome made it possible to clarify several points of the Accord before its

---

[52] On this subject, it is further discussed that Quebec still has not politically accepted the patriation of the Canadian Constitution and the adoption of the Act of 1982. See the "Future Possibilities for Constitutional Reform" sub-heading.

[53] Richard Johnston, "An Inverted Logroll: The Charlottetown Accord and the Referendum" (1993) 26 *PS: Political Science & Politics* 43.

[54] *Constitutional Referendum Act* RSA 2000, s 2; *Constitutional Amendment Approval Act* RSBC 1996, s 1.

conclusion on 3 June 1987. On this occasion, the government of Quebec was the only executive body to proceed in this manner. This way of proceeding, albeit likely to complicate matters, offers the advantage of associating parliamentarians and public opinion with the constitutional exercise underway, thus facilitating the passage of the resolution. In Manitoba, the holding of public hearings is required in order to encourage a debate prior to the adoption of a government motion to authorize a constitutional amendment by the legislature.[55]

Over the past several years, various interest groups and associations have expressed their willingness to intervene and articulate their concerns in constitutional discussions when their rights are likely to be affected. They have argued that the ratification process of the Meech Lake Accord and the negotiation of the Charlottetown Accord show the necessity of inviting them to such meetings. They have also insisted on their capacity to participate effectively at said deliberations.

Could the above precedents be foreshadowing the emergence of new constitutional conventions? The question is still unresolved. Regardless, one thing is certain: Aboriginal peoples, the territories, minorities, and the public in general henceforth want to have their say in the constitutional renewal process.

In light of this reality, it is evident that new political phenomena relating to constitutional amendments no longer fall exclusively under traditional executive federalism. In other words, more reconciliation between executive federalism and public participation should be pursued. This does not mean that future constitutional negotiations must take place entirely in the public arena; clearly, the emergence of compromises on certain subjects can only be facilitated during closed-door sessions. Nor does this mean that the presence at the negotiating table of a greater number of players is necessarily a solution. Within the context of Canada's federalism, the negotiation of constitutional amendments should essentially remain a matter for those whose interest and status in this process are provided for by the Constitution.

4. PARACONSTITUTIONAL ADAPTATION: ALTERNATIVE APPROACHES TO THE FORMAL AMENDMENT PROCEDURE

Undoubtedly, the difficulties presented by constitutional amendment in Canada before 1982 were due to the absence of a Canadian-based procedure. Still, even the current procedure remains complicated and cumbersome. Moreover, obstacles associated with political realities have been added to the already demanding requirements of this procedure. As a result, this general difficulty has certainly encouraged the development of

---

[55] *Rules, Orders and Forms of Proceedings of the Legislative Assembly of Manitoba*, s 47(1) and (2).

alternative approaches to the formal constitutional amendment procedure within the Canadian federation.

These approaches have an indirect effect on the system of government and its evolution. Without a doubt, resorting to these measures can bring about a "paraconstitutional" adaptation to the changing contexts in which state action takes place.

This adaptability may be a positive characteristic. However, it becomes problematic if it results in a blatant bypassing of the constitutional formalities or if it leads to a relativization or banalization of the basic principles of the Canadian political and institutional structure. It seems that more attention needs to be given to this type of risk to ensure that the main components of the Canadian regime are maintained and the authority inherent in the status of each of the partners is respected. It should be remembered that despite a British constitutional culture that is not particularly bound by formalism, the founders of Canada recognized the need for overarching rules from the outset. This necessity for rules thus justified the drafting of a supreme constitutional text,[56] which defined the formal division of legislative powers and the other key features of the country.

The need for rules is just as fundamental today. The difficulty of amending the Constitution does not diminish the importance thereof, nor preclude the reexamination of the constitutional amendment procedure. With that said, the following is an exploration of the different methods likely to serve as a substitute within Canadian practice for the formal constitutional amendment procedure.

A. Constitutional Interpretation

Notwithstanding the fact that the interpretation of the Constitution falls under the jurisdiction of the courts, their intervention does not involve the exercise of constituent authority, which lies with elected representatives via Parliament and legislatures. However, in Canada, legal interpretation can have major structural effects at the constitutional level; that is to say, court decisions can occasionally have tangible impacts similar to those of a constitutional amendment.

In the famous *Edwards* ruling of the Judicial Committee of the Privy Council, the importance of a dynamic interpretation of the Constitution was emphasized, comparing it with a living tree capable of growth and expansion within its natural limits.[57] The dynamic or progressive interpretation of jurisprudence makes a significant contribution to conferring the permanence and completeness that the constitutional order demands. However, there is a risk in relying too heavily on legal interpretation when modernising

---

[56] On the value of formal written amendment rules, see Richard Albert, "The Difficulty of Constitutional Amendment in Canada" (2015) 39 *Alberta Law Review* 26.

[57] *Edwards v Attorney-General for Canada* [1930] AC 124, at p. 136. Regarding "living tree" constitutional interpretation, see the chapter by W.J. Waluchow in this *Handbook*.

federalism.[58] It must not undermine the certainty of the constitutional text or its ability to provide guidance and limitations for government action. Moreover, the intervention of the courts within the context of constitutional judicial review most often occurs as a result of a unilateral parliamentary measure. It is possible that when jurisprudence plays a predominant role in constitutional change, unilateral legislative initiatives end up becoming the preferred means for influencing the evolution of the federal system. This might be to the detriment of the multilateral constitutional amendment process, in which everyone must seek mutual consent through reciprocal concessions.[59]

In any event, it is clear that the Canadian Constitution has an internal architecture.[60] It consists, among other elements, of underlying principles that permeate it and give it life.[61] Each of these principles, and each individual component of the Constitution, is related to others and must be interpreted according to the corpus of the Constitution.

In their decisions on constitutional matters, courts may consider unwritten elements that make up the foundation of the Constitution of Canada. These elements, and in particular those within the preamble to the Act of 1867, invite "the courts to turn those principles into the premises of a constitutional argument that culminates in the filling of gaps in the express terms of the constitutional text".[62] However, recognition of these structural principles should not be seen as an invitation to neglect the written text of the Constitution.

It is currently impossible to categorically declare that the underlying constitutional principles are covered by the amendment procedure under Part V of the Act of 1982, even though it is highly likely that such is the case, mainly because they are fundamental to the functioning of the Canadian state. If the Supreme Court of Canada were to give a precise meaning to each of these principles, it would ultimately evolve the Canadian Constitution by its own jurisprudence, without requiring the political actors to implement the constitutional amendment procedure.

The interpretation and definition of constitutional principles cannot however be called "para-constitutional" as such, because they are rather fully constitutional and form part of the delimitation of the "constitutional circumference". In other words, they are intimately linked to the determination of the scope of the Constitution itself.

---

[58]   Some experts have criticized the Supreme Court of Canada's tendency to favour a functional assessment of federal relational metamorphosis. See Henri Brun, Guy Tremblay, and Eugénie Brouillet, *Droit constitutionnel* (6th ed., Éditions Yvon Blais 2014), at para VI-2.221: "[Translation] [. . .] the Supreme Court positions itself before the federal government as a more convenient forum to obtain what it wants without compensation."

[59]   *Reference re* Employment Insurance Act *(Can), at ss. 22 and 23* [2005] 2 SCR 669, 699.

[60]   For more information on the Canadian constitutional architecture, see Warren J. Newman, "Of Castles and Living Trees: The Metaphorical and Structural Constitution" (2015) 9 *Journal of Parliamentary and Political Law* 471.

[61]   Recall that in *Reference re Secession of Quebec* [1998] 2 SCR 217, 240, the Supreme Court of Canada identified four constitutional principles in a non-exhaustive list: federalism, democracy, constitutionalism and the rule of law, and respect for minorities.

[62]   *Reference re Remuneration of Judges of the Provincial Court (P.E.I.)* [1997] 3 SCR 3, 75.

Furthermore, the aforementioned remarks on the underlying constitutional principles can easily apply, mutatis mutandis, to privileges and royal prerogatives, at least those which are considered entrenched into the Canadian Constitution, that is, formally protected by the latter. It is also the case with respect to the principles incorporated into the Canadian Constitution via the preamble to the Act of 1867, such as the principle of judicial independence,[63] the rule of law,[64] and freedom of speech.[65]

B. Federal Spending Power

A second alternative approach to constitutional reform consists of the multiplication of federal interventions in provincial jurisdiction by resorting to financial levers. Such interventions—which illustrate the federal claim of a broad spending power—might be problematic at the constitutional level.[66] They could also be facilitated by the existence of a structural fiscal imbalance between the federal government and the provinces.[67] This stems from a disparity between the distribution of fiscal resources on the one hand and the respective responsibilities of the governments on the other. Chapter 20 in this *Handbook* provides a full analysis of the issues surrounding the exercise of the spending power in Canada. Here, it is simply necessary to reiterate that the exercise of the federal spending power in provincial jurisdictions, especially when tied to conditions, could, over time, lead to an erosion of the constitutional autonomy of the provinces. Moreover, the exercise of this power could eventually allow the federal government to achieve most of its objectives without having to subject itself to the respect of the division of legislative powers and without having to proceed with a formal constitutional amendment.[68]

---

[63] The Supreme Court of Canada affirmed that the principle of judicial independence was incorporated into the Canadian Constitution as an unwritten norm via the preamble to the Act of 1867. On this point, see *The Queen v. Beauregard* [1986] 2 SCR 56, 72, and *ibid*, 75–76.

[64] In *Reference re Manitoba Language Rights* [1985] 1 SCR 721, 750, the Supreme Court of Canada said that the rule of law "[. . .] becomes a postulate of our own constitutional order by way of the preamble to the *Constitution Act, 1982*, and its implicit inclusion in the preamble to the *Constitution Act, 1867* by virtue of the words 'with a Constitution similar in principle to that of the United Kingdom' ". The rule of law is also explicitly mentioned in the preamble to the *Canadian Charter of Rights and Freedoms*, which is Part I of the Act of 1982.

[65] See *Fraser v. P.S.S.R.B.* [1985] 2 SCR 455, 462–463, where the Supreme Court affirmed what follows about freedom of speech: "It is a principle of our common law constitution, inherited from the United Kingdom by virtue of the preamble to the *Constitution Act, 1867*". Freedom of speech, or more precisely freedom of expression, is also recognized by s 2(*b*) of the *Canadian Charter of Rights and Freedoms, ibid.*

[66] Brun, Tremblay and Brouillet, above (n 58), at para VI-1.122.

[67] *Ibid*, at para VI-1.127.

[68] "[. . .] federal Parliament may spend or lend its funds to any government or institution or individual it chooses, for any purpose it chooses; and that it may attach to any grant or loan any conditions it chooses, for any purpose it chooses, including conditions it could not directly legislate", in Peter W. Hogg, *Constitutional Law of Canada*, (5th edition, Carswell, loose leaf 2015 update), 6-18 to 6-19; also see *Re* Canada Assistance Plan [1991] 2 SCR 525, 567, *Finlay v Canada (Minister of Finance)* [1993] 1 SCR 1080, dissent of Justice McLachlin, 1104–1105; *Winterhaven Stables Ltd. v Canada (Attorney General)* (1988), 53 DLR (4th) 413, at 433.

C. Administrative Agreements

Administrative agreements between governments constitute the third approach for modernizing Canadian institutions without formal constitutional amendment. These agreements fall under the heading of executive federalism. They may be bilateral or multilateral in nature and constitute an important tool for managing intergovernmental relations because they make it possible to ensure a certain complementarity of governments' actions in common sectors of intervention. They also eliminate, wherever possible, overlapping and duplication of programs.

In certain sectors of activity where both orders of government intervene, resorting to an administrative agreement makes it possible to specify the terms of intergovernmental relations without subjecting them to the rigidity inherent to formal constitutional provisions. For instance, in matters of immigration, the Quebec and federal governments have reached major agreements implementing, in a complementary and harmonious manner, their action in this concurrent field of jurisdiction since the 1970s.[69] At the multilateral level, mention may be made of the Agreement on Internal Trade reached in 1994.[70] Even if this Agreement is intergovernmental in nature, it falls within the continuity of the discussions on the development of the Canadian economic union, held under the context of the constitutional reform process associated with the Charlottetown Accord.

Administrative agreements thus add flexibility to the definition of intergovernmental relations. Such flexibility is favourable when there is a coherent relationship between the agreement and the existing constitutional order, but it can be problematic when it represents an attempt to achieve something that would otherwise require a constitutional amendment. However, because these administrative agreements are subject, as documents emanating from executive powers, to the principle of parliamentary sovereignty, their flexibility comes with a degree of fragility. Furthermore, several questions arise concerning their legal nature and their justiciability.[71]

---

[69] The governments of Canada and Quebec have had agreements on immigration for a long period of time. It began in 1971 with the Lang-Cloutier Agreement, which was followed in 1975 by the Andras-Bienvenue Agreement, which was replaced by the Cullen-Couture Agreement in 1979. Finally, this was substituted for by the McDougall-Gagnon-Tremblay Agreement of 1991.

[70] Canada, Government of Canada, Industry Canada, *Agreement on Internal Trade* (18 July 1994), online: http://www.ic.gc.ca/eic/site/ait-aci.nsf/eng/h_il00034.html.

[71] J. Poirier, "Les ententes intergouvernementales et la gouvernance fédérale: aux confins du droit et du non-droit", in J.F. Gaudreault-Desbiens and F. Gélinas (eds), *Le fédéralisme dans tous ses états: gouvernance, identité et méthodologie/The States and Moods of Federalism: Governance, Identity and Methodology* (Yvon Blais 2005) at pp. 441–474; J. Poirier, "Intergovernmental Agreements in Canada: At the Cross-roads between Law and Politics", in J.P. Meekison et al. (eds), *Canada: The State of the Federation 2002. Reconsidering the Institutions of Canadian Federalism*, (McGill-Queen's University Press, 2004) 425–462.

D. Infraconstitutional Political Declarations

Finally, mention should be made of the emergence of methods intended to inspire an eventual constitutional reform, but which remain infraconstitutional. The resolution of the House of Commons affirming that Quebec is a distinct society within Canada, passed on 11 December 1995 in the wake of the Quebec Referendum, is a case in point. The afore-mentioned *Act respecting constitutional amendments* is also a part of this phenomenon, as is the 2006 motion of the House of Commons recognizing that the *Québécois* form a nation within a united Canada,[72] and, to some extent, the creation of the Council of the Federation in 2003. The option to rely on infraconstitutional measures in matters so closely related to constitutional reform are proof of the difficulty experienced in relaunching this reform since the rejection of the Charlottetown Accord.

An example of an infraconstitutional attempt to bypass constitutional amendment rules was provided by the former Harper government's initiative with respect to the Senate. Beginning in 2006, there were several bills put forward by the Conservative government, a number of which were examined by the Supreme Court in its opinion rendered in 2014 in the *Reference re Senate Reform*.[73] Ultimately, the Court stated that Parliament could neither modify the essential characteristics of the Senate nor abolish it unilaterally. In order to do either of those things, Parliament and legislatures would have to apply the complex constitutional amending procedures, more specifically the unanimous procedure for the abolition of the Senate[74] and the 7/50 formula for changes that affect the Senate's essential or fundamental features. The Court even went as far as to require the application of the procedure set out in section 43 of the Act of 1982, with regards to the amendment of certain constitutional provisions concerning the qualifications of Senators from Quebec.[75]

---

[72] HC Deb 27 November 2006, vol 141, cols 1245–1250.

[73] *Reference re Senate Reform* [2014] 1 SCR 704.

[74] The Supreme Court of Canada concluded that "[a]bolition of the Senate would fundamentally change Canada's constitutional structure, including the procedures for amending the Constitution, and could only be done with unanimous federal-provincial consensus", *ibid*, 715–716.

[75] Section 23(6) of the Act of 1867 provides that, in the case of Quebec, Senators shall have their real property qualification in the Electoral Division for which they are appointed or shall be resident in that Division. The Supreme Court of Canada affirmed that any amendment that would repeal or that would render inoperative the provisions of said s 23(6) would constitute an amendment in relation to a "special arrangement applicable to a single province" and would therefore "fall within the scope of the special arrangement procedure" contained in s 43 of the Act of 1982: *ibid*, 751. For more on the scope of s 43 of the Act of 1982, see Dwight Newman, "Understanding the Section 43 Bilateral Amending Formula" in Emmet Macfarlane (ed), above (n 22) 155, where Newman states: "[o]verall, section 43 might offer the real possibility of developing some asymmetric relationships that have relatively specific legal shape, but these cannot be asymmetries that have any sort of legal knock-on effect on other provinces. So, there are real limits that must be acknowledged. That said, there are real possibilities here as well [. . .]".

E. Future Possibilities for Constitutional Reform

As noted above,[76] Quebec is still searching for constitutional reforms that would make the patriation of the Canadian Constitution and ensuing coming into force of the Act of 1982 acceptable in its view, politically-speaking. This situation persists despite the fact that, since the 1970s, a number of global proposals have been put forward or have been the subject of discussions within the context of constitutional reform, proposals which contained elements that certainly promoted the attainment of a number of Quebec's objectives. For example, the Victoria Charter of 1971 provided for a major broadening of linguistic rights and called for the participation of the provinces in the selection of the justices of the Supreme Court of Canada. Moreover, the constitutional amendment procedure of the Victoria Charter— a procedure founded on the concept of regional consent as previously discussed[77]—gave Quebec a veto right. Bill C-60 which was mentioned earlier in this Chapter, also contained interesting elements, including the proposal of participation by the provinces in the selection of Supreme Court justices. Regarding the Senate, the Bill proposed replacing it with a House of the Federation, half of whose members would have been appointed by the provinces, which would notably have had the power to approve the appointments to the Supreme Court and other federal bodies. The Bill also recommended amending the Constitution in order to incorporate a mechanism whereby the provinces would have been protected against a sudden and arbitrary termination of payments from the federal government.

Although they were likely to meet part of the demands of the Quebec government, all the proposals mentioned in the paragraph above—and many others—have not received the approval of the latter, because, according to Quebec, either they did not go far enough, or they contained other proposals which were deemed inadmissible.

Also, given the palpable complexity of the constitutional process in Canada, the lack of interest of the Canadian population in general to reform the Constitution, and Quebec's "challenging demands"[78] in the matter, the question arises as to whether such a reform has any future in this context.

It is impossible to predict the future, however it can be said without risk of being mistaken that the chances of a constitutional reform being accomplished in Canada over the next few years are extremely slim, to say the least.

Nonetheless, this does not prevent Canadian federalism from transforming gradually, either via the para-constitutional methods mentioned above,[79] or through

---

[76] Under the "Political Framework" sub-heading.

[77] Under the "Pre-patriation" sub-heading.

[78] Quebec's traditional requests in matters of reform of Canadian federalism are now perceived by federative partners as very demanding, if not impossible to meet. Even an agreement such as Meech Lake, where the content was nevertheless considered minimal by the Quebec government, would probably not, in the current political landscape, receive support from the federal government or a majority of provinces representing at least 50 percent of the population of all the provinces.

[79] Under heading III, "Paraconstitutional Adaptation: Alternative Approaches to the Formal Amendment Procedure".

governmental initiatives that do not require the implication of the complex procedure in Part V of the Act of 1982. For example, on 19 January 2016, the Government
of Canada announced the creation of an independent advisory committee on Senate
appointments.[80] On 2 August 2016, the same Government publicized the creation of
an independent advisory committee on the appointment of justices to the Supreme
Court.[81] None of these initiatives required the implementation of formal constitutional
amendment procedures. As for reform of the federal voting system, a concept which
the current Canadian government contemplated for a certain period of time,[82] it is less
clear that it could be achieved without constitutional amendment. However, it could be
argued that Parliament could act unilaterally for this purpose, under the powers conferred by section 44 of the Act of 1982.

5. Conclusion

After this brief historical overview, it is without question that the search for a constitutional amendment procedure has been shown to be an arduous and lengthy endeavour
in Canada. It culminated in 1982 with the adoption, without Quebec's consent, of a procedure which has strict requirements and has proven to be very difficult to implement
in its multilateral dimensions.[83] Indeed, almost all of the successful amendments have
been made bilaterally.

---

[80] Press Release, "Minister of Democratic Institutions Announces Establishment of the Independent
Advisory Board for Senate Appointments", 19 January, 2016, online: http://news.gc.ca/web/article-
en.do?crtr.sj1D=&crtr.mnthndVl=1&mthd=advSrch&crtr.dpt1D=&nid=1028349&crtr.lc1D=&crtr.
tp1D=&crtr.yrStrtVl=2016&crtr.kw=&crtr.dyStrtVl=19&crtr.aud1D=&crtr.mnthStrtVl=1&crtr.
page=2&crtr.yrndVl=2016&crtr.dyndVl=19.

[81] Letter from Prime Minister Justin Trudeau, 2 August, 2016: "Why Canada Has a New Way to
Choose Supreme Court Judges", in *The Globe and Mail,* online: http://www.theglobeandmail.com/
opinion/why-canada-has-a-new-way-to-choose-supreme-court-judges/article31220275/; Office of the
Prime Minister of Canada, Justin Trudeau, "Prime Minister Announces New Supreme Court of Canada
Judicial Appointments Process", *News Releases* (Ottawa, 2 August 2016), online: http://pm.gc.ca/eng/
news/2016/08/02/prime-minister-announces-new-supreme-court-canada-judicial-appointments-
process; Office of the Prime Minister of Canada, Justin Trudeau, "New Process for Judicial Appointments
to the Supreme Court of Canada," *News Releases* (Ottawa, 2 August 2016), online: http://pm.gc.ca/eng/
news/2016/08/02/new-process-judicial-appointments-supreme-court-canada.

[82] Press Release, "Government of Canada Proposes All-Party Parliamentary Committee on Electoral
Reform", 11 May 2016, online: http://news.gc.ca/web/article-en.do?nid=1063809&_ga=1.87200283.243318
583.1465820727.

[83] "Amending the Constitution of Canada is [. . .] much harder than its text suggests. The dialogic
interactions of Canadian political actors have given rise to extra-textual rules over and above the already
onerous formal amendment rules entrenched in the *Constitution Act, 1982.* These formal and extra-
textual rules make the Constitution exceedingly rigid, perhaps even more resistant to alteration than the
United States Constitution, long believed by scholars to be among the world's most difficult democratic
constitutions to amend.", in Richard Albert, above (n 56), 22.

The failure of the Meech Lake ratification process followed by the rejection of the Charlottetown Accord revealed factors of a political nature which today constitute key elements of the context in which constitutional renewal must be considered. Undeniably, there is the need to reconcile the tradition of executive federalism with the expectations related to public participation. Additionally, the substitution of different approaches to formal constitutional amendments has taken on greater significance. Since the rejection of the Charlottetown Accord, these approaches have partly been used in relation to questions which, up until then, were seen as requiring constitutional amendments.[84]

The conference that was supposed to be convened under section 49 of the Act of 1982 in the 15 years following the inception of the constitutional amendment procedure could have resulted in a suitable review of the amending process; however, it was all in vain. Hopefully, new opportunities for such a review will arise in the future.

Constitutional reform in Canada is difficult precisely because of the complexity of the constitutional amendment procedure stemming from the 1982 patriation and other added constraints of legislative, reglementary, or judicial nature.[85] Nevertheless, reform is not impossible. Its success rests first and foremost on the existence of a strong political will and sufficient popular support. It is now up to federalists to rehabilitate the word "Constitution", which is perceived as almost taboo by a portion of the Canadian population, and to make sure that constitutional amendment and reform in Canada recover their credibility, not to say their nobility.

Bibliography

Secondary sources

Albert, Richard, 'The Difficulty of Constitutional Amendment in Canada' (2015) 39 Alberta Law Review 1

Canada, Special Joint Committee on the Process for Amending the Constitution of Canada, *The Process for Amending the Constitution of Canada: The Report of the Special Joint Committee of the Senate and the House of Commons* (HC 1991, 3rd session, 34th Parliament)

Hogg, Peter W., *Constitutional Law of Canada*, 5th ed. (Toronto: Carswell 2007)

Hurley, James Ross, *Amending Canada's Constitution: History, Processes, Problems and Prospects* (Ottawa: Minister of Supply and Services Canada 1996)

Monahan, Patrick and Byron Shaw, *Constitutional Law*, 4th ed. (Toronto: Irwin Law 2013)

---

[84] For example, the recognition of Quebec as a distinct society within Canada by a motion adopted by the House of Commons, the recognition of regional vetoes by the adoption of a law by Parliament, and the recognition that the *Québécois* form a nation within a united Canada by a motion adopted by the House of Commons.

[85] On the role of the Supreme Court of Canada with regards to constitutional amendments, see Emmett Macfarlane, "Conclusion: The Future of Canadian Constitutional Amendment" in Emmett Macfarlane (ed), above (n 22), 297–298: "Even more significant is the extent to which judicial interpretation effectively can amount to judicial amendment of the Constitution. Admittedly, the line between judicial interpretation and judicial amendment is tricky to identify [. . .]".

Macfarlane, Emmett (ed), *Constitutional Amendment in Canada* (Toronto: University of Toronto Press 2016)

Macfarlane, Emmett, 'Architecture: Ambiguity, the *Senate Reference*, and the Future of Constitutional Amendment in Canada' (2015) 60 McGill LJ 883

Newman, Warren J, 'Defining the "Constitution of Canada" since 1982: The Scope of the Legislative Powers of Constitutional Amendment under Sections 44 and 45 of the *Constitution Act, 1982*' (2003) 22 SCLR 423

Newman, Warren J, 'Living with the Amending Procedures: Prospects for Future Constitutional Reform in Canada' in Peach and others (eds), *A Living Tree: The Legacy of 1982 in Canada's Political Evolution* (LexisNexis, 2007). Also in [2007] 37 SCLR 383.

Pelletier, Benoît, *La modification constitutionnelle au Canada* (Scarborough: Carswell 1996)

Régimbald, Guy and Dwight Newman, *The Law of the Canadian Constitution* (Markham: LexisNexis Canada 2013)

Cases

Reference re Authority of Parliament in relation to the Upper House [1980] 1 SCR 54

Reference re Secession of Quebec [1998] 2 SCR 217

Reference re Supreme Court Act, ss. 5 and 6 [2014] 1 SCR 433

Reference re Senate Reform [2014] 1 SCR 704

PART III

INDIGENOUS PEOPLES AND THE CANADIAN CONSTITUTION

A. Indigenous Sovereignty

CHAPTER 13

....

CONTENDING
SOVEREIGNTIES

....

JEREMY WEBBER[*]

1. INTRODUCTION

....

THE essential principles of Aboriginal law emerged out of a long process of interaction between Indigenous peoples and French, British, and then Canadian governments in North America. It is, fundamentally, a body of 'intersocietal law' developed out of the experience of living together, combined with reflection and experimentation to determine what might serve as workable principles of co-existence in this land.[1]

To say that the principles were intersocietal is not to idealize the interaction. The practices that were adopted were marked by power and even, at times, by brutal imposition. Indeed, it is useful to think in terms of periods with, in the earliest period, patterns of conduct established that assumed the identity of Indigenous peoples as substantially autonomous, self-governing peoples—patterns of conduct that were grounded in the collaborative relations of the fur trade and colonial powers' need for Indigenous allies in their competition with rival powers. Those relations, however, were substantially undermined, indeed forcibly displaced, as agricultural settlement took precedence over the fur trade and collaboration gave way to dispossession. In this second period, Indigenous peoples were pushed to the margins, land and treaty rights were eroded, the political

* Professor and Dean, Faculty of Law, University of Victoria. My thanks to Catherine George, Maegan Hough, and Vivian Lee for their able research assistance, and to Robert Gibbs, Martin Loughlin, Patrick Macklem, Brad Morse, Val Napoleon, Peter Oliver, Heidi Kiiwetinepinesiik Stark, and Jim Tully for their astute comments on previous versions of this chapter.

[1] Brian Slattery, 'Understanding Aboriginal Rights' (1987) 66 CBR 751; Jeremy Webber, 'Relations of Force and Relations of Justice: The Emergence of Normative Community between Colonists and Aboriginal Peoples' (1995) 33 Osgoode Hall LJ 623; Canada, Royal Commission on Aboriginal Peoples, *Report of the Royal Commission on Aboriginal Peoples, Volume 1: Looking Forward, Looking Back* (Supply and Services Canada, 1996) 99–132; *R v Van der Peet*, [1996] 2 SCR 507 [42] (Lamer CJ).

autonomy of Indigenous peoples was denied, and Canadian governments imposed an ostensibly paternalistic regime of land administration, community control, and child-rearing that subjected Indigenous peoples to the decision-making of non-Indigenous civil servants and the pervasive influence of non-Indigenous institutions.

The results were devastating, leaving in their wake a legacy of shattered lives and troubled communities. This prompted, beginning especially in the 1960s, a growing resurgence of Indigenous initiatives for cultural revitalization, the protection of Indigenous lands, and the re-assertion of Indigenous control over their peoples' futures. Thus began the third period, marked by increasing recognition on the part of Canadian citizens and governments of the miserable consequences of the period of dislocation, and an increasing willingness to explore whether a better relationship might be established on the basis of principles derived from the more productive relations of the first period. It was during this third period that the courts recognized the binding force of treaty rights and Aboriginal title in contemporary Canadian law,[2] that the first modern treaty was concluded,[3] that mechanisms (albeit imperfect) were put in place to address Indigenous claims based on treaty and Aboriginal title, that the phasing out of residential schools commenced, and that governments began to grapple with Indigenous demands to govern themselves.[4]

This resurgence of Indigenous advocacy occurred in the years immediately prior to the patriation of the Canadian Constitution and led to the inclusion within the patriation package of section 35 of the *Constitution Act, 1982*, the essential clause of which reads as follows:

> 35(1) The existing aboriginal and treaty rights of the aboriginal peoples of Canada are hereby recognized and affirmed.

This became the foundation for the constitutional protection of Indigenous rights. The content of the protected rights did not derive from section 35. By its very terms, section 35 recognized rights presumed already to exist. Moreover, those rights had been the subject of contestation over the course of Canadian history, with many of the most important developments occurring in the decade immediately prior to patriation. The engagement with the historical record therefore has to be critical, combining normative reflection and deliberation with close attention to the history of Indigenous/non-Indigenous interaction. It derives principles from that long experience, identifying constitutional norms, weighing them, and searching for the most compelling fit between principle and experience. Indigenous rights are, then, intersocietal law, but that law's identification and development has occurred through continual critical deliberation.

[2] *R v White and Bob* (1964) 50 DLR(2d) 613, aff'd [1965] SCR vi; *Calder v British Columbia (Attorney-General)* [1973] SCR 313.

[3] *The James Bay and Northern Quebec Agreement* (Éditeur official, 1976).

[4] For an overview, see Royal Commission above (n 1) especially 31–244 and, with respect to residential schools, Truth and Reconciliation Commission of Canada, *Canada's Residential Schools: The Final Report of the Truth and Reconciliation Commission of Canada* (McGill-Queen's UP 2015), vols 1–4.

This also means that the generation of Indigenous rights is not locked in the distant past. It is happening right now as participants reflect upon the course of the relationship and seek to develop principles appropriate to it.[5] Moreover, the critical actors in its emergence are not merely courts. Indigenous rights have been shaped by constitutional negotiations, treaties, legislative initiatives, executive action, judicial decision, academic reflection, and, above all, the principled self-assertion of Indigenous peoples.

Nowhere are these characteristics of Indigenous rights more pronounced than with respect to questions of sovereignty. The notion of Indigenous sovereignty has been invoked expressly only sparingly in Canada (unlike, for example, the United States, where a limited form of Indigenous sovereignty is expressly recognized in law[6]). In Canada, parties have tended to discuss political and legal authority using other terms, especially 'self-government', with some form of sovereignty apparently implicit in the use of the term 'inherent' to describe the right to self-government. One suspects that the parties have judged that the term 'sovereignty' itself—carrying, as it often does, an implication of ultimate decision-making authority—was more of an obstacle than an aid to reconciliation, especially as virtually all parties have accepted that viable solutions have to be secured through co-determination rather than imposition. And yet questions bound up with sovereignty run throughout the Indigenous dimensions of the constitution: questions about the grounding of governmental authority, the scope of Indigenous jurisdictions, the definition of Indigenous nations, the sources of Indigenous law, and relations of precedence and subordination between Indigenous and non-Indigenous institutions. Certainly Canadian governments have long claimed to be sovereign, not least in relation to Indigenous peoples. Perhaps in response, Indigenous peoples also have, from time to time, claimed sovereignty. As we will see, the courts too have been drawn to discuss sovereignty, albeit carefully and tentatively. Questions of sovereignty are inherent in the discussion of Indigenous rights, as one might expect given that those rights speak to relations of law and governance between societies.

This chapter begins by examining the ways in which sovereignty and related concepts—especially rights of self-government—have been invoked in constitutional negotiations, the courts, and legislative action. In that part, I attempt to reveal both the extent to which Indigenous sovereignty has been discussed within Canadian constitutional deliberation and the state of an Indigenous right of self-government generally. I then turn to the concept of sovereignty itself. Sovereignty is often used to express a number of claims. Those claims can be combined in a single, compound concept but they can also be held individually. It is worthwhile teasing apart the claims in order to identify precisely what is in issue in a particular case. Otherwise one can substantially misread a party's objectives, and opportunities for resolving conflicts can be

[5] Brian Slattery, 'The Generative Structure of Aboriginal Rights' (2007) 38 Supreme Court LR (2d) 595.
[6] Joanne Barker, 'For Whom Sovereignty Matters' in Joanne Barker (ed), *Sovereignty Matters: Locations of Contestation and Possibility in Indigenous Struggles for Self-Determination* (U of Nebraska Press, 2005), 12–16; N Bruce Duthu, *Shadow Nations: Tribal Sovereignty and the Limits of Legal Pluralism* (OUP, 2013).

missed. That is especially true, as we will see, when it comes to Canada's contending sovereignties.

2. INDIGENOUS SOVEREIGNTY AND SELF-GOVERNMENT IN THE CANADIAN CONSTITUTION

This section will focus on constitutional actors' engagement with sovereignty in the period following the adoption of the *Constitution Act, 1982*. Two aspects of the constitutional landscape prior to 1982 need to be mentioned, however.

First, although I will focus primarily on the positions adopted by state actors, the impetus that drove all these developments was Indigenous peoples' commitment to sustaining their existence as peoples, maintaining their law, and determining, to the greatest extent possible, their own collective fate. Indigenous peoples pursued that commitment with great tenacity even under heavy pressure. The 1885 ban on the potlatch, for example, outlawed the traditional government structures of many peoples of the Pacific Coast, and yet members did their best to sustain the meetings in secret and, when the ban was lifted in 1951, they restored them to their central place within their communities.[7] Indigenous peoples across Canada also fought successfully to remove federal Indian agents from their communities so that the structures of band government recognized under the Indian Act could exercise their powers without the agents' veto, eventually succeeding in the 1960s. Indigenous peoples' refusal to acquiesce in their subjection, and their attachment to their laws and institutions, preserved an Indigenous autonomy to which Canadian institutions, ultimately, were forced to respond.

Second, the long engagement with issues of Aboriginal title also was, in substantial measure, a struggle for Indigenous legal and governmental autonomy. Aboriginal title appears, superficially, to be about property rights but, rather than property, a better analogy is the claim of states to their territory in international law. One sees this if one examines the nature of Aboriginal title in Canadian law. There, Aboriginal title is treated as though it were held in undivided co-ownership by the people concerned. Within the communities themselves, however, the land tends to be held by particular families, lineage groups, or individuals, not by the people as a whole. Canadian law's insistence on the collective nature of Aboriginal title is not designed to displace these rights and impose communal ownership. It refers to the fact that, from the point of view of the Canadian state, the apportionment of land within the community is left to the laws and procedures of the people concerned. It recognizes a sphere of jurisdiction, not

---

[7] Douglas Cole and Ira Chaikin, *An Iron Hand upon the People: The Law against the Potlatch on the Northwest Coast* (Douglas & McIntyre, 1990).

property rights as such. Examples from the law of Aboriginal title might be multiplied.[8] The essential point is that in striving for the recognition of Aboriginal title, Indigenous peoples have sought to maintain autonomous spheres in which their law and governance could continue to function.

A. Indigenous Sovereignty and Self-Government in Constitutional Reform

Indigenous peoples have also worked to have their rights to self-government expressly recognized in the Constitution. As we saw above, section 35 of the *Constitution Act, 1982* recognized and affirmed 'existing aboriginal and treaty rights' without specifying their content. In fact, because of the vagueness of the section, because it was qualified by the term 'existing' (which Indigenous peoples worried might leave them merely with the remnants of rights), and because it was very uncertain whether 'recognized and affirmed' created any sort of constitutional guarantee, leaders of the National Indian Brotherhood (the principal representative of First Nations in Canada, later renamed the Assembly of First Nations) had rejected the clause and opposed patriation. In response, the framers had committed themselves, in section 37 of the *Constitution Act, 1982*, to hold a constitutional conference with Indigenous leaders, devoted to Indigenous issues, within one year of section 37 coming into force.

Between 1983 and 1987, four such conferences were held. It quickly became clear that the primary Indigenous demand was that the Constitution recognize that Indigenous peoples possessed an inherent right of self-government. Ultimately, the federal government and five provinces expressed their willingness to recognize such a right in principle, although they resisted having the right directly enforceable before the courts, arguing that the complexity of the issues involved in recognizing a third order of government—what should be the dimensions of Indigenous nations, who belonged to them, who was entitled to exercise their powers, by what process, over what matters—required that self-government be instituted through negotiations. In any case, the consent of five provinces was insufficient to adopt such an amendment and the negotiations ended in failure.[9]

The lack of progress on Indigenous self-government was one of the principal reasons for the 1990 failure of the Meech Lake Accord—the bundle of amendments designed

---

[8] See Jeremy Webber, 'The Public-Law Dimension of Indigenous Property Rights' in Nigel Bankes and Timo Koivurova (eds), *The Proposed Nordic Saami Convention: National and International Dimensions of Indigenous Property Rights* (Hart, 2013).

[9] Bryan Schwartz, *First Principles, Second Thoughts: Aboriginal Peoples, Constitutional Reform and Canadian Statecraft* (Institute for Research on Public Policy, 1986); David C Hawkes, *Aboriginal Peoples and Constitutional Reform: What Have We Learned?* (Institute of Intergovernmental Relations, 1989); Jeremy Webber, *Reimagining Canada: Language, Culture, Community and the Canadian Constitution* (McGill-Queen's, 1994), 122–125, 170–172; Peter Russell, *Constitutional Odyssey: Can Canadians Become a Sovereign People?* (3rd edn, U of Toronto Press, 2004), ch 10–12.

to secure Quebec's willing adherence to the Constitution. Meech's failure was followed by frantic efforts to conclude a new constitutional settlement, one that would retain the essence of Meech but also address matters that Meech had not included. The resulting Charlottetown Accord, agreed to by the federal government and all Canadian provinces and territories in 1992, would have recognized that '[t]he Aboriginal peoples of Canada have the inherent right of self-government within Canada'.[10] It also would have required what were, in effect, court-supervised negotiations regarding the implementation of the rights. The Charlottetown Accord also collapsed when it was rejected, for reasons too complex to be discussed here, in a national referendum. But Charlottetown nevertheless demonstrated significant acceptance by Canadian governments of the principle of Indigenous self-government.

Would that recognition, if adopted, have amounted to an acknowledgement of Indigenous sovereignty? The constitutional proposals avoided the term but, as we will see below, the description of the right as 'inherent' does evoke one of the principal meanings associated with sovereignty. Moreover, Charlottetown contemplated that Indigenous governments would be treated as 'one of three orders of government in Canada'.[11] That language clearly contemplated that Indigenous governments should have a status equivalent to that of the other two orders of government, the federal and provincial levels, which, in Canadian constitutional law, are considered to be sovereign in their spheres.[12]

That certainly was the interpretation given to that language by the Royal Commission on Aboriginal Peoples (RCAP). RCAP had been established in 1991 in the aftermath of the failure of the Meech Lake Accord and in the midst of severe tensions between the government of Canada and Indigenous peoples. Over the course of the next five years, it conducted a searching inquiry into all aspects of Indigenous/non-Indigenous relations, holding hearings throughout the country and issuing several interim reports and a multi-volume final report. It too recommended that Indigenous governments be treated as one of three orders of government, in which each order 'operates within its own distinct sovereign sphere, as defined by the Canadian constitution, and exercises authority within spheres of jurisdiction having both overlapping and exclusive components'.[13]

There have been no further attempts at comprehensive reform of the Canadian Constitution, but self-government rights for some peoples have been achieved piecemeal through contemporary treaties and self-government agreements. These can be very significant. The Inuit-majority territory of Nunavut, for example, was created as

---

[10] *Draft Legal Text: October 9, 1992,* proposed section 35.1(1) to be enacted by section 29. For a full discussion of the Meech Lake and Charlottetown Accords, see Webber, above (n 9) 125–175; Russell, above (n 9) 127–227.

[11] *Draft Legal Text,* above (n 9), proposed section 35.1(2).

[12] *Hodge v The Queen* (1883) 9 App Cas 117; *Maritime Bank of Canada (Liquidators of) v New Brunswick (Receiver-General)* [1892] AC 437.

[13] Canada, Royal Commission on Aboriginal Peoples, *Report of the Royal Commission on Aboriginal Peoples, Volume 2: Restructuring the Relationship* (Supply and Services Canada, 1996), 228–232, 310 (quotation at 232).

a result of the Nunavut Land Claims Agreement of 1993. There is, however, significant variation in the powers that Indigenous governments have been able to secure. Indeed, Indigenous peoples attempting to negotiate self-government often complain that the powers acceptable to Canadian provinces are closer to those of municipalities. It is also possible for these agreements to benefit from constitutional protection under section 35 as 'treaty rights'. The degree of protection is, however, subject to two important caveats: (1) the terms of the agreements themselves sometimes limit the rights and obligations that are created; and (2) the effective autonomy of Indigenous peoples depends heavily on rules, also contained within the agreements, for determining which rules take precedence in the case of a conflict. Principles regulating interjurisdictional conflicts exist in any federal system, including between the federal and provincial levels of government in Canada, but the rules contained within modern-day treaties are often particularly complex.

It is still the case, then, that the Canadian Constitution does not expressly contain an Indigenous right of self-government. The developments sketched above do suggest an emerging consensus in favour of the recognition of Indigenous governance rights (although the extent of those rights remains a matter of dispute) and perhaps also a willingness to treat Indigenous governments (at least rhetorically) as having a status similar to that of the federal and provincial levels of government. Canadian governments, however, remain cautious about creating an enforceable right of self-government expressed at a high level of generality, no doubt for the same reasons that they resisted an enforceable right during the constitutional negotiations of the 1980s, namely their conviction that detailed structures of governance need to be negotiated. There has been some progress in negotiating those agreements for particular peoples as part of modern-day treaties. And, quite apart from constitutional and treaty negotiations, there have been many intriguing governance initiatives pursued by Indigenous peoples on their own or, in the case of the co-management of resources, through non-treaty agreements between Indigenous peoples and Canadian governments. We will return to one striking example after examining the treatment of Indigenous governance before the courts.

B. Sovereignty and Self-Government in the Judicial Interpretation of Section 35

Indigenous parties have also attempted to establish a constitutional right to self-government through the courts. These have met with very limited success. The Supreme Court of Canada in *Pamajewon* held that claims to self-government could not be general in nature but (following the restrictive approach to Indigenous rights established in *Van der Peet*[14]) had to be made in relation to a specific field, with the claimant establishing that the power to regulate that field was integral to the distinctive culture of the

---

[14] *Van der Peet* above (n1).

people claiming the right. An example of just how specific is given by *Pamajewon* itself, where the Court held that the relevant area was 'the regulation of gambling'. It decided that the evidence was insufficient to establish the right.[15]

The question of self-government came before the Supreme Court of Canada again in *Delgamuukw*. In that case, the Court decided that the narrow *Van der Peet* approach was inappropriate for questions of Aboriginal title. It held that Aboriginal title was general in character, comprising virtually the entire beneficial interest in the land. It therefore put in place very different requirements from those applicable to more specific Aboriginal rights. Given the manner in which the case had been pleaded at trial, the Court held that it was unable to rule on the existence of Aboriginal title and referred the case back to trial (a trial that never occurred). With respect to self-government, its reasons were more ambiguous. Like Aboriginal title, it referred the question of self-government back to trial. As for the manner in which such a right should be framed, the Court referred to *Pamajewon* but did not specifically affirm that case's approach. Significantly, the Court commented on how difficult it was to determine 'the difficult conceptual issues which surround the recognition of aboriginal self-government', noting that RCAP had devoted 277 pages to the issues. One suspects that, given this complexity, the Court tends to share the view that negotiations would be required to establish acceptable government structures.[16]

But although the Supreme Court of Canada has been reluctant to be drawn into the adjudication of the structure of Indigenous governments, it has been willing, cautiously, haltingly, to pose fundamental questions regarding the contending sovereignties of Canadian constitutionalism. It has done so when articulating constitutional principle at the broadest level, specifically when describing the moral challenge at the foundation of the constitutional protection of Indigenous rights. It has not purported to answer the questions it has posed. Clearly it believes that they are too difficult for quick response. They are the kind of questions that one must attend to, but that can only be answered over time through dedicated, persistent, and self-critical deliberation.

That the Court should begin to pose such questions is striking. Twenty-five years ago, few judges would have thought there could be any doubt that the sovereignty of Canadian institutions excluded any rival sovereignty held by Indigenous peoples. In the Supreme Court's pathbreaking decision on section 35, *R v Sparrow* (1990), Dickson CJ and La Forest J spoke for a unanimous Court saying: 'there was from the outset never any doubt that sovereignty and legislative power, and indeed the underlying title, to such lands vested in the Crown'.[17] Indeed, I suspect that many Canadian judges would have agreed with the dictum of Jacobs J in the High Court of Australia in *Coe*

---

[15] *R v Pamajewon* [1996] 2 SCR 821.

[16] *Delgamuukw v British Columbia* [1997] 3 SCR 1010 [170–171].

[17] [1990] 1 SCR 1075 [49]; Michael Asch and Patrick Macklem, 'Aboriginal Rights and Canadian Sovereignty: An Essay on *R v Sparrow*' (1991) 29 Alberta LR 498.

v Commonwealth of Australia (1979) that a challenge to a nation's sovereignty was 'not cognisable in a court exercising jurisdiction under that sovereignty which is sought to be challenged'.[18]

Remarkably, however, the Supreme Court of Canada has ventured into that territory in its discussions of Indigenous/non-Indigenous reconciliation. In its first statements on the topic, it affirmed that the purpose of section 35 was to reconcile 'the pre-existence of aboriginal societies'—or, alternatively, 'prior Aboriginal occupation'—with the sovereignty of the Crown. In those formulations, it did not expressly attribute sovereignty to Indigenous societies.[19] It did do so in *Haida Nation* (2004), stating that treaties 'serve to reconcile pre-existing Aboriginal sovereignty with assumed Crown sovereignty'.[20] The Court has also begun to qualify its acknowledgement of Crown sovereignty: that sovereignty is said to be merely 'assumed', 'asserted', or in one striking decision 'de facto'.[21]

These statements do not themselves amount to an acceptance that Indigenous sovereignty continues into the present day, although they do not exclude that possibility. But they certainly state that Aboriginal rights are grounded in the search for reconciliation between societies, each of which is entitled to be included in the constitutional order; they acknowledge that notions of sovereignty are implicated in that encounter; and they suggest that until reconciliation is achieved, Canadian sovereignty is somehow imperfect, 'asserted', 'de facto'. A persuasive way to understand that last claim is that it is plausible to argue, in the case of non-Indigenous Canadians, that sovereignty is grounded in consent of the people; it is not in the case of Indigenous peoples. The task of the Indigenous provisions of the Constitution is to change that situation.

That is the extent of the Supreme Court of Canada's discussion, in majority judgements, of Indigenous sovereignty. In one concurring judgement, however, two members of the Court, Binnie and Major JJ, have gone further. They suggest that Indigenous self-government might be nested within an overarching Canadian sovereignty, so that Canada is conceived in terms of 'merged' or 'shared' sovereignty. That language draws upon the conclusions of RCAP and, like the invocation of 'a third order of government' in the failed Charlottetown Accord, implies that Indigenous governance might be seen as a species of federalism.[22] The majority of the Court did not join in their reasons, however. The Court clearly wants to stimulate the search for reconciliation; it genuinely sees reconciliation as the fundamental purpose of section 35, and has held that that purpose must shape the interpretation of Aboriginal rights, but it believes that the solution must

[18] [1979] HCA 68 (Jacobs J at [3]).
[19] *Van der Peet* (n 1) [31]; *Delgamuukw* (n 16) [186]; *Haida Nation v British Columbia (Minister of Forests)* [2004] 3 SCR 511 [17]; *Taku River Tlingit First Nation v British Columbia (Project Assessment Director)* [2004] 3 SCR 550 [42].
[20] *Haida Nation* (n 19) [20].
[21] See ibid [20] and [26]; *Taku River* (n 19) [24] and [42].
[22] *Mitchell v Canada (Minister of National Revenue)* [2001] 1 SCR 911 [125–135].

be devised by means that are more participatory, cross-cultural, flexible, and varied than are possible in proceedings before the courts.

C. Agonistic Constitutionalism

Analogies to federalism do offer a convincing analysis of how Indigenous governments ought to relate to Canadian institutions, but there is wisdom in the Court's caution. Reconciliation takes place against the backdrop of a troubled history. If it is to be reconciliation of the kind suggested by the Court—reconciliation that grounds the legitimacy of Canadian institutions upon Indigenous as well as non-Indigenous foundations— then Canadians need to undertake the challenges of listening, engagement, and translation across normative vocabularies. That process has hardly begun. It is likely in any case to involve trial and error. How then should we proceed? The attempt to tease apart the various strands that are often confounded in discussions of sovereignty—the task of the following section of this chapter—will, I hope, assist by clarifying what is in issue. In addressing those questions of constitutional theory, however, it will help to have before us a remarkable initiative, one that opens up possibilities that we often unknowingly foreclose.

The Haida Gwaii Reconciliation Act was adopted in 2010 by the British Columbia legislature.[23] It establishes a land management regime for Haida Gwaii (formerly the Queen Charlotte Islands; the act officially changed their name to the Haida name). The act creates a management structure with representation both from the Haida Nation and the province, and gives legislative effect to a protocol negotiated between the provincial government and the Haida. Co-management structures are common. What is novel is the framing of the initiative in the statute's preamble, especially its fifth recital. It says:

> AND WHEREAS the Kunst'aa guu—Kunst'aayah Reconciliation Protocol provides that the Haida Nation and British Columbia hold differing views with regard to sovereignty, title, ownership and jurisdiction over Haida Gwaii, under the Kunst'aa guu–Kunst'aayah Reconciliation Protocol the Haida Nation and British Columbia will operate under their respective authorities and jurisdictions;

Thus, in the introduction to a sovereign act of the British Columbia legislature, the province acknowledges the Haida's rival claims to sovereignty, title, ownership, and jurisdiction. It notes that the parties disagree on these matters, but then goes on to acknowledge that the province and the Haida will implement the agreement 'under their respective authorities and jurisdictions'. The Kunst'aa guu–Kunst'aayah Protocol is even more striking.[24] It states that '[t]he Parties hold differing views with regard to sovereignty,

---

[23] SBC 2010, c 17.
[24] Kunst'aa guu—Kunst'aayah Reconciliation Protocol (14 December 2009), online at http://www.llbc. leg.bc.ca/public/pubdocs/bcdocs2010/462194/haida_reconciliation_protocol.pdf.

title, ownership and jurisdiction over Haida Gwaii . . . ' and then sets out the differing views in two columns:

The Haida Nation asserts that:	British Columbia asserts that:
Haida Gwaii is Haida lands, including the waters and resources, subject to the rights, sovereignty, ownership, jurisdiction and collective Title of the Haida Nation who will manage Haida Gwaii in accordance with its laws, policies, customs and traditions.	Haida Gwaii is Crown land, subject to certain private rights or interests, and subject to the sovereignty of her Majesty the Queen and the legislative jurisdiction of the Parliament of Canada and the Legislature of the Province of British Columbia.

As constitutional lawyers, we tend to assume that fundamental questions—certainly so fundamental a question as the location of sovereignty—have to be settled before anything else can be done. But is that the case? Isn't it true that many of our foundational principles are disputed over a very long time, yet we nevertheless manage to collaborate in workable structures of government? The Haida Gwaii Reconciliation Act expressly recognizes that fact, states that the parties agree to disagree over fundamental notions of sovereignty and jurisdiction, and proceeds to implement an agreed structure of joint decision-making. It is an example of 'agonistic constitutionalism', in which constitutional government acknowledges the pervasiveness of fundamental political disagreement, accepts that it will persist, and proceeds to establish principles and processes that can sustain collaboration even in the face of disagreement.[25] Agonistic constitutionalism is more common than we tend to realize. In the Canadian context, the *Secession Reference*,[26] discussed in Chapter 47 of this *Handbook*, is a prime example.

3. The Interplay of Canada's Contending Sovereignties

Sovereignty is not just one thing. It generally is a bundle combining several distinct claims. Here I identify five that are relevant to the Indigenous context in Canada, explaining the extent to which these claims have figured in the debate over Indigenous rights in Canada.[27] It is worth distinguishing among them. Parties often mean very

---

[25] See Jeremy Webber, *The Constitution of Canada: A Contextual Analysis* (Hart, 2015) 259–266.

[26] *Reference re Secession of Quebec* [1998] 2 SCR 217.

[27] See also Jeremy Webber, 'We Are Still in the Age of Encounter: Section 35 and a Canada beyond Sovereignty' in Patrick Macklem and Douglas Sanderson (eds), *From Recognition to Reconciliation: Essays on the Constitutional Entrenchment of Aboriginal and Treaty Rights* (U of Toronto Press, 2016).

different things when they speak of sovereignty. The use of the term can therefore obscure more than it reveals.

A. Sovereignty 1: The Final Power of Decision

The first claim associated with sovereignty is perhaps the most familiar: the idea that sovereignty is the ultimate, ostensibly unconstrained, right to determine what is law—in the phrase that the English jurist Albert Venn Dicey applied to the sovereignty of Parliament, sovereignty is 'the right to make or unmake any law whatever.'[28] This is *Sovereignty 1*.

Sovereignty 1 has played an important role in relations between Indigenous peoples and the Canadian state. It is this absolute entitlement to make law, attributed to the Canadian state, that underpins the view, dominant until the adoption of the *Constitution Act, 1982,* that the Canadian Parliament could extinguish any Aboriginal right as long as its intention to do so were sufficiently 'clear and plain.'[29] It is also, one suspects, the principal reason that Canadian legislatures and courts have been reluctant to acknowledge that Indigenous peoples possess sovereignty. If Indigenous peoples are sovereign, are they able to decide matters without regard to Canadian law? Are Canadian institutions powerless to constrain them? Sovereignty 1 functions as the ultimate powerplay: an assertion of unlimited entitlement to make law. As such, it is resistant to compromise. To surrender any part of Sovereignty 1 is to lose it.

The adoption of section 35 of the *Constitution Act, 1982* might be said to have changed the nature of Sovereignty 1. The Supreme Court of Canada's decisions in *Delgamuukw* and *Tsilhqot'in Nation* make clear that infringements of Aboriginal title can only occur lawfully either with the consent of the Indigenous people concerned or following the tests of justification set out in those judgements.[30] In that sense, the application of section 35 has limited the freedom of action of Canadian legislatures. Section 35 might be seen, then, as an autolimitation of Canadian sovereignty. A Sovereignty 1 theorist, however, would not see it in this fashion. Rather, the theorist would see the change as a restructuring of the exercise of Sovereignty 1, shifting some authority to decide from the legislatures to the courts, all subject to the overriding power of the constitutional amending formula. Under modern conceptions of Sovereignty 1, sovereign power resides in the constitutional order as a whole; absolute power may therefore continue to exist in the whole order even if its exercise requires complicated procedures and the coordination of multiple institutions. On this view, despite the adoption of the *Constitution Act, 1982,* Sovereignty 1 continues to reside within the institutions of Canadian law.

---

[28] AV Dicey, *Introduction to the Study of the Law of the Constitution* (8th ed, Macmillan, 1915) 3–4.
[29] See *Sparrow* above (n 17) [37].
[30] *Delgamuukw* above (n 16) [168–169]; *Tsilhqot'in Nation v British Columbia*, 2014 SCC 44 [77].

B. Sovereignty 2: Status as a State in International Law

A second claim often associated with sovereignty focuses on the international sphere. *Sovereignty 2* is the ultimate entitlement to represent a population and territory in international law—the possession of the distinctive legal personality associated with states.

This conception of sovereignty has also had an influence, from time to time, on Indigenous rights. The courts' endeavour to determine the status of treaties with First Nations had to confront the question of whether these were treaties between international sovereigns, constituting treaties in international law. The courts decided that they were indeed treaties, but sui generis (of their own kind), having effect within domestic rather than international law.[31] The celebrated decisions of Marshall CJ of the United States Supreme Court in the early nineteenth century, from which the American acceptance of Indigenous sovereignty derives, also explored whether First Nations constituted separate states. He held that they were 'domestic dependent nations' existing under the suzerainty of other states, more akin to protectorates in international law.[32] The Marshall decisions have been influential in Canada, drawing as they do on a common colonial experience, although the Canadian courts have not embraced, as yet, Marshall's conception of restricted sovereignty.

Occasionally, although very rarely, an Indigenous people has claimed to be fully a sovereign state.[33] Much more commonly, indeed in Canada virtually universally, Indigenous peoples have claimed to have international legal personality as 'peoples', so that they have a measure of independent standing in international organizations and benefit from the right of self-determination in international law, but without asserting full statehood.[34] At least to this point, the great majority of Indigenous representatives have tended to argue that self-determination would be exercised internally, within states. The notion that Indigenous governments should be recognized as a third order of government within Canada, analogous to the federal and provincial orders of government, certainly conforms to that view. In all but the most exceptional situations, then, Sovereignty 2 is not in issue.

C. Sovereignty 3: The Originating Source of Law

Sovereignty 3 consists in the grounding of the ultimate authority for law and governance within one's own society, so that political power is, in a very real sense, self-authorized and self-determined—not dependent for its authority on the gift of any outside party.

---

[31] *Simon v The Queen* [1985] 2 SCR 387 [33]; *R v Sioui* [1990] 1 SCR 1025, 1037–1043.

[32] *Cherokee Nation v. Georgia*, 30 U.S. 1, 17 (1831).

[33] See Royal Commission above (n 13) 109.

[34] UN General Assembly, *United Nations Declaration on the Rights of Indigenous Peoples*, art 3, UN Doc. A/RES/61/295 of 13 September 2007, on-line http://www.un.org/esa/socdev/unpfii/documents/DRIPS_en.pdf.

The concept of popular sovereignty is an expression of Sovereignty 3, emphasizing as it does the anchoring of political legitimacy within the citizenry. If Sovereignty 1 focuses on the effects of political authority—on a government's entitlement to exercise ultimate power—Sovereignty 3 focuses on the origin of political authority—on a government's authority springing from within.

This, I suggest, is what most Indigenous leaders mean when they invoke sovereignty. Sovereignty 3 accords very closely with the language they use to express their aspirations. In RCAP's final report, the Commission summarized Indigenous representatives' testimony as follows:

> For many Aboriginal people, this is perhaps the most basic definition of sovereignty—the right to know who and what you are. Sovereignty is the natural right of all human beings to define, sustain and perpetuate their identities as individuals, communities and nations.
>
> . . .
>
> From this perspective, sovereignty is seen as an inherent attribute, flowing from sources within a people or nation rather than from external sources such as international law, common law or the Constitution.[35]

Sovereignty 3 captures the most natural meaning of self-government as an 'inherent right'. And it tracks the concept of self-determination so important in the negotiations leading to the United Nations Declaration on the Rights of Indigenous Peoples.[36]

It is also evident in the Haida Gwaii Reconciliation Act and the Kunst'aa guu—Kunst'aayah Reconciliation Protocol, where those instruments emphasize that British Columbia and the Haida Nation will operate 'under their respective authorities and jurisdictions'. That example also reveals that it is possible to assert Sovereignty 3 without insisting on Sovereignty 1. The instruments do not stipulate that either British Columbia or the Haida Nation must possess the ultimate authority to decide (although doubtless the province's representatives would assert that Canadian law applies; that is one of the aspects of sovereignty over which the parties disagree). Rather, they contemplate the operation of both sets of authorities and jurisdictions in parallel, without specifying that one needs to be subjected to the other.

Sovereignty 3 also fits nicely within the concept of reconciliation articulated by the Supreme Court of Canada. That approach emphasizes, above all, the need to found the legitimacy of Canadian institutions on principles that can plausibly appeal to all Canadians, Indigenous and non-Indigenous. That goal necessarily means that one must find some way to anchor the legitimacy of Canadian institutions both in the legal and political traditions of Indigenous peoples and those of other Canadians. That is why

---

[35] Royal Commission (n13) 105 and 107 (also 201–202). See also Heidi Kiiwetinepinesiik Stark, 'Nenabozho's Smart Berries: Rethinking Tribal Sovereignty and Accountability' 2013 Michigan State LR 339, 342–344; Wallace Coffey and Rebecca Tsosie, 'Rethinking the Tribal Sovereignty Doctrine: Cultural Sovereignty and the Collective Future of Indian Nations' (2001) 12 Stanford Law and Policy R 191.
[36] UN Declaration, above (n 34).

treaties exercise such a powerful force on the Canadian legal imagination. They embody the aspiration to found political community on principles acceptable to all.[37]

D. Sovereignty 4: A Unified and Rationalized Order of Law

Sovereignty 4 emphasizes that a society's legal order should be organized in a unified, consistent, and rationalized fashion, coherent and non-contradictory across the whole body of law. A corollary of this goal is that a society should have an institutional struc-ture that can guarantee this unity, notably mechanisms for the final adjudication of questions of law so that inconsistencies can be eliminated. To be sovereign, in other words, a society must be organized as a state.

This meaning of sovereignty is, I suspect, the least idiomatic of those presented here, primarily because we theorists are so used to working within state structures that we lose sight of their specificity. We can see the link to conceptions of sovereignty, however, if we ask, 'Can a nation truly be sovereign if it has no mechanisms for ensuring that decisions taken by agencies in the society conform to the law of the society?' Moreover, if one wanted to identify why the arena of international law and international organiza-tions lacked sovereignty in its own right, one would, I believe, fall back upon something like Sovereignty 4: there are insufficient mechanisms for imposing normative coher-ence. Indeed, I suspect that it is questions such as these that, for a very long time, led some jurists to doubt whether Indigenous peoples even had law or government (just as the status of international law was once a matter of controversy).

Canadian jurists have now conclusively rejected that blinkered conception of law, but Sovereignty 4 continues to generate problems in the area of Indigenous rights. North American Indigenous peoples are, traditionally, non-state peoples, and their structures of law and governance often maintain elements of a non-state character, such as the dis-tribution of legal authority among diverse units of political organization (nations, clans, villages, families), the persistence of distinct traditions of law and governance among these various units, and the lack of binding mechanisms for adjudicating among these variant traditions. One of the great challenges of Canadian constitutionalism is there-fore how to manage the interaction between state and non-state forms of social order-ing. Most of our mechanisms are premised on the centralization of authority and the crisp clarity of rules typical of states.

If we do succeed in meeting that challenge, we are likely to advance our understand-ing of law in non-Indigenous contexts as well. That certainly is true of the international realm—the legal order of which states are members but which is itself beyond the authority of any state. Something similar is true within domestic legal orders. Think for

---

[37] For an important discussion of the significance of treaties, see: Robert A Williams, *Linking Arms Together: American Indian Treaty Visions of Law and Peace, 1600–1800* (OUP, 1997).

a moment of the assertions made above with respect to Sovereignty 4. In what society is that degree of consistency truly guaranteed? If those values operate more at the level of aspiration than accomplishment, and if there is a plurality of normative orders operating within any complex society, then an understanding of non-state legal orders will help us to understand state legal orders as well.

E. Sovereignty 5: The Unified Representation of Political Community

The final form of sovereignty addressed here is *Sovereignty 5*, in which sovereignty is identified with the capacity to represent the society as a whole. This unified embodiment of the political order, this personification of the order, is classically identified with an individual. This is perhaps the oldest conception of sovereignty, captured in the idea of one's monarch as one's sovereign.

Sovereignty 5 has lost much of its prominence within contemporary Canadian constitutionalism, although it is retained within the institution of the head of state (as we have seen in Jennifer Smith's chapter on the Crown). A significant expression of this notion in the Indigenous context was evident at the time of patriation. Then, a central argument of some of the First Nations that opposed patriation was that their treaties had been concluded with the British monarch, and that they were dependent on the personal honour of the Crown, so that, when the constitutional connections to the United Kingdom were severed, the treaties themselves would be undermined. Their arguments were rejected by the Court of Appeal of England and Wales on the grounds that the Crown was now represented by its Canadian ministers.[38]

Such arguments are rarely if ever made with respect to constitutional rights of self-government, but it is still worth remembering Sovereignty 5. There are close affinities between it, the political theory of Thomas Hobbes, and, through Hobbes, the constitutional theories of the Nazi-era jurist Carl Schmitt—arguments that are influential in contemporary discussions of sovereignty.[39] Schmitt emphasizes the personalization of sovereign authority for at least three linked reasons: (1) because (in his view) the concentration of political authority in one person guarantees, as nothing else can, the unity of the political order; (2) because doing so maximizes the ability of governments to make clear decisions; and (3) because it also emphasizes personal political responsibility, for an identifiable person holds and wields political power. I do not accept Schmitt's analysis. Far from it.[40] But the challenges posed by his arguments need to be answered.

[38] *R v Secretary of State for Foreign and Commonwealth Affairs, ex parte Indian Association of Alberta* [1982] 2 All ER 118 (CA).

[39] Thomas Hobbes, *Leviathan* (Penguin, 1968) 227ff; Carl Schmitt, *The Concept of the Political* (Rutgers UP, 1976); Ulrich K Preuss, 'Political Order and Democracy: Carl Schmitt and His Influence' in Chantal Mouffe (ed), *The Challenge of Carl Schmitt* (Verso, 1999) 155.

[40] See Jeremy Webber, 'National Sovereignty, Migration, and the Tenuous Hold of International Legality: The Resurfacing (and Resubmersion?) of Carl Schmitt' in Oliver Schmidtke and Saime

Implicit in the Supreme Court of Canada's concept of reconciliation—and indeed in the dynamic of Indigenous societies' own constitutions—is that unity and stability is best achieved not by centralized imposition but by broadening the foundations of political legitimacy to secure members' willing adherence. The second concern with governments' ability to make decisions also deserves consideration. That capacity—the exercise of political agency—is the substance of the right of self-government. Indeed, I suspect that a concern with political agency underlies Sovereignty 1's chief appeal. If nothing else, Sovereignty 1 ensures that decision-making is not paralyzed by differences of opinion. The clear direction of this chapter has been towards greater co-determination founded on Sovereignty 3, not towards a reinforcement of Sovereignty 1, but, in moving in that direction, we must continue to attend to ways of fostering political agency.

Finally, the emphasis on personal political responsibility should stimulate reflection. Indigenous politics is sometimes criticized for being too personal, especially given the small size of many Indigenous societies and the role that familial relationships sometimes play in their governance.[41] Those criticisms sometimes are well-taken. But Indigenous legal traditions also have means of holding people to their responsibilities—of combining, in other words, an emphatically personal responsibility with insistence on obligations to the community as a whole. It would be worth considering and building upon those mechanisms.

4. CONCLUSION

What conclusions can we draw from this analysis for understanding Canada's contending sovereignties?

Often when sovereignty is invoked by constitutional lawyers, one suspects that the implicit form they have in mind is Sovereignty 1. That is a great pity, for if Sovereignty 3 does express Indigenous aspirations better than Sovereignty 1, an exclusive focus on the latter is likely to divert us from the parties' primary concerns. Moreover, Sovereignty 1 has the disadvantage of being all or nothing. It focuses our attention on who gets to win in the last analysis, distracting us from solutions that we might try short of that ever-receding horizon. And it encourages us to pick a single winner, distinguishing sharply between who gets to prevail and who does not. In a plural society, where one seeks to build institutions that are accepted as legitimate by all constituent groups, Sovereignty 1 is unhelpful, narrowing rather than broadening the foundations of constitutional

Ozcurumez (eds), *Of States, Rights, and Social Closure: Governing Migration and Citizenship* (Palgrave Macmillan, 2008).

[41] This is a principal theme of the Harvard Project on American Indian Economic Development. See, for example, Stephen Cornell and Joseph P Kalt, 'Successful Economic Development and Heterogeneity of Government Form on American Indian Reservations' Harvard Project PRS 95-4 (1995), online: http://www.hpaied.org/sites/default/files/publications/PRS95-4.pdf 9ff.

legitimacy. It is no wonder, then, that constitutional actors have tended to avoid sovereignty if Sovereignty 1 is the only game in town.

As I have argued, however, the focus of Indigenous arguments is Sovereignty 3, not Sovereignty 1. They are not arguing for an ultimate and unconstrained decision-making power. They seek, as RCAP said, the right 'to define, sustain and perpetuate their identities as individuals, communities and nations'.[42] They attempt to order their lives by drawing upon their own peoples' normative resources—their languages, their conceptual universe, their stories, their accounts of social interaction, their relationships to the land, their processes of memory, affirmation, correction, deliberation, and decision. This aspiration presupposes a substantial degree of autonomy, so that there are spheres in which Indigenous institutions and resources are able to be used, to be refined, and to flourish. Nevertheless, it does not exclude the possibility of collaboration as the Haida Gwaii Reconciliation Act makes clear. One can agree to disagree, work on the basis of one's own authorities and jurisdictions, and still find grounds upon which to act together. We constitutional theorists often write as if a community can only be sustained if its members agree to a set of canonical principles. But much more often, we find ourselves living in community, and we then seek, over long spans of time, to develop principles and procedures to organize our lives together. These principles can be plural in their origins, drawing upon different traditions and speaking different normative languages. They need not be perfectly rationalized.

The model of the Haida Gwaii Reconciliation Act suggests that those communities can be sustained without answering the questions of Sovereignty 1, and that we are therefore free to concentrate on the interplay of Sovereignty 3s. But how realistic is that position? Doesn't Sovereignty 1 always hover in the background, shaping the parties' conduct? There may indeed be circumstances in which the grounds for cooperation break down so thoroughly that the only solution is to determine who has the ultimate say—although when that happens one wonders whether sovereignty can do much work. Sovereignty is about the *entitlement* to govern; it is a claim of right, not simply an exercise of force. If the grounds for justifying governmental arrangements have broken down so convincingly, I suspect that arguments of right will hold little sway.

Most of the time, however, our societies are not at that extremity. We are not in 'the last analysis' but are acting in a zone in which justificatory arguments do have an impact. That need not be because we are especially moral (though we should not discount that possibility). It may be because we realize the cost of simply imposing our position, and we therefore have little alternative but to rely upon arguments of justification. I noted above, for example, that theorists of Sovereignty 1 would generally consider that section 35 has not in any way constrained sovereignty. An absolute power of decision continues in the system as a whole, if necessary through the use of the amending formula. But if the only way to overturn an ostensible right is by constitutional amendment, and if constitutional amendments are too costly to pursue (because of the extent of political capital

⁴² Royal Commission, above (n 35).

that must be expended, the potential for generating division within government, or, above all in the case of Indigenous rights, the cost in extreme disaffection if Indigenous rights are simply overrun), then the threat of constitutional amendment recedes into the background, a theoretical but not a practical option. Sovereignty 1 is bracketed by eminently practical concerns, and one is left with carrying on the debate within the more open territory of normative argument.

Sovereignty 1 is, in short, rarely a winning ploy, except in political orders in which there is already a substantial measure of consensus. In other situations, it is an argument appropriate only to the most extreme circumstances—and, when one is in such a situation, those who are on the receiving end of the decision are unlikely to see much difference between a claim of Sovereignty 1 and a threat of force. Most of the time, we operate in territory where Sovereignty 1 has little role to play.

Another way to state that argument is to draw on the work of theorists of law and government who emphasize that sovereignty is a relational concept.[43] They argue that the power of a government to act depends, in substantial measure, on its ability to carry the population along with it. Only then will it secure the benefit of the population's willing compliance with its laws. Only then will its soldiers and public servants invest their energies in the government's cause. On this view, sovereignty is the people's implicit authorization of the government to act on its behalf, an authorization that is always a work in progress. If that is true, then arguments for the justification of government are at the heart of sovereignty. The relevant form of sovereignty in most of its applications is Sovereignty 3.

This insight constructs the challenge of contending sovereignties in a distinctive form. It emphasizes the constructive dimension of sovereignty: its character as a work in progress. Moreover, in a complex, culturally-diverse polity such as Canada's, the work of sovereignty must be integrative, actively seeking to build the allegiance of all its constituent peoples, fashioning the political community so that it can attract the willing adherence of its members. And that, of course, is very much the work of reconciliation as the Supreme Court of Canada has envisaged it.

BIBLIOGRAPHY

Asch, Michael and Patrick Macklem, 'Aboriginal Rights and Canadian Sovereignty: An Essay on *R v Sparrow*' (1991) 29 Alberta LR 498.

Asch, Michael, *On Being Here to Stay: Treaties and Aboriginal Rights in Canada* (U of Toronto Press 2014).

Barker, Joanne (ed), *Sovereignty Matters: Locations of Contestation and Possibility in Indigenous Struggles for Self-Determination* (U of Nebraska Press 2005).

[43] See Martin Loughlin, *The Idea of Public Law* (OUP, 2003) 72–98; Lon Fuller, *The Morality of Law* (rev'd ed, Yale UP 1964) 48.

Bird, John, Lorraine Land, and Murray MacAdam, *Nation to Nation: Aboriginal Sovereignty and the Future of Canada* (Irwin Higher Education 2002).

Borrows, John, 'A Genealogy of Law: Inherent Sovereignty and First Nations Self-Government' (1992) 30 Osgoode Hall LJ 291.

Borrows, John, 'Sovereignty's Alchemy: An Analysis of *Delgamuukw v British Columbia*' (1999) 37 Osgoode Hall LJ 537.

Borrows, John, 'Tracking Trajectories: Aboriginal Governance as an Aboriginal Right' (2005) 38 UBC L Rev 285.

Borrows, John, *Canada's Indigenous Constitution* (U of Toronto Press 2010).

Christie, Gordon, 'The Court's Exercise of Plenary Power: Rewriting the Two Row Wampum' (2002) 16 Supreme Court LR 285.

Coffey, Wallace and Rebecca Tsosie, 'Rethinking the Tribal Sovereignty Doctrine: Cultural Sovereignty and the Collective Future of Indian Nations' (2001) 12 Stanford L & Policy R 191.

Cole, Douglas and Ira Chaikin, *An Iron Hand upon the People: The Law against the Potlatch on the Northwest Coast* (Douglas & McIntyre 1990).

Corntassel, Jeff and TH Primeau, 'Indigenous "Sovereignty" and International Law: Revised Strategies for Pursuing "Self-Determination"' (1995) 17:2 Human Rights Q 343.

Duthu, N Bruce, *Shadow Nations: Tribal Sovereignty and the Limits of Legal Pluralism* (OUP 2013).

Hawkes, David C, *Aboriginal Peoples and Constitutional Reform: What Have We Learned?* (Institute of Intergovernmental Relations 1989).

Hoehn, Felix, *Reconciling Sovereignties: Aboriginal Nations and Canada* (Native Law Centre, University of Saskatchewan 2012).

Loughlin, Martin, *The Idea of Public Law* (OUP 2003).

Macklem, Patrick, 'Distributing Sovereignty: Indian Nations and Equality of Peoples' (1993) 45 Stanford LR 1311.

Macklem, Patrick, *Indigenous Difference and the Constitution of Canada* (U of Toronto Press 2001).

McNeil, Kent, 'Aboriginal Rights in Canada: From Title to Land to Territorial Sovereignty' (1998) 5 Tulsa J Comp & Int'l L 253.

McNeil, Kent, 'Judicial Approaches to Self-Government since *Calder*: Searching for Doctrinal Coherence' in Hamar Foster, Heather Raven & Jeremy Webber (eds), *Let Right Be Done: Aboriginal Title, the Calder Case, and the Future of Indigenous Rights* (UBC Press 2007).

Royal Commission on Aboriginal Peoples, *Report of the Royal Commission on Aboriginal Peoples* (Minister of Supply and Services Canada 1996).

Russell, Peter, *Constitutional Odyssey: Can Canadians Become a Sovereign People?* (3rd edn, U of Toronto Press 2004).

Schwartz, Bryan, *First Principles, Second Thoughts: Aboriginal Peoples, Constitutional Reform and Canadian Statecraft* (Institute for Research on Public Policy 1986).

Slattery, Brian, 'Understanding Aboriginal Rights' (1987) 66 CBR 751.

Slattery, Brian, 'Aboriginal Sovereignty and Imperial Claims' (1991) 29 Osgoode Hall LJ 681.

Slattery, Brian, 'The Generative Structure of Aboriginal Rights' (2007) 38 Supreme Court LR (2d) 595.

Stark, Heidi Kiiwetinepinesiik, 'Nenabozho's Smart Berries: Rethinking Tribal Sovereignty and Accountability' 2013 Michigan State LR 339.

Truth and Reconciliation Commission of Canada, *Canada's Residential Schools: The Final Report of the Truth and Reconciliation Commission of Canada* (McGill-Queen's UP 2015).

Walters, Mark, 'British Imperial Constitutional Law and Aboriginal Rights: A Comment on *Delgamuukw v. British Columbia*' (1992) 17 Queen's LJ 350.

Webber, Jeremy, *Reimagining Canada: Language, Culture, Community and the Canadian Constitution* (McGill-Queen's UP 1994).

Webber, Jeremy, 'Relations of Force and Relations of Justice: The Emergence of Normative Community between Colonists and Aboriginal Peoples' (1995) 33 Osgoode Hall LJ 623.

Webber, Jeremy, 'The Public-Law Dimension of Indigenous Property Rights' in Nigel Bankes and Timo Koivurova (eds), *The Proposed Nordic Saami Convention: National and International Dimensions of Indigenous Property Rights* (Hart 2013).

Webber, Jeremy, *The Constitution of Canada: A Contextual Analysis* (Hart 2015).

Webber, Jeremy, 'We Are Still in the Age of Encounter: Section 35 and a Canada beyond Sovereignty' in Patrick Macklem and Douglas Sanderson (eds), *From Recognition to Reconciliation: Essays on the Constitutional Entrenchment of Aboriginal and Treaty Rights* (U of Toronto Press 2016).

Williams, Robert A, *Linking Arms Together: American Indian Treaty Visions of Law and Peace, 1600–1800* (OUP 1997).

B. Treaties

CHAPTER 14

....

TREATIES
AS CONSTITUTIONAL
AGREEMENTS

....

SÉBASTIEN GRAMMOND[*]

THE word 'treaty' usually designates agreements between states, governed by international law. That it should be used to describe agreements between the Indigenous peoples and the European colonial powers, and later the Canadian state, is indicative of the mindset of the parties: one makes treaties with one's equals. Yet there is a paradox in the continuing use of that term. Although the parties' bargaining power may have been roughly equal at the beginning of their encounter, British and, later, Canadian authorities eventually used treaties as a way to appropriate Indigenous lands, while pursuing an aggressive policy of assimilation.

Despite that sad history, the concept of the treaty stands out as embodying the political ideal of equal and respectful relationships. It is one concept that can be rescued from the past and 'rehabilitated,' so to speak, to sustain the current project of reconciliation. The treaty appears to be the privileged legal instrument to transform the relationship between the Indigenous peoples and the state in the manner suggested by modern political theory[1] as well as emerging norms of international law.[2] Treaties might 'serve to reconcile pre-existing Aboriginal sovereignty with assumed Crown sovereignty.'[3] From that viewpoint, treaties bear an obvious constitutional dimension, because they 'distribute constitutional authority. Treaties are thus as much a part of the constitutional history of Canada as the Constitution Act, 1867.'[4] The Canadian Constitution would find its

---

[*] DPhil, FRSC, AdE; Professor, Civil Law Section, University of Ottawa; counsel, Dentons Canada LLP.

[1] See eg J Tully, *Strange Multiplicity: Constitutionalism in an Age of Diversity* (Cambridge University Press, 1995).

[2] *Declaration on the Rights of the Indigenous Peoples*, UN GA Res 61/295 (2007).

[3] *Haida Nation v British Columbia (Minister of Forests)* [2004] 3 SCR 511 [20].

[4] P Macklem, *Indigenous Difference and the Constitution of Canada* (University of Toronto Press, 2001) 155; see also JY Henderson, 'Empowering Treaty Federalism' (1994) 58 Sask L Rev 241.

roots in the shared normative community initially established between the Indigenous peoples and the newcomers.[5] It would be a compact not only among the provinces or 'founding peoples,'[6] but also 'between the non-Aboriginal population and Aboriginal peoples.'[7]

This chapter analyzes how treaties may be said to be an integral part of the Constitution of Canada. It first reviews the patterns of treaty-making in Canada during the 'historic' and 'modern' periods, showing how disagreement has pervaded relationships that are meant to be consensual.[8] The current constitutional framework for the protection of treaty rights, in particular section 35 of the Constitution Act 1982, is then examined.[9]

1. Historic Treaties

The concept of 'historic' treaty includes treaties made from the early seventeenth century to approximately 1930, when the Government of Canada formed the belief that the Indigenous peoples had surrendered Aboriginal title to all of Canada. Agreements included in this category are extremely diverse; one convenient division is between those that sought to establish relationships of peace and friendship, on the one hand, and those that purported to transfer title to the land, on the other hand. Among the latter category, the 'numbered treaties' concluded in the Canadian West in the late nineteenth and early twentieth century stand out because of the importance of the area covered. These families of treaties will be studied in turn; but we will address first the indigenous perspectives and protocols which were crucial in their making.

A. Indigenous Treaty-Making

Indigenous groups had relationships with one another before the arrival of the Europeans in North America. There was a well-established diplomatic tradition, embedded in Indigenous philosophies and worldviews. Although it is impossible to give a full account of that tradition here, some of its features may be highlighted.[10]

---

[5] J Webber, 'Relations of Force and Relations of Justice: The Emergence of Normative Community between Colonists and Aboriginal Peoples' (1995) 33 Osgoode Hall LJ 623.

[6] S Grammond, 'Compact Is Back: The Supreme Court of Canada's Revival of the Compact Theory of Confederation' (2016) 53 Osgoode Hall LJ 799.

[7] *Beckman v Little Salmon/Carmacks First Nation* [2010] 3 SCR 103 [97] (Deschamps J); see also B Slattery, 'The Aboriginal Constitution' (2014) 67 Sup Ct L Rev (2d) 319.

[8] For a book-length history of treaties, see J Miller, *Compact, Contract, Covenant: Aboriginal Treaty-Making in Canada* (University of Toronto Press, 2009).

[9] For a more in-depth analysis, see S Grammond, *Terms of Coexistence: Indigenous Peoples and Canadian Law* (Carswell, 2013).

[10] RA Williams, *Linking Arms Together: American Indian Treaty Visions of Law and Peace, 1600–1800* (Routledge, 1997); Treaty Elders of Saskatchewan, *Our Dream Is That Our Peoples Will One Day Be*

First, treaties are mainly understood in terms of the relationships they create. Kinship vocabulary is often used to describe those relationships. A treaty, in that sense, might be described as the adoption of another nation into one's family.[11] One consequence of viewing treaties as creating relationships is that treaties must be constantly renewed, for example through yearly meetings. The idea of a one-off transaction appears incompatible with this tradition.

Second, treaties are considered to be sacred agreements. As such, they cannot be broken without incurring spiritual consequences. They establish relationships not only between the treaty partners, but also between the latter and the Creator. Moreover, treaties cannot be separated from the spiritual relationship between the Indigenous peoples and the lands they inhabit, where they consider they have been placed by the Creator.

Third, Indigenous protocols and ceremonies are central to treaty-making. Some of those ceremonies may be related to the sacred nature of treaties. Thus, in the Prairies, the ceremony of the pipe established a connection with the Creator and solemnized any agreement then made.[12] In Eastern North America, the exchange of wampum (belts or necklaces made of coloured seashell beads) was a manner of extending an invitation to negotiate or solemnizing a treaty.[13] Wampum was also used as a mnemonic device, as the designs formed by the beads symbolized the contents of the agreement. More generally, the exchange of gifts was a common feature of treaty relationships.

B. Peace and Friendship Treaties

Upon their arrival in North America, European colonizers were integrated in the existing treaty relationships. Negotiations were conducted according to Indigenous protocol, which the newcomers had to learn quickly.[14] These treaties were formed through feasts, exchange of wampum, and exchange of personnel between the partner groups. Kinship metaphors were extensively employed in the discussions. Parties often described each other as 'brothers', suggesting equality of status.[15]

Treaty relationships of that era were too numerous and complex to be described here.[16] They ranged from trading alliances such as the Covenant Chain with the

---

Clearly Recognized as Nations (University of Calgary Press, 2000); L Simpson, 'Looking After Gdoo-naaganinaa: Precolonial Nishnaabeg Diplomatic and Treaty Relationships' (2008) 23:2 Wicazo Sa Rev 29.

[11] Treaty Elders of Saskatchewan, *Our Dream* above (n 10) 33–34.

[12] Miller above (n 8) 20.

[13] Ibid., 39–41.

[14] BG Trigger, *Natives and Newcomers* (McGill-Queen's University Press, 1986) at 172–174; DH Fischer, *Champlain's Dream* (Simon & Schuster, 2008) 124–147, 227–253.

[15] MD Walters, ' "Your Sovereign and Our Father": The Imperial Crown and the Idea of Legal-Ethnohistory' in S Dorsett and I Hunter (eds), *Law and Politics in British Colonial Thought: Transpositions of Empire* (Palgrave Macmillan, 2010) 91; P Cook, 'Onontio Gives Birth: How the French in Canada Became Fathers to Their Indigenous Allies, 1645–73' (2015) 96 Can Hist Rev 165.

[16] For a thorough review see JY Henderson, *Treaty Rights in the Constitution of Canada* (Carswell, 2007).

Haudenosaunee[17] to peace treaties made by the British with the Indigenous peoples of Acadia after the conquest of that region from the French in 1713.[18] One prominent instance was the 1701 Great Peace of Montreal, which put an end to decades of warfare between the Haudenosaunee and the French and their allies.[19]

To be sure, the European powers involved in those treaty relationships were pursuing a colonial project. They envisioned the acquisition of sovereignty over North American lands. Nevertheless, they did not presume that this could be accomplished by mere declaration. This is in line with the thinking of that era, which recognized that the Indigenous peoples may hold sovereignty over their lands and that treaties were necessary to transfer that sovereignty to colonial powers.[20]

Colonial practice also pointed to a relationship of equality that assumed the sovereignty of the Indigenous peoples.[21] Indigenous peoples made war and peace independently of the wishes of the colonial power. The colonizers' criminal law was not applied to them.[22] In the words of legal historian Paul McHugh, 'whatever *imperium* was asserted over Indians rested on their agreement rather than the fact of their forced submission.'[23]

C. Land Treaties

Private purchases of land from the Indigenous peoples have taken place from the earliest stages of British presence in North America. For a number of reasons, colonial authorities sought to forbid this practice and to centralize in their hands the dealings with the Indigenous peoples.[24] Those actions gave rise to the idea that the Indigenous peoples owned the land until such lands were purchased in the name of the Crown. That fundamental rule was enshrined in the Royal Proclamation of 1763 that was issued by the British king upon the conquest of New France. Although it is better known for the initial

---

[17] F Jennings, *The Ambiguous Iroquois Empire: The Covenant Chain Confederation of Indian Tribes with English Colonies from Its Beginnings to the Lancaster Treaty of 1744* (W.W. Norton, 1984).

[18] Miller above (n 8) 60–65.

[19] G Havard, *The Great Peace of Montreal of 1701* (McGill-Queen's University Press, 2001).

[20] CH Alexandrowicz, *An Introduction to the History of the Law of Nations in the East Indies* (Clarendon Press, 1967); Michel Morin, 'Fraternité, souveraineté et autonomie des Autochtones en Nouvelle-France' (2013) 43 RGD 531. As late as 1840 the British acquired sovereignty over New Zealand through a treaty with the Maori: I Brownlie, *Treaties and Indigenous Peoples* (Clarendon Press, 1992) 31–34.

[21] J Hurley, *Children or Brethren: Aboriginal Rights in Colonial Iroquoia* (University of Saskatchewan Native Law Centre, 1985).

[22] DH Brown, 'They Do Not Submit Themselves to the King's Law: Amerindians and Criminal Justice during the French Regime' (2002) 28 Man LJ 377.

[23] PG McHugh, *Aboriginal Societies and the Common Law: A History of Sovereignty, Status and Self-Determination* (Oxford University Press, 2004) 103; see also *R v Sioui* [1990] 1 SCR 1025, 1052–1053.

[24] DK Richter, 'To "Clear the King's and Indians' Title:" Seventeenth-Century Origins of North American Land Cession Treaties' in Saliha Belmessous (ed), *Empire by Treaty: Negotiating European Expansion, 1600–1900* (Oxford University Press, 2014).

political organization of the new British colonies and the purported repeal of French law in Quebec, the crucial character of its Indigenous provisions, which have never been repealed,[25] has earned the Proclamation the nickname of 'Indian Bill of Rights.'[26] In the summer of 1764, William Johnson, the Superintendent of Indian Affairs, called a meeting of several Indigenous nations at Niagara, where he presented the Proclamation.[27] Some authors have thus argued that the Proclamation itself became a treaty.[28]

The preamble to the Proclamation stated that lands 'not having been ceded to, or purchased by Us, are reserved to' the Indigenous peoples. In its operative part, the Proclamation also stated that all purchases of Indigenous land would be made in the name of the Crown only, at a public assembly of the Indigenous peoples concerned. There was found the mandate to conclude land treaties in those parts of North America remaining under British rule.

Nevertheless, the Proclamation also signalled the Crown's assertion of sovereignty over Indigenous lands, whether or not ceded by treaty. The King speaks of 'Our Dominions and Territories' and considers that the Indigenous peoples are living 'under Our Protection.' In the British minds, the treaties envisioned by the Proclamation were not international treaties. They were instruments of domestic law, or perhaps colonial law, always subject to the overriding power of the Imperial Parliament. Indeed, throughout the nineteenth century, colonial authorities pursued a policy of treaty-making while taking an increasingly reductionist view of the legal status and capacity of the Indigenous peoples.[29]

The principles enshrined in the Proclamation were not uniformly applied in the territory that became Canada. In particular, land treaties were never signed in Quebec or in the Maritime provinces, where indigenous claims were settled by the allotment of reserves. The reasons behind this distinctive policy are unclear and may have more to do with the political or military power of the Indigenous peoples in different regions as well as a complex web of political relationships between colonial and Imperial authorities.[30] It may be argued that the requirement to make treaties laid out in the Proclamation applied in all British colonies, including Quebec.[31]

---

[25] *St Catharine's Milling & Lumber Co v The Queen* (1887) 13 SCR 577, 632, Strong J; *R v McMaster*, [1928] ExCR 68.
[26] See eg *R v Marshall; R v Bernard* [2005] 2 SCR 220, 257; MD Walters, 'The Aboriginal Charter of Rights: The Royal Proclamation of 1763 and the Constitution of Canada' in T Fenge and J Aldridge (eds), *Keeping Promises: The Royal Proclamation of 1763, Aboriginal Rights, and Treaties in Canada* (McGill-Queen's University Press, 2015) 49.
[27] Miller above (n 8) 72–73.
[28] J Borrows, 'Constitutional Law from a First Nation Perspective: Self-Government and the Royal Proclamation' (1994) 28 UBCLRev 1; *Chippewas of Sarnia Band v Canada (AG)* [2001] 1 CNLR 56, 195 DLR (4th) 135 (Ont CA) [54]; but see *Rice v Agence du revenu du Québec* 2016 QCCA 666 [55].
[29] Grammond above (n 9) 82–89, 109–120; McHugh (n 24) 117–214; SL Harring, *White Man's Law: Native People in Nineteenth-Century Canadian Jurisprudence* (University of Toronto Press, 1998).
[30] A Beaulieu, 'The Acquisition of Aboriginal Land in Canada: The Genealogy of an Ambivalent System' in Belmessous above (n 13) 101.
[31] Grammond, above (n 9) 67–77.

Nevertheless, a policy of making treaties for the acquisition of land was consistently applied in Upper Canada (now Ontario) since the end of the eighteenth century.[32] Initially, those treaties were for a narrow strip of land on the shores of Lakes Ontario and Erie, and the consideration was for a one-time payment in goods. As the need for land increased, the area covered increased as well, and the Indigenous parties, who were feeling less secure in this new environment, bargained for additional terms, such as a right to hunt and fish, and an annual payment in perpetuity instead of a lump sum, as well as the creation of reserves. The Robinson-Huron and Robinson-Superior treaties, made in 1850 and encompassing a large area north of Lakes Huron and Superior, constituted the capstone to this era of treaty-making as well as the prelude to the next.

D. The Numbered Treaties

The use of treaties to acquire land switched to high gear after Confederation. To prepare the settlement of the newly-acquired Prairies, the federal government made treaties, over a period of about 50 years, with the Indigenous peoples of what is now Northeastern British Columbia, Alberta, Saskatchewan, Manitoba, and Northern Ontario, as well as parts of the Northwest Territories and the Yukon. These treaties were assigned numbers, from 1 to 11, and became known collectively as the 'numbered' treaties.

The actual contents of the numbered treaties has given rise to an enduring controversy. Indigenous peoples have a solid oral tradition as to their meaning.[33] In the case of the later treaties, the direct testimony of persons present at the negotiations was recorded in the 1970s.[34] In many respects, their accounts are confirmed by transcripts or shorthand notes of the negotiations.[35] The picture that emerges is one of sharing. The Indigenous peoples agreed to share the land with the newcomers, but never intended to 'sell' it. The purpose of the sharing was understood to be agriculture. Oral history frequently refers to the idea of rights measured by the 'depth of a plough.' But according to Elders, treaties rested on deeper foundations. By the treaties, Indigenous peoples and the European settlers mutually adopted each other, so as to create 'a perpetual family relationship.'[36] From that relationship flowed a set of reciprocal obligations, such as caring, loyalty, non-interference, and respect.[37] The relationship aimed at providing a 'guarantee of each other's survival,'[38] in particular through ensuring the continuance of the

---

[32] Miller above (n 8) 79–122.

[33] Treaty Elders of Saskatchewan above (n 10); Aimée Craft, *Breathing Life into the Stone Fort Treaty: An Anishinabe Understanding of Treaty One* (Purich, 2013).

[34] See eg R Price (ed), *The Spirit of the Alberta Indian Treaties* (Institute for Research on Public Policy, 1979).

[35] A Morris, *The Treaties of Canada with the Indians of Manitoba and the North-West Territories* (Belfords, Clarke & Co 1880); JS Long, *Treaty No. 9: Making the Agreement to Share the Land in Far Northern Ontario in 1905* (McGill-Queen's University Press, 2010).

[36] Treaty Elders of Saskatchewan above (n 10), 33.

[37] Ibid., 34.

[38] Ibid.

Indigenous peoples' way of life. In this regard, the report of the government commissioners who negotiated Treaty 8 mentioned that they had to reassure the Indigenous peoples 'that the treaty would not lead to any forced interference with their mode of life' and that 'they would be as free to hunt and fish after the treaty as they would be if they never entered into it.'[39]

The English text of the treaties paints an entirely different picture. It begins with a surrender of all the rights and titles of the Indigenous party over a large expanse of territory. Three broad categories of rights constituted the consideration of this purported abandonment. First, 'reserves' were to be created where Indigenous communities could become sedentary and engage in agriculture. The area of those reserves was to be determined as a function of the population that would settle there, but in any event it was only a tiny fraction of the surrendered territory. Second, an annual payment, typically five dollars, was to be made to every person 'taking treaty.' Such payments are still made today, although the amount has never been adjusted for inflation. Third, the Indigenous party would keep a right to hunt, trap, and fish over such parts of the surrendered territory as are not taken by the government for purposes of settlement, mining, or other purposes.

Today, the Indigenous peoples say that they never intended to surrender title to their lands. What we know of the negotiations suggests that the meaning of that clause was not discussed. It is difficult to reconcile the idea of the surrender of all rights with the sacred link that the Indigenous peoples have with the territories they inhabit.

The Government's policy was to conclude treaties with First Nations (or 'Indians'). In the nineteenth century, an indigenous group called the 'Métis' emerged on the Prairies. They initially resisted the Canadian government's assertion of authority in 1869–1870, an event called the Red River 'Rebellion' or 'Resistance.' The Métis-led provisional government sent a delegation to Ottawa to negotiate the terms under which the territory would join Canada. Although the Government initially denied it, the *Manitoba Act 1870* was the result of a bargain with the delegates of the provisional government. The Supreme Court has now recognized the consensual character of the instrument, although it refrains from calling it a 'treaty.'[40] Under that arrangement, the Métis would not be treated like the First Nations, but would rather receive lands (through what became known as the 'scrip' system) on an individual basis. However, in many cases, Indigenous persons were allowed to choose between 'taking treaty' (and be considered as a member of a First Nation) or 'taking scrip' (and be considered as Métis).

Treaty-making continued until the 1920s, when the Government thought that the task of treaty-making had been completed and that Aboriginal title had been surrendered throughout Canada. In 1969, the federal government issued a new policy (called the 'White Paper') proposing the full integration of the indigenous peoples in mainstream Canadian society, the repeal of the Indian Act, and the end of any special legal

---

[39] Report of Commissioners for Treaty No 8 (22 September 1899) in *Treaty No 8 Made June 21, 1899 and Adhesions, Reports, and other Documents* (Department of Supply and Services, 1981) 6.

[40] *Manitoba Métis Federation Inc v Canada (AG)* [2013] 1 SCR 623; *Caron v Alberta* [2015] 3 SCR 511.

treatment. With respect to treaties, the Government proposed to find a way to equitably end 'the anomaly of treaties between groups within society and the government of that society.'[41] The forceful rejection of that policy by the Indigenous peoples would spur the revival of treaty-making.

2. MODERN TREATIES

The government's new policy, announced in 1973, was made necessary by the *Calder*[42] decision, in which the Supreme Court held that Aboriginal title existed even in the absence of explicit recognition by the Crown. The federal government would negotiate with Indigenous groups who asserted Aboriginal title. The aim was to replace such title, said to be 'undefined,' by a set of clearly defined rights and compensation.

The first 'modern' treaty (or 'land claim agreement') was the James Bay and Northern Quebec Agreement, signed in 1975. Although it contained a clause purporting to extinguish Aboriginal title in return for money, reserves, and a right to hunt, trap, and fish throughout the territory, it also contained many innovative provisions that went far beyond the old template of the numbered treaties and that served as a model for subsequent agreements. Those provisions are reviewed in more detail below.

Since 1975, treaties have covered most of the northern territories. Thus, Inuit groups across the Arctic have signed the Inuvialuit Final Agreement (1984), the Nunavut Land Claims Agreement (1993), and the Labrador Inuit Agreement (2005). Several First Nations in the Yukon and Northwest Territories have also done the same. Progress has been slower in British Columbia and southern Quebec, in particular because the federal government insisted on the presence of the province at the negotiating table and because of the initial reluctance of the province to acknowledge the existence of Aboriginal rights or title. In British Columbia, the Nisga'a Treaty (1999) was the first to be signed in the modern era and was followed by a small number of other treaties. However, negotiations have not yet come to fruition in the greater part of the province.[43] Likewise, negotiations with the First Nations of southern Quebec have proceeded at snail's pace.

A. Extinguishment Clauses

Reaching certainty as to the rights to the territory remains a central objective of the federal government. In truth, the government was prompted to resume treaty-making by the possibility that Indigenous groups could stop resource extraction projects by

---

[41] *Statement of the Government of Canada on Indian Policy* (1969), online: http://www.aadnc-aandc. gc.ca/eng/1100100010189/1100100010191 (accessed 11 April 2016).

[42] *Calder v British Columbia* [1973] SCR 313.

[43] C McKee, *Treaty Talks in British Columbia: Building a New Relationship*, 3rd ed (UBC Press, 2009).

invoking their Aboriginal rights. This explains why the government insisted firmly on the extinguishment of the Indigenous party's Aboriginal rights and title and their replacement by a set of rights defined in the treaty as well as monetary compensation. In fact, this was a replication of what the Government perceived to be the main feature of historic treaties, namely the extinguishment of Aboriginal title.

The policy of requiring Indigenous parties to consent to the extinguishment of their Aboriginal rights has come under constant attack.[44] From the perspective of the Indigenous peoples, it is unacceptable to surrender rights that represent their sacred ties to the land. Moreover, from a practical perspective, such a clause deprives an Indigenous people of the benefit of any future evolution in the definition of Aboriginal rights. In some treaties, a 'definitional' clause was substituted for the extinguishment clause.[45] This means that the Aboriginal rights of the Indigenous party are defined as being those expressly set forth in the treaty, and no other. In other cases, the Indigenous party undertakes not to exercise nor to assert rights not mentioned in the agreement.[46] In practice, however, the result is the same.

B. Land Regime and Co-management

Modern treaties have laid out a complex regime for the management of the territory covered. As with the numbered treaties, the central feature is the recognition of the Indigenous party's right of exclusive use of certain lands, which form a small portion of the territory covered, and the recognition of a right to hunt and fish over the balance of that territory. Those lands are not called 'reserves' and they are not subject to the Indian Act. In most cases they are granted in fee simple and they do not fall under federal jurisdiction.

The Indigenous peoples participate in the management of the rest of the territory, through detailed environmental assessment and co-management regimes. As a result, modern treaties are tantamount to a constitution of the region they cover; their provisions often replace legislation applicable elsewhere in the province or territory, or require the adoption of specific implementing legislation. Thus, the James Bay and Northern Quebec Agreement contains regimes for the assessment of environmental and social impact of major projects, as well as a regime for the co-management of hunting, trapping, and fishing. Treaties concluded in the northern territories also provide for the participation of the indigenous peoples in land use planning and water management.

---

[44] See eg Royal Commission on Aboriginal Peoples, *Treaty Making in the Spirit of Co-existence: An Alternative to Extinguishment* (Royal Commission on Aboriginal Peoples, 1995); *Concluding Observations of the Human Rights Committee: Canada*, UN Doc. CCPR/C/CAN/CO/5 (20 April 2006) at para. 8; *Concluding Observations of the Committee on Economic, Social and Cultural Rights: Canada*, UN Doc. E/C.12/CAN/CO/4 and E/C.12/CAN/CO/5 (22 May 2006) [16].

[45] Nisga'a Final Agreement c 2 s 23; Maa-Nulth First Nations Final Agreement s 1.11.

[46] Nunavik Inuit Land Claims Agreement s 2.29.

A number of treaties have also made explicit provision for the sharing of benefits arising from natural resource extraction in the region covered by the treaty. This may take the form of a share of the royalty payments received by the Crown as a result of resource extraction activities. Some treaties also require the signature of an 'impacts and benefits agreement' (or 'IBA') before major projects receive the green light.[47] Pursuant to those agreements, the Indigenous peoples may receive a number of benefits such as guaranteed employment and training, guaranteed subcontracts, a share in the profits of the project, access to project infrastructure, relationships with non-Indigenous employees, and so forth.

C. Self-Government

As we have seen above, the Indigenous peoples were self-governing entities before the arrival of the European settlers and as a matter of fact they have continued to govern themselves to this day, at least to a certain extent. It is arguable that, as a matter of Canadian law, they have an inherent right to self-government (i.e., without the need of formal acknowledgement from government) and that this is an Aboriginal right protected by section 35 of the *Constitution Act, 1982*.[48] Until that issue is settled, however, treaties remain a privileged means to entrench a self-government regime. This may happen in a number of ways.

First, the treaty may form part of a broader settlement that also includes a form of self-government. In the Yukon, for example, a number of First Nations have concluded treaties as well as companion self-government agreements that do not constitute a part of the treaty and that are implemented by federal legislation.[49] Those agreements confer jurisdictions upon First Nations that compare with those of a province or territory; these jurisdictions include education, health, child welfare, adoption, estates, cultural issues, and so forth. In Nunavut, the land claims agreement was accompanied by a political accord that provided for the division of the Northwest Territories and the creation of a new territory in which the Inuit would be a large majority of the population. This is a 'public' form of government, in the sense that non-indigenous persons may vote and be elected to the governing bodies of the territory, although they are a minority of the population. In both cases, the provisions regarding self-government are outside the treaty. Hence, they are not protected by section 35.

Second, self-government provisions may be contained in the treaty itself.[50] The James Bay and Northern Quebec Agreement, for instance, created local governments as well

---

[47] Nunavut Land Claims Agreement c 26.

[48] A federal policy document recognized as much: Government of Canada, *Federal Policy Guide: Aboriginal Self-Government* (Ottawa, 1995). However, in *R v Pamajewon* [1996] 2 SCR 821 and in *Delgamuukw v British Columbia* [1997] 3 SCR 1010, the Supreme Court declined to rule on the issue.

[49] Yukon First Nations Self-Government Act SC 1994 c 35.

[50] The validity of self-government provisions was confirmed in *Sga'nism Sim'augit (Chief Mountain) v Canada (AG)*, 2013 BCCA 49.

as Cree and Inuit regional school boards and health boards. More recent treaties, such as the Nisga'a Treaty, the Labrador Inuit Agreement, and the Tlicho Agreement, contain a broader self-government regime. The powers conferred may again be similar to those of a province, although there are often restrictions or standards as to how these powers may be exercised; for example, the Tlicho government may make laws on social assistance, "provided that such laws provide for standards, including standards for equitable access, portability and availability of appeal mechanisms."[51] Some of these treaties set up a two-level government structure, with regional and local governments. Certain treaties also provide for the creation of Indigenous courts or justice systems. However, it is made clear that the *Canadian Charter of Rights and Freedoms* applies to Indigenous treaty governments.[52] As the self-government regime is in the treaty, it is protected by the Constitution, and the federal or provincial governments cannot change it without the consent of the Indigenous party.[53]

One of the challenges of exercising self-government is funding. Certain treaties grant Indigenous governments a power to tax their citizens. However, the reality is that Indigenous governments depend on federal funding, which has proven insufficient to allow them fully to exercise their jurisdiction. As a result, many of the wide heads of jurisdiction described in the treaties remain in disuse.

D. Challenges of Implementation

It is often said that historic treaties were mainly honoured in the breach. In a sense, the challenge is even greater with modern treaties, given the broad array of benefits, programs, and structures that they mandate. Their implementation often requires changes in the day-to-day operations of several government departments and agencies. It also requires the government to fund adequately a number of programs, services, and activities. To avoid those pitfalls, modern treaties require their signatories to prepare implementation plans, which set out specific activities, responsibilities, and funding levels needed to ensure the carrying out of the obligations created by the treaty.[54] There are also monitoring and reporting mechanisms.

Yet, the Indigenous signatories to the modern treaties have persistently complained about inadequate implementation and insufficient funding to ensure that the promises made in the treaties are realized.[55] Certain Indigenous groups, such as the Cree of Eeyou Istchee and the Inuit of Nunavut, fought long court battles over the failure to implement large portions of their treaties. The Cree eventually reached an original solution: in

---

[51] Tlicho Agreement s 7.4.4(f).
[52] See eg Nisga'a Final Agreement c 9 s 2; Labrador Inuit Agreement s 2.18.1.
[53] See eg *Tłįcho Government v Canada (AG)*, 2015 NWTSC 9.
[54] See eg the Nunavut Land Claims Agreement c 37.
[55] T Fenge, 'Negotiation and Implementation of Modern Treaties between Aboriginal Peoples and the Crown in Right of Canada' in Fenge & Aldridge (eds) above (n 26) 105.

exchange for a fixed yearly payment, they assumed a number of federal and provincial obligations under the James Bay and Northern Quebec Agreement for a period of 20 years. Yet, the impression remains that too much is left at the discretion of the federal government.

3. TREATY LAW

So far, we have chronicled the conclusion of treaties during various periods of Canadian history. Those treaties, obviously, create law: they set forth binding legal rules governing the relationship between the Indigenous peoples and the settler state. But there is also a body of law about treaties: rules governing how treaties are made, how they are interpreted, and how they are protected. These rules may come from several legal systems. For example, international treaties are governed by international law, but the legal system of each state party may also have its specific set of rules. Thus, in a dualist country such as Canada, an international treaty might not be enforced by the domestic courts if it is not implemented by legislation, even though it would be perfectly valid and enforceable from the perspective of international law.

Over most of the twentieth century, Canadian law has asserted a monopoly over the legal status and interpretation of Indigenous treaties. Canadian courts have stated that those treaties were not regulated by international law[56] and have typically given little weight to the Indigenous perspectives on the meaning of those treaties.[57] Nevertheless, international law and Indigenous law are currently reasserting a legitimate role in providing a juridical foundation for the implementation of treaties. Thus, article 37 of the UN Declaration on the Rights of the Indigenous Peoples declares a 'right to the recognition, observation and enforcement of treaties . . . concluded with States.'[58] The breach of a treaty might also constitute a violation of international human rights law, for example of article 27 of the International Covenant on Civil and Political Rights.

As this chapter focuses on the Canadian Constitution, however, we will review how the Canadian legal system conceives of, and protects, Indigenous treaties. In Canadian law, treaties are conceptualized as 'analogous to contracts,'[59] because they are exchanges of promises or, to use civil law language, bilateral juridical acts. Contract law, however, is often insufficient to ensure the full implementation of treaties and does not recognize their constitutional significance.[60] Contracts may not constrain the exercise of statutory

---

[56] *Simon v R* [1985] 2 SCR 387, 404; *R v Sioui* [1990] 1 SCR 1025, 1037–38.

[57] See eg *R v Horse* [1988] 1 SCR 187, where evidence of the Indigenous understanding of the treaty was ruled inadmissible as the text was 'clear.'

[58] UN GA Res 61/295 (2007).

[59] *R v Badger* [1996] 1 SCR 771, 812; see also *Nunavut Tungavik Inc. v Canada (AG)* 2014 NUCA 2 [76] ('essentially a contractual relationship').

[60] Macklem above (n 1) 140–144.

powers and may be overridden by legislation. In practice, the protection of treaties derives from specific statutory provisions such as section 88 of the Indian Act or the legislation implementing modern treaties. Treaties finally received constitutional protection with the enactment of section 35 of the *Constitution Act, 1982*.

A. Scope of the Concept: What Counts as a Treaty?

The existence of legal protections afforded to 'treaties' generally begs the question of a comprehensive definition of the concept. As we have seen above, the agreements that have been called 'treaties' over the centuries are quite diverse. Hence, does Canadian law consider that the concept of treaty comprises all agreements between the state and the Indigenous peoples, or only a subset? The answer to that question is highly important, as it delineates the category of instruments that will receive constitutional protection. The debate about the definition of a treaty can thus be likened to the debate about whether the list of enactments forming part of the Constitution of Canada is opened or closed.[61]

The Supreme Court defined the term 'treaty' broadly. In *Badger*, it said that '[. . .] a treaty represents an exchange of solemn promises between the Crown and the various Indian nations. It is an agreement whose nature is sacred. [. . .] Treaties are analogous to contracts, albeit of a very solemn and special, public nature. They create enforceable obligations based on the mutual consent of the parties.'[62] Other decisions testify to this openness. In *Simon*, the Court held that a treaty need not contain land surrender clauses,[63] whereas in *Sioui*, a peace agreement concluded in haste and with little formality was characterized as a treaty.[64]

Nevertheless, judicial decisions and government practice have narrowed down the concept and excluded several categories of agreements from the protections afforded to treaties.[65] Thus, many agreements, including treaty implementation plans or certain self-government agreements, explicitly state that they do not constitute treaties or do not create treaty obligations within the meaning of section 35 of the *Constitution Act, 1982*.[66] The Supreme Court also appeared to consider that 'reserve surrenders' (i.e., agreements whereby a First Nation cedes a part of its reserve to the Crown) are not treaties and do not benefit from constitutional protection,[67] and refused to accept that funding agreements were treaties or even 'other agreements' giving rise to a exemption from seizure under the Indian Act.[68] Likewise, in a series of recent decisions, the Supreme

---

[61] Constitution Act 1982 s 52(2).

[62] *R v Badger* [1996] SCR 771, 793, 812.

[63] *Simon v R* [1985] 2 SCR 387, 408–410.

[64] *R v Sioui* [1990] 1 SCR 1025.

[65] See eg *Kaska Dene Council v R* [2007] 3 CNLR 28 (BCSC) aff'd on other grounds [2009] 1 CNLR 102 (BCCA); *Bear v Saskatchewan (Government of)*, 2016 SKQB 73.

[66] See eg the *Tsawwassen First Nation Final Agreement Act* S.C. 2008 c. 32 s 3, 9, 11.

[67] *Ermineskin Indian Band and Nation v Canada* [2009] 1 SCR 222 [46]–[48].

[68] *McDiarmid Lumber Ltd v God's Lake First Nation* [2006] 2 SCR 846.

Court avoided using the word 'treaty' to describe certain major agreements with the Métis Nation.[69] Although provinces are often parties to treaties made by the federal government, agreements made by the provinces alone have never been characterized as treaties.[70] In effect, all those 'non-treaty' agreements are de-constitutionalized and relegated to the nebulous category of intergovernmental agreements, always vulnerable to contrary legislation and to insufficient budgetary appropriations.

Agreements between Indigenous groups and private companies cannot be characterized as treaties. 'Impacts and benefits agreements,' often concluded to allow Indigenous groups to share in the benefits of resource extraction projects, would thus be considered as mere private contracts and outside the scope of section 35.

B. Interpretation

Treaties, like constitutions, are meant to establish long-term legal relationships. Because few words are used to convey a meaning that must adapt to changing circumstances, the application of treaties and constitutions often gives rise to what lawyers call problems of 'interpretation.' The well-known controversy about whether a constitution must be interpreted according to the 'original intent' of its authors or in a dynamic fashion also plays out with respect to treaties. In this regard, governments have usually insisted on the text of the treaties as proof of the original intent of the parties. However, several difficulties make a purely textual approach unrealistic. The parties who made the treaties spoke different languages and came from widely different cultural and legal traditions, so that the concepts used during the negotiations may not have had the same meaning for each of them. Moreover, it has become quite clear that several promises made during the negotiations were not recorded in the treaty text, even though they are mentioned in the treaty commissioners' report or other accounts of the negotiations.[71] Although the foregoing reasons suggest that the search for a common intention must go beyond the treaty text, there are also reasons to doubt that the meaning of a treaty must be defined forever by the intentions at the time of signing. The Indigenous peoples often made a treaty in unfavourable circumstances, where they did not have equal bargaining power. Most important, treaties were usually meant to define a long-term relationship, which by definition must be allowed to evolve over time.[72]

To address those concerns, courts have tried to use a number of interpretive devices designed to bring justice to other cases of unbalanced contractual relations.[73] First, it is often asserted that treaties must be given a liberal and generous interpretation.

[69] *Alberta (Aboriginal Affairs and Northern Development) v Cunningham* [2011] 2 SCR 670; *Manitoba Métis Federation Inc v Canada (AG)* [2013] 1 SCR 623; *Caron v Alberta* [2015] 3 SCR 511.

[70] See eg *Lovelace v Ontario* [2000] 1 SCR 950.

[71] *R v Badger* [1996] 1 SCR 771, 798; *R v Morris* [2006] 2 SCR 915 [24].

[72] On these issues, see J Borrows '(Ab)Originalism and Canada's Constitution' (2012) 58 Sup Ct L Rev (2d) 351.

[73] Grammond above (n 9) 297–305; LI Rotman, 'Taking Aim at the Canons of Treaty Interpretation in Canadian Aboriginal Rights Jurisprudence' (1997) 46 UNBLJ 11; JY Henderson, 'Interpreting Sui Generis

Ambiguities must be resolved in favour of the Indigenous peoples. Second, various techniques are used to ascertain the 'meaning understood' by the Indigenous peoples, for example through the use of extrinsic evidence or oral history.[74] Third, the court may imply terms in order to find a satisfactory compromise between the interests of both parties.[75] These guidelines are not binding, however, and courts sometimes fall back on a textual interpretation or ignore oral promises.[76]

But framing the issue as one of interpretation may obscure broader concerns. In many cases the intentions of the parties at the time of signing may have little relevance to the challenges of today. One must also contemplate the possibility that there was no genuine agreement on some of the treaty's important terms. In those circumstances, what is called for is a process that focuses on the spirit of the treaty and that finds practical ways to implement that spirit in the current context. One example is the Supreme Court's implication of a duty to consult and accommodate the Indigenous signatories to a treaty when the Crown intends to use the surrendered lands.[77]

Methods of treaty interpretation were developed mainly with respect to historic treaties. Their use with respect to modern treaties has been controversial. Although some courts have stated that a generous interpretation was mandated and even admitted extrinsic evidence,[78] the dominant tendency seems to be that the text is of paramount importance.[79] Nevertheless, the Supreme Court suggested that modern treaties must be interpreted in a generous and forward-looking manner, while bearing in mind that the parties intended to reach a certain degree of certainty.[80]

C. Statutory and Constitutional Protection

The first protections of treaty rights beyond contract law were statutory. Section 88 of the Indian Act, adopted in 1951, was interpreted as shielding treaty rights against provincial game laws.[81] Contrary to section 35, section 88 does not include a justification

---

Treaties' (1997) 36 Alta L Rev 46; G Christie, 'Justifying Principles of Treaty Interpretation' (2000) 26 Queen's LJ 142.

[74] See eg *R v Badger* [1996] 1 SCR 771; *R v Marshall* [1999] 3 SCR 433.

[75] See eg *R v Sioui* [1990] 1 SCR 1025.

[76] See eg *Benoit v Canada* [2003] 3 CNLR 20 (FCA).

[77] *Mikisew Cree First Nation v Canada (Minister of Canadian Heritage)* [2005] 3 SCR 388.

[78] *Cree School Board v Canada (AG)* [2001] RJQ 2128 (CA) 2152, 2155.

[79] *Eastmain Band v Canada (Federal Administrator)*, [1993] 1 FC 501 (CA) 515–516; *Tr'ondëk Hwëch'in v Canada* [2004] 2 CNLR 346 (Yukon CA); *Nunavut Tungavik Inc. v Canada (AG)* 2014 NUCA 2; J Jai, 'The Interpretation of Modern Treaties and the Honour of the Crown: Why Modern Treaties Deserve Judicial Deference' (2009) 26 NJCL 25.

[80] *Beckman v Little Salmon/Carmacks First Nation* [2010] 3 SCR 103 [9]–[12]; see also *First Nation of Nacho Nyak Dun v Yukon*, 2015 YKCA 18; D Newman, 'Contractual and Covenantal Conceptions of Modern Treaty Interpretation' (2011) 54 Sup Ct L Rev (2d) 475.

[81] See eg *R v Taylor and Williams* (1981) 34 OR (2d) 360 (CA); *R v Horseman* [1990] 1 SCR 901; *R v Sioui* [1990] 1 SCR 1025; but see *Dick v R* [1985] 2 SCR 309; for a more detailed analysis, see S Grammond, *Les traités entre l'État canadien et les peuples autochtones* (Yvon Blais 1995) 142–148.

test.[82] Moreover, each modern treaty is implemented by federal and provincial or territorial statutes that validate the treaty, make it binding on third parties, and make it paramount over conflicting statutes.[83]

However, the most effective protection of treaty rights today is found in section 35(1) of the *Constitution Act, 1982*, which states that '[t]he existing aboriginal and treaty rights of the aboriginal peoples of Canada are hereby recognized and affirmed.' To remove any doubt as to the application of this guarantee to modern treaties, section 35(3) provides that 'treaties' include existing or future 'land claims agreements.'

Section 35 prevents the state from extinguishing a treaty.[84] However, the protection afforded by section 35 is not absolute, even in the case of modern treaties.[85] As for *Charter* rights, restrictions on Aboriginal and treaty rights are valid if they satisfy a justification test, known as the *Sparrow* test.[86] The state must prove that a legislative or administrative measure curtailing such rights was adopted for a valid public purpose. It must also prove that the measure is compatible with the 'honour of the Crown,' which, according to the most recent restatement of the test, means that 'the benefit to the public is proportionate to any adverse effect on the Aboriginal interest.'[87] The state must also consult with the Indigenous group affected and accommodate its concerns. It is not possible to analyze the jurisprudence regarding the *Sparrow* test here. Suffice it to say that the practical result is to enable one party to a treaty, and not the other, to change the scope of its obligations.

* * *

For all intents and purposes, treaties with the Indigenous peoples are now recognized as part of the Constitution of Canada, both in formal terms—treaty rights are protected by section 35—and in substantive terms—treaties establish a significant portion of the terms of coexistence between Canada's founding peoples. Yet, it is difficult to see treaties as genuine instruments of reconciliation when they perpetuate a crucial component of the policy of dispossession, namely, extinguishment of Aboriginal rights. Moreover, the challenges of securing the full implementation of historic and modern treaties remain daunting. Together with the delays and costs of negotiation, this may explain why many Indigenous groups are having doubts about the treaty-making process and are pursuing alternatives, for example piecemeal agreements with respect to specific resource extraction projects or other 'interim' measures.

---

[82]   *R v Morris* [2006] 2 SCR 915 [55] (Deschamps and Abella JJ) [98] (McLachlin CJ and Fish J dissenting).

[83]   See eg the Nisga'a Final Agreement Act SC 2000 c 7.

[84]   See eg *R v Marshall* [1999] 3 SCR 456 [48]; see also *R v Van der Peet* [1996] 2 SCR 507 [28] with respect to Aboriginal rights.

[85]   *Sga'nism Sim'augit (Chief Mountain) v Canada (AG)*, 2013 BCCA 49 [71]; *Corporation Makivik v Québec (PG)*, 2014 QCCA 1455.

[86]   *R v Sparrow* [1990] 1 SCR 1075.

[87]   *Tsilhqot'in Nation v British Columbia* [2014] 2 SCR 256 [125].

This situation may illustrate what Jeremy Webber calls 'agonistic constitutional-ism,' namely the idea that although there exist widely diverging views of the nature of the country and the terms on which the various founding peoples agreed to join, it is possible to live together on the basis of more practical and day-to-day commitments which do not bring conflicting claims about the nature of the country into collision.[88] However, simply 'agreeing to disagree' or 'bracketing fundamental differences' raises important concerns. There is a risk that the institutions of the majority will continue to operate on the basis of premises not accepted by the Indigenous peoples. Indeed, one of the purposes of a constitution—including treaties—is to protect a minority against a powerful majority. This will likely not be accomplished unless and until there is a shared understanding about the meaning of treaties. This may require more effort than what has already been consented. After all, agreeing on a constitution may take a long time.

BIBLIOGRAPHY

Craft, Aimée. *Breathing Life into the Stone Fort Treaty: An Anishinabe Understanding of Treaty One*. Saskatoon: Purich, 2013.

Grammond, Sébastien. *Terms of Coexistence: Indigenous Peoples and Canadian Law*. Toronto: Carswell, 2013.

Henderson, James Youngblood. *Treaty Rights in the Constitution of Canada*. Toronto: Carswell, 2007.

Macklem, Patrick. *Indigenous Difference and the Constitution of Canada*. Toronto: University of Toronto Press, 2001.

McHugh, Paul G. *Aboriginal Societies and the Common Law: A History of Sovereignty, Status and Self-Determination*. Oxford: Oxford University Press, 2004.

Miller, Jim. *Compact, Contract, Covenant: Aboriginal Treaty-Making in Canada*. Toronto: University of Toronto Press, 2009.

Newman, Dwight. 'Contractual and Covenantal Conceptions of Modern Treaty Interpretation' (2011) 54 Sup Ct L Rev (2d) 475.

Treaty Elders of Saskatchewan. *Our Dream Is That Our Peoples Will One Day Be Clearly Recognized as Nations*. Calgary: University of Calgary Press, 2000.

Williams, Robert A. *Linking Arms Together: American Indian Treaty Visions of Law and Peace, 1600–1800*. New York: Routledge, 1997.

---

[88] J Webber, *The Constitution of Canada: A Contextual Approach* (Hart, 2015) 262–265.

C. *Indigenous Peoples and the* Constitution Act, 1982

CHAPTER 15

....

THE FORM AND SUBSTANCE
OF ABORIGINAL TITLE

Assimilation, Recognition, Reconciliation

....

PATRICK MACKLEM*

1. INTRODUCTION

....

THE patriation of the Constitution of Canada in 1982 brought far-reaching structural
changes to the Canadian constitutional order. Among the most prominent of these
changes, and addressed extensively elsewhere in this Handbook, were the introduction
of a complex set of amending formulas that release Canada from the need to request the
Parliament of the United Kingdom to enact legislation to amend Canadian constitutional norms, and the enactment of the *Canadian Charter of Rights and Freedoms,* which
places constitutional limits on the exercise of legislative, executive, and administrative
authority in the form of entrenched constitutional rights and freedoms. Patriation also
created the possibility of structural changes in the relationship between Indigenous
peoples and Canada, by recognizing and affirming, in section 35 of the *Constitution Act,
1982,* the 'existing aboriginal and treaty rights of the aboriginal peoples of Canada'—
changes that have the potential to promote reconciliation in the wake of a long and
punishing history of colonialism that structured and continue to structure Canadian-
Indigenous relations.

  This chapter seeks to highlight law's participation in the colonizing projects that
initiated the establishment of the Canadian constitutional order. Imperial and subsequently Canadian law refused to acknowledge the presence of a plurality of Indigenous
constitutional orders on the continent, laying instead the groundwork for a decidedly

  * William C. Graham Professor of Law, University of Toronto. I am grateful to David Schneiderman
and Peter Oliver for their comments on a previous version of this chapter.

monist conception of sovereign power, initially rooted in the sovereignty of the United Kingdom and ultimately grounded in the sovereignty of Canada. Imperial and subsequently Canadian law deemed legally insignificant the deep connections that Indigenous peoples had with their ancestral territories, and imposed alien norms of conduct on diverse Indigenous ways of life. In doing so, law legitimated the manifold political, social, and economic acts of dispossession and dislocation that collectively bear the label of colonialism. The constitutional entrenchment of Aboriginal and treaty rights in 1982 formally recognized a distinctive constitutional relationship between Indigenous peoples and Canada. The judiciary has begun to see the purpose of formal constitutional recognition to be a process of substantive constitutional reconciliation of the interests of Indigenous peoples and those of Canada. This chapter argues that constitutional reconciliation can only commence by comprehending Aboriginal rights and title as protecting Indigenous interests associated with culture, territory, treaties, and sovereignty in robust terms—terms, if met, which will have profound structural consequences for the relationship between Indigenous peoples and Canada.

2. LAW AND COLONIALISM

To grasp the nature and scope of Aboriginal rights and title in the contemporary Canadian constitutional order, it is necessary to go back in time to unearth how imperial powers comprehended their claims of sovereign authority on the continent. At the time of initial contact between Indigenous peoples and imperial powers and their colonial representatives, manifold Indigenous legal orders exercised lawmaking authority over territories and peoples in the Americas. The legal norms that constituted these legal orders specified and regulated the economic, social, and political practices of individuals and groups belonging to distinct Indigenous nations as well as relations between and among Indigenous nations. The legal validity of these norms lay in the nature of the legal orders from which they emanated. European settlement imported colonial legal norms whose validity ultimately depended on the legal systems of France and the United Kingdom. Colonial settlement also marked the genesis of a series of intersocietal encounters, some friendly, others hostile, with mistrust, trust, suspicion, and expectation alike participating in the formation of a pluralist ethos characteristic of their relations. In the words of Jeremy Webber, 'the distinctive norms of each society furnished the point of departure, determining the spirit of interaction, colouring the first interpretations of the other's customs, and shaping the beginning of a common normative language.'[1]

---

[1] Jeremy Webber, 'Relations of Force and Relations of Justice: The Emergence of Normative Community between Colonists and Aboriginal Peoples' (1995) 33 Osgoode Hall L.J. 623, 627.

The promise of a 'common normative language' informing this relationship, however, remains unfulfilled. There are many complex reasons for its absence—reasons that span many domains, including epistemology, economics, politics, and law. But one account merits attention, even though it glosses over the complexity of what it seeks to explain. The common normative language immanent in early encounters between and among Indigenous and colonial peoples failed to take root and was replaced by its antithesis: a monistic account of constitutional order, with decidedly non-Indigenous sources of legal authority initially grounded in British law and subsequently grounded in the Constitution of Canada.[2]

One contributing factor to the emergence of a monist conception of the Canadian constitutional order, addressed elsewhere in this *Handbook*, was a transformation of the Crown's objectives in entering into treaties with Indigenous peoples. Although the Crown initially entered into treaties with Indigenous peoples to secure its precarious legal and factual footing on Indigenous territories by acts of mutual recognition, the Crown began to negotiate treaties for different reasons. During the nineteenth century, perhaps as a result of the dramatic shift in demography and in the balance of military and economic power between Indigenous nations and the Crown, the treaty process from the Crown's perspective instead became a means of facilitating the relocation and assimilation of Indigenous people. The Crown increasingly saw the treaty process as a means of formally dispossessing Indigenous peoples of ancestral territory in return for reserve land and certain benefits to be provided by state authorities.

When law gradually emerged as a relatively autonomous sphere of social life, the judiciary began to address the legal consequences of the treaty process. Judicial interpretation of treaties only started to occur in Canada in the late 1800s, when courts held treaties to be political agreements unenforceable in a court of law. International law provides that an agreement between two 'independent powers' constitutes a treaty binding on the parties to the agreement.[3] But because courts regarded Indigenous nations as uncivilized and thus not independent, they refused to view Crown promises as legally enforceable obligations under international or domestic law.[4]

Moreover, with the establishment of British colonies in North America, there arose a need to extend legal validity to the emergent pattern of landholding occasioned by

---

[2] Compare P.G. McHugh, *Aboriginal Societies and the Common Law: A History of Sovereignty, Status, and Self-Determination* (Oxford University Press, 2004) 94 ('constitutional lawyers and courts intellectually cleaving to the unitary common law model of sovereignty—itself . . . largely a nineteenth-century model—were unable to recognize a shared or multiple version'). For a comparative perspective, see Peter C. Oliver, *The Constitution of Independence: The Development of Constitutional Theory in Australia, Canada, and New Zealand* (Oxford University Press, 2005) 27–42.

[3] See, eg, James Crawford, *Ian Brownlie's Principles of Public International Law* (Oxford University Press, 2012) 58–70. It should be noted that, even if treaties between the Crown and First Nations constituted treaties in international law, this fact alone would not render them enforceable in domestic courts; implementing legislation would be required: see *AG Canada v AG Ontario (Labour Conventions)* [1937] AC 326 (PC).

[4] *See, eg, R v Syliboy*, (1929) 1 DLR 307 (NS Co Ct).

colonization. Enter the fiction of underlying Crown title, with a particularly brutal twist. Canadian property law holds that the Crown enjoys underlying title to all of Canada.[5] Property owners possess and own their land as a result of grants from the Crown. Ownership confers a right to use and enjoy the land in question and a right to exclude others from entering onto one's land.

The fiction of original Crown occupancy was originally developed to legitimate feudal landholdings in England, along with another fiction that the actual occupants of the land enjoyed rights of ownership as a result of Crown grants. The law imagined the Crown as granting lands to landholders, with the result that ownership, or fee simple, passed as a result of these grants to landholders. As Kent McNeil has explained, this process never truly occurred; the Crown was not the original occupant and therefore not the original owner of the land, and by and large the Crown did not confer actual grants to landholders. These fictions were developed to rationalize the existing pattern of landholdings in England, and they served this purpose well.[6]

The fiction of underlying Crown title has had dramatically different consequences in the colonial context. Underlying Crown title in England was accompanied by legal recognition of initially fictional grants to actual occupants, thereby legitimating the existing pattern of landholdings. But only one-half of this equation was imported to Canada, thereby severely disrupting the existing pattern of Indigenous landholdings in Canada. Although the Crown was imagined as the original occupant of all of Canada, there were no fictional Crown grants vesting title in Indigenous peoples to their territories. The fiction of underlying Crown title became a legal technology of Indigenous dispossession, radically disrupting the actual pattern of Indigenous landholdings in British North America. The Crown was relatively free to grant third-party interests to whomever it pleased, which it did: to settlers, mining companies, forestry companies, and others.

To the extent that it refused to acknowledge the full legal significance of Indigenous occupancy, Canadian property law vested extraordinary proprietary power in the Crown. Proprietary authority flows from the fact that the federal and provincial governments possess title to certain public lands, often called Crown lands. Each level of government, as owner of Crown lands, possesses proprietary authority over its lands akin to the authority that a private property owner enjoys over his or her property. As owner, the federal or provincial government can exploit, sell, mortgage, lease, or license

---

[5] See *R. v Sparrow* [1990] 1 SCR 1075, 1103 ('while British policy towards the native population was based on respect for their right to occupy their traditional lands, . . . there was from the outset never any doubt that . . . the underlying title . . . to such lands vested in the Crown').

[6] See, generally, Kent McNeil, *Common Law Aboriginal Title* (Clarendon Press, 1989). On the utility of legal fictions, see Lon Fuller, *Legal Fictions* (Stanford University Press, 1967) 111 (legal fictions are in part a function of the 'inveterate hang of the human mind toward an organized simplicity'). See also Henry Maine, *Ancient Law* (1861, Dent and Sons Everyman ed., 1917) 76–77 ('[t]his conflict between belief or theory and notorious fact is at first sight extremely perplexing; but what it really illustrates is the efficiency with which Legal Fictions do their work in the infancy of society'); Duncan Kennedy, *A Critique of Adjudication* (Harvard University Press, 1997) 200–202 (examining legal fictions as modes of collective denial produced by specific conflicts).

activities on Crown lands, subject to any legislative or constitutional restrictions that constrain the exercise of such proprietary authority.[7] When coupled with its legislative power, the Crown's proprietary authority authorized a vast array of competing claims to ancestral territories.

In the late 1800s, Canadian law, with its belated acceptance of a tepid form of common law Aboriginal title, did acknowledge that Indigenous peoples lived on and occupied the continent prior to European contact and, as a result, possess certain interests worthy of legal protection.[8] This body of law prescribed ways of handling disputes between Indigenous and non-Indigenous peoples, especially disputes over the use and enjoyment of land. It recognized, in common law terms, Indigenous occupation and use of ancestral lands,[9] described rights associated with Aboriginal title in collective terms, as vesting in Indigenous communities,[10] and purported to restrict settlement on Indigenous territories until these territories had been surrendered to the Crown.[11] It prohibited sales of Indigenous land to non-Indigenous people without the approval of and participation by Crown authorities.[12] And it prescribed safeguards for the manner in which such surrenders can occur and imposed fiduciary obligations on government in its dealings with Indigenous lands and resources.[13]

The common law of Aboriginal title, however, historically failed to protect Indigenous territories from settlement and exploitation. Law's inability to protect Indigenous territories was in part a function of broader social and historical realities associated with colonial expansion. Governments and settlers either misunderstood or ignored the law of Aboriginal title. Crown respect for the law of Aboriginal title was eroded by the decline of the fur trade and the waning of Indigenous and non-Indigenous economic

---

[7] In 1867, the various assets and liabilities of the confederating colonies were apportioned between the federal and provincial governments by the *Constitution Act, 1867*. By s 117 of the Act, the four original provinces retained all their public property not otherwise disposed of by the Act, and s 109 confirmed this by stipulating that all lands, mines, minerals, and royalties belonging to the colonies at the time of union shall continue to belong to the provinces, subject to any trusts existing in respect thereof, and to any interest other than that of the province. Accordingly, when colonies joined Confederation as provinces, they possessed Crown title to all lands to which they previously possessed title as colonies. However, by s 109, such title continued to be subject to any trusts or interests, including Aboriginal title, other than that of the province: see *St Catherine's Milling and Lumber Co v The Queen* [1888] 14 AC 46 (PC); *Delgamuukw v British Columbia* [1997] 3 SCR 1010, 1117.

[8] See *St. Catherine's Milling and Lumber Co v The Queen*, above (n 7).

[9] See, eg, *Hamlet of Baker Lake v Minister of Indian Affairs and Northern Development* [1980] 1 FC 518 (FCTD).

[10] See, eg, *Amodu Tijani v Secretary, Southern Nigeria* [1921] 2 AC 399 (PC).

[11] See, eg, *Guerin v The Queen* [1984] 2 SCR 335, 383 ('[t]he purpose of this surrender requirement is clearly to interpose the Crown between the Indians and prospective purchasers or lessees of their land, so as to prevent the Indians from being exploited').

[12] See, eg, *Canadian Pacific Ltd v Paul* [1988] 2 SCR 654, 677 (Aboriginal title cannot be transferred, sold, or surrendered to anyone other than the Crown).

[13] See, eg, *Guerin v The Queen* above (n 11) 382 (Aboriginal title 'gives rise upon surrender to a distinctive fiduciary obligation on the part of the Crown to deal with the land for the benefit of the surrendering Indians'); see also *R. v Sparrow* above (n 5) 1108 ('the Government has the responsibility to act in a fiduciary capacity with respect to Aboriginal peoples').

interdependence. Increased demands on Indigenous territories occasioned by population growth and westward expansion, followed by a period of paternalistic administration marked by involuntary relocations, only exacerbated the erosion of respect.

In addition to these external factors, law's failure to protect Indigenous territories can also be internally traced to legal choices of the judiciary. On more than one occasion, the judiciary suggested that Indigenous territorial claims might not possess any independent legal significance at all.[14] The possibility that Indigenous territories might not generate legal recognition by the Canadian legal order served as a legal backdrop for almost a century of relations between the Crown and Indigenous peoples, shaping legal expectations of governments, corporations, citizens, and other legal actors. It contributed to a perception that governments and third parties were relatively free to engage in a range of activity on ancestral lands—a perception which, in turn, legitimated unparalleled levels of government and third-party development and exploitation of Indigenous territories, which continue relatively unabated today.

Moreover, until recently, the legal significance that the judiciary attached to Indigenous territorial interests was minimal. Courts resisted characterizing Aboriginal title in proprietary terms, preferring instead to characterize it as a right of occupancy or a personal or usufructuary right,[15] or, more recently, as a sui generis interest.[16] Constructing Aboriginal title as a non-proprietary interest enabled its regulation and indeed its extinguishment by appropriate executive action,[17] disabled Indigenous titleholders from obtaining interim relief,[18] and frustrated access to the common law presumption of compensation in the event of expropriation.[19] Courts also indicated a willingness to view Aboriginal title as a set of rights to engage only in traditional practices on Indigenous territory, that is, those practices that Indigenous people engaged

[14]   See, eg, *St. Catherine's Milling v The Queen*, above (n 7) (Aboriginal rights with respect to land and resources did not predate but were created by the Royal Proclamation and, as such, are 'dependent on the good will of the Sovereign').

[15]   *St. Catherine's Milling Co v The Queen*, ibid., 54; see also *Smith v The Queen* [1983] 1 SCR 554.

[16]   *Canadian Pacific Ltd v Paul* [1988] 2 SCR 654, 658 (Aboriginal title refers to an 'Indian interest in land [that] is truly *sui generis*'); see also *R v Sparrow*, above (n 5) 1112 ('[c]ourts must be careful . . . to avoid the application of traditional common law concepts of property as they develop their understanding of . . . the *sui generis* nature of aboriginal rights').

[17]   See, eg, *Ontario (AG) v Bear Island Foundation* [1991] 2 SCR 570, 575 ('whatever may have been the situation upon signing of the Robinson-Huron Treaty, that right was in any event surrendered by arrangements subsequent to that treaty by which the Indians adhered to the treaty in exchange for treaty annuities and a reserve').

[18]   A number of cases held that Aboriginal title does not constitute an interest in land sufficient to support the registration of a caveat or certificate of lis pendens, which would temporarily prevent activity on ancestral territory pending final resolution of a dispute. See, eg, *Uukw v AGBC* (1987) 16 BCLR (2d) 145 (BCCA); *Lac La Ronge Indian Band v Beckman* [1990] 4 WWR 211 (Sask CA); *James Smith Indian Band v Saskatchewan (Master of Titles)* [1994] 2 CNLR 72 (Sask QB); but see *Ontario (AG) v Bear Island Foundation*, above (n 17).

[19]   See, eg, *British Columbia v Tener* [1985] 1 SCR 533, 559, quoting *Attorney-General v De Keyser's Royal Hotel Ltd* [1920] AC 508, 542, per Lord Atkinson ('a statute is not to be construed so as to take away the property of a subject without compensation').

in at the time the Crown acquired territorial sovereignty.[20] Until recently, the judiciary also assumed that 'there has been all along vested in the Crown a substantial and paramount estate, underlying the Indian title, which became a plenum dominium whenever that title was surrendered or otherwise extinguished.'[21] Each of these legal choices had a profound effect on the ability of Indigenous peoples to rely on Canadian law to protect ancestral territories from non-Indigenous incursion. Aboriginal rights and title existed at the margins of the common law, meaningful only in geographic spaces left vacant by Crown or third party non-use.

3. Constitutional Recognition of Aboriginal Rights

With the constitutional entrenchment of Aboriginal and treaty rights in 1982, the Constitution of Canada now formally recognizes a distinctive constitutional relationship between Indigenous peoples and Canada. Section 35(1) of the *Constitution Act, 1982* provides that '[t] existing aboriginal and treaty rights of the aboriginal peoples of Canada are hereby recognized and affirmed.' The judiciary has begun to see the purpose of section 35 as a process of substantive constitutional reconciliation of the interests of Indigenous peoples and those of Canada.

The Supreme Court of Canada began to conceive of section 35 in these terms in its historic 1990 ruling in *R. v Sparrow*.[22] At issue in *Sparrow* was the constitutionality of federal fishing regulations imposing a permit requirement and prohibiting certain methods of fishing. The Musqueam First Nation, located in British Columbia, had fished since ancient times in an area of the Fraser River estuary known as Canoe Passage. According to anthropological evidence at trial, salmon is not only an important source of food for the Musqueam but also plays a central role in Musqueam cultural identity. The Musqueam regard salmon as a race of beings that had, in 'myth times,' established a bond with humans, which required the salmon to come each year to give themselves to humans, who in turn treated them with respect by performing certain rituals.

The Musqueam argued at trial that the federal fishing requirements interfered with their Aboriginal fishing rights and, as a result of section 35(1), were invalid. In its landmark decision, the Supreme Court of Canada found that fishing for food was central to the identity of the Musqueam nation. With respect to Aboriginal rights more generally, the Court reasoned that if such rights 'existed' as of 1982, that is, if such rights had

---

[20] See, eg, *Baker Lake v Minister of Indian Affairs* above (n 9) 559 ('the common law . . . can give effect only to those incidents of that enjoyment that were . . . given effect by the [Indigenous] regime that prevailed before'); *AG Ont v Bear Island Foundation,* above (n 17) 3 (Ont SC) ('the essence of Aboriginal rights is the right of Indians to live on the lands as their forefathers lived').

[21] *St Catherine's Milling v The Queen,* above (n 7).

[22] Above (n 5).

not been 'extinguished' by state action before 1982, then any law that unduly interferes with their exercise must meet relatively strict standards of justification. Specifically, such a law must possess a 'valid legislative objective,' and any allocation of priorities after implementing measures that secure the law's objective must give 'top priority' to Indigenous interests. The Court also indicated that in future cases it might require that such laws infringe the right in question as little as possible, and that infringements be accompanied by fair compensation.

Strictly speaking, the Court in *Sparrow* did not explicitly state that the practice of fishing among the Musqueam constituted an Aboriginal right because it forms an integral part of Musqueam culture; it merely described the significance of fishing to the Musqueam in these terms. But subsequent jurisprudence makes it clear that Aboriginal rights are designed to protect integral aspects of Indigenous cultures. In *R. v Van der Peet,* a member of the Sto:lo First Nation of British Columbia was charged with selling salmon contrary to federal law.[23] The trial judge held that fishing for food and ceremonial purposes was a significant and defining feature of Sto:lo culture and as such merited constitutional protection. He further held, however, that the Sto:lo, at the time of contact with European settlers, did not participate in a regularized market system in the exchange of fish. As a result, he found that the Sto:lo could not assert an Aboriginal right to fish for commercial purposes.

On appeal to the Supreme Court of Canada, a majority of the Court, per Lamer CJ, held that 'to be an aboriginal right an activity must be an element of a practice, custom or tradition integral to the distinctive culture of the aboriginal group claiming the right at the time of contact.'[24] He held this to be the case because the overarching purpose of section 35 is one of *reconciliation*. According to Lamer CJ, the purpose of section 35 is to reconcile Canadian sovereignty with the 'simple fact' that 'when Europeans arrived in North America, aboriginal peoples were already here, living in distinctive communities on the land, and participating in distinctive cultures, as they had done for centuries.'[25] But Lamer CJ spent relatively little time explaining why Canadian sovereignty needs to be reconciled with this 'simple fact,' what indigenous interests need protection to accomplish reconciliation, and why recognizing rights to engage in culturally significant practices (as opposed to, say, rights to territory) might further recognition.

But Lamer CJ's judgment nonetheless suggests, somewhat obliquely, that the 'simple fact' of Indigenous prior occupancy—that which is to be reconciled with Crown sovereignty—is more complex than it first appears. It suggests that the purpose of section 35 is to protect interests associated with culture ('participating in distinctive cultures'), territory ('living . . . on the land'), and sovereignty (living 'in distinctive communities'). As stated, elsewhere in his reasons, he defines an Aboriginal right in terms of an activity that is an 'element of a custom, practice, or tradition integral to the distinctive culture of the aboriginal group claiming the right.'[26] Thus he suggests specifically that,

23   [1996] 2 SCR 507.
24   Ibid, 549.
25   Ibid.
26   Ibid.

in the name of reconciliation, section 35 protects culturally significant practices, from which we can infer that part of the purpose of section 35 is to protect interests associated with Indigenous cultural identities.

Subsequent case law has also defined the nature and scope of Aboriginal rights in ways that assist in identifying the interests that the guarantee serves to protect and clarifies its overall purpose of reconciliation. In *R v Adams*, a majority of the Court held that Aboriginal title was a specific subset of Aboriginal rights recognized and affirmed by section 35(1) of the *Constitution Act, 1982*.[27] Lamer CJ outlined this principle as follows: 'while claims to aboriginal title fall within the conceptual framework of aboriginal rights, aboriginal rights do not exist solely where a claim to aboriginal title has been made out.'[28] If an Indigenous community has shown that a particular practice, custom, or tradition taking place on the land was integral to the distinctive culture of that community then, even if they have not shown that their occupation and use of the land was sufficient to support a claim of title to the land, they will have demonstrated that they have an Aboriginal right to engage in that practice, custom or tradition.

Indigenous peoples therefore possess Aboriginal rights to engage in culturally significant customs, practices, and traditions, and possess Aboriginal title to lands that they historically used and occupied. In *Delgamuukw v British Columbia*, for example, hereditary chiefs of the Gitksan and We'suwet'en nations claimed Aboriginal title to 58,000 square kilometres of the interior of British Columbia. The Gitksan sought to prove historical use and occupation of part of the territory in question by entering as evidence their 'adaawk,' a collection of sacred oral traditions about their ancestors, histories, and territories. The Wet'suwet'en entered as evidence their 'kungax,' a spiritual song or dance or performance that ties them to their territory. Both the Gitksan and Wet'suwet'en also introduced evidence of their feast halls, in which they tell and re-tell their stories and identify their territories to maintain their connection with their lands over time. The trial judge admitted the above evidence but accorded it little independent weight, stating that, because of its oral nature, it could not serve as evidence of a detailed history of extensive land ownership.[29] He concluded that ancestors of the Gitksan and Wet'suwet'en peoples lived within the territory in question prior to the assertion of British sovereignty, but predominantly at village sites already identified as reserve lands. As a result, he declared, the Gitksan and Wet'suwet'en did not own or possess Aboriginal title to the broader territory.[30]

On appeal, the Supreme Court of Canada ordered a new trial. Although its reasons for doing so were predominantly procedural in nature, it took the opportunity to provide a definition of Aboriginal title that swept away many of the procedural and substantive hurdles Indigenous peoples faced in their attempts to obtain legal recognition of their rights to ancestral territories. Specifically, the Court held that Aboriginal title is a

---

[27] [1996] 3 SCR 101.
[28] Ibid, [26].
[29] *Uukw v R*, above (n 18), 181.
[30] [1991] 3 WWR 97, 383 (BCSC).

communally held right in land and, as such, comprehends more than the right to engage in specific activities which may themselves constitute Aboriginal rights. Based on the fact of prior occupancy, Aboriginal title confers the right to exclusive use and occupation of land for a variety of activities, not all of which need be aspects of practices, customs, or traditions integral to the distinctive cultures of Aboriginal societies. The Court held further that the trial judge erred by placing insufficient weight on the oral evidence of the Gitksan and Wet'suwet'en appellants: 'the laws of evidence must be adapted in order that this type of evidence can be accommodated and placed on an equal footing with the types of historical evidence that courts are familiar with, which largely consists of historical documents.'[31]

4. Constitutional Recognition of Indigenous Law

Although the Court characterized Aboriginal title as a species of Aboriginal right, it is important to note that an Indigenous community possesses Aboriginal title not because its ancestral lands are integral to its cultural identity at the time of contact—although no doubt they were and continue to be so today. Title vests when an Indigenous community proves exclusive occupation and control of the lands in question, and *Delgamuukw* establishes that oral evidence and oral histories can be relied on in proving occupation. The Court refers to the role that oral evidence and oral histories play in this process as an instance of reconciling the common law mode of establishing title and its constitutional recognition with an 'Aboriginal perspective.'

Oral evidence about Indigenous legal norms can participate in establishing the requisite exclusive occupation and control on which Aboriginal title rests. In the words of Lamer CJ in *Delgamuukw*: 'if, at the time of sovereignty, an aboriginal society had laws in relation to land, those laws would be relevant to establishing the occupation of laws which are the subject of a claim of Aboriginal title. Relevant laws might include, but are not limited to, a land tenure system or laws governing land use.'[32]

Elsewhere in his reasons, Lamer CJ stated that Indigenous laws governing trespass and conditional land use by other Indigenous nations, as well as treaties between and among Indigenous nations, also might assist in establishing the occupation necessary to prove Aboriginal title.[33]

---

[31] *Delgamuukw v British Columbia*, above (n 7). For an extensive, anthropological analysis of Aboriginal title in general and *Delgamuukw* in particular, see Dara Culhane, *The Pleasure of the Crown: Anthropology, Law and First Nations* (Talonbooks, 1998).

[32] Above (n 7), [148].

[33] Ibid, [157].

These passages were instrumental to the Court's recent decision in *Tsilhqot'in Nation v British Columbia* to grant a declaration of Aboriginal title to the Tsilhqot'in people, a collectivity of six communities sharing a common culture and history, who live in a remote valley bounded by rivers and mountains in central British Columbia.[34] The Court held that the Tsilhqot'in manifested sufficient and exclusive occupation and exclusive control of the land in question required for a declaration of Aboriginal title. Sufficiency of occupation was established by evidence at trial of a strong presence on or over the land claimed, manifesting itself in acts of occupation that could reasonably be interpreted as demonstrating that the land in question belonged to, was controlled by, or was under the exclusive stewardship of the Tsilhqot'in. Exclusivity of occupation was established by evidence that Tsilhqot'in laws excluded others from the land, except when they were allowed access to the land with the permission of the Tsilhqot'in.

Constitutional recognition of Indigenous legal norms is not restricted to the proof of Aboriginal title. Elsewhere the Court has suggested that Indigenous laws compatible with the assertion of Crown sovereignty survived its assertion, were 'absorbed into the common law as rights,' and, if not surrendered or extinguished, received constitutional recognition as Aboriginal rights by section 35(1).[35] This suggests that at least part of the reason something is an Aboriginal right in Canadian law is because it was an Indigenous legal norm at the time of the assertion of Crown sovereignty. If this is the case, then logically other conclusions follow: for example, it renders section 35 capable of housing an Aboriginal right of self-government.

In this vein, the Court regularly refers to 'the pre-existing societies of aboriginal peoples,'[36] Indigenous 'legal systems,'[37] 'pre-existing systems of aboriginal law,'[38] and 'aboriginal peoples occupying and using most of this vast expanse of land in organized, distinctive societies with their own social and political structures.'[39] And, in the following passage, Chief Justice McLachlin, in her dissent in *Van der Peet,* clearly summoned the spirit of Indigenous sovereignty:

> The history of the interface of Europeans and the common law with aboriginal peoples is a long one. As might be expected of such a long history, the principles by which the interface has been governed have not always been consistently applied. Yet running through this history, from its earliest beginnings to the present time is a golden thread—the recognition by the common law of the ancestral laws and customs of the aboriginal peoples who occupied the land prior to European settlement.[40]

[34] *Tsilhqot'in Nation v British Columbia* [2014] 2 SCR 257.
[35] *Mitchell v MNR* 1 SCR 911, [10] per McLachlin CJ.
[36] *R v Van der Peet,* above (n 23), [39] per Lamer CJ.
[37] *R v Sappier; R v Gray* [2006] 2 SCR 686, [35] per Bastarache J.
[38] *Delgamuukw,* above (n 7), [145] per Lamer CJ.
[39] *Mitchell v MNR* [2001] 1 SCR 911, above (n 35), [9] per McLachlin CJ.
[40] *Van der Peet,* above (n 23), [263].

However, the Court has been circumspect about interpreting section 35 as recognizing and affirming an Aboriginal right of self-government, that is, an Aboriginal right
to make laws. In *R. v Pamajewon*,[41] the Eagle Lake First Nation unsuccessfully argued
that it possessed an Aboriginal right to manage its economic affairs and thus be constitutionally capable of operating a casino on its reserve land free of federal and provincial interference. According to Chief Justice Lamer, '[a]ssuming that section 35(1)
encompasses claims to self-government, such claims must be considered in light of the
purposes underlying the provision and must, therefore, be considered against the test
derived from consideration of those purposes.'[42] The 'test' to which he was referring is
the test he outlined in *Van der Peet*, namely, that Aboriginal rights protect culturally significant practices of Indigenous communities.

But the Court's decision in *Pamajewon* should be read in light of its subsequent decision in *Delgamuukw*, in which the Gitksan and Wet'suwet'en nations asserted not only
Aboriginal title but an Aboriginal right of self-government over lands to which they
possessed title. The Court in *Delgamuukw* held that errors of the trial judge made it
'impossible . . . to determine whether the claim to self-government has been made out.'[43]
Nonetheless, the Court also held that Aboriginal title confers an exclusive, collective right
to use and occupy land for a variety of activities that need not relate to customs, practices, or traditions that are integral to the distinctive culture of the Indigenous nation
in question. As a collective right, Aboriginal title presumably requires governance
mechanisms to determine the kinds of activities that can occur on the territory, and who
can engage in them and for what purposes. The Court held further that 'the same legal
principles governed the aboriginal interest in reserve lands and lands held pursuant to
aboriginal title.'[44] In other words, *Delgamuukw* contemplates the very possibility that
Pamajewon sought to foreclose: a First Nation successfully asserting a broad Aboriginal
right to regulate and engage in economic activity on reserve lands unrelated to traditional patterns of territorial use and enjoyment.[45] Viewed together, *Delgamuukw* and
Pamajewon suggest that the Constitution recognizes and affirms an inherent Aboriginal
right of self-government—specifically, a right to make laws in relation to the use of
reserve lands and lands subject to Aboriginal title.

Addressed in greater detail in Sébastien Grammond's chapter in this *Handbook*, section 35's explicit recognition of 'the treaty rights of the aboriginal peoples of Canada'
makes it relatively clear that the guarantee also protects interests relating to treaty processes. In *R. v Badger*, the Supreme Court of Canada stated that 'a treaty represents
an exchange of solemn promises . . . [and] an agreement whose nature is sacred.'[46] It

---

[41] [1996] 2 SCR 821. *R. v Pamajewon* also involved the trial and conviction of, and subsequent appeals
by, members of the Shawanaga First Nation for similar violations of the Criminal Code.

[42] Ibid, 832.

[43] *Delgamuukw v. British Columbia*, above (n 7), 1114.

[44] Ibid, 1085.

[45] See Brian Slattery, 'The Constitutional Dimensions of Aboriginal Title' (2015) 71 Supreme Court
Law Review 45.

[46] *R v Badger* [1996] 1 SCR 771.

reiterated that treaties should be interpreted in 'a manner which maintains the integrity of the Crown' and that ambiguities or doubtful expressions in the wording of the treaty should be resolved in favour of Indigenous peoples. *Badger* marks a significant transformation in the judicial understanding of a treaty's form and substance. No longer mere political agreements or contractual agreements, treaties now possess the formal status of constitutional accords. Their substance ought to be determined in a manner consistent with Indigenous understandings, flexible to evolving practices, and inclusive of reasonably incidental practices, and in a way that best reconciles the competing interests of the parties.

So we can infer that section 35 protects interests associated with culture, territory, sovereignty, and the treaty process from the kinds of activities that Court has seen fit to protect and from the purpose of reconciliation it has ascribed to the guarantee. Why then does it matter that the Court regards the purpose of section 35 to be the reconciliation of the fact of an Indigenous prior presence with Canadian sovereignty? It matters not because the purpose of recognition is reconciliation. Rather, it matters, first, because of how the Court's conception of reconciliation informs the nature and scope of the rights recognized by section 35. The way the Court conceives of reconciliation factors in countervailing state interests as well as Indigenous interests when determining the nature and scope of Aboriginal and treaty rights themselves. Second, the Court's conception of reconciliation affects also how the guarantee speaks to laws that interfere with the exercise of Aboriginal rights. Each is addressed in turn.

5. RECONCILIATION AND RIGHTS-DEFINITION

The Court's approach to reconciliation suggests that countervailing state interests will not only be taken into account when assessing whether a law justifiably interferes with an Aboriginal or treaty right but that they will affect the nature and scope of section 35 rights themselves. This concern partially reveals itself in the approach that the Court has taken in characterizing the nature of a right to engage in a culturally significant practice. Because the purpose of section 35 is to reconcile the fact that distinctive Indigenous societies existed prior to European contact with Crown sovereignty, an Aboriginal right to engage in a culturally significant practice is said to relate to a practice that makes the society in question distinctive.[47] This approach has two consequences, and both influence how the Court conceives of reconciliation as the purpose of section 35. First, it produces constitutional protection only for those practices that amount to 'defining and central attributes of the Indigenous society in question.'[48] Second, it forecloses a

---

[47] *R v Van der Peet,* above (n 23).
[48] Ibid.

conception of Aboriginal rights as 'general and universal; their scope and content must be determined on a case-by-case basis.'[49]

This concern also partially revealed itself in *R. v Gladstone*,[50] complicated somewhat because it overlapped with an assessment of whether an interference with an Aboriginal right is justifiable. In *Gladstone*, Lamer CJ drew a distinction between a right to fish for food for social and ceremonial reasons and a right to engage in commercial fishing. He held that the former type of right involves an internal limit as 'at a certain point the band will have sufficient fish to meet these needs.'[51] In contrast, the latter involves no such limit save for the 'external constraints of the demand of the market and the availability of the resource.'[52] In such a case, where a right to engage in commercial fishing is recognized, the government is nonetheless not required to respect an exclusive Aboriginal right to fish after conservation goals are met. Instead,

> the doctrine of priority requires that the government demonstrate that, in allocating the resource, it has taken account of the existence of aboriginal rights and allocated the resource in a manner respectful of the fact that those rights have priority over the exploitation of the fishery by other users. This right is at once both procedural and substantive; at the stage of justification the government must demonstrate both that the process by which it allocated the resource and the actual allocation of the resource which results from that process reflect the prior interest of aboriginal rights holders in the fishery.[53]

The concept of an internal limit allows governments, after conservation requirements have been met, to limit the extent to which Indigenous right-holders can rely on a commercial Aboriginal right in order to allocate shares in the resource to non-Indigenous harvesters. In other words, governments are authorized to interfere with constitutionally protected Aboriginal rights in order to protect non-Indigenous interests.

Left unexplained in *Gladstone* is how non-Indigenous interests, which do not correspond to any constitutional entitlement on the part of non-Indigenous harvesters, can trump ostensibly broad Indigenous interests that are protected as a matter of constitutional right. It may be that Lamer CJ was unwilling to regard the commercial Aboriginal right in question in exclusive terms, that is, as preventing others from participating in the fishery. But the Court's definition of an Aboriginal right does not foreclose constitutional recognition of a custom, practice, or tradition that contemplates exclusivity of access to and use of a resource. Nor does it explain why exclusivity is inappropriate in the context of a commercial right. The distinction between a right that possesses an 'internal limit' and a right that possesses no such limit does not help much. Although it may capture a descriptive difference between a right to fish for food and

---

[49]   Ibid.

[50]   [1996] 2 SCR 723.

[51]   *Gladstone*, ibid, 764.

[52]   Ibid.

[53]   *Delgamuukw*, above (n 7), 1109.

a right to fish for commercial purposes, it does not justify either the conclusion that a commercial Aboriginal right must be non-exclusive or the proposition that interests of non-Indigenous harvesters should take precedence over Indigenous interests that are otherwise entitled to constitutional protection. What it does signal, perhaps obliquely, is that countervailing state interests, in this case, the state's interest in legislating for the protection of non-Indigenous harvesters, will affect the nature and scope of Aboriginal rights.

The concern that reconciliation entails defining section 35 rights by reference to countervailing state interests is beginning to reveal itself more explicitly in recent cases. In *Mitchell v MNR*, at issue was whether section 35 protects a Mohawk practice of cross-border trade. The Court held that the Mohawk nation failed to establish that it was integral to their distinctive culture at contact to carry goods across the St. Lawrence River for trade purposes. It can be questioned whether the Court characterized the practice underpinning the right properly; the outcome may well have been different had the Court defined the practice at issue more broadly as the transportation of goods to and from Indigenous nations in the St. Lawrence River region.[54] More immediately relevant, however, is another dimension of the judgment alluded to in McLachlin CJ's majority decision and expressly addressed by Binnie J's concurring reasons. The government had contended that section 35(1) extends constitutional protection only to those Indigenous practices, customs, and traditions that are compatible with the historical and modern exercise of Crown sovereignty. Pursuant to what was referred to as the doctrine of 'sovereign incompatibility,' the government argued further that any Mohawk practice of cross-border trade, even if established on the evidence, would be barred from recognition under section 35(1) as it would be incompatible with the Crown's sovereign interest in regulating its borders.

McLachin CJ refused to address the merits of the doctrine of sovereign incompatibility as the respondent had not proven its claim to an Aboriginal right. Nonetheless, Binnie J, concurring, characterized British colonial law as presuming that the Crown intended to respect Aboriginal rights that were not incompatible with the sovereignty of the Crown. In his view, this notion of incompatibility with Crown sovereignty is a defining characteristic of sovereign succession and therefore operates as a limit on the scope of Aboriginal rights. A fundamental attribute and incident of sovereignty is a state's control over the mobility of persons and goods across its border. According to Binnie J, the international dimension of the asserted Aboriginal right thus is incompatible with the historical attributes of Canadian sovereignty, and cannot be said to be an 'existing' right within the meaning of section 35.

Binnie J regarded the doctrine of sovereign incompatibility to be consistent with the section 35's purpose of reconciliation. In his words, the government's 'claim relates to national interests that all of us have in common rather than to distinctive interests that

---

[54] See Mark Walters, *The Right to Cross a River: Aboriginal Rights and the* Mitchell *Case* (Canadian Business & Law Institute, 2001).

for some purposes differentiate an aboriginal community.' In other words, Binnie J saw the task of defining the nature and scope of the Aboriginal right as one that required reconciling competing sets of interests. On the one hand, the case implicates interests, associated with Canadian sovereignty, 'that all of us have in common'; on the other hand, it also implicates interests, associated with cross-border trading, that, for historical reasons, 'differentiate an aboriginal community' from other Canadians.[55] For Binnie J, the nature and scope of Aboriginal rights are to be determined by reconciling these competing interests, and 'reconciliation of these interests in this particular case favours an affirmation of our collective sovereignty.'[56] Countervailing governmental interests, in other words, not only justify limiting the exercise of aboriginal rights; they influence their nature and scope at the outset.

Binnie J is quick to argue that the doctrine of sovereign incompatibility does not foreclose constitutional protection of interests associated with Indigenous sovereignty in the form of an Aboriginal or treaty right of self-government. And although he is careful not to express any opinion on the subject, he discusses at length the concept of 'shared sovereignty,' and quotes the Royal Commission on Aboriginal Peoples as follows:

> Shared sovereignty, in our view, is a hallmark of the Canadian federation and a central feature of the three-cornered relations that link Aboriginal governments, provincial governments and the federal government. These governments are sovereign within their respective spheres and hold their powers by virtue of their constitutional status rather than by delegation. Nevertheless, many of their powers are shared in practice and may be exercised by more than one order of government.[57]

Given that '[t]he constitutional objective is reconciliation not mutual isolation,'

> Section 35 does not warrant a claim to unlimited governmental powers or to complete sovereignty, such as independent states are commonly thought to possess. As with the federal and provincial governments, Aboriginal governments operate within a sphere of sovereignty defined by the constitution. In short, the Aboriginal right of self-government in section 35(1) involves circumscribed rather than unlimited powers.[58]

If, in the future, the Court is willing to accept explicitly that section 35 recognizes an existing Aboriginal right of self-government, the doctrine of sovereign incompatibility may be one instrument it relies on to circumscribe the nature and scope of that right. The logic would be as follows: the nature and scope of an Aboriginal right of self-government must advance the purpose of section 35, that is, it must reconcile Canadian sovereignty

---

[55] Ibid.

[56] Ibid.

[57] Canada, Royal Commission on Aboriginal Peoples, *Final Report*, vol. 2 (Supply and Services Canada, 1993) 240–241.

[58] Quoting ibid, 214.

with interests associated with Indigenous sovereignty that stem from the fact that Indigenous self-governing societies existed prior to European contact. Any lawmaking authority such a right confers on an Indigenous community must not conflict with a fundamental attribute or incident of Canadian sovereignty. In other words, the assertion of Crown sovereignty circumscribed, but did not extinguish, Indigenous lawmaking authority. The United States Supreme Court has relied on a variant of this approach to place limits on the inherent sovereignty of Indian tribes, holding, for example, that their 'domestic, dependent nation' status deprives them of their authority to subject non-resident, non-Indians to tribal law.[59] Stated differently, the doctrine of sovereign incompatibility may empower the judiciary to restrict the scope of an Aboriginal right of self-government in a manner that reconciles interests associated with Indigenous sovereignty with those associated with Canadian sovereignty. Jeremy Webber's chapter in this *Handbook* explores in greater detail several ways of aligning Canadian and indigenous sovereignty consistent with constitutional reconciliation.

Assuming that a majority of the Court eventually accepts some version of the doctrine of sovereign incompatibility, the following question will, of course, present itself: Under what circumstances will national interests prevent Indigenous interests from achieving constitutional recognition in the form of an Aboriginal or treaty right? Binnie J suggests this will arise when the asserted right conflicts with 'a fundamental attribute and incident of sovereignty,' and cites the compelling example of an asserted Aboriginal right to engage in war. But more controversial possibilities also present themselves. Is the right to legislate a military draft 'a fundamental attribute and incident of Canadian sovereignty'? What about the establishment of military bases on or near ancestral lands? Does 'sovereignty' here refer to external attributes and incidents of sovereignty, that is, the sovereign face that Canada presents to the world? Or does it also include internal attributes and incidents, such as the power to legislate and the power to distribute legislative authority? If the latter, how might this square with the United Nations Declaration on the Rights of Indigenous Peoples,[60] endorsed by Canada, and its full embrace of Indigenous rights of internal self-determination?

More pointedly, is underlying Crown title a 'fundamental attribute' of Canadian sovereignty? If so, what is its relation to Aboriginal title? The British Columbia Court of Appeal in *Tsilhqot'in* held that, in the name of the 'well-being of all Canadians,' Crown title vests in Indigenous territories not 'extensively used' by Indigenous inhabitants.[61] Although the Court of Appeal's 'intensive use' requirement was rejected by the Supreme Court of Canada on appeal, the Court nonetheless held that the Crown acquired the 'radical or underlying title' to Tsilhqot'in lands 'at the time of the assertion of European sovereignty.'[62] This holding places the onus on an Indigenous community claiming

---

[59]   See, eg, *Oliphant v Squamish Indian Tribe*, 435 U.S. 191 (1978).

[60]   United Nations Declaration on the Rights of Indigenous Peoples, UNGA Res 61/295 (13 September 2007).

[61]   2012 BCCA 285.

[62]   Above (n 34), [12], [19]. For critique, see Felix Hoehn, 'Back to the Future—Reconciliation and Aboriginal Sovereignty after *Tsilhqot'in*' (2016) 67 University of New Brunswick Law Journal 109; John

Aboriginal title to ancestral territories to prove that it had exclusive occupation and control of the lands in question. Aboriginal title, if established, places a 'burden' on the Crown's underlying title, rendering Crown title inconsequential in constitutional terms. But if Aboriginal title is not established, then the Crown possesses full property rights in the territory without having to prove that it had exclusive occupation and control of such lands. With sovereignty came Crown title, and with Crown title came the presumption that the Crown is 'the original occupant of all the lands of the realm.' Left unanswered, of course, is how to characterize the legality of the assertion of Crown sovereignty that spans the gaping chasm between the Court's premise and conclusion.

One possibility not explicitly canvassed by the Court is that requiring the Crown to prove exclusive occupation and control of territory before Crown title vests is incompatible with Crown sovereignty. But this possibility of 'sovereign incompatibility' illustrates the dangers associated with treating national interests as relevant to proof of an Aboriginal right or title when their relevance properly only arises in the context of laws that interfere with Aboriginal title. Criticized by this Court in numerous Charter decisions,[63] 'definitional balancing' confuses interpretation and justification.[64] This approach also thrusts the judiciary into the uncomfortable and institutionally inappropriate role of determining, in the abstract, what the 'well-being of all Canadians' amounts to. Is it really in the best interests of all Canadians that the Crown is presumed to be 'the original occupant of all the lands of the realm'? The interests of all Canadians is a question best left to the democratic process, and to the legislative process of enacting legislation that defines and advances specific and democratically identified societal interests. If such a law interferes with an Aboriginal right or title, then the judiciary must engage this question, not by determining in the abstract the relevant societal interests but by weighing the significance of the societal interests identified by the legislature and specified in the law in question against the severity of the infringement, in accordance with the justification tests associated with section 35. Instead, definitional-balancing invokes vague and undefined societal interests—in the absence of democratic, legislative specification and in the absence of evidence and argument at trial and on appeal as to their existence and content—as reasons for limiting the scope of an Aboriginal right. This will be the case whether the Aboriginal right in question is an Aboriginal right of

Borrows, 'The Durability of *Terra Nullius: Tsilhqot'in Nation v British Columbia*' (2015) 48 UBC Law Review 701.

[63] See, eg, *Ref re BC Motor Vehicle Act* [1985] 2 SCR 486; *Edwards Books and Art Ltd v The Queen* [1986] 2 SCR 713; *R v Smith* [1987] 1 SCR 1045; *Andrews v. Law Society of British Columbia* [1989] 1 SCR 143; *Black v Law Society of Alberta* [1989] 1 SCR 591; *R v Turpin* [1989] 1 SCR 1296; *Ford v Quebec* [1988] 2 SCR 712; and *USA v Cotroni* [1989] 1 SCR 1469.

[64] See David Beatty, *Constitutional Law in Theory and Practice* (University of Toronto Press, 1995) 89–90 (criticizing 'definitional-balancing', ie, the inclusion of state interests in the definition of a constitutional right). The concept, 'definitional balancing', first appeared in the context of constitutional protection of free speech in the United States, in Melville B. Nimmer, 'The Right to Speak Times to Time: First Amendment Theory Applied to Libel and Misapplied to Privacy' (1968) 56 California Law Review 935.

self-government, as is the case in Binnie J's reasons in *Mitchell*, or proof of Aboriginal title, as in the case of the Court of Appeal's reasons in *Tsilhqot'in*. This approach unfairly tips the scales of reconciliation by defining Aboriginal rights by reference to vague, undefined, and judicially generated interests of all Canadians and then subsequently re-emphasizing these societal interests in the context of discrete violations.

6. Reconciliation and Rights-Limitation

The second concern with Lamer CJ's conception of reconciliation advanced in *Van der Peet*—that it affects the proportionality analysis that awaits laws that interfere with the exercise of Aboriginal rights—manifested itself immediately, in *R. v Gladstone*.[65] In *Gladstone,* Lamer CJ held that the purpose of reconciliation informs the justifiable limits of section 35 rights, by assisting in determining whether an infringement furthers a compelling and substantial governmental objective. In his view,

> objectives which can be said to be compelling and substantial will be those directed at either the recognition of the prior occupation of North America by aboriginal peoples or—and at the level of justification it is this purpose which may well be most relevant—at the reconciliation of the fact of Indigenous prior occupation with the assertion of the sovereignty of the Crown.
> ... Aboriginal rights are recognized and affirmed by s. 35(1) in order to reconcile the existence of distinctive aboriginal societies prior to the arrival of Europeans in North America with the assertion of Crown sovereignty over that territory; they are the means by which the critical and integral aspects of those societies are maintained. Because, however, distinctive aboriginal societies exist within, and are a part of, a broader social, political and economic community, over which the Crown is sovereign, there are circumstances in which, in order to pursue objectives of compelling and substantial importance to that community as a whole (taking into account the fact that aboriginal societies are a part of that community), some limitation of those rights will be justifiable. Aboriginal rights are a necessary part of the reconciliation of aboriginal societies with the broader political community of which they are part; limits placed on those rights are, where the objectives furthered by those limits are of sufficient importance to the broader community as a whole, *equally* a necessary part of that reconciliation.[66]

By defining a 'compelling and substantial purpose' in light of the need to reconcile Indigenous prior occupancy with Canadian sovereignty, Lamer CJ generated an expansive list of governmental objectives acceptable under the first stage of the justification inquiry,

---

[65] Above (n 23).
[66] Ibid, 774–775 (emphasis in original).

including 'the pursuit of economic and regional fairness, and the recognition of the histori-cal reliance upon, and participation in, the fishery by non-aboriginal groups.'[67] In his view, such objectives are constitutionally acceptable to the extent they are 'in the interests of all Canadians,' including Indigenous peoples, and because 'the reconciliation of aboriginal societies with the rest of Canadian society' may depend on their successful achievement.[68]

In *Delgamuukw v British Columbia*, Lamer CJ interpreted *Sparrow*'s earlier holding that conservation is an acceptable governmental objective[69] to be consistent with his view of the purpose of section 35(1)—namely, the reconciliation of Indigenous prior occupancy with Canadian sovereignty. In his words, '[t]he conservation of fisheries . . . simultaneously recognizes that fishing is integral to many aboriginal cultures, and also seeks to reconcile aboriginal societies with the broader community by ensuring that there are fish enough for all.'[70] Having established that reconciliation ought to inform a finding of whether a governmental objective is compelling and substantial, Lamer CJ proceeded to add to *Gladstone*'s list of acceptable governmental objectives:

> [I]n the wake of *Gladstone*, the range of legislative objectives that can justify the infringement of aboriginal title is fairly broad. Most of these objectives can be traced to the reconciliation of the prior occupation of North America by aboriginal peoples with the assertion of Crown sovereignty, which entails the recognition that 'distinc-tive aboriginal societies exist within, and are a part of, a broader social, political and economic community.' In my opinion, the development of agriculture, forestry, min-ing, and hydroelectric power, the general economic development of the interior of British Columbia, protection of the environment or endangered species, the build-ing of infrastructure and the settlement of foreign populations to support those aims, are the kinds of objectives that are consistent with this purpose and, in principle, can justify the infringement of aboriginal title.[71]

The expansive nature of this list makes it clear that few laws that interfere with the exer-cise of Aboriginal rights will be considered as insufficiently compelling or substantial to meet the first stage of the justification inquiry.

Two additional problems present themselves. First, the Court fails to explain why this list of acceptable governmental objectives follows from what it regards as the purpose of section 35(1), namely, reconciliation. If its purpose is to reconcile Indigenous prior occupancy with Crown sovereignty, why does reconciliation justify a law that inter-feres with the exercise of an Aboriginal or treaty right on the basis that it furthers the interests of the broader community? On the contrary, Aboriginal rights ought to oper-ate to prevent governments from interfering with their exercise for purposes of simply advancing interests of the broader community. 'Reconciliation' just as easily supports

---

[67] Ibid, 775.
[68] Ibid.
[69] *R. v Sparrow*, above (n 5), 1113.
[70] *Delgamuukw v British Columbia*, above (n 7), 1108.
[71] *Delgamuukw*, above (n 7), 1111, quoting *Gladstone*, above (n 50), 774.

the proposition that governmental objectives such as the development of agriculture, forestry, mining, and hydroelectric power and the general economic development of the interior of a province are *not* sufficiently compelling and substantial to warrant interfering with Aboriginal and treaty rights. Assuming that section 35(1) rights are not absolute, governments can no doubt pursue certain governmental objectives that limit their exercise. But authorizing such a wide range of acceptable governmental objectives defeats the very reconciliation said to be embedded in the constitutional recognition of existing Aboriginal and treaty rights.

Lamer CJ attempts to render his conception of reconciliation more determinate by claiming that it entails that 'distinctive aboriginal societies exist within, and are a part of, a broader social, political and economic community'.[72] But this merely restates the issue, namely, under what circumstances can governments interfere with the exercise of Aboriginal and treaty rights in the name of the 'larger, social, political and economic community'? That Indigenous people also belong to this broader community should not obscure the fact that this issue will arise exactly when Indigenous interests and those of the broader community are in conflict. The Court's list suggests that governments can compromise constitutional rights to satisfy community interests. It ignores the fact that Indigenous interests receive constitutional protection whereas community interests, generally speaking, do not. In other words, it ignores the fact that the Constitution recognizes and affirms existing Aboriginal and treaty rights precisely to protect certain Indigenous interests from governments seeking to satisfy community interests.[73]

In contrast, if reconciliation means the protection of Indigenous interests associated with culture, territory, governance, and treaty processes from the interests of the broader community, then laws that simply advance interests of the broader community would not be seen as sufficiently compelling to justify limiting the exercise of an Aboriginal or treaty right. The approach originally adopted in *Sparrow*—upholding a violation if it preserves section 35(1) rights, prevents the exercise of section 35(1) rights that would harm the general population or Indigenous people themselves, or ensures that the exercise of section 35(1) rights will be compatible with the rights (and not simply interests) of others—should be wedded to an alternative reading of *Van der Peet*, hinted at in the Court's reasons in *Tsilhqot'in*. In that case, the Court held that the governmental objectives at stake were insufficiently compelling to merit interfering with Aboriginal title. 'To constitute a compelling and substantial objective,' the Court held, 'the broader public goal asserted by the government must further the goal of reconciliation, having regard to both the Aboriginal interest and the broader public objective.'[74] The objective, in other words, must be one that *reconciles* Indigenous and public objectives. The list

---

[72] Ibid.
[73] Compare Kent McNeil, *Defining Aboriginal Title in the 90's: Has the Supreme Court Finally Got It Right?* (Toronto: Robarts Centre for Canadian Studies, 1998), at 19 (list of acceptable governmental objectives in *Gladstone* turns 'the Constitution on its head by allowing interests that are not constitutional to trump rights that are').
[74] Van der Peet, above (n 23), [82].

of public objectives might be lengthy, but to be sufficiently compelling, a public objective such as forestry development needs to take Indigenous interests into account by, for example, maintaining Indigenous access to title lands and providing an equity share to Aboriginal title-holders in development projects on their lands.

7. CONCLUSION

This chapter sought to highlight law's participation in the colonizing projects that initiated the process of the establishment of the Canadian constitutional order. Imperial and subsequently Canadian law refused to acknowledge the presence of a plurality of Indigenous constitutional orders on the continent, laying instead the groundwork for a monist conception of sovereign power, initially rooted in the sovereignty of the United Kingdom and ultimately grounded in the sovereignty of Canada. Imperial and subsequent Canadian law deemed legally insignificant the deep connections that Indigenous peoples had with their ancestral territories, and imposed alien norms of conduct on diverse Indigenous ways of life. In doing so, law legitimated the manifold political, social, and economic acts of dispossession and dislocation that collectively bear the label of colonialism. The constitutional entrenchment of Aboriginal and treaty rights in 1982 formally recognized a distinctive constitutional relationship between Indigenous peoples and Canada. The judiciary has begun to see the purpose of formal constitutional recognition to be a process of substantive constitutional reconciliation of the interests of Indigenous peoples and those of Canada. This chapter argued that constitutional reconciliation can only commence by comprehending Aboriginal rights and title as protecting Indigenous interests associated with culture, territory, treaties, and sovereignty in robust terms—terms, if met, which will have profound structural consequences for the relationship between Indigenous peoples and Canada.

BIBLIOGRAPHY

Secondary sources

Beatty, David, *Constitutional Law in Theory and Practice* (Toronto: University of Toronto Press, 1995)

Borrows, John, 'The Durability of *Terra Nullius: Tsilhqot'in Nation v British Columbia*' (2015) 48 *University of British Columbia Law Review* 701

Crawford, James, *Brownlie's Principles of Public International Law,* 8th edition (Oxford: Oxford University Press, 2012)

Culhane, Dara, *The Pleasure of the Crown: Anthropology, Law and First Nations* (Burnaby: Talonbooks, 1998)

Fuller, Lon, *Legal Fictions* (Stanford, CA: Stanford University Press, 1967)

Hoehn, Felix, 'Back to the Future—Reconciliation and Aboriginal Sovereignty after *Tsilhqot'in*' (2016) 67 *University of New Brunswick Law Journal* 109

Kennedy, Duncan, *A Critique of Adjudication* (Cambridge, MA: Harvard University Press, 1997)

Maine, Henry, *Ancient Law* (1861, Dent and Sons Everyman ed., 1917)

McNeil, Kent, *Common Law Aboriginal Title* (Oxford: Clarendon Press, 1989)

_____, *The Temagami Indian Claim: Loosening the Judicial Straight-Jacket*, in Matt Bray & Ashley Thomson, eds., *Temagami: A Debate on Wilderness* (Toronto: Dundurn Press, 1990), at 200–205

_____, *Defining Aboriginal Title in the 90's: Has the Supreme Court Finally Got It Right?* (Toronto: Robarts Centre for Canadian Studies, 1998)

McHugh, P.G., *Aboriginal Societies and the Common Law: A History of Sovereignty, Status, and Self-Determination* (New York: Oxford University Press, 2004)

Nimmer, Melville B., 'The Right to Speak Times to Time: First Amendment Theory Applied to Libel and Misapplied to Privacy' (1968) 56 *California Law Review* 935

Oliver, Peter C., *The Constitution of Independence: The Development of Constitutional Theory in Australia, Canada, and New Zealand* (Oxford: Oxford University Press, 2005)

Slattery, Brian, 'The Constitutional Dimensions of Aboriginal Title' (2015) 71 *Supreme Court Law Review* 45

Walters, Mark, 'The Right to Cross a River: Aboriginal Rights and the *Mitchell* Case' (Canadian Business & Law Institute, 2001)

Webber, Jeremy, 'Relations of Force and Relations of Justice: The Emergence of Normative Community between Colonists and Aboriginal Peoples' (1995) 33 *Osgoode Hall Law Journal* 623

Cases

Amodu Tijani v Secretary, Southern Nigeria [1921] 2 AC 399 (PC)

Canadian Pacific Ltd v Paul [1988] 2 SCR 654

Delgamuukw v British Columbia [1997] 3 SCR 1010

Guerin v The Queen [1984] 2 SCR 335

Hamlet of Baker Lake v Minister of Indian Affairs and Northern Development [1980] 1 FC 518 (FCTD)

Oliphant v Squamish Indian Tribe, 435 U.S. 191 (1978)

Ontario (AG) v Bear Island Foundation [1991] 2 SCR 570

R v Badger [1996] 1 SCR 771

R. v. Pamajewon [1996] 2 SCR 821

R v Sappier; R v Gray [2006] 2 SCR 686

R v. Sparrow [1990] 1 SCR 1075

R v Syliboy [1929] 1 DLR 307 (NS Co Ct)

R v Van der Peet [1996] 2 SCR 507

Ref re BC Motor Vehicle Act [1985] 2 SCR 486

St Catherine's Milling and Lumber Co v The Queen [1888] 14 AC 46 (PC)

Tsilhqot'in Nation v British Columbia [2014] 2 SCR 257

CHAPTER 16

....

THE SECTION 35 DUTY
TO CONSULT

....

DWIGHT NEWMAN*

1. INTRODUCTION

SECTION 35 of Canada's *Constitution Act, 1982* enacts that "existing aboriginal and treaty rights are hereby recognized and affirmed".[1] One particularly important doctrine that has developed in Canada's section 35 case law is the duty to consult doctrine. Although the section 35 case law alluded to the pertinence of consultation before—notably as part of the test for justified infringements of section 35 rights[2]—the duty to consult has taken on a new, proactive form since 2004. In a trilogy of cases over the course of 2004 and 2005, the Supreme Court of Canada enunciated that the Crown and thus Canadian federal and provincial governments were under a proactive duty to consult—and possibly accommodate—potentially affected Aboriginal communities. This duty applied prior to making administrative decisions that might adversely affect their asserted Aboriginal or treaty rights, with this duty applying even prior to final proof or settlement of their asserted claims.[3] In the treaty rights context, it will often apply in the context of the

 * Professor of Law & Canada Research Chair in Indigenous Rights in Constitutional and International Law, University of Saskatchewan. I am grateful to Bernie Roth for commenting on a draft version of this chapter and to students in my "Indigenous Rights and Resource Development" courses for many discussions.

 [1] *Constitution Act, 1982* (Can), s 35(1).
 [2] See *R v Sparrow* [1990] 1 SCR 1075; Sonia Lawrence & Patrick Macklem, 'From Consultation to Reconciliation: Aboriginal Rights and the Crown's Duty to Consult' (2000) 29 Cdn Bar Rev 252.
 [3] The first three cases were: *Haida Nation v British Columbia (Minister of Forests)* 2004 SCC 73, [2004] 3 SCR 511; *Taku River Tlingit First Nation v British Columbia (Project Assessment Director)* 2004 SCC 74, [2004] 3 SCR 550; and *Mikisew Cree First Nation v Canada (Minister of Canadian Heritage)* 2005 SCC 69, [2005] 3 SCR 388. For extended accounts of the doctrine, see: Dwight Newman, *The Duty to Consult: New Relationships with Aboriginal Peoples* (Purich 2009); Dwight Newman, *Revisiting the Duty to Consult Aboriginal Peoples* (Purich, 2014).

Crown exercising its rights under a historic treaty to "take up" land for development, so as to protect treaty rights that may be affected by the gradual taking up of land.[4]

In terms of the key parameters of the duty, the duty to consult would be triggered or engaged when there was a government decision at issue that would have a potential adverse impact on an asserted right of which the government had actual or constructive knowledge.[5] The contents, scope, or depth of that duty would vary in different circumstances, based on the prima facie strength of the asserted right and the degree of adverse impact on that right.[6] The legally required depth of the duty could range from limited notice requirements through to larger consultative processes, and on through to requirements of deep consultation which might well include accommodation of potentially affected Aboriginal or treaty rights.[7] It pertains to presently contemplated future conduct, rather than to historic infringements, which are to be dealt with under other doctrines.[8] It is also worth noting that the duty to consult is a doctrine that may proactively limit impacts on Aboriginal or treaty rights and thus that mandates consultation on those impacts rather than simply on Aboriginal views about particular decisions.

This one constitutional doctrine has enormous impacts, and not always those that had been foreseen by the nine justices sitting in Ottawa rendering the seminal cases on it. In the context of various governmental decisions, particularly considering provinces with significant resource industries, the legal duty to consult can be estimated to be triggered hundreds of thousands of time each year in Canada.[9] At the same time, although the duty to consult doctrine purports to further governmental consultation of Aboriginal communities, one of the major practical effects of the uncertainty it generates for resource companies is to incentivize direct negotiations between industry and Aboriginal communities. In the context of the most significant resource developments, there are now hundreds of Impact Benefit Agreements (IBAs) or other industry-community agreements in place in Canada. A typical format includes a so-called "support clause" under which, in exchange for benefits under the agreement, the community agrees to support the project, including by saying in all forums that the duty to consult has been met and thus avoiding any role for government.[10] There is evidence of some Aboriginal communities receiving as much as a hundred million dollars a year under IBAs, although with enormous variation between differently situated communities.[11]

---

[4] *Grassy Narrows First Nation v Ontario*, 2014 SCC 48, [2014] 2 SCR 447, at [52].

[5] *Haida* above (n 3) [35]; Newman, *New Relationships* above (n 3) passim; *Rio Tinto Alcan Inc. v Carrier Sekani Tribal Council* 2010 SCC 43, [2010] 2 SCR 650 at [39–50].

[6] *Haida* above (n 3) [43–45].

[7] *Ibid.*

[8] *Rio Tinto* above (n 5) [45–49].

[9] See Jean-François Tremblay, *Statement by the Observer Delegation of Canada delivered by Jean-François Tremblay, Senior Assistant Deputy Minister, Indian and Northern Affairs Canada, at the tenth session of the United Nations Permanent Forum on Indigenous Issues: Follow-Up to the Recommendations of the Permanent Forum on Free, Prior and Informed Consent*, New York (17 May 2011).

[10] See discussion in Dwight Newman, *Natural Resource Jurisdiction in Canada* (LexisNexis, 2013).

[11] See discussion in Ravina Bains & Kayla Ishkanian, 'Government Spending and Own-Source Revenue for Canada's Aboriginals: A Comparative Analysis' (Fraser Institute, 2016); Dwight Newman &

When we turn back, though, to the legal structure that contributes to these practical results, we see the duty to consult is subject to a number of fundamental legal complexities that raise ongoing questions on what its implications will be in the decades ahead. To understand these complexities, it is necessary first to develop further the purposes and origins of the duty to consult and how these purposes and origins shape the basic features of the duty. Thereafter, it will be possible to consider briefly what the duty to consult doctrine's interaction is with developing international norms on consultation and consent. With this background, it will be possible to think more about the boundaries of what decisions are and are not subject to the duty to consult and to consider ongoing controversies concerning the interaction of the duty to consult and the role of administrative boards and tribunals. In the concluding section on future prospects for the duty to consult, it will be worth considering the ways in which the presence of the duty to consult doctrine both pushes forward some substantive issues and simultaneously locks some issues into interim positions. These ideas will also show how some of the future challenges for the duty raise challenging questions on the ways that the judiciary struggles to foresee what comes from its decisions in the Aboriginal rights context by approaching issues from a constitutional or public law perspective that does not take full account of the ways various parties react to the law.

2. Purposes and Origins of the Duty

The "duty to consult" in its primary contemporary sense concerns the proactive duty to consult prior to acting in ways that may adversely affect Aboriginal or treaty rights. There had previously been a possible practical need for consultation when a government sought to argue a justification for an infringement on Aboriginal or treaty rights. Consultation was an element of the test for such justifications as enunciated in *Sparrow* in 1990 and expanded upon in 1997 in *Delgamuukw*.[12] Although the 2004 *Haida* decision purported to apply *Delgamuukw* in noting what it had said on consultation and then reasoning that its "words apply as much to unresolved claims as to intrusions on settled claims"[13]—an extension presaged by some insightful scholars[14]—the application to the pre-proof context is nonetheless different in some meaningful ways. Indeed, practitioners in the area sometimes refer specifically to *Sparrow* consultation and *Haida* consultation as two separate concepts, with *Haida* consultation the main referent of the term "duty to consult".

Kaitlyn Harvey, 'Stepping Into the Sunshine without Getting Burned: The *Extractive Sector Transparency Measures Act (ESTMA)* and Aboriginal Communities' (Macdonald-Laurier Institute, 2016).

[12] *Sparrow* (n 2); *Delgamuukw v British Columbia*, [1997] 3 SCR 1010.
[13] *Haida* above (n 3) [24].
[14] See especially Lawrence & Macklem above (n 2).

One notable distinction between *Sparrow* consultation and *Haida* consultation is in the different origins of the duty in the two contexts. In *Sparrow*, while developing the test for justified infringements on section 35 rights, the Supreme Court of Canada held that the fiduciary duty on the Crown when infringing on Aboriginal rights made consultation an appropriate part of the test for justifications of those infringements.[15] And that is the language that returns in other cases in discussions of justified infringements, most recently in the *Tsilhqot'in Nation* case in a discussion of justified infringements on Aboriginal title.[16] In *Haida*, by contrast, the Court explained the proactive duty to consult as arising from the honour of the Crown principle.[17] Aside from any issue of fiduciary duty, the Court reasons that it would not be in keeping with the honour of the Crown for the government to go ahead with an action that might affect Aboriginal or treaty rights if it had not consulted those asserting the claims. Although the point has not received sufficient attention, the Supreme Court of Canada has gone to great efforts in recent years to disentangle the concepts of fiduciary duty and honour of the Crown in the Aboriginal law context, with fiduciary duty having only rather narrow applications and honour of the Crown having the potential to guide the development of a number of doctrines.[18] Blurring *Sparrow* consultation and *Haida* consultation would ignore a fundamental conceptual distinction within Aboriginal law jurisprudence.

At the same time, more needs to be said about the interaction of *Haida* consultation and the *Sparrow* justified infringement test. Asking about that interaction supposes a consistency across various areas of Aboriginal law jurisprudence or, effectively, an expectation that the law would develop in a reasonably systematic manner. Here, the challenging situation that might arise would be in a circumstance where consultation was carried out on the *Haida* test during the interim period when rights were asserted but not yet established, but rights were later established, giving rise to a call for the strictures of the *Sparrow* test to be met.

The issue would have a particular bite in the context of Aboriginal title, where the *Tsilhqot'in* decision effectively adapts and develops the *Sparrow* test for justified infringements while also announcing that possible remedies in the case of an unjustified infringement would potentially sometimes include cancellation of a project that was later proven to infringe on Aboriginal title.[19] Would those proceeding in good faith based on *Haida* consultation and making their best efforts at meaningful consultation nonetheless be subject to the possibility of a later shift in expectations based on a transition from the *Haida* framework to a *Sparrow*-based framework upon the establishment of Aboriginal title?

---

[15] *Sparrow* above (n 2).

[16] *Tsilhqot'in Nation v British Columbia* 2014 SCC 44, [2014] 2 SCR 257, paras 87–88.

[17] *Haida* above (n 3) [16].

[18] See generally Jamie Dickson, *The Honour and Dishonour of the Crown: Making Sense of Aboriginal Law in Canada* (Purich, 2015).

[19] *Tsilhqot'in* above (n 16) [77–88], [92].

Fitting together these two frameworks requires, first, a realization that consultation continues to be part—but only part—of the test for justified infringements. In addition to consultation, the justified infringement test also looks to appropriate priority to Aboriginal rights, to compensation in appropriate circumstances, and to a proportionality analysis, with the last being even clearer after *Tsilhqot'in*.[20] Meaningful consultation will naturally tend to result in the other elements of the test being met, but based only on the depth mandated by the test for the scope of consultation, which is weighted down by the strength of the claim. Where the claim moves from something uncertain to something established, the expectations may rise. However, if various parties are to trust in *Haida* consultation processes, it would almost invariably be inappropriate to apply a remedy such as cancellation of a resource project where there had been good faith consultation that had met the applicable *Haida* requirements. To have an appropriate nexus between these two streams of related law, respect for *Haida* in the interim period must have meaning in a post-*Haida* transition, and a court considering what became an actual infringement rather than a potential adverse effect would most appropriately look instead to implications from other parts of the test, such as compensation, in those circumstances.

To say as much may, of course, seem to lend solace to certain of the more critical takes on the duty to consult. Some have expressed views that the duty to consult offers little protection to Aboriginal communities and is effectively window dressing on moves forward on resource development.[21] However, these perspectives, in addition to being overly skeptical from a descriptive point of view, may also be focused on a limited range of values and thereby negatively judging all efforts at the real world reconciliation of interests and values that must actually occur.

Apart from the honour of the Crown, the other principle the Supreme Court of Canada references in *Haida* and other cases to support the duty to consult is that of reconciliation, repeatedly identified as the underlying purpose of section 35.[22] For the Court, there is an aspect of the duty to consult that is generative, dynamic, and fundamentally "[c]oncerned with an ethic of ongoing relationships".[23] The *Haida* case itself avoided making the stark choice between granting an injunction against the government

---

[20] *Ibid* [87].

[21] Gordon Christie, 'Developing Case Law: The Future of Consultation and Accommodation' (2006) 39 UBC L Rev 139; Kaitlin Ritchie, 'Issues Associated with the Implementation of the Duty to Consult and Accommodate Aboriginal Peoples: Threatening the Goals of Reconciliation and Meaningful Consultation' (2013) 46 UBC L Rev 397. See also Lorne Sossin, "The Duty to Consult and Accommodate: Procedural Justice as Aboriginal Rights" (2010) 23 Cdn J Admin L & Pr 93 (implying such concerns, while avoiding entering into much actual detail on the duty to consult and instead discussing it within broader theoretical concepts on procedural justice).

[22] *Haida* above (n 3) [14]; *Mikisew* above (n 3) [1] ('The fundamental objective of the modern law of aboriginal and treaty rights is the reconciliation of aboriginal peoples and non-aboriginal peoples and their respective claims, interests and ambitions'); Dwight Newman, 'Reconciliation: Legal Conception(s) and Faces of Justice' in John Whyte (ed), *Moving Toward Justice: Legal Traditions and Aboriginal Justice* (Purich, 2008).

[23] *Haida* above (n 3) [38], citing Newman, *New Relationships* above (n 3) 21.

action at issue until all issues were resolved and offering no protection to the Aboriginal interests at stake, instead developing a proactive doctrine that requires efforts at good faith relationships.[24] In interpreting challenging facets of the duty to consult doctrine, this underlying ethic of ongoing relationships provides an important lodestar. Thus, in developing the doctrine, courts appropriately look to analyses that have the potential to be responsive to all interests at stake while furthering, so far as possible, better relationships among all rights-holders and stakeholders.

Many of these principles, of course, rapidly become more complicated in their application, with the result that the mere presence of the duty to consult doctrine may reshape various power relations in ways other than those that would have been more specifically contemplated by the courts. The doctrine has effects on power relations not just as between governments and Aboriginal communities but, for instance, within Aboriginal communities themselves. The duty to consult is owed to rights-bearing communities, and the judicial focus thus far on collectively held Aboriginal rights thus means that the doctrine leads to consultation with those identified as official representatives of rights-bearing communities. Challenges by those within Aboriginal communities who consider their interests to have been overridden have been rejected, and the courts have thus far declined to recognize any individually held Aboriginal rights,[25] so the duty to consult doctrine has certain effects in terms of strengthening the centralization of power within communities as one side effect of a doctrine developed to further the honour of the Crown and reconciliation.

3. Developing International Norms on Consultation and Consent

The Canadian doctrine of the duty to consult has, at least based on surface appearances, developed independently of developing international norms related to consultation and FPIC (free, prior, and informed consent). Indeed, many consultation cases have seen parties or intervenors seek to argue based on claims as to international norms only to see the courts never cite to those arguments. Considering an intervention application on such issues in 2015, the Federal Court of Appeal discussed the limited pertinence of international law to this area of constitutional law, noting that "[i]n the case of the duty to consult, decisions of the Supreme Court are binding on us and have defined the duty with some particularity. We are not free to modify the Supreme Court's law on the basis of international law submissions made to us. International law, at best, might be of limited assistance in interpreting and applying the law set out by Supreme Court".[26]

---

[24] *Haida* above (n 3) [12–15], [26–27].
[25] For some interesting engagement with this issue, see *Behn v Moulton Contracting Ltd.* 2013 SCC 26, [2013] 2 SCR 227.
[26] *Gitxaala Nation v Canada*, 2015 FCA 73, Stratas J.A.

Some might nonetheless interpret some of the case law development to be affected in some respects by international law. For example, in the Supreme Court of Canada's 2014 Aboriginal title determination in *Tsilhqot'in Nation,* the Court seemingly moved toward an ideal of consent in at least certain contexts of strong Aboriginal title claims.[27] Although the Court did not cite international sources in support of this alteration, many might be inclined to see this change as reflective of trends in international law.

That said, international law on consultation and consent is more complex than is commonly depicted. Although the United Nations Declaration on the Rights of Indigenous Peoples (UNDRIP) is often presented as the lead instrument on Indigenous rights in international law, there are many complexities on its actual legal status.[28] And although UNDRIP makes references to pertinent contexts giving rise to a need for consultation with Indigenous peoples "in order to obtain their free, prior, and informed consent",[29] there have been significant debates on the meaning of this phrase. It may well be interpreted as seeing consent only as a goal that good faith consultation processes aim at, without consent being required other than in certain limited circumstances of very severe impacts on Indigenous communities.[30] On such an analysis, Canadian law on the duty to consult has not been an international laggard but very much in step with international developments. How international law develops in the future and how this affects Canadian law—including in the context of varying government commitments around "implementation" of UNDRIP—remains to be seen.

4. THE SCOPE OF DECISIONS
SUBJECT TO CONSULTATION

In its initial applications, the duty to consult applied to administrative decisions by governments, such as to decisions on whether to issue a permit or licence under a statutory regime. The question was whether a particular administrative decision was such as to "trigger" the duty, with the test for that based on actual or constructive government knowledge of an asserted Aboriginal or treaty right that might be adversely affected by a contemplated government decision.[31]

---

[27] *Tsilhqot'in* above (n 16) [89–92].

[28] See eg Newman, *Revisiting the Duty to Consult* above (n 3) c 5; Mauro Barelli, *Seeking Justice in International Law: The Significance and Implications of the UN Declaration on the Rights of Indigenous Peoples* (Routledge, 2016) passim.

[29] United Nations Declaration on the Rights of Indigenous Peoples (UNDRIP), GA Res 61/295, UN Doc A/RES/47/1 (2007), arts 19, 32.

[30] See Dwight Newman, 'Norms of Consultation with Indigenous Peoples: Decentralization of International Law Formation or Reinforcement of States' Role?', in Andrew Byrnes, Mika Hayashi & Christopher Michaelsen (eds), *International Law in the New Age of Globalization* (Brill, 2013) 267.

[31] *Haida* (n 3) para 35.

However, the boundaries of the duty to consult have been tested in various ways, with some of the potential applications now inspired by the developing international norms just discussed. The question of in what ways the duty to consult extends to other types of decisions is a significant one and, indeed, one that has the potential to make the duty to consult something actually reshaping the structure of Canadian government to some extent.

Two separate developments that got underway in December 2012 have profound significance for this question. During that month, the Yukon Court of Appeal released its decision in a case called *Ross River Dena Council*,[32] with potentially profound legal significance, and the Idle No More movement gathered steam initially as a protest about a lack of government consultation with Aboriginal communities on a bill in the federal Parliament, Bill C-45.[33] Both of these developments related in different ways to the scope of the duty to consult.

The *Ross River Dena Council* case saw the Yukon Court of Appeal determine that the Yukon government had to rewrite its mining legislation to expand the opportunities available for consultation with Aboriginal communities. Under the longstanding prior legislation, the system in place was a so-called "free entry" system under which prospectors could enter onto public lands and stake claims, which they would then be automatically entitled to have registered in a way that gave rise to certain exploratory rights. The Court held that the lack of consultation at the time of registration was not in accordance with the constitutional expectations arising from the duty to consult doctrine, and the Supreme Court of Canada denied leave to appeal from this decision.[34]

Note here the transformed application of the duty to consult in this decision. A doctrine that applied to discretionary administrative decisions would have no application to an automatic registration. The Court said that the entire system of automatic registration effectively amounted to a system inconsistent with the emergent doctrine. Although there have not as yet been further applications exactly along these lines, if followed, this case stands as a notable precedent for a significantly expanded application of the duty to consult.

The Idle No More movement's protest against Bill C-45 reflected an emerging expectation for consultation prior to the adoption of legislation that could affect Aboriginal communities. During the Idle No More protests, in January 2013, a prominent Aboriginal law professor wrote a widely noted op ed piece in the *Toronto Star* in which he indicated that such an obligation already clearly existed in the law.[35] This was a highly peculiar claim in light of the legal determinations on this issue to that point in time,

---

[32] *Ross River Dena Council v Government of Yukon* 2012 YKCA 14, leave to appeal to SCC denied (19 September 2013).

[33] For a history of Idle No More, see Ken Coates, *#IdleNoMore: And the Remaking of Canada* (U of Regina Press, 2015).

[34] *Ross River* above (n 32).

[35] Kent McNeil, 'Idle No More Deserves Our Thanks: Movement Has Exposed Harper Government's Lack of Respect for Aboriginal and Treaty Rights', *Toronto Star* (27 January 2013).

combined with the simple reality that legislators are not the Crown. The Alberta Court of Appeal had issued an early post-*Haida* decision that seemed to indicate that there would be no such obligation, with some of the reasoning by one of the judges suggesting a basic incompatibility between a duty to consult applicable to legislative action and the parliamentary form of government.[36] In its 2011 decision in *Rio Tinto,* the Supreme Court of Canada went out of its way to comment on this decision and highlight the issue as one for future consideration.[37] But the latter certainly did not indicate a view one way or the other. Even if such an application does develop in the future, the question of whether there was a duty to consult on legislative action had not had any definitive resolution by 2013, and the claim that such a duty was legally clear at that point was actually highly questionable.

Litigation has moved forward on the issue and, indeed, a trial decision of the Federal Court in *Courtoreille v Canada* did find a duty to consult applicable at the moment just before the introduction of legislation in Parliament—after the judge went through some significant contortions over how the duty to consult interacted with the legislative process more broadly.[38] This was reversed, though, on appeal—with two different sets of reasons at the Federal Court of Appeal on why the duty to consult does not arise in legislative contexts—and this issue will be confronted by the Supreme Court of Canada.[39] It is worth noting that the practicalities of potentially constitutionally mandatory consultation with over six hundred First Nations on needed statutory reforms at the federal level, in addition to Métis and Inuit communities, are one particular challenge that renders more complicated whose interests such additional consultation serves in the context of needed statutory reforms. Given that section 35 rights are not limited to the resource context, this is an issue for many different areas of statutory reform that could have particular implications for Aboriginal communities.

The potential expectation of consultation on legislative action, though, is rooted in the developing international norms referenced earlier. In particular, Article 19 of the UNDRIP states that "[s]tates shall consult and cooperate in good faith with the indigenous peoples concerned through their own representative institutions in order to obtain their free, prior and informed consent before adopting and implementing legislative or administrative measures that may affect them".[40] The legal question of the duty to consult on legislative action will be one significant test of the domestic implications of UNDRIP in Canada.

The issue of consultation on legislative action also flowed from the principle that early, high-level strategic decisions could trigger the duty to consult. Where an early strategic

---

[36] *R v Lefthand* 2007 ABCA 206.

[37] *Rio Tinto* above (n 5) [44].

[38] *Courtoreille v Canada (Aboriginal Affairs and Northern Development)* 2014 FC 1244, rev'd by *Canada (Governor in Council) v. Mikisew Cree First Nation,* 2016 FCA 311; leave to appeal was granted by the Supreme Court of Canada in May 2017.

[39] For an examination of some of these complexities, along with an argument for such an application of the duty, see Zachary Davis 'The Duty to Consult and Legislative Action' (2016) 79 Sask L Rev 17.

[40] UNDRIP above (n 29).

decision has the effect of preconditioning or determining various later decisions that could impact on Aboriginal or treaty rights, it may be proper to consider that the early strategic decision actually triggers the duty.[41] Saying that it is triggered only later may, in effect, be too late. That said, an early strategic decision does not necessarily always precondition later decisions. Where there is genuine consideration later on, such that those decisions may or may not necessarily follow, there has been case law that holds that such early decisions do not then trigger the duty to consult.[42] The Supreme Court of Canada's reference to the ongoing openness of the question of whether legislative action triggers the duty to consult came in a paragraph mainly about early strategic decisions.[43]

Considering where that reference is, then, even if a doctrine did develop that subjected legislative action to the duty to consult, the application of the duty would arguably be analogously subject to nuance as to whether any particular legislative action triggered it. The question analogous to that with early strategic decisions would be whether the legislative action preconditioned or determined later decisions. That principle would support a determination of the duty to consult being triggered by legislation that created automatic results impacting on Aboriginal or treaty rights, such as in the *Ross River Dena Council* case referenced earlier. But it would not necessarily go farther. Where legislative action created statutory schemes under which there continued to be discretion on decisions that potentially impacted Aboriginal or treaty rights, such that consultation could effectively occur at a later stage, such legislative action would not necessarily trigger the duty to consult even if some legislative action could.

Apart from legislative action, some have argued for possibly even wider applications of the duty to consult to other types of government action as well. The Hupacasath First Nation pursued a case arguing that the federal government should have consulted with Aboriginal communities prior to entering into the Canada-China foreign investment treaty. The claim was unsuccessful, largely on the basis that no causation of any adverse impact on Aboriginal communities was demonstrated.[44] The idea of consultation being required before Canada would enter into treaties that specially affect Aboriginal populations actually has international precedents, and the *Hupacasath* case may ultimately come to be seen very much as a decision based just on a lack of causation and special impact.[45] That said, constitutional consultation requirements prior to entry into international treaties would also be a significant shift in Canadian governance.

The focus on the need to actually establish causation of an adverse impact in cases such as *Hupacasath* has been present in some other cases as well, putting into question

---

[41] *Dene Tha' First Nation v Canada (Minister of Environment)* 2006 FC 1354, aff'd 2008 FCA 20; *Rio Tinto* above (n 5) [44].

[42] *Buffalo River Dene Nation v Saskatchewan (Energy and Resources)* 2015 SKCA 31; *Hupacasath First Nation v Canada (Foreign Affairs and International Trade Canada)* 2015 FCA 4.

[43] *Rio Tinto* above (n 5) [44].

[44] *Hupacasath* above (n 42).

[45] See generally Dwight Newman & Wendy Elizabeth Ortega Pineda 'Comparing Canadian and Colombian Approaches to the Duty to Consult Indigenous Communities on International Treaties' (2016) 25 Const Forum 29.

the early conception that the duty to consult was going to be triggered relatively easily, with the legal analysis then to occur principally at the stage of the spectrum analysis. There is a renewed judicial focus on whether the duty is even triggered. Another prominent example comes from a northern Saskatchewan decision, *Buffalo River Dene*, in which the community challenged early-stage government disposition of mineral rights at auction and argued that this disposition ought to trigger the duty to consult as an early strategic decision that would set in motion subsequent effects on the community's treaty rights. The Saskatchewan Court of Appeal rejected this claim, holding that the mere disposition of mineral rights did not have any adverse impact on treaty rights and that consultation would properly occur at the later stage when applications were made for surface activities, given that all such activities required further application. The Court also noted that many mineral rights disposed of at auction did not lead to any subsequent activity, further bolstering the view that the initial disposition did not amount to an early strategic decision triggering the duty.[46]

However, other cases have seen courts offering profoundly broad readings of the duty to consult's application. For instance, a trial-level decision in British Columbia saw a court hold that even an omission can amount to action triggering the duty to consult, with the court making this pronouncement in the context of the province omitting environmental review of a pipeline project in the context of a joint agreement with the federal government concerning that review.[47] This particular decision, which also contradicted much traditional division-of-powers analysis, was highly singular and arguably must be described as an outlier case, but it nonetheless illustrates the tendencies of some courts to push the boundaries of the doctrine in various ways.

One particularly complicated question is how to deal with the duty to consult in the context of cumulative effects on an Aboriginal community from different project approvals in the same region over time. Consultation takes place on a decision-by-decision basis. Although few decisions have pronounced on this issue of cumulative effects, there has been a significant decision to the effect that when considering the required depth of consultation, it is relevant, and thus reviewing courts can potentially consider how a particular decision affects a community in the context of past impacts and potential future impacts.[48] Doing so is distinct from trying to analyze historic infringements under the duty to consult, which falls outside the purpose of the duty.[49] Rather, it pertains to considering fully the impacts of a particular decision, in light of the context in which it is made and reasonably predictable context in which the decision would operate. However, it is important to acknowledge that saying as much at a foundational level obviously does not overcome all the practical challenges to implementing such principles.

---

[46] *Buffalo River Dene* above (n 42).
[47] *Coastal First Nations v British Columbia (Environment)* 2016 BCSC 34.
[48] *West Moberly First Nations v British Columbia (Chief Inspector of Mines)* 2011 BCCA 247 at paras 117–119, 18 BCLR (5th) 234, leave to appeal to SCC refused [2011] SCCA No 399.
[49] *Rio Tinto* above (n 5) [45–49].

In theory, the duty to consult imposes obligations on the Crown when the Crown's conduct could impact on Aboriginal or treaty rights and thus pertains solely to Crown-Aboriginal interactions. Indeed, in the *Haida* decision, the Supreme Court of Canada specifically determined that the duty would not be imposed on third parties; however, the Court also permitted "delegation" of "procedural aspects" of the duty to third parties.[50] In the context of this possibility, some provinces have enacted provincial policies on consultation that either choose not to delegate to industry or to delegate to industry relatively explicitly on narrower or broader bases.[51] However, in the rather uneven development of government policies on the duty to consult, some provinces have left much ambiguity and have sometimes tried to suggest that companies were responsible for consultation even without any formal delegation and then failed to carry out governmental consultation. Some companies have worked within these sorts of ambiguities by entering into Impact Benefit Agreements (IBAs) or other similar arrangements. Other companies, standing on their legal rights, have seen devastating impacts to their businesses, including when some courts have granted legally peculiar orders, such as injunctions directly against companies based on a doctrine pertaining to Crown consultation.[52] Although provinces where such issues were arising have moved to adjust legislative obligations on companies, it would not overstate matters to say that the duty to consult, as applied in practice and amongst its many effects, has arguably had some corrosive effects on the rule of law in some contexts and has privatized some aspects of Canadian governance in complex ways.

There are complex arguments around some other applications as well. To mention two more, first in the context of modern treaties that contain their own codes on consultation, the Supreme Court of Canada has complicated the certainty of those agreements by suggesting that the constitutional duty to consult may continue to impose additional consultation requirements beyond those contained within the highly detailed negotiated agreements that spoke to consultation.[53] These issues, though, will return to the Court, as a series of lower court cases have been diverging on the principles applicable to modern treaty interpretation. Second, there have been arguments for the possibility of expanding the duty to consult beyond the section 35 Aboriginal and treaty rights context, such as to labour rights under the *Charter*.[54] The courts have rejected such

---

[50] *Haida* above (n 2) [52–53].

[51] For a survey, see Ravina Bains & Kayla Ishkanian, 'The Duty to Consult with Aboriginal Peoples: A Patchwork of Canadian Policies' (Fraser Institute, 2016).

[52] The complex cases involving Solid Gold in Ontario are an example. In *Wahgoshig First Nation v Ontario* 2011 ONSC 7708, an injunction was granted against the company's operations based on the duty to consult. Leave to appeal this injunction was granted in 2012 ONSC 2323 (Div Ct), with an extended set of reasons exploring why the injunction appeared legally problematic, though because of changed legislation in the province that appeal was then declared legally moot in *Wahgoshig First Nation v Solid Gold Resources Corp* 2013 ONSC 632 (Div Ct), leaving the company effectively no legal recourse.

[53] *Beckman v Little Salmon/Carmacks First Nation* 2010 SCC 53, [2010] 3 SCR 103.

[54] *Saskatchewan Federation of Labour v Saskatchewan* 2012 SKQB 62, rev'd 2013 SKCA 43, rev'd 2015 SCC 4 (with the trial decision rejecting this claim and it then not making its way further through the appellate decisions).

arguments, but the Supreme Court of Canada will likely need to comment on them in cases that see particular claims pursued as both section 35 claims and *Charter* claims at the same time.[55]

There are hints in some case law references to the duty to consult to a related but distinct "duty to negotiate", which would actually impose a constitutional duty on governments to enter into negotiations on unresolved Aboriginal claims.[56] To the extent that the honour of the Crown principle underlying the duty to consult can generate a variety of resulting legal doctrines,[57] such a duty to negotiate appears a plausible further application. Like the extended set of applications of the duty to consult discussed in this section, such a further duty would effect some fundamental changes in Canadian governance.

5. THE DUTY TO CONSULT AND ADMINISTRATIVE LAW DIMENSIONS

One distinct issue that has presented ongoing challenges is the relationship of the duty to consult to the vast array of administrative boards and tribunals that might be making decisions where the Crown's duty to consult could be at issue. That issue is one of how section 35 constitutional law bears on administrative law contexts, and it was seen as one on which there had been relatively little guidance from the *Haida* trilogy in 2004–2005. Several years later, the Supreme Court of Canada took up further leave applications so as to return to some unresolved questions on the duty to consult, including this issue of interaction with administrative boards and tribunals in the 2010 *Rio Tinto/ Carrier Sekani* decision.[58] What the Court enunciated there was effectively that governments choose how to organize themselves so as to meet the duty to consult. In different cases, particular administrative boards will actually carry out consultation, will review consultation efforts by other parts of government, or will have no relationship at all to consultation—what determines this is their statutory mandate as defined in their enabling legislation.[59] That said, the fact that a particular administrative board is not responsible for consultation does not mean that the duty to consult simply disappears but, rather, that government has chosen to organize itself to address the duty to consult through some other mechanism. If it has not, there is of course always the potential for a judicial challenge related to lack of required consultation.[60] So, administrative law does

---

[55] See *Ktunaxa Nation v British Columbia (Ministry of Forests, Lands, and Natural Resources)* 2015 BCCA 352, leave to appeal to SCC granted.

[56] See *Daniels v Canada (Indian Affairs and Northern Development)* 2016 SCC 12, [56].

[57] See Dickson above (n 18). For an example, see the establishment of a duty of diligent fulfillment in *Manitoba Metis Federation Inc v Canada (Attorney General)* 2013 SCC 14, [2013] 1 SCR 623.

[58] *Rio Tinto* above (n 5).

[59] *Ibid* [55–63].

[60] *Ibid* [63].

not override constitutional law, but governments' approach to administrative law bodies may determine how governments meet their constitutional duties.

Because of the sheer variety of administrative bodies whose decisions may concern matters triggering the duty to consult, it is to be expected that the role of these administrative bodies in relation to the duty to consult will vary. Indeed, even the same administrative body may have different responsibilities in light of different types of decisions under different parts of its enabling legislation. Some scholars have rushed to characterize alleged inconsistencies in the decisions of particular administrative bodies or alleged the inadequacy of their approaches to consultation,[61] but their approaches may well be overly hasty in doing so. Although their careful contributions to trying to analyze these complex questions are welcome, it is important not to lose sight of the sheer legal complexity of the structure the Supreme Court has effectively mandated.

Even some judicial decisions that have been critiqued by various activist scholars, such as the *Standing Buffalo* decision under which the Federal Court of Appeal had enunciated that the National Energy Board might end up engaging in no review of consultation in some circumstances where the Crown was not even a party to particular proceedings,[62] have genuine underlying logic within this legal structure. Such logic was recognized in that particular case by the denial of leave to appeal the decision even when the Supreme Court was actively and simultaneously considering issues related to administrative bodies during the same period in the *Rio Tinto* case.[63] Nonetheless, these issues ended up back at the Supreme Court of Canada again just a few years after *Rio Tinto* in several cases heard in late 2016.[64] That these particular cases ended up at the Court occurred after several chance factors and even procedural irregularities, perhaps again speaking to some tendencies of the courts' approach to Aboriginal issues somewhat corroding rule of law considerations.[65] It remains to be seen if the Supreme Court of Canada can shore up the logic of its framework so as to avoid repeated cases coming forward on these issues, which might actually be best advanced by offering clear statements of law that the Court will stand by to provide a predictable environment for all rights-holders and stakeholders.

[61] See eg Janna Promislow, 'Irreconcilable? The Duty to Consult and Administrative Decision Makers' (2013) 22 Const Forum 63; Sari Graben & Abbey Sinclair, 'Tribunal Administration and the Duty to Consult: A Study of the National Energy Board' (2015) 65 UTLJ 382.

[62] *Standing Buffalo Dakota First Nation v Enbridge Pipelines Inc.* 2009 FCA 308, leave to appeal to SCC rejected (2 December 2010).

[63] *Rio Tinto* above (n 5).

[64] *Ktunaxa Nation* above (n 55) is slightly different and considers consultation and religious freedom issues together. But two cases concern directly the National Energy Board and consultation: *Hamlet of Clyde River v TGS-NOPEC Geophysical Company ASA (TGS)* 2015 FCA 79, leave to appeal to SCC granted (10 March 2016); *Chippewas of the Thames First Nation v Enbridge Pipelines Inc.*, 2015 FCA 222, leave to appeal to SCC granted (10 March 2016).

[65] Dwight Newman, *Indigenous Rights, Canada's National Energy Board, and the Supreme Court of Canada*, JURIST—Academic Commentary, 11 April 2016, http://jurist.org/forum/2016/04/Dwight-Newman-indigenous-rights.php.

In light of considerations such as the enormous number of times the duty to consult is triggered each year and resulting inability of the courts to exercise supervision over even a fraction of these situations, as well as the inherent and appropriate flexibilities in the doctrine itself, there are strong reasons for judicial deference concerning the manner in which the duty to consult is carried out by governments in particular circumstances. Although some courts have wandered imprecisely in their language on the standard of review when consultations have been challenged, the correct approach is surely to consider the determination of the triggering of consultation based on the correctness of any decision on that issue, and to consider the carrying out of consultation based on a reasonableness standard, with appropriate deference part of that reasonableness analysis.[66]

Indeed, in many respects, the question at stake in complex cases may be whether there are reasonable processes in play to make a good faith effort at consultation. Contrary to some suggestions that consultation with Aboriginal communities must always be a distinct process, the *Taku River Tlingit* case released simultaneously with *Haida* determined on its particular facts that a general environmental assessment process had met the requirements of the duty to consult.[67] Later cases have similarly upheld reasonable processes as meeting the requirements of the duty to consult, with the question being simply whether meaningful consultation was available through the mechanisms available.[68] Though these processes must address Aboriginal and treaty rights issues and thus specific impacts on Aboriginal communities, they need not necessarily be processes specific to Aboriginal communities to meet the legal standards at issue.

As noted repeatedly by the Federal Court of Appeal in its dramatic 2016 decision quashing the approval of the Northern Gateway Pipeline for some inadequacies of consultation in one particular phase of the pipeline approval process, the standard in all of this is not "perfection" but good faith pursuit of meaningful consultation.[69] That said, in respect of that multi-billion dollar project, one might presume that the government would have been trying to fulfill the requirements of the duty. The case, quite possibly resulting in one of the largest practical impacts in a single case from the duty to consult doctrine to date, arguably stands as a dramatic indicator of a continuing lack of clarity in the doctrine given that the government was trying to fulfill the duty to consult but could not sufficiently determine its requirements. Although time will tell, within certain political realities, the case does not presently seem likely to be litigated as a further test of the possibilities for affected third parties to sue governments for inadequacies in their carrying out of the duty to consult. That said, there have been such lawsuits in some situations where those failures have cause significant harms to industry. Without appropriate compensatory possibilities, investors may of course, shy away from Canadian investment if the constitutional parameters of the duty to consult generate too much

---

[66] See eg *Gitxaala Nation v Canada* 2016 FCA 187, [128–155].
[67] *Taku River* above (n 3).
[68] See eg *Council of the Innu of Ekuanitshit v. Canada (Attorney General)* 2014 FCA 189.
[69] See *Gitxaala* above (n 66) passim.

uncertainty.[70] There may yet be interesting intersections of constitutional, administrative, and tort law at issue.

Aspects of the duty to consult clearly have analogies to administrative law principles, as some scholars have tried to emphasize.[71] However, it is an error to overemphasize those analogies. The duty to consult has a complex interrelationship with administrative law contexts, but it must also stand outside administrative law. The duty to consult is part of section 35 constitutional law, and treating it too much like administrative law may inadvertently diminish it. Although administrative law and the duty to consult share some of the same aims in offering protection against government action, some of the principles of section 35 constitutional law are diminished if the analogies to traditional Canadian administrative law are overplayed, including principles in the section 35 context of finding reconciliation between different legal conceptions in Western and Indigenous legal worldviews. The duty to consult, as constitutional law, will continue to develop in distinctive ways and it should not be subject to a leaden anchor of attempted administrative law empire-building weighing it down.

6. FUTURE PROSPECTS

The development since *Haida* of the duty to consult doctrine has in fact pushed forward many substantive discussions, in many cases as between industry and Aboriginal communities—though it has also put some other issues more on the table than they would have been, such as resource revenue sharing. At the same time, it can have unintended consequences. One of the very beneficial effects it has had, the promotion of Impact Benefit Agreements, was arguably not intended. Even more concerning are the ways in which the underpinnings of that development have partly been in legal ambiguities and some tendencies against the rule of law. Moreover, the duty to consult doctrine has arguably also had tendencies to lock some matters into interim positions. For many Aboriginal communities, continuing to work with the duty to consult has more beneficial consequences than actually having their longer-term issues resolved. The doctrine may thus sow the seeds of some of its own future problems. If a duty to negotiate doctrine does emerge from the honour of the Crown, as suggested earlier, and if the courts apply it to both sides, they may be doing so partly as a counterbalance to a doctrine that risks seeing many things left in a perpetual interim state.

The expanding scope of decisions subject to the duty to consult may spell some reworkings of Canadian governance. However, even while it is important to reject quick analogies to other areas of law, as in other areas of Aboriginal law, an overly specialized

---

[70] See eg Malcolm Lavoie & Dwight Newman, 'Mining and Aboriginal Rights in Yukon: How Certainty Affects Investor Confidence' (Fraser Institute, 2015).

[71] See eg David Mullan, 'The Supreme Court and the Duty to Consult Aboriginal Peoples: A Lifting of the Fog?' (2011) 24 Cdn J Admin L & Pr 233; Sossin above (n 21).

orientation of the courts when thinking about this area carries its own dangers and, in particular, neglect of the private law consequences of constitutional law reasoning may actually undermine some of what the courts are trying to do.[72] In so far as they seemingly did not anticipate how various parties would react to the emergence of the duty to consult doctrine, the courts have caused various effects. Many are clearly bargaining around what the courts have done, but others are facing unexpected breakdowns in the predictability of the legal environment.

The courts would properly take various steps to render clearer the duty to consult doctrine as applied. They must continue to offer clarity on some of the major sources of potential friction—such as the scope of the duty to consult, its applications in complex contexts such as modern treaty environments, and its interaction with administrative boards and tribunals—while also engaging with complex questions about its purposes, its effects on emerging philosophical questions concerning Aboriginal communities versus Aboriginal individuals, and its interaction with international norms. In all of this, it is also worth remembering that the duty to consult is an area of constitutional law with massive consequences for reconciliation with Aboriginal communities in Canada, for the economic prospects of Aboriginal and non-Aboriginal communities, and for Canada generally.

BIBLIOGRAPHY

Bains, Ravina & Kayla Ishkanian. 'The Duty to Consult with Aboriginal Peoples: A Patchwork of Canadian Policies'. Vancouver: Fraser Institute, 2016.

Davis, Zachary. 'The Duty to Consult and Legislative Action' (2016) 79 Saskatchewan Law Review 17.

Dickson, Jamie. *The Honour and Dishonour of the Crown: Making Sense of Aboriginal Law in Canada.* Saskatoon: Purich, 2015.

Isaac, Tom. *Aboriginal Law in Canada,* 5th edn. Toronto: Carswell, 2016.

Newman, Dwight. *The Duty to Consult: New Relationships with Aboriginal Peoples.* Saskatoon: Purich, 2009.

_____. *Revisiting the Duty to Consult Aboriginal Peoples.* Saskatoon: Purich, 2014.

Promislow, Janna. 'Irreconcilable? The Duty to Consult and Administrative Decision Makers' (2013) 22 Constitutional Forum 63.

Woodward, Jack. *Native Law.* Toronto: Carswell, 1994.

---

[72] Dwight Newman, 'The Economic Characteristics of Indigenous Property Rights: A Canadian Case Study' (2016) 95 Nebraska L Rev 432. See also Dwight Newman, 'Consultation and Economic Reconciliation', in Patrick Macklem & Douglas Sanderson (eds), *From Recognition to Reconciliation: Essays on the Constitutional Entrenchment of Aboriginal and Treaty Rights* (U of Toronto Press, 2016).

CHAPTER 17

....

MÉTIS CONSTITUTIONAL LAW ISSUES

....

LARRY CHARTRAND*

1. INTRODUCTION

THIS chapter is a selective analysis of certain significant constitutional issues concerning the Aboriginal and Treaty rights of the Métis peoples and their identity within Canada. Métis peoples possess certain Aboriginal and Treaty rights under various constitutional provisions as well as at common law.[1] Métis peoples evolved from intermarriages between English and French fur traders and Indigenous women throughout North America. In certain cases, the offspring of these unions developed their own unique cultures and societies distinct from their European and Indigenous forbearers. These groups were identified by various terms such as bois-brules (burnt wood), half-breeds, and country born. The term "Métis" has become the dominant term and is the one used in section 35 (2) of the *Constitution Act, 1982* that defines Aboriginal peoples in Canada as "including Indian, Inuit and Métis peoples".

Although Métis—Crown relations have existed since the 1700s, it is only relatively recent that the issue of Métis claims has led to the creation of uniquely Métis specific

---

* Full Professor, Faculty of Law, University of Ottawa.

[1] This chapter focuses on Métis Aboriginal rights claims based primarily on s. 35 of the Canadian Constitution. The scope of s. 35 remains uncertain, but such rights may include rights to lands, resources, cultural protections, and governance authority. The *Manitoba Act, 1870* S.C. 1870, c. 3 contains constitutional rights for land to be set aside for the benefit of Métis families. Whether the terms of this constitutional obligation born out of negotiations between the Métis of the present day region of southern Manitoba and the British colony of Canada were fulfilled is the subject of interpretation in *Manitoba Métis Federation v Canada* [2013] 1 S.C.R. 623. For an account of Métis Treaty rights claims see Larry Chartrand, "Métis Treaties in Canada: Past Realities and Present Promise" in Christopher Adams, Gregg Dahl and Ian Peach, eds, *Métis in Canada: History, Identity, Law and Politics* (2nd ed., University of Alberta Press, forthcoming).

legal doctrine warranting the necessity of a separate chapter on Métis constitutional law. This development of Métis specific legal principles, however, is not without controversy.

Foremost among the outstanding issues addressed in this chapter is the question over Métis identity and how to best determine when an assertion of Métis identity is legitimate. Of particular concern is the broad definition recently attributed to the term "Métis" by the Supreme Court of Canada in the *Daniels* decision and its failure to sufficiently contain the scope of Métis identity in deciding that Métis are Indians under section 91(24) of the Constitution.[2] In addition, there is a marked tension between the imposition of membership criteria by Canadian judicial intervention and the right to self-determine membership according to principles set out in the *United Nations Declaration on the Rights of Indigenous Peoples* that will be highlighted.[3] Although this tension is applicable to all Indigenous peoples in Canada, it has unique dimensions in the case of the Métis due to judicially imposed definitions of who is Métis compared to the experiences of First Nations who have been the subject of federal legislative definitions.[4] These issues are but only a few of the major concerns that the courts and policy makers must address in this emerging and growing field of law.[5] The concern over the imposition of a judicially defined definition of Métis identity is addressed first.

2. The Imposition of Judicially Constructed Métis Identity

The issue of Métis identity is controversial. There are strong differences of opinion as to who can qualify as "Métis" for the purposes of self-identification, especially in terms of asserting Métis rights in the Constitution. The academic literature reflects this debate. There are

---

[2] *Daniels v Canada (Indian Affairs and Northern Development)*, 2016 SCC 12.

[3] GA Res. 61/295 (Annex). UN GAOR, 61st Sess., No 49, Vol. III, UN Doc. A/61/49 (2008) 15 [hereinafter UNDRIP].

[4] The experiences of Métis and First Nations are not completely separate as there is overlap in terms of the fact that many Métis have been affected by legislative definitions of who is an Indian under the *Indian Act*, R.S.C. 1985, c. I-5, and likewise some First Nations (primarily none-status Indians) have been influenced by judicial definitions of who is a Métis according to case law defining Métis discussed *infra*.

[5] Other significant issues include concerns regarding the assessment of Métis title including the failure of the court to consider the negotiations that lead to the creation of the province of Manitoba as a treaty and the failure of the *Manitoba Métis Federation*, above (n 1) case to distinguish between Métis land-holding customs internal to the people as compared to the assertion of occupation for the purposes of external recognition of Aboriginal title under s. 35. There are also significant division-of-powers issues regarding the validity of provincial laws relating to the Métis by provinces such as Alberta including identity and membership in settlements of land collectively set aside for the Métis and the recognition of a regime of self-government on those settlements. Concerns of interjurisdictional immunity clearly arise since *Daniels* clarified that Métis are Indians and therefore under federal jurisdiction. It is beyond the scope of this chapter to deal with these and other significant issues within this field of Aboriginal constitutional law.

those who argue that the word "Métis" in section 35 is a proper name that refers only to the Métis Nation, the core of which has been said to be geographically located in Red River.

In 1870, under the leadership of Louis Riel, the Métis of the Red River territory (part of present day southern Manitoba) resisted Canada's attempt to take control of the territory. The Métis were the majority of the population of the area and had the military advantage. Negotiations between Canada and the Métis of the Red River area led to a peaceful resolution and the creation of the province of Manitoba. Section 31 of the *Manitoba Act, 1870* (which is part of the Constitution) included the promise of 1.4 million acres of land for the benefit of Métis families. For a short time the Métis were politically dominant in the new province, but due to an overwhelming influx of settlers from eastern Canada, the Métis lost the legislative majority and fell victim to Canada's failure to implement the land provisions in a timely way, resulting in most Métis not being able to benefit from the land promised. Negotiations are currently underway between Canada and the Manitoba Metis Federation as a result of the positive finding in the *Manitoba Metis Federation* case that the Crown breached its duty in delaying the effective implementation of the promise of lands.

As mentioned above, some scholars argue that the only legitimate Métis are those who are descendants of the historical Métis communities that have kinship, social, and economic connections to Red River.[6] Others interpret the term "Métis" conceptually as representing a state of identity based solely on mixed-ancestry heritage unburdened by any particular temporally rooted ethnogenisis trajectory of Métis collective belonging.[7] Still others conceive of the term as reflecting a category of self-identifying mixed-ancestry communities that evolved into distinct communities separate from their First Nation and European ancestral roots. According to this view, the "Métis Nation" is therefore not just a proper name for a specific "Métis people", but under the category approach the Métis Nation is also one among other potentially distinct Métis communities, nations, or peoples.

To the disappointment of those who advocated for a singular exclusive Métis Nation definition and to those who advocated for a more broader open-ended definition, the Supreme Court of Canada in *R. v Powley* instead opted to define the term "Métis" as a category representative of mixed-ancestry communities that have demonstrated continuity to a particular historical Métis community that existed prior to "effective European control" over the relevant territory.[8] The Court stated:

> The term "Metis" in section 35 does not encompass all individuals of mixed Indian and European heritage; rather, it refers to distinctive peoples who, in addition to

---

[6] Paul Chartrand, "The Constitutional Status and Rights of the Métis People in Canada" (2015) (University of Ottawa Conference on *Reconciliation and the Métis of Canada*) (unpublished: copy with author).

[7] For example, the definition of "Métis" used by the Eastern Woodland Métis Nation Nova Scotia does not place geographical limits on the ancestry of their members. See http://easternwoodlandMétisnation.ca/main.htm. As discussed below, the recent *Daniels* decision, above (n 2), appears to have adopted this kind of broad definition leading to concerns over the breadth of who can be legitimately Métis.

[8] *R. v Powley*, [2003] 4 C.N.L.R. 321 (SCC).

their mixed ancestry, developed their own customs, ways of life, and recognizable group identity separate from their Indian or Inuit and European forebears.[9]

The *Powley* decision also spoke to the issue of what an individual must prove in order to be considered a member of a Métis rights-bearing community. The Court identified three indicia. First, the claimant must self-identify as a member of a Métis community. Second, the claimant must present evidence of an ancestral connection to a historic Métis community. The Court did not restrict this connection to a test of blood-quantum, but also allowed for birth, adoption, or "other means" of becoming a member. Third, the claimant must show that "he or she is accepted by the modern community whose continuity with the historic community provides the legal foundation for the right being claimed".[10]

There has been critical commentary on the Court's indicia of proof of Métis belonging. Métis membership in Métis political organizations may include individuals who have been accepted by the community as Métis but for various reasons are unable to show an ancestral connection to a historic Métis community.[11] The *Powley* decision has the potential of dividing Métis communities between those who have rights and those who do not. Unless the community has set out a mechanism for inclusion of such individuals through "other means", they will become second-class Métis.[12]

Another concern with the judicially imposed *Powley* indicia relates to the imposition of identity criteria by a foreign institution from the perspective of Métis peoplehood independence. Such interference can be argued as a violation of Métis peoples' human rights according to international human rights standards as defined in the *United Nations Declaration on the Rights of Indigenous Peoples*.[13] Article 4 upholds the general right of self-determination of Indigenous peoples whereas Article 9 expressly recognizes the right of an Indigenous community to determine membership according to its

[9] *Ibid*, [10].
[10] *Ibid*, [31–33].
[11] For instance, a woman who married a non-status Indian would lose her Indian status according to the *Indian Act* before Bill C-31 was enacted in 1985 that allowed those who lost status to apply to regain it. However, this woman may have decided to join a Métis association and become an integral part of the Métis community, possibly for decades and that identity of being Métis may have been passed on to her children. She and her children for all intensive purposes had become Métis by long-time cultural association. Yet she or her children may not be able to benefit from Aboriginal rights belonging to the Métis community that she has become a part of because she, as an individual of that community, may not be able to prove the criteria of "Métis" ancestral connection through birth, adoption, or marriage. It is in circumstances such as these that Métis law-making authorities need to take advantage of the door left open in *Powley* to come up with "other means" for satisfying the criteria of ancestral connection.
[12] For a more detailed analysis of this issue, see Larry Chartrand, "Métis Identity and Citizenship" (2001) 12 Windsor Review of Legal and Social Issues 5.
[13] UNDRIP, above (n 3). For a useful review and analysis of the Declaration see Indigenous Bar Association, *Understanding and Implementing the UN Declaration on the Rights of Indigenous Peoples: An Introductory Handbook* (Indigenous Bar Association, 2011).

traditions and customs. Métis rights scholar Paul Chartrand insists that it is the Métis that have the right to decide who are Métis, and not the courts.[14] However, in the context of Canada, Paul Chartrand recognizes the reality that determining Métis identity and membership will most likely involve negotiations between political representatives of the Métis and the Crown.[15] But the determination of the boundaries of belonging must remain a political and not a judicial matter. Canadian courts have inappropriately assumed that they have a valid role in deciding questions of Indigenous peoplehood existence and whether an individual rightly or wrongly belongs to an Indigenous political collective in Canada.

Legal commentators often fall into the same limited colonial understanding. For example Thomas Isaac, in his monograph on *Métis Rights*, distinguishes the issue of Métis identity between its legal understanding and its political and social understandings.[16] In doing so, Isaac contrasts Métis leaders as concerned with the question as a social and political issue as opposed to Canadian law-making institutions that are concerned with the question as a legal matter. In making this distinction, Isaac has adopted a colonial and racialized approach to the issue. Nowhere does Isaac acknowledge that the issue of Métis citizenship and belonging is very much a legal question within Métis law-making institutions and political traditions. He fails to recognize that the Métis have a legal tradition that has something to say about who can or cannot be a citizen of their political community.[17] The legal determination of Métis identity is not the exclusive preserve of Canadian law as Isaac and others assume. Consequently his entire "legal" analysis, commendable as it is from within a colonial perspective, is found wanting, as such a limited colonial understanding of Métis identity and rights is of only marginal benefit to a comprehensive analysis of the issue expected in a post-colonial Canada.

To be fair, however, this is not a criticism that is applicable to only Isaac; it is an indictment of many legal scholars and their publishers that continue to comment on Aboriginal legal issues in Canada and fail to acknowledge its colonial and Euro-biased nature. This failure perpetuates an Aboriginal rights doctrine that does not address the racist heritage of governmental and judicial pronouncements. By putting on blinders, lawyers and judges can conveniently declare that the black letter law of Aboriginal doctrine is all that matters. It is beyond their professional competence, they may argue, to question the legitimacy of the law itself. Yet, there is no shortage of critical scholarship on Aboriginal rights doctrine.[18] Arguably

---

[14]   Paul Chartrand, "Defining the 'Métis' of Canada: A Principled Approach to Crown—Aboriginal Relations" in Frederica Wilson & Melanie Mallet (eds), *Métis—Crown Relations: Rights: Identity, Jurisdiction, and Governance* (Irwin Law, 2008) 27 at 35.

[15]   *Ibid*, at 36.

[16]   Thomas Isaac, *Métis Rights* (University of Saskatchewan, Native Law Centre, 2008) at 9.

[17]   For a thorough account of the complex nature of membership and community inclusion of Métis in Northwestern Saskatchewan communities see Brenda Macdougall, *One of the Family: Métis Culture in Nineteenth—Century Northwestern Saskatchewan* (UBC Press, 2010).

[18]   Such authors include Larry Chartrand, Justice Harry Laforme, Michael Asch, John Borrows, Gordon Christie, D'Arcy Vermette, Taiaiake Alfred, Darren O'Toole, Glen Coulthard, Joshu Nichols and many others who have consistently shown how Aboriginal law principles and doctrine are

serious ethical issues are raised if lawyers remain ignorant of such critical perspectives of the law they are "objectively" applying.

At the time *Powley* was decided, the criteria of membership paralleled closely to the criteria adopted by the Métis National Council.[19] Thus, the human rights concern over the courts determining membership criteria has not been a serious issue from the perspective of this national Métis political body. However, whether the membership criteria adopted by the Métis National Council reflects accurately Métis customs and traditions is debatable given the significance of membership movement between First Nation and Métis communities historically.[20]

Robert Innes notes that the Cree, Saulteaux, and Assiniboine were so closely intertwined that "multicultural" bands were common on the Prairies. Building alliances through marriage was encouraged, and the Métis welcomed their Indian kin into their buffalo hunting brigades and vice versa.[21] "Given the remarkable overlap between Métis and other peoples, contemporary political policies based on mutual exclusion should not be projected back onto the history of Métis, Cree, Assiniboine and Saulteaux relations".[22] Porous identity and membership boundaries were commonplace and economically encouraged.[23]

For instance, it is a troubling issue how certain strictly applied membership codes concerning Métis identity have affected individuals who have chosen to accept Indian status to obtain certain benefits available only to status Indians such as non-insured health care benefits, but in doing so have been wrongly criticised as crossing identity and cultural boundaries.

The *Indian Act* defines who is an Indian for the purposes of the Act and thus it determines who has access to various federal benefits programs aimed at Indians who have status under the Act. Up until 1985, however, the *Indian Act* through various "enfranchisement provisions" caused many status Indians to lose their status as Indians for the purposes of the Act. The most notorious provision was the one that resulted in the loss of Indian status when an Indian status women married a non-status man. She and her

---

fundamentally discriminatory and racist at their core. There are professional and ethical questions that are of concern here, but this discussion is beyond the scope of this chapter.

[19] Isaac, above (n 16) at 10.

[20] Robert Innes, "Multicultural Bands on the Northern Plains and the Notion of Tribal Histories" in Robin Jarvis Brownlie and Valerie J. Korinek (eds), *Finding a Way to the Heart: Feminist Writings on Aboriginal and Women's History in Canada* (University of Manitoba Press, 2012). Of course, Indigenous peoples traditions and customs should be allowed to evolve. I wonder whether the current criteria would be upheld under *Powley* if the claim was based on an Aboriginal right to determine membership instead of the right to hunt.

[21] Robert Innes, *Elder Brother and the Law of the People: Contemporary Kinship and Cowessess First Nation* (University of Manitoba Press, 2013) at 86.

[22] Adam Gaudy and Karen Drake. " 'The lands . . . belonged to them, once by the Indian title, twice for having defended them . . . and thrice for having built and lived on them': The Law and Politics of Métis Title" (2016) 54 Osgoode Hall Law Journal 1 at 4.

[23] Nicole St-Onge, "Uncertain Margins: Métis and Saulteaux Identities in St-Paul des Saulteaux—Red River 1821–1870" (2006) 53 Manitoba History 1 at 9.

children lost status. This provision was removed in the 1985 amendments known as Bill C-31. As a consequence many who lost status under the former provisions were entitled to regain status by individual application. Some Métis took advantage of this opportunity to gain benefits under the *Indian Act* if they were qualified to gain status under Bill C-31. However, Métis living on Métis settlements in Alberta, for example, did not realize the full implications of gaining Indian status.

This is particularly the case when Métis chose to apply for Indian status and are successful but are then denied membership in Métis communities for doing so.[24] In the *Cunningham* case, the plaintiff, Mr. Cunningham, was denied membership on one of the Alberta Métis Settlements because he obtained status under Bill C-31. Choosing Indian status in this context for the reasons explained by the plaintiff in the case had nothing to do with ethnic, cultural, or national identity. The Métis settlement was his home and he identified himself as Métis. Yet he was denied his right to be Métis and live in his own home on the settlement. Problematic still, is that if Cunningham chose to reject the status he received under the *Indian Act* and to regain membership in his long-time home community of Peavine, this culturally Métis individual would be unable to do so as there is no mechanism in the current legislation to voluntarily reject Indian status. In such scenarios, federal and provincial policy that view Aboriginal categories as closed and exclusionary become sources of personal and community injustice. Furthermore, I would argue that existing Métis political organizations should not exacerbate such injustices by insisting on strict membership boundaries, which are not consistent with Métis historical membership customs and traditions as noted above.

3. MÉTIS AS "INDIANS" WITHIN SECTION 91(24) OF THE *CONSTITUTION ACT*, 1982

To achieve reconciliation with the Métis peoples of Canada requires the federal government to recognize the Métis as distinct peoples in contemporary society and not a phenomenon of the past. Métis studies scholar Paul Chartrand made an interesting remark in a keynote address about reconciliation being like an "ingredient that can be added to any relationship or transaction to make it better. Like french fries, '*would you like some*

---

[24] *Alberta v Cunningham,* [2011] 2 SCR 670. Having acquired Indian status under the *Indian Act,* the plaintiff in *Cunningham* complained that his exclusion from membership in the settlement because of him acquiring Indian status amounted to discrimination contrary to s. 15 (1) of the *Charter.* The Court held that s. 15(2) provides a good answer to the charge of discrimination because s. 15 (2) is concerned with promoting substantive equality for disadvantaged groups. The Court held that those Métis who benefit from the *Métis Settlements Act,* RSA 2000, c. M-14 are part of an ameliorative program because the legislation at issue was part of a negotiated agreement between the government of Alberta and the Métis Settlements Federation to "establish a Métis land base to preserve and enhance Métis identity, culture and self-government, as distinct from Indian Identity, culture and modes of governance." ([69]).

reconciliation with that'?"[25] What has become apparent in Métis discussions of reconciliation is that you can't have reconciliation until you actually have a meaningful relationship to begin with. From the Métis perspective, the relationship with Canada has always been peripheral at best and non-existent at worse. Métis studies scholars have consistently noted that this denial of Métis peoplehood status has been the result of entrenched federal policy.[26]

Although 1982 marked a watershed moment in terms of Métis recognition due to their inclusion in section 35 of the Constitution, the federal government was nonetheless very reluctant to acknowledge the change in policy terms, claiming that the Métis are a provincial responsibility and not a federal responsibility. When Canada apologized to the victims of residential schools, on 11 June 2008, Clem Chartier, President of the Métis National Council, made it clear in his response to Parliament and Prime Minister Harper that the Métis are tired of being excluded; "the Métis Nation . . . wants in", he stated to the politicians and the public at large.[27] With the clarification that Métis are under federal jurisdiction, the Supreme Court of Canada in the *Daniels* case held that the federal government no longer has an excuse to deny jurisdictional responsibility for the Métis.[28] Unfortunately, it took 17 years of litigation to create the main course for the accompanying french fries.

Daniels is a watershed case, the implications of which will likely take many years to fully appreciate. In rendering its decision the Supreme Court upheld the Federal Court trial decision of Justice Phelan and recalled his conclusions on the purpose of section 91(24). Justice Phelan held that 91(24) was intended to "control Native people and communities where necessary to facilitate development of the Dominion; to honour the obligations to Natives that the Dominion inherited from Britain . . . [and] eventually to civilize and assimilate Native people".[29] The Trial Court stated that at the time of confederation the Dominion intended to develop the North-Western territory, and as Métis occupied the North-Western territory, it is consistent with the described purpose of section 91(24) to define "Indians" as inclusive of a "broad range of people sharing a Native hereditary base".[30] The Supreme Court decided that the Constitution would be more coherent by holding that section 91(24) is synonymous with section 35(2) which defines Aboriginal peoples as including "Indians, Inuit and Métis".

Given the decision, it is now clear which level of government has responsibility for policy involving the Métis. The jurisdictional uncertainty is finally resolved. Yet, Joseph

---

[25] Chartrand, above (n 6) at 8.

[26] For example see Michel Hogue, *Métis and the Medicine Line* (University of Regina Press, 2015) at 113.

[27] See Canada, House of Commons Debates, 11 June 2008, starting at page 1605. President Chartier's statement appears on page 1619. Quoted in Signa Daum Shanks, *Searching for Sakitawak: Place and People in Northern Saskatchewan's Ile-A La Crosse* (2015). Electronic Thesis and Dissertation Repository. Paper 3328. (University of Western Ontario) at 3.

[28] *Daniels*, above (n 2).

[29] *Ibid* [5] quoting Justice Phelan, [2013] 2 F.C.R. 268 (F.C. Trial Division) at para. 353.

[30] *Ibid* [566].

Magnet, lead counsel for Harry Daniels, was not assured that the federal government would necessarily act on its jurisdiction over the Métis if the court found them to be "Indians" under section 91(24). Hence he also asked the court for a declaration that the Crown has a positive obligation to negotiate and resolve outstanding claims rather than to await for Métis to assert them in a context where lack of financial recourses and alternative decision-making forums make it next to impossible to do so. He stated, "It is unlikely these negotiations will happen unless the court issues the third declaration, the obligation to negotiate with the representatives of the peoples concerned".[31] This declaration was not granted.[32]

However, the Supreme Court did emphasize the importance of Parliament's obligation to "reconcile with *all* of Canada's Aboriginal peoples".[33] Whether this translates into the federal government deciding to include the Métis within the existing comprehensive and specific claims processes remains uncertain.[34] However, given the likelihood of court action based on discrimination for non-inclusion and the current government's openness to working with the Métis, there is a good possibility that inclusion in existing processes or the creation of a new targeted process specifically for Métis and non-status claims will likely develop.[35]

Previously I had criticized the trial court decision of *Daniels* because of the implications on Métis peoplehood equality and self-determination.[36] I expressed the concern about the potential incompatibility of being subjected to unilateral federal regulation with the principle of self-determination and free prior and informed consent recognized in UNDRIP. In the past, the ability of the federal government to rely on section 91(24) has proved disastrous to Indigenous rights and governance and was the source of authority to impose the residential school system. The danger of colonial power and the corresponding vulnerability to unilateral legislation by the federal government poses a serious potential risk to the freedom and integrity of Aboriginal peoples. I had hoped that when the Supreme Court of Canada decided *Daniels*, it

[31] Joseph Magnet, Reconciliation and the Métis of Canada Conference, transcript of proceedings (University of Ottawa, October, 2015) at 5. Conference presentation videos are available on the Métis Treaties Project website. See http://www.Métistreatiesproject.ca/conference/.

[32] However, since the release of the *Daniels* decision in 2016, the Justin Trudeau government has expressed a willingness to engage with the Métis to discuss outstanding claims. See Angela Mulholland, "SCC Rules Métis, Non-Status Indians Are Federal Responsibility" CTV News, 14 April 2016. Online: http://www.ctvnews.ca/canada/scc-rules-Métis-non-status-indians-are-federal-responsibility-1.2858535.

[33] *Daniels*, above (n 2) [19].

[34] At time of writing the policy of the federal government has been to exclude the Métis from both the comprehensive claims process (except for Metis comprehensive claims in the Northwest Territories) and specific claims processes.

[35] For a review of current federal policy processes regarding Métis issues see Larry Chartrand, "Metis Land Claim Participation in the North: Implications for the Southern Canada" (2016) 4:2 Northern Public Affairs. Online: http://www.northernpublicaffairs.ca/index/magazine/volume-4-issue-2/Métis-land-claim-participation-in-the-north-implications-for-southern-canada/.

[36] Larry Chartrand, "The Failure of the *Daniels* Case: Blindly Entrenching a Colonial Legacy" (2013) 50 Alberta Law Review 1.

would reframe the nature of the power in section 91(24) to make it compatible with the principle of self-determination and UNDRIP's provisions regarding free prior and informed consent.

I argue that section 91(24) has been mistakenly interpreted and assumed to be plenary in nature by the jurisprudence and treated like the other heads of power in section 91 and s 92 of the Constitution. Rather, I argue that based on a more comprehensive review of the historical evidence combined with a progressive interpretation of the Constitution as a "living tree" that section 91(24) should be read in a way that is consistent with the principle of free prior and informed consent. This would mean that section 91(24) has a built in limitation, and its use is dependent on whether the Aboriginal peoples that would be affected by proposed federal legislation have provided consent. This interpretation of section 91(24) was not expressly addressed by the Supreme Court in *Daniels* and remains a concern.

Yet, interestingly the language used by the Court in characterizing section 91(24) in *Daniels* seems to have indirectly reframed its purpose to reflect a qualified understanding of the power. Without explicitly stating that section 91(24) is limited in its plenary nature, the Court carefully connects the reconciliatory purpose of section 35 of the Constitution with a characterization of section 91(24) as expressing a federal responsibility to Aboriginal peoples, and avoids using the language of power and jurisdiction normally associated with division-of- powers analysis.[37] The Court states that section 91(24) must be read in a broader contemporary societal context consistent with the purpose of section 35 as mandating the reconciliation of Aboriginal peoples' interests with the Canadian state. Moreover, the Court held that section 91(24) is about the "federal government's relationship with Canada's Aboriginal peoples" which is markedly distinct from previous articulations of the section being a power over Indians as a subject matter of jurisdiction.[38] This characterization of a federal head of power is qualitatively distinct from characterizations typical of other heads of power. For example it would be awkward to speak of the federal government as having a relationship with "navigation and shipping" or "Banking". More to the point, the Court speaks of section 91(24) as "Parliament's protective authority" in regards to Aboriginal peoples.[39] Thus, without explicitly stating that the plenary nature of section 91(24) is limited or conditional, the tone and approach the Court takes in describing this power certainly is very suggestive that it ought to be understood in the context of a relationship of respect and

---

[37] *Daniels*, above (n 2) [34].

[38] *Ibid*, [49]. Interestingly, the Court does not undertake the standard division-of-powers analysis that is typical of such cases except as a brief afterthought late in the judgment where it then promptly endorses cooperative federalism and the diminishing scope of interjurisdictional immunity by simply referencing *Canadian Western Bank v Alberta*, [2007] 2 S.C.R. 3 and *NIL/TU,O Child and Family Services v B.C. Government and Service Employee's Union*, [2010] 2 S.C.R. 696 in the judgment. This point was no doubt made in the contemplation of pending litigation that challenges the *Métis Settlements Act* of Alberta as *ultra vires* the power of the province as Métis are now clearly under federal jurisdiction.

[39] *Ibid*.

reconciliation that distinguishes it in a real and fundamental way from the other subject heads of power.

Although the potential exists (although very unlikely in today's political climate) for Parliament to legislate policy that is harmful, negative, and discriminatory (which would likely be subject to *Charter* and section 35 challenges), such a policy of that nature may be found outside the scope of its power as such harmful legislation would be found contrary to the colour given to section 91(24) by the Court's indirect reframing of its protective meaning. Restricting the power of the federal government this way would be a remarkable departure from the orthodox understanding of parliamentary supremacy where legitimacy in this context would be tested according to substantive understandings of justice and the rule of law in addition to the more accepted obligations of procedural legitimacy regarding the nature of the rule of law.

However, it is difficult to imagine a court, under a division-of-powers analysis, deciding that a clear legislative statement concerning Indian policy would be outside the scope of section 91(24) regardless of how harmful such legislation would be to the "Indian" population. Parliament has in fact relied on this power in the past in initiating a reign of discrimination, assimilation, and oppression for over 150 years.[40] Hopefully the past will not repeat itself again. I would have been more comforted had the Court been more concrete and decisive in limiting the power of section 92(24) rather than relying on the "noblesse oblige than on what is obliged by the constitution".[41] The magnanimous and colourful language of responsibility, protection, and reconciliation are simply not included in the text of section 91(24) and are open to reinterpretation in future cases.

It remains difficult to reconcile Indigenous peoples as a third order of government equal to federal and provincial governments when the relationship is tainted by one government having a potentially unlimited power over the other.[42] It conjures up images of the one group being inferior and dependent on the other. It is reparation for past harms and the rebuilding of Indigenous political independence and authority that should be the aim of Parliament's obligations.

---

[40] The Truth and Reconciliation Commission characterized the period from the mid-1800s to 1960s as the period of cultural genocide against Aboriginal peoples in Canada. Truth and Reconciliation Commission, *Honouring the Truth, Reconciling the Future: Summary of the Final Report of the Truth and Reconciliation Commission* (2015) at 1.

[41] *Daniels,* above (n 2) [12].

[42] The Canadian government announced in May 2016 that it would implement UNDRIP in Canada. See CBC News: http://www.cbc.ca/news/aboriginal/canada-adopting-implementing-un-rights-declaration-1.3575272 (last accessed May 10 2016). Importantly, there exists within UNDRIP an article that requires the free, prior, and informed consent by Indigenous peoples of any legislation that may impact their rights and interests. A recent announcement by the Minister of Justice, however, indicates that Canada will take a cautionary and case-by-case approach to implementing UNDRIP which cautionary approach has been the subject of criticism and concern by Indigenous peoples in Canada. See https://ipolitics.ca/2016/07/12/ottawa-wont-adopt-undrip-directly-into-canadian-law-wilson-raybould/ (last accessed July 12, 2016).

4. Métis as Ancestry: An Imprudent Definition of Indian

The definition of Métis identity for the purpose of claiming section 35 Aboriginal rights differs from how the Supreme Court defined "Métis" in reference to section 91(24). In *Daniels,* the Court interpreted "Métis" broadly in deciding that Métis are "Indians" for the purposes of section 91(24). The Court held that Métis "can refer to the historic Métis community in Manitoba's Red River Settlement or it can be used as a general term for anyone with mixed European and Indian Heritage". [43] Thus a person who can prove some Indian heritage could claim to be Métis and thus "Indian" for the purposes of federal jurisdiction. However, he or she would not necessarily be Métis for the purposes of section 35 without proving that he or she was also a descendant of a historic Métis community as defined in *Powley.*

There are serious concerns with the broad definition of Métis as including "anyone with mixed European and Aboriginal heritage" adopted by the Supreme Court in *Daniels.*[44] One relevant concern relates to whether the term "Indian" should be disconnected from the concept of Indigenous as embodying collective peoplehood experiences of colonization. The broad definition allows for "Indian" identity under section 91(24) based simply on Métis self-declaration and proof of mixed ancestry without showing any real connection to a distinctly Métis community or having been the victim of colonization policies of assimilation through increasingly restrictive Indian membership criteria or refusal of colonial governments to acknowledge any Indigenous identity. Simply declaring one is Métis because one has some distant ancestor that was Indigenous arguably should not result in such person, without more, being a constitutional Métis Indian under section 91(24).

Métis identity should not be based simply on ancestry alone. This is why noted Métis lawyer Jean Teillet is so critical of the trial decision in *Daniels* and preferred the Court of Appeal's analysis.[45] The Federal Court of Appeal commented on the identity criteria needed to be Métis for the purposes of being Indian in section 91(24):

> I accept the submission of the Intervener Métis Nation of Ontario that a progressive interpretation of section 91(24) requires the term Métis to mean more than individuals' racial connection to their Indian ancestors. The Métis have their own language,

---

[43] *Daniels,* above (n 2) [17]. This does not mean that anyone with mixed-blood is Métis or non-status and thus Indians under federal jurisdiction. The Court held at paragraph 47 that such determinations may need to proceed on a "case by case" basis.

[44] *Ibid.* One could, however, argue that the court was not adopting such a broad definition but simply pointing out the current divisions within the society over the meaning of Metis.

[45] Jean Teillet, *Métis Law in Canada* (Pape, Salter, Teillet, LLP, 2015) at 1–19.

culture, kinship connections and territory. It is these factors that make the Métis one of the Aboriginal peoples of Canada.[46] . . .

It follows that the criteria identified by the Supreme Court in *Powley* inform the understanding of who the Métis people are for the purpose of the division of powers analysis. The *Powley* criteria are inconsistent with a race-based identification of the Métis.[47]

Professor Sébastien Grammond argues that it is obvious

that ancestry alone is not enough to constitute indigenous identity. A person may have indigenous ancestry, but may not have been raised within an indigenous culture, may not have suffered the disadvantages and oppression flowing from the injustices suffered by the indigenous peoples and may not self-identify as indigenous. This is why acceptance by an indigenous group plays a major function in most definitions of indigenous identity.[48]

In contrast, the Supreme Court explicitly over-ruled the Court of Appeal's decision to narrow the scope of Métis for the purposes of section 91(14) by the addition of a community acceptance requirement. The Supreme Court justified its decision by distinguishing the purpose of section 91(24) from the purpose of section 35. Section 35 is about identifying rights-holders whereas section 91(24) is about the Government's relationship with Aboriginal peoples, noting that this "includes people who may no longer be accepted by their communities because they were separated from them as a result, for example, of government policies such as Indian Residential Schools".[49] However, this conclusion raises additional questions when, for example, the exclusion is based on the Indigenous community's own criteria of membership.

Such persons may be legitimately Métis, but it should not be because they are caught in an indeterminate broad net of who is an Indian. Rather their inclusion as Indian may be justified because of the impact colonization has had on their identity and membership choices and the socio-political context and history of the region or territory in

---

[46] *Daniels v Canada (Minister of Indian Affairs and Northern Development)*, [2014] C.N.L.R. 139 (FCA) [96].

[47] *Ibid* [99].

[48] Sébastien Grammond, *Terms of Coexistence: Indigenous Peoples and Canadian Law* (Thomson Reuters, 2013) at 12. Or if they do self-identify, it may be for opportunistic reasons unconnected to their lived experiences (including possible intergenerational effects) and heritage as some courts have determined. See for example, *Vautour*, [2011] 1 CNLR 283 (NB Prov. Ct) and *Québec (Procureur général) (Ministère des Ressources naturelles) v Corneau*, 2015 QCCS 482. English summary available online at: https://www.usask.ca/nativelaw/news/2015/qu%C3%A9bec-c.-corneau.php.

[49] *Daniels*, above (n 2) [49]. It is not apparent to me that a Métis community or political association would necessarily exclude those who went to residential schools from membership within the Métis community. In any event, the example of residential schools on membership inclusion reflects more the identity marker of negative impact of colonization on the individual's ability to belong, which may still justify that individual's legitimate identification as a Métis Indian under s. 91(24) even if such a person was not accepted by a Métis community as a member.

question. Forced identity migration due to restrictive definitions of who is or is not Métis by federal policy may have resulted in social, cultural, and family disconnection between such individuals and their ancestral roots and community. For instance, in the case of First Nation identity, the loss of Indian status due to assimilation policy in the *Indian Act* has seriously impacted cultural and community connection, as was noted in the *Lovelace* case.[50] Residential schools broke community connections for many Métis and First Nations children. The '60s scoop, which is the term given to the policy initiated in the 1960s of adopting Métis and First Nation children out of their home communities and placing them into White homes, was also significant in breaking cultural and community ties.

In term of Métis, federal policies that refused to accept Métis as distinct political and social polities forced some members to become First Nations or to become White.[51] Also to avoid racism and backlash from mainstream White society, Métis to the extent they could, would go underground or integrate into White society to avoid negative social and economic discrimination and prejudice.[52] Inclusion of such disaffected persons and communities within federal government responsibility under s. 91(24) may be appropriate as there are arguably moral and legal obligations that may exist in terms of repairing social and cultural connections and the harms that have resulted from federal identity polices.[53]

Although there is a need for a boundary marker of identity, it should not be limited to the requirement of "community acceptance" adopted by the Federal Court of Appeal in *Daniels*. Lack of community acceptance should not necessarily be a bar to falling under the protective authority of Parliament. However, there still needs to be some principled basis for restricting the scope of section 91(24) so as to exclude those that have not been negatively impacted by colonial identity policies. Evidence of such negative impact by colonial identity policies is arguably an alternative valid marker of indigeneity in a colonized societal context.[54] The adoption of the trial judge's broad definition by

---

[50] *Sandra Lovelace v Canada*, Communication No. 24/1977: Canada 30/07/81, UN Doc. CCPR/C/13/D/24/1977. The United Nations Human Rights Committee found Canada had discriminated against Sandra Lovelace because of the denial of her being able to maintain a cultural connection to her home community because of the impact of s. 12(1)(b) of the *Indian Act* which resulted in her loss of Indian status when she married a non-Indian and the right to live on the reserve where Mi'kmaq culture is most prominent.

[51] See Jacqueline Peterson, "Red River Redux: Métis Ethnogenesis and the Great Lakes Region" in Nicole St-Onge, Carolyn Podruchny and Brenda Macdougall (eds), *Contours of a People: Métis Family, Mobility and History* (University of Oklahoma Press, 2012) 22 and Larry Chartrand, above (n 1).

[52] *R. v Powley*, [2000] 2 CNLR 233 (Ont. SCJ). The Ontario Superior Court upheld the provincial court's finding "that the contemporary Métis community had always existed, except that it was, until the early 1970's, an invisible entity within the general population, an invisibility (to outsiders) caused by shame, ostracization, and prejudice" ([38]).

[53] The Truth and Reconciliation Commission has documented the impact of losing one's connection to culture and community and has concluded that reconciliation between Indigenous peoples and Canada must involve efforts at repairing community alienation and identity. Truth and Reconciliation Commission, above (n 40) at 1–3.

[54] Sébastien Grammond, Isabelle Lantagne and Natacha Gagné, "Non-status Indigenous Groups in Canadian Courts: Practical and Legal Difficulties in Seeking Recognition" in Patrick Macklem and

the Supreme Court of Canada is too simplistic. There is a need for some profundity to be attributed to the meaning of "Indian". To leave the definition open ended will cause much confusion and potential bitterness between Métis and First Nations who see limited financial resources being further divided among a growing category.[55] Moreover, the gate will be left wide open for ethnic fraud to result.[56]

On the other hand, individuals may be re-asserting Métis identity and community where there is a well-documented history of a distinct Métis presence in an area, where there is evidence of denial of this distinct Métis community by federal policy makers and where this occurred without choice.[57] In this context, it can be argued that such a reassertion of Métis identity could very well be a profound act of decolonization.

Whereas in other cases such as in the *Vautour* decision, the ethnic mobility choice from Acadian to Métis seemed opportunistic and not necessarily the result of imposed colonial policies sufficient to justify the inclusion of Vautour as a Métis for the purposes of claiming Aboriginal rights under section 35.[58] There was no direct historical evidence of a Métis community having existed, and thus no evidence of the community having experienced the negative impact of colonization or identity denial. In other words, the community identified as Acadian for most of its history and has not experienced the negative impact of colonization and assimilation to justify identifying the community as Métis in the Aboriginal sense notwithstanding the existence of mixed-ancestry in the defendant's distant lineage.[59]

Douglas Sanderson (eds), *From Recognition to Reconciliation: Essays on the Constitutional Entrenchment of Aboriginal & Treaty Rights* (University of Toronto Press, 2016) 259.

[55] In some cases First Nations have intervened against Métis claims for Aboriginal rights. In *R. v Hirsekorn*, [2013] 4 C.N.L.R. 244 (Alta. C.A.) the Blood Tribe and Siksika Nation both intervened against a Métis claim to hunt in the environs of the Cypress Hills in southern Alberta.

[56] Chris Andersen, "Peoplehood and the Nation Form: Tools for Thinking Juridically about Métis History" paper presented at Reconciliation and the Métis Conference, University of Ottawa, October 2015 at 18. Accessed online: http://www.Métistreatiesproject.ca/wp-content/uploads/2016/01/Peoplehood-and-the-Nation-Form.pdf.

[57] For example, the Red Sky Métis were originally beneficiaries of the Robinson Superior Treaty of 1850. At the time of treaty, the Métis wished to join as a Métis band, but were denied. Colonial officials said they can only benefit if they joined the Saulteaux bands which they had relations with. The Chief accepted them but several years later, the "Métis" descendants were excluded from the treaty annuity lists because they were ironically Métis and since being excluded, they now have re-formed as a distinct Métis community. See Chartrand, above (n 1).

[58] *Vautour,* above (n 48). The Superior Court of Quebec in the *Corneau* case came to a similar conclusion. In *Corneau*, the respondent asserted Aboriginal rights to occupy a hunting camp based on his Montagnais (Inuu) ancestry. The evidence did not support the existence of a historic Métis collective in the territory in question. In terms of Métis identity, "[t]he court found his self-identification to be primarily a recent phenomena driven by opportunism". *Corneau,* above (n 48).

[59] It may be fair to argue, given the concerns raised by Grammond et al., above (n 54) that there may be valid reasons for a presumption in law that colonization has impacted identity formation negatively and that recognition of Métis/Mi'kmaq identity should be provided to Vautour unless proof can be shown by the Crown that the defendant was not affected by colonization in this regard. It is difficult for me to be entirely confident given the history of colonization that it is fair or just to deny Vautour's Aboriginal identity even if Indigenous identity is a recent assertion.

Arguably, even apart from whether courts have failed to fully account for federal assimilation policy and its impact on Indigenous identity, there remains the question of which Indigenous identity is appropriately considered. What is more problematic for the defendants in my opinion is that both Vautour and Corneau showed genealogical evidence of either Mi'kmaq ancestry or Montagnais ancestry yet argued that because of this ancestry they were therefore "Métis". If they were supporting their claims based on Métis identity, would they not be claiming Métis ancestry instead of Mi'kmaq or Montagnais ancestry? What the defendants (or their lawyers) likely fail to realize is that being Métis is not reducible to whether one has some First Nation ancestry. Instead, the defendants should be claiming Aboriginal rights based on their belonging to the Mi'kmaq or Montagnais communities.[60] Chris Andersen would characterize these claims as misrecognition of who the Métis are as a distinct people by attributing Métisness to a hollow empty construct based on mere mixedness.[61]

Adopting a broad open-ended definition gives the impression that Métis are those that are in the "reject pile where you throw all the people who lost their Indian status. We are not a garbage can, and we are not the leftovers".[62] Yet the Supreme Court of Canada adopted Hogg's analysis that implies just that. According to Hogg, Métis are those who were "excluded from the charter group from whom Indian status devolved".[63] This is a very empty and insufficient understanding of the Métis peoples of Canada and must be rejected.

5. CONCLUSION

Defining Métis as anyone with Indian ancestry seriously diminishes the social and political dimensions of Métis and renders these essential characteristics of Indigenous peoplehood meaningless. One cannot be Métis without an attachment to community. Alternatively such attachment may have been disrupted by colonial policies, and

---

[60] There are cases where non-status Indians have been found to possess Aboriginal rights. In *R. v Lavigne* [2005] 3 C.N.I..R. 176 the court found a non-status Mi'kmaq to have a "sufficient and substantial connection with a tribe" ([59]). The court expressly choose not to apply *Powley* because the defendant was not Métis. Instead the court applied the *R. v Fowler*, (1993) 134 N.B.R. (2d) 361 test which requires a "sufficient and substantial connection with a tribe". Yet, more recent cases of non-status claimants have been applying *Powley* by requiring evidence of "community acceptance". In *R v Acker*, [2004] N.B.J. No. 525 (N.B. Prov. Ct.) and *R. v Vienneau*, [2014] N.B.J. 222 (N.B.Q.B.) there was evidence of Mi'Kmaq ancestry, but insufficient evidence of community acceptance and only recent evidence of Mi'kmaq self-identity. Arguably the *Fowler* approach is more sensitive to the negative colonial impact of federal identity policies and is preferred for those reasons.

[61] Chris Andersen, *Métis: Race, Recognition, and the Struggle for Indigenous Peoplehood* (UBC Press, 2014) at 176–179.

[62] Jean Teillet, Submission to Senate Standing Committee on Aboriginal Peoples, Issue 16, Evidence, 2 May 2012. http://www.parl.gc.ca/content/sen/committee/411%5CAPPA/16EV-49504-e.HTM.

[63] Peter Hogg, *Constitutional Law of Canada*, 5th ed. suppl. (Carswell, 2007) at 28–34.

therefore such individuals are justified in re-asserting a Métis identity notwithstanding lack of formal connection to a present Métis community. However, having some Indigenous ancestry without any connection to a present day Métis community nor any evidence of having been negatively impacted by federal policies should not automatically result in Metis recognition. Many Canadians likely have some First Nation ancestors if they search far enough back into their genealogy. Does that make half the Canadian population all of a sudden Métis and therefore Indians under federal jurisdiction?

According to *Daniels*, Vautour and Corneau could potentially argue that they ought to be classified as Métis even though they were unable to prove that they were accepted by a distinct Métis community or were negatively affected by federal policy denying or severing their Métis identity and heritage. Yet *Daniels* potentially leaves open the possibility that they may be found to be Indians under section 91(24). Are such "Metis" individuals now entitled to Indian programs (assuming the federal government expands the scope of beneficiaries beyond status Indians to all Indians)? Federal policy makers can obviously adopt a narrower category of Indian that relates to the experiences of Indigeneity in Canada and thus be more tailored to addressing the needs of those who have experienced the negative impacts of colonization because of their Indigeneity. However, these restrictions run the risk of being declared under-inclusive from a *Charter* equality perspective because of the arguably broad definition adopted by the Supreme Court of Canada in *Daniels*.

BIBLIOGRAPHY

Jurisprudence

Alberta v Cunningham, 2011 SCC 37, [2011] 2 SCR 670.
Daniels v Canada (Indian Affairs and Northern Development), 2016 SCC 12, [2016] SCJ No 12.
Daniels v Canada (Indian Affairs and Northern Development), 2014 FCA 101, 3 CNLR 139.
Manitoba Métis Federation, 2013 SCC 14, [2013] 1 SCR 623.
Québec (Procureur général) (Ministère des Ressources naturelles) v Corneau, 2015 QCCS 482, [2015] JQ No 1026.
R v Acker, 281 NBR (2d) 275, [2004] NBJ No 525.
R. v Fowler, 134 NBR (2d) 361, [1993] 3 CNLR 178.
R. v Hirsekorn, 2013 ABCA 242, [2013] 4 C.N.L.R. 244.
R. v Lavigne 2005 NBPC 8, [2005] 3 C.N.L.R. 176.
R. v Powley, 2003 SCC 43, [2003] 4 CNLR 321.
R. v Powley, 47 OR (3d) 30, [2000] 2 CNLR 233.
R. v Vautour, 2010 NBPC 39, [2011] 1 CNLR 283.
R. v Vienneau, 419 NBR (2d) 205, [2014] NBJ 222.

International Materials

Human Rights Committee, *Sandra Lovelace v. Canada*, Communication No. 24/1977: Canada 30/07/81, UN Doc. CCPR/C/13/D/24/1977.

United Nations General Assembly, *United Nations Declaration on the Rights of Indigenous Peoples,* GA Res. 61/295 (Annex), UN GAOR, 61st Sess, No 49, Vol. III, UN Doc. A/61/49 (2008) 15.

Books

Andersen, Chris, *Métis: Race, Recognition, and the Struggle for Indigenous Peoplehood* (Vancouver: UBC Press, 2014).

Chartrand, Larry, "Métis Treaties in Canada: Past Realities and Present Promise" in Christopher Adams, Gregg Dahl and Ian Peach, eds., *Métis in Canada: History, Identity, Law and Politics, 2nd Edition* (Edmonton: University of Alberta Press).

Chartrand, Paul, "Defining the 'Métis' of Canada: A Principled Approach to Crown—Aboriginal Relations" in Frederica Wilson and Melanie Mallet, eds., *Métis—Crown Relations: Rights: Identity, Jurisdiction, and Governance* (Toronto: Irwin Law, 2008).

Elder Pangman, Joe, Commentary, in Fred Shore and Lawrence Barkwell, *Past Reflects the Present: The Métis Elders Conference* (Winnipeg: Manitoba Métis Federation, 1997).

Grammond, Sebastien, Isabelle Lantagne and Natacha Gagne, "Non-Status Indigenous Groups in Canadian Courts: Practical and Legal Difficulties in Seeking Recognition" in Patrick Macklem and Douglas Sanderson, *From Recognition to Reconciliation: Essays on the Constitutional Entrenchment of Aboriginal & Treaty Rights* (Toronto: University of Toronto Press, 2016).

Grammond, Sebastien, *Terms of Coexistence: Indigenous Peoples and Canadian Law* (Toronto: Thomson Reuters, 2013).

Hogue, Michel, *Métis and the Medicine Line* (Regina: University of Regina Press, 2015).

Innes, Robert, *Elder Brother and the Law of the People: Contemporary Kinship and Cowessess First Nation* (Winnipeg: University of Manitoba Press, 2013).

Innes, Robert, "Multicultural Bands on the Northern Plains and the Notion of Tribal Histories" in Robin Jarvis Brownlie and Valerie J. Korinek, eds., *Finding a Way to the Heart: Feminist Writings on Aboriginal and Women's History in Canada* (Winnipeg: University of Manitoba Press, 2012).

Isaac, Thomas, *Métis Rights* (Saskatoon: University of Saskatchewan, Native Law Centre, 2008).

Macdougall, Brenda, *One of the Family: Métis Culture in Nineteenth-Century Northwestern Saskatchewan* (Vancouver: UBC Press, 2010).

Hogg, Peter, *Constitutional Law of Canada, 5th Edition* (Scarborough: Thomson Carswell, 2007).

Palmater, Pamela, *Beyond Blood: Rethinking Indigenous Identity* (Saskatoon: Purich Publishing, 2011).

Peterson, Jacqueline, "Red River Redux: Métis Ethnogenesis and the Great Lakes Region" in Nicole St-Onge, Carolyn Podruchny and Brenda Macdougall, eds., *Contours of a People: Métis Family, Mobility and History* (Norman: University of Oklahoma Press, 2012).

Teillet, Jean, *Métis Law in Canada* (Vancouver: Pape, Salter, Teillet, LLP, 2015).

Truth and Reconciliation Commission, *Honouring the Truth, Reconciling the Future: Summary of the Final Report of the Truth and Reconciliation Commission* (Winnipeg Truth and Reconciliation Commission of Canada, 2015).

Journals/Periodicals

Chartrand, Larry, "Métis Identity and Citizenship" (2001) 12 Windsor Review of Legal and Social Issues 5.

Chartrand, Larry, "Métis Land Claim Participation in the North: Implications for Southern Canada" (2016) 4:2 Northern Public Affairs, online: http://www.northernpublicaffairs.ca/index/magazine/volume-4-issue-2/Métis-land-claim-participation-in-the-north-implications-for-southern-canada/.

Chartrand, Larry, "The Failure of the Daniels Case: Blindly Entrenching a Colonial Legacy" (2013) 50 Alberta Law Review 1.

Gaudy, Adam and Karen Drake. "'The lands … belonged to them, once by the Indian title, twice for having defended them … and thrice for having built and lived on them': The Law and Politics of Métis Title" (2016) 54 Osgoode Hall Law Journal 1.

St-Onge, Nicole, "Uncertain Margins: Métis and Saulteaux Identities in St-Paul des Saulteaux— Red River 1821–1870" (2006) 53 Manitoba History 1.

Papers/Presentations

Andersen, Chris, "Peoplehood and the Nation Form: Tools for Thinking Juridically about Métis History" (Paper delivered at the Reconciliation and the Métis Conference, University of Ottawa, October 2015) online: http://www.Métistreatiesproject.ca/wp-content/uploads/2016/01/Peoplehood-and-the-Nation-Form.pdf.

Chartrand, Paul, *The Constitutional Status and Rights of the Métis People in Canada* (2015) [unpublished, University of Ottawa Conference on *Reconciliation and the Métis of Canada*].

Daum Shanks, Signa A.K, *Searching for Sakitawak: Place and People in Northern Saskatchewan's Ile-A La Crosse (PhD Thesis, The University of Western Ontario, 2015)*.

Grammond, Sebastien, "How Courts Perceive Aboriginal Communities" (Presentation delivered at the Reconciliation and the Métis of Canada conference, University of Ottawa, October, 2015).

Magnet, Joseph, *Transcript of proceedings of the Reconciliation and the Métis of Canada Conference, Ottawa, 2015* (Ottawa: University of Ottawa, 2015) online: http://www.Métistreatiesproject.ca/conference/.

Government Documents

Teillet, Jean, *Submission to Senate Standing Committee on Aboriginal Peoples*, Issue 16, Evidence, May 2, 2012.

Websites/News Sources

CBC News, "Canada Officially Adopts UN Declaration on Rights of Indigenous Peoples" (May 10, 2016), online: CBC http://www.cbc.ca/news/aboriginal/canada-adopting-implementing-un-rights-declaration-1.3575272.

Dawn, Manitou, "Eastern Woodland Métis Nation Nova Scotia", online: http://easternwoodlandMétisnation.ca/main.htm.

Mulholland, Angela "SCC Rules Métis, Non-status Indians Are Federal Responsibility" *CTV News* (14 April 2016), online: http://www.ctvnews.ca/canada/scc-rules-Métis-non-status-indians-are-federal-responsibility-1.2858535.

PART IV

FEDERALISM

A. Federalism in Canada

CHAPTER 18

....

FROM DUALISM
TO COOPERATIVE
FEDERALISM AND BACK?

Evolving and Competing Conceptions
of Canadian Federalism

....

JEAN-FRANÇOIS GAUDREAULT-DESBIENS* &
JOHANNE POIRIER**

1. INTRODUCTION
....

IN all federations, intergovernmental cooperation represents a practical necessity.
Canada is no exception in that regard. However, the institutional design, constitutional regime, and political and legal culture in which such cooperation takes place may
impact on how it is justified, and on how it concretely unfolds, both vertically and horizontally. The intensity of cooperation, as well as its level of formalization, institutionalization and "juridification", may vary considerably. These differences also affect the way
in which cooperation is justified from a normative standpoint (at least when "normative" is understood from a strict legal angle, i.e., as referring to a source of substantive
legal—or at least binding—obligations).[1] Moreover, transformations in the scope and

---

* Dean of Law, Université de Montréal and Canada Research Chair in North American and
Comparative Juridical and Cultural Identities, Faculty of Law, Université de Montréal: jf.gaudreault-
desbiens@umontreal.ca.

** Professor and Holder of the Peter MacKell Chair in Federalism, Faculty of Law, McGill
University: johanne.poirier3@mcgill.ca. The authors would like to acknowledge the effective assistance
of Maryna Polataiko in tracking sources for parts of this text.

[1] From that perspective, a constitutional convention can be characterized as normative as it is
binding, even if it is not judicially enforceable. See *Reference re Amendment of Constitution of Canada*
[1981] 1 SCR 753.

modes of intervention by public authorities may lead to significant evolution in how federalism is both conceptualized and lived. This is to some extent what happened in Canada, where cooperation, although always present, expanded as a result of a change in the role of state actors under the influence of Keynesian economics, particularly since the 1930s. That role's expansion inevitably propelled intergovernmental "encounters" and frictions in areas from which governments were previously absent, or where they previously intervened in a less ambitious and more autonomous fashion. In such areas, a form of cohabitation emerged, which sometimes led to duplication of legal regimes, and occasionally to outright rivalry. In order to reduce the occurrence of conflict, and to ensure better public policy planning and implementation, governments were somehow bound to collaborate "on the ground".

Oddly, the rich *practice* of intergovernmental collaboration collides with the fundamentally dualist nature of the Canadian federal architecture.[2] Faced with this contradiction, courts have adopted ambivalent and ambiguous solutions which reveal competing underlying conceptions of federalism. On the one hand, courts have gradually tended to lower constitutional and legal barriers to overlapping legislative action and administrative collaboration. On the other, the pragmatic and political imperative of collaboration was never translated into any form of legal obligation to cooperate, or for the various federal partners to take each other's interest into consideration in the exercise of their respective sovereign powers. While constitutionally encouraging cooperation, judges still overwhelmingly consider non-cooperation to be a matter of politics, which should be shielded from judicial intervention. In other words, unlike the evolution that can be observed in other federations which constitutionally enshrine principles of cooperation, or that are structurally "cooperative",[3] the political/legal dichotomy has remained a characteristic feature of the law of Canadian federalism.

This chapter seeks to document the evolution from a dualist—"watertight compartments"—conception of Canadian federalism, to one that has to acknowledge an increased number of intergovernmental cooperative ventures. It first examines Canada's fundamentally dualist federal architecture (Section 2) before surveying the empirical reality of cooperative federalism which frequently challenges this structural dualism (Section 3). It then looks at how the rise of cooperative federalism influenced the evolution of the interpretive doctrines underpinning the law of Canadian federalism (Section 4). Finally, it analyses the normative strength and scope of cooperative federalism (Section 5). It concludes that the impact of cooperative federalism in Canadian constitutional law remains tamed by the dualist conception of federalism that still underlies the Supreme Court of Canada's federalism case law.

---

[2] For a discussion of the judicial use of "building" metaphors (notably, "structure" and "architecture"), see Warren J. Newman, "Of Castles and Living Trees: The Metaphorical and Structural Constitution" (2015) 9 JPPL 471.

[3] See below, Section 2 of this text.

2. CANADA'S FUNDAMENTALLY DUALIST FEDERAL ARCHITECTURE

In the *Secession Reference*,[4] the Supreme Court of Canada emphasized that federalism was one of the structural, underlying principles of Canadian constitutional law, which should be interpreted alongside other equally important principles such as democracy, the protection of minorities, constitutionalism, and the rule of law.[5] Although the status of these "underlying" principles is debated, they minimally should inform constitutional,[6] and sometimes legislative,[7] interpretation.

Today, very few analysts doubt that Canada is a federal country.[8] Yet, the very term "federalism" is polysemous. Reduced to its simplest expression, it combines "self-rule and joint-rule", that is, the autonomy of constitutive units on the one hand, with joint action/participation of all actors on the other. Comparative law and politics teach us that there are as many shades of federalism as there are concrete incarnations of this arithmetic formula. From an empirical standpoint, each federal regime flows from its particular history, socio-demographic make-up, and internal institutional logic.[9]

Hence, when the Supreme Court reiterates the centrality of federalism to Canadian constitutional law and life, what underlying conception of federalism does it envisage? A multitude of possible characteristics immediately come to mind: multinational or not?, asymmetric or not?, "provincialist" or "centralist"?, egalitarian or hierarchical? A multifarious mixture of some of these attributes? What (implicit) conceptions of what federalism may mean or entail guide judges' determinations of the distribution of powers, or their assessment of the legality of complex cooperative schemes, or the constitutionality of unilateral actions by orders of government whose actions are sometimes, and in many ways, intertwined in joint and complex systems?

Obviously, in a pluralist society, particularly one in which the federal system was established in the nineteenth century (and has thus evolved, alongside the increased intervention of state institutions in most aspects of public and private life), unanimous conceptions of federalism are neither possible, nor desirable. Nor can the law of federalism be reasonably expected to capture all the layers of complexity inherent in this

---

[4] This section is adapted from Johanne Poirier, "Souveraineté parlementaire et armes à feux: le fédéralisme coopératif dans la ligne de mire?" (2015) 45 RDUS 47, 49–79.

[5] *Reference Re Secession of Quebec* [1998] 2 SCR 217, [49].

[6] *Reference re Senate Reform*, 2014 SCC 32, [2014] 1 SCR 704 [26]; *Reference re Assisted Human Reproduction Act*, 2010 SCC 61, [2010] 3 SCR 457 [184, 191, 196].

[7] *Lalonde v Ontario (Commission de restructuration des services de santé)* [2001] OJ No. 4767 (ONCA) [130].

[8] *Contra*: Andrée Lajoie argues that the process of centralisation that has plagued the Canadian Confederation since 1867 makes it a unitary state: Andrée Lajoie, "Le fédéralisme canadien: science politique fiction pour l'Europe?", *Lex Electronica*, vol. 10, no. 1, 2005, p. 2: available at: https://depot.erudit.org/bitstream/002578dd/1/Le%2Bfederalisme%2Bcanadien.pdf.

[9] Ronald L. Watts, *Comparing Federal Systems* (3rd edn, McGill-Queen's University Press, 2008) 1.

political regime, in Canada or elsewhere. Yet, bearing those caveats in mind, and since the Supreme Court's work is also about setting guidelines for the benefit of social and political actors, one could legitimately wish for greater clarity (as distinguished from unanimity) on its part as to the nature, scope, and possible uses of cooperative federalism.

A. Distinguishing between "Dualist" and "Integrated/Cooperative" Federations

Amongst the myriad of angles from which federalism can be examined, in this chapter we focus on the evolution, tension, and ambiguities that characterize one dimension of Canada's federal architecture and interpretive doctrines: that is the co-existence, not always harmonious, of both a "dualist" conception of federalism and a "cooperative" one. Both archetypes have their own internal and institutional logic. Shifts from one dominant conception to another may thus have an impact on the overall coherence and balance of the system.

In dualist federal systems, each order of government enjoys legislative and executive—and often judicial—powers. These powers are likely to be distributed on an exclusive basis, to maximize the autonomy and independence of each order of government. Formal legal norms are adopted in a parallel fashion, unilaterally, by each order of government. The official architecture is thus "compartimentalised", or, perhaps more tellingly "pillarized", that is, built on parallel vertical columns or "pillars". In this type of system, interaction between federal partners is not an integral part of the overall structure or logic. Rather, it takes the form of intergovernmental relations that are more "deliberate" and "optional", somewhat along the lines of diplomatic relations between independent states.[10] The American, Australian, Brazilian, or Belgian federations largely follow this dualistic logic, and so does Canada.[11]

This "pillarised" form of federal architecture is to be contrasted with systems in which constitutive units implement most of the legislative acts and programmes adopted by central authorities.[12] Such systems—known in Germany, Switzerland or, by analogy, the European Union, for instance—may be described as "administrative", "executive", "cooperative",[13] or "integrated".[14] In those regimes, cooperation is

---

[10] Richard Simeon, *Federal-Provincial Diplomacy: The Making of Recent Policy in Canada* (University of Toronto Press, 1972, reprinted 2006).

[11] Johanne Poirier & Cheryl Saunders, 'Conclusion: Comparative Experience of Intergovernmental Relations in Federal Systems' in Johanne Poirier, Cheryl Saunders & John Kincaid (eds), *Intergovernmental Relations in Federal Systems: Comparative Structures and Dynamics* (Oxford University Press, 2015) 440, 491–494.

[12] ibid.

[13] By contrast, Robert Schütze, *From Dual to Cooperative Federalism: The Changing Structures of European Law* (Oxford University Press, 2009) considers that cooperative federalism refers not to the "functional executive" dimension but rather to the legal authority that an order of government may have to adopt legislative norms that are complementary to more general ones adopted (normally) by central authorities.

[14] These adjectives can all be potentially confusing. For instance, although European federations will tend to describe such systems as "cooperative", this ignores the fact that dualist federal systems can also

more "organic" and structural than voluntary. Constitutive units contribute in a far more direct fashion in the adoption of federal norms which they will then have to implement (alongside their own). This form of "intrastate" federalism is, of course, an integral part of officially "administrative" federal regimes.[15] A lesser degree of legislative autonomy is thus somewhat compensated by greater participation. It is worthy of note that there is no empirical evidence suggesting that these official forms of "integrated" systems lead to more actual cooperation than dualist ones.[16] However, cooperation follows different channels, involves distinct institutions, and tends to rest on contrasting conceptions of the role of law in the life of specific federations. Formally "integrated" regimes have been more heavily influenced by European civil law, and are more likely to integrate constitutional rules and principles, legislative frameworks, and judicial oversight of "inter-federal behaviour" than their counterparts with roots in the English common law.[17]

B. Dualist Components of the Canadian Federation

Sections 3 and 4 of this chapter will canvass the diversity and the intensity of cooperative practices in Canada, as well as the increasing judicial endorsement of a particular, albeit vague, conception of "cooperative federalism". At this stage, we would like to underline a number of features which underpinned Canada's fundamentally dualist federal architecture from its inception, and which, with limited nuances, still provide its institutional backbone.

First, with very few exceptions, executive powers follow legislative ones, in a way which consolidates the "pillarization" of the federal structure.[18] In principle, each order

give rise to coordinated and collaborative mechanisms and structures. The term "administrative" is not quite suitable either, as the formation of intergovernmental agreements in a dualistic context can also be described as a form of "administrative" federalism. Similarly, the expression "executive federalism" could be confused with the use of this expression to describe federal regimes in which the executive branch of government dominates, regardless of the fundamental "dualist" or "integrated" federal architecture.

[15] "Intra-state" federalism refers to a formal institutional cooperative set up within the federation often through a second chamber, for instance. By contrast, "inter-state" federalism refers to relations between constitutive units, or the latter and central authorities, that are less "organic" or "structured", somewhat analogous to "international relations".

[16] Thomas O. Hueglin & Alan Fenna, *Comparative Federalism: A Systematic Inquiry* (2nd edn, University of Toronto Press, 2015) 243.

[17] Poirier & Saunders, above (n 11) 479–481.

[18] *Bonanza Creek Gold Mining Co. v Canada* [1916] 3 JCJ (UKPC) [16], [29]. There are two exceptions to this rule. The first relates to treaties, the conclusion of which rests with the federal executive, regardless of the issue at stake, whereas the implementation in the domestic legal order follows the internal division of powers. The second relates to the criminal law, as substantive and procedural norms fall under federal heads of power (s. 91(27) of the *Constitution Act, 1867* (UK), 30 and 31 Vict, c 3, s 92(10)(c) reprinted in

of government has a full-fledged public administration which implements the laws and programmes adopted by "its" order. Administrative inter-delegation, pursuant to which executive functions are (revocably) transferred to another order are relatively common, and have been held to be constitutional.[19] This form of delegation introduces a form of ad hoc "administrative" federalism, which represents an exception to the rule of dualism. [20]

Second, the formal division of powers is essentially grounded in two parallel lists of exclusive legislative heads of power. De jure concurrency is the exception, rather than the norm (as would more likely be the case in officially integrated/cooperative federal systems).[21] The "watertight compartments" metaphor[22] which best rendered this strict dualist conception of federalism has undoubtedly been largely discounted.[23] Yet, even contemporary doctrines which seek to limit the impact of the principle of jurisdictional exclusivity must take into account the very text of sections 91 and 92 of the *Constitution Act, 1867*, which still explicitly states that Parliament and the provincial legislatures have *exclusive* authority to make laws in relation to enumerated matters. To give but one example, the double aspect doctrine enables the two orders of government to legislate on distinct dimensions of a common matter, but from the standpoint of their own *exclusive* power.[24]

Third, basically every mechanism for control of executive action takes place along dualist lines. Hence, under Canadian parliamentary law, it is incumbent upon every legislative assembly to control the regulatory function of "its" executive branch, in a resolutely dualist vision.[25] Similarly, the executive branch's political accountability also reflects and consolidates the dualist model. Put simply, a federal minister may be called to account before Parliament, while her provincial counterpart would be responsible before her legislative assembly, even when they are acting in a collaborative way. There

---

RSC 1985, Appendix II, No 5.), whereas the implementation explicitly rests with the provinces (S 92(14) of the same Act). Hence, in *R. v Wetmore* [1983] 2 SCR 284 (SCC) 307, Dickson J., dissenting, opined that the complementarity between ss. 91(27) and 92(14) of the *Constitution Act, 1867*, evinced the intent of the drafters of the Constitution that cooperative federalism was in order in view of reconciling the national and local dimensions of a given issue.

[19] *P.E.I. Potato Marketing Board v Willis* [1952] 2 SCR 392 (SCC); *Reference Re Agricultural Products Marketing* [1978] 2 SCR 1198 (SCC); *Fédération des producteurs de volailles du Québec v Pelland*, 2005 SCC 20, [2005] 1 SCR 292.

[20] This ad hoc adoption of "administrative federalism" is clearly only partial, as it is not accompanied by structural measures guaranteeing the participation of provinces in federal law-making, which are inherent to formal "cooperative" or "administrative" federal regimes. See section I.1.

[21] Sections 94A and 95, *Constitution Act, 1867*.

[22] Lord Atkin in *Canada (A.G.) v Ontario (A.G.)* [1937] AC 326 (UKPC) 356.

[23] See Section 4 of this chapter.

[24] Jean Leclair, "The Elusive Quest for the Quintessential 'National Interest'" (2005) 38 UBCLR 355, 368–369.

[25] Although certain parliamentary committees may occasionally examine cooperative arrangements—in the framework of budgetary evaluation, for example—control over intergovernmental relations is in no way systematic, nor is it coordinated between federal partners.

are simply no structural mechanisms of political control that are adapted to "network" governance.

Even in the case of administrative inter-delegation, courts have held that it is the minister of the order of government which holds the formal legislative competence which remains politically accountable before his or her assembly for administrative acts and decisions taken by officials to which administrative functions have been delegated.[26] Although legally defensible, this solution is questionable from the perspective of transparency and democratic accountability. When officials simultaneously implement both federal and provincial laws (as is the case of agricultural products boards for instance), lines of ministerial accountability become particularly blurry, as the practice so clearly derogates from the dualist model, without adequate adaptation of parliamentary control mechanisms. The Supreme Court, however, seems to tolerate decreased administrative transparency and accountability which can result from cooperative action. Hence La Forest J., writing about the difficulty of identifying the precise normative basis of administrative decisions made by intergovernmental bodies, expressed the opinion that:

> In so far as it may be somewhat confusing for the citizen to sort out the question of jurisdiction because two levels of government are ultimately accountable for the appellant's actions, that is the very nature of a national marketing scheme. If we are going to tolerate joint delegation arrangements—permissible as a matter of constitutional law and desirable, in my view, as a matter of practice—then we must accept that the details of these arrangements will be implemented by marketing boards empowered from multiple sources. Citizens must look first to these boards to be accountable for their actions, and then to the two levels of government that have constituted them. In my view any potential loss in accountability that results in this situation is more than made up for by the benefits and practicalities of the joint delegation arrangement.[27]

The fourth marker of dualism is also related to control mechanisms. In Canada, judicial review of administrative action is essentially designed in a parallel fashion. Federal officials are subject to the supervision of the Federal Court,[28] whereas the actions of provincial civil servants are subject to the supervision of provincial administrative tribunals (or the Superior Court of the province). This separation of control powers can be a source of confusion for third parties challenging decisions taken by agencies acting pursuant to administrative delegation schemes, as well as for courts themselves. In other words, the rule of law, of which judicial review is a crucial component, remains anchored in a dualist structure, even when, on the ground, federal actors develop intertwined collaborative schemes which rest on normative networks.

---

[26] *Ricken Leroux Inc. v Québec (Ministère du Revenu)* [1997] JQ no 2953 (QCCA) [18], leave to appeal rejected, (1913/1998) by Rousseau-Houle J.A., for the majority.

[27] Concurring in *British Columbia (Milk Board) v Grisnich* [1995] 2 SCR 895, [30].

[28] Guy Régimbald, *Canadian Administrative Law* (LexisNexis 2008), 47–54.

Finally, and perhaps more importantly, judicial interpretation of the principle of parliamentary sovereignty, inherited from nineteenh century British constitutional law, clearly reinforces the dualist nature of the Canadian federation. Even in the face of cooperative practices, the Supreme Court has made it clear—and has recently reiterated—that Parliament and provincial/territorial legislatures are endowed with the same type and the same intensity of parliamentary sovereignty.[29] This maximalist conception of parliamentary sovereignty grants each order a similar—and very substantial—degree of legislative autonomy. This includes the power to unilaterally adopt or repeal any laws and programs, with two (important) caveats, however: respect for fundamental rights and for the formal division of powers. As we shall argue in the last section of this chapter, this reading of parallel sovereignties consolidates a strongly dualist conception of Canadian federalism, in a way that is clearly at odds with the notable, and simultaneous, judicial endorsement of "cooperative federalism".

Simply put, Canada's federal edifice, erected in 1867 was, and mostly remains, inherently dualist. In the next two sections, we explore how certain practices and evolving interpretive doctrines of the distribution of competences have challenged this dualist compartmentalization, without however entirely ousting it.

3. The Rich Practice of Intergovernmental Relations in the Canadian Federal System

A distribution of competences elaborated in the nineteenth century and essentially based on a principle of exclusivity became difficult to sustain from the 1930s on, with the advent of the welfare state. The involvement of the federal order in social protection led to a limited number of constitutional amendments.[30] However, with time, provinces and federal authorities have instead resorted to a number of cooperative techniques to limit duplication and articulate their respective intervention in similar policy areas. It has become trite to say that very few public policies are now developed and delivered by a single order of government. In other words, interaction between federal partners is no longer exceptional—as it was designed to be in the original dualist conception—but has become matter-of-course.

---

[29] *Reference Re Canada Assistance Plan (B.C.)* [1991] 2 SCR 525; *Québec (A.G.) v Canada (A.G.)* 2015 SCC 15, [2015] 1 SCR 693; *In the Matter of the Reference of the Government of Quebec in virtue of Order in Council 642-2015 Concerning the Constitutionality of the Implementation of pan-Canadian Securities Regulation*, 500-09-025430-158, May 10, 2017 (Quebec Court of Appeal).

[30] Section 91(2)A, *Constitution Act, 1867*: Added by the *Constitution Act, 1940*, 3-4 Geo. VI, c. 36 (U.K.). Section 94A: Amended by the *Constitution Act, 1964*, 12-13 Eliz. II, c. 73 (U.K.) and as originally enacted by the *British North America Act, 1951*, 14-15 Geo. VI, c. 32 (U.K.), repealed by the *Constitution Act, 1982*.

Some cooperative mechanisms involve the legislative branches, but most are designed and implemented by the respective executives. Hence, although the direct delegation of legislative competence from one order of government to another is not constitutionally permitted,[31] incorporating another order's legislation into one's legal order has been deemed acceptable,[32] as is making the application of one order's legislation conditional on the actions of another.[33] As mentioned earlier, by law, an order of government may also delegate to another order a number of its administrative functions, in a way which introduces, in an ad hoc manner, an "integrated" form of federalism, but without the intrastate mechanisms that allow for more systematic input of constitutive units.[34]

For their part, executive-led modes of cooperation are multi-dimensional. Some are "purely political". This is the case not only of informal and personal intergovernmental relations, but also of top-level inter-ministerial meetings, which take place outside any kind of formal legal framework.[35] Joint secretariats or administrative bodies have also been set up, occasionally endowed with regulatory powers.[36] Finally, thousands of intergovernmental agreements, with various degrees of—and often nebulous—legal status are concluded every year, as a means of bridging and structuring public action of federal actors in a way that clearly belie the dualist conception in its maximalist version.[37]

These executive-led schemes are sometimes, but not always, confirmed by (parallel) legislative norms. In theory, in a parliamentary regime, third parties should never be bound by norms taken in the absence of a legislative basis. However, a number of cooperative techniques have an undeniable degree of "effectivity", even when they contravene public law orthodoxy.[38] Such schemes are regarded with startling benevolence by

---

[31] *A.-G. of Nova-Scotia v A.-G. of Canada* [1951] SCR 31.

[32] *Coughlin v Ontario Highway Transport Board* [1968] SCR 569, 583–584.

[33] See, for instance, section 207(1) of the *Criminal Code*, RS C 1985, c C-46, regarding the regulation of lotteries.

[34] See sub-section 2 b).

[35] By contrast to what is generally the case in "European" federations, often grounded in the civil law tradition and which tend to "legalise" this form of interaction: Poirier & Saunders, above (n 11) 479-481.

[36] See, for example Bill 49, *An Act to Implement the Accord between the Government of Canada and the Government of Québec for the Joint Management of Petroleum Resources in the Gulf of Saint-Laurence*, 1st Sess, 41st Legislature, Quebec, 2015, ss. 15-30.

[37] On the legal status of intergovernmental agreements in Canada, see Johanne Poirier, "Les ententes intergouvernementales dans les régimes fédéraux: aux confins du droit et du non-droit" in Jean-François Gaudreault-Desbiens & Fabien Gélinas, (eds), *Le fédéralisme dans tous ses états: Gouvernance, identité et méthodologie/The States and Moods of Federalism: Governance, Identity and Methodology* (Carswell/Bruylant, 2005), 441; Johanne Poirier, "Intergovernmental Agreements in Canada: at the Cross-roads Between Law and Politics," in Peter Meekison, Hamish Telford & Harvey Lazar (eds), *Reconsidering the Institutions of Canadian Federalism, Canada: the State of the Federation 2002* (Institute of Intergovernmental Relations 2004); Johanne Poirier, "Une source paradoxale du droit constitutionnel canadien: les ententes intergouvernementales," (2009) 1 RQDI <http://aqdc.quebec/blog/volume-1-levolution-du-droit-constitutionnel-au-canada-et-au-quebec-un-retour-aux-sources/>

[38] One of us has analysed this practice as an odd form of state-based legal pluralism: Johanne Poirier, "Quand le non-droit fait la loi: les ententes entre partenaires fédéraux et l'hypothèse du pluralisme juridique," (*Le droit public existe-t-il?*, May 2009) <http://dev.ulb.ac.be/droitpublic/index.php?id=14&tx_ttnews[pointer]=1&cHash=bf631284b0>

courts, which are clearly at pains not to disrupt collaborative efforts displayed by the other two branches.[39] Judicial restraint arguably comes close to willful blindness, when courts show leniency in the face of violations of some traditional rules of administrative law that have clearly been developed in a dualist context, as we noted earlier.[40] This is, apparently, considered to be a tolerable price to pay for effective public policy in the Canadian federation. This judicial indulgence is, however, set aside when federal partners do not wish to collaborate, no longer wish to do so, or seek to ascertain their sovereignty through unilateral action.

The next section briefly reviews how the Supreme Court's recent case law has sought to curb the consequences of the official dualist federal structure, by extolling a conception of "cooperative", "flexible", and "modern" federalism, which largely legitimizes legislative—and thus administrative—overlap.

4. The Evolution of Interpretive Doctrines and the Rise of Cooperative Federalism

As discussed in the previous section, most federal and provincial competences are explicitly and mutually exclusive. This is certainly how the Judicial Committee of the Privy Council conceptualised them until 1949, that is, until that court ceased to be Canada's ultimate appellate tribunal. Textual indications in the *Constitution Act, 1867* could have led to a different conclusion,[41] but these were largely discounted. This conceptualization culminated in the famous metaphor of the "watertight compartments", which presupposed, or sought to identify, clear boundaries between federal and provincial jurisdictions.[42]

Yet, just like the Titanic's watertight compartments, those once found to exist in Canada's constitutional structure could not resist the pressure of external forces, such as the evolution of the state's role as a result of the rise of Keynesian economics after the Great Depression of 1929. A shift indeed took place, slowly but surely, under which what Ryder calls the "classical" interpretive paradigm of the federal division of powers, emphasising exclusivity, eventually receded.[43] A competing paradigm—the "modern"

[39] On this "benevolent" form of constitutional scrutiny, see: Jean-François Gaudreault-DesBiens, "The 'Federal Principle' and the Legacy of the *Patriation* and *Quebec Veto* References," (2011) 54 SCLR 78, 98.

[40] See Sub-section 2(B), notably the quote from La Forest J. in *Grisnich* above (n 27).

[41] See, generally John T. Saywell, *The Lawmakers: Judicial Power and the Shaping of Canadian Federalism* (Osgoode Society for Canadian Legal History & University of Toronto Press 2002).

[42] *Canada (AG) v Ontario (AG)* [1937] AC 326 (JCPC).

[43] Bruce Ryder, "The Demise and Rise of the Classical Paradigm in Canadian Federalism: Promoting Autonomy for the Provinces and First Nations," (1991) 36 McGill LJ 308.

one—emerged, which sought to better take stock of the growing interaction between federal and provincial actors in the public sphere.

Under that new paradigm, the courts' focus has moved away from abstractly identifying the boundaries of the matters assigned to either level of legislative authority, seeking instead to decipher the predominant characteristic of impugned statutes, that is, their "pith and substance". The underlying assumption is that, in many policy domains, one order of government may legislate over one aspect of a particular matter—or issue— while the other order of government may also legislate over that same matter, but regarding a different aspect. For example, addressing drug abuse problems may require federal action (pursuant to criminal law powers) as well as provincial action (in the areas of social assistance and health care).[44] Provided that both laws relate, in pith and substance, to the competences with which the respective orders of government that have enacted them are vested, both will be valid.[45]

Writing in 1987, Chief Justice Dickson of the Supreme Court of Canada captured that dynamic as follows:

> The history of Canadian constitutional law has been to allow for a fair amount of interplay and indeed overlap between federal and provincial powers. It is true that doctrines like interjurisdictional and Crown immunity and concepts like "watertight compartments" qualify the extent of that interplay. But it must be recognized that these doctrines and concepts have not been the dominant tide of constitutional doctrines; rather they have been an undertow against the strong pull of pith and substance, the aspect doctrine and, in recent years, a very restrained approach to concurrency and paramountcy issues.[46]

As our colleagues Eugénie Brouillet and Bruce Ryder examine the key doctrines that currently shape the interpretation of the federal division of powers in this *Handbook*,[47] we will not discuss these in any greater detail. It suffices to underline that the recent rise of cooperative federalism as an explicit interpretive principle of the division of powers has had an impact on how these traditional doctrines of interpretation—largely developed in the context of the "classic" paradigm based in the idea of exclusive powers—are applied. More precisely, the idea of limiting the scope of interpretive doctrines susceptible of unduly inhibiting legislative overlaps has infused the Supreme Court's case law, at least since the beginning of the new millennium.[48]

---

[44] *Canada (Attorney General) v PHS Community Services Society* 2011 SCC 44, [2011] 3 SCR 134; *Schneider v The Queen* [1982] 2 SCR 112.

[45] A valid legislative or regulatory measure may, however be inapplicable (pursuant to the doctrine of interjurisdictional immunity) or inoperative (in the case of a provincial law, pursuant to the doctrine of federal paramountcy).

[46] *Ontario (Attorney General) v OPSEU* [1987] 2 SCR 2, [27].

[47] See the chapter by Eugénie Brouillet & Bruce Ryder in this *Handbook*.

[48] See: *Rothmans, Benson & Hedges Inc. v Saskatchewan* 2005 SCC 13, [2005] 1 SCR 188, and more recently, *Alberta (A.G.) v Moloney* 2015 SCC 51, [2015] 3 SCR 327; *407 ETR Concession Co. v Canada (Superintendent of Bankruptcies)* 2015 SCC 52, [2015] 3 SCR 397; *Saskatchewan (A.G.) v. Lemare Lake*

However, that case law can at best be characterized as elevating cooperative federalism to the status of an interpretive principle that seeks to maximise the impact of the "double aspect doctrine" in a way that allows for legislative overlap over a similar "matter" (or policy issue). This development is combined with a tendency to limit as much as possible operational conflicts between federal and provincial legislations. Governments are under an obligation to facilitate the expression of the principle of cooperative federalism,[49] as they must take stock of the overlaps inherent to the post-watertight compartments era.[50] However, this is an obligation of means, not of results, and arguably a merely moral one.

Actually, the only cases where a formal *duty to cooperate* was found to exist are ones where the notion of comity was imported from international law to the domestic realm with a view to implementing valid provincial statutes having extra-territorial effects. Comity was envisaged in these cases as intrinsic to federalism,[51] the Supreme Court holding that it should *a fortiori* apply to domestic, inter-provincial, relations. These cases have not, however, had much percolating effect in other contexts.

Indeed, beyond judicial acknowledgements of the fact of cooperation, the status of cooperative federalism remains relatively weak in the Supreme Court's discourse. In fact, cooperative federalism appears to have a substantial normative effect only when non-governmental parties challenge cooperative measures elaborated by different orders of government, that the latter seek to defend. In those cases, courts tend to rely on the principle of cooperative federalism to reject arguments that some (often long-standing) intergovernmental schemes contravene certain more "traditional" rules of public law.[52] To put it bluntly, "cooperative federalism" has little normative scope to limit the freedom of government actors to act unilaterally, when they choose not to—or no longer to—cooperate. But the same principle will be given significant—even supra-legislative—weight in order to "save" cooperative schemes when governments are cooperating, and challenges are raised by affected third parties.

Logging Ltd. 2015 SCC 53, [2015] 3 SCR 419 [21–24]. This approach was reiterated by the majority in *Rogers Communications Inc. v Châteauguay (City)* [2016] SCC 23 [38, 85], despite the conclusion that in the case at bar, municipal norms related, in pith and substance, to the federal exclusive competence over telecommunications. By contrast, for Gascon J., concurring, the "modern" interpretation of the distribution of competences militated in favour of the double aspect doctrine. He concluded, however, that in the instant case, the valid municipal measure were inapplicable pursuant to the doctrine of interjurisdictional immunity.

[49] *Husky Oil Operations Ltd. v Minister of National Revenue* [1995] 3 SCR 453, [162] (Iacobucci J., dissenting with Sopinka and Major JJ, without being contradicted by the majority on the question of cooperative federalism). See also: *Canadian Western Bank v Alberta* 2007 SCC 22, [2007] 2 SCR 3; *British Columbia (A.G.) v Lafarge Canada Inc.* 2007 SCC 23, [2007] 2 SCR 86; *Reference re Securities Act* [2011] SCC 66, [2011] 3 SCR 837 [9].

[50] *Chatterjee v Ontario (A.G.)* 2009 SCC 19, [2009] 2 SCR 624 [32].

[51] *Morguard Investments Ltd v De Savoye* [1990] 3 SCR 1077; *Hunt v T & N plc* [1993] 4 SCR 289; *Tolofson v Jensen,* [1994] 3 SCR 1022.

[52] On this distinction, see Poirier, "Une source paradoxale du droit constitutionnel canadien: les ententes intergouvernementales," above (n 37).

An illustration can be found in *Fédération des producteurs de volailles du Québec v Pelland*, where the Court was faced with a federal-provincial agreement governing the marketing of chicken. This agreement granted a federal office the power to delegate to a provincial organization its authority to regulate the marketing of chicken in all markets. Upholding the constitutionality of this delegation mechanism, the Court merely observed that the impugned agreement "both reflects and reifies Canadian federalism's constitutional creativity and cooperative flexibility".[53] The Court did so despite the fact that the agreement had not been adequately transposed into formal law, binding on third parties.[54]

Cooperation, both as a fact inherent to federalism and as a virtue of that political regime, also influenced the Supreme Court's confirmation of the constitutionality of a tri-partite decision-making framework involving the federal and provincial governments as well as an aboriginal band.[55] In *NIL/TU,O*, the Court was called upon to determine whether labour relations in an agency created under the auspices of this agreement, and offering services to aboriginal families and children, fell under the federal power over "Indians", despite the fact that such services are usually deemed to fall under provincial jurisdiction. Cooperative federalism was somewhat used as a prism through which the impugned regime was seen in the best possible light, and the provincial competence confirmed:

> Today's constitutional landscape is painted with the brush of co-operative federalism [...] A co-operative approach accepts the inevitability of overlap between the exercise of federal and provincial competencies.
>
> NIL/TU,O's operational features are painted with the same co-operative brush. The agency exists because of a sophisticated and collaborative effort by the Collective First Nations, the government of British Columbia and the federal government to respond to the particular needs of the Collective First Nations' children and families. This effort has resulted in a detailed and integrated operational matrix comprised of NIL/TU,O's Constitution and by-laws, a tripartite delegation agreement, an intergovernmental memorandum of understanding, a set of Aboriginal practice standards, a federal funding directive and provincial legislation, all of which govern the provision of child welfare services by NIL/TU,O in a manner that respects and protects the Collective First Nations' traditional values.
>
> By virtue of the memorandum of understanding and the tripartite agreement, the federal government actively endorsed the province's oversight of the delivery of child

---

[53] *Fédération des producteurs de volailles du Québec v Pelland* 2005 SCC 20, [2005] 1 SCR 292 [15].

[54] To the same effect, see also *Boucher v Stelco* 2005 SCC 64, [2005] 3 SCR 279. Contrast with *UL Canada Inc. v Québec (A.G.)* 2005 SCC 10, [2005] 1 SCR 143 [*Unilever*], summarily confirming [2003] RJQ 2729 (QCA) in which both courts held that a major multilateral agreement did not supersede a prior provincial regulation. On these ambiguous—and hard to reconcile cases—, see section 2.2. of Poirier, "Une source paradoxale du droit constitutionnel canadien: les ententes intergouvernementales," above (n 37).

[55] *NIL/TU,O Child and Family Services Society v B.C. Government and Service Employees' Union* 2010 SCC 45, [2010] 2 SCR 696.

welfare services to Aboriginal children in the province, including those services pro-vided by NIL/TU,O to the Collective First Nations. I see this neither as an abdication of regulatory responsibility by the federal government nor an inappropriate usurpa-tion by the provincial one. It is, instead, an example of flexible and cooperative feder-alism at work and at its best.[56]

We are merely talking here of an interpretive framework, no more, no less. A year later, in *Reference re Securities Act*, the Supreme Court reiterated this hope that "the federal government and the provinces [would] exercise their respective powers over securi-ties harmoniously, in the spirit of cooperative federalism".[57] It did so, however, while also emphasizing the need to respect "the constitutional boundaries that underlie the division of powers"[58] and concluding that "[t]he 'dominant tide' of flexible federalism, however strong its pull may be, cannot sweep designated powers out to sea, nor erode the constitutional balance inherent in the Canadian federal state".[59]

In that case, the Supreme Court struck down the main provisions of proposed fed-eral securities legislation as massively trenching upon provincial jurisdiction over prop-erty and civil rights.[60] Interestingly, the Court used aspirational language, envisaging cooperative federalism as encouraging cooperation, but not imposing it.[61] It strongly relied on the principle of federalism to buttress its holding that cooperative federalism, although relevant, has no independent normative (legal/constitutional) weight to force orders of government to actually engage in cooperative schemes:

> It is not for the Court to suggest to the governments of Canada and the provinces the way forward by, in effect, conferring in advance an opinion on the constitutionality on this or that alternative scheme. Yet we may appropriately note the growing prac-tice of resolving the complex governance problems that arise in federations, not by the bare logic of either/or, but by seeking cooperative solutions that meet the needs of the country as a whole as well as its constituent parts.
>
> Such an approach is supported by the Canadian constitutional principles and by the practice adopted by the federal and provincial governments in other fields of activities. The backbone of these schemes is the respect that each level of govern-ment has for each other's own sphere of jurisdiction. Cooperation is the animating force. The federalism principle upon which Canada's constitutional framework rests demands nothing less.[62]

---

[56] ibid [42]–[44].
[57] *Reference re Securities Act* 2011 SCC 66, [2011] 3 SCR 837 [9].
[58] ibid [62].
[59] ibid [62]. Yet, as we will see *infra* in Section 5, the Court largely fails, in its case law, to take stock of the fact that "the constitutional balance inherent in the Canadian federal state" can also be upset by the way in which the legal holder of a power decides to exercise it, even when it exercises it in a valid manner from the standpoint of the division of powers.
[60] *Reference re Securities Act* 2011 SCC 66, [2011] 3 SCR 837 [7], [85].
[61] ibid [57], [130], [132].
[62] ibid [132]–[133].

Thus, although cooperation is an "animating force" which must induce federal actors to avoid disproportionately upsetting the federation's internal balance,[63] it cannot have the effect of upsetting the division of powers either. This clearly echoes the views of Laskin C.J. in *Reference re Anti-Inflation Act* that "[c]o-operative federalism may be consequential upon a lack of federal legislative power but it is not a ground for denying it".[64] In other words, cooperative federalism may *result* from a lack of legislative power (because an order of government would then have to rely on another one in order to realise a public policy objective), but it is not a ground for denying the existence of such a power.

Forty years later, in *Rogers* Communications, the majority opinion essentially reiterates Laskin C.J.'s view:

> [. . . A]lthough cooperative federalism has become a *principle* that the courts have invoked to provide flexibility for the interpretation and application of the constitutional doctrines relating to the division of powers, such as federal paramountcy and interjurisdictional immunity, it can neither override nor modify the division of powers itself. It cannot be seen as imposing limits on the valid exercise of legislative authority: *Quebec (Attorney General) v. Canada (Attorney General)*, at paras. 17–19. Nor can it support a finding that an otherwise unconstitutional law is valid.[65]

It follows from the above that cooperative federalism, even when it is described as a "principle", does not constitute an autonomous source for challenging the constitutionality of a particular legislative measure. It does not dissolve the constitutional jurisdictions of either level of government into a joint normative magma, nor does it constitutionally transform all de jure exclusive powers into de jure concurrent ones. It merely provides an interpretive tool to bridge the respect for each order of government's powers, on the one hand, and the latitude that they require for implementing public policies in a complex environment, on the other. It maintains constitutional boundaries, but makes them more porous.

It thus appears that judicial resort to interpretive tools in view of facilitating cooperation between federal partners arguably contributes, albeit incrementally and partially, to the transformation of Canada's dualist federal foundations. Yet, as we shall also see, "cooperative federalism" has limited normative teeth, which begs the question: Is cooperative federalism a mere mantra in the Supreme Court's discourse?

---

[63] *Canadian Western Bank v Alberta* 2007 SCC 22, [2007] 2 SCR 3; *Reference re Assisted Human Reproduction Act* 2010 SCC 61, [2010] 3 SCR 457.

[64] *Reference re Anti-Inflation Act* [1976] 2 SCR 373, 421. The statement is actually clearer in the French version: "Le fédéralisme coopératif peut résulter d'une absence de pouvoir législatif fédéral, mais il ne peut être invoqué pour le contester".

[65] *Rogers Communications Inc. v Châteauguay (City)* 2016 SCC 23, [2012] 2 SCR 283 [39]. [Emphasis added].

5. The Few Splendours and Many Miseries of Cooperative Federalism as a Normative Principle

Although the Canadian federation's daily life is rife with cooperative ventures,[66] be they vertical or horizontal, bilateral or multilateral, complex or mundane,[67] the status given to cooperation in the country's judicial discourse is ambiguous at best. Explicit resort to cooperative federalism is a relatively new phenomenon in Canadian constitutional law as is the reference to the principle of federalism at large.[68] In all likelihood, the emphasis that has long been placed on jurisdictional exclusivity in Canadian constitutional law has had the effect of restraining judicial impulses to invoke cooperative federalism. However, the decreasing importance of the dynamic of "watertight compartments" between the two orders of government has led to the emergence of a new, and competing, representation valuing their complementarity. This, in turn, paved the way to an increased mobilization of the notion of cooperative federalism in the discourse of the Supreme Court of Canada.

We do not wish to suggest here that courts had ignored the phenomenon of cooperative federalism in the past. Actually, the Supreme Court and its predecessor, the Judicial Committee of the Privy Council,[69] have long ago been called upon to acknowledge the empirical fact of cooperation in Canada's federal context. They first did it without even explicitly referring to the notion of "cooperative federalism", and always more as a question of fact than a question of law.

- **Cooperation as a finding of fact**

As early as 1912, the JCPC (Judicial Committee of the Privy Council) held that in exercising its own powers in relation to streetcars, a province was under no obligation to enter

---

[66] This section draws on these previous texts: J.-F. Gaudreault-DesBiens & J. Leclair, *Provinces, lutte contre la corruption et fédéralisme* (Éditions Thémis, 2016); J.-F. Gaudreault-DesBiens, "Cooperative Federalism in Search of a Normative Justification: Considering the Principle of Federal Loyalty," (2014) 23(4) Constit. Forum 1; J.-F. Gaudreault-DesBiens, "The Ethos of Canadian Aboriginal Law and the Potential Relevance of Federal Loyalty in a Reconfigured Relationship between Aboriginal and Non-Aboriginal Governments: A Thought Experiment," in G. Otis & M. Papillon (eds), *Fédéralisme et gouvernance autochtone/Federalism and Aboriginal Governance*, (Presses de l'Université Laval, 2013) 51.

[67] Marc-Antoine Adam, Josée Bergeron & Marianne Bonnard, "Intergovernmental Relations in Canada: Competing Visions and Diverse Dynamics," in Johanne Poirier, Cheryl Saunders & John Kincaid (eds), *Intergovernmental Relations in Federal Systems: Comparative Structures and Dynamics*, above (n 11) 135–173.

[68] See, generally: Jean-François Gaudreault-DesBiens, "The Federal Principle", above (n 39).

[69] Hereinafter "JCPC."

into an agreement with the federal order to set user rates. [70] However, the Privy Council stated that "(. . .) it cannot be assumed that either body [the provincial Legislature and the Dominion Parliament] will decline to cooperate with the other in a reasonable way to effect an object so much in the interest of both."[71] Although such a finding in no way imposes a formal constitutional duty to cooperate, it can be read as creating a rebuttable presumption of fact—not law—that orders of government will cooperate in the interest of effective and coordinated policy-making.

To say the least, such a timid endorsement of cooperative federative does not lead us very far. Yet, in the 1920s, the JCPC appeared ready to embrace cooperative federalism. But again, cooperation was merely deemed necessary to achieve the objective of an impugned federal statute in the absence of any federal power to enact it.[72] Thus, the JCPC's observations regarding cooperation did not stem from some strong adhesion to cooperative federalism as a normative principle. Rather, the Privy Council seemed simply to take stock of a practical necessity. It suggested that concerted action is sometimes needed to resolve problems that have an intergovernmental dimension, or that result from a jurisdictional overlap.[73]

Similarly, and more recently, the Supreme Court held that the voluntary harmonisation of environmental evaluation processes constituted a manifestation of cooperative federalism. By so doing, the Supreme Court acknowledged a fact; it did not iterate a normative principle.[74]

In other words, courts have noted concrete intergovernmental cooperation, and acknowledged its practical necessity, but have not necessarily drawn normative conclusions from this acknowledgement. At most, as we saw in the previous section, courts have resorted to cooperative federalism to shield collaborative schemes from challenges raised by third parties. They do so, however, without offering structured normative justification and reasoning.

- **Cooperative federalism does not curb the potential for unilateral action**

High courts have also been forced to respond to challenges questioning the constitutionality of various forms of unilateral actions which may impose negative externalities on others, or simply affect their interests, arguably the very anti-thesis of cooperative federalism. Here again, the underlying current of strong unilateralism, as permitted by a dualist federal structure, is clearly visible, despite another current favouring cooperation.

---

[70] *City of Montreal v Montreal Street Railway* [1912] AC 333, 345 (JCPC).
[71] ibid 346.
[72] *Re Board of Commerce* [1922] 1 AC 191, 201 (JCPC).
[73] See also *Reference re Validity of the Combines Investigation Act and of s. 498 of the Criminal Code* [1929] SCR 409, 413.
[74] *Québec (A.G.) v Moses* 2010 SCC 17, [2010] 1 SCR 557 [29].

Some of these cases had momentous constitutional consequences. One is the 1981 *Patriation Reference*,[75] in which the Supreme Court had to examine the constitutionality of a federal attempt to unilaterally patriate the Canadian Constitution from the United Kingdom in the absence of any pre-existing amending formula. The reference dealt with the normative consequences to be drawn from the federal structure of the country. The Court opined that although the federal government's initiative could be upheld on the basis of the *law* of the Constitution, it failed to respect a constitutional convention which required a substantial degree of provincial consent for the contemplated amendment as it affected federal-provincial powers.[76] The reason for such a convention was found to be the federal principle.[77]

The Court's advisory opinion in the *Patriation Reference* contributes to an understanding of the constitutionally problematic nature of unilateral changes, whether these result from federal or provincial initiatives, when these changes affect either the federal nature of central institutions such as Parliament,[78] or the political compromise on which Canada had been founded and which could not unilaterally be altered by a single province.[79]

That being said, certain cases deserve particular attention, as they send mixed signals as to what extent normative consequences can flow from the fact of cooperation, or lack thereof, in Canada's federal system. One such case directly addresses the scope of Parliament's unilateral and discretionary power to declare works that would normally fall under provincial competencies to be to "the general advantage of Canada".[80] Such a declaration has the effect of permanently transferring the legislative competence over some infrastructure or undertaking to the federal order. This "declaratory power" was used rather intensively in the early years of Confederation, and decried as an uncontrolled tool of centralisation.[81]

In *Ontario Hydro*, the majority seemed inclined to give some legal status to a principle of political morality limiting the ways in which an undisputed constitutional power can be exercised, which is reminiscent of holdings made in other federations on the basis of the doctrine of federal loyalty.[82] Yet, in retrospect, the actual influence of *Ontario*

---

[75]   *Re: Resolution to amend the Constitution* [1981] 1 SCR 753.

[76]   In a subsequent case, the Court did not find that Québec had to be included in the assessment of "substantial" provincial consent, despite a historic practice in which its approval was always obtained prior to petition to Westminster: *Re: Objection by Quebec to a Resolution to amend the Constitution* [1982] 2 SCR 793, 814.

[77]   *Re: Resolution to amend the Constitution* [1981] 1 SCR 753, 905.

[78]   *Reference Re Legislative Authority of the Parliament of Canada in Relation to the Upper House* [1980] 1 SCR 54; see also *Reference re Senate Reform* 2014 SCC 32, [2014] 1 SCR 704.

[79]   *Attorney General of Quebec v Blaikie et al.* [1979] 2 SCR 1016.

[80]   Section 92(10)(c) *Constitution Act, 1867*.

[81]   Andrée Lajoie, *Le pouvoir déclaratoire du Parlement* (Les Presses de l'Université de Montréal, 1969).

[82]   See: J.-F. Gaudreault-DesBiens, "The Ethos of Canadian Aboriginal Law and the Potential Relevance of Federal Loyalty in a Reconfigured Relationship between Aboriginal and Non-Aboriginal Governments: A Thought Experiment," above (n 66) and Poirier, 'Souveraineté parlementaire', above (n 4) 88–102.

Hydro has been rather limited with regard to the judicial review of the manner in which the uncontested holder of a constitutional competence may or may not exercise it. This is hardly surprising in light of a seminal case rendered just two years prior to *Ontario Hydro*, in which the very principle of federalism was unanimously hollowed. The *Canada Assistance Plan Reference* dealt with a unilateral change to the federal government's financial commitments to recipient provinces prior to the end of the agreement providing for such funding.[83] This case epitomizes the Supreme Court's staunch refusal to tangibly revisit the principle of parliamentary supremacy in view of the principle of federalism, and to acknowledge that the constitutional context in which the former operates in Canada is substantially different from that in which it operates in the United Kingdom, from which it originates. A substantial difference primarily lies, of course, in the fact that Canada is a federation, a crucial variable which the Court treated as if it were of no relevance. Moreover, the idea that recipient provinces, which had counted on federal installments in planning their budget, could entertain legitimate expectations as to the continuation of such installments for the duration of the agreement had no impact on the case's outcome. Nor was the Court ready to impose, on the basis of federalism (or cooperative federalism, for instance), any procedural obligation upon the federal executive—at least when it is acting in the legislative process—either to consult the provinces negatively affected by Parliament's legislation, or to better take into consideration their interests.[84]

Even without calling into question the power of the federal Parliament to alter its legislation concerning financial assistance to provinces, the Court could have considered imposing upon it additional requirements as to the manner in which it was exercising its power. In other contexts, this would be considered to be analogous to an "abuse of right" or to an "unconstitutional use of a constitutional competence."[85] It could have done so, for example, by forcing the government in question to reconsider the timeline for the implementation of its new policy so as to reduce to a reasonable extent the significant negative externalities caused by the policy change examined in the case at bar. By so doing, parliamentary supremacy would have been respected, and only some of its effects would have been postponed for a limited period of time. As it is, the Court did

---

[83] *Reference Re Canada Assistance Plan* [1991] 2 SCR 525. See also: *Québec (A.G.) v Moses* 2010 SCC 17, [2010] 1 SCR 557.

[84] The Court simply stated that no doctrine of legitimate expectation could limit the freedom of action of the executive *when it is introducing legislation*, as was the case in the factual context of the reference. Indeed although the provincial obligations deriving from the arrangement were contained in an intergovernmental agreement, the actual funding formula was included in a federal act, which Parliament was unilaterally modifying. One of us has argued elsewhere that this rejection of the idea that legislators may have some obligation to take into consideration the legitimate expectations of other parties, grounded in a maximalist conception of parliamentary sovereignty, may not necessarily extend to the Executive when it is not an actor in the legislative process: Poirier, "Souveraineté parlementaire", above (n 4) 92–94.

[85] See, by analogy, Laurent Eck, *L'abus de droit en droit constitutionnel* (L'Harmattan 2010) and Patrick Peeters, "Le principe de la loyauté fédérale: une métamorphose radicale," (1994) Administration publique (Belgium) 239, 241.

not even want to curb the Parliament's unilateral capacity in view of the federal context in which it was acting.[86] What may be even more surprising is that, following the *Quebec Secession Reference* in 1998, the Court has not even considered (re)interpreting the unwritten principle of parliamentary sovereignty in light of the principle of (cooperative) federalism.[87]

The Court's blindness to Canada's federal structure and context, and to the division of internal sovereignty that characterizes it, arguably amounts to condoning future clashes of absolute parliamentary sovereignties, provincial and federal. It entrenches even more firmly the dualist—or non-cooperative—nature of Canadian federalism, from a legal standpoint.[88]

The 2015 long-gun registry case clearly echoes and amplifies that logic.[89] The Court had to examine a provincial challenge to the destruction by the federal government of the long-gun registry it had previously established.[90] The Court held that the principle of cooperative federalism does not prevent the lawful holder of a plenary constitutional power from exercising that power in the way it sees fit, and this, even when that exercise frustrates policies promoted by another government, or imposes upon it unwanted negative externalities. In that case, Quebec was seeking to retrieve data collected about firearms on its territory in order to create its own registry, after the destruction of the federal one.

This case represented a true test for the principle of cooperative federalism. Would the Supreme Court decide to give it some muscle by transforming it into a full-fledged normative principle from which tangible legal consequences could flow? Could the exercise of an otherwise plenary constitutional power be, in some circumstances, submitted to broader structural limitations, notably emanating from the principle of federalism? Could parliamentary sovereignty be restricted so as to integrate in legal analysis federalism-related concerns, and this, beyond the formal division of powers? Implicitly, but still rather clearly, the Supreme Court answered these underlying questions in

---

[86] Another potential positivist justification for this state of law, that is, that one part of the constitution (federalism) cannot modify another part of the constitution (parliamentary sovereignty)—see *New Brunswick Broadcasting Co. v Nova Scotia (Speaker of the Legislative Assembly)* [1993] 1 SCR 319—would also hardly be intellectually satisfying. Since the *Secession Reference*, it is arguable that these principles should be interpreted in a dialogical manner. But even this, the Court seems to have rejected. See discussion of the Long-Gun Registry case where the Court refuses to interpret the principle of parliamentary sovereignty in light of the principle of federalism (and vice versa): Poirier, "Souveraineté parlementaire," above (n 4) 119–122.

[87] *Québec (A.G.) v Canada (A.G.)* 2015 SCC 14, [2015] 1 SCR 693; on this see Poirier, "Souveraineté parlementaire," above (n 4) 119–122.

[88] Interestingly, the need to adapt principles of British constitutional law to a federal environment was emphasized by the Supreme Court itself in *Aetna Financial Services Ltd. v Feigelman* [1985] 1 SCR 2 (SCC) [34]–[35], and reiterated by La Forest J. in both *Morguard* [1990] 3 SCR 1077 and *Hunt*, [1993] 4 SCR 289. Equally interestingly, these cases are not cited in *Reference Re Canada Assistance Plan*, rendered in 1991.

[89] *Québec (A.G.) v Canada (A.G.)* 2015 SCC 14, [2015] 1 SCR 693.

[90] A major disagreement between the majority of five and the minority of four judges turned on a question of fact: whether the registry and the data it contained had been the result of a federal-provincial partnership, or not.

the negative. In the end, despite the rhetoric of cooperative federalism in which most recent constitutional analysis basks, the majority of the Court resorted to a traditional dualist vision of federalism, one which maximises the unilateral power of each order of government when at least one party does not wish (or no longer wishes) to cooperate. The normative force of "cooperative federalism", understood as a shield against third party challenges, vanishes when opposition occurs between the orders of government themselves.

Actually, the Court's infatuation with cooperative federalism in the last decade or so, as discussed in Section 4, did not change its traditional position, according to which this concept could, at best, be relied upon as an interpretive principle in litigation involving the different orders of government in the Canadian federation. In doing so, the Supreme Court's case law has implicitly rejected at least the potential normative effect of the principle of cooperative federalism. First, the "principle" of cooperative federalism certainly cannot prevail over the formal provisions governing the distribution of powers. Second, it can hardly serve as a tool to monitor the way the holders of formal constitutional powers exercise them.[91] Finally, it appears that no inherent, federalism-based duty to cooperate exists, subject to the narrowly construed federal comity that may exceptionally arise in certain contexts.

The long-gun registry case provided the Supreme Court with an opportunity to revisit its traditional stance on the interplay between federalism and parliamentary sovereignty, a challenge that the Court refused to take on. As a result, the federal principle remains first and foremost an interpretive tool,[92] and the status of the "principle" of cooperative federalism is even more ambiguous, with all the inconsistencies or contradictions that may flow from such ambiguity. In practice, this risks turning cooperative federalism into a mere interpretive principle open to opportunistic appropriations by judicial and political actors.

6. CONCLUSION

It is fair to say that cooperative federalism, when envisaged from a normative standpoint, remains largely un-conceptualised in the law of Canadian federalism. The Supreme Court's reluctance to anchor it to a broader normative justification—federal loyalty could have provided one—has certainly not helped in this respect. Can this be attributed to an archetypical common law atavism of refusing to decide cases on the basis of general principles, and to remain faithful to precedents? Perhaps. However, in other areas of constitutional law, such as human rights protection, the same Supreme

---

[91] *Reference Re Canada Assistance Plan*, [1991] 2 SCR 525. See also Poirier, 'Souveraineté parlementaire', above (n 4).

[92] J.-F. Gaudreault-Desbiens, "The Federal Principle," above (n 39) 94.

Court has not shied away from general principles, from sometimes distancing itself from its own precedents, and from showing a great deal of legal creativity.

Could it be that the Court is more conservative when dealing with the institutional dimensions of Canadian constitutional law; that despite its endorsement of cooperative federalism allowing more legislative and executive overlap, the Court cannot negate the federation's fundamentally dualist structure?[93] These are plausible hypotheses which, however, are not entirely satisfying from the standpoint of the normative potential of cooperative federalism. In any event, the governance of Canada could arguably benefit from a better alignment of the country's constitutional law with the empirical evolution of the federation, an evolution which the Supreme Court itself has largely contributed to by facilitating legislative overlap and administrative normative networks. In the meantime, the Court's case law still embraces two divergent—and sometimes clearly competing—conceptions of federalism.

Bibliography

Secondary sources

Adam, Marc-Antoine, Josée Bergeron and Marianne Bonnard, "Intergovernmental Relations in Canada: Competing Visions and Diverse Dynamics," in Johanne Poirier, Cheryl Saunders and John Kincaid (eds), *Intergovernmental Relations in Federal Systems: Comparative Structures and Dynamics* (Oxford University Press 2015) 440, 135–173

Brouillet, Eugénie, "Le fédéralisme et la Cour suprême du Canada: quelques réflexions sur le principe d'exclusivité des pouvoirs", [2010] 3 *Revue québécoise de droit constitutionnel* 1

Gaudreault-DesBiens, Jean-François, "The 'Federal Principle' and the Legacy of the *Patriation* and *Quebec Veto* References," (2011) 54 SCLR 78

Gaudreault-DesBiens, Jean-François and Jean Leclair, *Provinces, lutte contre la corruption et fédéralisme* (Éditions Thémis 2016)

Gaudreault-DesBiens, Jean-François, "Cooperative Federalism in Search of a Normative Justification: Considering the Principle of Federal Loyalty," (2014) 23(4) Constit.Forum 1

Gaudreault-DesBiens, Jean-François, "The Ethos of Canadian Aboriginal Law and the Potential Relevance of Federal Loyalty in a Reconfigured Relationship between Aboriginal and Non-Aboriginal Governments: A Thought Experiment," in G. Otis and M. Papillon (eds), *Fédéralisme et gouvernance autochtone/Federalism and Aboriginal Governance*, (Presses de l'Université Laval 2013)

Hueglin, Thomas O. and Alan Fenna, *Comparative Federalism: A Systematic Inquiry* (2nd edn, University of Toronto Press 2015)

Leclair, Jean, "The Supreme Court of Canada's Understanding of Federalism: Efficiency at the Expense of Diversity", (2003) 28 Queen's L.J. 411–423

---

[93] This may explain the Québec Court of Appeal's conclusion that a complex intergovernmental scheme regarding the regulation of securities violated the parliamentary sovereignty of some provinces and was thus unconstitutional: see *In the Matter of the Reference of the Government of Quebec in virtue of Order in Council 642-2015 Concerning the Constitutionality of the Implementation of pan-Canadian Securities Regulation*, 500-09-025430-158, May 10, 2017 (Québec Court of Appeal).

Pigeon, Louis-Philippe, "The Meaning of Provincial Autonomy" (1951) 29 *Canadian Bar Rev.* 1126–1135

Poirier, Johanne and Cheryl Saunders, "Conclusion: Comparative Experience of Intergovernmental Relations in Federal Systems" in Johanne Poirier, Cheryl Saunders and John Kincaid (eds), *Intergovernmental Relations in Federal Systems: Comparative Structures and Dynamics* (Oxford University Press 2015) 440

Poirier, Johanne, "Les ententes intergouvernementales dans les régimes fédéraux: aux confins du droit et du non-droit" in Jean-François Gaudreault-Desbiens & Fabien Gélinas (eds), *Le fédéralisme dans tous ses états: Gouvernance, identité et méthodologie/The States and Moods of Federalism: Governance, Identity and Methodology* (Carswell/Bruylant 2005), 441

Poirier, Johanne "Intergovernmental Agreements in Canada: At the Cross-roads between Law and Politics," in Peter Meekison, Hamish Telford and Harvey Lazar (eds), *Reconsidering the Institutions of Canadian Federalism, Canada: The State of the Federation 2002* (Institute of Intergovernmental Relations 2004)

Poirier, Johanne "Une source paradoxale du droit constitutionnel canadien: les ententes intergouvernementales," (2009) 1 RQDI http://www.aqdc.org/volumes/pdf/poirier-une_source_ paradoxale.pdf

Poirier, Johanne, "Le partage des compétences et les relations intergouvernementales: la situation au Canada" in Fournier, Bernard & Reuchamps, Min (dir), *Le fédéralisme en Belgique et au Canada: Un dialogue comparatif*, de Boeck, 2009, pp. 103–118

Ryder, Bruce, "The Demise and Rise of the Classical Paradigm in Canadian Federalism: Promoting Autonomy for the Provinces and First Nations," (1991) 36 McGill LJ 308

Ryder, Bruce, "Equal Autonomy in Canadian Federalism: The Continuing Search for Balance in the Interpretation of the Division of Powers" (2011), 54 *S.C.L.R.* (2d), 565–600

Schütze, Robert, *From Dual to Cooperative Federalism: The Changing Structures of European Law* (Oxford University Press 2009)

Simeon, Richard, *Federal-Provincial Diplomacy: the Making of Recent Policy in Canada* (University of Toronto Press 2006)

Watts, Ronald L., *Comparing Federal Systems* (3rd edn, McGill-Queen's University Press 2008)

Case Law

A.-G. of Nova-Scotia v A.-G. of Canada [1951] SCR 31

Boucher v Stelco [2005] SCC 64

Canadian Western Bank v Alberta [2007] SCC 22, [2007] 2 SCR 3

Coughlin v Ontario Highway Transport Board [1968] SCR 569, 583–584

Fédération des producteurs de volailles du Québec v Pelland [2005] CSC 20, [2005] 1 SCR 292

In the Matter of the Reference of the Government of Quebec in virtue of Order in Council 642-2015 Concerning the Constitutionality of the Implementation of pan-Canadian Securities Regulation, 500-09-025430-158, May 10, 2017 (Quebec Court of Appeal)

P.E.I. Potato Marketing Board v Willis [1952] 2 SCR 392

Québec (A.G.) v Canada (A.G.) [2015] SCC 14, [2015] 1 SCR 693 (Abolition of Firearms Registry)

Reference re Anti-Inflation Act [1976] 2 SCR 373

Reference re Assisted Human Reproduction Act [2010] SCC 61, [2010] 3 SCR 457

Reference Re Canada Assistance Plan [1991] 2 SCR 525

Reference re Securities Act [2011] SCC 66, [2011] 3 SCR 837

Rogers Communications Inc. v Châteauguay (City) [2016] SCC 23, [2012] 2 SCR 283

CHAPTER 19

....

KEY DOCTRINES
IN CANADIAN LEGAL
FEDERALISM

....

EUGÉNIE BROUILLET &
BRUCE RYDER*

1. INTRODUCTION

AT the heart of Canada's constitutional design is its federal nature. The preamble to the *Constitution Act, 1867* announces the colonies' "Desire to be federally united into one Dominion". As the Privy Council put it in a classic formulation:

> The object of the Act was neither to weld the provinces into one, nor to subordinate provincial governments to a central authority, but to create a federal government in which they should all be represented, entrusted with the exclusive administration of affairs in which they had a common interest, each province retaining its independence and autonomy.[1]

The Supreme Court of Canada expressed itself in similar fashion in the *Secession Reference*, describing federalism as a "central organizational theme of our Constitution".[2] As one of the fundamental principles underlying the written Constitution, the federal principle can be used to guide the courts in the interpretation and application of the provisions of the constitutional text, and to fill any gaps in the text.[3]

---

* Eugénie Brouillet, Dean and Full Professor, Faculty of Law, Université Laval; Bruce Ryder, Associate Professor, Osgoode Hall Law School, York University.
[1] *Liquidators of the Maritime Bank of Canada v. Receiver-General of New Brunswick*, [1892] A.C. 437, 441.
[2] *Reference re Secession of Quebec*, [1998] 2 S.C.R. 217, [57].
[3] *Ibid* [53].

The creation of a federation required the adoption of a written constitution dividing legislative powers between the federal and provincial legislatures. The *Constitution Act, 1867* thus contains a number of provisions allocating law-making powers. The most important of these are sections 91 and 92, which set out two lists of subject matters that fall within the exclusive legislative domain of the federal Parliament and the provincial legislatures respectively. The courts have the responsibility of interpreting these provisions and thus determining the boundaries of the law-making powers of Canadian legislative bodies. When legislation is challenged on division-of-powers grounds, it is the courts which decide whether the measure falls within the enacting legislature's power, and is thus valid or invalid. Court rulings in federal matters have the same force and the same normative value as the constitutional texts. They are binding on all federal, provincial, and local political organs.

The appropriate division of sovereign legislative power and the validity of particular statutes passed by our elected assemblies are thus hotly contested issues with high stakes. The stakes are even higher because of the enormous difficulty of amending the Canadian Constitution. Constitutional interpretation by the judiciary becomes, by default, the preferred way of modifying the legal regime. It is essentially up to the courts, and ultimately the Supreme Court, to adapt the constitutional texts to new societal conditions. The gradual evolution in legal doctrine that results, less easily perceptible and less spectacular than formal amendments, nevertheless has had a determining influence.

Judicial decisions interpreting the constitutional division of legislative powers have attracted criticisms for being overly centralizing, or overly decentralizing, or for stifling the democratic expression of local or national sovereignty. In recent decades, the Supreme Court of Canada has responded to these concerns by favouring a "modern" or "co-operative" approach to federalism that interprets both federal and provincial legislative powers generously, and tolerates a high degree of overlap and interplay between them. On this vision, the primary responsibility for maintaining a healthy federation rests with political actors, especially those involved in intergovernmental relations. The Court sees its role as interpreting the Constitution in a manner that facilitates co-operation, maintains the federal balance, and provides equal protection to the autonomy of each order of government.[4] Despite these general statements highlighting the normative implications of the principle of federalism, the jurisprudence of Canada's highest court tends to have some asymmetric effects that favour the federal government.

We will first discuss the principles the courts have employed when interpreting the power-conferring provisions of the *Constitution Act, 1867*. These principles are used to determine the scope of the heads of legislative power allocated to the federal Parliament and the provincial legislatures.

We will then turn to a discussion of the principles used to determine the constitutional status of legislation challenged on division-of-powers grounds. These principles relate to three general inquiries posed by Canadian courts: (1) whether the challenged

---

[4] See, e.g., *Reference re Secession of Quebec*, above (n 2) [58]; *Reference re Securities Act*, [2011] 3 S.C.R. 837, [7]; *Reference re Assisted Human Reproduction Act*, [2010] 3 S.C.R. 457, [43], [74]; *Canadian Western Bank v Alberta*, [2007] 2 S.C.R. 3, [24].

law falls within the heads of power allocated to the enacting legislature's jurisdiction, and is therefore valid; (2) if so, whether the law is applicable in the circumstances or has to be read down to prevent it from impairing matters at the heart of the other level of government's exclusive jurisdiction; and (3) if the law is valid and applicable, whether it is operative or has to be suspended to avoid a conflict with a valid and applicable law passed by the other level of government.[5]

2. Principles Used in the Interpretation of Legislative Powers

As is the case with other parts of the Constitution, the power-conferring provisions of the *Constitution Act, 1867* are drafted in sparse and open-ended language. When disputes have arisen regarding the scope of particular legislative powers, the courts have faced the difficult task of assigning precise meaning to the words used in the text. For example, what is the scope of provincial jurisdiction to pass laws in relation to "property and civil rights" (s.92(13)) or "private and local matters" (s.92(16))? Or of Parliament's jurisdiction to pass laws in relation to "peace, order and good government" (opening language of section 91), "trade and commerce" (section 91(2)), or "criminal law and procedure" (section 91(27))? In answering these questions, the courts have been guided by the text of the provisions in question, as well as any clues that can be divined from associated provisions of the text. They have also drawn on historical understandings of the words used in the text and on fundamental norms or principles that undergird the Constitution as a whole. Text, history, structure, and principle have formed a rich interpretive tapestry that has guided the courts' constitutional jurisprudence.

The courts had to adapt one of the key principles of the UK Constitution, the principle of parliamentary sovereignty, to the Canadian federal reality where no legislative body has unlimited law-making powers. They did so by creating the principle of exhaustiveness, the notion that when the powers of Parliament and the provincial legislatures are combined, they are exhaustive or complete. The courts thus interpret the legislative powers as a whole so as to avoid any gaps by ensuring the totality of legislative power is possessed by Canadian legislatures.

When confronted with a dispute about the meaning of a particular head of legislative power, the courts have had to consider the words used in the text to define that power,

---

[5] We have set out these three inquiries into validity, applicability, and operability in the traditional and logical order in which the courts analyze them. However, as we will discuss below, in *Canadian Western Bank, ibid*, the Supreme Court indicated that it did not favour an "intensive reliance" [47] on the interjurisdictional immunity doctrine, which leads to a finding of inapplicability. The Court noted that a conclusion that a law is inapplicable "should in general be reserved for situations already covered by precedent". [77] If that's not the case, a court will generally be justified in "proceeding directly to the consideration" of its operability. [78]

but they have also considered its place in the text as a whole, as well as any foundational norms or historical evidence that should guide the meaning to be accorded to the text. A good example is the Privy Council decision in *Citizens Insurance v Parsons*,[6] which remarkably is still a leading case on legislative powers in relation to economic regulation almost a century and a half later. At issue in that case was whether the Ontario legislature had legislative jurisdiction to regulate the insurance industry in the province. Was the law at issue in relation to "property and civil rights", and thus validly enacted by the provincial legislature pursuant to section 92(13)? Or was it a law in relation to "trade and commerce", and thus an invalid invasion of Parliament's jurisdiction pursuant to section 91(2)? In defining these two heads of power for the first time, Sir Montague Smith articulated the principle of "mutual modification", the idea that the broad language in which a power is described in the text needs to be modified or limited to minimize conflict with other legislative powers. "It becomes obvious", he wrote, "as soon as an attempt is made to construe the general terms in which the classes of subjects of ss 91 and 92 are described, that both sections and other parts of the Act must be looked at to ascertain whether language of a general nature must not by necessary implication or reasonable intendment be modified and limited".[7] Drawing on the principle of mutual modification, as well as other provisions of the text and historical understandings,[8] the Privy Council concluded that the framers of the Constitution had intended that a broad meaning should be given to the phrase "property and civil rights". Sir Montague Smith held that the regulation of businesses within a province fell within provincial jurisdiction, whereas the regulation of international and interprovincial trade fell within federal jurisdiction.

The principle of "mutual modification" has helped shape the division of legislative jurisdiction in many other contexts. For example, the courts have reconciled federal jurisdiction in relation to "penitentiaries" [s.91(28)] and provincial jurisdiction in relation to "prisons" [s.92(6)] by limiting federal legislative responsibility to more serious offenders (defined as those sentenced to incarceration for two years or more).

Although the text, historical understandings, and fundamental norms such as the principle of federalism have influenced the interpretation of the division of powers ever since Confederation, difficult questions arise whenever new issues not anticipated by the framers must be resolved. The need to adapt the constitutional text to meet changing conditions in society cannot be questioned—the very preservation of the constitutional order depends on this ability. As formal constitutional amendments have been

---

[6] *Citizens Insurance Co. of Canada v Parsons* (1881), 7 A. C. 96 [hereinafter *Parsons*].

[7] *Ibid* at 110.

[8] Sir Montague Smith pointed out that if the federal "trade and commerce" power included the power to regulate all contractual transactions, then the inclusion of a specific kind of contract in s. 91, "bills of exchange and promissory notes" in s. 91(18), would have been unnecessary. *Ibid* at 110. Moreover, he noted that the words "property" and "civil rights" were used in a broad sense in s. 94 of the *Constitution Act, 1867*, as well as in the *Quebec Act, 1774* to restore the civil law as the private law of New France. Following these textual and historical guides to meaning, he found there was "no reason for holding" that these words should be given a different and narrower meaning in s. 92(13). *Parsons, ibid* at 111.

so difficult to achieve in Canada, the burden of adapting the Constitution to new social realities has fallen particularly heavily on the judiciary.

Thus, although history plays an important role in constitutional interpretation, the courts have rejected the idea that the meaning of the Constitution is "frozen in time" by the framers' "original intent" (even if a single intent could be ascertained). Rather, the courts have embraced a principle of progressive interpretation, one that allows the meaning of constitutional language to evolve over time. Indeed, the idea of the Constitution as a "living tree" is "the most powerful and enduring metaphor in modern Canadian constitutional jurisprudence".[9] The metaphor was first articulated in *Edwards v A.G. Canada* (the "Persons Case") when the Privy Council was considering whether women were "persons" eligible for appointment to the Senate pursuant to section 24 of the *Constitution Act, 1867*. Lord Sankey answered in the affirmative, stating that the Act "planted in Canada a living tree capable of growth and expansion within its natural limits".[10] By referencing both natural limits and growth, the Privy Council captured the need to balance original political intent and court-based adaptation. As Vicki Jackson has remarked, the living tree metaphor "suggests that constitutional interpretation is constrained by the past, but not entirely"; "it captures the idea of constraint, the role of text and original understanding in the roots of the constitutional tree and the role of precedent and new developments in its growth".[11]

The Supreme Court of Canada has relied heavily on the principle of progressive interpretation in recent decades when interpreting the Constitution as a whole, including the division of legislative powers. For example, the Court cited the living tree principle when concluding that the word "marriage" in section 91(26) should now encompass same-sex marriage,[12] and the words "unemployment insurance" in section 91(2A) should now include parental and pregnancy leave,[13] even though the understandings of these words at the time of their enactment would have excluded both.

3. THE KEY DOCTRINES

The powers conferred on the national and provincial legislatures by sections 91 and 92 are both described in the text as "exclusive". Defining the meaning of exclusivity has not been easy. Since the birth of the federation, two main trends can be identified in the approach taken by the courts to the principle of exclusivity. The Judicial Committee of

---

[9]   Robert J. Sharpe and Patricia I. McMahon, *The Persons Case: The Origins and Legacy of the Fight for Legal Personhood* (Toronto: University of Toronto Press, 2008), p. 6.

[10]   *Edwards v A.-G. for Canada*, [1930] A.C. 124, p. 136.

[11]   Vicki C. Jackson, "Constitutions as 'Living Trees'? Comparative Constitutional Law and Interpretive Metaphors" (2006) 75 *Fordham L. Rev.* 921–960 at 926.

[12]   *Reference re Same-Sex Marriage*, [2004] 3 S.C.R. 698.

[13]   *Reference re Employment Insurance Act (Can.), ss. 22 and 23*, [2005] 2 S.C.R. 669.

the Privy Council opted for a dualistic approach by seeking to limit overlaps of power between the two orders of government and by preserving each government's sphere of autonomy. The Judicial Committee used the nautical image of "watertight compartments" to illustrate the need to protect the autonomy of each order of government and balance their powers.[14] Beginning in the mid-twentieth century, however, the Supreme Court of Canada gradually moved away from the dualistic stance of the Judicial Committee to embrace a so-called "co-operative" approach to federalism, open to overlapping powers.[15] In a number of decisions, it stated that the principle of exclusive powers was not imperative, and that intergovernmental cooperation was the "dominant tide"[16] of modern federalism. The expressions "flexible", "co-operative", and "modern" federalism are used frequently in its jurisprudence, emphasizing the idea that the separation between the orders of government is not absolute. The Court "should favour, where possible, the ordinary operation of statutes enacted by *both* levels of government. In the absence of conflicting enactments of the other level of government, the Court should avoid blocking the application of measures which are taken to be enacted in furtherance of the public interest".[17] The adoption of a co-operative approach has led to an increase in the number of overlaps between equally valid provincial and federal statutes that then trigger the application of the doctrine of federal paramountcy if they prove incompatible. This will be discussed below.

In pursuit of this co-operative approach, the Supreme Court has affirmed the ability of each order of government to incidentally affect matters under the jurisdiction of the other order when both are legislating in their own area of jurisdiction (incidental effects rule).[18] It considers that certain matters may include both federal and provincial aspects, and it upholds legislation by both orders of government in relation to these matters (double aspect doctrine).[19] It also has maintained the constitutional validity of provisions that overlap with a matter falling under the jurisdiction of the other order of government if they are integrated into an otherwise valid legislative whole (ancillary powers doctrine).[20] We will discuss these doctrines in the first part of the next section.

---

[14] *A.-G. for Canada* v. *A.-G. for Ontario*, [1937] A.C. 326, p. 354, which included Lord Atkin's comment: "while the ship of state now sails on larger ventures and into foreign waters she still retains the watertight compartments which are an essential part of her original structure".

[15] Bruce Ryder, "Equal Autonomy in Canadian Federalism: The Continuing Search for Balance in the Interpretation of the Division of Powers" (2011) 54 *S.C.L.R.* (2d) 565–600.

[16] *Ontario (Attorney General)* v *OPSEU*, [1987] 2 S.C.R. 2, [27].

[17] *Canadian Western Bank* v *Alberta*, above (n 2), [37] and [42]. See also: *Quebec (Attorney General)* v *Canada (Attorney General)*, [2015] 1 S.C.R. 693; *Reference re Securities Act*, above (n 4), [9], [57], [131], [132]; *Reference re Assisted Human Reproduction Act*, above (n 4), [139], [152]; *Quebec (Attorney General)* v *Lacombe*, [2010] 2 S.C.R. 453 [119]; *Chatterjee v Ontario (Attorney General)*, [2009] 1 S.C.R. 624, [32].

[18] See particularly, *Attorney General (Que.)* v *Kellogg's Co. of Canada et al.*, [1978] 2 S.C.R. 211.

[19] *British Columbia (Attorney General)* v *Lafarge Canada Inc.*, [2007] 2 S.C.R. 86, [4].

[20] *General Motors of Canada Ltd.* v *City National Leasing*, [1989] 1 S.C.R. 641; *Quebec (Attorney General)* v *Lacombe*, above (n 17).

In the second part, we will analyse two principles that operate as limits on co-operative federalism, namely, the interjurisdictional immunity and the paramountcy doctrines.

A. The Pith and Substance Doctrine

Any constitutional challenge to the distribution of legislative powers begins with an examination of the validity of the contested laws or legislative provisions.[21] A law is valid when it falls within the powers (*intra vires*) of the legislative body that enacted it; in other cases it is invalid, or *ultra vires*. The validity of a law essentially turns on whether it qualifies under the powers conferred respectively on the federal Parliament and the provincial legislatures. The cardinal principle for classifying laws for this purpose is the "pith and substance" principle. We will look, below, at some of the supplementary notions it has engendered, and the concepts with which it combines to create a solution in specific cases.

Seeking the pith and substance of contested legislation involves an examination of its true nature, or essential character, in other words, identifying the "matter" to which it essentially applies, using the terminology of the introductory lines of sections 91 and 92. This characterization process must determine, as closely as possible, the true nature of the legislation. An overly broad or general formulation makes it difficult to attach to a specific area of jurisdiction.[22] As a result, "[l]ogically, except in cases of highly specific powers, the pith and substance of a provision or a statute will be less general than that of the power itself".[23]

In characterizing a statute's pith and substance, the courts are guided by the object of the law, as well as the effects it produces. The object is the goal or objective targeted by the legislative measure; the effects are its practical or legal consequences.[24] The focus is on the actual objective of the legislation, rather than its stated or apparent objective. It must not be "disguised" or colourable legislation.[25] Last, it is the law's original objective that counts, in the sense that the purpose of a given law cannot change over time.[26]

To identify the pith and substance of a contested law, it is necessary to focus on what it is about rather than all of its potential effects—in other words, at what it targets directly, and not what it could affect incidentally. What counts is the law's "dominant purpose".[27] Conversely, the secondary goals or effects of the law do not influence its validity.[28] The

---

[21] Henri Brun, Guy Tremblay and Eugénie Brouillet, eds, *Droit constitutionnel* (6e éd, Yvon Blais, 2014) pp. 462–472.

[22] *Reference re Assisted Human Reproduction Act*, above (n 4) (four judges uncontradicted on this point).

[23] *Ibid*, [par. 190].

[24] *Reference re Employment Insurance Act (Can.), sect. 22 and 23*, above (n 13), p. 679.

[25] *Re Upper Churchill Water Reversion Act*, [1984] 1 S.C.R. 297.

[26] *R. v Big M Drug Mart Ltd.*, [1985] 1 S.C.R. 295, p. 335.

[27] *Global Securities Corp. v British Columbia (Securities Commission)*, [2000] 1 S.C.R. 494.

[28] *Reference re Same-Sex Marriage*, above (n 12), p. 714.

logic of this approach is based on the impossibility of defining a clear line between jurisdictions. For example, the federal Parliament cannot legislate effectively on copyright if
it is unable to touch on the fields of property and civil rights, and the provinces cannot
legislate effectively on civil law if they are barred from touching incidentally on the status of foreigners.

In determining the pith and substance of a law, the courts seek its meaning using the
ordinary rules of interpretation.[29] They may also examine extrinsic evidence to assess
the factual context the legislation sought to address. Reports filed by commissions of
inquiry, white papers, scientific studies, reports by parliamentary committees, and even
transcripts of parliamentary debates may be considered.[30] However, the reliability and
weight given to parliamentary debates or political statements is limited.[31] The extrinsic
evidence of most interest in connection with the distribution of powers is the evidence
which, with regard to all the factual circumstances that led to the passage of the law,
allows its true objective to be determined, beyond all disguise and appearance.[32]

– *The double aspect doctrine*

As early as 1883,[33] the Judicial Committee of the Privy Council explained that "subjects"
could have a double aspect, in other words both a federal and a provincial aspect. This
occurs most frequently with subjects or matters that were not specifically allocated by
the *Constitution Act, 1867*, such as highway traffic, games and lotteries, youth protection,
and waterfront protection.[34] As the Supreme Court has put it: "This concept, known
as the double aspect doctrine, allows for the *concurrent application* of both federal and
provincial legislation, but it does not create *concurrent jurisdiction* over a matter".[35] For
example, the Court has found that nude dancing has a double aspect, one federal (the
criminal aspect) and the other provincial (the regulation of entertainment in association with liquor permits).[36]

A given law does not generally have a double aspect; once its pith and substance has
been determined, it either comes under or does not come under the jurisdiction of the
level of government that passed it. In addition, in our view it is important not to apply
the double aspect doctrine each time a few aspects of a matter could come under the

---

[29] See *Attorney General for Ontario v Attorney General for Canada*, [1894] A.C. 189, pp. 198–199; and
Proprietary Articles Trade Association v A.-G. Canada, [1931] A.C. 310, p. 317 et seq.

[30] *RJR-MacDonald Inc. v Canada (Attorney General)*, [1995] 3 S.C.R. 199, pp. 242–245; *Reference re
Assisted Human Reproduction Act*, above (n 4) [202 et seq] (four judges).

[31] *R. v Morgentaler*, [1993] 3 S.C.R. 463, p. 484.

[32] *R. v Hydro-Québec*, [1997] 3 S.C.R. 213, pp. 309–310.

[33] *Hodge v The Queen*, (1883–1884) 9 A.C. 117, p. 130.

[34] For example, see *O'Grady v Sparling*, [1960] S.C.R. 804, p. 811; *Law Society of British Columbia v
Mangat*, [2001] 3 S.C.R. 113, pp. 142–144; *Siemens v Manitoba (Attorney General)*, [2003] 1 S.C.R. 6, p. 21;
British Columbia (Attorney General) v Lafarge Canada Inc., above (n 19), [4].

[35] *Reference re Securities Act*, above (n 4), par. [66]. See also *Chatterjee v Ontario (Attorney General)*,
above (n 17); *Multiple Access v McCutcheon*, [1982] 2 S.C.R. 161, pp. 181–182.

[36] *Rio Hotel Ltd. v New Brunswick (Liquor Licensing Board)*, [1987] 2 S.C.R. 59.

jurisdiction of the other level of government, as an unbridled application of the doctrine would undermine the principle of exclusiveness that forms the foundation of the distribution of powers in Canada. The Supreme Court has specified that "The double aspect doctrine will apply whenever the contrast between the relative importance of the federal and provincial characteristics of a particular subject matter is not sharp".[37] In short, the double aspect doctrine targets legislative rules responding to different (but potentially overlapping) factual situations, that may be viewed from two different normative standpoints and whose "pith and substance" can be seen as coming under the legislative jurisdiction of either level of government.[38]

- *The incidental effects rule and the ancillary powers doctrine*

Although the distribution of subject matters can be circumscribed with a fair degree of precision in writing, the situation is less clear when it is time to apply the powers to actual real-life situations. The complexity of life in society necessarily involves a degree of overlapping of the exercise of legislative powers between different levels of government in a federation. This is why the Canadian courts have recognized that the federal and provincial legislatures can incidentally affect the powers of the other level of government when legislating in their own areas of jurisdiction.[39] In other words, if the pith and substance of a law is a matter within the enacting legislature's jurisdiction, the courts will not take into account the law's incidental effects on the powers of the other level of government.

However, it is a frequent occurrence for laws passed by one level of government to contain provisions that substantially affect matters under the jurisdiction of the other level, a situation that must be distinguished from the situations giving rise to the application of the "incidental effects rule". The typical case here is a provision whose "pith and substance" exceeds or falls outside the jurisdiction of the level of government that passed it, but whose constitutionality is preserved because of the link between the provision and the valid legislative whole of which it forms a part. This is what the Supreme Court considers a provision giving rise to the application of the "ancillary powers doctrine".[40] The doctrine has, so far, been applied primarily for the benefit of the federal Parliament. The possibility that a provincial provision could be found to be valid under this doctrine remained theoretical until comparatively recently,[41] but was confirmed a number of years ago.[42]

---

[37] *Ibid*, 65.

[38] *Reference re Assisted Human Reproduction Act*, above (n 4) [268 ff] (four judges).

[39] *General Motors of Canada v City National Leasing*, above (n 20) p. 670. In *Attorney General (Que.) v Kellogg's Co. of Canada et al.*, above (n 18), the Supreme Court ruled that Québec's *Consumer Protection Act* was valid even though it incidentally affected the area of television, an exclusive federal power.

[40] *Ibid*.

[41] *Global Securities Corp. v British Columbia (Securities Commission)*, above (n 27) p. 517.

[42] *Quebec (Attorney General) v. Lacombe*, above (n 17), [36], [58] a decision in which the Supreme Court concluded that a provincial provision was invalid because of the lack of a functional connection between the provision and the provincial law concerned.

In determining whether a provision of a law could be upheld by the ancillary powers doctrine, for around one hundred years, the Judicial Committee, followed by the Supreme Court, developed and applied a criterion of necessity: the federal government was required to demonstrate that Parliament's legislative intervention in a given matter under provincial jurisdiction was necessary and in fact indispensable to the effective exercise of one of its own powers. As a result, the traditional jurisprudence did not tolerate any encroachment by the federal Parliament on provincial powers unless its necessity could be shown.[43]

In 1988, the Supreme Court introduced a more flexible test to determine whether an encroachment on the powers of the other level of government was sufficiently integrated into a valid law. The choice of the test to apply depends on the context of the case and the degree of encroachment:

> The required degree of integration increases in proportion to the seriousness of the encroachment. Where the impugned legislation encroaches only slightly on the jurisdiction of the other level of government, a rational, functional connection is required. As the degree of intrusion grows more serious, the required degree of integration tends toward a test of necessity. A particularly serious encroachment will attract a standard of strict necessity.[44]

Applying these and other criteria,[45] the Supreme Court has in all of its majority opinions adopted the functional connection test.[46]

The functional connection approach tends to broaden the domain of federal powers to an inordinate degree, extending the areas of overlapping jurisdiction and multiplying the possibility of conflicting laws. In fact, as will be examined below, a conflict between a federal provision that is found to be valid under the ancillary powers doctrine, on the one hand, and a provincial provision or law that is also valid under the granting of a specific power, on the other, leads to the invocation of the federal paramountcy rule to suspend the operation of the provincial legislation to the extent of the conflict.

– *The principle of subsidiarity*

In the wake of its reliance on a co-operative approach to Canadian federalism, the Supreme Court has invoked the principle of subsidiarity on a number of occasions.[47]

---

[43] *Montreal v Montreal Street Railway*, [1912] A.C. 333; *Regional Municipality of Peel v Mackenzie et al.*, [1982] 2 S.C.R. 9, p.18.

[44] *Quebec (Attorney General) v Lacombe*, above (n 17), [42]. See also *General Motors of Canada v City National Leasing*, above (n 20) pp. 670–672 and *Kirkbi AG v Gestions Ritvik Inc.*, [2005] 3 S.C.R. 302.

[45] See *General Motors of Canada v City National Leasing, ibid*, pp. 671–674. See also *Reference re Assisted Human Reproduction Act*, above (n 4) [128ff] (four judges).

[46] Four judges nevertheless applied the criterion of necessity in *Reference re Assisted Human Reproduction Act ibid*, [275ff].

[47] *114957 Canada Ltée (Spraytech, Société d'arrosage) v Hudson (Town)*, [2001] 2 S.C.R. 241, [3] and [4]; *Canadian Western Bank*, above (n 17), [45]; *Quebec (Attorney General) v Lacombe*, above (n 17), [119]

The Court has defined subsidiarity as "the proposition that law-making and implemen-tation are often best achieved at a level of government that is not only effective, but also closest to the citizens affected and thus most responsive to their needs, to local distinc-tiveness, and to population diversity".[48] The principle aims to ensure that smaller enti-ties in a federation have all the rights and powers they need to regulate their own affairs freely and effectively, while limiting the responsibilities of the larger entities to matters that the smaller entities cannot address alone.

The principle of subsidiarity is not part of the federation's formal constitutional struc-ture. It is not mentioned in the text. In the *Reference re Assisted Human Reproduction Act*, a sharp division between justices of the Supreme Court was apparent. Four jus-tices found that subsidiarity is an "important component"[49] of Canadian federalism, an underlying principle that can help guide the courts in the interpretation and application of the express provisions of the Constitution. In their view, the principle supported the preservation of the provincial sphere of autonomy in the field of assisted human repro-duction and thus a finding that the federal legislative provisions at issue were invalid. The analysis of another group of four justices differed markedly. In their view, "subsid-iarity does not override the division of powers in the *Constitution Act, 1867*", and cannot prevent a level of government from legislating in its areas of competence.[50] These jus-tices would confine the role of the principle of subsidiarity to supporting the validity of provincial legislation in areas of concurrent power subject to federal paramountcy. This approach would neutralize the rebalancing potential that the principle of subsidiarity could bring to the law of Canadian federalism.

The role and status of the principle of subsidiarity in Canadian federalism is not yet clear. Its increasing invocation by members of the Supreme Court suggests that it could play an increasingly prominent role in the future. It certainly has the potential to exert a significant rebalancing influence on the centralizing asymmetries of Canadian federal-ism jurisprudence.

B. The Interjurisdictional Immunity Doctrine

As a result of the liberal and generous invocation of the pith and substance, double aspect and ancillary powers doctrines, the dominant tide of the Supreme Court's modern approach to interpreting the division of powers allows for a great deal of overlap and inter-play between federal and provincial powers. The result is a division-of-powers jurispru-dence aimed at maximizing the democratic space open to the federal Parliament and the

---

(dissenting opinion); and *Reference re Assisted Human Reproduction Act*, above (n 4) [72] (four judges) and [273] (four other judges); *Rogers Communications Inc. v Châteauguay (City)*, 2016 SCC 23, [84], [110] and [116] (concurring opinion of Gascon J.).

   48   *Spraytech*, above (n 47) [3]. See also *Canadian Western Bank*, above (n 4) [45].
   49   *Reference re Assisted Human Reproduction Act*, above (n 4) [183].
   50   *Ibid* [72] per McLachlin CJ.

provincial legislatures when exercising their powers to pass laws within their respective spheres of jurisdiction. However, two interpretive doctrines developed by the courts, the interjurisdictional immunity doctrine and the paramountcy doctrine, function to limit the application and operation of provincial legislation respectively. Because these doctrines are in tension with the Supreme Court's modern, flexible, and co-operative conception of federalism, the Court has stated that they should be applied with restraint.

The interjurisdictional immunity doctrine holds that provincial laws (notably those that are of general application) that are in pith and substance in relation to matters within exclusive provincial jurisdiction, and therefore valid, must nevertheless be read down, or restricted in their application, to the extent necessary to prevent them from impairing matters at the core of federal heads of power. This result applies whether or not the federal Parliament has exercised its power to pass a law in the area. The result of invoking the interjurisdictional immunity doctrine is that the general terms of a provincial statute are "read down" so as not to impair matters at the core of federal jurisdiction. The provincial law otherwise remains valid and applicable.

The doctrine has its origins in rulings that limited the application of valid provincial laws to prevent them from impairing the status or essential operations of federally-incorporated companies.[51] Over the years, this reasoning was extended to grant a similar immunity from the application of valid provincial laws to "works, such as federal railways, things, such as land reserved for the Indians, and persons, such as Indians, who are within the special and exclusive jurisdiction of Parliament" rendering them immune from the application of provincial laws that impair integral and vital elements of federally regulated subjects.[52]

The interjurisdictional immunity doctrine is rooted in the idea of exclusive jurisdiction. Sections 91 and 92 of the *Constitution Act, 1867* confer "exclusive" legislative powers on the federal Parliament and the provincial legislatures. The doctrine is premised on a strong interpretation of the meaning of exclusivity—one that renders the subject matters falling within the exclusive jurisdiction of one level of government immune from impairment by valid laws passed by the other level of government. In *Bell Canada*, a case that represented the high-water mark of the doctrine, and offers the most complete attempt to defend it, Justice Beetz wrote that the exclusive nature of federal and provincial powers in sections 91 and 92 requires that each head of power be assured a "basic, minimum and unassailable content" immune from the application of legislation enacted by the other level of government.[53] In upholding the immunity of a federally-regulated business from the application of a valid Quebec law on occupational health and safety, Justice Beetz observed that labour relations is "an integral and vital part of [Parliament's] primary legislative authority over federal undertakings. If this power is exclusive, it is because the Constitution, which could have been different but is not, expressly specifies this to be the case; and it is because this power is exclusive that it pre-empts that of the

---

[51] *John Deere Plow Co. v Wharton*, [1915] A.C. 330; *Great West Saddlery v The King*, [1921] 2 A.C. 91.
[52] *Bell Canada v Quebec (Commission de la Santé et de la Sécurité du Travail)*, [1988] 1 S.C.R. 749 [21].
[53] *Ibid*, p. 839.

legislatures both as to their legislation of general and specific application, in so far as such laws affect a vital part of a federal undertaking".[54]

The doctrine of interjurisdictional immunity is thus "directed to ensuring that the two levels of government are able to operate without interference in their core areas of exclusive jurisdiction".[55] As the role of the doctrine is to protect the exclusivity of legislative jurisdiction, and federal and provincial heads of power in sections 91 and 92 are both exclusive, the doctrine should be reciprocal, applying equally to protect core elements of federal and provincial powers from impairment. In practice, however, this has not been the case. The Court has resisted attempts to invoke the doctrine to protect the exclusivity of provincial heads of power.[56] As the doctrine has been applied only to federal heads of power, the unprincipled result is a jurisprudence that treats federal heads of power as "more exclusive" than provincial heads of power.

Moreover, the grounding of the doctrine in the idea of exclusivity is difficult to square with the modern approach to the interpretation of the federal division of legislative powers favoured by Canadian courts. The understanding of exclusivity as requiring immunity from even incidental encroachment has a greater affinity with the "watertight compartments" conception of federalism than it does with the modern, flexible federalism now favoured by the courts. In the modern paradigm, the courts employ the pith and substance, double aspect, and ancillary powers doctrines to interpret the meaning of exclusivity in a weaker manner: exclusivity means the exclusive ability to pass laws that deal predominantly with a subject matter allocated to the enacting legislature's jurisdiction. So long as the dominant or most important characteristic of a law falls within a class of subjects allocated to the jurisdiction of the enacting legislature, the law will be valid and applicable despite its incidental effects on subject matters outside of the enacting legislature's jurisdiction.

The Supreme Court has recognized that the interjurisdictional immunity doctrine is not in harmony with the dominant trends of its federalism jurisprudence. Indeed, in *Canadian Western Bank*, Justices Binnie and LeBel put forward a remarkably thorough critique of the doctrine. They stated that the interjurisdictional immunity doctrine is unpredictable in operation, at odds with the flexible federalism promoted by the pith and substance and double aspect doctrines, risks creating legal vacuums (because it is invoked whether or not a federal law is in existence), creates a centralizing tendency in constitutional interpretation, and is unnecessary because the paramountcy doctrine can be used to protect the primacy of federal legislation.[57] They concluded that the interjurisdictional immunity doctrine should be applied "with restraint".[58] Its application should "in general be reserved for those situations already covered by precedent"[59]

[54] *Ibid*, p. 840.
[55] *Tsilhqot'in Nation v British Columbia*, [2014] 2 S.C.R. 256 [141].
[56] *Canada (Attorney General) v. PHS Community Services Society*, [2011] 3 S.C.R. 134 [57–70]; *Carter v Canada (Attorney General)*, [2015] 1 S.C.R. 331 at [49–53].
[57] *Canadian Western Bank v Alberta*, above (n 4), [42–46].
[58] *Ibid*, [67].
[59] *Ibid*, [77].

within its "natural area of operation" regarding Parliament's power "over enumerated federal things, people, works or undertakings".[60]

The doctrine thus has a restricted role in contemporary federalism jurisprudence. It is invoked only when the application of a valid provincial law would significantly or seriously intrude on the exercise of a core element of federal jurisdiction, and even then, only when precedent supports the invocation of the doctrine.[61] Although the Supreme Court has since invoked the doctrine where these conditions are met in contexts where the invocation of the doctrine is supported by precedent,[62] attempts to rely on the doctrine in novel circumstances have been rejected.[63] In addition, the Court has been willing to pull back on the scope of the doctrine by overruling precedents.[64] The interjurisdictional immunity doctrine is thus likely to play an even more restricted role in future jurisprudence.

C. The Federal Paramountcy Doctrine

As we have seen, Canadian federalism jurisprudence allows for a great deal of overlap and interplay between laws passed by the federal Parliament and the provincial legislatures. Some legislative powers conferred by the Canadian Constitution are explicitly concurrent, or shared by both levels of government. Concurrent jurisdiction exists to pass laws in relation to the export of natural resources (section 91(2) and section 92A(2)), old age pensions (section 94A), agriculture (section 95), and immigration (section 95). Although the remainder of the legislative powers are described in the constitutional text as exclusive rather than concurrent, as we have seen the courts use the pith and substance, double aspect, and ancillary powers doctrines to uphold laws even though they may have significant impacts on matters within the other level of government's jurisdiction. The result is the creation of large areas of *de facto* concurrency.

In areas of *de jure* or *de facto* concurrency, a federal state needs a rule to deal with conflicts between validly enacted laws that apply to the same factual situations. Otherwise, those attempting to comply with the rule of law are put in an impossible situation.

In the few instances where the Canadian Constitution explicitly confers concurrent powers, it also specifies a rule for resolving potential conflicts. Section 94A provides

---

[60] *Ibid*, [67].

[61] *Marine Services International Ltd. v Ryan Estate*, [2013] 3 S.C.R. 53, [50–64].

[62] *Quebec (Attorney General) v Canadian Owners and Pilots Association*, [2010] 2 S.C.R. 536.

[63] *PHS Community Services*, above (n. 56); *Carter*, above (n. 56); *Bank of Montreal v Marcotte*, [2014] 2 S.C.R. 725, [63–69].

[64] Despite previous rulings to the contrary, in 2014 the Court held that the interjurisdictional immunity doctrine should no longer be used to limit the application of valid provincial legislation to protect Aboriginal or treaty rights. Henceforth, limits on validly enacted provincial legislation to affect Aboriginal or treaty rights will be imposed pursuant to the constitutional provision protecting those rights, s. 35(1) of the *Constitution Act, 1982*, rather than by the interjurisdictional immunity doctrine: *Tsilhqot'in Nation*, above (n 55) at [131–152]; *Grassy Narrows First Nation v Ontario (Natural Resources)*, [2014] 2 S.C.R. 447, [53].

that provincial laws will prevail over conflicting federal laws in the context of old age pensions; section 92A(3) and section 95 provide that federal laws will prevail over conflicting provincial laws in relation to export of natural resources, immigration, and agriculture.

The Canadian Constitution is silent, however, on what rule should be used for resolving a conflict between federal and provincial laws in areas of *de facto* concurrency. As a result, the courts have had to create a rule for resolving conflict. The rule they adopted is one of federal paramountcy: when a valid federal law and a valid provincial law apply to the same facts, and the requirements of the two laws conflict, the federal law is paramount. The effect of the paramountcy doctrine is that the federal law prevails; the provincial law is suspended, or rendered inoperative, to the extent it conflicts with the federal legislation.

The Court's embrace of the modern approach to federalism gives rise to large areas of legislation jurisdiction subject to *de facto* concurrency. When coupled with the rule of federal paramountcy, the modern federal paradigm results in an obvious threat to the autonomy of the provinces. Valid provincial laws are in danger of being suspended, or rendered inoperative, by the primacy of federal laws in the steadily expanding areas of *de facto* concurrency.

This concern is reflected in the large body of case law grappling with the question of how to define what counts as a "conflict" between a valid federal law and a valid provincial law giving rise to federal paramountcy. Some earlier case law supports a broad definition of conflict, one that would lead to the suspension of valid provincial laws whenever they overlap with a valid federal law that has "occupied the field". This approach has potentially dire consequences for provincial autonomy.

The Supreme Court recognized this concern at the time its modern conception of federalism was developing, and has sought to define conflict narrowly for the purposes of the paramountcy rule. In *Multiple Access*, a leading case on the paramountcy doctrine, Justice Dickson (as he then was) held that "in principle there would seem to me no good reason to speak of paramountcy and preclusion except where there is actual conflict in operation where one enactment says 'yes' and the other says 'no'. . . . compliance with one is defiance of the other".[65] This definition of conflict, known as the "impossibility of dual compliance" test, is the narrowest one that is compatible with the rule of law, and was justified by Dickson J. on the grounds that the resulting "untidiness" and "diseconomy" that results from overlapping federal and provincial laws "has to be subordinated to provincial autonomy".[66]

The "impossibility of dual compliance" understanding of conflict limits the threat posed by the federal paramountcy rule to the operation of valid provincial statutes. However, beginning in 1990, the Supreme Court has recognized a second kind of

---

[65] *Multiple Access Ltd. v McCutcheon*, above (n 35), at 191.
[66] *Ibid* at 190, quoting Peter W. Hogg, *Constitutional Law of Canada* (1977) 110.

conflict that can lead to the suspension of the operation of provincial laws.[67] Even when it is possible to comply with a valid federal law and a valid provincial law, the provincial law will be suspended to the extent necessary to prevent it from undermining the purpose of the federal law.

It is now settled doctrine that conflict for the purposes of the paramountcy doctrine may arise in two ways: (1) an impossibility of dual compliance, or (2) frustration of a federal legislative purpose by the provincial law.[68] The existence of either type of conflict is sufficient to give rise to federal paramountcy and thus the suspension of the operation of a valid provincial law to the extent of the conflict.

The second branch of the two-pronged definition of conflict, frustration of the federal legislative purpose, poses a more serious threat to provincial autonomy. It could even take the jurisprudence back to a "covering the field" test if the courts are too willing to attribute to federal legislation an implicit parliamentary intention to exclude the concurrent operation of provincial laws. It also makes it difficult to predict when the paramountcy doctrine will be invoked, given the uncertainties involved in identifying whether Parliament intended to limit the future operation of valid provincial laws, a question that is rarely addressed explicitly in federal legislation, and is often not discussed in the federal legislative process.

In an attempt to limit these concerns, the Supreme Court has stated that, like interjurisdictional immunity, the paramountcy doctrine should be applied with restraint. The party alleging the existence of a conflict has a high burden of proof.[69] The courts must be particularly careful "not to give too broad a scope to paramountcy on the basis of frustration of federal purpose".[70] The Court has cautioned that to impute to Parliament an intention to "occupy the field" in the absence of clear statutory language to that effect "would be to stray from the path of judicial restraint in questions of paramountcy".[71] It has also cautioned that the principle of co-operative federalism requires that "the purpose of federal legislation should not be artificially broadened beyond its intended scope".[72]

The restrained approach to the paramountcy doctrine is an essential component of the Supreme Court's commitment to a modern vision of federalism premised on relationships between equally autonomous levels of government. Without it, the principles of modern federalism may produce a hierarchical relationship between a dominant Parliament and subordinate provincial legislatures. Although the judges agree on the

---

[67] *Bank of Montreal v Hall*, [1990] 1 S.C.R. 121.

[68] See, e.g., *Law Society of British Columbia v Mangat*, [2001] 3 S.C.R. 113, [69-70]; *Rothmans, Benson & Hedges Inc. v. Saskatchewan*, [2005] 1 S.C.R. 188, [11–14]; *Quebec (Attorney General) v Canadian Owners and Pilots Association*, above (n 62), [64]; *Bank of Montreal v Marcotte*, [2014] 2 S.C.R. 725, [70]; *Alberta (Attorney General) v Moloney*, [2015] 3 S.C.R. 327, [18]; *Saskatchewan (Attorney General) v Lemare Lake Logging Ltd.*, [2015] 3 S.C.R. 419, [17].

[69] *Lemare Lake*, above (n 68) [26].

[70] *Marcotte*, above (n 63) [72].

[71] *Lemare Lake*, above (n 68) [27]; *Rothmans*, above (n 68) [21].

[72] *Lemare Lake*, above (n 68) [23].

general principles regarding the paramountcy doctrine, their application of the principles in particular cases often produces divergent and hotly contested positions. The paramountcy jurisprudence thus provides a useful prism through which to discern ongoing normative tensions related to the relative strength of judges' attachments to federal and provincial political communities.

4. Conclusion

The arbiter of the federal distribution of legislative powers plays an important role in the development of the federation and the maintenance of its legitimacy.[73] In a plurinational federation such as Canada, this is a critical role in the management of diversity and conflict.

Over the decades, the decisions of the Supreme Court in connection with the distribution of powers have created an asymmetric degree of protection for the autonomy of each order of government. Although the co-operative approach to federalism has allowed the federal Parliament to maximize, and even extend, its legislative domain, the Court has not always taken the same expansive approach to provincial legislative powers. The application and operation of valid provincial laws, unlike their federal counterparts, have been circumscribed by the interjurisdictional immunity and paramountcy doctrines.[74] At a time when state intervention is becoming more widespread and more complex, it is clearly impossible to avoid overlapping of powers between the two orders of government. However, federalism cannot survive over the long term if legislative powers are completely decompartmentalized. As a result, neither the classical "watertight compartments" approach nor the modern co-operative approach to federalism is entirely satisfactory.

The trend towards centralization that is generally apparent in the Court's constitutional jurisprudence is, perhaps, a reflection of the natural propensity of all organised societies to strengthen their centre.[75] However, it constitutes a problem in a plurinational federal context, which requires that particularly close attention be given to preserving the balance of power between the federal and provincial governments.

[73] Robert Schertzer, *The Judicial Role in a Diverse Federation* (University of Toronto Press, 2016) 8–18.

[74] As Peter W. Hogg wrote, "Judicial interpretation since the abolition of appeals [to the Privy Council] has permitted some growth of federal power, and this may well continue": Peter W. Hogg, *Constitutional Law of Canada*, loose-leaf edition (5th ed, Thomson Carswell, 2007) 5–18.

[75] Alain Delcamp, "Principe de subsidiarité et décentralisation" (1993) 23 Revue française de droit constitutionnel 609, p. 616.

SELECT BIBLIOGRAPHY

Secondary sources

Eugénie Brouillet, *La négation de la nation: l'identité culturelle québécoise et le fédéralisme cana-dien* (Septentrion, 2005)

Henri Brun, Guy Tremblay and Eugénie Brouillet, *Droit constitutionnel* (6e éd, Yvon Blais, 2014)

Peter Hogg, *Constitutional Law of Canada* loose-leaf edition (5th ed., Thomson Carswell, 2007)

Patrick Monahan, Byron Shaw and Padraic Ryan, *Constitutional Law* 5th ed. (Irwin Law, 2017)

Bruce Ryder, "Equal Autonomy in Canadian Federalism: The Continuing Search for Balance in the Interpretation of the Division of Powers" (2011) 54 SCLR (2d) 565

Robert Schertzer, *The Judicial Role in a Diverse Federation* (University of Toronto Press, 2016)

Katherine Swinton, *The Supreme Court and Canadian Federalism: The Laskin-Dickson Years* (Carswell, 1990)

Jeremy Webber, *The Constitution of Canada: A Contextual Analysis* (Hart, 2015)

Cases

A.-G. for Canada v A.-G. for Ontario, [1937] A.C. 326

Bank of Montreal v Marcotte, [2014] 2 S.C.R. 725

Bell Canada v Quebec (Commission de la Santé et de la Sécurité du Travail), [1988] 1 S.C.R. 749

Canada (Attorney General) v PHS Community Services Society, [2011] 3 S.C.R. 134

Canadian Western Bank v Alberta, [2007] 2 S.C.R. 3

Carter v Canada (Attorney General), [2015] 1 S.C.R. 331

Citizens Insurance Co. of Canada v Parsons (1881), 7 A. C. 96

Edwards v A.-G. for Canada, [1930] A.C. 124

General Motors of Canada Ltd. v City National Leasing, [1989] 1 S.C.R. 641

Hodge v The Queen, (1883–1884) 9 A.C. 117

Liquidators of the Maritime Bank of Canada v Receiver-General of New Brunswick, [1892] A.C. 437

Quebec (Attorney General) v Canada (Attorney General), [2015] 1 S.C.R. 693

Quebec (Attorney General) v Canadian Owners and Pilots Association, [2010] 2 S.C.R. 536

Quebec (Attorney General) v Lacombe, [2010] 2 S.C.R. 453

Reference re Assisted Human Reproduction Act, [2010] 3 S.C.R. 457

Reference re Employment Insurance Act (Can.), ss. 22 and 23, [2005] 2 S.C.R. 669

Reference re Same-Sex Marriage, [2004] 3 S.C.R. 698

Reference re Secession of Quebec, [1998] 2 S.C.R. 217

Reference re Securities Act, [2011] 3 S.C.R. 837

Rothmans, Benson & Hedges Inc. v Saskatchewan, [2005] 1 S.C.R. 188

Saskatchewan (Attorney General) v Lemare Lake Logging Ltd., [2015] 3 S.C.R. 419

CHAPTER 20

....

THE SPENDING POWER
IN CANADA

....

HOI L. KONG*

INTRODUCTION

....

THE federal spending power in Canada has long been the object of intense debate in constitutional circles. Scholars have disagreed about the extent of the power and its sources of authorization, and some have called into question the constitutionality and legitimacy of federal action in this area. In this chapter, I will provide an overview of this debate and propose a resolution of it. My central claim is twofold: (1) the Constitution authorizes the federal government to spend in areas of provincial jurisdiction and limits the scope of this power to spend, and (2) the effective enforcement of these limits requires that the judiciary recognize its institutional limits and that the political branches act with restraint.

In Part II, I will examine two sources of positive law that have given rise to significant disagreement about the nature and limits of the spending power: the (*Constitution Act, 1867*) and the case law. I will argue that the best interpretation of these sources leads to the conclusion that the federal order of government is authorized to spend in areas of provincial jurisdiction. In so doing, I will answer an argument that claims that the federal spending power should be limited to areas of federal legislative jurisdiction that are explicitly identified in the division of powers provisions of the Canadian Constitution (sections 91–95 of the *Constitution Act, 1867*).

In Part III, I will respond to a second theory of the federal spending power that claims it is unlimited and I shall argue that the spending power should be limited by an interpretation of a specific provision of the Canadian Constitution governing equalization and

* Associate Professor, Faculty of Law, McGill University. For outstanding research assistance, I thank Amy Preston-Samson, and for his meticulous final review of the citations, I thank Darius Bossé. I have previously published on the spending power in Canada, including most notably Hoi Kong, 'The Spending Power, Constitutional Interpretation and Legal Pragmatism' (2008) 34 Queen's LJ 305. This chapter draws on arguments and references from that previous work.

regional disparities within the federation (section 36 of the *Constitution Act, 1982*). Before I enter into these debates, I will in Part I specify what it means for the federal government to spend in areas of provincial jurisdiction, and why such spending is problematic.

PART I. WHAT IS THE PROBLEM?

Let us begin with some examples of exercises of the federal spending power that affect areas of provincial jurisdiction. The first case is when the federal government attaches conditions to the provinces' receipt of federal grants. For example, if federal legislation specifies that provinces will only receive funds if they meet federally-established standards in the area of health care, the federal government spends in order to influence the actions of the provinces, in an area of the latter's legislative jurisdiction.[1] A second case arises when the federal government directs spending to individuals or organizations for activities related to areas of provincial jurisdiction. For instance, if the federal government gives scholarships directly to university students, or sends funding directly to universities, it is spending on education, which is an area of provincial legislative jurisdiction.[2] These first two instances of federal intervention in areas of provincial jurisdiction are relatively straightforward. A third case is more complicated. Imagine if the federal government were to tax at a rate in excess of its spending needs, and thereby deprived provinces of their capacity to raise funds necessary to deliver essential services to their citizens. In this case, the federal government would be acting *in relation to* its spending power in a way that would influence provinces' capacity to act in areas within their competence.[3]

Let us now turn to examine why these examples of federal intervention are problematic. The case of conditional federal spending gives rise to problems of political accountability. Citizens in a province that received such spending would find it difficult to determine which order of government was ultimately responsible for policies directly affecting their interests. As a result of this confusion, governments would be unaccountable for their policy decisions.[4] There is a second, related concern with

---

[1] For a historical overview of these kinds of spending arrangements, including shared-cost programs, see Thomas J Courchene, 'Reflections on the Federal Spending Power: Practice, Principles, Perspectives' (2008) 34 Queen's LJ 75, 85–88.

[2] For an assessment of this kind of direct spending, see Tom Kent, 'The Federal Spending Power Is Now Chiefly for the People, not Provinces' (2008) 34 Queen's LJ 413.

[3] The concern about the fiscal capacity of provinces is not new. It arose as early as the 1880s when Quebec requested more federal transfers (see Ramsey Cook, *Provincial Autonomy, Minority Rights and the Compact Theory, 1867–1921* (Queen's Printer for Canada 1969)), and it came to the fore of public consciousness in the post-War period when the provinces entered into tax rental agreements with the federal government: Gerard V La Forest, *The Allocation of Taxing Power under the Canadian Constitution* (Canadian Tax Foundation 1967) 27–35.

[4] Andrew Petter, 'Federalism and the Myth of the Federal Spending Power' (1989) 68 Can Bar Rev 448. See also the political economic arguments for aligning jurisdiction with spending and taxing power: Michel Maher, 'Le défi du fédéralisme fiscal dans l'exercice du pouvoir de dépenser' (1996) 75 Can Bar Rev 403, 405–407.

conditional spending that also applies to direct spending by the federal government in areas of provincial jurisdiction. In both instances, the policy priorities of provincial governments are distorted.[5] In the case of conditional spending, provincial governments will act according to the priorities of the federal government in order to continue to receive funding.[6] And in the case of direct spending by the federal government without conditions, provincial governments will be incentivized to increase spending, and voters in the province receiving this funding will not be able to accurately evaluate the cost of provincial services.[7] In either case, there is a risk that the provinces will become dependent on the federal spending in their areas of jurisdiction, and if such spending is removed, will need to make policy choices that they would not otherwise choose to make.[8] Finally, in the case of the federal government's taxing at an excessively high rate, the provinces are deprived of the capacity to tax and spend in areas of their own jurisdiction, and therefore to govern in ways that they are constitutionally authorized to.[9]

Each of the preceding concerns about exercises of the federal spending power focuses on the *effects* of its exercise on the provinces and their polities. These are related to, but distinct from, a general disquiet about the constitutionality of some exercises of the federal spending power. Indeed, broad federal spending in areas within state or provincial jurisdiction may be constitutional, yet nonetheless give rise to concerns about the negative consequences just canvassed. This is the case in the two jurisdictions with which Canada is most frequently compared in respect of the federal spending power: Australia and the United States.[10] Where the constitutional limits of the spending power are controversial, however, analysis of potential negative consequences may assist in determining whether a particular exercise of it is unconstitutional.[11] Yet even in the absence of any such consequences, one might be concerned about questions of constitutionality as any violation of the Constitution undermines the rule of law. Authors in Canada have objected to some exercises of the federal spending power on precisely these grounds.[12] In order to assess the constitutionality of federal spending in areas of provincial legislative jurisdiction, I now turn to examine the relevant constitutional sources.

---

[5] Petter above (n 4) 467–468.

[6] For a description of these effects in Canada, see Robin Boadway, 'Recent Developments in the Economics of Federalism' in Harvey Lazar (ed), *Toward a New Mission Statement for Canadian Fiscal Federalism* (McGill-Queen's University Press, 2000) 69.

[7] For a summary of the literature on this "fiscal illusion" effect of unconditional spending, see Brian Dollery and Andrew Worthington, 'Fiscal Expenditure and Fiscal Illusion: A Test of the Flypaper Hypothesis in Australia' (1995) 25 Publius 23, 25–26.

[8] See eg Alan Fenna, 'Commonwealth Fiscal Power and Australian Federalism' (2008) 31 UNSWLJ 509, 515.

[9] This concern is articulated in Quebec, Commission on Fiscal Imbalance, *Fiscal Imbalance in Canada: Historical Background: Supporting Document 1* (Bibliothèque nationale du Québec 2002) 16.

[10] See eg Gabrielle Appleby, 'There Must Be Limits: The Commonwealth Spending Power' (2009) 37 Fed L Rev 93; Erwin Chemerinsky, 'Protecting the Spending Power' (2001) 4 Chapman L Rev 89.

[11] See eg Hoi Kong, 'The Spending Power, Constitutional Interpretation and Legal Pragmatism' (2008) 34 Queen's LJ 305, 337–344.

[12] See eg Marc-Antoine Adam, 'The Federal Spending Power, Co-operative Federalism and Section 94' (2008) 34 Queen's LJ 175, 196.

PART II. CONSTITUTIONAL INTERPRETATION, TEXT, AND DOCTRINE

In this Part, I will analyze two sources of constitutional law that have been understood to authorize exercises of the federal spending power, in areas of provincial jurisdiction: constitutional text, and the relevant case law. I will start with authors who have argued that the *Constitution Act, 1867* can be interpreted to authorize this kind of federal spending, before turning to various interpretations of the case law.

A. The *Constitution Act, 1867*

Peter Hogg has noted that the federal spending power is not explicitly mentioned in the *Constitution Act, 1867*, and claims that it "must be inferred from the power to levy taxes (s 91(3)), to legislate in relation to 'public property' (s 91(1A)), and to appropriate federal funds (s 106)."[13] He further notes that the federal government's power to provide subsidies to the provinces was expressly provided for by section 118 of the British North America Act 1867, which specified sums "in full settlement of all future demands on Canada."[14]

Roderick Macdonald adds to this gloss of the constitutional provisions a juxtaposition of relevant federal powers with their provincial counterparts. He writes:

> Nowhere is the federal power textually limited in purpose, while in sections 92(2) and 92(9) direct taxation and licensing fees may be imposed only to raise revenue for "provincial purposes," although provincial borrowing under section 92(3) is not so limited. Likewise, section 91 does not explicitly constrain the power of Parliament to authorize federal expenditures, although section 92 limits the authorization to disburse that may be granted to provincial government by provincial legislatures.[15]

We can situate Hogg's and Macdonald's interpretations of the constitutional text in what Philip Bobbitt has labelled the "modalities" of constitutional interpretation.[16] Both

---

[13] Peter W Hogg, *Constitutional Law in Canada* (5th edn, Carswell 2007) ch 6.8(a).

[14] Ibid ch 6.1.

[15] Roderick A Macdonald, 'The Political Economy of the Federal Spending Power' (2008) 34 Queen's LJ 249, 263–264.

[16] For the idea of constitutional modalities and an enumeration of them, see Philip Bobbitt, *Constitutional Interpretation* (Basil Blackwell 1991) ch 1. For an illustration of these modalities using Canadian examples, see Robin Elliot, 'References, Structural Argumentation and the Organizing Principles of Canada's Constitution' (2001) 80 Can Bar Rev 67. For an example of an author resolving problems of constitutional interpretation by appealing to the range of interpretive modalities and arguing for the relative weight of some of them, see Michael C Dorf, 'Integrating Normative and Descriptive Constitutional Theory: The Case of Original Meaning' (1997) 85 Geo LJ 1765.

authors aim to fill a lacuna in the constitutional text. Hogg does so, in part, by inferring from a repealed constitutional provision (s 118) an intention on the part of the drafters of the 1867 document to allow the federal government to spend in areas of provincial jurisdiction. One can therefore place his interpretation in the originalist mode of constitutional interpretation, which emphasizes the motivations of constitutional drafters.[17] By contrast, Macdonald adopts a tack that focuses on the text alone.[18] He contrasts the textual limits on the purposes for which provincial legislatures may make laws imposing taxes (s 92(2)) refers to the "raising of a Revenue for Provincial Purposes") with the corresponding federal power (s 91(3)), which is not limited. From this textual contrast, argues Macdonald, one may infer that the federal government is authorized to spend in areas beyond its legislative competence.

To these originalist and textualist arguments in favor of the federal power to spend in areas of provincial legislative jurisdiction may be added those inspired by living tree constitutionalism and constitutional structure. In the context of the federal spending power, these arguments are deployed in tandem. Consider, first, the relevant constitutional history. The provinces have legislative jurisdiction over matters—such as health and education—that at Confederation were not costly for governments.[19] Over time, these services have drawn ever-increasing amounts of government expenditures. In response, federal taxation powers have expanded, as has federal spending in these areas of provincial jurisdiction. These actions on the part of the federal government reflect its greater fiscal capacity, as well as a national interest in providing relatively equal levels of public services across the country.[20]

What significance might these developments have for the interpretation of the federal spending power? According to the dominant, modern interpretive approach in Canada, the Constitution is a living tree that must be interpreted to evolve with changing social, political, and economic circumstances.[21] In the context of the current discussion, this approach argues in favor of an interpretation that would enable federal spending in areas

---

[17] For a judicial statement of originalism, see Rhode Island v. Massachusetts 37 U.S. (12 Pet) 657, 721 (1838) and for academic developments of the idea, see Antonin Scalia, 'The Rule of Law as the Law of Rules' (1989) 56 U Chicago L Rev 1175; Vasan Kesavan and Michael Stokes Paulsen, 'The Interpretive Force of the Constitution's Secret Drafting History' (2003) 91 Geo LJ 1113. For a Canadian treatment of originalism and its presence in the Supreme Court of Canada's jurisprudence, see Bradley W Miller, 'Beguiled by Metaphors: The "Living Tree" and Originalist Constitutional Interpretation in Canada' (2009) 22 Can JL & Jur 331.

[18] For a description of textualism, as an approach to constitutional interpretation, see Richard A Posner, 'Legal Formalism, Legal Realism, and the Interpretation of Statutes and the Constitution' (1987) 37 Case W Res L Rev 179, 191. For notable instances of textualism in Canadian constitutional law, see the reasons of Beetz J in *Société des Acadiens v Association of Parents for Fairness in Education* [1986] 1 SCR 460 and those of Arbour J in *Gosselin v Québec (A-G)* 2002 SCC 84.

[19] Hogg above (n 13) ch 6.1.

[20] The Rowell-Sirois Commission recommended expansion of the federal taxing power, as well as equalization through federal spending: Canada, *Report of the Commission on Dominion Provincial Relation* (King's Printer, 1940). For a history of these developments, in the post-War period, see La Forest above (n 3) 27–35.

[21] See eg Reference re Same Sex Marriage 2004 SCC 79 [22].

of provincial jurisdiction as a response to the increasingly limited fiscal capacities of the provinces relative to their areas of legislative competence. This living tree approach to constitutional interpretation is bolstered by structural arguments.[22] Structuralism, in the context of constitutional interpretation, involves examining the constitutional order and offering prescriptions for how its institutions should fit together.[23] In the present context, an interpreter following the structural approach would insist that we should understand the federal spending power in light of the general constitutional relationship between the federal and provincial orders of government. This relationship is today characterized by expansive federal authority and considerable overlap between areas of federal and provincial jurisdiction.[24] Absent convincing arguments to the contrary, a structural reading, joined with a living tree approach, would lead one to conclude that the federal spending power should be read expansively and that, therefore, one should understand the Constitution as authorizing at least some exercises of the spending power in areas of provincial jurisdiction.

B. Case Law

Let us turn now from interpretations of the constitutional text to a reading of the relevant constitutional case law. This debate has turned on the relative weight of, on the one hand, a Privy Council decision about the relationship between the federal spending power and the legislative division of powers, and on the other hand, a line of cases in which the Supreme Court of Canada has reasoned that federal spending in areas of provincial jurisdiction is constitutional. The Privy Council case, *Reference Re Employment and Social Insurance Act (Can)*,[25] stands for the proposition that exercises of the federal spending power are ultra vires if in their purpose and effects, they invade areas of exclusive provincial jurisdiction.[26] More recently, the Supreme Court of Canada has repeatedly affirmed the constitutionality of conditional exercises of the spending power,[27] although it has not made a ruling about the constitutionality of such an exercise in a

---

[22] For the classic presentation of structuralism, see Charles Lund Black, *Structure and Relationship in Constitutional Law* (Louisiana State University Press, 1969).

[23] For a recent judicial example of this kind of structural argument, see Reference Re Senate Reform 2014 SCC 32, and for an analysis of it, see Kate Glover, 'Structure, Substance and Spirit: Lessons in Constitutional Architecture from the *Senate Reform Reference*' (2014) 67 Sup Ct L Rev (2d) 221.

[24] Wade K Wright, 'Facilitating Intergovernmental Dialogue: Judicial Review of the Division of Powers in the Supreme Court of Canada' (2010) 51 Sup Ct L Rev (2d) 625.

[25] *Reference Re Employment and Social Insurance Act (Can)* [1937] 1 DLR 684 (PC), sub nom Canada (A-G) v Ontario (A-G)) [1937] AC 326 (hereinafter *Unemployment Insurance Reference*).

[26] For this interpretation of the case, see Andrée Lajoie, 'Current Exercises of the 'Federal Spending Power': What Does the Constitution Say about Them' (2008) 34 Queen's LJ 141, 151.

[27] The Supreme Court of Canada has in several cases reasoned that conditional federal spending is constitutional. See *YMWA Jewish Community Centre v Brown* [1989] 1 SCR 1532, 1549; *Reference Re Canada Assistance Plan* [1991] 2 SCR 525; *Eldridge v British Columbia* [1997] 3 SCR 624 [24]; *Auton (Guardian ad litem of) v British Columbia (A-G)* [2004] 3 SCR 657, App B.

case where that was the central issue presented. Opponents of federal spending in areas of provincial jurisdiction claim that the Supreme Court of Canada has only spoken in obiter dicta about the validity of this kind of federal spending and has not expressly overruled the *Unemployment Insurance Reference*. These opponents conclude that that decision sets constitutional limits on the federal spending power.[28]

This argument can be challenged on several grounds. Consider first the claim that the Supreme Court of Canada's reasoning in favour of the federal spending power has only been articulated in obiter dicta. The line between obiter dicta and ratio decidendi is not as obvious in this area as it may appear to be at first glance. For example, according to Hogg, the unambiguous unanimous statement in *Reference Re Canada Assistance Plan*[29] validating conditional federal spending, responded to a specific constitutional argument advanced by the Attorney General of Manitoba.[30] It would seem, therefore, that the statement was pertinent to the determination of the case. Moreover, it is worth noting that the doctrinal context in which the *Unemployment Insurance Reference* was decided differs greatly from our own. The judgment reflects a theory of federalism that enforces a strict separation between federal and provincial jurisdictions.[31] But as we have seen above, that is not the view of federalism that currently prevails in Canadian courts. It therefore seems problematic to insist on the continuing authority of the Privy Council's statement of law, given that its underlying theory of federalism is no longer applicable, and the fact that the Supreme Court has repeatedly affirmed a contrary view.

There is a final reason that favours recognizing the constitutionality of past and present exercises of the federal spending power in areas of provincial jurisdiction. In general, government action benefits from a presumption of constitutionality.[32] The benefits of such a presumption are systemic: comity between the branches of government requires that all branches be presumed to be good-faith interpreters of the Constitution. Moreover, in the absence of such a presumption, the resources of the judiciary would be overextended, as courts would constantly be called upon to assess government action, and often in areas beyond their institutional competence.[33] In light of these

---

[28] See eg Lajoie above (n 26) 151; Marc-André Turcotte, *Le pouvoir fédéral de dépenser* (Éditions Yvon Blais, 2015) 126–132.

[29] [1991] 2 SCR 525 [567].

[30] Hogg above (n 13) ch 6.8(a).

[31] For an interpretation of the federal spending power in light of contemporary federalism doctrine, see Sujit Choudhry, 'Recasting Social Canada: A Reconsideration of Federal Jurisdiction over Social Policy' (2002) 52 UTLJ 163, 174–175.

[32] See eg McKay v R [1965] SCR 798. The arguments set out in this section can be understood as being "prudential" in Bobbit's sense of the term, as they expressly consider the consequences of exercises of constitutional interpretation. Bobbitt above (n 16) 13.

[33] See James Bradley Thayer, 'The Origin and Scope of the American Doctrine of Constitutional Law' (1893) 7(3) Harv L Rev 129, for a classic statement of these reasons for deference, and Mark Tushnet, 'Policy Distortion and Democratic Deliberation: Comparative Illumination of the Countermajoritarian Difficulty' (1995) 94(2) Mich L Rev 245, 300–301 for a contemporary argument for them. For an overview of the debate about the presumption of constitutionality in Canadian constitutional law, and an argument in favour of that presumption, see Nicolas Lambert, 'The Charter in Administrative Process: Statutory Remedy or Refounding of Administrative Jurisdiction?' (2007) 13 Rev Const Stud 21,

considerations, federal spending in areas of provincial jurisdiction should benefit from the presumption of constitutionality. If courts were to proceed otherwise, they would overturn much of the well-established policy architecture of the Canadian federation, ignore ongoing provincial and federal acceptance of such spending, and therefore upset the balance of inter-institutional comity and strain their institutional capacities.[34]

In this Part, we have considered two sources of authorization for federal exercises of the spending power in areas of provincial jurisdiction, namely the *Constitution Act, 1867* and the jurisprudence. My interpretation of the constitutional text and the relevant case law leads to the conclusion that some federal spending in areas of provincial legislative jurisdiction is constitutionally authorized. I therefore reject the arguments of those who would limit the federal spending power to areas of Parliament's legislative jurisdiction. These arguments should not, however, be taken to support an *unlimited* federal spending power. In the next Part, I will survey arguments in support of such an unlimited power, demonstrate that they are implausible, and conclude by offering an alternative set of limits, grounded in section 36(1) of the *Constitution Act, 1982*.

PART III. AGAINST THE GIFT THEORY AND FOR SECTION 36(1) LIMITS ON FEDERAL SPENDING

Peter Hogg is the contemporary scholar most closely associated with the "gift theory" of the spending power.[35] He argues that because spending is a private act of government, and thus distinct from legislating, the constitutional division of powers cannot limit federal exercises of the spending power. His arguments resonate with those offered decades ago by F.R. Scott, who found in the prerogative power constitutional authorization for an unlimited federal spending power.[36] It is worth quoting Scott in full on this point:

> All public monies that fall into the Consolidated Revenue Funds of the federal and provincial governments belong to the Crown. The Crown is a person capable of making gifts or contracts like any other person, to whomsoever it chooses to benefit. The recipient may be another government, or private individuals. The only constitutional requirement for Crown gifts is that they must have the approval of Parliament or legislature. This being obtained, the Prince may distribute his largesse at will. Such gifts,

---

57–60. And for a discussion of the presumption's relevance in the context of the federal spending power, see Kong, above (n 11) 337–38.

[34] See Andrew Petter, 'The Myth of the Federal Spending Power' (2008) 34 Queen's LJ 163, 168–169.

[35] Hogg, above (n 13) ch 6.8(a). This conception of the spending power is supported by, and consistent with, his interpretation of the relevant constitutional provisions, which were surveyed above.

[36] FR Scott, 'The Constitutional Background of Taxation Agreements' (1955) 2 McGill LJ 1.

of course, do not need to be accepted; the donee is always free to reject as the donor to offer. Moreover, the Crown may attach conditions to the gift, failure to observe which will cause its discontinuance. These simple but significant powers exist in our constitutional law though no mention of them can be found in the B.N.A. Acts. They derive from the doctrines of the Royal Prerogative and the common law. They operate equally for the Crown in right of the provinces as for the Crown in right of the Dominion.[37]

As others have noted, the analogy between the federal government and a private actor upon which the gift theory depends ignores the high political costs of permitting the federal government to act with the impunity of a private actor.[38] As we have seen above, when the federal government effectively regulates in areas of provincial jurisdiction, through its spending power, it undermines public law values: it confuses lines of authority, as even the best informed citizens will not be able to determine who is ultimately responsible for governmental action, and it permits the federal government to distort the legislative priorities of provincial governments.[39] Yet, in order for these concerns about political costs to be convincing as a matter of constitutional law, they need to be joined to arguments that refer to constitutional sources. More precisely, we will need to draw from the Constitution a limit on the federal government's spending power that is not evident in either the provisions of the *Constitution Act, 1867* surveyed above, or in Scott's presentation of the prerogative power. Section 36 of the *Constitution Act, 1982* provides such a limit and in what follows, I will offer an exegesis of it.

A. Section 36(1)'s Limitations on the Federal Spending Power

Section 36(1) states:

> Without altering the legislative authority of Parliament or of the provincial legislatures, or the rights of any of them with respect to the exercise of their legislative authority, Parliament and the legislatures, together with the government of Canada and the provincial governments, are committed to (a) promoting equal opportunities for the well-being of Canadians; (b) furthering economic development to reduce disparity in opportunities; and (c) providing essential public services of reasonable quality to all Canadians.[40]

---

[37] Ibid 6.

[38] Jean-François Gaudreault-DesBiens, 'The Irreducible Federal Necessity of Jurisdictional Autonomy, and the Irreducibility of Federalism to Jurisdictional Autonomy' in Sujit Choudhry, Jean-François Gaudreault-DesBiens and Lorne Sossin (eds), *Dilemmas of Solidarity: Rethinking Redistribution in the Canadian Federation* (University of Toronto Press 2006) 190–192.

[39] Petter above (n 4) 467–468.

[40] Constitution Act 1982, s 36(1) being Schedule B to the Canada Act 1982 (UK), 1982, c 11 [emphasis added].

On its face, section 36(1) applies to governmental action that does not alter the Constitution's distribution of legislative authority. The discussion in the previous Part suggests that federal spending is not limited by the division of powers and that therefore it is one plausible object of the section. Aymen Nader's history of section 36(1) supports this reading. He argues that the intention behind this section was to provide specific constitutional support for federal spending in areas of provincial jurisdiction.[41] This history suggests that section 36(1) authorizes federal spending that advances the section's objectives.

We have seen above that federal spending in areas of provincial jurisdiction can have negative consequences, including reducing political accountability and affecting the policy priorities of provinces. It is important, therefore, to note that the section 36(1) objectives prescribe *limits* on exercises of the federal spending power that can palliate some of these consequences. To understand the nature of one such limit, it is helpful to explore briefly the background conditions of redistribution, in the Canadian federation. In order to achieve the redistributive objectives identified in section 36(1), the federal government requires sufficient financial resources, and this in turn necessitates a difference in fiscal capacity between the federal and provincial governments.[42] Yet, at a certain point, the gap can become disproportionate to and unnecessary for the pursuit of section 36(1)'s objectives. Imagine that the federal government occupied an amount of tax room far in excess of its own budgetary needs and its section 36(1) obligations. Imagine further that if the federal government expanded its taxing activity, the provinces' capacity to tax would necessarily be reduced. Finally, imagine that the provinces' constitutional obligations were much more costly than those of the federal government and that the provincial governments, as a result of this excessive vertical fiscal gap, were to become entirely dependent upon federal government support to provide services that fell within their core constitutional competences.[43] In this hypothetical, the federal government would compromise the regulatory autonomy of the provincial governments in a way that was disproportionate to, and unnecessary for, legitimate redistributive objectives. As a consequence, its actions would exceed the limits set by section 36(1).[44]

---

[41] Aymen Nader, 'Providing Essential Services: Canada's Constitution under Section 36' (1996) 19 Dal LJ 306, 320–347, 354–355.

[42] See eg Harvey Lazar, 'Trust in Intergovernmental Fiscal Relations' in Harvey Lazar (ed), *Canadian Fiscal Arrangements: What Works, What Might Work Better* (McGill-Queen's Press, 2005) 12.

[43] Some commentators argue that the situation presented in hypothetical terms in the main text represents the current state of affairs in Canada today. See eg Alain Noël, 'Il suffisait de presque rien: Promises and Pitfalls of Open Federalism' in Keith Banting and others (eds), *Open Federalism: Interpretations, Significance* (Institute of Intergovernmental Relations 2006).

[44] A similar analysis would apply to conditional and direct federal spending that would compromise provincial interests. Any such negative consequences would need to be proportional and necessary for achievement of s 36 objectives. For the proportionality and necessity analysis in this paragraph, see also Kong (n 11) 350.

B. Answering Objections

There are three objections to this interpretation of section 36(1). According to the first objection, the interpretation is implausible because it implies that all federal spending in areas of provincial jurisdiction before 1982 was unconstitutional.[45] In response, one might note that, according to the above interpretations of the prerogative power and the *Constitution Act, 1867*, federal spending was constitutionally unlimited prior to 1982. The proponents of these interpretations would argue that section 36(1) therefore imposed novel constitutional limits on Parliament, in much the same way that the *Charter of Rights and Freedoms* imposed new rights-based constraints. As a consequence, just as it would be inaccurate to describe as unconstitutional pre-1982 state action that violated interests that were only subsequently protected by the *Charter*, it would be wrong to claim that pre-1982 federal spending that infringed section 36(1) was unconstitutional. The objection therefore misses its mark.

The remaining two objections address enforcement issues. One claims that section 36(1) is not justiciable because the phrase "committed to" renders the provision merely hortatory. The Nova Scotia Court of Appeal has answered this claim. According to MacDonald CJ, section 36(1) "may indeed, in appropriate circumstances represent an actionable obligation among the parties to the agreement that is being codified in s 36."[46] Given the express wording of the text, a claimant would need to show that the federal government did more than simply fail to achieve the section's objectives. In other words, the federal government could comply with the section if it attempted to achieve the relevant objectives, but failed to do so, as such action would arguably evidence the requisite level of commitment. The federal government would, however, be constitutionally barred from manifestly disregarding section 36(1), either by flagrant inaction or by acting in a way that was disproportionate to and unnecessary for the attainment of the section's objectives.

I close this Part by answering a final, related objection, which states that section 36(1)'s obligations are beyond the institutional capacity of the courts to enforce. One response might concede this point about limited judicial competence, but insist that governments are nonetheless under a constitutional obligation to comply with section 36(1). An analogy with constitutional conventions may illustrate the point. Conventions are enforced politically, rather than judicially, but nonetheless impose constitutional obligations on governments to whom they apply.[47] Similarly, section 36(1) may set out constitutional duties whose enforcement depends on political processes, rather than courts. In this view, the Constitution requires the federal government to act with self-restraint, rather than in anticipation of, or in response to, judicial commands. As a corollary, courts should recognize their institutional limits and therefore refrain from attempting to enforce and apply section 36(1).

---

[45] See Adam, above (n 12) 183.

[46] *Cape Breton v Nova Scotia* (2009) 277 NSR (2d) 350 (NSCA) 65. The Court arrived at this conclusion primarily by relying on the dictionary meaning of the word "committed" ([50]).

[47] See the discussion in *Re: Resolution to amend the Constitution* [1981] 1 SCR 753.

A second response to the concern about the institutional capacity of courts to enforce section 36(1) would propose a doctrinal rule that relies on significant inter-governmental cooperation and over-sight.[48] The rule would state that federal action is presumed to be in accordance with section 36(1)'s objectives unless an administrative agency constituted by the federal and provincial governments were to find the action to be disproportionate to, or unnecessary for, the achievement of those objectives.[49] In light of such a finding, the agency would issue recommendations on how the federal government should remedy the violation, and if the government decided to depart from those recommendations, it would be obliged to provide reasons, which a court would review on a reasonableness standard.[50] Finally, if the government's reasons were to fail on this review, it would be obliged to provide new reasons or comply with the agency determination. This proposed doctrinal rule would therefore encourage governments to act with self-restraint, according to an ethic of cooperation, and it would call upon the courts to acknowledge their institutional limitations.

This arrangement is modeled on the remedy ordered by Supreme Court of Canada in the *Remuneration Reference*.[51] There, the Court responded to a concern about judicial independence by directing that a commission set provincial court judges' salaries.[52] That order was designed to remove the possibility of improper political influence, to safeguard the decision-making process from self-dealing, and to ensure that objective information would be considered. The doctrinal rule and administrative oversight body that I have proposed for section 36(1) aim to achieve similar outcomes. The proposed rule allocates responsibility for settling a constitutional question among the branches of government, it responds to the risks of self-dealing that would arise from leaving the relevant constitutional questions exclusively to political actors, and it aims to ensure that empirical determinations which are beyond the institutional capacities of the courts will be competently made.

---

[48] The following two paragraphs draw on material previously published in Kong, above (n 11).

[49] Professors Albert Abel and Robin Boadway have proposed similar bodies: see Albert Abel, 'Albert Abel's Constitutional Charter for Canada' (1978) 28(3) UTLJ 261, 313–337; Boadway, above (n 6) 74.

[50] For the Court's statement of current judicial review standards, see Dunsmuir v New Brunswick 2008 SCC 9 [*Dunsmuir*]. The issues addressed by the proposed administrative agency are a hybrid: they require expertise *and* they implicate the constitutional division of powers. The former characteristic attracts deference whereas the latter typically compels close judicial scrutiny: *Dunsmuir* [51]–[62]. I suggest that the appropriate standard for s 36(1) review is deferential, because one of the reasons for the agency's existence is to make determinations that are beyond the expertise of a court. This level of review is consistent with that articulated in Reference Re Remuneration of Judges of the Provincial Court (PEI) [1997] 3 SCR 3, paras [183]–[184] [*Remuneration Reference*]; Provincial Court Judges' Association of New Brunswick v New Brunswick (Minister of Justice) 2005 SCC 44 [28]-[42] [*Provincial Court Judges' Association*].

[51] *Remuneration Reference*, above (n 50) [168]–[185].

[52] The reasoning in that case was refined in *Provincial Court Judges' Association*, above (n 50), and those refinements are reflected in the doctrinal rule I have proposed.

Conclusion

In this chapter, I have argued that the Canadian Constitution authorizes the federal government to spend in areas of provincial jurisdiction and constrains the scope of this power. I have, moreover claimed that effective enforcement of these limits requires that the judiciary recognize its institutional limits and that the political branches act with restraint. The arguments advanced have sought to occupy a middle ground, between proponents of an unlimited spending power and critics who would bind federal spending to the limits imposed by the legislative division of powers, strictly interpreted. In staking out this ground, I have undertaken an approach to constitutional interpretation that closely examines the sources of constitutional law and carefully considers issues of institutional competence and constitutional legitimacy. In the course of this discussion, I hope to have shown that what at first glance appears to be a narrow and technical question reveals itself to be a rich site of reflection about foundational questions of constitutional law.

Bibliography

Primary and secondary sources

Abel A, 'Albert Abel's Constitutional Charter for Canada' (1978) 28(3) UTLJ 261.

Adam M-A, 'The Federal Spending Power, Co-operative Federalism and Section 94' (2008) 34(1) Queen's LJ 175.

Appleby G, 'There Must be Limits: The Commonwealth Spending Power' (2009) 37(1) Fed L Rev 93.

Boadway R, 'Recent Developments in the Economics of Federalism' in Harvey Lazar (ed), *Toward a New Mission Statement for Canadian Fiscal Federalism* (McGill-Queen's University Press 2000).

Canada, *Report of the Commission on Dominion Provincial Relation* (King's Printer 1940).

Chemerinsky E, 'Protecting the Spending Power' (2001) 4 Chapman L Rev 89.

Choudhry S, 'Recasting Social Canada: A Reconsideration of Federal Jurisdiction over Social Policy' (2002) 52(3) UTLJ 163.

Courchene TJ, 'Reflections on the Federal Spending Power: Practice, Principles, Perspectives' (2008) 34(1) Queen's LJ 75.

Dollery B and Worthington A, 'Fiscal Expenditure and Fiscal Illusion: A Test of the Flypaper Hypothesis in Australia' (1995) 25(1) Publius 23.

Fenna A, 'Commonwealth Fiscal Power and Australian Federalism' (2008) 31(2) UNSWLJ 509.

Gaudreault-DesBiens J-F, 'The Irreducible Federal Necessity of Jurisdictional Autonomy, and the Irreducibility of Federalism to Jurisdictional Autonomy' in Sujit Choudhry, Jean-François Gaudreault-DesBiens and Lorne Sossin (eds), *Dilemmas of Solidarity: Rethinking Redistribution in the Canadian Federation* (University of Toronto Press 2006).

Hogg PW, *Constitutional Law in Canada* (5th edn, Carswell 2007).

Kent T, 'The Federal Spending Power Is Now Chiefly for the People, not Provinces' (2008) 34(1) Queen's LJ 413.

Kong H, 'The Spending Power, Constitutional Interpretation and Legal Pragmatism' (2008) 34(1) Queen's LJ 305.

La Forest GV, *The Allocation of Taxing Power under the Canadian Constitution* (Canadian Tax Foundation 1967).

Lajoie A, 'Current Exercises of the 'Federal Spending Power': What Does the Constitution Say about Them' (2008) 34(1) Queen's LJ 141.

Lazar H, 'Trust in Intergovernmental Fiscal Relations' in Harvey Lazar (ed), *Canadian Fiscal Arrangements: What Works, What Might Work Better* (McGill-Queen's Press 2005).

Macdonald RA, 'The Political Economy of the Federal Spending Power' (2008) 34(1) Queen's LJ 249.

Maher M, 'Le défi du fédéralisme fiscal dans l'exercice du pouvoir de dépenser' (1996) 75(3) Can Bar Rev 403.

Nader A, 'Providing Essential Services: Canada's Constitution under Section 36' (1996) 19(2) Dal LJ 306.

Noël A, 'Il suffisait de presque rien: Promises and Pitfalls of Open Federalism' in Keith Banting and others (eds), *Open Federalism: Interpretations, Significance* (Institute of Intergovernmental Relations 2006).

Petter A, 'Federalism and the Myth of the Federal Spending Power' (1989) 68(3) Can Bar Rev 448.

_____. 'The Myth of the Federal Spending Power' (2008) 34(1) Queen's LJ 163.

Quebec, Commission on Fiscal Imbalance, *Fiscal Imbalance in Canada: Historical Background: Supporting Document 1* (Bibliothèque nationale du Québec 2002).

Scott FR, 'The Constitutional Background of Taxation Agreements' (1955) 2(1) McGill LJ 1.

Turcotte M-A, *Le pouvoir fédéral de dépenser* (Éditions Yvon Blais 2015).

Cases

Auton (Guardian ad litem of) v British Columbia (A-G) [2004] 3 SCR 657.

Eldridge v British Columbia [1997] 3 SCR 624.

Reference Re Canada Assistance Plan [1991] 2 SCR 525.

Reference Re Employment and Social Insurance Act (Can) [1937] 1 DLR 684 (PC), sub nom *Canada (A-G) v Ontario (A-G))* [1937] AC 326.

YMWA Jewish Community Centre v Brown [1989] 1 SCR 1532.

B. Federalism in Context

....

CHAPTER 21

FEDERALISM AND HEALTH CARE IN CANADA

A Troubled Romance?

....

COLLEEN M. FLOOD, WILLIAM LAHEY &
BRYAN THOMAS*

1. Introduction

CANADA's efforts to offer a modern health care system to its people are shaped, complicated, and in many ways hindered, by interpretations of federal/provincial divisions of power laid out in the *Constitution Act, 1867* (the 1867 Act). Given its vintage, the 1867 Act has relatively little to say *directly* with respect to the health sector, which has since Confederation evolved into an enormously important area of the economy and of government activity. Consequently, the courts are forced to interpret more general provisions as to who governs with respect to the delivery and financing of health care and with respect to health more broadly.

With respect to the *delivery* of health care, Canada's 10 provinces have been interpreted to have primary jurisdiction, owing to two provisions of the 1867 Act. First, in the only direct mention of health care in the 1867 Act, provinces are assigned jurisdiction over the "establishment, maintenance, and management of hospitals, asylums, charities and eleemosynary institutions."[1] Second, the provinces are assigned general jurisdiction

* Colleen M. Flood is the Inaugural Director of the University of Ottawa, Centre for Health Law, Policy and Ethics and is a Professor and University of Ottawa Research Chair in Health Law & Policy; William Lahey is a Professor at Dalhousie's Schulich School of Law and President of University of King's College; Bryan Thomas is an Adjunct Professor and Senior Research Fellow with the University of Ottawa Centre for Health Law, Policy and Ethics. The authors would like to thank David Rodriguez for superb research assistance.

[1] *Constitution Act, 1867* (UK), 30 & 31 Vict, c 3, s 92(7), reprinted in RSC 1985, Appendix II, No 5. s. 92(7) [hereinafter *Constitution Act*]; Originally enacted in the UK as the *British North America Act, 1867* (30 & 31 Vict c 3).

over "property and civil rights," which has been interpreted as providing broad authority to regulate professional services—including the specific services of doctors, nurses,
and other health professionals.[2]

By contrast, jurisdiction over the *financing* of health care and over health more broadly
is divided. Court rulings from the 1930s found that the provinces have broad authority
under their jurisdiction over property and civil rights to enact programs of social insurance, including health insurance.[3] Subsequent rulings, however, recognized a federal
"spending power," allowing the federal government to fund social insurance programs
through financial grants to the provinces, and influence the design of those programs
through the attachment of conditions.[4] Some dispute the legal validity of the federal
spending power, as it has no explicit basis in constitutional text.[5] Notwithstanding,
the spending power is recognized by Court of Appeal[6] and Supreme Court of Canada
jurisprudence and has played a critical and longstanding role in Canadian federalism—
particularly in health care, as explained below in our discussion of the *Canada Health
Act (CHA)*.[7]

The federal Parliament has other important powers it can use to govern in relation
to health and to health care, including its criminal law powers, its powers and duties in
relation to Aboriginal people, its power over patents, and its (arguably under-utilized)
power to regulate in pursuit of "peace, order and good government." Using these powers, the federal order of government has made significant inroads into various facets
of health care—including establishing the conditions for a national medicare scheme;
regulating the approval of pharmaceuticals and medical devices; and enacting criminal
law provisions in areas such as assisted human reproduction, abortion, narcotics, and so
on. With respect to public health, it has also, for example, regulated the sale and advertising of tobacco and acted—insufficiently, as we discuss below—to track and prevent
the spread of contagious diseases across borders.

---

[2] See e.g., *Landers v N.B. Dental Society* (1957) 7 DLR (2d) 583 (N.B.C.A.) (affirming provincial powers
to regulate the practice of dentistry).

[3] See *Canada (Attorney General) v Ontario (Attorney General)*, [1934] ExCR 25, [1934] 3 DLR 483;
Reference re Employment and Social Insurance Act, [1936] SCR 427, [1936] SCJ No 30 (S.C.C.); *Reference re
Employment and Social Insurance Act*, [1937] AC 355 (J.C.P.C.) (affirming S.C.C.). The amendment of the
Constitution that reversed these rulings as regards the specific issue of unemployment insurance (but not
the general holding that schemes of social insurance were provincial) came in 1940, through the *British
North America Act, 1940* (3-4 Geo VI c 36) (renamed *Constitution Act, 1940* by *Constitution Act, 1982*),
which added s 91(2A), "Unemployment Insurance", to enumerated federal powers.

[4] *YMHA Jewish Community Centre of Winnipeg Inc. v Brown* [1989] 1 SCR 1532; *Reference Re Canada
Assistance Plan (B.C.)*, [1991] 2 S.C.R. 525. For a more detailed discussion of the federal spending power,
see below and the chapter by Hoy Kong in this *Handbook*.

[5] See Andrew Petter, 'Federalism and the Myth of the Federal Spending Power' [1989] 68 Can Bar
Rev 448.

[6] *Winterhaven Stables Limited v Canada (Attorney General)*, 1988 ABCA 334 [hereinafter
Winterhaven]; *Syndicat national des employés de l'aluminium d'Arvida Inc. v Canada (Attorney General)*
2006 QCCA 1453.

[7] RSC 1985, c C-6 [hereinafter *CHA*].

Below, we first describe in greater detail the ways in which the provinces have exercised jurisdiction in health (Section 2, below), before turning to the federal role (Section 3). We discuss how, in some cases, the courts have rebuked federal assertions of power, particularly the use of its criminal law powers, as an intrusion into provincial terrain (e.g., the regulation of IVF). We will also discuss some areas where the federal government could (and arguably should) exert greater regulatory muscle—such as in the area of infectious disease control.

We conclude with some general reflections on the troubled romance between federalism and health care, and how this contributes to a number of ongoing policy challenges. The federal government's role in health care is often portrayed as residual to that of the provinces, although as we will argue the federal authorities potentially have a far greater range of powers under the Constitution than is generally acknowledged or employed. The inability to track responsibility for health care, as between the federal and provincial governments, leaves a gap in accountability and results in political inertia in the face of mounting problems. In our conclusion, we analyze how federalism could be better employed to modernize Canadian health care. There is a need for bold federalism in health care, of the sort that spurred the creation of Medicare in the 1950s and 1960s, when federal-provincial cooperation expanded Saskatchewan's experiment with universal coverage into a national program of seminal importance to Canadians. To use the metaphor of our title, there is a need to work past the "troubled romance" that now characterizes federal-provincial relations in health care, to forge a vibrant and durable partnership adaptive to the twenty-first century.

2. Exercises of Provincial Jurisdiction in Health Care

To understand the limits upon direct federal action in health care, one must understand the extent to which health care has been interpreted to date as falling under provincial jurisdiction. For example, although the federal government can operate quarantine and military hospitals and health care facilities for Aboriginal Canadians,[8] the establishment, governance, regulation, and funding of hospitals and health care facilities falls under provincial jurisdiction. Health care providers, whether working in hospitals or in the community, and whether in the public or private system, generally operate under provincial jurisdiction. Similarly, health insurance, like other kinds of insurance, is within provincial jurisdiction, whether it is private insurance purchased in the market or public insurance provided by government.

Nonetheless, it is important to acknowledge, as the Supreme Court of Canada has, that health is a diffuse field of legislative responsibility in which Parliament and provincial

---

[8] See *Constitution Act*, ss 91(7), (11), (24).

legislatures can both pass valid laws.[9] For example, with respect to jurisdiction over prescription drugs, although provinces have authority over medicine and other prescribing professions, the federal government has the ability to regulate safety and approval of new drugs for general distribution and the price of prescription drugs still under patent.[10] The porousness of federal/provincial jurisdiction over health was nicely explained by Chief Justice McLachlin in *Canada v. PHS Community Services Society*, responding in this instance to an argument with respect to interjurisdictional immunity:

> [t]he federal role in the domain of health makes it impossible to precisely define what falls in or out of the proposed provincial "core". Overlapping federal jurisdiction and the sheer size and diversity of provincial health power render daunting the task of drawing a bright line around a protected provincial core of health where federal legislation may not tread.[11]

3. Exercises of Federal Power in Health Care: Successes, Failures, and Works-in-Progress

In this section we proceed through relevant federal powers and explain their role in Canadian health care. In some cases, the federal government has made forays into a given area of health care only to be pushed back by the courts—either because the move treaded on provincial jurisdiction, or due to conflicts with the *Charter of Rights and Freedoms*.[12] We start with the federal spending power, which despite its contested nature lies at the foundation of Canada's public health care system (Medicare).

A. The Federal Spending Power and the Foundations of Medicare

(i) How the Spending Power Is Applied to Health Care

The federal government flexes its implied "spending power" through provisions of the *CHA*,[13] which employs a carrot and stick approach to incentivize provinces to comply with national standards in their respective public insurance plans (see detailed

---

[9] *Schneider v British Columbia*, [1982] 2 SCR 112, [1982] SCJ No 64.

[10] *Patent Act*, RSC 1985, c P-4, ss 79-103.

[11] *Canada (Attorney General) v PHS Community Services Society*, [2011] SCC 44, [2011] 3 SCR 134 [68] [hereinafter *PHS*].

[12] Part I of the *Constitution Act, 1982*, being Schedule B to the *Canada Act 1982* (UK), 1982, c 11.

[13] *CHA* above (n 7).

discussion below). In theory, if provinces do not comply with *CHA* criteria (e.g., related to preventing out-of-pocket billing of patients at point-of-service), the federal government can in future years withhold funding from the offending province.[14]

In reality, direct enforcement of the *CHA* by the federal government (e.g., withholding dollars from transfers to the provinces as a result of non-compliance) rarely happens. The federal government's political leverage (and perhaps political will) to enforce the *CHA* has likely diminished as a result of the rapid decline in the amount of federal health transfers, from 50 percent of the total cost in 1968 to an estimated 15.5 percent in 2015.[15] Growth in health care expenditures, combined with an imperative to lower taxation rates, have resulted in some provinces seeing their share of expenditures on health care absorb nearly 50 percent of total governmental spending,[16] further diminishing the federal government's capacity under existing levels of federal funding to influence system reform.

Nonetheless, past federal governments have attempted to use negotiations over annual health transfers as an opportunity to buy real system change. For example, in 2000, 2003, and 2004, the federal government and most of the provinces, along with the territories, agreed to non-enforceable political accords under which the federal government committed to a decade of substantial increases in its health transfers to the provinces in exchange for promises to achieve or adopt certain basic reforms in their respective systems. The core outcome was to be the implementation of wait time benchmarks for five specified services (and the development and implementation of benchmarks for others). Other promises dealt with 24/7 access to multidisciplinary primary care teams, universal availability of catastrophic drug coverage, the development and implementation of a national pharmaceutical strategy, and a national system of electronic health records. Responsibility for reporting on progress was given to the Health Council of Canada[17]—a pale imitation of the strong, independent oversight and coordinating body recommended by Commissioner Romanow in his Royal Commission report on the Future of Medicare.[18]

---

[14] Gregory Marchildon and Haizhen Mou, 'A Needs-Based Allocation Formula for Canada Health Transfer' (2015) 40(3) Can Pub Pol'y 209 [hereinafter Marchildon].

[15] Department of Finance Canada, 'Federal Support to Provinces and Territories' (Department of Finance Canada 2016) www.fin.gc.ca/fedprov/mtp-eng.asp accessed 27 June 2016; Canadian Institute for Health Information, 'National Health Expenditure Trends, 1975 to 2015' (CIHI 2016) 6, https://www.cihi.ca/en/spending-and-health-workforce/spending/national-health-expenditure-trends accessed 27 June 2016 (CIHI NHEX 2015).

[16] Canadian Institute for Health Information, 'How Do the Provinces and Territories Compare?' (CIHI 2014) https://www.cihi.ca/en/spending-and-health-workforce/spending/health-spending-data/nhex-infographic-how-do-the-provinces accessed 27 June 2016.

[17] The Health Council of Canada was defunded and closed in 2014 by the Harper federal government on the rationale that the 10-year health accord started in 2004 had been completed. Steve Rennie, 'Tory Government Will End Funding of Body That Oversees Canada's Health Accord' (The Toronto Star, 2013) https://www.thestar.com/news/canada/2013/04/16/tory_government_will_end_funding_of_body_that_oversees_canadas_health_accord.html accessed 27 June 2016.

[18] Roy J Romanow, *Building on Values: The Future of Health Care in Canada* (Commission on the Future of Health Care in Canada 2002) http://publications.gc.ca/collections/Collection/CP32-85-2002E.pdf accessed 27 June 2016.

Like the parallel Kelowna Accord, which promised significant action on First Nation health, the accords were, at best, "soft law." They stressed respect for the jurisdiction of the provinces over health care and emphasized that provinces would be accountable to their residents, not to the federal government or to each other. So, it was perhaps unsurprising that although the federal money flowed, reform came unevenly, if at all. As Romanow and others have charged, the accords bought federal-provincial peace but not change that benefited patients.[19] Although this may have been predictable given their softness, it was foreordained once responsibility for their administration shifted in 2007 from the Chretien/Martin government, which at least asserted a federal role in health care, to the Harper government, which did not. Indeed, the latter would go on to recalculate the formula for the health transfer as a flat per capita amount, pegged to GDP growth—meaning that (e.g.) provinces with older populations receive no special assistance, significantly undermining national solidarity in the project of Medicare.[20] The Kelowna Accord dealing with funding for Aboriginal peoples in Canada fared worse: it was simply disowned by the Harper government.[21]

(ii) Constitutional Challenges to the Implied Spending Power

Though not explicitly enumerated in the constitutional text, the spending power is derived partly from the federal government's section 91 powers to raise revenues "by any mode or system of taxation." It has been suggested that the power garners additional support from the federal Parliament's section 91A powers related to "public debt and property" and its section 102 authority to make payments out of the Consolidated Revenue Fund.[22]

The federal government's use of the spending power to influence areas nominally under provincial jurisdiction has been subject to constitutional challenge. Thus, in *Winterhaven Stables Ltd. v Canada (Attorney General)*,[23] the appellants argued that the spending power was being used, through legislation such as the *CHA*, to "coerce" provinces into participating in federal programs, usurping their jurisdiction. In the health care context specifically, the case raises the example of Canadian restrictions on two-tier care, with the appellant contending that ". . . Parliament cannot directly prohibit extra-billing (over and above health care payments) by doctors, so it cannot achieve the same end by the conditions attached to funding."[24] The court rejected this argument

[19] See The Honourable Kelvin K Ogilvie and The Honourable Art Eggleton, 'Time for Transformative Change: A Review of the 2004 Health Accord' (Canada, Parliament, Standing Senate Committee on Social Affairs, Science and Technology, 2012) www.parl.gc.ca/content/sen/committee/411/soci/rep/repo7mar12-e.pdf accessed 27 June 2016 at 82.
[20] Marchildon above (n 14).
[21] Christopher Alcantra and Zac Spicer, 'Learning from the Kelowna Accord' (Policy Options 2015) http://policyoptions.irpp.org/magazines/clearing-the-air/alcantara-spicer/ accessed 27 June 2016.
[22] Constitutional Law Group, *Canadian Constitutional Law* (4th ed.) at 469.
[23] Above (n 6).
[24] Ibid [20].

on grounds that the federal authorities had not used "legislative force" to achieve their ends—provinces could refuse to accept the conditions of the *CHA*, and "there would be no effect on matters within provincial jurisdiction."[25] Subsequently, in *Reference Re Canada Assistance Plan*,[26] the province of Manitoba argued that a federal spending ceiling on the Canada Assistance Plan program was an unconstitutional interference with the provinces' jurisdiction over social services.[27] The argument was rejected along similar lines to *Winterhaven*, with Justice Sopinka writing for a majority of the Supreme Court that, "[t]he simple withholding of federal money which had previously been granted to fund a matter within provincial jurisdiction does not amount to the regulation of that matter."[28]

Moreover, in various *Charter* challenges concerning access to health goods and services, the Supreme Court of Canada has relied on the *CHA* for guidance in interpreting provincial health insurance acts, seeming to embrace the idea that health care is an area of federal/provincial cooperation.[29] Canadian legal scholars appear by and large to accept the spending power's constitutionality.[30] It is unclear whether *at some point* the strings attached to federal financial inducements become so irresistible as to be coercive. A majority of the US Supreme Court embraced this view for the first time in its history in 2012, as it rejected the US federal government's efforts to expand Medicaid eligibility on grounds that the massive financial stake used to incentivize state participation crossed the line from encouragement into coercion.[31]

---

[25] Ibid.

[26] [1991] 2 SCR 525 [hereinafter *Re Canada Assistance Plan*].

[27] The Canada Assistance Plan was introduced in 1966 as a cost-sharing arrangement for social assistance programs. It entitles provinces to federal funding on the condition of providing social assistance without provincial or territorial residency requirements. In 1995 the program was combined with the Established Programs Financing to create the Canada Health and Social Transfer program. This combined program has since been split into the Canada Social Transfer and Canada Health Transfer. Department of Finance Canada, 'History of Health and Social Transfers' (Department of Finance Canada 2014) https://www.fin.gc.ca/fedprov/his-eng.asp accessed 27 June 2016.

[28] *Re Canada Assistance Plan*, above (n 26) [92].

[29] *Eldridge v British Columbia (Attorney General)*, [1997] 3 SCR 624, 31; *Auton (Guardian ad litem of) v British Columbia (Attorney General)*, 2004 SCC 78, [2004] 3 SCR 657, 1.

[30] Peter W Hogg (ed), *Constitutional Law of Canada* (2015 Student Edition, Carswell 2015) 6-16–6-22, 32–34; William Lahey, 'The Legal Framework for Intergovernmental Health Care Governance: Making the Most of Limited Options' in Katherine Fierlbeck and William Lahey (eds), *Health Care Federalism in Canada: Critical Junctures and Critical Perspectives* (McGill-Queen's University Press) 75–77. Constitutional experts in Quebec are on the whole more skeptical. See, e.g., Henri Brun, Eugénie Brouillet and Guy Tremblay, *Droit constitutionnel* (4th ed Yvon Blais, 2002) and Marc-André Turcotte, *Le pouvoir fédéral de dépenser* (Yvon Blais, 2015).

[31] *National Federation of Independent Business v. Sebelius*, 132 S. Ct. 2566 (2012); Nicole Huberfeld, Elizabeth Weeks Leonard and Kevin Outterson, 'Plunging Into Endless Difficulties: Medicaid and Coercion in *National Federation of Independent Businesses v. Sebelius* (2013) 93 BUL Rev 1 http://papers.ssrn.com/sol3/papers.cfm?abstract_id=2128760 accessed 27 June 2016.

B. The *Canada Health Act* (*CHA*) and Challenges to It

In theory, to receive federal transfer payments for health care, the provinces must comply with five program criteria set out in the *CHA*:

  (i) public administration;
 (ii) comprehensiveness;
(iii) universality;
 (iv) portability; and
  (v) accessibility.[32]

The requirement of *public administration* refers to the insurance system for medically necessary care, but does not preclude private *delivery* of health care services, as is often mistakenly believed. In fact, most Canadian physicians operate as independent for-profit businesses, billing government on a fee-for-service basis. The principle of *comprehensiveness* requires that a province's public insurance scheme cover "all insured health services provided by hospitals, medical practitioners or dentists."[33] However, given that the *CHA* defines all "insured services" as being "medical necessary" physician services and "medically required" hospital services but defines neither term, it is effectively left to each province to determine the basket of health services actually insured.[34] The principle of *universality* requires that all insured persons receive uniform coverage. This would appear to preclude, for example, means testing for public coverage. The principle of *portability* ensures that Canadians retain coverage when moving from one province to another. Last, the principle of *accessibility* requires reasonable access on uniform terms and conditions. In furtherance of accessibility, the *CHA* also specifically forbids employment of user fees (requiring that patients make an out-of-pocket payment at point of service) and extra billing (physicians charging an additional fee above the amount paid by the public insurer), which might block people of limited means from making use of Medicare or otherwise cause inequalities of access. Arguably, the criteria of accessibility is violated by long wait times in the public system, though this has not been strongly tested by the federal government or in the courts.[35]

The *CHA* has undoubtedly played a critical role in establishing a core of public finance for important health care services and ensuring redistribution from the wealthy to the poor, and from the healthy to the sick.[36] However, it is showing its age and needs

---

[32] *CHA* above (n 7).

[33] Ibid s 9.

[34] Colleen M Flood, Mark Bernard Stabile and Carolyn Hughes Tuohy, 'What Is In and Out of Medicare? Who Decides?' in Colleen M Flood (ed), *Just Medicare: What's In, What's Out, How We Decide* (University of Toronto Press 2006).

[35] William Lahey, 'Medicare and the Law: Contours of an Evolving Relationship' in Jocelyn Downie, Tim Caulfield and Colleen M Flood (eds), *Canadian Health Law and Policy* (Lexis 2011) 43.

[36] Canadian Institute of Health Information, 'Lifetime Distributional Effects of Publicly Financed Health Care in Canada' (CIHI 2013) https://secure.cihi.ca/free_products/Lifetime_Distributional_Effects_AiB_EN.pdf accessed 27 June 2016.

modernization.[37] Drafted to protect a system of public health in the 1960s, the *CHA* focuses entirely on health care delivered by physicians and in hospitals.[38] This has meant, for example, that the *CHA* does nothing to ensure public coverage for the growing spending on pharmaceuticals in community settings or spending on long-term care. Health care has increasingly shifted out of hospitals and to different kinds of health care providers apart from physicians, eroding the public system in a process dubbed "passive privatization." We return to the question of how to expand and modernize public health insurance in our conclusion.

Apart from the need to expand, there is also a problem of actually *enforcing* the present provisions of the *CHA*. The broad provisions of the *CHA* mean the federal government has wide and virtually unreviewable discretion as to whether a province has complied with any of its criteria and then, further, whether to penalize a province. On both fronts, federal governments over the decades have taken a lenient if not a permissive approach to enforcement. The *CHA* does, however, have a stronger in-built mechanism for enforcing the ban on extra-billing and user fees: for every dollar patients or private insurers are billed for medically necessary care, the federal government *must* withhold a dollar from the transfer payment to the relevant province. However, this still leaves space for interpretation—for example, as to whether private clinics could charge a facility fee directly to patients or their insurers to cover the costs of running the clinic, and then separately bill the public system for the cost of the physician service. To clarify this practice, then federal Minister of Health Diane Marleau wrote to all provincial and territorial ministers of health on 6 January 1995, to announce that when a province pays the physician fee for a medically necessary service delivered at a private clinic, it must also pay the facility fee or have the sum treated as a user charge and deducted from their transfer payment.[39] More recently, even these more robust and ostensibly mandatory provisions of the *CHA* have fallen away, with anecdotal evidence of little or no enforcement through the last 10 years under a Conservative federal government which viewed health care as solely a matter of provincial jurisdictions. Into this void, private clinics have sprung up across the country, often only thinly disguising the fact that they are offering medically necessary care in contravention of the *CHA*.[40]

---

[37] Colleen M Flood and Bryan Thomas, 'Modernizing the Canada Health Act' (2017) 39 Dal LJ 397.

[38] See *CHA* above (n 7) s 2 for the definition of "insured services."

[39] See Canada, Health Canada, *Canada Health Act Annual Report 2014–2015* (Health Canada 2015) 7 www.hc-sc.gc.ca/hcs-sss/alt_formats/pdf/pubs/cha-ics/2015-cha-lcs-ar-ra-eng.pdf accessed 27 June 2016.

[40] See Kate McNamara, 'Alberta Government to Investigate Private Medical Clinic in Calgary' (CBC News 2016) www.cbc.ca/news/canada/calgary/copeman-clinic-investigation-alberta-government-1.3603242 accessed 27 June 2016; Kate McNamara, 'Both Province and Patients Pay for Tests at Copeman Clinic' (CBC News 2016) www.cbc.ca/news/canada/calgary/private-healthcare-copeman-overtesting-billing-1.3589748 accessed 27 June 2016; Kate McNamara, 'Copeman Clinic, Doctors Battle over How Private Health Care Should Be Delivered' (CBC News 2016) www.cbc.ca/news/canada/calgary/copeman-nedelmann-calgary-clinic-lawsuit-1.3530149 accessed 27 June 2016.

To be clear, the *CHA* does not itself entrench direct rights to health or health care for Canadians. As indicated, where a province for example violates the criteria of accessibility by allowing extra-billing, the federal government must respond by withholding a portion of transfer payments. However, on a plain reading, the *CHA* does not issue *citizens* a right to challenge their provincial government's noncompliance with the five principles.[41] Canadian patients have nevertheless found legal avenues for pursuing access to health care through litigation—for example, by launching mass tort claims, requesting administrative reviews, and bringing constitutional challenges. In the last-mentioned scenario, the courts are being used to launch attacks on provincial laws enacted to limit the private sale of medically necessary care. Depending on the province, these laws ban private health insurance for services covered by Medicare, forbid physicians from charging patients more than the public tariff they receive (extra-billing), and require physicians who wish to practice privately to opt out of the public system entirely.[42] These kinds of provincial laws have been largely successful in discouraging the emergence of a parallel private payment system of medicine in Canada but are now under sustained constitutional attack in a number of provinces on the basis that they violate the security of the person of those who would be able and willing to pay for faster access to medical care than is available to them under the public system. One such challenge has succeeded at the Supreme Court of Canada level, leading to the partial overturn of a Quebec law banning private insurance for medically necessary care. [43] Thus, counter-intuitively, the *Charter* and human rights legislation are being used to attack a Canadian social program that is, more than any other, based on a commitment to equity.[44]

These *Charter* challenges do not directly threaten the federal government's use of the spending power to create—or expand—a national medicare scheme. But it may be a genuine conundrum how Canada will maintain a single-payer system on a national scale if the courts overturn provincial statutes now in place. Meanwhile, because of the failure of the *CHA* to cover important areas of care such as prescription drugs outside of hospitals and because of the reluctance of the federal government to enforce the *CHA* against provinces, the system is being increasingly privatized contrary to the Act's clear intent.

[41] Cf Sujit Choudhry, 'The Enforcement of the Canada Health Act' (1996) 41 McGill LJ 462.

[42] Colleen M Flood and Tom Archibald, 'The Illegality of Private Health Care in Canada' (2001) 61 CMAJ 825, 825–830; See Colleen M Flood and Amanda Haugan, 'Is Canada Odd? A Comparison of European and Canadian Approaches to Choice and Regulation of the Public/Private Divide in Health Care' (2010) 5 Health Econ Pol'y & L 319 for a comparative overview of regulation of the public/private divide.

[43] *Chaoulli v Quebec (Attorney General)*, 2005 SCC 35, [2005] 1 SCR 791.

[44] Colleen M Flood, 'Litigating Health Rights in Canada: A White Knight for Equity' in Collen M Flood and Aeyal Gross (eds), *The Right to Health at the Public/Private Divide: A Global Comparative Study* (Cambridge University Press, 2014).

C. Other Uses of the Spending Power: Existing and Potential

In addition to the *CHA*, the federal spending powers are also used in pursuit of diverse health purposes including: health research, health information, health promotion and disease prevention and control, and other various health care initiatives undertaken in cooperation with the provinces.[45]

Both in these specific applications and in its core role in cost-sharing provincial health insurance, the federal spending power clearly has played a critical role in giving Canada the semblance of a national health care system. At the same time, the weak enforcement of the minimalist and narrow requirements of the *CHA*, discussed above, and the failure of three broader health accords to achieve meaningful reform, cast doubt on the potential for real reform in the health care system if the spending power is applied as it has been in the past. Something is required beyond narrowly-targeted and weakly-administered efforts to get each province to meet and maintain basic national standards or to achieve basic outcomes. This is a topic we return to in the conclusion.

D. First Nations and Inuit People

We have just discussed the general structure and financing of Medicare. For some populations, such as prisoners in federal institutions and members of the military, health care falls directly under federal jurisdiction. Here we focus on First Nations and Inuit People—arguably the most contentious group, because the federal Parliament has jurisdiction relating to "Indians," and provincial legislatures have jurisdiction more broadly with respect to health care, but neither level of government wants to take responsibility for the poor state of Aboriginal health, or admit of constitutional duties with respect thereto.

(i) Historical Perspective on First Nations Health

Aboriginal peoples enjoyed relatively good states of health prior to the arrival of European settlers in Canada,[46] who carried with them diseases that decimated Indigenous populations.[47] Subsequent colonization further detrimentally affected the health of First Nations, who were forced off resource- and agriculturally-rich land and

---

[45] *Canadian Institutes of Health Research Act*, SC 2006, c 6, ss 4, 5; *Public Health Agency of Canada Act*, SC 2006, c 5, preamble.

[46] We are indebted in this section to the research of Allison Nesbit and her excellent paper, 'Targeting High Rates of First Nations Youth Suicide: Exploring a Positive Right to Government-Funded Mental Health Care Services' (2016) (copy on file with authors) [hereinafter *First Nations Child*].

[47] First Nations Health Authority, *Our History, Our Health* (First Nations Health Authority 2016) www.fnha.ca/wellness/our-history-our-health accessed 27 June 2016.

onto small plots of reserve land, usually in remote areas with a high population density[48] and relatively poor access to health care services.[49] Conditions on many reserves continue to this day to be described as "third world," with insufficient access to clean drinking water, poor sanitation, food insecurity, and inadequate shelter.[50] Aboriginal heath was further threatened as a result of government assimilation policies: "The colonization of Indigenous Peoples . . . [has been recognized] as a fundamental underlying health determinant."[51]

The process of colonization and the resulting negative impact on health is exemplified by the policy of forcibly taking Aboriginal children from their families and incarcerating them in residential schools. Residential schools, which existed in Canada from the late nineteenth century until the late 1960s (although some remained until the 1990s), institutionalized more than 150,000 Aboriginal children. The policy goal was to entirely isolate the children from their Aboriginal culture, and assimilate them into the predominantly European culture that Canada wanted to recreate.[52] Subjected, at a minimum, to complete repression of their language and culture and, in some cases, physical and sexual abuse, generations suffered and continue to suffer the ill-effects, including a persistent gap in health outcomes compared to the rest-of-Canada and galloping rates of mental illness for both themselves and their children.[53] Nationwide, First Nations youth are seven times more likely to commit suicide in comparison to the non-First Nations youth population of Canada.[54] Within Northern Ontario, some First Nations have a suicide rate that is 50 times the Canadian average for children under 15 years.[55]

[48] Truth and Reconciliation Commission of Canada, *Canada's Residential Schools: The History, Part 1 Origins to 1939, Final Report of the Truth and Reconciliation Commission of Canada, vol 1* (McGill-Queen's University Press, 2015) 3.

[49] Canada, Royal Commission on Aboriginal Peoples, *Report of the Royal Commission on Aboriginal Peoples*, Vol 1, Part 2 (Communication Group, 1996) 396–400.

[50] Ben Spurr, 'First Nations Chief Blames 'Third World' Living Conditions for Fatal Fire on Reserve' (The Toronto Star 2016) http://www.thestar.com/news/canada/2016/03/31/chief-blames-third-world-living-conditions-on-first-nations-reserve-for-fatal-fire.html accessed 27 June 2016.

[51] International Symposium on the Social Determinants of Indigenous Health, 'Social Determinants and Indigenous Health: The International Experience and Its Policy Implications' (World Health Organization 2007) http://www.who.int/social_determinants/resources/indigenous_health_adelaide_report_07.pdf accessed 27 June 2016, at 2.

[52] Norah Keilland and Tonina Simeone, *Current Issues in Mental Health in Canada: The Mental Health of First Nations and Inuit Communities*, (Publication No 2014-02-E 6, Library of Parliament, Parliamentary Information and Research Service, Legal and Social Affairs Division, 2014).

[53] Truth and Reconciliation Commission of Canada, *Canada's Residential Schools: The History, Part 1 Origins to 1939, Final Report of the Truth and Reconciliation Commission of Canada*, Vol 1 (McGill-Queen's University Press, 2015) 152.

[54] Laura Eggertson, 'Aboriginal Youth Suicide Rises in Northern Ontario' (2015) 187:11 CMAJ 335, 355ff>. First Nations females aged 19 and under are five times more likely to commit suicide versus non-First Nations females; PA Peters, LN Oliver and DE Kohen, 'Mortality among Children and Youth in High-Percentage First Nations Identity Areas, 2000–2002 and 2005–2007' (2013) 13:2424 Rural and Remote Health 7 www.rrh.org.au/publishedarticles/article_print_2424.pdf accessed 27 June 2016.

[55] DPRA Canada, 'North West Local Health Integration Network Aboriginal Health Programs and Services Analysis & Strategies: Final Report' (DPRA 2010) www.northwestlhin.on.ca/resources/~/media/sites/nw/uploadedfiles/Home_Page/Report_and_Publications/NW%20LHIN%20

(ii) Current Division of Powers Problem Negatively Affects First Nations' Health

As mentioned, the *Constitution Act, 1867* is not explicit on whether the federal or provincial governments have jurisdiction over health care. Section 92(7) is the only constitutional provision that explicitly defines a branch of health care as a provincial matter, but it is restricted to the "[m]anagement of [h]ospitals."[56] Nevertheless, through judicial interpretation, health care has primarily (though not exclusively) been assigned to provincial jurisdiction. As stated in *R v Schneider*, "[the] view that the general jurisdiction over health matters is provincial . . . has prevailed and is . . . not seriously questioned."[57] However, the issue of Aboriginal health is further complicated as section 91(24) assigns "Indians" to federal jurisdiction.[58] Thus, whilst both levels of government may provide health care to Aboriginal peoples, it is yet to be determined whether either level of government *must* do so. It speaks volumes that with respect to Aboriginal health, both levels of government have sought to avoid rather than assume responsibilities in this area.

The federal government has interpreted its responsibility under section 91(24) to apply only to individuals registered as "Indians" under the *Indian Act* and to Inuit peoples.[59] The recent Supreme Court of Canada victory for Canada's Métis peoples, establishing their status as "Indians" under the Constitution, confirms the doubtfulness of this self-serving restriction.[60] What remains is the insistence of Health Canada (the federal government department) that the health benefits it delivers to Aboriginal peoples are discretionary, humanitarian efforts. In other words, the federal government claims that it is the provincial governments' constitutional responsibility to provide health care to First Nations persons as part of their pubic health insurance schemes:[61] to the extent the federal government provides services to First Nations peoples, it purports to do so on a discretionary basis and cannot be required to do so under section 91(24).[62] Obviously First Nations' peoples dispute this characterization.

One of the major health care initiatives launched by the federal government is the Non-Insured Health Benefits (NIHB) program, which provides a portion of Aboriginal

---

Aboriginal%20Health%20Programs%20and%20Services%20Analysis%20and%20Strategy.pdf accessed 27 June 2016, at 25.

[56]   *Constitution Act, 1867* above (n 1).

[57]   *Schneider v The Queen* [1982] 2 SCR 112, 137, 139 DLR (3d) 417.

[58]   *Constitution Act, 1867* above (n 1) s 91(24). "Indians" under this provision refers to Aboriginal peoples, First Nations, Inuit, and Métis.

[59]   Constance MacIntosh, 'Indigenous Peoples and Health Law and Policy: Responsibilities and Obligations' in Jocelyn Downie, Timothy Caulfield and Colleen M Flood (eds), *Canadian Health Law and Policy 4th Edition* (Markham, LexisNexis 2011) 587–588 [hereinafter *Indigenous Peoples*].

[60]   *Daniels v Canada (Indian Affairs and Northern Development)*, [2016] 1 SCR 99.

[61]   Kelly A Macdonald and Kylie Walman, 'Jordan's Principle: A Child First Approach to Jurisdictional Issues' in First Nations Child & Family Caring Society of Canada, *WEN: DE—We Are Coming to the Light of Day* (First Nations Child & Family Caring Society of Canada, 2005) https://fncaringsociety.com/sites/default/files/docs/WendeReport.pdf accessed 27 June 2016, at 90.

[62]   Romanow, 'The Future of Health Care in Canada' above (n 18) 212; *Indigenous Peoples* above (n 59).

peoples with select medically necessary health-related goods and services that are not covered by provincial or privately-held medical plans.[63] This includes pharmacy benefits, dental services, medical transport, and eye and vision services. The NIHB accounts for nearly half of Health Canada's expenditures for First Nations and Inuit health, with pharmacy costs alone making up nearly half of that amount.[64]

Aboriginal peoples may find themselves slipping through the cracks, as both federal and provincial governments look to avoid financial responsibility. In 1999, a First Nations boy named Jordan was born in Manitoba with complex medical needs, and hospitalized at birth. Although he could have been cared for in his home/community, he eventually died in hospital at five years of age, as neither the federal government (Health Canada) nor the Manitoba provincial government were willing to take responsibility for the costs involved in moving him from hospital. Although this case resulted in an agreement that Aboriginal children would not be subjected to these kind of jurisdictional disputes—"Jordan's Principle"—it seems that such disputes continue to arise.[65]

Canada's abysmal approach to First Nations' peoples has drawn international attention. The United Nations has called on Canada to "implement and reinforce its existing programmes and policies to supply basic needs to indigenous peoples."[66] The most hopeful response to this jurisdictional quagmire has come in the form of devolution: the passage of financial and governance authorities from federal and provincial and territorial governments to First Nations bands themselves. Although not without its own concerns—passage of authority without sufficient resources may only allow bands to "self-administer their own misery"—devolution potentially allows Aboriginal peoples the autonomy to craft health care systems that better reflect their own needs and culture. The British Columbian Tripartite Agreement marks the most comprehensive Aboriginal health self-governance agreement to date. It was signed on 13 October 2011 by the First Nations Health Society, the province of British Columbia (BC), and the federal government. Pursuant to this agreement, the federal government transferred all of its responsibilities, resources, and infrastructure for Aboriginal health in BC to a new First Nations Health Authority. Although BC's regional health authorities will continue to provide acute care to Aboriginal people, the First Nation Health Authority will be responsible for on-reserve programs, including primary care and public health initiatives. In total,

---

[63] The NIHB assumes that Aboriginal peoples who are accepted by the federal government as coming within federal jurisdiction are eligible persons under provincially and territorially administered medicare programs. This is consistent with the definition of "resident" found in the Canada Health Act, which includes Aboriginal persons. The effect is that provinces and territories must ensure Aboriginal people who live within their territory to satisfy the universality criteria of their eligibility for federal health transfers under the Act.

[64] Canada, Health Canada, *Non-insured Health Benefits Program: Annual Report 2008/2009* (Health Canada, 2010) 17.

[65] *Pictou Landing Band Council v Canada (Attorney General)*, [2013] FC 342, [2013] 3 CNLR 371.

[66] United Nations Human Rights Committee, *Concluding Observations on the Sixth Periodic Report of Canada* (International Covenant on Civil and Political Rights 2015) www.refworld.org/docid/5645a16f4. html accessed 27 June 2016.

the federal government is to transfer about $380 million per year to Aboriginal communities under the Tripartite Agreement, with the province of BC contributing an additional $83 million.[67] The new governance agreement ultimately marks an attempt to close the disparities that exist between First Nations and other British Columbians in, inter alia, the area of health, by increasing the capacity of First Nations communities to provide primary health care and by empowering them to take a much more active role in the formulation of Aboriginal health policy.[68]

Apart from devolution of responsibility there are also signs that courts are growing far more willing to order action on the part of governments vis-à-vis their responsibilities to Aboriginal peoples. The case law demonstrates that Canadian courts and tribunals have begun to recognize the importance of Aboriginal rights and the protection these groups deserve.[69] Thus courts may in the future be more willing to demand positive action by Canadian governments when it comes to the provision of adequate health and health care services to Aboriginal Canadians than they have been relative to Canadians more generally.

E. Criminal Law Power

Section 91(27) of the *Constitution Act, 1867* confers on the federal Parliament the exclusive power to legislate in relation to the criminal law. The Supreme Court of Canada has found this power to be plenary and broadly defined in scope; further, the Court has emphasized that the definition of a crime is not frozen in time nor confined to a fixed domain of activity. At first blush, such a broad jurisdiction could be used to achieve almost any regulatory purpose—which would lead to intolerable intrusions into provincial domains. Thus the courts have established tests for ascertaining whether a law is a valid exercise of the criminal law power, requiring that it "contain a prohibition

---

[67] Lauren Vogel, 'BC First Nations to Run Own Health System' (2011) 183(17) CMAJ E1227.

[68] The Supreme Court has broadly endorsed this approach of "cooperative federalism" in the context of delivering child welfare services to Aboriginal children and families in British Columbia. See *NIL/ TU,O Child and Family Services Society v B.C. Government and Service Employees' Union* [2010] 2 SCR 696 [42] (Abella J), (LeBel, Deschamps, Charron, Rothstein and Cromwell JJ concurring).

[69] For example, in *McIvor v Canada (Registrar of Indian and Northern Affairs)*, [2009] BCCA 153,165– 166, 306 DLR (4th), 190 CRR (2d) [hereinafter *McIvor*], the B.C.C.A. forced the federal government to amend the *Indian Act* to eliminate discrimination against wives and children of non-status Indians. The Canadian Human Rights Tribunal has found that the federal government discriminated against on-reserve First Nations children in failing to provide equal social assistance funding for children living on reserves, in comparison to off-reserve children. *First Nations Child and Family Caring Society of Canada et al. v Attorney General of Canada (for the Minister of Indian and Northern Affairs Canada)*, 2016 CHRT 2. The complainants are now seeking to have the decision enforced by the Federal Court. Kristy Kirkup, 'Trudeau Government on Notice in First Nations Child Welfare Dispute' (The Toronto Star 20 September 2016), online: https://www.thestar.com/news/canada/2016/09/20/trudeau-government-on-notice-in-first-nations-child-welfare-dispute.html.

accompanied by a penal sanction and must be directed at a legitimate public health evil."[70] Legislation that attempts to disguise a regulatory purpose as a prohibition runs the risk of being overturned.[71]

There are a host of issues in health care where the federal authorities have asserted their power to enact criminal law. For example, doctors and hospitals providing care under provincial jurisdiction can only use drugs and medical devices that have been licensed by federal regulators. Another example is federal tobacco control, including laws which impose advertising restrictions on tobacco companies and which work in combination with provincial laws, (e.g., Nova Scotia's requiring that retailers keep cigarettes "under an opaque front counter," out of customer's view). Federal advertising restrictions have been upheld by the Supreme Court as valid criminal law on the basis that "it is difficult to conceive what Parliament's purpose could have been in enacting this legislation apart from the reduction of tobacco consumption and the protection of public health."[72] Further, the Court found that Parliament's choice to prohibit tobacco *advertising* (rather than tobacco consumption) was not an attempt to colourably intrude on provincial jurisdiction, as the choice was driven by the reality that widespread use of tobacco made a direct ban on consumption simply impractical.[73]

There are however prominent examples of federal forays into health and health care based on the criminal law power being turned back by the courts, on grounds that they infringe *Charter* rights. Examples include cases striking down *Criminal Code* provisions imposing bureaucratic restrictions on access to abortion,[74] restrictions on the use of medical marijuana,[75] and a ministerial decision to revoke a previously granted exemption of a safe injection site from criminal prohibitions on possession contained in the *Controlled Drugs and Substances Act*.[76] Arguably, these cases show that criminal law can be a very blunt tool with which to regulate public health and health care. This no doubt limits the extent and manner of its possible use, particularly as a means of regulating health care financing and delivery. It also suggests that those subjected to this kind of

---

[70] *RJR-MacDonald Inc. v Canada (Attorney General)*,[1995] 3 SCR 199 [267], 111 DLR (4th) 385 [hereinafter *RJR*].

[71] *Reference re Assisted Human Reproduction Act*, [2010] 3 SCR 457.

[72] Ibid [33].

[73] In *RJR* above (n 70), the Supreme Court went on to find that the restrictions on brand advertising violated free speech rights under the *Charter*. A majority of the Court also found that the violation could not be justified, due to the federal government's failure to show that the legislation's limitations on advertising were reasonably necessary to achieving the legislation's objective of reducing tobacco consumption. This very disappointing result was largely reversed in the subsequent case of *Canada (Attorney General) v JTI-Macdonald Corp.* 2007 SCC 30, where the Court viewed the array of international evidence presented as now sustaining the government's approach to regulation. Very recently, the newly-minted Liberal federal government announced plans to introduce laws requiring plain packaging of all tobacco products. These laws are sure to result in further challenges to the authority of Parliament to use its criminal law powers to control the harms which tobacco poses to public health.

[74] *R. v Morgentaler*, [1988] 1 SCR 30, 63 OR (2d) 281.

[75] *Allard v Canada*, 2014 FC 280 (CanLII), 451 FTR 45.

[76] *PHS* above (n 11).

regulation can be expected to challenge the federal Parliament's constitutional authority to regulate them under criminal law. But challenges also occur because the provinces (frequently Quebec) believe the federal government is intruding into their areas of
jurisdiction, even in cases where the challenging province itself has failed to sufficiently
regulate an area.

This last point is illustrated by the fate of the federal government's attempt to regulate in the field of assisted human reproduction (AHR). In 2004, the federal Parliament
passed legislation regulating diverse aspects of AHR. The *Assisted Human Reproduction
Act (AHRA)*[77] broadly divided AHR technologies and therapies into two baskets—
controlling some and altogether *prohibiting* others. Sensing an intrusion into provincial
jurisdiction, Quebec asked the Quebec Court of Appeal to decide whether certain provisions of the *AHRA* dealing with "controlled activities," such as IVF, were ultra vires
federal jurisdiction. The Attorney General of Quebec argued these provisions were an
attempt to regulate medical practice, an area that has historically fallen within provincial jurisdiction under ss. 92(13) and 92(16) of the *Constitution Act, 1867*.[78] The Attorney
General of Canada defended the impugned provisions as a valid use of the federal criminal law power under s. 91(27) of the *Constitution Act, 1867*.[79]

In a 4–4–1 split decision released in December 2010, the Court ruled in part for
Quebec, striking down the provisions that empowered the federal Assisted Human
Reproductive Agency to license and regulate the practice of IVF.[80] Relying substantially
on the recommendations of the Baird Commission, which had prompted the legislation, Justices LeBel and Deschamps found the pith and substance of these provisions
to be regulatory, in joint reasons for judgment that Justices Abella and Rothstein concurred with and that Justice Cromwell agreed with in the result.[81] They argued that these
provisions of the Act did not target either a harm or a moral evil within the criminal
law power and that to find otherwise would make the criminal power too broad and
too encroaching on provincial jurisdiction over the practice of medicine.[82] For the
impugned provisions, no moral evil or harm had been identified; indeed, the Baird
Commission considered the "controlled" activities beneficial.[83]

---

[77] *Assisted Human Reproduction Act*, SC 2004, c 2 [hereinafter *Assisted Reproduction*].
[78] *Reference Re Assisted Human Reproduction Act*, 2010 SCC 61 [7], [327]. Sub-s 92(16) of the
Constitution Act, 1867 confers authority over "local matters" on provincial legislatures.
[79] Ibid [6], [327].
[80] Colleen M Flood and Bryan Thomas, 'Regulatory Failure: The Case of the Private-for-Profit IVF
Sector' in T Lemmens, C Milne and I Lee (eds), *Legal, Ethical and Policy Challenges of Assisted Human
Reproduction* (University of Toronto Press 2015) 438–475 [hereinafter Regulatory Failure].
[81] Ibid [227], [327].
[82] Ibid [236], [238], [243], [327].
[83] Ibid [250], [327]. The Act's "prohibited" activities, set out in sub-ss 5-7 were not challenged and
therefore remain in force. These include human cloning, screening for sex for non-medical purposes,
permanently altering the genome of an embryo so that the alterations would be passed down to
descendants, creating chimeras or animal hybrids, paying surrogates or intermediaries to a surrogacy
contract, using a surrogate mother under the age of 21, and the sale of gamete material: *Assisted
Reproduction* above (n 77) ss 5-7.

The Supreme Court essentially ruled that the regulation of the delivery of IVF services lies primarily in the hands of the provinces and that the federal authorities could not regulate using its criminal law powers, even in the absence of provincial action. Further, Justices LeBel and Deschamps were unmoved by the federal government's argument that a federal scheme was required in light of the difficulty the provinces would face in creating a uniform national scheme through coordinated legislative action.

Few would contest that, absent an overriding federal jurisdiction based on the criminal law power, it does lie within the power of provinces to regulate the provision of IVF services. Until recently however, none had taken up this challenge, making a national consensus that would see harmonization of such regulations across the country a very remote possibility. The first child conceived through in vitro fertilization was born in 1978, the first Canadian child in 1983.[84] It took 21 years for the federal authorities to attempt (unsuccessfully) to regulate the practice through the *AHRA*. In 2010, Quebec became the first province to directly regulate IVF, 27 years after the technology's appearance in Canada. To date, most provinces in Canada resemble Ontario in eschewing direct regulation of the IVF sector, taking instead a light and indirect approach. This "light" regulatory approach is especially problematic given the safety, quality, and consumer concerns arising from the delivery of IVF services in the context of private, for-profit clinics.[85]

The broader implications of the ruling in the *AHRA* reference should not be overstated. There was no majority consensus on the reason for the ruling. Four justices would have upheld the impugned provisions of the AHRA on reasoning which agreed with the federal government's argument—that criminal legislation was required in order to ensure uniform regulation in an emerging field of health technology which raised fundamental questions about the limits which society should place on technological manipulation of human reproduction. Moreover, the newly enacted federal legislation on medically assisted dying,[86] replacing laws struck down on *Charter* grounds in the *Carter* decision, shows that there is both jurisdictional competency and wide support for federal criminal law in some critical areas of medical practice.[87] Nevertheless, the fate of the AHRA shows how conflicts over division of power can limit optimal health care governance on issues of great importance to Canadians.

---

[84] Canadian Press, 'First Test-Tube Babies Born in Canada Turn 25' (CTV News 2007), www.ctvnews.ca/first-test-tube-babies-born-in-canada-turn-25-1.234615 accessed 27 June 2016.

[85] Regulatory Failure above (n 80).

[86] *An Act to amend the Criminal Code and to make related amendments to other Acts (medical assistance in dying)* S.C. 2016, c. 3.

[87] *Carter v Canada (Attorney General)*, 2015 SCC 5, [2015] 1 SCR 331.

F. Peace, Order, and Good Government

Under existing case law, Parliament's residual jurisdiction under section 91 of the *Constitution Act, 1867* to make laws for the "peace, order and good government of Canada" could conceivably authorize federal laws on or affecting health care in three situations. First, where a "gap" is found to exist in the jurisdiction over health care otherwise assigned to one of the two levels of government. Second, where an emergency situation of sufficient magnitude arises, requiring temporary federal encroachment on provincial jurisdiction. Third, where federal legislation addresses an aspect of health care, which would normally be within provincial jurisdiction, but which is found to have become a matter of "national concern."

Federal jurisdiction based on a gap in the jurisdiction over health care otherwise conferred seems a remote possibility, given the capacious interpretation of existing jurisdictional categories (e.g., the provinces' power to regulate health professionals, grounded in jurisdiction over 'property and civil rights'). The emergency branch will remain a vital ground for federal action: recent events, including the SARS outbreak in 2003 and the 2009 H1N1 flu pandemic, have demonstrated the importance of the federal role in ensuring readiness for and management of public health emergencies, including by exercising temporary authority over health care personnel, resources, and systems otherwise under provincial and territorial jurisdiction. A key concern here is the persistent unwillingness of the federal government to fully and proactively play its assigned role, apparently for fear of upsetting the provinces, and perhaps to avoid or limit its financial commitments. There have, for example, been sustained calls for the federal authorities to make more assertive use of their POGG powers to assist with the surveillance and reporting of infectious diseases.[88] Surveillance is crucial to limiting the spread of infectious disease across borders, both international and interprovincial. The existing reporting system, such as it is, relies on voluntary federal/provincial/territorial cooperation. Experience to date suggests that this strategy of "cooperative federalism" leads to breakdowns and unclear accountability, with Justice Archie Campbell complaining in the SARS Commission report of a "lack of any federal-provincial machinery of agreements and protocols to ensure cooperation."[89] To date—even in the wake of these rattling disease outbreaks and subsequent damning reports—only the province of Ontario has entered into a voluntary agreement with the Public Health Agency of Canada to exchange information on epidemic outbreaks. These failings put Canadians at greater

---

[88] Sina A. Muscati, 'POGG as a Basis for Federal Jurisdiction over Public Health Surveillance' (2007) 16 Constitutional Forum 41; Keri Gammon, 'Pandemics and Pandemonium: Constitutional Jurisdiction over Public Health' (2006) 15 *Dalhousie J Legal S* 1; Amir Attaran and Kumanan Wilson, 'A Legal and Epidemiological Justification for Federal Authority in Public Health Emergencies' (2007) 52 McGill LJ 381; Amir Attaran and Elvina C. Chow, 'Why Canada Is Very Dangerously Unprepared for Epidemic Diseases: A Legal and Constitutional Diagnosis' (2011) 5 *Journal of Parliamentary and Political Law* 287.

[89] *The Sars Commission Interim Report: SARS and Public Health in Ontario* (15 April 2004) (Commissioner: The Honourable Justice Archie Campbell) at 66, online: The SARS Commission http://www.sarscommission.ca/report/Interim_Report.pdf.

risk and invite sanctions under international law; Canada was subject to travel warnings by the WHO during the SARS crisis, suffering over a billion dollars in lost tourism and trade.

This is one of several emerging challenges where Canada lags behind other countries due to its disjointed health governance. For example, antimicrobial resistance is another area where the stakes are incalculably high—recent estimates are that, by 2050, superbugs will kill more people globally than currently die of cancer[90]—whereas the response by both levels of government has been slow and ineffectual. The key components of a response are well understood, and crucially involve careful stewardship of the existing cache of antimicrobials; currently, they are profligately overprescribed to patients and pumped into agricultural animals. As with infectious disease control, this issue demands national and indeed global coordination—yet key levers of governance (e.g., the regulation of prescribing practices) fall under provincial jurisdiction. Solutions to this problem, bringing forward concerted action by the various sectors of government involved (e.g., health, environment, agriculture) have scarcely been conceptualized, let alone set on a path to implementation.[91]

The "national concern" branch of the "POGG power" seems at first blush to offer the greatest prospects for use in the health sector. Regular comparisons between the Canadian system and that of other countries by the Commonwealth Fund show that the performance of the Canadian system is objectively a matter of national concern: in these comparisons, Canada has always ranked behind the United Kingdom, the Netherlands, Germany, Denmark, Australia, and New Zealand in health system performance and ahead of only the United States.[92] However, to satisfy the "national concern" test set out by the courts, one must meet more than its common-sense definition.

The leading case on what constitutes a "national concern" for the purposes of POGG is *Crown Zellerbach*.[93] There, the Court said a matter of national concern must have "a singleness, distinctiveness and indivisibility that clearly distinguishes it from matters of provincial concern and a scale of impact on provincial jurisdiction that is reconcilable with the fundamental distribution of legislative power under the Constitution."[94] This is typically referred to as the distinctiveness requirement. The Court further stated that in determining if a matter has the required degree of singleness, distinctiveness,

[90] Jim O'Neil, 'Foreword by Jim O'Neil' in Review on Antimicrobial Resistance, *Tackling Drug-Resistant Infections Globally: Final Report and Recommendations* (Review on Antimicrobial Resistance 2016) http://amr-review.org/Publications accessed 29 June 2016, at 1.

[91] Bryan Thomas and Colleen Flood, 'Why Aren't We Doing More about Superbugs and Over-Prescribing?' (Policy Options 2016), http://policyoptions.irpp.org/2016/03/29/arent-superbugs-prescribing/ accessed 27 June 2016.

[92] Canadian Institute for Health Information, 'How Canada Compares: Results from the Commonwealth Fund 2015 International Health Policy Survey of Primary Care Physicians' (CIHI 2016) https://www.cihi.ca/en/health-system-performance/performance-reporting/international/commonwealth-fund-survey-2015 accessed 27 June 2016, at 6–22.

[93] *R v Crown Zellerbach*, [1988] 1 SCR 401, 49 DLR (4th) 161.

[94] Ibid [33].

and indivisibility, courts should "consider what would be the effect on extra-provincial interests of a provincial failure to deal effectively with the control or regulation of the intra-provincial aspects of the matter."[95] This is typically referenced as the provincial inability requirement.

Together, these two requirements set a very high threshold for establishing federal jurisdiction under the national concern branch of POGG. This reflects the underlying judicial concern that federal jurisdiction based on POGG, unlike jurisdiction based on an enumerated power such as criminal law, gives Parliament "exclusive jurisdiction of a plenary nature to legislate in relation to that matter, including its intra-provincial aspects."[96] In other words, federal jurisdiction based on POGG is not, unlike other less-expansive federal jurisdiction based on enumerated powers, subject to the double aspect doctrine, which allows provincial jurisdiction on provincial aspects of the same matter to operate, subject to federal paramountcy. It also reflects the difference between the national concern and emergency branches of POGG: whereas the latter where triggered confers only a temporary jurisdiction on Parliament, the national concern branch provides a constitutional basis for what is necessarily legislation of a permanent nature. In these respects, there is judicial concern that applying the national concern branch has greater potential to reduce the jurisdiction of the provinces and to alter the fundamental balance of federalism between the federal government and the provinces. Thus the general approach of the courts with respect to this power is illustrated in *Ontario Hydro*, where the Supreme Court of Canada held that laws made under POGG must be "carefully described to respect and give effect to" the powers of the provinces.[97]

The consequence for health care is that the federal government has little jurisdiction to legislate directly on health care on the basis that it is a matter of national concern. Instead, it is limited to acting indirectly by making conditional grants to the provinces or to regulating aspects of health care that fall within its power to make laws on other subjects, such as the criminal law. A broader approach would require a federal government to challenge the restrictiveness of the national concern branch of POGG by asserting jurisdiction under over aspects of health about which the rationale for federal jurisdiction is strong and the consequences of splintered provincial jurisdiction demonstrably serious. For example, building on the soft jurisdiction it already exercises by operating the Canadian Institute for Health Information, the federal authorities could assert jurisdiction over monitoring, evaluating, and reporting on health system performance. More broadly, building on the jurisdictions it already exercises over pharmaceuticals and the growing national importance of pharmaceuticals in health care, the federal authorities might assert jurisdiction to launch national pharmacare.[98] In the latter regard, it can

[95] *Ontario Hydro v Ontario (Labour Relations Board)*, [1993] 3 SCR 327 [328], 107 DLR (4th) 431–432 [hereinafter *Ontario Hydro*].

[96] Ibid [433].

[97] Ibid [457].

[98] Roy Romanow and Greg Marchildon, 'The Time Has Come for Universal Pharmacare' (The Toronto Star 2015) https://www.thestar.com/opinion/commentary/2015/10/29/the-time-has-come-for-universal-pharmacare.html accessed 27 June 2016.

plausibly be argued that without a single purchaser of prescription drugs, Canada cannot ever achieve the price and cost savings and meet access goals as has been the case in many other developed countries. Further, in the absence of one pan-Canadian formulary and where provinces negotiate separately with large global providers of prescription drugs, this results in "whip-sawing," where provinces buckle under public pressure to fund drugs covered in other provinces.

These remain theoretical possibilities: to date federal authorities have been unwilling to assert jurisdiction in health care under the national concern branch of POGG, due to the power's uncertain but generally restrictive boundaries and a political unwillingness to test those boundaries.

4. Conclusion

The credibility of future reform strategies based on the spending power first requires federal insistence that provinces satisfy existing CHA conditions, preventing for example the privatization of medically necessary physician services. Second, as a quid pro quo, the provinces must be assured of a meaningful and predictable level of cost-sharing based on an evidence-based and transparent funding formula, built with provincial input, which honours the Constitution's concern for equalizing the capacity of the provinces to provide comparable services at comparable costs.[99] A third critical ingredient would be measures, including institutional arrangements, which build independence, objectivity, and transparency into the measurement and evaluation of provincial compliance with program criteria. This is vital, among other things, to avoiding a repeat of the past decade's failings, where the federal government has paid lip service to the CHA while allowing it to fizzle into obsolescence through lack of enforcement. A fair and objective dispute resolution process through a neutral institution is another key ingredient—having the federal government as the umpire of the *CHA* when it is one of the players is clearly insufficient to ensure fair enforcement.

But these reforms alone are insufficient, as true modernization requires expansion of the public system. For example, universal health insurance for prescription drugs is a glaring gap: Canada is the only country in the world with a universal health insurance program that does not include prescription drugs.[100] The lack of universal pharmacare results in severe access problems; to cite just one data point, an estimated 830 patients in Ontario under the age of 65 die each year for want of access to something as basic as insulin.[101] Without federal support, our provincial systems tend to regress to a US-style

[99] *Constitution Act* (n 1) s 36.
[100] Steven G Morgan and others, 'Estimated Cost of Universal Public Coverage of Prescription Drugs in Canada' (2015) 187 CMAJ 491.
[101] Gillian L Booth and others, 'Universal Drug Coverage and Socioeconomic Disparities in Major Diabetes Outcomes' (2012) 35 Diabetes Care 2257.

insurance system, insuring the elderly (or least the poor elderly) and those on social assistance, and leaving the rest of the system to private insurance and out-of-pocket payments. This messy mix of public and private insurers and heavy reliance on patients paying for treatment themselves is not only inequitable but inefficient, as it leads to higher drug prices. Canada has the fourth highest level of per capita drug spending across the OECD.[102]

There are essentially three constitutional options to help modernize Medicare by expansion to community-based pharmaceuticals. First, the federal government could assert authority under the POGG power to achieve reform, but as we discussed earlier, there is great reluctance on the part of both the federal government and the courts to liberalize this head of power. Second, the provinces could agree to delegate administrative responsibilities for pharmaceuticals to a pan-Canadian agency, funded by the federal government;[103] this is a real prospect given the increasing fiscal burden experienced by the provinces with respect to their pharmaceutical plans even for the limited populations covered.[104] The third option is the most familiar and arguably most feasible: it is for the federal government to use its spending power to give each province financial incentives to offer universal insurance for a core range of medically necessary drugs to all of its citizens. Here, the eligibility of each province should depend not only on its own pharmacare plan but also on its participation in the pan-Canadian governance schemes which are needed to ensure the affordability of universal pharmacare and the safety and efficacy of the drugs it funds. These schemes would include coordinated health technology assessment processes, collective bulk purchasing, optimal use of generics, and a national system of post-market surveillance, monitoring, and evaluation—overcoming the jurisdictional divide which currently exists between federal licensing for drug safety and provincial regulation, monitoring, and evaluation of their use.

It is clear the need for coordinated and cooperative health system governance, which transcends provincial boundaries, goes beyond pharmacare. The reasons include the constrained capacity of the smaller provinces and the common interest of all provinces—and their residents—in consolidation of purchasing power for human resources and other inputs, minimization of duplication and maximization of value derived from the large-scale investments required in areas such as information technology. More generally, there is a common interest in a more deliberate harnessing of federalism's potential for policy experimentation and learning across jurisdictional boundaries. There is, in other words, a need to rekindle the romance that once enabled bold action on health care within Canadian federalism. Aboriginal health, human resource planning,

[102] OECD, Health at a Glance 2015: OECD Indicators (OECD, 2015).
[103] Full-fledged delegation of legislative powers was declared unconstitutional by the Supreme Court of Canada in General of Nova Scotia v Attorney General of Canada, [1951] S.C.R. 31. However, it is open to the provinces to delegate administrative responsibility for a national arms-length agency, as is done for example with Canadian Blood Services.
[104] Aidan Hollis, 'Opinion: Time to End Haphazard Pharmacare Coverage' (Edmonton Journal 2015) http://edmontonjournal.com/news/politics/opinion-time-to-end-haphazard-pharmacare-coverage accessed 29 June 2016.

health professional regulation, electronic health information systems, health technology assessment, and system-level quality assurance are all areas of modern health system governance which could benefit from more coordinated and cooperative action by provinces and territories.

Various pan-Canadian initiatives show glimmers of hope for renewed health care federalism—many focused on specific diseases or on specific aspects of health care governance. More to the point, the provinces and territories have used the Council of the Federation as a forum to coordinate action on a number of specific reform priorities, ostensibly to fill the void created by the federal government's abandonment of the field over the past decade during the tenure of the last Conservative government. Individually and collectively, these initiatives are encouraging, as are the handful of federally funded supporting institutions, such as the Canadian Patient Safety Institute and the Canadian Institute for Health Information. They are however not big enough, durable enough, or sufficiently integrated to achieve fundamental reform. They are unlikely, in other words, to amount to more than the sum of their parts.

What is missing is what has been missing for decades: a general plan of sustained and integrated reform through coordination and cooperation among provinces and territories, with the active participation of the federal government, flexing not only its spending power but its full array of governance assets—its jurisdiction over aboriginal health, large dimensions of public health, health research, drug and medical devices licensing, and a number of the broader determinants of health, such as age-related income security. The accords of the first decade of this century were a vague and inadequate attempt to lay the foundations for such a plan and process of reform. Fresh efforts at righting this troubled romance must link eligibility for federal funding to ongoing participation in a process of reform, to achieve lasting transparency and accountability of a sort lacking in the health accords of the past.

BIBLIOGRAPHY

Secondary sources

Attaran A and Chow EC, 'Why Canada Is Very Dangerously Unprepared for Epidemic Diseases: A Legal and Constitutional Diagnosis' (2011) 5 *Journal of Parliamentary and Political Law* 287.

Attaran A and Wilson K, 'A Legal and Epidemiological Justification for Federal Authority in Public Health Emergencies' (2007) 52 McGill LJ 381.

Choudhry S, 'The Enforcement of the Canada Health Act' (1996) 41 McGill LJ 462.

_____. 'Recasting Social Canada: A Reconsideration of Federal Jurisdiction over Social Policy' (2002) 52:3 UTLJ 163.

Davis K, Stremikis K, Squires D. and Schoen C, 'Mirror, Mirror on the Wall—How the Performance of the U.S Health Care System Compares Internationally' (The Commonwealth Fund 2104) http://www.commonwealthfund.org/~/media/files/publications/fund-report/2014/jun/1755_davis_mirror_mirror_2014.pdf.

Fierlbeck K and Lahey W (eds), *Health Care Federalism in Canada: Critical Junctures and Critical Perspectives* (McGill-Queen's University Press 2013).

Flood CM, 'Litigating Health Rights in Canada: A White Knight for Equity' in Collen M Flood and Aeyal Gross (eds), *The Right to Health at the Public/Private Divide: A Global Comparative Study* (New York, Cambridge University Press 2014).

Flood CM and Archibald T, 'The Illegality of Private Health Care in Canada' (2001) 61 CMAJ 825.

Flood CM and Haugan A, 'Is Canada Odd? A Comparison of European and Canadian Approaches to Choice and Regulation of the Public/Private Divide in Health Care' (2010) 5 Health Econ Pol'y & L 319.

Flood CM, Stabile MB and Tuohy CH, 'What Is in and out of Medicare? Who Decides?' in Colleen M Flood (ed), *Just Medicare: What's In, What's Out, How We Decide* (University of Toronto Press 2006).

Flood CM and Thomas B, 'Regulatory Failure: The Case of the Private-For-Profit IVF Sector' in T Lemmens, C Milne and I Lee (eds), *Legal, Ethical and Policy Challenges of Assisted Human Reproduction* (Toronto, University of Toronto Press 2015) 438–475.

Flood CM and Thomas B, 'Modernizing the Canada Health Act' (2016) 39(2) Dal LJ [forthcoming].

Gammon K, "Pandemics and Pandemonium: Constitutional Jurisdiction over Public Health" (2006) 15 *Dalhousie J Legal S* 1.

Hogg PW, *Constitutional Law of Canada* (2015 Student Edition, Carswell 2015).

Jackman M, 'The Constitutional Basis for Federal Regulation of Health' (1996) 5(2) Health L Rev 3.

_____. 'Constitutional Jurisdiction over Health in Canada' (2000) 8 Health LJ 95.

Lahey W, 'Medicare and the Law: Contours of an Evolving Relationship' in Jocelyn Downie, Tim Caulfield and Colleen M Flood (eds), *Canadian Health Law and Policy* (Lexis 2011) 43.

Lahey W, "The Legal Framework for Intergovernmental Health Care Governance: Making the Most of Limited Options" in Katherine Fierlbeck and William Lahey, *Health Care Federalism in Canada: Critical Junctures and Critical Perspectives* (McGill-Queen's University Press 2013).

MacIntosh C, 'Indigenous Peoples and Health Law and Policy: Responsibilities and Obligations' in Jocelyn Downie, Timothy Caulfield and Colleen M Flood (eds), *Canadian Health Law and Policy 4th Edition* (Markham, LexisNexis 2011) 587–588 (Indigenous Peoples).

Marchildon G and Mou H, 'A Needs-Based Allocation Formula for Canada Health Transfer' (2015) 40(3) Can Pub Pol'y 209.

Morgan SG and others, 'Estimated Cost of Universal Public Coverage of Prescription Drugs in Canada'(2015) 187 CMAJ 491.

Muscati SA, 'POGG as a Basis for Federal Jurisdiction over Public Health Surveillance' (2007) 16 Constitutional Forum 41.

Ogilvie K and Eggleton A, 'Time for Transformative Change: A Review of the 2004 Health Accord' (Standing Senate Committee on Social Affairs, Science and Technology 2012) www.parl.gc.ca/content/sen/committee/411/soci/rep/rep07mar12-e.pdf accessed 27 June 2016, at 82.

Petter A, 'Federalism and the Myth of the Federal Spending Power' [1989] 68 Can Bar Rev 448.

Romanow RJ, 'Building on Values: The Future of Health Care in Canada' (Commission on the Future of Health Care in Canada 2002) http://publications.gc.ca/collections/Collection/CP32-85-2002E.pdf accessed 27 June 2016.

Select Cases

Canada (Attorney General) v PHS Community Services Society, [2011] SCC 44, [2011] 3 SCR 134 [68]

Chaoulli v Quebec (Attorney General), 2005 SCC 35, [2005] 1 SCR 791

Pictou Landing Band Council v Canada (Attorney General), [2013] FC 342, [2013] 3 CNLR 371.

R v Crown Zellerbach, [1988] 1 SCR 401, 49 DLR (4th) 161

Schneider v The Queen [1982] 2 SCR 112, 137, 139 DLR (3d) 417

Winterhaven Stables Limited v Canada (Attorney General), 1988 ABCA 334

CHAPTER 22

....

CRIMINAL LAW IN THE FEDERAL CONTEXT

....

MARK CARTER*

1. INTRODUCTION: THE INTRICATE DIVISION OF LEGISLATIVE POWERS RELATING TO CRIMINAL LAW

....

THE *Constitution Act, 1867*[1] establishes an intricate division of legislative powers in the area of criminal law, the implications of which are constantly evolving in response to federal and provincial (including municipal) policy agendas and shifting judicial temperaments. Under section 91(27) Parliament is given legislative authority over "criminal law . . . including the Procedure in Criminal Matters." Expressly excluded from this grant of powers is the jurisdiction to make laws in relation to "the Constitution of Courts of Criminal Jurisdiction." The power to constitute these courts—along with those of civil jurisdiction—is granted to the provincial legislatures in each province under section 92(14).[2] Section 92(14) also confers on the provincial legislatures the power to make laws in relation to "[t]he administration of Justice in the Province" which has significant implications for the federal criminal law power, particularly as it concerns jurisdiction to investigate and to prosecute crimes. Also of significance to an understanding of the ability to create laws that have criminal law characteristics in Canada is the provincial legislatures' jurisdiction to enforce provincial laws by the imposition of fines, penalties, or imprisonment under section 92(15). Finally, the expansively-worded provincial

---

* Professor, College of Law, University of Saskatchewan.

[1] (U.K.), 30 & 31 Vict, c 3, reprinted in RSC 1985, App II, No 5 [hereinafter *Constitution Act, 1867*].

[2] Although the provincial courts of appeal and superior courts are established by the provincial governments pursuant to these provisions, the judges of these courts are appointed by the federal executive pursuant to s. 96 of the *Constitution Act, 1867*.

power contained in section 92(16) to make laws in relation to "all Matters of a merely local or private Nature in the Province" would seem to have great potential significance for the provinces' powers to legislate in relation to what might otherwise be criminal law. In fact, however, section 92(16) has had little significance in this area.

2. Parliament's Plenary Jurisdiction over Criminal Law

A conventional starting point for discussions about criminal law in the Canadian federal context is the way that the grant of plenary jurisdiction to the federal Parliament contrasts with the situation in some other federal constitutions, the United States and Australia in particular, which share with Canada a British colonial and common law heritage. In the United States and Australia, as Peter Hogg suggests, "[t]he argument [was] accepted . . . that criminal law should reflect local conditions and sentiments."[3] In Confederation-era British North America, however, there was general consensus in favour of a federal or Canada-wide power to legislate in this area.[4] In the Confederation debates, speaking on 6 February 1865, shortly before the end of the American Civil War, John A. MacDonald asserted that having "the same criminal law throughout these provinces" was "a matter almost of necessity."[5] The lack of this unifying element was, in Macdonald's estimation, "one of the most marked instances in which we take advantage of the experience derived from our observations of the defects in the Constitution of the neighbouring Republic."[6]

To whatever degree that federal criminal law acts as the agent of national unity that MacDonald imagined—a "symbol of nationhood" that "state[s] fundamental values"[7]— the catalogue of provincial powers has allowed some of the adaptation to regional conditions and attitudes that exists where criminal law is a matter of state-level jurisdiction. As discussed below, the courts have recognized a considerable degree of provincial aspect in matters that are also of criminal concern, which has allowed provinces to pass laws that are often more restrictive than criminal laws. Also of significance is the fact that most *Criminal Code*[8] offences are prosecuted by provincial Crown attorneys, acting as agents for provincial Attorneys General. An issue that will be returned to is the question as to whether this practice reflects the provinces' jurisdiction over the "administration of justice" under section 92(14), or merely the fact that Parliament has delegated

---

[3] Peter Hogg, *Constitutional Law of Canada*, 5th ed., vol. 1, loose-leaf (Thomson Carswell, 2007) 18-2.

[4] Martin Friedland, *A Century of Criminal Justice: Perspectives on the Development of Canadian Law* (Carswell, 1984), 47.

[5] Canada, *Parliamentary Debates on the Subject of the Confederation of the British North American Provinces*, 8th Leg 3rd sess, No 35906 (6 February 1865) at 41 (Hon. John A. Macdonald)).

[6] ibid.

[7] Friedland, above (n 4) 48.

[8] *Criminal Code*, R.S.C. 1985, c C-46 [hereinafter *Criminal Code*].

its authority in this area to provinces through its definition of "Attorneys General" in the *Criminal Code*. One way or the other, when combined with the provincial power to create police forces, which falls less controversially within the power over the administration of justice in the province,[9] criminal law can be administered in a manner that recognizes some unique regional values and needs.

3. The Formal Characteristics of Criminal Laws

Laws that are characterized as criminal in nature under section 91(27) are expected at least to possess the requisite formal characteristics of, first, prohibiting some forms of activity and, second, setting out punitive sanctions for the commission of the prohibited acts.[10] The Supreme Court has recently remarked on the "liberal interpretation given to the formal component"[11] of criminal laws in its past decisions. As it relates to prohibitions, the "liberalization" that the Court alludes to has arisen in situations where federal legislation has been upheld under section 91(27) notwithstanding the fact that the conduct that some laws targeted was more regulated than prohibited. Characteristics of regulation include the licencing of the "prohibited" activity,[12] the exercise of administrative discretion in defining the important aspects of the prohibition,[13] exemptions from prohibitions[14] and provincial equivalency whereby federal legislation will not apply where provincial regulation of the activity is deemed adequate.[15] Legislation has also been upheld under section 91(27) notwithstanding the fact that it did not directly prohibit the objectionable activity—smoking—but, rather, the advertising that promotes it.[16] In relation to punishment, imprisonment and significant fines provide the standard criminal

---

[9] *Di Iorio v Warden of Montreal Jail*, [1976] 2 SCR 152.

[10] *R v Malmo-Levine*, [2003] 3 S.C.R. 571, [74] [hereinafter *Malmo-Levine*].

[11] *Reference re Assisted Human Reproduction Act*, SCC 61, [2010] 3 SCR 457 [234] [hereinafter *AHRA Reference*].

[12] For example the regime established by the *Firearms Act, S.C. 1995, c. 39*, upheld as criminal law in *Reference re Firearms Act (Can.)*, [2000] 1 SCR 783 [hereinafter *Firearms Reference*].

[13] This was a major issue for the dissent, which rejected as criminal law the regime established by the *Canadian Environmental Protection Act*, R.S.C., 1985, c. 16, in the Supreme Court's 5-4 decision in *R. v Hydro-Québec*, [1997] 3 SCR 213 [hereinafter *Hydro- Québec*].

[14] In Sopinka and Major JJ's dissent in *In RJR-MacDonald* [1995] 3 SCR 199 [hereinafter *RJR-MacDonald*], the broad-based exemptions from the tobacco advertising bans contained in *Tobacco Products Control Act*, SC 1988, c 20, undermined the prohibitory nature of the legislation and, therefore, its criminal law character. Similarly, in *AHRA Reference* above (n 11), LeBel and Deschamps JJ [217] found that the controlled activities were not exceptions or "carve-outs" from prohibitions as the Chief Justice asserted, but were instead "designed to promote beneficial practices" (as Justices LeBel's and Deschamps's position was characterized by McLachlin CJ [37]).

[15] For example the provision of the *Canadian Environmental Protection Act*, RSC, 1985, c16 which were at issue in *Hydro-Québec* above (n 13).

[16] *RJR-MacDonald* above (n 14).

sanctions. However, the courts have also recognized a preventive branch of the criminal law power which allows, for example, for the detention of people who are found not criminally responsible on account of mental disorder. [17]

4. The Substantive Characteristics of Criminal Laws

A. Narrow and Broad Definitions

The third prerequisite for criminal laws is the substantive one, requiring that they should serve a recognized criminal law purpose.[18] The courts' attempts to identify these purposes and, therefore, the kinds of conduct that are the appropriate subjects of Parliament's jurisdiction under section 91(27) fall along a spectrum of definitions from narrow to broad. The extreme ends of the spectrum were both provided by decisions of the Judicial Committee of the Privy Council. *Reference Re the Board of Commerce Act, 1919, & The Combines and Fair Prices Act, 1919*[19] concerned the validity of federal legislation aimed at restricting profiteering and unfair business practices in the post-World War I period. These objectives were pursued by, among other things, allowing the Board to make orders that limited profit margins on the sale of food and clothing. The Court rejected all of the bases on which the legislation's validity was defended. In relation to the scheme's characterization as criminal law, Lord Haldane held that the legislation did not deal with a matter "which by its very nature belongs to the domain of criminal jurisprudence. . . ." such as would be the case with "[a] general law . . . making incest a crime."[20] Lord Haldane's example is meant to speak for itself, but it may be concluded that in this view the fact that prohibitions addressed concerns about the moral nature of the activity was determinative of their appropriateness as subjects of criminal law.

At the other end of the spectrum, Lord Atkin provided the broadest understanding of Parliament's criminal law jurisdiction, in *Proprietary Articles Trade Association v A.G. Canada (PATA)*.[21] The case, once again, involved federal legislation aimed at unfair business practices.[22] In upholding the legislation as criminal law, Lord Atkin stated:

> Criminal law connotes only the quality of such acts or omissions as are prohibited under appropriate penal provisions by authority of the State. The criminal quality of

---

[17]   *R v Swain*, [1991] 1 SCR 933.

[18]   *Malmo-Levine* above (n 10) [74].

[19]   *In re the Board of Commerce Act, 1919, and the Combines and Fair Prices Act, 1919*, [1922] 1 AC 191 [hereinafter *Board of Commerce*].

[20]   ibid 198–199.

[21]   *Proprietary Articles Trade Association v AG Canada*, [1931] AC 310 (PC) [hereinafter *PATA*].

[22]   The legislation being challenged was amendments to the *Criminal Code* and the *Combines Investigation Act* aimed at participating in agreements to restrain competition.

an act cannot be . . . discovered by reference to any standard but one: Is the act prohibited with penal consequences?[23]

On the connection between criminal law and morality, Lord Atkin asserted that
"[m]orality and criminality are far from co-extensive; nor is the sphere of criminality
necessarily part of a more extensive field covered by morality."[24]

A place somewhere closer to the middle of the spectrum was provided by Justice
Rand's decision in *Margarine Reference*.[25] In assessing the proposed criminal nature
of federal prohibitions on the manufacture, possession, and sale of margarine, Justice
Rand interpreted Lord Atkin in *PATA* as only having rejected Lord Haldane's views
regarding criminal law's exclusive focus on acts that "carry some moral taint."[26] In Rand
J.'s view, however, it was still appropriate to require Parliament to address "some evil or
injurious or undesirable effect upon the public."[27] Along with morality, Justice Rand's
non-exhaustive list of "public purposes" of criminal law included public peace, order,
security, and health.[28] In an earlier passage Rand J. also indicated that criminal law could
be properly concerned with "social, economic or political interests."[29] Notwithstanding
the breadth of these purposes, however, Justice Rand held the margarine prohibitions to
be "insidious form[s] of encroachment" on provincial jurisdiction over the dairy industry,[30] a position with which a majority concurred.

Justice Rand's allusion to "insidiousness" suggests the tone of judicial disapproval
which, as Peter Hogg points out, often attends the invocation of the doctrine of "colourablility." Colourablility is invoked when courts determine that "a law [that] looks as
though it deals with a matter within jurisdiction . . . in essence is addressed to a matter
outside jurisdiction."[31] In fact, notwithstanding Rand J.'s efforts at reigning in the broadest definition of the criminal law power, until recently colourability seemed to have
emerged as the only significant qualifier of Lord Atkin's broad definition of the criminal
law power. This was Justice La Forest's interpretation for the majority in *R. v Hydro-
Québec*.[32] In recognizing that a clean environment is "a public purpose within Rand J.'s
formulation in the *Margarine Reference*"[33] he also emphasized that Justice Rand's "helpful" list of "the more usual purposes of a criminal prohibition" was not exhaustive.[34] This
remark was prefaced by the observation that "the *Charter* apart, only one qualification

---

[23] *PATA* above (n 21) 324.
[24] ibid.
[25] *Reference re Validity of Section 5(a) of the Dairy Industry Act* [1949] SCR 1 [hereinafter *Margarine
Reference*].
[26] ibid 49.
[27] ibid.
[28] ibid 50.
[29] ibid.
[30] ibid.
[31] *Starr v Houlden,* [1990] 1 SCR 1366 at p. 1403.
[32] *Hydro-Québec* above (n 13).
[33] ibid [123].
[34] ibid [122].

has been attached to Parliament's plenary power over criminal law. The power cannot be employed colourably . . ."[35] The Supreme Court also used a challenge to the offence of possessing marijuana for personal use to confirm the on-going validity of using the criminal law power to condemn forms of conduct for purely moral reasons, without requiring Parliament to prove that the proscribed conduct is otherwise harmful.[36]

Justice La Forest's expansive view of the criminal law power simultaneously advanced his argument against an overly "enthusiastic adoption of the 'national dimensions' doctrine"[37] under the peace order and good government power contained in the introductory clause of section 91. In a number of significant decisions, Justice La Forest argued that the enumerated classes of subjects under section 91, including the criminal law power, provide a better jurisdictional basis for Parliament's attempts to address environmental and health issues, than the national concern branch.[38] Arguments for national concern jurisdiction had achieved some success at the Supreme Court in relation to environmental jurisdiction[39] and at provincial courts of appeal in relation to health issues.[40] Justice La Forest argued that national concern jurisdiction "assign[s] full power to regulate an area to Parliament,' whereas criminal law merely "seeks by discrete prohibitions to prevent evils falling within a broad purpose, such as, for example, the protection of health."[41] A beneficial effect of locating Parliament's jurisdiction in section 91(27) or one of the other enumerated classes of section 91 is that the provinces retain jurisdiction to regulate the matter as well through the double aspect doctrine.[42]

For the reasons that Justice La Forest suggested, criminal law jurisdiction over a matter may be preferable to national concern from the perspective of provincial governments. Some commentators, however, have been concerned on the provinces' behalf about the expansive view being taken by Supreme Court majorities—as slim as they may have been[43]—in relation to both the formal and substantive characteristics of criminal law. Morris Manning, for example, suggested that the trend bore out Albert Abel's characterization of the criminal law power as the "floodplain clause which has enabled

---

[35] ibid [121].

[36] *Malmo-Levine* above (n 10).

[37] ibid [116].

[38] This was a theme of Justice La Forest's dissent in *R v Crown Zellerbach Canada Ltd*, [1988] 1 SCR 401 [hereinafter *Crown Zellerbach*], where the majority held that relevant sections of the *Ocean Dumping Control Act*, S.C. 1974-75-76, c. 55 were valid under the national concern branch of peace, order, and good government. See also his decision in *Friends of the Oldman River Society v Canada (Minister of Transport)*, [1992] 1 SCR 3 and *RJR-Macdonald* above (n 14).

[39] *Crown Zellerbach* above (n 38).

[40] The Quebec Court of Appeal upheld the legislation that was at issue *RJR-MacDonald* (n 14) under the national concern doctrine.

[41] *Hydro-Québec* above (n 13) [128].

[42] ibid [131]. See the chapter by Eugénie Brouillet & Bruce Ryder in this *Handbook* for an explanation of the double aspect doctrine.

[43] Jeremy Webber suggests that the fact that *Hydro-Québec* was decided by "the narrowest of majorities" (5-4) may be a sign "that the power is reaching its limit." *The Constitution of Canada: A Contextual Analysis* (Hart, 2015), 161.

the Dominion Parliament to engulf whatever it will."[44] Similarly, Graeme Mitchell commented that Justice La Forest's "loose reformulation" of the public purposes of criminal law in *Hydro-Québec*, combined with his tolerance for "an aggressive regulatory function of the criminal law power," would "invite increasingly intrusive forays by Parliament into areas of legitimate provincial jurisdiction."[45] Mitchell looked ahead to the decision in *Firearms Reference*,[46] then on appeal to the Supreme Court of Canada, as the case that would test the "greatly expanded regulatory aspect of the criminal law power" and "not only delineate the parameters of the criminal law's regulatory aspect but also test the elasticity of the balance of legislative powers in our federal system."[47] In the result, the *Firearms Act* with its extensive regulatory and licencing system was upheld as valid criminal law by a unanimous Supreme Court.

B. Renewed Interest in Judicial Review of the Purposes of Criminal Law

Reference Re Assisted Human Reproduction Act (the *AHRA Reference*)[48] signals an intention on the part of the Supreme Court once again to focus on the public purposes of criminal law in order to limit the scope of the criminal law power. The unprecedented aspect of this newest initiative is the Court's determination not only to be satisfied that Parliament is responding to, for example, moral concerns or the risk of harm, but also to assess how well-founded those concerns or risks may be. Furthermore, four of the justices writing for the majority informed their analysis with issues drawn from case law involving the *Canadian Charter of Rights and Freedoms*,[49] which represents a significant and problematic doctrinal development. Although four other justices, in a decision written by the Chief Justice, rejected the integration of *Charter* concerns into the federalism analysis, they nonetheless joined the majority in raising the standards that Parliament has to meet in order to satisfy the courts of the significance of the public purpose of criminal law that it may be relying on in support of a legislative initiative.

The legislation that was at issue in the *AHRA Reference* contained absolute prohibitions against certain uses of reproductive and genetic technologies.[50] The legislation also

---

[44] Morris Manning, "Criminalization by Regulation: The Outer Limits of Section 91(27) of the Constitution Act, 1867," (2002) 13 Nat'l J Const L 309 at 310 quoting Albert Abel, "The Neglected Logic of 91 and 92," (1969) 19 U of T LJ 487, 504.

[45] Graeme Mitchell, "Developments in Constitutional Law: The 1997–98 Term—Activism and Accountability," (1999), 10 SCLR 83, 158–159.

[46] *Firearms Reference* above (n 12).

[47] Mitchell above (n 45) 159.

[48] *AHRA Reference* above (n 11).

[49] *Canadian Charter of Rights and Freedoms*, Part I of the *Constitution Act, 1982*, being Schedule B to the *Canada Act 1982* (UK), 1982, c 11 [hereinafter the *Charter*].

[50] These included human cloning, creating hybrids of animals and humans, and the purchase and sale of women's and men's reproductive functions.

identified a range of controlled activities[51] that could only be undertaken pursuant to the regulations and the licencing regime that the act established. The Attorney General of Canada submitted that the dominant purpose of the act, including the regulated activities, was to prohibit practises that would "undercut moral values." The Attorney General also argued that the legislation was aimed at avoiding public health evils, and protecting the security of donors, donees, and people who would be conceived by use of the reproductive technologies.[52] The province of Quebec, which launched the reference, conceded the criminal character of the prohibitions but argued that the pith and substance of the controlled activities regime was the regulation and licencing of scientific activity and medical services, which are firmly established areas of provincial jurisdiction.[53]

In their decision for four members of the Court declaring the impugned provisions of the Act to be ultra vires, Justices LeBel and Deschamps asserted that because of the "liberal interpretation given to the formal component" of criminal laws in the case law mentioned above, "[t]he substantive criterion [for criminal law] assumes particular importance."[54] Returning, to the touchstone of Rand J.'s decision in the *Margarine Reference*, Justices LeBel and Deschamps read much significance into his characterization of the public purposes of criminal law as being addressed at an "evil to be supressed or a threatened interest to be safeguarded." Suggesting that the point is self-evident, they concluded that this implies that "the evil or threat must be real."[55] LeBel and Deschamps JJ. proceeded to identify for the Court a role in reviewing the significance of the risk of harm or the moral concern that, for its part, Parliament considered significant enough to legislate against.

LeBel and Deschamps JJ. relied on the majority's position in *Malmo-Levine* that the process of analyzing whether laws that infringe *Charter* protections can be upheld as reasonably justified is "somewhat related"—a conclusion that was not explained in *Malmo-Levine*—to the analysis of the purposes of criminal laws under section 91(27).[56] Thus, to the extent that laws that infringe freedom of expression will only be reasonably justified if they address harm that is "reasonably apprehended," criminal laws also have to meet the "reasonable apprehension of harm" standard in order to be upheld under section 91(27). Ultimately, this introduces into section 91(27) analysis the concept of a "concrete basis" as the standard that is to be met both in order to establish that a law reflects a reasoned apprehension of harm and "where the legislative action is based on morality."[57] LeBel and Deschamps JJ. proceeded to establish the newly-claimed

---

[51] These included manipulating, importing, exporting, and altering human reproductive material or in vitro embryos, and the combination of parts of the human genome with the parts of other species' genomes.

[52] *AHRA Reference* above (n 11) [20].

[53] LeBel and Deschamps JJ for the plurality identified these as falling within provincial jurisdiction over hospitals in s. 92(7), civil rights in s. 92(13), and matters of a local nature in s. 92(16), [158].

[54] ibid [237].

[55] ibid [236].

[56] *Malmo-Levine* above (n 10) [76].

[57] *AHRA Reference* above (n 11) [238].

jurisdiction to review the moral purposes of criminal legislation as the basis for pre-emptive judicial strikes against what would otherwise be *Charter* infringements. They use federalism review in this area to assist the *Charter* in its role in "freeing" the *Criminal Code* from the "fetters" of "Judeo Christian morality."[58] By exercising this enhanced level of review, Justices LeBel and Deschamps envision the courts being employed in saving the criminal law power from the "limitless definition"[59] that would result from allowing Parliament the last word in relation to the harm that it wishes to avoid and the moral standards that it wishes to enforce.

Chief Justice McLachlin and three others would have upheld the entire Act, resist-ing the incorporation of *Charter* issues into federalism analysis: "Whether a federal law falls within Parliament's criminal law power under section 91(27) of the *Constitution Act, 1867*, is a question of *which level* of government has jurisdiction to enact this law ... The degree to which the Act may impact on individual liberties is not relevant to this inquiry."[60] In her more deferential perspective, the Chief Justice was anxious to avoid "substitut[ing] a judicial view of what is good and what is bad for the wisdom of Parliament."[61] McLachlin C.J.C. did, however, recognize a standard of proof which is also potentially significant. Rather than giving Parliament the last word, she indicated that the courts will need to be satisfied that there is a reasonable apprehension that con-duct is a threat to central moral precepts, and also that there is "consensus in society" that the conduct "engages a moral concern of fundamental importance"[62] even in situa-tions where the "jury is still out."[63]

The "concrete basis" standard has arrived in our jurisprudence without guidance from the Court in relation to how it will be assessed, which will be a difficult task for the moral purposes of criminal law in particular.[64] As it applied to the controlled activities in the *AHRA*, Justices LeBel and Deschamps found "nothing in the record" to suggest that the controlled activities "should be regarded as conduct that is reprehensible or represents a serious risk to morality, safety or public health."[65] For her part, Chief Justice McLachlin was satisfied that the legislation met the lower standard of a "societal consensus" that a moral concern of fundamental importance was being addressed. In arriving at this con-clusion, the Chief Justice considered the validity of the Act as a whole before considering

---

[58] ibid [239].

[59] ibid.

[60] ibid [44]. Justice Cromwell split (some of) the difference between the factions by upholding three of the controlled activities as validly enacted under the criminal law power, while agreeing with LeBel and Deschamps JJ. that the rest fall within provincial legislative competence. ibid [287–288].

[61] ibid [76].

[62] ibid [51].

[63] ibid [50].

[64] Hoi Kong feels that the courts are up to the task. Kong suggests that the balancing tests that the judiciary has developed under, for example, the peace, order, and good government power and the general trade and commerce power have been applied by judges "without usurping legislative power or introducing an unacceptably high level of uncertainty into the constitutional framework." H. Kong, "Subsidiarity, Republicanism, and the Division of Powers in Canada," (2015) 45 RDUS 13, 45.

[65] *AHRA Reference* above (n 11) [251].

the controlled activities in particular.[66] Accordingly, it was not difficult to determine the existence of societal consensus—in fact, as far as the prohibitions were concerned, it was not in dispute—about the moral significance of such extraordinary activities, given the extent to which they had been the subject of public and parliamentary debate and expert study.[67] Since, in her estimation, the controlled activities were lesser variations of the prohibited practices, the need to regulate them was supported by the same consensus. That being said, evidence of "societal consensus" will be difficult to identify for legislation that deals with less extraordinary forms of activity, and it is not clear that the courts will be in a better position to assess this than Parliament.

Justices LeBel and Deschamps demonstrate admirable concern for the way that criminal law may compromise freedom and liberty interests, and their determination to let these concerns inform their federalism analysis is commendable. Such deprivations are, however, part of the definition of criminal law, some of the restrictive and punitive characteristics of which may be sanctioned by the Constitution.[68] The *Charter* is an important vehicle for assessing the (un)reasonableness of these sorts of deprivations that define criminal laws and the consequences of being found guilty of them. As Peter Hogg suggests, however, when validity is an issue, "the first question is whether the law is within the law making power of the enacting body and the second is whether the law is consistent with the *Charter*."[69] It may be added to this that, in cases that only involve the distribution of powers, the courts should avoid confusing these questions and attempting to address what might be future *Charter* arguments. Among other concerns[70] this form of premature substantive judicial review interferes with "an essential characteristic of the federal distribution of powers" which is the principle of exhaustiveness: "In essence, there is no topic that cannot be legislated upon, though the particulars of such legislation may be limited by, for instance, the *Charter*."[71]

---

[66] This was a point of contention between the two four-justice factions. LeBel and Deschamps JJ followed the framework for considering the validity of parts of legislation in situations where the entire act is not being challenged, which was established in *General Motors of Canada Ltd. v City National Leasing*, [1989] 1 SCR. 641. In this approach the first consideration is the validity of the impugned provisions and therefore, in the case at hand, the potential public criminal law purposes of these specific provisions. The Chief Justice, however, determined that the parts of the legislation being challenged were so significant that, in effect, the validity of the entire act was at issue. ibid [17].

[67] Canada, Royal Commission on New Reproductive Technologies, *Proceed with Care: Final Report of the Royal Commission on New Reproductive Technologies* (Minister of Government Services Canada, 1993).

[68] If, for example, imprisonment necessarily involves deprivations of liberty, freedom of association, and other liberties, then these deprivations are anticipated by the extent to which the *Constitution Act, 1867* anticipates the construction of federal penitentiaries in s 91(28) and prisons in s 92(6). I have called these "definitional deprivations" and expand on this point in Mark Carter, "Retributive Sentencing and the *Charter*: The Implications of *Sauvé v. Chief Electoral Officer*," (2005), 10 *Canadian Criminal Law Review* 43.

[69] Hogg above (n 3) 15-3.

[70] See Mark Carter, "Federalism Analysis and the Charter," (2011) 74 *SKLR* 5.

[71] *Reference re Same-Sex Marriage*, 2004 SCC 79, [2004] 3 S.C.R. 698 [34].

5. PROVINCIAL OFFENCES

The earlier discussion mentioned a theme of concern that the expansive interpretation of the federal criminal law power is seen by some as a threat to provincial legislative jurisdiction. It must be said, however, that the Supreme Court has also been liberal with its interpretation of provincial jurisdiction in relation to matters that are or could also be addressed by federal criminal legislation. This fact explains why the terrain that provincial jurisdiction shares with federal criminal law jurisdiction is probably the greatest example of the "double aspect" doctrine at work in Canadian constitutional law. Notwithstanding the references in sections 91 and 92 to the exclusivity of federal and provincial legislative competence over the matters that are enumerated in those sections, only 16 years after Confederation the Privy Council had already declared that a "subject[...] which for one purpose fall[s] within section 92, may in another aspect and for another purpose fall within section 91."[72] Two important examples from the case law discussed above are tobacco advertising[73] and the release of toxic substances into the environment.[74]

Provincial laws that regulate matters that have a double aspect are allowed to operate until those laws come into conflict with federal laws, at which point the provincial legislation becomes inoperative to the extent of the conflict pursuant to the doctrine of federal paramountcy.[75] A provincial law will be in conflict with a federal law when it is impossible to comply with both or when a provincial law frustrates the purpose of a federal law.[76] Working in favour of provincial laws in this area is the Supreme Court's holding that because criminal laws are "essentially prohibitory in character" it will be assumed that it is not the purpose of criminal legislation to provide a "freestanding right" to do whatever the law has not prohibited. Thus, in areas of double aspect, the provinces can legislate in ways that are more restrictive than Parliament's criminal legislation in relation to the same matter.[77] In *Rothmans, Benson & Hedges Inc. v Saskatchewan*, for example, provincial legislation that imposed an absolute ban on tobacco advertising was held not to be in conflict with federal criminal law that allowed a limited amount of advertising.[78]

---

[72] *Hodge v The Queen* (1983) 9 App Cas 117 at 130. More recently, see *Canadian Western Bank v Alberta* 2007 SCC 22, [2007] 2 SCR 3 [hereinafter *Canadian Western Bank*] [30] " . . . some matters are by their very nature impossible to categorize under a single head of power: they may have both provincial and federal aspects. Thus, the fact that a matter may for one purpose and in one aspect fall within federal jurisdiction does not mean that it cannot, for another purpose and in another aspect, fall within provincial competence . . . ."
[73] *RJR-Macdonald* above (n 14).
[74] *Hydro-Québec* above (n 13).
[75] *Alberta (Attorney General) v Moloney*, 2015 SCC 51, [2015] 3 SCR 327.
[76] *Rothmans, Benson & Hedges Inc v Saskatchewan*, 2005 SCC 13, [2005] 1 SCR 188 [15].
[77] ibid [19].
[78] ibid.

The courts' general willingness to uphold provincial laws that address moral considerations—the classic concern of criminal law—has been facilitated by the fact that such laws may be completely regulatory in nature which will detract from their characterization as "truly" criminal. For example *Nova Scotia Board of Censors v McNeil*[79] involved a challenge of provincial legislation that required all films to be submitted to the censor board before they were allowed to be shown in theatres. The board could permit or prohibit the exhibition of films, or require changes, based on the board's assessment of, among other things, whether the films were decent or obscene. Indecency and obscenity are matters of moral concern that are addressed by *Criminal Code* offences. In upholding this part of the legislation as validly enacted in relation to the regulation of an industry under sections 92(13) and (16), Ritchie J. for the majority emphasized the fact that the act did not create offences or provide for punishment and was preventive rather than penal in nature.[80] Justice Ritchie's reasons also provide an interesting inversion of Justice Rand's position in *PATA*. If, as Justice Rand observed, federal criminal laws did not have to be concerned with morality—"morality and criminality are far from coextensive"—then it followed that provincial regulation of morality "is not necessarily 'an invasion of the federal criminal field.'"[81] In this regard, although Justice Ritchie was satisfied that the legislation was "in pith and substance, directed at property and civil rights and therefore valid under s. 92(13)," in obiter he suggested that an alternative basis supporting "pure" moral regulation might be available: "In a country as vast and diverse as Canada. . . . the determination of what is and what is not acceptable for public exhibition on moral grounds may be viewed as a matter of a 'local and private nature in the Province' within the meaning of section 92(16)."[82]

Although the regulatory rather than punitive character of provincial laws counts in favour of their validity, another factor that explains why provincial legislatures' criminal-like enactments have so often been upheld is that the Constitution specifically allows such laws to contain the formal characteristics of criminal laws. It will be recalled that section 92(15) gives the provincial legislatures the power to "impose[. . .] punishment by fine, penalty, or imprisonment for enforcing any law of the province." This power is ancillary, and must be used to enforce laws that are otherwise "anchored" in one of the other section 92 enumerations.[83] However, given the courts' broad interpretation of the public purposes of criminal law, as discussed in the previous section of this chapter, it will be appreciated that the provinces' jurisdiction in such areas as health will make it very difficult to distinguish the substantive differences between some provincial and federal criminal law initiatives.

The phenomenon of overlapping provincial and federal criminal laws is well-illustrated in the area of automobile driving offences. It was established early in the

---

[79] *Nova Scotia Board of Censors v McNeil*, [1978] 2 SCR. 662 [hereinafter *McNeil*].
[80] ibid 691.
[81] ibid 692.
[82] ibid 699.
[83] ibid Laskin CJ (dissenting), 683.

twentieth century that the application of provincial legislation concerning the use of property could depend on convictions under the federal *Criminal Code*.[84] On this basis, and in recognition of the province's jurisdiction over highways and the use of property, a line of decisions upheld provincial laws that suspended the drivers' licenses of people who were convicted of impaired driving offences under the *Criminal Code*[85] and which did so in a manner that was more restrictive than the *Criminal Code* required.[86] In *Goodwin v British Columbia (Superintendent of Motor Vehicles)*[87] the Court upheld provincial legislation imposing automatic roadside licence suspensions, high fines, and the impounding of vehicles on the basis of lower blood alcohol levels than those that would trigger liability under the *Criminal Code*. The Court's finding of validity in *Goodwin* was made in full recognition that the law "targets, in part, specific criminal activity and imposes serious consequences, without the protections attendant on criminal investigations and prosecutions."[88] Keeping with the theme of its decisions in this area, however, the Court found that the pith and substance of the legislation was not to "oust the criminal law, but rather to prevent death and serious injury on public roads by removing drunk drivers and deterring impaired driving."[89] Using this same line of reasoning, the Supreme Court has upheld provincial legislation allowing for the forfeiture of property that officials establish, on a balance of probabilities, constitutes the proceeds of crime, without the need for proof that a crime has been committed or charged.[90]

The courts have, however, occasionally shown less willingness to recognize a provincial aspect in relation to matters that are otherwise the subject of criminal laws. In *McNeil*, for example, although the provisions discussed above were upheld, Justice Ritchie found that the sections of the act that prohibited live "indecent or improper" performances (again, as determined by the board), were ultra vires because they were "indistinguishable from the like provisions of the *Criminal Code*."[91] Similarly, although the courts have shown considerable tolerance for municipal by-laws[92] that regulate

---

[84] *Bédard v Dawson* [1923] SCR 681. The decision upheld Quebec legislation that allowed judges to order the closing of a "disorderly house"—where prostitution or gambling was carried on—as being within the province's authority over property and civil rights under s 92(13). The objection to the statute's validity was the fact that proof that a place was being used as a disorderly house was conviction for this offence under the *Criminal Code*.

[85] *Provincial Secretary of Prince Edward Island v Egan*, [1941] SCR 396.

[86] *Ross v. Registrar of Motor Vehicles*, [1975] 1 SCR 5. The decision upheld Ontario legislation imposing an absolute three-month driving suspension for anyone convicted of impaired driving and found that it was not in conflict with *Criminal Code* provisions allowing judges to allow convicted persons to drive at certain times (e.g., on the fact of the case, in the course of employment during the work week).

[87] *Goodwin v British Columbia (Superintendent of Motor Vehicles)*, 2015 SCC 46, [2015] 3 SCR. 250 [hereinafter *Goodwin*].

[88] ibid. [29].

[89] ibid.

[90] *Chatterjee v Ontario (Attorney General)*, 2009 SCC 19, [2009] 1 S.C.R. 624.

[91] *McNeil* above (n 79) 699.

[92] Section 92(8) of the *Constitution Act, 1867* gives the provincial legislatures jurisdiction over municipal institutions. Once created by provincial legislation, these institutions can exercise any of the provinces' powers that are delegated to them.

kinds of activity on city streets that could also be the bases for *Criminal Code* offences,[93] by-laws that are more clearly aimed at punishing than preventing criminal activity have been declared ultra vires.[94] The Supreme Court has also blocked attempts by provincial legislatures to, in effect, replace *Criminal Code* prohibitions that have been struck down on *Charter* grounds.[95]

6. THE ADMINISTRATION OF CRIMINAL JUSTICE

An earlier part of the discussion indicated that, although Parliament enjoys the plenary power over the creation of criminal law pursuant to section 91(27) of the *Constitution Act, 1867*, the provincial governments have the ability to affect the application of that law within their territories by the terms of section 92(14). That section gives the provincial legislatures jurisdiction over "The Administration of Justice in the Province, including the ... Constitution, Maintenance, and Organization of Provincial Courts ... Of Criminal Jurisdiction. ... " It is well accepted that the reference to justice in this section includes criminal justice,[96] and that the section gives the provinces the jurisdiction to establish police forces. The *Goodwin* decision provides some idea of the role of police and police discretion in modifying the application of criminal law in the provinces. In that case, the parties who were challenging the validity of the provincial roadside driving licence suspension scheme suggested that its true criminal nature was revealed by the fact that the police tended to enforce it instead of the *Criminal Code* provisions "effectively removing the more onerous and protective processes associated with criminal investigations and prosecutions."[97] In this regard, the Court recognized that "the fact that [the police] exercise their discretion to enforce one of these laws rather than another is consistent with police discretion generally."[98]

---

[93] *Dupond v City of Montreal et al.*, [1978] 2 SCR 770, upholding bylaws that prohibited and provided for fines and imprisonments for public gatherings and parades that could "endanger tranquility, safety, peace or public order," notwithstanding the bylaws' similarities to *Criminal Code* provisions prohibiting breaches of the peace.

[94] *Westendorp v The Queen*, [1983] 1 SCR 43, declaring ultra vires Calgary bylaws aimed at prostitution activities on city streets.

[95] In the wake of the Supreme Court of Canada's decision in *R v Morgentaler*, [1988] 1 SCR 30, which struck down the *Criminal Code* provisions relating to abortions, and with knowledge that Dr. Morgentaler intended to set up private abortion clinics in the province, the government of Nova Scotia passed legislation that prohibited the provision of certain kinds of medical services in private clinics. Regulations made under the legislation listed the prohibited procedures, one of which was non-emergency abortions. In *R v Morgentaler*, [1993] 3 SCR 463, the Court held that the legislation and the regulations were ultra vires the province as being in pith and substance criminal law.

[96] *Di Iorio v Warden of the Montreal Jail* (note 9) but see Laskin C.J.'s dissent (with de Grandpré J.).

[97] *Goodwin* above (n 87) [19].

[98] ibid [28].

The question as to whether the administration of justice in the provinces includes original jurisdiction to prosecute federal criminal laws is a matter of some debate.[99] Practically speaking, provincial Crown prosecutors and Crown attorneys do, in fact, prosecute most *Criminal Code* offences and, before it started to become expanded with amendments in 1969, the *Code's* definition of "Attorney General" was restricted to Attorneys General of the provinces where proceedings under the *Code* were taken.[100] From the provincial governments' perspective, this arrangement reflected what they understood to be their exclusive constitutional authority to prosecute criminal offences, which allowed for a measure of sensitivity to local conditions and attitudes in the application of the single national framework of criminal laws. Since that time, the federal government has successfully asserted its own jurisdiction to prosecute the criminal offences that it creates, whether they are included in the *Criminal Code* or in other statutes.[101] Accordingly, although commentators generally assume the existence of original provincial jurisdiction over the prosecution of federal criminal offences that is at least concurrent with federal jurisdiction,[102] some questions remain as to whether the provinces operate in this area only because Parliament has delegated that authority to them. There may, however, be some benefits to the possibility that the provinces prosecute as a matter "of grace and not as of right."[103] The "mere delegation" interpretation of their prosecutorial authority raises the possibility that the provinces could decline that responsibility in relation to some unpopular and/or expensive federal criminal law initiatives, leaving it up to the Attorney General of Canada to prosecute them if he or she wishes.[104]

7. CONCLUSION

The federal criminal law power and the terrain that it shares with areas of provincial jurisdiction promise to remain at the center of debates concerning the practice of Canadian federalism. Nowhere is the tension so sharp between Canadian federalism's traditional—indeed, definitional—need to retain some clear lines between areas of

---

[99] See Mark Carter, "Recognizing Original (Non-delegated) Provincial Jurisdiction to Prosecute Criminal Offences" (2007) 38 Ottawa Law Review 163.

[100] Where *Criminal Code* proceedings were undertaken in the territories, the Attorney General was defined as the Attorney General of Canada.

[101] *R. v Hauser*, [1979] 1 SCR 984; *A.G. Canada v CN Transportation*, [1983] 2 SCR 206; *R. v Wetmore*, [1983] 2 SCR 284.

[102] Hogg above (n 3) 19-18; Guy Régimbald & Dwight Newman, *The Law of the Canadian Constitution* (Butterworths, 2013), 268.

[103] William Henkel, "Case Comments and Notes: *R v Hauser*" (1980) 18 Alberta L Rev 265, 268.

[104] This suggestion (or threat) was made by some provincial Attorneys General in response to what may have been the expectation that they would handle prosecutions under the long-gun registry provisions of the federal *Firearms Act* (S.C. 1995, c. 39). See Carter above (n 99).

federal and provincial jurisdiction on the one hand, and on the other the siren call of the "dominant tide" of federalism[105] which seeks to maximize the ability of both levels of government to legislate in the public interest, unrestricted by jurisdictional boundaries and limited only by instances of conflict.[106] The nature and scope of the criminal law power is a necessarily dynamic subject, operating as something of a bellweather for the country's shifting needs for, and interest in, either more centralized or more regional responses to such things as moral, social, environmental, and health concerns. In whatever way that the courts decide to draw the lines to suit the current legal, political, and social contexts, it must be done in a manner that recognizes not only the lines that exist between sections 91 and 92, but those that separate the branches of government and the other parts of the Constitution as well.

BIBLIOGRAPHY

Articles, Chapters, and Books

Carter, Mark, "Recognizing Original (Non-delegated) Provincial Jurisdiction to Prosecute Criminal Offences" (2007), 38 Ottawa Law Review 163.

Carter, Mark, "Retributive Sentencing and the Charter: The Implications of *Sauvé v. Chief Electoral Officer*" (2005), 10 Canadian Criminal Law Review 43.

Carter, Mark, "Federalism Analysis and the Charter" (2011) 74 SKLR 5.

Duff, R.A. "Theorizing Criminal Law: A 25th Anniversary Essay" (2005) 25 OXJLS 353.

Friedland, Martin, *A Century of Criminal Justice: Perspectives on the Development of Canadian Law* (Toronto: Carswell, 1984).

Hogg, Peter, *Constitutional Law of Canada*, 5th ed., vol. 1, loose-leaf (Toronto: Thomson Carswell, 2007).

Kong, Hoi, "Subsidiarity, Republicanism, and the Division of Powers in Canada" (2015) 45 RDUS 13.

Leclair, Jean, "The Supreme Court of Canada's Understanding of Federalism: Efficiency at the Expense of Diversity" (2003) 28 Q LJ 411.

Manning, Morris, "Criminalization by Regulation: The Outer Limits of Section 91(27) of the *Constitution Act, 1867*", (2002) 13 Nat'l J Const L 309.

McConnell, Howard, *Commentary on the British North America Act* (Macmillan: Toronto, 1977).

Mitchell, Graeme, "Developments in Constitutional Law: The 1997–98 Term—Activism and Accountability" (1999), 10 SCLR 83.

Régimbald, Guy & Newman, Dwight, *The Law of the Canadian Constitution* (Butterworths: Toronto, 2013).

Ryder, Bruce, "The Demise and Rise of the Classical Paradigm in Canadian Federalism: Promoting Autonomy for the Provinces and First Nations" (1991) 36 McGill LJ 308.

Webber, Jeremy, *The Constitution of Canada: A Contextual Analysis* (Hart: Oxford, 2015).

---

[105] *Canadian Western Bank* (n 72) [37].
[106] ibid.

Cases

A.G. Canada v CN Transportation, [1983] 2 SCR 206.
Bédard v Dawson [1923] SCR 681.
Canadian Western Bank v Alberta, 2007 SCC 22, [2007] 2 SCR 3.
Chatterjee v Ontario (Attorney General), 2009 SCC 19, [2009] 1 S.C.R. 624.
Dupond v City of Montreal et al, [1978] 2 SCR 770.
Friends of the Oldman River Society v Canada (Minister of Transport), [1992] 1 SCR 3.
Goodwin v British Columbia (Superintendent of Motor Vehicles), 2015 SCC 46, [2015] 3 SCR 250.
In re the Board of Commerce Act, 1919, and the Combines and Fair Prices Act, 1919, [1922] 1 AC 191 (PC).
Nova Scotia Board of Censors v McNeil, [1978] 2 SCR. 662.
Proprietary Articles Trade Association v AG Canada, [1931] AC 310 (PC).
Provincial Secretary of Prince Edward Island v Egan, [1941] SCR 396.
R. v Crown Zellerbach Canada Ltd, [1988] 1 SCR 401.
R. v Hauser, [1979] 1 SCR 984.
R. v Hydro-Québec, [1997] 3 SCR 213.
R. v Malmo-Levine, [2003] 3 SCR 571.
R. v Morgentaler, [1993] 3 SCR 463.
R. v Wetmore, [1983] 2 SCR 284.
Reference re Assisted Human Reproduction Act, 2010 SCC 61, [2010] 3 SCR 457.
Reference re Firearms Act (Can.), [2000] 1 SCR 783.
Reference re Validity of Section 5(a) of the Dairy Industry Act (Margarine Reference) [1949] SCR 1.
RJR-MacDonald Inc. v Canada (Attorney General), [1995] 3 SCR 199.
Ross v Registrar of Motor Vehicles, [1975] 1 SCR 5.
Rothmans, Benson & Hedges Inc v Saskatchewan, 2005 SCC 13, [2005] 1 SCR 188.
Switzman v Elbing and the AG of Quebec [1957] SCR 285.
Westendorp v The Queen, [1983] 1 SCR 43.

CHAPTER 23

....

THE ENVIRONMENT, FEDERALISM, AND THE CHARTER

....

DAYNA NADINE SCOTT[*]

To understand environmental law in Canada is to come to terms with a complex and contested jurisdictional struggle often characterized as a "tug of war" between federal and provincial orders of government.[1] The jurisdictional struggle is performed in legal and policy arenas, but its effects are felt most acutely on the ground as environmental and health impacts unevenly affect Canadians in their daily lives. Although these struggles cannot be uniformly characterized as contests to fill nor vacate jurisdictional space, it is obvious that they have contributed to a collective failure to enact an effective and coordinated system of environmental law and regulation in Canada.[2] Contemporary movements for environmental justice, foregrounding how ordinary people experience environmental benefits and burdens, and how they are distributed, are increasingly turning to the *Canadian Charter of Rights and Freedoms* to challenge the inadequacy of this regime. Activists are claiming entitlements to clean air and clean water for everyone,

---

* Associate Professor, Osgoode Hall Law School and the Faculty of Environmental Studies at York University. Jacqui Hebert, 2L at Osgoode Hall Law School and a student in the joint MES/JD Program, was instrumental in the drafting of this chapter. She provided excellent research assistance and advice based on her own research into how Canadian federalism impacts environmental policy making in Canada.

¹ See for example, Kathryn Harrison, *Passing the Buck: Federalism and Canadian Environmental Policy* (UBC Press 1996); Meinhard Doelle and Chris Tollefson, *Environmental Law: Cases and Materials* (2nd edn, Carswell, 2013).

² Lynda Collins and Heather McLeod-Kilmurray, *The Canadian Law of Toxic Torts* (Canada Law Book, 2014): the question now is whether governments must step in to fill the breach, citing *British Columbia v Canadian Forest Products Ltd* 2004 SCC 38 at [81], 240 DLR (4th) 1. The federal "retreat" from its historical role in areas of environmental protection began in the early 2000s and intensified when the Harper government achieved a majority in 2011. See for example, G. Bruce Doern, Graeme Auld and Christopher Stoney, *Green-Lite: Complexity in Fifty Years of Canadian Environmental Policy, Governance, and Democracy* (McGill-Queens University Press, 2015).

and demanding that governments recognize a right to a healthy environment for all. Despite its limitations, the campaign for environmental rights in Canada has the potential to bring constitutional litigation about the environment out from the technical doldrums and into everyday politics—and this is a good thing.

This chapter reviews the key jurisprudential developments in relation to the division of powers, including the current trend towards local regulation of environmental matters according to the principle of "subsidiarity", and the growing recognition of the inherent jurisdiction of Indigenous peoples. I illustrate the contemporary dynamics by exploring two critical policy case studies from the perspective of barriers to environmental justice: safe drinking water on reserves, and climate change mitigation. Finally, I explore some promising *Charter* litigation motivated by environmental justice concerns and evaluate the utility of constitutionalizing "environmental rights" in Canada.

1. The Constitutional Contours of Canadian Environmental Law and Policy

Canada's Constitution, which formally includes the *Constitution Act, 1867*,[3] the *Constitution Act, 1982*,[4] the *Canadian Charter of Rights and Freedoms*,[5] and the body of jurisprudence that flows from their interpretation, exerts powerful control over the operation of Canadian environmental law, the practice of environmental policy-making, and thus the prospects for attaining environmental justice. Specifically, the division of powers laid out in sections 91 and 92 of the *Constitution Act, 1867* is at the core of Canadian debates and controversies over environmental issues, from litigation through to political struggle. This is often attributed to the fact that the powers distributed between the federal Parliament and the provincial legislatures in sections 91 and 92 at the time of Confederation did not, understandably, include the words "the environment". Thus, we are without a clearly delineated and distinct subject-matter of regulation allocated to a single level of government, making a definitive articulation of environmental regulatory jurisdiction a perennial challenge.

The environment is thus a matter of "shared" jurisdiction in Canada, which is to say, it is always already contested—legally, socially, and politically—with ecological and environmental health consequences. This is not to say that these consequences could be erased with a clear division of powers or singular jurisdiction in charge of regulating "the environment"; it is to emphasize that the particular contours of the legal and political mobilizations needed to achieve change are structured by the constitutional

---

[3] *Constitution Act, 1867* (UK), 30 & 31 Vict, c 3, reprinted in RSC 1985, Appendix II, No 5.
[4] *Canada Act 1982* (UK), 1982, c 11.
[5] *Canadian Charter of Rights and Freedoms*, Part I of the *Constitution Act, 1982*, being Schedule B to the *Canada Act 1982* (UK), 1982, c 11.

configuration. Although several commentators attribute Canada's "inefficient" and largely inadequate patchwork of environmental laws to this situation of shared jurisdiction,[6] it is also clear that much of this contestation is productive and appropriately politicizes questions of environmental justice.[7]

2. THE CONSTITUTIONAL DIVISION OF POWERS

The division of powers laid out in sections 91 and 92 of the *Constitution Act, 1867* is the starting point for determining legislative authority with respect to the environment, as it is for other policy areas. The failure of sections 91 and 92 of the *Constitution Act, 1867* to explicitly name and allocate legislative power over "the environment", as mentioned, is a defining and enduring feature of Canadian environmental law and policy.[8] In addition to the federal, provincial, and municipal authorities, the jurisdiction of Indigenous peoples over the environment is increasingly recognized in Canada, not only through self-government arrangements established in land claims negotiations, but also as exercises of inherent jurisdiction.[9]

A. Sources of Federal Authority

Section 91 of the *Constitution Act, 1867* enumerates the legislative powers of the Parliament of Canada. The following listed subject matters form the basis for the exercise of federal jurisdiction over the environment: federally-owned property (91(1A)), sea coast and inland fisheries (91(12)), navigation and shipping (91(10)), the criminal law

[6] See for example, Jamie Benidickson, 'The Constitutional Allocation of Environmental Responsibility and Interjurisdictional Coordination' in J. Benidickson, *Environmental Law* (4th edn, Irwin Law, 2013).

[7] ibid; Neil Hawke, 'Canadian Federalism and Environmental Protection' (2002) 14:2 J Envtl L 185; Irene Henriques and Perry Sadorky, 'Voluntary Environment Programs: A Canadian Perspective' (2008) 36:1 Policy Stud J 143; Melody Hessing, Michael Howlett and Tracy Summerville, *Canadian Natural Resource and Environmental Policy: Political Economy and Public Policy* (2nd edn, UBC Press, 2005); James Salzman and Barton H Thompson Jr, 'Perspectives of Environmental Law and Policy' in J. Salzman and B.H. Thompson, *Environmental Law and Policy* (3rd edn, Foundation Press, 2010).

[8] Benidickson, above (n 6).

[9] Canada, Environment and Climate Change Canada, *Shared Responsibility* (7 January 2016) www.ec.gc.ca/eau-water/default.asp?lang=En&n=035F6173-1 accessed 10 May 2016; Kent McNeil, *Emerging Justice? Essays on Indigenous Rights in Canada and Australia* (Native Law Centre 2001) 161–355; Canada, Indigenous and Northern Affairs Canada, *The Government of Canada's Approach to Implementation of the Inherent Right and the Negotiation of Aboriginal Self-Government* (15 September 2010) www.aadnc-aandc.gc.ca/eng/1100100031843/1100100031844 accessed 10 May 2016; Lorne Sossin, 'Indigenous Self-Government and the Future of Administrative Law' (2012) 45 UBC Law Review 595.

(91(27)), and Indians and lands reserved for Indians (91(24)).[10] Two of Canada's earliest environmental laws were created when the federal Parliament exercised its law-making powers under these sections. First, the *Navigable Waters Protection Act*,[11] which received Royal Assent in 1882 (and was only recently substantially "watered down" in 2012), was enacted on the basis of the federal Parliament's authority to regulate navigation under section 91(10). Second, in 1868, the federal Parliament introduced the *Fisheries Act*, which contained explicit provisions for the protection of fish and fish habitat. This instance of more direct regulation of environmental matters is derived from the federal Parliament's right to regulate sea coast and inland fisheries under section 91(12).

Canada's authority to make criminal law, enumerated in section 91(27), is another avenue by which the federal Parliament has more recently shaped environmental regulation. The seminal 1997 Supreme Court of Canada (SCC) decision in *R v Hydro-Québec*[12] upheld the constitutionality of the federal *Canadian Environmental Protection Act (CEPA)* as a valid exercise of the federal government's criminal law power.[13] The Court held that *CEPA* had a legitimate public purpose in providing protection for environmental and human health, and was therefore constitutional as per the federal Parliament's power to make laws relating to criminal matters. According to the majority's reasons, the federal use of the criminal law power in *CEPA* was justified because it constituted an attempt to implement *prohibitions coupled with penalties* for the purpose of preventing harm to human health, making it analogous to the criminal law. This was the case even though the *CEPA* was recognized to contain a very elaborate regulatory apparatus for assessing and managing the risks posed by toxic substances. As schemes become even more "regulatory" in nature, moving beyond the traditional command-and-control form, "deployment of the criminal law power becomes more controversial".[14]

Federal laws based on powers to regulate, for example, trade and commerce (s. 92(2)) or taxation (s. 92(3)), may be similarly utilized to support federal legislation that touches on environmental issues within those subject-matters even if that legislation incidentally touches on provincial matters.[15] These heads of power offer a more conceptual

---

[10] The residual "peace, order and good government" (POGG) power, grounded in the opening paragraph of section 91, is also a significant source of federal jurisdiction in relation to the environment, as described below.

[11] *Navigable Waters Protection Act*, RSC 1985, c N-22.

[12] *R v Hydro Quebec* [1997] 3 SCR 213, 151 DLR (4th) 32.

[13] La Forest J., writing for the five justices in the majority, stresses that the POGG power (discussed in more detail below) would also provide a valid grounding for federal Parliamentary action with respect to environmental protection, in certain circumstances.

[14] Doelle and Tollefson, above (n 1) 168.

[15] This approach to constitutional analysis of law was reiterated in *Reference Re: Assisted Human Reproduction Act* 2010 SCC 61 at [32], 327 DLR (4th) 257, where the Court explains that "the doctrine of pith and substance permits either level of government to enact laws that have "substantial impact on matters outside its jurisdiction": PW Hogg, *Constitutional Law of Canada* (5th edn, Carswell 2012) 15–19. The provincial and federal orders of government may make laws that incidentally touch on issues outside of their jurisdiction as long as the dominant purpose of the law falls within one of its listed heads of power.

means of justifying the exercise of federal law-making but nonetheless have the potential to contribute to a more holistic and expansive federal role in regulating for environmental protection.[16]

Finally, the federal Parliament's residual power to make laws consistent with "Peace, Order, and good Government", as per the opening paragraph of section 91, opens further space for environmental regulation under certain conditions.[17] Reaching all the way back to the Judicial Committee of the Privy Council, the jurisprudence established that where the subject matter of the legislation is such that it "goes beyond" local or private concerns then it will "fall within the competence of the Dominion Parliament as a matter affecting the peace, order, and good government of Canada, though it may in another aspect touch on matters specifically reserved to the provincial legislatures".[18] This became the basis for a constitutional doctrine known as "national dimension" or "national concern" which was later vigorously applied by the SCC to justify federal legislative action over environmental matters, only attracting limits in the 1970s and 1980s.[19] It is now well-established that the peace, order, and good government power ("the POGG power") has both a national concern branch and an emergency branch, giving the federal Parliament the authority to legislate with respect to quickly emerging threats. Eventually, in a case about whether the federal *Ocean Dumping Control Act* was properly within Parliament's jurisdiction, the SCC held that in order to qualify under the national dimension test a matter would have to have a "singleness, distinctiveness and indivisibility".[20] The majority of the Court explained that international commitments and the inability of provinces to effectively regulate waters beyond their borders meant that marine pollution must be a matter of national concern. Further, it was held that the subject-matter of the legislation was sufficiently defined so as not to produce a boundless incursion on provincial jurisdiction. Each of these factors remains an important consideration in division-of-powers jurisprudence: international treaty commitments, provincial "inability", and effect on provincial powers.[21]

---

[16] Kathryn Harrison, 'The Constitutional Framework: Constraints and Opportunities' in Harrison above (n 1) 39.

[17] Because it was recognized that all powers could not be expressly conferred, a "residual" power was given to the federal Parliament so as to arrive at an exhaustive distribution. This should not be confused with 'paramountcy', which holds that in cases of inconsistencies or conflict between federal and provincial laws, federal laws will prevail. Otherwise, the powers should be conceived as "coordinate", that is neither level of government is intended to be superior to the other or to be able to control the exercise of the other's legitimate authority to legislate within its sphere.

[18] *Ontario (Attorney General) v Canada Temperance Federation* [1946] AC 193 [7], 2 DLR 1 (JCPC) per Viscount Simon at 203. See also D. Paul Emond, 'The Case for a Greater Federal Environment Role in the Environmental Protection Field: An Examination of the Pollution Problem and the Constitution' (1972) 10 Osgoode Hall Law Journal 647–680.

[19] See, for example, *R. v, Fowler*, [1980] 2 S.C.R. 213 and the *Crown Zellerbach* decision of the Supreme Court of Canada in 1988, discussed below.

[20] *R v Crown Zellerbach Canada Ltd* [1988] 1 SCR 401 [33], 49 DLR (4th) 161.

[21] With respect to the effect on provincial powers, *Friends of the Oldman River Society v Canada (Minister of Transport)* [1992] 1 SCR 3 at [63–64], 88 DLR (4th) 1, held that federal environmental assessment is valid because "environment" is "amorphous and all-encompassing" and lacks the necessary

By way of further example, federal jurisdiction to regulate in areas of environmental protection was again upheld in *R v J.D. Irving Ltd*[22], a 2008 challenge to the constitutionality of the *Migratory Birds Convention Act (MBCA)*.[23] The *MBCA* was enacted in 1917 in accordance with the Migratory Birds Convention signed by the British Crown on behalf of Canada with the United States.[24] At the time, the *MBCA* was enacted under section 132 of the *Constitution Act, 1867* which granted authority to the federal Parliament to implement treaties signed by Britain as law. In *Irving*, the appellants argued that their actions, which resulted in the disturbance of several great blue herons and the destruction of their nest, were not unlawful because the *MBCA* was ultra vires the federal Parliament.[25] More specifically, counsel for J.D. Irving Ltd. argued that the Act was essentially hunting legislation, which falls under provincial jurisdiction over property and civil rights. In contrast, the Court held that the *MBCA* must be interpreted more broadly as environmental legislation, noting that it was initially created in accordance with section 132 of the *Constitution Act, 1867*, and that it can now be justified by the federal POGG power. The idea that the federal Parliament holds a stand-alone treaty-implementation power was rejected by the Privy Council in the Labour Conventions case of 1937. This holding has generated copious critiques in the years since and many commentators speculate that a modern challenge to a statute enacted on the basis of implementing a treaty could succeed.[26]

The constitutional distinction between Canadian provinces and territories represents another interesting consideration in relation to the division of powers. Where provinces have jurisdiction over the enumerated grounds in section 92 of the *Constitution Act, 1867* in their own right, the territories exercise powers delegated to them by Parliament.[27] The Northwest Territories Devolution Agreement, which came into effect 1 April 2014, shifted this highly centralized concentration of power as it gave the Northwest Territories jurisdiction to manage and develop its own land and resources

---

definition to be categorized as a head of power under section 91 or 92. The environment could not be treated as a unique head of power in any federalist government "because no system in which one government was so powerful would be federal". For distinctiveness and indivisibility "what seems to be required is that federal legislation be aimed at a matter that has defined boundaries, so that recognizing this matter as being subject to POGG will not unduly interfere with or negate existing provincial regulatory powers". Patrick J Monahan and Byron Shaw, 'Peace, Order, and Good Government (POGG) Power' in P. Monahan and B. Shaw, *Constitutional Law* (Irwin Hall, 2013) at 276.

[22] *R v JD Irving Ltd* 2008 37 CELR (3d) 200, PL Cumming Prov J (NB Prov Ct).

[23] *Migratory Birds Convention Act*, 1994 SC, c 22.

[24] Environment and Climate Change Canada, 'Acts and Regulations' (*Government of Canada*, 25 April 2016), www.ec.gc.ca/ap-pa/default.asp?lang=En&n=86E31D77-1 accessed 12 May 2016.

[25] A law that is ultra vires is one that is outside the jurisdiction of the enacting government. For example, a law is ultra vires provincial jurisdiction if it relates to a head of power attributed to the federal Parliament.

[26] See for example, Stewart Elgie, 'Kyoto, the Constitution, and Carbon Trading: Waking a Sleeping BNA Bear (or Two)' (2008) 13 Review of Constitutional Studies 67.

[27] The territorial governments of the Yukon, the Northwest Territories, and Nunavut exercise delegated jurisdiction acquired from the federal Parliament by legislation.

akin to what the provinces exercise via section 92(A). This devolution, which took more than a decade to negotiate, gives people in the north the ability to make decisions about things that affect them the most, including with respect to lands and resources, and therefore some aspects of environmental protection.

B. Sources of Provincial Authority Regarding the Environment

Section 92 of the *Constitution Act,1867* enumerates the matters in regard to which the provinces may make laws. It contains some heads of power that provide clear mandates to create environmental legislation, as well as others that present broad opportunities for regulation. Specifically, section 92(A), which was introduced with the 1982 slate of constitutional amendments, allocates jurisdiction to the provinces regarding the "development, conservation and management of [. . .] natural resources" as well as "sites and facilities [. . .] for the generation and production of electrical energy".[28] The powers allocated under section 92(A) have allowed provincial legislatures to regulate primary resource industries, such as forestry and mining, which have significant consequences for environmental integrity.

Prior to the 1982 amendment the provinces enjoyed a solid constitutional foundation for environmental law-making, though jurisdiction was more arbitrary. Although provincial environmental legislation found constitutional backing from section 92(13) "Property and Civil Rights"; 92(10) "Local works and Undertakings"; 92(16) "Matters of a local or private nature"; and 92(5) "The management of land and timber resources", the broad interpretations that were given to "property and civil rights" in early jurisprudence meant that a large share of what we would call "environmental law" across the country has been enacted under that source of authority.[29] The provinces are also constitutionally empowered to delegate aspects of their jurisdiction to municipalities by legislation, and this has opened up avenues for municipalities to step into the realm of environmental policy-making in many respects, as discussed below.

Further, as much of the public land in Canada is under provincial ownership, provincial policy thus naturally has significant capacity to influence environmental protection.[30] For example, Ontario's Greenbelt Plan is a piece of provincial developmental policy that directly addresses environmental concerns with its prevention of fragmentation, protection of environmental heritage, and preservation of rural interests.[31] The regulatory regime for environmental assessment in Canada is also influenced by the fact

---

[28] *Constitution Act, 1982*, being Schedule B to the *Canada Act 1982* (UK), 1982, c 11 at s 92(A).

[29] Peter W Hogg, *Constitutional Law of Canada*, Student Edition (Carswell, 2015) 5–13.

[30] Barry C Field and Nancy D. Olewiler, 'Environmental Policy and Institutions in Canada' in BC Field and ND Olewiler (eds), *Environmental Economics* (3rd edn, McGraw Hill, 1997).

[31] Ministry of Municipal Affairs and Housing, *Ontario's Proposed Greenbelt Plan* (May 2016), http://www.mah.gov.on.ca/Page13783.aspx.

that most Crown land is under control of the provinces. However, prior to the radical amendments to the *Canadian Environmental Assessment Act* in 2012, environmental assessment was a field to which we could point for examples of "cooperative federalism" in action. Coordination between provincial and federal environmental assessments was aimed at making two separate assessments under distinct provincial and federal legislative schemes work together to obtain the information required.[32] In the lead-up to the changes, notions of cooperation and coordination in this field were recast as "costly duplication".[33] Instead, under the 2012 Act, "substitution and equivalency" is the name of the game;[34] provincial processes for assessment can be substituted for federal ones, even in situations where the provincial assessment allows for a narrower scope and fewer opportunities for public involvement.[35]

Finally, municipalities draw power to regulate with respect to environmental matters from acts of provincial legislatures that delegate powers to pass by-laws, and specify the limits of those powers. The SCC made clear in its *Spraytech* decision of 2001 that it would interpret those powers purposively, as it does in constitutional litigation, so as to ensure that municipalities can deal effectively with emerging environmental and public health issues.[36] At the same time however, as "creatures of the province", municipalities cannot have delegated to them powers that are outside provincial jurisdiction.[37] In *Spraytech*, the SCC found that a municipal by-law seeking to limit the use of cosmetic pesticides according to the "precautionary principle" was valid and within the scope of the municipality's powers over public health and welfare. The Court also outlined a principle of "subsidiarity" which holds that "law-making and implementation are often best achieved at a level of government that is not only effective, but also closest to the citizens affected . . .".[38] As Neil Craik explains, the principle of subsidiarity is now well-established and is a factor in the "determination of whether a matter ought to be

---

[32] An Act to implement certain provisions of the budget tabled in Parliament on March 29, 2012 and other measures HC Bill (First Session, 41st Parliament) Chapter 19 at 51 para 32. Canada, Canadian Environmental Assessment Agency and Ministry of Environment, *Federal/Provincial Environmental Assessment Coordination in Ontario* (June 2007) www.ceaa-acee.gc.ca/ED4330AB-54FD-448B-B523-38B00187D618/Federal_Provincial_Guide_6260e.pdf accessed 13 May 2015.

[33] Canada, Canadian Environmental Assessment Agency, *Frequently Asked Questions* (20 November 2015) www.ceaa.gc.ca/default.asp?lang=en&n=CE87904C-1#wsoBF9A0BD accessed 13 May 2016.

[34] ibid. See for example, Robert B. Gibson, Meinhard Doelle and A. John Sinclair, 'Fulfilling the Promise: Basic Components of Next Generation Environmental Assessment' (2016) Journal of Environmental Law & Practice, forthcoming.

[35] Mark Winfield, 'A New Era of Environmental Governance in Canada: Better Decisions Regarding Infrastructure and Resource Development Projects', Metcalf Foundation, May 2016, online: http://metcalffoundation.com/wp-content/uploads/2016/05/Metcalf_Green-Prosperity-Papers_Era-of-Governance_final_web.pdf.

[36] *114945 Canada Ltée (Spraytech, société d'arrosage) v Hudson (Town)* 2001 SCC 40, 200 DLR (4th) 419.

[37] For a discussion of the origins of the persistent idea that municipalities are mere "creatures of the province", see Ron Levi and Mariana Valverde, 'Freedom of the City: Canadian Cities and the Quest for Governmental Status' (2006) 44 Osgoode Hall Law Journal 409.

[38] ibid [3].

considered to fall within the exclusive confines of a particular head of power, or whether the activity, in fact, has a double aspect".[39]

The idea of subsidiarity is in tension with the notion that environmental governance in Canada is undergoing a constant "rescaling"[40] in response to changing ecological and political circumstances. As an example, the vacating of regulatory space by the federal government that characterized the Harper government years, and has been the subject of much critique especially in the field of environmental assessment, might also be seen as an *assertion* of jurisdiction. In other words, the aims of "responsible resource development" that shaped the regulatory retreat also imposed norms, such as a priority on "timely decisions", into areas of conventional provincial jurisdiction as an example.[41]

C. Inherent Jurisdiction of Indigenous Peoples

The recognition of "existing Aboriginal and treaty rights" in section 35(1) incorporates into our constitutional framework the affirmation and protection of Indigenous peoples' inherent right to govern themselves and their territories according to certain judicially-defined terms.[42] This right arguably includes Indigenous peoples' jurisdiction over environmental management throughout their traditional territories. We are seeing an escalation in the frequency and profile of assertions of such inherent jurisdiction by Indigenous communities across the country in recent years.[43] As an example, there are

[39] Alastair Neil Craik, 'Subsidiarity and Environmental Federalism: The Emergence of 'New Governance' in Finfish Aquaculture in Canada' (2009), at 20, available on SSRN: https://papers.ssrn. com/sol3/papers.cfm?abstract_id=1468617. Thus far, the principle has only been applied in support of a finding of shared jurisdiction, not to dictate provincial over federal authority.

[40] Doern, Auld and Stoney, above (n 2) 349.

[41] See Winfield above (n 35).

[42] Although, with respect to upholding the inherent Aboriginal right of self-government, Canadian courts require Indigenous rights claimants to bring evidence regarding specific activities as "elements of practices integral to their distinctive culture" (see *R. v Pamajewon*, [1996] S.C.J. No. 20), the federal government recognizes the existence of a broad inherent right of self-government (see *Renewing the Comprehensive Lands Claims Policy*, September 2014, online at https://www.aadnc-aandc.gc.ca/DAM/DAM-INTER-HQ-LDC/STAGING/texte-text/ldc_ccl_renewing_land_claims_policy_2014_1408643594856_eng.pdf). See also K. McNeil, 'Challenging Legislative Infringements of the Inherent Aboriginal Right of Self-Government' (2003) 22 Windsor Yearbook of Access to Justice 329 and K. McNeil, "The Jurisdiction of Inherent Right Aboriginal Governments" (2007) Research Paper for the National Centre for First Nations Governance, 32pp. According to McNeil, this jurisdiction should be considered concurrent with federal and provincial powers such that Aboriginal nations may proceed to establish "self-government capacity and to extend the exercise of their jurisdiction into new areas at their own pace and in accordance with their own needs and priorities" (2007) at 28.

[43] As an example, see the Notice of Assertion presented by the Chiefs of Ontario to the Premier of Ontario on 11 July 2014. It states: "By this Notice of Assertion, the First Nations whose territories and lands are within the boundaries of the [Province of Ontario], give formal notice to the Province of Ontario and Canada, to other governments, to resource users and developers, to neighbours and the general public that First Nations inherent and Treaty rights are currently and will continue to be asserted over traditional and historical territory, and ancestral lands.", online: http://www.chiefs-of-ontario.org/sites/default/files/news_files/NOTICE-1.pdf.

now several regulatory processes designed by Indigenous peoples in Canada in relation to environmental approvals and permits for resource extraction, with different degrees of articulation depending on the community and the context.[44] These exercises of inherent jurisdiction institute processes incorporating elements of Indigenous worldviews, standards of legitimacy, and values.[45] Within them, Indigenous laws and traditions for stewardship are being used by Indigenous peoples to structure regulatory mechanisms and exercise jurisdiction in relation to the environment. Reflection and dialogue over the necessary reconciliation of Indigenous jurisdiction over the environment protected by s. 35(1)—whether this jurisdiction is delineated under a self-government agreement, a treaty or land claim agreement, delineated judicially, or has yet to be delineated at all—with the division of powers over the environment under sections 91 and 92 of the Constitution is an area of environmental law that will call for increased analysis over the coming years as more cases and implementation scenarios come to light.

The complex overlap of jurisdictional authorities and the collision of political and ecological factors in determining the most appropriate governance structure is illustrated below through the example of drinking water regulation on First Nations reserves.

3. Case Study: Kashechewan First Nation Water Crisis

Indigenous communities in Canada face major challenges in accessing clean and safe drinking water. "First Nations homes are 90 times more likely to be without running water than the homes of other Canadians",[46] and boil-water advisories, which are widespread, often last years if not generations. In the Northern Ontario community of Neskantaga First Nation, a boil-water advisory has been in place for 20 years and Shoal Lake 40, a First Nations community on the Manitoba-Ontario border, has been under a boil-water advisory for 17 years.[47] These conditions raise serious physical and psychological health risks, and present an obvious example of enduring environmental injustice.[48]

---

[44] See, for examples, Jessica Clogg et al, "Indigenous Legal Traditions and the Future of Environmental Governance in Canada" (2016) 29 J Envtl L & Prac 227.

[45] John Borrows, 'Stewardship and the First Nations Governance Act' (2003–2004) 29 Queen's Law Journal 103. See also the chapter by Patrick Macklem in this *Handbook* regarding Aboriginal rights including Aboriginal title.

[46] Kaitlyn Mitchell and Zachary D'Onofrio, 'Environmental Injustice and Racism in Canada' (2016) 29 J Envtl L & Prac 305 at 324.

[47] To add insult to injury, Shoal Lake 40 is also "without an all-weather road due to an aqueduct constructed to carry water to Winnipeg because the city's drinking water source is in Shoal Lake 40's traditional territory". ibid, 325. In March 2016, the City of Winnipeg and the federal government committed to funding an all-weather road into Shoal Lake, but debates over the cost continue: CBC News, 'Officials Formally Announce Manitoba Reserve to Get Its "Freedom Road" ', 11 June 11 2016: http://www.cbc.ca/news/canada/manitoba/shoal-lake-first-nation-freedom-road-cost-1.3630363.

[48] Nathalie J Chalifour, 'Environmental Discrimination and the *Charter's* Equality Guarantee: The Case of Drinking Water for First Nations Living on Reserves' (2013) 43 *REG* 183; Constance MacIntosh,

It is generally accepted that provincial and territorial governments in Canada are responsible for ensuring access to safe and clean drinking water as a function of their authority to regulate for public health. This is accomplished mostly through delegation of responsibility for water treatment and distribution to local municipalities by legislation. A critical exception to this general rule exists in relation to federal lands and institutions, including First Nations reserves, over which legislative authority rests with the federal government under section 91(24). Thus, the provision of safe drinking water on reserves is said to be a shared responsibility between First Nation band councils, and several federal departments including Indian and Northern Affairs Canada which provides funding for the construction and maintenance of water services, Health Canada (HC) which oversees monitoring of water supplies, and Environment and Climate Change Canada which has responsibility for source water protection. On this official account, band councils are responsible for the "design, construction, operation and maintenance of [their] water systems" and are expected to contribute 20 percent of the costs.[49]

On 14 October 2005, nearly 1,000 people from the Kashechewan First Nation, a remote, fly-in community on the shores of James Bay in Northern Ontario, were evacuated because their community's drinking water was contaminated by E. coli.[50] The alert was sounded by HC, who reported that the Kashechewan drinking water supply had tested positive for the deadly bacteria. Residents already knew something was wrong: many were suffering from diarrhea and painful stomach cramps, or skin conditions such as scabies and impetigo.[51] The crisis managed to catch the attention of the mainstream media and photos showing children covered in rashes and scabs provoked shock and anger across the country. The general public was being urged to understand the issue as one of mismanagement that stemmed from confusion over jurisdiction between the federal and provincial governments.[52]

There was plenty of room for confusion: the federal government had been testing the water for contaminants; they had also shipped over $250,000 worth of bottled water into

---

'Testing the Waters: Jurisdictional and Policy Aspects of the Continuing Failure to Remedy Drinking Water on First Nations Reserves' (2007) 39 Ottawa Law Rev 6.

[49] Tonina Simeone, *Safe Drinking Water in First Nations Communities* (Library of Parliament 08-43-E, 28 May 2010) 2.

[50] CBC News in Review, 'Toxic Water: The Kashechewan Story' (December 2005) https://media. curio.ca/filer_public/f8/4e/f84e2dd8-76c5-4fbf-b9b7-b9d053b4ac2f/kashechewan.pdf accessed 10 May 2016.

[51] The relationship of the skin conditions to the bacterial contamination is contested. In a more recent flare-up of the ongoing crisis, experts argued that the chronic skin conditions should be attributed to the very poor housing stock on the reserve, rather than to water contamination. Jane Philpott, 'Statement from Jane Philpott, Minister of Health, on the Situation in Kashechewan (*Government of Canada*, 24 March 2016) http://news.gc.ca/web/article-en.do?nid=1042399&tp=980 accessed 12 May 2016; John Dehaas, ' "Social Emergency": Kashechewan Skin Problems Blamed on Poverty, Overcrowding' (*CTV News*, 23 March 2016) www.ctvnews.ca/canada/social-emergency-kashechewan-skin-problems-blamed-on-poverty-overcrowding-1.2830199 accessed 13 May 2016.

[52] Mike Krebs, 'The Crisis in Kashechewan: Water Contamination Exposes Canada's Brutal Policies against Indigenous People' (*Socialist Voice*, 23 November 2005): http://www.socialistvoice.ca/?p=75.

Kashechewan by that point.[53] Many traced the E. coli contamination to the federal government's refusal a decade earlier to heed the community's concerns with respect to the location of the water treatment plant, built downstream of the sewage lagoon in a place where seasonal flooding is expected. Training of operators for the treatment plant, also a responsibility of the federal government, seems to have been inadequate, exacerbating the health effects as chlorine was routinely fed into the system to deal with bacterial contamination.

Understandably, then, the Ontario government "pointed the finger" at Ottawa.[54] But Ottawa fired back, noting that drinking water safety and public health were under provincial jurisdiction. And in fact, on 25 October 2005, after 11 days of so-called confusion over which government should act, the Ontario Minister of Aboriginal Affairs, calling Ottawa "missing in action", ordered the community's emergency evacuation. A staggering 50 percent of the population was airlifted to surrounding cities and towns at the province's expense.[55]

The Institute on Governance has said drinking water in Canada presents a "governance problem of major complexity"[56] and allocates at least some of the blame to the lack of an "effective legislative base".[57] In making the argument that the lack of access to safe drinking water on many First Nations' reserves is a violation of the right to equality under s. 15(1), Nathalie Chalifour states that the main challenge is "the fact that there is no single law which categorically excludes First Nations reserve communities from . . . protection. Instead, there is a national network of laws which provides clean drinking water to all Canadians . . . with one glaring exception: Aboriginal peoples living on reserves".[58]

[53] ibid.

[54] Lawrence Solomon, 'Kashechewan Woes Boil Down the Leadership' (*National Post*, 5 November 2006) https://urbanrenaissance.probeinternational.org/2006/11/05/kashechewan-woes-boil-down-leadership/ accessed 12 May 2016; Karen Howlett, 'Ontario Orders Survey of Water on Reserves' (*Globe and Mail*, 1 November 2005) www.theglobeandmail.com/news/national/ontario-orders-survey-of-water-on-reserves/article1130351/ accessed 12 May 2016; 'Aboriginals Must Wrest Healthcare Control from Ottawa Mandarins' (*National Review of Medicine*, 15 November 2015) www.nationalreviewofmedicine.com/issue/2005/11_15/2_editorial_19.html accessed 12 May 2016.

[55] CBC News, 'Ottawa "Missing in Action" over Reserve's Bad Water: McGuinty' (26 October 2005) www.cbc.ca/news/canada/ottawa-missing-in-action-over-reserve-s-bad-water-mcguinty-1.533290 accessed 13 May 2016.

[56] Institute on Governance, *Safe Water for First Nations Communities: Learning the Lessons from Walkerton* (15 September 2002) at 9.

[57] ibid at 1; Canada, Office of the Auditor General, 'Chapter 5: Drinking Water in First Nation Communities' in *Report of the Commissioner of the Environment and Sustainable Development to the House of Commons* (September 2005) at 10.

[58] Chalifour above (n 47) 188. In the aftermath of the tragedy that occurred in Walkerton, Ontario, the Walkerton Inquiry (an independent commission charged with investigating the events and circumstances that allowed the contamination to occur), along with the Honourable Dennis R. O'Connor, published a very detailed two-part report. Both parts of the Report can be accessed online at www.archives.gov.on.ca/en/e_records/walkerton/. Following the events in Walkerton, the Ontario provincial government passed the *Safe Drinking Water Act, 2002*, SO 2002, c 32 to address the legal and policy-related issues blamed for facilitating the tragedy.

4. Cooperative Federalism

Sometimes the federalism debates have the effect of reinforcing the idea of clean lines of demarcation, or "watertight compartments", between the responsibilities of the central and regional authorities.[59] But as the drinking water example demonstrates, and as Peter Hogg has remarked, "modern governmental involvement in social and economic matters has produced policies which require constant interaction" between officials at various levels of government, and often a high degree of cooperation.[60] In fact, for these complex and persistent policy problems, we are seeing an increasing reliance on mechanisms which can foster relationships between executives of the central, regional governments and Aboriginal governments, and which call out for more formalized collaborations.[61] One of these mechanisms is the joint federal-provincial-territorial committee that produces the Guidelines for Canadian Drinking Water Quality;[62] another is the First Minister's Conference, which entails periodic face-to-face meetings between the Prime Minister and all provincial and territorial leaders.[63] An area which this tool has recently been employed to deal with is another intractable policy problem, pressing environmental issue and a "constitutional puzzle": climate change.[64]

5. Case Study: Climate Change Mitigation in Canada

Many observers would agree that Canada's "divided environmental house" is standing in the way of a coordinated greenhouse gas (GHG) reduction strategy, and thus hampering efforts to mitigate climate change and to live up to our international commitments, most recently instantiated in the *Paris Accord*.[65] Several commentators have called

[59] See for example, Richard Simeon and Amy Nugent, 'Parliamentary Canada and Intergovernmental Canada: Exploring the Tensions' in Herman Bakvis and Grace Skogstad (eds), *Canadian Federalism* (Oxford University Press, 2012).

[60] Hogg above (n 29) 5–4.

[61] See for example, Patricia Hania, 'Uncharted Waters: Applying the Lens of New Governance Theory to the Practice of Water Source Protection in Ontario' (2013) 24(2) Journal of Environmental Law & Practice 177.

[62] Health Canada, Federal-Provincial-Territorial Committee on Drinking Water (CDW), (19 Sept 2006; last accessed 28 March 2017) http://hc-sc.gc.ca/ewh-semt/water-eau/drink-potab/fpt/index-eng.php.

[63] AFN.

[64] Allan Hutchinson, 'Climate Change: A Constitutional Puzzle" (*Globe & Mail* Opinion, 27 April 2016) www.theglobeandmail.com/opinion/climate-change-a-constitutional-puzzle/article29764807/ accessed 12 May 2015.

[65] Thomas Posyniak, 'A Constitutional Foundation for a Greenhouse Gas Reduction Policy', *Policy Options* (1 November 2010) policyoptions.irpp.org/magazines/afghanistan/

climate change "the most significant policy challenge" facing the Canadian federation.[66] Although there is no clear delineation of authority over international affairs within the Constitution, such authority has over time been conferred on the executive branch of the federal government.[67] As such, Canada's agreement to the *Paris Accord* is generally consistent with the principle that the federal Crown administers and is responsible for implementing commitments made by treaty.[68] In 2005, when Parliament added six GHGs to Schedule 1 under *CEPA*, it was taken as an indication that the federal order of government intended to exercise jurisdiction to regulate industrial emissions as part of a climate change mitigation strategy. In 2012, the federal government followed up with regulations to control CO_2 emissions from coal-fired utilities,[69] and then later for the transportation sector.[70] Regulations that would apply to the oil and gas sector, however, were promised but never delivered. The Harper government's allegiance to the oil and gas sectors led to years of stalling, and the lack of an effective federal plan for curbing GHG emissions became an obvious gap in Canadian environmental policy.[71]

Hopes were renewed in March 2016 when the new Liberal Prime Minister called a First Ministers' Conference to focus on climate change.[72] This was in the wake of statements at the Paris Climate Conference in late 2015 that the federal government wished to move forward with the support of the provinces.[73] Crucially, the provinces each came to the Conference with varying degrees of commitment to addressing climate change, and with a range of different approaches and existing programs in place.[74] Despite media

a-constitutional-foundation-for-a-greenhouse-gas-reduction-policy/ accessed 13 May 2016; see also Nathalie Chalifour, 'Climate Federalism—Parliament's Ample Constitutional Authority to Regulate GHG Emissions' (2016) University of Ottawa Working Paper Series: https://papers.ssrn.com/sol3/papers.cfm?abstract_id=2775370##.

[66] Ibid, posniak.

[67] Laura Barnett, *Canada's Approach to the Treaty-Making Process* (Library of Parliament 2008-45-E, 14 November 2008, revised 6 November 2012) 1.

[68] Elgie, above (n 26).

[69] Reduction of Carbon Dioxide Emissions from Coal-Fired Generation of Electricity Regulations, SOR/2012-167.

[70] Heavy Duty Vehicle and Engine Greenhouse Gas Emission Regulations, SOR/2013-24. These regulations are presumably justified according to the federal authority over international and interprovincial trade and commerce, as they deal with emissions standards for imported engines and vehicles that cross provincial borders.

[71] Shawn McCarthy, 'Harper Calls Climate Regulations on Oil and Gas Sector "Crazy Economic Policy"', The Globe and Mail (9 December 2014) www.theglobeandmail.com/news/politics/harper-it-would-be-crazy-to-impose-climate-regulations-on-oil-industry/article22014508/ accessed 12 May 2016.

[72] Canada, Canadian Intergovernmental Conference Secretariat, *Vancouver Declaration on Clean Growth and Climate Change* (3 March 2016) https://news.gov.bc.ca/files/Vancouver_Declaration_clean_Growth_Climate_Change.pdf accessed 28 April 28 2016.

[73] Gary Mason, 'Are the Provinces Ready for Trudeau's Climate Plan?' Globe and Mail (December 4, 2015) http://www.theglobeandmail.com/opinion/are-the-provinces-ready-for-trudeaus-climate-plan/article27585585/.

[74] As an example, British Columbia has instituted a carbon tax, and Alberta has announced plans to implement one; Quebec, Ontario, and Manitoba have opted for an emissions trading system (to be harmonised with California's); Ontario also has a Feed-in-tariff program. Links to individual

reports that the Prime Minister intended to achieve a national price on carbon (either through a carbon tax or a cap-and-trade scheme), little in the way of concrete commitments came out of the Conference: the First Ministers agreed merely that the transition to a low carbon economy should be "adapted to each province's and territory's specific circumstances".[75] The matter flared up again in the House of Commons in October 2016 when the Prime Minister apparently surprised the provinces with the announcement that the federal government would step in and impose a price on carbon if the provinces did not institute one by 2018—either by carbon tax or a "cap-and-trade" emissions trading model.[76]

Speaking strictly from a legal perspective, both levels of government have broad powers of taxation; either or both could institute a carbon tax.[77] The provincial jurisdiction over industry and commerce could easily justify regulations addressing GHG emissions from industrial development, such as mining, oil and gas, or energy generation, including an emissions trading scheme.[78] But there is also a strong argument for "provincial inability" to effectively regulate GHGs, as climate change presents almost the quintessential border-crossing problem, with GHG emissions having a global effect, rather than localized impacts.[79] Despite the fact that the industrial facilities that emit GHGs often have serious adverse environmental health impacts on local communities, climate change itself is undoubtedly beyond the ability of any one jurisdiction to manage effectively. This is true at the international level as well, of course, but under the *Paris Accord* nation-states have been tasked with meeting "Nationally Determined Contributions" (NDCs) for which the federal government is accountable.[80] This would lend weight to an argument that the federal government holds authority under its residual power, with climate change constituting a "matter of national concern".

provincial approaches to climate change policy can be located online: www.climatechange.gc.ca/default.asp?lang=en&n=64778DD5-1. One commentator calls it a "bewildering patchwork of inconsistent and incompatible regulations" (Robert MacNeil and Matthew Paterson, 'This Changes Everything: Canadian Climate Policy and the 2015 Election' (2016) 25(3) Environmental Politics 553 at 556).

[75] Outputs included the "pan-Canadian framework on clean growth and climate change" and the "Canadian Energy Strategy". CBC News, 'Trudeau, Premiers Agree to Climate Plan Framework, But No Specifics on Carbon Pricing' (3 March 2016) http://www.cbc.ca/news/politics/first-ministers-premiers-trudeau-1.3474380 accessed 28 April 2016.

[76] Kathleen Harris, 'Justin Trudeau Gives Provinces until 2018 to Adopt Carbon Price Plan', The Globe and Mail (3 October 2016), http://www.cbc.ca/news/politics/canada-trudeau-climate-change-1.3788825.

[77] Chalifour above (n 64).

[78] Alexis Bélanger, 'Canadian Federalism in the Context of Combating Climate Change' (2011) 20(1) Constitutional Forum 21 at 25: "The leadership shown to date by the provinces on the climate change front illustrates their ability to lead the way in combating climate change, based on powers attributed to them by the Constitution".

[79] Elgie, above (n 26).

[80] Canada, Environment and Climate Change Canada, *Canada's Second Biennia Report on Climate Change* (10 February 2016) www.ec.gc.ca/GES-GHG/default.asp?lang=En&n=02D095CB-1 accessed 13 May 2016.

In fact, most commentators agree that there is "ample authority" for Parliament to act under the national concern branch of the POGG power.[81] Although it is possible that entrenched regional differences, combined with significant economic interests, could prompt constitutional litigation, it is clear that the chief obstacles are political. One such obstacle, of course, is the continued economic reliance on the fossil fuel industry.[82] Still, although economic actors will continue to try to achieve their aims of slowing or stopping costly regulations by direct lobbying and political influence, the courts are always in the background of these negotiations, and constitutional litigation remains an option. In this sense, the jurisprudence on the division of powers provides a powerful bargaining chip.[83]

6. Getting Past the Division-of-Powers Problem

As illustrated through these examples, conventional analysis is that this situation of shared jurisdiction prevents effective, decisive legislative action on pressing environmental issues.[84] Accordingly, for a period through the 1990s, the solution to the complex and overlapping authorities to regulate with respect to environmental matters in Canada became a project of "harmonization".[85] To be sure, there are plenty of examples in which the lack of a clear legislative mandate falling to one identifiable level of government has exacerbated problems on the ground for people struggling to achieve environmental justice in Canadian communities. But most of the jurisprudence on the division of powers in the environmental context has arisen from situations in which the applicant is seeking to challenge a legislative enactment as *ultra vires* because it creates compliance burdens for industry. In the context of the recent federal retreat from environmental regulation, however, we have seen provincial legislatures attempt to fill the void in some cases. Where these regimes are seen as too lax, they may be challenged by

---

[81] Chalifour, above (n 64); Thomas Posyniak, 'A Constitutional Foundation for a Greenhouse Gas Reduction Policy' *Policy Options* (1 November 2010) policyoptions.irpp.org/magazines/afghanistan/a-constitutional-foundation-for-a-greenhouse-gas-reduction-policy/ accessed 13 May 2016; Elgie, above (n 26); Bélanger, above (n 77).

[82] MacNeil and Paterson, above (n 73).

[83] Hutchinson, above (n 63).

[84] Harrison, above (n 1); FL Morton, 'The Constitutional Division of Powers with Respect to the Environment in Canada' in Kenneth M Holland, FL Morgan and Brian Galligan (eds), *Federalism and the Environment: Environmental Policymaking in Australia, Canada, and the United States* (Greenwood Press, 1996); Benidickson, above (n 6).

[85] Canada, Standing Committee on Environment and Sustainable Development, *Harmonization and Environmental Protection: An Analysis of the Harmonization Initiative of the Canadian Council of Ministers of the Environment* (HC December 1997) www.parl.gc.ca/HousePublications/Publication.aspx?DocId=1031507&Language=E&Mode=1&Parl=36&Ses=1 accessed 13 May 2016.

environmentalists or First Nations (on other grounds) as *ultra vires* the province.[86] More often, however, the ability of each level of government to deny that they hold legislative authority results in a "jurisdictional wasteland": certain areas where assuming jurisdiction entails direct financial costs, lost resource revenues, or indirect political costs, into which governments are reluctant to take legislative steps. With respect to safe drinking water on reserves, and the regulation of GHG emissions, this dynamic has contributed to on-the-ground needs and demands not being met, and compromised environmental integrity. In other words, federalism in Canada sometimes produces a "jurisdictional tug of war" that governments are trying to lose, rather than win. Often, the dispute is really about who is going to pay. The problem is not actually a technical failure of legal architecture, but an enduring political one.

Politicization of environmental law is an aim of the environmental justice movement.[87] Although these activists may engage in strategic litigation, they often prefer to achieve their aims through other tactics.[88] Demands include access to clean air and clean water for everyone, regardless of race, income, indigeneity, gender, or location. In recent years, the *Canadian Charter of Rights and Freedoms* has provided a focal point for organizing around environmental justice in Canada, especially by members of Indigenous communities.

A. The *Canadian Charter of Rights and Freedoms*

An innovative judicial review application filed by two members of the Aamjiwnaang First Nation in 2012 inspired environmental justice activists across Canada. The application was ultimately withdrawn, but its demands for what the *Charter* should guarantee hit a nerve across the country.[89] The *Charter* rights enshrined in section 7, the right to life, liberty, and security of the person, and section 15, the right to equality,

---

[86] See *Morton v British Columbia (Minister of Agriculture and Lands)* 2010 BCSC 100—"Section 26(2)(a) of Fisheries Act (note: provincial statute), ss. 1(h) and 2(1) of Farm Practices Protection (Right to Farm) Act, and Aquaculture Regulation were found to be **ultra vires** provincial Crown with respect to finfish and to apply only to cultivation of marine plants—Finfish Aquaculture Waste Control Regulation was found to be **ultra vires** provincial Crown in its entirety and invalid"; See also *Grassy Narrows First Nation v Ontario (Natural Resources)*, 2014 SCC 48, [2014] 2 S.C.R. 447.

[87] Cheryl Teelucksingh and Andil Gosine, *Environmental Justice and Racism in Canada*, (Emond Montgomery, 2008).

[88] See Luke W Cole and Sheila R Foster. *From the Ground Up: Environmental Racism and the Rise of the Environmental Justice Movement* (New York University Press, 2001). As a recent Canadian example, consider the Idle No More movement: Adam J Barker, ' "A Direct Act of Resurgence, a Direct Act of Sovereignty": Reflections on Idle No More, Indigenous Activism, and Canadian Settler Colonialism' (2014) Globalizations, http://dx.doi.org/10.1080/14747731.2014.971531.

[89] The application has been recently withdrawn, with the claimants' counsel, Ecojustice, indicating that Ontario is now taking steps towards addressing the issues raised by Ron and Ada's application. EcoJustice, 'Changing Course in Chemical Valley' (25 April 2016) www.ecojustice.ca/changing-course-chemical-valley/ accessed 13 May 2016.

created the foundation for Ada Lockridge and Ron Plain's application for judicial review, which became known as the "Chemical Valley Charter challenge".[90] The application questioned the constitutionality of permits granted to Suncor, which operates a refinery in the petrochemical cluster near Sarnia, Ontario. The industrial emissions from Sarnia's Chemical Valley, with several refineries and heavy industries accounting for approximately 40 percent of Canada's chemical production, flow downwind towards the Aamjiwnaang First Nation reserve.[91] The high air pollution burden in Aamjiwnaang and the devastating environmental health impacts on the community have been well documented.[92] In the judicial review, Lockridge and Plain contended that the decision by Ontario's Ministry of Environment to allow Suncor to increase its emissions, without proper consideration for the cumulative effects from all industrial emissions in the area, violates their *Charter* rights.[93] They argued that the decisions and practices of the ministry contribute to exceedingly high levels of emissions that threaten their health and force them to confront risks and trade-offs that non-Indigenous Canadians do not face, engaging the *Charter*'s equality guarantee. This is in line with persuasive accounts by leading environmental law scholars who argue that section 7 is "available to strike down laws that allow pollution at levels that interfere with human health and well-being".[94]

The SCC has, for over a decade, been placing consistent emphasis on environmental protection as a central value in Canadian society.[95] This, in combination with the expansive jurisprudence interpreting section 7, gives rise to considerable optimism.[96] Courts

[90] *Lockridge v Ontario (Director, Ministry of the Environment)* 2012 ONSC 2316, 350 DLR (4th) 720 (Div Ct).

[91] Ecojustice, 'Defending the Rights of Chemical Valley Residents—Charter Challenge' (7 April 2016) www.ecojustice.ca/case/defending-the-rights-of-chemical-valley-residents-charter-challenge/ accessed 13 May 2016.

[92] Ecojustice, 'Exposing Canada's Chemical Valley: An Investigation of Cumulative Air Pollution Emissions in the Sarnia, Ontario Area' (October 2007) www.environmentalhealthnews.org/ehs/news/2012/2007-study.pdf accessed 13 May 2016; Constanze A Mackenzie, Ada Lockridge and Margaret Keith, 'Declining Sex Ratio in a First Nation Community' (2005) 113:10 Environmental Health Perspectives 1295; Environmental Commissioner of Ontario, 'MOE Continues to Fail the Aamjiwnaang First Nation' in *Managing New Challenges: Annual Report 2013/2014* (October 2014) 114–115; World Health Organization, 'Urban Outdoor Air Pollution Database' www.who.int/phe/health_topics/outdoorair/databases/cities-2011/en/ accessed 13 May 2016; CBC News, 'First Nations Exposed to Pollutants in "Chemical Valley"' (24 November 2013) www.cbc.ca/news/canada/windsor/first-nations-exposed-to-pollutants-in-chemical-valley-1.2438724 accessed 13 May 2015.

[93] *Lockridge v Ontario (Director, Ministry of the Environment,* 2012 ONSC 2316 [1], 350 DLR (4th) 720 (Div Ct).

[94] Chalifour, above (n 47), at 103, citing Lynda Collins, 'An Ecologically Literate Reading of the Charter' (2008) 26 Windsor Rev Legal Soc Issues 7 and David R Boyd, *The Environmental Rights Revolution: A Global Study of Constitutions Human Rights, and the Environment* (UBC Press 2011).

[95] *Friends of the Oldman River Society v Canada (Minister of Transport)* [1992] 1 SCR 3, 88 DLR (4th) 1; *R v Crown Zellerbach Canada Ltd* [1988] 1 SCR 401, 49 DLR (4th) 161; *Canada (Procureure générale) c Hydro-Québec,* (sub nom *R v Hydro-Québec*) [1997] 3 SCR 213, 151 DLR (4th) 32; *114957 Canada Ltée (Spraytech, Société d'arrosage) v Hudson (Town)* [2001] 2 SCR 241, 200 DLR (4th) 419.

[96] See for example, Avnish Nanda, 'Heavy Oil Processing in Peace River, Alberta: A Case Study on the Scope of Section 7 of the Charter in the Environmental Realm' (2015) 27 JELP 109.

have held that section 7 means that the state must not unreasonably increase one's risk of death, interfere with people's right to make important decisions, or threaten bodily integrity, and that people have a right to be free from state-imposed psychological and emotional stress.[97] The current statement of the "purpose" of section 7 emphasizes that "the sanctity of life is one of our most fundamental societal values" and that "[s]ection 7 is rooted in a profound respect for the value of human life".[98] As Chalifour asks: "What is more essential to human life than the ability to breathe clean air and drink safe water, and to keep harmful toxins out of our bodies?"[99]

One concern with using section 7 to deal with questions of environmental injustice, however, is that it is not explicitly aimed at, nor particularly well-equipped for, tackling disproportionate burdens or addressing environmental inequities.[100] But, as Chalifour notes, the SCC jurisprudence repeatedly emphasizes the importance of the *Charter*'s equality guarantee and its influence on the interpretation of *all Charter* rights, including section 7.

An upcoming test of this formula is the litigation launched by the Grassy Narrows First Nation in northwestern Ontario. After decades of struggle trying to protect their homelands from the incursions and impacts brought by industrial logging, this application argues that the Government's forest management plan will cause existing methylmercury (that was dumped in the English-Wabigoon river system in 1960 by a pulp and paper mill in Dryden, Ontario) to be released from soil into waters across their territory.[101] Specifically, the First Nation claims a violation of their section 7 rights to life, liberty, and the security of person as a result of illness from the mercury contamination of food sources relied upon by its members, as well as their section 15 rights to equality on the basis that the plan will disproportionately affect the health of the First Nations people who rely on fish from local waters as a primary source of food.[102]

The combination of section 7 and section 15 seems to accord well with the aims of the environmental justice movement, which strives to ensure that individuals and communities from marginalized groups are not burdened with greater environmental risks and harms, and that members of marginalized communities are able to participate fully and meaningfully in environmental decision-making.[103] If and how these *Charter*

---

[97] *Chaoulli v Quebec (AG)* 2005 SCC 35, 254 DLR (4th) 577; *Carter v Canada (AG)* 2015 SCC 5, 384 DLR (4th) 14; *R v Morgentaler* [1988] 1 SCR 30 at 32, 44 DLR (4th) 385.

[98] *Carter v Canada (AG)* 2015 SCC 5, 384 DLR (4th) 14.

[99] Above (n 77) at 104.

[100] This is in part because the jurisprudence has not imposed a positive obligation on states to be proactive in this regard.

[101] Jody Porter, 'Mercury Contamination at Grassy Narrows First Nation Will Get Worse with Logging, Deputy Chief Says' (*CBC News*, 17 June 2015) www.cbc.ca/news/canada/thunder-bay/mercury-contamination-at-grassy-narrows-first-nation-will-get-worse-with-logging-deputy-chief-says-1.3115932 accessed 13 May 2016.

[102] *Grassy Narrows First Nation v Ontario* (1 September 2015), Toronto, Ont Div Ct, 446/15 (Notice of Application).

[103] Chalifour, above (n 77) at 105.

challenges will impact environmental regulation in Canada is yet to be seen, however.[104] The skepticism of environmental justice activists towards litigation strategies is well-founded: litigation favours repeat players and parties with deep-pockets. It can draw attention away from local concerns and channel disputes into pre-formed legal boxes. It can muffle the voices of activists in favour of legal and scientific "experts" etc.[105] Nonetheless, these cases are ground-breaking examples of how the *Charter* is being called on to remedy pressing matters of environmental injustice, and they illustrate how contemporary movements strategically navigate these obstacles. Although there is no way in established constitutional jurisprudence to challenge the failure of a government to fill a legislative void, these cases illustrate how the *Charter* can be used to challenge governments that regulate in an area if the manner by which they do so creates unfairness in environmental burdens.

B. A Constitutional Right to a Healthy Environment?

Several scholars, most prominently David Boyd, have put forward the idea in recent years that constitutional reform is needed to formally enshrine a "right to a healthy environment" in Canada.[106] Recognizing that constitutional amendment is a long and complicated process that would require significant political will across the country,[107] these advocates have put together a compelling list of reasons for why it might be worth the trouble. Both David Boyd and Lynda Collins have demonstrated that industrialized countries that recognize environmental rights have better environmental records than Canada, including stronger enforcement of environmental laws, and more citizen involvement in environmental decision-making.[108] Further, there are material consequences for Canadians: our poor environmental record translates into thousands of premature deaths and millions of preventable illnesses.[109]

---

[104] John Borrows has argued that environmental degradation in traditional territories could also violate the guarantee of religious freedom in section 2A of the *Charter*: "Proponents could show that [First Nations] spiritual beliefs concerning the Earth are holistic, deeply held, linked to their self-definition and fulfillment, and foster a connection with the subject of their faith", thus meeting the definition of religious belief under s. 2(a). John Borrows, *Canada's Indigenous Constitution* (University of Toronto Press, 2010) 253.

[105] See for example, Scott L Cummings and Ingrid V Eagly, 'A Critical Reflection on Law and Organizing' (2001) 48 UCLA L Rev 443.

[106] David R Boyd, *The Right to a Healthy Environment: Revitalizing Canada's Constitution* (UBC Press 2012).

[107] Requires the agreement of Parliament and 2/3 of the legislatures of the provinces equalling 50 percent of the population of the provinces. As Benoît Pelletier explains in the chapter in this *Handbook* regarding constitutional amendment in Canada, the federal *Act Respecting Constitutional Amendments* adds further legislated hurdles.

[108] Boyd, above (n 93); Lynda M Collins, 'Safeguarding the Longue Durée: Environmental Rights in the Canadian Constitution' (2015) 71 SCLR (2d) 519.

[109] Boyd, above (n 93).

Worse, these environmental burdens are not borne equally. Disproportionate pollution burdens affect low income, racialized, and marginalized communities in Canada, and often, within those communities, women, children, and people with disabilities are also likely to bear more than their fair share of the impacts. As Mitchell and D'Onofrio note, a right to a healthy environment would recognize the "human right to an environment that is adequate for health and well-being".[110] It would not, as its critics contend, "guarantee a pristine environment free from chemicals or pollution", but instead, would highlight the vital role of the environment in the "promotion of human dignity and welfare".[111] Now, as Boyd has shown, in many of the countries with a constitutionally recognized right to a healthy environment, the right was recognized initially by courts, and subsequently enshrined in the nation's constitution.[112] In fact, Boyd argues that a human right to live in a healthy environment is supported by 181 of the 193 countries belonging to the United Nations, meaning Canada is one of only 12 countries that have not recognized this right.[113]

The greatest strike against the argument for constitutionalizing a right to a healthy environment might be that it will effect little practical change: it is hard to imagine how achieving this language through a constitutional amendment could promptly improve the drinking water situation on reserves for example, or clear the roadblocks to effective GHG emission reductions. The right to water enshrined in South Africa's post-apartheid constitution, as an example, could not overcome the persistent, race-based inequities in water distribution in that country.[114] But, on a concrete level, advocates for this approach argue that a constitutional right to a healthy environment may result in judicial application of the "standstill" principle, or principle of non-regression in the environmental law context.[115] Emerging from the human rights law context, and with echoes of the debate in South Africa, this principle is based on the idea of "progressive realization". In other words, it would mean that existing environmental laws are to be treated as a baseline or floor—they could be strengthened, but not weakened. As Mitchell and D'Onofrio note: "This principle takes on heightened significance in Canada where, in recent years, we have seen many key federal and provincial environmental laws rolled back. Given that the trend toward environmental deregulation has in many instances had a disproportionate impact on Aboriginal peoples in particular, the non-regression doctrine could be an additional tool to promote environmental justice and equity".[116]

---

[110] Mitchell and D'Onofrio, above (n 45) 334.

[111] ibid.

[112] David R Boyd, 'The Implicit Right to Live in a Healthy Environment' (2011) 20 RECIEL 171 at 171–172.

[113] Ibid. See also Mitchell and D'Onofrio, above (n 45) at 335.

[114] See for example, P Bond and J Dugard 'The Case of Johannesburg Water: What Really Happened at the Pre-paid 'Parish Pump'' (2008) 12 Law, Democracy and Development 1; K Bakker, 'The "Commons" versus the "Commodity": Alter-Globalization, Anti-privatization and the Human Right to Water in the Global South' (2007) 39 Antipode 430.

[115] Mitchell and D'Onofrio, above (n 45) at 335.

[116] ibid at 337.

There are various potential sources of environmental rights.[117] First, we may find them embedded in the existing rights explicitly stated within the *Charter*, as explored above. Lynda Collins argues that this requires an "ecologically literate" reading of the constitutional documents, which reveals that high quality environmental conditions are necessary for full enjoyment of our existing rights; or, in other words, that protection of the environment is required for the protection of people.[118] Second, according to Collins, the same ecologically literate reading of the Constitution may reveal a more robust free-standing right to a healthy environment. This view asserts that understanding environmental rights as a derivative of existing human rights is fundamentally backward; that is, instead environmental rights should be seen as primary. Indeed, the SCC has alluded to a deeply entrenched free-standing environmental right by emphasizing the importance of intergenerational equity and the precautionary principle in cases that engage s. 35 and s. 7 of the Charter.[119]

Finally, as Collins argues, section 35 of the Constitution recognizes and affirms the existence of "Aboriginal environmental rights". The argument is that Aboriginal and treaty rights to hunt, fish, and trap; to carry out integral spiritual and cultural practices; and to self-govern (among others) are "meaningless" without protection of the ecosystems that support them.[120] And further, Aboriginal title appears to encompass an even broader right to conservation of the subject lands: the SCC decision in *Tsilhqot'in Nation v British Columbia* held that even the title-holders themselves must respect environmental quality and maintain the "benefit of the land" for future generations.[121]

---

[117] Collins above (n 107).

[118] Collins above (n 93) 8. See also Lynda M Collins, 'The United Nations, Human Rights and the Environment' in Louis Kotze and Anna Grear (eds), *Research Handbook on Human Rights and the Environment* (Edward Elgar 2015).

[119] Collins, above (n 93).

[120] Lynda M Collins and Meghan Murtha, 'Indigenous Environmental Rights in Canada: The Right to Conservation Implicit in Treaty and Aboriginal Rights to Hunt, Fish and Trap' (2010) 47 Alta L Rev 959 at 970, 984; John Borrows, 'Living Law on a Living Earth' in Moon (ed), *Law and Religious Pluralism in Canada* (UBC Press 2008); Theresa A McClenaghan, 'Why Should Aboriginal Peoples Exercise Governance over Environmental Issues?' (2002) 51 UNBLJ 211 at 220–222. See also Randy Kapashesit and Murray Klippenstein, 'Aboriginal Group Rights and Environmental Protection' (1991) 36 McGill LJ 925 at 957; Borrows above (n 103); John Borrows, 'Living between Water and Rocks: First Nations, Environmental Planning, and Democracy' (1997) 47 UTLJ 417; L Little Bear, 'Relationship of Aboriginal People to the Land and the Aboriginal Perspective on Aboriginal Title' in CD-ROM: *For Seven Generations: An Information Legacy of the Royal Commission on Aboriginal Peoples* (Minister of Supply & Services 1996); James (Sakej) Youngblood Henderson, Marjorie L Benson, and Isobel M Findlay, *Aboriginal Tenure in the Constitution of Canada* (Carswell, 2000) at 410–420, 256; Patrick Macklem, 'The Impact of Treaty 9 on Natural Resource Development in Northern Ontario' in Michael Asch (ed), *Aboriginal and Treaty Rights in Canada* (UBC Press 1997); *R v Nikal* [1996] 1 SCR 1013 at [94], 133 DLR (4th) 658.

[121] *Tsilhqot'in Nation v British Columbia* 2014 SCC 44 at [15], 374 DLR (4th) 1.

7. CONCLUSION

Despite the sense that we have experienced in Canada an "overt federal resiling from environmental law"[122] over recent years, it is important to keep in mind also that jurisdiction over the environment is a perennial contestation that cannot be uniformly characterized as a contest to fill nor vacate jurisdictional space, nor is it always straightforward to determine the jurisdictional balance that would produce optimal results in terms of achieving environmental justice. I have argued in this chapter that a politicization of these questions is appropriate and necessary, and thus I welcome the way that new movements for environmental justice have been turning increasingly to the *Canadian Charter of Rights and Freedoms* to challenge the inadequacy of environmental law and regulation in Canada. Activists are claiming entitlements to clean air and clean water for everyone, and demanding that governments recognize a fundamental human right to a healthy environment for all. Despite all they are up against, these campaigns have the potential to draw constitutional debates over authority to regulate the environment out of the exclusive domain of lawyers and into everyday politics—and this is a good thing.

BIBLIOGRAPHY

Secondary sources

Jamie Benidickson, 'The Constitutional Allocation of Environmental Responsibility and Interjurisdictional Coordination' in J. Benidickson, *Environmental Law* (4th edn, Irwin Law 2013).
John Borrows, *Canada's Indigenous Constitution* (University of Toronto Press 2010).
David R Boyd, *The Right to a Healthy Environment: Revitalizing Canada's Constitution* (UBC Press 2012).
Lynda Collins, 'An Ecologically Literate Reading of the Charter' (2008) 26 *Windsor Rev Legal Soc Issues* 7.
Kathryn Harrison, *Passing the Buck: Federalism and Canadian Environmental Policy* (UBC Press 1996).

Cases

R v Hydro Quebec [1997] 3 SCR 213, 151 DLR (4th) 32.
Friends of the Oldman River Society v Canada (Minister of Transport) [1992] 1 SCR 3, 88 DLR (4th) 1.

---

[122] Deborah Curran, 'Water Law as a Watershed Endeavour: Federal Inactivity as an Opportunity for Local Initiative' (2015) 28 JELP 53.

R v Crown Zellerbach Canada Ltd [1988] 1 SCR 401 [33], 49 DLR (4th) 161.

114945 Canada Ltée (Spraytech, société d'arrosage) v Hudson (Town) 2001 SCC 40, 200 DLR (4th) 419.

Grassy Narrows First Nation v Ontario (Natural Resources), 2014 SCC 48, [2014] 2 S.C.R. 447.

Tsilhqot'in Nation v British Columbia 2014 SCC 44 at [15], 374 DLR (4th) 1.

CHAPTER 24

....

CONSTITUTIONAL ASPECTS OF COMMERCIAL LAW

....

ANITA ANAND[*]

1. INTRODUCTION

....

ALTHOUGH scholars debate the scope of the term "commercial law," many would agree that it encompasses the legal aspects of the purchase and sale of goods and services and can involve a diversity of subjects including banking, securities and bankruptcy law.[1] This chapter will explore Canadian constitutional issues pertaining to commercial law as well as other related areas essential to the work of the commercial lawyer. For example, corporations are frequent parties in transactions for the purchase and sale of goods (whether, for instance, those goods are securities, household items, or real estate), and therefore many areas of commercial law require an understanding of corporate law.

Commercial law, and particularly the law that relates to corporations, is not an area dominated by burning constitutional questions. Corporations are considered to be private actors in that they are, generally, non-governmental bodies, and the *Canadian Charter of Rights and Freedoms* does not apply to common law disputes between private litigants—though the Supreme Court of Canada has said that courts should apply and develop principles of the common law in a manner consistent with fundamental

[*] J.R. Kimber Chair in Investor Protection and Corporate Governance, University of Toronto. Thanks to Raeya Jackiw, Dov Kagan, and Samreen Beg for excellent research assistance funded by the Social Sciences and Humanities Research Council of Canada.
[1] For example, Professor Roy Goode defines commercial law as the "branch of law which is concerned with rights and duties arising from the supply of goods and services in the way of trade." RM Goode, *Commercial Law* (3rd edn, LexisNexis 2004) 8. See also TGW Telfer, 'Justice Rand's Commercial Law Legacy: Contracts and Bankruptcy Policies' (2010) 61 UNBLJ 243, 244.

constitutional values.[2] Furthermore, corporations have relatively fewer *Charter* rights than natural persons despite their separate legal personality. For example, the Supreme Court has held that the section 7 right to life, liberty, and security of the person is restricted to human persons.[3]

The key constitutional issues that have arisen in commercial law relate to the division of powers, although the *Constitution Act, 1867* does not use the term "commercial law" per se.[4] Rather, it delineates particular enumerated fields of jurisdiction that apply to each level of government. These areas do not necessarily correspond directly with areas of commercial law.

Whether an area of law falls under federal or provincial jurisdiction is dictated by the *Constitution Act, 1867* and the manner in which this Act has been interpreted by Canadian courts. With reference to a number of sub-areas of commercial law, I argue that generally speaking, issues relating to constitutional jurisdiction in this domain are uncontroversial with one main exception in the area of securities regulation. In the securities field, jurisdictional wrangling between the federal government and various provinces has occurred over the past number of decades culminating in the 2011 *Securities Reference* case.[5] Over time, this case has given rise to yet another proposal to regulate securities markets, which both Quebec and Alberta oppose.

In addition, I will argue that although most areas of commercial law are well settled as being either in the federal or provincial domain constitutionally speaking, at the same time, the legislation of the other level of government remains relevant. For example, although bankruptcy law is exclusively federal, certain provincial legislation affects individuals and corporations in bankruptcy. This chapter will illuminate this nuance in commercial law: provincial law and federal law tend to interact in a number of areas, with no one level of government completely and singularly occupying a given field of law.

Section 2 sets the background for the chapter by examining the division of powers set forth in the *Constitution Act, 1867* focusing specifically on the powers that apply to corporations. Section 3 analyzes jurisprudence regarding the content and scope of federal and provincial powers in areas of commercial law in which constitutional jurisdiction is relatively settled: the areas of corporate, banking, and bankruptcy law. Section 4 turns to the securities realm, exploring the intense debate that has occurred recently regarding federal and provincial jurisdiction in this area of law. Section 5 concludes.

---

[2] *RWDSU v Dolphin Delivery Ltd* [1986] 2 SCR 573.

[3] *Irwin Toy Ltd v Quebec (Attorney General)* [1989] 1 SCR 927 [1004]. There are many examples of *Charter* cases involving corporations that do not pertain to commercial law. See e.g., *R v Big M Drug Mart Ltd* [1985] 1 SCR 295.

[4] *Constitution Act, 1867*, 30 & 31 Vict c 3 [hereinafter *Constitution Act, 1867*].

[5] *Reference re Securities Act* 2011 SCC 66, [2011] 3 SCR 837 [hereinafter *Securities Reference*].

2. DIVISION OF POWERS

In a treatise about constitutional jurisdiction, it seems trite to say that the key sections of the *Constitution Act, 1867* governing the division of legislative powers are sections 91 and 92, which enumerate the federal and provincial governments' powers. The federal Parliament has exclusive jurisdiction over matters enumerated in section 91, including: the regulation of trade and commerce, the raising of money by taxation, navigation and shipping, currency and coinage, banking, incorporation of banks, and the issue of paper money, bills of exchange and promissory notes, interest, bankruptcy and insolvency, and the criminal law.[6] Matters enumerated under section 91 are beyond the legislative competence of the provinces with some exceptions.[7]

Section 91(2), which gives the federal Parliament exclusive jurisdiction over trade and commerce, was the focal point of the recent jurisdictional tussle pertaining to securities regulation, to be discussed below (see Section 4). It is enough for now to say that courts have attempted to define the scope of the vastly broad term "trade and commerce" through the establishment of two branches within 91(2): (1) interprovincial and international trade and commerce, and (2) general trade and commerce "affecting the whole dominion."[8]

The courts have avoided giving a very expansive interpretation of the second category in order to protect the provinces' jurisdiction over section 92 matters. In *General Motors of Canada Ltd. v City National Leasing*[9] the Supreme Court of Canada affirmed five indicia to determine what properly falls within the general trade and commerce category, including (1) whether the impugned law is part of a general regulatory scheme; (2) whether the scheme is under the oversight of a regulatory agency; (3) whether the legislation is concerned with trade as a whole rather than with a particular industry; (4) whether it is of such a nature that provinces, acting alone or in concert, would be constitutionally incapable of enacting it; and (5) whether the legislative scheme is such that the failure to include one or more provinces or localities in the scheme would jeopardize its successful operation in other parts of the country. The overarching principle in defining the general trade and commerce category is that all matters touching upon "trade and commerce" cannot be included in the category.[10]

The provincial legislatures also have exclusive jurisdiction over certain matters. These are enumerated in section 92 and include: the incorporation of companies with provincial objects, property and civil rights in the province, and all matters of merely local or private nature in the province.[11] Apart from the powers enumerated under sections

---

[6] *Constitution Act, 1867*, ss 91(2), 91(3), 91(10), 91(14), 91(15), 91(18), 91(19) and 91(21).
[7] John D Honsberger and Vern W DaRe, *Bankruptcy in Canada* (4th edn, Canada Law Book 2009) 24.
[8] *Citizens Insurance Co. of Canada v Parsons* (1881), 7 App. Cas 96 (PC).
[9] [1989] 1 SCR 641.
[10] See also *Securities Reference* for a more recent discussion.
[11] *Constitution Act, 1867*, ss 92(11), 92(13) and 92(16).

91 and 92, the federal Parliament also has residual jurisdiction, known as the "residual power" or the "POGG power," over lawmaking for the peace, order, and good government of Canada. The POGG power is derived from the opening statement of section 91.[12] Occasionally, a matter may fall simultaneously under federal and provincial jurisdiction.[13] In such cases, both federal and provincial legislatures can validly enact laws relating to the subject with a "double aspect" so long as they remain within the area of authority assigned to them by sections 91 and 92, and so long as the laws they enact do not conflict.[14]

Federal and provincial legislatures can validly enact conflicting laws and there are two approaches for identifying conflicting legislation. First, the impossibility-of-dual-compliance approach—the narrower of the two—applies in situations where compliance with a provincial law would necessarily involve breaching the federal law.[15] Second, the broader frustration-of-purpose approach considers whether compliance with a provincial law would effectively frustrate the purpose of the underlying federal law.[16] Under either approach, when conflict is identified, the federal law will prevail over the provincial law to the extent of the conflict, sometimes rendering part or all of the provincial law inoperative.[17] This resolution of legislative conflict is known as the doctrine of federal paramountcy;[18] essentially, federal legislation relating to a matter enumerated in section 91 is of paramount authority, even when it intrudes upon matters assigned to the provincial legislatures by section 92.[19]

3. SETTLED AREAS OF COMMERCIAL LAW

Although sections 91 and 92 of the *Constitution Act, 1867* set forth the division of legislative authority, the content and scope of the enumerated classes of power have been left entirely to judicial interpretation. Over time, courts have attempted to delineate where and how these legislative powers apply within various areas of commercial law. As discussed in this section, in most areas of commercial law, issues relating to constitutional jurisdiction are quite settled as resting either with the federal Parliament alone or with

---

[12] The opening words of s. 91 of the *Constitution Act, 1867* state that: 'It shall be lawful for [the Parliament of Canada] to make laws for the Peace, Order and Good government of Canada, in relation to all Matters not coming within the Classes of Subjects by this Act assigned exclusively to the Legislatures of the Provinces.'

[13] *Hodge v R* [1883] UKPC 59, [1883] 9 AC 117 (PC).

[14] *Ontario (AG) v Canada (AG)* [1896] UKPC 20, [1896] AC 348 (PC) [hereinafter *Prohibition Reference*].

[15] *Multiple Access v McCutcheon* [1982] 2 SCR 161, 190 (Justice Dickson).

[16] *Bank of Montreal v Hall* [1990] 1 SCR 121, 153–155 (Justice La Forest).

[17] *Prohibition Reference* above (n 14) 366.

[18] *Rothmans, Benson & Hedges Inc v Saskatchewan* 2005 SCC 13, [2005] 1 SCR 188 [11].

[19] Honsberger and DaRe above (n 7) 24.

both the provincial legislatures and the federal Parliament. Even where constitutional jurisdiction is settled, however, the legislation of the other level of government remains relevant to purchasers' rights and to corporations' obligations, as we will now see.

A. Bankruptcy and Insolvency Law

Falling squarely in the federal constitutional domain is bankruptcy and insolvency law. Section 91(21) of the *Constitution Act, 1867* gives the federal government exclusive jurisdiction over bankruptcy and insolvency, and the bankruptcy and insolvency power has been broadly interpreted in favor of the federal government by the courts.[20] For legislation to be valid under the bankruptcy power, it should generally provide for the sale and division of the assets of a debtor, or be used for liquidation purposes.[21] There is no dispute that federal Parliament exercises constitutional authority in the insolvency area.

The Bankruptcy and Insolvency Act (BIA) is at the foundation of federal law enacted pursuant to section 91(21).[22] This statute governs bankruptcy proceedings of both insolvent persons and corporations. Under the BIA, a bankrupt's assets are vested in a trustee-in-bankruptcy, who distributes the property to creditors according to priority rules set out in the Act. During this process, there is an automatic stay of proceedings over the claims of unsecured creditors. In addition to traditional bankruptcy proceedings, the BIA also governs both the appointment of receivers as well as consumer and commercial proposals, which are offers by debtors to modify their obligations to creditors.

The Companies Creditors' Arrangement Act (CCAA) is another example of valid federal legislation affecting distressed firms.[23] The CCAA is designed to prevent struggling, insolvent (or near insolvent) companies from becoming bankrupt and having to "declare bankruptcy." It allows insolvent corporations that owe creditors more than $5 million dollars to restructure their business pursuant to a highly flexible court-driven process.[24] Debtor corporations remain in possession of their property while they develop a plan of compromise or "arrangement" that both their creditors and the court must approve. Stelco, Canwest, and Air Canada are notable examples of large corporations that have utilized the CCAA.[25]

Notwithstanding these two pieces of federal legislation relating to financially distressed firms, pieces of provincial legislation also serve to impact a firm or individual in bankruptcy. For example, provincial legislation allows creditors to make claims for

---

[20]   ibid 23.

[21]   ibid 28; *Reference re Companies' Creditors Act* [1934] SCR 659 (SCC) [hereinafter *CCAA Reference*].

[22]   Bankruptcy and Insolvency Act RSC 1985 c B-3 [hereinafter BIA].

[23]   Companies' Creditors Arrangement Act RSC 1985 c C-36 [hereinafter CCAA]; *CCAA Reference* (n 21).

[24]   See CCAA, s 3(1).

[25]   'When a Company Tries to Reorganize' (*CBC News*, 14 Jan 2009) http://www.cbc.ca/news/business/when-a-company-tries-to-reorganize-1.790181 accessed 10 May 2016.

fraudulent preferences and conveyances.[26] Although federal legislation also contains provisions relating to fraudulent preferences,[27] the Supreme Court has affirmed the provinces' right to enact concurrent preferences legislation under their jurisdiction over property and civil rights.[28] Furthermore, the priority of secured creditors' claims is also generally a matter of provincial law.[29] That said, the Supreme Court has had a less favorable view of provincial legislation that reorders the priorities of other creditors during bankruptcy. For example, the Supreme Court held that provincial legislation that had the effect of increasing the priority of worker's compensation board payments was inapplicable.[30]

Federal bankruptcy legislation itself explicitly recognizes the validity of related provincial laws. For instance, the BIA states that it does not derogate from the substantive provisions of laws relating to property and civil rights, provided that those laws do not conflict with the BIA.[31] The rights and remedies created by those laws are thus available to a trustee-in-bankruptcy.[32] The BIA also clarifies that property exempt from seizure under provincial law is not subject to division among the bankrupt's creditors.[33] In Ontario, for example, this is an incorporation of the general exemptions against seizure of property found in the Execution Act.[34]

B. Banks and Financial Institutions

Banks and banking activities also fall exclusively under federal jurisdiction. Section 91(15) of the *Constitution Act, 1867* gives the federal government jurisdiction over "Banking, Incorporation of Banks, and the Issue of Paper Money." Other powers enumerated in section 91, including the regulation of trade and commerce, currency and coinage, promissory notes, and interest, contribute to the general federal power over banks and banking.[35] Banks can only be incorporated federally with the permission of the Minister of Finance and the Office of the Superintendent of Financial Institutions (OSFI), the regulator of all federally incorporated Canadian financial institutions.[36]

---

[26] Assignments and Preferences Act RSO 1990 c A.33; Fraudulent Conveyances Act RSO 1990 c F.29. A fraudulent preference is a transfer of property by a debtor to a creditor designed to improve that creditor's position relative to other creditors. A fraudulent conveyance is a transfer of property by a debtor that impedes the ability of his or her creditors to recover their debts.

[27] BIA, s 95.

[28] *Robinson v Countrywide Factors Ltd* [1978] 1 SCR 753.

[29] See BIA, s 136(1): "Subject to the rights of secured creditors." See e.g. Personal Property Security Act RSO 1990 c P.10, s 30(1).

[30] *Husky Oil Operations Ltd v Minister of National Revenue* [1995] 3 SCR 453.

[31] BIA, s 72(1).

[32] ibid.

[33] ibid s 67(1)(b).

[34] Execution Act RSO 1990 c E.24, s 2(1).

[35] MH Ogilvie, *Bank and Customer Law in Canada* (2nd edn, Irwin Law Inc 2013) 7.

[36] Scott R Hyman, Carol D Pennycook, Derek RG Vesey, and Nicholas C Williams, 'The Banking Regulation Review: Canada' in Jan Putnis (ed), *The Banking Regulation Review* (6th edn, Law Business

Although the *Bank Act* theoretically permits mergers of Canadian banks after review by the Competition Bureau and other oversight bodies, these regulators have not actually allowed any mergers to occur.[37]

Section 91(15) does not define "banking" and courts have disagreed on the scope and definition of a "bank" and the activities of "banking."[38] The most commonly used jurisprudential definitions of "bank" and "banking" are outlined in *Canadian Pioneer Management Ltd v Labour Relations Board of Saskatchewan*: "banks" are those institutions authorized pursuant to the federal *Bank Act*, and banking simply refers to the activities in which banks are permitted by the federal Parliament to engage.[39] Furthermore, "banking" is a dynamic bundle of activities[40] that must be interpreted in light of current legislation and circumstances.[41]

One of the most distinctive characteristics of Canada's banking system is that only a handful of banks exists in Canada. The largest bank in Canada in terms of assets and market capitalization is the Royal Bank of Canada, followed by the Toronto-Dominion Bank, the Bank of Nova Scotia, the Bank of Montreal, the Canadian Imperial Bank of Commerce, and the National Bank of Canada.[42] Collectively, these banks are known as "the Big Six" and comprise more than 90 percent of Canada's total banking assets as of 2015.[43] In addition to the Big Six, Canada has another 22 domestic or "Schedule I" banks[44]—domestic banks that are authorized to accept deposits under the *Bank Act*[45]—and 24 foreign bank subsidiaries[46] or "Schedule II" banks—subsidiaries controlled by foreign institutions, authorized to accept deposits under the *Bank Act*.[47]

Research 2015) 114. Note that the federal Parliament's various banking powers also allow for federal incorporation of the Bank of Canada.

[37] Bank Act SC 1991 c 46. For example, in 1998 the Competition Bureau reviewed the proposed mergers of the Royal Bank and Bank of Montreal, and the Canadian Imperial Bank of Commerce and Toronto Dominion Bank respectively. During the merger review process, both the Competition Bureau and the OSFI expressed concerns regarding the potential consequences of the mergers, including the stifling of competition between Canadian banks, resulting in higher transaction prices and lower levels of service and choice for Canadian customers. Ultimately, the then Minister of Finance Paul Martin rejected the mergers because of the public interest override.

[38] Ogilvie above (n 35) 6.

[39] [1980] 1 SCR 433. Therefore, when courts determine the scope and content of s. 91(15) they generally begin by examining the *Bank Act*, and if the provincial legislation being challenged is not specifically addressed by the Act, conduct a pith and substance analysis to see if the legislation falls within the elusive "core" of the banking power.

[40] *Woods v Martin Bank* [1959] 1 QB 55.

[41] *Attorney-General of Alberta v Attorney-General of Canada* [1939] AC 117 (PC).

[42] Hyman, Pennycook, Vesey and Williams above (n 36) 113.

[43] ibid.

[44] ibid.

[45] 'Banks Operating in Canada' (*Canadian Bankers Association*, 14 July 2015) http://www.cba.ca/banks-operating-in-canada accessed 10 May 2016.

[46] Hyman, Pennycook, Vesey and Williams above (n 36) 113.

[47] Canada also has 26 full-service branches and 3 lending branches or "Schedule III" banks—foreign bank branches of institutions authorized to conduct banking in Canada by the *Bank Act*.

As we saw with bankruptcy law, provincial legislation affects banks in numerous important ways despite section 91(15). First, other than banks, Canada has a variety of financial institutions, and the federal Parliament has never attempted to assert jurisdiction over all of them.[48] The courts have consistently upheld the validity of the provincial regulation of "near banks"[49] which include a multitude of financial institutions such as trust companies,[50] credit unions,[51] and treasury offices[52] operating within provincial boundaries.

Second, the provinces are involved in the regulation of certain individuals employed by banks. Under provincial securities law, investment advisors and dealers are subject to registration requirements and other regulation by both the securities commissions and self-regulatory organizations such as the Investment Industry Regulatory Organization of Canada (IIROC) and the Mutual Fund Dealers Association (MFDA).[53] Third, banks—indeed all financial institutions—that have issued securities to the public are subject to provincial securities law and stock exchange requirements including, for example, the requirement to make periodic and timely disclosure of material information.[54] Finally, financial institutions that are involved in the insurance business can be subject to provincial regulations governing the promotion of insurance.[55]

C. Corporate Law

Corporate law does not regulate the rules relating to the exchange of goods between parties, but governs the formation and conduct of a ubiquitous entity involved in commercial transactions. Both provincial and federal legislatures have authority over corporations and as a result each province, territory as well as the federal government has passed a corporations statute. These statutes tend to be similar but not identical.[56]

The provinces' powers of incorporation stem from section 92(11) of the *Constitution Act, 1867* which gives provinces jurisdiction over the incorporation of companies with "provincial objects." The federal government's jurisdiction over incorporation is

---

[48] Ogilvie above (n 35) 23.

[49] Through legislation enacted pursuant to ss. 91(11), (13), and (16), see Ogilvie above (n 35) 11.

[50] *Re Dominion Trust Company and US Fidelity Claim* [1918] 3 WWR 1023 (BCSC); *Re Bergethaler Waisenamt* [1948] 1 DLR 761 Man KB rev'd [1949] 1 DLR 769 (Man CA); *Canadian Pioneer Management* above (n 39) 25.

[51] *Caisse Populaire Notre Dame Ltee v Moyen* [1967] 61 DLR (2d) 118 (Sask QB).

[52] *Provincial Treasurer of Alberta v Long* [1973] 49 DLR (3d) 695 (Alta SC).

[53] Ontario Securities Commission, 'Self-Regulatory Organizations' (*Ontario Securities Commission*) http://www.osc.gov.on.ca/en/Marketplaces_sro_index.htm accessed 11 May 2016.

[54] *Continuous Disclosure Obligations* OSC NI 51-102 (30 March 2004).

[55] *Canadian Western Bank v Alberta* 2007 SCC 22, [2007] 2 SCR 3 [hereinafter *Canadian Western Bank*].

[56] For example, both the British Columbia and Nova Scotia corporate statutes differ from statutes in most other provincial jurisdictions. Business Corporations Act SBC 2002 c 57; Companies Act RSNS 1989 c 81.

expressly stated only as regards to the incorporation of banks under s. 91(15). But in the seminal case of *John Deere Plow v Wharton*, the court held that the federal Parliament has implicit jurisdiction over the incorporation of companies through its POGG power,[57] and over the incorporation of companies carrying on activities that fall under an enumerated federal power.[58] *John Deere Plow* implied that the federal Parliament could validly incorporate companies with objects, other than provincial objects, with the right to carry on business anywhere in Canada.[59] However, the federal Parliament can also validly incorporate a company with a provincial object, as long as the company is not limited in its objects to operating within a single province.[60]

Thus, a federal corporate statute is alive and well in Canada and firms seeking to incorporate can choose to do so under the federal statute or under a provincial statute. The federal power extends beyond incorporation and encompasses authority over all aspects of the status of a corporation.[61] It includes the nature and terms of corporate share capital,[62] as well as aspects of the internal affairs of the corporation, including the power to provide for the management and constitution of the corporation,[63] the responsibility of members of the corporation for corporate debt,[64] and inquiries into the manner in which corporate matters are conducted.[65] Yet, federal jurisdiction to incorporate does not extend to the regulation of the business in which the corporation engages,[66] or corporate labour relations unless the corporation's field of business constitutes a federal undertaking.[67]

A government cannot extend its jurisdiction over subject matters not enumerated in its list of powers simply by incorporating a corporation that carries on business related to that subject.[68] Jurisprudence following *John Deere Plow* has developed the interpretation of the residual POGG power to include the authority to regulate federal corporations.[69] The federal Parliament may regulate activities carried on by a provincially incorporated company to the extent prescribed by the federal Parliament's general legislative jurisdiction.[70] Similarly, a province may validly regulate the conduct of a federally

---

[57] *John Deere Plow v Wharton* [1915] AC 330 (PC).

[58] Kevin P McGuinness, *Canadian Business Corporations Law* (2nd edn, LexisNexis Canada 2007) 144.

[59] *John Deere Plow* above (n 57).

[60] *Colonial Building and Investment Association v AG Quebec* [1883] 9 App Cas 157 (PC).

[61] See e.g. Canada Business Corporations Act RSC 1985 c C-44, ss 6(1)–(4), 24(1)–(4), 102(1); *Letain v Conwest Exploration Co* [1961] SCR 98 (SCC) 105-6.

[62] *Rathie v Montreal Trust Co* [1952] 5 WWR (NS) 675, 683.

[63] *Montel v Groupe de consultants PGL Inc* [1982] 20 BLR 159 (Que CA).

[64] *Multiple Access* above (n 15) 178.

[65] *Restrictive Trade Practices Commission* [1983] 7 DLR (4th) 524, 529–530.

[66] *Re Board of Commerce Act* [1921] UKPC 107, [1922] 1 AC 191.

[67] *Canadian Pioneer Management* above (n 39) 1. Banks and federal (cross-border) transportation and communications undertakings fall under federal labour relations legislation.

[68] *Lymburn v Mayland* [1932] AC 318, [1932] 2 DLR 6 (PC) 11.

[69] Mary G Condon, Anita I Anand and Janis P Sarra, *Securities Law in Canada: Cases and Commentary* (2nd edn, Emond Montgomery 2010) 86.

[70] McGuinness above (n 58) 161.

incorporated company as long as that conduct falls within one of the fields of provincial jurisdiction,[71] and as long as it does not hinder the federally incorporated company's operation or lead to its destruction.[72]

The test for whether a provincial legislature has valid regulatory jurisdiction over a federally incorporated company is whether its regulatory legislation addresses the "corporate activity," or the "regulatory activity" associated with the corporation.[73] If the provincial legislation extends to corporate activity, and conflicts with the federal legislation, then the federal legislation is paramount and the provincial legislation is inoperative; but if the provincial legislation concerns regulatory activity in a field over which the province has jurisdiction, the legislation is valid even if it "destroys" the business of the federal company. Provincial legislation regulating corporate activities over which the provinces have jurisdictional authority will be held to be inoperative if, once again, the doctrine of federal paramountcy applies: where federal and provincial laws are incompatible either because it is impossible to comply with both laws or because applying a provincial law would frustrate the purpose of the federal law.[74]

In the corporate area it is insufficient to simply observe that both the federal and provincial legislatures have constitutional jurisdiction over corporations without understanding the potential for overlapping and possibly conflicting laws in this area. By and large, however, the constitutional domains of each level of government are well-established in law and infrequently debated.

4. SECURITIES LAW: AN UNSETTLED AREA OF COMMERCIAL LAW

Unlike bankruptcy and banking law, areas which seem to be incontrovertibly within federal constitutional jurisdiction, securities law has until now been primarily enacted through provincial authority, although federal legislation exists which overlaps with securities law.[75] The provinces have historically enacted legislation relating to the purchase and sale of securities under their jurisdiction over "property and civil rights,"

---

[71] *Re Insurance Act of Canada* [1932] AC 41 (PC).

[72] *Commission de transport de la communaute urbaine de Quebec v Canada (Commission des champs de bataille nationeaux)* [1988] RL 146 (Que CA); Note that the destruction of a federal company does not mean the destruction of its business. Provincial regulation—for example environmental regulation—can validly "destroy" a federal company's line of business. See *Lymburn* above (n 68) 11.

[73] See McGuinness above (n 58) 166.

[74] If the federally incorporated company is, for example, a bank or a federal (cross-border) transportation or communication undertaking then provincial legislation may be inapplicable if it impairs the core of federal jurisdiction over such undertakings. *Canadian Western Bank* above (n 55).

[75] For example, the *CBCA* contains provisions regarding proxy solicitation and financial disclosure, topics that are also discussed in provincial securities acts. See Mark R Gillen, *Securities Regulation in Canada* (3rd edn, Thomson Carswell 2007) 77.

which the courts have interpreted to include property and contract deals, as well as the regulation of business and professional trades.[76] Over time, courts have come to include the regulation of securities market transactions as an element of property and civil rights.[77] Historically, courts have tended to uphold the validity of provincial jurisdiction over securities laws,[78] even when there were overlapping (but not conflicting) federal laws under the trade and commerce and POGG powers.[79] For example, in *Multiple Access v McCutcheon* federal corporate laws and provincial securities laws regarding securities overlapped almost identically. The Court interpreted the federal power to incorporate and regulate the management of federal corporations as allowing the federal Parliament to regulate insider trading, and held that the provincial legislation was valid as the federal and provincial laws could operate concurrently—in other words, as they did not conflict.[80]

Early cases held that provincial securities legislation prohibiting the sale of securities by federal companies without a licence was invalid, because federal companies have the right to operate throughout Canada, and preventing a federal company from obtaining funding in a province effectively prevents the company from operating in that province.[81] However, later in *Lymburn v Mayland,* provincial legislation requiring that securities trade by federal companies be conducted through a registered provincial broker was upheld as it did not prevent federal companies from obtaining financing through securities entirely.[82] *Lymburn* left open the possibility that securities regulations could infringe on federal jurisdiction in certain cases. Other provincial laws regulating the trading of securities by federal companies should correspondingly be held valid if they do not prevent a federal company from operating within a province.[83]

In 2010, the federal government brought a reference to the Supreme Court of Canada asking if its proposed Canada Securities Act[84] was within the jurisdiction of the

---

[76] *Constitution Act, 1867,* s 92(13); *Citizens Insurance Co of Canada v Parsons* [1881] UKPC 49, [1881] 7 AC 96; *Canada (AG) v Alberta (AG)* [1916] 1 AC 588 (PC). See also Gillen (n 75) 77.

[77] Condon, Anand and Sarra, above (n 69) 86.

[78] *Lymburn* above (n 68); *R v Layton* [1970] 10 CRNS 290 (BCCA); *International Claim Brokers Ltd v Kinsey* [1966] 57 DLR (2d) 357 (BCCA).

[79] *Multiple Access* above (n 15); *Duplain v Cameron* [1961] SCR 693 (SCC); *Smith v. R* [1960] SCR 776.

[80] *Multiple Access* above (n 15).

[81] *Lukey v Ruthenian Farmers' Elevator Co* [1924] SCR 56, [1924] 1 DLR 706, [1924] 1 WWR 577 (SCC); *Manitoba (Attorney General) v Canada (Attorney General)* [1929] 1 DLR 369 (PC).

[82] *Lymburn* above (n 68).

[83] Gillen above (n 75) 79. The Supreme Court of Canada has also held that provisions in securities legislation relating to other jurisdictions are *intra vires* of the province. In *Global Securities Corp. v British Columbia (Securities Commission),* [2000] 1 SCR 494, the Supreme Court held that a provision enacted in the British Columbia *Securities Act* allowing it to order a registrant to produce records to assist "in the administration of securities law" in another jurisdiction (in this case, the Securities and Exchange Commission in the United States) was valid. The Court held that the provision furthered the enforcement of British Columbia's securities laws by reciprocating co-operation that it expected from securities regulators in other jurisdictions, and also by helping uncover misconduct abroad, which would ultimately impact the fitness of domestic registrants to trade in the province.

[84] Canada Securities Act Order in Council PC 2010-667 (26 May 2010) [hereinafter CSA].

Parliament of Canada. However, the Supreme Court ruled in the *Reference Re Securities Act*[85] that the CSA was ultra vires Parliament's constitutional authority. The Court pointed to the federal Parliament's authority under the trade and commerce power and held that the proposed statute was intended to be "comprehensive" (exclusively federal) and therefore ultra vires as its objectives were similar to those proposed in provincial legislation.[86] The Court also held that the legislation regulated a particular industry and thus was not valid under the general trade and commerce power test set forth in *City National Leasing Ltd. v General Motors of Canada Ltd.*[87]

Prior to the 2011 *Securities Reference* decision, the Court had not opined on whether the federal regulation of securities is constitutional.[88] Some suggest that federal securities regulation legislation could be validly enacted given that the 2011 decision related only to the proposed Securities Act.[89] For instance, additional federal powers remain open to justify the enactment of national securities legislation, such as the power to regulate international and interprovincial trade (under s. 91(2)) and the power to legislate with respect to interprovincial works and undertakings (under s. 91(10)).[90] Importantly, although the Supreme Court was unwilling to accord the federal government the constitutional authority to establish national securities regulation over the provinces and territories in the *Securities Reference*, it did acknowledge Parliament's role as guardian over market systemic risk and national data collection. This left available the option of establishing a cooperative regulatory approach to market regulation between the federal, provincial, and territorial governments.

This option was pursued, and Canadian jurisdictions are now in the process of establishing a new Cooperative Capital Markets Regulatory System (CCMR). To date, participating jurisdictions include Ontario, British Columbia, New Brunswick, Prince Edward Island, Saskatchewan, and the Yukon Territory;[91] however, the remaining provinces and territories appear to be unwilling or reluctant to join the system. The CCMR contemplates a single independent Capital Markets Regulatory Authority (CMRA) with regulatory, enforcement, and adjudicative functions that has the authority to identify and manage systematic risk in capital markets.[92]

---

[85] *Securities Reference* above (n 5).

[86] Ian B Lee, 'The General Trade and Commerce Power after the Securities Reference' in Anita Anand (ed), *What's Next for Canada? Securities Regulation after the Reference* (Irwin Law 2012) 59.

[87] *City National Leasing Ltd v General Motors of Canada Ltd* [1989] 1 SCR 641 (SCC) [643].

[88] Anita Anand, 'Introduction' in Anita Anand (ed), *What's Next for Canada? Securities Regulation after the Reference* (Irwin Law 2012).

[89] Lee above (n 86) 66.

[90] ibid 71.

[91] 'About' (*Cooperative Capital Markets Regulatory System*) http://ccmr-ocrmc.ca/about/ accessed 10 May 2016.

[92] 'Agreement in principle to move towards a cooperative capital markets regulatory system' (*Cooperative Capital Markets Regulatory System*, 19 September 2013) http://ccmr-ocrmc.ca/wp-content/uploads/2014/04/CCMRWebSept19AIPPDF.pdf 2.

As part of the CCMR implementation, the participating provincial and territorial jurisdictions agreed to seek the enactment of uniform Capital Markets Acts (CMA), which would harmonize and address aspects of capital markets regulation particular to provincial and territorial jurisdiction.[93] As a participant in the CCMR, the federal government seeks to implement a national Capital Markets Stability Act (CMSA) to address regulatory matters under federal authority including criminal matters, matters relating to management of systemic risk in national markets, and national data collection.[94] In 2014, the federal Minister of Finance along with participating jurisdictions released draft Provincial and Territorial CMAs and a federal CMSA for consultation.[95] The Department of Finance recently released a revised draft of the CMSA.[96] The final pieces of legislation on the provincial and territorial fronts have not yet been released.[97]

Quebec and Alberta are both hostile towards the proposed CCMR regime and, as before, are opposed to federal involvement in the area of securities regulation. Quebec has already referred two constitutional questions concerning the proposed CMSA to the Court of Appeal of Quebec.[98] The reference asks whether the Canadian Constitution authorizes the pan-Canadian securities regulation regime contemplated by the CCMR, and whether the federal CMSA is within the federal government's constitutional power over general trade and commerce under s. 91(2).[99]

Thus, when compared to other areas of commercial law in Canada, securities regulation is in a state of flux regarding the roles of the federal and provincial orders of government. Some would argue that the *Securities Reference* decision firmly established provincial constitutional authority over the day-to-day trading of securities. Yet, there continues to be pushback from the provinces regarding the appropriate scope of federal jurisdiction in this area, if any.

[93] ibid.

[94] ibid.

[95] Davies Ward Phillips & Vineberg LLP, *Canadian Capital Markets Report 2015: Looking Back, Looking Forward, Ch 2: The Cooperative Capital Markets Regulator: To Be or Not to Be?* (Davies 2015) 4.

[96] 'Statement on the Release of a Revised Consultation Draft of the Capital Markets Stability Act' (*Cooperative Capital Markets Regulatory System*, 5 May 2016) http://ccmr-ocrmc.ca/statement-release-revised-consultation-draft-capital-markets-stability-act/ accessed 6 May 2016.

[97] 'Cooperative Capital Markets Regulatory System Provincial—Territorial Capital Markets Act September 2014 Consultation Draft: Summary of Comments Received and Ministerial/Regulatory Responses' (*Cooperative Capital Markets Regulatory System*, 13 October 2015) http://ccmr-ocrmc.ca/wp-content/uploads/2015-10-13-CMA-Comments-Chart.pdf accessed 10 May 2016. Note that several commentators have participated in the consultation process and have raised concerns regarding the proposed drafts of the legislation. See Davies above (n 95).

[98] Government of Québec, 'Reference concerning the constitutionality of the implementation of pan-Canadian securities regulation under the authority of a single regulator' (*Government of Québec*, 6 January 2016) https://www.saic.gouv.qc.ca/affaires-intergouvernementales/institutions-constitution/dossiers-judiciaires/valeurs-mobileres-en.asp accessed 10 May 2016.

[99] ibid.

5. Conclusion

With one main exception in the area of securities regulation, the broader constitutional issues in the commercial law area have been litigated and settled.[100] The above analysis allows for a consideration of the *Constitution Act, 1867* itself—a document that contains broad principles relating to jurisdictional powers. The *Constitution Act, 1867* is (obviously) authoritative legally, but it does not and cannot address the realities of economic markets in a federal state. These realities include both vendors and consumers as parties to the economic transaction at issue, as well as multiple provincial jurisdictions that are generally wary about ceding authority to the federal government. The resulting legal system has at its base the *Constitution Act, 1867* itself but also multiple layers of legislation that provide the legal and regulatory framework within which economic markets will function. The framework is without question comprehensive, containing protections for consumers, creditors (both secured and unsecured), and depositors while also regulating the entities with whom they interact on a daily basis.

Bibliography

Anand, Anita. (ed), *What's Next for Canada? Securities Regulation after the Reference* (Irwin Law, 2012).

Honsberger, John D. and DaRe, Vern W. *Bankruptcy in Canada* (4th edn, Canada Law Book, 2009).

McGuinness, Kevin P. *Canadian Business Corporations Law* (2nd edn, LexisNexis Canada, 2007).

Cases

Attorney-General of Alberta v Attorney-General of Canada [1939] AC 117 (PC).

Bank of Montreal v Hall [1990] 1 SCR 121.

Caisse Populaire Notre Dame Ltee v Moyen [1967] 61 DLR (2d) 118 (Sask QB).

Canadian Pioneer Management [1980] 1 SCR 433.

Canadian Western Bank v Alberta 2007 SCC 22, [2007] 2 SCR 3.

Citizens Insurance Co. of Canada v. Parsons (1881), 7 App. Cas 96 (PC).

City National Leasing Ltd v General Motors of Canada Ltd [1989] 1 SCR 641 (SCC) [643].

Colonial Building and Investment Association v AG Quebec [1883] 9 App Cas 157 (PC).

Continuous Disclosure Obligations OSC NI 51-102 (30 March 2004).

Duplain v Cameron [1961] SCR 693.

General Motors of Canada Ltd. v. City National Leasing [1989] 1 SCR 641.

Hodge v R [1883] UKPC 59, [1883] 9 AC 117 (PC).

---

[100] Of course, the boundaries between provincial and federal jurisdiction are never perfectly clear and some litigation continues. See e.g. *407 ETR Concession Co v Canada (Superintendent of Bankruptcy)* 2015 SCC 52, [2015] 3 SCR 397; *Bank of Montreal v Marcotte* 2014 SCC 55, [2014] 2 SCR 725.

Husky Oil Operations Ltd v Minister of National Revenue [1995] 3 SCR 453.

International Claim Brokers Ltd v Kinsey [1966] 57 DLR (2d) 357 (BCCA).

Irwin Toy Ltd v Quebec (Attorney General) [1989] 1 SCR 927 (SCC) [1004].

John Deere Plow v Wharton [1915] AC 330 (PC).

Letain v Conwest Exploration Co [1961] SCR 98 (SCC) 105-6.

Lukey v Ruthenian Farmers' Elevator Co [1924] SCR 56, [1924] 1 DLR 706, [1924] 1 WWR 577.

Lymburn v Mayland [1932] AC 318, [1932] 2 DLR 6 (PC) 11.

Manitoba (Attorney General) v Canada (Attorney General) [1929] 1 DLR 369 (PC).

Montel v Groupe de consultants PGL Inc [1982] 20 BLR 159 (Que CA).

Multiple Access v McCutcheon [1982] 2 SCR 161.

Ontario (AG) v Canada (AG) [1896] UKPC 20, [1896] AC 348 (JCPC).

Provincial Treasurer of Alberta v Long [1973] 49 DLR (3d) 695 (Alta SC).

R v Layton [1970] 10 CRNS 290 (BCCA).

Rathie v Montreal Trust Co [1952] 5 WWR (NS) 675.

Re Bergethaler Waisenamt [1948] 1 DLR 761 Man KB rev'd [1949] 1 DLR 769 (Man CA).

Re Board of Commerce Act [1921] UKPC 107, [1922] 1 AC 191.

Re Dominion Trust Company and US Fidelity Claim [1918] 3 WWR 1023 (BCSC).

Re Insurance Act of Canada [1932] AC 41 (PC).

Reference re Companies' Creditors Act [1934] SCR 659.

Reference re Securities Act 2011 SCC 66 [2011] 3 SCR 837.

Restrictive Trade Practices Commission [1983] 7 DLR (4th) 524.

Robinson v Countrywide Factors Ltd [1978] 1 SCR 753.

Rothmans, Benson & Hedges Inc v Saskatchewan 2005 SCC 13, [2005] 1 SCR 188 [11].

RWDSU v Dolphin Delivery Ltd [1986] 2 SCR 573.

Smith v. R [1960] SCR 776.

Woods v Martin Bank [1959] 1 QB 55.

CHAPTER 25

THE EXPLOITATION OF NATURAL RESOURCES IN THE FEDERATION

LUANNE A. WALTON[*]

1. INTRODUCTION

OWNERSHIP of and jurisdiction over natural resources has been an area of interjurisdictional dispute since Canada's Confederation in 1867. This chapter focuses on the ways in which the dispute has shifted over time, adapting and changing as necessary. In the years immediately following Confederation, the principal focus was establishing resource ownership for all provinces. Once that was established, legislative jurisdiction over resources became the issue. The caselaw from the first century or so after Confederation resulted in the resource amendment, which was the only change to the federal-provincial division of powers constitutionally entrenched in the *Constitution Act, 1982*. Issues of ownership and legislative jurisdiction were settled just in time for the courts to turn their focus to environmental protection. All of this has led us to the situation which exists today, when environmental protection and the desire for profit are going head to head in the courts.

* General Counsel, Constitutional, Administrative and International Law Section, Justice Canada. The views expressed in this chapter are the author's and do not necessarily reflect the views of the federal Department of Justice.

2. PROVINCIAL STRUGGLE FOR OWNERSHIP

Jurisdiction over resources was distinguished from ownership of those resources at a very early point in Canada's history. In the *Fisheries Reference*,[1] the Judicial Committee of the Privy Council was faced with this question in respect of provincial fisheries. The Court found that

> . . . there is a broad distinction between proprietary rights and legislative jurisdiction. The fact that such jurisdiction in respect of a particular subject matter is conferred on the Dominion Legislature, for example, affords no evidence that any proprietary rights with respect to it were transferred to the Dominion.
>
> . . .
>
> At the same time, it must be remembered that the power to legislate in relation to fisheries does necessarily to a certain extent enable the Legislature so empowered to affect proprietary rights. An enactment, for example, prescribing the times of the year during which fishing is to be allowed, or the instruments which may be employed for the purpose . . . might very seriously touch the exercise of proprietary rights, and the extent, character, and scope of such legislation is left entirely to the Dominion Legislature.

Having achieved judicial recognition of the fact that federal legislative jurisdiction does not carry ownership with it, provincial ownership of public lands and their accompanying mineral rights became the issue. Section 109 of the *Constitution Act, 1867* specified that the original four provinces were each granted control of the public "lands, mines, minerals and royalties" found within their borders. This practice was not continued as other provinces joined Canada. When Manitoba became a province in 1871, section 2 of its Terms of Union provided that the relevant portions of the *Constitution Act, 1867* would also apply to Manitoba. However, section 30 of the Terms made an exception to this general principle: all ungranted and waste lands in the province would be held by the federal Crown "for the benefit of the Dominion". As La Forest J. points out,[2] this would include base mines and minerals[3] and water rights,[4] but would leave in provincial control minerals and other resources which would fall within the meaning of the term "royalties" in section 109.[5] Section 2 of the British Columbia Terms of Union is almost identical to that of Manitoba. However, the land grant to that province was subject only to the railway belt of land granted back to the Dominion by section 11. This

---

[1] *AG Canada v AG Ontario et al* [1898] AC 700 at 709–710 and 713 [hereinafter *Fisheries Reference*].
[2] GV La Forest, *Natural Resources and Public Property under the Canadian Constitution* (University of Toronto Press, 1969) 30–31.
[3] *Attorney General of British Columbia v Attorney General of Canada* (1889) 14 AC 295.
[4] *Burrard Power Co Ltd v R* [1911] AC 87; [1911] CCS No 60.
[5] *Ibid.*

grant back to the Dominion was subsequently found not to have included royalties, just as in Manitoba.[6] Prince Edward Island had no public lands when it joined Canada, so although section 109 applied to it, there was no real impact.

When they became provinces in 1905, Alberta and Saskatchewan can be considered to have received the worst deal of all of the provinces. Section 21 of their respective Terms of Union retained for the Dominion "all Crown lands, mines, minerals and royalties incident thereto" as well as all of the water rights.

As of 1905, with all provinces except Newfoundland within Confederation, it is clear that Manitoba, Saskatchewan, and Alberta were at a definite disadvantage. They alone did not have control and ownership over their own natural resources. After many years of unsuccessful complaints to Ottawa and two years of negotiations, this problem was solved through the three Natural Resources Transfer Agreements. An agreement was entered into between each of the prairie provinces and Canada, and all three agreements were given constitutional status by the *Constitution Act, 1930*. The effect was to put all provinces on the same footing as regards the control of the natural resources found within their boundaries.

3. LEGISLATIVE TUG OF WAR

Post-1930, the provinces were faced with a new federal-provincial situation— capitalizing on the ownership of those resources in the face of the significant legislative powers of Parliament. The most urgent concerns in the 1930s with respect to oil and gas centred on physical conservation of the resources. "The Turner Valley field was being rapidly depleted by furiously unregulated drilling for oil and the flaring of vast quantities of natural gas".[7] In an effort to address the problem, the Alberta legislature adopted first the *Oil and Gas Wells Act*[8] and then the *Turner Valley Conservation Act* by virtue of its powers over property and civil rights and matters of a local nature.[9]

There was also increasing government involvement on the federal side. In 1907, perhaps in anticipation of exports from Canada's then newest provinces, Parliament enacted the *Electricity and Fluid Exportation Act* by virtue of the international/interprovincial branch of the trade and commerce power.[10] However, it was only in the 1930s that the first licences were issued pursuant to this legislation.

Jurisdictional conflicts began in earnest in 1947 when significant deposits of oil were found at Leduc, Alberta. The federal and provincial governments had divergent interests

---

[6] *Ibid.*
[7] S Blackman, J Keeping, M Ross, JO Saunders, 'The Evolution of Federal/Provincial Relations in Natural Resources Management' (1994) 32 Alta L Rev 511, 513.
[8] SA 1931 c 46.
[9] SA 1932 c 6.
[10] SC 1907 c 16.

in the find: Alberta saw the oil as an opportunity to transform its economy from its agricultural base, hoping to avoid another disaster like the Great Depression, and the federal government wanted to use the oil to assist in building the country following the end of World War II. Parliament fired the first salvo, introducing the *Pipelines Act* in 1949 in reliance on its federal power over interprovincial undertakings. Although it did not become law until 1952, the Bill signalled the federal intention to "exercise control over all interprovincial and international oil and gas pipelines in the country".[11] Alberta's response was to require a permit for the removal of gas from the province. Given its relatively recent acquisition of ownership of its natural resources, the province's prime motivator was seen to be the fear that it would once again lose control—this time through extra-provincial ownership:

> Fear of outside monopoly under federal jurisdiction was behind the enactment of the *Gas Resources Preservation Act* in 1949, and it was also the dominant consideration underlying the idea for a provincial monopoly over gas-gathering within the province. A single integrated gathering system would act as a common carrier inside Alberta, distributing pooled gas to export companies . . . at the provincial border. This would keep the export companies—and Ottawa—out, and prevent encroachments on the province's jurisdiction.[12]

As the 1950s went on, energy policy became an increasingly high priority for the federal government. In an effort to develop a comprehensive approach to these issues, the Royal Commission on Energy (the Borden Commission) was established by Order-in-Council on 15 October 1957. The Commission's mandate was to recommend

> . . . the policies which will best serve the national interest in relation to the export of energy and sources of energy from Canada; the problems involved in, and the policies, which ought to be applied to, the regulation of the transmission of oil and natural gas between provinces or from Canada to another country . . . the extent of authority that might best be conferred on a National Energy Board . . . ;[13]

Perhaps the Commission's most significant recommendation was the National Oil Policy. Essentially, it was recommended that the oil pipeline which was being built east from Alberta would stop in the Ottawa Valley. The Commission members felt that Montreal refineries should continue to rely on foreign crude, which was lower in price than Canadian crude once the pipeline costs were factored in. This recommendation was adopted, and the National Oil Policy remained in effect until the dramatic changes of the 1970s. The Commission's recommendations also led to the procedure of active surveillance of oil and gas exports as to quantity and price, and overall regulation of

---

[11] S Blackman et al. above (n 7).
[12] GB Doern and G Toner, *The Politics of Energy: The Development and Implementation of the NEP* (Methuen, 1985) 66.
[13] P.C. 1957-1386.

the oil and gas industry through the National Energy Board which it recommended be established and which was subsequently created by Parliament in 1959. By enacting the *National Energy Board Act*,[14] Parliament asserted regulatory jurisdiction at the federal level over oil and gas pipelines and international power lines together with jurisdiction over the export and import of gas and the export of electric power.[15]

> By all these means, the federal government sought to ensure security of supply to Canadian industry, in the medium term, and to carry out its other responsibilities (including the funding of its equalization obligations). The producing provinces, in what they perceived to be a temporary situation of advantage as owners of a depleting resource, considered the federal measures to be broad-based threats to their long-term development as well as to their short-term interests.[16]

4. The 1970s

In 1973, the Organization of Petroleum Exporting Countries (OPEC) increased the price of oil to unprecedented levels. The result was long lineups at gas stations and concerns regarding domestic dependence on foreign oil. Throughout this period, Canadian intergovernmental energy negotiations reflected the very opposite of cooperative federalism at both levels of government.

Alberta and Saskatchewan responded to the energy crisis with policies and legislation designed to ensure that new resource wealth would accrue to them rather than to the federal government.[17] They also wanted to control the pace of resource development in order to combat the "boom and bust" cycles familiar to the primarily agricultural prairie economies. They needed breathing space to attract and maintain secondary and manufacturing industries.

The Saskatchewan legislature enacted the *Oil and Gas Conservation, Stabilization and Development Act, 1973*.[18] The Act imposed a mineral income tax on oil and gas produced in the province and imposed a royalty surcharge on oil and gas produced from Crown lands. Canadian Industrial Gas and Oil Ltd (CIGOL) opposed the new legislation, arguing that the tax was beyond provincial jurisdiction. In 1978, a majority of the Supreme Court[19] agreed and found that the measures were ultra vires the taxation

---

[14] SC 1959, c 46 [hereinafter *NEB Act*].

[15] Ralph Toombs, Canadian Energy Chronology, 1998 http://geoscan.nrcan.gc.ca/starweb/geoscan/servlet.starweb?path=geoscan/downloade.web&search1=R=297918.

[16] RD Cairns, MA Chandler, WD Moull, 'The Resource Amendment (Section 92A) and the Political Economy of Canadian Federalism' (1985) 23 Osgoode Hall LJ 253, 260.

[17] R Romanow, 'Federalism and Resource Management', in J Owen Saunders (ed), *Managing Natural Resources in a Federal State* (Carswell, 1986) 2, 3.

[18] SS 1973-74 c 72. Amended by SS 1973-74 c 73.

[19] *Canadian Industrial Gas and Oil Ltd v Saskatchewan* [1978] 2 SCR 545 [hereinafter *CIGOL*].

power of the provincial legislature as they did not constitute direct taxation. The majority also found that the measures interfered with federal powers over international trade and commerce. Of note is the finding by Dickson J., in dissent, that "[s]ubject to the limits imposed by the Canadian Constitution, the power of the Province to tax, control and manage its natural resources is plenary and absolute".[20]

In 1979, the Supreme Court rendered another pivotal decision concerning natural resources: *Central Canada Potash v Saskatchewan*.[21] The focus of this case was Saskatchewan's *Potash Conservation Regulations*.[22] The Regulations addressed potash overproduction and dumping and the associated price implications. The provincial government "strenuously contended" that "the natural resources, the mineral wealth of the Province was subject to provincial regulatory control alone, and that production controls or quotas were peculiarly matters within exclusive provincial legislative authority".[23] The Supreme Court found that the situation may be different where a province establishes a marketing scheme with price fixing as its central feature. Provincial legislative authority does not extend to the control or regulation of the marketing of provincial products outside of the province.[24] The Court concluded that the pro-rationing scheme was a marketing scheme to fix prices. Given that the potash was marketed outside of the province, the legislation was found to be unconstitutional as infringing on federal jurisdiction over international and interprovincial trade and commerce.

The decisions in *CIGOL* and *Canada Potash* made it clear that although provincial ownership of natural resources was clearly established, legislative jurisdiction over exported natural resources remained firmly in Parliament's grasp. The federal government was prepared to defend and to exercise this jurisdiction. For the federal government, the energy crisis foretold "traumatic adjustment and transformation for the world economy, supply uncertainties and unpredictable oil prices".[25] In addition, there were concerns that the distribution of benefits from oil and gas were "extra-ordinarily unfavourable" to the federal coffers.[26] From 1973 to 1980, the federal government developed a series of policies to address natural resource exploitation and energy consumption.[27] By far the most notorious of Parliament's unilateral actions was the National Energy Program (NEP). Particularly high profile aspects of the NEP were the federal freeze on

---

[20] *Ibid* 574.
[21] *Central Canada Potash Co v Saskatchewan* [1979] 1 SCR 42 [hereinafter *Canada Potash*].
[22] *Potash Conservation Regulations*, 1969, Sask. Reg. 287/69.
[23] *Central Canada Potash* above (n 21) 73.
[24] *Ibid* 74.
[25] Minister of Energy, Mines and Resources Canada, *The National Energy Program, 1980* (Energy, Mines, and Resources Canada 1980) referred to by the majority in *Reference re Proposed Federal Tax on Exported Natural Gas* [1982] 1 SCR 1004, 1058 [hereinafter *Exported Natural Gas*].
[26] *Exported Natural Gas* above (n 25) 1059.
[27] J Peter Meekison: 'Negotiating the Revenue-Sharing Agreements' in JO Saunders, *Managing Natural Resources in a Federal State* (Carswell, 1985) 84.

the price of domestic oil, and the imposition of an export charge on oil and natural gas for the purpose of increasing the federal share of resource revenues.

The NEP was announced in the October 1980 Budget as a tax on all natural gas and gas liquids produced in Canada. On 12 November 1980, Alberta put a reference to the Alberta Court of Appeal challenging the constitutional validity of the tax.[28] Alberta argued that natural gas owned by the province is shielded from the kind of charges imposed under the *Petroleum Administration Act*.[29] When the case reached the Supreme Court of Canada[30] a majority of six agreed with the Alberta Court of Appeal that the levy proposed under the law was not intended to act as a regulatory mechanism of an industry operating throughout Canada "but was to attain, in the eyes of the federal government, a more equitable sharing of gas revenues".[31]

The majority concluded that federal taxation legislation could bind a province if the legislation was, in pith and substance, enacted incidental to another head of power. However, due to the operation of section 125,[32] no provincial lands or property could be taxed pursuant to section 91(3).[33] It fell to the federal government to show that the measures related to some other legislative function. The federal government could not. The majority found that the measures were, "purely and simply" taxation, "imposed for revenue purposes". Of import to this conclusion were:

- There was no language to indicate that the tax was imposed as a regulatory device or to reduce or eliminate the export of natural gas;
- The tax was imposed in a uniform manner, whether the natural gas was consumed outside or inside Alberta;
- It applied equally to distributors, to exporters, to consumers;
- It was recoverable from anyone who sold or used natural gas.

The impugned legislation was a revenue raising statute.[34] On a plain reading of the text, the proposed tax added nothing to the existing structure of regulation but revenue.[35]

---

[28] *Exported Natural Gas* above (n 25) 1062–1063.

[29] 1974-75-76, c. 47 (PAA). The Act enabled the federal government to authorize charges on exported oil, to regulate distribution, to set the price of oil and natural gas entering international trade, and to set the price of oil and gas entering interprovincial trade. PAA powers to set the price of oil and natural gas were not exercised until the federal government attempted to do so under the NEP. See Romanow above (n 17).

[30] *Exported Natural Gas* above (n 25).

[31] *Ibid* 1046.

[32] "No Lands or Property belonging to Canada or any Province shall be liable to Taxation". S. 125, *Constitution Act 1867*.

[33] "The raising of Money by any Mode or System of Taxation" Section 91(3), *Constitution Act 1867*.

[34] *Exported Natural Gas* above (n 25) 1072–1073.

[35] *Ibid* 1073–1074.

5. THE RESOURCE AMENDMENT

Section 92A was added to the *Constitution Act, 1867* in 1982 to respond to provincial concerns following the *CIGOL, Canada Potash,* and *Exported Natural Gas* cases. Entrenchment of this provision resulted in the provinces gaining concurrent power with Parliament to impose indirect taxes and make laws in relation to interprovincial trade in resources. Subsection 92A(3) preserves federal jurisdiction and paramountcy in this area. Regulatory jurisdiction over international resources export is also left to Parliament. Subsection 92A(1)(c) confirmed exclusive provincial jurisdiction over electrical generation and production facilities (except nuclear generators and interprovincial undertakings).

In 1985, Roy Romanow wrote that "[t]here can be no doubt that section 92A has enhanced the scope of provincial legislative jurisdiction over natural resources".[36] It was anticipated, at least by some, that section 92A would provide greater scope for provincial legislation on land-use planning and environmental standard-setting, and that the scope for federal rule-making would be correspondingly diminished.[37] Despite these high hopes, Professor Hogg characterizes the provision as "declaratory of the pre-1982 law".[38]

That section 92A essentially reaffirmed pre-existing provincial jurisdiction was confirmed by La Forest J. in *Ontario Hydro v Ontario (Labour Relations Board)*:

> It may be, however, that s. 92A(1) is merely preliminary to the provisions that follow, although, as I will indicate, it, at a minimum, fortifies the pre-existing provincial powers. . . .
>
> In a general sense, the interventionist policies of the federal authorities in the 1970s in relation to natural resources, particularly oil and other petroleum products, were a source of major concern to the provinces. . . .
>
> It was to respond to this insecurity about provincial jurisdiction over resources— one of the mainstays of provincial power—that s. 92A was enacted. Section 92A(1) reassures by restating this jurisdiction in contemporary terms, and the following provisions go on, for the first time, to authorize the provinces to legislate for the export of resources to other provinces subject to Parliament's paramount legislative power in the area, as well as to permit indirect taxation in respect of resources so long as such taxes do not discriminate against other provinces.[39]

Perhaps the most significant indicator that section 92A served only to codify existing law is the fact that there has been no significant caselaw focusing on section 92A.

---

[36] Romanow above (n 17) 5.

[37] Alastair R Lucas, 'Harmonization of Federal and Provincial Environmental Policies: the Changing Legal and Policy Framework' in JO Saunders, *Managing Natural Resources in a Federal State* (Carswell, 1985) 84.

[38] Peter W Hogg, *Constitutional Law of Canada* (looseleaf ed, Carswell, 1992) s 29–18.

[39] [1993] 3 SCR 327 [81].

Following the entrenchment of the resource amendment, the focus of natural resources litigation shifted to the protection of the environment.

6. THE RISE OF ENVIRONMENTAL PROTECTION

In the 1980s and 1990s, the protection of the environment emerged as an increasing focus for natural resources litigation. The issue of legislative jurisdiction over environmental protection was at the heart of this growing area of the law. Provincial jurisdiction over such matters of wildlife and resource management, property and civil rights, and local land use (among others) was fairly obvious. Not so obvious was the degree to which federal jurisdiction might come into play.

Perhaps the most significant statement from the Supreme Court of Canada addressing this issue was *R. v Crown Zellerbach*.[40] This was the first case in which a majority (4-3) of the Supreme Court upheld the use of the peace, order, and good government power (POGG)[41] as the jurisdictional underpinning for a federal measure concerning the environment. In issue was the *Ocean Dumping Control Act* which prohibited the dumping of any substance into the sea without a permit.

Although differing in the result in the particular case, the entire court concurred in identifying a number of analytical indicators to be used in determining whether a particular subject matter qualifies as a matter of the national concern branch of POGG. The Court in *Crown Zellerbach* emphasized that the doctrine applies to legislative subject-matters that either did not exist at the time of Confederation (such as aeronautics) or to matters that, although otherwise of a local and private nature, have now attained national dimensions (such as marine pollution).[42] For a matter to so qualify it must have "a singleness, distinctiveness and indivisibility that clearly distinguishes it from matters of provincial concern and a scale of impact on provincial jurisdiction that is reconcilable" with the federal-provincial balance of powers. In making a determination on the latter point, one must consider issues such as the potential failure or incapacity of one or more provinces to deal effectively with the prohibition or regulation of the matter.

Although the dissenting judgment concluded that marine pollution did not satisfy the test, its author, La Forest J., did make some helpful statements regarding legislative jurisdiction in respect of the environment. He states clearly that environmental pollution as a whole is not a matter for either level of government:

> To allocate environmental pollution exclusively to the federal Parliament would, it seems to me, involve sacrificing the principles of federalism enshrined in the

---

[40] [1988] 1 SCR 401 [hereinafter *Crown Zellerbach*].
[41] Introductory words s 91, *Constitution Act 1867*.
[42] *Crown Zellerbach* above (n 40) 431–432.

Constitution. As Professor William R. Lederman has indicated in his article, "Unity and Diversity in Canadian Federalism: Ideals and Methods of Moderation" (1975), 53 *Can. Bar Rev. 597*, at p. 610, environmental pollution "is no limited subject or theme [it] is a sweeping subject or theme virtually all-pervasive in its legislative implications". If, he adds, it "were to be enfranchised as a new subject of federal power by virtue of the federal general power, then provincial power and autonomy would be on the way out over the whole range of local business, industry and commerce as established to date under the existing heads of provincial powers". And I would add to the legislative subjects that would be substantially eviscerated the control of the public domain and municipal government.[43]

Although La Forest J. did not say that POGG has no role to play in controlling pollution, his concern was that that role be appropriately circumscribed to preserve the federal-provincial balance. This position was subsequently adopted by the entire Court in *Friends of the Oldman River Society v Canada (Minister of Transport)*:[44]

It must be recognized that the environment is not an independent matter of legislation under the *Constitution Act, 1867* and that it is a constitutionally abstruse matter which does not comfortably fit within the existing division of powers without considerable overlap and uncertainty. A variety of analytical constructs have been developed to grapple with the problem, although no single method will be suitable in every instance. . . .

In my view the solution to this case can more readily be found by looking first at the catalogue of powers in the *Constitution Act, 1867* and considering how they may be employed to meet or avoid environmental concerns. When viewed in this manner it will be seen that in exercising their respective legislative powers, both levels of government may affect the environment, either by acting or not acting.

The federal criminal law power[45] is the other area of jurisdiction which the Supreme Court has found to be an option to ground legislation dealing with environmental protection. The debate was brought into focus in *Attorney General of Canada v Hydro-Quebec*.[46] At issue in this case was the toxic substances regulatory scheme in the *Canadian Environmental Protection Act*. Writing for the 5-4 majority, La Forest J. found that the scheme could be supported by the criminal law power.

The accumulated case law dealing with the criminal law power has established several requirements for the exercise of this power. First, there must be an act which is prohibited with accompanying penal sanction. Second, the legislation must not encroach on areas of provincial jurisdiction—it must not be colourable. Finally, the legislation in question must have a "typically criminal purpose". The classic statement of what would

[43] *Ibid* [71].
[44] [1992] 1 SCR 3 [94–95].
[45] Section 91(27) *Constitution Act 1867*.
[46] *Attorney General of Canada v Hydro-Quebec* [1997] 3 SCR 213 [hereinafter *Hydro-Quebec*].

be considered such a purpose was made by Rand J. in Reference Re Validity of Section 5(a) of the Dairy Industry Act (the *Margarine Reference*):[47]

> Is the prohibition then enacted with a view to a public purpose which can support it as being in relation to criminal law? Public peace, order, security, health, moral-ity: these are the ordinary though not exclusive ends served by that law. . . .

A major impact of the decision in *Hydro-Quebec* is the following determination by the majority

> I entertain no doubt that the protection of a clean environment is a public purpose within Rand J.'s formulation in the *Margarine Reference* . . . sufficient to support a criminal prohibition. It is surely an "interest threatened" which Parliament can legit-imately "safeguard", or to put it another way, pollution is an "evil" that Parliament can legitimately seek to suppress.[48]

This was a major breakthrough for environmental legislation. In the past, attempts had been made to tie criminal jurisdiction in the environment field to the protection of health and public safety, two traditional "criminal purposes". However, having endorsed the protection of the environment as such a purpose, the *Hydro-Quebec* decision has cer-tainly broadened the scope for environmental law supported by the criminal law power.

The other significant impact of the decision addressed the extent to which a criminal prohibition could be supported by significant "regulatory like" legislation. Parliament cannot call something a crime and proscribe a penalty when it is really attempting improperly to regulate an area of provincial jurisdiction. However, the majority in the *Hydro-Quebec* decision was quite willing to allow significant latitude in this respect.

> In summary, as I see it, the broad purpose and effect of Part II is to provide a pro-cedure for assessing whether out of the many substances that may conceivably fall within the ambit of s. 11, some should be added to the List of Toxic Substances in Schedule I and, when an order to this effect is made, whether to prohibit the use of the substance so added in the manner provided in the regulations made under s. 34(10) subject to a penalty. These listed substances, toxic in the ordinary sense, are those whose use in a manner contrary to the regulations the Act ultimately prohib-its. This is a limited prohibition applicable to a restricted number of substances. The prohibition is enforced by a penal sanction and is undergirded by a valid criminal objective, and so is valid criminal legislation.
>
> . . .
>
> It is precisely what one would expect of an environmental statute—a procedure to weed out from the vast number of substances potentially harmful to the envi-ronment or human life those only that pose significant risks of that type of harm. Specific targeting of toxic substances based on individual assessment avoids resort

---

[47] [1949] 1 DLR 433 (SCC) 473 [hereinafter *Margarine Reference*].
[48] *Hydro-Quebec* above (n 46) 293.

to unnecessarily broad prohibitions and their impact on the exercise of provincial powers.[49]

Based on the *Crown Zellerbach* and *Hydro-Quebec* decisions, it was clear that both the criminal law power and the national concern branch of POGG would have a significant role to play in the enactment of federal environmental protection legislation. And in turn, that legislation would have a significant impact on natural resources exploitation.

7. PROFIT VERSUS ENVIRONMENT: THE FUTURE?

Money has always been a significant motive underlying natural resources litigation in Canada. However, with the rise in oil prices in the 1990s and 2000s, this became a more significant aspect. "Canada is on record as a strong supporter of sustainable development, yet the environmental costs of projects like the oil sands are justified by the creation of economic wealth."[50]

As is discussed in the preceding section, this is the same period in which the goal of environmental protection increased in public support. At the same time, Canada witnessed a deliberate move on the part of the federal government to encourage the development of Canada's resource industries and exports.

> According to Jacques Leslie, "from 2008 to 2012, oil industry representatives registered 2,733 communications with [Canadian] government officials, a number dwarfing those of other industries. The oil industry used these communications to recommend changes in legislation to facilitate tar sands and pipeline development. In the vast majority of instances, the government followed through."
>
> As the Commissioner of the Environment and Sustainable Development recently observed, "[i]n 2006, the government first announced its intent to regulate GHG emissions from the oil and gas industry but has not yet done so even though emissions are growing fastest in this sector." This failure to regulate the oil and gas industry is all the more striking given that "detailed proposals have been available internally for over a year," but the government has only consulted privately, largely through "a small working group of one province [Alberta] and selected industry representatives."[51]

Nowhere has that tension between economic development and environmental protection been manifest more clearly than in the ongoing struggle to build pipelines for oil and gas products in order to improve access to world markets.

---

[49] *Ibid* 308.

[50] Heather McLeod-Kilmurray and Gavin Smith, 'Unsustainable Development in Canada: Environmental Assessment, Cost-Benefit Analysis, and Environmental Justice in the Tar Sands' (2010) 21 J Env L & Prac 65, 65–68.

[51] Jason MacLean, 'Striking at the Root Problem of Canadian Environmental Law: Identifying and Escaping Regulatory Capture' (2016) 29 J Env L & Prac 111 at 123.

Section 92(10)(a) exempts from provincial jurisdiction (therefore placing within federal jurisdiction)

(a) Lines of Steam or other Ships, Railways, Canals, Telegraphs, and other Works and Undertakings connecting the Province with any other or others of the Provinces, or extending beyond the limits of the Province.

This provision has been interpreted to apply only to interprovincial works and undertakings of transportation or communication. Interprovincial pipelines have been found to fall within the category of transportation undertakings. Perhaps the most comprehensive decision addressing this jurisdiction in the pipeline context was *Westcoast Energy Inc. v Canada (National Energy Board).*[52] At paragraph 46 Iacobucci and Major JJ., writing for the 6-1 majority, identified the chief issue in the case as

Whether the Westcoast mainline transmission pipeline, gathering pipelines and processing plants, including the proposed facilities, together constitute a single federal work or undertaking.

They also identified the factors which lead to a determination of section 92(10)(a) jurisdiction:

In our view, the primary factor to consider is whether the various operations are functionally integrated and subject to common management, control and direction. The absence of these factors will, in all likelihood, determine that the operations are not part of the same interprovincial undertaking, although the converse will not necessarily be true. Other relevant questions, though not determinative, will include whether the operations are under common ownership (perhaps as an indicator of common management and control), and whether the goods or services provided by one operation are for the sole benefit of the other operation and/or its customers, or whether they are generally available.[53]

The majority compared two cases to illustrate the impact of common management and operational control: *Luscar Colliers, Ltd. v McDonald*[54] and *United Transportation Union v Central Western Railway Corp.*[55] In *Luscar*, the Court found that a short line of railway located entirely within the province of Alberta formed a part of the CNR federal railway undertaking. This finding was based on that fact that, although the line was owned by Luscar, it was operated by CN. In *Central Western*, Central Western owned the line, but CN did not operate it. The Court found that the operational control necessary for the two to be part of the same undertaking was not present.

[52] *Westcoast Energy Inc v Canada (National Energy Board)* [1998] SCR 322 [hereinafter *Westcoast*].
[53] *Ibid* [65].
[54] [1927] AC 925.
[55] [1990] 3 SCR 1112.

In *Westcoast*, the Court concluded that physical connection between the processing plants and the mainline transmission pipeline and the fact that Westcoast owns both were insufficient by themselves. What determined the issue for the Court was the fact that it was clear that Westcoast managed them "in common as a single enterprise which is functionally integrated."[56] Key in this conclusion were the following facts:

– facilities and personnel subject to common control, direction and management and operated in coordinated and integrated manner;
– management personnel in Vancouver direct all field personnel;
– all facilities operated by the same field personnel;
– all facilities served by the same support services;
- Vancouver personnel control flow in both gathering and main transmission pipelines;
– processing plants operated by different people, but all directed from Vancouver; and
– system connected by sophisticated telecommunications system.

In decisions concerning section 92(10)(a) the courts have emphasized over and over that although some guidance can be obtained from previous cases, each situation will be determined on its facts and on the actual nature of the operations in question. One clear principle does emerge: to the extent that the system is more integrated, more of the factors noted above will be present; to the extent that the system is less integrated, fewer of these factors will be present. Where sufficient integration is found, interprovincial transportation undertakings including pipelines fall within federal jurisdiction.

Although the subject matter was freight forwarding, the decision of the Supreme Court of Canada in *Consolidated Fastfrate Inc. v Western Canada Council of Teamsters*[57] is relevant to a discussion of pipeline jurisdiction. The issue in this case was whether the employees of Fastfrate, a freight forwarder, were subject to provincial or federal labour laws. As provincial jurisdiction over labour relations is the default position, the company would only fall within federal jurisdiction if it was found to be an interprovincial transportation undertaking within the meaning of section 92(10)(a). Rothstein J. wrote for the 6-3 majority, with Binnie J. writing the dissent. The ultimate decision was that Fastfrate would not fall within federal jurisdiction because it was not found to be an interprovincial undertaking. In making this finding, Rothstein J. made some significant changes to the previously established test under section 92(10)(a). It is these changes which are relevant in the pipeline context.

Rothstein J. began with the text of the section, and the way in which the various terms were understood by the Constitution's framers. He concluded that there was a common thread evident in the transportation undertakings given as examples in that provision.[58] He

---

[56] *Westcoast* above (n 52) [68].
[57] [2009] SCC 53, [2009] 3 SCR 407 [hereinafter *Fastfrate*].
[58] "Lines of Steam or other Ships, Railways, Canals . . . "

identified this common thread as the fact that actual transport of goods or people must take place for a business to be considered to be an interprovincial transportation undertaking.

Rothstein J. used the necessity of actual transport to distinguish between transportation and communication undertakings:

> It is true that in the communications context, the constitutional inquiry has at times focused on "the service that is provided and not simply . . . the means through which it is carried on": *Public Service Board v. Dionne* [1978] 2 SCR 191, at p. 197. The difference between the communications and transportation contexts, however, is that communications undertakings can *operate* and *provide* international and interprovincial communication services from a fixed point. . . . [emphasis original][59]
>
> In the transportation context, it is not possible for an undertaking to operate an interprovincial transportation service where it does not itself perform the interprovincial carriage. A business can, of course, act as an intermediary between interprovincial carriers and consumers who want to access those carriers at a reduced price. This does not mean that such a business becomes the operator and provider of the interprovincial carriage, however. . . .[60]

On the basis of this distinction, Rothstein J. elaborated a separate test for interprovincial transportation undertakings. He made no mention of the fact that the previous jurisprudence had established one test for a section 92(10)(a) undertaking, regardless of whether it was in the transportation or communication fields. On behalf of the majority, he found that it was not enough for the company to be both the consolidator of the cargo at the beginning and the distributor of the cargo at the end. Rather, in order to be considered an interprovincial undertaking, a company must also physically transport the goods across provincial borders. Fastfrate did not pass this test because it contracted with other shippers to move the consolidated load from one province to another.

In dissent, Binnie J. rejected the proposition that separate tests are appropriate for transportation and communication undertakings:

> In my view, the relevant distinction in the s. 92(10)(*a*) jurisprudence is not between undertakings engaged in transportation and those engaged in communications, but between local undertakings within the province and undertakings whose service (whether transportation or communication) extends beyond the province. In this respect, there is no difference between the test for transportation cases and the test for communications cases. This was confirmed (again) by Dickson C.J. in the last of his series of "interprovincial undertaking" cases where he made a direct comparison between the scope of the intraprovincial transportation "service" offered in *Central Western Railway* with the interprovincial communications "service" offered by AGT

---

[59] *Fastfrate* above (n 57) [60].
[60] *Ibid* [61].

(p. 1135). On this point, I agree with Watson J.A., speaking for the majority in the court below:

> In our view, the jurisprudence does not give trumping status to, let alone mandate, the factor of physical transition as a pre-condition to finding an interprovincial work or undertaking. . . . More important than a *physical* connection is whether the *functional* nature of the operation is to connect the provinces. [Emphasis original.][61]

He acknowledged that the technology is different between communications and transportation undertakings, but stated that "the legal test was (and is) the same."[62]

Fastfrate is the new normal. In order to rely on section 92(10)(a) to support federal regulation of cross-border oil and gas pipelines, it will be necessary to satisfy the *Fastfrate* test.

It is settled law that federal jurisdiction will prevail where pipelines extend across provincial boundaries. However, natural resources litigation is not disappearing from the Canadian landscape any time soon. The essence of the litigation challenges which lie ahead is found in the decision of the British Columbia Supreme Court in *Coastal First Nations—Great Bear Initiative Society and Gitga'at First Nation v Minister of Environment for British Columbia, NGP et al.*[63] This case focused on the construction of the Northern Gateway Pipeline (NGP) which is proposed to be constructed from the Alberta oil fields to the coast of British Columbia with the greatest portion to be built in British Columbia. At its heart, the issue in this case was whether federal jurisdiction to regulate interprovincial pipelines (manifest in the National Energy Board) is so exclusive that it cannot be touched by any provincial legislation at all. The trial judge points out that no head of jurisdiction—federal or provincial—carries this sort of immunity from laws of general application:

> As the Court held in *Canadian Western Bank*, at para. 29, the doctrine of pith and substance "is founded on the recognition that it is in practice impossible for a legislature to exercise its jurisdiction over a matter effectively without incidentally affecting matters within the jurisdiction of another level of government." It is not enough for NGP to argue that s. 17 of the EAA affects matters beyond the Province's jurisdiction. As long as the "dominant purpose" of the legislation is intra vires, any secondary effects are not relevant to the question of constitutional validity. . . .[64]

This view is consistent with a long line of Supreme Court jurisprudence concluding that matters falling within federal jurisdiction do not become federal enclaves, immune from all provincial legislation. As La Forest J. stated in *Air Canada v British Columbia*,

---

[61] *Ibid* [88] citing the Alberta Court of Appeal decision: [2007] ABCA 198, [2007] 79 Alta LR (4th) 201, [53].

[62] *Ibid* [85].

[63] [2016] BCSC 34, [2016] BCWLD 1415 [hereinafter *Coastal First Nations*].

[64] *Ibid* [56].

"[b]y and large federal undertakings, like other private enterprises functioning within the province, must operate in a provincial legislative environment."[65]

Koenigsberg J. proceeded to an assessment of the validity of the BC *Environmental Assessment Act (EAA)* She concluded that: "Given that the dominant purpose of the *EAA* is regulation of the environment within British Columbia . . . , the statute represents a valid exercise of provincial power even inasmuch as it may affect certain aspects of an interprovincial pipeline."[66]

As the justice points out, there can be no doubt that the BC *Environmental Assessment Act*[67] is valid provincial legislation, standing on its own. It is a law of general application throughout British Columbia which addresses environmental impacts of construction and other projects occurring in British Columbia.

Given that the validity of the provincial legislation is clear, the legislation must be examined to determine whether its operation or application would be problematic. This directs the analysis to the issues of paramountcy and interjurisdictional immunity.[68]

Koenigsberg J looks first at the *EAA* itself and determines that there is nothing on the face of the Act which would raise issues of paramountcy or interjurisdictional immunity, without more:

> I do not find that at this point any aspect of British Columbia's laws or environmental protection regime amount to a prohibition, or are in anyway rendering the Project inoperative. I agree with the petitioners' submissions that it is premature to engage in this analysis until the parties know whether the Province chooses to issue any conditions and, if it does, until it becomes clear what those conditions are.[69]

It is likely that the situation would be different if the *EAA* stated that no pipelines could be built in BC or alternatively, that no pipelines could be built unless the proponents can demonstrate no environmental effects. It would also be different if the province had enacted a statute addressing only the environmental effects of pipelines. In both situations, the result would very likely be a finding of invalidity, given that the provincial legislature would be dealing with pipelines, qua pipeline. The issue is different in the current situation because the law is one of general application.

For the trial judge, the issue of whether the *EAA* will be relevant to the construction of the pipeline can only be determined once the provincial process has taken place and conditions have been placed on the pipeline's construction. Only with actual

---

[65] [1989] 1 SCR 1161 1191.

[66] *Coastal First Nations* above (n 63) [75].

[67] SBC 2002, c 43.

[68] For further discussion of paramountcy and interjurisdictional immunity, see the chapter by Eugénie Brouillet and Bruce Ryder in this *Handbook*.

[69] *Coastal First Nations* above (n 63) [65].

conditions will it be possible to conduct a paramountcy or interjurisdictional immunity analysis.

> I agree that absent concrete conditions imposed by the Province in conjunction with an EAC, it would be premature to make a finding based on hypothetical conditions. The constitutional doctrines of inter-jurisdictional immunity and paramountcy cannot be adequately determined on merely speculative provincial conditions. As such, for the reasons that follow, there is currently no factual basis to make such a determination.[70]

This is entirely consistent with the Supreme Court jurisprudence elaborating the tests for paramountcy and interjurisdictional immunity.

The central proposition is that pipelines are not completely immune from any provincial regulation. Once that proposition is accepted, then it is clear that the paramountcy and interjurisdictional analyses cannot take place until any conditions are imposed as a result of the provincial process. The actual conditions will be used in the paramountcy analysis to determine if a conflict exists with the federal legislation or orders made in reliance on that legislation. In the interjurisdictional immunity analysis, the actual provincial conditions will be examined to determine if they impair the core of the undertaking's ability to build and operate the pipeline.

Based on the trial judge's analysis, we are left with the result that both the National Energy Board (NEB) and provincial legislation will have a role to play in the planning, approval, and construction of interprovincial pipelines.

> While I agree that the Province cannot go so far as to refuse to issue an EAC and attempt to block the Project from proceeding, I do not agree with the extreme position of NGP that this invalidates the *EAA* as it applies to the Project.[71]

As with so much of Canadian division-of-powers law, the heart of the issue is where to draw the line. What is the meaning of "block the Project from proceeding"? Is it only refusal to issue the appropriate certificate in the provincial process which will result in "blocking" a project? Or can overly onerous conditions placed on that certification also be considered to "block" the project? Will "blocking" take place if the conditions impose such a financial burden on the project's proponent that the project is no longer financially viable?

These questions are likely to be answered only through future litigation emerging from the imposition of actual conditions. There are arguments on both sides. If the provincial conditions effectively prevent the pipeline from being built, there would certainly be a good argument that interjurisdictional immunity would be engaged.

---

[70] *Ibid.* [47].
[71] *Ibid* [55].

Interjurisdictional immunity requires that federal jurisdiction or a federally regulated undertaking is impaired by the application of provincial legislation.[72] It is difficult to envision a more significant impairment than preventing the construction of the project at all.

Weighed against the interjurisdictional immunity argument is the relatively recent trend of the Supreme Court of Canada toward cooperative federalism. An excellent example of this trend is manifest in the opinion rendered in the *Reference re Securities Act*.[73] The Court concluded that

> ... we may appropriately note the growing practice of resolving the complex governance problems that arise in federations, not by the bare logic of either/or, but by seeking cooperative solutions that meet the needs of the country as a whole as well as its constituent parts.
>
> Such an approach is supported by the Canadian constitutional principles and by the practice adopted by the federal and provincial governments in other fields of activities. The backbone of these schemes is the respect that each level of government has for each other's own sphere of jurisdiction. Cooperation is the animating force. The federalism principle upon which Canada's constitutional framework rests demands nothing less.[74]

Going forward, the tension between these two arguments is likely to be the focus of most natural resources litigation.

BIBLIOGRAPHY

Secondary Sources

Blackman S, Keeping J, Ross M, Saunders JO, 'The Evolution of Federal/Provincial Relations in Natural Resources Management' (1994) 32 Alta L Rev 511

Cairns RD, Chandler MA, Moull WD, 'The Resource Amendment (Section 92A) and the Political Economy of Canadian Federalism' (1985) 23 Osgoode Hall LJ 253

Doern GB, and Toner G, *The Politics of Energy: The Development and Implementation of the NEP* (Methuen 1985)

Hogg PW, *Constitutional Law of Canada* (looseleaf ed, Carswell 1992)

La Forest GV, *Natural Resources and Public Property under the Canadian Constitution* (University of Toronto Press 1969)

Lucas AR, 'Harmonization of Federal and Provincial Environmental Policies: The Changing Legal and Policy Framework' in JO Saunders, *Managing Natural Resources in a Federal State* (Carswell 1985)

[72] *Canadian Western Bank v Alberta* [2007] SCC 22, [2007] 2 SCR 3 [48].
[73] [2011] SCC 66, [2011] 3 SCR 837 132.
[74] *Ibid* [132–133].

MacLean J, 'Striking at the Root Problem of Canadian Environmental Law: Identifying and Escaping Regulatory Capture' (2016) 29 J Env L & Prac 111

McLeod-Kilmurray H, and Smith G, 'Unsustainable Development in Canada: Environmental Assessment, Cost-Benefit Analysis, and Environmental Justice in the Tar Sands' (2010) 21 J Env L & Prac 65

Meekison JP: 'Negotiating the Revenue-sharing Agreements' in JO Saunders, *Managing Natural Resources in a Federal State* (Carswell 1985)

Minister of Energy, Mines and Resources Canada, *The National Energy Program, 1980* (Energy, Mines, and Resources Canada 1980)

Romanow R, 'Federalism and Resource Management', in Saunders JO (ed), *Managing Natural Resources in a Federal State* (Carswell, 1986)

Toombs R, Canadian Energy Chronology, 1998 http://geoscan.nrcan.gc.ca/starweb/geoscan/servlet.starweb?path=geoscan/downloade.web&search1=R=297918

Cases

Attorney General of British Columbia v Attorney General of Canada (1889) 14 AC 295

Canadian Industrial Gas and Oil Ltd v Saskatchewan [1978] 2 SCR 545

Central Canada Potash Co v Saskatchewan [1979] 1 SCR 42

Consolidated Fastfrate Inc. v Western Canada Council of Teamsters [2009] SCC 53, [2009] 3 SCR 407

Friends of the Oldman River Society v Canada (Minister of Transport) [1992] 1 SCR 3

R. v Crown Zellerbach [1988] 1 SCR 401

Reference re Proposed Federal Tax on Exported Natural Gas [1982] 1 SCR 1004

United Transportation Union v Central Western Railway Corp. [1990] 3 SCR 1112.

Westcoast Energy Inc v Canada (National Energy Board) [1998] SCR 322

CHAPTER 26

....

MINORITY LANGUAGES, EDUCATION, AND THE CONSTITUTION

....

LINDA CARDINAL* &
PIERRE FOUCHER**

1. INTRODUCTION

....

SINCE the nineteenth century, minority education language rights have been at the centre of many constitutional and political debates in Canada.[1] Those debates have contributed to define Canada's national identity and discourse. Federalism and constitutionalism have also been central to our understanding of minority education language rights. This chapter discusses institutional constraints to minority language education rights in Canada since 1867, such as constitutionalism and federalism. Its objective is to provide an overview of the situation, examine some of the key debates in the area, and identify future directions for research.

Simply put, we argue that since 1867, both constitutionalism and federalism guide the development and implementation of minority education language rights. For example, because of federalism, in 1867 education was confirmed as a head of provincial

* Linda Cardinal is Professor of Politics and Holder of the University of Ottawa Research Chair in Francophone Studies and Public Policy. Her research interests includes comparative language regimes and policies, Canadian and Quebec constitutional politics, and federalism. In 2015, she coedited *State Traditions and Language Regimes* (with Selma Sonntag) (McGill-Queen's University Press).

** Pierre Foucher is Law Professor at the University of Ottawa and Director of the Research Center on French-Canadian Civilisation (2017-2019). His research interests are minority education language rights, constitutionalism, and federalism in Canada.

[1] P. Carignan, "Les Résolutions de Québec et la compétence législative en matière d'éducation." (1989) 23 *Revue juridique Thémis* 67; P. Carignan, "La raison d'être de l'article 93 de la Loi constitutionnelle de 1867 à la lumière de la législation préexistante en matière d'éducation." (1986) 20 *Revue juridique Thémis* 375.

jurisdiction. Section 93 of the Canadian Constitution recognized the right of Catholics and Protestants to run their own school systems. As for language *per se*, the Constitution was silent about who had jurisdiction. The particular demands for French-language education in the provinces were not explicitly addressed in the Constitution at the time. Language rights were subordinated to religious schooling rights as it was generally understood that Catholics were French and Protestants were English.[2] However, the approach was asymmetrical. In the absence of any protection for the French language in the provinces, English became the de facto official language of the provincial school systems. In Quebec, where French is and remains the predominant language, religious schooling rights for Protestants were synonymous with the English language.

It took a hundred years after Confederation for the English-speaking provinces to start addressing the language rights of their French-speaking minorities, especially in the area of education. In 1969, New Brunswick was amongst the first provinces to accommodate the demands for French-language education. At about the same time, the Ontario government accepted the principle of establishing French schools where reasonable and practical. No other provinces volunteered to advance the language rights or education language rights of their French-speaking minority at the time.

In 1969, with the adoption of the *Official Languages Act*[3] at the federal level, English and French were confirmed as Canada's official languages; however, this legislation could not reach provincial competence over education. In the 1970s English language education became the object of debate in Quebec, especially in the Montreal area, because of the growing popularity of English schooling amongst the predominantly Catholic immigrant population. The result was a legislated obligation to have children of immigrant backgrounds attend French-only schools. As of 1982, the *Canadian Charter of Rights and Freedom*[4] recognized the constitutional right of children of some English-speaking parents in Quebec to schooling in their own language, as well as the constitutional right of children of French-speaking parents outside of Quebec to schooling in their mother tongue under some conditions. The *Canadian Charter* also embodied a constitutional recognition of French and English as official languages of the federal as well as New Brunswick's jurisdictions and asserted some rights in that regard.

The constitutional recognition of minority education language rights represents a critical moment for official languages minorities in Canada, as important if not even more so than the recognition of official bilingualism federally because of the specific history of language schooling in the provinces.[5] How has Canada moved from a de facto

---

[2] M. Bastarache, "Le rôle des tribunaux dans la mise en œuvre des droits linguistiques au Canada." (2010) 40 *Revue générale de droit* 221.

[3] *Official Languages Act*, (1969) 17-19 Eliz II, c. 54 (Can.) [*Official Languages Act (Can.)*]

[4] *Canadian Charter of Rights of Freedoms*, being Part I of Annex B of the *Canada Act*, 1982, c. 11 (U.K.) [hereinafter the *Canadian Charter*].

[5] L. Cardinal, (2015), "Language Regime and Language Politics in Canada" in *Language Regimes and State Traditions* (L. Cardinal and S. Sonntag eds), (McGill-Queen's University Press) pp. 29–43 [hereinafter Cardinal (2015)]; P. Foucher, "Droits et lois linguistiques. Le droit au service du Canada français" in *L'espace francophone en milieu minoritaire au Canada. Nouveaux enjeux, nouvelles*

unilingual English language schooling system to one which recognizes minority language education rights? How did Canada address its linguistic duality? What have been the key constitutional issues in this particular area?

The study of minority education language rights in Canada belongs to a multidisciplinary field which includes education experts, sociolinguists, applied linguists, historians, political scientists, and legal experts. Briefly, most studies within this field focus on the history and legal dimensions of minority language education rights, their impact on community activism and on youth identity, especially within French-speaking minorities.[6] Our chapter builds on those studies and proposes a discussion of minority language education rights from a historical, institutional, and constitutional perspective.

First we define the concept of official and minority languages in the Canadian context. Second, we discuss constitutionalism and federalism and the development of official minority language rights since 1867; third, we look at the particular history of minority language education rights in Canada. Fourth, we provide a discussion of the rich body of Canadian jurisprudence in the area of minority language education rights, in particular how it addresses a first generation of issues pertaining to the implementation of minority language education rights in Canada. We conclude by explaining why the relationship between constitutionalism and federalisms remains important to any discussion of the development and future of minority education language rights.

2. DEFINING OFFICIAL LANGUAGES AND MINORITY LANGUAGES

Francesco Carpotorti defines a minority as "a group numerically inferior to the rest of the population of a state, in a non-dominant position, whose members—being nationals of the state—possess ethnic, religious or linguistic characteristics differing from

mobilisations, (J.-Y. Thériault, A. Gilbert and L. Cardinal eds) (Fides, 2008), pp. 463–513 [hereinafter Foucher (2008)].

   [6] M. Behiels, *Canada's Francophone Minority Communities: Constitutional Renewal and the Winning of School Governance* (Montreal: McGill-Queen's University Press, 2003) [hereinafter Behiels]; R. Landry, K. Deveau and R. Allard, "Engagement identitaire francophone en milieu minoritaire" in *L'espace francophone en milieu minoritaire au Canada. Nouveaux enjeux, nouvelles mobilisations*, (J.-Y. Thériault, A. Gilbert and L. Cardinal, eds) (Fides, 2008) pp. 275–317 [hereinafter Landry, Deveau & Allard 2008]; R. Landry and S. Rousselle, *Éducation et droits collectifs*. (Les Éditions de la Francophonie, 2003) [hereinafter Landry and Rousselle, 2003]; M. Normand (2013), "De l'arène politique à l'arène juridique: les communautés francophones minoritaires au Canada et la Charte canadienne des droits et libertés." In *Le nouvel ordre constitutionnel canadien*, (F. Rocher and B. Pelletier, eds) (Montréal: Les Presses de l'Université du Québec à Montréal, 2013) 179–204 [hereinafter Normand (2013)]; A. Pilote and M.-O. Magnan, L'école de la minorité francophone au Canada: L'institution à l'épreuve des acteurs." In *L'espace francophone en milieu minoritaire au Canada. Nouveaux enjeux, nouvelles mobilisations* (J.-Y. Thériault, A. Gilbert and L. Cardinal, eds) (Fides, 2008) 275–317. [hereinafter Pilote (2008)].

those of the rest of the population and show, if only implicitly, a sense of solidarity, directed towards preserving their culture, traditions, religion or language".[7] A particular group of people speaking a specific language becomes a linguistic minority for political and social reasons.[8] It involves power relations and situations of domination. Any language group, even speakers of internationally recognized languages such as English and French, can become a linguistic minority group for political reasons. For example, Quebec is a predominantly French-speaking province, but it is considered a "national minority" or a "minority nation" in the Canadian context.[9] The French language is also a minority language in Canada both in terms of numbers and power dynamics. French does not have the same power of attraction as English, in particular as a language of business or as a community language. There are French-speaking communities in all the provinces but they also witness high rates of assimilation to the English language. Both English and French are official languages, which means that they have "equality of status and equal rights and privileges as to their use in all institutions of the Parliament and government of Canada".[10]

The status of official language is of importance because it recognizes formal equality between the two major linguistic groups in the country. However, because of federalism, provinces in Canada do not need to adopt the same approach in their own jurisdictions. French is the official language of Quebec. As already mentioned English and French are the official languages of New Brunswick.[11] In Ontario, English and French are the official languages of the justice system,[12] but not of the whole province, although provincial legislation grants some rights to French-language services.[13] English is de facto the official language in all the other provinces. Manitoba, for historical reasons, has a limited constitutional recognition of French and English in legislation, parliamentary debates, and courts.[14]

From a federal government perspective, French-speakers outside of Quebec are members of an official language minority and English-speakers in Quebec are also considered an official language minority. There is a symmetrical legal relation between both minority groups despite the fact that English is not a threatened language in Canada. The concept of official language minority is formally found in the *Canadian Charter*, in the section on minority language education rights (section 23) as well as in Part VII

---

[7] F. Carpotorti, *Study on the Rights of Persons Belonging to Ethnic, Religious or Linguistic minorities* E/CN.4/Sub.2/384/Rev.1. (United Nations, 1977), [578].

[8] D. Juteau, *Les frontières de l'ethnicité.* (Presses de l'Université de Montréal, 2015) [hereinafter Juteau (2015)].

[9] A.-G. Gagnon, *Minority Nations in the Age of Uncertainty: New Paths to National Emancipation and Empowerment.* (University of Toronto Press, 2014) [hereinafter Gagnon (2014)]; W. Kymlicka, (1998), *Finding Our Way.* (Oxford University Press, 1998) [hereinafter Kymlicka (1998)].

[10] S. 16 of the *Canadian Charter.*

[11] S. 16(2) of the *Canadian Charter; Official Languages Act* (New-Brunswick), R.S.N.-B. ch O-0.5.

[12] S. 125 of the *Courts of Justice Act, Courts of Justice Act*, R.S.O. c. C-43 (Ont.).

[13] *French Language Services Act*, R.S.O. 1990 c. F-32 (Ont.), ss 2 and 5.

[14] S. 23 of the *Manitoba Act*, 1870, S.C. 1870, c. 3 (Can.)

of the 1988 *Official Languages Act* (Can). It states the role of the federal government as one of "enhancing the vitality and supporting the development of English and French linguistic minority communities, as an integral part of the two official language communities of Canada". It also confirms respecting "the constitutional guarantees of minority language educational rights", which are the English language in Quebec and the French language in the rest of Canada.

Even though there are many other linguistic groups in Canada, historical and political reasons explain why they do not qualify as linguistic minorities in sociological, political, or legal terms. Their rights as citizens, despite Canada's commitment to multiculturalism, are not defined in relation to language. For example, the 1988 *Canadian Multiculturalism Act*[15] refers to the concept of "other languages", not minority languages.

Canada relies on statistical data to implement official language rights. Its main body for collecting data, Statistics Canada, defined statistical categories that governments use to determine who qualifies as right-holders of those rights and to insure service delivery in both official languages where numbers warrant. The most relevant statistical categories in Canada are: "mother tongue", "language most often spoken at home", and the "first official language spoken". Simply put, the category "mother tongue" means the first language learned at home during childhood and still understood, whereas "language most often spoken at home" is used to collect data on the language in which the person is the most comfortable with at home.[16] There is also a category called "first official language spoken", which has been conceived to provide information on the capacity of the individual to conduct a conversation in Canada's two official languages.[17] The category of first official language spoken is preferred by many agencies because it helps capture the use of official languages in the public domain by individuals who do not have English or French as mother tongue. The category also provides some measure of the power of attraction of both official languages amongst immigrants.

Even if English or French is a first language spoken for many Canadians, it does not grant them an automatic right to education in either language. In every province, all children of school age have the right to an education in the language of the majority of that province. Access is more restricted for minorities. Minority language education rights in the *Canadian Charter* are limited to three specific categories of Canadian citizen, as we will explain below, one of which consists of those who have English or French as their mother tongue. Therefore, interpreting statistical data correctly is crucial especially when right-holders insist on exercising their right. As already mentioned, defining a linguistic minority is not a natural process. It is a historical, social, and political process characterized by power relations; but once officially recognized, linguistic minorities can and will expect state action.

---

[15] *Canadian Multiculturalism Act*, R.S.C. 1985 c. 24 (4th Supp.).

[16] See definition of Language most spoken at home, Statistic Canada, on line: http://www.statcan.gc.ca/eng/concepts/definitions/language02 (accessed 3 March 2016).

[17] See definition of First Official Language Spoken, Statistic Canada, on line: http://www.statcan.gc.ca/eng/concepts/definitions/language05 (accessed 3 March 2016).

3. MINORITY LANGUAGE RIGHTS, ASYMMETRY, AND THE CONSTITUTION

Canada has moved incrementally from colonial status into a fully independent country while keeping the Westminster regime and its status as a constitutional monarchy. It is a federation where legislative sovereignty is divided between federal and provincial institutions since 1867. However, constitutional rights in Canada are the result of a fairly recent change in attitude towards rights in general.

Minority language education rights in Canada are the product of such historical and institutional contexts informed by federalism and constitutionalism. In 1867, four British colonies joined together to form the initial Canada—today known as the provinces of New Brunswick, Nova Scotia, Ontario, and Quebec—with the understanding that the western territories, so far the property of the Hudson's Bay Company, and the other British colonies of the time would eventually join in. The constitutional protection of French and English thus varies in time and geography. No province would have the same obligation in the area of language rights while the federal government adopted a limited and asymmetrical approach to those rights. The main representation of language in Canada at the time rested on the principle of Anglo-conformity, which increased pressure on provincial governments not to recognize any language rights to their French-speaking minorities.[18]

As a result, the only section of the Constitution which addressed directly the status of French and English is section 133 of the *British North America Act, 1867*.[19] It stated that English or French may be used in the debates of the Canadian Parliament and the Quebec legislature and their courts, and that it "shall" be used in legislation and parliamentary proceedings. Section 133 was imposed on Quebec to protect the English language in the province. In return, the French language was timidly recognized at the federal level. In 1979, in *Blaikie No 1*,[20] section 133 was interpreted by the Supreme Court of Canada as an intangible measure that neither the province nor the federal Parliament could amend unilaterally.

When Manitoba was carved out of the vast western territories in 1870, section 133 was extended to the new provincial institutions under the same model, becoming section 23 of the *Manitoba Act, 1870*, confirmed by the *British North America Act, 1871*,[21] and thus acquiring a constitutional status. Twenty years later, Manitoba adopted the *Official Language Act* making English the only language of legislation and courts, and in

---

[18] C. Berger, *The Sense of Power: Studies in the Ideas of Canadian Imperialism, 1867–1914* (University of Toronto Press, 1970).

[19] *Constitution Act, 1867*, 30-31 Victoria, c. 3 (U.K.) The former name was the *British North America Act, 1867*, but it was replaced by this one by s. 53 of the *Constitution Act, 1982*, being Annex B of the *Canada Act*, above (n 4).

[20] *Attorney General of Quebec v. Blaikie* (no. 1), [1979] 2 SCR 1016 [hereinafter *Blaikie no. 1*].

[21] *Manitoba Act, 1870*, above (n 14); *Constitution Act, 1871*, 34-35 Victoria, c, 28 (R.-U.).

Forest,[22] published the same day as *Blaikie No1*,[23] the Supreme Court gave section 23 the same status as section 133 of the *Constitution Act, 1867*: it was entrenched and could not be modified unilaterally by the province. Nevertheless, Manitoba had ceased to adopt its laws in French from 1891 onwards, and in 1985, amidst an acute language crisis in the province,[24] the Supreme Court of Canada, in the *Manitoba Language Rights Reference*, concluded that the consequence was to render all unilingual laws unconstitutional.[25] But to preserve the rule of law in the province, the Court suspended its declaration of unconstitutionality for the time required to translate and re-enact its unilingual statutes.

In 1870, the North-West Territories were annexed to Canada by a royal decree. In 1875, Parliament adopted the *Northwest Territories Act, 1875*.[26] When adopted the *NWT Act* had no provision concerning language; however, it was amended in 1877 to include what became section 110 of the *NWT Act*, extending the rights and obligations of section 133 mentioned above to territorial institutions.[27] Section 110 was prolonged when Saskatchewan and Alberta were created out of the Northwest Territories by federal legislation in 1905[28] even though the new provinces, while part of the Territory, had not complied with section 110 since 1891 and still didn't comply after becoming provinces. In 1988, the Supreme Court in *R v Mercure* declared that section 110 was indeed still in force in Saskatchewan.[29] Given that those provinces had not adopted their laws in French since 1891 while they were part of the Northwest Territories, these laws were ultra vires. The difference between Manitoba and Quebec was that Saskatchewan and Alberta provided only legislative protection to the French language, and that protection was thus subject to modification by the relevant legislature, whereas in Manitoba and Quebec the protection was included in the Constitution and therefore entrenched, as we just saw. Both provinces legislated in the summer of 1988 to abrogate section 110. *Mercure* was confirmed in 2015 in *Caron v Alberta*,[30] when a divided Supreme Court of Canada concluded that language rights needed to be explicitly recognized in order to exist. As no language rights had been enshrined in the documents annexing the Northwest Territories or, later, creating the two provinces, they could not be claimed regardless of any promises made by the authorities at the time. *Caron v Alberta* represents an important setback to the demands for French-language rights in the western provinces.

---

[22] *Attorney General of Manitoba v. Forest*, [1979] 2 SCR 1032 [hereinafter *Forest*)].

[23] *Blaikie no. 1*, above (n 20).

[24] J. Blay, *L'article 23: Les péripéties législatives et juridiques du fait français au Manitoba* (Les éditions du Blé, 1987); R. Hébert, *Manitoba's French Language Crisis: A Cautionary Tale* (McGill-Queens University Press, 2005).

[25] *Reference re Manitoba Language Rights*, [1985] 1 SCR 721 [hereinafter *Manitoba Language Rights Reference*].

[26] *North-West Territories Act, 1875*, S.C. 1875, c. 49 (Can.) [hereinafter *NWT Act*].

[27] *North-West Territories Act, 1877*, S.C. 1877, c. 7, s. 11 (Can.).

[28] *Saskatchewan Act*, S.C. 1905, c. 42 (Can.); *Alberta Act*, S.C. 1905, c. 3 (Can.).

[29] *R. v Mercure*, [1988] 1 SCR 234 [hereinafter *Mercure*]. By way of consequence, Alberta inherited the same legal situation as both provinces were created on the same date by the same legal instrument.

[30] *Caron v Alberta*, [2015] 3 SCR 511 [hereinafter *Caron*].

In the 1960s Quebec's growing independence movement and nationalism were viewed as posing a threat to Canadian unity. The new situation prompted the rest of Canada to move gradually out of its model of Anglo-conformity and to embrace bilingualism and linguistic equality. In 1963, the federal government launched the Royal Commission on Bilingualism and Biculturalism, which recommended that English and French be made official languages of Canada, and that guarantees be enshrined in the Constitution, along with the same for New Brunswick and Ontario,[31] while recognizing the right to minority language education where numbers warranted.[32] Both the federal government and New Brunswick enacted an *Official Languages Act* in 1969.[33] In 1975, in the *Jones* case,[34] the Supreme Court confirmed that section 133 was a "floor" and not a complete code, and that jurisdiction over language policy was legally shared between the federal and the provincial jurisdictions as an accessory to any other field of legislative power. The Supreme Court thus confirmed that there would be no uniformity in the area of official languages in Canada, outside of the constitutional provisions. As a result, Canada now has 14 different languages policies (the federal, the 10 provinces, and the 3 territories)—Aboriginal languages and culture are also increasingly recognized in modern treaties.[35]

In 1974, the Quebec government promoted French as its official language (*Bill 22*).[36] In 1977, after the election of the *Parti Québécois*, the *French Language Charter*, better known as *Bill 101*, was adopted,[37] thus confirming the official status of French in Quebec in all areas of political, social, cultural, and economic life falling under its jurisdiction. As the policy ran contrary to the federal thrust towards bilingualism, protracted constitutional negotiations (also fueled by issues other than language) led to the adoption of sections 16 to 23 of the *Canadian Charter* in 1982. Sections 16 to 20 recognized official bilingualism at the federal level. And early in the process, New Brunswick asked to be bound by similar measures, so each of sections 16 to 20 now includes a paragraph (2) which mirrors the same obligations for that province. There is only one difference between the federal and New Brunswick linguistic regime with

---

[31] Canada, *Royal Commission on Bilingualism and Biculturalism* (1967), Book I, p.134 par. 418, rec. 1.1, 1.3 and par. 420.

[32] Canada, Royal Commission on Bilingualism and Biculturalism (1968), Book 3, p.156, rec. 8.

[33] *Official Languages Act (Can.)*, above (n 3); *Official Languages Act (New-Brunswick)*, S.N.-B. 1969, c. 14.

[34] *Jones v Attorney General of New-Brunswick*, [1975] 2 SCR 182 [hereinafter *Jones*].

[35] See, for example, *Tla'amin Final Agreement*: "The Tla'amin Nation has the right to practise the Tla'amin culture, and to use the Tla'amin language, in a manner consistent with this Agreement."; and s. 4(1): "The Tla'amin Nation may make laws applicable on Tla'amin Lands in relation to: a. the preservation, promotion and development of Tla'amin culture and Tla'amin language; Ottawa, Department of Northern Affairs, 2014, on line: https://www.aadnc-aandc.gc.ca/DAM/DAM-INTER-HQ-LDC/STAGING/texte-text/tla_1397237565325_eng.pdf. The website provides all the modern treaties with various nations, and similar clauses are now often included.

[36] *Official Language Act,* L.Q. 1974 c. 6 (Qc) [known as "Bill 22"].

[37] *Charter of French Language,* L.R.Q. c. C-11 (Qc) [known and hereinafter referred to as "Bill 101"].

regard to language of government services: in New Brunswick the right, under section 20(2), is granted throughout the province, whereas at the federal level the right is limited to central offices of government, or where there is "significant demand", or if the nature of the office warrants providing services in both official languages.[38] Both in New Brunswick and at the Federal level, legislation provides details as to how the right is implemented.

Finally, between 1986 and 1992, New Brunswick sought and obtained federal consent to have section 16.1 included in the *Canadian Charter*. That provision expressly recognized the equality of status of the French-speaking and the English-speaking linguistic communities and their right to distinct institutions in specific fields. It also recognized the role of the provincial government and legislature to promote such duality in all its programs.[39]

In the end, due to the aftermath of the *Jones* case in 1975,[40] most Canadian jurisdictions have adopted some language measures, Quebec having the most extensive approach, followed by New Brunswick, Ontario, and Manitoba, and smaller interventions elsewhere. Furthermore, in 1986, in both *MacDonald*[41] and *Société des Acadiens*,[42] the Supreme Court of Canada relied on the theory that contrary to other fundamental and more universal human rights, language rights were the product of a political compromise and therefore must be interpreted literally. It was up to the legislative process to advance official languages equality in Canada. Then the *Secession Reference* of 1998 elevated the protection of linguistic minorities to the status of an unwritten constitutional principle.[43] In 1999, in *R v Beaulac*,[44] the Supreme Court reversed *Société des Acadiens* and concluded that regardless of their political nature, language rights must in all cases be interpreted in a manner consistent with their object and purpose, which is the enhancement and development of minority language communities. But then again in *Caron* in 2015 the Court seemed to revert to its previous approach and treat language rights as a political compromise that needs to be explicitly spelled out to exist: the courts cannot, by a liberal and purposeful interpretation, create new rights. Federalism, as the Court explicitly says, is still a major feature of the Canadian Constitution, and asymmetry in constitutionally protected language rights is a reflection of that powerful structure.

We will now turn to minority education language rights more specifically because of their special interaction with constitutionalism and federalism.

---

[38] *Canadian Charter*, s. 20(1)a) and b) for the Federal level, s. 20(2) for New-Brunswick.

[39] *Canadian Charter*, s. 16.1a) and b).

[40] *Jones*, above (n 34).

[41] *MacDonald v City of Montreal*. [1986] 1 SCR 460 [hereinafter *MacDonald*].

[42] *Société des Acadiens et als v Association of Parents for Fairness in Education*, [1986] 1 SCR 549 [hereinafter *Société des Acadiens*].

[43] *Refererence re Secession of Quebec*, [1998] 2 SCR 217 [hereinafter *Secession Reference*].

[44] *R. v Beaulac*, [1999] 1 SCR 768.

4. Minority Language
Education Rights

As with official languages and bilingualism, education needs a historical presentation. Two defining moments need to be addressed: the constitutional recognition of limited rights in education in 1867; and section 23 of the *Charter,* at which point Canada's approach to official languages became court-driven,[45] leading to major advancements in the area of official minority language education rights.[46]

In a spirit of reciprocity between Protestants and Catholics, the Canadian Constitution protected the rights that denominational schools had acquired, by law, at the time of Confederation (section 93 of the *Constitution Act, 1867*) but remained silent on the subject of minority language education rights. The reference in section 93 to rights that were recognized *by law, before* the colony joined Confederation, prompted in each case a study of pre-Confederation legislation concerning education, and of course it triggered the question of the regulation of the language of education within denominational schools.

At the time, religion was intertwined with language. Being a Protestant was synonymous with speaking English. Catholics were both French speakers and English speakers (albeit in a minority within the Catholic world) because of the growing Irish immigration to Canada in the aftermath of the famine.[47] There were fierce debates during Confederation as to whether the rights of Protestants and Catholics should be specifically granted in the new constitution.[48] In a spirit of compromise, acquired legal rights to denominational schools were confirmed and no provincial law could affect them negatively. In 1871, when New Brunswick decided to create a public school system, complete with school taxes, it excluded any particular arrangements towards Catholics. New Brunswick Catholics took the government right up to the Judicial Committee of the Privy Council, the highest court in the judicial system of the time, which decided that because colonial legislation had not recognized denominational schools, the rights of the Catholics were not protected under the Constitution.[49] Riots ensued and a political compromise was reached.[50] Manitoba followed the same route in 1891, and again

---

[45]   Cardinal (2015) above (n 5).

[46]   Pierre Foucher "Qui peut le plus peut le moins: Fédéralisme et droits linguistiques au Canada" in *Langues, constitutionnalisme et minorités,* (edited by A. Braën, P. Foucher, and Y. Lebouthillier) (Butterworth, 2005), pp. 325–350; Foucher (2008) above (n 5).

[47]   Linda Cardinal, Simon Jolivet et Isabelle Matte (dir.), *Le Québec et l'Irlande. Histoire, culture, identité* (Septentrion, 2014.

[48]   Carignan (1989) above (n 1).

[49]   *Ex Parte Renaud* (1873), 14 NBR 298 (Q.B.); conf. by Privy Council in *Maher v Town of Portland* (1874) (P.C.), cited in Gerald John Wheeler, *Confederation Law of Canada* (1894) p. 364.

[50]   G. Migneault, *La crise scolaire de 1871 à 1875 au Nouveau-Brunswick: un produit de la Confédération* (Éditions du BeauBassin, 2013).

the Privy Council confirmed the right of the province to create a public school system;[51] Catholic rights were not prejudicially affected, according to the Privy Council, as Catholics still could, if they so wished, open, finance, and operate private Catholic schools, even if they had to pay for public school taxes. At the same time, Manitoba also prohibited teaching in a language other than English. The judicial decisions did not address the question of language prohibition, but the Government compromised on that issue and proposed a limited form of bilingual education by way of a political compromise. The compromise lasted until 1919, when English became anew the sole language of schools. In Ontario, Regulation XVII also prohibited the use of French in schools, public as well as separate, after the second grade; the Ottawa Roman Catholic School Board disobeyed the regulation, prompting a Protestant board member to seek an injunction to force compliance. In the ensuring litigation, the Privy Council decided that section 93 protected only rights pertaining to religion, not language.[52] Legally, the Constitution had done nothing to guarantee minority language education rights. Those decisions did raise questions about whether Confederation was fair towards its French-language speaking minorities. Quebec politicians in both the federal and provincial legislatures as well as local associations outside of Quebec were adamantly opposed to the prohibition of French as a language of schooling. Their protests were not heard and French language education remained a contentious issue until the 1980s.[53]

Provinces started to change their policies in the 1970s. New Brunswick and Ontario restored French language education; in the other provinces, some bilingual education was also implemented but more timidly. With the prohibition of French in schooling in the early twentieth century, school board amalgamations in the 1960s had the effect of transforming local and regional school boards which belonged to Catholic francophones into English ones. This prompted new demands for control over school boards by French-speaking minorities. In the 1980s, this became a major issue amongst French-speaking minorities and in Canada as a whole. In contrast, in Quebec, the government had not interfered with the Protestant (English) system. Anglo-Quebecers already had the right to schools and school boards. However, *Bill 101* limited the right to English language schooling to children of Canadian citizens who did the major part of their primary instruction in English in Quebec (the so-called Quebec clause). It imposed the obligation on both immigrants and the French majority to attend French language schools. That ran contrary to the federal thrust towards official bilingualism and led to protracted constitutional negotiations, resulting in the adoption of section 23 of the *Canadian Charter*, which Quebec strenuously opposed.

Although provinces reacted differently to section 23, the importance of the new section outside of Quebec is not to be undermined. It meant, finally, that religious and

---

[51] *City of Winnipeg v. Barrett*, [1892] A.C. 445.

[52] *Ottawa Roman Catholic Separate School Trustees v Mackell*, [1917] 1 AC 63 (P.C.).

[53] P. Foucher, "Le Règlement 17 devant la justice. Les aléas d'une protection constitutionnelle" in *Le siècle du Règlement 17. Regards sur une crise scolaire et nationale*, (edited by M. Bock and F. Charbonneau) (Prise de parole, 2015), pp. 301–328.

linguistic constitutional protections would be separated for good, thus putting an end to almost a hundred years of discrimination in schooling against the French language outside of Québec. In Quebec, section 23 enlarged the categories of persons who could claim a constitutional right of access to English language education, while the Anglo-Quebec community remained in control of its schooling system.

Obviously, section 23 of the *Canadian Charter* represents a second major turning point in the area of education. Where section 93 of the *Constitution Act, 1867* failed in preventing provincial legislative assaults on French language education, section 23 of the *Charter* granted a specific, constitutional, positive right, of which minority language communities could and would seek the full realization in Court, therefore curtailing provincial autonomy in the field of education—the spirit of 1982 took away some of the powers from the provinces to decide how they addressed official language minority education in Canada. Section 23 also redefined constitutionalism in Canada, forcing numerous court interventions in order to implement official language minority education rights in all the provinces. Courts have since then been struggling between the need to preserve provincial autonomy consistent with Canadian federalism, with the concurrent and equally compelling need to give full force and effect to a constitutional right. This challenge was compounded by the effect that section 23 would have on Quebec's language policy, curtailing its margin of appreciation as much as in the other provinces in the name of equal rights.

5. Minority Language Education Rights, Federalism and the Courts

Section 23 of the *Canadian Charter of Rights and Freedom* defines the right to a minority language education in the following terms: "(1) Citizens of Canada (a) whose first language learned and still understood is that of the English or French linguistic minority population of the province in which they reside, or (b) who have received their primary school instruction in Canada in English or French and reside in a province where the language in which they received that instruction is the language of the English or French linguistic minority population of the province"; or (2) who has a child having received or receiving its instruction in French or English and is residing in a province where it is the minority language. Under section 23(3)a), this right to instruction applies in any area within a province "where numbers warrant" that instruction out of public funds, and under section 23(3)b) it includes, "where numbers warrant", a right to minority language educational facilities.

Obviously, section 23 as a whole was open to interpretation, and courts have played a major role in its implementation. In Quebec, section 23 somehow enlarged access to English language education to new categories of right-holders, although, as will be seen, section 59(2) of the *Constitution Act*, 1982, provided that section 23(1)a) of the *Charter* (the clause granting a right to English Mother Tongue speakers to send their children to English schools in Quebec) will not apply to Quebec unless the National Assembly or the Quebec Government consents to it; outside of Quebec, section 23 helped franco-phone minorities to create new schools, gain control over school boards, and address the financing formulas of provinces for French-language education and the need to have appropriate infrastructure to restore minority language education in provinces where it had legally disappeared since the dawn of the twentieth century, although it had never-theless continued, even with limited means.

Section 23 is not easy to explain. It has generated most of the jurisprudence on lan-guage rights in Canada and there are still many unanswered questions around it. To facilitate comprehension, the following structure will be followed: rules of interpreta-tion of section 23; constitutional definition of right-holders and treatment of non-right-holders; meaning of the right to "minority language instruction"; meaning of "minority language educational facilities"; right to management and control of such instruction and facilities; and built-in conditions related to numbers warrant and to costs of instruc-tion and facilities.

Contrary to other constitutional language rights in Canada, section 23 has been inter-preted very generously by courts. In *Mahe*, Chief Justice Dickson laid the ground for that jurisprudential trend. He styled section 23 as " . . . a linchpin of this nation's com-mitment to the values of bilingualism and biculturalism".[54] In the same paragraph he emphasized "the vital role of education in preserving and encouraging linguistic and cultural vitality".[55] In a now-famous excerpt, Chief Justice Dickson stated that the pur-pose of section 23 was to "preserve and promote the two official languages of Canada, and their respective cultures".[56] He added "Language is more than a mere means of communication, it is part and parcel of the identity and culture of the people speaking it".[57] He went on to add that section 23 had a remedial purpose,[58] and he endorsed the concept of equality between the majority and the minority in education.[59] In *Arsenault-Cameron*, in 2000, the Supreme Court went further and asserted that even if the rights are granted to individuals, the official language minority " . . . *is itself a true beneficiary under s. 23*".[60] And in 2005 in *Solski*, the Court again acknowledged the dual nature of section 23, written as an individual right but aimed at a collective interest.[61] In *Rose-des-vents*, in 2015, the Court used this purposive interpretation to coin the notion that "equivalence in the context of s. 23 may mean something other than formal equiva-lence",[62] and that "[r]ather, what is paramount is that the educational experience of the

[54] *Mahe v Alberta*, [1990] 1 SCR 342, 350.
[55] *Ibid.*
[56] *Ibid* 362.
[57] *Ibid.*
[58] *Quebec Association of Protestant School Boards v Attorney General of Quebec*, [1984] 2 SCR 66.
[59] *Mahe*, above (n 54).
[60] *Arsenault-Cameron v Prince-Edward Island*, [2000] 1 SCR 3, [29] (emphasis added).
[61] *Solski v Quebec*, [2005] 1 SCR 201 [23].
[62] *Association des parents de l'école Rose-des-vents v. British Columbia*, [2015] 2 SCR 139, [32].

children of s. 23 rights holders at the upper end of the sliding scale be of meaningfully similar quality to the educational experience of majority language students".[63]

But federalism considerations are never far away. In *Commission scolaire francophone du Yukon* in 2015 the Court was faced with a challenge to a government policy restricting admission to minority language schools.[64] The francophone school board of Yukon[65] argued that this power should be part of their right to management and control, (*infra*) but the Court rejected that claim and emphasized the importance of federalism even in language rights cases.[66] So even in section 23 jurisprudence, the inherent tensions between federalism and minority rights are at play.

It is with these rules of interpretation in mind that we shall discuss some of the issues concerning minority language education rights and the application of section 23 since the 1980s. These issues include: how does the *Charter* define who is a right-holder; what can provincial legislatures do concerning non-right-holders; what is "minority-language instruction"; what are "minority language educational facilities"; what control, if any, do the minority have over such instruction and facilities; and what are the conditions of implementation of the rights granted,[67]

Section 23 does not grant a general right to minority language instruction. It has defined very carefully who is entitled to exercise that right. And as we saw, the constitutional definition of who are legitimate right-holders is fraught with questions. Some of them were answered by courts, others remain to be solved.

A few conditions are common to all categories of right-holders. Claimants must be Canadian citizens. This creates discrimination where non-citizens are concerned, albeit a justifiable one according to the courts.[68] Right-holders also have to be parents; one parent is deemed to be sufficient to trigger the right. Arguably, adoptive parents should be included. Finally, claimants must be residents of the province where they seek admission for their child. That also raises the question of military or diplomatic personnel living outside Canada.

Over and above these conditions, three specific categories of right-holders have been devised based upon language. They are mirrored from *Bill 101*'s categories. The first one uses the Mother Tongue criterion (first language learned and still understood). It is the language of the parent and not the child. It does not apply to Quebec and will not until

[63] *Ibid.*, [33].

[64] *Commission scolaire francophone du Yukon v. Yukon (Attorney General)*, [2015] 2 SCR 282 [hereinafter *CSFY*].

[65] Although, technically, Yukon is not a province but a Federal Territory, Federal legislation has devolved exclusive legislative powers concerning education to the Legislative Assembly. In all practical purposes, its situation is similar to that of a province. See s. 18(1)o) of the *Yukon Act*, S.C. 2002, c. 7.

[66] *CSFY* above (n 64) [68].

[67] M. Power and P. Foucher, "Language Rights and Education" in *Canadian Charter of Rights and Freedoms*, 4th ed., edited by G.-A. Beaudoin and E. Mendes, (LexisNexis Canada, 2005) p. 1095; P. Foucher, "Éducation, langues d'instruction et droit constitutionnel" in *Jurisclasseur Québec, Droit constitutionnel*, fascicule 13. (LexisNexis Canada, 2011).

[68] S. Grammond, *Identity Captured by Law: Membership in Canada's Indigenous Peoples and Linguistic Minorities* (McGill-Queens, 2009).

the Assemblée nationale or the Quebec government gives its assent.[69] It was added at the request of French language minorities, who could not benefit from the two other criteria in many instances. It includes children who do not speak the minority language, which creates a special challenge for minority language schools who have to provide resources to have admissible children develop sufficient language proficiency.[70]

The second criterion is called the "Canada-clause". It is a direct answer to the Quebec-clause of *Bill 101*.[71] It encompasses parents who received their primary education in Canada, in French or English. The Supreme Court concluded that the Canada clause had superseded the Quebec clause of *Bill 101*. And the third criterion relates to a child who has been or is receiving minority language instruction. In *Solski*, in 2005, the Supreme Court said that although a major part of that education was sufficient, it should not be calculated mathematically and need not to be consecutive; a case-by-case evaluation is required and has to take into account "a genuine commitment to a minority language educational experience".[72] And in *Nguyen*, in 2009, the Court said that the nature of minority language education previously received did not matter: even if it was received in a private, non-subsidized school, it should count towards minority language education and enable children to switch from private English schools to public English schools.[73]

As section 23 is limited to three very specific categories of persons, this begs the question: What happens to non-right-holders such as francophone immigrants outside Québec or anglophone immigrants in Québec? Should they be allowed to register for minority language education if they so choose? And more importantly, who should decide? This leads to the question of having the power to self-identify as a legitimate member of the minority community, but it also involves administrative and financial considerations. This is a particularly sensitive issue in Québec, because the government is active in directing everyone into French schools, save some exceptions, in circumstances where a majority of immigrants—and a substantial proportion of francophones wishing their children to learn English—would have them registered in English schools. The Supreme Court of Canada has finally ruled that absent an explicit delegation from the provincial legislation to minority language school boards, the latter did not have, under section 23, the intrinsic power to decide upon eligibility nor to open up their schools to non-right-holders Nevertheless, if the minority could prove that the provincial admissions policy run contrary to the object and purpose of section 23, it could challenge provincial legislation.[74] In reality, except for Quebec who applies strictly section 23

---

[69] S. 59(2) of the *Constitution Act, 1982*.

[70] *Abbey v Essex County Board of Education*, (1999) 42 OR (3d) 481 (Ont. C.A.); *Northwest Territories (Attorney General) v Commission scolaire francophone des Territoires du Nord-Ouest* (2015), 78 Admin. L.R. (5th) 343, [2015] 5 W.W.R. 60 (C.A.) [hereinafter CSF TNO].

[71] *Quebec Association of Protestant School Boards*, above (n 58).

[72] *Solski*, above (n 61), [47].

[73] *Nguyen v Québec (Éducation, Loisirs et Sports)* [2009] 1 SCR 308.

[74] *CSFY*, above (n 64) [74].

criteria, many provinces have delegated the authority to admit non-right-holders to the minority language school board or to schools themselves.[75]

Once right-holders have been identified, the nature and content of the rights themselves must be determined. Three aspects of section 23 rights must be studied: the right to a minority language instruction at the primary or secondary level, the right to minority language educational facilities, and the right to manage and control the above.

Because of the popularity of language acquisition by immersion schooling (a method by which the children are "immersed" in the language to be learned), the question arose as to whether this right was really part of section 23, especially when school boards, for financial reasons, decided to cut back on those programs. The courts decided that minority language instruction meant that the instruction must be objectively seen as belonging to the minority community, thus excluding immersion programs and schools from its ambit.[76] These decisions only concern the vindication of the right itself, but they have not touched upon the status of right-holders under section 23(1) or (2). The courts would probably rule similarly that having received instruction in an immersion program does not count to qualify one as a right-holder.

Another issue concerns the territory of Nunavut, where Inuktitut is the majority language but where both francophones and anglophones can, arguably, claim section 23 rights because both languages are the minority languages of the territory. Where Aboriginal nations have gained authority over education within their territory, the same argument could be made, involving a possible clash between section 23 of the *Canadian Charter* and section 35 of the *Constitution Act, 1982*, over the supremacy of treaty rights.

Another aspect of "instruction" covers the nature of the programs. When section 23 was adopted, it probably referred to the classical setting of a classroom full of children receiving courses from an instructor. In the twenty-first century, the classroom is being transformed with online courses flourishing; specialized schools (sports and education, music and education, international programs, exchange programs, etc.); adult learning, special programmes for dropouts, and prisoners, as well as for Aboriginal communities; vocational training; home schooling; and special schools for students with handicaps. Are all these issues within the ambit of section 23? Most of these issues still await judicial determination. Finally, school buses can also be an issue.

As education must be provided somewhere, section 23(3)b has added a specific recognition of minority language educational facilities. This is central to minority language rights, as it refers to the sociological theory of institutional completeness,[77] where a minority group needs to have control of its own institutions as much as possible. The Supreme Court has acknowledged that homogeneous schools are the ideal model for

[75] *Ibid.* [71–74].

[76] *Whittington v Saanich School Dist. 63*, [1987] 44 D.L.R. (4th) 128 (B.C.S.C.); *Reference Re Education Act of Ontario and Minority Language Education Rights*, [1984] 10 D.L.R. (4th) 491 (Ont.); *Mahe*, above (n 54).

[77] R. Breton, "Institutional Completeness of Ethnic Communities and the Personal Relations of Immigrants" (1964) 70 *American Journal of Sociology* 193–205.

linguistic minorities[78] and that a school must preferably be established within a community,[79] transportation being a last resort.[80] Sharing spaces with the majority is also to be avoided,[81] but where language rights and denominational rights co-exist, there could be a debate about sharing spaces between French Catholic schools and French public schools.

The quality of educational facilities must be comparable to what the linguistic majority gets, and assessed from the perspective of the reasonable minority parent, in a local context: if the parent is faced with having to choose between less favourable schools in French or more favourable schools in English or in French immersion within his neighbourhood, then there is unconstitutional inequality in facilities.[82]

The right to instruction and to educational facilities is meaningless if it is not accompanied with a right of management and control of such. This right directly goes to the heart of the classical federalist theory according to which sovereign governments can legislate to organize the school system as they see fit. They are not free to organize minority language education: they must provide for management and control of minority language education by official language minorities themselves. This begs many questions, such as: Who is entitled to run for election? How may the representatives be selected? Which powers must be delegated? To what extent can the government control those powers? And as education is publicly funded, how are these minority language boards rendered accountable for the monies received?

In *Mahe* 1990, the Supreme Court acknowledged that where numbers are not sufficient to warrant a full-fledged school board, linguistic minorities should at least have proportional and guaranteed representation on majority school boards with exclusive powers on five subject-matters: spending the monies allocated to minority language instruction, hiring teachers, hiring administrative staff, developing specific programs on language and culture, and concluding agreements to provide their services.[83] In *Arsenault-Cameron* 2000, that list was expanded to also include deciding upon the location of new schools, subject to numbers.[84] But "The province can also regulate this area, as previously mentioned, by fixing legitimate parameters to the exercise of the right of management by the Board". In *CSFY*, 2015, the Supreme Court decided that it did not include the power to decide upon admission of non-right-holders.[85]

Finally, two conditions have been built in section 23 to limit its implementation: the "numbers warrant" test, and the costs.

---

[78] *Reference re Public Schools Act (Man.), s. 79(3), (4) and (7)*, [1993] 1 SCR 839.

[79] *Arsenault-Cameron*, above (n 60).

[80] *Chubbs v Newfoundland and Labrador* (2004), 237 Nfld. & P.E.I.R. 146 (S.C.)

[81] *Conseil scolaire fransaskois de Zenon Park v. Saskatchewan*, [1999] 3 W.W.R. 743, 170 Sask. R. 103 (Q.B.).

[82] *Rose-des-vents*, above (n 62); *Northwest Territories (Attorney General) v Association des parents ayants-droit de Yellowknife*, [2015] 3 W.W.R. 490 (C.A.).

[83] *Mahe*, above (n 54).

[84] *Arsenault-Cameron*, above (n 60), 58.

[85] *CSFY*, above (n 64).

The *Charter* does not provide for an absolute and unlimited right to minority language education. The right to instruction is related to numbers. And according to the Courts, numbers cannot be fixed in advance (so that x students trigger the right but x-1 students don't). In *Mahe*, the Court concluded that ". . . it is more sensible, and consistent with the purpose of section 23, to interpret section 23 as requiring whatever minority language educational protection the number of students in any particular case warrant".[86] The numbers test must be put in relation to what is asked from the government. It is impossible to determine in advance what a proper number would be. The Courts have also added that illegally admitted students should not count in the numbers,[87] as well as out-of-province students as each province must only pay for their own residents.[88]

Education is paid out of public funds. Section 23 does not include private, non-subsidized education. There is no constitutional right to establish such schools, and provinces may allow them, forbid them, or ignore them and not recognize their diplomas.

Costs are related to numbers and to whatever facilities are asked to provide instruction. Section 23 grants to official language minorities the same right as that given to linguistic majorities: a right to a free, public education, financed by taxes. That is why costs have to be considered by courts, in relation to numbers and to quality of education, in order to decide if what the right-holders are asking is constitutionally mandated. Furthermore, costs are not evaluated on a strictly formal equality basis between the minority and the majority: "Special circumstances may warrant an allocation for minority language schools that exceeds the per capita allocation for majority schools".[89] Many cases have acknowledged that costs might be higher because scale economies are not possible due to smaller numbers. The federal government has also recognized the problem and offers financial aid, through its constitutionally valid spending power, to help provinces shoulder the supplementary costs of minority language education. This leads to another federalism problem: minority language communities sometimes complain that federal monies are diverted from minority language education to other purposes, to which the provinces retort that education is within their own constitutional responsibility and the federal government has no useful legal means to force accountability upon provincial civil servants.[90] In 2011, a trial judge recognized a fiduciary duty of the territorial government with regard to federal monies destined to minority language education where the evidence had shown that the territory had diverted 1.9 million dollars to French immersion without the express consent of the French language school board.

---

[86] *Mahe*, above (n 54), 367; *Re Ontario Minority Language Education Rights*, (1984), 10 DLR (2^d) 491 (Ont. C.A.)

[87] *CSF TNO*, above (n 64).

[88] *Commission scolaire francophone du Yukon v. Yukon (Attorney General)*, [2015] 2 SCR 282.

[89] *Mahe*, above (n 54), 378.

[90] M. Power (with A. Poulin-Denis, A. Nolette, D. Lozis, D. Morin, J. Wirz and E. LeBlanc) "*Le soutien financier accordé par le Ministère du Patrimoine canadien pour l'enseignement dans la langue de la minorité: constats et proposition de réforme.*" (2010) 12 *Revue de common law en français* 163.

The Supreme Court has returned the case to trial as it decided that the trial judge's atti-tude created a reasonable apprehension of bias.[91] The parties finally settled out of court.

As can be seen, courts have had to struggle with questions surrounding the definition of right-holders, and the nature of minority language education as well as the extent of the right to management and control and the numbers warrant tests. This constitutes the first generation of issues surrounding minority language education rights in Canada. Three points should be stressed. First, constitutionalism has proven to be fundamental to the implementation of minority language education rights, both in Quebec and in the rest of Canada. Second, federalism remains a dominant feature and an important state tradition which informs jurisprudence. Third, the relationship between both is a troubled one because of the separation of powers.

6. Conclusion

When Canada was created, two school systems coexisted: a Protestant one, de facto English, and a Catholic one, de facto French. But as it developed under a federal struc-ture, the initial constitutional recognition of that earlier compromise was unable to protect the Catholic and French systems outside Quebec from the pressures towards moving to a public and English-speaking school system; whereas in Quebec a policy of laissez-faire allowed the Anglo-Protestant school system to grow. Thus a legal asym-metry was created by the use each province made of its constitutional power. Federalism and political compromise were the driving forces behind that evolution. Then in 1982 the enactment of the *Canadian Charter* and its section 23, and the interpretation given to it by the Supreme Court of Canada, replaced that with a strong statement in favour of minority language rights: three categories of right-holders were identified, one of which did not apply in Quebec; the rights granted were interpreted in a liberal and purposive fashion, including separate educational facilities and rights of management and control through autonomous school boards; and conditions related to numbers and costs were interpreted generously, in favour of the linguistic minorities. The courts acknowledged the collective aspect of minority language educational rights even if the wording of the guarantee refers to individuals. Language policy in the field of education, until that point left to the will of provincial governments under the initial compromise, became driven by the courts. The language provisions of the Canadian Constitution generally reflected some form of asymmetrical treatment. Section 23 also has a pan-Canadian or national perspective, which creates some difficulties in Quebec where there is a will to restrict access to minority language education in order to preserve the French majority within Quebec.

---

[91] *CSFY*, above (n 64) [55].

Thus, in the first century of its legal existence, Canada had adopted a constitutional posture based on federalism and initial compromises which left language regulation outside the constitutional realm, save for some exceptions for language of laws, parliaments, and courts, applicable in some but not all jurisdictions. Since 1982, the introduction of minority language constitutional rights in the realm of education presented a new set of issues, having to do with the proper judicial interpretation of these rights, the importance of symmetry or asymmetry in language and education policies, and the interplay between judicial and political interventions in order to further the cause of minority language communities, in particular minority language education rights.

We are now in an era where a second generation of issues is arising in the area of minority language education rights. Demographic trends prompted by new patterns of immigration in Canada and exogamy (French-English) are forcing a new debate on the very definition of the three categories of right-holders mentioned above. There is a need to better understand and to adjust to the changing demographic reality of minority language communities. This also entails reviewing the relationship between language and culture. Whereas the older rationale underpinning section 23 referred to traditional minority language communities, centered around a village, a parish, and a local school, thus building a homogeneous culture, the changing realities of the modern times require us to take a new look at the mission of official language minority schooling around issues of diversity and belonging.[92]

Another set of issues deal with the extent of the reach of section 23 to capture new forms of public education that happen outside traditional ways to teach, such as online education, specialized programs, and many more. A third category concerns financial aspects and the need to fund properly official language minority education in order to enable its artisans to fulfill their mandate. A fourth category involves a look at how responsibilities are divided between decentralized school boards and the provincial ministers of education, as management and control of education is now constitutionally mandated to be shared between government and minority language representatives. This will involve some rethinking of the interaction between federalism, including the concept of provincial sovereignty, and constitutional rights and the extent of the judicial power. More research is needed in the classical field of federalism and constitutionalism in both political science and law in order to address the proper role of courts and governments in implementing minority language education rights. Institutional constraints to official minority language protection remains an important dimension of any discussion on the future development of the country as well as in understanding Canadian identity and national discourse.

---

[92] See also Pilote (2008) above (n 6).

Bibliography

Books and Articles

Behiels, M. *Canada's Francophone Minority Communities: Constitutional Renewal and the Winning of School Governance* (Montreal: McGill-Queen's University Press, 2003).

Berger, C. *The Sense of Power: Studies in the Ideas of Canadian Imperialism, 1867–1914* (Toronto: University of Toronto Press, 1970).

Breton, R. "Institutional Completeness of Ethnic Communities and the Personal Relations of Immigrants." (1964) *American Journal of Sociology* 70(2) 193–205.

Cardinal, L. "Language Regime and Language Politics in Canada." In *Language Regimes and State Traditions*, edited by L. Cardinal and S. Sonntag, pp. 29–43. (Montréal: McGill-Queen's University Press, 2015).

Carpotorti, F. *Study on the Rights of Persons Belonging to Ethnic, Religious or Linguistic Minorities* E/CN.4/Sub.2/384/Rev.1. (New-York: United Nations, 1977).

Foucher, P. "Éducation, langues d'instruction et droit constitutionnel." In *Jurisclasseur Québec, Droit constitutionnel*, fascicule 13. (Markham, Ont.: LexisNexis Canada, 2011).

Gagnon, A.-G. *Minority Nations in the Age of Uncertainty: New Paths to National Emancipation and Empowerment.* (Toronto: University of Toronto Press, 2014).

Grammond, S. (2009). *Identity Captured by Law: Membership in Canada's Indigenous Peoples and Linguistic Minorities.* (Montreal: McGill-Queens University Press).

Hébert, R. (2005). *Manitoba's French Language Crisis: A Cautionary Tale.* (Montreal: McGill-Queens University Press).

Kymlicka, W. *Finding Our Way.* (Oxford: Oxford University Press, 1998).

Power, M. and Foucher, P. "Language Rights and Education." In *Canadian Charter of Rights and Freedoms*, 4th ed., edited by G.-A. Beaudoin and E. Mendes, p. 1095. (Markham, Ont.: LexisNexis Canada, 2005).

Legislation

Alberta Act, S.C. 1905, c. 3 (Can.)

British North America Act, 1867, 30-31 Vict., c. 3 (U.K.)

British North America Act, 1871, 34-35 Vict., c. 28 (U.K.)

Canadian Charter of Rights and Freedoms, being Part I of Annex B of the *Canada Act*, 1982, c. 11 (U.K.)

Constitution Act, 1982, enacted as Annex B of the *Canada Act*, 1982, c. 11 (U.K.)

Manitoba Act, 1870, S.C. 1870 c. 3 (Can.)

North-West Territories Act, 1875, S.C. 1875, c. 49 (Can.)

North-West Territories Act, 1877, S.C. 1877, c. 7, s. 11 (Can.)

Rupert's Land and North-Western Territory Order, 23rd day of June, 1870

Saskatchewan Act, S.C. 1905, c. 42 (Can.)

Cases (Supreme Court of Canada and Judicial Committee of the Privy Council only)

Arsenault-Cameron v Prince-Edward Island, [2000] 1 SCR 3

Association des parents de l'école Rose-des-vents v British Columbia, [2015] 2 SCR 139

Attorney General of Quebec v Blaikie (no. 1), [1979] 2 SCR 1016

Attorney General of Manitoba v Forest, [1979] 2 SCR 1032

Caron v Alberta, [2015] 3 SCR 511

Commission scolaire francophone du Yukon v Yukon (Attorney General), [2015] 2 SCR 282

Ex Parte Renaud (1873), 14 NBR 298 (Q.B.); conf. by Privy Council in *Maher v Town of Portland* (1874) (P.C.), cited in Wheeler. (1894). *Confederation law of Canada*. p. 364.

Jones v Attorney General of New-Brunswick, [1975] 2 SCR 182.

MacDonald v City of Montreal. [1986] 1 SCR 460

Mahe v Alberta, [1990] 1 SCR 342

Nguyen v Québec (Éducation, Loisirs et Sports) [2009] 1 SCR 308

Ottawa Roman Catholic Separate School Trustees v Mackell, [1917] 1 AC 63 (P.C.)

Quebec Association of Protestant School Boards v Attorney General of Quebec, [1984] 2 SCR 66

R. v Beaulac, [1999] 1 SCR 768

R. v Mercure, [1988] 1 SCR 234

Reference Re Education Act of Ontario and Minority Language Education Rights, [1984] 10 D.L.R. (4th) 491 (Ont.)

Reference re Manitoba Language Rights, [1985] 1 SCR 721

Reference re Public Schools Act (Man.), s. 79(3), (4) and (7), [1993] 1 SCR 839

Refererence re Secession of Quebec, [1998] 2 SCR 217

Société des Acadiens et als v Association of Parents for Fairness in Education, [1986] 1 SCR 549

Solski v Quebec, [2005] 1 SCR 201

CHAPTER 27

....

MARRIAGE, FAMILY, AND FEDERAL CONCERNS

....

ROBERT LECKEY* &
CAROL ROGERSON**

1. INTRODUCTION

....

WHERE is the family in a federal state? Textbooks of the Canadian Constitution locate it in the distribution of legislative powers between the two orders of government.[1] We take a broader understanding, including other parts of our constitutional structure such as the entrenched guarantee of equality. This richer story about the place of marriage, families, and family law in our federation looks beyond formal constitutional text to consider institutional structures and practices. More sociologically, it acknowledges the effect of overlapping legal traditions, two official languages, and the dramatic social changes that have driven reform of family law across recent decades. Here as in other chapters, the distinctiveness of Quebec will emerge as significant—although one should not exaggerate it.

After an overview of the constitutional framework for family law and policy, we take up federalism's conceptual tensions between centralization and decentralization and between unity and diversity. Centralizing, unifying forces in family law include: the Parliament of Canada's power over marriage and divorce, entrenched fundamental rights, and principles of modern family law, such as the welfare or best interests of the child. Decentralizing, diversifying forces include the provinces' broad legislative powers in relation to the family, as well as constitutionally enshrined elements of legal pluralism, chiefly the coexistence of the common law, civil law, and Aboriginal legal

---

* Dean and Samuel Gale Professor, Faculty of Law, McGill University, Montreal.
** Professor of Law, Faculty of Law, University of Toronto.
[1] E.g. Peter W Hogg, *Constitutional Law of Canada*, vol 1 (5th edn, Thomson/Carswell, 2007); Henri Brun, Guy Tremblay & Eugénie Brouillet, *Droit constitutionnel* (6th edn, Yvon Blais, 2014) 506 at paras VI-2.136 to VI-2.144.

traditions. Furthermore, the language barrier between the French-speaking majority of Quebec and the English-speaking majorities of the other jurisdictions inhibits the cross-fertilization of family norms across provincial boundaries. Ultimately, these elements of uniformity and diversity, which find their sources both within and outside of our constitutional structure,[2] coexist and interact in ways that defy easy categorization.

2. History, Background, and Constitutional Texts

We begin with federalism and the division of powers in sections 91 and 92 of the *Constitution Act, 1867* (originally the *British North America Act, 1867*)—the only explicit reference to family matters in our constitutional texts. Authority to legislate with respect to the family is divided, in a complicated way, between our two orders of government. Section 91(26) places 'Marriage and Divorce' within federal jurisdiction, thus allowing for uniform legislation on these matters, whereas section 92(12) enables the provincial legislatures to make laws respecting the 'Solemnization of Marriage in the Province'.

The drafting history of these provisions indicates a desire to ensure uniformity in the status of persons across the country, thereby avoiding the domestic recognition issues plaguing the United States, where marriage and divorce fall within state jurisdiction.[3] Concerns about religion also played a role. Making marriage and divorce a federal head of power was intended to minimize the role of religion in laws defining the institution of marriage. Specifically, doing so would protect the Protestant minority in Lower Canada (which became the province of Quebec) from laws influenced by a Roman Catholic majority. However, in response to countervailing concerns from Lower Canada that the federal power over marriage might eventually recognize a purely civil marriage, solemnization was carved out as a separate power for the provinces.[4]

On the conventional reading of the 1867 Act, the bulk of family law—apart from the federal powers over marriage and divorce—falls within provincial jurisdiction under section 92(13) (property and civil rights) or section 92(16) (matters of a 'local or private' nature in the province). Peter Hogg, who has written the leading English language text on the Canadian Constitution, confidently defends the wisdom of this allocation on the

---

[2] See John Dewar, 'Family Law and Its Discontents' (2000) 14 International Journal of Law, Policy and the Family 59 for a discussion of the tensions between uniformity and diversity within modern family law systems across a number of Western jurisdictions.

[3] A few years later, Australia followed the Canadian model: the Australian Constitution gives the Commonwealth the power to make laws with respect to 'marriage' (s 51(xxi)) and 'divorce and matrimonial causes and in relation thereto, parental rights and the custody and guardianship of children' (s 51(xxii)).

[4] F J E Jordan, 'The Federal Divorce Act (1968) and the Constitution' (1968) 14 McGill Law Journal 209.

basis that the ordering of people's lives is a private matter likely to reflect values that differ from one part of the country to another.[5]

However, these assumptions about the inherently 'private' nature of family law and the inevitability of significant regional diversity are open to question. Practice in Canada and other federal jurisdictions has shown that ideas about the nature of family law are shaped by social and political context: it is possible to understand family law as having a public dimension and as reflecting the evolution of national norms. In what follows, we will recount the complex, evolving pattern of shared provincial and federal responsibility over family law and family policy since Confederation. The federal order of government has come to play a larger role than the text of the 1867 Constitution might have suggested. Our constitutional evolution has not, however, centralized power over family law as much as in federations such as Australia[6] and Germany.[7] There are thus interesting questions about what explains the stronger centrifugal forces in our systems of constitutional and family law.[8] Moreover, as we will show, patterns of uniformity and diversity in Canadian family law do not necessarily track the distribution of powers.

The 1867 Constitution also divides power over the judicial system, complicating the resolution of family law disputes. Section 96 authorizes the federal government to name the judges of the superior courts and makes it responsible for their remuneration. This provision has been interpreted as guaranteeing an exclusive core jurisdiction to those courts, one that includes the determination of property rights. For their part, the provinces have exclusive power over the administration of justice in the provinces (section 92(14)), including the establishment of provincial courts. Jurisdiction over family matters is spread across the superior and provincial courts, with legislative choices about jurisdiction constrained by section 96. Conversely, the constitutional order also secures elements of unity. Superior courts can hear matters under both federal and provincial law and the Supreme Court of Canada, which serves as the final court of appeal for all courts, is the final interpreter of federal and provincial law.

This initial inventory of constitutional provisions affecting the family must mention two arising from the reforms of 1982. First, the *Canadian Charter of Rights and Freedoms*, particularly the guarantee of equality in its section 15, has significantly shaped

---

[5] Hogg above (n 1) at 27-1.

[6] In Australia, the Commonwealth enacted the Family Law Act, 1975 with the intention of assuming as plenary a jurisdiction over family law as the Constitution would allow. The Act, which dealt with all of the incidents to marriage and divorce, including matrimonial property rights, withstood constitutional challenge. In addition, with the exception of Western Australia, the states have used the referral power in the Australian Constitution (s 51(xxxviii)) to refer to the Commonwealth their powers over children born to unmarried parents and, more recently, their powers over unmarried couples.

[7] Under the German Constitution family law, as an aspect of civil law, is a matter of concurrent jurisdiction, but state legislative power is pre-empted when the federal government has acted. Family law seems firmly controlled by the federal Parliament, governed by Book 4 of the German Civil Code, a federal statute that deals comprehensively with family law matters.

[8] At the other end of the spectrum is the United States. Even there the federal role in shaping family policy has grown over time, but remains far less significant than in Canada: Ann Laquer Estin, 'Sharing Governance: Family Law in Congress and the States' (2009) 18 Cornell J Law and Public Policy 267.

our family law, federally and provincially. But as we show below, it is important to not exaggerate the unifying effect of the *Charter*. Second, section 35 of the *Constitution Act, 1982*, which recognizes Aboriginal rights, pulls towards legal pluralism and diversity by affirming and reinforcing the distinctive Aboriginal laws governing family status and relationships.

3. CENTRALIZING/UNIFYING FORCES

A. Federal Jurisdiction

Looking only at section 91(26), one might conclude that the federal role in regulating families is a limited one, with the national interest confined to providing uniform rules for the recognition of marriage and divorce—matters of legal status. However, as we further examine the federal powers over marriage, divorce, and the family, we find a more complex story. In the exercise of its divorce power, the federal government has led in developing family law policy, and federal norms have influenced the enactment of provincial laws and their judicial interpretation. At the same time, federal authority does not necessarily translate into uniformity, either because the central government has abstained from exercising its powers or from testing their limits or because it has used its powers in a way that leaves room for expressions of provincial diversity.

Provincial power over 'The Solemnization of Marriage in the Province' limits the scope of the federal power over marriage. Guided by classifications used in private international law, judges have interpreted these provisions as placing matters relating to marriage's *essential validity* (i.e., the capacity to marry) within federal jurisdiction and matters related to its *formal validity* (i.e., the ceremonial and procedural requirements) within provincial jurisdiction. The provincial power has been interpreted generously to include the granting of marriage licenses and the imposition of requirements regarding minimum age and parental consent.[9] In practice, there is a certain amount of jurisdictional 'fuzziness' as it is often provincial officials who monitor compliance with federal requirements.

All of the common law provinces have enacted comprehensive Marriage Acts dealing with matters such as the requirement of a license, the authority of officiants, the form of the ceremony, and the need for witnesses.[10] For its part, the Parliament of Canada has enacted no similarly comprehensive law setting out the requirements for marriage's essential validity. Absent federal legislation, pre-Confederation law in a province governs the essential validity of marriage.[11]

---

[9] *Ross v MacQueen* [1948] 2 DLR 536 (Alta SC); *Kerr v Kerr* [1934] SCR 72.

[10] In Quebec see Rules respecting the solemnization of civil marriages and civil unions, CQLR c CCQ, r 3. In Ontario see the Marriage Act, RSO 1990, c M.3.

[11] *Constitution Act, 1867,* s 129. For the history of post-Confederation marriage laws in Canada, see Jordan above (n 4).

Parliament's first major exercise of its power over marriage came in 1990, modifying the common law's 'prohibited degrees of consanguinity and affinity' (restrictions on marriage between closely related persons).[12] Further reform followed in 2005 with the legalization of same-sex marriage.[13] Although the constitutional drafters in the nineteenth century had obviously not contemplated legislation regarding same-sex marriage, the Supreme Court of Canada relied on the 'living tree' doctrine of constitutional interpretation to interpret the federal marriage power as not confined to the historical definition of marriage.[14] Initially, the *Civil Marriage Act* only removed the common law's requirement that spouses be of different sexes for their marriage to be valid. In 2015, amendments fuelled by a political agenda focussing on forced marriage and polygamy added requirements of 'free and enlightened consent', a minimum age of 16, and the dissolution of any prior existing marriage.[15]

Unlike its Australian counterpart,[16] the Parliament of Canada has never tried to see whether its marriage power would sustain legislation dealing with the consequences of marriage. Nor has it claimed a general power to regulate marriage-like relationships such as civil unions and conjugal cohabitants.[17]

The Parliament of Canada has used its power over divorce more extensively, although only after leaving that power dormant for a century. Following Confederation, a patchwork of pre-Confederal law and federal laws enacted by request for a particular province prevailed. Until 1968, there was no judicial divorce in Quebec or Newfoundland and the only means to terminate a marriage in those provinces was a private member's bill in Parliament. In 1968, the first federal *Divorce Act* introduced no-fault divorce across the country, based on spouses having lived separate and apart for three years.[18] In 1985, our current *Divorce Act* further liberalized divorce by shortening that period to one year.[19] Significantly, both laws also dealt with 'corollary relief' sought in the context of divorce—support for children and a former spouse (previously termed 'maintenance') and the exercise of parental authority (e.g. custody and access) regarding children of the marriage. This exercise of federal power over matters falling *prima facie* within provincial jurisdiction was justified on the basis that these provisions could be characterized as 'ancillary' to divorce.[20] Significantly, there was no federal attempt to treat matters of matrimonial property in this way.

---

[12] This was accomplished by the Marriage (Prohibited Degrees) Act, SC 1990, c 46.

[13] Civil Marriage Act, SC 2005, c 33.

[14] Reference re Same-Sex Marriage, 2004 SCC 79, [2004] 3 SCR 698.

[15] Zero Tolerance for Barbaric Cultural Practices Act, SC 2015, c 29, discussed in Martha Bailey, 'Setting Boundaries' in Bill Atkin (ed), *The International Survey of Family Law 2015 Edition* (Jordans 2015) 21.

[16] In Australia the federal marriage power has been interpreted expansively to allow the federal government to deal with the property rights and maintenance obligations that attach to marriage; see n 6.

[17] It likely does not have such a power; see *Same-Sex Marriage Reference* above (n 14) at para 33.

[18] Divorce Act, 1968, RSC 1970, c D-8.

[19] Divorce Act, RSC 1985, c 3 (2nd Supp).

[20] See *Papp v Papp* [1970] 1 OR 331 (CA) and *Zacks v Zacks* [1985] 1 SCR 851.

We thus have two sets of laws dealing with child support, spousal support, and custody and access. As a general rule, federal law applies to couples who are divorcing or have divorced, whereas provincial laws on these matters apply to unmarried couples and parents and to married couples who are not seeking a divorce. The dividing line is not always clear and there may be situations where both laws are potentially applicable. Where provincial and federal laws or judicial orders made under them conflict, the doctrine of federal paramountcy renders the provincial law or order inoperative to the extent of the conflict. Although one could imagine significant variation between federal and provincial laws and between the laws in one province and those in another, in practice the federal presence in these fields has had a unifying effect, with the exception of Quebec.

Federal and provincial governments worked together during the 1990s to standardize child support. Under the authority of the *Divorce Act*, the federal government promulgated the Federal Child Support Guidelines,[21] which despite their name are a binding instrument that quantifies the support payable. Soon afterwards, all provinces except Quebec enacted virtually identical rules for determinations under provincial legislation. Quebec created its own regime, which applies to cases regulated by the province's Civil Code and, by virtue of an accommodation built into the federal legislation, to cases in Quebec under the *Divorce Act*.[22] We thus see co-operative federalism at work, with federal law creating space for provincial diversity. This is an example of a mechanism fairly common in Canadian federalism, that of allowing provinces to opt out of a federal scheme if they can demonstrate that they have an equivalent. However, despite the near uniformity achieved respecting the amount of child support, variation persists with respect to the basis for entitlement. For instance, provincial laws differ from the *Divorce Act* and from one another in their determination of when children over the age of majority receive child support.

Spousal support has taken a different path to uniformity. Some provinces have copied the language of the *Divorce Act*, but even where the statutory language differs, great weight is accorded to judgments on spousal support rendered by the Supreme Court of Canada in cases under the *Divorce Act*. A further unifying force has been the Spousal Support Advisory Guidelines (SSAG),[23] a set of informal, advisory guidelines developed to assist in determining the amount and duration of spousal support under the *Divorce Act*. The SSAG have reduced the differences between the local cultures of family law that had developed under the *Divorce Act*'s highly discretionary provisions. Although a federal initiative for use under the *Divorce Act*, the SSAG have also been applied in cases under provincial legislation—although their uptake in Quebec has been relatively low.

---

[21] SOR/97-175.

[22] Divorce Act (n 19), ss. 2(1) and 2(5), allowing provincial guidelines to be designated as 'applicable guidelines'.

[23] Carol Rogerson & Rollie Thompson, 'The Spousal Support Advisory Guidelines' (Department of Justice Canada 2008) available at http://www.justice.gc.ca/eng/rp-pr/fl-lf/spousal-epoux/spag/index.html accessed 23 August 2016.

Springboarding from its foothold in the area of divorce, the federal government has led in developing family law policy, often cooperating with the provinces. The federal–provincial relationship has been institutionalized in the form of the Federal-Provincial-Territorial Family Law Working Group, coordinating the development of policy across a number of issues, including the child support guidelines. Despite provincial responsibility for the administration of justice, the federal government has provided extensive funding to the provinces for court services to support families experiencing separation and divorce.

Consideration of the federal role in regulating families must also look to other powers that have allowed the Parliament of Canada to shape family policy. Under the Immigration and Refugee Protection Act,[24] the federal government defines eligible family relationships for sponsorship purposes, a power recently driven by concerns about sham marriages and polygamous unions. Through its powers to tax and spend, the federal government distributes significant benefits to citizens based upon their family status. The power over criminal law allows the Parliament of Canada to define the basic contours of family relationships, for example by prohibiting bigamy, polygamy, and incest as well as the failure to provide the necessaries of life to a child or spouse. This power does not, however, allow Parliament to enact a detailed regulatory scheme, such as one regulating assisted reproduction.[25]

B. The *Charter*

The entry into force of the *Canadian Charter of Rights and Freedoms* in 1982 presaged greater respect for fundamental rights across the federation. The converse of this respect for individual rights is a constraint on legislative policy. Commentators eager to protect provincial autonomy have expressed concern with the prospect of the *Charter*'s potential unifying force.[26] At the same time, the *Charter* incorporates two mechanisms that might make space for interprovincial variation. Its derogation clause (section 33) allows the Parliament of Canada and provincial legislatures to make a law effective 'notwithstanding' the law's incompatibility with one or more *Charter* rights. Furthermore, section 1 contemplates 'reasonable limits prescribed by law as can be demonstrably justified in a free and democratic society'. At the outset, nobody knew how often elected lawmakers would resort to the notwithstanding clause or how much judges would defer to governmental determinations as to what limits are reasonable. Over the decades, the experience of the *Charter* has consisted of movement between the poles of uniformity and diversity—including in relation to marriage and family.

---

[24] SC 2001, c 27.

[25] *Reference re Assisted Human Reproduction Act* 2010 SCC 61, [2010] 3 SCR 457.

[26] E.g. José Woehrling, 'La *Charte canadienne des droits et libertés* et ses répercussions sur la vie politique' in Réjean Pelletier & Manon Tremblay (eds), *Le parlementarisme canadien* (5th edn, Presses de l'Université Laval 2013) 89 at 122.

The *Charter* appears to have played a major role in bringing about reforms typical of Western democracies over the past 40 years—or in accelerating their spread to each province and territory.[27] Three broad issues represent the *Charter's* involvement in changing family law and achieving greater uniformity. One concerns the identity and status of children born outside a traditional different-sex marriage. In the first years of the *Charter*, the courts several times addressed provincial legislation that disadvantaged the children of unmarried parents. Some such laws were held to unjustifiably limit the guarantee of equality in section 15. In 2003, the Court found unjustifiable discrimination—this time against fathers—in a provincial birth registration regime that, for unmarried parents, gave the mother the sole authority to decide whether the father would appear on the child's birth certificate.[28] Changes regarding same-sex couples as parents have drawn impetus from *Charter* rulings. In the mid-1990s, an Ontario court concluded that denying the partners of lesbian mothers the opportunity to have a 'step-parent' adoption unjustifiably violated the *Charter's* equality guarantee.[29] Courts have also found unjustifiable discrimination where a regime for birth registration provides no means for the same-sex partner of a child's mother to declare her parentage.[30] Although some jurisdictions had started recognizing same-sex couples as parents, these judgments have prompted legislative reforms. Principles of equality emerging from these judgments plainly apply across the federation.

The second issue concerns unmarried cohabitants. In 1995 the Supreme Court of Canada recognized marital status as analogous to the suspect grounds for governmental decision making listed in the *Charter's* equality guarantee. The majority viewed as unjustifiably discriminatory a provincial law that provided for accident indemnities for married but not unmarried couples.[31] Although some public regimes such as welfare, workers' compensation, and taxation already recognized unmarried cohabitants as spouses, further legislative changes after *Miron* reflected the notion that the *Charter* might prohibit distinctions on the basis of marital status.

The third issue concerns gay and lesbian couples. Starting in the 1990s, authoritative interpretations of the equality guarantee have required legislatures to recognize same-sex couples. Initially, successful challenges bore on distinctions between different-sex and same-sex cohabitants.[32] Ultimately, however, courts have interpreted the *Charter* as requiring a definition of marriage—a matter of exclusive federal competence—that permits same-sex couples to marry.[33]

---

[27] See generally Nicholas Bala & Robert Leckey, 'Family Law and the Charter's First 30 Years: An Impact Delayed, Deep, and Declining but Lasting' (2013) 32 Canadian Family Law Quarterly 21.

[28] *Trociuk v British Columbia (Attorney General)* 2003 SCC 34, [2003] 1 SCR 835.

[29] *K (Re)* (1995), 23 OR (3d) 679 (Ont Ct (Prov Div)).

[30] E.g. *Fraess v Alberta* 2005 ABQB 889; *Rutherford v Ontario (Deputy Registrar General)* (2006), 81 OR (3d) 81 (Ont SCJ).

[31] *Miron v Trudel* [1995] 2 SCR 418.

[32] E.g. *M v H* [1999] 2 SCR 3.

[33] E.g. *Halpern v Canada (Attorney General)* (2003), 65 OR (3d) 161 (Ont CA).

We said above that the *Charter* 'appears' to have played a major role. The qualifier is appropriate because isolating causation is difficult. We know that *Charter* litigation played a high-profile part on the path to reform, but we cannot be certain that elected lawmakers would not have made those reforms but for the *Charter*. For example, as discussed below, every provincial legislature modified its approach to matrimonial property in order to advance a conception of women's equal role in marriage before the advent of the *Charter*.

Further features caution against exaggerating the *Charter*'s unifying effects in the family field. The courts have developed the liberty interest and parents' rights, such as their freedom of religion, less than some observers had predicted. Indeed, in some contexts the unifying impulse has proceeded not via the *Charter*, but by ordinary family law's principle of the best interests of the child.

Next, although the courts have to a degree used the equality guarantee to refashion family law, they have also recognized countermanding values in the *Charter*. Some observers had read the equality decision in *Miron* on cohabitants broadly, as indicating the unconstitutionality of all legislative distinctions based on marital status.[34] In 2002, however, a majority of the Supreme Court of Canada offered another view. It upheld a matrimonial property law restricted to married spouses on the basis that such a policy respected cohabitants' autonomy and choice. The judges associated the absence of coercion and the ability to make fundamental choices with the *Charter* value of liberty.[35] The idea that legislation withholding rights and obligations from cohabitants might legitimately respect their autonomy and choice returned, a decade later, when the Court heard an equality challenge against Quebec's family policy. The *Civil Code* in that province imposes no rights or obligations on unmarried couples. A majority of the Court upheld that state of affairs as constitutionally compliant.[36]

Finally, courts occasionally signal respect for federalism and diversity in family policy across the federation. Consider again the challenge to Quebec's restrictive approach towards cohabitants. The tie-breaking judge agreed with the claimant that excluding cohabitants from the protections enacted for married spouses was discriminatory. Under section 1 of the *Charter*, however, that judge upheld the limit on rights as reasonably justifiable. In doing so, she emphasized that values of federalism inform the test for minimum impairment.[37] When weighing the benefits of pursuing the state objective against the impact on infringing the claimant's rights, she underscored the 'need to be sensitive to the constitutional responsibility of each province to legislate for its population'.[38]

[34] Brenda Cossman & Bruce Ryder, 'What Is Marriage-Like Like? The Irrelevance of Conjugality' (2001) 18 Canadian Journal of Family Law 269, at 275.
[35] *Nova Scotia (Attorney General) v Walsh* 2002 SCC 83, [2002] 4 SCR 325.
[36] *Quebec (Attorney General) v A* 2013 SCC 5, [2013] 1 SCR 61.
[37] *Ibid* at para 440.
[38] *Ibid* at para 449.

Nor were these statements the first to express concern about using the *Charter*'s equality guarantee to attack Quebec's distinctive family policy. Another challenge concerned the federal executive's decision to designate Quebec's child support guidelines as applicable for *Divorce Act* cases in that province. The complainants challenged the federal recognition of Quebec's distinctive instrument, noting that they would receive more support under the federal guidelines. The trial judge agreed with the litigants that the Quebec guidelines discriminated against divorced or divorcing single mothers. She held, however, that 'in a free and democratic society, cooperative federalism must have effect'.[39]

The suggestion that fundamental rights interpreted by judges threaten the distinctiveness of Quebec civil law exemplifies the concerns of those who fear centralization. An opposing view sees fundamental rights as enriching Quebec's civil law, not as a disruption from the outside, but as an internal resource for positive change.[40]

C. Best Interests of the Child

The unifying features of our family law system also derive from sources outside of our constitutional framework, reflected in the basic norms and principles that have come, over the course of the last 50 years, to structure Canadian family law.[41] Gender equality is one such principle—at work in family law long before the advent of the *Charter*. Another is the best interests of the child. Now recognized as a central principle of international law in Article Three of the United Nations Convention on the Rights of the Child (1989), to which Canada is a signatory, the principle began to take root in Canada during the 1960s.[42] Across a wide range of federal and provincial legislation affecting matters such as adoption, child protection, the exercise of parental authority, and consent to care, the best interests of the child is now recognized as the primary (if not sole) consideration when making decisions about children.

Although the principle is one of fundamental importance—recognizing children's personhood and the priority of their interests over the rights of parents and other adults—its indeterminacy, even incoherence inspires criticism. The unity provided by the principle exists at a high level of generality and abstraction, while the term undergoes widely varying interpretations. Often it is understood as precluding the application of fixed rules, and requiring discretionary, highly individualized decision-making

---

[39] *Droit de la famille—111526* 2011 QCCS 2662, [2011] RJQ 907 at para. 280, aff'd on other grounds, *Droit de la famille—139* 2013 QCCA 15, [2013] RJQ 9.

[40] E.g. Mélanie Samson & Louise Langevin, 'Revisiting Québec's *Jus Commune* in the Era of the Human Rights Charters' (2015) 63 American Journal of Comparative Law 719.

[41] For an overview of this evolution, see Robert Leckey, 'Families in the Eyes of the Law: Contemporary Challenges and the Grip of the Past' (2009) 15:8 IRPP *Choices* 2.

[42] See Nicholas Bala, 'The Best Interests of the Child in the Post-Modern Era: A Central but Paradoxical Concept' in Harold Niman & Gerald Sadvari (eds), *The Best Interests of the Child—Special Lectures 2000* (Law Society of Upper Canada 2001) 1.

tailored to a particular child's circumstances.[43] Moreover, the principle's discretion may make it the vehicle for dominant ideologies, reflecting the judiciary's or experts' sense of what is best for children. In the Canadian context, as in other settler states, the welfare of children has justified massive intrusions into Indigenous communities, including the institutionalization of vast numbers of children.[44] Best interests of the child presents the somewhat paradoxical combination of near universality of principle with highly individualized, 'decentralized' decision-making. It thus serves as an apt transition between the forces we characterize as centralizing and those we see as decentralizing.

4. DECENTRALIZING/ DISHARMONIZING FORCES

A. Provincial Jurisdiction

In the exercise of its powers under the 1867 Constitution, each province has enacted legislation dealing with matters such as solemnization of marriage, child and spousal support, matrimonial property, domestic contracts, maintenance enforcement, birth registration, parentage, custody and access of children, adoption, and child protection. Further to the unifying influences discussed above, some inter-jurisdictional copying occurs. For example, two smaller jurisdictions, Prince Edward Island and the Northwest Territories, modelled their matrimonial property statues on Ontario's *Family Law Act*. In some areas one can see the influence of model uniform laws developed by the Uniform Law Conference of Canada, a volunteer organization composed largely of government policy lawyers. Finally, the Supreme Court of Canada also plays a unifying role. Its interpretation of one province's legislation will typically govern that of another, while its decisions under the *Divorce Act* can affect the interpretation of provincial legislation.

Nonetheless, there remains significant variation between provincial family laws, at the level of principle as well as of detail. Three areas stand out as examples: matrimonial property, unmarried couples, and legal parentage.

All provinces during the 1970s or 1980s adopted schemes for sharing matrimonial property. The schemes incorporate the basic concept of marriage as an equal partnership, entitling spouses to a presumptive equal division of marital assets when the partnership ends. But the schemes differ with respect to the pool of assets subject to this presumption. Major differences of principle exist between those provinces where the

---

[43] See Robert Leckey, 'Particular Justice: Michel Bastarache and Family Law' in Nicholas C G Lambert (ed), *À l'avant-garde de la dualité: Mélanges en l'honneur de Michel Bastarache* (Éditions Yvon Blais 2011) 117.

[44] Marlee Kline, 'Child Welfare Law, "Best Interests of the Child" Ideology, and First Nations' (1992) 30 Osgoode Hall Law Journal 375.

basic premise is that all wealth generated during the marriage is shared equally and those that distinguish 'family' assets from 'business' assets, sharing only the former. At the level of detail, provinces deal variously with pre-marital property and gifted or inherited property and in the distribution mechanism—whether through an equaliza-tion payment or a proprietary interest in the assets. Given the increased mobility of per-sons across the country and the relative uniformity with respect to the other financial aspects of divorce and separation, is having 10 different schemes of matrimonial prop-erty justifiable? The explanation lies in our constitutional history, which has put prop-erty rights at the tenaciously guarded core of provincial jurisdiction.

The treatment of unmarried couples varies across the country and reflects a con-tentious issue of social policy: to what degree should the state respect the 'choice' such couples have made to not marry, and how meaningful are such 'choices'? Although Canadian law as a whole accords significant legal recognition to unmarried couples, we have no uniform definition of the non-marital relationships treated as 'spousal' and no uniform set of consequent rights and obligations. As the federal marriage power does not extend to unmarried couples, the Parliament of Canada is restricted to dealing with spouses in the exercise of another power, as over taxation, bankruptcy, and immigra-tion. Rights and obligations of unmarried couples fall chiefly under provincial jurisdic-tion and vary substantially from province to province.

All of the common law provinces have imposed a spousal support obligation on unmarried couples, but the definitions of eligible relationships differ. Fewer than half of the common-law provinces have included unmarried couples in their matrimonial property legislation. In Quebec, which has the highest rate of cohabitation outside of marriage, unmarried couples are subject to none of the rights and obligations entailed by marriage regarding spousal support and family property.

A distinguishing feature of Canadian family law is its broad recognition of de facto parent-child relationships under federal and provincial laws. In further evidence of interprovincial difference, the exception is again Quebec. However, this widespread recognition of de facto parentage contrasts with substantial variation in laws determin-ing *legal* parentage, an exclusively provincial domain. Although all of the provinces have removed the status of illegitimacy, they have been slow to undertake comprehen-sive reform to take account of assisted reproduction. Here provincial unwillingness to exercise jurisdiction coexists with the absence of federal power to fill the legislative vacuum. Although Quebec and several other provinces have tackled these issues, the majority of provinces have left courts to address them or adopted piece-meal reform.[45] It remains unclear whether there will be significant provincial take-up of the Uniform Law Conference of Canada's Uniform Child Status Law, 2010.

A final point about provincial jurisdiction and diversity in family law policy is neces-sary. Provincial power over the administration of justice gives the provinces control of

---

[45] See Carol Rogerson, 'Determining Parentage in Cases Involving Assisted Reproduction: An Urgent Need for Provincial Legislative Action' in Trudo Lemmens et al. (eds), *Regulating Creation: The Law, Ethics and Policy of Assisted Human Reproduction* (University of Toronto Press, 2017) 91.

court procedure in family law cases, including those under the federal *Divorce Act*. The upshot is wide variation across provinces in forms and procedures for dispute resolution and in the support services available to families experiencing separation and divorce.[46] Furthermore, the division of power over the justice system has slowed the introduction of unified family courts (UFCs) competent to address all aspects of a family dispute. The robust interpretation of the federal government's appointment power for the judges of the superior courts, noted above, means that any UFC must be established at that level, requiring the federal government to appoint and pay those judges.[47] Some provinces have undergone an arduous process of bargaining with the federal government to achieve such a UFC. In others, though, specialized courts created by the province deal with some family matters, while the federally appointed superior courts of general jurisdiction maintain exclusive competence regarding matrimonial property and matters under the *Divorce Act*.

B. Legal Pluralism/Multiple Legal Traditions

Diversity does not arise only from the Constitution of Canada's divided jurisdiction in relation to marriage and the family. Pluralism also arises from the multiplicity of legal sources within the Canadian constitutional order.

The distinction recognized most classically is that between the traditions of the common law and the civil law.[48] The common law, received from England, establishes the general private law in the provinces and territories other than Quebec. The civil law, received from France, provides the general private law in Quebec. The Imperial Parliament at Westminster recognized this ongoing role for the civil law in the *Quebec Act, 1774* and again in the *Constitution Act, 1867*. Of course, centuries of legislative and judicial developments have substantially altered the received law in Quebec and the common-law provinces. Canada now has living traditions of the common law and the civil law.

Here we identify several ways by which the coexistence of these traditions inherited from Europe contributes to diversity within the Canadian federation. One is the sources and forms of law. In the common-law provinces, the chief sources of family law are statutes and case law. Provincial regulation of families runs across different statutes and the residual common law plays a relatively minor role. By contrast, in Quebec, family law is set out in the civil code, first the *Civil Code of Lower Canada* (1866) and now the *Civil Code of Québec* (1991).

---

[46] Even in unitary states or federations where legislative powers over family law are highly centralized, such as Germany, similar decentralizing forces are at work, such that much of the actual administration of the family justice system is delegated to the regional and local level.

[47] See *Re BC Family Relations Act* [1982] 1 SCR 62.

[48] H Patrick Glenn, *Legal Traditions of the World: Sustainable Diversity in Law* (5th edn, Oxford University Press, 2014).

Differences across the two legal traditions condition the approach to families. The generalization by which the common law focuses on facts and remedies and the civil law on substantive rights applies here. The drafters' ambition for the Civil Code is that it exhaustively elaborate all the institutions, rules, and concepts that govern interpersonal relationships and property rights. It aims to fix the meaning of these elements for the entire legal system.[49] In keeping with this task, the Code defines the core family relationships—marriage and filiation, the institution connecting a child to his parents—and their legal consequences. In general, family law's key terms—'spouse', 'parent', 'child'—retain the same meaning across the Civil Code. This fixity and ambition for coherence contrast with the approach of the legislative drafters in the common-law provinces. Common-law drafters will adjust a term's reach in specific contexts. Thus the classes of 'parent', 'child', and 'spouse' are larger in some contexts, such as maintenance and child custody, than in others, such as intestate successions.

Relatedly, although both traditions regulate using a mix of functional and formal bases, Quebec's approach to family regulation is more formal than that of the common-law provinces. That is, family law in Quebec is based on formally recognized family statuses of marriage and filiation, whereas the common-law provinces grant more legal effects to lived family relationships on a factual basis, following a functional approach.[50] This matter of style affects substance. For example, in Quebec, only formally recognized spouses owe one another support. In the common-law provinces, as noted above, the support obligation attaches to married spouses and to cohabitants who satisfy legislated criteria. Similarly, in Quebec, the obligation to support a child is an effect of the formal status of parent. In most common-law provinces, a legal parent owes support to a child, but so may a person having acted parentally towards the child.

The focus on formalism in Quebec goes hand in hand with a focus on individual freedom and a reluctance to attribute obligations absent consent. We see this connection in the approach to adult conjugality, which centres on marriage—a contract freely entered by informed consenting parties. The focus on formalism explains—whether or not it justifies—Quebec's repeated decision against ascribing spousal rights and duties to unmarried couples.[51] This approach contrasts with the common-law jurisdictions' recognition of a reciprocal duty of spousal support and, in some cases, access to the regime of matrimonial property. In addition, the civil law's emphasis on freedom of contract—and its relatively more restrained role for the judge, developed apart from the common law's equitable jurisdiction—underpins the approach to prenuptial agreements. In the common-law provinces, such contracts may have effect, but legislation provides scope for judges to set them aside, for instance if unconscionable. On

---

[49] John E C Brierley & Roderick A Macdonald (eds), *Quebec Civil Law: An Introduction to Quebec Private Law* (Emond Montgomery Publications, 1993) 99 at para 87.

[50] Robert Leckey, 'Family outside the Book on the Family' (2009) 88 Canadian Bar Review 545; Nicholas Bala & Rebecca Jaremko Bromwich, 'Context and Inclusivity in Canada's Evolving Definition of the Family' (2002) 16 International Journal of Law, Policy and the Family 145.

[51] Robert Leckey, 'Cohabitation and Comparative Method' (2009) 72 Modern Law Review 48.

the contrary, in Quebec, a validly formed marriage contract that does not offend public order is binding. Faithful to its preference for regulating via formal means, Quebec recognized same-sex couples by adopting a form of civil union, whereas some common-law provinces extended the class of cohabitants defined functionally.

The interaction of federal and provincial law merits mention. Across the country, federal family law, such as the *Divorce Act*, interacts with provincial regimes, such as laws dividing matrimonial property. The general view is that federal legislation in family matters, as on many other topics, reflects a common-law more than a civil-law perspective. Accordingly, there is little discussion in the common-law provinces about conceptual conflict between federal and provincial law or about federal law as intruding into provincial law. On several matters, though, the *Divorce Act* introduces concepts that depart from their equivalents in Quebec civil law. For example, the *Divorce Act*'s concept of 'custody'—drawing from the common law—includes major decision-making power. This approach contrasts with the civil law's definition of 'custody' as merely an attribute of parental authority. Under the Civil Code of Québec, even if custody of the child is given to someone else, the holder of parental authority retains the rights and duties of education and supervision.[52] Another point of difference concerns spousal support. The *Divorce Act* contemplates support as a lump sum, and judicial interpretations have emphasized its compensatory aim.[53] Both contrast with the civil law's conception of support as a pension to cover current needs. Finally, the *Divorce Act* provides that, where conditions are met, an individual may owe support to the child of his former spouse. A judge of the Quebec Court of Appeal has expressed the view that courts in that province should require clear evidence before finding the conditions satisfied. His basis was that the federal statute derogates from the general private law of Quebec, which imposes no such obligation on step-parents.[54] We do not have data measuring the degree to which outcomes reflect this reticence about points on which federal family law differs from Quebec civil law. What we can observe is that characterizing federal family law as making exception to a province's general private law is a move distinct to Quebec.

Differences arising from the legal traditions are amplified by linguistic dynamics. Whatever the constitutional guarantees for French and English, our concern here is sociological. The community of legal scholars and practitioners working in French in Quebec and the community of legal scholars and practitioners working in English in the other jurisdictions are divided by language. Distinct bodies of scholarship on constitutional law and family law have relatively little crossover. To be sure, there are exceptions, largely grounded in the law faculties that teach the common law in French or the civil law in English. But the separation remains.

Before we close on the common law and the civil law, it is important to acknowledge the risk of essentialism. Such rich traditions cannot be homogeneous. As confirmed

---

[52] Michelle Giroux, 'Le partage des responsabilités parentales après une rupture: Une matière à débat' (1998) 77 Canadian Bar Review 354.

[53] *Moge v Moge* [1992] 3 SCR 813.

[54] *A (V) v F (S)* [2001] RJQ 36 (Qc CA).

by comparison with other jurisdictions, present arrangements regarding the family in the Canadian jurisdictions do not represent the sole possible approach under the common law or the civil law. Indeed, in Quebec and the common-law provinces, minority voices may call for reform, advancing alternative readings of their tradition's resources. Nevertheless, the different legal traditions include robust patterns of thought manifested in the regulation of family.[55] The upshot is abiding diversity within the Canadian federation.

Pluralism also arises from the place of Canada's Indigenous peoples. One element of such pluralism stems from the federal distribution of powers. The provinces generally regulate family law in the exercise of their exclusive competence relating to property and civil rights in the province. Under section 91(24) of the 1867 Constitution, the Parliament of Canada enjoys exclusive competence relating to 'Indians, and Lands reserved for the Indians'. Courts have held that provincial regimes of matrimonial property do not apply on First Nations reserves. For decades, Parliament failed to address the resultant legal vacuum. It was only in 2013 that it legislated to address family homes and matrimonial property rights on reserves.[56] The statute empowered First Nations to enact laws for their reserves, and provided default rules that would apply in the event that First Nations failed to do so. Accordingly, the legal pluralism in relation to official family law includes provincial and territorial regimes, regimes adopted by a First Nation, and the federal default rules.

Another element of pluralism arises from the abiding normative force of Aboriginal law. Section 35 of the *Constitution Act, 1982* recognizes and affirms the 'existing aboriginal and treaty rights of the aboriginal peoples of Canada'. One practice relevant in the family domain is customary adoption. Although the modalities of the practice vary significantly, Aboriginal customary adoption generally proceeds informally. It departs radically from state adoption's focus on the judge, herself acting on a bureaucratic assessment of the child's best interests. Arguably, section 35 requires provinces to recognize Aboriginal customary adoptions without distorting the custom and subordinating it to the dominant legal culture.[57] For example, British Columbia has legislated to provide that a court may recognize an adoption effected by Aboriginal custom, but on critical views that recognition process distorts the custom.[58] Giving full scope to the constitutional protection of Aboriginal rights might call for attributing effect to customary adoptions without passing through a court, and for better acknowledging customary adoption's differences from state adoption.

---

[55] Pierre Legrand, 'Foreign Law: Understanding Understanding' (2011) 6:2 Journal of Comparative Law 67, at 110.

[56] Family Homes on Reserves and Matrimonial Interests or Rights Act, SC 2013, c 20.

[57] Ghislain Otis, 'La protection constitutionnelle de la pluralité juridique: le cas de "l'adoption coutumière" autochtone au Québec' (2011) 41 Revue Générale de Droit 567.

[58] Cindy L Baldassi, 'The Legal Status of Aboriginal Customary Adoption across Canada: Comparisons, Contrasts, and Convergences' (2006) 39 University of British Columbia Law Review 63.

Before closing, we may observe that religion serves as an engine of state-recognized legal pluralism less than in some other jurisdictions and less than it might in Canada. In relation to children, the best interests of the child trumps a parent's freedom of religion.[59] Under legislation addressing consent to care, the court's duty to act in the best interests of the child allows it to override a young person's refusal of life-saving treatment—and her fundamental rights to freedom of religion and equality.[60] Although private ordering in family matters may open space for religious norms, Quebec excludes family matters from its scheme of binding arbitration.[61] For its part, Ontario requires that, to be binding, a 'family arbitration' be conducted exclusively in accordance with the law of Ontario or of another Canadian jurisdiction.[62] The province enacted this measure in response to a crisis triggered by the prospect of Muslim arbitrators applying religious law.[63] Arguably, attempts to prevent the turn to religious norms in family matters are incoherent in the light of the liberal space that the *Divorce Act* and provincial laws open for private ordering in deviation from default entitlements.[64] In any event, spouses may conclude effective separation agreements—based on advice from religious advisors. Practically speaking, for many cases, efforts to deny the legal force of family arbitration based on religious principles may be 'a matter of form rather than normative substance'.[65]

5. CONCLUSION

From a family law perspective, we can see that federalism further complicates an area of law already under pressure to meet the overwhelming legal and social needs created by the dramatic changes in marriage and family life since the 1960s. Federalism's complications affect both policy makers and individuals seeking to resolve family disputes. A federal division of legislative powers produces line-drawing exercises that would not arise in a unitary state—such as that between the solemnization of marriage and the capacity to marry. In areas of overlapping jurisdiction, it can introduce confusion and complexity, raising questions as to which laws or orders apply and how to resolve conflicts between them. Implementing a Unified Family Court or UFC—what many

---

[59] *Young v Young* [1993] 4 SCR 3.

[60] *AC v Manitoba (Director of Child and Family Services)* 2009 SCC 30, [2009] 2 SCR 181.

[61] Art 2639 CCQ.

[62] Arbitration Act, 1991, SO 1991, c 17, s 1 'family arbitration'.

[63] Sherene H Razack, 'The "Sharia Law Debate" in Ontario: The Modernity/Premodernity Distinction in Legal Efforts to Protect Women from Culture' (2007) 15 Feminist Legal Studies 3.

[64] Audrey Macklin, 'Multiculturalism Meets Privatisation: The Case of Faith-Based Arbitration' (2013) 9 International Journal of Law in Context 343.

[65] Annie Bunting, 'Family Law's Legal Pluralism: Private Opting-out in Canada and South Africa' in Albert Breton and others (eds), *Multijuralism: Manifestations, Causes and Consequences* (Ashgate, 2009) 77, at 83.

view as the optimal institutional structure—requires an uncertain, arduous process of federal–provincial bargaining. The constitutional drafters in 1867 entrusted power over marriage to Parliament to assure uniformity regarding status, but they could not have foreseen the consequential variation across provinces regarding the treatment of parentage and unmarried couples. Conversely, the Federal Child Support Guidelines attest that inter-governmental co-operation can vault over federalism's hurdles when all players recognize the value of harmonization.

More generally, our chapter holds four lessons for comparative constitutionalists. First, researchers should not examine the division of powers on its own, but must understand its interactions with other parts of the Constitution, such as the guarantees of fundamental rights. The interactions can centralize and decentralize: the *Charter* has exercised some unifying effect on family law, but judges will sometimes take federalism into account when applying it. Second, it is critical to look beyond the constitutional text, as the unfolding of governance will not always track what the federal constitution would lead observers to predict. Powers can be granted but not exercised. The exercise of federal authority may create space for provincial diversity, and provincial laws can mirror federal laws. Mechanisms of inter-governmental co-operation can ease the rigidities of the formal distribution of power, as can exercises of a spending power.[66] Third, institutional structures merit serious attention. Diversity in court structures and procedures and in the services provided can affect the implementation and effectiveness of national laws. Moreover, regionally variable interpretations of national laws can give rise to local family law cultures. Fourth, what we think of as constitutional norms may have their anchorage outside the constitutional text. Although the *Charter* guarantee of equality has undoubtedly prompted legislative change, equality values began to shape family law long before the advent of the *Charter*. Our case study of the family in the Canadian federation thus attests to the dynamic potential of the federal model—as well as to the benefits for lawyers of enriching their accounts with the insights of others such as political scientists and sociologists.

BIBLIOGRAPHY

Bala, Nicholas and Rebecca Jaremko Bromwich. "Context and Inclusivity in Canada's Evolving Definition of the Family." *International Journal of Law, Policy and the Family* 16 (2002): 145–180.
Bala, Nicholas and Robert Leckey. "Family Law and the Charter's First 30 Years: An Impact Delayed, Deep, and Declining but Lasting." *Canadian Family Law Quarterly* 32 (2013): 21–52.
Baldassi, Cindy L. "The Legal Status of Aboriginal Customary Adoption across Canada: Comparisons, Contrasts, and Convergences." *University of British Columbia Law Review* 39 (2006): 63–100.

---

[66] Regarding the spending power, see the chapter by Hoi L. Kong in this *Handbook*.

Brierley, John E C and Roderick A Macdonald (eds). *Quebec Civil Law: An Introduction to Quebec Private Law*. Toronto: Emond Montgomery Publications, 1993.

Brun, Henri, Guy Tremblay and Eugénie Brouillet. *Droit constitutionnel*, 6th edn. Cowansville, Québec: Éditions Yvon Blais, 2014: 506–509.

Castelli, Mireille D. and Dominique Goubau. *Le droit de la famille au Québec*, 5th edn. Sainte-Foy: Presses de l'Université Laval, 2005.

Glenn, H Patrick. *Legal Traditions of the World: Sustainable Diversity in Law*, 5th edn. Oxford: Oxford University Press, 2014.

Hogg, Peter W. *Constitutional Law of Canada*, 5th edn. Toronto: Thomson/Carswell, 2007: ch. 27.

Hovius, Berend and Mary-Jo Maur. *Hovius on Family Law: Cases, Notes and Materials*, 8th edn. Toronto: Carswell, 2013.

Jordan, F J E. "The Federal Divorce Act (1968) and the Constitution." *McGill LJ* 14 (1968): 209–271.

Kline, Marlee. "Child Welfare Law, 'Bestinterests of the Child' Ideology, and First Nations." *Osgoode Hall Law Journal* 30 (1992): 375–425.

Leckey, Robert. "Families in the Eyes of the Law: Contemporary Challenges and the Grip of the Past." IRPP *Choices* 15:8 (2009): 2–42.

Mossman, Mary Jane, Natasha Bakht, Vanessa Gruben and Karen Pearlston. *Families and the Law: Cases and Commentary*, 2nd edn. Concord, ON: Captus Press, 2015.

Payne, Julien. "Divorce and the Canadian Constitution." *Conciliation Courts Review* (now *Family Court Review*) 18:1 (1980): 57–60.

Payne, Julien D and Marilyn A Payne. *Canadian Family Law*, 6th edn. Toronto: Irwin Law, 2015.

Pineau, Jean and Marie Pratte. *La famille*. Montréal: Thémis, 2006.

Rogerson, Carol. "Canada: A Bold and Progressive Past but an Unclear Future." In *The Future of Child and Family Law: Future Predictions*, edited by Elaine E Sutherland. Cambridge: Cambridge University Press, 2012: 77–111.

Rogerson, Carol. "Determining Parentage in Cases Involving Assisted Reproduction: An Urgent Need for Provincial Legislative Action." In *Regulating Creation: The Law, Ethics and Policy of Assisted Human Reproduction*, edited by Trudo Lemmens and others. Toronto: University of Toronto Press, 2017: 91–123.

Tétrault, Michel. *Droit de la famille*, 4th edn. Cowansville, Québec: Éditions Yvon Blais, 2010.

Cases

AC v Manitoba (Director of Child and Family Services) 2009 SCC 30, [2009] 2 SCR 181

A (V) v F (S) [2001] RJQ 36 (Qc CA)

Droit de la famille—111526 2011 QCCS 2662, [2011] RJQ 907

Fraess v Alberta 2005 ABQB 889

Halpern v Canada (Attorney General) (2003), 65 OR (3d) 161 (Ont CA)

In re Marriage Legislation in Canada [1912] AC 880

Kerr v Kerr [1934] SCR 72

Lamb v Lamb [1985] 1 SCR 851

M v H [1999] 2 SCR 3

Miron v Trudel [1995] 2 SCR 418

Moge v Moge [1992] 3 SCR 813

Nova Scotia (Attorney General) v Walsh 2002 SCC 83, [2002] 4 SCR 325

Papp v Papp [1970] 1 OR 331 (CA)
Quebec (Attorney General) v A 2013 SCC 5, [2013] 1 SCR 61
Re BC Family Relations Act [1982] 1 SCR 62
Reference re Adoption Act [1938] SCR 398
Reference re Assisted Human Reproduction Act 2010 SCC 61, [2010] 3 SCR 457
Reference re Same-Sex Marriage, 2004 SCC 79, [2004] 3 SCR 698
Ross v MacQueen [1948] 2 DLR 536 (Alta SC)
Rutherford v Ontario (Deputy Registrar General) (2006), 81 OR (3d) 81 (Ont SCJ)
Trociuk v British Columbia (Attorney General) 2003 SCC 34, [2003] 1 SCR 835
Young v Young [1993] 4 SCR 3
Zacks v Zacks [1973] SCR 891

CHAPTER 28

......

INTERNATIONAL TREATY-MAKING AND TREATY IMPLEMENTATION

......

HUGO CYR* &
ARMAND DE MESTRAL**

1. INTRODUCTION

TREATIES have always been a contentious subject in Canadian law. Although for many countries treaty-making may be a straight-forward endeavour, in Canada it is rife with uncertainty brought on by Canada's unique brand of federalism. The very limited references to treaty-making in Canada's constitution have resulted in disagreement between some provincial governments, which claim they possess treaty-making capacity, and the Government of Canada, which has consistently rejected these claims. Moreover, the issue of treaty implementation is central to any discussion on treaties within Canada, given that Canada is a dualist country.

The first broad section of this chapter deals with the current *modus vivendi* of treaty-making in Canada and discusses constitutional issues, political pragmatism, executive versus legislative powers, and the division of powers. The second section addresses

* Hugo Cyr, LL.B., B.C.L. (McGill), LL.M. (Yale), LL.D. (U. de Montréal), is Dean and Professor of Public Law and Legal Theory at the Université du Québec à Montréal and a member of the Québec Bar. He is a member of the *Centre de recherche interdisciplinaire sur la diversité et la démocratie* (CRIDAQ). He has been a Boulton Fellow at McGill University, a law clerk to the Honourable Justice Ian C. Binnie of the Supreme Court of Canada, a Visiting Researcher at the European Academy of Legal Theory, a Visiting Professor at McGill University, and a Schell Fellow at Yale Law School.
** Armand de Mestral, C.M., A.B. (Harvard), BCL, (McGill), LLM. (Harvard), Emeritus Professor, Jean Monnet Professor of Law, McGill University.
The authors wish to express their thanks to Robin Morgan, LL.B, BCL. (McGill), LL.M. candidate Harvard Law School for his invaluable assistance in preparing this manuscript.

treaty implementation in the Canadian federation. The twin issues with respect to implementation deal with the division of powers' impact on implementation, and when legislative implementation will actually be necessary.

2. ENTERING INTO TREATIES

A. Background and the Current *Modus Vivendi* of Federal-Provincial Collaboration

Due to Canada's unique history, there is no explicit treaty-making provision to be found in the *Constitution Act, 1867*.[1] At the time of Canadian Confederation in 1867, the Fathers of Confederation, as well as the British Parliament, did not expect that Canada or the provinces would engage in international relations independently from London's Foreign Office.[2] Interestingly, almost 30 years later when the Australian Constitution was enacted it included, under s. 51(xxix), a provision giving the Parliament of Australia the power to legislate with respect to external affairs.[3] Nevertheless, throughout the course of subsequent Canadian history, despite several efforts, it has proven politically impossible to agree on the addition of language governing the conduct of foreign relations or treaty-making and implementation.[4] These matters are now largely governed by the law of Crown prerogatives and constitutional conventions and practices.

The one exception to the general lack of treaty-related provisions in the *Constitution Act, 1867* is s. 132. S. 132 does not deal with treaty-making but rather with the implementation of treaties entered into by the British Empire, and it reads:

> The Parliament and Government of Canada shall have all Powers necessary or proper for performing the Obligations of Canada or of any Province thereof, as Part of the British Empire, towards Foreign Countries, arising under Treaties between the Empire and such Foreign Countries.[5]

Although this provision only applies to implementation, it has also been restrictively interpreted to only applying to treaties entered into by the British Empire. Thus, it is simply a relic of Imperial times.[6]

---

[1] See Peter Hogg, *Constitutional Law of* Canada (loose-leaf 5th ed Carswell 2007) 11–12; *Constitution Act, 1982*, ss 91–92, being Schedule B to the *Canada Act 1982* (UK), 1982 c 11; Hugo Cyr, *Canadian Federalism and Treaty Powers* (P.I.E Peter Lang SA, 2009).

[2] Cyr, above (n 1), 35.

[3] *Commonwealth of Australia Constitution Act 1900* Chapter 12.

[4] This was seen in the two failed attempts to amend the Canadian Constitution, namely, the *Charlottetown Accord* and the *Lake Meech Accord*. For details see Hogg above (n 1) at ch 4.

[5] *Constitution Act, 1867* s 132.

[6] *AG Canada v AG Ontario (Labour Conventions)* [1937] AC 326.

There are four distinct steps in the Canadian treaty process: negotiation, signing, ratification, and implementation. In the first stage—negotiation—the federal government has adopted an official position that it will not enter into treaties dealing with matters falling under provincial jurisdiction without prior consultation with the provinces.[7] However, this does not mean that the federal government consults the provinces in all matters which may relate to provincial jurisdiction. For example, the provinces were not consulted when the federal government ratified the *Kyoto Protocol*.[8] Conversely, two areas where the federal government has extensively sought consultation are trade agreements and human rights instruments. Especially noteworthy is the creation of an information-sharing forum for stakeholders (including federal, provincial, and others) in relation to trade,[9] and a Continuing Committee of Officials on Human Rights for federal consultations with provincial entities on human rights-related issues.[10]

Moreover many Canadian delegations sent to negotiate treaties on behalf of Canada include provincial participation. For example, despite the federal government not having consulted the provinces prior to ratifying the *Kyoto Protocol*, several provincial representatives (including Alberta's Energy Minister) formed part of the Canadian delegation to Kyoto.[11] Likewise, Canada's delegation to the Third United Nations Conference on the Law of the Sea saw extensive federal consultation with the provinces, industry (especially fishing and mining industries), and trade unions.[12] The actual delegation to the conference included representation of diverse interests and skills that included provincial, trade, and industry representation, and at one point the Canadian delegation was the third largest in the conference.[13] The support across industries, governments, and unions enjoyed by the delegation to the conference was perhaps exceptional. However, both the *Kyoto Protocol* and the Conference on the Law of the Sea are examples of a dominant trend where the federal government allows for provincial participation in Canadian delegations where the subject matter involves matters within provincial jurisdiction.[14] Provincial participation in major diplomatic negotiations varies extensively, but the inclusion of provincial representatives (and other stakeholders) in a Canadian delegation has been an exclusively political decision with no real formal or legal basis.[15] Thus,

---

[7] Edward G Lee, "Canadian Practice in International Law at the Department of External Affairs" [1986] Can YB Int'l Law 386, 397.

[8] Cyr above (n 1) 212–213.

[9] See Christopher Kukucha, *The Provinces and Canadian Foreign Trade Policy* (UBC Press 2008) 53–58.

[10] See for example Canada, Final Report of the Standing Senate Committee on Human Rights, *Children: The Silenced Citizens* (April 2007) xi–xii.

[11] Bruce Wallace and Danylo Hawaleshka, "Inside the Kyoto Deal" *Macleans* (22 Dec 1997) http://www.thecanadianencyclopedia.ca/en/article/inside-the-kyoto-deal/ accessed 23 June 2016.

[12] Armand de Mestral and LHJ Legault, "Multilateral Negotiation—Canada and the Law of the Sea Conference" (1979–1980) 35 Int'l J 47, 51–52.

[13] Ibid 53.

[14] Armand de Mestral, "The Province and International Relations in Canada" in Jean-Francois Gaudreault-DesBiens and Fabien Gélinas, *The States and Moods of Federalism* (Éditions Yvon Blais, 2005) 309, 317–318.

[15] Ibid 318.

although there may be little formal law on treaty-making in Canada, there certainly seems to be significant pragmatism which allows for rich and complex Canadian foreign policy and further empowers the provinces to fulfill their own domestic missions.

Nevertheless, a constitutional convention—or, at least, an accepted practice—exists allowing the provinces to exercise some limited foreign representation. Québec has been the most active in maintaining representation abroad, though each province engages in some form of foreign relations.[16] Furthermore, it is common practice for the provinces to sign "administrative agreements" with foreign states to maintain relations and collaborate on a variety of issues.[17] For example, Ontario is a signatory of the *Great Lakes Charter (1985)*, and the *Great Lakes-Saint Lawrence River Basin Sustainable Water Resources Agreement*.[18] But while the federal government has accepted these administrative agreements, it has likewise long taken the view that the provinces are unable to enter into treaties.[19] The current *modus vivendi* is that the federal government tolerates—and even appears to promote—administrative agreements on matters within provincial jurisdiction between the provinces and foreign governments.

On the rare occasions when a province has dealt with a foreign state in ways Ottawa deemed inappropriate, the federal government threatened to cut diplomatic ties. One example comes from 1968, when Gabon's National Minister of Education officially invited his Québec counterpart to participate in the annual conference of education ministers of francophone countries.[20] The invitation was sent directly to Québec instead of going through Ottawa. Québec's then-education minister accepted, took part in the conference, and was treated with all the honours usually bestowed upon representatives of sovereign states, causing Canada to sever diplomatic ties with Gabon. As for treaties, the federal government has adopted the same approach. Although Canada has never challenged in court the validity of provincial administrative agreements, it has condemned the inclusion of an arbitration clause purporting to be governed by international law in an agreement between Québec and the Federal Republic of Germany.[21] Following Canada's objection, Germany quickly withdrew the clause.[22] The current *modus vivendi* thus appears to be that the provinces can exercise limited foreign relations—provided they do so with Ottawa's explicit, or tacit, consent.

---

[16] See Cyr above (n 1) 186–196.

[17] Ibid 186–196. See also de Mestral above (n 14) generally.

[18] *Great Lakes Charter*, (Council of Great Lakes Governors 1985); *Great Lakes-St Lawrence River Basin Sustainable Water Resources Agreement*, (Council of Great Lakes Governors 2005).

[19] See Paul Martin, *Federalism and International Relations* (Queen's Printer 1968); see also de Mestral above (n 14) [322–323].

[20] A summary of these events can be found in Prof. Jean-Herman Guay's historical project *Bilan du siècle: une base intégrée d'information sur le Québec* (Anonymous, "1968 Participation du Québec à la conférence de Libreville" in Jean-Herman Guay et al., *Bilan du siècle: une base intégrée d'information sur le Québec*, online: Université de Sherbrooke, Faculté des lettres et sciences humaines, Bilan du siècle http://bilan.usherbrooke.ca/bilan/pages/evenements/1934.html).

[21] De Mestral above (n 14) 323.

[22] Ibid 323.

B. Executive and Legislative Powers: Parliament and the Democratic Deficit

In Canada, the executive branch has extensive power during the treaty-making stage: according to the federal government, the signing and ratification stages are "wholly controlled by the executive."[23] This has led to criticisms that the treaty-making process in Canada suffers from a profound democratic deficit.[24] Indeed, unlike the Westminster tradition, there is no requirement that the Executive consult the legislature prior or after entering a treaty.[25] Despite these criticisms and calls for reform, it is well recognized that the executive branch exercises exclusive treaty-making power.

The legislature has little say in the treaty-making process until implementation. There is simply no Canadian equivalent to Article II, section 2 of the United States Constitution granting a "power, by and with the consent of the Senate, to make treaties, provided two-thirds of the Senators present concur."[26] This has heavily restricted Parliament's role in the treaty-making process, although prior to the Pierre Elliott Trudeau years, the federal government would often submit major treaties for parliamentary scrutiny.[27] One famous example of this is the *General Agreement on Tariffs and Trade (GATT)*, which entered into force in Canada in 1948.[28] At the time, it was customary for the Executive to seek parliamentary approval for important multi-lateral instruments.[29]

Beginning in 1968 with P.E. Trudeau's election, the government ceased submitting treaties for Parliamentary approval.[30] The fact that his terms coincided with a fierce battle between Québec and the federal government over provincial capacity to engage in international relations likely contributed to his Cabinet asserting treaty-making as the exclusive function of the federal executive.[31] Indeed, prior to his becoming Prime Minister, tensions ran high following provincial Education Minister Paul Gérin-Lajoie's statement that Québec had the desire and capacity to be an international actor.[32] Although Québec's international aspirations likely influenced P.E. Trudeau's stance on executive power over treaty-making, such speculation is ultimately immaterial. Suffice

---

[23] Laura Barnett, "Canada's Approach to the Treaty-Making Process" (Parliament Background Paper, 6 November 2012) http://www.lop.parl.gc.ca/content/lop/researchpublications/2008-45-e.htm accessed 02/06/2016.

[24] Armand de Mestral and Evan Fox-Decent, "Implementation and Reception: The Congeniality of Canada's Legal Order to International Law" in Oonagh Fitzgerald (ed), *The Globalized Rule of Law* (Irwin Law, 2006) 31.

[25] Ibid 56.

[26] Art II US Constitution.

[27] De Mestral and Fox-Decent above (n 24) 36–37.

[28] See Canada, House of Commons, *Debates,* 20th Leg, 4th Sess, (1948).

[29] De Mestral and Fox-Decent above (n 24) 36–37.

[30] Ibid.

[31] Ibid 36; Pierre Elliott Trudeau, *Memoirs* (first published in 1993, McClelland & Stewart, 1994).

[32] Québec, *Ministere des Relations internationales, Paul GL speech delivered at Montreal to the Consular Corps on April 12, 1965,* online: https://www.saic.gouv.qc.ca/documents/positions-historiques/positions-du-qc/part2/PaulGuerinLajoie1965_en.pdf, accessed 2 June 2016.

to say that during the P.E Trudeau years, the legislature had no role in the treaty-making process, as reflected in the official policy statements of Canada's Secretaries of State for Foreign Affairs.[33] This view has greatly influenced Canada's legal landscape, and is now the judicially-accepted position.[34]

Following the P.E. Trudeau years, parliamentary approval has been occasionally sought for controversial treaties. It would appear that although there is no legal requirement for legislative approval of treaties, the federal government has accepted that parliamentary approval can add democratic legitimacy to the treaty-making process. An example of this recognition was the *Kyoto Protocol*, signed in 1997.[35] Prior to ratification in 2002 the *Protocol* was submitted to and approved by Parliament.[36] Despite ratification in 2002,[37] and federal implementation through the *Kyoto Protocol Implementation Act* in 2007,[38] the federal government exercised its executive power to withdraw from the treaty in 2011.[39] This unilateral withdrawal was contested in *Turp v Canada*, where the Federal Court had to determine whether parliamentary implementation and approval meant that the Executive's treaty-making powers were somehow transferred, in whole or in part, to Parliament. [40] Justice Noël rejected this argument, stating that "it is up to Parliament to pass a law that would force the House of Commons to be consulted before a treaty is ratified or withdrawn from."[41] As this was not done, he continued, the power to conclude and withdraw from treaties remained with the executive branch of government—thus, he recognized the Executive's exclusive treaty-making jurisdiction.[42]

(i) Moving Forward: The 2008 Treaty Policy

However, in recent years the Executive has recognized the need for more parliamentary input in the treaty-making process. In 2008, then-Prime Minister Stephen Harper announced a new policy to enhance parliamentary involvement in the treaty process by requiring that all treaties be tabled in the House of Commons before ratification.[43] This policy grants the House the ability to debate and recommend action pursuant to the treaty, but no real power was transferred and the policy remains "courtesy on the part of the executive, which retains full authority to decide whether to ratify the treaty."[44] In short, the legislature still has no real treaty-making power.

[33] Martin above (n 19).
[34] See *Turp v Canada* 2012 1 FCR 439.
[35] *Kyoto Protocol to the United Nations Framework Convention on Climate Change*, 11 December 1997, UN Doc FCCC/CP/1997/L7/Add.1, 37 ILM 22 [hereinafter *Kyoto Protocol*].
[36] See the debates: Canada, *Hansard* 37th Leg, 2nd Sess, (2 December 2002).
[37] See the *Kyoto Protocol Implementation Act*, SC 2007 c 30 [repealed 28 June 2012].
[38] *Kyoto Protocol Implementation Act* SC 2007 c 30, repealed 2012 c 19 s 699.
[39] Hogg above (n 1) [11-5].
[40] *Turp* above (n 34).
[41] Ibid 31.
[42] Ibid.
[43] Barnett above (n 23); Foreign Affairs and International Trade Canada, "Canada Announces Policy to Table International Treaties in House of Commons," News Release No 20, 25 January 2008.
[44] Barnett above (n 23).

The 2008 policy has certainly improved the democratic process in treaty-making, but does not go very far. According to Campbell McLachlan, out of all former British colonies, Canada has the least developed process for parliamentary involvement in treaty-making.[45] In effect, the 2008 policy imports the Ponsonby Rule into parliamentary procedure without making it law, meaning the policy has no real substance.[46] This was seen by executive ratification of the *Amendment to the Convention on Future Multilateral Cooperation in the Northwest Atlantic Fisheries* in 2009, despite Parliament having voted by way of resolution against ratification.[47] Thus, although the 2008 policy has definitely increased Parliament's role in the treaty-making process, it would seem that this role is largely symbolic.

C. The Division of Powers: Federal and Provincial Treaty-Making Powers

The federal government is the primary treaty-making authority. Although many would suggest that it is the only treaty-making authority in Canada, in this chapter we argue that Canadian provinces also have some limited capacity to enter into treaties. Both topics shall now be addressed.

(i) Federal Powers

It is well established that the federal government has treaty-making powers. But although many, such as Bora Laskin,[48] Peter Hogg,[49] and Stephane Beaulac[50] have claimed that this power is plenary, it is impossible to identify a constitutional source to support this claim. Because the *Constitution Act, 1867* is silent on the matter, proponents of the exclusive federal power cite the *Letters Patent* 1947 as the source of plenary

---

[45] Campbell McLachlan, *Foreign Relations Law* (Cambridge University Press, 2014) 172.

[46] Ibid.

[47] Ibid; Canada, *Eighth Report of the Standing Committee on Fisheries and Oceans*, Vote No 158 40th Parliament, 2nd Session, Sitting No 128 (1 December 2009).

[48] Bora Laskin, "The Provinces and International Agreements" in Ontario, Ontario Advisory Committee on Confederation, *Background Papers and Reports*, Vol. 1 (Queen's Printer 1967). Bora Laskin argued that treaty-making was necessarily associated with sovereignty. However, since the time when Laskin wrote this article, it is now well-known that this is certainly not the case (see Cyr above (n 1) 150).

[49] Hogg above (n 1) at ch 11. Of the three authors cited here Hogg is the most blunt in his proposition about the *Letters Patent*, stating that the source is necessarily and entirely the *Letters Patent*. He then goes on to echo Bora Laskin's arguments concerning sovereignty.

[50] Stephane Beaulac, "The Myth of *Jus Tractatus* in *La Belle Province*" [2012] 35 Dalhousie LJ 237; Cyr above (n 1) 196–199. Beaulac's position is not quite that the *Letters Patent* were the transfer, but rather that they officialised the transfer of plenary powers to the federal government. However, he does claim that it is the *de jure* confirmation of the *de facto* plenary treaty-making powers, and thus does in fact argue that the legal source of the transfer is the *Letters Patent*.

federal treaty-making power.[51] The *Letters Patent* certainly reveal a formal transfer of treaty-making powers possessed by the British Crown in 1947 to the Governor General of Canada, but it is wrong to suggest that the *Letters Patent* are the source of all treaty-making powers.[52] Indeed, if the *Letters Patent* were the only source of the federal treaty-making power, then Canada would not have been able to enter into treaties prior to 1947, including the *Charter of the United Nations*.[53] As the validity of Canada's adherence to these treaties is not in doubt, the federal treaty-making power must have some other source.

Although the *Letters Patent* transferred King George VI's remaining treaty-making powers to the Governor General, the scope of his remaining powers in 1947 is difficult to ascertain. To be sure, the *Letters Patent* were far from purely declaratory, and the King certainly transferred the ability to enter into "Head of State" treaties, such as peace treaties, to the Governor General.[54] However, the federal government had already entered into treaties of its own accord, meaning that Canadian treaty-making powers over now-dominant "intergovernmental treaties" pre-existed the *Letters Patent*. Some of these inter-governmental treaties included Canadian-ratified ILO Conventions that formed the basis for the *Labour Conventions Reference*.[55] In the *Labour Conventions Reference*, the provinces challenged federal legislation which sought to implement several ILO conventions, and the dispute ultimately reached the Privy Council. There, Lord Atkin accepted the provinces' arguments that the federal government has no explicit implementation power, ruling that the "watertight compartments" of Canadian federalism cannot be trenched simply because the federal government had come to some agreement with foreign nations.[56] His conclusion was therefore that treaties were to be implemented in Canada according to the usual division of powers under sections 91 and 92 of the *Constitution Act, 1867*.

Although it is impossible to pinpoint the precise source of the treaty-making power in Canada, we do know that treaty-making forms part of the royal prerogative.[57] As a British Dominion, Canada inherited the same law governing prerogatives as existed in the United Kingdom. Importantly, royal prerogatives are understood as always having existed or having been lost by devolution, but as never being *acquired*.[58] Thus, what occurred in Canada was not the acquisition of royal prerogatives, but rather a devolution of the treaty-making power from the Imperial Crown as the latter was divided into the

---

[51] *Letters Patent Constituting the Office of the Governor General of Canada, 1947*, reproduced at R.S.C. 1985, Appendix II, No. 31 (Letters Patent). For proponents of the exclusive power see Laskin above (n 48), Hogg above (n 1), Beaulac above (n 50).

[52] Hogg above (n 1) 11-2;

[53] *Charter of the United* Nations, 26 June 1945, Can TS 1945 No 7.

[54] Cyr above (n 1) 107.

[55] See, for example, the *Weekly Rest in Industrial Undertakings Act* 1935, St. Can. (25 & 26 Geo. 5, c. 14).

[56] *Labour Conventions* above (n 6) 354.

[57] Beaulac above (n 50); Cyr above (n 1) 196–199.

[58] Albert V Dicey, *An Introduction to the Study of the Constitution* (10th ed Macmillan 1967) 424.

Canadian Crowns. Although many considered the Crown to be a single, indivisible crea-ture,[59] Confederation strained the idea of an indivisible Crown. Indeed, in Canada the Crown was a single entity, but, similarly to the Holy Trinity, split in three: the Imperial Crown in London, the Crown in right of Canada, and the Crown in right of each of the provinces.[60] Importantly, the Privy Council in *Liquidators of the Maritime Bank of Canada v New Brunswick* confirmed that each of these entities exercised royal pre-rogatives, and that their jurisdiction parallels that of the division of legislative powers.[61] Similarly, the Privy Council also recognized that each provincial "Lieutenant-Governor, when appointed, is as much the representative of Her Majesty for all purposes of pro-vincial government as the Governor-General himself is for all purposes of Dominion government."[62] Thus there can hardly be any doubt that in 1867 the "Crown" in Canada had three heads: one imperial, one federal, and one provincial.

At the time of Confederation only the Imperial Crown possessed treaty-making prerogatives.[63] Sometime between Canadian Confederation and the *Letters Patent*, these royal prerogatives began to be exercised by the Crown in right of Canada and the Crown in right of the provinces. Nobody seriously argues that the Crown in right of Canada, now assuming the exercise of certain prerogative powers formerly enjoyed by the Imperial Crown, does not enjoy some treaty-making power. The real issue is not whether the federal government can exercise treaty-making powers, but whether the provinces also enjoy some treaty-making capacities.

(ii) Provincial Powers: Background

A useful starting point is international law, specifically, the *Vienna Convention on the Law of Treaties*.[64] There is no provision in the *Vienna Convention* which expressly allows component states of Federations to enter into treaties.[65] Instead, the *Vienna Convention* leaves that question to domestic constitutional law. Many federated entities currently exercise treaty-making powers despite not exercising all of the attributes of statehood, and states that have authorized their constituent entities to enter into treaties include Germany,[66] Switzerland,[67] Belgium,[68] and Argentina.[69] However, the Canadian experi-ence has resulted in considerably more tension between the federal government and the provinces.

---

[59]   Cyr above (n 1) 109 and 293n.
[60]   Ibid. 109.
[61]   *Liquidators of the Maritime Bank of Canada v New Brunswick* [1892] AC 437.
[62]   Ibid 442.
[63]   See generally Cyr above (n 1) at ch 1.
[64]   *Vienna Convention*, (1969) 1155 UNTS 331.
[65]   De Mestral above (n 14).
[66]   See the *Grundgesetz fur die Bundesrepublik Deutschland* 2001, Art 32.3.
[67]   *Constitution fédérale de la Confédération Suisse du 18 avril 1999*, Art 56.
[68]   Texte coordonné de la Constitution du 17 février 1994 (Moniteur belge, 2nd ed. Feb. 17, 1994) updated 31 January 2014, art. 167.
[69]   *Constitutión Nacional de la República Argentina* 1994, Art 124(1).

It was not by coincidence that the province most actively arguing for the right to enter into treaties—Québec—did so during a period where it experienced a profound rise in nationalism often referred to as the "Quiet Revolution."[70] The Quiet Revolution was the explicit political fuel that resulted in the Gérin-Lajoie doctrine, which argued that Québec was a member of the Canadian federation but nonetheless capable of entering into treaties.[71] Other members of Québec society did not share Gérin-Lajoie's view that Québec was an integral part of Canada, which led to two unsuccessful sovereignty referendums in 1980 and 1995.[72] This, in turn, has led some to fear that recognizing provincial treaty-making powers would be a step towards an independent Québec. However, federalist governments in Québec since Gérin-Lajoie have all taken the opposite view: recognizing a certain provincial autonomy eases the desire for independences and thus reinforces the Canadian federation.[73]

Many Canadian authors argue that the federal government has exclusive treaty-making powers.[74] Apart from the *Letters Patent* argument examined above, some commentators have also argued that Lord Atkin, in the *Labour Conventions Reference*, ruled that the federal government has exclusive treaty-making power.[75] However, this position is rather curious as the Privy Council clearly distinguished between treaty implementation and treaty formation.[76] In fact, the Privy Council expressly refused to answer the argument that the federal government did not have exclusive treaty-making capacity:

> [It] will be seen that the Provincial contention 1.(b) *relates only to the formation of the treaty obligation* [...] as their Lordships have come to the conclusion that the reference can be decided upon the question of legislative competence alone [treaty implementation], in accordance with their usual practice in constitutional matters *they refrain from expressing any opinion upon the questions raised by the contention 1.(b)* [emphasis added].[77]

There is thus nothing in the *Labour Conventions Reference* to ground any plenary federal treaty-making power.

Although some have argued that the federal practice of acting as if it had plenary treaty-making powers might have evolved into a rule of law, this contradicts the Supreme Court of Canada's view expressed in the *Reference Re Québec Secession* about the so-called "principle of effectivity." The Court clearly rejected the idea that "a party

---

[70] Michael Gauvreau, *The Catholic Origins of Québec's Quiet Revolution 1931–1970* (McGill-Queen's Press, 2005).

[71] Paul Gérin-Lajoie speech, above (n 32).

[72] Lysiane Gagnon, *Chroniques référendaires: les leçons des référendums de 1980 et 1995* (Québec Amérique, 2015).

[73] Québec Liberal Party, *A Project for Québec: Affirmation, Autonomy and Leadership; Final Report of the Special Committee on the Political and Constitutional Future of Québec Society*, (Montreal 2001).

[74] Hogg above (n 1) at ch 11; Beaulac above (n 50); Laskin above (n 48).

[75] See Beaulac above (n 50).

[76] *Labour Conventions* above (n 6); Cyr above (n 1) 82–84.

[77] *Labour Conventions* above(n 6) 348–349.

may act without regard to the law, simply because it asserts the power to do so."[78] The alleged principle of effectivity was declared "contrary to the rule of law"[79] and thus rejected. Likewise, the same must be said about the argument according to which the federal plenary treaty-powers would be the result of a constitutional convention that would have developed over the years and that would have "crystalized" into law. Not only does this view not take into account the long-standing opposition of certain key actors that would negate the possibility of creating such a convention, it does not take into consideration the long analysis and clear rejection of the "crystallization of constitutional conventions into law" theory by the Supreme Court in the *Patriation Reference*.[80]

(iii) Provincial Powers: The Case for Jurisdiction over Treaty-Making

Although under the current *modus vivendi* the provinces do not enter into treaties with foreign states, there is nonetheless a case for provincial treaty-making capacity. According to this theory, provinces can enter into treaties on matters that fall under their jurisdiction under section 92 of the *Constitution Act, 1867*. Whether this capacity will ever be practicable is a question we do not seek to answer, but it does follow the normal assumption of the Constitution of Canada that executive powers mirror legislative powers, even if this does not seem in line with the current *modus vivendi*.

The argument for provincial treaty-making powers is premised on the fact that there was never a complete transfer of the treaty-making power from the Imperial Crown. As seen above, the commonly accepted view is that Canada's independence from the United Kingdom meant a "Canadianisation" of the Crown; the Crown continues to hold its prerogatives no longer in the name of the United Kingdom, but rather for Canada. The trouble is that seamless transformation of the Crown occurred in favour of a federation and not a unitary state. But Canadian constitutional law had long developed rules specifying how Crown prerogatives have to be divided between the Crown in right of Canada and the Crown in right of provinces. A long line of jurisprudence holds that royal prerogatives reflect the constitutional division of powers under sections 91 and 92.[81] Chief Justice Laskin stated in 1978 in *Alberta v Canadian Transport Commission*: "The Constitution of Canada distributes legislative power between a central Parliament and provincial Legislatures and prerogative or executive power (which is formally vested in the Queen) is similarly distributed to accord with the distribution of legislative power."[82]

---

[78] *Reference re Secession of Québec* [1998] 2 SCR 217 [107].

[79] Ibid [108].

[80] *Re: Resolution to amend the Constitution* [1981] 1 SCR 753, 774–784. Incidentally, the majority of the Supreme Court commented (p. 779): "There is nothing in the other judgments delivered in the *Labour Conventions* case, either in the Supreme Court or in the Privy Council that takes the matter there beyond its international law setting or lends credence to the crystallization proposition urged by counsel for the Attorney General of Manitoba."

[81] Examples include *Liquidators of the Maritime Bank of Canada* [1892] A.C. 437; *Bonanza Creek Gold Mining Co v Regem* [1916] 1 AC 566; *Alberta v Canadian Transport Commission* [1978] 1 SCR 61, 71; see also Cyr above (n 1) 111–112.

[82] *Alberta v Canadian Transport Commission*, above (n 80) 71.

Thus it is possible to argue that as there was a devolution of royal prerogatives, and as royal prerogatives are distributed according to the division of legislative power, then it follows that the treaty-making prerogative was distributed according to sections 91 and 92.

Treaty-making, like language, is not a distinct matter under sections 91 or 92 of the *Constitution Act, 1867* but is rather "ancillary" to the exercise of jurisdiction with respect to some class of subject matter assigned to Parliament or legislatures. For example, in *Devine v Québec*, the Supreme Court confirmed that statutes broaching language rights will be classified for constitutional purposes as laws in relation to the sections 91 or 92 powers which they affect, such as employment.[83] The same reasoning applies to treaty-making, especially as the Privy Council in the *Labour Conventions* case stated that "[f]or the purposes of sections 91 and 92, i.e., the distribution of legislative powers between the Dominion and the Provinces, there is no such thing as treaty legislation as such."[84] Thus, as the federal government does not exercise plenary treaty-making powers, and as it is impossible to pinpoint an explicit transfer of treaty-making power to the federal government, it naturally follows that the provinces possess some treaty-making capacity.

3. TREATY IMPLEMENTATION IN THE CANADIAN FEDERATION

In Canada, following the dualist tradition inherited from the United Kingdom, "performance of [the state's] obligations, if they entail alteration of the existing domestic law, requires legislative action."[85] However, the executive branch can fulfil treaty obligations of the state in such matters as national defence and diplomatic relations without legislative action if fulfilling its obligations does not require a modification of domestic law.[86] All this flows from Canadian constitutional traditions and is explained particularly by the principle that the Executive cannot make the law. Unlike the United States[87] or France[88], the legislature seldom has a role in treaty ratification. The situation is however quite different when it comes to treaty implementation. Here, as explained by the Privy Council in the *Labour Conventions Reference,*[89] and more recently by Justices

---

[83] *Devine v Québec (Attorney General)* [1988] 2 SCR 790; Hogg above (n 1) 56-3.

[84] *Labour Conventions* above (n 6) 351.

[85] Ibid 347.

[86] Francis Rigaldies and Jose Woehrling, "Le juge interne canadien et le droit international" (1980) 21 C. de D. 293, 314 reported that around 1980, 296 treaties ratified by Canada did not require any legislative action for their implementation. For a list of treaties falling within the exclusive jurisdiction of the executive branch, see *Francis v R.*, [1956] S.C.R. 618 at 625ff.

[87] See John Norton Moore, *The National Law of Treaty Implementation* (Carolina Academic Press, 2001).

[88] See Monroe Leigh and Merritt R. Blakeslee, *National Treaty Law and Practice: France, Germany, India, Switzerland, Thailand, and the United Kingdom* (American Society of International Law, 1995).

[89] *Labour Conventions* above (n 6) 348.

L'Heureux-Dubé and McLachlin (as she then was) in *Thomson v Thomson*,[90] the normal division of powers governs the implementation of all treaties, and any action taken to enforce a treaty must be justified by law.

A. Treaty Implementation Requiring Changes to Domestic Law

The leading case on the matter is the *Labour Conventions Reference*, where the federal government invoked section 132 of the *Constitution Act, 1867* to argue that it had a general power to implement treaties. Reproduced above, it confers upon Parliament the authority to implement all treaties signed between the British Empire and foreign nations on behalf of Canada.[91] However, this section was interpreted restrictively by the Privy Council, and no expansion of this power by analogy has ever been accepted subsequently by the courts. In the 1937 *Labour Conventions Reference*, Lord Atkin wrote that treaties signed by Canada as an independent international person do not fall under section 132.[92] Instead, he decisively ruled that treaties must be implemented according to the head of power under which their subject matter falls.[93] For example, the *ILO Conventions* subject to the reference had to be implemented by the provinces because labour relations fell mainly under provincial jurisdiction over property and civil rights under section 92(13).[94] Despite academic criticism,[95] judicial *obiter*,[96] and *ex cathedra* statements[97] that the *Labour Conventions Reference* may require revisiting, it remains good law. Indeed, this is true as it protects Canadian federalism from the risk of gutting provincial powers in an era where most domestic issues may be subject to international agreements. This means that section 132 has become nothing more than a historic relic of Canada's Imperial legacy.[98]

---

[90] *Thomson* [1994] 3 SCR 551, 612. The opinion of the judges is otherwise rather confused, claiming erroneously, at 610, that the power of the Canadian government to *make* treaties flows from section 132 of the *Constitution Act, 1867*, a provision that, as we have seen earlier, clearly only refers to the *implementation* of *Imperial* treaties.

[91] See above "Background and the Current *Modus Vivendi*" at n 5 and accompanying text.

[92] *Labour Conventions* above (n 6).

[93] Ibid.

[94] *Constitution Act, 1867*.

[95] Hogg above (n 1) at ch 11; FR Scott, "Labour Conventions Case" (1956) 34 Can Bar Rev 114; Torsten Strom and Peter Finkle, "Treaty Implementation: The Canadian Game Needs Australian Rules" (1993) 25 Ottawa LR 39.

[96] *Francis v Canada*, [1956] SCR 618; *Macdonald v Vapor Canada Ltd.* [1977] 2 SCR 134.

[97] Lord Wright, "Rt. Hon. Sir Lyman Poore Duff" (1955) 33 Can Bar Rev 1123; Ivan Rand, "Some Aspects of Canadian Constitutionalism" (1960) 38 Can Bar Rev 135.

[98] A few acts of Parliament enacted under s. 132, such as the *Boundary Waters Act* RSC 1985 c I-17 made pursuant to the *Treaty Relating to Boundary Waters and Questions Arising with Canada*, United States and United Kingdom, 11 Jan 1901, 36 US Stat 2448 are still in force.

Several notable judicial pronouncements have been made since the *Labour Conventions Reference*. First, in *Francis v the Queen*, the Supreme Court of Canada was asked whether a person deemed an "Indian" under the *Indian Act* could rely on the *Treaty of Amity, Commerce, and Navigation* to avoid paying duties on goods he imported from the United States under the *Customs Act*.[99] As the treaty was never implemented by legislation, the question was whether implementation was required. The Court ruled that implementation was indeed necessary, but Justice Rand, in his concurring opinion, also reflected on the current state of the law with respect to treaties:

> [Treaty] implementation may call for both legislative and judicial action. Speaking generally, provisions that give recognition to incidents of sovereignty or deal with matters in exclusively sovereign aspects, do not require legislative confirmation: for example, the recognition of independence, the establishment of boundaries and, in a treaty of peace, the transfer of sovereignty over property, are deemed executed and the treaty becomes the muniment or evidence of the political or proprietary title.[100]

Second, Chief Justice Laskin in *Vapor Canada* suggested that an explicit statement incorporated into a federal law to the effect that the purpose of the law was to implement a treaty could be seen as the exercise of the general power under section 91 and thereby provide constitutional justification for Parliament to implement the treaty.[101] It is not clear whether he intended this statement to apply to treaties covering matters under provincial jurisdiction.[102] In any case, this position has not been subsequently endorsed by the courts.

B. Treaty Implementation: Canadian Practice

Implementation in Canada may take different forms. In very rare cases, it may involve giving the treaty text itself the force of law or giving "direct effect" to the treaty, but in most cases involves legislation translating the treaty into law or various forms of subordinate legislation, executive, or even judicial action. Thus, treaty implementation is effected in Canada by many different means. These include the application of a rule of the common law, executive action under the prerogative, or legislation by Parliament or the provincial legislatures. In fact, implementation is accomplished by at least 13 different approaches in current Canadian practice.[103]

The first form of implementation is textual incorporation, in whole or in part, of a treaty. This makes the text of the treaty itself part of Canadian law, and is often used in relation to definitions found in treaties.[104] The second form of implementation is

---

[99] *Francis* above (n 96).
[100] Ibid (per Justice Rand) 625.
[101] *Vapor Canada* above (n 96); see also *Capital Cities Communications v CRTC* [1978] 2 SCR 141, 171–177.
[102] Ibid.
[103] De Mestral and Fox-Decent (n 24) 45–46.
[104] Ibid 46–47. For an example see the *Tax Conventions Implementation Act* SC 2005 c 8.

attaching the text of the treaty as a schedule to legislation, which typically gives effect only to certain articles of a treaty. An example is the incorporation of Article 1Fc of the *Refugee Convention* into the *Immigration and Refugee Protection Act*.[105] Third, there may be specific implementation by reference to particular treaty provisions.[106] The fourth form is the transposition of the treaty into Canadian statutory language. This is the most popular approach, most likely since it allows for the transposition of treaties into Canadian legal language, thus ensuring consistency among related statutes.[107] Fifth, some acts include statements of intention to implement a treaty. Unfortunately, it would seem that these types of statements are treated by courts as merely declaratory, and will not be given direct effect.[108] The sixth type relates to statements of intention to approve treaties, which occurs rarely due to the Executive's power over ratification.[109] Thus, this is also seen as purely declaratory.

The seventh way of implementing treaties is by adopting legislative or judicial instructions for interpretation that give priority to a treaty. This method requires that laws be interpreted consistently with the treaty in question.[110] Similarly, the eighth form of implementation involves adopting legislative provisions which provide for the adoption of implementing measures by regulations or decisions by the Governor-in-Council, a minister, or an independent tribunal. However, it does not seem that the failure to respect the treaty's terms has ever successfully been invoked vis-à-vis this method of implementation.[111] Ninth, the government sometimes adopts regulations with the purpose of implementing a treaty, and regulatory agencies whose authority is broad enough may adopt regulations implementing treaties.[112] The tenth form is by reliance upon a rule or provision of the Constitution. Indeed, since *Slaight Communications v Davidson* in 1989, the law is clear that the Canadian *Charter* is presumed to be as generous as the international human rights treaty obligations that Canada has undertaken to protect.[113]

The eleventh form of implementation is reliance upon pre-existing federal or provincial legislation or rules of the common law. Although this was a more controversial argument several decades ago, since then the Supreme Court has repeatedly stated that "where possible statutes should be interpreted in a way that makes their provisions consistent with Canada's international treaty obligations,"[114] and that "it is presumed that the legislature acts in compliance with Canada's obligations as a signatory of international

---

[105] See the *Immigration and Refugee Protection Act* SC 2001 c 27. See also *Pushpanathan v Canada* [1998] 1 SCR 982.

[106] See *An Act to Amend the Patent Act and the Food and Drugs Act* SC 2004 C 23 s 21.02.

[107] De Mestral and Fox-Decent above (n 24) 48–49.

[108] Ibid 49–50.

[109] Ibid 50–51.

[110] Ibid 50–51. See also the *North American Free Trade Agreement Implementation Act* SC 1993 c 44 s 21.

[111] De Mestral and Fox-Decent above (n 24) 52. For an example see the *Chemical Weapons Convention Implementation Act* SC 1995 c 25.

[112] De Mestral and Fox-Decent above (n 24) 52–53.

[113] *Slaight Communications v Davidson* [1989] 1 SCR 1038. See also *Health Services and Support— Facilities Subsector Bargaining Assn. v British Columbia* 2007 SCC 27 at [70], [79].

[114] *Németh v Canada* 2010 SCC 56, [34].

treaties and as a member of the international community."[115] However, a treaty will only have domestic legal effect if it does not contradict express statutory language. As held in *Németh v Canada*, the presumption that domestic law reflects international treaty obligations or customary international law is a rebuttable one, and unambiguous legislation which contradicts a treaty will be given legal effect.[116] Similarly, the twelfth form of implementation involves implementation through the common law including the royal prerogative.[117] Finally, the thirteenth form is reliance upon the intention of the treaty as self-executing or non-self-executing to determine its effects on the domestic legal system.[118] Since under current law it is understood that statutes should, where possible, be interpreted in conformity with Canada's international obligations, it is important to identify which treaties are actually self-executing. Some treaties aim to have direct effect, and thus should be used in statutory interpretation once they are ratified. Others do not, and require governmental discretionary action.

The leading decision with respect to the interpretation of treaties under Canadian law is *National Corn Growers Association v Canada (Import Tribunal)*.[119] In *National Corn Growers* the Canadian Import Tribunal conducted an investigation into whether subsidies paid to American producers substantially lowered Canadian corn prices, causing material injury to the domestic industry pursuant to section 42 of the *Special Import Measures Act*.[120] In deciding whether injury occurred, the Tribunal interpreted section 42 in light of the *GATT*. This approach was contested both before the Federal Court of Appeal[121] and before the Supreme Court. Justice Gonthier, writing for the majority, made several important statements about the law. First, he stated that "in circumstances where the domestic legislation is unclear it is reasonable to examine any underlying international agreement."[122] Second, he wrote that "[i]n interpreting legislation which has been enacted with a view towards implementing international obligations, as is the case here, it is reasonable for a tribunal to examine the domestic law in the context of the relevant agreement to clarify any uncertainty."[123] Finally, and most importantly, he rejected the idea that recourse to a treaty may only be made where domestic legislation is ambiguous:

> It is reasonable to make reference to an international agreement at the very outset of the inquiry to determine if there is any ambiguity, even latent, in the domestic legislation. The Court of Appeal's suggestion that recourse to an international treaty is only available where the provision of the domestic legislation is ambiguous on its face is to be rejected.[124]

---

[115] *R v Hape* 2007 SCC 26, [53].
[116] *Németh* above (n 114) 35.
[117] De Mestral and Fox-Decent above (n 24) 55.
[118] Ibid 56.
[119] *National Corn Growers Association v Canada (Import Tribunal)* [1990] 2 SCR 1324.
[120] *Special Import Measures Act* RSC 1985 c S-15.
[121] *National Corn Growers Association v Canada (Import Tribunal)* [1989] FCJ No 1159.
[122] *National Corn Growers Association* above (n 119) (Gonthier J).
[123] Ibid.
[124] Ibid.

A more recent, widely-cited but somewhat confusing decision is *Baker v Canada (Minister of Citizenship and Immigration)*.[125] In *Baker* the appellant contested her deportation under the *Immigration Act*, which would have resulted in the fact that she would have had to leave her Canadian-born children behind, and invoked the *International Convention on the Rights of the Child*, a treaty which was ratified by Canada after years of review by the federal and provincial governments but which, according to Justice L'Heureux-Dubé, was not yet implemented.[126] Justice L'Heureux-Dubé, writing for a majority of the Supreme Court of Canada, emphatically stated that "[i]nternational treaties and conventions are not part of Canadian law unless they have been implemented by statute."[127] However, she continued by writing that "[n]evertheless, the values reflected in international human rights law may help inform the contextual approach to statutory interpretation and judicial review," and in doing so interpreted the *Immigration Act* consistently with Canada's obligations under the *Convention*.[128] Although the principle enunciated by Justice L'Heureux-Dubé concerning the utility of interpreting Canadian law in the light of treaty obligations is a sound approach, her assumption that treaties must be implemented by specific statute and that the *Convention* was an "unimplemented" treaty have led to considerable confusion. The *Convention* had arguably been implemented by the common law and a host of federal and provincial enactments already in force at the time of ratification, as well as judicial pronouncements, and it is by no means clear that further legislative action was needed to ensure that Canadian domestic law conformed to the provisions of the treaty.

Furthermore, treaties are now regularly cited to support judicial pronouncements. The Supreme Court of Canada recently invoked international law to great effect in *Saskatchewan Federation of Labour v Saskatchewan* to reverse the long-standing position that the freedom of association under section 2(d) of the *Charter* does not protect the right to strike.[129] In this decision the Court came to its conclusion citing, among other things, ILO instruments and other labour-related conventions to which Canada is a party.[130] Similarly, the Court has also been adamant in interpreting *Charter* rights consistently with Canada's international human rights obligations. Justice LeBel and Chief Justice McLachlin said as much in *Health Services and Support—Facilities Subsector Bargaining Association v British Columbia*: "the *Charter* should be presumed to provide at least as great a level of protection as is found in the international rights documents that Canada has ratified."[131] According to Justice LeBel and Chief Justice McLachlin, it is ratification, not implementation, which lends legal authority to international human rights documents. Furthermore, this authority appears to be binding rather than merely

---

[125] [1999] 2 SCR 817.
[126] *Immigration Act* (IRPA); *Convention on the Rights of the Child*, UNGA, Treaty Series vol 1577 p 3.
[127] *Baker* above (n 125) [69].
[128] Ibid [70].
[129] *Saskatchewan Federation of Labour v Saskatchewan* 2015 SCC 4.
[130] Ibid [67–75].
[131] *BC Health Services* above (n 113) 70.

persuasive: they place a presumption in favour of the treaty which can only be displaced pursuant to clear statutory language. Indeed, this presumption was turned into an injunction to the Courts: "in interpreting the scope of application of the *Charter*, the courts should seek to ensure compliance with Canada's binding obligations under international law where the express words are capable of supporting such a construction."[132]

Finally, it may be argued that not having legislative implementation as the only means of implementation undermines Canadian democracy. Considering that Parliament only exercises power over treaties at the implementation phase, eliminating pure legislative implementation as a requirement for treaties to have force of law in Canada in some instances seemingly places all power at the hands of the Executive.[133] Although this argument may have been persuasive several decades ago, its persuasive force is largely non-existent today. The reason for this is that ratified treaties will only influence Canadian law if they do not contradict express statutory language or established rules of the common law. Following the 2008 Policy, there is no reason a diligent Parliament would be caught unaware by a treaty. Thus, although Parliament may have less of a formal role in the treaty-making process, it could always pre-empt the Executive, thereby eliminating the democratic deficit. Arguably, what is still required in Canada is the granting of a more explicit role to Parliament in the oversight of treaty negotiations and the formal approval of a treaty. This is even truer of the need to formalise provincial executive and parliamentary involvement in federal treaty-making dealing with provincial matters in order to ensure that such treaties are implemented effectively and without any democratic deficit.

4. Conclusion

The constitutional nuances that drive treaty-making and implementation within Canada are far from simple. First, it was seen that the Executive possesses all treaty-making power within Canada. Second, the much more controversial issue of provincial powers over treaty-making was addressed, and we conclude that the provinces could, in fact, exercise limited treaty-making capacity despite focusing on the use of administrative agreements in the face of staunch opposition from Ottawa to recognize a full *jus tractus* to the provinces.

Treaty implementation benefits greatly from the existence of many more judicial pronouncements on the matter when compared to treaty-making. First, as has been seen, there are at least 13 different forms of implementation in Canada. Unlike Justice L'Heureux-Dubé's view in *Baker*, a treaty does not necessarily need to be implemented by statute to have effect under Canadian law. This has become increasingly apparent

---

[132] *Hape* above (n 115) 56.
[133] See above under "legislative powers."

from the Supreme Court of Canada's judgments rendered after *Baker*, and it shows the richness of treaty law with respect to implementation in Canada. Second comes the question of which jurisdiction can properly implement treaties. The leading case on the matter is the *Labour Conventions Reference*, which still remains good law, and holds that implementation is to be done according to the division of powers—federal or provincial.

Chief Justice Laskin came very close to overturning the *Labour Conventions* case in *Vapor Canada*, but ultimately stated that "although the foregoing references would support a reconsideration of the *Labour Conventions* case, I find it unnecessary to do that here."[134] Chief Justice Laskin was a devoted centralist, and one of the staunchest advocates of increased authority for the federal government.[135] During his early career as an academic, he was a particularly outspoken critic of the Privy Council's restriction of the general power under s. 91.[136] Some have pointed to his struggles as a young man from an immigrant family during the depression of the 1930s, where the provinces had insufficient funds to provide adequate social and economic benefits, being the source of his views about the necessity of a strong federal government.[137] *Tempora mutantur et nos mutamur in illis*, but subsequent courts have not seen fit to take up Chief Justice Laskin's lead, and there seems to be no likelihood that this will happen. This is particularly true in light of the drastic changes it would bring to the federal equilibrium between Ottawa and the provinces in an era where domestic matters are increasingly subject to international agreements.[138]

BIBLIOGRAPHY

Books

Bernier, Ivan, *International Legal Aspects of Federalism*. London: Longman, 1973.

Brossard, Jacques, Patry, André and Weiser, Elisabeth, eds., *Les pouvoirs extérieurs du Québec*, Montréal: Presses Universitaires de l'Université de Montréal, 1967.

Cyr, Hugo. *Canadian Federalism and Treaty Powers*. Brussels: P.I.E Peter Lang SA, 2009.

Gotlieb, Allan E. *Canadian Treaty Making*. Toronto: Butterworths, 1968.

Jacomy-Millette, Anne-Marie. *Treaty Law in Canada*. Ottawa: University of Ottawa Press, 1975.

Martin, Paul. *Federalism and International Relations*. Ottawa: Queen's Printer, 1968.

Morissette, France. *Les procédures canadienne et communautaire de conclusion des traités. Démocratie, équilibre institutionnel et principe fédéral: leçons à tirer de la Communauté européenne*. Montréal: Wilson & Lafleur, 2008.

---

[134]   *Vapor Canada* above (n 96) 169.
[135]   The Constitutional Law Group, *Canadian Constitutional* (Emond Montgommery, 2012) 295.
[136]   Ibid.
[137]   Ibid 296.
[138]   On the major constitutional difficulties that would arise in the different parts of the Canadian Constitution from a judicial reversal of the *Labour Conventions*, see Cyr above (n 1), at ch. III.

Sharp, Mitchell William. *Federalism and International Conferences on Education: A Supplement to Federalism and International Relations*. Ottawa: Queen's Printer, 1968.

Van Ert, Gib. *Using International Law in Canadian Courts*. Toronto: Irwin Law, 2008.

Articles and Chapters in Books

Atkey, Ronald G. "The Role of the Provinces in International Affairs." 26 International Journal (1970), 249.

Beaulac, Stephane. "The Myth of *Jus Tractatus* in *La Belle Province*." Dalhousie Law Journal 35 (2012), 237.

Cyr, Hugo. "Les souverainistes canadiens et québécois et la conclusion des traités internationaux: ce qu'en dit le droit international public." Revue québécoise de droit constitutionnel 3 (2010).

De Mestral, Armand. "Le Québec et les relations internationales." In Québec—Communauté française de Belgique edited by Pierre Patenaude. Montréal: Wilson & Lafleur, 1991, 209.

De Mestral, Armand and Fox-Decent, Evan. "Rethinking the Relationship between International and Domestic Law." McGill Law Journal 53 (2008), 573.

De Mestral, Armand. "The Province and International Relations in Canada." In *The States and Moods of Federalism* edited by Jean-Francois Gaudreault-DesBiens and Fabien Gélinas, 309. Montreal: Éditions Yvon Blais, 2005.

De Mestral, Armand & Fox-Decent, Evan. "Implementation and Reception: The Congeniality of Canada's Legal Order to International Law." In *The Globalized Rule of Law* edited by Oonagh Fitzgerald, 31. Toronto: Irwin Law, 2006.

Giroux, Lorne. "La capacité internationale des provinces en droit constitutionnel canadien." Cahiers de Droit 9 (1967–1968), 241.

Harrington, Johanna. "Redressing the Democratic Deficit in Treaty Law Making." McGill Law Journal 50 (2005), 465.

Jacomy-Millette. "L'État fédéré dans les relations internationales contemporaines: le cas du Canada." Canadian Yearbook of International Law 14 (1976), 20.

Laskin, Bora. "The Provinces and International Agreements." In *Background Papers and Reports, Vol. 1* published by the Ontario Advisory Committee on Confederation. Ottawa: Queen's Printer, 1967.

Lee, Edward G. "Canadian Practice in International Law at the Department of External Affairs." Canadian Yearbook of International Law 386 (1986).

Levy, Thomas A. "Provincial International Status Revisited" Dalhousie Law Journal 3 (1976–1977), 70.

McWhinney, Edward. "Canadian Federalism and the Foreign Affairs and Treaty Power: The Impact of Québec's Quiet Revolution." Canadian Yearbook of International Law 7 (1969), 3.

Morin, Jacques-Yvan. "La conclusion d'accords internationaux par les provinces canadiennes à la lumière du droit comparé" Canadian Yearbook of International Law 3 (1965), 127.

Morin, Jacques-Yvan. "La personnalité internationale du Québec" Revue québécoise de droit international 1 (1984), 163.

Morris, Gerald. "The Treaty-Making Power: A Canadian Dilemma" Canadian Bar Review 45 (1967), 478.

Paquin, Stéphane. "Quelle place pour les provinces canadiennes dans les organisations et les négociations internationales du Canada à la lumière des pratiques au sein d'autres fédérations?" Administration publique du Canada/Canadian Public Administration 48 (2005), 477.

Scott, F.R. "Labour Conventions Case: Lord Wright's Undisclosed Dissent." Canadian Bar
    Review 34 (1956), 114.
Van Ert, Gib. "The Legal Character of Provincial Agreements with Foreign Governments"
    Cahier de droit 24 (2001), 1093.

Jurisprudence

AG Canada v AG Ontario (Labour Conventions) [1937] AC 326
Baker v Canada (Minister of Citizenship and Immigration), [1999] 2 SCR 817
Bonanza Creek Gold Mining Co v Regem [1916] 1 AC 566
Capital Cities Communications v CRTC [1978] 2 SCR 141
Francis v Canada, [1956] SCR 618
Global Securities Corp v British Columbia (Securities Commission), [2000] 1 SCR 494
Liquidators of the Maritime Bank of Canada v New Brunswick [1892] AC 437
Macdonald v Vapor Canada Ltd. [1977] 2 SCR 134.
National Corn Growers Association v Canada (Import Tribunal) [1990] 2 SCR 1324
Németh v Canada 2010 SCC 56
Ontario (A.-G.) v. Scott, [1956] S.C.R. 137
R v Hape 2007 SCC 26
Refernce re Ownership of Offshore Mineral Rights, [1967] S.C.R. 792
Reference re Newfoundland Continental Shelf, [1984] 1 S.C.R. 86
Reference re Resolution to amend the Constitution [1981] 1 SCR 753
Reference re Secession of Québec [1998] 2 SCR 217
Reference Re Weekly Rest in Industrial Undertakings Act (Canada), [1936] S.C.R. 461
Saskatchewan Federation of Labour v Saskatchewan 2015 SCC 4.
Slaight Communications v Davidson [1989] 1 SCR 1038

Legislation

*An Act respecting the exercise of the fundamental rights and prerogatives of the Québec people
    and the Québec State* R.S.Q. c. E-20.2, art. 7.
An Act respecting the Ministère des Relations internationales, R.S.Q. c. M-25.1.1, s. 22.1
Canadian Charter of Rights and Freedoms, Part I of the Constitution Act, 1982, being Schedule
    B to the *Canada Act 1982* (U.K.), 1982
Constitution Act, 1982, ss 91–92, being Schedule B to the *Canada Act 1982* (UK), 1982

Government Documents, Websites

Inter-Imperial Relations Committee, Report, Proceedings and Memoranda (Balfour
    Declaration), E (IR/26) Series, p 2.
Letters Patent Constituting the Office of the Governor General of Canada, reproduced at R.S.C.
    1985, Appendix II, no. 31.

PART V

RIGHTS AND FREEDOMS

A. *Litigating and Interpreting the* Charter

CHAPTER 29

INTERPRETING THE *CHARTER*

JOANNA HARRINGTON[*]

1. INTRODUCTION

BILLS of rights, by their nature, contain abstract statements of guarantee that inevitably require interpretation when those guarantees are applied to particular facts and specific policies. The *Canadian Charter of Rights and Freedoms*[1] is no different in this respect, although like other bills of rights, the national context also plays a role in influencing and guiding the interpretive approach. Indeed, despite various influences at play, and a desire to share its approach with others, Canada's *Charter* remains emphatically a Canadian instrument,[2] interpreted by jurists and non-jurists alike as a national statement of Canada's most enduring legal and societal values.

The aim of this chapter is to identify the general approaches to *Charter* interpretation embraced by the judiciary, and in particular the Supreme Court of Canada, given its role as the independent third party tasked with the resolution of interpretation disputes. The chapter begins by reviewing the key considerations that underpinned the *Charter*'s adoption in 1982, suggesting that there is a spirit of 'constitutional nationalism'[3] that animates the post-1982 interpretive approach. The inclusion of several internal aids to interpretation within the *Charter*'s text is then discussed, noting their embrace of

---

[*] Professor of Law, Faculty of Law, University of Alberta.

[1] Part I of the *Constitution Act, 1982*, being Schedule B to the *Canada Act, 1982* (UK), c 11.

[2] Indeed, it has been described by the Chief Justice of Canada as 'a made in Canada document' that 'truly reflects the ethos of Canada': Beverley McLachlin, 'Defining Moments: The Canadian Constitution', The Dickson Lecture, Ottawa 2014 http://www.scc-csc.ca/court-cour/judges-juges/spe-dis/bm-2014-02-13-eng.aspx.

[3] On the rise of 'constitutional nationalism' prior to 1982, see Eric M Adams, 'Constitutional Nationalism: Politics, Law, and Culture on the Road to Patriation' in Lois Harder and Steve Patten (eds) *Patriation and Its Consequences: Constitution Making in Canada* (UBC Press, 2015) 49–71.

certain key Canadian values, including respect for Canada's multicultural and bilingual heritage, as well as equality between the sexes. I then examine the general interpretive techniques developed by the courts, including the use of progress, purpose, generosity, and context, with each technique discussed in turn so as to avoid their conflation. I also consider the judicial use of external aids to interpretation, including both foreign and international law, before closing with a brief mention of the vexing issue of the role for the court and the determination of institutional boundaries. Throughout, there is a sense of 'give and take', of rights protection and limitation, and of accommodation and balance, that may itself constitute a key national value, and thus serve as the overarching guidepost for interpreting the *Charter*.

2. NATIONAL CONSIDERATIONS

The *Charter* is a nation-building instrument. Its adoption was part of a package of reforms intended to solidify a national identity through the cutting of ties to the British Parliament and the provision of an agreed set of rights for all, regardless of their province of residence. Rights were not, however, absent from Canada prior to the *Charter*, with protections provided by convention, the common law, and a number of provincial and federal anti-discrimination codes.[4] Indeed, in Canada, these anti-discrimination statutes are often called 'human rights codes' even though they do not protect the full range of human rights, reflecting a strong Canadian cultural practice of equating human rights with equality rights.[5] These statutes prohibit discrimination within the context of employment, accommodation, and publicly available services. They also continue to thrive in the post-*Charter* era, having been elevated in status to quasi-constitutional instruments, with consequential implications for the appropriate interpretative approach.[6]

The *Charter* is also not Canada's first bill of rights. An earlier effort entitled the 'Canadian Bill of Rights' was enacted in 1960,[7] but its ineffectiveness as an ordinary statute applicable only to federal laws has been widely acknowledged as a factor in the push for the *Charter*'s development. Ordinary in form, and thus suspect as to mandate, the Bill failed to engender a culture of rights within the judiciary, and as lamented by its

---

[4] See, for example, the Canadian Human Rights Act, RSC 1985, c H-6, first enacted in 1977. The first 'human rights code' to consolidate various anti-discrimination provisions into one Act was adopted by Ontario in 1962.

[5] Speaking extra-judicially, the Chief Justice of Canada has described equality as 'a value that was to become central to the nation's conception of itself': McLachlin, 'Defining Moments', above (n 2).

[6] See, for example, *New Brunswick (Human Rights Commission) v Potash Corporation of Saskatchewan Inc* 2008 SCC 45, [2008] 2 SCR 604 [19] per Abella J, and more robustly [65–70] per McLachlin CJC.

[7] SC 1960 c 44, now RSC 1985 App III. This Act was preceded by an earlier effort of provincial application: Saskatchewan Bill of Rights Act, SS 1947 c 35.

drafter, it 'received a poor reception from the legal profession'.[8] It also launched Canada on a distinct path. There are not many countries that have tried and failed, and then tried again, with respect to the enactment of a bill of rights—England being a sui generis case with the adoption of the English Bill of Rights of 1688[9] and the much later passage of a modern bill of rights in 1998.[10] There are, of course, countries that have amended an original bill of rights, with the United States being Canada's neighbouring example, and with the American Bill of Rights[11] also originally of application only to the federal government. By contrast, the *Charter* has applied to all levels of government since its adoption.[12] It is also part of Canada's 'supreme law',[13] with the constitutional embrace of a clear mandate to declare 'any law that is inconsistent' to be 'of no force and effect'[14] seen as signaling support for a more robust judicial interpretive approach. The Canadian Bill of Rights, however, remains in force, now fully embraced as having quasi-constitutional status.[15]

At age 35, the *Charter* is also a young bill of rights, with its drafters aware of experiences elsewhere with older instruments. Indeed, the structure of the *Charter* shares certain genealogical links with the Universal Declaration of Human Rights of 1948,[16] which has served as a source of inspiration for many of the bills of rights adopted by newly independent states since the 1950s.[17] Like the Declaration, the *Charter* eschews the absolutist approach to listing rights often associated with the American Bill of Rights, itself inspired by the English Bill of Rights, among other sources. Such absolutism is, however, tempered in practice by the inevitability that judges will read in some limitations to some otherwise unqualified rights; a point often made with reference to the opinion of Justice Oliver Wendell Holmes, Jr. on 'falsely shouting fire in a theatre' as a limitation

---

[8] EA Driedger, 'The Meaning and Effect of the Canadian Bill of Rights: A Draftsman's Viewpoint' (1997) 9 Ottawa L Rev 303, 303. See also Brian Dickson, 'The Canadian Charter of Rights and Freedoms: Context and Evolution' (2013) 61 Sup Ct L Rev (2d) 3, 8–9.

[9] The Bill of Rights 1688 (UK), c 2; 1 Will & Mar Sess 2. The Act received Royal Assent on 16 December 1689.

[10] Human Rights Act, 1998 (UK), c 42, giving domestic legal effect to the Convention for the Protection of Human Rights and Fundamental Freedoms, 4 November 1950, 213 UNTS 221, ETS No 5, in force 3 September 1953 (known as the 'European Convention on Human Rights' or 'ECHR'), which for Britain 'as a European nation . . . represents our bill of rights': *Brown v Stott (Procurator Fiscal, Dunfermline)* [2000] UKPC D3, [2003] 1 AC 681, 706–707 per Lord Steyn. This Act may in the future be replaced with what is often termed a 'British Bill of Rights'.

[11] U.S. Constitution, amend. I–X.

[12] *Canadian Charter of Rights and Freedoms*, above (n 1), s 32(1).

[13] *Constitution Act, 1982*, above (n 1), s 52(1).

[14] Ibid.

[15] *Hogan v R* [1975] 2 SCR 574, 597–598 per Laskin J (as he then was) in dissent. For post-*Charter* recognition, see *Singh v Minister of Employment and Immigration* [1985] 1 SCR 177 [83] per Beetz J.

[16] GA Res 217A(III), UN GAOR, 3rd Sess, Part 1 at 71–77, UN Doc A/810 (1948). Mention is often made in Canada of the role played by a Canadian lawyer in assisting with the Declaration's drafting. See further John P Humphrey, *Human Rights and the United Nations: A Great Adventure* (Transnational, 1984).

[17] The Declaration was also a model for the Canadian Bill of Rights and the Quebec Charter of Human Rights and Freedoms RSQ c C-12, adopted in 1975. See further William A Schabas, 'Canada and the Adoption of the Universal Declaration of Human Rights' (1998) 43 McGill LJ 403, 405–406.

on freedom of speech.[18] Thus once agreement is reached on the rights to include, the key issue of concern for the drafters of any new bill of rights is the degree of guidance to be provided within the text itself with respect to their limitation.

To this end, the drafters of the *Charter* opted for a qualified approach that would expressly embrace the balancing of rights protection with respect for wider societal concerns. The heart of this approach is the limitations provision found in section 1, which makes clear that the *Charter*'s guarantees are 'subject only to such reasonable limits prescribed by law as can be demonstrably justified in a free and democratic society'. Although often touted as a Canadian innovation, section 1 is clearly a descendent of the general limitations clause used in the 1948 Declaration,[19] with the latter's influence somewhat surprising given that the treaties adopted to give legal force to the Declaration's aspirations embraced a more tailored approach.[20] There is, for example, no 'one-size-fits-all' general limitations clause in either the European Convention on Human Rights, or the International Covenant on Civil and Political Rights (ICCPR),[21] with their drafters having recognized that some human rights are indeed unqualified and absolute.[22]

The *Charter*'s drafters were aware of these texts, with Canada's accession to the ICCPR six years before the *Charter*'s adoption leading to its use as inspiration for some *Charter* rights.[23] However, civil society groups hoping for a robust *Charter* were worried about the judicial use of a text containing multiple grounds of exception. The inclusion of an 'across-the-board' limitation clause was thus a compromise intended to convey strong support for fundamental rights, while also reassuring provinces that there remained some scope for legislative sovereignty.[24] Given the similarities between the *Charter*'s

---

[18] *Schenck v. United States* 249 U.S. 47, 52 (1919).
[19] Article 29(2) of the Declaration provides that: 'In the exercise of his rights and freedoms, everyone shall be subject only to such limitations as are determined by law solely for the purpose of securing due recognition and respect for the rights and freedoms of others and of meeting the just requirements of morality, public order and the general welfare in a democratic society'.
[20] But see Peter W Hogg, *Constitutional Law of Canada* (5th edn supplemented Carswell, 2015) s 38.1 stating that section 1 reflects the influence of the ECHR and the ICCPR. In Britain, the qualified approach to rights recognition is considered 'the direct descendant of the Universal Declaration of Human Rights which in Art. 29 expressly recognized the duties of everyone to the community and the limitation on rights in order to secure and protect respect for the rights of others': *Brown v Stott* above (n 10), 707 per Lord Steyn.
[21] 16 December 1966, 999 UNTS 171, Can TS 1976 No 47, in force 23 March 1976, in force for Canada by accession 19 August 1976.
[22] The consequence of a general limitations clause is the suggestion made in *Suresh v Canada (Minister of Citizenship and Immigration)* 2002 SCC 1, (2002) 1 SCR 3 [78] that an exception to the absolute prohibition on deportation to face torture can arise in Canadian law as a consequence of the balancing process mandated by the *Charter*. Some find comfort in the Court's reference to the 'exceptional' nature of this 'discretion to deport to torture', but in more tailored instruments, the right to be free from torture has no exceptions.
[23] Article 12 of the ICCPR above (n 21), for example, has been acknowledged as the inspiration for section 6(1) of the *Charter: Divito v Canada (Public Safety and Emergency Preparedness)* 2013 SCC 47, [2013] 3 SCR 157 [24].
[24] As acknowledged by the former Assistant Deputy Minister of Justice and active participant in the *Charter*'s drafting: Barry L Strayer, 'The Evolution of the Charter' in Harder and Patten, above (n 3),

limitation clause and the Declaration's final clause, albeit instruments of a different nature, the true Canadian innovation was its placement at the front of the text,[25] although a number of *Charter* rights did emerge with their 'own internal qualifications' and their 'own method of internal balancing'.[26] A legal-political culture still supportive of the British constitutional tradition of parliamentary sovereignty also led to the inclusion of a legislative override provision.[27]

3. INTERPRETIVE AIDS WITHIN THE *CHARTER*

Any interpretation of the *Charter* must begin with a textual analysis, since 'without some link to the language of the Charter, the legitimacy of the entire process of Charter adjudication is brought into question'.[28] The text shows that the *Charter* protects six categories of rights, a conclusion supported by reference to the headings that form an 'integral' part of the *Charter*'s provisions.[29] These rights range from classic liberties from state interference, now labeled as 'fundamental freedoms', to democratic and mobility rights for citizens; legal rights, including the 'right to life, liberty and security of the person'; robust equality rights; and linguistic rights relating to the use of English and French. The rights are listed one after the other, ostensibly with equal force and effect, with the courts having confirmed that there is no hierarchy between *Charter* rights.[30] The *Charter* is 'to be read as a whole, so that one right is not privileged against another',[31] and as part of the wider Canadian constitution, even though not all *Charter* rights are at risk with respect

---

82–84. See also Barry L Strayer, *Canada's Constitutional Revolution* (University of Alberta Press, 2013), 252–256. On the drafting of the content of the clause, see Adam M Dodek, 'Where Did (Section) 1 Come From?' (2010) 27 NJCL 77–91.

[25] The practice continues within the UN when drafting declaratory instruments to place the general limitations clause after the agreed listing of rights. See, for example, the United Nations Declaration on the Rights of Indigenous Peoples, GA Res 61/295, UN Doc A/61/49 (vol III) at 15–25 (2007), art 46(2).

[26] As recognized with respect to section 23 on minority language educational rights in *Mahe v Alberta* [1990] 1 SCR 342, 369. Section 7 concerning 'the right to life, liberty and security of the person and the right not to be deprived thereof except in accordance with the principles of fundamental justice' is another example.

[27] *Canadian Charter of Rights and Freedoms*, above (n 1), s 33. Commonly known as the 'notwithstanding clause', section 33 permits the federal Parliament and provincial Legislatures to override many but not all *Charter* provisions on a temporary five-year basis, with the possibility of renewal. For its predecessor, see Canadian Bill of Rights, above (n 7), s 2. See the chapter by Janet Hiebert in this *Handbook*.

[28] *Gosselin v Quebec (AG)* 2002 SCC 84, [2002] 4 SCR 429, [214], [336].

[29] *Law Society of Upper Canada v Skapinker* [1984] 1 SCR 357, 370 and 376.

[30] *Dagenais v Canadian Broadcasting Corporation* [1994] 3 SCR 835, 877.

[31] *Trinity Western University v British Columbia College of Teachers* 2001 SCC 31, [2001] 1 SCR 772 [31].

to the legislative override.[32] Language rights are one example, with respect for Canada's official bilingual character itself an interpretive factor, with the English and French versions of the *Charter* considered equally authoritative.[33] Discrepancies are resolved by appealing to the meaning that best reconciles the two texts, taking into account the purpose of a particular guarantee with a degree of generosity.[34]

The *Charter* also contains a number of internal aids to interpretation, which serve to affirm that certain Canadian cultural values are taken into consideration when interpreting the rights provisions as well as their limitation. Section 27, for example, recognizes Canada to be a multicultural society where immigrants from diverse nations are encouraged to retain their heritage and distinct cultural identities, whereas section 28 emphasizes a commitment to equality between the sexes. These provisions do not themselves confer any rights, although it has been argued that section 28 was intended to be 'rights enhancing',[35] and even as interpretive aids, the provisions are not without their own limitations. Section 27 must be read so as not to detract from the *Charter's* specific protections for French and English linguistic communities (sections 16–23), whereas section 28 must be read with the *Charter's* express protection for affirmative action programs (section 15(2)). Initially deemed as 'meaningless' by the doyen of Canadian statutory interpretation,[36] these provisions have attracted judicial mention, but in a general way and without any discernible impact.[37] However, not all cultural and religious practices will be considered compatible with other Canadian values embedded within the fabric of the legal system, as illustrated by reference to the wearing of a face-covering veil while testifying in circumstances where there is a serious risk to trial fairness.[38]

Several additional internal aids also serve to emphasize that it is not the goal of the *Charter* to remove any pre-existing rights and freedoms (section 26), nor is the *Charter* to be construed so as to 'abrogate or derogate' from any rights or freedoms held by

---

[32] A point made by Hogg, *Constitutional Law of Canada* above (n 20), s 36.8(e), who goes on to explain at s 36.8(f) that 'differences in the vulnerability of the right to legislative abridgement . . . does not imply' that one *Charter* right must take priority over another when they come into conflict.

[33] *Constitution Act, 1982* above (n 1), s 57. See further RM Beaupré, 'Vers l'Interpretation d'une Constitution Bilingue' (1984) 25 C de D 939–958; JP McEvoy, 'The Charter as a Bilingual Instrument' (1986) 64 Can Bar Rev 153–171. There is, however, some truth to the criticism that scholars, if not others, tend to work within their language silos. See further Robert Leckey, 'Prescribed by Law/Une Règle de Droit' (2007) 45 Osgoode Hall LJ 571–620.

[34] See, for example, *R v Collins* [1987] 1 SCR 265, 287, where 'the less onerous' French text of section 24(2) was preferred because it 'better protected' the right at issue.

[35] See further Beverley Baines, 'Section 28 of the *Canadian Charter of Rights and Freedoms*: A Purposive Interpretation' (2005) 17 CJWL 45–70.

[36] Elmer A Driedger 'The Charter of Rights and Freedoms' (1982) 14 Ottawa L Rev 366, 373–374.

[37] See, for example, the mention of section 27 in the hate speech case of *R v Keegstra* [1990] 3 SCR 697, 757 per Dickson CJC. For a critique of the judicial approach, see Natasha Bakht, 'Reinvigorating Section 27: An Intersectional Approach' (2009) 6 J L & Equality 135–161.

[38] *R v NS* 2012 SCC 72, [2012] 3 SCR 726, although only Lebel J referred expressly to section 27, which he balanced against Canadian values in relation to open courts and public trials in securing trial fairness [72–78]. See also Ayelet Shachar, 'Interpretation Sections (27 and 28) of the Canadian Charter' (2013) 61 Sup Ct L Rev (2d) 147.

Aboriginal peoples (section 25). The *Charter* also does not take away any rights or privileges guaranteed by the Constitution in respect of 'denominational, separate or dissentient schools' (section 29). Notwithstanding the *Charter*'s embrace of multiculturalism, the public funding of minority Protestant and Catholic schools in some Canadian provinces remains constitutionally protected, as it has since Confederation.[39] It is also permissible for a province to fund only these schools and deny public funds to private religious schools of other denominations,[40] a compromise that has attracted international criticism in relation to Canada's obligations under the ICCPR.[41]

4. Interpretive Techniques

Although the starting point for *Charter* analysis remains the language of the text, the courts have also developed a number of interpretive techniques to help guide the application of the *Charter*'s guarantees to specific facts and circumstances. These techniques support the use of a progressive, purposive, generous, and contextual approach, with Justice Brian Dickson (as he then was) having emphasized that the 'task of expounding a constitution is crucially different than interpreting a statute'.[42] An ordinary statute may be repealed by future legislation, but 'a constitution, by contrast, is drafted with an eye to the future',[43] with the *Charter* to be interpreted as a continuing framework for constraining government actions and protecting fundamental rights. By their nature, however, these techniques can only offer guidance of a general nature, with critics noting that there are limits to progress and generosity, and an array of purposes available for judicial endorsement whether or not contextual factors are taken into account.

A. Progressive Interpretation

It is well settled in Canada that the *Charter* is a dynamic and evolving instrument with the courts having long embraced what is called a progressive interpretive approach. As a text entrenched within a constitution that is highly resistant to change, the *Charter* must be interpreted, in the words of Justice Dickson, so as to be 'capable of growth and development over time to meet new social, political and historical realities often unimagined by the framers'.[44] This evolutive approach to interpretation is viewed as the

---

[39] *Constitution Act, 1867* (UK), 30 & 31 Vict, c 3, s 93.
[40] *Adler v Ontario* [1996] 3 SCR 609.
[41] *Waldman v Canada*, Merits, Communication No 694/1996, UN Doc CCPR/C/67/D/694/1996, (1999) 7 IHRR 368 (UNHRC).
[42] *Hunter v Southam* [1984] 2 SCR 145, 155.
[43] Ibid.
[44] Ibid.

logical extension of an understanding expressed long ago that the *British North America Act*, now renamed the *Constitution Act, 1867*, 'planted in Canada a living tree capable of growth and development within its natural limits'.[45] Despite having arisen within the imperial context of a British court's rejection of a Canadian court's decision concerning the eligibility of 'qualified' persons to sit in the Senate, this notion of the Constitution as a 'living tree' remains a strong and enduring one. Its embrace of a 'progressive interpretation [that] accommodates and addresses the realities of modern life' has been described as one of the 'most fundamental principles of Canadian constitutional interpretation'.[46]

It is also a metaphor with intuitive appeal, particularly if the alternative is a 'dead' constitution,[47] or a frozen conception of rights,[48] and there are parallels in other jurisdictions, both domestic and international,[49] including those with cultural-legal ties to Canada. The European Court of Human Rights, for example, has long embraced what it calls a 'living instrument' approach to ensure that the protection of rights throughout Europe accords with present-day conditions. This concept, first expressed in a 1978 case concerning the judicial use of corporal punishment,[50] has become a central feature of the Court's approach to the interpretation of an instrument that bears many similarities to the *Charter*.[51] The Human Rights Committee has also made use of an evolutive approach, making clear in a case critical of Canadian actions that the ICCPR 'should be interpreted as a living instrument and the rights protected under it should be applied in context and in the light of present-day conditions'.[52]

Metaphors, however, have their limits, and trees indeed have roots, spurring on various tree-related aphorisms about the risks of trees toppling if left to grow beyond their 'natural limits' or in soil bereft of the nutrients provided by history and tradition. Canadians are not unaware of the debates within the United States concerning a 'living constitution' versus an 'originalist' one,[53] including the existence of competing

---

[45] *Edwards v Attorney-General for Canada* [1930] AC 124, 136 per Lord Sankey LC. See also *Attorney General of Ontario v Attorney General of Canada* [1947] AC 127, 154 per Lord Jowitt LC ('it is . . . irrelevant that the question is one that might have seemed unreal at the date of the British North America Act. To such an organic statute the flexible interpretation must be given that which changing circumstances require. . . .').

[46] *Reference Re Same-Sex Marriage* 2004 SCC 79, [2004] 3 SCR 698 [22].

[47] William H Rehnquist, 'The Notion of a Living Constitution' (1976) 54:4 Texas L Rev 693–706, 693; revised and published in (2006) 29:2 Harv J L & Pub Pol'y 401–415.

[48] Referring to a narrow interpretive approach that is associated with the Canadian Bill of Rights: *Reference Re Public Service Employee Relations Act (Alta)* [1987] 1 SCR 313, 338 per Dickson J dissenting.

[49] See further Vicki C Jackson, 'Constitutions as "Living Trees"? Comparative Constitutional Law and Interpretive Metaphors' (2006) 75 *Fordham Law Review* 921–960.

[50] *Tyrer v United Kingdom*, App No 5856/72, Ser A No 26, (1979–1980) 2 EHRR 1 [31].

[51] See further George Letsas, 'The ECHR as a Living Instrument: Its Meaning and Legitimacy' in Andreas Føllesdal, Birgit Peters and Geir Ulfstein (eds) *Constituting Europe: The European Court of Human Rights in a National, European and Global Context* (Cambridge University Press, 2013), 106–141.

[52] *Judge v Canada*, Merits, Communication No 829/1998, UN Doc CCPR/C/78/D/829/1998, (2003) 11 IHRR 25 (UNHRC) [10.3].

[53] See, for example, the contributions by Justices Ian Binnie and Antonin Scalia in Grant Huscroft and Ian Brodie (eds), *Constitutionalism in the Charter Era* (LexisNexis, 2004).

originalist approaches.[54] But these battles have less purchase in a jurisdiction where the bill of rights was adopted after the planting of the 'living tree', even if the tree was not watered by Canada's highest court until the 1980s.[55] The key issue of concern is where and when to draw the limits, suggesting a balance to be achieved between the twin-goals of legal certainty and flexibility. The former is secured by a fidelity to past precedent whereas the latter embraces a change in course, for a good reason, ideally clearly stated, much like judge-made law in the common law tradition can evolve to address new realities.[56] Criticisms about whether a reason is 'good', or 'good enough', suggest a need for principles to guide the application of the progressive approach, but not an end to the approach itself.

B. Purposive Interpretation

As for the determination of the content and scope of specific *Charter* rights, here it has been emphasized that the proper interpretive approach is a purposive one.[57] This approach requires the interpreter to determine the underlying purpose of each *Charter* guarantee, taking into account 'the nature of the interests it is meant to protect'[58] while recognizing the instrument's character and origins. Using a purposive approach, the interpreter must examine the text of the rights provision, and likely that of any other associated rights, as well as 'the character and larger objects of the Charter itself' and 'the historical origins of the concepts enshrined'.[59] Often the underlying purpose of a right is grounded in such cultural values as respect for equality and the inherent dignity of the human person, but for some *Charter* guarantees, such as freedom of association, the underlying purposes can include both individual and collective goals.[60] A purposive approach may also lead to an analysis that includes among the provision's aims the honouring of Canada's international human rights obligations,[61] although these obligations are likely not determinative, with a Canadian purposive approach being the ultimate aim.[62]

---

[54] See further Grant Huscroft and Bradley W Miller (eds), *The Challenge of Originalism: Theories of Constitutional Interpretation* (Cambridge University Press, 2011).

[55] *Attorney General of Quebec v Blaikie* [1979] 2 SCR 1016, 1029.

[56] A comparison recognized by the Chief Justice of Manitoba in the 1950s: *Reference re Validity of Section 198 of Railway Act, RSC 1952, c 234* (1956) 2 DLR (2d) 93, 108, reversed on other grounds [1958] SCR 285 ('Constitutions change, as does the common law, and develop with times and circumstances, growth of constitutional and political conventions, and national and international evolution and requirements').

[57] *Hunter v Southam* above (n 42), 157.

[58] Ibid.

[59] *R v Big M Drug Mart Ltd* [1985] 1 SCR 295, 344.

[60] *Dunmore v Ontario (AG)* 2001 SCC 94, [2001] 3 SCR 1016 [30]; *Ontario (AG) v Fraser* 2011 SCC 20, [2011] 2 SCR 3 [32 and 63–66].

[61] *Dunmore* ibid, [13].

[62] *Keegstra* above (n 37), 837 per McLachlin J dissenting.

Once determined, the purposes of a *Charter* right or freedom are then cast in 'large and liberal' terms,[63] absent any specific language of restriction within the *Charter* provision, and 'absent any particular historical, political or philosophic context capable of providing an obvious gloss on the meaning of the guarantee'.[64] Flexibility is also encouraged so as to ensure that the meaning and scope of a *Charter* guarantee is not exhaustively defined, given the continuing role for the Charter to serve as a framework within which to address new and future circumstances. It is also important to consider both the purpose and effect of the legislation under challenge in *Charter* cases,[65] with this approach being one that differs substantially from that used in division-of-powers cases where spillover effects are tolerated.[66] This method of 'purpose and effect' is not, however, the same as the 'purposive approach' since the first is focused on the legislation being impugned, while the second focuses on the content of the *Charter*. However, the underlying rationale for both methods is the same, with both techniques considered vital to ensuring that individuals are given what is often called the 'full benefit' of the *Charter*'s guarantees.

To this end, the purposive interpretation of a *Charter* guarantee, whether cast as a right or a freedom,[67] may impose a positive obligation on the state to provide some process for the full enjoyment of that 'large and liberal' guarantee. The development of a 'positive rights' jurisprudence in Canada has been both notable and not without opposition, as the *Charter* is ordinarily viewed as a 'negative rights' instrument imposing constraints on government action, rather than an instrument imposing affirmative duties to enact protective legislation.[68] There are cases where the courts have required governments to address a situation of under-inclusion in an existing scheme that resulted in the denial of effective protection for persons in a situation of vulnerability,[69] but a majority of the court was not ready to accept the more radical argument of a positive obligation to the basic necessities for survival, in essence establishing a right to welfare assistance.[70] However, within the context of labour relations, the development of a positive rights dimension to the purposive approach to *Charter* interpretation has now led

[63] *Reference re Same-Sex Marriage* above (n 46), [23]; *Caron v Alberta* 2015 SCC 56, [2015] 3 SCR 511 [35]. It would hardly be otherwise since ordinary statutes are given a 'fair, large and liberal' construction to ensure that they attain their remedial goals. See, for example, Interpretation Act, RSC 1985, c I-21, s 12.
[64] *Hunter v Southam* above (n 42), 155.
[65] *Big M Drug Mart* above (n 59), 331–334.
[66] As noted by Wilson J in *Big M Drug Mart* ibid, 357.
[67] A 'bright line between freedoms and rights seems to us impossible to maintain . . . The freedom to do a thing . . . implies a right to do it': *Ontario (AG) v Fraser* above (n 60), [67].
[68] Compare *Delisle v Canada* [1999] 2 SCR 989 [33] with *Dunmore* above (n 60), [19–29].
[69] See, for example, *New Brunswick (Minister of Health and Community Services) v G(J)* [1999] 3 SCR 46 requiring the provision of state-funded counsel in child custody proceedings; a holding reminiscent of the European case of *Airey v Ireland* No 6289/73, Ser A No 32, (1980) 2 EHRR 305.
[70] *Gosselin* above (n 28), [82–83]. See also Strayer, 'The Evolution of the Charter' above (n 24), 78–79, indicating that the *Charter*'s drafters did not consider Canada's political culture to be ready for the inclusion of economic rights, particularly those imposing positive obligations.

to the judicial recognition of a right to a process of collective bargaining,[71] and a right to strike,[72] notwithstanding past precedents to the contrary that were decided within the *Charter* era.[73]

C. Generous Interpretation

As is often stated, a constitutional bill of rights should also be given a 'generous interpretation', with generosity requiring the absence of rigid and pedantic formalism so as to give individuals the full measure of their rights. One of the more famous expositions of this principle is that found in Lord Wilberforce's speech in *Minister of Home Affairs v Fisher* concerning the Bermudian Constitution, which gave judicial voice to the exhortation by Professor Stanley de Smith to 'bring out the general purpose of the guarantees and avoid the austerity of tabulated legalism'.[74] This approach is strongly supported in Canada, where it has long been held that the interpretation of the *Charter*'s rights and freedoms should be 'a generous rather than a legalistic one'.[75]

Generosity, however, also has its limits, with Chief Justice Dickson having cautioned that it is important when using a generous approach 'not to overshoot the actual purpose of the right or freedom in question'.[76] Indeed, it has been argued that the use of a generous approach, without subordination to purpose, upsets the balance between rights protection and rights limitation that is at the heart of the *Charter*'s scheme. The worry is that the widest possible reading of a *Charter* right, as encouraged by a generous interpretation, leads to the inclusion of a variety of legal entitlements, not all of which deserve constitutional protection, which in turn places pressure on the court to relax its approach when evaluating the government's justifications for limiting these rights under section 1.[77] Long ago enunciated by Professor Peter Hogg, this position has received express judicial endorsement, with Canada's highest court expressly warning against the conflation of the purposive and generous approaches, such that 'the purpose of a right must always be the dominant concern in its interpretation; generosity of

---

[71] *Health Services and Support—Facilities Subsector Bargaining Assn v British Columbia* 2007 SCC 27, [2007] 2 SCR 391. See also *Ontario (AG) v Fraser* above (n 60), [34–43].

[72] *Saskatchewan Federation of Labour v Saskatchewan* 2015 SCC 4, 2015 1 SCR 245.

[73] *Reference Re Public Service Employee Relations Act (Alta)* above (n 48); *Public Service Alliance of Canada v Canada* [1987] 1 SCR 424; *Retail, Wholesale and Department Store Union v Saskatchewan* [1987] 1 SCR 460.

[74] See Stanley A de Smith, *The New Commonwealth and Its Constitutions* (Stevens & Sons 1964), 194, cited without attribution in *Minister of Home Affairs v Fisher* [1980] AC 319, 328, but later with attribution in *Matthew v The State (Trinidad and Tobago)* [2004] UKPC 33, [2005] 1 AC 433 [34] and *Mist v The Queen* [2005] NZSC 77 [45].

[75] *Hunter v Southam* above (n 42), 156 per Dickson J citing *Fisher* ibid.

[76] *Big M Drug Mart* above (n 59), 344 per Dickson J (Chief Justice at the date of the judgment).

[77] Peter W Hogg, 'Interpreting the Charter of Rights: Generosity and Justification' (1990) 28 Osgoode Hall LJ 817–838.

interpretation is subordinate to and constrained by that purpose'.[78] Purpose may, however, be subordinate to a progressive interpretation, with the location of a right to strike within the *Charter's* guarantee of freedom of association being a generous interpretation that is only restrained by purpose if that purpose is itself interpreted in an evolutive manner to accord with contemporary views.[79]

D. Contextual Interpretation

Flexibility in *Charter* interpretation has also been encouraged by the embrace of context as an additional tool to be used to determine the scope and content of a *Charter* right, and in particular, the reasonableness of any justifications for its limitation. The use of a contextual approach means that 'a particular right or freedom may have a different value depending on the context', and thus *Charter* rights and freedoms may have 'different meanings in different contexts'.[80] For example, freedom of expression within a political context has greater value in a democracy than say expression for commercial purposes or for the purposes of disclosing the intimate aspects of an individual's private life. A contextual approach enables these different values to be taken into account, particularly at the section 1 stage in a *Charter* analysis. In such cases, context is viewed as a means to secure a 'sensitive case-oriented' analytical approach, which is necessary since Canadian jurisprudence does not embrace specific tests for different kinds of expression.[81] The requirements of fundamental justice relevant to a section 7 analysis may also vary according to context, resulting in different values to be attributed to interests such as privacy.[82]

There is, however, another use for context, where the broader political and social realities are used to 'set the scene' before engaging with the specific steps in *Charter* analysis now required by settled jurisprudence. This kind of broad contextual approach has been used to highlight the impact of trials on child victims of abuse, allowing the use of social science research to establish the reluctance of young victims to testify against their abusers.[83] It has also been used to highlight the prevalence and impact of discriminatory beliefs in trials for sexual conduct.[84] However, judicial engagement with a wide-ranging contextual inquiry does raise concerns for the focused nature and preparation costs of litigation, with some judges appearing to question the need for extensive

---

[78] *R v Grant*, 2009 SCC 32, [2009] 2 SCR 353 [17], citing Hogg, *Constitutional Law of Canada* above (n 20), s 36.8(b)–(c).

[79] Indeed, the dissent in *Saskatchewan Federation of Labour* above (n 72), [114], suggests that the majority has adopted an analysis that 'overshoots the actual purpose of the right or freedom'.

[80] *Edmonton Journal v Alberta (AG)* [1989] 2 SCR 1326, 1355–1356.

[81] *Rocket v Royal College of Dental Surgeons of Ontario* [1990] 2 SCR 232, 246–247.

[82] *R v Jarvis* 2002 SCC 73, [2002] 3 SCR 757 [67].

[83] *R v Levogiannis* [1993] 4 SCR 475, 483, concerning the use of screens to allow a young complainant to testify against an accused.

[84] *R v Seaboyer; R v Gayme* [1991] 2 SCR 577, 647 per L'Heureux-Dubé J dissenting.

external sources when one can give judicial notice to such matters as the power imbalance between adults and children 'by virtue of their age'.[85] Given its declining use as an overarching or preliminary consideration, many judges appear to have heeded the warning to be careful 'not to allow the discussion of context to pre-empt the analysis itself'.[86]

5. EXTERNAL AIDS TO INTERPRETATION

Canadian appellate courts have shown a willingness to consider an array of external aids to *Charter* interpretation, ranging from scholarly writings, newspaper commentary, and parliamentary reports, to foreign laws and the judgments of foreign courts, as well as a variety of international reports, treaties, and formally non-binding declarations. The writings of legal philosophers and political theorists have also been cited, with John Stuart Mill being a particular favourite. It is, however, often difficult to discern the weight given to any one particular external source, with a series of citations typically used to bolster a position rather than to suggest that any one external source had a determinative impact. Although at times akin to the wearing of a 'belt with suspenders', the liberality of the judicial approach suggests an openness to legal pluralism that extends well beyond the coexistence in Canada of the common law and civil law traditions; however, it is also an approach that at no time sacrifices the national voice.

On the use of comparative law, Canada's appellate courts have exhibited a willingness to cite persuasive decisions of other high courts, whether or not the principles or lessons embraced come from a court with close legal-cultural ties. In the early days of *Charter* jurisprudence, the decisions of the U.S. Supreme Court were often cited, notwithstanding clear differences between the *Charter* and the American Bill of Rights, but the courts also continued to make reference to the decisions of the Judicial Committee of the Privy Council. Since then, one can find citations to decisions from a variety of jurisdictions, including Australia, France, India, Israel, New Zealand, and the United Kingdom. Canadian courts have also found interpretive assistance in the recommendations of the former European Commission on Human Rights and the judgments of the European Court of Human Rights, with the latter treated as if it were a European constitutional court. Indeed, European Convention jurisprudence is viewed, in essence, as a source of comparative constitutional law, rather than a source of international human rights jurisprudence.

As for Canada's own international obligations, the treaties to which Canada is a party, as well as their interpretation by international bodies, are considered a 'relevant

---

[85] *R v L (DO)* [1993] 4 SCR 419, 428–429 per Lamer J, as compared with 438–442 per L'Heureux-Dubé J, concerning the evidentiary use of videotaped interviews with young complainants.

[86] *R v Lucas* [1998] 1 SCR 439, 486 per McLachlin J dissenting.

and persuasive' source for *Charter* interpretation.[87] However, the judicial use of these sources is more in the nature of comparative law, or foreign law, with the material to be considered 'in much the same way that … decisions of the courts of other jurisdictions are relevant and may be persuasive'.[88] Canadian courts are not obliged to consider the views of the international supervisory bodies responsible for monitoring Canada's treaty performance,[89] unlike in Britain and Ireland, where the courts must 'take into account' the decisions of the European supervisory bodies, whether judicial or recommendatory.[90] In South Africa, a court 'must' consider international law and 'may' consider foreign law.[91] The eclecticism of the Canadian approach has, however, led to the consideration of a variety of 'relevant and persuasive' sources, including treaties to which Canada is not a party. It has also led to the judicial consideration of declarations, interpretive guidelines, and other non-binding texts, a phenomenon that is often praised as being progressive in nature.[92] Indeed, rarely does a Canadian judge draw a distinction between a binding and non-binding text, preferring instead to group all international materials together as possibly persuasive. The downside of this approach is that it accords no weight to a government's decision to become bound, or not, to perform a treaty obligation in good faith.

Canadian courts have, however, given short shrift to the use of the historical record as an external interpretive aid to determine legislative intent. One cannot, for example, argue with any success that the framers of the *Charter* intended the words in the text to have meanings fixed by judicial decisions available at the time of the Charter's enactment.[93] There is also little scope for the use of testimony given before Parliament concerning the intention of the framers, with the courts having rationalized that 'the Charter is not the product of a few individual public servants, however distinguished, but of a multiplicity of individuals who played major roles in the negotiating, drafting and adoption of the *Charter*'.[94] The parliamentary record concerning the hopes and intentions for a particular *Charter* provision may be admitted as evidence, but the courts have 'consistently taken the view that they are of minimal relevance'.[95]

---

[87] *Reference Re Public Service Employee Relations Act* above (n 48), 348–349 per Dickson CJC dissenting, but see *Slaight Communications Inc v Davidson* [1989] 1 SCR 1038, 1056–1057 per Dickson CJC.

[88] Ibid, 348.

[89] Resulting in a lack of domestic judicial engagement with a notable series of international cases concerning Canada, extradition, and the death penalty: see Joanna Harrington, 'The Absent Dialogue: Extradition and the International Covenant on Civil and Political Rights' (2006) 32 Queen's LJ 82–134.

[90] Human Rights Act above (n 10), s 2; European Convention on Human Rights Act 2003 (Irl), No 20 of 2003, s 4.

[91] Constitution of the Republic of South Africa 1996 s 39(1).

[92] A non-binding text may, however, be 'more progressive' precisely because its negotiators knew it would be non-binding, with many years of further negotiation often required to transform a declaration into a treaty text.

[93] *R v Therens* [1985] 1 SCR 613, 638 per Le Dain J.

[94] *Re BC Motor Vehicle Act* [1985] 2 SCR 486, 506–507 per Lamer J.

[95] *Mahe v Alberta* above (n 26), 369.

6. *CHARTER* INTERPRETATION
AND THE ROLE FOR THE COURTS

The *Charter* has had a profound effect in Canada, with the wider historical context suggesting that its adoption was intended to encourage a strong judicial role in the protection of rights; a role the judiciary has embraced as 'a guardian of the constitution'.[96] As a result, Canada's legal culture has moved closer to the United States, prompting greater interest in the judicial appointment process and encouraging judges to undertake a larger public engagement role. Indeed, it was the *Charter*'s resemblance to U.S.-style judicial review that led to its rejection 15 years later as a model for a new British bill of rights.[97] Britain opted instead to combine judicial rights protection with continuing respect for parliamentary supremacy by denying courts the power to invalidate primary legislation. Notwithstanding the *Charter*'s 'notwithstanding clause',[98] and the intended general nature of its limitations provision, it is the power to invalidate the output of the legislature that underlines the *Charter*'s impact. It is also a power that has led to much academic writing, as well as judicial discussion, on the question of whether the judiciary really has the last word, or whether a decision striking down a law as non-*Charter* compliant initiates a 'dialogue' between the legislature and the courts, permitting space for the legislature to make a response.[99]

How a court should respond to these 'second-look' cases is a difficult task, but it remains the work of the courts to 'find' the purpose of a *Charter* right, to give it a generous and expansive interpretation, and to evaluate the reasonableness of any government limitations. *Charter* interpretation must never be a mechanical exercise, and it does require care. At base is the need for the recognition of balance, both within the very structure of the *Charter* and between the judiciary and the legislature in determining the boundaries of their institutional roles. Situations of inequality and vulnerability, and situations falling directly within the expertise of a judge, such as the fairness of a trial, are likely to fall on the judicial side of that boundary.

Here, however, the approach of others with a 'living' instrument may also be instructive, with European jurisprudence suggesting that the limits are reached if an evolutive approach leads to the creation of a new right that was not included at the outset within

---

[96] *Hunter v Southam* above (n 42), 155 per Dickson J. It has also been judicially mentioned that the role was placed upon them by the political actors of the day: *Re Motor Vehicle Act* above (n 94), 497.

[97] *Rights Brought Home: The Human Rights Bill* (Cm 3782 1997) [2.10–2.15]. See also Francesca Klug, *Values for a Godless Age: The Story of the United Kingdom's New Bill of Rights* (Penguin Books, 2000) 165–166.

[98] A political-legal culture that places greater confidence in judges than politicians has made it very difficult for legislatures to make use of the override provided by section 33.

[99] See further Peter W Hogg, Alison A Bushell Thornton and Wade K Wright, 'Charter Dialogue Revisited or "Much Ado about Metaphors"' (2007) 45 Osgoode Hall LJ 1–65.

the text, especially if deliberately so,[100] being an approach that admittedly requires more openness to the historical record than present in Canada. As for the interpretation of rights within the text, European jurisprudence suggests that the limits of a 'living instrument' are reached when there is an absence of consensus among European states as to present-day conditions.[101] Although it is a doctrine developed by an international court responsible for supervising a culturally diverse range of member-states, Canadian courts have, at times, made implicit use of this approach by 'taking note of factual developments in Canada and in relevant foreign jurisdictions', both in law and in public opinion.[102] A new consensus, whether domestic or international, may also justify the overturning of a prior consensus;[103] with this approach encapsulated in Canada as a 'change in circumstances or evidence that fundamentally shifts the parameters of the debate'.[104]

7. CONCLUSION

Charter interpretation is inevitably a matter of interpreting text, purpose, and context, often with some assistance gained from a review of developments elsewhere, but always with a view to 'developing a jurisprudence that is truly Canadian in scope, sensibility and outlook'.[105] Over the years, the courts have embraced several interpretive techniques designed to ensure a large and liberal interpretation for the *Charter*'s guarantees. There remains, however, the ever-present need for some 'give and take' in the balancing of rights protection with reasonable limitation, with the desire for a progressive approach, and the question of who shall determine that a *Charter* guarantee no longer accords with present-day realities, likely to be the area of future challenge for the balance achieved between the courts and the legislature as to their institutional roles.

---

[100] *Johnston and Others v Ireland*, App No 9697/82, Ser A No 112, (1987) 9 EHRR 203 [53] concerning a right to divorce. The intentional exclusion of property rights from the Charter would be a Canadian parallel: *Irwin Toy v Quebec (Attorney General)* [1989] 1 SCR 927, 1003–1004.

[101] See, among other cases, *Marckx v Belgium*, App No 6833/74, Ser A No 31, (1980) 2 EHRR 330 [41] concerning equality between legitimate and illegitimate children.

[102] See, for example, *Burns v United States* 2001 SCC 7, [2001] 1 SCR 283 [144], in effect overturning a past precedent with reference to prevailing views within Canada, and internationally, concerning the death penalty.

[103] See *Goodwin v United Kingdom*, App No 28957/95, ECHR 2002-VI, (2002) 35 EHRR 447 [79-85] (Grand Chamber), concerning the legal recognition of the sexual identity of post-operative transsexuals.

[104] *Carter v Canada (AG)* 2015 SCC 5, [2015] 1 SCR 331 [6–10 and 42–47, esp 44], concerning physician-assisted dying; *Canada (Attorney General) v Bedford*, 2013 SCC 72, [2013] 3 SCR 1101 [42], concerning prostitution.

[105] Dickson, above (n 8), 20.

BIBLIOGRAPHY

Secondary sources

Abella, J, 'Public Policy and the Judicial Role' (1989) 34 *McGill Law Journal* 1021–1035

Alford, RP, 'In Search of a Theory for Constitutional Comparativism' (2005) 52:3 *UCLA Law Review* 639–714

Binnie, I 'Constitutional Interpretation and Original Intent' (2004) 23 *Supreme Court Law Review* (2d) 345–382

Choudhry, S (ed), *The Migration of Constitutional Ideas* (Cambridge University Press, 2007)

Cohen M and AF Bayefksy, 'The Canadian Charter of Rights and Freedoms and Public International Law' (1983) 61 *Canadian Bar Review* 265–338

Gardbaum, S, 'The New Commonwealth Model of Constitutionalism' (2001) 49 *American Journal of Comparative Law* 707–760

Goldsworthy J (ed), *Interpreting Constitutions* (Oxford University Press 2006)

Harrington, J, 'The Democratic Challenge of Incorporation: International Human Rights Treaties and National Constitutions' (2007) 38 *Victoria University at Wellington Law Review* 217–235

Huscroft, G, 'A Constitutional "Work in Progress"? The Charter and the Limits of Progressive Interpretation' (2004) 23 *Supreme Court Law Review* (2d) 413–438

Huscroft, GA, ' "Thank God We're Here": Judicial Exclusivity in Charter Interpretation and Its Consequences' (2004) 25 *Supreme Court Law Review* (2d) 241–267

Huscroft, G and I Brodie (eds), *Constitutionalism in the Charter Era* (LexisNexis, 2004)

Huscroft, G and BW Miller (eds), *The Challenge of Originalism: Theories of Constitutional Interpretation* (Cambridge University Press, 2011)

Huscroft, G and P Rishworth (eds) *Litigating Rights: Perspectives from Domestic and International Law* (Hart, 2002)

Hogg, PW, *Constitutional Law of Canada* (5th edn supplemented Carswell, 2015)

Hogg, PW and AA Bushnell, 'The Charter Dialogue between Courts and Legislatures' (1997) 35 *Osgoode Hall Law Journal* 75–124

Hogg, PW, AA Bushnell Thornton and WK Wright, 'Charter Dialogue Revisited or "Much Ado about Metaphors"' (2007) 45 *Osgoode Hall Law Journal* 1–65

Iacobucci, F, ' "Reconciling Rights": The Supreme Court of Canada's Approach to Competing Charter Rights' (2003) 20 *Supreme Court Law Review* (2d) 137–164

Jackson, VC, 'Constitutions as "Living Trees"? Comparative Constitutional Law and Interpretive Metaphors' (2006) 75 *Fordham Law Review* 921–960

La Forest, AW, 'Domestic Application of International Law in Charter Cases: Are We There Yet?' (2004) 37:1 *University of British Columbia Law Review* 157–218

Manfredi, CP, *Judicial Power and the Charter: Canada and the Paradox of Liberal Constitutionalism* (Oxford University Press 2000)

Oliphant, B, 'Interpreting the Charter with International Law: Pitfalls & Principles' (2014) 19 *Appeal* 105–129

Oliphant, BJ, 'Taking Purposes Seriously: The Purposive Scope and Textual Bounds of Interpretation under the Canadian Charter of Rights and Freedoms' (2015) 65 *University of Toronto Law Journal* 239–283

Rothstein, M, 'Checks and Balances in Constitutional Interpretation' (2016) 79 *Saskatchewan Law Review* 1–15

Sharpe, RJ, 'The Impact of a Bill of Rights on the Role of the Judiciary: A Canadian Perspective' in P Alston (ed), *Promoting Human Rights through Bills of Rights: Comparative Perspectives* (Oxford University Press, 1999) 431–453

Strayer, BL, *Canada's Constitutional Revolution* (The University of Alberta Press, 2013)

Sugunasiri, SM, 'Contextualism: The Supreme Court's New Standard of Judicial Analysis and Accountability' (1999) 22 *Dalhousie Law Journal* 126–184

Cases

Edmonton Journal v Alberta (AG) [1989] 2 SCR 1326

Edwards v Attorney-General for Canada [1930] AC 124

Hunter v Southam [1984] 2 SCR 145

Minister of Home Affairs v Fisher [1980] AC 319

R v Big M Drug Mart [1985] 1 SCR 295

Reference Re Same-Sex Marriage 2004 SCC 79, [2004] 3 SCR 698

Saskatchewan Federation of Labour v Saskatchewan 2015 SCC 4, [2015] 1 SCR 245

Tyrer v United Kingdom, App No 5856/72, Ser A No 26, (1979–1980) 2 EHRR 1

....

CHAPTER 30

ACCESS TO *CHARTER* JUSTICE

....

CARISSIMA MATHEN[*]

A complete discussion of the Canadian Constitution, and of the *Charter of Rights*[1] in particular, must consider how constitutional issues come before courts. The topics covered in this chapter—standing, intervention, costs, and advisory opinions—inform how access to justice operates in the constitutional context. They are also interdependent. A generous approach to standing means little if individual litigants are unable to shoulder the burden of litigation. The doctrines of public interest standing and advance costs are possible responses to that challenge. The federal Court Challenges Program represents a different but related principle: the state does not occupy a purely adversarial relationship to its rights-bearing citizens.[2] Next, to the extent that constitutional litigation requires a personal claim, the courts are at risk of only receiving arguments that reflect that claimant's experience. Such a narrow record is unsuitable for confident resolution of deeply contested issues that invariably affect many other persons. The doctrine of public interest intervention provide some assurance that other relevant arguments have been considered. Finally, the advisory or reference function provides additional opportunities for the litigation and development of constitutional law.

The large and liberal approach to individual rights that has marked the *Charter* era is mirrored in the approach developed with respect to many of the issues canvassed in this chapter. The liberal approach has produced a vibrant sense of citizen ownership over, and investment in, the country's constitutional values. Although that is a great social good, there are costs to abdicating rights discussion entirely to the courts. Nevertheless, constitutional litigation and the process issues that ensue have been critically important to the development of Canadian constitutionalism.

---

[*] Associate Professor, Faculty of Law, University of Ottawa.

[1] *Canadian Charter of Rights and Freedoms*, Part I of the *Constitution Act, 1982*, being Schedule B to the *Canada Act 1982* (U.K.), 1982, c.11 [hereinafter *Charter*].

[2] The word "citizens" is used in its political rather than the legal or constitutional sense, that is, constituent members of a particular community. Most *Charter* rights apply to all persons in Canada regardless of legal citizenship.

1. STANDING

Initiating a legal proceeding is not open to just anyone. In order to trigger the courts' adjudicative function, a person must demonstrate that she has a cognizable legal interest known as "standing". With respect to constitutional cases, Canadian standing rules have been amplified to permit more types of challenges, in greater circumstances, and by different types of plaintiffs.

A. Direct Standing

The easiest way to establish standing is by alleging a direct injury. For example, an individual who asserts an economic loss as a result of someone else's tortious conduct will generally have standing to sue to recover those monies. Applied to constitutional cases, this would require that a plaintiff has suffered (or risks suffering) a violation of her constitutional rights. Such a test would render many laws immune from review for lack of an easily identifiable litigant. As well, it is inconsistent with the idea that in a system governed by the rule of law, citizens have an interest in the validity of *all* laws irrespective of whether, at any given moment, those laws interfere with their discrete rights.

The limited approach described above has not prevailed in Canada. Instead, the Constitution's supremacy clause[3] has been interpreted to mean that a person subject to a law may challenge its validity on any basis. That is how Big M Drug Mart, a corporation, successfully challenged a federal criminal law prohibiting commercial activity on Sunday on the basis that the law infringed the freedom of religion of natural persons.[4] Similarly, in *R. v Morgentaler*,[5] a male physician successfully challenged a criminal abortion law on the basis that it violated the *Charter* rights of pregnant women.

The breadth of the direct standing rule is also demonstrated in challenges to minimum sentences of imprisonment.[6] The Supreme Court has upheld such challenges in cases where the actual sentence imposed on the petitioner was found to be neither cruel nor unusual.[7] The challenge was, nonetheless, vindicated because the Court concluded

---

[3] *Constitution Act, 1982*, being Schedule B to the *Canada Act 1982* (U.K.), 1982, c.11 [hereinafter *Constitution Act, 1982*], s. 52.

[4] *R. v Big M Drug Mart Ltd.*, [1985] 1 S.C.R. 295 [hereinafter *Big M*], successfully challenging the *Lord's Day Act*, R.S.C. 1970, c. L-13, s. 4. Since then, the Supreme Court has affirmed that religious freedom has an organizational aspect and may be exercised by legal entities acting on the behalf of individuals. It has not yet endorsed the idea that the right may be enjoyed by corporations. See *Loyola High School v Quebec (Attorney General)*, 2015 SCC 12, [2015] 1 S.C.R. 613.

[5] [1988] 1 S.C.R. 30 [hereinafter *Morgentaler*].

[6] Such provisions tend to arise under the *Charter*'s section 12, which provides: "Everyone has the right not to be subjected to any cruel and unusual treatment or punishment". The *Criminal Code* speaks of "minimum sentence[s] of imprisonment", but they are commonly referred to as "mandatory minimums".

[7] For example, in *R. v Smith*, [1987] 1 SCR 1045, the petitioner received an eight-year sentence for an offence which imposed a minimum of seven years. As he received more than the minimum, Smith

that the impugned provisions created the risk that a "hypothetical offender" would receive a grossly excessive punishment. Thus, in *R. v Smith*, a seven-year minimum sentence for importing narcotics was judged cruel and unusual because of the possibility that it might capture "a young person who, while driving back into Canada from a winter break in the U.S.A." is caught with "his or her first 'joint of grass.'"[8] That such a person would be subject to such a lengthy term of imprisonment, the majority held, would "outrage standards of decency".[9]

The *Smith* case was excoriated as fanciful and divorced from reality.[10] It spurred debate over the parameters of such hypothetical reasoning and, indeed, whether it should be used at all. Although the Supreme Court did not abandon the approach, it has since emphasized that a given hypothetical must be reasonable.[11] Of course, what counts as "reasonable" is open to debate. But, given the problems that result when laws are rendered immune to meaningful review,[12] it is both sensible and principled to permit courts to adjudicate cases in which the claimed constitutional injury relates to persons other than the immediate litigant.

B. Public Interest Standing

Even with the relaxed direct standing rules described above, laws may remain resistant to review. Consider, for example, persons in immigration and refugee proceedings. The state may find it expedient to avoid judicial scrutiny by granting claimants individual relief. Such a result may avoid individual injustice, but it entrenches executive discretion without diminishing the possibility of future harm to others. Therefore, in order to ensure that persons have the necessary access to the courts "to resolve matters of

---

could not argue that the statute imposed cruel and unusual punishment on him personally. See also *R. v Nur*, 2015 SCC 15, [2015] 1 S.C.R. 773 which struck down the statutory minimums but upheld original sentences of three and five years imposed on two petitioners; and *R. v Lloyd*, 2016 SCC 13 which did the same in relation to a 12-month minimum.

[8] *Smith*, above (n 7) [2].

[9] *Ibid* [54].

[10] See the dissenting reasons of McIntyre J. in *Smith, ibid* [79], as well as the comments by Peter Hogg, *Constitutional Law of Canada* loose-leaf (consulted on 8 August 2016), (Thomson Reuters Canada, 2007) ch 53 at 4–5.

[11] *R. v Goltz*, [1991] 3 SCR 485; *R. v Morrissey*, 2000 SCC 39—[2000] 2 SCR 90.

[12] The Court has rejected using constitutional exemptions (which would leave the sentence in place but permit individual relief under section 24 of the *Charter*) to remedy minimum sentences that are found to infringe section 12: *R. v Ferguson*, 2008 SCC 6, [2008] 1 SCR 96. The nature of a minimum sentence (which is intended to eliminate the discretion to impose a lesser punishment) also removes the possibility of "reading down" the statute, or what in the U.S. context is known as an "as applied" challenge. One of the factors that makes mandatory minimum sentences less amenable to review is that severe sentences may create an incentive on defendants to accept a guilty plea in return for a lesser charge. Of course, this is only available when there are lesser included, or additional, offences available. Where a defendant is charged with a single offence, a minimum sentence actually removes a common motivation to plead.

consequence to the community as a whole",[13] the Supreme Court has recognized a concept of public interest standing which requires no direct link between the litigant and the impugned law.

Originally, the framework for public interest standing required demonstration of three things: (1) a serious issue about the invalidity of the impugned legislation, (2) a litigant with a "genuine interest" in the question, and (3) the lack of any other manner in which the question might arise before a court.[14]

The constitutional entrenchment of individual rights in the *Charter* opened up many laws to potential challenge.[15] Initially, the Supreme Court expressed concern that a broad approach to public interest standing would overwhelm the courts with well-meaning but misguided "busybodies".[16] In consequence, it endorsed a stringent approach to standing.[17] So long as there was a potential direct litigant, it ruled, courts should not award standing to others.[18] As a result, public interest standing became difficult to achieve.[19]

The first sign of a thaw came in *Chaoulli v Quebec (Attorney General)*.[20] The case involved a challenge to provincial laws prohibiting the purchase or sale of private insurance for publicly funded medical services.[21] Two plaintiffs, a patient (but not one at imminent risk) and a doctor, argued inter alia that the law violated s.7 of the *Charter*. The Attorney General of Quebec argued that neither claimant had suffered any direct injury. The Supreme Court found that argument irrelevant because, in its view, both plaintiffs merited an award of public interest standing.

One might have expected the third factor in the public interest standing test to pose a challenge for the *Chaoulli* plaintiffs. It was, after all, quite plausible that a person who had suffered actual harm from being unable to purchase private insurance could initiate a claim. Justice Marie Deschamps addressed that argument by simply stating that "there is no effective way to challenge the validity of the provisions other than by recourse to

---

[13]   *B.C. v Okanagan Indian Band*, [2003] 3 SCR 371, [27].

[14]   *Thorson v Canada (Attorney General)*, [1975] 1 S.C.R. 138; *Nova Scotia (Board of Censors) v McNeil*, [1976] 2 S.C.R. 265; *Canada (Minister of Justice) v Borowski*, [1981] 2 S.C.R. 575; and *Finlay v Canada (Minister of Finance)*, [1986] 2 S.C.R. 607.

[15]   Indeed, the anticipation of a flood of suits was one of the factors leading to the decision to delay for three years the coming into force of section 15 of the *Charter*, which guarantees equality rights. The delay was intended to give federal and provincial governments an opportunity to review their respective laws for inconsistency with the section.

[16]   *Hy and Zel's Inc. v Ontario (Attorney General); Paul Magder Furs Ltd. v Ontario (Attorney General)*, [1993] 3 S.C.R. 675.

[17]   *Canadian Council of Churches v Canada (Minister of Employment and Immigration)*, [1992] 1 S.C.R. 236.

[18]   *Ibid.* at 254.

[19]   The Canadian Council for Refugees (CCR) failed to obtain standing in a challenge against the *Safe Third Country Agreement (STCA)*. [2008] F.C.A. 40 leave to appeal ref'd [2008] S.C.C.A. No. 422. See also *Canadian Bar Association v British Columbia*, [2008] B.C.J. No. 350 (test case concerning the provision of legal aid in British Columbia).

[20]   [2005] 1 S.C.R. 791 [hereinafter *Chaoulli*].

[21]   *Health Insurance Act* R.S.Q. c.A-29; *Hospital Insurance Act* R.S.Q., c.A-28.

the courts".[22] That comment implied that the third criterion for public interest standing is more focussed on whether *litigation* is the only effective way to proceed, rather than on whether a proposed litigant is the most effective moving *party*. In a separate opinion, Justice Ian Binnie provided more detailed reasons. He noted that the claimants sought to make a "systemic" challenge that was not limited to "the circumstances of any particular patient".[23] He continued:

> From a practical point of view, while individual patients could [bring their own cases to court], it would be unreasonable to expect a seriously ailing person to bring a systemic challenge to the whole health plan, as was done here. The material, physical and emotional resources of individuals who are ill, and quite possibly dying, are likely to be focussed on their own circumstances. In this sense, there is no other class of persons that is more directly affected and that could be expected to undertake the lengthy and no doubt costly systemic challenge to single-tier medicine.[24]

Justice Binnie's remarks acknowledge that pursuing constitutional litigation involves a myriad of costs, and that potential litigants may be vulnerable in ways that make it inappropriate to thrust upon them the burden of initiation.

The more generous approach hinted at in *Chaoulli* received full support in *Canada (Attorney General) v Downtown Eastside Sex Workers United Against Violence Society*.[25] A non-profit organization and a former sex worker sought to challenge several prostitution-related offences in the *Criminal Code*.[26] Once again, under the traditional test, the plaintiffs seemed poor candidates for public interest standing. Not only were sex workers commonly charged under the impugned criminal provisions, but a similar (though not identical) challenge was already underway in Ontario.[27]

Despite the foregoing hurdles, the Court awarded standing. It confirmed comments in previous cases that standing is a necessary component of the principle of legality.[28] The Court maintained the basic rules but with some modifications. It rejected applying a necessity standard under the third criterion. Instead, it held, the proper question is "whether the proposed suit is, in all of the circumstances and in light of a number of considerations, a reasonable and effective means to bring the case to court".[29] The Court identified several such circumstances and considerations. One is the capacity of the proposed litigant to manage the claim, indicated by such things as past litigation experience, legal expertise, and resources. Another is whether the suit can "provide access to

---

[22] *Chaoulli*, above (n 20), [35].
[23] *Ibid* [189].
[24] *Ibid*.
[25] 2012 SCC 45, [2012] 2 S.C.R. 524 [hereinafter *SWUAV*].
[26] *RSC*, 1985, c C-46.
[27] *Canada (Attorney-General) v Bedford* 2013 SCC 72, [2013] 3 S.C.R. 1101 [hereinafter *Bedford*]. The plaintiffs in *Bedford* challenged fewer criminal provisions, and did not rely on sections 2(d) (freedom of association) or 15 (equality) of the *Charter*.
[28] *SWUAV*, above (n 25) [35] citing *Thorson*, above (n 14).
[29] *SWUAV*, ibid [2].

justice for disadvantaged persons in society whose legal rights are affected".[30] A court should consider whether, taking a "practical and pragmatic approach",[31] it is possible to identify a more efficient and effective use of judicial resources that will present a context more suitable for adversarial determination. Finally, it is relevant whether others "who are equally or more directly affected"[32] by the law have indicated a disinclination towards litigation. The latter comment is striking—it affirms that public interest advocacy decisions require some sensitivity to broader social interests and well-being.

The *SWUAV* case embodies a contextual, open-ended and permissive approach to public interest standing. By expanding on the analysis in *Chaoulli*, the *SWUAV* decision reflects a profound shift on the Supreme Court that is rooted in modern Canadian constitutionalism.

2. INTERVENTION

Another notable feature of *Charter* litigation is public interest intervention. The public interest intervener is different in kind from both the third-party intervener[33] and amicus curiae.[34] It is separate, too, from the standing enjoyed by various Attorneys General to intervene in constitutional cases.[35] Although public interest interveners do not have a personal interest to vindicate, they are not disinterested in a case's outcome. The public interest intervener wishes to influence the decision, often to further the interests of a specific group, and it generally asserts a particular expertise in the subject matter.[36]

The test for granting public interest intervention is whether it can lend a fresh perspective to an issue before the court. Although interveners occasionally introduce new evidence, they normally are expected to take the record as is and are rarely permitted to raise new issues.[37] Public interest intervention falls under the courts' discretionary powers; indeed, when they decide such applications the courts rarely issue reasons.

---

[30] *Ibid* [51].

[31] *Ibid.*

[32] *Ibid.*

[33] A third-party intervener is one for whom a case has a direct (usually economic) impact: *Norcan v Lebroc*, [1969] S.C.R. 665. Such an intervener can seek to admit fresh evidence and in appellate cases may be permitted to argue issues that have not been considered by the lower courts.

[34] The amicus curiae is invited by the court to provide a perspective on an issue that is not likely to be addressed by the other parties but about which the court requires dispassionate assistance. Amici are not common in Canadian cases; but see *R. v O'Connor*, [1995] 4 S.C.R. 411 (relevance and admissibility of personal records of witnesses in sexual offence proceedings); and *Reference re Senate Reform*, 2014 SCC 32 (process by which the Senate of Canada may be altered or abolished).

[35] *Rules of the Supreme Court of Canada* Rule, 60(3) [hereinafter *SCC Rules*].

[36] For example, in *Law Society of British Columbia v Andrews*, [1989] 1 S.C.R. 342, the Women's Legal Education and Action Fund (LEAF) made the first of dozens of interventions before the Supreme Court of Canada to urge a particular interpretation of section 15 of the *Charter*.

[37] See the discussion *infra* note 50 and associated text. A public interest intervener may be granted leave to intervene as an added party, though this is an exceptionally uncommon occurrence. The

For many decades, Canadian courts frowned on intervention.[38] The "public interest intervener" did not emerge until the mid-1970s.[39] Passage of the *Charter* did not immediately produce a change; indeed, the Supreme Court at first reduced access.[40] Beginning in 1987, the Court reversed course, and such applications were increasingly accepted.[41] The Court appears to have viewed relaxing the standards for intervention as one way to respond to the perceived "flood" of *Charter* claims initiated by public interest litigants.[42] The more generous approach to intervention was also consistent with the Court's purposive approach to *Charter* interpretation overall.[43] Public interest intervention is now a common feature of *Charter* litigation.[44]

Interveners can elaborate certain points of law or present evidence when parties are ill-equipped or unwilling to do.[45] For example, the courts have recognized that social science evidence, which can illuminate such things as conflicts between and among groups and individuals, and broader socio-economic trends and patterns, can be important to properly adjudicating *Charter* claims.[46] Yet it may be unrealistic to expect non-state parties to adduce adequate social science information concerning very broad or complex questions.[47] In such situations, public interest interveners may be able to assist.[48]

Women's Legal Education and Action Fund intervened as an added party in *Schachter v Canada*, [1992] 2 SCR 679.

[38] A rare exception is *Re Drummond Wren*, [1945] 4 DLR 674 which dealt with racially restrictive covenants. The Ontario Supreme Court permitted an intervention by the Canadian Jewish Congress.

[39] *A.G. (Canada) v Lavell* [1974] S.C.R. 1349; *Morgentaler v R.*, [1976] 1 SCR 616.

[40] Kenneth P. Swan, "Intervention and Amicus Curiae Status in Charter Litigation" in Robert J. Sharpe, ed., *Charter Litigation* (Butterworths, 1987) 27.

[41] Carissima Mathen, "The Expanding Role of Interveners: Giving Voice to Non-parties", in *Competence and Capacity: New Directions* (Law Society of Manitoba, 2000) 85–119.

[42] In *Canadian Council of Churches*, above (n 17) at 256, the Court explicitly mentioned intervention as a counterbalance to the stringent requirements of the public interest standing test, noting that the former procedure allowed for "the proper balance between providing for the submissions of public interest groups and preserving judicial resources".

[43] *Big M*, above (n 4); *Hunter et al. v Southam Inc.*, [1984] 2 SCR 145; *R. v Therens*, [1985] 1 SCR 613.

[44] At the Supreme Court, intervention is governed by Part 11 of the *Rules of the Supreme Court of Canada* SOR/2002–156. An application for intervention is treated as a motion, and is made to a single judge. An intervener must first make a motion for leave to file a factum. In 2017, the Court advised prospective interveners, including Attorneys General, that leave to file a factum would include a 5-minute oral argument—a significant reduction from past practice.

[45] Like-minded interveners also tend to coordinate among themselves on the points of law they will advance so as to avoid duplication, and maximize effectiveness, in their submissions.

[46] *Edmonton Journal v A.G. Alberta*, [1989] 2 SCR 1327.

[47] *Ford v Quebec (Attorney General)*, [1988] 2 SCR 712 [777].

[48] See the evidence cited in *Winnipeg Child and Family Services v G*, [1997] 3 SCR 925 by the Women's Health Rights Coalition. The case concerned whether pregnant women may be forcibly subjected to medical treatment to prevent harm to their fetuses. The record was particularly poor, as the parties (a child welfare agency and the pregnant woman under confinement) introduced virtually no evidence about the impact of such state interventions. The Coalition cited studies showing both the disproportionate impact of state interference on women from marginalized communities, and the unsuitability of a coercive approach to dealing with addiction during pregnancy. A majority of the Court referred to several of the health policy concerns, and ultimately declined to expand either tort law or parens patriae jurisdiction to permit the judicial apprehension of such women.

At the same time, *Charter* plaintiffs have performed extraordinary amounts of evidence-gathering on their own. In recent years, such copious records have provided the bedrock for trial-level success that proved very difficult to dislodge on appeal.[49] Increasingly, the Supreme Court has warned interveners against going beyond the confines of their proposed argument, or commenting on factual issues.[50] That attitude tends to restrict *Charter* analysis to the choices made by litigants. A plaintiff may, for example, decline to address equality rights issues out of a determination to focus the case on their legal rights, despite the fact that both sets of rights are in play.[51] Litigants may frame evidence in a way that deprives the Court of a complete picture. Such choices tend to be motivated by the simple, and understandable, desire to win. The moving party deserves some latitude to frame the challenge, but where their case has the potential to affect thousands or, even, millions of other persons it is unwise to cede them all control. In such cases, courts should consider permitting interveners to go further.

Equally as important as such functional concerns is the intervener's symbolic role. The intervener can remind both the court and society of a case's broader impact. In *Vriend v Alberta*, a ground-breaking equality rights case, the Court decided that Alberta's *Individual Rights Protection Act*[52] violated section 15(1) of the *Charter* because it excluded "sexual orientation" as a prohibited ground of discrimination.[53] On one level, the case might be viewed as a gay rights case. But it attracted all sorts of interveners. One, the Canadian Jewish Congress, powerfully articulated the case's importance for its own constituency:

> As a target of racism and a victim of the Holocaust, the Jewish community uniquely appreciates the importance of being vigilant in the fight against racism and all forms of discrimination. [Congress] views the issues raised in this case not only as issues pertaining to gays and lesbians, but also as human rights issues relevant to all minorities and all Canadians. Congress recognizes that it has an obligation to object wherever discrimination exists.[54]

Vriend involved 16 interveners. The plethora of participants is observed in other cases involving disparate but socially important issues: national security and terrorism,[55] hate speech,[56] the criminal regulation of sex work[57] and physician-assisted dying.[58]

---

[49] *Bedford*, above (n 27); *Carter v Canada (Attorney General)*, 2015 SCC 5, [2015] 1 SCR 331 [hereinafter *Carter*]; *Tsilhqot'in Nation v British Columbia*, 2014 SCC 44, [2014] 2 S.C.R. 256.

[50] Comments to this effect were made to some of the interveners presenting oral arguments in both *Bedford* and *Carter*, above (n 49).

[51] The legal rights are found in sections 7–14 of the *Charter*.

[52] *Individual's Rights Protection Act*, RSA 1980, c. I-2.

[53] [1998] 1 SCR 493 [hereinafter *Vriend*].

[54] *Vriend, ibid*, factum of the Canadian Jewish Congress [1].

[55] *Charkaoui v Canada (Citizenship and Immigration)* 2008 SCC 38, [2008] 2 SCR 326, (seven interveners).

[56] *Saskatchewan (Human Rights Commission) v Whatcott* 2013 SCC 11, [2013] 1 SCR 467 (23 interveners not including Attorneys General; some of the interveners made joint submissions).

[57] *Bedford*, above (n 27) (22 interveners not including Attorneys General; some of the interveners made joint submissions).

[58] *Carter*, above (n 49) (24 interveners not including Attorneys General; some of the interveners made joint submissions).

The intervener's presence suggests that the judicial process can accommodate, and even welcome, diverse views. A multiplicity of interveners in cases dealing with *Charter* rights (or, indeed, other constitutional issues) suggests that access to forums of debate over critical constitutional norms is reasonably available. In addition, interveners must clearly articulate their respective positions in advance, present them in a public forum, and, if invited, respond to questions.[59] There is, thus, an important deliberative element to public interest intervention that is not only consistent with, but positively promotes, the exercise of public reason.

3. Costs

Litigation is costly. The lack of a stable source of funding for *Charter* cases is a serious impediment to rights advocacy and vindication.[60] Individuals, lawyers, and organizations must shoulder the burden. Funding uncertainty tends to inhibit the development of comprehensive litigation strategies, collaboration, and compromise. That is counterproductive since such activities can facilitate selective litigation strategies, and, as a result, the more efficient use of resources.

The Canadian state faces numerous demands for funds. It is challenging to attract public support for constitutional litigation, especially if it feeds a perception that the government is lining the pockets of lawyers. Yet, a lack of funding ensures that for many persons, the ability to seek redress for wrongs done is illusory.

A. Judicial Discretion

A most interesting development in Canadian constitutional law is the doctrine of interim costs, under which a court orders the government to pay costs in advance. The concept was articulated in *British Columbia (Minister of Forests) v Okanagan Indian Band*.[61] In that case, four Aboriginal bands claimed the right to log on Crown lands by virtue of a right of Aboriginal title recognized by section 35 of the *Constitution Act, 1982*.[62] Responding to the Crown's attempt to have the issue remitted for trial, the bands argued that such action was appropriate only if the court made a costs award. In

---

[59] These aspects, though, are entirely dependent upon the scope of the leave application, particularly, whether the court permits oral argument.

[60] For further discussion of the distorting effect of lack of funding on rights and remedies, see the chapter by Kent Roach in this *Handbook*.

[61] *Okanagan* above (n 13).

[62] Section 35(1) states: "The existing aboriginal and treaty rights of the aboriginal peoples of Canada are hereby recognized and affirmed".

a 6-3 decision, the Supreme Court of Canada upheld a lower court decision to award interim costs.

According to the Court, the following factors will favour (but not mandate) an interim costs award: (1) impecuniousness together with the unlikelihood that the case could otherwise proceed, (3) a prima facie meritorious claim, and (3) unresolved issues of public importance which transcend a particular litigant's interests.[63] The Court stated that society is not served when fiscal concerns deter ordinary citizens from bringing forward constitutional cases. The "public interest" that underlies all constitutional litigation, the Court said, is one that should govern judicial responses to such requests.[64]

The power to award interim costs is discretionary; it does not support a corresponding right to funding.[65] After *Okanagan*, some queried whether indigenous rights cases might be more amenable than *Charter* cases to such awards. The subsequent decision in *Little Sisters Book and Art Emporium* did nothing to alleviate such concerns. There, the Court struck out an interim costs award to a bookstore in the midst of a long-standing battle with Canada Customs.[66] In a legal proceeding several years earlier, the bookstore established that Customs agents charged with reviewing its shipments had engaged in systemic discrimination on the basis of sexual orientation.[67] The Supreme Court confirmed the discrimination. But, because the government claimed that it had fixed the problem, a majority provided only declaratory relief as opposed to an injunction or an order of invalidity.[68]

Believing that it continued to be the subject of disproportionate and discriminatory seizures of its materials, Little Sisters launched a new action. It sought interim costs, successfully, in the B.C. Supreme Court.[69] The B.C. Court of Appeal set the order aside. A majority of the Supreme Court of Canada affirmed that decision. It found that,

---

[63]   *Okanagan*, above (n 13) [46].

[64]   The Court did emphasize that although all public law cases are "special" there must be a particular degree of importance or urgency before interim costs will be appropriate. *Ibid*, [38].

[65]   In *R. v Caron*, 2011 SCC 5, [2011] 1 SCR 78, a language rights case, the Court confirmed the power of provincial inferior courts to grant interim costs.

[66]   *Little Sisters Book and Art Emporium v Canada (Commissioner of Customs and Revenue)*, [2007] 1SCR 38 [hereinafter "*Little Sisters 2*"].

[67]   *Little Sisters Book and Art Emporium v Canada (Commissioner of Customs and Revenue)*, [2000] 1 S.C.R. 38 [hereinafter "*Little Sisters 1*'] [6] citing (1996), 18 BCLR (3d) 241.

[68]   On behalf of the majority, Justice Binnie wrote:

> [. . .I]t would serve the interests of none of the parties for this Court to issue a formal declaratory order based on six-year-old evidence supplemented by conflicting oral submissions and speculation on the current state of affairs. The views of the Court on the merits of the appellants' complaints as the situation stood at the end of 1994 are recorded in these reasons . . . These findings should provide the appellants with a solid platform from which to launch any further action in the Supreme Court of British Columbia should they consider that further action is necessary.

Ibid [158].

[69]   [2004] BCJ No. 1241.

because the new litigation was focussed on the seizure of specific publications, the *Okanagan* framework was not satisfied.

Justice Binnie, the author of the earlier decision declining to grant more structured relief, issued a strong dissent. Noting that the case was "not the beginning of a litigation journey, but 12 years into it,"[70] he wrote:

> The present application for advance costs comes before us precisely because the appellant says that the Minister's assurances proved empty in practice, that the systemic abuses established in the earlier litigation have continued, and that (in its view) Canada Customs has shown itself to be unwilling to administer the Customs legislation fairly and without discrimination. . . . The question of public importance is this: was the Minister as good as his word when his counsel assured the Court [in the earlier litigation] that the appropriate reforms had been implemented?[71]

Given the case's prior history, it seems clear that the public interest would have been better served by an interim costs award.

Another mechanism to ease the burden of litigation, of course, is to award costs at its conclusion. Given the ordinary rule that "costs follow the event,"[72] they generally are awarded to successful *Charter* plaintiffs. Courts have also awarded costs against a provincial Attorney General who, as an intervener, played a "full and active role" in the unsuccessful defence of a *Criminal Code* provision, for which the Attorney General of Canada was the named respondent.[73]

The role of costs in failed constitutional challenges is more delicate. In private litigation, costs perform a necessary check on frivolous or vexatious claims. In constitutional cases, such concerns must be weighed differently. That is especially true of *Charter* claims which, because of the requisite balancing and proportionality analysis,[74] can be difficult to predict or to characterize as so devoid of merit as to be vexatious. Although some unsuccessful *Charter* litigants probably should face the risk of an adverse costs award, an aggressive posture by the government will exert a serious chilling effect.[75] Perhaps in recognition of that reality, the courts have declined government's requests for costs even when it prevailed in the cause,[76] and have even granted costs to unsuccessful litigants.[77]

---

[70] *Little Sisters 2*, above (n 66) [114].

[71] *Ibid* [120].

[72] *Okanagan*, above (n 13) [30].

[73] *Carter*, above (n 49) [33]. Note that the plaintiffs succeeded in their challenge and were awarded special costs.

[74] Section 1 of the *Charter*, and the various internal limits in specific *Charter* rights (such as "the principles of fundamental justice" in section 7), contribute to the indeterminacy.

[75] *Gosselin (Tutor of) v Quebec (Attorney General)*, [2005] 1 SCR 238, 2005 SCC 15.

[76] *Canadian Foundation for Children, Youth and the Law v Canada (Attorney General)*, [2004] 1 SCR 76, 2004 SCC 4.

[77] *B. (R.) v Children's Aid Society of Metropolitan Toronto*, [1995] 1 SCR 315.

B. Government Innovation

Throughout the *Charter* era, various government departments have funded constitutional challenges. The best known initiative is the Court Challenges Program. Originally set up in 1978 but given real life in 1985, the program is an arm's-length organization that dispenses funds to support challenges against federal laws based on the *Charter*'s equality and language rights provisions. It has also funded research and development, as well as certain initiatives to promote civil society cooperation.

The Program was limited in scope. It rarely covered the full cost of litigation. It applied only to particular *Charter* rights. And, its limitation to federal laws ignored the many provincial laws that might be inconsistent with the Constitution.

The Program was cancelled twice: in 1992 (it was relaunched in 1994) and in 2006. In 2008, after threats of lawsuits, the government led by Prime Minister Stephen Harper decided to reinstate a modified version of the program that would fund language rights litigation. No funding was restored to equality rights litigation, although cases previously selected for support continued to be administered. In 2017, the Liberal government led by Prime Minister Justin Trudeau announced the restoration of the Program.[78]

The Program did not just fund litigation; it supported research and analysis on issues important to marginalized communities. Providing opportunities for organizations to develop analytical and strategic approaches to rights advocacy, the Program showed how constitutionalism not only sets limits on state power, but can channel and direct that power in positive ways. It demonstrated that the *Charter* is not simply an obstacle to be manoeuvred around but, potentially, a tool to enable the state to do more.

From the beginning, the Program attracted criticism. When the Conservative government cancelled the Program in 2006, a Crown minister said that it did not make sense to subsidize lawyers to challenge the government's own laws.[79] Clearly, the Program struck some as strategically unsound. To view the program solely through the lens of winning or losing litigation, though, is a deeply impoverished view. More than any other initiative, the Program has encapsulated the particular nature of the constitutional rights project in Canada. In a modest yet profoundly symbolic way, it recognizes that constitutional limits on the state require independent, proactive, and effective enforcement. It embodies the belief that the protection and promotion of rights is a collective project, not a battle between state and citizen.

---

[78] Court Challenges Program—Reinstatement News: http://www.ccppcj.ca/en/news.php.
[79] John Sossin, "An Axe That Harms Democracy" *Toronto Star* (28 September 2006), A23.

4. REFERENCE OPINIONS

Since the founding of the Supreme Court in 1875,[80] the federal executive has enjoyed the power to refer questions to the Court in the absence of a live case.[81] Provincial governments exercise a similar power with respect to provincial courts.[82] The function is traceable to English law[83] but its use in Canada has far surpassed any in that country. References—also known as advisory opinions—have been extremely significant to the development of Canadian constitutional jurisprudence.

References do not engage the court's remedial powers.[84] As they do not bind anyone to their result, such opinions seem to lack the basic character of a legal rule. In Canada, however, reference opinions are treated as having the force of law.[85] No government has ever regarded a reference opinion as mere "advice".[86] That is not surprising since, in their content and style of reasoning, reference opinions are indistinguishable from decisions. In both, the court appears to perform the same function: identifying applicable legal principles which produce a rule or rules capable of settling a particular question. The

[80] The Court was originally established by ordinary federal law passed under the authority of section 101 of the *Constitution Act, 1867*, 30 & 31 Victoria, c.3 (U.K.): *Supreme and Exchequer Court Act* S.C., 1875, c.11. In 2014, the Supreme Court ruled that its composition and "essential features" had evolved so as be protected against change except by formal amendment of the Constitution: *Reference re ss. 5 and 6 of the Supreme Court Act*, 2014 SCC 21, [2014] 1 SCR 433 [hereinafter *Supreme Court Act Reference*].

[81] *Supreme Court Act*, RSC 1985, c. S-26, s.53 [hereinafter *Supreme Court Act*)]. Where a federal reference concerns the validity of provincial legislation, the relevant Attorney General is to be advised: section 53(5). Section 54 provides a power for either chamber of the House of Commons to refer "private bills" for report by any two judges. It has not been used in a century, and is clearly of a different character than a reference opinion.

[82] References issuing from provincial courts of appeal can be appealed to the Supreme Court as of right: *ibid*, section 36. There have been very dramatic lower court references, such as the opinion on polygamy issued by the B.C. Supreme Court in 2011: see Carissima Mathen, "Reflecting Culture: The Charter and Polygamy" in Benjamin L. Berger and James Stribopoulos (eds), *Unsettled Legacy: Thirty Years of Criminal Justice under the Charter* (Lexis Nexis, 2013) 391. The discussion in this chapter focuses on references at the Supreme Court of Canada.

[83] The first instance of such a power appeared in the *Judicial Committee Act* of 1833.3 & 4 Wm. IV, c.41.

[84] In *Reference Re Criminal Code (Canada), s. 873(A)* (1910), 43 SCR 434 at 436, Justice Girouard stated that "as our advice has no legal effect, does not affect the rights of parties, nor the provincial decisions, and is not even binding upon us", he had no objection to answering a question about the federal jurisdiction over criminal law. Justice Davies made the same point in *Re References by the Governor-General in Council* (1910), 43 SCR 536 at 561:"Being advisory only and not binding upon the body to whom they are given [the Governor General in Council] or upon the judges who give them they cannot be said to be in any way binding upon the judges of any of the provincial courts".

[85] As referred to in *Reference Re Criminal Code*, above (n 84) at 550, the Chief Justice of the Supreme Court of Canada implied that the Court would never consider itself bound by its reference opinions. Yet, this is precisely what has happened over the intervening century.

[86] The Supreme Court itself refers to reference holdings as being "persuasive": *Manitoba v Canada*, [1981] 1 S.C.R. 753 (*per* Martland J. referring to the *Reference Re Legislative Authority of the Parliament of Canada in Relation to the Upper House*, [1980] 1 SCR 54.

Government is presumed to not want an unconstitutional law to stand. Thus, references generate significant legal authority.

Given that they are initiated by political actors, references appear to be inconsistent with the separation of powers between the Executive and the Judiciary.[87] The *Supreme Court Act* states that it is "the duty" of the Court to answer all reference questions.[88] It can be difficult too, to constrain a reference's scope (normally, a power the Court enjoys when it sets constitutional questions).[89] Perhaps in response, the Supreme Court has developed parameters under which it may refuse to answer certain questions. Over the years, the Court has cited the following reasons as justifying a refusal: insufficient factual context,[90] mootness,[91] lack of specificity,[92] vagueness,[93] and the risk that the opinion will produce legal uncertainty.[94] Given the mandatory wording of the *Supreme Court Act,* the most reasonable explanation for this jurisprudence is that the Court has concluded that the reference function is subordinate to the (unwritten) constitutional principle of judicial independence.[95]

Between 1867 and 1986, reference opinions accounted for one-quarter of the Supreme Court's constitutional decisions.[96] Since the enactment of the *Charter of Rights,* there have not been nearly as many, no doubt because of the expanded scope for *inter partes* constitutional litigation. Still, numerous references have contributed to *Charter* jurisprudence on a host of issues, including fault for crimes,[97] prostitution,[98] religious education,[99] and same-sex marriage.[100]

Indeed, the very first opinion of the Supreme Court in relation to the *Constitution Act, 1982* (which includes the *Charter*) was a reference.[101] The matter arose out of provincial objections to Prime Minister Pierre Trudeau's decision to seek approval from the United

---

[87] Admittedly, as a Westminster-style parliamentary democracy, Canada does not enjoy a robust separation of powers.

[88] *Supreme Court Act*, above (n 81), s.53(4).

[89] At the Supreme Court, constitutional questions are governed under R60–61 of the *SCC Rules,* above (n 35).

[90] *Attorney General (Ontario) v Attorney General (Canada)*, [1896] AC 348.

[91] *Re Objection by Que. To Resolution to Amend the Constitution*, [1982] 2 SCR 793, 806 [hereinafter *Quebec Veto*].

[92] *Re Authority of Parliament in relation to the Upper House*, [1980] 1 SCR 54.

[93] *McEvoy v Attorney General (New Brunswick)*, [1983] 1 SCR 704.

[94] *Reference re Same-sex Marriage*, [2004] 3 SCR. 698.

[95] For a discussion of the principle, see *Reference re Remuneration of Judges of the Provincial Court (P.E.I.)*, [1998] 2 S.C.R. 443. Note that the Court has never specified the underlying justification for its discretion to refuse.

[96] Barry L. Strayer, *The Canadian Constitution and the Courts* (Butterworths, 1988) 331.

[97] *Reference Re s. 94(2) of Motor Vehicle Act (British Columbia)*, [1985] 2 SCR 486.

[98] *Reference re ss. 193 and 195.1(1)(C) of the criminal code (Man.)*, [1990] 1 SCR 1123.

[99] *Reference re Bill 30, An Act to Amend the Education Act (Ont.)*, [1987] 1 S.C.R. 1148.

[100] *Reference re Same-Sex Marriage*, 2004 SCC 79, [2004] 3 SCR 698.

[101] *Reference re Resolution to Amend the Constitution*, [1981] 1 SCR 753 [hereinafter *Patriation Reference*].

Kingdom Parliament for a series of constitutional amendments even if the provinces did not agree. In the *Patriation Reference*,[102] a majority of the Supreme Court advised that, although the federal government was legally entitled to seek such approval, the specific nature of the amendments triggered a constitutional convention requiring a substantial degree of provincial consent.[103]

The reference's political impact was momentous. The Prime Minister resumed federal-provincial negotiations, and the resolution ultimately forwarded to Westminster reflected the consent of the federal Parliament and nine provincial legislatures.[104] The *Patriation Reference* had an equally powerful legal impact. It foreshadowed the rejection of a political questions doctrine,[105] embraced the progressive approach to constitutional interpretation, demonstrated the breadth of the declaratory power, and thrust the Court to the center of constitutional inquiry. In a number of respects, the reference provided a template for the modern constitutional method.[106]

The role of advisory opinions have been critical to Canadian constitutional law. But the exclusive executive power to initiate references means that they are vulnerable to political manipulation. As well, in 2014 the Court stated that its composition and "essential features" are protected under Part V of the *Constitution Act, 1982* and cannot be altered by ordinary law.[107] Should the reference function be found to be one of the Court's "essential features", which seems plausible, changing it would require the consent of Parliament and at least 7 of Canada's 10 provinces.[108] Of course, it may be that the essence of the reference function is not how or by whom it is initiated, but what it does. Still, it seems unlikely that Parliament will be eager to wade into that debate—which might well trigger litigation—in the near future.

There have been calls to use the advisory function pre-emptively—to put highly contested questions to the court in advance of a legislative decision. References occasionally have been initiated in this manner. The advisory proceedings initiated with respect to securities regulation,[109] assisted human reproduction,[110] Senate reform,[111] and same-sex marriage[112] could all be described as "pre-emptive". For the most part, though, both

---

[102]   Until the *Canada Act 1982*, changes to the Constitution required formal legislation enacted by the U.K. Parliament: *Statute of Westminster*, 1931, 22 Geo. V, c. 4 (U.K.) s.7.

[103]   *Patriation Reference*, above (n 101) 905.

[104]   The province of Quebec did not consent. One year later, the Supreme Court of Canada rejected the argument that Quebec enjoyed a veto over constitutional amendment: *Quebec Veto*, above (n 91).

[105]   *Operation Dismantle v The Queen*, [1985] 1 SCR 441 [52–54].

[106]   For discussion, see Carissima Mathen, "'The Question Calls for an Answer, and I Propose to Answer It': The *Patriation Reference* as Constitutional Method" [2011] 54 SCLR 143, 163–166.

[107]   *Supreme Court Act Reference*, above (n 72). For further discussion, see the chapter by Adam Dodek and Rosemary Cairns Way in this *Handbook*.

[108]   *Constitution Act, 1982*, s. 41(1)(d).

[109]   *Reference re Securities Act,* 2011 SCC 66, [2011] 3 S.C.R. 837.

[110]   *Reference re Assisted Human Reproduction Act,* 2010 SCC 61, [2010] 3 S.C.R. 457.

[111]   Above (n 34).

[112]   Above (n 100).

federal and provincial governments tend to wait for individuals or groups to initiate constitutional challenges.

Would greater recourse to reference opinions be a good thing? Certainly, reference opinions may facilitate the development of constitutional law. Given that the Constitution empowers judges to lay down rules obligating members of the legislative and executive branches, it seems desirable for them to do so pre-emptively. And, allowing the government to obtain a Supreme Court pronouncement on an important issue could be more economical than requiring a case to proeed through various levels of court. Pre-emptive use of references can also produce certainty and coordination—values that hold particular force in a federal system that is likely to produce multiple rules and interpretations of rules.

Against those arguments lie several counter-claims. One might object, first, that references do not provide a proper factual context for resolving deeply contested legal questions.[113] That objection has some force, particularly if a reference involves a new social problem, or very broad questions. But a reference concerning: a law that has been in force for some time, draft legislation that builds on or responds to an existing regime, or a question that has already been the subject of considerable study would not appear to be as problematic. The court can structure the hearing to address many gaps, including by appointing amicus curiae or public interest interveners. In any event, if a question remains unacceptably vague or outside the court's sense of propriety, it can decline to answer it.

Another objection is that references are grounded in executive discretion. The executive is the only body[114] that can initiate the advisory opinion process. It also enjoys sole authority to decide which questions to pose and how those questions are to be framed. It is unrealistic to think that political considerations would not weigh on such decisions. No doubt, such considerations are unavoidable, but given the degree to which the reference function is dependent upon the courts, increasing their use will increase the extent to which the judiciary is drawn into political disputes.

A third objection is that greater use of the reference function could encourage a political malaise. It could provide additional temptation for political actors to avoid difficult issues by tossing them to the courts. This could lessen the incentive for deliberative assemblies such as Parliament to do the hard but necessary work of debating questions that go to the heart of the nation's values and core political agreements.

It is true, of course, that the Canadian Parliament is no longer supreme. Its will must bow to constitutional limits.[115] But, within the broad confines of the Constitution, and the *Charter* in particular, there are many legitimate ways to achieve legislative objectives. It is possible that a court might rule out some of those alternatives, from the

---

[113] Lawrence Tribe, *American Constitutional Law* (The Foundation Press, 1988) 73 footnote 4; Note, *Advisory Opinions on the Constitutionality of Statutes*, [1956] 69 Harv L Rev 1302.

[114] As discussed, above (n 83), there is a modest power for legislative referrals, but it is not at all of the same character, and has fallen into disuse.

[115] The same, of course, applies to the provincial and territorial legislative assemblies.

outset, as unconstitutional. But, in such cases, one would expect that information to emerge during democratic deliberation. Parliament would then face a choice: either jettison such alternatives altogether, or to press ahead believing that it could defend the regime's validity.[116] Pressing ahead would be a calculated risk. But it is not at all clear that taking such a risk is so intolerable that an executive actor should be prevented from doing so, particularly at the cost of decreased enthusiasm for constitutional debate in non-judicial fora.

As demonstrated in this chapter, traditional legal process doctrines have responded to the unique challenges of *Charter* litigation in a number of ways. If there is a unifying theme to these distinct rules, practices, and policies, it is their acknowledgement of the critical importance, to Canada's constitutional order, of the principle of legality. Given that all laws must be consistent with the Constitution, judicial review should not be foreclosed by reasons that have little to do with the merits of a claim. The doctrines discussed in this chapter do not completely mitigate the challenges associated with *Charter* litigation.[117] But they have facilitated the development of a robust jurisprudence and constitutional culture that sustains the protection of individual rights. They are indispensable to Canada's *Charter* identity.

Bibliography

Secondary sources

Bryden, Phil. "Public Interest Intervention in the Courts", (1987) 66 Can. Bar. Rev. 490.
Hogg, Peter W. *Constitutional Law of Canada* (Toronto: Thomson Reuters 2007) Ch. 59.
Mathen, Carissima. "'The Question Calls for an Answer, and I Propose to Answer It': The *Patriation Reference* as Constitutional Method" [2011] 54 SCLR 143.

Cases

British Columbia (Minister of Forests) v Okanagan Indian Band [2003] 3 SCR 371.
Canada (Attorney General) v Downtown Eastside Sex Workers United Against Violence Society 2012 SCC 45, [2012] 2 S.C.R. 524.
Carter v Canada (Attorney General), 2015 SCC 5, [2015] 1 SCR 331.
R. v Big M Drug Mart Ltd., [1985] 1 S.C.R. 295.
Reference re Same-Sex Marriage, 2004 SCC 79, [2004] 3 SCR 698.

---

[116] It may also, in certain circumstances, invoke the notwithstanding clause under section 33, but this has become exceedingly rare. For further discussion of section 33, see Janet Hiebert's chapter in this *Handbook*.

[117] Further discussion of these challenges are found in the chapter by Kent Roach in this *Handbook*.

CHAPTER 31

....

THE JUSTIFICATION OF
RIGHTS VIOLATIONS

Section 1 of the Charter

....

CHARLES-MAXIME PANACCIO[*]

1. INTRODUCTION

....

SECTION 1 of the *Canadian Charter of Rights and Freedoms* states that the *Charter* 'guarantees the rights and freedoms set out in it subject only to such reasonable limits prescribed by law as can be demonstrably justified in a free and democratic society'. It thus simultaneously guarantees the rights set out in the following provisions and acknowledges that they can be subject to limits if these are prescribed by law, reasonable, and justified in a free and democratic society.

Rights, reason, justification, liberal-democratic political morality . . . these are fundamental, controversial notions. Do constitutional rights have special moral force? When can their infringement be reasonable and justified in a free and democratic society? To what extent can non-elected judges cast aside decisions made by other branches of government? These questions constantly haunt the application of section 1. Moreover, they have to be addressed through a methodology suitable for public understanding and judicial application.

Charter decision-making is an exercise in moral reasoning. It aims at determining whether the state has acted in a morally permissible way. Moral reasoning has substantive (*moral*) and formal (*reasoning*) aspects. The Supreme Court of Canada has structured the application of section 1 around a proportionality framework. Proportionality is a formal notion. In moral reasoning contexts, it essentially requires that action be the

[*] Associate Professor, Civil Law Section, Faculty of Law, University of Ottawa.

source of more moral good than bad. The political morality presupposed by the proportionality framework is a non-specific liberal-democratic political morality. We will see that although the Supreme Court of Canada had initially flirted with the view that rights reflect special moral considerations, it has not retained it. It has also been mindful of the limited institutional legitimacy of the judiciary.

Moral reasoning is not deductive reasoning. It cannot be encapsulated by lists of specific rules of absolute validity. It can be structured around formal and substantive principles, but will always leave room for weighing and pondering in practice. Section 1's proportionality framework properly amalgamates these elements of form, substance, and pragmatism.

2. GENESIS

The *Charter* became part of the Canadian Constitution in 1982 as a result of the process of constitutional 'patriation'. Patriation was the culmination of two decades of constitutional discussions which featured, among many other topics, a debate over constitutional rights judicial review i.e. the judicial power to strike down state action, including parliamentary legislation, that affects certain fundamental constitutional rights.[1] In that debate, those in favor of judicial review relied on ideals of fundamental human rights, arguing that these had to be protected against the tyranny of majorities, and extolled the judicial virtues of independence, impartiality, and rationality.[2] Those

---

[1] For good journalistic accounts of the events that have surrounded the patriation of the Canadian Constitution and, more particularly, negotiations over the *Charter of Rights*, see: Robert Sheppard and Michael Valpy, *The National Deal, The Fight for a Canadian Constitution* (Fleet Books, 1982), esp ch 7; Roy Romanow, John Whyte and Howard Leeson, *Canada . . . Notwithstanding: The Making of the Constitution, 1976–1982* (Methuen, 1984), esp. ch 8. See also the chapter by Janet Hiebert in this *Handbook*.

[2] E.g., Pierre Elliott Trudeau, 'A Constitutional Declaration of Rights' in P.E. Trudeau, *Federalism and the French Canadians* (MacMillan, 1968) 52, 56; Honourable Pierre Elliott Trudeau Minister of Justice, *A Canadian Charter of Human Rights* (Queen's Printer, 1968); The Right Honourable Pierre Elliott Trudeau Prime Minister of Canada, *The Constitution and the People of Canada: An Approach to the Objectives of Confederation, the Rights of People and the Institutions of Government* (The Queen's Printer 1969); Canada, Parliament, Special Joint Committee of the Senate and the House of Commons on the Constitution of Canada, "Final Report" (16 March 1972), 18–19; Canada, Parliament, *Minutes of Proceedings and Evidence of the Special Joint Committee of the Senate and of the House of Commons on the Constitution of Canada*, 30th Parl. 3d sess., Nos. 1-20 (1978), 12:12 (Prof. W. Tarnopolsky, 12 September 1978), 20:10 (Report to Parliament, 10 October 1980); Canada, Parliament, *Minutes of Proceedings and Evidence of the Special Joint Committee of the Senate and of the House of Commons on the Constitution of Canada*, 32 Parl.1st sess., No 13, 13:5, 13:21, 13:24 (National Association of Japanese Canadians, 26 November 1980); 14:66–67 (Representative for Ukrainian-Canadians, 27 November 1980); 22:104–123 (British Columbia Civil Liberties Association, 9 December 1980); Canadian Intergovernmental Conference Secretariat, Verbatim Transcript (Unverified Text) of the

who were against it praised parliamentary democracy and emphasized the limited legitimacy of the judicial branch.[3]

Similar arguments reverberated into the discussions surrounding the limitations
clause (as well as into the application of section 1, as we shall see): those in favor of judicial review preferred a limitations clause with restrictive language (or no limitations
clause at all),[4] whereas those suspicious of it (most provinces) favored a more permissive
one.[5] One version elaborated during the 1980 constitutional negotiations used very for-
giving language, stating that rights could be subject to 'reasonable limits as are generally
accepted in a free and democratic society with a parliamentary system of government'.[6]
This formula, suggesting that whatever had been decided by parliamentary legislatures or was in line with conventional social morality would be an appropriate limit to
constitutional rights, attracted withering criticism.[7] It was soon replaced by the more
demanding language of section 1, signalling a shift from a conventional-majoritarian
analysis to an ideal-justificatory one.

Federal-Provincial Conference of First Ministers on the Constitution, vol. I, (Ottawa: 8–13 September
1980) 506–508, 562–563.

[3] E.g., Ontario, *Royal Commission of Inquiry into Civil Rights, Report No. 2*, vol. 4 (Frank Fogg
Queen's Printer, 1969) 1588–1593; Minutes, *Special Joint Committee on the Constitution 1978* ibid 18:51–52
(K. Rafe Mair, Chairman Cabinet Committee on Confederation, Government of British Columbia, 27
September 1978); Minutes, *Special Joint Committee on the Constitution 1980*, ibid 12:100–101 (Canada
West Foundation, 25 November 1980), 14:81–82 (Premier MacLean, Prince Edward Island, 27 November
1980); Minutes, *Special Joint Committee on Constitution of Canada*, 32 Parl.1st sess., No 33 (7 January
1981) 33A-23 (Appendix, Alberta Government Position Paper on Constitutional Change, October
1978), 34:117–121 (Campaign Life Canada, 8 January 1981)), 34:131, 34:148–149, 34:168 (Peter Russell,
University of Toronto, 8 January 1981); Verbatim Transcript of Federal-Provincial Conference of First
Ministers, ibid 476–482, 485–492 (Premiers Lyon of Manitoba and Blakeney of Saskatchewan); *Canada
Notwithstanding* above (n 1) 218–220.

[4] Minutes, *Special Joint Committee on the Constitution 1978* (n 2) 20:14 (Report to Parliament);
Minutes, Special Joint Committee on the Constitution 1980 (n 2), 5-5A (14 November 1980), 5:8, 5:24,
5A:3 (Chief Commissioner Canadian Human Rights Commission); No 9 (20 November 1980), 9:129
(Advisory Council on the Status of Women), No 4 (13 November 1980), 4:92 (MP Svend Robinson),
No 9 (20 November 1980) at 9:58 (National Action Committee on the Status of Women), No 22 (9
December 1980), 22:32-33 (Coalition for the Protection of Human Life), No 7 (18 November 1980) 7:9
(Canadian Civil Liberties Association); No 14 (27 November 1980) 14:59–60 (Representatives of
Ukrainian Canadians). No 22 (9 December 1980) 22:105–106, 22:112 (British Columbia Civil Liberties
Association).

[5] *Canada Notwithstanding* above (n 1) 244.

[6] Ibid 245; *Federal-Provincial First Ministers' Conference, Ottawa, Ontario, September 8–12, 1980: The
Canadian Charter of Rights and Freedoms, Revised Discussion Draft, Federal, September 3, 1980* in Anne
F Bayefsky, *Canada's Constitution Act 1982 & Amendments: A Documentary History* (vol. I, McGraw-Hill
Ryerson Limited, 1989) 704.

[7] *The National Deal*, above (n 1) 135, 139–140; *Canada Notwithstanding*, above (n 1) 250. See also the
references to the Minutes, *Special Joint Committee on the Constitution 1980*, above (n 4).

3. INTERPRETATION

The basic elements of section 1's proportionality framework were established by the Supreme Court in 1986 in the *Oakes* case.[8] *Charter* reasoning usually proceeds in two distinct steps: first, it must be determined whether a rights-provision has been infringed; if that analysis yields a positive answer, it must then be determined, pursuant to section 1, whether the infringement constitutes a reasonable, justified limit in a free and democratic society.[9] From the first step to the second, the onus of 'demonstration' shifts from the plaintiff to the government.[10]

A. Proportionality

The proportionality framework is a framework for moral reasoning. Moral reasoning is a kind of practical reasoning. Practical reasoning is reasoning about how one ought to act, hence moral reasoning is reasoning about how one ought to morally act. The proportionality framework helps determine whether it was morally permissible for the state to infringe a *Charter* right in the way that it has. The infringement of a *Charter*-protected right is taken to signal morally negative features of the state's action, and the proportionality framework helps determine whether these morally negative features are outweighed by morally positive ones. It thus has a 'calculative', consequentialist aspect, but it is perfectly capable of incorporating less calculative, 'deontological', moral demands.

The proportionality analysis begins with an examination of the *ends* or objectives underlying the state's action. These must be sufficiently important—'pressing and substantial' said Chief Justice Dickson in *Oakes*. It then turns to an examination of the rationality and proportionality of the means and effects of the state's action. The state must satisfy both the ends and means/effects parts of the analysis, as well as every step of the means/effects part.

(i) Good Ends

To be justified, the state's action had to be motivated by acceptable ends. If state organs generally navigate morally suitable waters, this requirement should be met in most cases. Nevertheless, in some circumstances, it may prove impossible for the state to point to morally acceptable objectives. For instance, it may be impossible to conjure satisfactory ends to explain why an anti-discrimination statute

---

[8]   *R. v Oakes* [1986] 1 SCR 103. The main inspiration for the framework seems to have been the European Court of Human Rights' case law: Robert J. Sharpe and Kent Roach, *Brian Dickson: A Judge's Journey* (University of Toronto Press, 2003) 334.

[9]   Note however that 'qualified rights' provisions such as ss. 7, 8, and 15(1) leave a more limited role for s. 1 since their application already requires extensive balancing of various considerations.

[10]   *Oakes* above (n 8) [66].

does not protect the LGBT community.[11] Even more unusually, some motives for action are prohibited by particular constitutional rights doctrines. For example, if Sunday-as-a-day-of-rest legislation is being scrutinized under section 1 because it infringes the right to freedom of religion, it becomes crucial to determine whether it was adopted for religious or secular motives, because the former are strictly prohibited by the Canadian equivalent of the American no-establishment doctrine.[12]

(ii) Proportional Means/Effects

Even if it is found that the state's action was motivated by morally acceptable objectives, it may still not be justified. The means and effects of the state's action must also be rational and proportional. This assessment has three different branches: (1) 'Rational Connection', (2) 'Minimal Impairment' and (3) 'General Proportionality'.

(a) Rational Connection

'Rational Connection' requires that the state measures be minimally capable of achieving the valid objective(s) isolated in the ends part of the analysis.[13] It is a test of instrumental rationality, looking only at the relationship between means and ends, to the exclusion of side-effects and alternative options.[14] It is usually easily met by the state because only absurd actions would fail it. Rational Connection could thus be described, to borrow the colourful words of Felix Cohen, as asking courts to act as 'lunacy commissions sitting in judgment upon the mental capacity of legislators'.[15] It is indeed difficult to imagine state action which is thoroughly incapable of achieving its underlying objectives. Some

[11] *Vriend v Alberta* [1998] 1 SCR 493 [114]–[115]. For other examples of objectives not being found to be pressing and substantial or in accordance with the values of a free and democratic society, see *Thomson Newspapers Co. v Canada (Attorney General)* [1998] 1 SCR 877 [101]–[102]; *M. v H.* [1999] 2 SCR 3 [356] (Bastarache J., concurring); *Dunmore v Ontario (Attorney General)* [2001] 3 SCR 1016 [180]–[182] (L'Heureux-Dubé J., concurring); *R v Hall* [2002] 3 SCR 309 [112]–[115] (Iacobucci J., dissenting); *Nova Scotia (Attorney General) v Walsh* [2002] 4 SCR 325 [182]–[183] (L'Heureux-Dubé J., dissenting).

[12] Compare *R v Big M. Drug Mart Ltd.* [1985] 1 SCR 295 and *R v Edwards Books and Art Ltd* [1986] 2 SCR 713. See the chapter by Benjamin Berger in this *Handbook*.

[13] *Oakes* above (n 8) at 139; *Osborne v Canada (Treasury Board)* [1991] 2 SCR 69, 98; *Lavigne v Ontario Public Services Employees Union* [1991] 2 SCR 211, 291–292 (Wilson J., concurring); *R v Laba* [1994] 3 SCR 965, 1007–1008; *Harvey v New Brunswick* [1996] 2 SCR 876 [40]–[41]; *Alberta v Hutterian Bretheren of Wilson Colony* [2009] 2 SCR 567 [48], [51].

[14] Rationality can be conceived purely instrumentally or more substantively, however. This was noted by Paul G Murray in 'Section One of the *Canadian Charter of Rights and Freedoms*: An Examination at Two Levels of Interpretation' (1989) 21 Ott L R 631, 643–646. See also *R v Downey* [1992] 2 SCR 10, 36–37, 42–47 (the majority applies the minimal instrumental rationality version of the test while the minority applies a version which incorporates added balancing). For an account of the trend towards minimal instrumental rationality see Christopher M Dassios and Clifton P Prophet, 'Charter Section 1: The Decline of Grand Unified Theory and the Trend towards Deference in the Supreme Court of Canada' (1993) 15 Advocates Q 289, 297–301.

[15] Lucy Kramer Cohen (ed), *The Legal Conscience: Selected Papers of Felix S. Cohen* (Yale University Press, 1960), 44.

state actions may sabotage their own objectives to some extent,[16] but they are practically never completely instrumentally irrational or utterly self-defeating.[17] One would have to imagine an absurd situation, say a legislature banning criticism of the government in order to prevent the extinction of the beaver or some kind of 'destroying the city in order to save it' argument.

(b) Minimal Impairment

State measures should not only be rationally connected to their underlying objectives, they should also impair the infringed right or freedom as little as possible. This is the 'Minimal Impairment' component of the effects analysis. It is a prescription to minimize the (negative) 'rights-affecting' side-effects of action: if the state could have achieved its objectives without affecting rights to the same extent, it should have done so. This requires that less rights-impairing alternatives be considered.

Strictly construed, Minimal Impairment implies that the attainment of the state's objectives is not, to any extent, put into question; it should be satisfied if a less impairing solution were to jeopardize the realization of the objectives to whatever extent. Thus, strictly construed, it is not a full-fledged assessment of proportionality, involving a full evaluation of moral 'positives' and 'negatives'.[18] What is to be determined is whether the *same* positives could be achieved with less of the negative. Therefore, if this strict construal were to be dutifully applied, it would not be overly difficult to satisfy. And if it failed to be satisfied, it would amount to a gentle slap on the wrist of the state, suggesting that it ought to go back to the drawing board and pursue the very same aims through a path more respectful of rights. In practice, however, a more general assessment of proportionality has often been smuggled into the Minimal Impairment analysis.[19]

---

[16] *R v Keegstra* [1990] 3 SCR 697 [305]–[311] (McLachlin J., as she then was, for the minority) (making hate propagandists into heroes while attempting to stigmatize them); *Lavoie v Canada*, [2002] 1 SCR 769 [10] (McLachlin C.J. and L'Heureux Dubé J for the minority) (undermining citizenship while trying to promote it). *Sauvé v Canada (Chief Electoral Officer)*, [2002] 3 SCR 519 [30]–[44] (McLachlin C.J. for the majority) (undermining democracy and the rule of law while trying to protect it).

[17] And yet . . . see *Figueroa v Canada (Attorney General)*, [2003] 1 SCR 912 [75] (Iacobucci for majority) (party fielding a minimum of 50 candidates has little to do with genuine interest in electoral process); *R v Advance Cutting and Coring Ltd.* [2001] 3 SCR 209 [47] (Bastarache J. for the minority) ('regional quotas have little if anything to do with the professional competence of workers in the construction industry').

[18] That stripped down version of Minimal Impairment was most recently favoured by the Court in *Canada (Attorney General) v JTI-Macdonald Corp.* [2007] 2 SCR 610, 2007 SCC 30 [43]; *Hutterian Brothers* (n 13) [54]–[55]; *Saskatchewan (Human Rights Commission) v Whatcott* 2013 SCC 11, [2013] 1 SCR 467 [101].

[19] For a similar observation, see Murray (n 14) 647, 652, 663. For examples of the 'pure' and 'balancing' versions of minimal impairment, compare the majority (balancing) and minority (pure) reasons in *R v Hess; R v Nguyen*, [1990] 2 SCR 906 [24]–[32], [112]–[116]. See also *Osborne* (n 13) [55]–[61] (Sopinka J., for the majority—balancing), [91]–[94] (Stevenson J., dissenting—pure); *R v Seaboyer; R v Gayme*, [1991] 2 SCR 577 [83] (McLachlin J., as she then was, for the majority—balancing), [272]–[276] (L'Heureux-Dubé J. for the minority—pure); *R v Wholesale Travel Group Inc*, [1991] 3 SCR 154 [58]–[62], [80]–[91] (Lamer C.J. for the minority—balancing), [244]–[245] (Iacobucci J. for the majority—pure); *R v Mills*,

(c) General Proportionality

Even if the state meets the Rational Connection and Minimal Impairment components, for a rule to be justified the effects of the measure on the rights and freedoms must also, overall, be proportional to the objective sought and potential benefits.[20] We can call this last component of the effects analysis 'General Proportionality'. This, it must be noted, is the only requirement which consists in an overall balancing of the negative and positive moral aspects of state action. This was aptly picked up by Bastarache J. in *Thomson Newspapers*. He said:

> The third stage of the proportionality analysis performs a fundamentally distinct role. Determining whether there is a pressing and substantial objective behind the provision under scrutiny necessarily occurs in the abstract, before the specific nature of the legislation and its impact on the *Charter* right has been analysed. Of course, ascertaining that objective requires a consideration of what the provision actually does, as well as documentary evidence as to what the legislator thought it was doing. Moreover, the relevant purpose is the purpose specific to the provision which limits the *Charter* right. But the purpose must, nevertheless, be articulated abstractly because a purpose is a goal or outcome which, by definition, may be achieved in different ways. Before the specific effects of the measure in question have been scrutinized and concretized through the first two steps of the proportionality analysis, it is often difficult to assess, in the abstract, the possible impact on *Charter* freedoms of a laudable legislative objective. The focus of the first and second steps of the proportionality analysis is not the relationship between the measures and the *Charter* right in question, but rather the relationship between the ends of the legislation and the means employed. Although the minimal impairment stage of the proportionality test necessarily takes into account the extent to which a *Charter* value is infringed, the ultimate standard is whether the *Charter* right is impaired as little as possible given the validity of the legislative purpose. *The third stage of the proportionality analysis provides an opportunity to assess, in light of the practical and contextual details which are elucidated in the first and second stages, whether the benefits which accrue from the limitation are proportional to its deleterious effects as measured by the values underlying the Charter.* As Professor Jamie Cameron states ("The Past, Present, and Future of Expressive Freedom Under the *Charter*" (1997), 35 *Osgoode Hall L.J.* 1, at p. 66):
> ... this branch of the section 1 analysis asks an important question. By assessing the proportionality of its deleterious effects and salutary benefits it considers, in direct and explicit terms, whether the consequences of the violation are too great when measured against the benefits that may be achieved. As such, it is the only part

---

[1999] 3 SCR 668 [11] (Lamer C.J., dissenting—balancing); *R v Sharpe*, [2001] 1 SCR 45 [96]–[97] (McLachlin C.J. for majority—pure); *Harper v Canada*, [2004] 1 SCR 827 [32]–[39] (McLachlin C.J. and Major J., for the dissent—balancing). American courts also tend to apply different versions of the 'least drastic means test": Note, 'Less Drastic Means and the First Amendment' (1969) 78 Yale LJ 464, 471–473.

[20] A more complete formulation of the final proportionality test than the one described in *Oakes* was put forward by Chief Justice Lamer in *Dagenais v Canadian Broadcasting Corp.*, [1994] 3 SCR 835, 887–888.

of the current analysis to acknowledge the harm or cost of justifiable limits: that a constitutional right has been violated.[21]

If every step of the proportionality of means/effects analysis were strictly applied, truly controversial cases should almost always be settled at this very last stage. Yet, the reality is that General Proportionality is rarely used by itself to strike down legislation.[22] Courts seem to be more comfortable when they appear to be reaching their decisions on less controversial grounds, such as Rational Connection and Minimal Impairment. This may have rhetorical benefits, but it comes at the price of a certain kind of deception.

Be that as it may, the proportionality framework unveiled in *Oakes* and refined in later cases quite carefully manages the intrusion of the judiciary into the affairs of the other branches of government. As it progresses, the analysis becomes more and more fine-grained. It is only at the very last stage that it truly requires an all-encompassing exercise in moral balancing.

B. Taking Rights More or Less Seriously

In *Oakes*, Chief Justice Dickson had emphasized that the section 1 inquiry must be premised on an understanding that rights and freedoms which are part of the supreme law of Canada had been *violated*.[23] He added that the state had the burden of showing that a limit was justified according to a *rigorous* 'balance of probabilities' standard. And recall that he had insisted that the state's objective(s) had to be 'pressing and substantial' for a limit to be justified.

A few months earlier, in *Singh*, Justice Wilson had expressed doubts that 'utilitarian considerations' (in that case administrative convenience in the context of decisions

---

[21] *Thomson Newspapers* (n 11) [125] [Emphasis added]. The same point is made by L Wayne Sumner in *The Hateful and the Obscene: Studies in the Limits of Free Expression* (University of Toronto Press, 2004), 66–67. See also Pierre Blache, 'The Criteria of Justification under Oakes: Too Much Severity Generated through Legal Formalism' (1991) 20 Manitoba LJ 437, 444; David M Beatty, *The Ultimate Rule of Law* (Oxford University Press 2004) 163; Aharon Barak, 'Proportional Effect: The Israeli Experience' (2007) UTLJ 369, 374, 380–381; Dieter Grimm, 'Proportionality in Canadian and German Constitutional Jurisprudence' (2007) 57 UTLJ 383, 393–394, 396; Alan Brudner, 'What Theory of Rights Best Explains the *Oakes* Test?' in Luc B. Tremblay and Grégoire C.N. Webber (eds), *La limitation des droits de la Charte: essais critiques sur l'arrêt R. c. Oakes/The limitation of Charter Rights: Critical Essays on R. v. Oakes* (Thémis, 2009) 59, 60.

[22] See for instance *Ramsden v Peterborough (City)*, [1993] 2 SCR 1084 where General Proportionality is coupled with Minimal Impairment in order to show that the law is not justified. Apparently, courts in Germany tend to be more willing to declare laws unconstitutional *solely* on the basis of an absence of General Proportionality: Grimm ibid 389, 393.

[23] *Oakes* (n 8) 135; *Singh v Minister of Employment and Immigration*, [1985] 1 SCR 177, 218. See also the dissenting reasons of Dickson C.J. and Wilson J. in *Reference Re Public Service Employee Relations Act (Alta.)*, [1987] 1 SCR 313 [102].

concerning refugee status) could ground the justification for a limitation on *Charter* rights. She said:

> Certainly the guarantees of the *Charter* would be illusory if they could be ignored because it was administratively convenient to do so. No doubt considerable time and money can be saved by adopting administrative procedures which ignore the principles of fundamental justice but such an argument, in my view, misses the point of the exercise under s. 1.[24]

These statements are reminiscent of Ronald Dworkin's views on fundamental rights— particularly influential in the 1980s—according to which, generally, rights may not be outweighed by general social goals. Put differently, in general, fundamental rights have a certain threshold weight and may only be defeated by goals of special urgency, not by the routine goals of political administration.[25]

But the Supreme Court's statements of rights-enthusiasm were almost immediately qualified. At the end of his discussion of proportionality in *Oakes*, Chief Justice Dickson had cautioned that the inquiry into effects must be far reaching, as some limits to rights will be more serious than others 'in terms of the nature of the right or freedom violated, the extent of the violation, and the degree to which the measures which impose the limit trench upon the integral principles of a free and democratic society'.[26] He had also left some space for flexibility by suggesting that the standard of demonstration for justification would be 'commensurate with the occasion'.[27]

Furthermore, in *Edwards Books*, a decision released less than a year after *Oakes*, Chief Justice Dickson and Justice La Forest reiterated that the nature of the proportionality test would vary with the circumstances, adding that its application should be context-sensitive and that rigid and inflexible standards should be avoided.[28] Justice La Forest also insisted that the business of government is *practical* rather than theoretical, often requiring a complex exercise of adjudication between conflicting interests.[29] Such admonitions in favor of flexibility and pragmatism were repeated in several other cases. For instance, in *Keegstra*, Chief Justice Dickson said:

> The analytical framework of *Oakes* has been continually reaffirmed by this Court, yet it is dangerously misleading to conceive of s. 1 as a rigid and technical provision, offering nothing more than a last chance for the state to justify incursions into the realm of fundamental rights. From a crudely practical standpoint, *Charter* litigants sometimes may perceive s. 1 in this manner, but in the body of our nation's

[24] *Singh*, above (n 23) 218–219.
[25] They may nonetheless be overridden in order to 'protect the rights of others, or to prevent a catastrophe, or even to obtain a clear and major public benefit'. Ronald Dworkin, 'Taking Rights Seriously' in *Taking Rights Seriously* (New Impression with a Reply to Critics, Duckworth, 1978) 184, 191.
[26] *Oakes* above (n 8) 139–140.
[27] Ibid 138.
[28] *Edwards Books* (n 12) 768–769. See also *United States of America v Cotroni; United States of America v El Zein*, [1989] 1 SCR 1469.
[29] *Edwards Books* above (n 28) 795.

constitutional law it plays an immeasurably richer role, one of great magnitude and sophistication.[30]

The demand for 'pressing and substantial' objectives was also relaxed. In 1989, in *Andrews*, Justice MacIntyre stated that it may be 'too stringent for application in all cases [and] would frequently deny the community-at-large the benefits associated with sound social and economic legislation'. Hence, the question should be 'whether the limitation represents a legitimate exercise of the legislative power for the attainment of a desirable social objective'.[31]

Minimal Impairment, for its part, has generally been interpreted as determining whether there was no *reasonable* alternative that would have allowed the state to achieve its objective with fewer detrimental rights-related effects. In other words, the question became 'has the state made a "genuine and serious attempt to minimize adverse effects" and struck a legitimate compromise'?[32] Finally, the opposition between rights and collective 'utilitarian' considerations was re-visited and softened in later cases.[33] Hence, in general orientation, the Court quickly moved away from a 'Taking Rights Seriously' ethos and embraced a less demanding discourse of reasonableness.

4. DISCUSSION

A. Form and Substance

The 'formalism' of s. 1's proportionality framework has regularly been under attack.[34] The characterization is quite accurate: proportionality is, at base, a formal, mathematical concept. Proportionality is not a value—it is a relation between values. It thus requires

---

[30] *Keegstra* above (n 16) 735. See also La Forest J. in *McKinney v University of Guelph,* [1990] 3 SCR 229, 280; La Forest J. (dissenting) in *RJR-MacDonald Inc. v Canada (Attorney General),* [1995] 3 SCR 199 [60]–[64]; Gonthier J. (dissenting) in *Sauvé* above (n 16) [79]–[83]; *Hutterian Bretheren* above (n 13) [37] (McLachlin C.J. for the majority).

[31] *Andrews v Law Society of British Columbia,* [1989] 1 SCR 143, 184. Justice MacIntyre's reasons on s. 15 were agreed with by a majority of the court, but he was only joined by Lamer J. on s. 1 and on the result. Justice Wilson, joined by Dickson C.J. and L'Heureux Dubé J., expressly disagreed with that aspect of Justice MacIntyre's reasons, ibid 154. Justice La Forest (in agreement with Wilson J. as to the result) substantially agreed with Justice MacIntyre on this point, ibid 198.

[32] *Edwards Books* above (n 12) [144]; *Irwin Toy Ltd. v Quebec (Attorney General),* [1989] 1 SCR 927, 989–990.

[33] *R. v. Lee,* [1989] 2 S.C.R. 1384, 1391; *Newfoundland (Treasury Board) v N.A.P.E.,* [2004] 3 SCR 381 [66]–[68].

[34] For instance: Jamie Cameron, 'The Forgotten Half of Dolphin Delivery: A Comment on the Relationship between the Substantive Guarantees and Section 1 of the Charter' (1988) 22 UBC LR 147, 152; Blache above (n 21); Pamela A Chapman, 'The Politics of Judging: Section 1 of the *Charter of Rights*

independent values to be put to work. In a context of practical-moral reasoning, it prescribes that an action be morally right, which often means that it is the source of more good than bad. But proportionality is devoid of moral substance. Substance must be sought in substantial principles of political morality.[35]

In *Oakes*, Chief Justice Dickson did say that '[t]he Court must be guided by the values and principles essential to a free and democratic society' which embody

> respect for the inherent dignity of the human person, commitment to social justice and equality, accommodation of a wide variety of beliefs, respect for cultural and group identity, and faith in social and political institutions which enhance the participation of individuals and groups in society.[36]

Hence, *Oakes* contained both the formal idea of proportionality and a snapshot of substantive values essential to a free and democratic society. Should something more be expected? Can this framework be significantly improved upon?[37] This is doubtful. It may be tempting to blame the results of cases on proportionality, but precisely because proportionality is formal, it does not condition results. The better suggestion would be to say that judges are substantially wrong, but then that displaces the discussion to substantive political morality, and those who disagree have to argue for their views on that particular terrain.[38] However, in the practical context of public decision-making, abstract theories of political morality are of little help. The most that can be done is to provide a general survey of important, recurring considerations, as the Supreme Court of Canada has done.

and Freedoms' (1986) Osgoode Hall LJ 867; Errol P Mendes, 'In Search of a Theory of Social Justice: The Supreme Court Reconceives the Oakes Test' (1990) 24 RJT 1, 3, 6; Norman Siebrasse, 'The Oakes Test: An Old Ghost Impeding Bold New Initiatives' (1991) 23 Ott LR 99; Joel C Bakan, 'Constitutional Arguments: Interpretation and Legitimacy in Canadian Constitutional Thought' (1989) 27 Osgoode Hall LJ 123, 163–168, 180.

[35] Robert Alexy, perhaps the most well-known exponent of proportionality theory, seems to acknowledge that value attribution is not displaced by proportionality analysis: Robert Alexy, *A Theory of Constitutional Rights* (trans. Julian Rivers, Oxford University Press, 2002) 100, 105, 366, 397–414. See also, Mattias Kumm, 'Political Liberalism and the Structure of Rights: On the Place and Limits of the Proportionality Requirement' in George Pavlakos (ed), *Law, Rights, Discourse: The Legal Philosophy of Robert Alexy* (Hart, 2007) 131.

[36] *Oakes* above (n 8) 136.

[37] Eg Blache, above (n 21); Siebrasse, above (n 34) (who would drop the whole structure of *Oakes* and go for immediate balancing), and Leon E Trakman et al., 'R. v. Oakes, 1986-1997: Back to the Drawing Board' (1998) 36 Osgoode Hall LJ 83.

[38] Some suggestions as to the kind of normative political philosophy which should be adopted under s. 1: Mendes above (n 34) 12–13, 26, 30, 33–34; Ruth Colker, 'Section 1, Contextuality and the Anti-disadvantage Principle' (1992) 42 UTLJ 77.

B. Putting Rights in Their Place

It has been suggested earlier that some parts of Chief Justice Dickson's reasons in *Oakes* can be read as expressing a 'Taking Rights Seriously' view of constitutional rights. This requires further discussion.

First, recall that the Chief Justice had claimed that all infringements of *Charter* rights were *violations*. However, moral philosophers tend to define violations of moral rights as *unjustified* infringements. Mere infringements may or may not be justified all things considered. If they are not, they become violations. If they are, they remain benign infringements. Thus, by conceiving all infringements as violations, Chief Justice Dickson was using a term ('violation') that tends to be used only at the very end of an analysis of justification all things considered. But he was using it to describe the situation *before* the application of section 1, under which justification all things considered is examined. [39]

The philosophical defenders of the 'Taking Rights Seriously' perspective conceive rights as protecting morally basic attributes of persons such as autonomy, reason, or dignity. This explains why they see these rights as being quasi-absolute or very weighty and why they consider infringements to be justified only in exceptional circumstances. [40] But this is perhaps not the most perspicacious perspective to adopt in regards to constitutional rights. In practice, constitutional rights-infringements certainly do not map on violations of 'dignity' or 'autonomy'. Most generally, a right is infringed when state action can be described as interfering with protected interests. This generates a moral concern and triggers an analysis of whether the action is justified all things considered. But some interferences with rights-protected interests are more morally concerning

---

[39] This was noted by Henri Brun, Guy Tremblay, and Eugénie Brouillet, *Droit constitutionnel* (6th ed Yvon Blais 2014) 1010:

> À tort [. . . La Cour suprême du Canada] parle souvent de violation et même parfois de suppression de droit dès le début de cette deuxième étape de l'analyse, alors qu'il ne s'agit encore, en réalité, que d'une atteinte; en conséquence, elle soumet la deuxième étape à un régime complètement différent de la première, régime qui correspond davantage à un contexte de violation des droits. [The Supreme Court of Canada] often refers, wrongly, to a violation, and sometimes even to the suppression of a right at the very beginning of this second step of the analysis, whereas in reality it remains a mere infringement; consequently, the second step methodology is completely different from that of the first, and corresponds more to a violation of rights context.

See also Siebrasse, above (n 34) 118–119, 127.

[40] Robert Nozick has famously described rights as 'side-constraints' upon the actions to be done. This picture notably implies that one cannot violate the rights even in order to lessen their total violation in society, thereby rejecting what Nozick had called a 'utilitarianism of rights'. Robert Nozick, *Anarchy, State and Utopia* (Basic Books, 1974) 28–33; see also Ronald Dworkin, 'Rights as Trumps' in Jeremy Waldron (ed), *Theories of Rights* (Oxford University Press, 1984) 153. But recall that even Dworkin acknowledges that rights will give way to social-utilitarian considerations in some cases: Dworkin, above (n 25).
In Canada, something like the Taking Rights Seriously position was defended by Lorraine Eisenstat Weinrib in 'The Supreme Court of Canada and Section 1 of the Charter' (1988) 10 Sup Ct LR 469.

than others (contrast, for instance, political and commercial expression). And on the other side of the balance, important rights-protected interests and other weighty moral considerations may be protected by state action. Hence, calling for a 'stringent' justificatory threshold based on the supposed specialness of rights seems inapposite in the *Charter* context.[41] Each case of infringement and purported justification must be examined on its own merits. Indeed, this was recognized by Chief Justice Dickson in *Oakes* when he said that some limits to rights are more serious than others 'in terms of the nature of the right or freedom violated, the extent of the violation, and the degree to which the measures which impose the limit trench upon the integral principles of a free and democratic society'.[42]

Oakes had also established that the state bears the burden of demonstrating that an infringement is justified. This may be taken as signalling the Taking Rights Seriously view, but the use of the notion of 'burden' is somewhat awkward in this context. In law, burdens are usually burdens of proof, and burdens of proof relate to material facts, not normative justification.[43] Now, the notion of 'burden' may have a certain place in normative argumentation when the balance of arguments usually favors a particular position and there remains uncertainty after exhaustive consideration of the whole situation.[44] But in the *Charter* context, as discussed in the previous paragraph, the primary determination that a right has been infringed does not strongly and invariably suggest the conclusion that the balance of arguments weighs on the side of the plaintiff. More importantly, at that stage, the whole situation has not been analysed since this is just what remains to be done under section 1! Finally, even when there remains uncertainty following the application of section 1, it is far from clear that it should be resolved in favor of rights. In fact, considerations of institutional legitimacy point in the opposite direction, and deference to the other branches of government may well be appropriate.[45]

C. Institutional Self-Awareness

As mentioned before, the pre-patriation debate over the legitimacy of constitutional rights judicial review echoed into the application of section 1. Considerations of institutional legitimacy are an important element in the explanation of the Supreme Court's

---

[41] Blache above (n 21) 447.

[42] *Oakes* above (n 8) 139–140.

[43] For a similar observation see Brun, Tremblay, and Brouillet, above (n 39) 1015.

[44] See Giovanni Sartor, 'Defeasibility in Legal Reasoning' in Zenon Bankowski, Ian White and Ulrike Hahn (eds), *Informatics and the Foundations of Legal Reasoning* (Kluwer, 1995) 119, 122.

[45] Default rules in favor of rights or deference can be conceived as potential 'distancing devices', that is devices on which public institutions may rely to settle issues involving incommensurability of reasons and which cannot be settled by reason. Then we are faced with a choice of distancing devices. Joseph Raz 'On the Authority and Interpretation of Constitutions: Some Preliminaries' in J. Raz, *Between Authority and Interpretation: On the Theory of Law and Practical Reason* (Oxford University Press, 2009) 323, 368–369.

move toward a standard of reasonableness.[46] Starting in *Edwards Books* and in many cases thereafter, the relatively limited legitimacy and institutional capacities of courts were put forward as reasons to leave the other branches of government a 'margin of appreciation'.[47] In fact, very early on in the *Charter* era, in the *Operation Dismantle* case, Justice Wilson had clearly stated that such considerations were to be incorporated in the application of section 1. She said:

> Section 1 [. . .] embodies through its reference to a free and democratic society the essential features of our constitution *including the separation of powers,* responsible government and the rule of law. It obviates the need for a "political questions" doctrine and permits the Court to deal with what might be termed "prudential" considerations in a principled way without renouncing its constitutional and mandated responsibility for judicial review.[48]

Justice Binnie reiterated the point almost 20 years later in *Newfoundland (Treasury Board) v. N.A.P.E.*, saying:

> . . . it is nevertheless clear that there is built into the *Oakes* test a healthy respect for legislative choices in areas of economic and social policy.
> [. . .]
> the s. 1 test set out in *Oakes* and the rest of our voluminous s. 1 jurisprudence already provides the proper framework in which to consider what the doctrine of separation of powers requires in particular situations [. . .][49]

5. CONCLUSION

In *Oakes* and the following case law, the Supreme Court of Canada has relied on the language of section 1 to develop a general 'proportionality' framework aimed at determining whether a right-infringement was justified in a free and democratic society. That

[46] Aileen Kavanagh's work offers a particularly sophisticated and well-balanced analysis of the constitutional role of courts: 'The Role of Courts in the Joint Enterprise of Governing' in Nicholas W. Barber, Richard Ekins and Paul Yowell (eds), *Lord Sumption and the Limits of the Law* (Hart, 2016) 212; 'Defending Deference in Public Law and Constitutional Theory' (2010) 126 LQR 222; 'Judicial Restraint in the Pursuit of Justice' (2010) 60 UTLJ 23; 'Constitutional Review, the Courts and Democratic Scepticism', (2009) 62 CLP 102; 'Deference or Defiance? The Limits of the Judicial Role in Constitutional Adjudication' in G. Huscroft (ed), *Expounding the Constitution: Essays in Constitutional Theory* (Cambridge University Press, 2008) 184.
[47] *Edwards Books* (n 12), Dickson C.J. [147], La Forest J. [181]–[183]; *Irwin Toy* (n 32). See also Guy Tremblay and Stéphane Marsolais, 'Reconnaître aux pouvoirs politiques une marge d'appréciation aux fins de l'article premier de la Charte canadienne' (1992) 52 Can Bar Rev 841.
[48] *Operation Dismantle v The Queen*, [1985] 1 SCR 441, 491. [emphasis added]
[49] *Newfoundland (Treasury Board) v N.A.P.E.* (n 33) [114]–[116].

framework has become influential in other jurisdictions.[50] Proportionality is formal and calculative, but it applies within liberal democratic parameters and is fully capable of incorporating considerations associated with fundamental human rights. It has also consistently been mindful of institutional concerns.

The philosopher Kurt Baier said:

> Moral deliberation, like all kinds of deliberation, is a sort of calculus, a method of reckoning, of working out something—which course of action is supported by the best moral reasons. All that can be expected by moral philosophers is the clarification of the calculus, the statement of the general rules, and the methods of using them in particular calculations. It cannot be expected that philosophers should answer all moral questions or problems beforehand, or that, after the elucidation of this calculus, its users will find solving their problems much easier, or even that all problems will now be capable of solution. The procedure is much like weighing. One can only explain the weighing machine and check the weights: the weighing itself has still to be done on each particular occasion.[51]

'Moral deliberation' could easily be replaced by 'section 1 deliberation' in that quote. Section 1 reasoning is practical-moral reasoning. Inevitably, it has deployed itself through a flexible framework, not a strict recipe, leaving space for judgment, controversy, and disagreement.

BIBLIOGRAPHY

Secondary sources

Grimm, Dieter. 'Proportionality in Canadian and German Constitutional Jurisprudence' (2007) 57 UTLJ 383
Sweet, Alec Stone and Jud Mathews, 'Proportionality Balancing and Global Constitutionalism' (2008) 47 Colum. J. Transnat'l L. 72
Tremblay, Luc B. and Grégoire C.N. Webber (eds), *La limitation des droits de la Charte: essais critiques sur l'arrêt R. c. Oakes/The limitation of Charter Rights: Critical Essays on R. v. Oakes* (Thémis, 2009)
Webber, Grégoire C.N., *The Negotiable Constitution: On the Limitation of Rights* (Cambridge, 2009)
Weinrib, Jacob. *Dimensions of Dignity: The Theory and Practice of Modern Constitutional Law* (Cambridge, 2016), c. 7 'The Moral Structure of Proportionality'

Cases

R. v Oakes [1986] 1 SCR 103
R v Edwards Books and Art Ltd [1986] 2 SCR 713

---

[50] Eg in South Africa, Israel, Ireland, and New Zealand. See Alec Stone Sweet and Jud Mathews, 'Proportionality Balancing and Global Constitutionalism' (2008) 47 Colum. J. Transnat'l L. 72, 123–135.

[51] Kurt Baier, *The Moral Point of View: A Rational Basis of Ethics* (Cornell University Press, 1958), 172.

R v Keegstra [1990] 3 SCR 697
RJR-MacDonald Inc. v Canada (Attorney General), [1995] 3 SCR 199
Sauvé v Canada (Chief Electoral Officer), [2002] 3 SCR 519
Newfoundland (Treasury Board) v N.A.P.E., [2004] 3 SCR 381
Alberta v Hutterian Bretheren of Wilson Colony [2009] 2 SCR 567

CHAPTER 32

....

CHARTER REMEDIES

....

KENT ROACH[*]

1. INTRODUCTION

....

CONSTITUTIONAL commentators have long appreciated the importance of the relationship between rights and remedies. Albert Venn Dicey stressed the close connection between rights and remedies in the English Constitution. This connection was
tied to his sense that the Constitution only prevented "definite wrongs" which could be
repaired by the award of damages.[1] Daryl Levinson, however, has argued that too much
modern constitutional law scholarship has ignored the influence of remedies. This has
led to a form of "rights essentialism" that fails to see how remedies influence and shape
rights and the very institution of judicial review.[2] Some commentators influenced by the
experience of *Brown v. Board of Education*[3] have noted the frequent disjunction between
right and remedy and the need for remedial creativity and even experimentation. Some
remedies such as declarations and suspended declarations of invalidity can also facilitate dialogue between courts and legislatures.[4] All of this suggests that any study of the
Charter that does not include remedies will be radically incomplete.

  [*] Professor and Prichard Wilson Chair in Law and Public Policy. I thank Ravi Amarnath, Peter Hogg
and Don Stuart for helpful comments on an earlier draft. I also thank the Pierre Trudeau Foundation for
generous financial support.
  [1] A.V. Dicey *An Introduction to the Study of the Law of the Constitution* 10th ed (MacMillan,
1959) at 199.
  [2] Daryl Levinson "Rights Essentialism and Remedial Equilibration" (1999) 99 Colum.L.R. 857
  [3] Abram Chayes "The Role of the Judge in Public Law Litigation" (1976) 89 Harv.L.Rev. 1281; Owen
Fiss *The Civil Rights Injunction* (Bloomington: Indiana University Press, 1978). For similar recognition of
the disjunction between rights and remedies in the context of socio-economic rights see Jeff King *Judging
Social Rights* (Cambridge University Press, 2012).
  [4] See chapter by Ravi Amarnath and Peter Hogg in this *Handbook*; Kent Roach *The Supreme Court on
Trial: Judicial Activism or Democratic Dialogue* revised ed (Irwin Law, Law, 2016) chs 8, 16, and 17.

The *Canadian Charter of Rights and Freedoms* departed from both the *Constitution Act, 1867* and the 1960 Canadian Bill of Rights by placing a much greater emphasis on the role of the judiciary in providing remedies for rights violations. Section 52(1) of the *Constitution Act, 1982* contains Canada's first formal constitutional supremacy clause providing that laws are of no force and effect to the extent of their inconsistency with the *Charter*. This contemplates immediate declarations of invalidity, but the Supreme Court uses a broad range of remedies, including interpretative remedies and suspended, partial, or prospective declarations of invalidity. These alternatives to an immediate declaration of invalidity are often designed to recognize various reliance interests on unconstitutional laws and to respect the role of the legislature in enacting new laws. These remedial innovations, however, should still produce an overall result that is fair to the litigants.[5]

Section 24(1) of the *Charter* contemplates that courts and tribunals of competent jurisdiction will grant remedies for various governmental acts that violate the *Charter*. Remedial discretion is to be exercised to ensure that remedies are appropriate and just in the circumstances. This includes the need to ensure effective and meaningful remedies that respond to the circumstances of the violation and the claimant while also respecting the roles of different branches of government. Again the overall result should be fair to all litigants.[6]

Section 24(2) mandates the exclusion of unconstitutionally obtained evidence but only if its admission would bring the administration of justice into disrepute. Reflecting the prevalence of criminal litigation under the *Charter*, the Supreme Court has decided more cases under this section than under the general remedies clause in section 24(1) or the supremacy clause in section 52(1).[7] This underlines how the availability of remedies affects litigation and ultimately the substance of the Charter rights that are the subject of litigation.

A. Outline

The chapter will demonstrate how the Supreme Court has qualified judicial review under the *Charter* through the exercise of remedial discretion. It will first examine how the Court has brought nuance to an otherwise unequivocal supremacy clause by inventing the new remedy of a suspended declaration of invalidity and by using interpretative remedies as an alternative to an immediate declaration that an unconstitutional law is of no force and effect. Both remedies have tempered what could have been even more controversial *Charter* decisions on issues ranging from child pornography and the correction of children to prostitution and assisted dying.

[5] *Hislop v. Canada* [2007] 1 SCR 429 at para 78ff.
[6] *Doucet-Boudreau v. Nova Scotia* [2003] 3 SCR 3.
[7] Kent Roach *Constitutional Remedies in Canada* (2nd ed., Canada Law Book, 2013 and as updated) ch 10.

This chapter will next examine the Court's remedial jurisprudence under section 24 with special attention to how remedies may affect the degree to which rights are both recognized and enforced. For example, rights against unnecessary strip searches are most likely to be enforced under section 24(2) when an accused attempts to have evidence excluded rather than through civil litigation which in one landmark case resulted in section 24(1) damages of $5,000 for an unconstitutional strip search.[8]

One of the challenges in understanding the Constitution is to appreciate cases that have not been litigated, often for reasons related to lack of access to justice and effective remedies. Although the Supreme Court has affirmed that judges can order mandatory injunctions against the government and retain jurisdiction to enforce them under section 24(1), it did so in a narrowly divided 5-4 judgment.[9] Judicial hesitancy in using such remedies help explain the lack of *Charter* cases concerning unconstitutional conditions of confinement.

2. REMEDIES FOR LAWS THAT VIOLATE THE *CHARTER*: THE QUALIFIED SUPREMACY CLAUSE

On its face, section 52(1) of the Constitution Act is clear and simple in mandating that laws that are inconsistent with the *Charter* are of no force and effect to the extent of their inconsistency. Section 52 was placed in the *Constitution Act, 1982* as part of the patriation process and to indicate both that the *Charter* was no mere statutory bill of rights and that it was expected to result in the striking down of laws. In the first decade of the *Charter*, the Court honoured this expectation and often concluded that it should simply strike laws down and allow Parliament to exercise its role in deciding whether and how to reconstruct them to comply with the Charter.[10]

A. The Rise of Interpretative Remedies

By the *Charter*'s second decade, however, judicial review had become more controversial and the Court's approach to laws that might violate the *Charter* more nuanced.[11]

---

[8] *Ward v. Vancouver* [2010] 2 SCR.28. The author represented the British Columbia Civil Liberties Association in this case.

[9] *Doucet-Boudreau* above (n 6).

[10] *Hunter v Southam* [1984] 2 SCR 145, *Osborne v Canada* [1991] 2 SCR 69.

[11] For an account of some of these controversies see Kent Roach *The Supreme Court on Trial: Judicial Activism or Democratic Dialogue* (rev. ed., Irwin Law, 2016). For a defence of the Court's increased reliance on interpretative remedies see Hamish Stewart "A Defence of Constitutionalized Interpretation" (2016) 36 NJCL 195. For my response see Kent Roach "Constitutionalized Interpretation, Reading Down/ In and the Wisdom of *Schachter*" (2016) 36 NJCL 211.

In 1992, the Court read down obscenity provisions in the Criminal Code to only apply to violent, child or degrading pornography before holding that the offence was justified under section 1 of the *Charter*.[12] This avoided a repeat of political controversy that had previously made it impossible for Parliament to modernize Canada's obscenity law. Although Parliament can in theory amend legislation to revise the Court's interpretative remedy, this will often not occur because of the implicit suggestion that the Court has with its interpretative remedy reconciled the statute with the demands of the *Charter*.

In 2001, the Court upheld an overbroad child pornography offence but only by interpreting it in light of the *Charter* and by reading in exemptions for some self-created pictures and writing that would otherwise be caught by the broadly worded offence enacted in 1993.[13] In both pornography cases, however, the use of interpretative or reading in remedies created a disjunction between broad laws written by Parliament and the narrower interpretations provided by the courts. Such remedies avoid the political controversy that would have been caused by a declaration of invalidity, but created the risk that freedom of expression would be chilled by the lack of clear notice to people about exactly what form of expression could be prohibited under the *Charter*.

In other cases, the Court was unwilling to save legislation from invalidation by interpretation or reading down. In a case dealing with a criminal offence for spreading false news,[14] only a minority of the Court would have saved the archaic Criminal Code offence by reading in new restrictions similar to those that Parliament had imposed on a more modern hate speech offence. In the result the offence was struck down and a person who denied the Holocaust was allowed to go free. Similarly only a minority of the Court would have read down an old vagrancy offence to require that convicted sexual offenders be loitering in a park with an intent to offend against children. The striking down of this offence allowed a person to go free, but also forced Parliament to enact a more modern offence better tailored to its aim of preventing the sexual abuse of children.[15]

The most dramatic incident of interpretative remedies so far came in 2004 when the Court upheld an old Criminal Code provision that allowed parents and teachers to use "reasonable" force when correcting children.[16] The Court again modernized the Criminal Code provision and saved it from *Charter* invalidation by imposing categorical and quasi-legislative limits on the use of force. For example, the judicially reformed offence would not apply to children under two years of age or teenagers and would not allow the use of objects. These are praiseworthy restrictions from a policy perspective. Nevertheless, they created a large discrepancy between the law as enacted by Parliament and the law as interpreted by the Supreme Court. Reliance on interpretative remedies in this case raised concerns about fair notice to potential accused just as the pornography cases raised concerns about chilling legitimate expression. Indeed in

---

[12] *R. v Butler* [1992] 1 SCR 452.
[13] *R. v Sharpe* [2001] 1 SCR. 45.
[14] *R. v Zundel* [1992] 2 SCR 731.
[15] *R. v Heywood* [1994] 3 SCR 761.
[16] *Canadian Foundation for Children v Canada (Attorney General)* [2004] 1 SCR 76.

a different remedial context of rejecting the use of constitutional exemptions to save potentially unconstitutional law, the Court has noted that "the divergence between the law on the books and the law as applied . . . impairs the right of citizens to know what the law is in advance and govern their conduct accordingly—a fundamental tenet of the rule of law."[17]

In a number of the cases discussed above, the Court applied strong interpretative remedies similar to that used under section 3 of the UK's Human Rights Act, 1998 or s.6 of the New Zealand Bill of Rights.[18] A critical difference, however, is that UK and New Zealand courts use these remedies to ensure that affected individuals, especially the accused, received a remedy.[19] In Canada, such interpretative remedies were not necessary to give the accused a remedy. Why? The Court could and should have simply struck the laws down and allowed Parliament to go through the public and perhaps painful process of reconstructing them as a form of dialogue.[20]

Reading down is a legitimate *Charter* remedy but one that should be justified and disciplined by principles based on respect for institutional role and the broader purposes of the *Charter*. Following the basic remedial principles articulated by the Court in *Schachter*,[21] courts should not engage in reading down or reading in if there is a range of constitutionally appropriate policy choices available to the legislature. Such an approach respects the institutional strengths of legislatures even if it means that the Court strikes down more laws under section 52. As will be discussed below, the availability of a suspended declaration of invalidity also means that the court can minimize the disruptive effects of employing a strike down as opposed to relying on an interpretative remedy.

The official doctrine governing choice of remedies for unconstitutional laws under section 52 of the *Constitution Act, 1982* was articulated in *Schachter*; it is reasonably clear and follows from the jurisprudence governing severance or partial declarations of invalidity. The Court should only save a potentially unconstitutional law by reading in or an interpretative remedy if that is the only way to reconcile the purposes of the impugned law with the *Charter*. In all other cases, the Court should simply strike down unconstitutional laws subject to a suspension if necessary.[22] This allows the legislature to make policy choices between different ways to reconcile its objectives with the Charter.

Remedies depend on context. They are not amenable to automatic rules. It is thus not surprising that remedial discretion is exercised even under the seemingly mandatory terms of section 52(1) of the *Constitution Act, 1982*. For example, the Court read in sexual orientation to save Alberta's human rights code from invalidation rather than to strike

---

[17] *R. v Ferguson* [2008] 1 SCR 96 at para 72.

[18] Compare *R. v Laba* [1994] 3 SCR 965 with *R. v DPP ex parte Keblene* [2000] 2 AC 326 both reading down persuasive to evidential burdens. But see *R. v Hansen* [2007] NZSC 7 where the New Zealand Supreme Court refused to read down a persuasive burden to a less onerous evidential burden.

[19] Aileen Kavanagh *Constitutional Review under the UK Human Rights Act* (Cambridge University Press, 2009) ch 5.

[20] See the chapter by Ravi Amarnath and Peter Hogg in this *Handbook*.

[21] [1992] 2 SCR 679.

[22] *Ibid.*

down the entire human rights code.[23] The very next year, however, the Court did not use an interpretative remedy when it came to the need to include same-sex couples in a welter of complex statutes governing the benefits and burdens of spousal relationships. Instead it struck the offending sections down subject to a suspended declaration of invalidity.[24] Remedies are the place where the ideal world of Charter rights meet the more messy practical world.

B. Remedies and Dialogue between Courts and Legislatures

Remedies are an important site of dialogue between the court and legislatures.For example, the Court in *M v H* suspended the declaration of invalidity for six months, and during that time Ontario enacted legislation that equalized benefits and burdens for same-sex partners but stopped short of defining same-sex partners as spouses.[25] Unfortunately, the law was also enacted with prospective effect that deprived the successful litigant in the case of a remedy.[26] Ontario's new law was subsequently challenged as still infringing equality rights, but was upheld[27] before it was subsequently amended by a different government to define same-sex couples as spouses.[28] The lower courts approached the issue of same-sex marriage in a similar manner to give legislatures an opportunity to address the matter until the Ontario Court of Appeal provided the applicants with an immediate remedy.[29] I have argued elsewhere that this approach disturbed the dialogic balance of the *Charter* by limiting Parliament's option should it have wished to preserve the traditional definition of marriage perhaps through the use of the s.33 override, or to have attempted to justify an alternative to same-sex marriage.[30] Immediate strike downs in some cases can create entitlements and expectations that cannot easily be undone through the enactment of new legislation.

The tension between dialogic remedies that provide legislatures with policy-making opportunities and the traditional judicial role of providing successful litigants with immediate remedies is real but manageable. Robert Leckey has aptly described this tension as one between constitutional enforcement and legislative engagement.[31] My own

---

[23] *Vriend v Alberta* [1998] 1 SCR 493.

[24] *M. v H* [1999] 2 SCR 3.

[25] Amendments because of the Supreme Court Decision in M v H.S.O. 1999 c 9.

[26] Sujit Choudhry and Kent Roach "Putting the Past behind Us?" (2003) 21 SCLR (2d) 205.

[27] *Vincent v Ontario* (1999) 70 CRR (2d) 365 (Ont. SCJ).

[28] Spousal Relationships Statute Law Amendment S.O. 2005 c.5.

[29] *Halpern v Ontario* (2003) 225 DLR 4th) 529 (Ont. CA).

[30] See Kent Roach "Dialogic Judicial Review and Its Critics" (2004) 23 SCLR (2d) 49 at 75–88 stressing that the s. 33 override cannot be used retroactively. My point was that courts should exercise their remedial discretion in a manner consistent with the larger architecture of the constitution and not that same-sex marriage should not have been recognized.

[31] Robert Leckey *Bills of Rights in the Common Law* (Cambridge University Press, 2015) ch 7; For arguments that suspended declarations of invalidity harm litigants and the rule of law see Robert Leckey

view is this tension can often be resolved by applying a two-track approach which continues in appropriate to use the dialogic remedy of a suspended declaration of invalidity
while also exempting applicants and those who would suffer irreparable harm from the
unconstitutional law during the period of the suspension.[32]

C. The Rise of the Suspended Declaration of Invalidity

The suspended or delayed declaration of invalidity was first created by the Court to
avoid having all of Manitoba's unilingual statutes rendered of no force and effect. The
Court gave the unconstitutional laws temporary effect for the minimum time necessary
to translate them into French as required by section 23 of the *Manitoba Act, 1870*.[33] The
Court subsequently used the novel remedy in cases where an immediate declaration of
invalidity would present a threat to public safety or achieve equality with a vengeance by
depriving people such as single mothers of benefits only because they were not extended
to others. In the still leading 1992 *Schachter* case, the Court appeared to confine the suspended declaration to these three limited factual categories. The Court even appeared
to reject the principle that courts should employ the suspended declaration of invalidity for reasons related to the comparative institutional competence of legislatures over
courts in selecting the precise means by which to comply with the *Charter*.[34] This under-
cuts one of the great advantages of the suspended declaration of invalidity which is to
allow Parliament to develop policies to implement the *Charter* that would not otherwise
be available to the courts.

Since 1992, the Court has increased its use of suspended declaration well beyond the
limited factual categories outlined in *Schachter*. In 2007, it appropriately recognized that
respect for the role of the legislature, as well as respect for reliance interests, was one of
the justifications for the use of suspended declarations of invalidity. This case provided
a test that allowed the government to justify departures from fully retroactive remedies
while warning that the overall result should be fair to all parties.[35] In cases dealing with
the *Indian Act*, labour relations, workers compensation, and security certificates under
immigration law, the Court has used suspended declarations of invalidity of 6, 12, or
18 months in order to give governments ample time to consult and develop policies that

"Enforcing Laws That Infringe Rights" [2016] Public Law 206; Robert Leckey "The Harms of Remedial
Discretion" (2016) 14 International Journal of Constitutional Law 584.

[32]   *Carter v Canada* 2016 SCC 4. For an argument in favour of this two-track approach see Kent Roach
"Remedies for Laws That Violate Human Rights" in John Bell et al. eds *Public Law Adjudication in
Common Law Systems* (Hart Publishing, 2016) at 287–299.

[33]   *Reference Re Manitoba Language Rights* [1985] 1 SCR.721.

[34]   *Schachter v Canada* [1992] 2 SCR 679 at 715–717. For criticism of this "pigeon hole" as one that
was based on inevitably over- or under-inclusive rules but that has subsequently degenerated into
unpredictable strong discretion while ignoring principles related to comparative institutional role see
Kent Roach "Principled Remedial Decision-Making under the Charter" (2004) 25 SCLR (2d) 101.

[35]   *Hislop v Canada* above (n 5).

would comply with the *Charter* though this also meant that the successful litigants did not receive an immediate remedy.[36]

An important suspended declaration of invalidity that often escapes notice is the Court's one year suspension in *Chaoulli*.[37] This suspension allowed Quebec to introduce legislation designed to achieve efficiencies in the delivery of health services even while it followed the Court's ruling and allowed individuals to purchase private health insurance. The result appears to have dampened the demand for private health insurance and broadened the dialogue between the court and the legislature over health care.[38]

Many suspended declaration of invalidity cases implicitly recognize that legislatures have expertise in highly regulated environments and that they can conduct research and engage in consultations. Moreover, legislatures can select among a broad range of possible remedial responses in a way that would be difficult for the court to do. For example, in cases concerning unconstitutionally underinclusive benefits, legislatures retain the option of reducing, restructuring or perhaps even eliminating the benefits in question. Legislatures can accept a court's ruling on a particular point, but then pursue a legislative and regulatory objective by enacting new measures. An immediate declaration of invalidity is often a blunt remedy that ignores the role of the positive state.

D. Suspended Declarations of Invalidity under Stress

The suspended declaration of invalidity have featured in two recent and controversial decisions, the first declaring three prostitution-related Criminal Code provisions to be unconstitutional because they aggravated dangers to the lives of sex workers,[39] and the second declaring an assisted suicide offence unconstitutional to the extent it deprived competent adults with irremediable medical conditions from having assistance in ending their lives.[40] In both cases, litigants who had won in court expressed dissatisfaction that they ultimately lost in Parliament.

The suspended declaration of invalidity used in the prostitution case sits in tension to the Court's own conclusions that the unconstitutional laws placed sex workers' security of the person unnecessarily at risk, something the Court acknowledged in its judgment.[41] At the same time, the Court ultimately came down in favour of a one-year suspension because "immediate invalidity would leave prostitution totally

---

[36] *Corbiere v Canada* [1999] 2 SCR 203; *Dunmore v Ontario* [2001] 3 SCR 1016; *Health Services v British Columbia* [2007] 2 SCR 391; *Saskatchewan Federation of Labour v Saskatchewan* [2015] 1 SCR 245; *Mounted Police Association v Canada* [2015] 1 SCR.3; *Martin v Nova Scotia* [2003] 2 SCR 504.

[37] [2005] 1 SCR 791

[38] Kent Roach "Polycentricity and Queue Jumping in Public Law Remedies: A Two Track Response" (2016) 66 UTLJ 3 at 38–42.

[39] *Bedford v Canada* [2013] 3 SCR 1101.

[40] *Carter v Canada* [2015] 1 SCR 331.

[41] *Bedford v Canada* above (n 39) [168].

unregulated."[42] This raises concerns that the Court may have strategically acted to minimize criticism of its judgment and that it may have imposed harms on sex workers who remained vulnerable to prosecutions for solicitation or keeping a bawdy house or for hiring people from their earnings to provide services including protection to them.[43] It also illustrates that "remedial discretion adds one more step, like proportionality on the substantive question of compliance with rights, at which judges balance the claimant's rights against other factors."[44]

The suspended declaration provided Parliament with an opportunity to respond. In the prostitution case, the Court left much room for dialogic response by concluding that it was only making determinations that the existing laws were overbroad and disproportionate on the basis of facts found by the trial judge and by prefacing its judgment with a statement that it was not deciding "whether prostitution should be legal or not."[45] Parliament responded in an aggressive manner by criminalizing for the first time the purchase, but not the sale of sex. It also created new offences against advertising the sale of sexual services and providing services to commercial enterprises that offer sexual services. The government rejected arguments that the new offence would still leave sex workers in danger even though this had been the premise of the Court's original decision striking down the prostitution-related offences. The new offences may well be challenged again under the Charter.

The Court in the prostitution case was more concerned about engaging the legislature in dialogue than providing an immediate remedy perhaps because the applicants were more interested in law reform. Only one applicant still engaged in sex work and she was not charged under any of the unconstitutional laws during the one-year suspension. At the same time, the Court can be criticized for not providing clear guidelines about how or if the unconstitutional laws should have been enforced throughout the country during the one-year suspension. The South African Constitution has an explicit power under section 172 of its 1996 Constitution to suspend declarations, and the South African Constitutional Court has been more active than the Canadian court in providing guidelines to govern what should happen during suspensions.

In the assisted suicide case, the Court initially rejected allowing case-by-case constitutional exemptions from the overbroad law for competent persons on the basis that "Parliament must be given the opportunity to craft an appropriate remedy . . . Complex regulatory regimes are better created by Parliament than by the courts."[46] The Court also

[42] *Ibid.* [167]
[43] Emmett MacFarlane, *Governing from the Bench* (University of British Columbia Press, 2013) at 171 (stressing strategic nature of the suspension); Robert Leckey "The Harms of Remedial Discretion" above (n 31) at 591-596 (stressing harms to litigants and others similarly situated during the suspension and the creation of uncertainty about whether the law will be applied during the suspension).
[44] Robert Leckey *Bills of Rights in the Common Law* above (n 31) at 148.
[45] *Bedford v Canada* above (n 39) [2].
[46] *Carter v Canada* above (n 40) [125].

recognized that assisted dying might be subject to provincial as well as federal regulation. It refused to order exemptions during its initial one-year suspension. It was able to
avoid confronting whether successful litigants should be exempted from the law during the suspension because both lead applicants had passed away by the time the Court
rendered its decision. The 12-month time frame proved too short because Parliament
did not sit for four months during the 2015 federal election campaign. The Court subsequently gave the new government a four-month extension, but on the conditions
that individuals could obtain court-ordered exemptions during the additional months
and that Quebec be exempted from the extension so that its new legislation governing
physician-assisted dying would apply.[47]

The courts were able to grant a significant number of exemptions to competent adults
during the remaining four months of the suspension. In this context at least, the judiciary could manage and administer case-by-case exemptions in a manner that provided
successful litigants with remedies while allowing Parliament to create a new regulatory
regime[48] A dispute between the House of Commons and the Senate was not settled
before the additional four-month suspension expired. At this point, the Court's initial
tailored or partial declaration of invalidity applied and allowed competent adults with
grievous and irremediable medical conditions and enduring and intolerable suffering
to receive physician assistance in their death.[49] Later in June, 2016, Parliament enacted
a controversial new law that imposed the additional requirement that a person's death
must be foreseeable.[50]

The result has allowed Parliament to exercise its policy making function while also
allowing the courts to enforce *Charter* rights of those seeking assistance in dying.
Consistent with a dialogue where courts and legislatures play distinct roles, Parliament
has stressed its regulatory ambitions in protecting the vulnerable and discouraging suicide while the courts have focused on the facts of particular cases where the existing
overbroad offence would have severe and unconstitutional effects. As with the prostitution case, the dialogue over assisted dying between courts, legislatures and society is
not over. In the future, the new law will be subject to judicial interpretation and another
Charter challenge. The suspended declaration of invalidity has emerged as an important
feature of dialogue between courts and legislatures.

[47] *Carter v. Canada* 2016 SCC 4.
[48] For example, the Alberta Court of Appeal approved an exemption during the period of the
suspension on the basis that the Supreme Court's decision in *Carter* did not require that a person be
terminally ill. *Canada (Attorney General) v E.F.*, 2016 ABCA 155 [33–41].
[49] *Carter v. Canada* above (n 40) [127]. One justice, however, ruled that *Carter v Canada* 2016 SCC 4
meant even after the suspension expired, an assisted suicide could only be conducted with a court order.
O.P. v Canada (Attorney General), 2016 ONSC 3956. This seems erroneous given the mandatory nature of
s.52 and the expiry of the period of suspension.
[50] S.C. 2016 c. 3.

E. Reform of Suspended Declarations of Invalidity

Robert Leckey has argued that the Canadian courts use of a suspended declaration in the assisted suicide issue resembles the non-enforceable declaration of incompatibility under section 4 of the Human Rights Act.[51] I agree that the suspended declaration has tempered judicial review under the *Charter* to facilitate dialogue, but a critical difference is that the Canadian court will enforce the Constitution should Parliament be unable or unwilling to legislate. The Canadian approach could not result in an issue being held in indefinite limbo as has occurred with prisoner voting rights in the United Kingdom.

One problem with suspended declarations of invalidity is that the successful *Charter* applicant is often left without an immediate remedy. The Supreme Court recently refused to suspend a declaration involving the use of medical marijuana on the basis that it "would leave patients without lawful medical treatment and law enforcement in limbo"[52]. The applicant may also potentially be left without any remedy if the legislature follows its general practice of only legislating prospectively in response to the suspended declaration of invalidity.

The assisted dying case illustrates that even a 12-month suspension may be too short for Parliament to consult and deliberate in some circumstances. Nevertheless, the suspended declaration of invalidity should be reformed rather than abandoned. The tension between enforcing the Constitution and providing the legislature with an opportunity to engage in dialogic law-making can be overstated. One reform might be to allow longer periods of suspension. This could be balanced with other reforms: namely Canadian courts could follow South African practice by both providing guidelines to govern the suspension or they could follow Canada's second assisted dying case and allow for exemptions from unconstitutional laws when needed to prevent people from suffering irreparable harm during the suspension. The former reform would provide more certainty for all those potentially affected by an unconstitutional law during the suspension while the latter approach would mitigate the danger of the court's quasi-legislative interim guidelines influencing the legislative debate. Moreover, it would stress the court's traditional function celebrated since the time of Blackstone and Dicey of providing successful litigants with remedies.

In the assisted dying and other cases,[53] the Court seems to be aware that Parliament might not be able or willing to enact legislation before the suspension expires. In the assisted dying case, the Court tailored the judicial declaration of invalidity more narrowly to invalidate only those parts of the legislation that are unconstitutionally overbroad. This follows the severance and interpretative remedy jurisprudence discussed above by preserving as much of the impugned law that is consistent with the Constitution. These tailored declarations of invalidity are a remedy guided by the

---

[51] Leckey recognizes this but stresses the similarity between the suspended declaration of invalidity and the s.4 declarations of incompatibility. Leckey, "Enforcing Laws that Infringe Rights", above (n 31).

[52] R. *v Smith* 2015 SCC 34 [32].

[53] *R v. Appulonappa*, [2015] 3 S.C.R. 754 [67–74].

purposes of the Charter in the sense that they track the Court's use of proportionality reasoning under sections 7 and 1 of the Charter.

The Court should revisit its jurisprudence and articulate the general principles that will govern its decision whether to suspend a declaration of invalidity. The focus should not be on whether a case satisfies discrete categories where suspended declarations of invalidity have been used in the past.[54] It seems inevitable and consistent with other remedial jurisprudence stressing the need to respect institutional roles[55] that consideration of the respective roles of courts and legislatures will be relevant in determining whether a declaration of invalidity should be suspended. The focus should be on whether the Government can justify a suspension in terms of reliance and social interests that could be harmed by an immediate declaration of invalidity. Suspended declarations of invalidity may be particularly appropriate when the government demonstrates serious harms that would be caused by an immediate strike down and its interest and ability in enacting a new law that selects between multiple ways to comply with the *Charter*. The Court should also use general principles of proportionality to ensure that the harms caused by a suspension are minimized and the overall result is fair. As in other areas, general principles of proportionality can help guide the exercise of remedial discretion and make it more transparent.[56]

3. REMEDIES FOR ACTS THAT VIOLATE THE *CHARTER*: HOW REMEDIES AFFECT RIGHTS

One of the main messages of this chapter is that remedies often perform an important and under-appreciated function in calibrating rights as interpreted by the Court. Levinson calls this process one of equilibration.[57] As discussed above, suspended declarations of invalidity can facilitate dialogue between courts and legislatures but also avoid some of the disruption and perhaps controversy caused by an immediate declaration of invalidity.

Remedies issued under section 24 of the *Charter* for unconstitutional acts will be examined in the remainder of this chapter, and it will be suggested that they, no less than

---

[54] The Court has used suspended declarations far beyond the categories of threats to the rule of law and public safety and underinclusive benefits that it recognized in *Schachter* above (n 34) at 715–717 where it also stated that the use of the suspended declaration should not turn on consideration of the respective roles of courts and legislatures.

[55] See for example *Doucet-Boudreau v. Nova Scotia* above (n 6).

[56] For further discussion of the role of proportionality in guiding remedial discretion see Grant Hoole "Proportionality as a Remedial Principle: A Framework for Suspended Declarations of Invalidity" (2011) 49 Alta L Rev 107; Roach *Constitutional Remedies in Canada* above (n 7) at 3.970ff.

[57] Levinson above (n 2).

remedies for unconstitutional law, qualify and mediate judicial review and influence how rights are recognized and enforced.

A. The Remedial Tail and Its Influence on Rights

One feature of the rights essentialism that Levinson criticizes is that most scholars and commentators conceive of remedies as derivative and instrumental to rights. But remedies and particularly drastic or difficult remedies can shape rights. One example is the Court's decision in the early years of the *Charter* to hold that the drastic remedy of a stay of proceedings was the minimum remedy for the violation of the right to a trial in a reasonable time under section 11(b).[58] This approach sits uneasily with the Court's subsequent jurisprudence on stays of proceedings under section 24(1), which stresses the need for proportionality between violations and remedy, including consideration of alternative remedies, and allows social interests in prosecuting criminal cases to be considered at least in cases where the accused can still receive a fair trial.[59] Moreover, as Justice La Forest accurately predicted when he dissented from early cases, the drastic minimal remedy has led courts to interpret the section 11(b) right in a less generous manner.

The Court learned the lesson about the interdependence of rights and remedies the hard way. It experimented in *R. v Askov*[60] with a generous approach to section 11(b) only to find that over 50,000 criminal charges had to be stayed in Ontario as a result of its decision. The *Askov* crisis was caused by a number of systemic factors related to inefficiencies in the system. The wholesale stays of proceedings generated a systemic response that both increased the number of judges and prosecutors and encouraged them to resolve more cases through charge screening and plea bargaining. This was in many respects a positive systemic outcome, albeit one that was achieved by a perhaps unanticipated number of individual remedies that allowed many accused to go free without a trial. In any event, the Court became more cautious and less generous in interpreting section 11(b) rights in subsequent years[61] indicating that the strong and sometimes unpopular remedy of a stay was influencing its approach to rights.

In 2016, however, the Court returned to the methodology of *Askov*. It again established presumptive ceilings for trial delay. At the same time, the Court tried to avoid another *Askov* crisis. It devised longer presumptive ceilings and stressed that even in cases beyond these ceilings, the Crown can avoid a section 11(b) violation and a stay if it establishes "exceptional circumstances." Four judges dissented and warned that the Court was pursuing a quasi-legislative approach that could result in thousands of stays of proceedings. The majority of the Court stated that it would not revisit the question

---

[58] *Rahey v The Queen* [1987] 1 SCR 588.
[59] *R. v Regan* [2002] 1 SCR 97; *R. v Babos* [2014] 1 SCR 309.
[60] [1990] 2 SCR 1199.
[61] *R. v Morin* [1992] 1 SCR 771 (imposing less onerous s.11(b) standards).

of the minimal remedy for a section 11(b) violation because it was not asked to do so. Nevertheless, it is clear that its approach, as well as that of the minority, was influenced by the spectre of wholesale stays.[62] In short, remedies can impact the interpretation of rights. The *Askov* saga also demonstrates how Canadian courts remain more comfortable with ordering individual remedies than directly tackling the institutional and systemic nature of *Charter* violations.

Another example of remedies influencing rights is the Court's rejection of constitutional exemptions as a permanent remedy for laws that may only be unconstitutional in some of their applications. Exemptions or narrow "as applied" declarations of invalidity are frequently used in the United States. They can be seen as a form of constitutional minimalism that leaves space for legislative policies even when in some cases they may have unconstitutional effects. In contrast, the constitutionality of laws under the *Charter* is more of an all or nothing affair. For example, the Supreme Court in *Seaboyer*[63] struck down an overbroad rape shield law rather than save it through a constitutional exemption (as in the United States) or an interpretative remedy (as in the UK).[64] The result was public criticism of the Court, consideration of the use of the section 33 override to re-enact the law the Court struck down, and eventually fundamental reform of sexual assault law. The Supreme Court has refused to use constitutional exemptions on the basis that such remedies are inconsistent with the mandate in section 52(1) and the rule of law. This reluctance to use exemptions may also explain some of the Court's previous acceptance of mandatory minimum sentences that might otherwise have warranted exemptions in particularly sympathetic cases[65] and why four justices dissented from the Court's recent decision to allow exemptions when it extended the suspended declaration of invalidity in the assisted-dying case.[66] Remedies can be important to understanding the Court's rights jurisprudence.

B. The Under-Enforcement of Legal Rights?

Although they tend not to be central to most constitutional law scholarship, legal rights designed to protect those accused or suspected of crime are central to *Charter* litigation. One reason is the economics of *Charter* litigation. Most public legal aid is spent on

---

[62] *R. v Jordan* 2016 SCC 27 [92–97] noting special transitional circumstances in an attempt to avoid another *Askov* crisis. In his dissent, Justice Cromwell criticizes the transitional approach as a "Charter amnesty" (*ibid.* at para 287) while also warning that the case could result in thousands of stays. Clearly, the remedial consequences of the ruling were a pre-occupation of the Court.

[63] [1991] 2 S.C.R. 577.

[64] As discussed in Roach above (n 32).

[65] *R. v Ferguson* above (n 17) (upholding four-year mandatory minimum sentence and refusing to sanction constitutional exemptions.) But see *R. v Nasogaluak* [2010] 1 SCR 206 contemplating use of sentence reductions perhaps even below statutory minimums as a possible remedy. For a narrow reading of this possible exemption see *R v Donnelly* 2016 ONCA 988.

[66] *Carter v Canada* 2016 SCC 4.

criminal matters where the accused faces a risk of imprisonment. In addition, accused not eligible for legal aid have more incentives to seek *Charter* remedies when facing criminal charges. The end result is that there are many more cases involving criminal rather than non-criminal cases. The criminal accused has every incentive to seek remedies such as exclusion of evidence, stays of proceedings, and sentence reductions.

The incentives that persons accused of crimes have to seek remedies as opposed to those who are not charged criminally can skew the nature of rights that are enforced and the context in which the remedy is sought. In 2001, the Supreme Court in a 5-4 decision in *R. v Golden*[67] imposed new restrictions on the police use of strip searches. The Court found an unreasonable search and seizure but did not have to decide whether to exclude 10 grams of crack cocaine found in the accused's buttocks because the accused had already served his 14-month sentence by the time the Court decided the case. Four justices in dissent would not have imposed new restrictions or excluded the evidence under section 24(2) of the Charter. They recognized that the violation was serious (the accused was strip searched in a Subway sandwich shop and had his buttocks and genitals publicly exposed) but stressed the seriousness of the offence and the importance of the evidence. Subsequent developments under section 24(2) gave judges more flexibility in balancing competing interests before deciding whether evidence obtained during an unconstitutional strip search should be excluded because its admission would bring the administration of justice into disrepute.[68] The appellate record since that case on the exclusion of evidence in unconstitutional strip search cases is mixed.[69]

Remedies, and in particular the trial judge's exercise of remedial discretion, provide an often unappreciated flexibility in the process of *Charter* review. Remedies can provide another opportunity to balance the competing interests. In other words, there is a danger of under-enforcement of legal rights such as restrictions on the use of strip searches when a requested remedy such as exclusion of evidence is frequently denied because of its social costs of preventing a criminal trial on the merits. That said, a number of empirical studies have found high rates of exclusion of evidence under section 24(2).[70] These findings likely reflect that defence lawyers are generally careful in only litigating cases where there are strong arguments for exclusion of evidence.[71]

---

[67] [2001] 3 SCR 679.

[68] *R. v Grant* [2009] 2 SCR 353.

[69] The Ontario Court of Appeal in *R. v McGuffie*, 2016 ONCA 365 held that the trial judge had erred in refusing to exclude drugs obtained as a result of an unconstitutional strip search and indicated that "courts, as representatives of the community, cannot be seen to condone the blatant disregard of the appellant's rights that occurred in this case. The only way the court can effectively distance itself from that conduct is by excluding the evidentiary fruits of that conduct." *Ibid.* [78]. To similar effects see *R v Poirer* 2016 ONCA 582. But see *R v Saeed*, 2014 ABCA 238 admitting DNA evidence obtained by an unconstitutional strip search in a sexual assault case.

[70] See the chapter by Don Stuart in this *Handbook*.

[71] But see *R. v Cheng* 2014 BCCA 342 for a case where a defence lawyer did not pursue a strip search claim and the Court found no ineffective assistance of counsel.

The incentives are quite different when a person is subject to an unconstitutional stop or search but is not charged because no incriminating evidence is discovered. Such a person will only obtain a *Charter* remedy if they bring costly *Charter* litigation against the police and face the down side risk of having to pay a significant portion of the state's legal costs if they are unsuccessful. Such cases do happen, but they require litigants who are not risk adverse and perhaps not economically rational actors. One such case involved a landmark litigation brought against the City of Vancouver and the province of British Columbia. Vancouver civil rights lawyer Cameron Ward was strip searched in a detention centre when he was arrested at a protest before being released without charge. Many people would have simply done nothing, but assisted by counsel acting pro bono, Ward commenced litigation. The governments appealed the case to the Supreme Court, which upheld the $5,000 in *Charter* damages for the unconstitutional strip search. On the other hand, damages will not automatically be awarded for all *Charter* violations. The Court reversed a $100 Charter damage award for a related unconstitutional seizure of Ward's car on the basis that the mere declaration of a violation would be just satisfaction.[72]

Damages would have to be justified on a purposive basis as necessary to provide pecuniary or non-pecuniary compensation for the *Charter* violation, to vindicate *Charter* rights or to deter future *Charter* violations. In this case, all three rationales applied because the strip search was conducted after and without apparent regard to restrictions the Court had placed on strip searches. The Court was not persuaded that the award of $5,000 damages would overdeter officials in their performance of their public duties in part because unlike in the United States, the state as opposed to individual officials would have to pay the award. Even when damages were justified to compensate, vindicate, or deter, the government would still have an opportunity to demonstrate that damages were not appropriate because the award would harm good governance, or an alternative remedy would be adequate.

Although *Ward* presents a principled and even elegant framework for awarding damages and reconciling individual and collective interests under the *Charter*, the Court has taken more restrictive approaches to *Charter* damages in other contexts. Damages caused by unconstitutional legislation will not be awarded unless the government was at fault for enacting the law,[73] and damages will not be awarded for prosecutorial non-disclosure in the absence of proven fault.[74] These forms of qualified immunity will affect the already skewed incentives facing those who are not charged and may lead to under-enforcement of some Charter rights. At the same time, qualified immunity is not the same as absolute liability and Ivan Henry was awarded $7.5 million to vindicate his

---

[72]   *Ward v Vancouver (City)* [2010] 2 SCR 28.

[73]   *Mackin v New Brunswick* [2002] 1 SCR 405.

[74]   *Henry v British Columbia* [2015] 2 SCR 214. See also *Ernst v. Alberta Energy Regulator* 2017 SCC 1 where all members of the Court seemed united that quasi-judicial administrative tribunals would enjoy a qualified immunity from Charter damages with four judges even suggesting that they enjoyed an absolute immunity. Ibid at [24-31]

Charter rights when the prosecutor intentionally denied him disclosure that could have prevented his wrongful conviction.[75] This is an unprecedented *Charter* damage award, but the government has made a decision not to appeal it. Another area to watch is the award of *Charter* damages through class actions. One class action is ongoing in relation to the mass detentions at the 2010 G20 summit in Toronto.[76] The aggregation of *Charter* damage claims in class actions may make such litigation more attractive.

Even when the accused is charged, the accused's right to disclosure and the Crown's obligation to provide such disclosure may be under-enforced given the reluctance of courts to stay proceedings or exclude evidence as a remedy for disclosure violations.[77] The result, especially combined with possible reluctance to exclude evidence of serious crime obtained through unconstitutional stops, searches, or interrogations, is the likely under-enforcement of certain legal rights. In short, a full picture of the impact of judicial review is not likely to emerge in the absence of a detailed understanding of the exercise of remedial discretion and the incentives for *Charter* litigation.

4. THE CHOICE BETWEEN DECLARATORY AND INJUNCTIVE RELIEF

Another area where remedies have affected the substance of rights is the choice between declarations or injunctions as a remedy. With some exceptions, the Supreme Court has demonstrated a preference for declaratory relief over mandatory or injunctive relief. The Court has often relied on the idea that Canadian governments have a long tradition of complying with declarations and that such a remedy provides governments with flexibility in selecting among a variety of options for complying with the Constitution. Declarations allow governments to determine the exact means to implement *Charter* rights.

The results of the Court's frequent use of declarations have been uneven. In some cases such as those involving minority language schools rights under s.23 of the *Charter* or the right of hearing-impaired patients to sign language interpretation[78], the Court has been able to make clear the requirements of *Charter* compliance in terms of

---

[75] *Henry v British Columbia* 2016 BCSC 1038. Before this case the highest *Charter* damage award was $230,000 but with most cases awarding $10,000 or less. W.H. Charles *Understanding Charter Damages* (Irwin Law, 2016) at 140–141.

[76] *Good v Toronto* (Police Service Board) 2016 ONCA 250. See also *Ogiamien v Ontario*, 2016 ONSC 3080 awarding $60,000 in *Charter* damages instead of a systemic remedy in a case dealing with conditions and lock downs in remand cases. I am indebted to Don Stuart for bringing this case to my attention.

[77] *R. v Dixon* [2003] 3 SCR 307. See Roach *Constitutional Remedies in Canada* 2nd ed above (n 7) at 9.520–9.780.

[78] *Mahe v Alberta* [1990] 1 SCR 342; *Eldridge v British Columbia* [1997] 3 SCR 624.

outcomes while leaving governments free to select from a variety of means in achieving those outcomes. Nevertheless there are concerns that some provinces have been slow to act on the Court's declaration especially in cases where they were not the direct defendant.[79] Some commentators have defended this approach on the basis that governments retain their ability to act on their interpretations of the Constitution[80] but such arguments discount the persuasive force of Supreme Court decisions and the burdens that such an approach would place on individuals to litigate their *Charter* rights on a province-by-province basis.

In any event, other cases that have relied on declarations have had unsatisfactory results. In a case brought by a small gay and lesbian book store, the Court relied on declarations of past freedom of expression and equality rights violations that did not specify remedial steps or even goals for the Government to take to prevent similar violations.[81] The book store continued to experience problems with customs officials and had to start another round of litigation. This costly litigation was abandoned seven years after the first Supreme Court "victory" when the Court refused to order advance costs that were necessary to fund the litigation.[82]

The Court similarly relied on declarations of past violations in the Omar Khadr case and reversed a trial judge who had issued a mandatory order that Canada should request that the Canadian citizen be released from Guantanamo Bay and allowed to return to Canada.[83] The Court's use of a declaration as opposed to a mandatory order left the Government free to decide what steps should be taken. The federal government initially proposed to do nothing in response to the violation. It subsequently requested that the United States not use in Khadr's military commission trial the fruits of the Canadian interrogation of the teen-aged Khadr while he was held without charge at Guantanamo Bay.[84] The Government's grudging compliance with the *Khadr* declaration may help explain why the next year the Supreme Court issued a mandatory order to require a

---

[79] Kent Roach "Remedial Consensus and Dialogue under the Charter" (2002) 35 UBC Law Rev 211 (outlining apparent lack of robust response to the *Eldridge* declaration in some provinces); Doucet-*Boudreau* above (n.6) (finding delay in Nova Scotia's implementation of s. 23 minority language rights as declared in *Mahe.*)

[80] Dennis Baker *Not Quite Supreme* (McGill Queens Press, 2012) ch 7. Professor Baker defends the ability of the executive as well as the legislature to interpret the Charter in a manner different from the courts. For my own arguments that only the legislature can reject a judicial interpretation of the Charter and only if it uses the s.33 override see Roach *The Supreme Court on Trial* (n 4).

[81] *Little Sisters v Canada* [2000] 2 SCR 1120.

[82] *Little Sisters v Canada* [2007] 2 SCR 38.

[83] *Canada (Prime Minister) v Canada* [2010] 1 SCR 44.

[84] A judge in subsequent litigation found that because the United States refused not to use the evidence Canadian officials had obtained, Khadr had still not received an effective remedy, and retained jurisdiction to allow the government and Khadr to propose alternative remedies. This judgment was stayed pending appeal with concerns being expressed about whether it was beyond judicial competence. This is consistent with the caution that Canadian courts have demonstrated towards retention of jurisdiction but has also been subject to criticism in Amir Attaran and Jon Khan "Solving the "Khadr Problem": Retention of Jurisdiction—A Comparative Analysis" (2015) 34 NJCL 145 and K. Roach "The Supreme Court at the Bar of Politics" (2010) 28 NJCL 115.

reluctant Minister of Health to grant an exemption from drug laws to allow the successful Insite safe injection centre to continue to operate on Vancouver's downtown eastside.[85]

By 2013, however, the Court reverted to its preference for general declarations. It declared that Manitoba had breached the honour of the Crown in its discharge of its obligations under section 31 of the Manitoba Act to distribute land to the Métis between 1870 and 1890.[86] Again this left the Government maximum flexibility in deciding what to do, but invited additional delay. It took the Government two years to appoint a representative to negotiate a land claims and self-government agreement. At the same time, a framework agreement for such negotiations was reached in May 2016.[87] This demonstrates how declarations allow the Government much flexibility in deciding precisely how to respond to judicial decisions. In some cases where the government will respond in good faith and after consulting those affected, the flexibility of declarations can produce good results. In other contexts, however, declarations can result in prolonged delay and even a lack of full compliance.

The use of mandatory relief as an alternative to declarations has been controversial. In the 2003 case of *Doucet-Boudreau*,[88] a majority of the Court deferred to a trial judge's decision that a remedy stronger than a simple declaration was necessary to deal with Nova Scotia's long standing delay in building French language schools that had been the subject of declaratory relief in other provinces in the early 1990's. The trial judge did not attempt to solve all the problems or issue detailed relief. Rather he made a "best efforts" order accompanied by the retention to hear progress reports filed by the Government subject to adversarial challenge by the successful applicants. A few of these reporting sessions were held and the necessary facilities were constructed and made available so that by the time the case reached the Supreme Court, the Nova Scotia government had complied, and the case was moot.

The Nova Scotia government objected to the trial judge's actions and challenged them on the ground that he had no continuing role once he found a violation of the *Charter* and made the "best efforts" order. This argument found favour with four justices dissenting in the Court. They concluded that the trial judge should only have retained jurisdiction if he had made clear orders that could be enforced by contempt and argued that the trial judge was acting in an illegitimate political manner if he was retaining jurisdiction to hold the government's feet to the fire. In a subsequent case, an unanimous Court stressed that retention of jurisdiction was extraordinary and should be accompanied with clear and enforceable orders.[89] Trial judges will often and perhaps rightly be

---

[85] *Canada v PHS Community Services Society* [2011] 3 SCR 134.

[86] *Manitoba Metis Federation v Manitoba* [2013] 1 SCR 623.

[87] See K. Roach "The Role of Courts, Executive and the Legislature in Enforcing the Constitution: Three Manitoba Stories" in R. Albert and D. Cameron, *Canada in the World* (Cambridge University Press, forthcoming).

[88] [2003] 3 SCR 3.

[89] *Thibodeau v Air Canada* [2014] 3 SCR 340.

reluctant to micro-manage the Executive to ensure compliance with the *Charter*. The result is that with a few exceptions there have been very few cases where judges have retained jurisdiction to ensure that the Executive complies with the *Charter*. [90]

The reluctance of Canadian courts to retain jurisdiction influences the development of *Charter* rights. For example, Canada does not have many cases that revolve around institutional conditions in prisons despite reports of overcrowding and other deficient conditions in such institutions. To the extent that prison conditions in Canada have been challenged and litigated, it has tended to be in the form of individual claims for damages[91] or habeas corpus[92] or through non-*Charter* mechanisms such as complaints to human rights commissions or prisoner investigators. Indeed even attempts to ensure equality for female prisoners[93] focused on individual judicial and extra-judicial remedies. The focus on individual remedies provides some response for the worst Charter abuses, but may be deficient in articulating general standards that should govern governmental conduct in the future.

5. CONCLUSION

Remedies are often a neglected part of the *Charter*, but they are critical to understanding the full nature of judicial review under Canada's constitutional bill of rights. The 1982 constitutional changes highlighted remedies in terms of including a constitutional supremacy clause that invalidates unconstitutional laws and provisions for granting an open-ended range of appropriate and just remedies for unconstitutional governments acts.

The courts have developed an extensive and nuanced jurisprudence on *Charter* remedies. Despite the mandatory words of section 52 that unconstitutional laws shall be of no force and effect, courts exercise remedial discretion to select among interpretative remedies and partial, prospective, suspended, or immediate declarations of invalidity.

The suspended declaration delays invalidation to allow dialogic legislative responses, but it does promise that the Court's declaration of invalidity will ultimately take effect should Parliament not act. The recent assisted suicide case is promising because it underlines that it is possible to both defer systemic and policy issues to Parliament while allowing exemptions from unconstitutional laws to ensure that litigants do not suffer irreparable harm during the suspension period. It also provides for the ultimate judicial

---

[90] Roach *Constitutional Remedies in Canada* above (n 7) ch 13.
[91] *Canada v McArthur* [2010] 3 SCR 626.
[92] *May v Ferndale Institute* [2005] 3 SCR 809.
[93] *R. v Daniels* [1990] 4 CNLR 51 rev'd (1991) 65 CCC (3d) 366 (Sask CA) leave denied 69 CCC (3d) vi (SCC) (trial judge attempting to prohibit the imprisonment of an Indigenous woman in what was then Canada's only federal prison for women, thousands of miles from the woman's home).

enforcement of the *Charter* should Parliament not be able to occupy the field with new and constitutional legislation.

Interpretative remedies are acceptable when they reconcile a statute with the *Charter* in the only way possible, and they avoid the Court needlessly having to strike legislation down. At the same time, interpretative remedies are more problematic if the court chooses among different ways to comply with the *Charter* or if they open up a significant discrepancy between the law as enacted by the legislature and as interpreted by the Court to ensure *Charter* compliance.

Section 24(1) remedies influence the type of rights that are judicially recognized. The right to a trial in a reasonable time under section 11(b) of the *Charter* has been affected by the Court's early decision to require the drastic remedy of a stay of proceedings for all violations. This strong remedy has affected the content of the section 11(b) rights by raising the social costs of interpreting that right in a generous manner. The Court's approach in *Askov* and now *Jordan* is consistent with a general preference for individual remedies, but it also suggests that multiple individual remedies may have perhaps unanticipated social costs and systemic effects. Canadian courts have used multiple individual remedies to achieve systemic reforms while they have been much more cautious in ordering systemic remedies consciously designed to achieve systemic reform.

People will have the most incentive to seek *Charter* remedies when they face criminal charges, but this will often require the court to grapple with social interests that may be harmed by remedies such as stays of proceedings, exclusion of evidence, and sentence reductions. At the same time, if no evidence is discovered as a result of an unconstitutional search or interrogation, it will be a rare person who will face the costs of litigation in an attempt to obtain typically modest *Charter* damages even though there may be a strong case that a remedy is needed to compensate, vindicate, and deter *Charter* violations. Despite its promising start in *Ward*, Charter damages have been restrained by the high costs and financial risks compared to generally low quantum of awards. It has also been restrained by the Court's frequent imposition of qualified immunity requirements in various contexts that require plaintiffs to establish fault in addition to Charter violations in order to obtain damages.

Finally, the choice under section 24(1) between declaratory and mandatory remedies remains controversial and has likely shaped *Charter* rights. Declarations leave government with much flexibility in determining exactly how to implement a variety of rights such as minority language and equality rights. The reluctance of Canadian judges to retain jurisdiction means that most *Charter* claims relating to institutional conditions have been litigated through requests for individual remedies such as damages or habeas corpus. These remedies may be effective for some individuals but unless, as after *Askov*, they are ordered on a wholesale basis, they may not address the underlying systemic and institutional causes of the *Charter* violation and may not be successful in ensuring that similar *Charter* violations are not repeated in the future.

Important issues in the future will include whether *Charter* damage claims can be aggregated in a manner that will increase the incentives to litigate and whether Canadian judges become more comfortable with the retention of jurisdiction. If the

Jordan case results in another *Askov* crisis producing thousands of stays of proceedings, the Court will likely revisit its early decision that the drastic remedy of a stay of proceeding is the minimal remedy for a violation of the right to a trial in a reasonable time. The high profile use of suspended declarations of invalidity in the assisted dying and prostitution cases may also inspire courts to re-visit its jurisprudence and hopefully to reform suspended declarations of invalidity to provide greater protections for *Charter* rights during the period of suspension. Decreased use of suspended declarations of invalidity might also make the courts less willing to recognize Charter rights in controversial areas where legislatures have important social and regulatory interests. The future of remedies remains difficult to predict. Nevertheless, it can be confidently concluded that Charter remedies have affected Charter rights and that the future evolution of *Charter* rights will depend in no small part on the evolution of *Charter* remedies.

Bibliography

Secondary sources

Attaran, A & Khan, J, "Solving the "Khadr Problem": Retention of Jurisdiction—A Comparative Analysis" (2015) 34 Nat'l J. Const. L. 145

Charles, CH, *Understanding Charter Damage Claims* (Toronto: Irwin Law, 2016)

Cooper-Stephenson, KD, *Charter Damage Claims* (Calgary: Carswell, 1990)

Hoole, G, "Proportionality as a Remedial Principle: A Framework for Suspended Declarations of Invalidity" (2011) 49 Alta L Rev 107

Leckey, R, *Common Law Bills of Rights* (Cambridge: Cambridge University Press, 2015)

Leckey, R, "Enforcing Laws That Infringe Rights" [2016] Public Law 206

Leckey, R, "The Harms of Remedial Discretion" (2016) 14 International Journal of Constitutional Law 584

Pinard, D, "A Plea for Conceptual Consistency in Constitutional Remedies" (2006) 18 NJCL 105

Roach, K, *Constitutional Remedies in Canada*, 2d ed (Aurora, ON: Canada Law Book, 2013)

Roach, K, "Principled Remedial Decision-Making under the *Charter*" (2004) 25 Sup Ct L Rev (2d) 101

Roach, K, "Polycentricity and Queue Jumping in Public Law Remedies: A Two-Track Reponse" (2016) 62 UTLJ 3

Rogerson, C, "The Judicial Search for Appropriate Remedies under the *Charter*" in RJ Sharpe, ed, Charter *Litigation* (Toronto: Butterworths, 1987)

Ryder, B, "Suspending the *Charter*" (2003) 21 Sup Ct L Rev (2d) 267

Sharpe, RJ, "Injunctions and the *Charter*" (1984) 22 Osgoode Hall LJ 474

Sharpe, RJ, and Roach, K, *The Canadian Charter of Rights and Freedoms* 6th ed (Toronto: Irwin Law, 2017) ch. 17

Stuart, D, *Charter Justice in Canadian Criminal Law* 6th ed (Toronto: Carswell, 2014) ch 11

Cases

Doucet Boudreau v. Nova Scotia [2003] 3 SCR 3

Schachter v. Canada [1992] 2 SCR 679

Ward v. Vancouver 2010 SCC 27

CHAPTER 33

THE NOTWITHSTANDING CLAUSE

Why Non-use Does Not Necessarily Equate with Abiding by Judicial Norms

JANET L. HIEBERT[*]

THE *Canadian Charter of Rights and Freedoms* includes the notwithstanding clause in section 33, which allows provincial and federal parliaments to pre-empt judicial review or set aside the effects of a judicial ruling for most of the *Charter*'s protected rights[1] on a temporary but renewable basis. The notwithstanding clause was agreed to in the late stages of federal/provincial negotiations to broker agreement for a complex set of constitutional proposals to patriate the Canadian Constitution, adopt an amending formula, and entrench a constitutional bill of rights. For more than a decade a majority of provincial premiers rejected the merits of a constitutional bill of rights and the judicial remedial powers it authorized. However, by 1981 they were on the defensive when arguing against the *Charter* and envisaged the notwithstanding clause as a mechanism to temper the effects of judicial rulings on the legal validity of legislation.[2] The notwithstanding clause is also the *Charter*'s most explicit recognition of federalism, another fundamental pillar of the Canadian Constitution. By invoking this power, provincial legislatures can temporarily give priority to local or provincial interests that conflict with judicial interpretations of the *Charter*.

Despite the importance of the notwithstanding clause in securing agreement for the *Charter*, it has emerged as its most controversial provision. The notwithstanding clause was not the product of any grand normative theory about constitutional design and was

* Professor, Department of Political Studies, Queen's University. I would like to thank Emmett Macfarlane and Erin Crandall for their insightful and helpful comments on an earlier version of this chapter.
[1] The notwithstanding clause can be invoked with respect to section 2 and sections 7 to 15 of the *Charter*.
[2] Janet L. Hiebert, *Limiting Rights. The Dilemma of Judicial Review* (McGill-Queen's, 1996), 24–26.

given so little attention in negotiations that the framers were initially of different opinions as to whether it could be invoked to both pre-empt judicial review and to set aside the effects of a judicial ruling.[3]

Critics of this power worry its use could frustrate what they believe is the primary purpose of the *Charter*; to ensure that judicial interpretations of rights prevail over political judgment and, by implication, to prevent majority opinion infringing upon minority rights.[4] So potent has criticism of the notwithstanding clause become that many believe it is important to solicit from political leaders a commitment to never invoke the clause—as if the ideas of respecting the *Charter* and using the notwithstanding clause are mutually exclusive.[5]

Strong criticism of the clause does not mean it has not had its defenders. Scholars have championed it as constituting a 'distinctive constitutional partnership' between the judiciary and Parliament;[6] a safety valve to allow Parliament a lawful way to temporarily overturn the effects of judicial rulings for which they strongly disagree,[7] a way to protect equality rights should judicial rulings reflect gender bias,[8] an opportunity to benefit from judicial review without abandoning parliamentary processes for settling difficult questions of social policy,[9] and as an element of inter-institutional dialogue that allows Parliament to insist on the primacy of its judgment in cases of profound disagreement with courts.[10] Yet, support is likely tenuous for the idea that the notwithstanding clause is an important element of a dialogic conception of the *Charter*. Many subscribe to a court-centric version of dialogue and anticipate that the notwithstanding clause will be used only rarely; thus it is questionable how many would continue supporting this power (or its inclusion in their dialogic conception of the *Charter*) if politicians were to regularly invoke the notwithstanding clause after legislation is declared invalid.

This chapter analyses the political life of the notwithstanding clause. It begins in Section 1 by examining the origins of the notwithstanding clause and its uses. Section

---

[3] Janet L. Hiebert, "Compromise and the Notwithstanding Clause: Why the Dominant Narrative Distorts Our Understanding," in James B. Kelly and Christopher Manfredi (eds.) *The Charter at 25* (UBC Press 2009), 129–144.

[4] See for example, John D. Whyte, "On Not Standing for Notwithstanding," (1990) 28 *Alberta Law Review* 347.

[5] In the 2004 federal election, a handful of prominent Canadians published an open letter to then Conservative leader Stephen Harper to elicit a commitment to respect rights, which was defined in part by promising not to invoke the notwithstanding clause "Can We Trust You, Sir, to Defend the Charter?" Globe and Mail, 5 June2004, p A21.

[6] Paul Weiler, "Rights and Judges in a Democracy: A New Canadian Version," (1984) 18:1 *University of Michigan Journal of Law Reform* 51, 86.

[7] Peter H. Russell, "Standing Up for Notwithstanding," (1991) 29 *Alta. L Review* 293.

[8] Lois G. MacDonald, "Promoting Social Equality through the Legislative Override" (1994) 4 NJCL 1.

[9] Peter H. Russell, "The Effect of a Charter of Rights on the Policy-Making Role of the Canadian Courts" (1982) 25 *Can Public Administration* 1, 32.

[10] Kent Roach, *The Supreme Court on Trial. Judicial Activism or Democratic Dialogue?* (Irwin Law, 2001); Peter W. Hogg and Allison Bushell, 'The Charter Dialogue between Courts and Legislatures (Or Perhaps the Charter of Rights Isn't Such a Bad Thing after All),' (1997) 35 *Osgoode Hall Law Journal* 75.

2 analyses the influence of the notwithstanding clause on constitutional ideals beyond Canada. Section 3 discusses important consequences associated with deeply entrenched political reticence to use the notwithstanding clause, followed by a conclusion.

1. Origins of the Notwithstanding Clause and Its Uses

Despite the earlier introduction of the statutory Canadian Bill of Rights in 1960, the idea that a Westminster-based parliamentary system would adopt a constitutional bill of rights that authorizes strong judicial remedies represented a substantial challenge to the constitutional principle of parliamentary sovereignty in place before the *Charter's* adoption (as modified in Canada by judicial review on federalism grounds). Strong remedial power to strike down or refuse to apply inconsistent legislation contradicts the principle that Parliament has the final word on the legality of otherwise duly enacted legislation. From the time a constitutional bill of rights was included on the Canadian constitutional agenda in 1967 by Pierre Trudeau (then Federal Justice Minister) the provincial premiers expressed strong opposition to altering constitutional principles in this way, indicating their preference to retain the principle of parliamentary supremacy (subject to federalism-based review by the courts).

Provincial resistance engaged a two-track strategy, with positions moving between the two positions. The dominant track was to reject in its entirety the proposal for a constitutional bill of rights, engaging parliamentary supremacy and principles of democracy as opposing arguments. Many provincial premiers also insisted that more pressing constitutional amendments warranted attention, including changes to the division of powers, Senate reform, and appointment procedures to the Supreme Court of Canada. The second track focused on how to mitigate the effects of judicial review on legislation in the event that the provincial premiers agreed to a constitutional bill of rights. Provincial premiers predicated their possible support for a bill of rights, in part, on the adoption of a broadly constructed limitation clause explicitly conceived as an instrument to encourage judicial deference to legislation that might restrict rights. However, by the final round of formal constitutional negotiations in November 1981, many of the premiers were no longer confident that they could continue rejecting the *Charter* and were under increased pressure to engage the second track of their strategy: to conceive of ways to mitigate the effects of rights-based judicial review on provincial legislative agendas. Although the idea of a notwithstanding clause had been raised earlier and supported by provincial opponents of the proposed Charter, by 1981 its inclusion had become more important to the opposing provincial premiers as federal government changes to the proposed limitation clause promised to make it considerably more difficult for governments to justify legislation that restricts rights. In the late stages of constitutional negotiations, the notwithstanding clause was considered the best option available to moderate the impact of judicial review on legislative decision-making.[11]

To date, the notwithstanding clause has been invoked in an omnibus and retroactive fashion as well as in 16 specific instances.[12] These uses fall into one of four categories: (1) a form of political protest, (2) an exercise of risk aversion in the face of constitutional uncertainty about how protected rights would be interpreted, (3) an exercise in risk aversion as a result of uncertainty about how s. 1 arguments would be interpreted, or (4) an expression of political disagreement with Supreme Court jurisprudence.

A. Political Protest of the 1982 Constitutional Changes

The first use of the notwithstanding clause was as political protest of the decision to adopt the *Charter* and other constitutional reforms without Quebec's consent. A strongly held view in Quebec is that constitutional changes that affect Quebec, as a founding partner, should not be made without that partner's consent. However, as the Bélanger-Campeau Commission reported, "far from revising" the original Canadian Constitution of 1867, the 1982 constitutional reforms contain "a new definition of Canada which has altered the spirit of the 1867 Act and the compromise established at the time."[13] Within three months of the *Charter*'s adoption, the Quebec National Assembly invoked the notwithstanding clause in a retroactive as well as omnibus fashion to repeal and reenact all legislation passed before the *Charter* was enacted, so as to make a symbolic statement that this legislation would operate notwithstanding the *Charter*, and also to ensure that all future legislation would contain this provision. As Christopher Manfredi characterizes Quebec's response, the invocation of the notwithstanding clause in this manner "forcefully confirmed Quebec's continued opposition" to how the *Charter* was adopted as well as its substance.[14]

Although the omnibus use of the notwithstanding clause ended after the Liberal government of Robert Bourassa replaced the Parti Quebecois in 1985, both the retroactive and omnibus uses of the notwithstanding clause were subject to constitutional challenge in *Ford v Quebec*;[15] a case better known for its treatment of the Quebec's controversial signs law that prohibited advertising on business signs in languages other than French. The Quebec Court of Appeal ruled that the omnibus manner in

---

[11] Hiebert, *Limiting Rights*, above (n 2) 10–31; Hiebert, 'Compromise and the Notwithstanding Clause', above (n 3) 107.

[12] Tsvi Kahana, "The Notwithstanding Mechanism and Public Discussion: Lessons from the Ignored Practice of Section 33 of the Charter," (2001) 44:3 *Canadian Public Administration* 255.

[13] Quebec, *Report of the Commission on the Political and Constitutional Future of Quebec* (Éditeur officiel du Québec, 1991), 30.

[14] Christopher P. Manfredi, *Judicial Power and the Charter; Canada and the Paradox of Liberal Constitutionalism* (Oxford Universit Press 2001), 176.

[15] *Ford v Quebec (Attorney General)* [1988] 2 SCR 712.

which section 33 was invoked was not valid.[16] However, the Supreme Court rejected this argument, along with the position that there is a substantive requirement for invoking section 33. Although the Supreme Court ruled that the retroactive nature of the use of this power was not valid,[17] the Supreme Court's judgment was surprisingly thin on normative requirements for invoking the notwithstanding clause.[18]

B. Risk Aversion because of Constitutional Uncertainty about the Scope of Protected Rights

Several pre-emptive uses of the notwithstanding clause were to protect legislation from constitutional uncertainty when case law on the subject matter in question was under-developed. In the early days of the *Charter*, a serious challenge for legislative decision-making was to anticipate how the Supreme Court would interpret equality and, in particular, to predict when a distinction with respect to social policy benefits constitutes constitutionally invalid discrimination under section 15. The equality rights did not come into force for three years after the *Charter* was adopted, and it would not be until 1989 that the Supreme Court would first outline its method for interpreting equality. Quebec invoked the notwithstanding clause six times because of uncertainty about whether legislation affecting pension eligibility and criteria for receiving government grants violate equality.[19] Yukon also used section 33 once but the legislation did not come into force.

Saskatchewan also invoked the notwithstanding clause in 1986 with respect to back-to-work legislation for the public sector after a series of rotating strikes.[20] At the time the Supreme Court had not dealt with whether the *Charter* protects the right to strike. The Court's rulings two years later confirmed that the use of the notwithstanding clause would not have been required at the time, as the Court rejected the right to strike as constitutionally protected[21]—a position subsequently reversed.[22]

These pre-emptive uses of the notwithstanding clause can be interpreted as a form of risk aversion to protect legislation in the face of constitutional uncertainty about how equality would be interpreted and also whether there is a constitutional right to strike.

---

[16] *Alliance des professeurs de Montreal v Procureur général du Québec*, [1985] C.A. 376, (1985) 21 DLR (4th) 354.

[17] *Ford* above (n 15) [35].

[18] Lorraine Weinrib is critical of the Court's willingness to focus solely on the formal requirements of this power, rather than develop more substantive requirements for its use. Lorraine Eisenstat Weinrib "Learning to Live with the Override," (1990) 35 *McGill Law Journal* 553, 541.

[19] Kahana, above (n 12), 258.

[20] *An Act to Provide for Settlement of a Certain Labour-Management dispute between the Government of Saskatchewan and the Saskatchewan Governments' Employees Union*, s. 9, SS 1984-85-86, c. 111.

[21] *Reference re Public Service Employee Relations Act (Alta)*, [1981] 1 SCR 313

[22] *Saskatchewan Federation of Labour v Saskatchewan* (2015) SCC 4.

C. Risk Aversion because of Uncertainty about How Section 1 Arguments Would Be Interpreted

Similar to the above pre-emptive uses as a form of risk aversion because of uncertainty about the scope of protected *Charter* rights, the notwithstanding clause has also been used as a form of insurance given uncertainty about how the Court would interpret a government's s. 1 arguments to justify restrictions on rights.[23] The *Charter* has significantly enhanced the role of government lawyers who, amongst other responsibilities, advise governments on the likely risks of litigation and the potential consequences of possible judicial remedies, and also advise departments on how to minimize that risk. Over time, the popularity of the *Charter* and broad public disdain for the notwithstanding clause have discouraged reliance on the clause as a means for dealing with potential consequences of *Charter* litigation. Nevertheless, in the early days of the *Charter*, the notwithstanding clause was used in several instances to avoid *Charter* litigation because of uncertainty of about how a government's argument that legislation should be upheld would fare under s. 1.

The notwithstanding clause was invoked in this manner six times by Quebec with respect to education policy that offered Catholic or Protestant moral and religious instruction in public schools.[24] In so doing, Quebec insulated legislation from the kinds of challenges that occurred in other provinces as to whether the denominational character of Canadian public education violates *Charter* guarantees of religious freedom or equality in a manner not justified under s. 1.[25]

D. Political Disagreement about Judicial Interpretations of the *Charter*

The most controversial use of the notwithstanding clause is as a form of political disagreement with respect to how the Supreme Court has interpreted the *Charter*. The best-known example occurred during the midst of the ratification process for the Meech Lake Accord, which was initiated by the desire to redress Quebec's earlier grievances

---

[23] A controversial proposed use of the notwithstanding clause as a way of avoiding litigation (although eventually rescinded because of strong public criticism) was Alberta's decision to invoke the notwithstanding clause in Bill 26, *The Institutional Confinement and Sexual Sterilization Compensation Act*. Then-Premier Ralph Klein admitted that the government's consideration of the notwithstanding clause was a mistake, and implied that his government had been badly advised by its own legal advisers. Alberta Government Press Release, 10 March 1998; "Alberta, the Notwithstanding Clause and the Weak," *Vancouver Sun*, 12 March 1998, A10; "Klein Backs Off on Sterilization Deal," *Calgary Herald*, 12 March 1998, A1, 3.

[24] Kahana, above (n 12), 262–263.

[25] William F. Foster, "Moral and Religious Instruction in Quebec: Some Legal Issues," (1993) 28 *McGill Journal of Education* 33.

with the 1982 constitutional changes that were passed without its consent. Quebec invoked the notwithstanding clause to insulate new signs law legislation from judicial review following a Supreme Court ruling that declared a more extreme and earlier version of that policy unconstitutional. In the *Ford* ruling, the Court struck down part of Bill 101, enacted by the earlier Parti Quebecois government, which banned on public signs the use of languages other than French. A new Liberal government led by Robert Bourassa had promised English voters that his government would allow bilingual signs. However, following the Supreme Court ruling in *Ford*, Bourassa was under intense pressure to set aside the effects of the Court's ruling. Faced with a divided Cabinet and caucus, Bourassa decided to restore French-only requirements for commercial signs outdoors, but to allow multilingual signs indoors as long as they were out of sight from the street. This new law, Bill 178, invoked the notwithstanding clause in a pre-emptive fashion.[26] This use of the notwithstanding clause triggered significant public furor and a weakening of political support for the Meech Lake Accord, to the point of there being "virtually no chance that the Meech Lake Accord would be ratified."[27]

A second example of use of the notwithstanding clause to protest judicial interpretations of the *Charter* occurred in Alberta in 2000 when the legislature passed the Marriage Amendment Act, which invoked the notwithstanding clause to signal that the Alberta legislature did not approve of altering the definition of marriage so as to comply with equality. This action can be considered a largely symbolic gesture as Alberta (like other provinces) lacks jurisdiction over marriage.

(i) Potential Use of the Notwithstanding Clause

Although not yet utilized in this manner, a potential use of the notwithstanding clause is to give Parliament more time to revise legislation following a change to a common law rule or a suspended judicial declaration of invalidity.[28] Often when legislation is found to be inconsistent with the *Charter*, instead of declaring legislation as invalid immediately, the Court will suspend the effect of this ruling for a period of time, usually 12 months, to allow Parliament to address the identified *Charter* deficiencies. However, this time frame may be insufficient for Parliament, particularly if the government has been unwilling to act promptly (likely due to political disagreement with the Court's ruling), if the issue involves extensive consultation with the provincial governments, or if an election has delayed the effective period for legislative redress. When unable to legislate within the time frame granted by the Court, governments have gone to the Court to request additional time to pass the revised legislation. Two prominent examples occurred following the rulings of *R. v Feeney*[29] (involving new rules for warrantless

---

[26] Peter H. Russell, *Constitutional Odyssey. Can Canadians Become a Sovereign People?* 3rd edition (University of Toronto Press 2004), 145–148.

[27] Patrick Monahan, *Meech Lake. The Inside Story* (University of Toronto Press, 1991), 164.

[28] I have Emmett Macfarlane to thank for suggesting this possible use of the notwithstanding clause.

[29] *R. v Feeney* [1997] 2 S.C.R. 13. A 5-4 majority reversed itself on the validity of a common law rule that had allowed police, under certain conditions, to enter and search a home without a warrant.

police searches of domestic residences) and *Carter v Canada (Attorney General)*[30] (which ruled that an absolute prohibition on physician-assisted suicide is unconstitutional).[31] However, the Court may be unwilling to grant extensions to remedy *Charter* restrictions. Declarations of invalidity can be controversial because they suspend the remedial effects of judicial review.[32] By seeking yet more time, a government is effectively asking the Court to bear institutional responsibility for further delaying remedies. Yet, depending on Parliament's response, it is entirely possible that the revised legislation would be declared constitutionally valid, in which no remedy is owed.[33] When federal Justice lawyers were seeking an extension of the declaration of invalidity to enact a regulatory framework for physician-assisted suicide, Supreme Court Justice Russell Brown suggested that the Government ask Parliament to invoke section 33.[34] Nevertheless, a divided Supreme Court agreed to give the federal Parliament an additional four months.

2. The Influence of the Notwithstanding Clause Elsewhere

Despite considerable controversy within Canada about the merits of the notwithstanding clause, reformers elsewhere and many comparative constitutional scholars look more favourably upon it—or more accurately, on the ideas they associate with this power. Elsewhere, many conceptualize the notwithstanding clause as effectively rebutting more conventional orthodoxy that a bill of rights necessarily requires or presumes that judicial rulings will operate as binding constraints on democratically elected legislatures.[35] This idea of constraining the effects or scope of judicial remedial powers is

---

The Court's new rule required extensive negotiations between all levels of government, complicated by a federal election, and resulted in not only requests for a rehearing to delay the effects of the ruling, but also a further request for additional time to enact legislation. Janet L. Hiebert, *Charter Conflicts. What Is Parliament's Role?* (McGill-Queen's University Press, 2002) 148–154.

[30] *Carter v Canada (Attorney General)*, 2015 SCC 5.

[31] On 6 February 2015, the Court ruled that the complete ban on physician-assisted suicide is unconstitutional and suspended the effects of the ruling for 12 months so new legislation could establish regulatory guidelines. However, the Harper Conservative government did little towards developing new legislation on this issue, and the new Liberal government when faced with the nearing deadline, asked the Court in January 2016 to request an extension of the declaration of invalidity.

[32] Robert Leckey, *Bills of Rights in the Common Law* (Cambridge University Press, 2015).

[33] I am grateful to Grégoire Webber for this argument, which occurred in the course of a private conversation in February 2016 about judicial remedies and delayed legislative responses.

[34] Tonda MacCharles, "Ottawa Surprises Top Court Judges by Allowing Assisted Suicide to Proceed in Quebec", *Toronto Star*, 11 January 2016. http://www.thestar.com/news/canada/2016/01/11/ottawa-surprises-top-court-judges-by-asking-for-more-time-on-assisted-suicide.html.

[35] Although the notwithstanding clause demonstrated to other parliamentary systems the possibility of distinguishing the concept of judicial review from judicial supremacy it is not accurate to equate the

not only considered an essential way of bridging what has long been thought of as com-peting and mutually exclusive constitutional paradigms—those of parliamentary ver-sus judicial supremacy—but for some it also represents an alternative model of a bill of rights characterized in varying ways including the Commonwealth model,[36] hybrid approach,[37] weak-form model,[38] and parliamentary rights model.[39]

It is difficult to pinpoint when this idea of constrained judicial remedial powers gained currency. Unlike the *Charter* debate, where Canadian political participants struggled with the question of how to temper the impact of judicial remedial powers within the compressed and intensely political terrain of a looming deadline in a late spurt of con-stitutional negotiations, and in an intellectual and comparative context that situated the choices as being mutually exclusive (either parliamentary supremacy or judicial supremacy), reform-minded politicians elsewhere have had the luxury of time and the *Charter*'s example when considering the appropriate scope of judicial remedial power.

Unlike Canada, these other Westminster-based systems have adopted statutory rather than constitutional bills of rights that do not allow courts to set aside the legal effects of legislation. Political reluctance in New Zealand, the UK, the Australian Capital Territory, and the state of Victoria to conceive of strong judicial remedial pow-ers negated the need for an explicit mechanism such as the notwithstanding clause[40] to reverse the effect of a judicial ruling.[41] For this reason, the trigger mechanism for legisla-tive disagreement with judicial rulings differs. Unlike in Canada, where Parliament is required to act assertively to lawfully dissent from a judicial ruling by passing legisla-tion that invokes the notwithstanding clause, or to invoke this power in a pre-emptive manner to (temporarily) insulate legislation from judicial review when reasonably con-fident of losing in a *Charter* challenge, these other parliaments can voice their disagree-ment with judicial rulings passively: by ignoring them and refusing to amend legislation

---

notwithstanding clause with the retention of parliamentary supremacy in Canada. Use of this power displaces temporarily, rather than replaces permanently, judicial authority about constitutional validity.

[36] S. Gardbaum, "The New Commonwealth Model of Constitutionalism", (2001) 49 *American Journal of Constitutional Law* 707; "Reassessing the New Commonwealth Model of Constitutionalism" (2010) 8 *International Journal of Constitutional Law* 167; *The New Commonwealth Model of Constitutionalism. Theory and Practice* (Cambridge University Press, 2013).

[37] P. Rishworth, "The Birth and Rebirth of the Bill of Rights", in G. Huscroft and P. Rishworth (eds.), *Rights and Freedoms: The New Zealand Bill of Rights Act 1990 and the Human Rights Act* (Brookers, 1995), 4; J. Goldsworthy, "Homogenizing Constitutions", (2003) 23 *Oxford Journal of Legal Studies* 483.

[38] Mark Tushnet, 'New Forms of Judicial Review', (2003) 38 *Wake Forest Law Review* 813–838; Mark Tushnet, *Weak Courts, Strong Rights. Judicial Review and Social Welfare Rights in Comparative Constitutional Law* (Princeton University Press, 2008).

[39] Janet L. Hiebert, "New Constitutional Ideas: Can New Parliamentary Models Resist Judicial Dominance When Interpreting Rights?", (2004) 82 *Texas Law Review* 1963; Janet L. Hiebert "Constitutional Experimentation: Rethinking How a Bill of Rights Functions" in T. Ginsburg and R. Dixon (eds.) *Comparative Constitutional Law* (Edward Elgar, 2011) 298.

[40] The Victoria Charter of Rights and Responsibilties Act does contain a legislative override, despite the fact that courts do not have the authority to set aside the legal effects of duly enacted legislation.

[41] This argument was made earlier by Hiebert, "Constitutional Experimentation: Rethinking How a Bill of Rights Functions," above (n 39).

to comply with judicial interpretations of rights (either as inferred from those rulings where the judiciary is unable to render a rights-compliant interpretation of legislation or more directly indicated through a judicial declaration of incompatibility or inconsistency in the UK, ACT, or Victoria).

Disagreement will inevitably occur on where final legal authority should reside for determining the validity of legislation that restricts rights. Such disagreements reflect philosophical assumptions about the reasons for preferring a more juridical or political form of constitutionalism. However, whatever position one takes in this debate, it is important to recognize that bills of rights are not self-enforcing. Compliance will occur under a bill of rights that constrains the scope of judicial remedies if political behaviour assumes that compliance with judicial rulings is an important norm,[42] and non-compliance can occur regardless of the scope of judicial remedial powers when legislatures genuinely or intentionally misinterpret whether new legislation is compatible with relevant jurisprudence.[43] The latter point is demonstrated by Martin Sweet's assessments of how American legislatures have ignored, evaded, or overridden judicial rulings on a range of issues such as affirmative action, flag burning, hate speech, and school prayer,[44] even though the U.S. Bill of Rights is thought to be the quintessential example of a strong form system of judicial review[45] and does not contain a notwithstanding mechanism. As will be argued below, non-compliance with judicial norms about the meaning of constitutional principles likely occurs in Canada despite a failure to invoke the notwithstanding clause.

3. Impact of Public Disdain for the Notwithstanding Clause on Government Strategies

Strong political reticence to invoke the notwithstanding clause has effectively removed use of this power from federal political consideration. Interviews with federal government lawyers confirm that the notwithstanding clause is not considered an option when developing legislative initiatives and approving the government's legislative agenda.[46]

---

[42] Tushnet, *Weak Courts, Strong Rights,* above (n 38), 43–76.

[43] Mark Tushnet "Policy Distortion and Democratic Debilitation: Comparative Illumination of the Countermajoritarian Difficulty" (1995) 94:2 *Michigan Law Review* 270

[44] M.J. Sweet, *Merely Judgment. Ignoring, Evading, and Trumping the Supreme Court* (University of Virginia Press, 2010).

[45] Tushnet, *Weak Courts,* above (n 38).

[46] All interviews were conducted on the basis of anonymity, unless this condition was explicitly waived. The interviews were conducted with lawyers in the Human Rights Centre at the Department of Justice (Ottawa), between 1999 and 2000; with former justice officials (1994–1995), (1998–1999), and (2013–2015); and with former Minister of Justice Irwin Cotler (2015) [hereinafter "Interviews"].

One way of interpreting this presumption against invoking the notwithstanding clause is to assume that legislative initiatives are evaluated and revised to ensure they are compliant with judicial norms of the *Charter* (thus negating the need to invoke the not-withstanding clause). However, as argued below, this is not a compelling interpretation because it falsely equates failure to invoke this power with a commitment to ensure that legislation, as passed, complies with judicial norms.

The federal government is well equipped with the necessary legal resources to identify the likelihood that proposed legislation is vulnerable to a successful *Charter* challenge and pro-vide advice about how to make it more *Charter*-compliant. Legislative initiatives are system-atically subject to risk-based assessments of their chances of being litigated, the policy and fiscal consequences that would arise from an adverse judicial outcome,[47] and the expected litigation costs.[48] The regularity of this exercise and the crucial role government lawyers play has led James Kelly to characterize the Department of Justice's general influence on legis-lation as analogous to that of a central agency.[49] In short, the centrality of *Charter* vetting makes it difficult to believe that government is unaware of the risk level that legislation will be declared unconstitutional, or that it lacks the necessary advice to revise these initiatives to ensure that they stand a much stronger chance of withstanding a *Charter* challenge.

However, being forewarned that a proposed legislative bill bears a high risk of being declared constitutionally invalid does not necessarily discourage government leaders from supporting it, despite the political refusal to enact the notwithstanding clause. Government lawyers confirm both that political decisions to pursue proposed bills that carry warnings they incur a high-risk of judicial invalidation often boil down to a government's risk tolerance, and also that government has proceeded with high-risk bills.[50] The likelihood that successive federal governments have knowingly engaged in high-risk behaviour is also supported by the frequency in which the Supreme Court has found legislation unconstitutional, despite the extensive pre-legislative evaluations for *Charter* consistency that systematically occur, and that evaluations for Charter compli-ance were conducted for legislation that pre-dated the *Charter*. Between 1984 and 2012, 45 federal (and 27 provincial) acts have been invalidated.[51] In its last few years in office, the Harper government (which was defeated in October 2015) presided over a substan-tial number of high-profile Charter losses including sections of the federal anti-terrorist financing law,[52] mandatory minimum sentences for gun crimes,[53] criminal prohibitions

[47] Interviews, above (n 46).

[48] Mary Dawson, "The Impact of the Charter on the Public Policy Process and the Department of Justice," (1992) 30 *Osgoode Hall Law Journal* 30, 595.

[49] James B. Kelly, "Legislative Activism and Parliamentary Bills of Rights," in James B. Kelly and Christopher P. Manfredi, *Contested Constitutionalism. Reflections on the Canadian Charter of Rights and Freedoms*, (UBC Press, 2009), 93.

[50] Interviews, above (note 46).

[51] Janet L. Hiebert and James B. Kelly, *Parliamentary Bills of Rights. The Experiences of New Zealand and the United Kingdom* (Cambridge University Press, 2015), 73.

[52] *Canada (Attorney General) v Federation of Law Societies of Canada*, 2015 SCC 7.

[53] *R v Nur*, 2015 SCC 15.

against assisted suicide,[54] restrictions on judicial discretion to give offenders sentencing discounts,[55] repeal of early parole,[56] and the government's attempt to terminate a complex agreement allowing for a safe-injection facility for drug addicts.[57] The Harper government also suffered several high-profile non-*Charter* constitutional losses.[58]

Politically, it is not difficult to understand why government leaders are unwilling to invoke the notwithstanding clause to insulate high-risk legislation from a potentially negative judicial ruling. To invoke the notwithstanding clause essentially challenges the primacy of judicial norms about how *Charter* rights should constrain legislation. However, the *Charter's* popularity and public confidence in the Supreme Court's role interpreting constitutional values ensures that any political *Charter* judgment to disagree with the Court will likely be controversial and place pressure on the Government to explain and justify its reasons—a task made extremely difficult by the equation many make between invoking the notwithstanding clause and "overriding' rights" It is for this reason that some lament the wording of the notwithstanding clause, preferring instead that it refer to political disagreements with judicial interpretations of section 1.[59]

Rather than invoke the notwithstanding clause and defend politically what would likely be a highly contested action, federal government leaders apparently prefer to present high-risk legislation to Parliament and the public as consistent with the *Charter* and gamble on its constitutional fate. The gamble is either that the legislation will survive a *Charter* challenge (even when forewarned that the chances of this are fairly remote) or more likely than not, that the Government will benefit politically from pursuing legislation even if it is ultimately declared constitutionally invalid. Politically, it is far easier for a government to "roll the dice" by introducing high-risk legislation than to enact the notwithstanding clause, even if the Government ultimately loses. The actual impact of a judicial ruling for a government's legislative agenda will occur several years after legislation is enacted. When considered against the backdrop of the electoral cycle, this risk-taking is likely considered too far in the future to worry about immediately, particularly as there is no guarantee that the government responsible for introducing rights-offending legislation will still be in office after the many appeal options are exhausted. Even if a government is faced with pressure to pass remedial legislation, it can engage in rhetorical campaigns that blame the judiciary for forcing government to take a position that may be unpopular with its electoral base. A government can also pursue "creative" responses to a prior negative judicial ruling so as to preserve the basic legislative goals that have been impugned, but in ways that do not necessarily comply with the spirit of a

---

[54] *Carter v Canada (Attorney General)*, 2015 SCC 5.

[55] *R v Summers*, [2014] 1 SCR 575.

[56] *Canada (Attorney General) v Whaling*, 2014 SCC 20.

[57] *Canada (Attorney General) v PHS Community Services Society*, [2011] 3 SCR 134.

[58] Amongst the most significant of these were the Supreme Court rejecting the validity of the federal government's Supreme Court appointment and its proposal for Senate reform. *Reference re Supreme Court Act, ss. 5 and 6*, 2014 SCC 21, and *Reference re Senate Reform*, 2014 SCC 32.

[59] Christopher P. Manfredi, *Judicial Power and the Charter*, 2nd edition (Oxford University Press 2001) 191–193.

judicial ruling (or what James Kelly and Matthew Hennigar refer to as notwithstanding by stealth).[60] This strategy may again lead to legal challenges if individuals or groups believe it is a non-compliant response. However, even if this revised legislation is challenged, government leaders might calculate there could be judicial reticence to censure legislation a second time around. In contrast, use of the notwithstanding clause will not only be subject to criticism in the immediate circumstance, but criticism can also resurface in future election campaigns by critics willing to engage in rhetorical insinuations suggesting that a government's previous support for the notwithstanding clause indicates a lack of support for the *Charter*.

Although not widely known, the notwithstanding clause is not the only instrument through which the federal government is expected to announce if it intends to pursue legislation that patently contradicts judicial norms about protected rights or what constitutes a reasonable limit under s. 1. The federal Minister of Justice (who in Canada also functions as the Attorney General) has a statutory obligation to alert Parliament when government is introducing legislation that is inconsistent with the *Charter*.[61] This statutory reporting obligation was adopted in 1985, and is authorized by section 4.1 of the Department of Justice Act.[62] This reporting requirement is similar to an earlier obligation enacted under the Canadian Bill of Rights. As initially conceived, this statutory reporting obligation was expected to serve three purposes: (1) to introduce a more critical focus on rights when evaluating the merits of legislative objectives and identifying compliant ways to achieve these, (2) to influence how government conceives and pursues its legislative agenda, and (3) to encourage parliamentary evaluations of legislation from a rights perspective.[63]

Two streams of *Charter* assessments occur before legislative initiatives are approved as bills for introduction to Parliament. One functions as an advisory role for policy development purposes (as referred to above). The other is to assist the Minister of Justice's

---

[60] James B. Kelly and Matthew A. Hennigar, "The Canadian Charter of Rights and the Minister of Justice: Weak-Form Review within a Constitutional Charter of Rights" (2012) 10:1 I-CON 35.

[61] Information about how this statutory obligation is interpreted, normally highly confidential, became available to the public as a result of the legal challenge by Edgar Schmit of the standards used for determining whether the statutory reporting obligation for *Charter* inconsistency is engaged under s. 4.1 of the Department of Justice Act. Department of Justice, Extracts from "Effective Communication of Legal Risk", 15 December 2006; Department of Justice, "Legal Risk Management in the Public Sector, 26 November 2007. Redacted versions of both documents were provided as evidence in *Edgar Schmidt v The Attorney General of Canada*, 2016 FC 269.

[62] This requirement is: 4.1 (1) ... [T]he Minister shall, in accordance with such regulations as may be prescribed by the Governor in Council, examine every regulation transmitted to the Clerk of the Privy Council for registration pursuant to the *Statutory Instruments Act* and every Bill introduced in or presented to the House of Commons by a minister of the Crown, in order to ascertain whether any of the provisions thereof are inconsistent with the purposes and provisions of the *Canadian Charter of Rights and Freedoms* and the Minister shall report any such inconsistency to the House of Commons at the first convenient opportunity. *Department of Justice Act* R.S., 1985, c. J-2, s. 4.1(1); 1992, c. 1, s. 144(F).

[63] Janet L. Hiebert and James B. Kelly, *Parliamentary Bills of Rights. The Experiences of New Zealand and the United Kingdom* (Cambridge University Press 2015) 4.

section 4.1 statutory reporting obligation for *Charter* inconsistency. Yet although the statutory reporting obligation for *Charter* inconsistency has been in place for three decades, no report of *Charter* inconsistency has ever been made. The absence of any such report amounts to a tacit message regularly given to Parliament: that all legislative bills introduced since 1985 have been deemed by successive Ministers of Justice as being consistent with the *Charter*, and that rights are either not implicated or that the prescribed limitations satisfy judicial norms for section 1. This message of *Charter* compliance was explicitly delivered under the Conservative government of Stephen Harper following an opposition member's query about the criteria and processes used for assessing whether this reporting obligation is engaged.[64]

However, some Justice officials have suggested that it would be a serious mistake for Parliament to infer from the absence of a section 4. 1 report that there is no need to question *Charter* compliance or ask about whether legislation is so risky that it is vulnerable to judicial censure.[65] This skepticism is reinforced by what appears to be reliance on low standards for determining whether the reporting requirement is engaged to alert Parliament that legislative bills are inconsistent with the Charter. According to Department of Justice guidelines for Charter evaluations, a report of *Charter* inconsistency is not required if the bill is considered "not manifestly unconstitutional" and where "a credible argument exists in support" of the bill. However, a bill is considered to be not manifestly unconstitutional even if it is identified as having a high risk of being declared unconstitutional,[66] and a credible argument simply means one that is capable of being argued; not one that will necessarily be a successful argument.[67] In short, there is a very weak connection between judgments of Charter consistency for section 4.1 reporting purposes and confidence that legislation can be successfully defended. The sustained use of what appears to be an exceptionally low threshold for determining whether the reporting mechanism is engaged to alert Parliament about *Charter* consistency prompted a senior Justice lawyer to take legal action to challenge how the Department of Justice interprets this statutory reporting obligation.[68]

In a lengthy ruling, the Federal Court ruled against his claim, and upheld the validity of the "credible" *Charter* argument. One of the many arguments the Court made was that Parliament itself must assume responsibility to ensure *Charter* rights are protected, and thus "must not place its duties on the shoulders of the other branches, notably on those of the Minister of Justice."[69] However, the Court did not address substantial difficulties this responsibility presents for Parliament within a political setting where

---

[64] Statement provided by the Parliamentary Secretary to the Minister of Justice, read into the proceedings of the Justice and Human Rights Committee, Meeting 59, 13 February 2013, Evidence.

[65] Interviews, above (n 46).

[66] Department of Justice, Extracts from "Effective Communication of Legal Risk", 15 December 2006, above (n 61).

[67] *Edgar Schmidt v The Attorney General of Canada*, 2016 FC 269 [250–252].

[68] Ibid.

[69] Ibid. [276].

Parliament has been explicitly informed that the absence of a section 4.1 report should be interpreted as a judgment that the legislation is consistent with rights[70] (despite the high tolerance of risk that the Department of Justice Guidelines for interpreting the reporting obligation seemingly allow), is prevented from learning more about the criteria or processes that are used by the Minister of Justice when determining that no report of *Charter* inconsistency is required,[71] and lacks independent legal advice that specializes in issues of *Charter* compliance.

In short, notwithstanding the Court's willingness to uphold the standards used by the Minister of Justice when interpreting the s. 4.1 statutory reporting obligation, the political interpretation of this obligation parallels the willingness to pass high-risk legislation without invoking the notwithstanding clause. Both actions suggest governmental willingness to portray legislation as being constitutionally valid, even when apprised that this judgment involves an interpretation of the *Charter* that clearly contradicts judicial norms and thus the legislation stands a high chance of being declared constitutionally invalid. Both forms of political behaviour also demonstrate a lack of respect for Parliament by interpreting the statutory reporting obligation in a manner that bears little resemblance to the intent or wording of this reporting mechanism in section 4.1, and by placing Parliament in the unfortunate position of unknowingly approving high-risk legislation. Arguably, these forms of political behaviour are also inconsistent with what could be construed as the normative obligation implicit in the *Charter*—of invoking section 33 to signal legislative disagreement with judicial norms, thereby inviting debate about the appropriateness of this action—and also inconsistent with the normative ideals that underlie the statutory reporting requirement of section 4.1 of the Department of Justice Act (as referred to above).

It is not certainly not my intent to suggest that government should either avoid introducing legislation whenever uncertain about its chances of successfully defending legislation should it be subject to litigation, or that it is obliged to invoke the notwithstanding clause whenever it cannot be confident that legislation will survive a *Charter* challenge. This form of risk-averse behaviour would result in an overly cautious approach to defining a government's legislative agenda that would have a chilling effect on legislative development and unduly cede to courts sole responsibility to contribute to judgment about the meaning of protected rights or the scope of permissible limitations on rights under section 1.[72]

---

[70] Standing Committee on Justice and Human Rights, Meeting 59, 13 February 2013, Evidence.

[71] NDP Justice critic Francoise Boivin put forth a motion to the Justice and Human Rights Committee that a "thorough study" be conducted into how s. 4.1 was being interpreted. The Conservative-dominated committee defeated the motion, 6-5. A few months later, Brent Rathgeber resigned from the Conservative Party and acknowledged that intense pressure had been exerted on government members to defeat the motion. Standing Committee on Justice and Human Rights, Meeting 59, 13 February 2013, Evidence; "MP Brent Rathgeber's stand is a principled one that should give the Tories pause," http://o.canada.com/news/mp-brent-rathgebers-stand-is-a-principled-one-that-should-give-the-tories-pause, 7 June 2013.

[72] Janet L. Hiebert, *Charter Conflicts. What Is Parliament's Role*, above (n 29) 52–72.

However, a significant and important difference exists between "good-faith" interpretations of the *Charter* and actions that appear to be more akin to "rolling the dice" by pursuing legislation for which the government and its Minister of Justice have been fully apprised of contradicting judicial norms, and thus standing a significant chance of being declared invalid, particularly in situations where case law is reasonably settled. In those circumstances where government leaders knowingly support and promote legislation that is clearly inconsistent with judicial norms, and for which they have been apprised stands a strong likelihood of being declared constitutionally invalid, they should respect the legal mechanisms intended to support their political judgments to knowingly proceed: by enacting the notwithstanding clause and also informing Parliament via the statutory reporting obligation that legislation is inconsistent with the *Charter* (both actions that, although controversial, appropriately place government in the position of having to defend and convince Parliament and Canadians of the merits and justification of its judgment).

4. CONCLUSION

Both the origins of the notwithstanding clause and the infrequency of theoretical or normative discussions about its function or use have contributed to unease and suspicion about what role this power plays in a constitutional bill of rights that otherwise authorizes strong judicial remedies. Nevertheless, Canadians are not well served by either "wishing away" this clause or assuming they can equate its lack of use as an indication of compliance with judicial norms about the *Charter*. Faced with strong apprehension that use of the notwithstanding clause will have long-term negative consequences for political parties, government leaders prefer to roll the dice by passing high-risk legislation, and face whatever consequences arise from litigation. Although this may be understandable as a form of rational political behaviour, this does not negate the fact that it also reflects deeply ingrained cynicism about the importance of constitutional and statutory rules: a concern compounded by the extent to which the Attorney-General (who in Canada does double duty as Minister of Justice) is complicit in activities that lend the appearance of constitutional and statutory misbehavior.

It is well beyond time for a thoughtful discussion of the notwithstanding clause to dismantle the myths that its use signals disregard for the *Charter*, or that its lack of use implies respect and agreement for judicial norms about the *Charter*. Similarly, it is time to pay more attention to the interpretation and criteria used for the statutory reporting obligation of *Charter* inconsistency in section 4.1 of the Department of Justice Act.

These discussions will inevitably have to address the following question: When does the Minister of Justice cross the line between uncertainty about how legislation will fare if litigated, and a duty to invoke the notwithstanding clause or engage the section 4.1 statutory reporting obligation to alert Parliament that legislation is not consistent with the *Charter*? This question in turn invites many others, including: How much influence does and should the Minister of Justice have within Cabinet when advising his or her colleagues that legislative bills as approved are inconsistent with the *Charter*? Should the Minister of Justice be expected to alert Parliament or the public that legislation has a relatively high likelihood of being declared invalid, even when he/she believes that legislation is worth pursuing and represents a normatively compelling interpretation of the *Charter*? If so, what form should this notice take: reporting under section 4.1 and/or invoking the not-withstanding clause in a pre-emptive fashion? Should the statutory reporting obligation be amended to require explanations for all bills, rather than a bald statement of *Charter* inconsistency (that for the reasons explained above is unlikely to ever occur?) And should Parliament constitute a specialized committee and/or appoint an independent legal advi-sor to report on whether all bills introduced are consistent with the *Charter*?

Bibliography

Articles and Chapters

Dawson, Mary. "The Impact of the Charter on the Public Policy Process and the Department of Justice," (1992) 30 *Osgoode Hall Law Journal* 595–603

Foster, William F. "Moral and Religious Instruction in Quebec: Some Legal Issues," (1993) 28 *McGill Journal of Education* 33–44

Gardbaum, Stephen. "Reassessing the New Commonwealth Model of Constitutionalism," (2010) 8 *International Journal of Constitutional Law* 167–206

Gardbaum, Stephen. "The New Commonwealth Model of Constitutionalism," (2001) 49 *American Journal of Comparative Law* 707–761

Goldsworthy, J. "Homogenizing Constitutions," (2003) 23 *Oxford Journal of Legal Studies* 483–505

Hiebert, Janet L. 'Compromise and the Notwithstanding Clause: Why the Dominant Narrative Distorts Our Understanding,' in James B. Kelly and Christopher Manfredi (eds.) *The Charter at 25* (UBC Press 2009), 129–144

Hiebert, Janet. 'Constitutional Experimentation: Rethinking How a Bill of Rights Functions' in T. Ginsburg and R. Dixon (eds.) *Comparative Constitutional Law*, (Edward Elgar 2011), 298–320

Hiebert, Janet L. 'New Constitutional Ideas: Can New Parliamentary Models Resist Judicial Dominance When Interpreting Rights?' (2004) 82 *Texas Law Review* 1963–1987

Hogg, Peter W. and Allison Bushell, "The Charter Dialogue between Courts and Legislatures (Or Perhaps the Charter of Rights Isn't Such a Bad Thing after All)," (1997) 35 *Osgoode Hall Law Journal* 75–124

Kahana, Tsvi. "The Notwithstanding Mechanism and Public Discussion: Lessons from the Ignored Practice of Section 33 of the Charter," (2001) 44 *Canadian Public Administration* 255–291

Kelly, James B. "Legislative Activism and Parliamentary Bills of Rights," in James B. Kelly and Christopher P. Manfredi, *Contested Constitutionalism. Reflections on the Canadian Charter of Rights and Freedoms* (UBC Press 2009), 86–106

Kelly James B. and Matthew A. Hennigar, "The Canadian Charter of Rights and the Minister of Justice: Weak-Form Review within a Constitutional Charter of Rights" (2012) 10 I-CON 35–68

MacDonald, Lois G., "Promoting Social Equality through the Legislative Override" (1994) 4 NJCL 1–27

Rishworth, Paul. "The Birth and Rebirth of the Bill of Rights'" in G. Huscroft and P. Rishworth (eds.) *Rights and Freedoms: The New Zealand Bill of Rights Act 1990 and the Human Rights Act* (Brookers, 1995)

Russell, Peter H. "The Effect of a Charter of Rights on the Policy-Making Role of the Canadian Courts" (1982) 25 *Can Public Administration* 1–33

Russell, Peter H., "Standing Up for Notwithstanding," (1991) 29 *Alta. L Review* 293–309

Tushnet, Mark. "New Forms of Judicial Review" (2003) 38 *Wake Forest Law Review* 813–838

Tushnet, Mark. "Policy Distortion and Democratic Debilitation: Comparative Illumination of the Countermajoritarian Difficulty" (1995) 94:2 *Michigan Law Review* 245–301

Weiler, Paul, "Rights and Judges in a Democracy: A New Canadian Version," (1984) 18:1 *University of Michigan Journal of Law Reform* 51–92

Whyte, John D. "On Not Standing for Notwithstanding," (1990) 28 *Alberta Law Review* 347–357

Weinrib, Lorraine Eisenstat. "Learning to Live with the Override," (1990) 35 *McGill Law Journal* 553–571

Books

Gardbaum, Stephen. *The New Commonwealth Model of Constitutionalism. Theory and Practice* (Cambridge University Press 2013)

Hiebert, Janet L. *Charter Conflicts. What Is Parliament's Role?* (McGill-Queen's University Press, 2002)

Hiebert, Janet L. *Limiting Rights. The Dilemma of Judicial Review*, (McGill-Queen's University Press, 1996)

Hiebert, Janet L. and James B. Kelly, *Parliamentary Bills of Rights. The Experiences of New Zealand and the United Kingdom* (Cambridge University Press 2015)

Leckey, Robert. *Bills of Rights in the Common Law* (Cambridge University Press 2015)

Manfredi, Christopher P. *Judicial Power and the Charter; Canada and the Paradox of Liberal Constitutionalism* (Oxford University Press 2001)

Monahan, Patrick. *Meech Lake. The Inside Story* (University of Toronto Press, 1991)

Quebec, *Report of the Commission on the Political and Constitutional Future of Quebec*, (Éditeur officiel du Québec, 1991)

Roach, Kent. *The Supreme Court on Trial. Judicial Activism or Democratic Dialogue?* (Irwin Law, 2001)

Russell, Peter H., *Constitutional Odyssey. Can Canadians Become a Sovereign People?* 3rd edition (University of Toronto Press 2004)

Sweet, MJ. *Merely Judgment. Ignoring, Evading, and Trumping the Supreme Court.* (University of Virginia Press, 2010)

Tushnet, Mark. *Weak Courts, Strong Rights. Judicial Review and Social Welfare Rights in Comparative Constitutional Law* (Princeton University Press, 2008)

Cases

Alliance des professeurs de Montreal v Procureur général du Québec, [1985] C.A. 376, (1985) 21 DLR (4th) 354.

Canada (Attorney General) v Federation of Law Societies of Canada, 2015 SCC 7.

Canada (Attorney General) v PHS Community Services Society, [2011] 3 SCR 134.

Carter v Canada (Attorney General), 2015 SCC 5.

Edgar Schmidt v The Attorney General of Canada, 2016 FC 269.

Ford v Quebec (Attorney General) [1988] 2 SCR 712.

Reference re Public Service Employee Relations Act (Alta), [1981] 1 SCR 313.

Saskatchewan Federation of Labour v Saskatchewan (2015) SCC 4.

Reference re Supreme Court Act, ss. 5 and 6, 2014 SCC 21, and *Reference re Senate Reform,* 2014 SCC 32.

R. v Feeney [1997] 2 S.C.R. 13.

R v Nur, 2015 SCC 15.

B. Rights and Freedoms under the Charter

CHAPTER 34

··

DEMOCRATIC RIGHTS

··

YASMIN DAWOOD[*]

1. INTRODUCTION

DEMOCRATIC rights, such as the right to vote, are an essential component of any constitutional order. The right to vote is considered to be a preservative right because it allows for the protection of all other rights through the mechanisms of political participation, democratic representation, and accountable government. The right to vote thus encompasses more than the right to drop a ballot in a voting booth; it both presupposes and protects the right to participate in a fair electoral system.

This chapter examines the scope and extent of constitutionally protected democratic rights in Canada. It begins in Part 2 by outlining the source of democratic rights. Part 3 then analyzes how the Supreme Court of Canada and lower courts have interpreted the right to vote, focusing in particular on voter qualifications, residency rules, and voter identification requirements. Part 4 describes how the Court has interpreted the right to vote as being comprised of a bundle of democratic rights, thus enabling it to regulate a wide array of democratic institutions and processes. It discusses the Court's decisions on electoral redistricting, political parties, campaign finance, and the dissemination of electoral information. Part 5 concludes with an analysis of current and future challenges facing democratic rights and their protection by the courts.

* Canada Research Chair in Democracy, Constitutionalism, and Electoral Law, and Associate Professor of Law and Political Science, University of Toronto. I would like to thank Jennifer Che for excellent research assistance. The research for this chapter was supported by the Social Sciences and Humanities Research Council.

2. Sources of Democratic Rights

Democratic rights in Canada have three main sources. The first source is the constitutional text. Section 3 of the *Charter of Rights and Freedoms* provides that "every citizen of Canada has the right to vote in an election of the members of the House of Commons or of a legislative assembly and to be qualified for membership therein."[1] Prior to the adoption of the *Charter* in 1982, there was no constitutionally protected right to vote. The *Charter* contains two additional provisions that protect democratic rights. Section 4 sets a maximum duration of five years for the life of the House of Commons or a provincial legislature, although this period can be extended in the event of a national crisis.[2] Section 5 guarantees a sitting of Parliament and the legislatures at least once every year.[3] The democratic rights protected under sections 3, 4 and 5 of the *Charter* cannot be overridden by the legislative exercise of the notwithstanding clause in section 33,[4] although they are subject under section 1 to "such reasonable limits prescribed by law as can be demonstrably justified in a free and democratic society."[5]

The second source of democratic rights is statutory. The *Canada Elections Act*[6] sets forth a vast array of rules governing federal elections. These rules determine the eligibility of voters and candidates, the mechanics of voting and vote counting, the registration of political parties, and the raising and spending of campaign money, among other topics. Many of these provisions either determine or have a significant impact on democratic rights. Provinces and municipalities have their own electoral statutes, which also influence democratic rights at the local level.

The third source of democratic rights is found in judicial decisions. The Supreme Court has issued several decisions about democratic rights and the electoral process.[7]

---

[1] Canadian Charter of Rights and Freedoms, s 3, Part I of the Constitution Act, being Schedule B to the Canada Act 1982 (UK), 1982 c 11 [hereinafter *Charter*].

[2] ibid s 4.

[3] ibid s 5.

[4] ibid s 33.

[5] ibid s 1.

[6] SC 2000 c 9.

[7] *Reference re Provincial Electoral Boundaries (Saskatchewan)* [1991] 2 SCR 158, 81 DLR (4th) 16 [*Saskatchewan Reference*] (electoral boundary drawing); *Sauvé v Canada (AG)* [1993] 2 SCR 438, 64 CRR (2d) 1 [hereinafter *Sauvé I*] (inmate voting rights); *Haig v Canada (Chief Electoral Officer)* [1993] 2 SCR 995, 105 DLR (4th) 577 [hereinafter *Haig*] (residency requirements during referenda); *Harvey v New Brunswick (AG)* [1996] 2 SCR 876, 137 DLR (4th) 142 [hereinafter *Harvey*] (membership in provincial legislatures); *Libman v Quebec (AG)* [1997] 3 SCR 569, 151 DLR (4th) 385 [hereinafter *Libman*] (referendum spending limits); *Thomson Newspapers Co. v Canada (AG)* [1998] 1 SCR 877, 159 DLR (4th) 385 [hereinafter *Thomson Newspapers*] (public opinion polls); *Sauvé v Canada (AG)*, 2002 SCC 68 [2002] 3 SCR 519 [hereinafter *Sauvé II*] (inmate voting rights); *Figueroa v Canada (AG)* 2003 SCC 37, [2003] 1 SCR 912 [hereinafter *Figueroa*] (benefits for political parties); *Harper v Canada (AG)*, 2004 SCC 33 [2004] 1 SCR 827 [hereinafter *Harper*] (third-party election spending); *R v Bryan*, 2007 SCC 12 [2007] 1 SCR 527 [hereinafter *Bryan*] (distribution of election results); *Opitz v Wrzesnewskyj* 2012 SCC 55, [2012] 3 SCR 76 [hereinafter *Opitz*] (contested elections and the entitlement to vote).

These decisions have addressed a number of topics which bear directly on democratic rights, including the disenfranchisement of prisoners and the entitlement to vote, but they have also addressed other issues, such as electoral redistricting, campaign finance, and the rules regulating political parties that have an impact on citizens' democratic rights more broadly construed. Many of these cases have arisen under the section 3 right to vote as protected by the *Charter*.[8] Other cases have arisen under sections 2(b) and 2(d) of the *Charter*, which protect the freedoms of expression and association, respectively, and section 15, which guarantees equality. This area of constitutional law is commonly referred to as the "law of democracy."

There is a rich scholarly literature on the Supreme Court's law of democracy decisions. Some commentators have argued that the Court has adopted a relatively coherent approach to its cases. Colin Feasby argues, for example, that some of the Court's decisions reveal a commitment to an "egalitarian model" of the democratic process.[9] The role of the Court under this approach is to promote political equality by establishing a level playing field among participants. Other commentators have observed, by contrast, that the Court's approach to these cases is inconsistent. According to Christopher Bredt and Markus Kremer, the Court's section 3 jurisprudence does not provide much predictive guidance for the resolution of future cases.[10]

3. THE RIGHT TO VOTE

In its law of democracy jurisprudence, the Court has developed a multifaceted approach to democratic rights and democracy more generally.[11] It has identified the principle of democracy as a "fundamental value in our constitutional law and political culture" and as one of four principles that "inform and sustain the constitutional text."[12] Even though the principle of democracy is not explicitly mentioned in the Constitution, it has, according to the Court, "always informed the design of our constitutional structure,

---

[8] *Charter*, s 3.

[9] Colin Feasby, '*Libman v. Quebec (A.G.)* and the Administration of the Process of Democracy under the *Charter*: The Emerging Egalitarian Model' (1999) 44 McGill LJ 5 [hereinafter Feasby, 'Egalitarian Model']. In more recent work, Feasby has argued that the egalitarian model explains most, but not all, of the Court's decision-making. See Colin Feasby, 'Constitutional Questions about Canada's New Political Finance Regime' (2007) 45 Osgoode Hall LJ 514, 540 [hereinafter Feasby, 'Constitutional Questions']. But see Christopher D Bredt & Laura Pottie, 'A Comment on Colin Feasby's "Freedom of Expression and the Law of the Democratic Process"' (2005) 29 Sup Ct L Rev (2d) 291, 292 (arguing that the egalitarian model does not provide a comprehensive model nor is it consistently applied in the cases).

[10] Christopher D Bredt & Markus F Kremer, 'Section 3 of the *Charter*: Democratic Rights at the Supreme Court of Canada' (2005) 17 Nat J Const L 19, 20.

[11] Yasmin Dawood, 'Democracy and the Right to Vote: Rethinking Democratic Rights under the Charter' (2013) 51 Osgoode Hall LJ 251, 258–260 [hereinafter Dawood, 'Democratic Rights'].

[12] *Reference re Secession of Quebec*, [1998] 2 SCR 217, 161 DLR (4th) 385 [61].

and continues to act as an essential interpretive consideration to this day."[13] The Court has also highlighted the importance of the constitutionally protected right to vote, stating that the "right of every citizen to vote . . . lies at the heart of Canadian democracy."[14]

A. Voter Qualifications

Although section 3 applies to "every citizen," a number of qualifications have been established in electoral laws that limit the scope of the right to vote. For example, the *Canada Elections Act* provides that voters must be 18 years or older.[15] A lower court found that the minimum age requirement infringed the right to vote but was nonetheless justified under section 1.[16] Certain voter qualification rules have, however, been struck down by courts. For instance, a lower court held that individuals cannot be excluded from the right to vote on the basis of a mental illness.[17] Judges, who were traditionally deprived of the vote in order to preserve their independence, were granted the franchise after this disqualification was challenged as a violation of the *Charter*.[18] Historically, the right to vote was denied to women,[19] to Indigenous peoples,[20] and to certain individuals on the basis of racial or ethnic origin.[21]

The Supreme Court's most important voter qualification cases have concerned the right of penitentiary inmates to vote. The disenfranchisement of inmates was justified on the basis that convicted criminals are not worthy of participating as citizens in the political process. In *Sauvé v Canada* (*Sauvé I*),[22] the Court struck down a blanket prohibition on inmate voting as provided for in section 51(e) of the *Canada Elections Act* on the ground that the limitation was an unjustifiable violation of the section 3 right to vote. In response to this ruling, the Government amended the Act to prohibit inmates who had been sentenced to a term of two years or more from voting. In the Court's second decision on the issue, *Sauvé v Canada* (*Sauvé II*),[23] a closely divided Court struck down

---

[13] ibid [62].

[14] *Sauvé II* above (n 7) [1].

[15] *Canada Elections Act*, SC 2000 c 9, s 3.

[16] A lower court found that although the minimum voting age of 18 violated section 3, it was justified under section 1. See *Fitzgerald v Alberta* 2002 ABQB 1086, [2003] 3 WWR 752.

[17] *Canadian Disability Rights Council v Canada*, [1988] 3 FC 622 (FCTD).

[18] *Muldoon v R*, [1988] 3 FC 628 (FCTD).

[19] Women gained the right to vote in 1918 by statute. See *An Act to Confer Electoral Franchise upon Women*, SC 1918 c 20.

[20] Members of the First Nations gained the right to vote in 1960. See *Canada Elections Act*, SC 1960 c 39.

[21] *Cunningham v Homma* [1903] AC 151 (PC). The statute in British Columbia, which was upheld, barred individuals of Japanese and Chinese origin, and Indigenous individuals, from voting. *Provincial Elections Act*, RSBC 1897, c 67, s 8.

[22] *Sauvé I* above (n 7).

[23] *Sauvé II* above (n 7). For an analysis of the case, see David M Brown, 'Sauvé and Prisoners' Voting Rights: The Death of the Good Citizen?' (2003) 20 Sup Ct L Rev (2d) 297.

the limitation on inmate voting.[24] A five-member majority found that the limitation was an unjustified violation of section 3.[25] The Court stated that denying the right to vote to inmates was not a legitimate form of punishment and, in addition, it undermined the principles of democracy and the rule of law.[26] The *Sauvé II* case has been generally understood as establishing the proposition that courts will be protective of the right to vote.

B. Voter Identification Requirements

Voter identification requirements also place limitations on the right to vote. In 2007, Parliament passed new legislation requiring voters to provide proof of identity and residence in order to vote in federal elections. Prior to this legislation, voters did not have to produce any identification at the voting booth. The constitutionality of these new voter identification rules was challenged in court. The British Columbia Superior Court held that although the voter identification rules infringed the right to vote, they were demonstrably justified under section 1 as a reasonable limit.[27] The court found that the Government's objectives of preventing voter fraud and maintaining confidence in the electoral system were pressing and substantial. The decision was affirmed by the BC Court of Appeal, which upheld the constitutionality of voter identification requirements.[28]

C. Residency Rules

The right to vote is also restricted by residency requirements. Such requirements have been treated by courts as justifiable limitations on voting rights because of the territorial nature of representation.[29] Residency ensures that voters have a connection to their constituencies, in addition to having knowledge of the local issues. Non-residents also have a right to vote in federal elections provided that they have been absent for less than five years. The constitutionality of this five-year rule, however, was recently challenged in court. The Ontario Superior Court struck down the five-year rule on the grounds that residence is not a fundamental precondition of voting.[30] The basis of the right to vote is citizenship. According to the court, objections of fairness to resident voters and concerns of electoral fraud were not sufficiently pressing or substantial to warrant the

---

[24] *Canada Elections Act*, RSC 1985, c E-2, s 51(e).
[25] *Sauvé II* above (n 7) [62].
[26] ibid [40], [58]–[59].
[27] *Henry v Canada (AG)* 2010 BCSC 610.
[28] *Henry v Canada (AG)* 2014 BCCA 30, 301 CRR (2d) 216.
[29] *Reference re Yukon Election Residency Requirement* (1986), 27 DLR (4th) 146 (YTCA).
[30] *Frank v Canada (AG)* 2014 ONSC 536, 372 DLR (4th) 681.

restriction of the right to vote. The Ontario Court of Appeal reversed this decision on the basis that permitting expats to vote undermines the social contract which undergirds Canadian democracy.[31]

D. Scope of Application

The scope of section 3 has also been restricted by the kind of process to which it applies. Lower courts have held that section 3 does not apply to municipal elections,[32] nor to school board elections.[33] In addition, the Supreme Court has held that the section 3 right to vote does not apply to referenda. In *Haig v Canada*,[34] the Court considered the question of whether section 3 guaranteed the right to vote in the national referendum on the Charlottetown Accord.[35] In all provinces and territories except Quebec, the referendum took place under federal legislation.[36] The referendum in Quebec, however, was governed by provincial legislation which imposed a six-month residency requirement on all voters.[37] Graham Haig, who had moved from Ontario to Quebec during the relevant period, was not eligible to vote in Quebec because he did not meet the six-month residency requirement. He was also ineligible to vote in Ontario because he no longer resided there.[38] A majority of the Court, in an opinion by Justice L'Heureux-Dubé, found that section 3 was clearly limited to the election of representatives to the provincial and federal legislatures, and hence did not guarantee the right to vote in a referendum.[39] It also found that a referendum is not subject to section 2(b) of the *Charter*, which protects the right to freedom of expression. Because a referendum is a "creation of legislation," it is not subject to section 2(b) or to the *Charter* in general.[40] In a dissenting opinion, Justice Iacobucci argued that the effect of the federal *Referendum Act* did infringe Haig's section 2(b) rights, and moreover that the infringement could not be saved under section 1.[41] Although the Government is not obliged to hold a referendum, if the Government "chooses to conduct a referendum, it must do so in compliance with the Charter."[42] For Justice Iacobucci, the two referenda, taken together, had a "national character" that was intended to involve all Canadians.[43]

---

[31] *Frank v Canada (AG)* 2015 ONCA 536.
[32] *Jones v Ontario (AG)* 1988 53 DLR (4th) 273 (Ont HC).
[33] *Baker v Burin School Board District #7* (1999), 178 DLR (4th) 155 (Nfld SC).
[34] *Haig* above (n 7).
[35] ibid [30].
[36] See *Referendum Act*, SC 1992, c 30.
[37] See *Referendum Act*, RSQ c C-64.1.
[38] *Haig* above (n 7) [13].
[39] ibid [80].
[40] ibid [81].
[41] ibid [141] Iacobucci J dissenting.
[42] ibid [152] Iacobucci J dissenting.
[43] ibid [143] Iacobucci J dissenting.

E. The Entitlement to Vote

The Court has also tackled the question of how the entitlement to vote, as defined in the *Canada Elections Act*, ought to be determined. The case, *Opitz v Wrzesnewskyj*,[44] arose out of a contested election result in the federal election in 2011. The lower court set aside the election result because the margin of victory (a mere 26 votes) was smaller than the number of ballots that displayed procedural irregularities.[45] There was no evidence of fraud or corruption. A divided Supreme Court overturned the lower court, thus avoiding the need for a new election. In a 4-3 decision, the Court majority refused to disqualify the votes of citizens who were in fact entitled to vote just because there were administrative mistakes in the balloting process.[46] The majority drew a distinction between administrative mistakes and "irregularities," which it defined as "serious administrative errors that are capable of undermining the electoral process."[47] After examining the contested ballots, the Court majority found that the original winner had won the election by a six-vote margin. The dissenting justices argued that to protect the integrity of the electoral system, citizens who are entitled to vote must also meet the registration and identification standards set out in the legislation.[48] For this reason, some of the mistakes made were sufficiently serious to annul the election result.[49] Although *Opitz* was not a constitutional case, it sets out important standards with respect to the statutory requirements for the entitlement to vote.

F. The Right to Run for Office

Section 3 of the Charter also protects the right to run for office at the federal and provincial levels. In *Harvey v New Brunswick (A.G.)*, the Court considered whether provisions of the *New Brunswick Elections Act* violated section 3 of the Charter.[50] Fred Harvey, who was a member of the New Brunswick Legislative Assembly, was convicted of violating the *Act*, and according to the terms of the *Act*, he lost his seat and was also disqualified from running as a candidate for five years.[51] He argued that the *Act* was unconstitutional because section 3 provided an unqualified right to run for office.[52] A majority of the Court upheld the relevant provisions of the *Act* on the basis that they constituted a justifiable infringement of section 3.[53]

---

[44] *Opitz* above (n 7).
[45] 2012 ONSC 2873, 110 OR (3d) 350.
[46] *Opitz* above (n 7) [1].
[47] ibid [24].
[48] ibid.
[49] ibid [140] [147] McLachlin CJ dissenting.
[50] *Harvey* above (n 7) [4].
[51] ibid [6].
[52] ibid [21].
[53] ibid [28].

4. Beyond Voting: The Supreme Court's Regulation of the Political Process

In addition to considering the constitutionality of various restrictions on the right to vote, the Supreme Court has also issued decisions that have had a profound impact on the processes and institutions of democracy. These decisions have not only been based upon a certain interpretation of democratic rights, but they have also affected the scope and meaning of these rights.

A. The Right to Vote as a Bundle of Rights

The most distinctive aspect of the Court's approach to the law of democracy, I suggest, is that it has interpreted the right to vote as a plural right. That is, the Court has adopted what I refer to as a "bundle of rights" approach which recognizes multiple democratic rights, each of which is concerned with a particular facet of democratic participation and representation.[54] The Court has recognized four democratic rights in its law of democracy cases: (1) the right to effective representation, (2) the right to meaningful participation, (3) the right to equal participation, and (4) the right to a free and informed vote.[55] The first two rights—the right to effective representation and the right to meaningful participation—are described by the Court as the purposes of the section 3 right to vote.[56] The two additional rights—the right to equal participation and the right to a free and informed vote—appear to be derived from the right to meaningful participation and from an overarching constitutional commitment to the principle of democracy.[57] Although these two rights are not described as the purpose of section 3, they are relevant to the Court's understanding of voters' participatory rights.

The Court's multifaceted "bundle of rights" approach, I claim, has given it considerable scope and flexibility in its law of democracy cases. The bundle of rights approach provides the Court not only with the ability to protect the right to vote as provided for in section 3 of the *Charter*, but also to regulate the structure and process of the democratic system as a whole. The Court has used the bundle of rights to adjudicate a wide array of issues, including the regulation of political parties, campaign finance, and electoral redistricting. By treating the right to vote as a plural concept, the Court has been able

---

[54] Dawood, 'Democratic Rights' above (n 11) 254–255.

[55] ibid 255.

[56] *Saskatchewan Reference* above (n 7) [26]; *Figueroa* above (n 7). When determining the scope and meaning of a *Charter* right, the Court employs a "purposive approach," which focuses on the purpose underlying the right or the interests that the right was meant to protect. *R v Big M Drug Mart* [1985] 1 SCR 295 [116].

[57] Dawood, 'Democratic Rights' above (n 11) 255.

to intervene in various facets of the political process. The remainder of Part 4 examines four of these areas: electoral redistricting, political parties, campaign finance, and the dissemination of electoral information.

B. Electoral Redistricting

Canada has a first-past-the-post electoral system in which the country is divided geographically into a number of electoral districts, which are also known as constituencies or ridings. Voters in each federal electoral district elect a representative to the House of Commons; a similar system exists for provincial and territorial legislatures. Seats in the House of Commons are allocated along regional lines. A formula is used to initially allocate seats to each province. This allocation is subsequently adjusted to account for the "Senate floor" rule found in section 51A of the *Constitution Act, 1867*, which provides that no province will have fewer members in the House of Commons than in the Senate. The "grandfather clause" is also applied, which guarantees that each province will have no fewer seats than it had in 1985.[58]

In addition to the allocation of seats among the provinces and territories, there is also a process by which the individual electoral districts are determined. The Constitution requires that the boundaries of the electoral districts be redrawn after every decennial census to take account of changes and movements in population. The drawing of electoral districts is conducted by independent boundary commissions in each province.[59]

The Supreme Court's first law of democracy case concerned the question of how these electoral boundaries ought to be drawn. The case arose in Saskatchewan when the governing Progressive Conservative party passed the Electoral Boundaries Commission Act (*EBCA*), which imposed certain restrictions on the independent boundary commission that was tasked with redrawing the provincial electoral map.[60] The *EBCA* imposed a strict quota on the number of urban and rural ridings that could be created. In addition, the urban ridings had to coincide with municipal boundaries. The legislation also allowed variances in the population sizes of the electoral districts that were within plus or minus 25 percent from the provincial quotient.[61] As a result of these restrictions, urban voters were under-represented and rural voters were over-represented in

---

[58] *Representation Act of 1985*, S.C. 1986,C. 8, s. 2.

[59] For a discussion of independent boundary commissions, see John C Courtney, *Commissioned Ridings: Designing Canada's Electoral Districts* (McGill-Queen's University Press, 2001); RK Carty, 'The Electoral Boundary Revolution in Canada' (1985) 15 Am Rev Can Stud 273; John C Courtney, 'Redistricting: What the United States Can Learn from Canada' (2004) 3 Election LJ 488; Ron Levy, 'Regulating Impartiality: Electoral Boundary Politics in the Administrative Arena' (2008) 53 McGill LJ 1.

[60] *Electoral Boundaries Commission Act*, SS 1986-87-88, c E-6.1.

[61] *Saskatchewan Reference* above (n 7) [44]. The provincial quotient is calculated by dividing the total voting population in the province by the number of ridings.

the legislature.[62] The *EBCA* enhanced the Progressive Conservatives' electoral support, which at the time was located primarily in the rural districts.

In *Reference re Provincial Electoral Boundaries (Saskatchewan)*, the Court considered whether Saskatchewan's electoral boundaries violated the right to vote as protected by section 3 of the *Charter*.[63] A divided Supreme Court held that the electoral districts in Saskatchewan did not infringe the *Charter*. In a 5-3 decision, the Court stated that electoral districts do not have to adhere to the one-person, one-vote principle, which was the standard that had been adopted in the United States. Writing on behalf of the majority, Justice McLachlin (as she was then) stated in a key passage that the "purpose of the right to vote enshrined in s. 3 of the *Charter* is not equality of voting power *per se*, but the right to 'effective representation.'"[64] The relative parity of voting power is one of the main conditions for effective representation,[65] but additional considerations include "geography, community history, community interests and minority representation."[66]

In addition, the Court majority did not think that the involvement of the legislature in the work of the independent boundary commission rendered the process "arbitrary or unfair."[67] By contrast, Justice Cory argued in a dissenting opinion that the government had not justified why it imposed various limits on the independent commission that had the effect of diminishing the rights of urban voters.[68] According to Justice Cory, the legislature's interference with the right to vote risked "bringing the democratic process itself into disrepute."[69]

C. Political Parties

The bundle of democratic rights also contains the right to "play a meaningful role" in the electoral process. This right was first recognized in the *Haig* decision and elaborated at length in *Figueroa v Canada*.[70] In *Figueroa*, the head of the Communist Party of Canada challenged the constitutionality of a requirement that political parties nominate

---

[62] ibid [50].
[63] For a discussion of the *Saskatchewan Reference* decision, see Kent Roach, 'One Person, One Vote? Canadian Constitutional Standards for Electoral Distribution and Districting' in David Small, ed, *Drawing the Map: Equality and Efficacy of the Vote in Canadian Electoral Boundary Reform* (Dundurn Press, 1991) vol 11; Ronald E Fritz, 'The Saskatchewan Electoral Boundaries Case and Its Complications' in John C Courtney, Peter MacKinnon & David E Smith, eds, *Drawing Boundaries: Legislatures, Courts and Electoral Values* (Fifth House Publishers, 1992); Mark Carter, 'Reconsidering the *Charter* and Electoral Boundaries' (1999) 22 Dal LJ 53; David Johnson, 'Canadian Electoral Boundaries and the Courts: Practices, Principles and Problems' (1994) 39 McGill LJ 224.
[64] *Saskatchewan Reference* above (n 7) [26].
[65] ibid [28]
[66] ibid [31].
[67] ibid [53].
[68] ibid [92], Cory J, dissenting.
[69] ibid [87], Cory J, dissenting.
[70] *Figueroa* above (n 7).

candidates in at least 50 electoral districts in order to register as a political party.[71] Registered political parties are granted a number of benefits under the *Canada Elections Act*.[72] The Supreme Court held that the 50-candidate rule violated section 3 and was not justifiable under section 1.[73] Writing for the six-member majority, Justice Iacobucci stated that section 3 includes "the right of each citizen to play a meaningful role in the electoral process."[74] The majority also found that political parties act "as both a vehicle and outlet" for the participation of citizens in the electoral process.[75] Political parties are essential to participation "[i]rrespective of their capacity to influence the outcome of an election."[76] Thus, the rules governing political parties have a direct impact on the ability of citizens to play a meaningful role in the democratic process.[77]

The Court's bundle of democratic rights approach became apparent in the *Figueroa* decision. Justice Iacobucci stated that "the *democratic rights entrenched in s. 3* ensure that each citizen has an opportunity to express an opinion about the formation of social policy and the functioning of public institutions through participation in the electoral process."[78] The decision frames the right to vote as a composite of multiple democratic rights. The right to meaningful participation, which is one strand in the bundle of rights, was used by the Court to regulate political parties.

D. Money and Politics: Regulating Campaign Finance

There are two main approaches to the issue of regulating campaign finance—the libertarian approach and the egalitarian approach. The libertarian approach holds that the state should not impose limits on campaign finance because such limitations violate the freedom of expression. The egalitarian approach holds, by contrast, that the state regulation of speech is required to prevent the wealthy from monopolizing political discourse. The Supreme Court has considered the issue of campaign finance in two cases involving spending limits.

At issue in *Libman v Quebec (AG)*[79] was the constitutionality of the independent spending limits set out in Quebec's *Referendum Act*. The president of the Equality Party, Robert Libman, did not wish to join either the "yes" or the "no" position for the

---

[71] ibid [3].

[72] ibid [4].

[73] ibid [90].

[74] ibid [25].

[75] ibid [39].

[76] ibid.

[77] For a discussion of the *Figueroa* decision and its impact on the role of political parties in a democracy, see Heather MacIvor, 'Judicial Review and Electoral Democracy: The Contested Status of Political Parties under the Charter' (2002) 21 Windsor YB Access Just 479; Heather MacIvor, 'The *Charter* of Rights and Party Politics: The Impact of the Supreme Court Ruling in *Figueroa v. Canada (Attorney General)*' (2004) 10:4 IRPP Choices 1.

[78] *Figueroa* above (n 7) [29] [emphasis added].

[79] *Libman* above (n 7).

referendum on the Charlottetown Accord.[80] Instead, he wished to advocate the view that people should abstain from participating in the vote.[81] But the referendum legislation required that regulated expenses could be incurred only through a national committee. Libman was thus faced with the choice of either joining one of the national committees (whose views he did not support) or limiting the Equality Party to unregulated expenses only, which would have severely limited its ability to engage in advocacy.[82] Libman argued that these independent spending restrictions infringed the freedoms of expression and association and the right to equality.[83]

The Court held that the restrictions on independent spending infringed the freedom of expression and were not justified under section 1 of the *Charter*.[84] According to the Court, the restrictions failed the minimal impairment test because they amounted to a total ban.[85] Although the Court struck down the restrictions, it acknowledged the value of an "egalitarian" approach to the rules governing spending during an election or a referendum.[86] It was important to prevent "the most affluent members of society from exerting a disproportionate influence by dominating the referendum debate through access to greater resources."[87] To ensure electoral fairness, it "cannot be presumed that all persons have the same financial resources to communicate with the electorate."[88] Differences in the personal wealth of citizens should not be translated into disparities of political influence.[89]

In *Libman*, the Court first recognized a "right of equal participation in democratic government,"[90] which is another strand in the bundle of democratic rights. The Court returned to this right in *Harper v Canada*,[91] which considered the constitutionality of third-party spending limits as provided for in the *Canada Elections Act*.[92] Third-party spending refers to campaign spending that is conducted by individuals, corporations, or groups—essentially any person or entity that is neither a candidate nor a political party. The third-party spending limits at issue had been struck down by lower courts.[93]

---

[80] ibid [1].

[81] *Harper* above (n 7) [60].

[82] *Libman* above (n 7) [14].

[83] ibid [2], [27].

[84] ibid [35], [85].

[85] ibid [82].

[86] ibid [41]. Feasby, 'Egalitarian Model' above (n 9) 8, 31–32.

[87] *Libman* above (n 7) [41].

[88] ibid [47].

[89] Cass Sunstein, *Democracy and the Problem of Free Speech* (2nd ed, Free Press, 1995); Owen Fiss, *The Irony of Free Speech* (Harvard University Press, 1996).

[90] *Libman* above (n 7) [47].

[91] *Harper* above (n 7).

[92] See *Canada Elections Act*, SC 2000, c 9. For a discussion of the *Harper* decision, see Andrew Geddis, 'Liberté, Egalité, Argent: Third Party Election Spending and the *Charter*' (2004) 42 Alta L Rev 429 [18]–[25]; Jamie Cameron, 'Governance and Anarchy in the s. 2(b) Jurisprudence: A Comment on *Vancouver Sun* and *Harper v. Canada*' (2005) 17 Nat J Const L 71, 73. Yasmin Dawood, 'Freedom of Speech and Democracy: Rethinking the Conflict between Liberty and Equality' (2013) 26 Can J Law & Juris 293, 307–309.

[93] [2001] 93 Alta LR (3d) 281; [2002] 14 Alta LR (4th) 4.

A six-to-three majority of the Court, however, upheld the constitutionality of these spending limits. In an opinion by Justice Bastarache, the majority held that although the spending limits infringed the freedom of expression guarantee, the provisions were nonetheless justifiable under section 1.[94] The Court majority stated that Parliament had adopted an egalitarian model of elections, which treats wealth as the main obstacle to ensuring equal participation in the electoral process.[95] Spending limits are required to prevent the most affluent citizens from "monopolizing election discourse" and thereby preventing other citizens from participating in the political process on an equal basis.[96] The Court stated that to ensure "a right of equal participation in democratic government, laws limiting spending are needed to preserve the equality of democratic rights and ensure that one person's exercise of the freedom to spend does not hinder the communication opportunities of others."[97]

Chief Justice McLachlin and Justice Major wrote a dissenting opinion in which they argued that the spending limits amounted to a "virtual ban" on citizens who wished to participate in the political deliberation during the election period.[98] The limits were set so low that citizens would not be able to advertise in the national media. In addition, the dissenting justices saw no evidence that wealthy individuals in Canada were "poised to hijack this country's election process."[99] For this reason, the presumed dangers were "wholly hypothetical,"[100] and the impairment of the right to free expression was correspondingly severe.

E. The Dissemination of Information prior to an Election

In *Harper*, the Court also recognized "the right of electors to be adequately informed of all the political positions advanced by the candidates and by the various political parties,"[101] which it described as a right to a free and informed vote. This right was also at issue in *R v Bryan*.[102] In *Bryan*, a closely divided Court upheld the constitutionality of section 329 of the *Canada Elections Act* which prohibited the transmission of election results between electoral ridings before the closing of all polling stations in Canada.[103] The case arose when the claimant made election results from Atlantic Canada available on the Internet before the polls had closed in other ridings.[104] The five-member majority

---

[94] *Harper* above (n 7) [66], [121].
[95] ibid [62], citing Feasby, 'Egalitarian Model' above (n 9).
[96] ibid [61].
[97] ibid [emphasis added].
[98] ibid [35], McLachlin CJ and Major J dissenting. For a discussion, see Janet L Hiebert, "Money and Elections: Can Citizens Participate on Fair Terms amidst Unrestricted Spending?" (1998) 31 Can J Pol Sc 91, 108.
[99] ibid.
[100] ibid.
[101] ibid [61].
[102] *Bryan* above (n 7).
[103] ibid. Section 329 is no longer in effect.
[104] ibid [2].

held that although section 329 infringed the freedom of expression as protected by section 2(b) of the *Charter*, it could nonetheless be upheld under section 1. In the opinion for the majority, Justice Bastarache characterized the objective of the provision as "ensur[ing] informational equality by adopting reasonable measures to deal with the perception of unfairness created when some voters have general access to information that is denied to others, and the further possibility that access to that information will affect voter participation or choices." [105] The majority found that the government's objective of ensuring informational equality was pressing and substantial, and that the provision satisfied the proportionality stage of the *Oakes* test.[106] The four dissenting justices concluded, however, that section 329 did not meet the proportionality test under section 1. The publication ban was an "excessive response," particularly given the insufficiency of the evidence of harm.[107] On their view, Parliament must reach a higher standard of justification for violating the right of freedom of expression.[108]

The right to an informed vote also appeared in an earlier case, *Thompson Newspapers*,[109] which considered whether an opinion poll ban violated the right to vote in section 3 and the freedom of expression in section 2(b) of the *Charter*.[110] The *Canada Elections Act* banned the publication or dissemination of opinion poll results in the last three days of an election period.[111] The government's objectives behind the ban were, first, to ensure that the opinion polls did not distort public opinion so close to the election, and second, to prohibit the release of poll data that could not be verified in the three days before an election.[112] The Court majority held that the opinion poll ban infringed the freedom of expression, and moreover, that it could not be justified under section 1.[113] The Court concluded that opinion poll data clearly constituted political speech and thus lay at the core of the freedom of expression guarantee.[114]

5. CURRENT CHALLENGES AND FUTURE DEVELOPMENTS

In this section, I briefly address two topics—judicial deference and partisan self-entrenchment—that raise particular challenges to the judicial review of the electoral process.

---

[105] ibid [14].
[106] ibid [35], [41]–[51].
[107] ibid [133] Abella J dissenting.
[108] ibid [107] Abella J dissenting.
[109] *Thomson Newspapers* above (n 7).
[110] ibid [65].
[111] See *Canada Elections Act*, RSC 1985, c E-2, s 322.1.
[112] *Thompson Newspapers* above (n 7) [65].
[113] ibid [131].
[114] ibid [92].

A. Judicial Deference and Democratic Rights

The Supreme Court has generally played a vital role in protecting the fairness and legiti-macy of the democratic process.[115] It has distinguished, however, between electoral laws that place limitations on the right to vote, and electoral laws that regulate other aspects of the democratic system. The Court has usually subjected limitations on the right to vote to greater judicial scrutiny, stating, for instance, that the "right to vote is funda-mental to our democracy and the rule of law and cannot be lightly set aside. Limits on it require not deference, but careful examination."[116]

Laws that regulate other aspects of the political process tend to be treated with greater judicial deference. In *Harper*, for example, the Court majority was highly deferential to Parliament because it saw the electoral process as being presumptively "political." The majority stated that the workings of the electoral system are a "political choice, the details of which are better left to Parliament."[117] As Parliament has the right to "choose Canada's electoral model," it is incumbent on the Court to defer to Parliament.[118] The Court was also very deferential to the government's social science evidence.[119] Similarly in *Bryan*, the majority stated that the Court ought to take a "natural attitude of deference" with respect to election laws.[120] The Court has viewed the electoral process as "political" but nonetheless subject to certain constitutional limits.[121] The electoral process has thus been treated by the Court as having a dual constitutional-political nature.[122]

Despite these general trends, the justices often have divergent approaches to the ques-tion of whether the Court should defer to Parliament with respect to electoral laws.[123] The Court's election law cases tend to be divided, and the difference between the posi-tions of the majority and dissenting justices often turns on the issue of judicial defer-ence.[124] One reason for this is the challenge presented by social science evidence in the

---

[115] Yasmin Dawood, 'Electoral Fairness and the Law of Democracy: A Structural Rights Approach to Judicial Review' (2012) 62 Univ Toronto LJ 499, 504 [hereinafter Dawood, 'Electoral Fairness'].

[116] *Sauvé II* above (n 7) [9].

[117] *Harper* above (n 7) [87].

[118] ibid.

[119] Yasmin Dawood, 'Democracy and Deference: The Role of Social Science Evidence in Election Law Cases' (2014) 32 Nat J Const L 173, 188–191 [hereinafter Dawood, 'Social Science Evidence'].

[120] *Bryan* above (n 7) [9].

[121] *Harper* above (n 7) [87].

[122] I have elaborated this argument in Yasmin Dawood, 'Democracy and Dissent: Reconsidering the Judicial Review of the Political Sphere' 63 Sup Ct L Rev (2d) 59–87 (2013).

[123] ibid 84–87.

[124] ibid. This issue is part of a larger debate about the role of judicial review in democracy. For a discussion, see Patrick J Monahan, 'Judicial Review and Democracy: A Theory of Judicial Review' (1987) 21 UBC L Rev 87; Peter W Hogg & Allison Bushell, 'The Charter Dialogue between Courts and Legislatures' (1997) 35 Osgoode Hall LJ 75; Kent Roach, *The Supreme Court on Trial: Judicial Activism or Democratic Dialogue* (Irwin Law, 2001); FL Morton & Rainer Knopff, *The Charter Revolution and the Court Party* (Peterborough, ON: Broadview Press, 2000); Grant Huscroft & Ian Brodie, eds, *Constitutionalism in the Charter Era* (LexisNexis Butterworths, 2004); Rosalind Dixon, 'The Supreme Court of Canada, Charter Dialogue, and Deference' (2009) 47 Osgoode Hall LJ 235.

electoral realm.[125] Democratic systems are highly complex with a wide array of institutions and actors. It is very difficult, if not impossible, to scientifically test the effects of many of the laws that regulate the political system. Although social science evidence can provide very precise data for certain issues that pertain to the electoral process, it is less helpful for broader questions concerning the system-wide distribution of power or equality. Because the Court's decisions about the constitutionality of various electoral rules often do consider these broader system-wide issues, the justices have to determine whether the Government's restriction on the right to vote is "demonstrably justified" given the available social science evidence. Some justices defer to the legislature's assessment of the social science evidence, while other justices demand a more rigorous empirical standard in order to allow the infringement of rights.[126] The issue of whether the Court ought to defer to Parliament, or not defer, with respect to electoral laws is one of the main areas of disagreement among the justices.

B. Partisan Self-Entrenchment

Another issue which presents a significant challenge is partisan self-entrenchment, which refers to the propensity of elected officials to engage in partisan rule-making. There are significant incentives for the governing political party to craft election laws to provide it with an advantage at the next election. The Supreme Court, however, has yet to address the problem of partisan rule-making with respect to electoral laws.

Many commentators have argued that courts in the United States should adopt the "political markets" or "structural" approach, under which courts would intervene to prevent the partisan self-entrenchment of parties.[127] Several scholars in the Canadian law of democracy literature have also argued for a political markets/structural approach.[128] As described in Part 4 above, the electoral boundaries at issue in *Saskatchewan Reference* involved partisan rule-making, despite the existence of an independent boundary commission.[129]

---

[125] Dawood, 'Social Science Evidence' above (n 119).

[126] ibid 183–187.

[127] Richard H Pildes, 'Foreword: The Constitutionalization of Democratic Politics' (2004) 118 Harv L Rev 29, 41.

[128] Colin Feasby, 'Freedom of Expression and the Law of the Democratic Process' (2005) 29 Sup Ct L Rev (2d) 237, 288; Colin Feasby, 'The Supreme Court of Canada's Political Theory and the Constitutionality of the Political Finance Regime' in Keith Ewing & Samuel Issacharoff, eds, *Party Funding and Campaign Financing in International Perspective* (Hart Publishing, 2006) 243; Heather MacIvor, 'Do Canadian Political Parties Form a Cartel?' (1996) 29 Can J Pol Sci 317; Christopher Manfredi & Mark Rush, *Judging Democracy* (Broadview Press, 2008); Michael Pal, 'Breakdowns in the Democratic Process and the Law of Canadian Democracy' (2011) 57 McGill LJ 299; Yasmin Dawood, 'Democracy, Power, and the Supreme Court: Campaign Finance Reform in Comparative Perspective' [2006] 4 Int'l J Const L 269; Dawood, 'Electoral Fairness' above (n 115).

[129] Ronald Fritz, 'Challenging Electoral Boundaries under the *Charter*' (1999–2000) 5 Rev Const Stud 1, 4; Mark Carter, 'Ambiguous Constitutional Standards and the Right to Vote,' (2011) 5 J Parl & Pol L 309, 320–321.

More recently, critics of the 2014 *Fair Elections Act* (FEA) pointed out that the legislative changes benefitted the governing political party at the expense of the other political parties.[130] For example, the FEA tightened voter identification rules by prohibiting the Chief Electoral Officer from authorizing the use of Voter Information Cards (VICs) to establish a voter's identity and by replacing vouching with a narrower attestation procedure that could be used to establish a voter's address but not her identity. These changes raised barriers to voting for various groups that were viewed as being less likely to vote for the incumbent political party, including students, homeless electors, Indigenous electors, and elderly electors in long term care facilities. In 2015, a challenge was brought against the FEA provision prohibiting the use of VICs. The objective of the lawsuit was to permit the use of VICs so that voters would not be disenfranchised at the October 2015 federal election. The Ontario Superior Court declined to issue an injunction against the VIC prohibition, on the basis that a full hearing on the merits was required.[131]

Given the propensity of elected officials to enact laws that perpetuate their own power, courts should treat electoral laws with a certain amount of scepticism. Instead of deferring to the legislature, the Court could use a rights-based approach to ensure the fairness and integrity of the electoral process. An alternative structural approach, one that is based on democratic rights, could be used by the Court to address the problem of partisan rule-making.[132] The Court has already observed that section 3 "imposes on Parliament an obligation not to interfere with the *right of each citizen to participate in a fair election*."[133] I suggest that this "right to participate in a fair election" offers a promising way for the Court to ensure the fairness and legitimacy of the electoral process. By recognizing a right to a fair and legitimate democratic process as one of the purposes of the right to vote, the Court would send a signal to Parliament that partisan rule-making is constitutionally impermissible. In this way, the Court could signal the broad standards of electoral integrity and fairness that Parliament must meet.

6. Conclusion

The Supreme Court plays a fundamentally important role in safeguarding the fairness and legitimacy of the electoral process. It has adopted a multifaceted approach to the law of democracy, which has enabled it not only to protect the right to vote but also to regulate various aspects of the democratic process. By recognizing a bundle of democratic rights, the Court has been able to intervene in such issues as campaign finance, the regulation of political parties, and electoral redistricting. As partisan rule-making becomes

---

[130] Remarks of Professor Yasmin Dawood on Bill C-23, An Act to Amend the Canada Elections Act, before the Standing Committee on Procedure and House Affairs, Parliament of Canada (31 March 2014).
[131] *Council of Canadians v Canada (AG)* 2015 ONSC 4601.
[132] Dawood, 'Electoral Fairness' above (n 115) 503–508.
[133] *Figueroa* above (n 7) [51].

increasingly evident in the electoral arena, however, courts will have to confront the problems posed by legislation that is designed to advantage incumbent political parties. In addition to the challenge of partisan rule-making, courts will continue to face the issue of judicial deference. An overly deferential posture on the part of the courts significantly diminishes their ability to hold Parliament to account for its regulation of the democratic process. The constitutional protection of democratic rights depends to no small degree on the continued vigilance of the judicial branch.

BIBLIOGRAPHY

Secondary Sources

Bredt CD & Kremer MF, 'Section 3 of the *Charter*: Democratic Rights at the Supreme Court of Canada' (2005) 17 Nat J Const L 19.

Jamie Cameron, 'Governance and Anarchy in the s. 2(b) Jurisprudence: A Comment on *Vancouver Sun* and *Harper v. Canada*' (2005) 17 Nat J Const L 71.

Carter M, 'Reconsidering the *Charter* and Electoral Boundaries' (1999) 22 Dal LJ 53.

Courtney JC, MacKinnon P & Smith DE eds, *Drawing Boundaries: Legislatures, Courts and Electoral Values* (Fifth House Publishers 1992).

Courtney JC, *Commissioned Ridings: Designing Canada's Electoral Districts* (McGill-Queen's University Press, 2001).

Dawood Y, 'Democracy and the Right to Vote: Rethinking Democratic Rights under the Charter' (2013) 51 Osgoode Hall LJ 251.

Dawood Y, 'Electoral Fairness and the Law of Democracy: A Structural Rights Approach to Judicial Review' (2012) 62 Univ Toronto LJ 499.

Dawood Y, 'Freedom of Speech and Democracy: Rethinking the Conflict between Liberty and Equality' (2013) 26 Can J Law & Juris 293.

Feasby C, 'Constitutional Questions about Canada's New Political Finance Regime' (2007) 45 Osgoode Hall LJ 514.

Feasby C, '*Libman v. Quebec (A.G.)* and the Administration of the Process of Democracy under the *Charter*: The Emerging Egalitarian Model' (1999) 44 McGill LJ 5.

Fritz R, 'Challenging Electoral Boundaries under the *Charter*' (1999–2000) 5 Rev Const Stud 1.

Geddis A, 'Liberté, Egalité, Argent: Third Party Election Spending and the *Charter*' (2004) 42 Alta L Rev 429.

Johnson D, 'Canadian Electoral Boundaries and the Courts: Practices, Principles and Problems' (1994) 39 McGill LJ 224.

Levy R, 'Regulating Impartiality: Electoral Boundary Politics in the Administrative Arena' (2008) 53 McGill LJ 1.

MacIvor H, 'Do Canadian Political Parties Form a Cartel?' (1996) 29 Can J Pol Sci 317.

MacIvor H, 'The *Charter* of Rights and Party Politics: The Impact of the Supreme Court Ruling in *Figueroa v. Canada (Attorney General)*' (2004) 10:4 IRPP Choices 1.

Manfredi C & Rush M, *Judging Democracy* (Broadview Press 2008).

Pildes RH, 'Foreword: The Constitutionalization of Democratic Politics' (2004) 118 Harv L Rev 29.

Roach K, 'One Person, One Vote? Canadian Constitutional Standards for Electoral Distribution and Districting' in David Small, ed, *Drawing the Map: Equality and Efficacy of the Vote in Canadian Electoral Boundary Reform* (Dundurn Press 1991) vol 11.

Small D ed, *Drawing the Map: Equality and Efficacy of the Vote in Canadian Electoral Boundary Reform* (Dundurn Press 1991).

Cases

Figueroa v Canada (AG) 2003 SCC 37, [2003] 1 SCR 912.

Haig v Canada (Chief Electoral Officer) [1993] 2 SCR 995, 105 DLR (4th) 577.

Harper v Canada (AG) 2004 SCC 33, [2004] 1 SCR 827.

Harvey v New Brunswick (AG) [1996] 2 SCR 876, 137 DLR (4th) 142.

Libman v Quebec (AG) [1997] 3 SCR 569, 151 DLR (4th) 385.

Opitz v Wrzesnewskyj 2012 SCC 55, [2012] 3 SCR 76.

R v Bryan 2007 SCC 12, [2007] 1 SCR 527.

Reference re Provincial Electoral Boundaries (Saskatchewan) [1991] 2 SCR 158, 81 DLR (4th) 16.

Reference re Secession of Quebec, [1998] 2 SCR 217, 161 DLR (4th) 385.

Sauvé v Canada (AG) 2002 SCC 68, [2002] 3 SCR 519.

Thomson Newspapers Co. v Canada (AG) [1998] 1 SCR 877, 159 DLR (4th) 385.

Legislation

Canada Elections Act, RSC 1985, c E-2.

Canadian Charter of Rights and Freedoms, s 3, Part I of the Constitution Act, 1982, being Schedule B to the Canada Act 1982 (UK), 1982 c 11.

Electoral Boundaries Commission Act, SS 1986-87-88, c E-6.1.

CHAPTER 35

....

THE RIGHT TO PROTEST, FREEDOM OF EXPRESSION, AND FREEDOM OF ASSOCIATION

....

JAMIE CAMERON[*] &
NATHALIE DES ROSIERS[**]

1. INTRODUCTION

....

LONG before their constitutionalization by the *Charter*, freedom of expression and association were core commitments with a strong pedigree in Canada's legal and political tradition.[1] These freedoms are guaranteed independently by section 2(b) and (d) of the *Charter* but are closely related, conceptually and philosophically.[2] Despite sharing those bonds, each presents a distinctive journey in the first 30 years of *Charter* interpretation.

Whereas section 2(b) generated a deep jurisprudence, section 2(d) produced a discrete number of issue-specific decisions.[3] From the outset, the Supreme Court of Canada treated the guarantees differently, granting freedom of expression a generous interpretation while constraining the scope of associational freedom. In recent years,

---

[*] Professor, Osgoode Hall Law School, York University.
[**] Full Professor, Common Law, Faculty of Law, University of Ottawa.
[1] *Canadian Charter of Rights and Freedoms,* Pt 1 of the *Constitution Act 1982,* being Sch B to the *Canada Act 1982* (UK), 1982, c 11 [hereinafter "*Charter*"].
[2] *Ibid,* s 2 states: "Everyone has the following fundamental freedoms: . . . (b) freedom of thought, belief, opinion and expression, including freedom of the press and other media of communication; . . . and (d) freedom of association".
[3] The Supreme Court of Canada has decided more than 80 cases under s 2(b) and less than a third as many under s 2(d).

the momentum has shifted and though section 2(b) is quiet at present, section 2(d) has livened and is now an active site of rights protection.

This chapter follows the rhythm of the jurisprudence, as it is unrealistic to canvas expressive freedom comprehensively in this setting. Furthermore, any discussion of freedom of association under the *Charter* must reflect section 2(d)'s focus on labour rights.[4] Though section 2(d) has been dedicated, in the main, to the associational freedom of workers and labour unions, section 2(b) has addressed a variety of issues but, in doing so, has shown solicitude for labour expression. That cross-fertilization enables us to examine the two freedoms together and comment briefly on the status of protest and dissent under these guarantees.

The test of a constitution's commitment to freedom is whether and how well it protects the voices of those who are discontent and marginalized. In an early section 2(b) landmark, the Court stated that the *Charter*'s definition of expressive freedom must "ensure that everyone can manifest their thoughts, opinions, beliefs, indeed all expressions of the heart and mind, however unpopular, distasteful or contrary to the mainstream".[5] Much later, it reflected in 2015 on section 2(d)'s purposes, observing that "[h]istorically, those most easily ignored and disempowered have staked so much on freedom of association precisely because association was the means by which they could gain a voice".[6] Bonding the two is a recognition that to be meaningful the *Charter*'s guarantees of freedom must protect those who provoke and challenge the status quo.

Despite endorsing freedom values, the Supreme Court's section 2(b) and section 2(d) jurisprudence has been selective and uneven. Under section 2(b), the Court upheld limits on objectionable expression but adopted a different and more protective approach to labour picketing and related activities. In comparison, section 2(d) is unbalanced because the *Charter*'s general guarantee of associational freedom has been almost exclusively concerned with labour union issues. These dynamics prompt us to propose a more even-handed approach—one that protects expressive and associational freedom in and outside the labour domain, and especially when the right to protest or dissent from majoritarian views is at stake. Noting, as well, that section 2(d)'s standard of breach is strict, we also call for a generous and consistent interpretation to bring this guarantee into alignment with the other fundamental freedoms. More generally, our view is that for section 2's promise to be fulfilled, expression and association must be guaranteed equally, and limits under section 1 must be subject to an evidentiary threshold that applies in a consistent way across guarantees and issues. We explore these themes briefly in sections discussing expressive and associational freedom under the *Charter*.

---

[4] For a more comprehensive assessment of s 2(b) see Jamie Cameron, "A Reflection on Section 2(b)'s Quixotic Journey, 1982–2013" in Jamie Cameron & Sonia Lawrence (eds) *Constitutional Cases 2011* (2012) 58 SCLR (2d) 163 http://sclr.journals.yorku.ca/index.php/sclr/article/view/36529/33194 28 April 2016.

[5] *Irwin Toy Ltd v Quebec (Attorney General)* [1989] 1 SCR 927, 58 DLR (4th) 577, 968.

[6] *Mounted Police Association of Ontario v Canada (Attorney General)* 2015 SCC 1, [2015] 1 SCR 3 [57].

2. FREEDOM AND LIMITS UNDER SECTION 2(b) OF THE *CHARTER*

The *Charter's* framework contemplates a form of equilibrium between the protection of constitutional rights and the demands of democratic society. Calibrating that equilibrium engages the relationship between the scope of the guarantees and the standard of reasonable or justified limits under section 1.[7]

Under section 2(b) it was unknown, for instance, whether the Supreme Court would grant expressive freedom a generous interpretation or restrict the scope of entitlement. Some thought the guarantee should only protect expressive activity that was traditionally valued the most, such as political speech on matters of parliamentary government.[8] That conception would have excluded much communicative activity from the *Charter*, including artistic and commercial expression. In *Irwin Toy*, the Supreme Court chose instead to extend prima facie protection to all expressive activities.[9] In doing so, the Court embraced a principle of content neutrality, essentially in recognition that a restrictive definition would invite discrimination against unpopular ideas and lead to a blinkered conception of freedom. Under *Irwin Toy's* definition of expression as "any attempt to convey meaning", the content or value of expression was irrelevant to the threshold question under section 2.[10]

By the time *Irwin Toy* was decided, a stringent judge-made test ("the *Oakes* test") was in place to determine whether a *Charter* violation could be saved or justified as a reasonable limit under section 1.[11] A combination of section 2(b)'s broad scope and section 1's strict test meant that most violations could not survive reasonable limits review. The Court's decision to adjust section 1's standard downward, and introduce a content- or value-based approach, marked an early turning point in section 2(b)'s development.[12] This methodology, which was designed to uphold limits on "valueless" expression,

---

[7]   *Charter* s 1 states: "The *Canadian Charter of Rights and Freedoms* guarantees the rights and freedoms set out in it subject only to such reasonable limits prescribed by law as can be demonstrably justified in a free and democratic society".

[8]   See *e.g. Re Klein and Law Society of Upper Canada* (1985) 50 OR (2d) 118, 16 DLR (4th) 498 (Div Ct).

[9]   *Irwin Toy* above (n 5) 969 (stating that "[w]e cannot exclude human activity from the scope of guaranteed expressive activity on the basis of the content or meaning being conveyed").

[10]   *Ibid* 978–979. But note that *Irwin Toy* excludes "violent forms of expression" from s 2(b) and added a purpose-effect step to the test for determining breaches of s 2(b). Both are problematic; on violent expression see *infra* note 34.

[11]   *R v Oakes* [1986] 1 SCR 103, 53 OR (2d) 719 (prescribing a complex two-step test, with three elements of proportionality, to determine the justifiability of reasonable limits under s 1). See the chapter by Charles-Maxime Panaccio in this *Handbook*.

[12]   Initially, the Court proposed different standards under s 1, depending on whether the state acted as the singular antagonist of the individual, which would attract strict review, or mediated competing interests or protected the vulnerable, which would invite a more deferential application of *Oakes: Irwin Toy* above (n 5) 993–995.

created unavoidable tension between section 2(b)'s freedom-based definition, which was egalitarian and content-neutral, and section 1's "contextual" approach, which was hierarchical and content-based in nature.

The contextual approach modified the *Oakes* test by providing a doctrinal mechanism for measuring expressive activities against section 2(b)'s abstract and aspirational values.[13] The Court applied this approach in key decisions to conclude that controversial and undesirable expression does not serve section 2(b)'s values, and therefore should receive little or no *Charter* protection.[14] The result was a doctrinal framework that entrenched overt conflict between section 2(b)'s content-neutral definition of expression and a section 1 standard of justification that relied on content distinctions to justify limits. Without the *Charter*'s textual separation of rights and limits, this about-face in the Court's conception of expressive freedom—from section 2(b)'s definition of the right to section 1's question of limits—would not have been plausible. Despite the structural rationale, the contextual approach lacked analytical credibility, and in practice transformed section 2(b)'s principle of content neutrality into a false promise.[15]

Moreover, section 1's requirement of evidence-based limits was a casualty of the contextual approach, because the standard of proof was less pressing for low-value expression. Once the Court tempered the elements of the *Oakes* test, limits on expression could be based on a "reasoned apprehension of harm", common sense and logic, and uncritical deference to the legislature.[16] The attenuation of section 1 review in section 2(b) cases reached an apex when the Court combined these rationales to uphold proactive limits on core political expression; in *Harper v Canada*, it held that Parliament could regulate political expression, in the absence of evidence, to prevent the prospect of speculative

---

[13] See *Edmonton Journal v Alberta (Attorney General)* [1989] 2 SCR 1326, 64 DLR (4th) 577 (introducing the contextual approach), and *R v Keegstra* [1990] 3 SCR 697, 114 AR 81 (developing a core-values test for expressive activity under s.1, which asks whether expression advances the pursuit of truth; participation in social and political decision-making; or individual self-fulfillment and human flourishing; *Irwin Toy* above (n 5) 976).

[14] A partial list includes *R v Keegstra, ibid* (upholding hate propaganda provisions); *Canada (Human Rights Commission) v Taylor* [1990] 3 SCR 892, 75 DLR (4th) 577 (upholding human rights limits on expressive freedom); *R v Butler* [1992] 1 SCR 452, 89 DLR (4th) 449 and *R v Sharpe* 2002 SCC 2, [2001] 1 SCR 45 (upholding the criminalization of obscenity, pornography, and child pornography); and *Hill v Church of Scientology* [1995] 2 SCR 1130, 24 OR (3d) 865 and *R v Lucas* [1998] 1 SCR 439, 157 DLR (4th) 423 (refusing to protect defamatory statements). But see *R v Zundel* [1992] 2 SCR 731, 95 DLR (4th) 202 (invalidating a criminal prohibition against spreading false news).

[15] For further comment see Cameron, "Quixotic Journey" above (n 4) 167–173; see also Jamie Cameron, "The Past, Present and Future of Expressive Freedom under the *Charter*" (1997) 35 OHLJ 1 (explaining and critiquing the introduction and establishment of the contextual approach).

[16] See *R v Butler* above (n 14) (introducing the "reasoned apprehension of harm" standard); *RJR-MacDonald Inc v Canada (Attorney General)* [1995] 3 SCR 199, 127 DLR (4th) 1 [137] (stating that the "balance of probabilities may be established by the application of common sense to what is known"); and *Harper v Canada* 2004 SCC 33, [2004] 1 SCR 827 [88] (applying a deferential approach to Parliament's legislation restricting political expression).

and future harm.[17] The decision to uphold limits on high-value expression without proof of harmful consequences represented a low point in section 2(b)'s evolution.

In brief, that is how the Court demonstrated superficial respect for expressive freedom under section 2(b) and invoked content discrimination to justify limits under section 1. It is a methodology that misconceives the guarantee's objectives: section 2(b)'s purpose is not to monitor the content of expression and choose which views are valuable enough to protect; its central goal, instead, is to safeguard an inclusive process of freedom in which expressive activities are free, subject only to an evidentiary standard of harm and rigorous threshold of justification. Contrary to the Court's section 1 methodology, freedom is not a matter of compromise, context, and common sense; it is a matter of principle which, to be meaningful, must protect all expressive activities, including and especially those that are considered objectionable and valueless.

A pocket of section 2(b) jurisprudence resists this pattern. After upholding limits on picketing in two early cases, the Court consistently granted labour expression significant protection under section 2(b).[18] Less troubling than the outcome is the double standard that emerges from a comparison of the Court's labour and non-labour decisions on expressive freedom.

3. PROTEST AND DISSENT UNDER SECTION 2(b)

Juxtaposing protest activities by individuals and labour unions is instructive because it exposes the inconsistency of a content-based approach. A few examples are sufficient to show that individuals engaged in unpopular or protest activities have not fared well under section 2(b).

In *R. v Lucas*, two placard-carrying protestors went to jail for making defamatory statements about a police officer.[19] Their goal was to expose and draw attention to a miscarriage of justice involving wrongful criminal charges against members of a foster family, and the sexual betrayal of young children in foster care.[20] The protestors picketed

---

[17] *Harper v Canada, ibid* [98] (stating, *per* the majority opinion, that "[s]urely, Parliament does not have to wait for the feared harm to occur before it can enact measures to prevent the *possibility* of the harm occurring"; emphasis added); see also *R. v Bryan*, [2007] 1 SCR 527 (upholding a temporary ban on publication of federal election results).

[18] Compare *RWDSU v Dolphin Delivery Ltd* [1986] 2 SCR 573, 33 DLR (4th) 174; *BCGEU v British Columbia (Attorney General)* [1988] 2 SCR 214, 53 DLR (4th) 1 (upholding limits on picketing) and *KMart Canada Ltd v UFCW Local 1518* [1999] 2 SCR 1083, 176 DLR (4th) 607; *Pepsi-Cola Canada Beverages (West) Ltd v RWDSU Local 558* 2002 SCC 8, [2002] 1 SCR 156; and *UFCW, Local 401 v Alberta (Information and Privacy Commissioner)* 2013 SCC 62, [2013] 3 SCR 733 (protecting labour activities under s. 2(b)).

[19] *R v Lucas* above (n 14).

[20] *Ibid* [2]–[6] (outlining the background to the demonstration).

outside a provincial courthouse and police headquarters wearing placards that were crude and potentially misleading.[21] Their objective was to publicize a dereliction of duty on the officer's part—failing to protect female siblings from their brother, a sexual predator. Though the protest was grounded in the Crown's disclosure documents, the Lucases were unable or unwilling to conform their protest to standards of civility. The police halted the demonstration, arresting and charging the protestors with defamatory libel under the *Criminal Code*.[22]

The Supreme Court upheld the criminalization of libel, without dissent, and confirmed jail sentences for both Lucases.[23] Its decision acknowledged the demonstration's foundation in a plea for accountability, but held that the placards were without value and entitled to little or no protection under section 1.[24] In endorsing the use of the criminal law as a substitute for tort law, the Court found that the police officer was vulnerable and that the criminal sanction was necessary because he might not be able to recover damages through a civil action in defamation.[25]

R. v Lucas represents a startling betrayal of section 2(b)'s freedom values, because the criminal law was used to silence the Lucases, who spoke for those who had been falsely accused, and to prevent them from speaking truth to power.[26] Imprisoning them for exposing a profound miscarriage of justice constituted a serious setback for section 2(b)'s rationales of transparency and accountability.

A more recent example suggests that expressive freedom may have lost ground over the first 30 years of *Charter* interpretation. The issue in *Whatcott v Saskatchewan* was whether provincial human rights legislation prohibiting hate speech as a form of discrimination violated section 2(b) of the *Charter*. The appeal concerned a complaint arising from the distribution of anti-gay flyers near a school. Though closely divided in its earlier hate speech jurisprudence, the Supreme Court unanimously upheld the provision and found that Whatcott's flyers were hateful.[27] Although accepting that his ideas

---

[21] *Ibid* [7]–[8] (providing the text on the placards).

[22] RSC 1985 c C-46, ss 300, 301.

[23] *R v Lucas* above (n 14); McLachlin and Major JJ dissenting in part (to acquit Mrs. Lucas).

[24] Cory J described defamatory libel as "inimical to the core values" of s 2(b); as "so far removed" from those values as to merit "but scant protection"; and as having "negligible value" which "significantly reduces the burden of justification under s 1. *Ibid* [93], [94], [57].

[25] *Ibid* [74].

[26] Dozens of sex offence charges against members of the foster family were baseless, and it emerged that the officer and others were aware throughout that the problem was one of intra-familial sexual violence, not abuse by members of the foster family. See *Kvellv Miazga* 2009 SCC 51, [2009] 3 SCR 339 (action in malicious prosecution by the foster family against public officials, including the police officer who did not appeal an award against him at trial).

[27] *Whatcott v Saskatchewan (Human Rights Tribunal)* 2013 SCC 11, [2013] 1 SCR 467 (upholding s 14(1) (b) of the *Saskatchewan Human Rights Code* but severing unconstitutional language, and concluding that although two flyers were discriminatory, two others were not). See *Canada (Human Rights Commission) v Taylor* above (n 14) upholding a human rights provision limiting expressive freedom by a 4-3 margin; *R. v Keegstra* above (n 13). More generally, the Court has recognized and enforced rights of access to public property for s. 2(b) purposes. See *Ramsden v Peterborough (City)* [1993] 2 SCR 1084 (recognizing that posters have historically been an effective and relatively inexpensive means of communicating

could not be banned, the Court maintained that the hate speech provision prohibited the manner and not the content of expression.[28] In the Court's view, Whatcott's flyers were subject to regulation because they could lead to acts of discrimination by third parties at some date in the future.[29]

The Court's methodology relied on a "double discount" to attenuate the standard of review under section 1. First, *Whatcott* declared that restrictions are easier to justify because hate expression "contributes little to the values underlying freedom of expression".[30] In this way, the low-value designation enabled the Court to discount section 1's evidentiary requirements. Second, then, the Court stated that it was "entitled to use common sense and experience in recognizing that certain activities, hate speech among them, inflict societal harms", and to take notice that the "discriminatory effects of hate speech are part of the everyday knowledge and experience of Canadians".[31] In other words, common knowledge was sufficient evidence of harm to ground "a reasonable apprehension of societal harm" and allow objectionable views to be regulated.[32] *Whatcott's* approach to content, harm, and evidence are worrying, especially when set against the Court's earlier hate-speech landmarks, which engaged the justices in high-level debate about expressive freedom and led to strong dissenting opinions.

The same year—2013—*R. v Khawaja* unanimously upheld a *Criminal Code* provision that explicitly targeted section 2 activity. The question there was whether the definition of terrorist activity, which criminalized actions undertaken in part or whole for religious, political, or ideological objectives, violated section 2(a), (b), and (d) of the *Charter*.[33]

Most striking is the Court's dismissive response to the chilling effects of a provision that singled religious, political, and ideological objectives out for criminalization.[34] The Court departed from its position in other decisions, which took notice of such effects, stating in *Khawaja* that direct proof of a chill was required.[35] The Court also discounted

---

political, cultural, and social information). ' See also *Committee for the Commonwealth of Canada v Canada*, [1991] 1 SCR 139 (protecting section 2(b) leafleting at a public airport); and *Greater Vancouver Transportation Authority v Canadian Federation of Students*, [2009] SCR 295 (invalidating restrictions on political advertising on municipal buses).

[28] *Ibid* [51] (stating that "[h]ate speech legislation is not aimed at discouraging repugnant or offensive ideas").

[29] *Ibid* [52], [11], [191] (discussing the potential to lead to discrimination).

[30] *Ibid* [120], [114].

[31] *Ibid* [132], [135].

[32] *Ibid.*

[33] *R. v Khawaja*, 2012 SCC 69, [2012] 3 S.C.R. 555. Section 83.01 (1) of the Criminal Code defines "terrorist activity" as . . . an act or omission, in or outside Canada, that is committed in whole or in part for a "political, religious or ideological purpose, objective or cause".

[34] Note also that the Supreme Court has excluded violence and threats of violence from the *Charter*, without defining the exclusions or providing a rationale. The vagueness, overbreadth, and potential chill of this approach is another worrying aspect of the s. 2(b) jurisprudence and of the decision in *Khawaja*.

[35] *Ibid.* [79–80] (accepting generally that a chilling effect can be inferred from known facts and experience and concluding that such an inference is *impossible* in the case of the motive clause; emphasis added).

the argument of a chill, declaring that any adverse effects for the *Charter*'s fundamental freedoms should be attributed either to the events of 9/11 or to the targeted community's misunderstanding of the clause.[36] In other words, those potentially chilled from exercising their section 2 rights are at fault for not understanding that the motive clause only affects those engaged in criminal activities. Because the motive clause is neutral, it cannot deter the justifiable exercise of section 2 freedoms, and any adverse consequences are the result of "self-chilling". Ironically, this analysis failed to appreciate that the purpose of this doctrine is to prevent self-censorship. Finally, the Court speculated that prejudicial consequences for the Muslim community were due to a general climate of suspicion or to profiling by the police, and did not arise from the provision's criminalization of constitutionally protected motives.[37] *Khawaja*'s unwillingness to engage the *Charter* and protect members of a community that were subject to prejudice and suspicion could not have been more pronounced.

The Court's response to compelled expression is also indicative. Though individuals who seek freedom from the demands of conformity are by definition engaged in an act of protest or dissent, their claims have been considered trivial and unimportant. In *Lavigne v OPSEU*, the Court held that a non-union employee's objection to the use of mandatory union dues to support non-workplace causes did not engage section 2(b).[38] More recently, the Ontario Court of Appeal held in *McAteer v Canada* that principled objection to a mandatory oath to the Queen, which is a requirement for Canadian citizenship, did not violate section 2(b).[39] Finally, *Bernard v Canada* held that a non-union employee can be compelled to provide private, personal information to a union that represents workplace employees.[40] Only two claims have succeeded—once when the Court invalidated the compulsory use of the French language in outdoor signage, and a second time when the Court agreed that mandatory, unattributed warnings on cigarette packages violated section 2(b).[41]

In contrast, the Court's decisions on labour expression under section 2(b) look very different. After conservative responses in two early cases, the Supreme Court set a high-water mark for expression in decisions on leafleting, picketing, and other picket line activity.[42] This pocket of jurisprudence is small but important because of the way the Court shifted the key variables of value and harm. In place of the discount that governs in other section 2(b) cases, the Supreme Court applied a "double upgrade": first, it

---

[36] *Ibid* [81] [82] (stating, in particular, that there would only be a chilling effect on those having "cursory or incomplete" knowledge of the clause).

[37] *Ibid* [83] (stating that the provision is clearly drafted in a manner "respectful of diversity" and does not encourage or allow targeting or stereotyping).

[38] *Lavigne v OPSEU* [1991] 2 SCR 211, 81 DLR (4th) 545; all members of the panel rejected the s 2(b) claim and proposed a narrow test for freedom from compelled expression.

[39] *McAteer v Canada (Attorney General)* 2014 ONCA 578, 121 OR (3d) 1; leave to appeal denied, 26 February 2015.

[40] *Bernard v Canada* [2014] 1 S.C.R. 227.

[41] *Devine v. Quebec (Attorney General)* [1988] 2 SCR 790; *RJR-MacDonald v Canada* above (n 16).

[42] See *Kmart, Pepsi-Cola,* and *Information and Privacy Commissioner* above (n 19).

assigned labour expression the highest value, paradoxically relying on its then-narrow section 2(d) jurisprudence to do so; and then it concluded, as a result, that limits on this activity are subject to a strict standard of justification.[43]

The Court's treatment of harm in this context is revealing. Picketing and related activities are designed to cause serious consequences; a strike is "not a tea party" and can—indeed is intended to—cause serious disruption and economic harm to the employer and to other social actors.[44] Collateral damage and harm to third parties, including members of the public, is not only commonplace but the direct and immediate object of the exercise. Picketing can become violent and unruly, and is aimed at intimidating workers and third parties from crossing union lines. The Court nonetheless accorded these activities a higher degree of protection than any other form of expression under section 2(b).[45] Paradoxically, labour expression has received more favourable treatment than activities whose harmful consequences, as discussed above, are unknown or speculative.

4. Toward a Conception of Meaningful Freedom under Section 2

Though the Supreme Court's conception of expressive freedom under section 2(b) is sound in principle, the relationship between value and harm under section 1 is problematic. When value serves as a proxy for harm, the *Charter*'s protection for expression depends less on evidence of the consequences of the legislation than on the Court's perception of content. As our discussion demonstrates, this approach has consistently disadvantaged expression the Court deems to be low in value, and privileged expression it prefers—such as labour expression, which, for now, is treated more favourably than expressive activities around democratic elections.[46]

What is at stake in this methodology are competing visions, separated and represented by the *Charter*'s structural concepts of breach and justification. A freedom-based conception, which is reflected in the Court's commitment to content neutrality under section 2(b), rests on an egalitarian approach which extends the *Charter*'s protection without discrimination, including to those who express crude, unpopular, and

---

[43] See *e.g. Pepsi-Cola* above (n 19) [33], [32], [67], [68] (stating that free expression is "particularly critical" in the labour context and declaring that picketing engages "one of the highest constitutional values"), and [37] (indicating that freedom of expression is the starting point and presumption, and warning that limits are only permitted where reasonable and demonstrably necessary).

[44] *A.L. Patchett & Sons Ltd. v Pacific Great Eastern Railway Co.* [1959] SCR 271, 17 DLR (2d) 449 [276].

[45] See *Pepsi-Cola* above (n 19) [106]. Otherwise under s. 2(b) see *Dagenais v Canadian Broadcasting Corp.*, [1994] 3 SCR 835; *Canadian Broadcasting Corp.*, [1996] 3 SCR 480 (setting strong doctrinal standards on publication bans and open courtrooms to protect the open justice principle).

[46] *Harper, Bryan* above (n 17).

objectionable ideas. The alternative view features a content- or value-based approach, which prevails under section 1, where the contextual approach trumps section 2(b) egalitarianism and the requirements of *Oakes*, replacing both with an analysis which ensures that only valuable expression will be protected. Though content regulations are permissible, limits on expression should not depend on the low value of expression's content, on appeals to common sense, or on deference to the legislature, but should instead be evidence-based. In our view, section 2(b)'s principle of content neutrality must be followed by a section 1 analysis that takes seriously the requirement that limits must be demonstrably justified. A constitutional guarantee of expressive freedom demands no less.

We acknowledge that it is not self evident why the *Charter* should provide a safe haven to those who espouse and promote reprehensible views. Instinct and common sense confirm that expressive activity has impact and can be injurious. Constraining expressive activity that risks discord or discomfort insulates the community from unsettling points of view and serves to promote or maintain social harmony. As laudable as those objectives may be, they lead to a conception that dismisses alternative voices, impoverishes critical discussion, and does not protect freedom in a meaningful way. Excluding alternative voices promotes a static social harmony where new views—critical harsh, or unsettling—are silenced and cannot threaten the comfort of the status quo.

Tolerating the intolerable requires democratic humility—a willingness to recognize those who speak in a different and even jarring voice, as equal participants in collective political and social decision-making. That humility, and its processes of speech and counter-speech, is the hallmark of a free society, mindful that today's democratic values were forged in a crucible of freedom. That crucible allowed yesterday's outsiders to advocate change and claim their place as self-governing members of the democratic community. Some of those outsiders include women, the gay community, minority groups, aboriginals, Communist sympathizers in the Cold War, and political and religious dissidents of all stripes. Just as their activities and movements shaped current mores, their successors should be free to forge new pathways in the ongoing process of social and democratic renewal.

Meanwhile, it is no exaggeration to say that the courts have struggled to define the scope and role of section 2(d). The *Charter*'s concept of associational freedom has evolved in a singular and anomalous direction, which has been almost exclusively identified and concerned with labour relations. To some extent, associational freedom's central purposes have been sidelined because the guarantee's concern with unions' protection has dominated section 2(d)'s evolution. Normalizing this freedom within the framework of section 2 will depend, initially, on restoring a general conception of associational freedom. It follows that the guarantee's methodology must also be reconsidered, to bring section 2(d) doctrinally into alliance with the standards of breach and justification that define section 2's other guarantees.

For these reasons, section 2(d) differs from and, in certain respects, has been a lesser guarantee than section 2(b) and section 2(a). Still, it shares common bonds with section 2(b): here, as well, the Court has adopted a conception of the guarantee that is selective, and based on a particular view of what is valuable enough to warrant the *Charter*'s protection. Under section 2(d), it is labour union activity and, whatever one's view may be of labour and the *Charter*, section 2(d)'s broader objectives and aspirations have regrettably become invisible as a result.

Section 2(d)'s history is idiosyncratic, and can be divided into periods marked by two landmark developments: the *Labour Trilogy* and *Dunmore v Ontario*.[47] Between 1987 and 2001, the *Trilogy* governed, compromising section 2(d) through a narrow interpretation of the guarantee, with the result that a claim based on associational freedom succeeded just once in this period, and then only as a supplement to section 2(b).[48] Beginning with *Dunmore v Ontario* in 2001, the Supreme Court began to retreat from the *Trilogy*, and by 2015 would overrule section 2(d)'s threshold precedents. Our brief consideration of this unusual jurisprudence focuses on the impact and significance of section 2(d)'s evolution, essentially, as a labour guarantee.

5. LABOUR UNIONS AND ASSOCIATIONAL FREEDOM

In 1987, the Supreme Court issued a series of decisions on freedom of association which became known as the *Labour Trilogy*. The key landmark, the *Alberta Reference*, tested the constitutionality of a mandatory labour arbitration scheme, as well as a prohibition on public sector strikes. The majority result, that neither collective bargaining nor the right to strike is protected by the *Charter*, was resisted by a strong dissent which supported a generous conception of the guarantee and of labour union objectives under section 2(d).

Though the Court considered in abstract terms how freedom of association should be defined, its conception of section 2(d) was dominated by the labour context. The *Alberta Reference*'s plurality and concurring opinions revealed deep skepticism about the wisdom of constitutionalizing collective endeavours, in general, and labour union activities, in particular. No view of the guarantee attracted majority support, and Justice McIntyre's sole concurrence, which provided an extended discussion of section 2(d), became the leading opinion. His view of associational freedom as an individual, and not a collective, entitlement, was challenged by Chief Justice Dickson's forceful dissent, as well as by a host of academic commentators.[49] In addition, the prevailing but contested

---

[47] *Reference Re Public Service Employee Relations Act (Alta)*, [1987] 1 SCR 313 [hereinafter the "*Alberta Reference*"]; *PSAC v Canada*, [1987] 1 SCR 424, 38 DLR (4th) 249; *RWDSU v Saskatchewan*, [1987] 1 SCR 460, 38 DLR (4th) 277 [hereinafter "the *Labour Trilogy*"]. *Dunmore* v *Ontario (Attorney General)*, [2001] 3 SCR 1016, 2001 SCC 94.

[48] *Libman v. Quebec*, [1997] 3 SCR 569.

[49] See Judy Fudge, "Labour Rights as Human Rights: Turning Slogans into Legal Claims" (2014) 37 Dalhousie Law Journal 601; Dianne Pothier, "Twenty Years of Labour Law and the Charter" (2002) 40

view then and, for many years afterward, was that the courts should show almost complete deference to the legislatures on labour relations matters.[50]

The foundation for an alternative view of collective associational action and labour union activities is found in the Chief Justice's *Alberta Reference* dissent. There, he spoke in emphatic terms of the valuable role trade unions have played as instruments of the public good: "while trade unions also fulfill other important social, political and charitable functions, collective bargaining remains vital to the capacity of individual employees to participate in ensuring fair wages, health and safety protections, and equitable and humane working conditions".[51] The Chief Justice's approach to associational freedom endorsed collective purposes and the labour union imperative to empower workers and democratize the workplace; in the result he would have constitutionalized collective bargaining and the right to strike.[52]

In the years after the *Labour Trilogy*, a Court that was divided and apprehensive of section 2(d)'s implications for labour relations proved unable to agree on the meaning of associational freedom. Subsequent decisions went no further than to acknowledge a minimal definition protecting the right to form and maintain an association, and to undertake activities in association that are independently protected by other *Charter* guarantees.[53] Albeit for different reasons, a majority of justices was reluctant to endorse a definition that would protect activity in association that can lawfully be undertaken by individuals. Under these conditions of doctrinal hardship, section 2(d) generated a modest jurisprudence in which few claims proceeded and those that did predictably failed.[54]

Osgoode Hal L.J. 369; Ravi Malhotra, "Karl Klare's Vision of Democratization in the Workplace and the Contradictory Evolution of Labour Law Jurisprudence in the Supreme Court of Canada" (2014) 45 Ottawa Law Review 303; Brian Langille, "The Freedom of Association Mess: How We Got Into It and How We Can Get Out of It" (2009) 54 McGill L.J. 177; Nitya Iyer "Disadvantaged Unions: The Merging ss. 2(d) and 15(1) of the Charter" (2005) 12 CLELJ 1; Patrick Macklem, "Developments in Employment Law: The 1990–91 Term" 3 Sup Ct L Rev (2d Ser) 227; Judy Fudge, "Labour, the New Constitution and Old Style Liberalism" (1988) 13 Queen's L.J. 61; David Beatty & Steven Kennett, "Striking Back: Fighting Words, Social Protest and Political Participation in Free and Democratic Societies" (1988) 67 Can Bar Rev 573.

[50] This view was shared by many commentators and governed the work of labour arbitrators and specialized tribunals. Under this view, courts are structurally more sympathetic to employers and to the protection of property rights than they are to workers' rights. See Harry Arthurs, "Constitutionalizing the Right of Workers to Organize, Bargain and Strike: The Sight of One Shoulder Shrugging" (2010) 19 Social & Legal Studies 403–422 and Harry Arthurs, "Labour Law without the State" (1996) 46 University of Toronto Law Journal 1–45; Michael Mandel, The Charter of Rights and the Legalization of Politics in Canada (Toronto, Wall & Thompson, 1989).

[51] *Alberta Reference*, above (n 47) [92].

[52] Note that a collective approach to associational freedom is consistent with the Court's interpretation of the *Charter*'s minority language rights and the Constitution's entrenchment of Aboriginal rights.

[53] See *Professional Institute of the Public Service of Canada v Northwest Territories (Commissioner)*, [1990] 2 SCR 367, [1990] SCJ No 75 (*per* Sopinka J., proposing a four-point framework for s. 2(d) which was unable to attract majority support).

[54] See, e.g., *Black v Law Society of Alberta*, [1989] 1 SCR 591 (invalidating restrictions on interprovincial law firm partnerships under s. 6, not s. 2(d)); *R. v Skinner*, [1990] 1 SCR 1235 (rejecting a s. 2(d) challenge to the *Criminal Code*'s solicitation provision); *Professional Institute*, above (n 53); *Canadian Egg Marketing*

Starting in 2001, section 2(d) began to experience a reversal of jurisprudential fortune. In *Dunmore v Ontario*, the Court took a dramatic step away from its diffidence toward the guarantee by endorsing the Dickson dissent and its collective conception of the guarantee.[55] Specifically, the Court held that excluding agricultural workers from the statutory framework for labour relations was unconstitutional because it violated the workers' fundamental right to engage in meaningful associational activities. Though it stopped short of overruling the *Trilogy* and constitutionalizing collective bargaining, the Court stated that "certain union activities, such as making collective representations to the employers, adopting a majority political platform or federating with other unions, were central to freedom of association."[56] Not only did *Dunmore* validate a collective conception of section 2(d), it re-energized the relationship between labour and the *Charter*, and intimated that the Court might be prepared to reconsider the *Trilogy*.

In 2007, in *Facilities Subsector Bargaining Association v British Columbia* ("*Health Services*"), the Court dramatically overruled a core ruling of the *Trilogy* by declaring that collective bargaining is constitutionally protected.[57] *Health Services* was a monumental decision, but one that tied section 2(d) more explicitly to the circumstances of labour activities, and although the outcome was applauded in many quarters, the resulting doctrine was anomalous. First, the Court failed to address section 2(d)'s status as a general guarantee, treating associational freedom and its requirements primarily as a function of labour relations. Second, to minimize the consequences for public sector bargaining, the Court stated that the content of section 2(d) is procedural rather than substantive in nature. Third, to further deter the constitutionalization of bargaining in this sector, *Health Services* qualified the entitlement by setting a substantial interference test to determine the question of breach under section 2(d).[58] This standard is strict, and bears little resemblance to the analogous tests for expressive and religious freedom under section 2(b) and (a).[59]

The impact of *Health Services* was initially unclear but, after taking one step backward, the Court overruled precedent again in 2015, holding that the right to strike is protected by section 2(d).[60] It is also significant, in our view, that *Mounted Police*

Agency v Richardson, [1998] 3 SCR 157 (rejecting a s. 2(d) challenge to the exclusion of some from an egg producers marketing scheme); *Delisle v Canada*, [1999] 2 SCR 989 (rejecting the claim that excluding the RCMP from the federal government's labour relations scheme violated s. 2(d)); and *Suresh v Canada*, [2002] 1 SCR 1 (rejecting a s. 2(d) challenge to deportation provisions).

[55]   *Dunmore* above (n 47).

[56]   *Ibid* [17].

[57]   *Health Services and Support—Facilities Subsector Bargaining Assn v British Columbia*, [2007] 2 SCR 391 (stating, [2], that s. 2(d) "protects the capacity of members of labour unions to engage in collective bargaining on workplace issues").

[58]   For a comment see J. Cameron, "Due Process, Collective Bargaining, and s. 2(d) of the *Charter*: A Comment on *BC Health Services*", 13 *CLELJ* 233.

[59]   For s. 2(a), see, e.g., *Hutterian Brethren of Wilson Colony v Alberta*, 2009 SCC 37, [2009] 2 SCR 567 [32], 310 DLR (4th) 193.

[60]   The step backward was *Fraser v Ontario (Attorney General)*, 2011 SCC 20, [2011] 2 SCR 3 (applying an impossibility test to reject the s. 2(d) claim in the next collective bargaining case after *BC Health*

Association of Ontario proposed a definition of associational freedom that applies outside the labour context. In doing so, the Court confirmed that section 2(d) extends to the right to join with others and form associations, the right to join with others in the pursuit of other constitutional rights, and the right to join with others to *meet on more equal terms the power and strength of other groups or entities*.[61] We highlight the latter addition, which has the potential to expand the freedom of peaceful assembly and protect the right to protest and dissent in a meaningful way. The ability to join to make one's message heard resonates in the labour context to support a right to real and meaningful collective bargaining and the right to strike as a tool of action. Though it has not yet been articulated or applied outside the labour context, this element of associational freedom can ground a right to engage in collective action such as boycott or peaceful demonstration.[62] Still, and despite the promise of this definition, our lingering concern is that the focus on labour issues has distorted section 2(d); a standard of breach that is issue-specific and customized to the context of labour relations separates this guarantee from its analogues under section 2(b) and (a).

On the labour side, recognizing the right to strike as an element of freedom of association has changed the landscape of collective bargaining rights in Canada, and lower courts are moving on controversial labour issues to protect the rights of workers and unions.[63] It is too early to predict how *Charter* supervision of labour relations in the public sector will evolve, whether the Supreme Court will maintain its pro-union stance,

---

Services). See Steven Barrett, "The Supreme Court of Canada's Decision in *Fraser*: Stepping Forward, Backward or Sideways" (2012) 16 Canadian Lab & Emp LJ 331 at 338.] See also the essays collected in Fay Faraday, Judy Fudge & Eric Tucker (eds), *Constitutional Labour Rights in Canada: Farm Workers and the Fraser Case* (Toronto: Irwin Law, 2012). The 2015 decisions are *Mounted Police Association of Ontario v Canada (A.G.)*, 2015 SCC 1 (overruling *Delisle*, above (n 6), and declaring the exclusion of RCMP officers from the federal labour relations scheme unconstitutional); and *Saskatchewan Federation of Labour v Saskatchewan*, 2015 SCC 4, [2015] 1 SCR 245 (constitutionally protecting the right to strike).

[61]   [66] and [47–66] [emphasis added].

[62]   See *Daishowa Inc. v Friends of the Lubicon*, (1998) 39 O.R. (3d) 620, where the court denied a permanent injunction to stop picketing designed to educate the public about a dispute between a commercial enterprise and the Lubicon Cree and to induce consumers to boycott the products from this commercial enterprise. The court considered that s. 2(b) protects consumer boycotts.

[63]   See *Canadian Union of Postal Workers v Her Majesty in Right of Canada*, (2016) ONSC 418 (CanLII), http://canlii.ca/t/gpq4z, (2016) 130 OR (3d) 175 where the Ontario Superior Court issued a retroactive declaration striking down the *Restoring Mail Delivery for Canadians Act* which sought to oblige postal workers to go back to work. The Court considered that the legislative abrogation of the right to strike interfered with the collective bargaining process in a substantial way and violated s. 2(d). The violation could not be saved under s. 1 since the Act did not provide for a fair, independent, and impartial process to resolve the labour relations impasse and determine unilaterally the issue of wage increases. Similarly, in *OPSEU v Ontario (Ministry of Education)*, 2016 ONSC 2197, the Ontario Superior Court concluded that the process followed by the Ontario government with the teachers' unions represented a substantial violation of the right to collective bargaining and of s. 2(d)), which could not be saved under section 1 because it was unfair and arbitrary. It concluded that the legislative enactment which established a process to potentially remove the right to strike was also a substantial interference with s. 2(d).

and how legislatures might respond. In explaining section 2(d)'s trajectory, we suggest that the lack of options for social and economic rights under other guarantees, such as section 15's equality rights and section 7's liberty and security entitlements, may have influenced the Court's interpretation of associational freedom. It serves as a proxy or substitute for positive socio-economic rights, in part because labour unions historically have acted as agents of socio-economic change and equality. The Court's support of the institutional capacity and actions of unions is consistent with an instrumental, or communitarian-based conception of freedom, and a focus on collective rather than individual objectives. It is also consistent, in broad terms, with the value section 2(b) assigns labour expression, the Court's response to the question of compelled expression and association, and section 1's reliance on a general conception of societal harm to uphold limits on expression.

On its face, section 2(d)'s guarantee of associational freedom is broad in scope. Whether the guarantee will play a more generous role in protecting associational freedom in other contexts is unknown at present. What matters at the level of methodology is a principled conception of freedom: one that protects the associational activities of labour unions, but other associations as well, and does so according to standards of breach and justification that are supported by sound and rigorous analysis.

6. CONCLUSION

This brief account of sections 2(b) and (d) has shown that the *Charter*'s concept of freedom under these guarantees is grounded in instrumental virtues, where the communitarian values identified by the Court predominate and define the scope of *Charter* protection. Under section 2(b), expression that threatens community values, including ideological, racist, homophobic, or discriminatory speech, is discounted under section 1. Meanwhile, and despite the gains for labour union activities, associational freedom is subject to unstable and ad hoc standards; in addition, the guarantee remains divisive within the Court and the jurisprudence has been characterized, from its inception, by a strong pattern of dissenting opinions. These dynamics make it difficult to predict section 2(d)'s pathway in the future.

The *Charter*'s protection of freedoms will always be subject to contextual considerations. Even so, the section 1 analysis is applied erratically to limit expression that is incompatible with community values. At the same time, the section 2(d) jurisprudence has identified labour unions and their activities as the main beneficiary of this guarantee, and up to now, has glossed over opportunities to deepen its concept of associational freedom, protect those who may be associating for undesirable purposes, or recognize freedom from forms of compelled association.[64] To summarize, the Court's section 2(b)

---

[64] *Najafi v Canada (Minister of Public Safety and Emergency Preparedness)*, [2013] FC 876 where the court finds that membership in a protest party in Iran (the Kurdish Democratic Party of Iran) is

and (d) jurisprudence is not governed by coherent and analytical standards applied in an even-handed way across issues and guarantees, but it is primarily a matter of balancing that is based on the Court's assessment of expressive and associational values. To its credit, the Court took the unusual step of overruling the *Trilogy* and other section 2(d) precedents. That said, we do not expect the Court to undertake a reconceptualization of either guarantee. Despite the drawbacks we have discussed, the current concepts of expressive and associational freedom are likely to remain entrenched for the foreseeable future.

Looking ahead, it is also hard to predict the short term prospects for expressive and associational freedom. Section 2(b) has lost vitality, and has not generated a strong or positive precedent in some time. Despite regular and ongoing news headlines which confirm the visibility of expressive freedom issues, the section 2(b) jurisprudence is stalled. Section 2(d) is on a different trajectory, which will generate case law as courts and governments work through the implications of a constitutionalized labour relations scheme in public sector employment. We see room for cautious optimism that section 2(d) might offer a generous interpretation of associational freedom, in labour and other settings. As for section 2(b) and, quite apart from the jurisprudence, we observe that the *Charter* and its fundamental freedoms have had a clear and strong impact on public debate and discussion; moreover, these guarantees condition the work of legislatures and agencies at all levels of government and state action. In closing, we emphasize that the role of academic commentary in this process of evolution is to keep the principles at stake in protecting these fundamental freedoms at the forefront of discussion and debate.

Bibliography

Secondary Material

Arthurs, Harry, "Constitutionalizing the Right of Workers to Organize, Bargain and Strike the Sight of One Shoulder Shrugging" (2010) 19 Social & Legal Studies 403–422.

Arthurs, Harry, "Labour Law without the State" (1996) 46 University of Toronto Law Journal, 1–45.

Barrett, Steven, "The Supreme Court of Canada's Decision in *Fraser*: Stepping Forward, Backward or Sideways" (2011) 16 Canadian Lab & Emp LJ 368.

Cameron, J, "A Reflection on Section 2(b)'s Quixotic Journey, 1982–2013" in Jamie Cameron & Sonia Lawrence eds Constitutional *Cases 2011* (2012) 58 SCLR (2d) 163.

Cameron J, "The Past, Present and Future of Expressive Freedom under the *Charter*" (1997) 35 OHLJ 1.

Fudge, Judy, "Labour, the New Constitution and Old Style Liberalism" (1988) 13 Queen's L.J. 61.

not protected under the freedom of association and can lead to deportation. See also *Stables v Canada (Minister of Citizenship & Immigration)*, [2011] FC 1319 where the court refused to recognize membership in Hell's Angels as a protected form of association and proceeded to deport a man who had lived in Canada for 40 years.

Mandel, Michael, *The Charter of Rights and the Legalization of Politics in Canada* (Toronto, Wall & Thompson, 1989).
Roach, K. & D. Schneiderman, "Freedom of Expression in Canada" (2013) 61 S.C.L.R. (2d) 429.

Cases

A.L. Patchett & Sons Ltd. v Pacific Great Eastern Railway Co [1959] SCR 271, 17 DLR (2d) 449.
BCGEU v British Columbia (Attorney General) [1988] 2 SCR 214, 53 DLR (4th) 1.
Canada (Human Rights Commission) v Taylor [1990] 3 SCR 892, 75 DLR (4th) 577.
Canadian Union of Postal Workers v Her Majesty in Right of Canada, (2016) ONSC 418 (CanLII), (2016) 130 OR (3d) 175.
Daishowa Inc. v Friends of the Lubicon, (1998) 39 O.R. (3d) 620.
Edmonton Journal v Alberta (Attorney General) [1989] 2 SCR 1326, 64 DLR (4th) 577.
Harper v Canada 2004 SCC 33, [2004] 1 SCR 827.
Hill v Church of Scientology [1995] 2 SCR 1130, 24 OR (3d) 865.
Irwin Toy Ltd v Quebec (Attorney General) [1989] 1 SCR 927, 58 DLR (4th) 577.
KMart Canada Ltd v UFCW Local 1518 [1999] 2 SCR 1083, 176 DLR (4th) 607.
Kvell v Miazga 2009 SCC 51, [2009] 3 SCR 339.
Lavigne v OPSEU [1991] 2 SCR 211, 81 DLR (4th) 545.
McAteer v. Canada (Attorney General) 2014 ONCA 578, 121 OR (3d) 1.
Mounted Police Association of Ontario v Canada (Attorney General) 2015 SCC 1, [2015] 1 SCR.
Najafi v Canada (Minister of Public Safety and Emergency Preparedness), [2013] FC 876.
Pepsi-Cola Canada Beverages (West) Ltd v RWDSU Local 558 2002 SCC 8, [2002] 1 SCR 156.
OPSEU v Ontario (Ministry of Education), 2016 ONSC 2197.
R v Butler [1992] 1 SCR 452, 89 DLR (4th) 449.
R v Keegstra [1990] 3 SCR 697, 114 AR 81.
R v Lucas [1998] 1 SCR 439, 157 DLR (4th) 423.
R v Oakes [1986] 1 SCR 103, 53 OR (2d) 719.
R v Sharpe 2002 SCC 2, [2001] 1 SCR 45.
R v Zundel [1992] 2 SCR 731, 95 DLR (4th) 202.
Re Klein and Law Society of Upper Canada (1985) 50 OR (2d) 118, 16 DLR (4th) 498 (Div Ct).
RJR-MacDonald Inc v Canada (Attorney General) [1995] 3 SCR 199, 127 DLR (4th) 1.
RWDSU v Dolphin Delivery Ltd [1986] 2 SCR 573, 33 DLR (4th) 174.
Saskatchewan Federation of Labour v Saskatchewan, 2015 SCC 4, [2015] 1 SCR 245.
Stables v Canada (Minister of Citizenship & Immigration), [2011] FC 1319.
UFCW, Local 401 v Alberta (Information and Privacy Commissioner) 2013 SCC 62, [2013] 3 SCR 733.
Whatcott v Saskatchewan (Human Rights Tribunal) 2013 SCC 11, [2013] 1 SCR 467.

CHAPTER 36

....

FREEDOM OF RELIGION

....

BENJAMIN L. BERGER*

1. RELIGION AND CANADIAN CONSTITUTIONAL LIFE

....

RELIGION has shaped the distinctive character of Canadian constitutional life since well before Confederation. The *Treaty of Paris*,[1] which marked the end of the Seven Years' War and Imperial hostilities in Canada, acknowledged the political and practical realities of British rule over a substantial French Catholic population with the following guarantee, something of an early protection of religious freedom: "His Britannick Majesty, on his side, agrees to grant the liberty of the Catholick religion to the inhabitants of Canada: he will, in consequence, given the most precise and most effectual orders, that his new Roman Catholic subjects may profess the worship of their religion according the rites of the Romish church, as far as the laws of Great Britain permit." The *Quebec Act, 1774*,[2] another crucial step in the constitutional history of Canada, included similar provisions providing special rights to the Roman Catholic Church, and the *Constitutional Act, 1791*[3] extended privileges and protections to the Anglican Church in recognition of its special status in England.[4] This formative relationship between French and English communities, refracted through their constitutive religious identities and

* Professor and Associate Dean (Students), Osgoode Hall Law School, York University. The author wishes to thank Kate Glover for her insightful comments as this chapter took shape, Nathalie Des Rosiers and Peter Oliver for their helpful editorial guidance, and Amy Brubacher, Rachel Devon, and Caroline Sanders for their excellent research assistance.

[1] *Treaty of Paris* (1763), France, Britain, and Spain, 10 February 1763.

[2] (UK), 14 Geo III, c 83.

[3] (UK), 31 Geo III, c 31.

[4] See Janet Epp Buckingham, *Fighting over God: A Legal and Political History of Religious Freedom in Canada* (McGill-Queen's University Press, 2014); MH Ogilvie, *Religious Institutions and the Law in Canada* (3rd edn, Irwin Law, 2010).

interests, was again recognized when the modern Canadian state took form with its first Constitution, the *British North America Act, 1867*.[5] Included in that Constitution was section 93, a provision that gave authority to the provinces to legislate in respect of education and afforded distinct status to religious education, protecting Catholic and Protestant minority schools in English and French Canada, respectively. Over a century later, reflecting the constitutional significance of this provision, the Supreme Court of Canada explained that "[t]he protection of minority religious rights was a major pre-occupation during the negotiations leading to Confederation because of the perceived danger of leaving the religious minorities in both Canada East and Canada West at the mercy of overwhelming majorities."[6] In a decision effectively immunizing this histori-cal compromise from *Charter* scrutiny, the Court would explain that "[w]ithout this 'solemn pact,' this 'cardinal term' of Union, there would have been no Confederation."[7] Religion thus marked one of the fundamental themes that would define Canadian con-stitutionalism: the relationship between French and English Canada.

Religion—both its use and its suppression—was also central in shaping the founda-tional relationship between the Canadian state and the Indigenous peoples of Canada. The early colonial project was one in which religious missionaries played a crucial role, sometimes extending state power and sometimes aligning with Indigenous com-munities in advocating for the recognition of Aboriginal rights and sovereignty.[8] With the expansion of the Canadian state into the west, the Federal government banned Indigenous religious rituals and practices such as the potlatch as part of its effort to consolidate political and economic control over Indigenous peoples and their territo-ries. And in a devastating project aimed at cultural extinguishment, the Canadian state worked with the churches in administering the residential school system, the ruinous effects of which are still felt by Indigenous communities and continue to condition the political and legal relationship between the Canadian state and Indigenous peoples.[9] Religion was again tightly imbricated in one of the central dynamics that has shaped Canadian constitutionalism.

To reflect on the status, treatment, and role of religion was, thus, always an avenue into understanding the deeper tensions, ideologies, and politics at work in the Canadian state, and the history and logic of its constitutional order. Despite the profound consti-tutional and societal changes since these early days in the history of the country, this diagnostic, central role for religion in understanding key themes in Canadian constitu-tionalism persists. Over this period of Canadian history there has been a diminishment in the overt role of religion in the structures of state authority. Nowhere is this more

---

[5] (UK), 30 & 31 Vict, c 3.

[6] *Reference Re Bill 30* [1987] 1 SCR 1148, 1173.

[7] *Adler v Ontario* [1996] 3 SCR 609, [29].

[8] Hamar Foster and Benjamin L Berger, 'From Humble Prayers to Legal Demands: The Cowichan Petition of 1909 and the British Columbia Indian Land Question' in Hamar Foster and Benjamin L Berger (eds), *The Grand Experiment: Law and Legal Culture in British Settler Societies* (UBC Press, 2008).

[9] See JR Miller, *Shingwauk's Vision: A History of Native Residential Schools* (University of Toronto Press, 1996).

evident than in Quebec, where the Quiet Revolution of the 1960s has led to a funda-mental repositioning of the Catholic Church in the province's politics and culture. And with the introduction of the *Charter* in 1982, the frame of constitutional regard for indi-vidual and community rights and interests radically expanded in Canada. Religion and religious freedom would now be but one constitutionally recognized interest amongst many. Yet, in Canada as elsewhere in the world, freedom of religion is still serving as a singularly valuable site for the disclosure of the deeper challenges, politics, and par-adoxes of constitutionalism at large. It is a microcosm of constitutional themes and a bellwether of constitutional trends. One can still discern much about the deep character and culture of Canadian constitutionalism by studying freedom of religion.

What is it about the constitutional protection of freedom of religion that gives it this diagnostic function? The central role of religious freedom in revealing general trends and patterns in contemporary Canadian constitutionalism is not just a matter of a surge in cases on point or, in any straightforward way, a function of increased religious plural-ism. The answer is more structural and intrinsic to the relationship of law and religion, and to the unique constitutional task assigned to freedom of religion.

Constitutions offer themselves as normative frameworks for our political and legal lives. This is the character of the project of modern constitutionalism and, in the hands of some, a description of the constitutional rule of law. Religion, for its part, serves as a normative frame for the lives of individuals and communities, shaping meaning, belonging, conduct, and identity. Freedom of religion is the modern constitutional meeting place of these normative and cultural frameworks; it is tasked with reconcil-ing the salience and importance of both. But in its efforts to do so, the law of freedom of religion must adopt a particular vision of religion and its relationship to the political— an approach to and conception of its subject that will make religion digestible within the constitutional order.[10] And yet religion as experienced and lived by individuals and communities will always overflow the constitutional categories and assumptions used to attempt to manage it legally. Religion is never just what law imagines it to be, or wishes it were. In terms offered by Elizabeth Shakman Hurd in *Beyond Religious Freedom*, "lived religion" will always elude and exceed "governed religion."[11] In resist-ing those categories, assumptions, and commitments drawn from the logic of Canadian constitutionalism, it makes them visible. Through this friction, religion displays the tensions, paradoxes, and instabilities that bedevil that logic. The cases and controver-sies generated in the field of freedom of religion are thus uniquely adept at exposing the issues and dynamics that affect and afflict contemporary Canadian constitutional law more generally.

---

[10] I explore both the character of religion and constitutionalism as cultural forms, as well as the crucial role of law's definition or "rendering" of religion, in Benjamin L Berger, *Law's Religion: Religious Difference and the Claims of Constitutionalism* (University of Toronto Press, 2015).

[11] Elizabeth Shakman Hurd, *Beyond Religious Freedom: The New Global Politics of Religion* (Princeton University Press, 2015). See also Winnifred Fallers Sullivan, *The Impossibility of Religious Freedom* (Princeton University Press, 2005).

The next section of this chapter will offer a general overview of the Supreme Court of Canada's approach to analysing claims of religious freedom made under section 2(a) of the *Charter of Rights and Freedoms*, exploring how the Court has interpreted that right and how it has defined the religion that the right purports to make free. In the subsequent section, this chapter takes up some of the key themes that have emerged as central in the section 2(a) jurisprudence but that reflect broader issues within the structure and politics of Canadian constitutionalism: the instability of the public/private divide as a means of analysing constitutional problems, the tension between individual rights and regard for collective and community interests, and the paradoxes involved in the aspiration for state neutrality.

2. INTERPRETING RELIGIOUS FREEDOM
AND DEFINING RELIGION

As the history outlined at the start of this chapter shows, even before the introduction of a constitutional right protecting freedom of religion, religious liberty and equality was long a concern in Canadian constitutional life. Although some characterize this regard for religion as essentially pragmatic and the fruit of political compromise, this framing effaces the formative role of religion in shaping social and political life, a role that the Constitution reflected and honoured. Even without an explicit free exercise principle and, as the history shows, quite distant from any non-establishment principle such as that found in the United States, a concern with the constitutional status of religion has always been a part of the deep ethical structure of the Canadian Constitution. Indeed, in the half-century prior to the introduction of the *Charter of Rights and Freedoms*, the Supreme Court of Canada used principles of federalism, division of powers,[12] and the rule of law[13] to protect religious liberties, and in the process of so doing, the Court expressed the key role that religious freedom had played in the formation of the Canadian state. In *Saumur v City of Quebec*,[14] the Court invalidated a municipal bylaw that prohibited the distribution of pamphlets, books, and other literature without the consent of the Chief of Police, a measure aimed at limiting the proselytizing efforts of Jehovah's Witnesses. In holding that the provinces (and therefore municipalities) lacked authority to restrict religious freedom, Justice Rand drew (albeit selectively) from the history of religion in Canada to describe religious freedom as "a principle of fundamental character."[15] He explained, "although we have nothing in the nature of an established church, that the untrammelled affirmations of religious belief and its propagation,

---

[12] See, e.g., *Chaput v Romain* [1955] SCR 834.
[13] *Roncarelli v Duplesis* [1959] SCR 121.
[14] [1953] 2 SCR 299.
[15] ibid 327.

personal or institutional, remain as of the greatest constitutional significance through-out the Dominion is unquestionable."[16] Unlike civil rights, which "arise from positive law," freedom of religion was properly understood, along with freedom of speech, as one of the "original freedoms which are at once the necessary attributes and modes of self-expression of human beings and the primary conditions of their community life within a legal order."[17]

It was against this backdrop, and with the emergence of protections for religious free-dom and equality in human rights instruments over the second half of the twentieth century,[18] that the entrenchment of the *Canadian Charter of Rights and Freedoms* in 1982 introduced an explicit constitutional protection for religious freedom. Section 2 of the *Charter* states that "everyone has the following fundamental freedoms" and section 2(a) lists "freedom of conscience and religion." The Court would have to articulate the pur-pose and scope of this fundamental freedom, and that task first fell to it in a case that remains a touchstone in the jurisprudence, *R v Big M Drug Mart Ltd.*[19]

Big M involved a challenge to Sunday closing legislation, the Federal *Lord's Day Act*. Chief Justice Dickson, writing for the Court, reviewed the history discussed above. Importantly, he addressed the argument advanced by the government that the absence of a "non-establishment" clause similar to that found in the United States meant that leg-islation that advanced religious purposes would not contravene section 2(a). Although he conceded that there was no such principle in the Canadian Constitution, and that forms of government involvement in religion were, in fact, a part of Canada's constitu-tional history, he held that this did not dispose of the *Charter* issue. Chief Justice Dickson explained that the purpose of freedom of conscience and religion under the *Charter* was to ensure that "every individual be free to hold and to manifest whatever beliefs and opinions his or her conscience dictates, provided *inter alia* only that such manifestations do not injure his or her neighbours or their parallel rights to hold and manifest beliefs and opinions of their own."[20] "Religious belief and practice," he explained, "are histori-cally prototypical and, in many ways, paradigmatic of conscientiously-held beliefs and manifestations and are therefore protected by the *Charter*. Equally protected, and for the same reasons, are expressions and manifestations of religious non-belief and refusals to participate in religious practice."[21] In this respect, the Court's framing of religious free-dom involved a strong non-coercion principle reflective of a central concern for indi-vidual autonomy and choice. "The essence of the concept of freedom of religion," Chief Justice Dickson explained, "is the right to entertain such religious beliefs as a person chooses, the right to declare religious beliefs openly and without fear of hindrance or reprisal, and the right to manifest religious belief by worship and practice or by teaching

---

[16] ibid.
[17] ibid 329.
[18] See *Robertson and Rosetanni v R* [1963] SCR 651.
[19] [1985] 1 SCR 295.
[20] ibid 346.
[21] ibid 346–347.

and dissemination."[22] But the right also ensures that "subject to such limitations as are necessary to protect public safety, order, health, or morals or the fundamental rights and freedoms of others, no one is to be forced to act in a way contrary to his beliefs or his conscience."[23] The *Lord's Day Act* offended section 2(a) in part because it coerced individuals to behave in a fashion antithetical to their religious commitments.[24]

Yet there is another thread in the Court's reasons in *Big M*, one that runs parallel to this non-coercion principle. Chief Justice Dickson also explained that a free society seeks to "accommodate a wide variety of beliefs, diversity of tastes and pursuits, customs and codes of conduct" and "aims at equality with respect to the enjoyment of fundamental freedoms and I say this without any reliance upon s. 15 of the *Charter*."[25] Section 15 is the equality provision of the *Charter*, a provision that includes religion as a prohibited ground of discrimination. Chief Justice Dickson's care in not relying on section 15 is a consequence of the fact that this provision did not take force until three years after the other rights enumerated in the *Charter*. The decision in *Big M* injected an equality or non-discrimination principle into the basic purpose and logic of section 2(a); indeed, the Court held that one of the reasons that the *Lord's Day Act* offended section 2(a) is that "[t]he theological content of the legislation remain a subtle and constant reminder to religious minorities within the country of their differences with, and alienation from, the dominant religious culture."[26] This "communicative" effect—communicating a preference for one religion at the expense of another—sounds in the register of equal treatment rather than non-coercion.[27] The insertion of this equality principle into the heart of religious freedom is likely responsible for the virtual absence of religion cases decided under section 15 of the *Charter*. Whether the deep logic of religious freedom is respect for autonomy or equal protection is debated in the literature;[28] what is certainly true is that both are at work in the contemporary jurisprudence. As I will return to later, this conceptual tension—whether religious freedom is concerned with autonomy and coercion or equality and identity—haunts the area.

The Court's judgment in *Big M* seeded a set of other tensions or themes that would grow to be central in the jurisprudence. Reference to the scope of religious freedom

---

[22] ibid 336.

[23] ibid 337.

[24] Shortly after *Big M*, the Court upheld Sunday closing legislation with a less overt religious purpose in *R v Edwards Books* [1986] 2 SCR 713. Although the Court found that the legislation restricted the religious practice of those who did not observe a Sunday Sabbath, the limit was justified as reasonable and proportionate under s. 1.

[25] *Big M* above (n 19) 336.

[26] ibid 337.

[27] Mary Anne Waldron is highly critical of this line of reasoning from *Big M* and the early cases, which she considers having set the s. 2(a) jurisprudence "off on the wrong foot." See Mary Anne Waldron, *Free to Believe: Rethinking Freedom of Conscience and Religion in Canada* (University of Toronto Press, 2014) 22–53.

[28] See Bruce Ryder, 'The Canadian Conception of Equal Religious Citizenship' in Richard Moon (ed), *Law and Religious Pluralism in Canada* (UBC Press, 2008); Richard Moon, 'Government Support for Religious Practice' in Richard Moon (ed), *Law and Religious Pluralism in Canada* (UBC Press, 2008).

being subject to important public interests prefigures the crucial role that section 1 of the *Charter*—the limit-justifying provision of the *Charter*—would come to play in this area. Mention of limits to religious freedom based on the rights and freedom of others anticipates the central place that conflicts of rights would play in the jurisprudence in Canada. And the Court's nod to non-belief and freedom *from* religion anticipates the conundrums involved in the aspiration to state neutrality, discussed below.

In the first 15 years following *Big M*, cases raising questions of religious freedom were relatively episodic and, in comparison with other rights in this early phase in the life of the *Charter,* sparse, with no unified or structural approach to analysing claims under section 2(a).[29] The cases in this period addressed a range of questions, including the religious rights of parents with respect to their children,[30] issues surrounding public and religious education,[31] and the permissibility of public prayer in various settings.[32]

The analytic approach to section 2(a) took its modern form in *Syndicat Northcrest v Amselem*.[33] *Amselem* involved a dispute between Jewish residents of a condominium and the condominium association regarding whether religious freedom under the provincial human rights statute allowed the Jewish residents to construct a succah on their balconies during the festival of Succoth, despite condominium rules that prohibited alterations to the exterior of the building. The condominium association was prepared to allow a common succah on the grounds, but religious authorities were divided on whether Jewish law required a personal succah. In ruling that the prohibition was an improper interference with freedom of religion, Justice Iacobucci, writing for a majority of the Court, made two moves crucial to understanding Canada's approach to freedom of religion.

Recall my claim in the introduction to this chapter that the legal governance of religion will always depend on a conception of its subject. In *Amselem*, Justice Iacobucci stated that "[i]n order to define religious freedom, we must first ask ourselves what we mean by 'religion.'"[34] And what was the Court's definition?

> Defined broadly, religion typically involves a particular and comprehensive system of faith and worship. Religion also tends to involve the belief in a divine, superhuman or controlling power. In essence, religion is about freely and deeply held personal convictions or beliefs connected to an individual's spiritual faith and integrally linked to one's self-definition and spiritual fulfilment, the practices of which allow

---

[29] For description and analysis of these cases, see Richard Moon, *Freedom of Conscience and Religion* (Irwin Law, 2014).

[30] *RB v Children's Aid Society of Metropolitan Toronto* [1995] 1 SCR 315; *Young v Young* [1993] 4 SCR 3.

[31] *Adler* above (n 7); *R v Jones* [1986] 1 SCR 103.

[32] *Zylberberg v Sudbury Board of Education* (1988) 52 DLR 4th 577 (Ont CA); *Freitag v Penetanguishene* (1999) 47 3d 301 (Ont CA).

[33] 2004 SCC 47. Although the claim in *Amselem* was brought under the Quebec *Charter of Human Rights and Freedoms*, the Court held that the principles it would enunciate would equally guide claims under the Canadian *Charter*.

[34] ibid [39].

individuals to foster a connection with the divine or with the subject or object of that spiritual faith.[35]

Religion is notoriously difficult to define and, as I suggest in this chapter, the unruliness of the category of "religion" is one of the elements that makes its constitutional regulation so revealing. The Court's conception of religion reflected in this passage has a number of notable features: although it mentions religious practice, it is highly propositional and interior, emphasizing religion as rooted in beliefs and convictions; in emphasizing belief, it centralizes choice and autonomy; and this definition emphasizes the individual as the entity of principal salience in religion. Some scholars have referred to this understanding of religion as "protestant" in character.[36] As the jurisprudence develops in the years after *Amselem*, it is this understanding of what we might call "constitutional religion" that religion-as-lived overflows and resists, exposing the deep themes and tensions that I will examine in the latter part of this chapter.

In *Amselem*, this definition of religion fed the Court's second key move, which was to articulate an analytical approach to assessing claims made under section 2(a). Based on this definition, and drawing from Chief Justice Dickson's reasons in *Big M*, Justice Iacobucci explained that freedom of religion "revolves around the notion of personal choice and individual autonomy and freedom"[37] and that the analytical emphasis should be "on personal choice of religious beliefs."[38] This was important in *Amselem* because it bore on the crucial question of whether one's claim that one's religious freedom has been engaged should be tested against the views of the religious community or experts—in this case, whether the views of the Rabbis should dictate whether a personal succah was required by Judaism—or whether the test should be subjective, turning on the sincerely held views of the claimant him- or herself. In the face of dissenting opinions that would have required objective validation of a claimant's assertion that a religious belief or practice is at stake, the majority of the Court adopted a subjective sincerity test. Justice Iacobucci based this conclusion on the conception of religious freedom as "integrally linked with an individual's self-definition and fulfilment"[39] and his view that "the State is in no position to be, nor should it become, the arbiter of religious dogma."[40] He explained that any non-trivial interference by the state in a belief or practice sincerely held by the claimant to be religious in nature will offend section 2(a).[41] As the Court would later summarize the test: "in order to establish that his or

---

[35] ibid.
[36] See Sullivan above (n 11); Berger, *Law's Religion* above (n 10) 100–101.
[37] *Amselem* above (n 33) [40].
[38] ibid [43].
[39] ibid [42].
[40] ibid [50].
[41] Moreover, the Court emphasized that "[r]eligious beliefs, by their very nature, are fluid and rarely static" and so "it is it is inappropriate for courts rigorously to study and focus on the past practices of claimants in order to determine whether their current beliefs are sincerely held." ibid [53].

her freedom of religion has been infringed, the claimant must demonstrate (1) that he or she sincerely believes in a practice or belief that has a nexus with religion, and (2) that the impugned conduct of a third party interferes, in a manner that is non-trivial or not insubstantial, with his or her ability to act in accordance with that practice or belief."[42]

This analytical approach to section 2(a) is so capacious as to leave it almost analytically vacant. The Court has subsequently emphasized that the second part of the analysis—determining whether there is a non-trivial interference in the sincerely held belief or practice—is objective in nature.[43] But the result of this avowedly "broad and expansive approach to religious freedom"[44] is to push most issues of religious freedom in Canada to some form of a proportionality analysis to assess whether the limit on or interference with section 2(a) interests—so easily established—is justifiable. When the interference with section 2(a) flows from a law, that proportionality analysis will take place under section 1, the great "saving" provision of the *Charter* that permits the justification of "such reasonable limits prescribed by law as can be demonstrably justified in a free and democratic society."[45] When the interference with section 2(a) flows from actions or decisions made by other state actors, the prevailing approach to addressing *Charter* interests in administrative law holds that the decision-maker "is required to proportionately balance the *Charter* protections to ensure that they are limited no more than is necessary given the applicable statutory objectives that she or he is obliged to pursue."[46] In either case, freedom of religion is finally governed by the central logic of modern Canadian constitutionalism: proportionality.

"Proportionality," Paul Kahn has written, "is nothing more than the contemporary expression of reasonableness."[47] What does it mean to constitutionally govern religion with a metric of reasonableness? The perceived reasonableness of a limit on religious freedom will turn on legal ideas about the nature of religion, of the relationship between the personal and the political, and of the normative character of the modern "secular" state, each in turn inspired by deeper constitutional assumptions about personal, social, and political life. It is these assumptions and categories that the experience of lived religion will always challenge and resist. And it is for this reason that the study of religious freedom reveals so much of thematic interest to constitutionalism at large.

---

[42] *Multani v Commission scolaire Marguerite-Bourgeoys* 2006 SCC 6, [34].

[43] *SL v Commission scolaire des Chênes* 2012 SCC 7, [49]. For a discussion of this "non-triviality" requirement, see Howard Kislowicz, '*Loyola High School v Attorney General of Quebec*: On Non-Triviality and the Charter Value of Religious Freedom' (2015) 71 Sup Ct L Rev (2d) 331.

[44] *Amselem* above (n 33) [62].

[45] For an example to which I will return below, see *Alberta v Hutterian Brethren of Wilson Colony* 2009 SCC 37.

[46] *Loyola High School v Quebec (Attorney General)* 2015 SCC 12, [4]. This approach to analysing rights in administrative law settings using "*Charter* values" was established in *Doré v Barreau du Québec* 2012 SCC 12. For a discussion of "*Charter* values" and religious freedom, see Kislowicz above (n 43).

[47] Paul W Kahn, 'Comparative Constitutionalism in a New Key' (2003) 101 Mich L Rev 2677, 2698.

3. CONSTITUTIONAL THEMES IN FREEDOM OF RELIGION

A. The Instability of the Public/Private Divide

A crucial organizing idea in the logic of modern Canadian constitutionalism is the distinction between the private and the public. Commitment to this division as a means of arranging the social world for the purposes of constitutional analysis is found in central features of constitutional law. The doctrine of applicability, arising from section 32(1) of the *Charter*, means that the *Charter* binds only government actions and decision-making, leaving the realm of private power and social ordering to regulation through other mechanisms.[48] One also sees this commitment to the analytic utility and importance of this public/private divide expressed through the juridical deployment and potency of concepts of choice: to describe an experience, arrangement, or condition as a product of "choice" is to assign it, as a constitutional matter, to the realm of the private and, hence, to exempt it from constitutional analysis.[49]

Key to feminist and critical insights about the limits of *Charter* adjudication has been challenging the cogency of this distinction and exposing its political effects. Critical legal scholars have pointed to the forms of social and political injustice that are left untouched by virtue of doctrines of applicability.[50] Feminist scholars have explored the ways in which liberal constitutional ideas about choice fail to take seriously the way in which public ordering conditions private choice, showing the instability of this division that has so often frustrated an equality-seeking conception of the *Charter*.[51]

For reasons that flow from the gap between lived religion and law's religion, freedom of religion has emerged in recent years as a singularly potent site for challenging and destabilizing the public/private divide as a means of organizing constitutional law and analysis. It is, of course, a trope in liberal political theory that religion is best contained within the private sphere. This is the heart, for example, of Rawls's idea of a division between public reason and comprehensive doctrines.[52] Religion is properly a matter of personal belief and preference—at least that is the vision that makes religion most liberally tame and digestible. Religion is thus managed by assigning it to the private; its public dimensions become problematic. In Canadian constitutional law, this assignation is

---

[48] These include other non-constitutional legal and informal mechanisms, and, of course, the market. See Gavin W Anderson, 'Social Democracy and the Limits of Rights Constitutionalism' (2004) 17 CJLJ 31.

[49] See Patricia Hughes, 'The Intersection of Public and Private under the Charter' 52 UNBLJ 201. See also *Nova Scotia (Attorney General) v Walsh* 2002 SCC 83.

[50] See Anderson above (n 48).

[51] See Hughes above (n 49); Rebecca Johnson, *Taxing Choices* (UBC Press, 2002).

[52] John Rawls, *Political Liberalism* (2nd edn, Columbia University Press, 2005).

achieved through a particular description of religion and, in consequence, the adoption of certain categories as natural to analysing religion.

Think back to the account of the nature of religious freedom in *Big M* and the definition of religion offered in *Amselem*. The focus on autonomy, interiority, belief, and sincerity in those cases reflects this assignation of religion to the private realm. Despite the threads of identity/equality-based reasoning, the priority given to conceptions of choice and autonomy in the Court's understanding of religion participates in that privatizing function of "choice" discussed earlier.[53] Indeed, the characterization of religious belonging as a dimension of choice has served precisely to allow the Court to treat the effects of limitations on religious freedom as consequences of private decisions—not matters of constitutional concern—rather than the outcomes of public policy. *Alberta v Hutterian Brethren of Wilson Colony*[54] involved legislation that imposed a requirement for photographs on driver's licenses, contrary to the religious convictions of a small Hutterite community. Accepting that the legislation limited the community's religious freedom under section 2(a), the majority of the Court held that the justifiability of such a limit turns on whether it "leaves the adherent with a meaningful choice to follow his or her religious beliefs and practices."[55] Although not being able to drive would impose costs, disruption, and inconvenience on the community, these were all results of the choice exercised by the religious adherents.

Or consider the common legal and political habit of understanding religion in terms of belief rather than conduct, apparent in the definition offered in *Amselem*. This is another way that law shifts religion into a private register. The appeal of this approach was evident in the *TWU*[56] case, which considered whether the BC College of Teachers was entitled to deny certification to a private religious school's teachers training program on the basis that the school required students to sign a discriminatory code of conduct that prohibited "homosexual behaviour." In concluding that the BCCT had overreached in its decision, the Court held that the apparent conflict between equality and religious freedom would be avoided by drawing the line "between belief and conduct."[57] For the Court, signing the code was a reflection of religion as belief; it was, hence, essentially private and therefore solidly within the scope of constitutional protection.

And yet, however neatly and comfortably the deployment of such categories and understandings of religion serves to map religion within the logic of liberal constitutionalism, the lived character of religion consistently overflows and resists them. When religion is understood as a normative frame for one's life, the division between conduct and belief becomes unstable: not only does conduct "manifest" belief but, as critical religious studies scholarship shows, beliefs are often themselves shaped and constituted by

---

[53] On Canadian constitutional law's understanding of religion as primarily a matter of autonomy and choice, see Berger, *Law's Religion* above (n 10) 78–91.

[54] *Wilson Colony* above (n 45).

[55] ibid [88].

[56] *Trinity Western University v British Columbia College of Teachers* 2001 SCC 31.

[57] ibid [36].

practices.[58] Religion is not just, or even principally, experienced as chosen; and when it is seen as an aspect of identity, the fair treatment of religion has far-reaching constitutional implications that follow from a commitment to inclusion and equality. The use of a public/private divide to describe the political and social world ultimately depends on the insistence on such a division *within* the individual, sometimes with agonizing consequences. And so when same-sex marriage became legal in Canada and the question was raised as to whether a public marriage commissioner who objected on religious grounds to performing same-sex marriage should be accommodated, the analytical utility of the public/private divide for constitutionally digesting religion was placed under enormous stress.[59] The instability of a private conception of religion was nakedly displayed, the consequence being a fierce debate about the constitutional treatment of religion.[60]

A range of Canadian cases display the way in which the character of religion grates on its assignation to the private domains of social life.[61] Shaping conduct, affecting relationships, and informing political action, religion is insistent in pointing to the porousness of the boundary line between the private and public. The Court has itself gestured to this problem in its jurisprudence: "Religion is an integral aspect of people's lives, and cannot be left at the boardroom door."[62] Religion is far from alone in troubling this divide, but its structural capacity to overflow those containers makes the study of freedom of religion a tremendous critical resource for testing the cogency, stability, and justness of the public/private divide as a tool in the constitutional regulation of the social world.

B. The Individual and the Collective

Canadian constitutionalism is characterized, in part, by a structural tension between a deep regard for political and cultural collectivities and an emphasis or priority given to individual rights and liberties. This tension is one of the outgrowths of the "two logics" that shape Canadian constitutional life, one reflecting the "ancient" sense of constitutions as a political project of binding particular communities together into a common political life, and the other participating in the modern universal logic of rights protection.[63]

One finds a range of Canadian constitutional features that reflect a serious concern with the group and with the particularities of the political relationships between

---

[58]   See Mayanthi Fernando, 'Reconfiguring Freedom: Muslim Piety and the Limits of Secular Law and Public Discourse in France' (2010) 37 American Ethnologist 19.

[59]   *Re Marriage Commissioners Appointed under the Marriage Act* 2011 SKCA 3.

[60]   See, e.g., Ryder above (n 28); Richard Moon, 'Conscientious Objections by Civil Servants: The Case of Marriage Commissioners and Same-Sex Civil Marriages' in Benjamin L Berger and Richard Moon (eds), *Religion and the Exercise of Public Authority* (Hart Publishing, 2016).

[61]   See Berger, *Law's Religion* above (n 10) 91–98.

[62]   *Chamberlain v Surrey School District No 36* 2002 SCC 86, [19].

[63]   Benjamin L Berger, 'Children of Two Logics: A Way into Canadian Constitutional Culture' (2013) 11 ICON 319.

communities. The history of protections afforded to the French-speaking community outlined earlier in this chapter is, of course one such feature, one that led to the education provisions of the 1867 Constitution. Canadian federalism is itself an outgrowth of this history and a reflection of this constitutional regard for communities. Language rights and the constitutional protection of Aboriginal rights through sections 25 and 35 of the *Constitution Act, 1982* are also distinctive Canadian markers of the constitutional salience of the group.

And yet in 1982 the *Charter* introduced a frame of liberal rights constitutionalism that sees the individual far more clearly than the group. Since its early days, this has been a critique levelled about the political effects and limits of the *Charter*: that, by virtue of its informing liberal political ideology, it atomizes and pixelates human experience by prioritizing the individual as the primary unit of constitutional analysis.[64] The jurisprudence under the section 15 equality guarantee has tended to extract the individual from her meaningful group context, and equality claims with strong group dimensions have failed under *Charter* analysis.[65] Read in light of the near-sacred status of public health care in Canadian political life, *Chaoulli*[66]—a case in which a wealthy doctor successfully challenged legislative restrictions on private health insurance that were designed to protect a public health care system—is an emblem of the extent to which the dedicated individualism of *Charter* rights obscures the collective dimensions of public policy. Even when dealing with rights that would seem to have clear collective dimensions, such as freedom of association, the Court has struggled to give deep regard to these group elements within the frame of *Charter* analysis.[67]

Freedom of religion has become a microcosm of this abiding constitutional tension between the venerable state interest in the liberty and autonomy of the individual and due recognition that these individual lives are socially embedded and take place within communities. The constitutional protection of group-based religious education rights persists and there have always been notes of regard for the collective aspect of religion in the *Charter* jurisprudence. And yet a heavy priority on the individual has characterized much of the case law. One sees this in *Big M*, in which Chief Justice Dickson describes the core of freedom of religion as "the right of every Canadian to work out for himself or herself what his or her religious obligations, if any, should be".[68] It is also evident in the way in which the Court defines religion in *Amselem*, emphasizing the

---

[64] See, e.g., Joel Bakan, *Just Words: Constitutional Rights and Social Wrongs* (University of Toronto Press, 1997).

[65] See, e.g., *Newfoundland (Treasury Board) v NAPE* 2004 SCC 66.

[66] *Chaoulli v Quebec (AG)* 2005 SCC 35.

[67] The Court has showed an increased appetite to attend to these collective dimensions of freedom of association by recognizing a right to strike and to "meaningful collective bargaining" in *Saskatchewan Federation of Labour v Saskatchewan* 2015 SCC 4; *Mounted Police Association of Ontario v Canada (AG)* 2015 SCC 1. For an insightful treatment of the constitutional protection of collective rights see Dwight Newman, *Community and Collective Rights: A Theoretical Framework for Rights Held by Groups* (Hart Publishing, 2011).

[68] *Big M* above (n 19) 351.

internal, individual, and "believed" dimensions of religion. But it is the Court's choice in *Amselem* to adopt a subjective sincerity test under section 2(a) that is the most telling marker of this individualism. When deciding whether a belief or practice is part of "religion," the choice to defer to the subjective views of the claimant, rather than turning to text, tradition, or the views of religious officials, aligns the right with—and empowers—the individual, rather than the group.

A series of cases under section 2(a) bear the imprint of this individualism,[69] but the high-water mark came with the *Wilson Colony* decision, discussed above, involving the photograph requirement on driver's licenses.[70] Although she acknowledged a "collective aspect" of religion, Chief Justice McLachlin, writing for the majority, framed the "essential claim" as individual in nature and assessed the impacts on the community as incidental costs associated with this universal photo requirement.[71] Because individuals were still able to make a meaningful choice to practice their religion, the limit could be justified. By contrast, in her dissenting judgment Justice Abella emphasized the collective dimensions of the claim for an exemption, explaining the way in which the community's self-sufficiency and autonomy was central to the nature of the religious freedom claim. Taking seriously the impact of not having driver's licenses on the collective religious life of the community meant that the limitation on religious freedom was disproportionate and unjustifiable.

As *Wilson Colony* and the critiques that followed it showed, too much about the character of religion and religious life is obscured by a narrow focus on the individual.[72] Eventually the irrepressible fact of the collective dimensions of lived religion expressed itself in the Court's section 2(a) jurisprudence. Perhaps unsurprisingly, given the history, it did so in a case concerning religion and education. *Loyola High School v Quebec (Attorney General)*[73] is the Court's most ambitious attempt to acknowledge the collective aspects of religion within the section 2(a) analysis. The case concerned a mandatory religious education curriculum in Quebec that required teachers to adopt a "neutral and objective perspective" when teaching the beliefs and ethics of world religions. Loyola High School, a private Catholic school founded in 1840, objected to this neutrality requirement, specifically claiming that requiring a Catholic school to teach about Catholicism and the ethics of other traditions in a "neutral way" impaired its religious freedom. Collecting the jurisprudential threads acknowledging the collective aspects of religion, Justice Abella, writing for the majority, explained that "[r]eligious freedom under the *Charter* must . . . account for the social embedded nature of religious

---

[69] See Berger, *Law's Religion* above (n 10) 66–78.

[70] *Wilson Colony* above (n 45).

[71] ibid [31].

[72] See, e.g., Benjamin L Berger, 'Section 1, Constitutional Reasoning, and Cultural Difference: Assessing the Impacts of *Alberta v Hutterian Brethren of Wilson Colony*' (2010) 51 Sup Ct L Rev (2d) 25; Richard Moon, 'Accommodation without Compromise: Comment on *Alberta v Hutterian Brethren of Wilson Colony*' (2010) 51 Sup Ct L Rev (2d) 95; Sara Weinrib, 'An Exemption for Sincere Believers: The Challenge of *Alberta v Hutterian Brethren of Wilson Colony*' (2011) 56 McGill LJ 729.

[73] *Loyola* above (n 46).

belief, and the deep linkages between this belief and its manifestation through communal institutions and traditions."[74] Although she concluded that a requirement to teach other traditions from as objective a posture as possible did not offend religious freedom, requiring a "neutral" presentation of Catholicism was another matter: "[t]o tell a Catholic school how to explain its faith undermines the liberty of the members of its community who have chosen to give effect to the collective dimension of their religious beliefs by participating in a denominational school."[75] In granting a footing within section 2(a) for the intergenerational project of transmitting religion, *Loyola* is thus a jurisprudential reclamation of some of the collective aspects of religion.[76] And yet the larger tension remains: in the Court's rendering, the nature and value of these collective dimensions seem indexed to the individual, with these collective aspects understood as "manifestations" of individual religious beliefs and the interests of members. This tension will remain an important axis of development in freedom of religion in Canada, developments that will no doubt be informed by what we see as other countries explore the implications of the granting of collective and corporate religious rights.[77]

Even when framed by a priority on the individual, religion cannot really be analysed or understood without regard for the communities in which it is lived and that sustain it over time. Perhaps this aspect of the phenomenology of religion—that it is highly personal but also fundamentally relational and generational—is what makes it so well fitted to exposing the dialectic between the individual and the collective that is an architectural feature of modern Canadian constitutionalism. As religion exceeds the individualist analytic gaze so natural to liberal rights constitutionalism, we are reminded of that older constitutional logic that puts a concern for communities at the heart of the constitutional project. We are also reminded that groups can be sites of repression and discrimination. The study of religious freedom can thus encourage us to see the collective, and its complicated role in constitutional justice, more clearly.

C. Neutrality and the Normative Character of the Liberal State

In its claims for authority, liberal constitutionalism relies on a powerful myth of its autonomy from culture, from the influence of local history, and from larger claims about the good life. This is one aspect of presenting rights constitutionalism as an essentially universalist enterprise, founded in reason rather than politics and particularity; it works

---

[74] ibid [60].

[75] ibid [62].

[76] Chief Justice McLachlin and Justice Moldaver would have gone further by recognizing that religious organizations themselves could enjoy religious freedom under s. 2(a), a step that the majority demurred from taking in this case.

[77] See, e.g., *Hosanna-Tabor v EEOC*, 132 S Ct 694 (2012); *Burwell v Hobby Lobby Stores, Inc.*, 134 S Ct 2751 (2014).

by depoliticizing law's rule sufficiently to attract broad assent,[78] working on the assumption that, if sufficiently arid, law and legal reason could be an environment hospitable to all. So presented, law and legality offer themselves as a meeting ground amidst normative and cultural difference[79]—a particularly seductive offer in a highly multicultural setting.

One of the most potent instances of the capacity of the field of freedom of religion to reveal deep and general themes in Canadian constitutional law has arisen from religion's ability to expose and draw critical attention to the cultural nature of the project of liberal constitutionalism, repoliticizing it by highlighting its normative and historical character. This function has come into focus as the concept of state neutrality in matters of religion has settled in as the governing ideal in the constitutional management of religion. Although the demand for state neutrality has been interpreted and applied differently across constitutional orders, this is a transnational phenomenon.[80] As the Supreme Court of Canada has observed, "[r]eligious neutrality is now seen by many Western states as a legitimate means of creating a free space in which citizens of various beliefs can exercise their individual rights."[81] The seeds of this focus on state neutrality in Canada can be found in the Court's description of the purpose of religious freedom in *Big M*, but the early freedom of religion jurisprudence tended to focus on notions of toleration. Recent years have seen the ascendancy of the concept of state neutrality, arguably eclipsing notions of toleration.[82]

The Court's most elaborated articulation of this principle of state neutrality came in *Mouvement laïque québécois v Saguenay (City)*,[83] a case in which an organization seeking the "complete secularization of the state in Quebec"[84] challenged a local practice of opening municipal council meetings with a discernibly Christian prayer.[85] The Court found that the practice breached the state's duty of neutrality in religious matters, which, though not explicitly imposed by the *Charter*, "has become a necessary consequence of enshrining the freedom of conscience and religion".[86] Justice Gascon explained that "[t]he state is required to act in a manner that is respectful of every person's freedom

---

[78] See Courtney Bender and Pamela E Klassen (eds), *After Pluralism: Reimagining Religious Engagement* (Columbia University Press, 2010); Wendy Brown, *Regulating Aversion: Tolerance in the Age of Identity and Empire* (Princeton University Press, 2006).

[79] See Jean Comaroff and John Comaroff, *Theory from the South: Or, How Euro-America Is Evolving toward Africa* (Paradigm Publishers, 2012) 145.

[80] See, e.g. *Leyla Sahin v Turkey* ECHR 2005-XI 819, 44 EHRR 5; *Lautsi and Others v Italy* ECHR 2011-III 2412, 54 EHRR 3; *Dahlab v Switzerland* ECHR 2001-V 449.

[81] *SL* above (n 43) [10].

[82] See Benjamin L Berger, 'Religious Diversity, Education, and the "Crisis" in State Neutrality' (2014) 29 Can JL & Society 103; Richard Moon, 'Liberty, Neutrality, and Inclusion: Freedom of Religion under the Canadian Charter of Rights' (2003) 41 Brandeis L Rev 563.

[83] 2015 SCC 16.

[84] ibid [9].

[85] It is an interesting comparative constitutional exercise to compare *Saguenay* with the roughly contemporaneous U.S. municipal prayer case *Town of Greece v Galloway*, 134 S Ct 1811 (2014).

[86] *Saguenay* above (n 83) [76].

of conscience and religion" and that the "corollary is that the state must remain neutral in matters involving this freedom."[87] Picking up a thread first introduced in *Big M*, the Court held that for the purposes of freedom of religion, "the concepts of 'belief' and 'religion' encompass non-belief, atheism and agnosticism."[88] Building upon past jurisprudence,[89] the Court articulated this duty of state neutrality as requiring "that the state neither favour nor hinder any particular belief, and the same holds true for non-belief. . . . It requires that the state abstain from taking any position and thus avoid adhering to a particular belief."[90] Because the prayer in question "resulted in a distinction, exclusion and preference based on religion,"[91] it breached the duty of state neutrality.

The appeal of a duty or principle of state neutrality as the governing ideal for the management of religious difference is clear: as I explain elsewhere, "[i]t rhetorically positions law outside the 'us' and 'them' of political conflict; it casts law in the role of disinterested conciliator rather than boundary-setter; and its invocation relieves the legal system of the burden of its own cultural and historical contingency."[92] The duty of state neutrality reflects some important principles and aspirations regarding even-handedness and equality as between individuals and groups irrespective of religious belief.[93] Yet the ambition for depoliticization through adherence to this standard of state neutrality— that it will extract law from history and politics in matters of religion—is consistently and necessarily frustrated, collapsing in ways that gesture evocatively to the character of the constitutional project more generally.

Cases about prayer and historical symbols show one way in which this frustration occurs. Be it the crucifix that generated the *Lautsi* controversy,[94] reference to the "supremacy of God" in the preamble of the *Constitution Act, 1982*,[95] or legislative prayer,

---

[87] ibid [1].

[88] ibid [70].

[89] *SL* above (n 43); *Congrégation des témoins de Jéhovah de St-Jérôme-Lafontaine v Lafontaine (Village)* 2004 SCC 48.

[90] *Saguenay* above (n 83) [72]. In his dissenting opinion in *Lafontaine* (n 89) on which the Court in *Saguenay* relied heavily, Justice LeBel reasoned that the duty of neutrality also requires that the state "avoid placing unnecessary obstacles in the way of the exercise of religious freedoms" [71].

[91] *Saguenay* above (n 83) [120].

[92] Berger, 'Religious Diversity, Education' above (n 82) 119.

[93] For a review of a variety of justifications for a principle of state neutrality in matters of religion, see Moon, *Freedom of Conscience and Religion* above (n 29) 19–24.

[94] *Lautsi* above (n 80).

[95] For an account of the history leading to the inclusion of this reference in the preamble, see George Egerton, 'Trudeau, God, and the Canadian Constitution: Religion, Human Rights, and Government in the Making of the 1982 Constitution' in David Lyon and Marguerite Van Die (eds), *Rethinking Church, State, and Modernity: Canada between Europe and America* (University of Toronto Press, 2000). See also Lorne Sossin, 'The "Supremacy of God", Human Dignity and the Charter of Rights and Freedoms' (2003) 52 UNBLJ 227. In *Saguenay* above (n 83), and endorsing Sossin's interpretation of this clause, the Court stated that "[t]he preamble, including its reference to God, articulates the 'political theory' on which the *Charter*'s protections are based" [147], explaining that it "does not limit the scope of freedom of conscience and religion and does not have the effect of granting a privileged status to theistic religious practices" [149].

the political institutions and constitutions of the modern state are thick with the deposits of their religious histories. However, in *Saguenay*, Justice Gascon made clear that "the state's duty of neutrality does not require it to abstain from celebrating and preserving its religious heritage."[96] Translating these artefacts of the state's relationship with particular religions into matters of heritage and culture legally insulates them from the demands of state neutrality, but their presence and preservation is a reminder that the liberal state and its constitution are more religiously particular and historically conditioned than the language of "state neutrality" seeks to communicate.

But a clear-eyed reflection on the character of religion itself unsettles and frustrates the ideal of state neutrality in a more foundational way. For all of its virtues, the cogency of a duty of state neutrality floats on a naïve confidence in the divisibility of "matters involving" religion and those of a civic nature.[97] No such neat distinction can be drawn. If one understands religion as a normative and cultural system that produces claims about ethics, has implications for conduct, and advances a vision of a good society, religion will have much to say about matters of broad public policy import. The state's inescapable adoption of positions on such matters will thus involve position-taking on matters of deep religious interest. We have seen this in Canada as it relates to questions of abortion, same-sex marriage, doctor-assisted dying, and civic education, to name just a few, issues on which the adoption of a constitutional position is experienced by some communities as position-taking on matters of religion. The point is not that more work must be done to get the approach to state neutrality "right." It is that state neutrality, understood as abstention on position-taking, is dependent on a legal view of the nature of religion that fails and, in failing, consigns the legal demand for state neutrality to inconsistency and paradox. Faced with this reality, the Court has conceded what it must: that "the state always has a legitimate interest in promoting and protecting" values such as equality, human rights and democracy.[98] But, of course, each of these values and controversies is a ground for interpretation, debate, and contestation about which religion might have much to say. Whatever state neutrality may mean, it does not mean that the state must be neutral about the nature of a good society.[99]

What begins, then, as troubling the ideal of state neutrality as an adequate response to the deeper dynamics involved in the relationship between law and religion becomes a way into something of broader thematic import. The conundrums of pursuing state neutrality in matters of religion end up disclosing the particular and normative character of liberal constitutionalism and the state that it constitutes. The protection of freedom of religion becomes an important site of reflection for the larger critical enterprise of challenging the conceit of law's neutrality and autonomy from culture. Again, religion

---

[96] *Saguenay* above (n 83) [116].

[97] Richard Moon and Benjamin L Berger, 'Introduction: Religious Neutrality and the Exercise of Public Authority' in Benjamin L Berger and Richard Moon (eds), *Religion and the Exercise of Public Authority* (Hart Publishing, 2016) 6.

[98] *Loyola* above (n 46) [47].

[99] Berger, 'Religious Diversity, Education' above (n 82).

is not alone in being able to show this truth—from their own distinctive perspective, scholars of Indigenous law and Aboriginal justice have pointed to this fact about the Canadian constitutional project[100]—but it is a resource well fitted to exposing ways in which, as Charles Taylor put it years ago, "liberalism is also a fighting creed."[101]

4. CONCLUSION

As this chapter has shown, the conceptual containers and techniques drawn from the logic of modern liberal constitutionalism to legally govern religion inevitably come up short when met with religion as actually lived and experienced. Otherwise put, the social and political character of religion exceeds law's efforts to make religion manageable as a subject of constitutional regulation. It is this surplus that makes the study of religious freedom such a rich resource for reflection on the nature and politics of constitutional law—indeed, on the character of modern law. As the jurisprudence has shown, the specific ways in which these constitutional categories fall short in the field of freedom of religion highlights themes and patterns endemic to contemporary Canadian constitutional life. Religion resists the public/private divide, it lays bare the constitutional tension between the individual and the collective, and it upsets concepts of state (and legal) neutrality. With this, freedom of religion serves as a window into deeper and more general constitutional dynamics.

However, freedom of religion in Canada is haunted by a basic conceptual uncertainty. We remain fundamentally unresolved about what it is about religion, if anything, that calls for specific constitutional protection. The jurisprudence and scholarship is afflicted by ambivalence, framing freedom of religion as centrally designed to protect autonomy and choice, while at other moments evincing a sense that equality and inclusion are what drive the right. Either of these accounts generates a difficult question: If these are the essential interests, could religious freedom not be folded into robust protections for equality and liberty, thereby steering clear of the paradoxes and conundrums incumbent on the state involving itself in the definition of religion?[102] Perhaps, then, the protection

[100] See, e.g., John Borrows, *Freedom and Indigenous Constitutionalism* (University of Toronto Press, 2016); John Borrows, *Canada's Indigenous Constitution* (University of Toronto Press, 2010); Michael Asch, *On Being Here to Stay: Treaties and Aboriginal Rights in Canada* (University of Toronto Press, 2014); Andrée Boisselle, 'Beyond Consent and Disagreement: Why Law's Authority Is Not Just about Will' in Jeremy Webber and Colin M Macleod (eds), *Between Consenting Peoples: Political Community and the Meaning of Consent* (UBC Press, 2010).

[101] Charles Taylor, 'The Politics of Recognition', *Philosophical Arguments* (Harvard University Press, 1995) 249.

[102] See Christopher L Eisgruber and Lawrence G Sager, *Religious Freedom and the Constitution* (Harvard University Press, 2007); Sullivan above (n 11).

is not so generic, instead marking a positive societal valuation of religion itself.[103] The question then becomes: What is it about this particular aspect of the social world that attracts constitutional regard and care?

This underlying uncertainty has significant consequences for the *Charter* protection of religion. It troubles the defining feature of Canadian rights constitutionalism, proportionality reasoning, and its central role in freedom of religion: without a firm sense of the social and constitutional good marked by this right, it is unclear how one can engage in the principled balancing of competing interests required by proportionality analysis. The response to this uncertainty is also pivotal to the development of emerging issues in this area, such as the status of various forms of corporate and collective religious entities and interests, and the conceptual and practical relationship between Indigenous justice and freedom of religion. The 2013–2014 controversy involving the unsuccessful proposal for a "*Charter* of Secularism" in Quebec suggests that this uncertainty is also at work in debates about the meaning and implications of "secularism" as a description of the modern relationship among law, politics, and religion, a conversation that tends to conceal more than it illuminates.[104] In short, as the politics of religious difference continue to be a central feature of contemporary public life, reckoning with this underlying uncertainty within freedom of religion will take on both urgency and complexity.

Bibliography

Secondary Sources

Beaman LG and Sullivan WF (eds), *Varieties of Religious Establishment* (Routledge 2013)

Bender C and Klassen PE (eds), *After Pluralism: Reimagining Religious Engagement* (Columbia University Press 2010)

Berger BL, 'Religious Diversity, Education, and the "Crisis" in State Neutrality' (2014) 29 Canadian Journal of Law and Society 103

_____. 'Belonging to Law Religious Difference, Secularism, and the Conditions of Civic Inclusion' (2015) 24 Social and Legal Studies 47

_____. *Law's Religion: Religious Difference and the Claims of Constitutionalism* (University of Toronto Press 2015)

Berger BL and Moon R (eds), *Religion and the Exercise of Public Authority* (Hart Publishing 2016)

Bouchard G and Taylor C, 'Building the Future: A Time for Reconciliation' (Commission de consultation sur les pratiques d'accomodement reliées aux différences culturelles 2008)

Choudhry S, 'Rights Adjudication in a Plurinational State: The Supreme Court of Canada, Freedom of Religion, and the Politics of Reasonable Accommodation' (2013) 50 Osgoode Hall Law Journal 575

---

[103] See Jeremy Webber, 'Understanding the Religion in Freedom of Religion' in Peter Cane, Carolyn Evans and Zoe Robinson (eds), *Law and Religion in Theoretical and Historical Context* (Cambridge University Press, 2008).

[104] See Berger, *Law's Religion* above (n 10) 14, 195–197.

Eisenberg A, *Reasons of Identity: A Normative Guide to the Political and Legal Assessment of Identity Claims* (Oxford University Press 2009)

Epp Buckingham J, *Fighting over God: A Legal and Political History of Religious Freedom in Canada* (McGill-Queen's University Press 2014)

Hurd ES, *Beyond Religious Freedom: The New Global Politics of Religion* (Princeton University Press 2015)

Kislowicz H, 'Sacred Laws in Earthly Courts: Legal Pluralism in Canadian Religious Freedom Litigation' (2013) 39 Queen's Law Journal 175

_____. 'Law, Religion, and Feeling Included/Excluded: Case Studies in Canadian Religious Freedom Litigation' (2015) 30 Canadian Journal of Law and Society 365

Lefebvre S and Beaman LG (eds), *Religion in the Public Sphere: Canadian Case Studies* (University of Toronto Press 2014)

Moon R, 'Freedom of Religion under the Charter of Rights: The Limits of State Neutrality' (2012) 45 University of British Columbia Law Review 495

_____. *Freedom of Conscience and Religion* (Irwin Law 2014)

Ogilvie MH, *Religious Institutions and the Law in Canada* (3rd edn, Irwin Law 2010)

Shipley H, 'Religious Freedom and Sexual Orientation: Equality Jurisprudence and Intersecting Identities' (2015) 27 Canadian Journal of Women and the Law 248

Sullivan WF, *The Impossibility of Religious Freedom* (Princeton University Press 2005)

Sullivan WF, Hurd ES, Mahmood S, and Danchin PG (eds), *Politics of Religious Freedom* (University of Chicago Press 2015)

Waldron MA, *Free to Believe: Rethinking Freedom of Conscience and Religion in Canada* (University of Toronto Press 2014)

Cases

Alberta v Hutterian Brethren of Wilson Colony 2009 SCC 37

Chamberlain v Surrey School District No 36 2002 SCC 86

Loyola High School v Quebec (Attorney General) 2015 SCC 12

Mouvement laïque québécois v Saguenay (City) 2015 SCC 16

Multani v Commission scolaire Marguerite-Bourgeoys 2006 SCC 6

R v Big M Drug Mart Ltd [1985] 1 SCR 295

R v NS 2012 SCC 72

SL v Commission scolaire des Chênes 2012 SCC 7

Syndicat Northcrest v Amselem 2004 SCC 47

Trinity Western University v British Columbia College of Teachers 2001 SCC 31

CHAPTER 37

....

SECTION 7: THE RIGHT TO LIFE, LIBERTY, AND SECURITY OF THE PERSON

....

MARGOT YOUNG[*]

1. INTRODUCTION

....

SECTION 7 of the *Canadian Charter of Rights and Freedom*[1] is a site of rich activism potential. As more "ambitious" and strategic litigation under the *Charter* is launched in relation to section 7 rights, some of the "most contested political issues in Canada"[2] have landed in this corner of courts' constitutional dockets. The rights set out in section 7—life, liberty, and the security of the person—allow, because of their abstract and "protean" nature,[3] potential applicability to a wide range of normative claims and aspirations for a just and free society. Jurisprudence thus charts a growing and variable set of circumstances that fall within section 7 oversight.[4] Moreover, the stages of review under section 7 have, at first glance at least, a beguiling simplicity that other sections to which activists might turn, such as the section 15 equality rights, do not. One result is a line of high profile cases that leverage section 7 to target some of Canada's most intransigent systemic social justice issues. At the same time, section 7 persists as the workhorse of *Charter* rights, responsible for a large number of changes to both substantive and

  [*] Professor, Allard School of Law, University of British Columbia. Thanks for comments and collegiality to Martha Jackman and Jocelyn Stacey, and, for research assistance, to Mandev Mann.
  [1] Part I of the *Constitution Act 1982*, being Schedule B to the *Canada Act 1982* (UK), 1982, c 11.
  [2] Peter W. Hogg, 'The Brilliant Career of Section 7 of the *Charter*' (2012) 58 SCLR (2d) 195.
  [3] Hamish Stewart, *Fundamental Justice: Section 7 of the Canadian Charter of Rights and Freedoms* (Irwin Law 2012) 307.
  [4] For a discussion of this, see Hogg, 'Brilliant Career' above (n 2).

procedural criminal and regulatory law, most of which arise from the context of non-constitutional proceedings.[5]

The text that follows attempts to give a flavour of both these section 7 "personalities" in relation, specifically, to the scope and import allowed for the three rights in the section. Much of this discussion reflects the more established face of section 7, reviewing the basic structure of jurisprudence on section 7, and then adumbrating those areas of state action marked by potential section 7 stricture. The remaining text sketches out some thoughts on how to understand why the larger role activists wish to claim for section 7 has yet to be fully realized. I argue that expansion has been stymied by judicial reticence to engage critically with central aspects of the liberal legalism underpinning our system of constitutional rights, a liberal legalism that, ironically, is also responsible for the ways in which section 7 has already been powerful.[6] The result is a bounded but potent constitutional jurisprudence, entailing important victories for section 7 claimants but, at the same time, cementing a judicial approach at odds with broader social justice ambitions for section 7 rights. Strategic litigation runs up against two sturdy doctrinal barriers, forging in this contest the jurisprudential frontiers under strain in the evolution of section 7.

2. Section 7: The Text and Test

As prelude to my more substantive argument, I provide a brief overview of the full analysis required by section 7, useful, I hope, for non-Canadian readers.

Section 7 leads off the *Charter*'s list of legal rights. The text of section 7 reads as follows:

> Everyone has the right to life, liberty and security of the person, and the right not to be deprived thereof except in accordance with the principles of fundamental justice.

Jurisprudence is now clear that the section establishes a two-stage test for claimants.[7] The claimant must, first, show that at least one of the rights to life, liberty, and security of

---

[5] Canadian law allows broad standing for constitutional challenges in relation to a statute under which the challenger is being prosecuted. (*R v Big M Drug Mart Ltd* [1985] 1 SCR 295 [hereinafter *Big M*]. The text of section 7 grants the rights to 'everyone,' referencing individuals only, excluding corporations from coverage. (*Irwin Toy v Quebec (Attorney General)* [1989] 1 SCR 927 [97] [hereinafter *Irwin Toy*] Corporations can, however, challenge criminal charges levied against them on the basis of section 7. (*R v Wholesale Travel Group* [1991] 3 SCR 154) Further, section 7 protects all individuals "physically present in Canada and by virtue of such presence amenable to Canadian law." (*Singh v Canada (Minister of Employment and Immigration)* [1985] 1 SCR 177 [hereinafter *Singh*].

[6] Thanks to Jocelyn Stacey for reminding me of this.

[7] At different points, judges and commentators have contemplated the argument that the section actually establishes two distinct sets of rights, rather than a single set of rights modified by the notion of fundamental justice. See the dissent by Justice Arbour in *Gosselin*. (*Gosselin v Quebec (Attorney General)* [2002] 4 SCR 429 [338] [hereinafter *Gosselin*]. This notion of section 7 rights has not been taken up.

the person has been infringed.[8] Second, the claimant must then show that the infringement is not in accordance with the "principles of fundamental justice." In *Carter v
Canada (Attorney General)*, a case about criminal prohibition of physician-assisted suicide, the Court summarized this process:

> In order to demonstrate a violation of s. 7, the claimants must first show that the law
> interferes with, or deprives them of, their life, liberty or security of the person. Once
> they have established that s. 7 is engaged, they must then show that the deprivation in
> question is not in accordance with the principles of fundamental justice.[9]

Each stage places a distinct and separate onus on the claimant; contravention of section
7 results only when both stages have been successfully passed. Thus, the principles of
fundamental justice qualify the rights, resulting in a narrower scope of protection than
reference to the rights alone might accomplish. To paraphrase the Supreme Court of
Canada, section 7 does not hold out that the state can never interfere with an individual's
life, liberty, or security of the person—laws do this often. Instead, the guarantee is that
the state will not do so in a manner contrary to the principles of fundamental justice.[10]

The rights guaranteed by section 7 cast obligations upon the full range of government
actors and actions.[11] In *Operation Dismantle v The Queen*, the Court applied section 7 to
the executive branch of government: "the cabinet has a duty to act in a manner consistent
with the right to life, liberty and security of the person and the right not to be deprived
thereof except in accordance with the principles of fundamental justice."[12] More recently
in *Canada (Attorney General) v PHS Community Services Society*, the Supreme Court
found that a decision by the federal Minister of Health to deny an exemption from the
Controlled Drug and Substance Act[13] to the staff and clients of a Vancouver supervised
safe injection site was reviewable under section 7; indeed, it was, ultimately, held unconstitutional under those obligations.[14]

The Supreme Court's early statements about *Charter* interpretation set the stage for
ambitious deployment of this analytical structure. The purposive interpretation courts

---

[8] Only real persons can claim the rights. *Irwin Toy* above (n 5).

[9] *Carter v Canada (Attorney General)* 2015 SCC 5 [55] [hereinafter *Carter*].

[10] Ibid [71].

[11] For example, outside of the criminal law context, section 7 has been relied on to initiate review of
statutes that deal with, for example, immigration (*Charkaoui v Canada (Citizenship and Immigration)*
[2007] 1 SCR 350; private health insurance (*Chaoulli v Quebec (Attorney General)* [2005] 1 SCR 791
[hereinafter *Chaoulli*]; welfare payment levels (*Gosselin* above (n 7)); child apprehension (*Winnipeg
Child and Family Services v KLW* [2000] 2 SCR 519); adoption records (*Cheskes v Ontario (Attorney
General)* 87 OR (3d) 581(ONSC)); municipal bylaws (*Victoria (City) v Adams* 313 DLR (4th) 29
[hereinafter *Adams*]. Similarly, the following examples of regulatory acts have been the subject of section
7 obligations: assisted conception (*Doe v Canada (Attorney General)* 84 OR (3d) 81); health insurance
(*Flora v Ontario (Health Insurance Plan, General Manager)* 295 DLR (4th) 309).

[12] *Operation Dismantle v The Queen* [1985] 1 SCR 441 [28].

[13] *Controlled Drug and Substance Act* SC 1996, c 19.

[14] *Canada (Attorney General) v PHS Community Services Society* [2011] 3 SCR 134 [117] [hereinafter
PHS], citing *Suresh v Canada (Minister of Citizenship and Immigration)* [2002] 1 SCR 3 [hereinafter *Suresh*].

give to rights is to be generous and liberal: a rights enhancing approach.[15] In an early section 7 case, Chief Justice Lamer stated that development of section 7 itself should reflect the metaphor of the *Charter* as a "newly planted 'living tree,' "[16] committing the Court, at least rhetorically, to an expansive and evolving interpretation.[17]

Although not a direct source of legal obligation in Canada,[18] international human rights agreements are relevant to section 7.[19] In *R v Hape*, the Court stated that the *Charter*'s must be presumed to comply with Canada's obligations under international law.[20] Commentary frames international human rights as an "invaluable ... point of reference in the search for meaning in the ambiguous language of the section 7 right to life, liberty and security of the person."[21]

Section 15 of the *Charter*, the equality rights provision,[22] adds an additional interpretive lens that asks courts to develop section 7 obligations with an eye to issues specific to marginalized individuals in Canadian society. In the first equality case to reach the Court, *Andrews v Law Society of British Columbia*, Justice McIntyre wrote: "The section 15(1) guarantee is the broadest of all guarantees. It applies to and supports all other rights guaranteed by the *Charter*."[23] In *New Brunswick v G(J)*, Justice L'Heureux-Dubé underscored this in reference to section 7:

> ... it is important to ensure that the analysis takes into account the principles and purposes of the equality guarantee in promoting the equal benefit of the law and

---

[15] See, *Big M* above (n 5).

[16] *Re BC Motor Vehicle Act* [1985] 2 SCR 486, 24 DLR (4th) 536 [60] (Lamer J) [hereinafter *Motor Vehicle Reference*].

[17] Hester Lessard, 'Liberty Rights, the Family and Constitutional Politics' (2002) 6:2 Rev Const Stud 213, 12, 221. The Court has also said that section 7 is only triggered by interests that are more than trivial: they "must be serious." ' *Chaoulli* (above (n 11)) [123]; *R v Morgentaler* [1988] 1 SCR 30, 63 [hereinafter *Morgentaler*]; *Blencoe v British Columbia (Human Rights Commission)* [2000] 2 SCR 307 [4] [hereinafter *Blencoe*]; *New Brunswick v G(J)* [1999] 3 SCR 46 [60] [hereinafter *G(J)*].

[18] Direct obligation exists only if such conditions have expression in domestic legislation: *Re Arrow River and Tributaries Slide & Boom Co.* [1932] SCR 495.

[19] *Baker v Canada (Minister of Citizenship and Immigration)* [1999] 2 SCR 817, 174 DLR (4th)193 [69]–[71]; *Reference Re Public Service Employee Relations Act (Alta)* [1987] 1 SCR 313, 78 AR 1 [57] (Dickson CJ in dissent), quoted with approval in *Slaight Communications v Davidson* [1989] 1 SCR 1038, at 1056–1057; *Suresh* above (n 14) [46]; *Health Services and Support—Facilities Subsector Bargaining Assn. v British Columbia* [2007] 2 SCR. 391 [69]. See Martha Jackman and Bruce Porter, 'International Human Rights and Strategies to Address Homelessness and Poverty in Canada: Making the Connection' (2013) *Working Paper Series*, online http://www.socialrightscura.ca/documents/publications/Porter-Jackman%20 making%20the%20connection-can.pdf.

[20] The presumption of conformity in this context references the United Nations human rights treaties to which Canada is signatory. (*R v Hape* [2007] 2 SCR 292 (LeBel J) [53]).

[21] Martha Jackman, 'The Protection of Welfare Rights under the *Charter*' (1988) 20 Ottawa Law Review 257, 290.

[22] See the chapter by Sonia Lawrence on equality in this *Handbook*.

[23] *Andrews v Law Society* [1989] 1 SCR 143, 56 DLR (4th) 1 [185] (McIntyre J).

ensuring that the law responds to the needs of those disadvantaged individuals and groups whose protection is at the heart of s. 15.[24]

In sum, this interpretative framework beckons to activist rights deployment, promising to seed more transformation interpretations of section 7. Yet, substantial restraints on what will be recognized as an infringement of the section 7 rights persist, despite a (gradually) expansive approach to the scope of life, liberty, and the security of persons. What follows is structured to give a general sense of successful litigation relying on section 7. My focus is on the first stage of section 7 analysis—the finding of rights infringement—and somewhat out of step with recent commentary, much of which highlights emerging jurisprudence on the second part of section 7—the principles of fundamental justice.[25] But, establishing deprivation of section 7 rights is the substantive threshold to the section, a juncture central to the kind of rights protection the section provides. As such, the initial or prima facie rights infringement deserves some focused treatment.

3. The Three Rights: An Evolving Scope

This portion of my discussion aims to convey the range of section 7 protection and to capture, as well, the gradual judicial expansion of this range through interpretation of the scope of life, liberty, and security of the person. In this section I point out where section 7 is a significant site of *Charter* expansion, providing, I hope, a sense of the potential for a more encompassing scope for section 7 rights.

To begin, the Court has acknowledged that "the concepts of the right to life, the right to liberty, and the right to security of the person are capable of a broad range of meaning."[26] These rights inform and reinforce each other and are of equal importance.[27] In *Blencoe v British Columbia (Human Rights Commission)*, the Court noted that section 7, although clearly applicable to the criminal law, extended beyond that sphere to "state action which directly engages the justice system and its administration."[28] In the subsequent case of *Gosselin v Quebec (Attorney General)*, Chief Justice McLachlin explained that: " '[t]he justice system and its administration' refers to 'the state's conduct in the

---

[24] *G(J)* above (n 17) 115]. For an extension of this argument, see Patricia Hughes, 'Recognizing Substantive Equality as a Foundational Constitutional Principle' (1999) 22 Dal LJ 5.

[25] For example, Alana Klein, 'The Arbitrariness in Arbitrariness (and Overbreadth and Gross Disproportionality): Principle and Democracy in Section 7 of the *Charter*' (2013) Supreme Court Law Review 63.

[26] *Singh* above (n 5).

[27] *Rodriguez v British Columbia* [1993] 3 SCR 519, 107 DLR (4th) 342 [388] (Sopinka J) [hereinafter *Rodriguez*].

[28] *Blencoe* above (n 17) [45]–[46], citing *G(J)* above (n 17) [66].

course of enforcing and securing compliance with the law.' "[29] Thus, a broad range of state action is potentially subject to review under section 7 rights.[30]

Notably, section 7 omits mention of a right to property.[31] The omission was purposeful but its significance is much contested, both on and off the bench. In *Irwin Toy Ltd v Quebec (AG)*,[32] Chief Justice Dickson held that economic rights lie outside section 7.[33] However, he elaborated: "This is not to declare . . . that no right with an economic component can fall within 'security of the person.'"[34] Justice Arbour, in her dissenting judgment in *Gosselin*, explained: "On its face, [Chief Justice Dickson's] statement purports to rule out of s. 7 only those economic rights that are generally encompassed by the term 'property.'"[35] Although not all commentators and lower court judges agree,[36] it appears that the Supreme Court of Canada has not ruled out section 7 coverage of, at least, some significant economic interests. After all, the omission of property rights was due, at least in part, to concern that their protection would open the door to challenges to Canada's social programmes and to state regulation of corporate interests.[37] It would be ironic if reliance on the absence of property protections ruled out coverage of welfare interests, concern for which motivated the omission of property rights from the text in the first place.[38]

A. Life, Liberty, Security of the Person

The right to life is rooted in "a profound respect for the value of human life," and is most clearly engaged by the threat of death or an increased risk of death, either directly or indirectly.[39] Thus, in *Chaoulli v Quebec (Attorney General)*, a case in which the Quebec government's prohibition of private health insurance was challenged, the Court allowed invocation of the right to life where evidence showed that absence of timely health care

---

[29] *Gosselin* above (n 7) [77], citing *G(J)* above (n 17) [65].
[30] *Chaoulli* above (n 11) [194]–[197], (Binnie and LeBel JJ, dissenting, but not on this point). Binnie and LeBel argue that the real check on the range of state action section 7 rights cover is the requirement that an infringement of fundamental justice be shown. Showing this infringement is increasingly difficult as the range of the scope of the rights expands [199].
[31] Sujit Choudhry, 'The Lochner Era and Comparative Constitutionalism' (2004) 2:1 ICON 17; Martha Jackman, 'Poor Rights: Using the Charter to Support Social Welfare Claims' (1993) 19 Queens LJ 64.
[32] *Irwin Toy* above (n 5).
[33] Ibid.
[34] Ibid.
[35] *Gosselin* above (n 7) [311] (Arbour J in dissent).
[36] See, for example, Philip Bryden, 'Section 7 of the *Charter* outside the Criminal Context' (2005) 38:2 UBC LR 507.
[37] Choudhry, 'Lochner' above (n 31) 17-18; Jackman 'Poor Rights' above (n 31) 76.
[38] Choudhry, 'Lochner' above (n 31).
[39] *Carter* above (n 9) [62]–[63].

could result in death.[40] And, in *PHS*, the Court found that deprivation of medical care engaged the right to life.[41] The Court in *Carter* was clear that the right to life "is no longer seen to require that human life be preserved at all costs."[42] An individual's choice about the end of their life is "entitled to respect."[43] This links the right to life and the right to liberty.

Carter also saw the Court refuse to adopt a broader, more qualitative understanding of the right to life: "concerns about autonomy and quality of life have traditionally been treated as liberty and security rights."[44] Although not rejecting outright that such concerns might lodge in the right to life, the Court stated that it had "no reason to alter that approach in this case."[45] This line of argument is in tension with both academic commentary and lower courts' statements that the right to life guarantees the necessities of life. For example, Justice Taylor of the British Columbia Supreme Court in *Federated Anti-Poverty Groups of BC v Vancouver (City)* wrote: "the ability to provide for one's self . . . is an interest that falls within the ambit of the s. 7 provision of the necessity of life. Without the ability to provide for those necessities, the entire ambit of other constitutionally protected rights becomes meaningless."[46]

B. Liberty

As one commentator has written, " 'liberty' . . . has a long reach." [47] Its scope covers most obviously instances of physical restraint by the state. More broadly, it protects "the right to make personal choices free from state interference."[48] In *Carter*, the right to liberty was paraphrased as the right to "decide one's own fate."[49] It has been held to not encompass "pure economic interests" that do not engage fundamental life choices or that are not fundamentally "personal."[50]

Most liberty challenges involve criminal or penal provisions where a relatively uncontroversial sense of liberty is engaged: freedom from state-imposed detention or incarceration.[51] Section 7 is implicated anytime imprisonment is threatened.[52]

[40] *Chaoulli* above (n 11) [38], [50] (Deschamps J); [123] (McLachlin CJ and Major J); [191], [200], (Binnie and LeBel JJ). See also *PHS* above (n 14) [91].
[41] Ibid. [91].
[42] *Carter* above (n 9) [63], quoting *Rodriguez* above (n 27) 595 (Sopinka J).
[43] Ibid. [63].
[44] *Carter* above (n 9) [62]. See, Jackman, 'Welfare Rights' above (n 21) 326.
[45] *Carter* above (n 9) [62].
[46] *Federated Anti-Poverty Groups of BC v Vancouver (City)* 40 Admin LR (3d) [201]–[202].
[47] Hogg, 'Brillant Career' above (n 2) 196.
[48] *Blencoe* above (n 17) [54].
[49] *Carter* above (n 9) [67].
[50] *Siemens v. Manitoba (Attorney General)* [2003] 1 SCR 6 [45].
[51] Lessard, 'Liberty Rights' above (n 17) 216. This freedom also includes protection from things incidental to detention, such as fingerprinting. For more discussion of this, see Carissima Mathen, 'Section 7 and the Criminal Law' in Errol Mendes (ed), *Canadian Charter of Rights and Freedoms*, 5th ed (LexisNexis 2013).
[52] *Motor Vehicle Reference* above (n 16); *R v Smith* [2015] 2 SCR 602 [17].

Certain immigration proceedings have been ruled to implicate the section 7 liberty right: those in which an individual faces deportation and consequent possible torture are caught by section 7,[53] as are extradition proceedings[54] and refugee determination hearings.[55] Such cases reflect "[c]lassical liberalism's binary account of . . . the freedom-seeking individual and the potentially repressive state."[56] Consequently, they have a powerful presence in section 7 case law. Because invocation of liberty is thus uncontroversial, the second stage of the inquiry—the requirements of fundamental justice—bears the weight of these challenges.

But broader notions of liberty are increasingly relevant to an expanding number of constitutional challenges. Justice Bastarache argued in *Blencoe* that section 7 liberty entails more than "mere freedom from physical restraint," protecting "decisions of fundamental importance."[57] Justice Wilson, in dissent in *R v Jones*, captured this idea at more length:

> the freedom of the individual to develop and realize his potential to the full, to plan his own life to suit his own character, to make his own choices for good or ill, to be non-conformist, idiosyncratic and even eccentric—to be, in to-day's parlance, "his own person" and accountable as such. John Stuart Mill described it as "pursuing our own good in our own way."[58]

This conceptualization of liberty rests on familiar ideas of "self-ownership and self-realization,"[59] (and introduces squarely the theoretical underpinning of liberal legalism referenced in the section that follows.) Justice La Forest in *B (R.) v Children's Aid Society of Metropolitan Toronto* elaborated: "liberty does not mean mere freedom from physical restraint. In a free and democratic society, the individual must be left room for personal autonomy to live his or her own life and to make decisions that are of fundamental personal importance."[60] From another angle, Justice La Forest, this time in *R v Dyment*, observed that "privacy is at the heart of liberty in a modern state."[61] Thus, the "privacy" aspect of section 7 protects "'inherently private choices' of fundamental personal importance."[62] Section 7 accordingly fences off "an irreducible sphere of personal autonomy wherein individuals may make inherently private choices free from state

---

   [53] *Suresh* above (n 14) [19].
   [54] *Canada v Schmidt* [1987] 1 SCR 500; *Kindler v Canada (Minister of Justice)* [1991] 2 SCR 779; *United States v Burns* [2001] 1 SCR 283.
   [55] Bryden, 'Section 7' above (n 36) 513.
   [56] Ibid 223.
   [57] *Blencoe* above (n 17) [49].
   [58] *R v Jones* [1986] 2 SCR 284, 73 AR 133 [318]–[319] (Wilson J in dissent) [*Jones*].
   [59] Lessard, 'Liberty Rights' above (n 17) 12, 227.
   [60] *B(R) v Children's Aid Society of Metropolitan Toronto* [1995] 1 SCR 315 [80] [hereinafter *Children's Aid Society*].
   [61] *R v Dyment* [1988] 2 SCR 417 427.
   [62] *R v Clay* [2003] 3 SCR 735 [3] (Gonthier and Binnie JJ).

interference."[63] This does not signal protection for every personal action but, rather, for those sufficiently important and distinct from mere "lifestyle" choices.[64]

The conditions that inform personal choices need not be of the claimant's own making. The BC Court of Appeal in *Victoria (City) v Adams*, a case in which municipal bylaws prohibiting temporary overnight shelter on public lands were challenged, held that responses to homelessness were personal decisions protected by the right to liberty, despite the fact that homelessness was not itself necessarily the result of personal action alone: "The fact that a claimant has not chosen their underlying situation does not mean that a decision taken in response to it is not protected by the s. 7 liberty interest."[65]

A range of substantive personal choices has been protected. For example, constraints on medical and religious choices made for one's children trigger the right to liberty.[66] Similarly, "reasonable" personal medical choices are also protected from criminal proscription.[67] In *Godbout v Longueuil (City)*,[68] the Supreme Court considered a municipal resolution that all new permanent employees reside within the city's territorial limits an affront to employees' liberty rights. The right to choose the location of one's home fell within the scope of the liberty interest, implicating: ". . . basic choices going to the core of what it means to enjoy individual dignity and independence."[69] Likewise, in *Adams*, the BC Court of Appeal stated: "The choice to shelter oneself in this context [where there is no practicable shelter alternative] is properly included in the right to liberty under s. 7."[70]

However, liberty as protected by section 7 is not without limits:

> liberty does not mean unconstrained freedom. . . . Freedom of the individual to do what he or she wishes must, in any organized society, be subjected to numerous constraints for the common good. The state undoubtedly has the right to impose many types of restraints on individual behaviour, and not all limitations will attract *Charter* scrutiny.[71]

Liberty is not equivalent to license—and operates under constraints necessitated by collective values and the common good. But its protection resonates with the central place individual freedom—in at least its more formal variant—occupies in all strands of liberalism. And, judicial rendering of this notion is under pressure, as is true also of the

---

[63] *Godbout v Longueuil (City)* [1997] 3 SCR 844 (La Forest J) [hereinafter *Godbout*].

[64] *R v Malmo-Levine* [2003] 3 SCR 571 [hereinafter *Malmo-Levine*] In that case the Supreme Court characterized the consumption of marihuana as a lifestyle choice that was not protected under section 7. However, in the recent *Smith* case above (n 52), the Court found that restrictions on access to medical marihuana did engage section 7 interests.

[65] *Adams* above (n 11) [107].

[66] *Children's Aid Society* above (n 60); *R v Jones* above (n 58).

[67] *Smith* above (n 52) [18].

[68] *Godbout* above (n 63).

[69] Ibid [66].

[70] *Adams* above (n 11) [109].

[71] *Children's Aid Society* above (n 60) [368]–[369] (La Forest J).

right to life, from more substantive and material understandings of what make enjoyment of liberty possible.[72]

C. Security of the Person

This third right is, arguably, where the section's most expansive potential resides. A broad sense of security of the person invokes a full range of socio-economic rights. Although courts have been unwilling to go this far, significant scope for the right to security of the person has been established. Security of the person is engaged by state interference with an individual's physical or psychological integrity. In an oft-repeated statement, Justice Sopinka in *Rodriguez v British Columbia (Attorney General)* wrote that:

> personal autonomy, at least with respect to the right to make choices concerning one's own body, control over one's physical and psychological integrity, and basic human dignity are encompassed within security of the person, at least to the extent of freedom from criminal prohibitions which interfere with these.[73]

In *R v Bedford*, criminal prohibitions against bawdy-houses, living on the avails of prostitution, and public communication for the purposes of prostitution were found to infringe the right to security of the person: the laws imposed "*dangerous* conditions on prostitution; they prevent[ed] people engaged in a risky—but legal—activity from taking steps to protect themselves from the risks."[74] In another case, the threat of deportation to a jurisdiction where the person might face torture infringed the right to security of the person.[75]

Chief Justice Lamer in *G(J)* expanded on the scope of this protection outside of the criminal law context:

> For a restriction of security of the person to be made out, then, the impugned state action must have a serious and profound effect on a person's psychological integrity . . . This need not rise to the level of nervous shock or psychiatric illness, but must be greater than ordinary stress or anxiety.[76]

---

[72] See, for example, arguments made in *Tanudjaja v Canada (Attorney General)* 2013 ONSC 5410, aff'd 2014 ONCA 852, leave to appeal to SCC refused, 36283 (25 June 2015).

[73] *Rodriguez* above (n 27) [136] (Sopinka J).

[74] *R v Bedford* 2013 SCC 72 [60] [hereinafter *Bedford*] [emphasis in original].

[75] *Suresh* above (n 14). See also, *Singh* above (n 5) where security of the person was implicated in relation to risks less extreme than torture.

[76] *G(J)* above (n 17) [60] (Lamer J).

Thus, the Government's failure to ensure that an individual had legal representation in a process that could have resulted in loss of custody of her children imposed serious psychological stress, stigmatization, loss of privacy, and disruption of family life that interfered with her security of the person.[77] In *Winnipeg Child and Family Services v KLW*, state action resulting in the apprehension of the claimant's baby was similarly caught.[78]

The Supreme Court in *Carter* ruled that the law's denial of physician-assisted suicide for patients with intolerable suffering from irremediable medial conditions impinged such patients' security of the person.[79] And, in *Morgentaler*, a challenge to the federal *Criminal Code's*[80] therapeutic abortion scheme, the Court found that state-imposed delay and health risk in obtaining an abortion offended security of the person.[81] State action that is likely to impair an individual's health implicates both the right to security of the person and, as already noted, the right to life under section 7.[82]

I want to conclude this generally positive overview of the scope of section 7 rights with some indication of where courts have pulled back. Courts have stopped short of recognizing claims that might obligate the state to provide such things as health care and adequate social assistance benefits. Thus, in *Chaoulli*, Chief Justice McLachlin and Justice Major stated, in obiter, that: "The *Charter* does not confer a freestanding constitutional right to health care."[83] The state's foray into "a scheme to provide health care" did instantiate *Charter* obligations in relation to that scheme's structure,[84] but a more expansive obligation to provide health services was denied. And, in *Gosselin*, the majority similarly rejected a challenge to inadequate, discriminatory social assistance rates.[85] The recent housing rights case, *Tanudjaja v Canada (Attorney General)*,[86] was dismissed on preliminary motion as disclosing no viable cause of action and no reasonable prospect of success. These examples mark a general refusal on the part of courts to recognize substantive social and economic rights under section 7.

Pressure on section 7 has from another direction also faces judicial resistance. Advocates are increasingly seeking expansion of section 7, particularly security of the

---

[77] Ibid [5], [61], [97] (Lamer J).

[78] *KLW* above (n 11) 14.

[79] *Carter* above (n 9) [66].

[80] RSC 1970, c C-46 ss. 251, 605, 610(3).

[81] *Morgentaler* above (n 17).

[82] *PHS* above (n 14) [93]; *Rodriguez* above (n 27) [136]; *Chaoulli* above (n 11) 13. See also the discussion in *Toussaint v Attorney General of Canada* where the Federal Court of Appeal, in finding against the claimant, implied that exposure to serious health risks was protected against under the rights to life and security of the person (2011 FCA 213). For a critical exposition of *Chaoulli*, see Martha Jackman, 'The Last Line of Defence for [Which?] Citizens': Accountability, Equality and the Right to Health in *Chaoulli*' (2006) 44 Osgoode Hall LJ 349.

[83] *Chaoulli* above (n 11) [104] (McLachlin CJ and Major J).

[84] Ibid [104] For critical commentary on the case, see, generally, the collection of articles in Colleen M Flood, Kent Roach and Lorne Sossin (eds), *Access to Care, Access to Justice: The Legal Debate over Private Health Insurance in Canada* (University of Toronto Press 2005).

[85] *Gosselin* above (n 7). For a collection of critiques of this case, see Margot Young et al. (eds), *Poverty: Rights, Social Citizenship, and Legal Activism* (University of British Columbia Press 2007).

[86] *Tanudjaja* above (n 72).

person, to protect against "unreasonable risks or impacts to human health" from the hazards of environmental degradation,[87] arguing for an "ecological literate approach to ... [existing] human rights instruments."[88] Environmental rights cases have been launched, although all have been dismissed on other grounds.[89] One can anticipate that future environmental cases will not necessarily involve the rights of a specific individual but, rather, reference a larger number of, not identifiable, often future, individuals, adding to the conceptual challenge these claims pose to existing jurisprudence.[90]

Socio-economic and environmental issues are among the most pressing society faces. What is it about these claims that seems to guarantee their defeat? The next section takes up this question, looking not to the specifics of a particular claim but rather to the ideological frames in which section 7 (and all *Charter*) rights are embedded.

4. THE TAMING OF SECTION 7: LIBERAL LEGALISM AND RIGHTS

Liberal legalism limits in non-random ways the range of challenges that succeed under section 7. More pointedly, the ideological framing lent by liberalism to rights law explains recurring resistance by courts to challenges that target serious economic and social injustices in Canadian society. This is not the only ideological lens that influences constitutional law, but it is an important one:[91] it is a consistent thread across *Charter*

---

[87] Nickie Vlavianos, 'Intersection of Human Rights & Environmental Law' (Paper delivered at a Symposium on Environment in the Courtroom: Key Environmental Concepts and the Unique Nature of Environmental Damage, University of Calgary 2012) 8; Nickie Vlavianos, 'The Applicability of Section 7 of the Charter to Oil and Gas Development in Alberta' (2008) 13:3 Const Forum 123. But, see, Jocelyn Stacey, *The Constitution of the Environmental Emergency* (forthcoming) (manuscript on file with author).

[88] Lynda M Collins, 'An Ecologically Literate Reading of the *Canadian Charter of Rights and Freedoms*' (2009) 26 Windsor Rev Legal & Social Issues 7, 17; David Boyd, *A Right to A Healthy Environment: Revitalizing Canada's Constitution* (University of British Columbia Press 2012).

[89] See for example, *Metropolitan Authority v Coalition of Citizens for a Charter Challenge* (1993) 108 DLR (4th) 145 (NSCA), leave to SCC refused [1999] 1 SCR vii; *Manicom v Oxford* (1985) 52 OR (2d) 137 (ON Div Ct); *Energy Probe v Canada (Attorney General)* (1989) 58 DLR (4th) 513 (ONCA) [hereinafter *Energy Probe*]; *Locke v Calgary* (1993), 15 Alta LR 70 (ABQB); *Millership v British Columbia* 2003 BCSC 82; *Ada Lockridge and Ronald Plain v Ontario (Director, Ministry of the Environment) et al.* (2012) 350 DLR (4th) 720 [hereinafter *Lockridge*]; *Domke v Alberta (Energy Resources Conservation Board)* 432 AR 376; *Kelly v Alberta (Energy and Utilities Board)* (2008) 167 CRR (2d) 14.

[90] Indeed, even their framing as individual rights ill suits: Indigenous community claims of environmental rights claims will demand a different rights paradigm. For a sophisticated discussion of environmental rights in the neo-liberal era, see, Natasha Affolder, 'Square Pegs and Round Holes: Environmental Rights and the Private Sector' in Ben Boer (ed), *Environmental Dimension of Human Rights* (Oxford University Press 2015) 11.

[91] See, David Schneiderman, Joel Bakan, Bruce Ryder, and Margot Young, 'Developments in Constitutional Law: The 1993–94 Term' (1995) 6 Supreme Court Law Review 67.

law and, in relation to section 7, structures how courts treat challenges that ask for certain sorts of section 7 protection.

The term "liberal legalism" is shorthand for the role that the political philosophy of liberalism plays in our legal system.[92] And, although the content of the values and assumptions referenced by the term may be the "enormously plastic, loose congeries of ideas" Duncan Kennedy derides,[93] my argument is that a small set of elements, central to liberal legalism, tell powerfully in the context of section 7. These elements represent specific understandings of such things as the individual, the state, and the role of law— central, organizing concepts of liberalism.[94] Of course, my discussion renders simple what evolution of liberal thought has made more subtle and complex. But, my point is that these familiar constructs power section 7 jurisprudence—in both expansive and restrictive ways. This results in some very meaningful victories and some deeply discouraging losses. From the perspective of the latter, key ideological assumptions create dilemmas for rights enforcement that explain the doctrinal hesitations that plague progressive rights activism under section 7.

The individual of liberal thought is, in its simplest incantation, that willful, rational, self-actualizing person whose freedom is most threatened, not by other individuals, but by the centralized power of the state.[95] One commentator has described this outlook as "highly individualistic and anti-state."[96] The state is "presumptively illegitimate" when it threatens to intervene in, and thus to reset, private forms of ordering.[97] Individual freedom demands immunity from state coercion in those aspects most intimate and most critical to realization of the individual's own diverse and unique choices. (We can see this in the evolution of the scope of the three section 7 rights.) Thus, a private sphere is identified and sanctified.[98]

---

[92] Rosemary Hunter, 'Contesting the Dominant Paradigm: Feminist Critiques of Liberal Legalism' in Margaret Davies and Vanessa Munro (eds), *The Ashgate Research Companion to Feminist Legal Theory* (Ashgate 2013) 13. Brown and Halley write of the liberalism 'scribed' into our legal system. Wendy Brown and Janet Halley, 'Introduction' in Wendy Brown and Janet Halley (eds), *Left Legalism/Left Critique* (Duke University Press 2002) 1, 17.

[93] Duncan Kennedy, 'The Critique of Rights in Critical Legal Studies' in Brown and Halley, *Left Legalism* above (n 92) 178, 217.

[94] Brown and Halley, 'Introduction' above (n 92) 6.

[95] Rosemary Hunter and Sharon Cowan, 'Introduction' in Rosemary Hunter and Sharon Cowan (eds), *Choice and Consent: Feminist Engagements with Law and Subjectivity* (Routledge Cavendish 2007) 1. See, generally, Hester Lessard, Bruce Ryder, David Schneiderman, and Margot Young, 'Developments in Constitutional Law: The 1994–95 Term' (1996) 7 Supreme Court Law Review 81.

[96] Allan C Hutchinson, 'Condition Critical: The Constitution and Health Care' in Flood et al., *Access* above (n 84) 101, 110. See also, Andrew Petter, 'Wealthcare: The Politics of the Charter Revisited' in Flood et al, ibid 116, 120.

[97] Schneiderman et al, 'Developments' above (n 91) 69.

[98] What the concepts "public" and "private" signal has wide variance: "a complex family of them, neither mutually reducible nor wholly unrelated." Jeff Weintraub, 'The Theory and Politics of the Public/Private Distinction' in *Public and Private in Thought and Practice: Perspectives on a Grand Dichotomy* (University of Chicago Press 1997) 1.

The public/private distinction weighs heavily in debates over rights in liberal democracies. Launched by individuals against the state, rights protect freedom. This is Justice Wilson imagery when she strikes down limits on abortion in *R v Morgentaler*: "the rights guaranteed in the Charter erect around each individual, metaphorically speaking, an invisible fence over which the state will not be allowed to trespass."[99] Yet, when wielded by the state against non-state actors, rights threaten freedom: the application of collective (public) norms, in the guise of rights, to the private sphere becomes the "visible hand"[100] of government, a coercive collective correction of individual choice.[101] To avoid the coercive face of rights, the public/private opposition must, in some form, structure rights application. This is most obvious in case law about section 32, the application provision of the *Charter*, and the line courts draw there between state and non-state action.[102]

But the distinction is powerful, too, in scaling rights scope and infringement, once the application hurdle is leapt. More specifically, liberal anxiety about protecting individual freedom, a concern crystalized in the public/private distinction, helps explain two other features of rights law: the distinction between negative and positive rights and a concern about causation of the harm at issue. These aspects of section 7 jurisprudence channel liberal discomfort with those rights claims that seek to reorder the private sphere, as opposed to simply restrain discrete state action, and keep more activist claims, say, socioeconomic and environmental cases, at bay.

5. Economic Interests:
The Push to Positive Obligation

The distinction between public and private spheres inflects the distinction between negative and positive rights with rigid doctrinal significance. If rights are legitimate shields against state interference yet, as suggested above, problematic when used to require state action that reorders the private sphere, then judicial acceptance of negative obligations but rejection of positive obligations makes sense. "Negative rights ban and exclude government; positive ones invite and demand government. The former require the hobbling of public officials, while the latter require their affirmative intervention."[103] And, state intervention rings liberal legalism's alarm bells, for the reasons articulated above.

The problem of positive obligation is acute in relation to social and economic rights and, foreseeably, equally central to environmental claims. I have already noted the

---

[99] *Morgentaler* above (n 17) (Wilson J) [284].
[100] Weintraub, "Pubic/Private' above (n 98) 8–9; Hunter, 'Contesting' above (n 92) 18.
[101] Stephen Holmes and Cass Sunstein, *The Cost of Rights: Why Liberty Depends on Taxes* (WW Norton & Company Ltd 1999).
[102] See, as the foundational case, *RWDSU v Dolphin Delivery Ltd.* [1986] 2 SCR 573.
[103] Holmes and Sunstein, *The Cost* above (n 101) 40.

debate over protection of economic interests under section 7.[104] The subtext of this debate is, at least in part, concern about the positive nature of socio-economic rights and their redistributive (state interventionist) consequences.[105] Commentators (including me) have criticized the negative rights/positive rights distinction for its ambiguity and incoherence.[106] After all, it is well recognized that most rights require a mix of positive and negative obligation and that the state action/inaction opposition is itself conceptually indeterminate.[107] Canadian courts, however, continue to rely on the distinction. Judges are hesitant to explicitly recognize positive rights except in the abstract, as some sort of possible, future development seemingly never realizable in the case at hand.[108] Thus, in the *Adams* case the British Columbia Court of Appeal was clear that the section 7 claim was successful because it did not engage positive obligation.[109] The Supreme Court in *PHS* similarly favourably noted that the claims at issue in that case were negative.[110] The general tenor of the Canadian judicial response to socio-economic rights claims has been conservative, cautious, and unfriendly, precisely because of the claims' calls for positive obligations.[111]

6. COMPLEX HARM: CAUSATION CONCERNS

Insistence on the divide between public and private spheres also manifests in a reductive judicial focus on causation issues: From whose action does the harm at the centre of the case result? Judicial concern seeks to avoid using rights as corrective to private action. Recall my earlier discussion: rights are bulwarks against oppression when used

---

[104] See text accompanying footnote 31.

[105] Courts also cite concern about the separation of powers, phrased in the language of inappropriate judicial activism or non-justiciability. They fear turning the court into a "super-legislature." (Choudhry, 'Lochner' above (n 31) 29.) Separation of roles for the judiciary and the legislature reflects similar worries about the exercise of state power; insistence on the separation of law and politics that is part of this debate tracks, albeit in different language, the same liberal concerns that animate the distinction between negative and positive rights. See, also, Stacey, 'Constitution' above (n 87).

[106] Margot Young, 'Charter Eviction: Litigating Out of House and Home' (2015) 24 OHLJ 46; Martha Jackman, 'Charter Remedies for Socio-Economic Rights Violations: Sleeping under a Box?' in Justice Robert J Sharpe and Kent Roach (eds), *Taking Remedies Seriously* (Les Editions Yvon Blais 2009); Cass Sunstein, 'Social and Economic Rights? Lessons from South Africa' (1999) 11 Const Forum 123.

[107] Justice Bastarache implicitly accepted these points when, in *Gosselin*, he wrote: "The appellant and several of the interveners made forceful arguments regarding the distinction that is sometimes drawn between negative and positive rights . . . arguing that security of the person often requires the positive involvement of government in order for it to be realized. This is true. The right to be tried within a reasonable time, for instance, may require governments to spend more money in order to establish efficient judicial institutions." Above (n 7) 218.

[108] See, for example, ibid (McLachlin CJ).

[109] *Adams* above (n 11) [37], [95].

[110] *PHS* above (n 14).

[111] See, *Tanudjaja* ONSC above (n 72), for a stark example of this.

against the state, but instances of (at least potential) coercion when deployed in relation to individual private action. Simply put, this perspective maintains that rights are not a fix to individual bad choice; using them as such distorts rights protection. Requiring state implication in the harm at the centre of the complaint is to say that individuals are otherwise responsible for what they do to themselves, by themselves. Insistence on individual responsibility is flip side to respecting individual freedom. And, it is argued, harm that is the result of individual action—say, some lifestyle choice (the charge levelled by the Government in many socio-economic rights challenges[112])—ought not to call forth state obligations under a *Charter* right.

Thus, in *Bedford,* the Court held that there must be "sufficient causal connection" between the state and the prejudice suffered by the claimant.[113] This causation question is "the port of entry" to section 7 claims, and the Court has held that the standard employed must constitute a "fair and workable threshold."[114] This does not require that the state action be the only or even dominant cause—if a reasonable inference can be drawn, on the balance of probabilities, that the state action is connected to the harm, the test is met.[115] But, the link must be real, not speculative, with regard to the context of the case.

This doctrinal hurdle may be lower than the bar raised by the positive rights concerns discussed above. A recent group of cases is encouraging. In these, the abstract individual rights holder of classical liberalism gained some "flesh." Thus, the *Adams,*[116] *Abbotsford (City) v Shantz,*[117] *Bedford,*[118] and *PHS* judgments detail quite extensively the social context out of which the challenges arose, resulting in more nuanced understanding of causation. The "texture and meaning"[119] of the claimants' circumstances derailed government arguments of individual responsiblity. Not inconsequential, however, was the fact that, in each of these cases, the claim was for negative rights, constraining the import of the challenge. Of course, other high profile socio-economic challenges with issues of causation have failed—but, for some, they were also cases invoking positive government obligations.[120] We can also expect environmental cases where the issue of causation (both in terms of present and future harm) is prominent to be bellwethers for judicial progress (or intransigence) on this front.[121]

The legacy of liberal legalism for section 7 cases is complex. Powerful and effective assertions of section 7 rights are fuelled by the imagery of liberalism—individual

---

[112] See, for example, the discussion in *Adams* above (n 11) [104].
[113] *Bedford* above (n 74) [75].
[114] Ibid [78].
[115] Ibid [76], citing *Canada (Prime Minister) v Khadr* [2010] 1 SCR 44 [21].
[116] *Adams* above (n 11).
[117] *Abbotsford (City) v Shantz* 2015 BCSC 1909.
[118] *Bedford* above (n 74).
[119] Lessard et al., 'Developments' above (n 95) 87.
[120] *Gosselin* above (n 7); *Tanudjaja* above (n 72).
[121] Collins, 'Ecologically Literate' above (n 88); *Energy Probe* above (n 89); *Lockridge* above (n 89).

freedom and choice under threat. Yet, these rights are also curtailed by restricting their scope to negative obligations and by a focus on causation issues.

7. The Principles
of Fundamental Justice

Of course, infringement of section 7 requires also finding that deprivation of the rights to life, liberty, and security of the person is not in accordance with the principles of fundamental justice. Importantly, the principles of fundamental justice have a different profile, in terms of expansive or limited reading. Early on, the Supreme Court discarded the distinction between process and substance in relation to articulation of these principles. The Court held, contrary to the clear intentions of the drafters of section 7, that the principles are both substantive and procedural.[122] This development significantly displaced tensions around the scope of section 7—its activist potential—to the question of initial rights infringement. Courts sidestepped a difficult formalistic distinction, allowing "judicial scrutiny of governmental objectives as well as of governmental means for accomplishing those objectives"[123] and ensuring that "a wide range of laws would be scrutinized under section 7."[124] But judicial ecumenicalism towards the principles of fundamental justice is not out of step with a classical liberal vision of negative rights targeting clear state action: both protect the individual rights holder from an overzealous and aggressive state.[125] Were section 7 rights to engage more positive obligations, the balance set between current restrictions on the scope of rights and wider possibilities for principles of fundamental justice might be under pressure to shift.

8. Conclusion

Perhaps not only section 7 but this chapter, as well, has two personalities. Discussion has focused on an overview of section 7 in action—the effective scope of the rights to life, liberty, and security of the person. But, I have tried also to chart how courts refuse more transformative deployment of these rights. Judicial reluctance to question the distinction between positive and negative rights and the attention paid to possible rights holder complicity in the harm at issue in a challenge constrain the jurisprudence. A larger view

---

[122] *Motor Vehicle Reference* above (n 16) 546, (Lamer J).

[123] Lessard, 'Liberty Rights' above (n 17) 220.

[124] Stewart, above (n 3) 101. Peter Hogg notes that, despite expansion to include substantive principles, the best known invocation of the principles was in the *Morgentaler* case where the law was struck down mostly because of procedural defects. Hogg, 'Brilliant Career' above (n 2) 197.

[125] Lessard, 'Liberty Rights' above (n 17) 220.

that makes some (perhaps not complete) sense of these two concerns is the familiar liberal obsession with the divide between the public and private spheres.

So, where does such a conceptual unpacking of section 7 get us? Unfortunately, not far. The dilemma of rights for liberalism—that rights can both protect and threaten individual freedom—is unavoidable from within liberal legalism. The best we can expect is judicial "redrawing" but not erasure of the line between the public and the out-of-bounds private. This will take pushing by ambitious litigation. It will require more institutional risk-taking by judges. If this redrawing of the line succeeds, some significant redistribution of state resources will result. The payoff will not be trivial.[126] We must challenge judges on their lip service to the negative and positive rights distinction and demand better recognition of the contextual complexity of individual action. This will be controversial in the current cocktail of *Charter* politics. But the reward will be a section 7 jurisprudence that renders judgment more transparently, albeit not less politically. It will also enlarge the potential of section 7 to effect meaningful social change.

SELECT BIBLIOGRAPHY

Secondary Sources

Hogg, Peter W. 'The Brilliant Career of Section 7 of the *Charter*' SCLR (2d) 58 (2012) 195–210.
Klein, Alana. 'The Arbitrariness in "Arbitrariness" (And Overbreadth and Gross Disproportionality): Principle and Democracy in Section 7 of the Charter' SCLR 63 (2013) 377–402.
Mathen, Carissima. 'Section 7 and the Criminal Law' in Errol Mendes (ed). *Canadian Charter of Rights and Freedoms*, 5th ed (Toronto: LexisNexis Canada, 2013).
Young, Margot. 'Social Justice and the *Charter*: Comparison and Choice' Osgoode Hall Law Journal 50 (Spring 2013) 669–698.
Young, Margot. 'The Other Section 7' in Errol Mendes (ed). *Canadian Charter of Rights and Freedoms*, 5th ed (Toronto: LexisNexis Canada, 2013).

Cases

Re BC Motor Vehicle Act [1985] 2 SCR 486
Canada (Attorney General) v PHS Community Services Society [2011] 3 SCR 134
Singh v Canada (Minister of Employment and Immigration) [1985] 1 SCR 177
Carter v Canada (Attorney General) [2016] 1 SCR 13
R v Bedford [2013] 2 SCR 1101

---

[126] See, for example, perhaps, *Urgenda v Netherlands* (2015) C/09/456689/HA ZA 13-1396 (Hague District Court).

CHAPTER 38

THE *CHARTER* AND CRIMINAL JUSTICE

DON STUART[*]

THE enactment of the *Canadian Charter of Rights and Freedoms* in 1982 has without doubt had its biggest impact on the Canadian criminal justice system. Although no panacea, in my view 35 years of *Charter* jurisprudence, particularly from the Supreme Court of Canada, has produced a better balance against the expedient lure of "law and order politics". It has also helped to wrestle longstanding and entrenched criminal laws from outdated values.

Given the torrent of case law interpreting and applying *Charter* standards, this review will be highly selective.[1] Section 1 will identify basic principles of our *Charter* and the Supreme Court's activist approach. Section 2 will focus on the *Charter*'s Legal Rights sections 7–13 and their most significant impact on substantive law, police powers, trial fairness, and sentencing. Most Legal Rights standards expressly establish rights of accused. To complete the picture the review will also address the controversial issue of victim's rights.

1. BASIC PRINCIPLES

A. Structure of Charter

The *Canadian Charter of Rights and Freedoms* was entrenched by the Constitution Act on 17 April 1982. The *Charter*, expressly made applicable to both provincial and federal laws, sets out a number of rights and freedoms, notably a range of rights relevant to criminal justice.

---

[*] Professor, Faculty of Law, Queen's University.
[1] For a detailed analysis see Don Stuart, *Charter Justice in Canadian Criminal Law* (6th edn, Thomson Reuters 2014).

Of particular interest in the criminal context are the "Legal Rights" contained in sections 7 through 14. The broadest provision is that in section 7, which reads,

> Everyone has the right to life, liberty and security of the person and the right not to be deprived thereof except in accordance with the principles of fundamental justice.

The Supreme Court of Canada sees sections 8 to 14 as specific examples of the umbrella "principles of fundamental justice" to be asserted in the context of criminal or penal law. The drafters thought that "fundamental justice" in section 7 was limited to procedural justice and did not include substantive review. Speaking for the Supreme Court, future Chief Justice Lamer rejected this view given the wording of "fundamental principles of justice" in section 7, and he also decided not to follow the complex United States jurisprudence on due process.[2]

Unlike its predecessor, the Canadian Bill of Rights, the *Charter* not only declares rights but expressly confers remedies for breaches. Under s. 24

(1) Anyone whose rights or freedoms, as guaranteed by this Charter, have been infringed or denied may apply to a court of competent jurisdiction to obtain such remedy as the court considers appropriate and just in the circumstances.

(2) Where, in proceedings under subsection (1), a court concludes that evidence was obtained in a manner that infringed or denied any rights or freedoms guaranteed by this Charter, the evidence shall be excluded if it is established that, having regard to all the circumstances, the admission of it in the proceedings would bring the administration of justice into disrepute.

The availability of effective remedies for *Charter* breaches, particularly the possibility of exclusion of evidence under section 24(2), undoubtedly accounts for the *Charter*'s considerable impact on criminal justice in Canada. *Charter* motions occurring in criminal courts are far less often challenges to the constitutionality of laws but rather to state conduct found to violate a *Charter* right.

However the Constitution also authorizes challenges to the law. Independently of section 24, section 52(1) makes it quite clear that the *Charter* constitutes a significant inroad on the principle of parliamentary supremacy. Section 52(1) mandates courts to measure legislation against the now-entrenched yardstick of human rights and freedoms:

> The Constitution of Canada is the supreme law of Canada, and any law that is inconsistent with the provisions of the Constitution is, to the extent of the inconsistency, of no force or effect.

---

[2] *Re BC Motor Vehicle Act* [1985] 2 SCR 486, 48 CR (3d) 289.

Part of the political compromise that made possible the entrenchment of a *Charter* was the recognition that if a law violated a *Charter* right it might sometimes be demonstrably justified under section 1:

> The Canadian Charter of Rights and Freedoms guarantees the rights and freedoms set out in it subject only to such reasonable limits prescribed by law as can be demonstrably justified in a free and democratic society.

In the criminal law context section 1 has proved to be a high hurdle for the state. The Supreme Court has yet to save a section 7 violation.

B. Purposive Interpretation

In *Hunter et al. v Southam Inc*[3] Justice Dickson, later to be Chief Justice, first asserted a "purposive" approach which has been consistently asserted ever since:

> The task of expounding a constitution is crucially different from that of construing a statute. A statute defines present rights and obligations. It is easily enacted and as easily repealed. A constitution, by contrast, is drafted with an eye to the future. Its function is to provide a continuing framework for the legitimate exercise of governmental power and, when joined by a bill or a charter of rights, for the unremitting protection of individual rights and liberties . . . The judiciary is the guardian of the constitution and must, in interpreting its provisions, bear these considerations in mind.
>
> . . . .
>
> . . . The Canadian Charter of Rights and Freedoms is a purposive document. Its purpose is to guarantee and to protect, within the limits of reason, the enjoyment of the rights and freedoms it enshrines. It is intended to constrain governmental action inconsistent with those rights and freedoms; it is not in itself an authorization for governmental action.

2. The Impact of Legal Rights on the Criminal Justice System

A. Substantive Law

In the last 36 years the Supreme Court has relied on section 7 to convert a number of common law substantive principles into the following constitutional standards:

1. Subjective mens *rea* for a few crimes such as murder, attempted murder and war crimes;[4]

---

[3] [1984] 2 SCR 145, 41 CR (3d) 97, pp 110–111.

[4] *R v Martineau* [1990] 2 SCR 633, 79 CR (3d) 129; *R v Logan* [1990] 2 SCR 731, 79 CR (3d) 169; *R v Finta* [1994] 1 SCR 701, 28 CR (4th) 265.

2. A marked departure standard for crimes based on objective fault;[5]
3. Due diligence with the onus reversed for regulatory offences which affect the liberty interest;[6]
4. Physical voluntariness for acts;[7] and
5. Moral involuntariness for justifications and excuses.[8]

Canada should be particularly proud of its often quite distinctive and nuanced constitutional standards of fault. There is no evidence of rampant acquittals as a result. Fault standards are, however, in place to avoid injustice in borderline cases and to allow judges on occasion to use the criminal sanction with restraint. The policy foundations for these standards were laid by Chief Justice Dickson in the pre-*Charter* case of *R v Sault Ste Marie*.[9] Policy arguments in favour of some form of fault for even minor offences outweighed those favouring administrative and enforcement expediency. Later Chief Justice Lamer led the Court in striking down a constructive murder provision that had been in place since 1892. For a murder conviction in Canada there must now be proof of subjective knowledge of the likelihood of death.[10] The subjective standard is only a *Charter* standard for a few crimes in the Criminal Code, although the Court recently affirmed a common law presumption of subjective mens rea.[11] Our Criminal Code has always relied on objective fault standards for some crimes but the Court has imposed a unique *Charter* standard of a marked departure from the objective norm on the basis that

The law does not lightly brand a person as a criminal.[12].

Even for provincial offences there is now a *Charter* standard of a due diligence defence with the onus reversed where there is a risk to the liberty interest where a gaol sentence is possible.

The Supreme Court has also interpreted section 7 to put in place broad new *Charter* standards for challenge to criminal laws:

1. Laws must not be too vague and must allow sufficient room for legal debate;[13]
2. Laws must not be overbroad in using means more than necessary to achieve their objects;[14]

---

[5] *R v Beatty* 2008 SCC 5, [2008] 1 SCR 49. The ruling to acquit of a charge of dangerous driving on the facts was remarkably generous to the accused. The accused veered into the wrong lane, killing three persons and offered no real explanation other than that he might have nodded off after a day working in the sun.

[6] *Re BC Motor Vehicle Act* (n 2); *R v Pontes* [1995] 3 SCR 44, 41 CR (4th) 201.

[7] *R v Daviault* [1994] 3 SCR 63, 33 CR (4th) 165; *R v Ruzic* 2001 SCC 24, [2001] 1 SCR 687.

[8] *Ruzic* above (n 7).

[9] [1978] 2 SCR 1299, 3 CR (3d) 30, re-asserted as a common law principle in *Lévis (City) v Tetreault; Lévis (City) v 2629-4470 Québec Inc* 2006 SCC 12, [2006] 1 SCR 420.

[10] *Martineau* above (n 4).

[11] *R v ADH* 2013 SCC 28, [2013] 2 SCR 269.

[12] *R v Creighton* [1993] 3 SCR 3, 23 CR (4th) 189 [p. 47].

[13] *Canadian Foundation for Children, Youth and the Law v Canada (Attorney General)* 2004 SCC 4, [2004] 1 SCR 76.

[14] *Canada (Attorney General) v Bedford* 2013 SCC 72, [2013 3 SCR 1101.

3. Laws must not be arbitrary;[15] and
4. Laws must not be grossly disproportionate.[16]

As early as 1988 the Court struck down a narrow abortion prohibition.[17] In the last five years Chief Justice McLachlin has led the Court, mostly relying on the no overbreadth standard, to declare unconstitutional and inoperative a minister's refusal to grant an exemption to a supervised drug injection site,[18] prostitution laws,[19] a human smuggling offence,[20] and a criminal prohibition against doctor-assisted suicide.[21]

Some accuse the unelected judiciary of having been too activist and having exceeded its original *Charter* mandate. One senior judge, who wished to remain anonymous, was quoted[22] as saying the Court had "opened up a can of worms", and that many judges were "uncomfortable" in the role of assessing the effectiveness of governmental policy. It is true that the tests for finding breaches of fundamental justice under section 7 have been lowered, may seem unruly, and may be seen as giving unelected judges too much power. However, in my judgment, these major *Charter* victories have been firmly based in evidence tendered at the trial court and have provided salutary checks and balances against controversial and blunderbuss criminal prohibitions that politicians of all stripes were too timid to touch. *Charter* rights are in place not to curry popular favour but, as Chief Justice Lamer put it, to protect minority against the majority.[23]

There are many provisions still in the Criminal Code which have been declared unconstitutional and should be formally deleted by Parliament. For political reasons governments have been loath to be seen to support *Charter* rulings favourable to accused. Persons within and without Canada should be accurately informed by our Criminal Code as to our operating justice system which no longer has, for example, a felony murder provision nor severe limits on abortion choices.

B. Police Powers

(i) *Charter Limits on Police Powers to Search, Stop, Arrest, and Detain*

In the 1970s detailed recommendations by the now-defunct federal Law Reform Commission to clarify and declare police powers were eventually rejected in response

---

[15] ibid.
[16] ibid.
[17] *R v Morgentaler* [1988] 1 SCR 30, 62 CR (3d) 1.
[18] *Canada (Attorney General) v PHS Community Services* 2011 SCC 44, [2011] 3 SCR 134.
[19] *Bedford* above (n 14).
[20] *R v Appulonappa* 2015 SCC 59, [2015] 3 SCR 754.
[21] *Carter v Canada (Attorney General)* 2015 SCC 5, [2015] 1 SCR 331.
[22] Kirk Makin, "Landmark Insite Decision Threatens Peace between Judges and Legislators" *The Globe and Mail* (11 October 2011).
[23] *R v Collins* [1987] 1 SCR 265, 56 CR (3d) 193.

to police lobby groups which preferred to retain their wide and often unfettered powers. Since 1982 new *Charter* standards, particularly those under sections 8, 9, and 10, have been thoroughly litigated in criminal courts and have resulted in significant new limits being placed on policing.

> 8. Everyone has the right to be secure against unreasonable search or seizure.
> 9. Everyone has the right not to be arbitrarily detained or imprisoned.
> 10. Everyone has the right on arrest or detention
>   (*a*) to be informed promptly of the reasons therefor;
>   (*b*) to retain and instruct counsel without delay and to be informed of that right

In *Hunter v Southam*[24] Chief Justice Dickson applied his newly-announced purposive approach to the interpretation of the section 8 guarantees against unreasonable search or seizure. Far from a literal interpretation of "unreasonable" he led the Court to a number of important new *Charter* standards:

> 1. Section 8 applies wherever there is a reasonable expectation of privacy;
> 2. Prior authorisation by a warrant is required except where this is not feasible;
> 3. Prior authorisation must be authorised by someone neutral, impartial and capable of acting judicially and
> 4. The standard is one where "credibly-based probability replaces suspicion".

We saw earlier that in *Hunter* Chief Justice Dickson established the judiciary as the "guardian of the Constitution", and that the *Charter* was in place to constrain rather than authorise governmental power. Thirty-one years later there is no doubt that in resorting to a common law "ancillary powers doctrine" the Supreme Court has sometimes decided section 8 challenges by authorising new police powers. This occurred, for example, in the case of the limited power of investigative detention,[25] the roadblock stop power,[26] emergency entries,[27] strip searches,[28] and the use of sniffer dogs.[29]

Some argue[30] that the problem with the ancillary powers doctrine is that it is a fact-specific ex post facto inquiry that is vague and speculative, and that the matter of police powers should be left to Parliament to allow for full democratic processes. Both citizens and the police officer need to know what powers the state possesses in advance. But what of Parliament's record of almost always favouring arguments of law-and-order

---

[24] *Hunter* above (n 3).
[25] *R v Mann* 2004 SCC 52, [2004] 3 SCR 59.
[26] *R v Clayton* 2007 SCC 32, [2007] 2 SCR 725.
[27] *R v Godoy* [1999] 1 SCR 311, 21 CR (5th) 205.
[28] *R v Golden* 2001 SCC 83, [2001] 3 SCR 679.
[29] *R v Kang-Brown* 2008 SCC 18, [2008] 1 SCR 456.
[30] See, for example, Steve Coughlan, *Criminal Procedure* (2nd edn, Irwin Law 2012) 17–20 and James Stribopoulos, "In Search of Dialogue: The Supreme Court, Police Powers and the Charter" (2005) 31 Queen's L J 1.

expediency and listening only to police and prosecutor lobby groups? There is now a significant record of case law since the enactment of the *Charter* to suggest that our courts do a better job than Parliament in their non-political forum in balancing civil liberties of accused against the need for effective police powers.

Consider, for example, the issues of investigative detention, strip searches, and the use of dog sniffers. For years Parliament had not moved to regulate or authorise any of these powers although they were widely used by police and other state agents. In the case of investigative detention stops, the Supreme Court now requires individualised reasonable suspicion of a suspected crime and reasonable grounds for public safety concerns to permit any search.[31] Confronting strip searches, the Supreme Court put in place a number of new *Charter* standards including that a strip search can never be authorised as a matter of police routine.[32] In the case of police use of dog sniffers, the Court decided on a test of individualized reasonable suspicion.[33] The choice of a reasonable suspicion standard is indeed a reduction in the *Hunter* standard of reasonable and probable grounds. But the important and key aspect of an individualized standard is that police cannot just rely on police hunches and "Spidey senses".[34] These may mask arbitrariness and discriminatory behaviour. There are still concerns[35] that our courts should do more to address the well documented and corrosive aspect of racism in our justice system.

Importantly the Court has decided that an illegal search always violates section 8 and that an illegal detention always violates section 9.[36] These two rulings make it clear that under the *Charter* police conduct must be authorised by Parliament or the courts.

One of the key and often litigated *Charter* rights is the section 10(b) right of anyone under arrest or detention to be advised of the right to counsel and the right to consult a lawyer without delay. Chief Justice Lamer decided for the Court[37] that the information duty is automatic and must include advice as to how to obtain legal aid. However, an early compromise the Supreme Court made was that implementation duties, such as the requirement for police to stop questioning before a reasonable opportunity to consult counsel has been provided, only arise where the right to counsel is asserted. Those rights may also be lost if the detainee does not continue to assert it with reasonable diligence. This means that assertive and criminal-law-savvy suspects get a full panoply of right to counsel rights whereas the most vulnerable—those who are ignorant of their rights,

---

[31] *Mann* above (n 25) and *R v MacDonald* 2014 SCC 3, [2014] 1 SCR 37. The British Columbia Court of Appeal has been particularly firm in excluding evidence found as a result of stops that do not meet these *Charter* standards; see *R v Reddy* 2010 BCCA 11,71 CR (6th) 327 and *R v Dhillon* 2012 BCCA 254, 93 CR (6th) 260.

[32] *Golden* above (n 28). There are enforcement concerns addressed by Kent Roach in his chapter in this *Handbook* on *Charter* remedies.

[33] *Kang-Brown* above (n 29) and *R v Chehil* 2013 SCC 49, [2013] 3 SCR 220.

[34] This explanation for a police stop was rejected by LaForme J (as he then was) in *R v Ferdinand* (2004) 21 CR (6th) 65, 62 WCB (2d) 466 (Ont Sup Ct J) as lacking an objective basis for reasonable suspicion.

[35] See especially David Tanovich, *The Colour of Justice. Policing Race in Canada* (Irwin Law 2006).

[36] *Collins* above (n 23) and *R v Grant* 2009 SCC 32, [2009] 2 SCR 353.

[37] See the summary of jurisprudence by Lamer CJ in *R v Bartle* [1994] 3 SCR 173, 33 CR (4th) 1.

naïve, or just plain scared—get nothing. This compromise is thoroughly ingrained but needs to be re-considered.

(ii) Remedy of Exclusion of Evidence under Section 24(2)

Of course there are ongoing concerns as to whether these *Charter* standards for policing are in fact being applied by police and implemented by courts. Fortunately a strong discretionary remedy of exclusion of evidence under section 24(2) emerged with the bell-weather rulings of the Supreme Court in *R v Grant*[38] and *R v Harrison.*[39]

In *Grant* a 6-1 majority asserted a discretionary approach with revised criteria free of rigid rules. The Court placed special emphasis on the factor of seriousness of the breach rather than the seriousness of the offence or the reliability of the evidence. The same criteria are to be applied to all cases of *Charter* breach. Furthermore the Court emphasized that where the trial judge has considered the proper factors, appellate courts should accord "considerable deference".

In a joint judgment for the 6-1 majority Chief Justice McLachlin and Justice Charron settled on the following revised template:

> When faced with an application for exclusion under s. 24(2), a court must assess and balance the effect of admitting the evidence on society's confidence in the justice system having regard to:
> (1) the seriousness of the Charter-infringing state conduct (admission may send the message the justice system condones serious state misconduct),
> (2) the impact of the breach on the Charter-protected interests of the accused (admission may send the message that individual rights count for little), and
> (3) society's interest in the adjudication of the case on its merits.
> The court's role on a s. 24(2) application is to balance the assessments under each of these lines of inquiry to determine whether, considering all the circumstances, admission of the evidence would bring the administration of justice into disrepute[40].

According to the Court, the words of section 24(2) capture its purpose: to maintain the good repute of the administration of justice. Viewed broadly, the term "administration of justice" embraces maintaining the rule of law and upholding *Charter* rights in the justice system as a whole. The phrase "bring the administration of justice into disrepute" must be understood in the long-term sense of maintaining the integrity of, and public confidence in, the justice system. The inquiry is objective. It asks whether a reasonable person, informed of all relevant circumstances and the values underlying the *Charter*, would conclude that the admission of the evidence would bring the administration of

[38] *Grant* above (n 36).
[39] 2009 SCC 34, [2009] 2 SCR 494. See too *R v Coté* 2011 SCC 46, [2011] 3 SCR 215.
[40] *Grant* above (n 36) [71]. In *R. v McGuffie* 2016 ONCA 365 Doherty J.A. recently wrote that "If the first and second inquiries make a strong case for exclusion, the third inquiry will seldom, if ever, tip the balance in favour of admissibility".

justice into disrepute. Deterring police misconduct is not the aim although it could be a happy windfall.[41]

After some seven years there can be no doubt now that *Grant* has put in place a robust discretionary exclusion remedy for section 24(2). Surveys now indicate that across the country trial judges are likely to exclude for *Charter* violations in roughly two out of every three cases for all types of *Charter* breaches and whatever the type of evidence.[42] Appeal courts are much less likely to exclude. The *Grant* requirement of "considerable deference" to trial judges where there is no error in principle is not always followed.[43] The discrepancy between trial and appeal courts may be explained by the reality that courts of appeal are more likely to be confronted by selective Crown appeals against exclusion decisions by trial judges based on unreasonable errors.

The importance of these exclusion realities should not be exaggerated. In the vast majority of criminal trials across the country *Charter* issues are not even raised by defence counsel and often, where they are, *Charter* violations are not found. But it is the reality that in hundreds of rulings each year where *Charter* violations are found the section 24(2) remedy of exclusion is now regularly invoked. In section 24(2) cases it is clear that trial judges are to be concerned not only about truth concerning guilt or innocence, but also regarding the truth that police officers are often shown to be deliberately flouting, careless, or ignorant about *Charter* standards. If there is a concern about exclusion of highly probative evidence the question should be directed against the apparently lax and ineffective training of police officers respecting *Charter* standards, even where they are clearly established. If the police learned to apply *Charter* standards there would be no possibility of exclusion.

In the United States Supreme Court case, *Hudson v. Michigan*,[44] Justice Scalia, writing for a 5-4 majority, refused to apply the exclusionary rule to a violation of the Fourth Amendment "knock-and-announce" rule. He suggested that the exclusion remedy may no longer be necessary because of the increasing professionalism of police forces, with

---

[41] ibid [73]. Compare the pro-state view of the majority of the U.S. Supreme Court that the exclusionary remedy in that jurisdiction requires evidence that exclusion will deter this type of police conduct in the future (*Herring v. United States*, 555 U.S. 135 (2009)).

[42] See Mike Madden, "Empirical Data on Section 24(2) under *R. v. Grant*" (2010) 78 CR (6th) 278 (and see also Mike Madden, "Marshalling the Data: An Empirical Analysis of Canada's Section 24(2) Case Law in the Wake of *R. v. Grant*" (2011) 14 Can Crim L Rev 229) and, for similar findings in Quebec, see Thierry Nadon, "Le paragraphe 24(2) de la Charte au Québec depuis Grant: si la tendance se maintient" (2011) 86 CR (6th) 33). The most comprehensive survey is now that of Ariane Asselin, "Trends for Exclusion of Evidence in 2012" (2013), 1 CR (7th) 74 which reports the major findings of her LL.M. thesis at Queen's "The Exclusionary Rule in Canada: Trends and Future Directions"; http://hdl.handle.net/1974/8244. Asselin analysed all 24(2) rulings in Canada for the year 2012 where *Charter* violations were found. She found an overall exclusion rate at trials of 73 percent.

[43] Justin Milne, "Exclusion of Evidence Trends post Grant: Are Appeal Courts Deferring to Trial Judges" (2015) 19 Can Crim L Rev 373 surveyed appeal decisions between 2011 and 2014. He found that there was deference in only 60 percent of the cases and a preference to defer where the trial judge had admitted the evidence.

[44] 547 U.S. 586 (2006).

wide-ranging reforms in education, training, and supervision; better internal discipline; and various forms of citizen review.

Policing and review standards have also improved in Canada as well. However those preferring alternative remedies, such as civil suits and police complaints procedures, now bear a heavy burden of demonstrating their comparative efficacy. In Canada they have thus far generally proved to be a poor and low visibility response to systemic problems of police abuse or ignorance of their powers under an entrenched *Charter*. Police are rarely, if ever, disciplined for *Charter* breaches. Civil litigation is expensive, uncertain in outcome, and, if successful, likely to be subject to confidentiality agreements. Civil litigation is also highly unlikely where the plaintiff is in prison. The Supreme Court has recognized[45] a new right to sue civilly for compensation for a *Charter* breach but pragmatically restricted the remedy to superior courts.

Thankfully, the Canadian Supreme Court in *Grant* and *Harrison* saw the need for a vigorous remedy of exclusion for serious *Charter* breaches however serious the crime. In this area as in others our Supreme Court has given our criminal justice system a welcome balance against law-and-order expediency. In considering exclusion remedies courts must be especially concerned with the long-term integrity of the justice system if *Charter* standards for the accused are ignored and/or operate unequally against vulnerable groups, such as persons of colour and those who are young.

(iii) Few Charter *Limits on Police Interrogation*

There is no express *Charter* right to silence. However a pre-trial right to silence was first recognized by McLachlin J. in *R v Hebert*[46] under section 7. The Court used strong language. There was a need in the *Charter* era to move beyond the old common law voluntary confession rule's focus on reliability to allow judicial control of police interrogation, abuses, and tricks. The detainee had a fundamental right to choose whether to speak to police. The Court held that the police trick of sending an undercover officer into a cell to overcome the assertion of the right to silence violated section 7 and should result in exclusion. There was no consideration of involuntariness. The Court was pragmatic in limiting the right in that context to arise only on detention and to preclude only active eliciting "functionally equivalent to interrogation".[47] The majority in *Hebert* refused to require that the detainee be advised of the right to silence. In this context of undercover officers this decision seems wise, as otherwise all types of undercover work would have been effectively outlawed.

It has long been accepted that advising the accused of a right to remain silent is not a requirement of the voluntary confession rule, but a lack of warning may be taken into account in determining voluntariness. At common law the right to silence operates, per

[45] *Vancouver (City) v Ward* 2010 SCC 27, [2010] 2 SCR 28. See further Kent Roach in his chapter in this *Handbook* on *Charter* remedies.

[46] [1990] 2 SCR 151, 77 CR (3d) 145.

[47] *R v Broyles* [1991] 3 SCR 595, 9 CR (4th) 1.

Justice Abella for a unanimous Supreme Court in *R v Turcotte*,[48] to allow no adverse inferences to be drawn from pre-trial silence lest it be a "snare and delusion" to advise the accused of the right to remain silent and then to use it against someone who exercises it.

In 2002 in *R v Oickle*[49] the Supreme Court re-considered the voluntary confession rule. It voiced strong concerns about the dangers of coerced confessions leading to unreliable statements and wrongful convictions. It confirmed that an accused's confession to a person known to be in a position of authority is only admissible at common law if the Crown proves that it was voluntary beyond a reasonable doubt. The Court identified four factors to be considered: threats or promises, oppression, operating mind, and "other police trickery": the first three categories require a factual determination as to whether there has actually been an impact on the suspect's will. However the fourth category has a more specific object in maintaining the integrity of the criminal justice system and could lead to exclusion where those tricks in the view of the trial judge would shock the community.

The main disappointment in *Oickle* lies in its ruling on the facts. A confession by a suspected arsonist was held to have been voluntary despite numerous coercive police techniques such as inducements to go easy on his girlfriend, spiritual inducements, a promise of psychiatric help, and, especially, the police use of the polygraph test and lying about its accuracy. This amounts to a police manual for coercive interrogation.

Those of us hoping that the Court would interpret the *Charter* to provide further limits on police interrogation were disappointed. In *R v Singh*[50] a 5-4 majority of the Court decided that the *Charter* right to silence is subsumed by the voluntary confession rule. During hours of interrogation a person accused of murder had asserted his right to silence 18 times. The Court decided that he had in the end voluntarily chosen to speak and could not argue that, irrespective of the issue of voluntariness, he should have a *Charter* remedy for breach of his right to silence. Later in *R v Sinclair*[51] the Court decided in contrast to the position in the United States that section 10(b) does not mandate the presence of defence counsel during a custodial interrogation. A 5-4 division also decided that the right to counsel ends with initial consultation with counsel, including duty counsel, unless there is an objective change in the circumstances requiring another consultation.

The vehemence of the protests of the dissenters in *Singh* and *Sinclair* is palpable and, in my view, justified. In *Sinclair* Justice Binnie fired the most direct salvo:

> What now appears to be licensed as a result of the "interrogation trilogy"—Oickle, Singh, and [now Sinclair]—is that an individual (presumed innocent) may be detained and isolated for questioning by the police for at least five or six hours without reasonable recourse to a lawyer, during which time the officers can brush aside

---

[48]   2005 SCC 50, [2005] 2 SCR 519.
[49]   2000 SCC 38, [2000] 2 SCR 3.
[50]   2007 SCC 48, [2007] 3 SCR 405.
[51]   2010 SCC 35, [2010] 2 SCR 310.

assertions of the right to silence or demands to be returned to his or her cell, in an endurance contest in which the police interrogators, taking turns with one another, hold all the important legal cards.[52]

When the decisions are read together the resulting latitude allowed to the police to deal with a detainee, who is to be presumed innocent, disproportionately favours the interests of the state in the investigation of crime over the rights of the individual in a free society[53]

According to LeBel and Fish JJ (with Abella J. concurring) the suggestion of the majority

that our residual concerns can be meaningfully addressed by way of the confessions rule thus ignores what we have learned about the dynamics of custodial interrogations and renders pathetically anaemic the entrenched constitutional rights to counsel and to silence.[54]

The hope for a better balance may well lie with trial judges presiding over voluntary confession voir dires. Under *Oickle*, it should be recalled, and this was not emphasized in *Sinclair*, a confession must be excluded if oppressive conditions resulted in involuntariness *or*, irrespective of involuntariness, if the police tricks were "shocking". The latter is a high hurdle but it does give judges a direct remedy of exclusion for egregious interrogations. Prior to *Oickle,* Justice Ketchum in *R v S (MJ)*[55] excluded a confession in part because the videotape revealed Calgary police were using the oppressive atmosphere and psychological brainwashing Reid method pioneered in the United States, which should not, he held, be accepted in Canada. That method is currently in widespread use and emphasized in police training. It should result in judicial controls in egregious cases. Some judges might wish to resort to the little known automatic exclusion rule for evidence obtained by mental or physical torture found in section 269.1(4) of the Criminal Code.

In the case of undercover officers, the small *Hebert* right to silence has no application to undercover activities in the field as there is no detention, nor is the voluntary confession rule applicable given that there is no known person in authority. There seem to be few if any legal or *Charter* controls on such undercover tactics.

This has even proved true in the case of the use of the "Mr. Big" strategy where undercover agents pretend to be organised crime bosses and then allow the suspect to "join" as long as the suspect gains "respect" by admitting to a serious crime such as murder. The Supreme Court recently in *R v Hart*[56] asserted a new presumption of inadmissibility at common law but allowed for admission where the Crown can establish that the probative value exceeds the prejudicial effect, and furthermore noted that confirmatory

[52]   ibid [98].
[53]   ibid [77].
[54]   ibid [184].
[55]   2000 ABPC 44, 32 CR (5th) 378. See now similarly *R. v Thaher* 2016 ONCJ 113.
[56]   2014 SCC 52, [2014] 2 SCR 544. See too *R v Mack* 2014 SCC 58, [2014] 3 SCR 3.

evidence of reliability would point to admissibility. The Court added that more egregious uses of the Mr. Big strategy could result in a stay as an abuse of process.

Subsequent rulings in lower courts applying *Hart* now point to a wide path to admission of Mr. Big-induced confessions. This has led several academics to suggest that the Supreme Court did not do enough to control or prohibit this highly coercive and costly method of investigation.[57] In the United Kingdom or the United States principles against the admission of coerced statements wisely apply equally to confessions to known person in authority *and* to undercover agents.[58] Our own voluntary confession rule does not overlook police threats to persons other than the accused nor does it have a corroboration route to admission. We have seen that our test for exclusion of evidence obtained in violation of a *Charter* right under section 24(2) does not pivot on reliability. The Mr. Big regime certainly appears to be a pro-state anomaly.

(iv) Trial Fairness

The Supreme Court has relied on section 7 to declare the following procedural standards for a fair trial:

1. A residual right to stay as an abuse of process[59]
2. A right to disclosure of Crown case[60]
3. A right to have evidence preserved[61]
4. A right to effective assistance of counsel[62]; and
5. A duty to give reasons to allow for appellate review[63]

The *Charter* duty of full Crown disclosure established in *Stinchcombe* is one of the best demonstrations of the power of an entrenched *Charter* to produce positive change. For years prosecutors and Attorneys General had resisted disclosure rights and regimes, but we now know that full disclosure encourages guilty pleas and that non-disclosure has been a major factor in wrongful conviction cases.[64] There are strong arguments that disclosure requirements are costly and cumbersome in mega trials. However these can often be avoided or lessoned by sound prosecutorial discretion to sever trials into smaller groups and by forceful management strategies by experienced trial judges.

---

[57] Adriana Popoz, "Motive to Lie? A Critical Look at the 'Mr. Big' Investigative Technique" (2015) 19 Can Crim L Rev 231; Adelina Iftene, "The Hart of the (Mr.) Big Problem" (2016) 63 Crim L Q 178; and Jason Maclean and Frances Chapman, "Au Revoir, Monsieur Big? Confessions, Coercion and the Courts" (2015) 23 CR (7th) 184.

[58] See Chris Hunt and Micah Rankin, "*R. v. Hart*: A New Common Law Confession Rule for Undercover Operations" (2015) 14 Oxford University Commonwealth L J 322. The authors urge that the new Canadian Mr. Big model not be followed in other jurisdictions.

[59] *R v O'Connor* [1995] 4 SCR 411, 44 CR (4th) 1.

[60] *R v Stinchcombe* [1995] 1 SCR 754, 38 CR (4th) 42; *R v McNeil* 2009 SCC 3, [2009] 1 SCR 66.

[61] *R v La* [1997] 2 SCR 680, 8 CR (5th) 155.

[62] *R v B(GD)* 2000 SCC 22, [2000] 1 SCR 520.

[63] *R v Sheppard* 2002 SCC 26, [2002] 1 SCR 869.

[64] See, for example, *Royal Commission on the Donald Marshall Jr. Prosecution* (1989) vol 1, 238–242.

Section 11 lists a number of rights for any person charged with an offence including the right to be tried within a reasonable time (subsection (b)), the right not to be compelled to testify (subsection(c)), the right to be presumed innocent (subsection (d)), and the right not to be denied reasonable bail without just cause (subsection (e)). Section 12 protects everyone from being subjected to cruel and unusual treatment or punishment. Section 13 protects a witness from self-crimination, and section 14 concerns the right to the assistance of an interpreter.

One of the most important *Charter* checks is the enforcement of the section 11(b) right to be tried within a reasonable time.

> 11. Any person charged with an offence has the right
> * (*b*) to be tried within a reasonable time;

After the decision in *R v Askov*[65] on institutional delay, thousands of trials were stayed, particularly in Ontario. The Supreme Court got cold feet given the public outcry. In *R v Morin*[66] the Court adjusted the tests to include consideration of the factor of seriousness of the offence, with no strict comparison of better jurisdictions, putting the burden of proof on the accused and deciding that prejudice to the accused was the controlling factor. Section 11(b) stays were quickly reduced to a trickle.

In the last 10 years or so stays are on the rise again across the country with an *Askov*-like crunch looming in B.C. and in Montreal in recent mega gang trials.[67] The reality of lengthy unconstitutional delays due to lack of resources in the form of too few judges, too few Crown attorneys, and insufficient legal aid, is a powerful indicator that law-and-order rhetoric to toughen criminal laws is easy and effective politics but seldom accompanied by allocating sufficient resources to the judicial or prison systems. Without the infusion of adequate resources victims will undoubtedly suffer in not having a chance to see justice done. Section 11(b) stays bring this hypocrisy to a head, and a delay crisis, as in the aftermath of *Askov*, will force governments to find new resources for the justice system.

On 8 July 2016 a 5-4 majority of the Supreme Court in *R. v Jordan*[68] radically reversed its approach in *Morin*. The majority announced presumptive ceilings of 18 months for trials in Provincial Court and 30 months for those in Superior Courts. Prejudice and seriousness of the offence are no longer factors. Exceptional circumstances arising from a discrete unexpected event or complexity is declared to be the only bases upon which the Crown can discharge its burden of justification of a delay exceeding a ceiling. Nor can chronic institutional delay be relied on. It remains to be seen whether this bold decision will lead to substantial improvements in the growing and seemingly intractable

[65] [1990] 2 SCR 1199, 79 CR (3d) 273.

[66] [1992] 1 SCR 771, 12 CR (4th) 1.

[67] Gangsterism charges were stayed against 31 of 155 alleged Hells Angels members in *R v Auclair* 2011 QCCS 2661, 86 CR (6th) 155.

[68] 2016 SCC 27, 29 CR (7th) 235.

reality of court delays due to lack of resources, overly complex administration and what the Court called a "culture of Complacency".

The Supreme Court's current interpretation of section 11(e)'s protection against unreasonable denial of bail is distressing. At first the Court in *R v Morales*[69] commendably accepted that bail can be justifiably denied on the grounds of a flight risk or a risk to public safety, but it wisely struck down a third ground of denying bail in the "public interest" as too vague. Unfortunately 10 years later in *R v Hall*[70] a narrow 5-4 majority upheld a revised third ground of "maintaining confidence in the administration of justice". This criterion seems equally and dangerously vague and broad and is not found in bail laws in other jurisdictions. Furthermore the Court in *R v St-Cloud*[71] has now unanimously held that this controversial third ground should not be used "rarely" or "sparingly" as so many Courts of Appeal and bail judges had previously determined. The Supreme Court's position is here now unabashedly law and order in its orientation and has exacerbated one of the most serious issues facing the criminal justice system— that of burgeoning pre-trial detention in poor conditions at a time when crime rates are falling.

C. Victims' Rights

Although there are often calls in recent years to recognize new legal and constitutional rights for victims, and complaints that accused have too many rights, there is room for considerable caution and concern. The Supreme Court has avoided recognizing general *Charter* rights for victims. This is as it should be. A criminal trial is about determining guilt and just punishment of accused, not about personal redress for victims. For example, what if the input of victims were to be determinative on the issue of sentence? It surely would be unjust to have the length of a prison sentence determined by whether the victim wants revenge or compassion. It also seems clear that a general right of representation of victims at trial, even on the determination of guilt, would hopelessly burden and confuse an already overtaxed and under-resourced criminal justice system.

Thus far the enforceable *Charter* rights for victims are those of privacy and equality for complainants, but only in sexual assault cases. The recognition of enforceable section 15 equality rights came in the context of access to medical records in *R v Mills*.[72] In *R v Shearing*[73] however, a 7-2 majority of the Supreme Court ruled that defence counsel ought to have been allowed to cross-examine a complainant in a sexual assault trial as to a lack of reference to abuse in her diary, of which the accused had gained possession. According to Justice Binnie for the majority, the view of the B.C. Court of Appeal that

---

[69] [1992] 3 SCR 711.
[70] 2002 SCC 64, [2002] 3 S.C.R. 309.
[71] 2015 SCC 27, [2015] 2 S.C.R. 328.
[72] [1999] 3 SCR 668, 28 CR (5th) 207.
[73] 2002 SCC 58, [2002] 3 SCR 33.

the balance had shifted from the rights of accused to the equality rights of complainants was wrong "even in the context of production of third party records". In *Shearing* the language of privacy and equality rights for complainants is deliberately softened to that of "interests" and "values". The general approach in *Shearing* is a welcome re-calibration of the balance of the rights of accused and those of complainants in favour of the right to a fair trial.

The implications of an enforceable section 15 right for complainants in sexual assault cases has been left unexplored. The policy issues are far wider than establishing rights for protection of therapeutic and other records of complainants. Can complainants now seek status to be represented throughout a sexual assault trial? Why is representation allowed in the case of access to records but not rape shield hearings? What of such rights for principal witnesses in other gendered crimes such as domestic assault?

In the context of criminal law the enshrinement of section 15 equality rights has had a far greater impact when there is no attempt to claim an enforceable right but reliance is instead on "equality-lite" arguments of the need to be respectful of "equality values". This has, for example, allowed the Supreme Court in *R v Tran*[74] to rule respecting the partial provocation defence to murder that the individualized approach to the ordinary person test must be respectful of *Charter* values against discrimination so that homophobia and so-called honour killings cannot ground provocation defences.

The balance needs to be re-addressed in the context of our rape shield laws. Unlike most countries in the Western world, Canada's rape shield protection applies equally to prior sexual history with the accused, ever since a further assertion by Justice McLachlin in *R v Seaboyer*[75] and later enacted into the Criminal Code. The Supreme Court in *R v Darrach*[76] upheld the statutory regime as constitutional but left ambiguities such that the law is not clear. A problem is that *Darrach* is contradictory, indicating at one point that such evidence would never be admissible on the issue of consent as it is not relevant and at another that such evidence is rarely admissible to show consent. In *R v A (No.2)*[77] the House of Lords somehow read *Darrach* as not applying rape shield principles equally to prior sexual history with the accused. The Law Lords unanimously declared that new U.K. rape shield laws offended fair trial rights in the European Convention for the Protection of Human Rights and Fundamental Freedoms in applying with equal force to prior sexual history with the accused. My sympathy is with trial judges attempting to ensure in appropriate cases that sexual assault trials are fair to both the accused and the accuser.

---

[74] 2010 SCC 58, [2010] 3 SCR 350.
[75] [1991] 2 SCR 577, 7 CR (4th) 117.
[76] 2000 SCC 46, [2000] 2 SCR 443.
[77] [2001] UKHL 25, [2001] 2 WLR 1546.

D. Sentencing

In *R v Smith*[78] Chief Justice Lamer for the Supreme Court resorted to section 12 of the *Charter* to strike down, on the basis that it was grossly disproportional, a seven-year minimum sentence for importing any amount of a narcotic.

> **12.** Everyone has the right not to be subjected to any cruel and unusual treatment or punishment.

However in subsequent years the Supreme Court's approach was one of retreat and timidity, rejecting challenges to the few mandatory sentences then in effect. However judicial attitudes have changed in response to the former Harper government's recent orgy of enacting mandatory minimum sentences in the name of victim's rights. There are now over one hundred to be found in the Criminal Code. This initiative came at a time when policy makers in the United States courts appear, finally, to be questioning the danger, injustice, and costs of such sentencing rigidity. A strong candidate for being struck down is the simplistic and ridiculous grid scheme for sentencing for possession of marihuana for trafficking—mandatory six months for five plants, nine months for 6–200 plants, one year for 201–500 plants, and two years for 501 or more plants found at the time of the police raid.

In *R v Nur*[79] Chief Justice McLachlin led a 6-3 majority of the Supreme Court in invoking section 12 and its gross disproportionality standard to strike down minimum sentences for gun crimes. Again in *R v Lloyd*[80] she found a 6-3 majority to strike down a one-year minimum for a repeat drug offender. In both cases the Court confirmed that the minimum was appropriate for the offender before the court but reached its conclusion of unconstitutionality by considering reasonable hypotheticals of the possible use of such minimums in other situations.

In *Lloyd* the full Supreme Court of nine justices firmly rejected the notion that a *Charter* challenge on mandatory minimum sentences can be based on proportionality as a principle of fundamental justice under section 7 of the *Charter*. The view that gross proportionality under section 12 rather than proportionality under section 7 is the approach to be adopted for mandatory minimums appears to be pragmatic rather than principled. The Court reached that position without even acknowledging the weight of Canadian academic opinion that a higher standard of proportionality should be recognized.[81] The fundamental principle of sentencing declared in section 718.1 of the

---

[78] [1987] 1 SCR 1045, 58 CR (3d) 193.

[79] 2015 SCC 15, [2015] 1 SCR 773.

[80] 2016 SCC 13, [2016] BCWLD 2876.

[81] See, for example, Palma Paciocco, "Proportionality, Discretion and the Roles of Judges and Prosecutors at Sentencing" (2014) 18 Can Crim L Rev 241, David Paciocco, "The Law of Minimum Sentences: Judicial Responses and Responsibility" (2015) 19 Can Crim L Rev 173 and T. Quigley, "Pre-trial Sentencing Credit Rule Contrary to Section 7 Charter Proportionality Standard for Sentencing" (2014) 13 CR (7th) 63.

Criminal Code—the "cardinal" principle of sentencing as Wagner J. put it for the Court in *R v Lacasse*[82]—has been applied by our courts on a daily basis for almost 20 years following Parliament's acceptance of the work of the Sentencing Commission. Surely that principle as time passed had a strong claim to be recognized as a principle of fundamental justice in section 7 as

> a legal principle, about which there is a significant societal consensus that is fundamental to the way in which the legal system ought fairly to operate and . . . identified with sufficient precision to yield a manageable standard.[83]

The Court in *Lloyd* was clearly intent on giving Parliament room to manoeuver by suggesting it could narrow minima or give judges power to depart from minima in exceptional circumstances. The Court noted that a statutory exemption was the solution in many countries and had been recommended by the Canadian Bar Association. The Court here implicitly reneges on the strong policy arguments previously advanced by Chief Justice McLachlin in *R v Ferguson*[84] against a constitutional exemption solution to minimum sentences. Chief Justice McLachlin there suggested that it would be hard to judge claims of exceptional circumstances and that such an exemption would be contrary to the rule of law on the ground of uncertainty. The unruly ball is now tossed into the Government's court.

Federal governments have consistently said they will not re-introduce the death penalty which Canada formally abolished in 1976. Yet a 2012 poll[85] found that 49 percent of Canadians support the death penalty "for dangerous offenders". In its impressive per curiam judgment in *United States v Burns*[86] in 2001 the Court was unanimous in deciding that the Minister of Justice should not have agreed to the extradition of Canadian citizens on aggravated first degree murder charges in the State of Washington without obtaining assurances the death penalty would not be imposed. The issue was decided under section 7. However the Court added the following comment:

> We are not called upon in this appeal to determine whether capital punishment would, if authorized by the Canadian Parliament, violate s. 12 of the *Charter* ("cruel and unusual treatment or punishment"), and if so in what circumstances. It is, however, incontestable that capital punishment, whether or not it violates s. 12 of the *Charter*, and whether or not it could be upheld under s. 1, engages the underlying values of the prohibition against cruel and unusual punishment. It is final. It is irreversible. Its imposition has been described as arbitrary. Its deterrent value has been doubted. Its implementation necessarily causes psychological and physical suffering.[87]

---

[82] 2015 SCC 64, [2015] 3 SCR 1089.
[83] *R v Malmo-Levine; R v Caine* 2003 SCC 74, [2003] 3 SCR 571 [113].
[84] 2008 SCC 6, [2008] 1 SCR 96.
[85] *Leger Sun Media Poll*, 13 March 2012.
[86] 2001 SCC 7, [2001] 1 SCR 283.
[87] ibid [132].

It is salutary and another sign of the power of the *Charter* that the Supreme Court is on record that it would likely find that the death penalty would violate section 12.

3. CONCLUSION

Active judicial interpretation of *Charter* rights has put in place distinctive constitutional standards relating to fault, police powers to stop and detain, full Crown disclosure, and mandatory minimum sentences. Canada has a strong exclusionary remedy of evidence obtained in violation of a *Charter* standard. Oppressive Criminal Code provisions against abortion, prostitution, and medically-assisted suicide have been struck down for arbitrariness and overbreadth. The *Charter* is no panacea, and in some contexts, such as police interrogation and bail, our courts have been too protective of state interests. The picture of the criminal justice system in Canada is not all rosy under the *Charter*. But on balance Canada has been very fortunate to have had a Supreme Court, led by three outstanding Chief Justices (Brian Dickson, Antonio Lamer, and Beverley McLachlin), which has used the judiciary's *Charter* mandate to achieve a generally fairer system for those facing the blunt instrument of the criminal sanction and to balance the expedient lure of law and order politics.

BIBLIOGRAPHY

Secondary Sources

Coughlan, Stephen. *Criminal Procedure* (2nd edn, Irwin Law 2012).
Penney S., Rondinelli V. and Stribopoulos J. *Criminal Procedure in Canada* (LexisNexis, 2011).
Quigley, Tim. *Procedure in Canadian Criminal Law* (2nd edn, Thomson Reuters 2005).
Roach, Kent. *Criminal Law* (6th edn, Irwin Law 2015).
Stuart, Don. *Canadian Criminal Law: A Treatise* (7th edn, Thomson Reuters 2014).
Stuart, Don. *Charter Justice in Canadian Criminal Law* (6th edn, Thomson Reuters 2014).
Tanovich, David. *The Colour of Justice. Policing Race in Canada* (Irwin Law, 2006).

CHAPTER 39

EQUALITY AND
ANTI-DISCRIMINATION

The Relationship between Government Goals
and Finding Discrimination in Section 15

SONIA LAWRENCE[*]

WHAT does it mean to guarantee the right to equality but then suggest that this right is subject to limits? In 2001, the Hon. Beverley McLachlin, Chief Justice of the Supreme Court of Canada, labelled the equality section of the *Charter*, section 15, "the most difficult right".[1] In the years since the provision came into force in 1985,[2] disputes over precisely how to identify and rectify violations of equality have often resulted in split decisions and vigorous dissents in the rulings of the Supreme Court. At the core of this confusion lies the critically important commitment made in the very first section 15 case to a substantive understanding of equality-in-context, and the unique, two-step system of constitutional rights adjudication in Canada. Sheila Martin, also writing in 2001, argued that section 15 might present unique questions at the section 1 stage, as the cases, often seeking redistributive rather than corrective justice, raise different kinds of considerations for balancing. Martin also pointed out that since the business of the legislature is the business of categorization, the "distribution of benefits and burdens", equality cases will be particularly likely to provoke anxiety and conflict over institutional competence.[3] In her article, she set out to analyze this balancing of

* Associate Professor at Osgoode Hall Law School, York University. With gratitude to Andri Schudlo (Osgoode Hall 2016) for his able assistance with this chapter, and to Andrée Boisselle, Ruth Buchanan, and Dayna N. Scott, for their generous advice and companionship at the writing retreat that set this work in motion. All errors are mine alone.

[1] Beverley McLachlin "Equality: The Most Difficult Right" (2001) 14 SCLR 17.

[2] Section 15 came into effect three years after the other provisions, in order to allow governments time to bring laws into compliance with the requirements of the *Charter. Canadian Charter of Rights and Freedoms*, Part I of the *Constitution Act, 1982*, being Schedule B to the *Canada Act 1982* (UK), 1982, c 11.

[3] Sheila Martin, "Balancing Individual Rights to Equality and Social Goals." (2001) 80 Canadian Bar Rev 301.

equality rights and social goals, concluding that the cases revealed a poorly justified, overly deferential approach to section 1 review.

In this chapter, I consider the impact on the content of the equality right itself of the presence of section 1 in the *Canadian Charter of Rights and Freedoms,* a section which allows rights violations when they can be "demonstrably justified" in a "free and democratic society".[4] Fifteen years later, I pick up on some aspects of Martin's work, considering developments in section 15 and section 1. I trace the evolving test for section 15 violations, focusing on state goals within that analysis. Following this review, I canvass various positions and issues which arise in doctrine and scholarship about the appropriate relationship between sections 1 and 15, concluding that there are unique doctrinal, textual, normative, and institutional competence concerns which may drive a tendency for judges to resolve cases without serious engagement at section 1. Illustrating these themes through three post-2001 cases in which discrimination was justified, I conclude by asking about the role that the unique nature of the relationships between section 15 and section 1—rather than just doctrinal moves—has played in the development of an equality section more suited to providing recognition than redistribution. The work of the Court in this area reveals a preoccupation on the part of judges to avoid institutional competence conflicts with legislatures in order to preserve a broad zone in which governments can do their work. The Court struggles to fulfill its duty to the *Charter* while respecting institutional competence. I argue here that this anxiety has pushed the Court towards resolving these problems inside section 15, protecting a version of equality that is narrow and formalistic, quite different from that presented in the Court's expansive statements about equality's scope, and far from the powerful and transformative interpretations advocates dreamed of for this most complicated right.

1. DOCTRINAL DEVELOPMENTS

A. Substantive Equality, Analytic Silos

The text of section 15 reads:

15. (1) Every individual is equal before and under the law and has the right to the equal protection and equal benefit of the law without discrimination and, in particular, without discrimination based on race, national or ethnic origin, colour, religion, sex, age or mental or physical disability.

   (2) Subsection (1) does not preclude any law, program or activity that has as its object the amelioration of conditions of disadvantaged individuals or groups

---

[4] *Canadian Charter of Rights and Freedoms,* above (n 2).

including those that are disadvantaged because of race, national or ethnic origin, colour, religion, sex, age or mental or physical disability.[5]

It is, like all the rights protections in the *Charter*, modified by section 1:

1. The *Canadian Charter of Rights and Freedoms* guarantees the rights and freedoms set out in it subject only to such reasonable limits prescribed by law as can be demonstrably justified in a free and democratic society.[6]

The section 15 equality rights provisions first came to the Supreme Court for interpretation in 1987. Mark David Andrews might seem to be an unlikely equality claimant; a white male lawyer who married a Canadian and emigrated from the UK with an Oxford degree under his arm. He sought a call to the Bar in British Columbia so that he could practice law. However, the Law Society of British Columbia, regulator of lawyers in the province, prohibited non-citizens from being called to the bar in the province. Andrews challenged this rule as contrary to section 15.[7]

The decision in his case set a basic framework for section 15 analysis, a three-stage inquiry. Despite some twists and turns of the intervening decades, this analysis has re-emerged as the core of section 15 analysis, 30 years later. Claimants, who bear the burden of proof at this stage, need to establish that there has been *differentiation*, related to a recognized *ground*, with a *discriminatory* result. The somewhat spare decision was considered a clear victory for equality advocates in Canada, because the Court rejected a formal model of equality (sometimes described as an anti-differentiation approach) in favour of an approach which recognizes "that every difference in treatment between individuals under the law will not necessarily result in inequality and, as well, that identical treatment may frequently produce serious inequality". Under this approach, differentiation was required, but it could be either direct differentiation or indirect differentiation, in which application of the same rule to everyone produced "adverse effect" or "adverse impact" differentiation. There was no requirement that the state *intend* to differentiate. At this phase, at least, any reasons that a government might have for the way the law treats people differently seem to be entirely irrelevant—they do not make the claim any stronger or any weaker.

Differentiation must be related to an enumerated or analogous "ground" of discrimination. A key feature of the section 15 text is the open ended language of the section

---

[5] ibid. The wording of section 15 was influenced by both the Canadian Bill of Rights and the US experience of constitutional equality protection. The former was seen as overly narrow in its conception of equality, whereas the latter had, at the time of the *Charter*'s drafting, begun to reveal the ways in which it could be used to thwart movement towards meaningful equality through a fixation on formal equality that prevented recognition of or direct action to improve underrepresentation of minority groups. These kinds of concerns carried over into the first interpretation of the section by the Supreme Court of Canada. See Jim Hendry, "The Idea of Equality in Section 15 and Its Development" (2002) 21 Windsor Y.B. Access Just. 153, 184.

[6] *Canadian Charter of Rights and Freedoms*, above (n 2).

[7] *Andrews v Law Society of British Columbia*, [1989] 1 SCR 143.

around the prohibited grounds of discrimination.[8] This text informs the doctrine of analogous grounds, which holds that grounds similar to the enumerated grounds may also be recognized. In accepting a variety of "analogous" grounds, and rejecting others, the Court has tended to indicate that the purpose of having grounds is "to identify a type of decision making that is suspect because it often leads to discrimination and denial of substantive equality . . . The enumerated and analogous grounds stand as constant markers of suspect decision making or potential discrimination."[9]

The heart of the section 15 analysis is the third and final step, in which the claimant must establish that the differentiation on the enumerated or analogous ground(s) was discriminatory. It is this part of the analysis which has provoked the most disputes and dissents, and for which clear doctrinal resolution remains elusive. From *Andrews* forward, it is in this part of the analysis that the Court has tried to operationalize an equality often described as substantive as opposed to formal,[10] an effort which has occupied most of the many critics of this jurisprudence.

It is only after a finding that section 15 has been violated that section 1 come into play, formally. Justice McIntyre described a bright line between the violation of section 15 and the analysis required at the "saving" provision, section 1:

> Where discrimination is found a breach of s. 15(1) has occurred and—where s. 15(2) is not applicable—any justification, any consideration of the reasonableness of the enactment; indeed any consideration of factors that could justify the discrimination and support the constitutionality of the impugned enactment would take place under s. 1.[11]

In practice, however, this and other pronouncements by the Court have not held up and the bright lines have blurred. Part of the problem, as Peter Hogg notes, is that *Andrews* did not offer much explanation about how the discrimination inquiry proceeds.[12] But the battle over "discrimination" is connected to the question of section 1. As justificatory

---

[8] In the words of section 15, " . . . in particular, without discrimination based on race, national or ethnic origin, colour, religion, sex, age or mental or physical disability". *Canadian Charter of Rights and Freedoms* above (n 2).

[9] *Corbiere v Canada (Minister of Indian and Northern Affairs)* [1999] 2 SCR 203 [7–8].

[10] This term was not used in *Andrews v Law Society of British Columbia,* [1989] 1 SCR 143 by McIntyre J., though he did write: "that every difference in treatment between individuals under the law will not necessarily result in inequality and, as well, that identical treatment may frequently produce serious inequality" (p. 193). The first appearance of the term "substantive equality" in Supreme Court jurisprudence is in L'Heureux-Dubé's dissenting reasons in *Symes v Canada,* [1993] 4 SCR 695. It next appears in *Eldridge v British Columbia (Attorney General),* [1997] 3 SCR 624 [61], then in *Vriend v Alberta,* [1998] 1 SCR 493, and subsequently makes regular repeat appearances in all of the major section 15 Supreme Court decisions (e.g., *Lovelace v Ontario,* 2000 SCC 37, [4], [5].; Corbiere, above (n 9) [8], [18]. For a thorough consideration of the meaning of the term in the Canadian context, see B. Ryder, E. Lawrence, and C. Faria. "What's Law Good For? An Empirical Overview of Charter Equality Rights Decisions." (2004) 24 SCLR (2d) 103.

[11] *Andrews v Law Society of British Columbia,* above (n 7).

[12] Peter Hogg, "What Is Equality? The Winding Course of Judicial Interpretation" (2005) 29 SCLR (2d) 39, 56–57.

arguments fit into section 1, they are not part of section 15. That is the simple answer. But in a contextual analysis of inequality, how do we draw the line between context and justification in deciding whether differentiation is discriminatory? Furthermore, does it even matter? If the claimant succeeds in establishing a violation of section 15, the government will be given the opportunity to demonstrate, under section 1, that the limit on the right is reasonable and can be "demonstrably justified in a free and democratic society". If the state succeeds, the rights violation can continue. Still, there is arguably a real difference between a finding of discrimination which is then found justified under section 1, and a finding that no violation of the equality right occurred at all. This could matter both for policy making going forward, and in terms of maintaining the symbolic importance of violations of the equality right.[13] Justice McIntyre, in *Andrews*, had hoped that a strictly siloed approach would provide a "workable solution". In hindsight, that was probably overly optimistic.

B. The Workable Solution Proves Somewhat Unworkable

A very visible rift between members of the Court on this question appeared in *Egan v Canada*, released in May 1995. Part of a trilogy of section 15 cases (the other two were *Miron v Trudel* and *Thibaudeau v Canada*), *Egan* revealed both disagreement and confusion in the ranks, and the 4-1-4 decision left lower courts acting without clear guidance until 1999.[14] Three justices used what they called a "functional relevance" test to dismiss the appeal. Where the claimant challenged the exclusion of same-sex spouses from the Old Age Pension Act, these justices reasoned that the ground alleged was relevant to the Government's objectives in creating the law. Those objectives were described as:

> firmly anchored in the biological and social realities that heterosexual couples have the unique ability to procreate, that most children are the product of these relationships, and that they are generally cared for and nurtured by those who live in that relationship. In this sense, marriage is by nature heterosexual.[15]

Sexual orientation, the alleged ground, was clearly a ground of differentiation through the operation of this law. However, as the ground was relevant to the government

---

[13] On the issue of government intention and object in the section 1 analysis, see Sheila McIntyre, "Deference and Dominance: Equality without Substance" in S. McIntyre and S. Rodgers (eds), *Diminishing Returns: Inequality and the Canadian Charter of Rights and Freedoms* (LexisNexis Canada, 2006). On the "communicative power" of a rights violation, even one justified by section 1, see Claire Truesdale, "Section 15 and the *Oakes* Test: The Slippery Slope of Contextual Analysis (Symposium Issue: Commemorating the 25th Anniversary of R v Oakes [1986] 1 SCR 103)" (2011) 43 Ottawa L Rev 511.

[14] *Egan v Canada*, [1995] 2 SCR 513. Four justices (Lamer C.J. and La Forest, Gonthier, and Major JJ.) found no violation of section 15. Justice Sopinka found a violation that was saved at section 1. Justices L'Heureux-Dubé, Cory, McLachlin, and Iacobucci found a violation of section 15 not saved at section 1.

[15] ibid 536 (La Forest J).

objective, La Forest J concluded that the differentiation was not discriminatory. The dissenting justices took quite a different approach. That difference might be illustrated by the way that the reasons of Justice Cory and Iacobucci, in the section 1 analysis, defined the purpose of the law not as 'the support of heterosexual couples for the purpose of child rearing', but rather as an effort towards alleviating poverty in households of the elderly. This definition of the purpose left the Government with no arguments about how excluding same-sex couples served the purpose of the law. Thus section 15 was violated and the same issue—given the purpose of the law, what could the purpose of the exclusion be, other than to discriminate?—would lead to the Government's failure at section 1.

The divisions revealed in *Egan,* and the split on the Court, understandably caused real problems for potential litigants and for lower courts, and a great deal of ink was spilled criticizing Justice La Forest's relevancy test.[16] Finally, in 1999, the Court (Sopinka and La Forest JJ. having retired) unanimously rejected Nancy Law's section 15 claim, and used the opportunity to outline a doctrinal process that looked exhaustive, and created the impression of clarity. In the third stage, the Court embellished their description of discrimination by adding the concept of human dignity:

> Does the differential treatment discriminate, by imposing a burden upon or withholding a benefit from the claimant in a manner which reflects the stereotypical application of presumed group or personal characteristics, or which otherwise has the effect of perpetuating or promoting the view that the individual is less capable or worthy of recognition or value as a human being or as a member of Canadian society, equally deserving of concern, respect, and consideration?[17]

This language, of "human dignity" became the lynchpin of the new approach to section 15 discrimination. The Court followed with a non-exhaustive list of four "contextual factors" to be considered as part of the discrimination analysis, or the analysis of human dignity violation:

(A) Pre-existing disadvantage, stereotyping, prejudice, or vulnerability experienced by the individual or group at issue. . . .

(B) The correspondence, or lack thereof, between the ground or grounds on which the claim is based and the actual need, capacity, or circumstances of the claimant or others. . . .

---

[16] See for instance, R. Wintemute, "Discrimination against Same-Sex Couples: Sections 15(1) and 1 of the Charter: *Egan v. Canada,*" (1995) 74 Canadian Bar Rev. 682; R. Wintemute, "Sexual Orientation and the Charter: The Achievement of Formal Legal Equality (1985–2005) and Its Limits." (2003) 49 McGill LJ 1143; Lori G. Beaman, "Sexual Orientation and Legal Discourse: Legal Constructions of the 'Normal' Family" (1999) CJLS 173; B. Cossman, "Lesbians, Gay Men, and the Canadian Charter of Rights and Freedoms" (2002) 40 Osgoode Hall Law Journal 223–250 at 229–231.

[17] *Law v Canada (Minister of Employment and Immigration),* [1999] 1 SCR 497.

(C) The ameliorative purpose or effects of the impugned law upon a more disadvantaged person or group in society. . . .

(D) The nature and scope of the interest affected by the impugned law.[18]

In Nancy Law's case, these factors almost all worked against her claim (she was a young widow who, owing to her youth, was not eligible for a survivors pension after her elderly husband passed away).[19]

If the question that observers wanted answered by *Law* was about the continued relevance of relevance, the introduction of human dignity as central to the doctrine came as a surprise. It was mercilessly skewered by Peter Hogg who labelled it "vague", "confusing", and "burdensome to claimants". [20] The "contextual factors" fared no better, as they were, after all, a non-exhaustive list, and the Court had provided no guidance on how they were to be weighted. The correspondence factor came in for particular critique, with many seeing it as a revival of the much critiqued "relevancy" test from *Egan*. An empirical analysis of caselaw by Ryder, Lawrence and Faria in the years after *Law* illustrated how many claims were foundering on this particular factor.[21] Hogg described the work of the correspondence factor in Supreme Court cases:

> The correspondence factor has become the key to the impairment of human dignity. . . . Stripped of unnecessary verbiage, I suggest that the correspondence test, as it has been applied by the Court, comes down to an assessment by the Court of the legitimacy of the statutory purpose and the reasonableness of using a listed or analogous ground to accomplish that purpose. If I am right, this leaves very little work for section 1 to do.[22]

Even the Supreme Court could not produce consistent results with the *Law* recipe, splitting badly in *Gosselin* on whether there was "correspondence" and therefore on whether there was a negative impact on human dignity.[23]

In 2008, the Court continued the section 15 tradition of replacing without overruling in *Kapp*, a challenge to a federal program that offered special access to a 24-hour fishery on the Fraser River to members of three First Nations bands. Kapp and his supporters, who were not members of these bands, challenged the program as discriminatory on the basis of race.[24] A unanimous Court retreated from some of the more problematic

---

[18] ibid [88].

[19] ibid.

[20] Hogg, "What Is Equality?" (n 12) 56–57; See also Martin above (n 3); Sonia Lawrence, "Harsh, Perhaps Even Misguided: Developments in Law", (2003) 20 SCLR (2d) 93; Sophia R. Moreau, "The Promise of *Law v. Canada*" (2007) 57 UTLJ 415. For an effort to support the doctrinal use of human dignity, see Denise G. Réaume, "Discrimination and Dignity" (2003) 63 Louisiana L. Rev. 645.

[21] Ryder, Lawrence, and Faria, above (n 10).

[22] Hogg, "What Is Equality?" above (n 12) 59.

[23] *Gosselin v Quebec (Attorney General)*, [2002] 4 SCR 429, 2002 SCC 84.

[24] Unfortunately this chapter does not have room for a discussion of other issues raised by this case. In particular, I would argue that the Supreme Court's conclusion that there was differentiation on the basis of *race* was a grave and meaningful mistake, regardless of the fact that Kapp's challenge ultimately failed.

aspects of *Law*, notably pulling back from the articulation of human dignity as the lynchpin of constitutional equality:

> ... as critics have pointed out, human dignity is an abstract and subjective notion that, even with the guidance of the four contextual factors, cannot only become confusing and difficult to apply; it has also proven to be an additional burden on equality claimants, rather than the philosophical enhancement it was intended to be.[25]

The solution was another attempt to describe the core elements of *Andrews* in ways which would better avoid the formalism and rigidity that seems to keep creeping back into our jurisprudence, to refocus on the purpose of section 15. The Court rather narrowly described that purpose as "combatting discrimination, defined in terms of perpetuating disadvantage and stereotyping".[26] The other significant outcome of *Kapp* for the purposes of this chapter was with respect to section 15(2). Whereas an earlier case, *Lovelace*, had suggested that the role of section 15(2) was to provide guidance in the section 15(1) analysis, and the *Law* contextual factors had included a consideration of "the ameliorative purpose or effects of the impugned law upon a more disadvantaged person or group in society"(Law para 72, 73), in *Kapp* the Court moved to describe a more independent role for section 15(2) as a way of enabling governments to develop programs to remedy disadvantage without immediately becoming vulnerable to claims of discrimination.[27]

The decision to offer "independent force" to section 15(2) means that government objects and intentions figure in the analysis before the turn to section 1. But it also means that these are considered not in section 15(1) (which would contradict the letter of the siloing in *Andrews*) but in a "distinct and separate" provision.[28]

The cases after *Kapp* suggest that the revision of *Law*, and the return to *Andrews*, has offered some improvement in the clarity of section 15 judgments. However, this is mainly through clearing away the unhelpful doctrinal embroidery from *Law*, rather than from providing a new, clearer, analytic model. And the change does not seem to be improving the outcome for claimants. *Withler*, for instance, found the Court doing away with the much critiqued notion that each claim required a mirror comparator group (a group of people differing on a particular characteristic from the claimant group, illustrating the differential treatment). But unlike the earlier cases which failed without a mirror group, in *Withler* the mirror comparator group might have supported the claimants. Rejecting mirror comparison as "formalistic", the Court instead described the focus of the discrimination analysis as:

> the object of the measure alleged to be discriminatory in the context of the broader legislative scheme, taking into account the universe of potential beneficiaries. The

---

[25] *R. v Kapp* [2008] 2 SCR 483, 2008 SCC 41 [22], footnotes omitted.
[26] ibid [24].
[27] ibid [33] [40].
[28] ibid [40]

question is whether, having regard to all relevant factors, the impugned measure perpetuates disadvantage or stereotypes the claimant group.[29]

This approach *requires* the Court to consider what the government was trying to do—by looking at the panoply of other age-related financial program and the differential needs amongst plan beneficiaries. Having done so, they concluded that "the package of benefits, viewed as a whole and over time, does not impose or perpetuate discrimination".[30]

The thrust of *Withler*, then, is that the differentiation on the basis of age in the legislation is not discriminatory, because it is designed to meet differential needs which can be broadly construed as related to age. But the Court in *Withler* does not, as Jennifer Koshan and Jonette Watson Hamilton point out in their very thorough critique of the decision, explain why these arguments are appropriately considered in the section 15 analysis.[31] Even a return to the language of relevance is not explained by the Court or integrated into the revival of *Andrews* which was supposedly heralded by *Kapp*:

> Substantive equality . . . asks not only what characteristics the different treatment is predicated upon, but also whether those characteristics are relevant considerations under the circumstances. The focus of the inquiry is on the actual impact of the impugned law, taking full account of social, political, economic and historical factors concerning the group.[32]

Readers of *Withler* will note the striking flexibility of the analysis the Court is using, and the way this is justified by the need for contextual analysis in seeking to protect substantive equality. But this approach cannot assist lower courts, claimants, and litigators in building arguments. With regard to the central question in this analysis, *Withler* says nothing directly about the appropriate division between items for consideration at section 15 and those to be considered at section 1. Indirectly, it speaks volumes about the Court's unwillingness to move to section 1 in this kind of case.

There are some cases in which the Court, or some members of the Court, have moved to section 1 following the conclusion that section 15 has been violated. The majority of these cases find the violation unjustified by section 1, and I will not directly address those cases in this analysis.[33] However, there are a small number of cases in which section 15 violations are upheld by section 1—either by the majority, or by a significant set of justices. After describing some unique features of section 15 which might warrant attention in the next section, I will turn to three of these post 2001 cases.

---

[29] *Withler v Canada (Attorney General)*, 2011 SCC 12, [2011] 1 SCR 396 [3].

[30] ibid [71].

[31] Jennifer Koshan and Jonnette Watson Hamilton, "Meaningless Mantra: Substantive Equality after *Withler*" (2011) 16 Review of Constitutional Studies 31–62.

[32] *Withler* above (n 28) [39].

[33] For pre-2001 cases, see Martin above (n 3) for a very thorough analysis. Post-2001, examples include for instance, *Trociuk v British Columbia (Attorney General)*, [2003] 1 SCR 835, 2003 SCC 34, *Nova Scotia (Workers' Compensation Board) v Martin; Nova Scotia (Workers' Compensation Board) v Laseur*, [2003] 2 SCR 504, 2003 SCC 54.

2. A RIGHT APART: UNIQUE FEATURES
OF SECTION 15

This chapter aims to focus on section 15's relationship to section 1. Yet the Court often purports to treat the application of section 1 as if it is applied in the same way regardless of the right to which it is being applied. It is always the *Oakes* test, and the list of features of a law which call for deference to the government in the application of the *Oakes* test is a standard list.[34] Without calling into question the standard features of the application of section 1, I here describe some specific features of section 15 that may give it a unique relationship to section 1: the onerousness of section 15 for claimants, the treatment of government goals in section 15(2), worries about strangling government, and the normative mismatch between what section 15(1) seems to protect and the impact of section 1's focus on the needs of the larger collective.

Unlike most other *Charter* rights, most notably section 2(b), the development of s.15 doctrine has made it very difficult to establish a successful claim.[35] Scholarly critique tends to focus on cases in which the equality claim fails and there is no section 1 analysis, a significant subset of the existing cases. This leads to a body of work which could be read to argue that the problem is only the *placement* of attention to government goals, or "justification".[36] It seems, however, unlikely that many of these critics would be content if government goals operated at section 1 to uphold the law, rather than operating at section 15 to support a conclusion that the right had not been violated.

Comparison reveals that indeed some other rights have been interpreted extremely broadly, with no attention to government goals or intention in the analysis.[37] The focus is instead on the activity of the claimant and the way in which this is affected by the government law or action. The limitation of these rights, particularly section 2(b) rights, is, at this point in the history of the *Charter*, relatively commonplace (this is of course quite apart from the question of particular cases in which rights have been limited, which have raised significant controversy). As Sheila Martin has written with respect to section

---

[34] See, for instance, S. Choudhry, "So What Is the Real Legacy of *Oakes*? Two Decades of Proportionality Analysis under the Canadian Charter's Section 1" (2006) 34 SCLR 501.

[35] For some empirical approaches to this question, illustrating the challenges, see: Sujit Choudhry and Claire E. Hunter, "Measuring Judicial Activism on the Supreme Court of Canada: A Comment on *Newfoundland (Treasury Board) v. NAPE*" (2003) 48 McGill LJ. 525 at 549. (Choudhry and Hunter note the complications created by section 1 for empirical testing of win rates and the sampling bias that case reviews create.) See also Ryder, Lawrence, and Faria, above (n 10). Of course, section 7 also has an onerous process, but at least some of this could be heavily attributed to the text of section 7 as opposed to judicial choice about the development of the section.

[36] I have written in this vein myself. I should also say that there is far more nuance in this category of work by others than my simplified version here.

[37] Generally, Canadian rights analysis proceeds on the basis that rights can be violated by government purpose or by the effect of government action—in other words, government intent is not required for rights violations generally, and that tends to keep these discussions confined to section 1.

2(b), "[t]he purpose of the right . . . informs its limitation but the level of appropriate limitation is entirely a function of section 1". [38] The context of the violation, and the concept of deference (when appropriate) to the legislature then help the "Court to scrutinize the importance of the impugned expression under section 1".[39]

Section 15, in contrast and as we have seen, has a complex, multistep analysis, which results in a large number of claims failing at this part of the analysis. In this respect it is more similar to section 7, which also involves a multistage analysis, one directly mandated by the text.[40] It is often said of section 7 claims, as it is of section 15 claims, that they will only very rarely be the subject of successful government arguments at section 1.[41] But the text of section 7 does seem to require a two-stage analysis in a way that, textually, at least, is quite different from section 15.

The relatively complex and (arguably overly) onerous interpretation that section 15 has been given was not inevitable. Other options were canvassed in the period before *Andrews*, and before the three steps of grounds, differentiation, and discrimination started to feel cemented into section 15. Discussions at the time and since suggest that there is some important *symbolic* meaning to the decision to place government goals either in section 15 or in section 1. Would some additional damage to the value of equality accrue if the courts were repeatedly finding violations of the equality right to be "reasonably and demonstrably justified" as state action?[42]

Leading constitutional scholar Peter Hogg raised a version of this concern when he suggested in the mid-1980s that one way to deal with the complexity of section 15 analysis would be to ask only one question: Is there differentiation?[43] There would not even be a grounds inquiry in this approach, and Hogg notes that this simplicity would render the equality provision similar in analytic process to section 2(b), in that in virtually every case, the meat of the inquiry would be in section 1. As we have seen above,

---

[38] Martin, above (n 3) 361.

[39] ibid.

[40] *Canadian Charter of Rights and Freedoms* above (n 2). "7. Everyone has the right to life, liberty and security of the person and the right not to be deprived thereof except in accordance with the principles of fundamental justice".

[41] *New Brunswick (Minister of Health and Community Services) v G. (J.)*, [1999] 3 SCR 46 [99]; *Reference Re BC Motor Vehicle Act*, [1985] 2 SCR 486 [85], 24 DLR (4th) 536. No case in which section 1 has "trumped" a section 7 violation yet exists. In cases such as *Canada (Attorney General) v Bedford*, 2013 SCC 72, [2013] 3 SCR 1101, the Attorneys General involved in the case did not even seriously argue that section 1 could uphold the impugned laws if the section 7 challenge was successful [161]. In fact, K. Selick et al., arguing from a very different theoretical perspective, write that "[t]he courts in Canada have defined away a vast portion of the word 'liberty' to avoid applying the test contained in section 1 of the Charter". K. Selick, D. From, and C. Schafer 'The Evisceration of Liberty in Canadian Courts' in F. McMahon (ed), *Towards a Worldwide Index of Human Freedom* (Fraser Institute & Liberales Institut 2012), 250.

[42] On equality as a "value" rather than a "right" in constitutional jurisprudence, see Peter Hogg, "Equality as a Charter Value in Constitutional Interpretation" (2003) 20 Sup Ct L Rev (2d) 113 at 117.

[43] Peter W. Hogg, *Constitutional Law of Canada*, 2d ed (Carswell, 1985) at 799–801.

Justice McIntyre in the inaugural section 15 case, *Andrews*, rejected this approach, arguing that it "virtually denies any role for s. 15(1)".[44]

In fact, McIntyre J. took a rather deferential approach to the section 1 analysis, differentiating section 15 from other sections also subject to section 1,

> given the broad ambit of legislation which must be enacted to cover various aspects of the civil law dealing largely with administrative and regulatory matters and the necessity for the Legislature to make many distinctions between individuals and groups for such purposes.[45]

However, for the majority on this question, Justice Wilson argued "[g]iven that section 15 is designed to protect those groups who suffer social, political and legal disadvantage in our society, the burden resting on the government to justify the type of discrimination against such groups is appropriately an onerous one".[46] Justice La Forest, who would have accepted a somewhat less "onerous" version of *Oakes*, found that the Government could not meet even that standard, providing a result that, 4-2, favoured the claimant.[47] The lesson of *Andrews* seemed to be, as Justice Wilson wrote, "cases will be rare where it is found reasonable in a free and democratic society to discriminate".[48] Rare—but not non-existent.

In addition to relative complexity of a section 15 challenge compared to some other *Charter* rights, Section 15(2) also supports the idea that there is a symbolic significance to the gap between non-discrimination and justified discrimination. From the beginning, s. 15(2) has been understood to protect the government's ability to remedy inequality through targeted programs which treat people differently based on ascriptive characteristics (gender, race, disability, for instance). Such programs are not a form of justified discrimination—rather they do not violate section 15, according to section 15(2). The existence of this section seems to support a substantive equality approach to section 15(1), but in *Lovelace* and *Law*, it was treated as *part* of the section 15 analysis, a reminder that these state efforts form part of the context that helps determine whether the differentiation at issue is actually discriminatory.[49] This interpretation clearly treats public policy goals as a key part of the section 15 analysis, if only in this limited sense. However, the Court's latest interpretation of this section, in *Kapp*, holds that s.15(2) shields programs created to try to promote equality from the full operation of section 15, and creates a distinct role for section 15(2):[50]

> once the s.15 claimant has shown a distinction made on an enumerated or analogous ground, it is open to the government to show that the impugned law, program or

---

[44] *Andrews*, above (n 8). For a further critique of Hogg's suggested approach, see R. Moon, "Discrimination and Its Justification: Coping with Equality Rights under the Charter" (1988) 26 Osgoode Hall LJ 673.

[45] *Andrews* above (n 8).

[46] ibid 154 (Wilson J).

[47] ibid.

[48] ibid (Wilson J) 154.

[49] *Lovelace v Ontario*, 2000 SCC 37; *Law v Canada (Minister of Employment and Immigration)* above (n 17).

[50] *R. v Kapp* [2008] 2 SCR 483, 2008 SCC 41, [40].

activity is ameliorative and, thus, constitutional. This approach has the advantage of avoiding the symbolic problem of finding a program discriminatory before "saving" it as ameliorative, while also giving independent force to a provision that has been written as distinct and separate from s.15(1).[51]

Does this add yet another stage to the whole rights and justification analysis, or does it import public policy goals into section 15? On either interpretation, section 15(2) illustrates that government explanations of policy choice are not always doctrinally relegated to section 1. It also, I think, indicates that even in a two-step system such as Canada's, we have to pay attention to the symbolic importance of precisely how claimants fail.[52] The complexity of the section 15 analysis (which might both justify an onerous section 1 analysis and ensure that cases in which discrimination can be established will have features which make a section 1 argument very difficult for the government), along with the existence of section 15(2), might help us understand some of the reasons that applying section 1 to equality cases demands particular attention. Institutional competence concerns fill out this understanding. How can the Court best respect the pragmatics of law-making in its approach to section 15? And how can it cope with the normative mismatch created by the dual role the Court must play—both guarding the rights enshrined in the *Charter* and respecting institutional competence in determining their reasonable limits?

3. Law-Making as Line Drawing and the Problem of Normative Mismatch

Early in discussions of section 15, a vision of law-making emerges in which the role of the legislator is understood to be fundamentally engaged with line drawing, differentiation, and categorization. Treating all of these things as violations of section 15 would result in an enormous number of violations, and so early discussions of how to interpret the section included concerns that taking the approach suggested by Hogg would have the effect of distorting the section 1 analysis.[53] In *Andrews*, the idea of a wide open section 15, one more like section 2(b), prompted some anxiety over the Court being forced to produce some kind of section 1 justification, lest the country fall into "anarchy":

> . . . courts would be obliged to look for and find section 1 justification for most legislation, the alternative being anarchy . . .[54]

---

[51] ibid.

[52] For a discussion of the communicative function of a court finding a section 15 violation justified at s. 1 as opposed to no violation at all, see Claire Truesdale, "Section 15 and the Oakes Test: The Slippery Slope of Contextual Analysis: Symposium Issue: Commemorating the 25th Anniversary of R v Oakes, [1986] 1 SCR 103" (2011) 43 Ottawa L Rev 511 at 537–538.

[53] See discussion above (n 42), (n 43).

[54] McIntyre J. (quoting from the judgment of Hugessen J.A. in *Smith, Kline & French Laboratories Ltd. v Canada (Attorney General)*, [1987] 2 F.C. 359 (C.A.), at pp. 367–368, *Andrews*, above (n 8) 180). Recall

The idea of being "obliged" to look for justification lest all rules be thwarted points to a kind of pragmatic limit on the transformative powers of section 15—the *Charter* can only take on so much. If masses of contemporary legislation violate section 15 and are therefore unconstitutional, then it must be the *Charter* that bends.[55] That the *Charter* must not be used to invalidate massive amounts of legislation might be either counter-intuitive or obvious, depending on one's political convictions about rights review, but either way it is relatively rare to see judges overtly referencing this aspect of their decision-making, let alone treating it as the main factor in their choice.

Ultimately the Court chose an interpretation of discrimination which eliminated the extremes of this challenge, but similar concerns continue to surface. For instance, section 15(2) has been interpreted with an eye towards allowing government some freedom in developing ameliorative programs. A fear that equality will strangle government if not contained *somewhere* in the march through sections 15 and 1 has been an overt concern in terms of both the development of section 15 and the application of section 1 to these cases. Beside this pragmatic concern sits another, which takes the *location* of the containment very seriously, positing a critical if somewhat symbolic importance to the gap between non-discrimination and justified discrimination.

This critical-but-symbolic importance most obviously appears in discussions of section 15(2), often explained as a reaction to U.S. jurisprudence treating "affirmative action" programs as discriminatory.[56] These explanations are credible in terms of what the drafters were thinking, but they do not often note that the existence of section 1 *already* provides a route around such a finding (albeit not a clear textual instruction). Of course, the failure of a claim via section 1 would involve "justified discrimination", where the failure of a claim at a section 15 finding means non-discrimination. What is the significance of this, whether or not a program discriminates, *in a system where that is not the final word on the survival of the law?* This could be distinct from concerns about strangling government, or it could hint at the way even a finding of justified discrimination will constrain policy development. Refusing the language of "reverse discrimination", insisting that there is a category of programs which differentiate but do not discriminate because they are intended to improve equality, must surely suggest something about the power of the claim that a program *is* discriminatory. This in turn may illuminate why some judges resist the language of discrimination by pointing to government goals, or seem to want to stretch the concept of ameliorative program to include

---

however that under discussion in *Andrews* was the possibility of a section 15 test which left out both the grounds analysis *and* the discrimination analysis. Justice Arbour's concern in *Lavoie* was, in contrast, that the human dignity test was so subjective that it consumed the whole discrimination analysis, and belied the substantive equality commitment of *Andrews*.

[55] It may seem that the concern raised by McIntyre J. in Andrews is unclear as to whether the problem is too many cases being *brought* or too many cases being *won*, but I believe that the words "find section 1 justification" means that the problem is not cases being brought—it is how to confine the number of cases in which the claimants succeed at section 15 and section 1.

[56] Hendry above (n 3).

almost any benefit program provided by the state. These approaches avoid the finding that section 15 has been violated.

Finally, we can think about whether the anxiety which seems to attach to the very notion of justified discrimination might be attributed to a kind of what I will call a "normative mismatch" between section 15 and section 1, in the way that section 15 could be seen as an attempt to protect from the "tyranny of the majority" (even when it is an unintentional tyranny, a tyranny of non-attention, for instance), and section 1 brings back the idea that the needs of the whole might, on balance, justify discrimination. As Sheila Martin notes:

> [i]f a "commitment to social justice and equality" is a core value of a free and democratic society it may be logically difficult to hold that a breach of equality rights is a reasonable limitation.[57]

This potential "normative mismatch" may build pressure for judges to resolve cases by finding no violation rather than having to directly engage with the question of when discrimination (which was at one time dramatically defined as an affront to basic human dignity) is justified in a free and democratic society. It is perhaps not surprising that the courts relatively rarely accept the tension such a confrontation would generate.

In outlining these three themes—law-making as line drawing, the symbolic importance of whether there is justified discrimination or no discrimination at all, and "normative mismatch"—I am aiming to unpack some of the challenges that Canadian courts face in trying to work out how to apply section 1 to section 15 cases, and how these challenges shape doctrines and reasons. This unpacking does not, I think, illustrate what the Court should be doing. Rather it is meant to point out how looking at section 15 and section 1 in isolation or looking only at a section 15 win/loss record may obscure the complicated interrelationship between the two—especially as the justices of the Supreme Court have been quite inconsistent in terms of directly addressing this relationship.

4. Three Cases of "Justified Discrimination"

In this section, in an effort to illustrate the themes and concerns described above, I will consider the only three cases of "justified discrimination" released since 2001, when Martin's article was published. Two brief notes before turning to these cases. First, I am using a working hypothesis that the low number of cases is due to the symbolic tensions raised by these decisions. However, this has to be read alongside the forces that shape which challenges even make it into the court system, let alone to our

---

[57] Martin above (n 3) 364 (on section 1 and section 15).

830   OXFORD HANDBOOK OF THE CANADIAN CONSTITUTION

country's court of last resort. Quantitative approaches can be useful in filling out this picture. For instance, Choudhry and Hunter suggest there is empirical support for the hypothesis that the very difficult nature of establishing a section 15 claim means that any violations are usually found unjustifiable at section 1.[58] As such, the cases I highlight below must be seen as exceptions. Second, I have not, for reasons of space, considered the companion group of cases—post-2001 section 1 assessments in equality challenges where the government was *unsuccessful*.[59] Although more work on these cases could be useful (for instance, Sheila Martin's article considers a large number of such cases pre-2001),[60] the section 1 analyses in these cases are, in my view, perfunctory and undifferentiated from the kinds of approaches taken in cases involving other *Charter* rights. Their cursory nature is interesting—the details of it less so. With these caveats, I turn below to the three cases.

A. *Lavoie*

The decision in *Lavoie* is the most unruly of the three I will consider here, with four sets of reasons. The case involves a civil service hiring rule which creates a preference for citizens in open job competitions. The plurality upheld the law. Three justices, dissenting, found a violation of section 15, not justified under section 1, while four justices found a violation of section 15, justified under section 1. Finally, two justices found no violation at all, including Justice Arbour, whose forcefully written judgement demanded that all the others at least consider the relationship between section 15 and section 1. Her approach echoes the anxieties about overly broad approaches to section 15, and the way they either hamper legislatures or involve perverting the section 1 analysis to ensure justification. She took issue with the (then current) human dignity test from *Law*, arguing that it replicated the path rejected in *Andrews*, one in which there was a straight line from differentiation to the finding of a section 15 violation.[61] Her concern was the creation of a paradox resulting from an overly broad interpretation of section 15.

> . . . only by continually loosening the strictures imposed under the test that s. 1 can discharge the onerous burden that it has been placed under. The problem is that in thus discharging its burden s. 1 effectively denudes the equality rights guaranteed

[58] Choudhry and Hunter, above (n 34).

[59] *Trociuk v British Columbia (Attorney General)*, [2003] 1 SCR 835, 2003 SCC 34; *Nova Scotia (Workers' Compensation Board) v Martin; Nova Scotia (Workers' Compensation Board) v Laseur*, [2003] 2 SCR 504, 2003 SCC 54; *Canada (Attorney General) v Hislop*, [2007] 1 SCR 429, 2007 SCC 10.

[60] Martin above (n 3).

[61] *Lavoie v Canada*, [2002] 1 SCR 769, 2002 SCC 23 [80], [81] (Arbour J, concurring in the result). Most problematically, later in her discussion, without reference to section 15(2), she suggests that distinctions based on race might be treated as presumptive infringements ([83]), whereas others require a more searching analysis.

under s. 15(1) of their meaning and content while paying lip service to a broad and
generous concept of equality.

In other words, judges who are too generous at section 15 will be forced by institutional
competence concerns to reject the appropriate "uncompromising rigour" of section 1
in order to "guard the integrity of the legislative process".[62] This possibility, and the
word "anarchy", is the one that surfaced in *Andrews*.[63] The judges in *Lavoie* who went
the "justified discrimination" discrimination route found the law violated human dignity, a "sacrosanct" right[64] and then, in the section 1 analysis, said the impact was a mere
"inconvenience".[65] Like Justice McIntyre in *Andrews*, Justice Arbour wanted to avoid this
by tightening the section 15 analysis. In describing a narrower role for section 15 in the
name of saving it, she breaches the wall between section 15 and section 1, arguing that our
equality rights cannot be understood without attention to the realities of governance:

> No longer will keeping the legislatures functional necessitate tolerating violations of
> Charter rights, the embodiments of our freedom and of this society's most cherished
> values, in favour of less valued state objectives such as the one at issue in this case. [66]

Justice Arbour here offers her articulation of the role of the Court, and the dilemma that
the normative mismatch can produce. Her comments may speak to not only the doctrinal significance, but the symbolic significance, of designating a law "discriminatory".
However, she failed to bring any colleagues along with her.

Instead, dissenting Justices McLachlin, L'Heureux-Dubé, and Binnie took the position that there was a violation of section 15 here essentially indistinguishable from
Andrews.[67] Applying the "onerous" test for section 1 as set out in *Andrews*, they found
that it failed the rational connection requirement:

> A law that favours the relatively advantaged group of Canadian citizens over the
> relatively disadvantaged group of non-citizens serves to undermine, not fur-
> ther, the value of Canadian citizenship, based as it is on principles of inclusion and
> acceptance.[68]

---

[62] ibid (Arbour J) [91].

[63] See the concern about "anarchy" raised in *Andrews v Law Society of British Columbia*, above (n
8) discussed above (n 54). Recall however that under discussion in *Andrews* was the possibility of a
section 15 test which left out both the grounds analysis *and* the discrimination analysis. Justice Arbour's
concern in *Lavoie* was, in contrast, that the human dignity test was so subjective that it consumed the
whole discrimination analysis, and belied the substantive equality commitment of *Andrews*.

[64] Lavoie (n 60) (Arbour J) [85].

[65] ibid [79].

[66] ibid [92] (Arbour J). Although LeBel J. agreed with Justice Arbour on section 15, he felt that some of
her comments about *Oakes*, particularly about minimal impairment, went too far.

[67] ibid [1] (McLachlin & L'Heureux-Dubé JJ).

[68] ibid [11] (McLachlin and L'Heureux-Dubé JJ). Other section 15 cases which failed the rational
connection requirement under *Oakes* include *M. v H.*, [1999] 2 SCR 3 and *Vriend v Alberta*, [1998] 1 SCR 493.

They also held that it was "crucial not to elide the distinction between the claimant's onus to establish a prima facie section 15 violation and the state onus to justify . . . ".[69] The pragmatics of law-making cannot trump the institutional role of the Court. They are far less concerned about normative mismatch, pointing to the existence of a seemingly slim, but real, slice of cases in which section 15 is violated but section 1 could be invoked:

> While there is a point at which granting privileges to citizens may be unjustifiable under s. 1—banning immigrants from social housing, perhaps—that point is not the same as the point at which this Court finds a s. 15(1) violation.[70]

The other four justices, however, found justified discrimination. That justification was mainly won through the tailoring of the impugned provision to constitute "minimal impairment" of the right. The same factors that Justice Arbour relied upon to find no violation were used by these four justices to find the right had been minimally impaired. These justices held that the relative disadvantage created was "minor", an "inconvenience", a situation which left certain individuals to "fall through the cracks".[71] These things are justifiable when there is no less impairing way of meeting the Government's objective—and the Government had carefully considered a range of options. They took an approach relatively deferential to the legislative process, a standard method of responding to institutional competence concerns, though not prominent in the history of section 15.

In *Lavoie*, Justice Arbour's reasons throw the choices being made by all the members of the Court into high relief. I say this despite the fact that I think that, doctrinally and otherwise, the justices of the dissent have the correct answer in the case.[72] It is Justice Arbour who illustrates the significance of the choices and articulating the impact on section 15 of different approaches to discrimination and justification—not so much a doctrinal impact, but a symbolic and institutional impact. This analysis is worth considering for the ways that it may provide insight into the kinds of long-range thinking judges are keeping under wraps as they go through the somewhat mechanical steps and stages of the section 15 *Law* analysis and the section 1 *Oakes* test.

---

[69] *Lavoie* (n 60) [23] [47] (Bastarache J).
[70] ibid [59].
[71] ibid [69].
[72] I thank a reviewer of this chapter for pointing out that I appear to be supportive of Justice Arbour's disposition of the case. I have made efforts to be clearer that I am not. Instead, I am intrigued, or perhaps unsettled is a better word, by the way that she positions the significance of the choices judges make, and by all claims, including hers, that too open an approach to equality at section 15 is ultimately harmful to the larger cause of equality at section 15, and harmful to the *Charter* itself, as it renders equality violations less meaningful, and necessitates a loosening of the section 1 analysis. I disagree with this claim, but I wonder about the power it holds over judges picking their way through the thicket of section 15 and section 1.

B. *Newfoundland (Treasury Board) v Newfoundland and Labrador Association of Public and Private Employees*

The 2004 Supreme Court docket produced a rare, if somewhat ugly, unicorn—a unanimous case in which all members of the Bench agreed there was a section 15 violation, and all members agreed the violation was justified. In *Newfoundland (Treasury Board) v Newfoundland and Labrador Association of Public and Private Employees* (N.A.P.E.), the Supreme Court unanimously used section 1 to "save" a decision to eliminate a $24 million pay equity settlement to largely female public sector workers, after finding that section 15 was violated by the government action.[73] The critique of the decision was fairly vociferous, focusing on the extreme deference offered upon the invocation by Newfoundland of "fiscal crisis".[74] The Court appears to have tried to fend off some of this criticism, with Justice Binnie's reasons insisting they would "continue to look with strong scepticism at attempts to justify infringements of Charter rights on the basis of budgetary constraints".[75] But the opening paragraphs of the section 1 analysis signal fairly clearly what is about to happen:

> It should be stated at the outset that legislation aimed at perpetuating pay inequity is a very serious matter. Counsel for the respondent acknowledged at the hearing that this is so, but argued that this is one of those "exceedingly rare cases" where the issue is not about "administrative convenience or cost *simpliciter* or majorit[arian] [p]reference". It is, he says, about "the province's ability to deliver on some of its most basic social programs, such as education, health and welfare".[76]

This came after a relatively easy conclusion that section 15 had been violated:

> The effect of the *Public Sector Restraint Act* in 1991 was to affirm a policy of gender discrimination which the provincial government had itself denounced three years previously. The Act draws a clear formal distinction. . . . The adverse impact of the legislation therefore fell disproportionately on women, who were already at a disadvantage relative to male-dominated jobs as they earned less money.[77]

---

[73] See also those four justices in *Lavoie* who would have found a section 15 violation saved at section 1. *Lavoie,* above (n 60) [21–72] (Gonthier, Iacobucci, Major, and Bastarache JJ).

[74] See especially H Lessard, "Dollars versus [Equality] Rights: Money and the Limits on Distributive Justice" 2012 SCLR 58 (2d); J Koshan, "*Newfoundland (Treasury Board) v N.A.P.E.*" (2006) 18 C.J.W.L. 327; Judy Fudge, "Substantive Equality, the Supreme Court of Canada, and the Limits to Redistribution" (2007) 23 S.A.J.H.R. 235.

[75] *Newfoundland (Treasury Board) v N.A.P.E.*, 2004 SCC 66 [72].

[76] ibid [52].

[77] ibid [42] [emphasis added].

Compare this to Justice McLachlin's reasons in the B.C.C.A. decision in *Andrews*, many years before, where she wrote:

> Circumstances may arise where discriminatory measures can be justified. For exam-
> ple, in times of war, the internment of enemy aliens might be argued to be justifiable
> under s. 1, notwithstanding the fact that this is discriminatory and would not be tol-
> erated in peace time.[78]

Maybe fiscal crisis is the new war. In rendering the section 1 decision it is apparent that the Court paid scant attention to the section 15 context of the case. If anything, that context was overshadowed by the epic, 231-page 642-paragraph judgment delivered by the Newfoundland Court of Appeal in the case, a gauntlet thrown down defending defer-
ence through a proposal to change the *Oakes* test to more clearly honour the separation of powers.[79] In rejecting that proposal, and in mollifying those judges and governments outraged at the prospect of the Supreme Court rearranging the budgetary decisions of the province, the reasons say very little about equality per se. Rather they concentrate on defining the Spring 1991 situation in the province as "exceptional", and articulating a margin of deference for budgeting.

The specific, violated right was buried in a welter of other concerns brought into the section 1 analysis, one which does not advert to the normative mismatch at all. It focuses solely on the need for legislative room to manoeuver—in this case, in almost purely fis-
cal terms—and treats it as uncontroversial. Binnie J's reasons do focus on the precedents in so called "money versus rights" cases, but without attention to section 15. Instead he analogizes the claim of the Association to a s. 2(d) case from 1987 (it also challenged public sector restraint legislation—but only two justices even found a violation), erasing the section 15 context and the reasons that it might raise different issues requiring attention. Then the violated right is placed alongside other implications of the fiscal crisis, in ways which instantly minimize its significance. The Court's unwillingness to interfere in this process is palpable, but it is not really placed into specific conversation with the right being violated. Rather other rights are brought up to do the work:

> The government in 1991 was not just debating rights versus dollars but rights versus
> hospital beds, rights versus layoffs, rights versus jobs, rights versus education and
> rights versus social welfare. The requirement to reduce expenditures, and the allo-
> cation of the necessary cuts, *was* undertaken to promote other values of a free and
> democratic society.[80]
>   The women hospital workers were a disadvantaged group, but so in reality were
> the medical patients who lost access to 360 hospital beds, students of school boards

---

[78] *Andrews v Law Society of British Columbia*, (BC CA) 27 DLR (4th) 600; [1986] 4 WWR 242; 2 BCLR (2d) 305; [1986] BCJ No 338; 23 CRR 273 [31].
[79] *Newfoundland Assn. of Public Employees v R.*, 2002 NLCA 72. For a full description of the fracas, see Choudhury and Hunter above (n 34) 527–529.
[80] *Newfoundland (Treasury Board)*, above (n 74) [75].

whose transfers were frozen, and those who relied on other government programs that were reduced or eliminated (*although it is true that in their case Charter rights were not implicated*). As was pointed out in the House, "there was enough misery to go around".[81]

The rights claimants, in this analysis, are just another group who lost out in this cataclysm, in which the government had to act to preserve basic social goods. This is an approach that would seem to have many potential applications especially in those many section 15 claims that look to redistribution rather than recognition. Scholars have contested the Court's analysis of the level of crisis, and of course, the language of crisis as a justification for austerity is a phenomenon of neo-liberal politics writ large, rather than being confined to arcane constitutional balancing exercises.[82] But *N.A.P.E.* illustrates the potency of this language, building a section 1 argument that clearly signposts an institutional competence minefield that judges ought to walk very carefully around. Hester Lessard's consideration of *N.A.P.E.* along with the larger group of cases (many argued under section 7) which engage with rights in the context of fiscal restraint leads her to conclude:

> The tension between scarcity and justice is an abiding theme in liberal societies. Most of us accept that "money" and the scarcity of other sorts of resources limit justice. The bleakness lies in the failure of the jurisprudence to yield a workable framework for navigating the justice/scarcity tension in a principled way. The history of equality rights provides a particularly disheartening overview of this failure.[83]

C. *Quebec v A.*

The latest case to provide evidence of the treatment of section 15 claims at section 1 is *Quebec v A.*, in which splits on the Court illustrate divergent views of both section 15 and its treatment at section 1. The majority decision, finding a violation of section 15 in the Quebec laws which do not provide access to spousal support or "patrimonial property" to unmarried spouses, was written by Abella J. joined by four other judges.[84] Of these,

---

[81] ibid [93] [emphasis added].

[82] See Lessard; Koshan; Fudge above (n 74).

[83] Lessard above (n 74) 395 (She notes: "As the record since the first benefit case in 1991 indicates, only inexpensive substantive equality claims or ones in which the budgetary impact is conceded by the Crown to be insignificant—*Tétreault-Gadoury, Schachter, Eldridge, Martin* and *Hislop*—succeed.").

[84] In *Quebec (Attorney General) v A*, 2013 SCC 5, [2013] 1 SCR 61, both the lower courts and the SCC tended to split the challenge to the *Civil Code of Québec*, S.Q. 1991, c. 64 provisions into two parts, and I have done the same here. First, the challenge to the non inclusion of unmarried spouses in the obligation of spousal support (art. 585) and second, to what is variously described in English as "patrimonial property" ([41] per Lebel J), "rights of ownership" ([400]), "division of assets"([404]) or "patrimonial measures" ([408]) (all per Deschamps J.) which actually has four parts, a compensatory allowance, (arts. 427 *et seq.*), partnership of acquests (arts. 432 *et seq.*) protection of family patrimony patrimony (arts. 414 *et seq.*), and a provision dealing with the family residence (arts. 401 *et seq.*).

one found both violations justified under section 1, three found the spousal support exclusion unjustified and the property division exclusion justified, and Abella J. herself found both exclusions unjustified. In the result, the appeal was lost, as four other justices found no violation of section 15 had occurred. These latter justices saw "personal autonomy" as one of the important pieces of equality:

> The principle of personal autonomy or self-determination, to which self-worth, self-confidence and self-respect are tied, is an integral part of the values of dignity and freedom that underlie the equality guarantee. . . .[85]

This concern with autonomy, along with the 2002 case, *Walsh* (a failed equality claim by an unmarried separated spouse),[86] and a narrow view of the mischief that section 15 prevents ("a disadvantage by expressing or perpetuating prejudice or by stereotyping"[87]) was clearly one of the driving factors towards their conclusion that the provisions—far from violating section 15—were equality supporting. In stark contrast, Justice Abella found all of the impugned provisions violated section 15, and in this she carried the majority of the Court. She then concluded that none of the sections could be saved by section 1, in language which might respond to the claim of those justices in *Lavoie* who held that the Government's long engagement with the question of citizenship preferences supported the section 1 case:

> . . . the degree of legislative time, consultation and effort cannot act as a justificatory shield to guard against constitutional scrutiny. . . . Neither the deliberative policy route—nor the popularity of its outcome—is a sufficient answer to the requirement of constitutional compliance.[88]

Deschamps J. wrote for three justices who found that lack of access to support was an unjustified limit on the equality right,[89] but the limitation on property obligations was justified. Like the justices who found no violation, in her justification analysis she focused on the justificatory power of the legislature's efforts to validate individual "choice to marry", but was clear that this should function as justification of discrimination rather than an indication of non-discrimination.[90] In contrast to Justice Abella, she concluded that the limitation on the right in terms of property obligations was minimally impairing, noting a variety of ways that unmarried people could secure some aspects of property division should they choose to do so, and the way access to support

[85] ibid [139] (Lebel J).
[86] *Nova Scotia (Attorney General) v Walsh* [2002] 4 SCR 325, 2002 SCC 83.
[87] *Quebec (Attorney General) v A*, above (n 84) [281] (Lebel J).
[88] ibid [363] (Abella J).
[89] ibid [399] (Deschamps J) "A total exclusion from the right to support benefits only de facto spouses who want to avoid the obligation of support, and it impairs the interests of dependent and vulnerable former spouses to a disproportionate extent".
[90] ibid [384] (Deschamps J).

provisions (which her reasons would have created) lessened the urgency of access to the property provisions.[91] Here, other legal provisions, somewhat external to the case being argued, are raised at section 1 to illustrate how the claimants can secure some relief from the impact of the violation, an approach we might remember from *Withler*. Finally, Chief Justice McLachlin provided the swing vote by finding that *all* of the provisions were justified limits on the equality right, all of it falling into the category of "justified discrimination". She is categorical in her analysis of where the argument about "choice" belongs, and it is not at section 15:

> ... [one] difficulty with Quebec's argument is that it imports public interest considerations—the goal of maximizing choice and autonomy for conjugal partners as a whole—into the s. 15 analysis. Such interests, as I discussed above, should not be considered at the first stage of determining whether a right has been limited, but at the second stage of determining whether the limitation on the right is justified.[92]

She has chosen the strict siloing of the original *Andrews* formulation and, as Justice Arbour warned about in *Lavoie*, she then pairs it with some deferential approaches to section 1. Most tellingly, in her minimal analysis, she continues an approach seen in the *Hutterian Brethren of Wilson Colony* freedom of religion challenge.[93] In denying A's argument that an "opt out" scheme, whereby unmarried couples could opt out of these regimes, would be a lesser impairment, she set the test as "whether the limit imposed by the law goes too far *in relation to the goal the legislature seeks to achieve*".[94] She then noted that an opt-out approach would:

> require agreement and positive action on the part of *de facto* spouses. The Quebec scheme, by contrast, allows couples to avoid state-imposed obligations simply by not marrying. The state-free zone created by the Quebec scheme is thus broader than under a presumptive regime.[95]

Thus although choice does not negate the inequality problem here, the Government's wish to promote a regime based on choice to avoid potentially "paternalistic" measures "by instead allowing spouses to weigh the consequences of their choices and to make decisions accordingly"[96] is strong enough to balance the impact on those in A's position: ". . . left unprotected because their partner did not consent to marriage".[97] Looking beyond the approach from *Hutterian Brethren* we might wonder whether the reason for this approach in this case lies in some margin of extra appreciation allowed to the *Quebec* government,

---

[91] ibid [404] (Deschamps J).
[92] ibid [431] (McLachlin CJ).
[93] ibid [438] (McLachlin CJ).
[94] ibid [442] (McLachlin CJ) [emphasis in original].
[95] ibid [443] (McLachlin CJ).
[96] ibid [444] (McLachlin CJ).
[97] ibid [441] (McLachlin CJ).

given the uniqueness of this scheme in Canada, the way in which its legislative history was linked to the period of time in which the population of Quebec moved with remarkable alacrity away from very close associations with the Catholic Church, to the point where Quebec now boasts the highest percentage of unmarried couples in Canada.[98]

Moving to the final stages of the balancing test, the Chief Justice accepts that the impact of this regime on the equality right as "significant". Against this, she sets the pragmatics of law-making: "the need to allow legislatures a margin of appreciation on difficult social issues and the need to be sensitive to the constitutional responsibility of each province to legislate for its population."[99] If avoiding the strangulation of governments is a consideration, in this case we might be seeing how some governments are (perceived to be) more sensitive to choking than others.

This is a very different approach from the one that the Chief Justice proposed decades ago from her position on the British Columbia Court of Appeal in *Andrews*, where she stated that the equality right could be justifiably violated very rarely, for instance, in times of war.[100] But the Chief Justice's moves with regard to the minimal impairment test in *Hutterian Brethren*,[101] her enthusiasm for engaging with concepts such as autonomy and liberty throughout her judicial career, and, I suggest, her pragmatic concern for the potential implications for the national Court of even a partial invalidation of Quebec's unique regime in the context of Canadian federalism, are all important keys to understanding her decision. As precedent, *Quebec v A*. is important in terms of section 15 doctrine because of the way that the plurality essentially repudiated 2002's *Walsh*, and the treatment in that case of the "choice to marry".[102] With respect to section 1, however,

---

[98] See the chapters in this *Handbook* in the Part on federalism.

[99] *Quebec (Attorney General) v. A* above (n 84) [449] (McLachlin CJ).

[100] *Andrews v. Law Society of British Columbia*, (BC CA) 27 DLR (4th) 600; [1986] 4 WWR 242; 2 BCLR (2d) 305; [1986] BCJ No 338 (QL) (McLachlin J.A. as she then was) [31] ("Circumstances may arise where discriminatory measures can be justified. For example, in times of war, the internment of enemy aliens might be argued to be justifiable under s. 1, notwithstanding the fact that this is discriminatory and would not be tolerated in peace time. Viewed thus, s. 1 plays a vital role in the determination of the validity of legislation impugned on the basis of s. 15. The role, while essential, is limited; most cases may not disclose circumstances which can be argued to justify discriminatory legislation. This, in my view, is as it should be.")

[101] *Alberta v Hutterian Brethren of Wilson Colony*, 2009 SCC 37, [2009] 2 SCR 567 [53–62] (writing for the majority, the Chief Justice held that, in the section 1 analysis, the legislative goal was to be accepted into the analysis without change. In this particular case, that meant the goal was a blanket requirement of pictures on drivers licences. The working of the proportionality analysis then tended to favour the government, as the photographic requirement was what violated the religious right. However all efforts to suggest alternatives which would make space for the religious beliefs were held by the Court to deviate from the actual legislative goal. The majority concluded that, given this goal, the law "minimally impaired" the right).

[102] *Quebec (Attorney General) v. A* above (n 84) [341–347] (Abella J) (majority on this issue; dissenting in the result); *Nova Scotia (Attorney General) v Walsh*, above (n 85); for critiques of *Walsh*, see D. Majury, "Women Are Themselves to Blame: Choice as a Justification for Unequal Treatment" in F. Faraday, M. Denike, and M.K. Stephenson (eds), *Making Equality Rights Real: Securing Substantive Equality under the Charter* (Irwin Law, 2006) 209–244; S. Lawrence, "Choice, Equality and Tales of Racial Discrimination: Reading the Supreme Court on Section 15" in S. McIntyre and S. Rodgers (eds),

Quebec v A serves to illustrate the way in which successfully arguing that such considerations ("choice") are not properly part of the section 15 analysis does not change the
outcome. The Chief Justice's swing vote here referenced deliberative work on the part of
the legislature, and the need to allow not just room to legislate at all (the anarchy concern) but room in a federal system for provinces to legislate differently—even if in more
rights-restricting ways.

These three cases offer a glimpse into the ways that the Supreme Court is making
sense of the relationship between section 15 and section 1. They illustrate the scarcity of
justified discrimination decisions, and the way that such decisions contain both silences
and vigorous argument about the appropriate relationships between differentiation and
state goals—as well as between courts and governments. There is only a limited anxiety
about normative mismatch in these reasons, raised by dissenters. What these cases do
not do, I think, is help us see any particular trajectory. They can, though, help us identify
gaps and themes in the way that the Supreme Court is willing to decide that equality
rights must be sacrificed to social—or rather state—goals.

5. Conclusion

The place of government objectives in *Charter* equality claims is far from the only
challenge that burdens our understanding of this right. A short list of other problems
include many that I hinted at above—remaining confusion about how intersectional
grounds claims will be analysed,[103] a tendency to fixate on individual choice where contextual analysis might suggest more caution in using the concept of choice and liberty
to dismiss equality claims,[104] difficulties around operationalizing equality without let-
ting its comparative aspect over-determine the results,[105] and significant access to justice
issues related not only to those which arise in almost all rights claims, but specifically to
section 15 requirements that look very onerous for individual claimants.[106] In spite of
these other pressing issues, as the *Charter* promise of equality is one which is made in

Diminishing Returns: Inequality and the Canadian Charter of Rights and Freedoms (LexisNexis
Butterworths, 2006).

[103] See D. Gilbert, "The Silence of Section 15: Searching for Equality at the Supreme Court of Canada
in 2007" (2008) 42 SCLR (2d), 2008.

[104] S. Lawrence, "Choice, Equality and Tales of Racial Discrimination: Reading the Supreme Court on
Section 15" (2006). SCLR, Vol. 33, 2006.

[105] See for instance, H. Lessard, "Mothers, Fathers, and Naming: Reflections on the Law Equality
Framework and *Trociuk v. British Columbia (Attorney General)*" (2004) 16 Can. J. Women & L. 165;
S.R. Moreau, "Equality Rights and the Relevance of Comparator Groups" (2006) 5 Journal of Law &
Equality 81–96.

[106] J. Watson Hamilton and J. Koshan. "*Kahkewistahaw First Nation v. Taypotat*: An Arbitrary
Approach to Discrimination" (2016) 76 SCLR (2d) 219; Julie Jai and Joseph Cheng, "The Invisibility
of Race in Section 15: Why Section 15 of the *Charter* Has Not Done More to Promote Racial Equality"
(2006) 5 J L & Equality 125.

relation to the Canadian state, the struggle of the courts to understand the role of state goals and intentions in determining violations of section 15 is a critical area of study. Placing our attention on this question offers insight into the core questions of rights review in a democratic state, and illustrates the significance of constitutional form and text in interpreting the specifically Canadian form of a relatively abstract guarantee such as the equality provision. It reveals the shaky and limited nature of agreement amongst judges as to the content of the guarantee, illustrates the shifting ways in which government goals have repeatedly helped structure the scope of our right to equality itself, and provides insight into how observers of the Canadian experiment might answer the ultimate question about section 15: Has it made our society more equal? We are now asking that question amidst a chorus of warnings about (rising) inequality at every level of analysis. A focus on the significance of state intent may help us identify the doctrinal moves which have helped recognition as a remedy for inequality flourish, even as redistribution, and the kind of equal society it seems to promise, continues to stay largely out of the reach of constitutional law.

Bibliography

Dawson, Mary. "The Making of Section 15 of the Charter" (2006) 5 JL & Equal 25.

Dixon, Rosalind. "The Supreme Court of Canada and Constitutional (Equality) Baselines (Special Issue: Rights Constitutionalism and the Canadian Charter of Rights and Freedoms)" (2012) 50 Osgoode Hall L J 637.

Faraday, Fay, Margaret Denike, and M. Kate Stephenson. *Making Equality Rights Real: Securing Substantive Equality under the Charter.* (Irwin Law, 2006).

Fudge, Judy. "Substantive Equality, the Supreme Court of Canada, and the Limits to Redistribution" (2007) 23 S.A.J.H.R. 235.

Greschner, Donna. "The Purpose of Canadian Equality Rights" (2001) 6 Rev Const Stud 291.

Hendry, Jim. "The Idea of Equality in Section 15 and Its Development" (2002) 21 Windsor Y.B. Access Just. 153, 184.

Hogg, Peter. "What Is Equality? The Winding Course of Judicial Interpretation" (2005) 29 S.C.L.R. (2d) 39.

Hogg, Peter. "Equality as a Charter Value in Constitutional Interpretation" 20 Sup Ct L Rev (2d) 113.

Koshan, Jennifer and Jonnette Watson Hamilton. "Meaningless Mantra: Substantive Equality after *Withler*" (2011) 16 Rev Const Stud 31.

Lessard, Hester. "Dollars versus [Equality] Rights: Money and the Limits on Distributive Justice" (2012) 58 SCLR 299.

Macklem, Timothy. "Defining Discrimination" (2000) 11 KCLJ 224.

Majury, Diana. "The Charter, Equality Rights, and Women: Equivocation and Celebration" (2002) 40 Osgoode Hall LJ 297.

Martin, Sheila. "Balancing Individual Rights to Equality and Social Goals" (2001) 80 Canadian Bar Review 301.

McIntyre, Sheila and Sanda Rodgers, eds., *Diminishing Returns: Inequality and the Canadian Charter of Rights and Freedoms* (LexisNexis Canada, 2006).

McLachlin, Beverley. "Equality: The Most Difficult Right" (2001) 14 Sup. Ct. L. Rev. 17.

Moon, Richard. "Discrimination and Its Justification: Coping with Equality Rights under the Charter" (1988) 26 Osgoode Hall LJ 673.

Moreau, Sophia R. "The Wrongs of Unequal Treatment" (2004) 54 U Toronto LJ 291.

Reaume, Denise G. "Discrimination and Dignity" (2002) 63 La L Rev 645.

Ryder, Bruce, Emily Lawrence and Cidalia Faria. "What's *Law* Good For? An Empirical Overview of Charter Equality Rights Decisions" (2004) 24 Supreme Court Law Review (2d) 103.

Watson Hamilton, Jonnette and Jennifer Koshan. "*Kahkewistahaw First Nation v. Taypotat:* An Arbitrary Approach to Discrimination" (2016) 76 Supreme Court Law Review (2d) 219.

Wintemute, Robert. "Sexual Orientation and the Charter: The Achievement of Formal Legal Equality (1985–2005) and Its Limits" (2003) 49 McGill LJ 1143.

Cases

Andrews v Law Society of British Columbia, [1989] 1 S.C.R. 143.

Canada (Attorney General) v Hislop, [2007] 1 S.C.R. 429, 2007 SCC 10).

Corbiere v Canada (Minister of Indian and Northern Affairs) [1999] 2 S.C.R. 203 para 7–8.

Egan v Canada, [1995] 2 S.C.R. 513.

Gosselin v Quebec (Attorney General), [2002] 4 S.C.R. 429.

Lavoie v Canada, [2002] 1 S.C.R. 769, 2002 SCC 23.

Law v Canada (Minister of Employment and Immigration), [1999] 1 S.C.R. 497.

M. v H., [1999] 2 S.C.R. 3.

Newfoundland (Treasury Board) v N.A.P.E., 2004 SCC 66.

Nova Scotia (Workers' Compensation Board) v Martin [2003] 2 S.C.R. 504, 2003 SCC 54.

Quebec (Attorney General) v A, 2013 SCC 5, [2013] 1 S.C.R. 61.

R. v Kapp [2008] 2 S.C.R. 483, 2008 SCC 41.

Trociuk v British Columbia (Attorney General), [2003] 1 S.C.R. 835, 2003 SCC 34.

Vriend v Alberta, [1998] 1 S.C.R. 493.

Withler v Canada (Attorney General), 2011 SCC 12, [2011] 1 S.C.R. 396.

....

CHAPTER 40

SOCIAL AND ECONOMIC RIGHTS

....

MARTHA JACKMAN* &
BRUCE PORTER**

1. INTRODUCTION

....

THE constitutional status of socio-economic rights in Canada is an unresolved issue, connected to historic expectations and continuing struggles by marginalized groups for access to justice and social inclusion, as much as it is to evolving jurisprudence under the *Canadian Charter of Rights and Freedoms*.[1] Since the enactment of the *Charter*, in every case addressing the effects of poverty, homelessness, or other forms of socio-economic deprivation, judges have been confronted with two opposing paradigms of constitutional rights. Governments have argued that the absence of explicit constitutional protection for socio-economic rights reflects a political choice to leave social and economic policy exclusively to legislatures, largely immune from *Charter* review. They have characterized Canada's international human rights commitments as aspirational goals that are beyond the competence of the courts. And they have alleged that the *Charter* imposes no positive obligations on governments to implement social programs or to take action necessary to protect the life, security of the person, or equality rights of the most disadvantaged members of Canadian society.

Those who are homeless, refugees and migrants, people with disabilities, and others living in poverty, have advanced a different view of the *Charter*. They maintain that all aspects of government decision-making must be subject to *Charter* scrutiny and that broadly framed *Charter* guarantees should be read to include, rather than exclude, human rights violations experienced by disadvantaged individuals and groups. They argue the

* Full Professor, Faculty of Law, University of Ottawa.
** Director, Social Rights Advocacy Centre.
1 Part I of the *Constitution Act, 1982*, being Schedule B to the *Canada Act 1982* (UK), 1982, c 11.

Charter must do more than restrain government action: it must also require governments to adopt measures to protect *Charter* rights to life, security of the person, and equality including, where necessary, health care, housing, food security, or social assistance. People living in poverty contend that the *Charter* must be interpreted in light of Canada's obligations under the *International Covenant on Economic, Social and Cultural Rights (ICESCR)*,[2] in a manner that recognizes social and economic rights not simply as aspirational goals, but as human rights that courts are competent to adjudicate and enforce.

As this chapter documents, judicial responses to these opposing constitutional paradigms have been inconsistent. Lower courts, including in several recent cases, have often sided with governments in dismissing *Charter* claims to positive measures in the context of access to health care, housing, or adequate income. For its part, the Supreme Court of Canada has resisted efforts to circumscribe the positive scope of *Charter* guarantees and it has refused to rule that socio-economic rights fall beyond the ambit of the *Charter*. At the same time, the Supreme Court has shied away from engaging the key issues raised in cases involving socio-economic rights and it has dismissed applications to appeal lower court decisions in which the *Charter* rights claims of people living in poverty have been rejected.[3] The new millennium has seen significant international, regional, and comparative law developments in advancing access to justice for socio-economic rights claimants, disproving earlier suggestions that socio-economic rights are beyond the competence of courts to adjudicate or enforce.[4] These advances have not, as yet, been absorbed in Canadian jurisprudence, where the constitutional status of socio-economic rights remains an open question.

This chapter will first present the historical context and legislative history of the *Charter* as a source of socio-economic rights protection. It will then describe the Supreme Court of Canada's approach to interpreting the *Charter* in light of Canada's international human rights obligations, including those set out in the *ICESCR*. The chapter will next consider sections 7 and 15 of the *Charter* in particular, with specific reference to the positive versus negative rights debate to which social and economic rights claims have frequently given rise. The chapter will go on to discuss several recent *Charter* challenges in two of the most active areas of current socio-economic rights litigation in Canada: housing and health.[5] In conclusion, the chapter will refer to the recommendations of the UN Committee on Economic, Social and Cultural Rights (CESCR), in its

---

[2] *International Covenant on Economic, Social and Cultural Rights*, 16 December 1966, 993 UNTS 3, Can TS 1976 No 46 (entered into force 3 January 1976, accession by Canada 19 May 1976).

[3] Martha Jackman, 'Constitutional Castaways: Poverty and the McLachlin Court' (2010) 50 Supreme Court Law Review (2d) 297.

[4] Malcolm Langford et al. (eds), *The Optional Protocol to the International Covenant on Economic, Social and Cultural Rights: A Commentary* (Pretoria University Law Press, 2016) also online http://www.pulp.up.ac.za/edited-collections/the-optional-protocol-to-the-international-covenant-on-economic-social-and-cultural-rights-a-commentary.

[5] Although minority language education, labour, and Indigenous rights also engage important socio-economic rights issues, these constitutional guarantees are addressed in other chapters of this *Handbook*.

latest review of Canada's compliance with the *ICESCR*, for resolving the opposing paradigms that characterize this important area of constitutional rights.

A. Historical Context and Legislative History of the *Charter*

Acceptance of a positive role for governments in the promotion of human rights is a key feature of Canadian rights culture. Since the Second World War, Canadians have come to expect governments to act affirmatively to support and expand individual and collective freedom and welfare, and the view that socio-economic rights are integral to rights to life, security of the person, and equality is firmly rooted in the human rights movement in Canada.[6] Prior to the adoption of the *Charter* in 1982, positive measures to accommodate needs of disadvantaged groups and to address systemic inequality in housing, employment, and private sector and government services had already been recognized as components of the right to non-discrimination under federal and provincial human rights legislation in place across Canada by 1977.[7] In Quebec, socio-economic rights were explicitly included in the Quebec *Charter of Human Rights and Freedoms* when it was enacted in 1975.[8] Unlike the United States, Canada ratified the *ICESCR* in 1976, at the same time as the *International Covenant on Civil and Political Rights (ICCPR)*,[9] shortly before the Trudeau government began the federal-provincial constitutional reform discussions that culminated in the adoption of the *Constitution Act, 1982*.

No proposal to include social and economic rights in the *Charter* was made during the 1980–1981 hearings of the Special Joint Committee of the Senate and the House of Commons on the Constitution of Canada. An amendment was put forward to what is now section 36 of the *Constitution Act, 1982* to add a "commitment to fully implementing the *International Covenant on Economic, Social and Cultural Rights* and the goals of a clean and healthy environment and safe and healthy working conditions."[10] Although the Special Joint Committee members expressed agreement on the "principles embodied

---

[6] Martha Jackman and Bruce Porter, 'Introduction: Advancing Social Rights in Canada' in Martha Jackman and Bruce Porter (eds), *Advancing Social Rights in Canada* (Irwin Law, 2014); Martha Jackman, 'The Protection of Welfare Rights under the Charter' (1988) 20 Ottawa Law Review 2.

[7] See eg, *CN v Canada (Canadian Human Rights Commission)* [1987] 1 SCR 1114.

[8] *Quebec Charter of Human Rights and Freedoms*, RSQ 1977, c C-12; see generally Pierre Bosset and Lucie Lamarche (eds), *Droit de cité pour les droit économiques, sociaux et culturels: La Charte québécoise en chantier* (Éditions Yvon Blais, 2011); David Robitaille, *Normativité, interprétation et justification des droits économiques et sociaux: les cas québécois et sud-africain* (Éditions Bruylant, 2011).

[9] *International Covenant on Civil and Political Rights*, 19 December 1966, 999 UNTS 171, Can TS 1976 No 47 (entered into force 23 March 1976, accession by Canada 19 May 1976).

[10] Special Joint Committee of the Senate and the House of Commons on the Constitution of Canada, *Minutes of Proceedings and Evidence*, First Session of the Thirty-second Parliament, 1980–1981, Issue no. 49 (30 January 1981) 65–71.

in the amendment," it was noted that Canada was already committed to implementing the *ICESCR* and the amendment was not adopted.[11] Rather than pressing for explicit inclusion of socio-economic rights in the *Charter*, human rights experts and equality-seeking organizations generally referred to Canada's obligations under the *ICESCR* as components of the right to equality. They argued that *Charter* equality guarantees should be framed to impose clear governmental obligations to address socio-economic disadvantage through positive measures, including adequate social programs. They underscored the importance of providing strong interpretive direction to the Canadian courts to apply the *Charter* to take into account not only the potential harms but also the benefits of government action. In a sharp departure from their *Canadian Bill of Rights* record,[12] courts were expected to interpret section 15 of the *Charter* to require governments to address the needs of vulnerable groups, to remedy systemic inequality, and to maintain and improve social programs on which the enjoyment of equality and other *Charter* rights was seen to depend.[13]

Following an unprecedented lobbying campaign by women's, disability, and other human rights organizations, in and beyond the Special Joint Committee hearings, section 15 "non-discrimination rights" were renamed "equality rights" and significantly expanded to guarantee both equality "before and under" the law, and the equal "protection and benefit" of the law. This wording was designed to make it clear that equality rights applied to social benefit programs, such as welfare and unemployment insurance, and that governments' positive obligations toward disadvantaged groups were constitutionally affirmed.[14] As a result of concerted efforts by disability rights organizations, newly organized in the ferment of the International Year of Persons with Disabilities in 1981, Canada also became the first constitutional democracy to include mental and physical disability as a constitutionally prohibited ground of discrimination.[15] In their submissions to the Special Joint Committee, disability rights advocates made explicit reference to the rights to education, work, and social security under the *ICESCR*, in support of the need to add disability as a prohibited ground of discrimination under the *Charter*.[16]

The wording of section 7 of the *Charter*, which guarantees the "right to life, liberty and security of the person" drew on the text and unified framework of article 3 of the *Universal Declaration of Human Rights*.[17] A proposed amendment to add a right to "the enjoyment of property" to section 7 was rejected in part because of fears that property rights would conflict with Canadians' commitment to social programs and could give

---

[11] Ibid 49: 68–70.

[12] *Bliss v Attorney General of Canada* [1979] 1 SCR183 [191]–[194].

[13] Bruce Porter, 'Expectations of Equality', (2006) 3 Supreme Court Law Review 23.

[14] Ibid 25–29.

[15] See generally Yvonne Peters, 'From Charity to Equality: Canadians with Disabilities Take Their Rightful Place in Canada's Constitution', in Deborah Stienstra and Aileen Wight-Felske (eds), *Making Equality—History of Advocacy and Persons with Disabilities in Canada* (Captus Press, 2003) 119–136.

[16] Special Joint Committee (n 10), No. 10 (21 November 1980) 10:10.

[17] Annex to GA Res 2200A, 21 UN GAOR, supp (No 16) 52, UN Doc A/6316, (1976).

rise to challenges to government regulation of corporate interests, including environmental protection measures and provincial control over natural resources.[18] The wording of the section 7 requirement that any deprivation of life, liberty, or security of the
person be "in accordance with the principles of fundamental justice" was preferred over
a reference to "due process of law" because of concerns around the use of the due process
clause in the United States during the *Lochner* era as a means for propertied interests to
challenge the regulation of private enterprise and the promotion of social rights.[19]

In the period leading up to and following its adoption, women's, anti-poverty, disability, and other human rights and equality-seeking organizations became vocal
advocates for their interpretive expectations of the *Charter*.[20] In submissions to a parliamentary sub-committee charged with examining the new constitutional responsibilities imposed on governments by section 15,[21] women's organizations asserted that "the
poverty of women in Canada is a principal source of inequality in this country" and that
"the goal of the section is equality, a positive concept, as opposed to non-discrimination,
a negative concept."[22] People with disabilities affirmed that equality meant a decent
place to live, access to meaningful work and an adequate income, and a full range of
social opportunities.[23] In short, the interdependence between socio-economic and
Charter rights was widely accepted by disadvantaged groups from the *Charter*'s inception, although, as outlined below, this rights paradigm has met with significant resistance from governments and in the courts.

2. THE INTERNATIONAL
HUMAN RIGHTS FRAMEWORK

Rights contained in the *ICESCR* and other international human rights treaties ratified
by Canada are not directly enforceable by Canadian courts unless they are incorporated
into Canadian law by Parliament or provincial legislatures—something that has not
been seriously considered in Canada.[24] As the CESCR explains, Canada's obligation as a
State party is not to incorporate but rather to implement *ICESCR* guarantees: "Covenant
norms must be recognized in appropriate ways within the domestic legal order,

---

[18] Martha Jackman, 'Poor Rights: Using the Charter to Support Social Welfare Claims' (1993) 19
Queen's LJ 65, 76.

[19] Sujit Choudhry, 'The *Lochner* Era and Comparative Constitutionalism', (2004) 2 *International
Journal of Constitutional Law* 1, 16–24.

[20] Porter, 'Expectations of Equality' above (n 13) 23.

[21] Canada, The Sub-committee on Equality Rights of the Standing Committee on Justice and Legal
Affairs, *Minutes of Proceedings* First Session of the 33rd Parliament, Vol. 3 (17 April 1985).

[22] Porter, 'Expectations of Equality', above (n 13) 30.

[23] Ibid 33.

[24] *Baker v Canada (Minister of Citizenship and Immigration)* [1999] 2 SCR 817 [69]–[71].

appropriate means of redress, or remedies, must be available to any aggrieved individual or group, and appropriate means of ensuring governmental accountability must be put in place."[25]

In his dissenting judgment in *Reference Re Public Service Employee Relations Act (Alberta)*, Chief Justice Dickson declared that "the *Charter* should generally be presumed to provide protection at least as great as that afforded by similar provisions in international human rights documents which Canada has ratified."[26] This interpretive presumption, which has been reiterated by the majority of the Court,[27] applies not only to rights with direct counterparts in the *Charter*, such as the right to life or to non-discrimination under the *ICCPR*, but has also been invoked in cases involving socio-economic rights guaranteed under the *ICESCR*.

For example, in its 1989 decision in *Slaight Communications*, the Court pointed to Canada's ratification of the *ICESCR* as evidence that the right to work is a fundamental human right, that had to be balanced against the section 2(b) *Charter* right to freedom of expression in that case.[28] In its 2015 ruling in *Saskatchewan Federation of Labour*, the Court reversed its previous jurisprudence on the right to strike as a component of the right to freedom of association under section 2(d) of the *Charter*, relying, inter alia, on the CESCR's interpretation of the right to strike under the *ICESCR*.[29] Referring to the *ICESCR* as one of the most important sources for the interpretation of section 2(d), Chief Justice McLachlin and Justice Lebel explained in *Health Services Bargaining Assn* that "the *Charter*, as a living document, grows with society and speaks to the current situations and needs of Canadians. Thus Canada's *current* international law commitments and the current state of international thought on human rights provide a persuasive source for interpreting the scope of the *Charter*."[30]

3. SECTIONS 7 AND 15 AS A SOURCE OF PROTECTION FOR SOCIO-ECONOMIC RIGHTS

The Supreme Court has explicitly left open the possibility that the *Charter* may protect a range of socio-economic rights. In its 1986 decision in *Irwin Toy*, the Court rejected a section 7 challenge to government regulation of corporate activities on the grounds that

---

[25] Committee on Economic, Social and Cultural Rights, *General Comment 9, The domestic application of the Covenant* (Nineteenth session, 1998), E/C.12/1998/24 (1998), [2].

[26] *Reference Re Public Service Employee Relations Act (Alberta)* [1987] 1 SCR 313 [59].

[27] See eg *Health Services and Support—Facilities Subsector Bargaining Assn v British Columbia* 2007 SCC 27 [70]; *Ontario (Attorney General) v Fraser* 2011 SCC 20 [92]; *Saskatchewan Federation of Labour v Saskatchewan* 2015 SCC 4 [62]–[65].

[28] *Slaight Communications v Davidson* [1989] 1 SCR 1038, 1056–1057.

[29] *Saskatchewan Federation of Labour*, above (n 27) [65], [68].

[30] *Health Services Assn*, above (n 27) [78].

private property rights had been intentionally excluded from the *Charter*.[31] However, the Court was careful to distinguish what it characterized as "corporate-commercial economic rights" from "such rights, included in various international covenants, as rights to social security, equal pay for equal work, adequate food, clothing and shelter."[32] The Court found that it would be "precipitous" to exclude the latter class of rights at so early a moment in *Charter* interpretation.[33]

Despite the Supreme Court's caution, most Canadian lower courts called upon to consider poverty, homelessness, or other socio-economic rights claims during the first two decades of the *Charter* rejected such challenges on the basis that economic rights were excluded from section 7 and so beyond the purview of the courts.[34] At the Supreme Court level, however, the question left unanswered in *Irwin Toy*, about the status of *ICESCR* rights under section 7, lay essentially dormant until the 2003 *Gosselin* case. In *Gosselin*, the Court considered the constitutionality of a Quebec regulation that dramatically reduced benefits for welfare recipients under the age of 30 who were not participating in training or work experience programs.[35] In her dissenting judgment, Justice Arbour found that the section 7 right to security of the person imposed a positive obligation on governments to provide those in need with an amount of social assistance adequate to cover basic necessities.[36] The majority of the Court left open the possibility of such an interpretation in a future case, but it concluded there was insufficient evidence to make this finding on the facts of *Gosselin*, as compensatory "workfare" provisions were available and, in the majority's view, "the evidence of actual hardship is wanting." [37] As Chief Justice McLachlin explained:

> The question therefore is not whether s. 7 has ever been—or will ever be—recognized as creating positive rights. Rather, the question is whether the present circumstances warrant a novel application of s. 7 as the basis for a positive state obligation to guarantee adequate living standards. I conclude that they do not.[38]

Although the Supreme Court's approach to section 7 has been inconclusive, in its early section 15 jurisprudence the Court played a leading role, internationally, in affirming

---

[31]   *Irwin Toy Ltd v Quebec (Attorney General)* [1989] 1 SCR 927, 1003.

[32]   Ibid 1003–1004

[33]   Ibid.

[34]   David Wiseman, 'Methods of Protection of Social and Economic Rights in Canada' in Fons Coomans (ed), *Justiciability of Economic and Social Rights: Experiences from Domestic Systems* (Intersentia, 2006) 173; Jackman, 'Poor Rights', above (n 18).

[35]   *Gosselin v Quebec (Attorney General)* 2002 SCC 84.

[36]   Ibid [82]–[83].

[37]   Ibid [83].

[38]   Ibid [82]. For critiques of *Gosselin* and the Court's post-*Gosselin* record see Sanda Rodgers and Sheila McIntyre (eds), *The Supreme Court of Canada and Social Justice: Commitment, Retrenchment or Retreat?* (LexisNexis, 2010); Kerri Froc, 'Is The Rule of Law the Golden Rule? Accessing "Justice" for Canada's Poor' (2008) 87 Canadian Bar Review 459; Margot Young et al. (eds), *Poverty: Rights, Social Citizenship, and Legal Activism* (University of British Columbia Press, 2007).

and developing a notion of substantive equality that includes important dimensions of socio-economic rights as well as positive governmental obligations to remedy disadvantage. The Court recognized that programs such as social assistance for single mothers are "encouraged" by section 15 and it ordered positive remedies to under-inclusive benefit programs on that basis.[39] Following the Supreme Court's lead, in the 1993 *Sparks* case, the Nova Scotia Court of Appeal extended security of tenure protection to approximately 10,000 public housing tenants, after finding that restrictions on the scope of the province's residential tenancies legislation discriminated on the grounds of poverty, race, sex/marital status, and public housing residence.[40] Likewise, in the 2002 *Falkiner* case, the Ontario Court of Appeal found that "spouse-in-the-house" rules limiting social assistance eligibility of single mothers living with male partners was discriminatory based on sex and receipt of public assistance, and the Court ordered that benefits be extended to include this group.[41] In these cases appellate courts recognized the existence of systemic discrimination on the grounds of poverty, or reliance on social assistance or public housing, and accepted these as analogous grounds of discrimination that are prohibited under section 15.

However, even in its most progressive judgments, the Supreme Court has stepped back from explicitly affirming a key element of equality that was advanced by human rights advocates and equality-seeking organizations during pre-*Charter* debates over the wording of section 15, and that is also at the core of Canada's international human rights obligations. Although repeatedly declaring its commitment to substantive equality the Court has yet to rule that, in the absence of an under-inclusive program or benefits scheme, the *Charter* imposes a positive obligation on governments to provide benefits or social programs necessary to address the needs of disadvantaged groups.[42] The Court has also failed to address the question of whether socio-economic status, or the "social condition of poverty" should be recognized as a prohibited ground of discrimination under section 15, having refused leave to appeal a number of lower court decisions in which this argument was made and rejected.[43]

---

[39] *Schachter v Canada* [1992] 2 SCR 679 [41].

[40] *Dartmouth/Halifax (Country) Regional Housing Authority v Sparks* (1993) 119 NSR (2d) 91 (NS CA).

[41] *Falkiner v Ontario (Ministry of Community and Social Services)* (2002) 59 OR (3d) (ON CA).

[42] See generally Sanda Rodgers and Sheila McIntyre (eds), *Diminishing Returns: Inequality and the Canadian Charter of Rights and Freedoms* (LexisNexis Butterworths, 2006); Porter, 'Expectations of Equality', above (n 13) 40–41; David Wiseman, 'Managing the Burden of Doubt: Social Science Evidence, the Institutional Competence of Courts, and the Prospects for Anti-poverty *Charter* Claims' (2014) 33 National Journal of Constitutional Law 1.

[43] See eg *Boulter v Nova Scotia Power Assn Inc* 2009 NSCA 17, leave to appeal to SCC refused, 33124 (10 September 2009); Claire McNeil and Vincent Calderhead, 'Access to Energy: How Form Overtook Substance and Disempowered the Poor in Nova Scotia' in Jackman and Porter, *Advancing Social Rights*, above (n 6) 253. For a review of socio-economic status as an analogous ground see Wayne MacKay and Natasha Kim, *Adding Social Condition to the Canadian Human Rights Act* (Canadian Human Rights Commission, 2009); Kerry Froc, 'Immutability Hauntings: Socio-economic Status and Women's Right to Just Conditions of Work under Section 15 of the *Charter*' in Jackman and Porter, *Advancing Social Rights*, above (n 6) 187.

4. POSITIVE AND NEGATIVE DUTIES
IN RELATION TO SOCIO-ECONOMIC RIGHTS

The Supreme Court has acknowledged that the *Charter* places duties on governments that can be categorized as both positive and negative. In its 1998 ruling in *Vriend*, that the Alberta government's failure to prohibit discrimination based on sexual orientation under its human rights legislation was unconstitutional, the Court addressed the argument that government inaction could not be subject to *Charter* review:

> The relevant subsection, s. 32(1) (b), states that the *Charter* applies to "the legislature and government of each province in respect of all matters within the authority of the legislature of each province". There is nothing in that wording to suggest that a posi-tive act encroaching on rights is required . . . Dianne Pothier has correctly observed that s. 32 is "worded broadly enough to cover positive obligations on a legislature such that the *Charter* will be engaged even if the legislature refuses to exercise its authority" . . . The application of the *Charter* is not restricted to situations where the government actively encroaches on rights.[44]

In the 1997 *Eldridge* case the claimants, who were born deaf, argued that the government of British Columbia's failure to fund sign language interpretation services within the publicly funded health care system violated section 15.[45] In response, the Attorney General of British Columbia and other government interveners insisted that "s. 15(1) does not oblige governments to implement programs to alleviate disadvantages that exist independently of state action."[46] Writing for a unanimous Court, Justice La Forest stated that "this position bespeaks a thin and impoverished vision of s. 15(1). It is belied, more importantly, by the thrust of this Court's equality jurisprudence."[47]

Similarly, the Supreme Court has recognized that section 7 of the *Charter* has both negative and positive dimensions. In the health care context, for example, the Court found in the 1988 *Morgentaler* case,[48] dealing with women's access to reproductive health services; in the 2015 *Carter* case,[49] dealing with access to physician-assisted death; and in the 2015 *Smith* case, dealing with access to medical marihuana,[50] that section 7 imposes negative duties on governments to refrain from adversely affecting individual physical or psychological health or security. From a positive rights perspective, in the 1999 *G.(J.)*

---

[44] *Vriend v Alberta* [1998] 1 S.C.R. 493 [60], citing Dianne Pothier, 'The Sounds of Silence: *Charter* Application When the Legislature Declines to Speak' (1996) 7 Constitutional Forum 113, 115.

[45] *Eldridge v British Columbia (AG)* [1997] 3 SCR 624. In particular, one of the applicants underwent an emergency caesarean section with no hospital staff able to communicate with her about the procedure or her newborn twins' survival or state of health.

[46] Ibid [72].

[47] Ibid [73].

[48] *R v Morgentaler* [1988] 1 SCR 30.

[49] *Carter v Canada (Attorney General)* 2015 SCC 5.

[50] *R v Smith* 2015 SCC 34.

case, the Court rejected the New Brunswick government's argument that it had no obligation to provide legal aid to the appellant, a single mother in receipt of social assistance who was unable to afford a lawyer to represent her in child welfare proceedings.[51] The Court found that in circumstances where her security of the person was under threat, section 7 imposed "a positive constitutional obligation to provide state-funded counsel" so that the appellant could participate meaningfully in the proceedings in conformity with section 7 principles of fundamental justice.[52] Justice Arbour summarized the Court's position on the justiciability of the positive rights claim in *Gosselin*:

> This Court has never ruled, nor does the language of the Charter itself require, that we must reject any positive claim against the state—as in this case—for the most basic positive protection of life and security. This Court has consistently chosen instead to leave open the possibility of finding certain positive rights to the basic means of subsistence within s. 7.[53]

In the 2011 *PHS Community Services (Insite)* case, the claimants challenged the Government's refusal to grant an exemption from federal narcotics control legislation that the Insite supervised safe injection clinic required in order to offer services to intravenous drug users in Vancouver's Downtown Eastside.[54] The Supreme Court found that, by putting their lives and health at risk, the Government had violated the claimants' rights to life and security of the person.[55] Given clear evidence of the benefits of Insite's safe injection and related health services, both for individual and community health and safety, the Court concluded that the Government's failure to grant the exemption was arbitrary and so in violation of section 7 principles of fundamental justice.[56] On that basis, the Court ordered the federal Minister of Health to act immediately to provide the exemption that Insite needed to continue offering its services.[57]

At the same time, the negative rights paradigm that human rights advocates and equality-seeking organizations criticized during pre-*Charter* debates, and that textual changes to the language of the *Charter* were designed to overcome, remains a serious obstacle in socio-economic rights litigation. For instance, in the 2004 *Auton* case, the claimants relied on the Supreme Court's earlier decision in *Eldridge* to argue that the British Columbia government's failure to fund their autistic children's intensive behavioural treatment violated section 15 of the *Charter*.[58] In rejecting that claim, Chief Justice McLachlin stated that: "this Court has repeatedly held that the legislature is under no obligation to create a particular benefit. It is free to target the social programs it wishes

---

[51] *New Brunswick (Minister of Health and Community Service) v G(J)* [1999] 3 SCR 46.

[52] Ibid [81], [108].

[53] *Gosselin* above (n 35) [309] (Arbour J), [83] (McLachlin CJ).

[54] *Canada (Attorney General) v PHS Community Services Society* 2011 SCC 44 [hereinafter *Insite*].

[55] Ibid [93].

[56] Ibid [130]–[132].

[57] Ibid [150], [156].

[58] *Auton (Guardian ad litem of) v British Columbia (Attorney General)* 2004 SCC 78.

to fund as a matter of public policy, provided the benefit itself is not conferred in a discriminatory manner."[59]

In the 2005 *Chaoulli* case, the appellants, backed by interveners representing a number of private clinics, argued that Quebec's prohibition on private health insurance deprived them of access to timely care, thereby violating their section 7 rights to life and security of the person as well as their right to life under section 1 of the *Quebec Charter*.[60] In response to the dissenting justices' concern that "[t]he resolution of such a complex fact-laden policy debate does not fit easily within the institutional competence or procedures of courts of law"[61] Chief Justice McLachlin and Justice Major argued that:

> While the decision about the type of health care system Quebec should adopt falls to the Legislature of that province, the resulting legislation, like all laws, is subject to constitutional limits, including those imposed by s. 7 of the *Charter*. The fact that the matter is complex, contentious or laden with social values does not mean that the courts can abdicate the responsibility vested in them by our Constitution to review legislation for *Charter* compliance when citizens challenge it.[62]

In their view, although the *Charter* "does not confer a freestanding constitutional right to health care" nevertheless, "where the government puts in place a scheme to provide health care, that scheme must comply with the *Charter*."[63] The Chief Justice and Justice Major went on to find that delays in obtaining health care posed a threat to life, and to physical and psychological security, and that the government's failure to ensure timely access to health care of reasonable quality triggered the application of section 7.[64] Emphasizing that the appellants were not seeking "an order that the government spend more money on health care" or "that waiting times for treatment under the public health care scheme be reduced" but only that "they should be allowed to take out insurance to permit them to access private services" Chief Justice McLachlan and Justice Major agreed with Justice Deschamps that Quebec's ban on private insurance must be struck down.[65] In contrast, the three dissenting justices referred to evidence accepted by the trial judge that the prohibition was necessary to protect the publicly funded system, upon which everyone relies,[66] and they warned that: "the *Canadian Charter* should not become an instrument to be used by the wealthy to 'roll back' the benefits of a legislative scheme that helps the poorer members of society."[67]

---

[59] Ibid [41].
[60] *Chaoulli v Quebec (Attorney General)* 2005 SCC 35.
[61] Ibid [164].
[62] Ibid [107].
[63] Ibid [104].
[64] Ibid [102], [111]–[119].
[65] Ibid [103]. Four of seven justices ruled the ban violated the *Quebec Charter* [100] (Deschamps J), [102] (McLachlin CJ, Major and Bastarache JJ); three of seven justices found it also offended section 7 [159] (McLachlin CJ, Major and Bastarache JJ).
[66] Ibid [240]–[241].
[67] Ibid [274].

5. Recent Socio-economic Rights Litigation in the Areas of Health and Housing

Charter claims by disadvantaged individuals in need of publicly funded health care or protection from the consequences of homelessness, although raising similar life and security of the person interests to those recognized by the Supreme Court in *Chaoulli*, have been treated very differently by lower courts. The recent *Toussaint*[68] and *Canadian Doctors for Refugee Care*[69] health care challenges, and the *Adams*,[70] *Abbotsford*,[71] and *Tanudjaja*,[72] decisions in the homelessness context, illustrate the tension between competing constitutional paradigms that continues to underlie socio-economic rights adjudication in Canada.

In the 2010 *Toussaint* case the applicant, who had worked in Canada for a number of years as an undocumented migrant, developed several life-threatening medical conditions related to untreated diabetes and hypertension.[73] Her application under the Interim Federal Health Benefit Program (IFHP) was denied, on the grounds that she did not fall within the four classes of immigrants eligible for coverage.[74] On a judicial review application to the Federal Court, the applicant alleged that the denial of health care violated sections 7 and 15 of the *Charter*. Citing *Chaoulli* the Attorney General of Canada claimed that, as there is no freestanding right to publicly funded health care under the *Charter*, "it clearly follows that non-citizens residing illegally in Canada certainly do not" possess such rights. [75] Justice Zinn rejected the Government's argument that section 7 cannot be applied to the denial of publicly funded health care and instead found that, by "expos[ing] her to a risk to her life as well as to long-term, and potentially irreversible, negative health consequences," exclusion from the IFHP violated the applicant's rights to life and to security of the person.[76]

Nevertheless, Justice Zinn went on to decide that denying health care benefits to the applicant and others who have chosen to enter or remain in Canada illegally was not arbitrary as, "to grant such coverage to those persons would make Canada a health-care safe haven for all who require health care and health care services."[77] In response to the

---

[68]   *Toussaint v Canada* 2011 FCA 213, aff'g *Toussaint v Canada* 2010 FC 810.
[69]   *Canadian Doctors for Refugee Care v Canada* (AG) 2014 FC 651.
[70]   *Victoria (City) v Adams* 2009 BCCA 172, aff'g *Victoria (City) v Adams* 2008 BCSC 1363.
[71]   *Abbotsford (City) v Shantz* 2015 BCSC 1909.
[72]   *Tanudjaja v Canada (Attorney General)* 2013 ONSC 5410, aff'd 2014 ONCA 852, leave to appeal to SCC refused, 36283 (25 June 2015).
[73]   *Toussaint* (FC), above (n 68).
[74]   Ibid [19].
[75]   Ibid [73].
[76]   Ibid [91].
[77]   Ibid [94].

applicant's reliance on the right to health guaranteed under article 12(1) of the *ICESCR*, Justice Zinn stated that: "This application cannot succeed on the basis of the alleged international law obligations of Canada because Canada has not expressly implemented them."[78] On appeal, the Federal Court of Appeal accepted Justice Zinn's finding that "the appellant was exposed to a . . . risk significant enough to trigger a violation of her rights to life and security of the person."[79] However, the Court of Appeal ruled that the appellant's own conduct was the "operative cause" of any injury to her section 7 rights,[80] and it agreed with the trial court that the appellant's exclusion from the IFHP did not violate section 7 principles of fundamental justice.[81]

Less than three weeks after the Supreme Court refused leave to appeal the decision in *Toussaint*, the federal government announced revisions to the IFHP to exclude further classes of migrants from health care coverage, including refugee claimants from designated countries of origin, and failed refugee claimants.[82] These IFHP changes were challenged by a number of individuals and organizations in the 2014 *Canadian Doctors for Refugee Care* case.[83] In her decision at the Federal Court trial level, Justice Mactavish found that the deliberate exclusion of the targeted groups constituted "cruel and unusual treatment or punishment" under section 12 of the *Charter*, and was also discriminatory on the ground of national or ethnic origin under section 15.[84]

However, Justice Mactavish dismissed the applicants' claim that the IFHP cuts violated section 7.[85] She pointed out that, in *Chaoulli*, the applicants were not asking the court to order the Government to pay for, but rather were challenging limits on their ability to obtain their own private care.[86] With reference to the *Insite* case, although Insite's safe injection program was publicly funded, she suggested that "there is . . . a world of difference between requiring the state to grant an exemption that would allow a health care provider to provide medical services funded by others and requiring the state itself to fund medical care."[87] After reviewing a series of cases in which positive rights-based claims had, as in *Toussaint*, been unsuccessful,[88] Justice Mactavish concluded that

---

[78] Ibid [70].

[79] Ibid [61].

[80] Ibid [72]–[73].

[81] Ibid [82].

[82] Ibid leave to appeal to SCC refused, 17813 (5 April 2012). The changes to the IFHP were announced on 25 April 2012. *Canadian Doctors for Refugee Care* above (n 69) [54]. After the Supreme Court denied her leave to appeal, Toussaint filed a petition to the UN Human Rights Commission under the *Optional Protocol* to the *ICCPR; Nell Toussaint v Canada* HRC No 2348-2014 http://www.socialrightscura.ca/eng/legal-strategies-right-to-healthcare.html.

[83] *Canadian Doctors for Refugee Care*, above (n 69).

[84] Ibid [12]–[14].

[85] Ibid [510].

[86] Ibid [533]–[534].

[87] Ibid [538].

[88] Ibid 539–570.

"the Charter's guarantees of life, liberty and security of the person do not include the positive right to state funding for health care."[89]

Litigation with respect to the right to adequate housing under section 7 is in a similar state of uncertainty—claims against interference with the right to shelter under section 7 having been upheld by lower courts whereas claims to positive measures to ensure access to housing have been rejected.[90] In the 2008 *Adams* case, residents of a tent city in Victoria successfully challenged the constitutionality of a municipal bylaw that prohibited the erection of temporary structures in public parks at night.[91] At trial, Justice Ross found that the shortage of shelter spaces in Victoria meant that "hundreds of people are left to sleep in public places in the City"[92] and that the Government's interference with the ability of homeless people to provide themselves with temporary shelter while sleeping outdoors exposed them to a risk of serious harm, including death by hypothermia.[93] On that basis she found that the prohibition on erecting temporary shelter violated section 7 of the *Charter*.[94]

In arriving at her decision, Justice Ross underlined the fact that the defendants were not seeking to compel the government to provide them with adequate shelter, but instead were challenging restrictions on their ability to shelter themselves, akin to the situation in *Chaoulli*.[95] Likewise, in upholding Justice Ross's ruling on appeal, the British Columbia Court of Appeal emphasized that it was applying section 7 as a negative "restraint" on government action, rather than as a source of positive obligations to address the problem of homelessness or the rights of the homeless.[96] Whereas the Court of Appeal recognized that the trial court's decision would likely require some responsive action by the City to deal with the inadequate number of shelter beds and the lack of housing options available to homeless people in Victoria, the Court declared "[t]hat kind of responsive action to a finding that a law violates s. 7 does not involve the court in adjudicating positive rights."[97]

The British Columbia Supreme Court relied on the *Adams* decision in coming to a similar finding in the 2015 *Abbotsford* case, that a bylaw prohibiting the erection of

---

[89] Ibid 571. Following the electoral defeat of the Conservative government in 2015, the new Liberal government announced that it would withdraw the appeal to Justice Mactavish's ruling and review the Government's position in future *Charter* litigation. Statement from the Minister of Immigration, Refugees and Citizenship and the Minister of Justice and Attorney General of Canada Ottawa, 16 December 2015 http://news.gc.ca/web/article-en.do?nid=1025029.

[90] See generally Martha Jackman, '*Charter* Remedies for Socio-economic Rights Violations: Sleeping under a Box?' in Robert J Sharpe and Kent Roach (eds), *Taking Remedies Seriously* (Canadian Institute for the Administration of Justice, 2010) 279; Margot Young, '*Charter* Eviction: Litigating out of House and Home' (2015) 24 Journal of Law & Social Policy 46.

[91] *Adams* (SC), above (n 70).

[92] Ibid [58].

[93] Ibid [142].

[94] Ibid [216].

[95] Ibid [119]–[120].

[96] *Adams* (CA) (n 70) [95].

[97] Ibid [96]. See also *British Columbia v. Adamson*, 2016 BCSC 584.

temporary shelter or sleeping in parks overnight violated section 7.[98] The challenge arose following the City of Abbotsford's efforts to evict residents from homeless encampments, using "displacement tactics" that included damaging tents and personal property and spreading chicken manure.[99] In response to the City's submission that many of those who are homeless have a "disinclination . . . to rules" and prefer to sleep outside "over other viable options"[100] Chief Justice Hinkson pointed out that, "to assert that homelessness is a choice ignores realities such as poverty, low income, lack of work opportunities, the decline in public assistance, the structure and administration of government support, the lack of affordable housing, addiction disorders, and mental illness."[101] In striking down the bylaw, Chief Justice Hinkson underlined the fact that the claimants were "not seeking to impose any positive obligations on the City"[102] and that "the obligation to provide housing for the homeless, if it exists, is not a burden that the City must discharge in these proceedings."[103]

In the 2013 *Tanudjaja* case the applicants, who had experienced inadequate housing and homelessness, challenged the federal and Ontario governments' failure to take positive measures to address the problem of homelessness.[104] In particular, in collaboration with a number of human rights, anti-poverty, and housing organizations participating as public interest interveners, the applicants argued that the federal government's failure to implement a national strategy to address homelessness violated sections 7 and 15 of the *Charter*.[105] The Attorneys General of Ontario and Canada brought a successful motion before the Ontario Superior Court to dismiss the claim, on the grounds that section 7 does not require governments to adopt positive measures, and that the right to housing is non-justiciable. In granting the motion to strike, Justice Lederer held that the *Charter* imposes neither positive obligations on governments in general, nor any particular requirement to provide "affordable, adequate, accessible housing."[106] In Justice Lederer's view:

> The *Charter* does nothing to provide assurance that we all share a right to a minimum standard of living. Any Application built on the premise that the *Charter* imposes such a right cannot succeed and is misconceived . . . General questions that reference, among many other issues . . . the levels of housing supports and income supplements, the basis on which people may be evicted from where they live and the treatment of those with psycho-social and intellectual disabilities are important, but the courtroom is not the place for their review.[107]

---

[98] *Abbotsford*, above (n 71).
[99] Ibid [94]–[115].
[100] Ibid [76]–[77].
[101] Ibid [81].
[102] Ibid [148].
[103] Ibid [271].
[104] *Tanudjaja* (ONSC) above (n 72).
[105] Ibid [2].
[106] Ibid [59].
[107] Ibid [120].

Justice Lederer's dismissal of the *Tanudjaja* application was upheld by a 2-1 majority of the Ontario Court of Appeal. In her dissenting judgment, Justice Feldman found that the motions judge had characterized the applicants' claim "in an overly broad manner," that he erred in finding that the section 7 jurisprudence on whether positive obligations can be imposed on governments to address homelessness was settled, and that the issues raised in the case should not have been determined without a full hearing on the evidence.[108] Writing for herself and Justice Strathy, Justice Pardu did not comment on the issue of positive obligations. Instead she found that that the applicants' failure to challenge a specific law meant there was "no sufficient legal component to engage the decision-making capacity of the courts."[109] As she saw it, the application amounted to a claim to a "free-standing right to adequate housing"[110] which "is not a question that can be resolved by application of law, but rather it engages the accountability of the legislatures"[111] and was therefore non-justiciable.[112]

The lower courts' decisions in *Tanudjaja* amounts to a finding that some violations of the right to life and equality—those involving interconnected laws, policies, and programs in complex areas of social and economic policy—are beyond the scope of the *Charter*. With the denial of a hearing on the evidence, and the Supreme Court of Canada's refusal to grant leave to appeal the motion to dismiss in *Tanujaja*, socio-economic rights remain in the unsettled state that has prevailed since *Gosselin*: caught between two contrasting constitutional rights paradigms. Unless there is a significant change in the way governments defend against such claims, government lawyers will continue to insist that socio-economic rights ought not to be "read in" as components of sections 7 and 15 of the *Charter*. Claimants, for whom deprivations of life, security of the person, and equality result from government action and inaction in the socio-economic sphere will continue to maintain that their rights should not be "read out."[113]

6. CONCLUSION

In other states where the protection of socio-economic rights relies on the interpretation and application of rights to life and to non-discrimination, efforts to secure remedies for social and economic rights violations as components of these rights have sometimes been criticized as attempts to supplement inadequate constitutional provisions through

---

[108]   Ibid [52].
[109]   Ibid [27].
[110]   Ibid [33].
[111]   Ibid [33].
[112]   Ibid [36].
[113]   Gwen Brodsky, 'The Subversion of Human Rights by Governments in Canada' in Jackman and Porter, *Advancing Social Rights* above (n 6) 355; Bruce Porter, 'Inclusive Interpretations: Social and Economic Rights and the Canadian Charter' in Helena Alviar García, Karl Klare and Lucy A Williams (eds), *Social and Economic Rights in Theory and Practice: Critical Enquiries* (Routledge, 2014) 215.

expansive judicial interpretation. Given the historical context and legislative history of the *Charter*, this critique is especially misplaced in Canada. Such strategies are better understood as claims to the same rights advanced in different circumstances, calling for equal protection and benefit of *Charter* guarantees of life, liberty, security of the person, and equality without discrimination based on socio-economic disadvantage. This was indeed the expectation of human rights advocates and equality-seeking organizations when the content of the *Charter* was being negotiated 35 years ago.

During her tenure as UN High Commissioner for Human Rights, Justice Louise Arbour observed that: "the potential to give economic, social and cultural rights the status of constitutional entitlement represents an immense opportunity to affirm our fundamental Canadian values, giving them the force of law."[114] Yet, as Justice Arbour acknowledged from her experience on the Supreme Court of Canada, section 15 has yet to fully deliver on its promise of substantive equality for disadvantaged groups seeking remedies not only for inequitable but for inadequate social programs and policies. The question, left open by the Supreme Court in *Irwin Toy*, of whether section 7 should be interpreted to include social and economic rights such as the right to food, housing, or social security, also remains unanswered.

The status of socio-economic rights under the *Charter* and the related demand for equal recognition of the rights to life, security of the person, and equality of the most disadvantaged need not, however, be left exclusively to the courts to decide. Civil society groups have begun to take up the issue of rights interpretation in a manner reminiscent of their role in the pre-*Charter* debates over the scope of the new Canadian Constitution. In the most recent CESCR review of Canada in February 2016, dozens of organizations representing Indigenous people, people with disabilities, women, those living in poverty, and racialized and other disadvantaged groups, appeared before the Committee to reassert that access to justice for violations of socio-economic rights in Canada relies on inclusive interpretations of existing *Charter* rights. In its *Concluding Observations*, the CESCR held both Canadian governments and courts responsible for their respective roles in denying access to effective remedies for socio-economic rights violations within the domestic constitutional framework.[115]

As in previous reports,[116] the Committee underscored the need to improve the accountability of the judiciary and administrative decision-makers to socio-economic rights norms, recommending that Canada: "improve human rights training programmes in order to ensure better knowledge, awareness and application of the Covenant, in particular among the judiciary, law enforcement and public officials."[117] In

---

[114] Louise Arbour, '"Freedom from Want"—From Charity to Entitlement', LaFontaine-Baldwin Lecture, Quebec City (2005) 7. Accessed at: https://www.icc-icc.ca/site/site/uploads/2016/11/LaFontaineBaldwinLecture2005_LouiseArbour.pdf .

[115] United Nations Committee on Economic, Social and Cultural Rights, *Concluding Observations on the Sixth Periodic Report of Canada*, UN Doc E/C.12/CAN/CO/6 (4 March 2016) [5].

[116] Porter, 'Inclusive Interpretations', above (n 113).

[117] CESCR, *Concluding Observations*, above (n 115).

addition, the Committee urged Canadian governments to engage directly with rights-claiming constituencies and to alter their own approach to the justiciability of social and economic rights under the *Charter*, in order to better reflect and respect Canada's international human rights undertakings and to promote a more inclusive and democratically accountable engagement with this fundamental issue of constitutional interpretation:

> The Committee recommends that the State party implement its commitment to review its litigation strategies in order to foster the justiciability of the economic, social and cultural rights. The State party should engage civil society and organizations of indigenous peoples in this revision with a view to broadening the interpretation of the Canadian Charter of Rights and Freedoms, notably sections 7, 12 and 15, to include economic social and cultural rights, and thus ensure the justiciability of Covenant rights.[118]

The Committee's recommendations remind us that the constitutional status of socio-economic rights in Canada remains a matter of choice. If Canadian governments decided to affirm such rights in courts, if Canadian courts attended to their role in ensuring effective implementation of international human rights through the interpretation and application of domestic law, and if Canada's legal culture were to better align with the views and expectations of civil society and Indigenous peoples, socio-economic rights would achieve more equal constitutional recognition and the most disadvantaged Canadians more equal benefit of Canada's post-*Charter* democracy.

Bibliography

Secondary Sources

Froc, Kerri. "Is the Rule of Law the Golden Rule? Accessing 'Justice' for Canada's Poor" (2008) 87 Canadian Bar Review 459.

Jackman, Martha and Bruce Porter (eds). *Advancing Social Rights in Canada*. Toronto: Irwin Law, 2014.

Langford, Malcolm (ed). *Social Rights Jurisprudence: Emerging Trends in International and Comparative Law*. Cambridge: Cambridge University Press, 2008.

Porter, Bruce. "Expectations of Equality" (2006) 3 Supreme Court Law Review 23.

Rodgers, Sanda and Sheila McIntyre (eds). *The Supreme Court of Canada and Social Justice: Commitment, Retrenchment or Retreat?* Markham, ON: LexisNexis, 2010.

Young, Margot et al. (eds). *Poverty: Rights, Social Citizenship, and Legal Activism*. Vancouver: UBC Press, 2007.

---

[118] Ibid [6].

Cases

Canada (Attorney General) v PHS Community Services Society 2011 SCC 44.
Chaoulli v Quebec (Attorney General) 2005 SCC 35.
Eldridge v British Columbia (AG) [1997] 3 SCR 624.
Gosselin v Quebec (Attorney General) 2002 SCC 84.
New Brunswick (Minister of Health and Community Service) v G(J) [1999] 3 SCR 46.
Tanudjaja v. Canada (Attorney General), 2014 ONCA 852 (CanLII), http://canlii.ca/t/gffz5
Victoria (City) v. Adams, 2009 BCCA 563; 2008 BCSC 1363.

PART VI

··

CONSTITUTIONAL THEORY

··

A. Constitutional Interpretation

CHAPTER 41

···

CONSTITUTIONAL
INTERPRETATION
On Issues of Ontology and of Interlegality

···

STÉPHANE BEAULAC*

FROM a theoretical viewpoint, two contemporary dimensions of constitutional interpretation are of particular interest in Canada. First is a purely ontological issue: whether
or not, by its nature, the interpretation of a constitution is fundamentally different than
legal interpretation or, more specifically, statutory interpretation. The second is the
problematics of interlegality, or the domestic use of international law, which has caused
much ink to flow as of late, here and elsewhere in liberal democracies.

1. ONTOLOGY: NO EXCEPTIONALISM
IN CANADA'S CONSTITUTIONAL
INTERPRETATION

···

The specificity of constitutional interpretation, compared to the methodology of legal
interpretation in general, has long been stated and affirmed in legal circles, although few
scholars have actually conducted a demonstration to show that the claim is actually accurate.[1] For instance in *Re Residential Tenancies*,[2] Justice Dickson (as he then was) wrote:

> A constitutional reference is not a barren exercise in statutory interpretation. What is
> involved is an attempt to determine and give effect to the broad objectives and purpose

---

* PhD (*Cantab*). Full Professor, Faculty of Law, Université de Montréal and Flaherty Visiting Professor,
University College Cork (2016–17).
[1] See: Alain-François Bisson, "La Charte québécoise des droits et libertés de la personne et le dogme
de l'interprétation spécifique des textes constitutionnels" (1986) 17 *RD U Sherbrooke* 19.
[2] *Re Residential Tenancies Act, 1979,* [1981] 1 SCR 714.

of the Constitution, viewed as a "living tree", in the expressive words of Lord Sankey in *Edwards and Others v Attorney-General for Canada and Others*, [1930] A.C. 124.[3]

A few years later, the Supreme Court reiterated in *Re Upper Churchill*[4]—in the same context involving the use of parliamentary debates—that constitutional interpretation is fundamentally different from statutory interpretation. Incidentally, it is noteworthy that, since the yearly 1980s, the "exclusionary rule"[5] regarding parliamentary debates has been set aside across the board, that is to say, not only in constitutional interpretation, but also for the construction of ordinary statutes. This suggests that insisting on the specific context of constitutional interpretation to relax the exclusionary rule for parliamentary debates in *Re Residential Tenancies* and in *Re Upper Churchill* was perhaps unnecessary. But the damage was done, in a sense: the splitting of interpretative methodology became the dominant narrative.

With respect to the construction of the *Canadian Charter of Rights and Freedoms*, there seems to be another underlying reason that the Supreme Court of Canada spoke in terms of exceptionalism in constitutional interpretation, namely the disappointing experience with the 1960 *Canadian Bill of Rights*,[6] which the judiciary reduced to an instrument of little impact. There were indeed some authors in legal writings who predicted the same inglorious fate for the *Charter*.[7] Surely it was in the back of the justices' mind, if not at the forefront, when they considered the first few cases of *Charter* interpretation. For instance, in the 1985 case of *Singh*,[8] Justice Wilson wrote:

> It seems to me rather that the recent adoption of the *Charter* by Parliament and nine of the ten provinces as part of the Canadian Constitutional framework has sent a clear message to the courts that the restrictive attitude which at times characterized their approach to the *Canadian Bill of Rights* ought to be re-examined.[9]

The same year in *Therens*,[10] Justice Le Dain emphasised that, when interpreting the *Charter*, unlike the *Canadian Bill of Rights*, there is a "clear constitutional mandate to make judicial decisions having the effect of limiting or qualifying the traditional sovereignty of Parliament".[11]

---

[3] *Ibid*, 723.

[4] *Reference re Upper Churchill Water Rights Reversion Act*, [1984] 1 SCR 297, 318.

[5] An ancient and firmly established interpretative tool in the common law tradition, the exclusionary rule prohibited the use of parliamentary debates and other *travaux préparatoires* in ascertaining legislative intent. See Stéphane Beaulac, "Parliamentary Debates in Statutory Interpretation: A Question of Admissibility or of Weight?" (1998) 43 *McGill LJ* 287.

[6] SC 1960, c 60, reprinted in RSC 1985, App III.

[7] See, for example, Berend Hovius and Robert Martin, "The Canadian Charter of Rights and Freedoms in the Supreme Court of Canada," 61 *Canadian Bar Rev* 354.

[8] *Singh v Minister of Employment and Immigration*, [1985] 1 SCR 177.

[9] *Ibid*, 209.

[10] *R v Therens*, [1985] 1 SCR 613.

[11] *Ibid*, 639.

But this begs the question: Does the constitutional nature of the instruments to be interpreted, such as the *Canadian Charter*, warrant a completely different and novel methodology when it comes to ascertaining the normative content of a provision? The first authoritative judicial statement to support this proposition came in the 1984 case of *Skapinker*.[12] At the outset, Justice Estey described the interpretation and application of the *Charter* as a "new task";[13] he later highlighted that, in deciding the role of headings in interpretation, neither the federal nor the provincial interpretation Acts applies to the *Charter*.[14] In the following, Estey J explained why a different methodology is needed for constitutional instruments:

> The *Charter* comes from neither level of the legislative branches of government but from the Constitution itself. It is part of the fabric of Canadian law. Indeed, it "is the supreme law of Canada": *Constitution Act, 1982*, s. 52. It cannot be readily amended. The fine and constant adjustment process of these constitutional provisions is left by a tradition of necessity to the judicial branch. Flexibility must be balanced with certainty. The future must, to the extent foreseeably possible, be accommodated in the present. The *Charter* is designed and adopted to guide and serve the Canadian community for a long time. Narrow and technical interpretation, if not modulated by a sense of the unknowns of the future, can stunt the growth of the law and hence the community it serves.[15]

Later that year, while emphasising the need to interpret the constitution in a dynamic and evolving fashion, Chief Justice Dickson was quite categorical in *Hunter v Southam*[16] regarding exceptionalism in constitutional interpretation: "The task of expounding a constitution is crucially different from that of construing a statute".[17] The same reasons are identified by Dickson CJ: namely (1) a constitution is drafted to be perennial; (2) its functions relate to government powers and, with a *Charter*, to protections of human rights; (3) such an entrenched document is complicated to change; and (4) consequently, it must, in the Chief Justice's words, "be capable of growth and development over time to meet new social, political and historical realities often unimagined by its framers".[18]

Just as he had done three years earlier in *Re Residential Tenancies*, then for the *Constitutional Act, 1867*, Dickson CJ invoked in *Hunter v Southam* the metaphor of the "living tree", from the classic speech of Viscount Sankey in the 1930 Judicial Council case of *Edwards v Canada*.[19] The reason is clear: to historically root the need to have a broad perspective in approaching constitutional instruments, which translates into

[12] *Law Society of Upper Canada v Skapinker*, [1984] 1 SCR 357.
[13] *Ibid*, 365.
[14] *Ibid*, 370.
[15] *Ibid*, 366–367.
[16] *Hunter v Southam Inc*, [1984] 2 SCR 145.
[17] *Ibid*, 155.
[18] *Ibid*.
[19] *Edwards v Attorney-General for Canada*, [1930] AC 124, 136.

exceptionalism in the constitutional interpretation of the *Charter*.[20] What is this methodology of a particular kind? Not only is this methodology not new, dating back to the 1930s, not only does it exist also in Great Britain and the United States,[21] but even the name given to it has nothing original: *purposive interpretation* or "*interpretation téléologique*" in French.[22] Déjà vu, all over again (perhaps?).

It was a year later, in *Big M Drug Mart*,[23] that Chief Justice Dickson fleshed out what "purposive interpretation" means in constitutional interpretation. Referring to both *Hunter v Southam* and *Skapinker*, the following became solemn instructions for the construction of the *Charter*:

> This Court has already, in some measure, set out the basic approach to be taken in interpreting the *Charter*. In *Hunter v. Southam Inc.* [. . .] this Court expressed the view that the proper approach to the definition of the rights and freedoms guaranteed by the *Charter* was a purposive one. The meaning of a right or freedom guaranteed by the *Charter* was to be ascertained by an analysis of the <u>purpose</u> of such a guarantee; it was to be understood, in other words, in the light of the interests it was meant to protect.
>
> In my view this analysis is to be undertaken, and the purpose of the right or freedom in question is to be sought by reference to the character and the larger objects of the *Charter* itself, to the language chosen to articulate the specific rights or freedoms, to the historical origins of the concepts enshrined, and where applicable, to the meaning and purpose of the other specific rights and freedoms with which it is associated within the text of the *Charter*. The interpretation should be, as the judgment in *Southam* emphasizes, a generous rather than a legalistic one, aimed at fulfilling the purpose of the guarantee and securing for individuals the full benefit of the *Charter*'s protection. At the same time it is important not to overshoot the actual purpose of the right or freedom in question, but to recall that the *Charter* was not enacted in a vacuum, and must therefore, as this Court's decision in *Law Society of Upper Canada v. Skapinker* [. . .] illustrates, be placed in its proper linguistic, philosophic and historical contexts.[24]

I shall come back to these two paragraphs, specifically, to bring to light each of the points made in regard to *constitutional* interpretation, with a view to comparing these elements with the methodology of *statutory* interpretation.

---

[20] See Dale Gibson, "Interpretation of the Canadian Charter of Rights and Freedoms: Some General Considerations", in WS Tarnopolsky and G-A Beaudoin (eds), *The Canadian Charter of Rights and Freedoms—Commentary* (Carswell, 1982), 25, 39.

[21] In *Hunter v Southam*, above (n 16), 156, indeed Dickson J refers to the British case of *Minister of Home Affairs v Fisher*, [1980] AC 319 (HL) and to the American old case of *M'Culloch v Maryland*, 17 U.S. (4 Wheat) 316 (1819).

[22] See, in general, Luc B Tremblay, "L'interprétation téléologique des droits constitutionnels" (1995) 29 *Revue juridique Thémis* 460, 462.

[23] *R v Big M Drug Mart Ltd*, [1985] 1 SCR 295.

[24] *Ibid*, 344 [emphasis in original].

It needs to be emphasized that these interpretative directives, with no interruption or exception, have been followed in *Canadian Charter* case law, just as the general idea of exceptionalism in constitutional interpretation, as well as the metaphor of the "living tree", continue as an unchallenged mantra (even an incantation) every time the Supreme Court of Canada addresses issues of construction in constitutional law. Along with some important cases from the 1980s and 1990s—*Motor Vehicle Act*,[25] *Saskatchewan Electoral Boundaries*[26]—recent judgments such as *Doucet-Boudreau*[27] (2003) and *Reference re Same-Sex Marriage*[28] (2004), as well as the *Nadon case*[29] (2014) and the *Caron case*[30] (2015), confirm a sort of *orthodoxy* in constitutional interpretation concerning the purposive construction of the *Charter*.

* * *

The hypothesis at the centre of this section of the chapter is that, in spite of the claims of ontological exceptionalism, there is nothing inherently and fundamentally different about constitutional interpretation in Canada—not anymore, in any event—when compared with the general methodology of statutory interpretation. Previous work I conducted—including with Professor Emeritus Pierre-André-Côté[31]—shows that the "modern principle" in statutory interpretation has created a convergence of approaches, where the construction of regular legislation and of constitutional instruments such as the *Canadian Charter* follows one and the same logical reasoning or analytical scheme. Put another way, empirically, one cannot observe any real or essential distinctions in the methodology applicable to constitutional interpretation and statutory interpretation; the difference that remains is one of weighting (*pondération*) of the different interpretative elements.

The first element to support this argument is the timing of the Supreme Court of Canada's call for purposive interpretation for the *Charter*—in 1984–1985 as noted above—and the implementation of Professor Elmer Driedger's "modern principle" in regard to statutory interpretation. Let us recall the famous quote from the second edition of Driedger's *Construction of Statutes*:

> Today there is only one principle or approach, namely, the words of an Act are to be read in their entire context and in their grammatical and ordinary sense harmoniously with the scheme of the Act, the object of the Act and the intention of Parliament.[32]

---

[25] *Re British Columbia Motor Vehicle Act*, [1985] 2 SCR 486.
[26] *Re Provincial Electoral Boundaries (Saskatchewan)*, [1991] 2 SCR 158.
[27] *Doucet-Boudreau v Nova Scotia (Minister of Education)*, [2003] 3 SCR 3, [24].
[28] *Reference re Same-Sex Marriage*, [2004] 3 SCR 698, [23].
[29] *Reference re Supreme Court Act, ss. 5 and 6*, [2014] 1 SCR 433, [19].
[30] *Caron v Albert*, [2015] 3 SCR 511, [35] and [218].
[31] See Stéphane Beaulac and Pierre-André Côté, "Driedger's 'Modern Principle' at the Supreme Court of Canada: Interpretation, Justification, Legitimization" (2006) 40 *Revue juridique Thémis* 131.
[32] Elmer A Driedger, *The Construction of Statutes*, 2nd ed. (Butterworths, 1983), 87.

The official endorsement of the "modern principle" in Canadian case law has a date: 1984, in *Stubart v The Queen*,[33] a case in tax law. Since then, it has become the most popular legal commentator's citation in the Supreme Court of Canada's history,[34] with major reiterations of the principle in *Rizzo Shoes*[35] and *Bell Express Vu*.[36] As we also highlighted: "Driedger's quote is used in all areas of the law and, in fact, in all facets of legal interpretation: from tax law to human rights law, from criminal law to family law, as well as to qualify legislation in constitutional challenges [. . .]".[37]

The Supreme Court of Canada, be it by means of a direct quote, a reference to the passage, or an indirect endorsement via previous cases, has referred to Driedger's modern principle as the "prevailing and preferred" or the "traditional and correct" approach, and as a "definitive formulation", which "best captures or encapsulates" their interpretative approach, even the "starting point" for addressing issues of interpretation.[38] The latter point was again made, very recently, in the 2014 case of *Conception*,[39] involving the interpretation of the Canadian *Criminal Code*. In fact, Driedger's quote, often in tandem with the cases of *Rizzo Shoes* and/or *Bell Express Vu*, was, in 2015 alone, again used numerous times, five times to be precise: *Loyola High School*[40] (education law), *ATCO Gas and Pipelines*[41] (regulatory law), *Wilson v British Columbia*[42] (administrative law), *Canadian Broadcasting*[43] (copyright law), and *CIBC v Green*[44] (securities law). It is also worth noting that in the very recent case of *World Bank Group v. Wallace*,[45] handed down 20 April 2016, the Supreme Court of Canada associated the "modern approach to statutory interpretation", along with the *Rizzo Shoes* decision, with the methodology of treaty interpretation under sections 31 and 32 of the *Vienna Convention on the Law of Treaties*, for the purpose of interpreting implementing legislation.[46]

In sum, since 1984, the consistent message from the Supreme Court of Canada, which has been heard loud and clear by lower courts, is that the methodology involved in the construction of statutes has changed substantially.[47] The old Anglo-Saxon approach of

[33] *Stubart Investments Ltd v The Queen*, [1984] 1 SCR 417.
[34] Stéphane Beaulac and Pierre-André Côté, above (n 31), 135.
[35] *Rizzo & Rizzo Shoes Ltds. (Re)*, [1998] 1 SCR 27.
[36] *Bell Express Vu Limited Partnership v Rex*, [2002] 2 SCR 559.
[37] Stéphane Beaulac and Pierre-André Côté, above (n 31), 137 [footnotes omitted].
[38] *Ibid*, 139 [footnotes omitted].
[39] *R v Conception*, [2014] 3 R.C.S. 82.
[40] *Loyola High School v Quebec (Attorney General)*, [2015] 1 SCR 613.
[41] *ATCO Gas and Pipelines Ltds v Alberta (Utilities Commission)*, [2015] 3 SCR 219.
[42] *Wilson v British Columbia (Superintendent of Motor Vehicles)*, [2015] 3 SCR 300.
[43] *Canadian Broadcasting Corp. v SODRAC 2003 Inc*, [2015] 3 SCR 615.
[44] *Canadian Imperial Bank of Commerce v Green*, [2015] 3 SCR 801.
[45] *World Bank Group v. Wallace*, 2016 SCC 15.
[46] *Ibid*, [47].
[47] See Louis LeBel, "La méthode d'interprétation moderne: le juge devant lui-même et en lui-même," in S Beaulac and M Devinat (eds), *Interpretatio non cessat—Essays in honour of Pierre-André Côté* (Éditions Yvons Blais, 2011), 103.

strict and restrictive interpretation of legislation,[48] articulated around the so-called literal rule (or plain meaning rule)—often put in terms of interpretation only if the statute is ambiguous or obscure—is no longer acceptable in Canada and beyond.[49] The negative prejudice vis-à-vis statutory law, when it was considered that "Parliament changes the law for the worse",[50] as suggested by Sir Frederick Pollock in the nineteenth century, or that legislation is "an alien intruder in the house of the common law",[51] as once quipped by Harland Stone in the early twentieth century, is now a thing of the past in the common law world. To give but one example from abroad, witness the position expressed by Lord Griffiths in the famous British case *Pepper v Hart*: "The days have long passed when the courts adopted a strict constructionist view of interpretation which required them to adopt the literal meaning of the language. The courts now adopt a purposive approach which seeks to give effect to the true purpose of legislation [. . .]".[52]

* * *

The main point here is that the general methodology of statutory interpretation, infused with Driedger's modern principle, corresponds with the approach favoured for constitutional interpretation, including for the *Canadian Charter*. The convergence between the two can be observed both in terms of the spirit of the method and the very language used to describe the interpretative directives.

First, as regards the spirit behind the methodology of construction, the underlying message is the same for ordinary statutes and for constitutional instruments: the judge in a case must ascertain the intention of the legislative authority based on the language used in the provisions, but always considered in context and in harmony with other relevant statutes, and most importantly in light of the purpose that the provision and the statute as a whole want to accomplish The strategy behind such an approach is twofold: (1) out goes the preliminary condition of ambiguity or obscurity; (2) in comes, always, the full arsenal of interpretative tools for the judge to work with, in order to realise the actual legislative intent. This is encapsulated in section 12 of the federal *Interpretation Act*:[53] "Every enactment is deemed remedial, and shall be given such fair, large and liberal construction and interpretation as best ensures the attainment of its objects". It took a long while, but the full strength of this commandment from the *Interpretation Act*—with equivalents in provincial interpretation acts[54]—was embraced by courts, along with Driedger's modern principle.

---

[48] See, in general, Roderick Munday, "The Common Lawyer's Philosophy of Legislation" (1983) 14 *Rechtstheorie* 191.

[49] See, in general, Stéphane Beaulac and Frédéric Bérard, *Précis d'interprétation legislative*, 2nd ed. (LexisNexis, 2014), 1.

[50] Frederick Pollock, *Essays in Jurisprudence and Ethics* (Macmillan, 1882), 85.

[51] Harlan F Stone, "The Common Law in the United States" (1936) 50 *Harvard L Rev* 4, 15.

[52] *Pepper v Hart*, [1993] AC 593 (HL), 617. See also Francis AR Bennion, *Statutory Interpretation—A Code*, 4th ed (Butterworths, 2002), 500.

[53] RSC 1985, c I-21.

[54] See, for instance, s 41 of the Quebec's *Interpretation Act*, RSQ, c I-16, and s 10 of the Ontario's *Interpretation Act*, RSO 1990, c I.11.

A forceful example comes from the 1993 case of *Hasselwander*[55] at the Supreme Court of Canada, where the majority resorted to section 12 of the *Interpretation Act* to assist in interpreting a provision of the *Criminal Code*, legislation which was traditionally seen as requiring a strict and restrictive construction. However, Justice Cory explained: "The apparent conflict between a strict construction of a penal statute and the remedial interpretation required by section 12 of the *Interpretation Act* was resolved by according the rule of strict construction of penal statutes a subsidiary role."[56] As a consequence, the pragmatic argument involving a presumption of legislative intention favoring a strict and restrictive construction of criminal law provisions comes into play "only when attempts at the neutral interpretation suggested by section 12 of the *Interpretation Act* still leave reasonable doubt as to the meaning or scope of the text of the statute."[57] Similarly in 1984, while endorsing in general terms Driedger's modern principle, the *Stubart case*[58] had rejected a priori strict interpretation in tax law, an area of statutory law that used to epitomise strict and restrictive construction.

These decisions, as I have argued elsewhere,[59] explicitly confirm how the literal rule (or plain meaning rule) is no longer a valid approach in Canada. With regard to the *Canadian Charter*, one can sense the same spirit behind these interpretative directives—informed by both Driedger's modern principle and section 12 of the *Interpretation Act*—namely the rationale which similarly animates the purposive approach in constitutional interpretation, favouring a large and liberal, as well as dynamic, interpretation.[60]

In fact, this common interpretive approach to ordinary statutes and constitutional instruments was highlighted by the Supreme Court of Canada in a few cases. In *Blais*,[61] for example, at issue was a provision of the Manitoba *Natural Resources Transfer Agreement*, incorporated as Schedule 1 to the *Constitution Act, 1930*[62] and thus a constitutional document; specifically, whether the word "Indians" in paragraph 13 of the Agreement included Métis. Interestingly, the Court wrote: "The starting point in this endeavour is that a statute—and this includes statutes of constitutional force—must be interpreted in accordance with the meaning of its words, considered in context and with a view to the purpose they were intended to serve: see E.A. Driedger, *Construction of Statutes* (2nd ed. 1983), at p. 87".[63] Similarly, in *Lavigne v Canada*,[64] Justice Gonthier for the Court had to consider so-called "quasi-constitutional" legislation—namely the

[55] *R v Hasselwander*, [1993] 2 SCR 398.
[56] *Ibid*, [29].
[57] *Ibid*, [30].
[58] Above (n 33).
[59] See Stéphane Beaulac, "Les dommages collatéraux de la Charte canadienne en interprétation législative" (2007) 48 *Cahiers de droit* 751.
[60] See A Wayne Mackay, "Interpreting the Charter of Rights: Law, Politics and Poetry", in G-A Beaudoin (ed), *Causes invoquant la Charte, 1986–87—Actes de la Conférence de l'Association du Barreau canadien tenue à Montréal en octobre 1986* (Cowansville: Éditions Yvon Blais, 1987), 347.
[61] *R v Blais*, [2003] 2 SCR 236.
[62] Reprinted in RSC 1985, App II, No. 26.
[63] *R v Blais*, above, (n 61), [16].
[64] *Lavigne v Canada (Commissioner of Official Languages)*, [2002] 2 SCR 773.

Official Languages Act[65] and the *Privacy Act.*[66] According to Gonthier J, "that status does not operate to alter the traditional approach to the interpretation of legislation, defined by E.A. Driedger in *Construction of Statutes* (2nd ed. 1983), at p. 87". Recently, in the 2015 *Caron case*,[67] under the heading "Guiding Principles of Interpretation" and after referring to the relevant case law, including the *Blais case*,[68] the majority *per* Justices Cromwell and Karakatsanis summed up the methodology of constitutional construction by referring to "the ordinary meaning of the language used in each document, the historical context, and the philosophy or objectives lying behind the words and guarantees,"[69] essentially paraphrasing Driedger's modern principle. This was followed by a qualification, also applicable across the board in the methodology of legal interpretation: "The Court must generously interpret constitutional linguistic rights, not create them."[70]

In terms of the spirit, but also in the very wording used by the judiciary, we can see an obvious parallel between the directives in constitutional interpretation, especially with regard to the *Charter*, and the general approach in the construction of regular statutes. For this demonstration, let us go back to the (long) excerpt from *Big M Drug Mart*,[71] reproduced above, summarizing the method of constitutional interpretation of the *Charter*, and compare it with the formulation found in Driedger's modern principle with respect to legislative interpretation. The first thing to note is that the idea of *purpose* is central, hence the name given to the method in *Charter* interpretation. Chief Justice Dickson even underlined the word "purpose" in the first paragraph of the quote: "The meaning of a right or freedom guaranteed by the *Charter* was to be ascertained by an analysis of the <u>purpose</u> of such a guarantee; [. . .]".[72] The same general idea of purpose is also at the heart of Driedger's modern principle, endorsed by courts, and embodied in section 12 of the Federal *Interpretation Act*,[73] and its provincial equivalents.

But there is much more to say about purpose. In *Big M Drug Mart*, Chief Justice Dickson distinguished two types of purpose, one specific to the *Charter* provision at issue, and the other general to the entire *Charter*: "The purpose of the right or freedom in question is to be sought by reference to the character and the larger objects of the Charter itself".[74] This dual use of purpose is very common in statutory interpretation. Pierre-André Côté (with S Beaulac and M Devinat) summarizes the two forms of what is called teleological interpretation as follows: "[S]ometimes, the objectives of the specific provision being considered are invoked, and sometimes those of the statute as a

[65] RSC 1985, c 31 (4th Supp).
[66] RSC 1985, c P-21.
[67] Above (n 30).
[68] Above (n 61).
[69] *Caron v Alberta*, above (n 30), [38].
[70] *Ibid*
[71] Above (n 23).
[72] *Ibid*, 344 [emphasis in original].
[73] Above (n 53).
[74] *Big M Drug Mart*, above (n 23), 344.

whole."[75] The case of *Abrahams v Canada*[76] is a classic illustration of how legislative purpose can be considered in relation to the specific provision at issue and/or in relation with the act as a whole. In *Abrahams*, Justice Wilson for the Court was not only interested in the purpose of fraud prevention in the provision of the employment insurance legislation, but also in the overall purpose of the Act, namely, to provide benefits to entitled workers. It is thus apparent that Dickson CJ's instructions in *Big M Drug Mart* concerning the dual role of purpose in *Charter* interpretation, far from unique, are found on a regular basis in cases involving the interpretation or ordinary statutes.[77]

Similarly, Chief Justice Dickson's discussion of the role of the wording employed by the constituting authority in *Charter* provisions, as accurate as it may be, says nothing new in terms of interpretative methodology. The relevant passage in *Big M Drug Mart* speaks of "the language chosen to articulate the specific rights or freedoms" and, later in the same paragraph, after referring to the *Skapinker case*,[78] of the "proper linguistic context".[79] In general statutory interpretation, of course, the letter of the law (the text) is the crucial element with which any process of ascertaining legislative intent begins. With the rejection of the plain meaning (or literal) rule and the acceptance of the Driedger's modern principle in statutory interpretation, the textual interpretative moment is not the "whole story"—that is, one that ends the process of interpretation because the provision is allegedly clear and unambiguous. Instead, it is the "beginning of the story", namely, the first element that the judge considers to identify the intention of Parliament.[80] A recent illustration comes from the constitutional case of *Caron case*,[81] where the majority of six justices started off interpretation with the wording employed by the constituting authority and gave it high importance in determining the meaning of the provision.

Recalling the interpretative text-context-object trilogy,[82] as captured in Driedger's modern principle, there remains contextual interpretation, or what is also referred to as the systematic and logical method of construction.[83] Here again, the directive is echoed by Chief Justice Dickson in *Big M Drug Mart*, when, after referring to the historical origins of the concepts enshrined in the *Charter,* he emphasizes the "meaning and purpose of the other specific rights and freedoms with which it is associated within the text of the

---

[75] Pierre-André Côté (coll Stéphane Beaulac and Mathieu Devinat), *The Interpretation of Legislation in Canada*, 4th ed (Carswell, 2011), 415.

[76] *Abrahams v Attorney General of Canada*, [1983] 1 SCR 2.

[77] See Stéphane Beaulac, "L'interprétation de la Charte: reconsidération de l'approche téléologique et réévaluation du rôle du droit international", in G.-A. Beaudoin and E. Mendes, (eds), *Canadian Charter of Rights and Freedoms*, 4th ed (LexisNexis Butterworths, 2005), 27.

[78] Above (n 12).

[79] *Big M Drug Mart*, above (n 23), 344.

[80] See Stéphane Beaulac, *Handbook on Statutory Interpretation: General Methodology, Canadian Charter and International Law* (LexisNexis, 2008), 51.

[81] *Caron v Alberta*, above (n 30).

[82] This is another expression of my own making in statutory interpretation: see Stéphane Beaulac, above (n 80), 49.

[83] See Pierre-André Côté (coll Stéphane Beaulac and Mathieu Devinat), above (n 77), 325 *ff.*

Charter".[84] Put another way, a right or freedom at issue must not be construed in isolation, but rather in the normative context of the other provisions, and the *Charter* as a whole. Pierre-André Côté (with S Beaulac and M Devinat)[85] and Ruth Sullivan[86] (who took up Driedger's work) divide up context into several categories: immediate context, comprised of all the words in the actual provision; the wider context of the whole Act (other provisions, the components such as headings and preambles, as well as empowered regulations); related legislation or statutes *in pari materia* and other external context such as judge-made-law (or common law), historical and philosophical context, and international law.

In sum, Dickson CJ in *Big M Drug Mart*, just like the Supreme Court of Canada in all cases of constitutional interpretation, resorts to the three pillars of construction: text, context, and object. There is nothing novel here, just as Driedger did not re-invent the wheel with the modern principle of interpretation, which in fact was based on the traditional Liberal Rule,[87] Golden Rule,[88] and Mischief Rule.[89] Though the restrictive flavor of these rules has disappeared, their essence remains.[90] Driedger's famous principle, found in chapter 4 of his book,[91] was in fact a recapitulation of the three traditional English "rules" of statutory interpretation.[92] Recall his instructions that a judge should resort to the "grammatical and ordinary sense" of the words in an Act (text), "read in their entire context" (context) and considering them "harmoniously with the scheme of the Act" (context), and in light of the "object of the Act and the intention of Parliament" (object or purpose).

Thus the novelty with Driedger's modern principle is not with regard to the use of text-context-object in legal interpretation. It lies instead in the fact that all three facets are always relevant and ought to be, at a minimum, considered by the decision-maker. In turn, this implies that there is no such thing as a preliminary condition of ambiguity or obscurity, as the literal rule (or plain meaning rule) used to suggest, before resorting to these interpretative tools in ascertaining legislative intent. Then it becomes a matter of weighting the different elements of construction in the particular case at hand. The same novelty was said to flow from Justice Dickson's directives for *Charter* interpretation in *Big M Drug Mart*, also with a view to avoiding strict and restrictive construction in human rights law, an approach set aside in constitutional interpretation since

---

[84] *Big M Drug Mart*, above (n 23), 344.

[85] Pierre-André Côté (coll Stéphane Beaulac and Mathieu Devinat), above (n 77).

[86] Ruth Sullivan, *Sullivan and Driedger on the Construction of Statutes*, 4th ed (Butterworths, 2002), as well as the following editions.

[87] See the classic British cases: *Vacher and Sons Ltd v London Society of Compositors*, [1913] AC 107; *Hill v East and West India Dock Co.* (1844), 9 AC 448, and *Sussex Peerage* (1844), 8 ER 1034.

[88] See the classic British cases: *River Wear Commissioners v Adamson*, [1877] 2 AC 743, and *Grey v Pearson* (1857), 10 ER 1216.

[89] See the famous British decision in the *Heydon's case* (1584), 76 ER 637.

[90] See John M Kernochan, "Statutory Interpretation: An Outline of Methods" (1976) *Dalhousie LJ* 333.

[91] Elmer A Driedger, above (n 32), 81 *ff.*

[92] Stéphane Beaulac and Pierre-André Côté, above (n 31), 141–142.

the "living tree" in the 1930 *Edwards case*,[93] though it had been highly problematic in the 1960s and 1970s with regard to the *Canadian Bill of Rights*.[94]

In any event, the main point in this section of the chapter is that, because of the general endorsement of Driedger's modern principle by the Court, what has happened in the last 30 years is a convergence of methodology. The same elements of text-context-object are to be considered in all instances, be it to interpret a constitutional instrument such as the *Canadian Charter* or to ascertain legislative intent in an ordinary statute. Interestingly, Sidney Peck highlighted this commonality as early as 1987: "These factors [in *Charter* construction]—purpose, language, history, and context—are central to the well-established 'rules' of statutory construction".[95] To be sure, the relevant interpretative elements may be weighted differently in constitutional and statutory interpretation, but the nature of both methodologies is one and the same. "*Blanc bonnet, bonnet blanc*".

2. Interlegality: The Enduring Normative Divide of the Westphalian Paradigm

In addition to the convergence of interpretative methodology, interlegality, or the domestic use of international law by Canadian courts, has also become a distinctive trait of contemporary constitutional construction. Here again, recent developments in judicial practice have taken place simultaneously in regard to the interpretation of the Constitution and of ordinary statutes. The following discussion revisits the international theory behind the problematics of interlegality.

Although there were times, within international circles, when it was fashionable to speak of national sovereignty as a dying metaphor,[96] recent scholarship acknowledges the enduring role of this *idée-force* which, in its international dimensions,[97] was codified in Article 2, paragraph 1 of the *Charter of the United Nation* as the principle of "sovereign equality" of states. Thus in Canada, as in most common law jurisdictions, the matrix within which state affairs take place and according to which international law is indeed understood continues to be based on the so-called *Westphalian model* of international

---

[93] Above (n 19).

[94] Above (n 6).

[95] Sidney R Peck, "An Analytical Framework for the Application of the Canadian Charter of Rights and Freedoms" (1987) 25 *Osgoode Hall LJ* 1, 13.

[96] See Stephen J Toope, "The Uses of Metaphor: International Law and the Supreme Court of Canada" (2001) 80 *Canadian Bar Rev* 534, 540. This was, of course, reminiscent of the empty claims of the "end of history", associated to Francis Fukuyama, *The End of History and the Last Man* (Free Press, 1992).

[97] See, for instance, Stephen D Krasner, "The Hole in the Whole: Sovereignty, Shared Sovereignty, and International Law" (2004) 25 *Michigan J Int'l L* 1075, 1077.

relations.[98] The traditional stance has constantly held that, following the paradigm of Westphalia, governed by the Vattelian legal structure—from Emer de Vattel's work *Droit des Gens*[99]—the international legal plane is distinct and separate from the internal legal realms. Janne Nijman and André Nollkaemper, although attempting to justify a different perspective, address the problematics of interlegality in terms of a "divide" between national law and international law.[100] Similarly, though suggesting the situation was perhaps changing, Geoffrey Palmer used this image: "[I]nternational law and municipal law have been seen as two separate circles that never intersect".[101] In Canada, John Currie writes: "Public International law is not so much an area or topic of the law as it is an entire legal system that is conceptually distinct from the national legal systems".[102] Karen Knop puts it schematically as follows: "domestic law is 'here' and international law is 'there' ".[103]

The continuing distinct and separate legal realities of our modern state system of international relations explain two fundamental principles.[104] First, on the international plane, a state cannot invoke its internal law—including constitutional law[105]—to justify a breach of its international obligations.[106] At the Supreme Court of Canada, in *Zingre v The Queen*,[107] Justice Dickson adopted the statement by the (then) Canadian Department of External Affairs stating that "it is a recognized principle of international customary law that a state may not invoke the provisions of its internal law as justification for its failure to perform its international obligations".[108] Indeed, within the paradigm of Westphalia, a state cannot rely on its domestic law to justify a breach of *pacta sunt servanda*—as per section 26 of the *Vienna Convention*[109]—because these norms and duties are part of two distinct and separate legal spheres.

---

[98] See Stéphane Beaulac, "The Westphalian Legal Orthodoxy—Myth or Reality" (2000) 2 *J History Int'l L* 148.

[99] Emer de Vattel, *Le droit des Gens; ou Principes de la loi naturelle appliqués à la conduite & aux affaires des Nations & des Souverains*, 2 vols (n.b., 1758). See also Stéphane Beaulac, "Emer de Vattel and the Externalization of Sovereignty" (2003) *J History Int'l L* 237.

[100] Janne Nijman and André Nollkaemper, *New Perspectives on the Divide between National and International Law* (Oxford University Press, 2007).

[101] Geoffrey Palmer, "Human Rights and the New Zealand Government's Treaty Obligations" (1999) 29 *Victoria U Wellington L Rev* 27, 59.

[102] John H Currie, *Public International Law*, 2nd ed (Irwin Law, 2008), 1.

[103] Karen Knop, "Here and There: International Law in Domestic Courts" (2000) 32 *New York U J Int'l L & Pol* 501, 504.

[104] This part borrows from Stéphane Beaulac, "National Application of International Law: The Statutory Interpretation Perspective" (2003) 41 *Canadian YB Int'l L* 225, 234–236.

[105] See Robert Jennings and Arthur Watts, *Oppenheim's International Law*, 9th ed, vol 1 (Longman, 1992), 254.

[106] This rule was codified in section 27 *Vienna Convention on the Law of Treaties*; it was first articulated in the arbitration decision in the *Alabama Claims case* (US/UK) (1872), Moore, Arbitrations, i. 653.

[107] *Zingre v The Queen*, [1981] 2 SCR 392.

[108] *Ibid*, 410.

[109] Above (n 106).

The other core principle flowing from the international-internal divide is the need to manage the relationship between these two legal realities. John Currie refers to this scheme as the "international-national law interface",[110] whereas I prefer the expression "interlegality",[111] to refer to the national use of international law. As in other common law countries, the rules on the status of international law in Canada are domestics ones, deemed fundamental enough to form part of its constitutional law. As Francis Jacobs explained: "Indeed international law is generally uninformative in this area since it simply requires the application of treaties in all circumstances. It does not modify the fundamental principle that the application of treaties by domestic courts is governed by domestic law".[112] In that regard, Mattias Kumm is right that: "The very idea that the national constitution is decisive for generating the doctrines that structure the relationship between national and international law is dualist [in a meta-structuring way]".[113] In fact, the continuing apprehension of interlegality based on national constitutions—in spite of or even beyond the binary logics of dualism and monism—brings us back, inexorably, to the Westphalian paradigm and the international/national divide.

This traditional stance is being challenged by what is dubbed the internationalist conception of the relation between international law and domestic law, advocated by an increasing number of commentators, according to which "the incorporation and status of international law in the [domestic] legal system should be determined, at least to some extent, by international law itself".[114] Anne-Marie Slaughter took the lead in the 1990s,[115] suggesting that there ought to be global normative integration and noting the increasing use of international law domestically. However, her caveat, to the effect that there is a continuing divide between the two (at least conceptually), was lost by too many of her followers.[116] International commentators in constitutional legal theory, such as Neil Walker, have also considered what Anne-Marie Slaughter presented as "a new world order",[117] attempting to make sense of a "disorder of orders",[118] as regards interlegality. Drawing from the terminology developed by Jürgen Habermas,[119] in 2010, Nico

---

[110] *Above* (n 115), 220.

[111] Stéphane Beaulac, "La problématique de l'interlégalité et la méthodologie juridique," in JY Chérot et al. (eds), *Le droit entre autonomie et ouverture—Mélanges en l'honneur de Jean-Louis Bergel* (Bruylant, 2013), 5.

[112] Francis G Jacobs, "Introduction", in FG Jacobs and S Roberts (eds), *The Effect of Treaties in Domestic Law* (Sweet and Maxwell, 1987), xxiii, xxiv.

[113] Mattias Kumm, "Democratic Constitutionalism Encounters International Law: Terms of Engagement", in S Choudhry (ed), *The Migration of Constitutional Ideas* (Cambridge University Press, 2007), 256, 258.

[114] Curtis A Bradley, "Breard, Our Dualist Constitution and the Internationalist Conception" (1999) 51 *Stanford L Rev* 529, 531.

[115] See Anne-Marie Slaughter, "A Typology of Transjudicial Communication" (1994) 29 *U Richmond L Rev* 99.

[116] See Anne-Marie Slaughter and William Burke-White, "The Future of International Law Is Domestic (or, The European Way of Law)" (2006) 47 *Harvard Int'l LJ* 327, 349–350.

[117] See Anne-Marie Slaughter, *A New World Order* (Princeton University Press, 2004).

[118] Neil Walker, "Beyond Boundary Disputes and Basic Grids: Mapping the Global Disorder of Normative Orders" (2008) 6 *Int'l J Constitutional L* 373.

[119] Jürgen Habermas, *Die postnationale Konstellation* (Suhrkamp Verlag, 1998).

Krisch coined a new expression: "postnational law", that is, normativity where the line between domestic and international legal spheres is blurred, "with a multitude of formal and informal connections taking the place of what once were relatively clear rules and categories".[120] Similarly, in light of recent case law especially on freedom of association, Patrick Macklem examined what he called, "the nature of Canadian constitutionalism in an age of post-dualism".[121]

The question to address here is this: Is the paradigm of Westphalia really outdated and obsolete? Can we seriously suggest that the concept of national sovereignty is dead and buried? In this country, can we observe in the practice of the Supreme Court of Canada a fundamental change in the use of international law? In that regard, the most significant development in the last 30 years is the decision of the Supreme Court of Canada in the 1999 case of *Baker*.[122]

Baker considered whether the order to deport a woman with Canadian-born dependent children should be judicially reviewed. She had asked for an exemption from the requirement to leave the country to apply for Canadian citizenship, based on humanitarian and compassionate considerations under section 114(2) of the *Immigration Act*.[123] In order to determine the scope of this legal norm, namely "compassionate or humanitarian considerations", the majority *per* L'Heureux-Dubé J considered Canada's international treaty obligations. Central to her analysis was the 1989 *Convention on the Rights of the Child*, and its notion of the "best interests of the child",[124] because the interests of the applicant's children to have her continue providing for them would be a humanitarian and compassionate reason for an exemption.

Canada had ratified the *Convention on the Rights of the Child*, but has yet to implement it within its domestic legal system. Pursuant to the dualist logic, there is no direct effect possible and courts should not resort to the international norms therein to help interpret and apply the domestic legal rules regarding an exemption to the immigration requirement in section 113(2) of the *Immigration Act*. This is where L'Heureux-Dubé J made what is generally deemed a groundbreaking statement in *Baker* on the normative interaction between the national and international:

> I agree with the respondent and the Court of Appeal that the Convention has not been implemented by Parliament. Its provisions therefore have no direct application within Canadian law.

---

[120] Nico Krisch, *Beyond Constitutionalism—The Pluralist Structure of Postnational Law* (Oxford University Press, 2010), 4.

[121] Patrick Macklem, "The International Constitution", in F Faraday, J Fudge and E Tucker (eds), *Constitutional Labour Rights in Canada—Farm Workers and the Fraser Case* (Irwin Law, 2012), 261, 263.

[122] *Baker v Canada (Minister of Citizenship and Immigration)*, [1999] 2 SCR 817. This part borrows from Stéphane Beaulac, "International Law Gateway to Domestic Law: Hart's 'Open Texture', Legal Language and the Canadian Charter" (2012) 46 *Revue juridique Thémis* 443.

[123] *Immigration Act*, RSC 1985, c I-2; now replaced by the *Immigration and Refugee Protection Act*, SC 2001, c 27.

[124] *Ibid*, article 3.

Nevertheless, the values reflected in international human rights law may help inform the contextual approach to statutory interpretation and judicial review.[125]

She then referred to legal scholarship on statutory interpretation[126] for the proposition that international law (treaties, customs) is part of the legal context relevant to ascertain the normative content of a legislative provision. As well, it was acknowledged that the role of international human rights in interpreting domestic legislation had been recognised in other common law countries.[127]

Accordingly, Justice L'Heureux-Dubé considered the values and principles underlying the international legal norm of the best interests of the child, pursuant to the *Convention of the Rights of the Child*, even though this treaty remains unimplemented in the Canadian legal order. The convention contributed greatly, along with other soft-law instruments—the *Universal Declaration of Human Rights* and the *Declaration of the Rights of the Child*—to a large and liberal interpretation of the legal norm expressed by the phrase "compassionate or humanitarian considerations".

The reason the *Baker* decision has been considered so important on these issues is straightforward: Justice L'Heureux-Dubé, by saying that both implemented and unimplemented treaties may be utilised in interpreting domestic statutes, quite clearly opened the door wide to the use of international normativity. Be it in regard to ordinary legislation or, as we will see, constitutional instruments such as the *Canadian Charter*, the position in this country is to allow international legal norms a great deal of influence on the interpretation and application of domestic law. Having said that, is permitting the use of unimplemented treaty norms revolutionary, as far as interlegality is concerned? Is it at least a meaningful change, a sort of "creeping monism"[128]—as an author once put it to describe a definite trend in common law countries with regard to the domestic use of international human rights law? Conversely, is *Baker* vulnerable to criticism for enabling "to achieve indirectly what cannot be achieved directly, namely, to give force and effect within the domestic legal system to international obligations undertaken by the executive alone that have yet to be subject to the democratic will of Parliament"?[129] This was the main point made in the minority opinion by Iacobucci and Cory JJ.

In terms of the operationalization of international normativity by means of legal interpretation, I have demonstrated elsewhere that Justices Iacobucci and Cory's point is exaggerated, if not plain wrong, for two reasons.[130] First, L'Heureux-Dubé J maintains

---

[125] *Baker*, above (n 122) [69–70].

[126] Ruth Sullivan, *Driedger on the Construction of Statutes*, 3rd ed. (Butterworths, 1994), 330.

[127] *Baker*, above (n 122), [70].

[128] Melissa A Waters, "Creeping Monism: The Judicial Trend toward Interpretive Incorporation of Human Rights Treaties" (2007) 107 *Columbia L Rev* 628.

[129] *Baker*, above (n 122), [70].

[130] See Stéphane Beaulac, "Interlégalité et réception du droit international en droit interne canadien et québécois," in S Beaulac and J-F Gaudreault-DesBiens (eds), *JurisClasseur—Droit constitutionnel* (LexisNexis, 2011), 23/1, 23/102.

the theoretical status quo by reaffirming the applicability of the dualist logic with regard
to the incorporation of international treaty norms. Second, and more important, the
majority in *Baker* resorts to international law via the contextual method of interpretation which, as the reference to legal scholarship demonstrates,[131] falls within Driedger's
modern principle of interpretation: International law, indeed, "constitute[s] a part of
the legal context in which legislation is enacted and read".[132] Resorting to these norms
as an argument of context allows courts to exercise their interpretative discretion and
give appropriate persuasive force to international law, that is to say to evaluate its weight
based, inter alia, on its domestic status within Canadian law.

Put another way, since *Baker* the operationalization of international conventional
law has been refined (not revolutionized): it is no longer a simple all-or-nothing-type
of reasoning, on/off based on a dualist logic only, treaty norms being implemented or
not, black or white, as it once was.[133] Instead, the analysis now involves a sliding scale
of persuasive force which, by means of the contextual argument of interpretation, can
be assessed on a case-by-case basis by the court, depending on many discretionary
factors—as in any process of legal construction—including whether the treaty norm has
been implemented.[134] The dualist logic as regards treaty norms remains highly material
to the analysis, but it is not determinative by itself anymore. This being so, does *Baker*
short-circuit the need for treaty implementation? More generally, does *Baker* contribute to the "'normalization' of international law and global standards in regional and
national law, quite in contrast with—or at least circumventing—the classical picture
of separate spheres,"[135] as suggested by one author recently? I believe not. By reiterat-
ing dualism, *Baker* refuses to throw the baby out with the bathwater, maintaining the
Westphalian paradigm and the international/national divide.[136]

Many other cases involving international law have been at the Supreme Court of
Canada since *Baker* was decided in 1999. They confirm not only the more sophisticated
analysis of the issue based on the circumstantial evaluation of the persuasive force of
international law (not simply an on/off switch), but also that the epistemological matrix
founded on the divide between international and national law is still highly relevant.
A few years later in the 2001 case of *Spraytech v Hudson*,[137] a generous interpretation was

[131] *Baker*, above (n 122), [70].
[132] Ruth Sullivan, above (n 126), 33.
[133] See Hugh M Kindred, "Canadians as Citizens of the International Community: Asserting
Unimplemented Treaty Rights in the Courts," in SG Coughlan and D Russell (eds), *Citizenship and
Citizen Participation in the Administration of Justice* (Éditions Thémis, 2002) 263.
[134] See Stéphane Beaulac, "International Law and Statutory Interpretation: Up with Context, Down
with Presumption," in OE Fitzgerald *et al.* (eds), *The Globalized Rule of Law—Relationships between
International and Domestic Law* (Irwin Law, 2006), 331.
[135] Nico Krisch, above (n 12), 10.
[136] Accordingly, I have a very different reading than Patrick Macklem, above (n 121), 264, when he
suggests that: "In recent years, [. . .] the Supreme Court of Canada has effectively rendered obsolete
Canada's dualist engagement with international law".
[137] *114957 Canada Ltée (Spraytech, Société d'arrosage) v Hudson (Town)*, [2001] 2 SCR 241.

given to the enabling statutory provision under which a municipal by-law (prohibiting certain pesticides) was adopted on the basis of international law, among other factors. Referring to her reasons in *Baker*, L'Heureux-Dubé J relied again on values reflected in international normativity, this time not for unimplemented treaty norms, but for a rule of customary international law; the so-called "precautionary principle", which was resorted to as an element of context deemed relevant to the interpretation of the relevant statutory provision.[138] A similar argument of contextual interpretation was employed in 2002 in *Suresh*,[139] dealing with torture under the *Canadian Charter*; in 2005 in *Mugesera*,[140] dealing with Canadian criminal law and international crimes; and again in the 2013 case of *Ezokola*,[141] regarding immigration and refugee law.

Of course, international law can also be utilized by means of another argument of statutory interpretation, namely the presumption of conformity with international law[142] (the "Charming Betsy" rule,[143] as it is known in the United States). Articulated in Canada by Justice Pigeon in the 1968 case of *Daniels v White*,[144] it continues to be a favored way, even after *Baker* in 1999, by which to operationalize international normativity through interpretation, whether for regular statutes or for constitutional instruments.[145] Witness, for instance, *Schreiber v Canada*[146] in 2002 on state immunity law, *Canadian Foundation for Children*[147] in 2004 on corporal punishment in criminal law, and *Hape*[148] in 2007 on the application of the *Canadian Charter*, as well as *Health Services and Support*[149] in 2007 on freedom of association under the *Charter*.

Again recently in the 2014 case of *Kazemi v Iran*,[150] the Supreme Court of Canada was faced with a problem of interlegality, as customary international law was invoked to create a new statutory exception for state immunity under the applicable Canadian federal

---

[138] *Ibid*, [31–32].

[139] *Suresh v Canada (Minister of Citizenship and Immigration)*, [2002] 1 SCR 3.

[140] *Mugesera v Canada (Minister of Citizenship and Immigration)*, [2005] 2 SCR 100.

[141] *Ezokola v Canada (Citizenship and Immigration)*, [2013] 2 SCR 678.

[142] See the classic formulation, from British author Peter Maxwell, *On the Interpretation of Statutes* (Sweet & Maxwell, 1876), 173: "every statute is to be so interpreted and applied, as far as its language admits, as not to be inconsistent with the comity of nations, or with the established rules of international law".

[143] From the case *Murray v The Charming Betsy*, 6 U.S. 64 (1804).

[144] *Daniels v White and the Queen*, [1968] SCR 517.

[145] See Stéphane Beaulac and John H. Currie, "Canada", D Sherton (ed), *International Law and Domestic Legal Systems—Incorporation, Transformation, and Persuasion* (Oxford University Press, 2011), 116, 145 *ff*.

[146] *Schreiber v Canada (Attorney General)*, [2002] 3 SCR 269.

[147] *Canadian Foundation for Children, Youth and the Law v Canada (Attorney General)*, [2004] 1 SCR 76.

[148] *R v Hape*, [2007] 2 SCR 292.

[149] *Health Services and Support—Facilities Subsector Bargaining Assn. v British Columbia*, [2007] 2 SCR 391.

[150] *Kazemi Estate v Islamic Republic of Iran*, [2014] 3 SCR 176.

legislation.[151] Writing for the majority, Justice LeBel rejected the interpretative argument based on the presumption of conformity, pointing out the following:

> The current state of international law regarding redress for victims of torture does not alter the [legislation], or make it ambiguous. International law cannot be used to support an interpretation that is not permitted by the words of the statute. Likewise, the presumption of conformity does not overthrow clear legislative intent (see S. Beaulac, "'Texture ouverte', droit international et interprétation de la Charte canadienne", in E. Mendes and S. Beaulac, eds., Canadian Charter of Rights and Freedoms (5th ed. 2013), at pp. 231–35). Indeed, the presumption that legislation will conform to international law remains just that—merely a presumption.[152]

This latest case shows how clearly the divide between the international and the national legal realms is maintained when courts consider such norms by means of the presumption of conformity with international law. Of course, this separating line is even more blatant when the argument of legal interpretation is rejected in the end, as in the Kazemi case.

The same margin of appreciation, with a sort of sliding scale-type of reasoning, is favoured by the Supreme Court of Canada when it comes to resorting to international law in constitutional interpretation, to construe and apply the Canadian Charter. In Re Public Service Employee Relations Act,[153] Chief Justice Dickson expressed a point of view that set the tone for resorting to international law in Charter interpretation:

> The Charter conforms to the spirit of this contemporary international human rights movement, and it incorporates many of the policies and prescriptions of the various international documents pertaining to human rights. The various sources of international human rights law—declarations, covenants, conventions, judicial and quasi-judicial decisions of international tribunals, customary norms—must, in my opinion, be relevant and persuasive sources for interpretation of the Charter's provisions. [. . .] I believe that the Charter should generally be presumed to provide protection at least as great as that afforded by similar provisions in international human rights documents which Canada has ratified. [. . .] In short, though I do not believe the judiciary is bound by the norms of international law in interpreting the Charter, these norms provide a relevant and persuasive source for interpretation of the provisions of the Charter, especially when they arise out of Canada's international obligations under human rights conventions.[154]

Chief Justice Dickson draws a distinction between two categories of international legal instruments: (1) those that, although not necessarily binding upon Canada as a

---

[151] Indeed, the law of state immunity in Canada, with specific exceptions (such as for commercial activities), is codified by federal legislation: State Immunity Act, RSC 1985, c S-18.

[152] Kazemi Estate, above (n 150), [60].

[153] Re Public Service Employee Relations Act [1987] 1 SCR 313.

[154] Ibid, 348–350.

question of law, fit generally into the category of contemporary international human rights law; and (2) those that actually bind Canada as a matter of international law. The first category includes treaties such as *the European Convention on Human Rights* and *the American Convention on Human Rights*; declarations and other inherently non-binding norms, such as the *Universal Declaration of Human Rights*, and the *Helsinki Final Act*, and documents such as the *Organization for Security and Cooperation in Europe*, the *Standard Minimum Rules for the Treatment of Prisoners*, the *Declaration on the Rights of Persons Belonging to National or Ethnic Religious and Linguistic Minorities*, and the *Declaration on the Rights of Indigenous Peoples*. Such non-binding or soft law norms are said to be relevant and persuasive to the interpretation of the *Charter*, probably because they are sources of comparative law, more than international law proper.[155]

The second category identified by the Chief Justice—instruments that are legally binding upon Canada—includes documents such as the *International Covenant on Civil and Political Rights*; the *International Convention on the Elimination of All Forms of Racial Discrimination*; the *Convention on the Elimination of Discrimination Against Women*; the *Convention Against Torture and Other Cruel, Inhuman and Degrading Treatment or Punishment*; the *Convention on the Rights of the Child*; and the *Rome Statute of the International Criminal Court*. The provisions of these instruments are similar to those of the *Charter*, and they have been ratified or acceded to by Canada. According to Dickson CJ, Canada is bound by international law to protect such rights within its borders. Interestingly, he did not specifically base his conclusion on the classic rule of interpretation by which domestic legislation is presumed to be consistent with international obligations. Rather, he wrote that "general principles of constitutional interpretation require that these international obligations be a <u>relevant and persuasive</u> factor in *Charter* interpretation".[156]

Although initially in dissent, Chief Justice Dickson's views on international law has been very influential. In a 1988 speech, former justice of the Supreme Court of Canada Gérard La Forest said the following about the Chief Justice's position in *Re Public Service Employee Relations Act*: "Though speaking in dissent, his comments on the use of international law generally reflect what we all do".[157] In 2000, another former justice of Canada's highest court, Michel Bastarache, opined similarly: "While Chief Justice Dickson rejected the implicit incorporation of international law doctrine in a dissenting judgment, his opinion reflects the present state of the law".[158] Although the "relevant and

---

[155] See Karen Knop, above (n 103).

[156] *Re Public Service Employee Relations Act*, above (n 153), 350 [emphasis added].

[157] Gérard V La Forest, "The Use of International and Foreign Material in the Supreme Court of Canada" in *Proceedings, XVIIth Annual Conference* (Ottawa: Canadian Council on International Law, 1988) 230, 232.

[158] Michel Bastarache, "The Honourable GV La Forest's Use of Foreign Materials in the Supreme Court of Canada and His Influence on Foreign Courts," in R Johnson & JP McEvoy (eds), *Gérard V La Forest at the Supreme Court of Canada, 1985–1997* (Canadian Legal History Project, 2000) 433, 434.

persuasive" passage has been cited on numerous occasions in subsequent cases, the distinction suggested by the Chief Justice between binding and non-binding instruments has generally been ignored. As a matter of fact, judges in Canada rarely, if ever, consider international law sources by taking into account whether they have a legally binding effect. Instead, they tend to consider *all sources* of international human rights law as "relevant and persuasive".[159]

Recent examples at the Supreme Court of Canada include the 2007 case of *Health Services and Support*[160] on freedom of association under section 2(d) of the *Charter*, which affirmed Dickson CJ's approach to international law. Writing for the majority in this case, Chief Justice McLachlin and Justice LeBel referred to the *International Covenant on Economic, Social and Cultural Rights*; and the *International Covenant on Civil and Political Rights*, as well as the *Convention (No. 87) concerning Freedom of Association and Protection of the Right to Organize*, adopted at the International Labour Organization. The status of these instruments—binding or not, implemented or not— was not specified, only that "Canada has endorsed all three of these documents".[161] It is worth noting that a few years before, in the 2001 case of *Dunmore*,[162] the majority per Justice Bastarache had gone more broadly because, in addition to the above instruments used to interpret freedom of association, reference was also made to two treaties that Canada has in fact not even ratified: ILO *Convention (No. 11) concerning the Rights of Association and Combination of Agricultural Workers*, and ILO *Convention (No. 141) concerning Organizations of Rural Workers and Their Role in Economic and Social Development*. Be they binding or not, implemented or not, ratified or not, all that mattered was that these international instruments represented "international human rights law",[163] norms deemed relevant and persuasive to the construction of section 2(d) of the *Charter*.

This generality of terms in the use of international law in *Charter* interpretation goes in line not only with Dickson CJ's call for resorting to such normativity in *Public Service Employee Relations Act*—although dispensing with the two categories of binding and not binding norms—but also with L'Heureux-Dubé J's message of flexibility and openness in *Baker*. More importantly for the central point of this second section of the chapter, both these decisions confirm that the paradigm of Westphalia is alive and strong in Canada and that the international/national divide remains highly relevant for constitutional and statutory interpretation. The new era of postnational law or post-dualism is aspirational at best, probably just a *"vue de l'esprit"*.

---

[159] See William A Schabas and Stéphane Beaulac, *International Human Rights and Canadian Law— Legal Commitment, Implementation and the Charter*, 3rd ed (Thomson Carswell, 2007), 84–90.

[160] Above (n 149), [70].

[161] *Ibid*, [71].

[162] *Dunmore v. Ontario (Attorney General)*, [2001] 3 SCR 1016.

[163] *Ibid*, [27].

3. CONCLUSION

By way of concluding remarks, it is appropriate to tie up these two issues and to insist on how they represent contemporary challenges not only in Canada, but also in a lot of liberal democracies, whatever their legal traditions. Talks of convergence in interpretative methodology have been going on for some time now, not merely within the common law world in regard to constitutional and statutory interpretation. Indeed, although Brexit may signal a reorientation of the debates, the European Union has provided a most interesting legal ground where, as legal commentators have highlighted,[164] there are mighty forces for the convergence, not only in legal methodology among the different member states, but also more generally in regard to the two legal systems, civil law and common law.[165]

With respect to the problematics of interlegality, we saw that the same feature distinguishes our Canadian experience, as recent developments on the domestic use of international law do not differentiate whether courts are involved in constitutional or statutory interpretation. Furthermore, when the focus is put on the operationalization of international normativity by means of legal interpretation, it becomes clear that both the contextual argument and the presumption of conformity with international law now allow the judiciary greater flexibility and, at the end of the day, additional opportunities for interlegality, meanwhile keeping intact, indeed reaffirming the paradigm of Westphalia. Numerous jurisdictions around the globe are having similar debates; witness the *Oxford Reports on International Law in Domestic Courts*,[166] a web-based resource led by André Nollkaemper at the Amsterdam Centre for International Law,[167] which have compiled and analyzed the domestic cases resorting to international law from nearly a hundred countries. Unlike the trendy argument in the field, however, this chapter shows how the empirical data—at least those from Canada—do not support the proposition suggesting the end of the international/national divide, when it comes to interlegality.[168]

---

[164] See Xavier Lewis, "L'Européanisation du *common law*," in P Legrand (ed), *Common law d'un siècle à l'autre* (Éditions Yvon Blais, 1992), 275; H Patrick Glenn, "La civilisation de la common law," in E Capparo (ed), *Mélanges Germain Brière* (Wilson & Lalfeur, 1993), 595; and also the different contributions in Baris S Markesinis (ed), *The Gradual Convergence: Foreign Ideas, Foreign Influences, and English Law on the Eve of the 21st Century* (Clarendon Press, 1993). *Contra*, see Pierre Legrand, "European Legal Systems Are Not Converging" (1996) 45 *Int'l & Comp LQ* 52.

[165] On the methodological convergence in the Canadian bijural context, see: Louis LeBel and Pierre-Louis Le Saunier, "L'interaction du droit civil et de la common law à la Cour suprême du Canada", (2006) 47 *Cahiers de droit* 179, 230–231.

[166] See: http://opil.ouplaw.com/page/ILDC/oxford-reports-on-international-law-in-domestic-courts.

[167] For the sake of disclosure, I am myself involved with *Oxford Reports on International Law in Domestic Courts*, as well as with research projects at the Amsterdam Centre for International Law, between 2004 and 2010.

[168] See the recent diagnostic, to the similar effect, by Machiko Kanetake and André Nollkaemper, "The International Rule of Law in the Cycle of Contestations and Deference", in M Kanetake and A Nollkaemper (eds.), *The Rule of Law at the National and International Levels—Contestations and Deference* (Hart Publishing, 2016), 445.

BIBLIOGRAPHY

Beaulac, Stéphane, "La problématique de l'interlégalité et la méthodologie juridique," in JY Chérot *et al.* (eds), *Le droit entre autonomie et ouverture—Mélanges en l'honneur de Jean-Louis Bergel* (Brussels: Bruylant, 2013), 5

Beaulac, Stéphane, "Les dommages collatéraux de la Charte canadienne en interprétation législative" (2007) 48 *Cahiers de droit* 751

Beaulac, Stéphane, "Interlégalité et réception du droit international en droit interne canadien et québécois," in S Beaulac and J-F Gaudreault-DesBiens (eds), *JurisClasseur—Droit constitutionnel* (Montreal: LexisNexis, 2011), 23/1

Beaulac, Stéphane, "International Law and Statutory Interpretation: Up with Context, Down with Presumption," in OE Fitzgerald *et al.* (eds), *The Globalized Rule of Law—Relationships between International and Domestic Law* (Toronto: Irwin Law, 2006), 331

Beaulac, Stéphane, "International Law Gateway to Domestic Law: Hart's 'Open Texture', Legal Language and the Canadian Charter" (2012) 46 *Revue juridique Thémis* 443

Beaulac, Stéphane, "L'interprétation de la Charte: reconsidération de l'approche téléologique et réévaluation du rôle du droit international", in G.-A. Beaudoin and E. Mendes (eds), *Canadian Charter of Rights and Freedoms*, 4th ed (Toronto: LexisNexis Butterworths, 2005), 27

Beaulac, Stéphane, "National Application of International Law: The Statutory Interpretation Perspective" (2003) 41 *Canadian YB Int'l L* 225

Beaulac, Stéphane, *The Power of Language in the Making of International Law—The Word Sovereignty in Bodin and Vattel and the Myth of Westphalia* (Leiden and Boston: Martinus Nijhoff, 2004)

Beaulac, Stéphane and Frédéric Bérard, *Précis d'interprétation legislative*, 2nd ed. (Montreal: LexisNexis, 2014)

Beaulac, Stéphane and Pierre-André Côté, "Driedger's 'Modern Principle' at the Supreme Court of Canada: Interpretation, Justification, Legitimization" (2006) 40 *Revue juridique Thémis* 131

Beaulac, Stéphane and John H. Currie, "Canada", in D Sherton (ed), *International Law and Domestic Legal Systems—Incorporation, Transformation, and Persuasion* (Oxford: Oxford University Press, 2011), 116

Bradley, Curtis A, "Breard, Our Dualist Constitution and the Internationalist Conception" (1999) 51 *Stanford L Rev* 529

Côté, Pierre-André, (coll Stéphane Beaulac and Mathieu Devinat), *The Interpretation of Legislation in Canada*, 4th ed (Toronto: Carswell, 2011), 415

Driedger, Elmer A, *The Construction of Statutes*, 2nd ed. (Toronto: Butterworths, 1983)

Kanetake, Machiko and André Nollkaemper, "The International Rule of Law in the Cycle of Contestations and Deference", in M Kanetake and A Nollkaemper (eds.), *The Rule of Law at the National and International Levels—Contestations and Deference* (Oxford: Hart Publishing, 2016), 445

M Kindred, Hugh M, "Canadians as Citizens of the International Community: Asserting Unimplemented Treaty Rights in the Courts," in SG Coughlan and D Russell (eds), *Citizenship and Citizen Participation in the Administration of Justice* (Montreal: Éditions Thémis, 2002) 263

Knop, Karen, "Here and There: International Law in Domestic Courts" (2000) 32 *New York U J Int'l L & Pol* 501

Krisch, Nico, *Beyond Constitutionalism—The Pluralist Structure of Postnational Law* (Oxford: Oxford University Press, 2010)

Kumm, Mattias, "Democratic Constitutionalism Encounters International Law: Terms of Engagement", in S Choudhry (ed), *The Migration of Constitutional Ideas* (Cambridge: Cambridge University Press, 2007), 256

LeBel, Louis, "La méthode d'interprétation moderne: le juge devant lui-même et en lui-même," in S Beaulac and M Devinat (eds), *Interpretatio non cessat—Essays in honour of Pierre-André Côté* (Cowansville: Éditions Yvons Blais, 2011)

Mackay, A Wayne, "Interpreting the Charter of Rights: Law, Politics and Poetry", in G-A Beaudoin (ed), *Causes invoquant la Charte, 1986–87—Actes de la Conférence de l'Association du Barreau canadien tenue à Montréal en octobre 1986* (Cowansville: Éditions Yvon Blais, 1987), 347

Macklem, Patrick, "The International Constitution", in F Faraday, J Fudge and E Tucker (eds), *Constitutional Labour Rights in Canada—Farm Workers and the* Fraser *Case* (Toronto: Irwin Law, 2012), 261

Nijman, Janne and André Nollkaemper, *New Perspectives on the Divide between National and International Law* (Oxford: Oxford University Press, 2007)

Peck, Sidney R, "An Analytical Framework for the Application of the Canadian Charter of Rights and Freedoms" (1987) 25 *Osgoode Hall LJ* 1

Schabas, William A and Stéphane Beaulac, *International Human Rights and Canadian Law—Legal Commitment, Implementation and the Charter*, 3rd ed (Toronto: Thomson Carswell, 2007)

Slaughter, Anne-Marie, *A New World Order* (Princeton: Princeton University Press, 2004)

Slaughter, Anne-Marie, "A Typology of Transjudicial Communication" (1994) 29 *U Richmond L Rev* 99

Toope, Stephen J, "The Uses of Metaphor: International Law and the Supreme Court of Canada" (2001) 80 *Canadian Bar Rev* 534

Tremblay, Luc B, "L'interprétation téléologique des droits constitutionnels" (1995) 29 *Revue juridique Thémis* 460

Walker, Neil, "Beyond Boundary Disputes and Basic Grids: Mapping the Global Disorder of Normative Orders" (2008) 6 *Int'l J Constitutional L* 373

Waters, Melissa A, "Creeping Monism: The Judicial Trend toward Interpretive Incorporation of Human Rights Treaties" (2007) 107 *Columbia L Rev* 628

CHAPTER 42

....

THE LIVING TREE

....

W.J. WALUCHOW[*]

In 1929, the Judicial Committee of the United Kingdom's Privy Council decided one of the most famous and influential cases in Canadian legal history: *R v Edwards*, commonly referred to as "The Persons Case."[1] In addition to setting a landmark precedent regarding the legal status of women, *Edwards* addressed key questions surrounding the nature and interpretation of constitutions. In addressing these questions, the Privy Council introduced, into Canadian constitutional theory, rhetoric, and practice, a powerful metaphor, the Constitution as a *living tree*, that has continued to exert its influence throughout the decades. In a relatively recent case, *Reference re Same-Sex Marriage*, the Supreme Court of Canada was quite explicit about its continued commitment to the living tree metaphor when it dealt with the question whether the meaning of *marriage* is constitutionally fixed so as to preclude same-sex marriages. "The 'frozen concepts' reasoning runs contrary to one of the most fundamental principles of Canadian constitutional interpretation: that our Constitution is a living tree which, by way of progressive interpretation, accommodates and addresses the realities of modern life."[2]

In this chapter, I shall begin with a brief, and of necessity selective, history of the living tree metaphor as it has played out in the interpretive practices of Canadian courts since *Edwards*. I shall then briefly consider to what extent the Canadian living tree approach really is different from its contemporary rival, originalism. Originalism, which seeks to tie the meaning of a constitutional provision to history and intent, in particular to the meaning the provision bore at the time of its adoption, is thought to stand in stark contrast to living constitutionalism. The latter views constitutional meaning as continually evolving in response to changing moral and political views, new social circumstances, and the necessity of allowing a measure of flexibility in interpreting and applying an

---

[*] Professor and Senator William McMaster Chair in Constitutional Studies, McMaster University.
[1] *Edwards v A.G Canada* [1930] AC 124. In 1927 the Judicial Committee of the Privy Council was the highest court of appeal under Canadian law.
[2] *Reference re Same-Sex Marriage*, [2004] 3 S.C.R. 698, 2004 SCC 79, [22].

entrenched constitution, one intentionally designed to last a very long time.[3] As we shall see, however, things are not as clear as this simple picture suggests. Originalism, as it has come to be understood in theoretical treatments of constitutional interpretation, is arguably much closer to the type of living constitutionalism introduced in *Edwards* and practiced by Canadian courts thereafter. It is to this question that we will turn briefly at the end of the chapter.

1. *EDWARDS*

In 1929, Canada's constitution consisted mainly of *the British North America Act, 1867* (*BNA Act*), an Act of the UK Parliament that created the Dominion of Canada and defined its various government bodies and offices.[4] In 1916, Alberta social activist Emily Murphy was appointed the first female police magistrate in Alberta, an appointment that was later challenged on the ground that women did not qualify as *persons* under the *BNA Act*. In 1917, the Alberta Supreme Court expressed its disagreement, ruling that women were indeed persons. However, the ruling applied only within the province of Alberta. Many years later, Murphy allowed her name to stand as a candidate for the Canadian Senate and once again encountered resistance. Section 24 of the *BNA Act* specified that "The governor general shall from time to time, in the Queen's name, by instrument under the Great Seal of Canada, summon qualified persons to the Senate . . ." Prime Minister Robert Borden rejected Murphy's candidacy on the ground that she was not, for purposes of the *BNA Act*, a *person*. Thus she did not qualify for Senate membership. In 1927, Murphy, together with four other prominent Alberta women's rights activists, now immortalized as "The Famous Five," challenged Borden's decision before the Supreme Court of Canada.[5] In rejecting Murphy's claim, the Court ruled that Murphy, though perhaps qualified in every other respect, was ineligible for appointment to the Senate.[6] The common law meaning of the word *person* would not, at the time of the *BNA Act*'s enactment, have been thought to extend to women—and it was this understanding that must inform any attempt to interpret section 24.

Undeterred by this result, the Famous Five appealed to the UK's Judicial Committee of the Privy Council, at the time the final court of appeal in Canada. The women continued

---

[3] Originalism is commonly contrasted with living constitutionalism, of which Canada's living tree theory is an instance. Living constitutionalism is defended in, among other places, David Strauss, *The Living Constitution* (Oxford University Press, 2010) and W.J. Waluchow, *A Common Law Theory of Judicial Review: The Living Tree* (Cambridge: Cambridge University Press, 2007). In this chapter the terms *living tree constitutionalism* and *living constitutionalism* (and their cognates) will be used interchangeably.

[4] Now called the *Constitution Act, 1867*, U.K., 30 & 31 Victoria, c.3.

[5] In addition to Emily Murphy, the Famous Five included Henrietta Muir Edwards, Irene Parlby, Louise McKinney, and Nellie McClung.

[6] See *Edwards v Canada (Attorney General)*, [1928] S.C.R. 276.

to face two substantial hurdles in making their case. First, nowhere in the *BNA Act* does one actually find mention of women or female persons. Indeed, the statute used the word *persons* when the intention had clearly been to refer to more than one person, and the word *he* was employed when the intended referent was a single person. Second, and perhaps more important, under nineteenth century common law women were, with a few notable exceptions, generally deemed incapable of exercising public functions. "In England no woman under the degree of a Queen or a Regent, married or unmarried, could take part in the government of the state. A woman was under a legal incapacity to be elected to serve in Parliament and even if a peeress in her own right she was not, nor is, entitled as an incident of peerage to receive a writ of summons to the House of Lords." Hence, the Committee agreed with the Canadian Supreme Court that the original, common law understanding of *persons* in 1867 was such as to preclude women from holding public office.[7]

For a variety of reasons the Committee refused, however, to base its decision on this original understanding. Most notable were: the Committee's views concerning the special nature of constitutions, even those of ordinary statutory origin as this one was; its belief that such instruments are deliberately designed to facilitate evolution so as to meet changing social circumstances, and moral and political views; and its observation that the place of women within society had evolved considerably since the nineteenth century.

> The *British North America Act* planted in Canada a living tree capable of growth and expansion within its natural limits. The object of the Act was to grant a Constitution to Canada. Like all written constitutions it has been subject to development through usage and convention. . . . Their Lordships do not conceive it to be the duty of this Board—it is certainly not their desire—to cut down the provisions of the Act by a narrow and technical construction, but rather to give it a large and liberal interpretation so that the Dominion to a great extent, but within certain fixed limits, may be mistress in her own house . . .

Quoting from *Clement's Canadian Constitution*, the Committee went on to add that

> The Privy Council, indeed, has laid down that Courts of law must treat the provisions of the *British North America Act* by the same methods of construction and exposition

---

[7] Whereas Justice Anglin of the Supreme Court had emphasized that the authors of the BNA Act could not have intended to depart from the common law understanding of the word *person* as of 1867, Justice Duff relied on a somewhat different argument. Though alluding to the absence of intent to depart from the common law understanding of *person*, in the end he relied on a structural argument that the Senate, a body created by the BNA Act in the image of an earlier government body called the *Legislative Council*, was meant to be more impervious to change than the House. "It seems to me to be a legitimate inference, that the *British North America* Act contemplated a second Chamber, the constitution of which should, in all respects, be fixed and determined by the Act itself, a constitution which was to be in principle the same, though, necessarily, in detail, not identical, with that of the second Chambers established by the earlier statutes. That under those statutes, women were not eligible for appointment, is hardly susceptible of controversy."

which they apply to other statutes. But there are statutes and statutes; and the strict construction deemed proper in the case, for example, of a penal or taxing statute or one passed to regulate the affairs of an English parish, would be often subversive of Parliament's real intent if applied to an Act passed to ensure the peace, order and good government of a British Colony.

And finally, the Committee added, "The Act should be on all occasions interpreted in a large, liberal and comprehensive spirit, considering the magnitude of the subjects with which it purports to deal in very few words." Such an approach, the Committee reasoned, demanded the following conclusions. "[T]he word 'persons' in sec. 24 *does* include women, and ... women are eligible to be summoned to and become members of the Senate of Canada." In commenting on their conclusion, the Committee added "that the exclusion of women from all public offices is a relic of days more barbarous than ours." And to those "who would ask why the word ['persons'] should include females, the obvious answer is, why should it not."

This living tree conception introduced in *Edwards* continued, over the decades, to exert its influence in Canada, up to and including the time when efforts were being made to introduce a new constitution.[8] Distinct echoes of *Edwards* can be detected in the *Patriation Reference*, which dealt with whether the Federal Government was constitutionally entitled to introduce a new Canadian constitution, absent substantial agreement on the part of Canada's provincial governments.[9] They can also be found in *Skapinker*, the very first case decided under the new constitutional regime. *Skapinker*, together with a number of key cases that followed in its wake, required of the Canadian Supreme Court that it come to terms with the judiciary's role as official interpreter of Canada's new constitution, particularly its incorporated *Charter of Rights and Freedoms*. In each of these cases, one sees the Court endeavouring to articulate clearly the interpretive approach they thought appropriate. These cases reveal the extent to which the living tree metaphor continued to shape Canada's approach to its constitutional practices.

2. The *Patriation Reference*

During the period 1867–1982, Canadian constitutional law revolved mainly around the *BNA Act*. It is important to recognize the somewhat peculiar status of this constitutional instrument. The *BNA Act* was an ordinary statute of the UK Parliament, one that, to be sure, had the rather extraordinary task of establishing a new nation, albeit one with strong colonial ties to the mother country. Though for all practical purposes Canada

---

[8] These efforts were eventually successful and culminated in the adoption of the *Constitution Act, 1982*, which included a newly minted *Charter of Rights and Freedoms*.

[9] *Re: Resolution to amend the Constitution*, [1981] 1 S.C.R. 753 commonly known as the *Patriation Reference*.

evolved into a fully independent state in the decades that followed adoption of the *BNA Act*, strictly speaking the country owed its continued legal existence to the good graces of the UK's Parliament and courts. In 1931, an Empire Conference was convened that included the leaders of all the countries within the (then) British Empire. Among the notable results was general agreement on the Statute of Westminster, formally adopted by the UK Parliament later that year.[10] The Statute aimed to grant full independence to all existing dominions within the Empire and, in the case of Canada, to sever the *BNA Act* from its British roots. The Canadian Parliament requested a delay in implementing the Statute (in Canada), however, because it could not secure the agreement of all provincial governments on the addition to the *BNA Act* of an amending formula. It would be another 50 years before (near unanimous) agreement on a new constitution could be achieved—before, that is, the *BNA Act* with an amending formula and charter of rights, could be *patriated* to its new Canadian home as *The Constitution Act, 1982*.[11]

The process leading up to patriation was far from easy. The Federal Government, led by Prime Minister Pierre Trudeau, experienced considerable resistance, not only because of the newly proposed amending formula but also, and principally because of, the Government's proposal to include a new charter of rights and freedoms. This additional element would have radically transformed the Canadian system from one based largely on the Westminster model of unlimited parliamentary sovereignty (within spheres of federal and provincial jurisdiction, duly defined by the Constitution) to one incorporating substantive limits of political morality on the powers of both Parliament and the provincial legislatures. The objections were predictable. Such a transformation would accord far too much political power to the judges, who would of necessity be the final, authoritative voice as to the meaning and import of the charter's abstract rights provisions, thereby threatening the rule of law and undermining the principles of democracy. Despite considerable effort on the part of the Trudeau government to negotiate settlement of the patriation question, sufficient agreement among the provinces could not be mustered. As a result, the Government seriously contemplated the possibility of unilateral action, that is, formally requesting on its own that the UK Parliament patriate the Constitution duly amended. Resistance continued, bolstered by the claim that any such step, without prior agreement on the part of the provinces whose powers would be seriously affected, would be in serious violation of constitutional law. The end result was the *Patriation Reference*, in which a number of provinces petitioned the Canadian Supreme Court to declare the Trudeau government's proposed unilateral move unconstitutional. The Court ruled that such a request, though not in violation of Canadian constitutional law, would nonetheless be *unconstitutional*.

---

[10] Statute of Westminster, 1931 (22 & 23 Geo. V c. 4, 11 December 1931).

[11] As the BNA Act never resided in Canada, one could not strictly speaking refer to it as being subject to *repatriation*—that is, being brought back. Instead, the relevant political actors invented a new term, *patriation*, which served to designate the process of bringing the Act home to Canada for the very first time.

In coming to this somewhat paradoxical decision, the Court drew on A.V. Dicey's distinction between *constitutional laws* and *constitutional conventions*.

> The one set of rules are in the strictest sense "laws," since they are rules which (whether written or unwritten, whether enacted by statute or derived from the mass of custom, tradition, or judge-made maxims known as the common law) are enforced by the courts; these rules constitute "constitutional law" in the proper sense of that term, and may for the sake of distinction be called collectively "the law of the constitution."[12]

According to the law of the Canadian Constitution, so construed, the Trudeau government was not constitutionally barred from taking its formal request to the UK Parliament. Nor was there anything to prevent the UK Parliament from acceding to that request. But there is more to a constitution than constitutional law, the Court opined. The justices once again turned to Dicey.

> The other set of rules consist of conventions, understandings, habits, or practices which, though they may regulate the conduct of the several members of the sovereign power, of the Ministry, or of other officials, are not in reality laws at all since they are not enforced by the courts. This portion of constitutional law may, for the sake of distinction, be termed the "conventions of the constitution," or constitutional morality.[13]

Given its endorsement of Dicey's views on the nature and role of constitutional conventions, it was open to the Court simply to note the distinction and leave it at that. In other words, having ruled that there is nothing in constitutional *law* to prevent the Trudeau government from having its way, the Court could have declined to deal with the further question whether such an action would nonetheless be in violation of constitutional convention. After all, as the Court noted, such conventions are political entities, and as such are not enforceable in courts. But the Court chose not to take this easy route and instead expressed its view that the Trudeau government's proposed course of action would violate an important constitutional convention, thus rendering the action unconstitutional. No doubt the Court took this route because of its stated belief that some constitutional conventions are in fact more important than some constitutional laws—and that a convention bearing directly on this case was one of them.

> It should be borne in mind however that, while they are not laws, some conventions may be more important than some laws. Their importance depends on that of the value or principle which they are meant to safeguard. Also they form *an integral part of the constitution* and of the constitutional system. . . .
>   That is why it is perfectly appropriate to say that *to violate a convention is to do something which is unconstitutional although it entails no direct legal consequence.* But

---

[12] *Ibid.*, 855, quoting A.V. Dicey, *The Law of the Constitution*, 10th ed. (Macmillan, 1959), at 23–24.
[13] C.f. *Edwards*, above (n 1), where the Privy Council remarked that written constitutional documents are "subject to development through usage and convention . . ."

the words "constitutional" and "unconstitutional" may also be used in a strict legal sense, for instance with respect to a statute which is found *ultra vires* or unconstitutional. The foregoing may perhaps be summarized in an equation: *constitutional conventions plus constitutional law equal the total constitution of the country.*[14]

Later, the Court added this observation, one particularly relevant to the issue of whether constitutions are living trees: "The main purpose of constitutional conventions is to ensure that the legal framework of the constitution will be operated in accordance with the prevailing constitutional values or principles of the period."[15] In the Court's view, among the most important of Canada's constitutional conventions was the long-standing requirement that "the Canadian Parliament will not request an amendment directly affecting federal-provincial relationships without prior consultation and agreement with the provinces."[16] The Court added that the "nature and the degree of provincial participation in the amending process, however, have not lent themselves to easy definition."[17] But it was clear that by no reasonable measure of substantial agreement did the Trudeau government have it. As a result, the government went back to the drawing board and once again attempted to garner support from the provinces. An agreement was ultimately reached, one that incorporated certain key features into the new constitution designed to placate the most forceful and influential critics. Among the most notable of these were two provisions, commonly referred to as the *reasonable limitations* and *notwithstanding* clauses. The former, found in section 1, states that the *Charter* "guarantees the rights and freedoms set out in it subject only to such reasonable limits prescribed by law as can be demonstrably justified in a free and democratic society." This provision is designed to leave Parliament and the provincial legislatures room to pursue valid social objectives without the looming threat of judicial interference motivated by an inflated concern for the protection of individual rights. The notwithstanding or override clause provides, at least in theory, an even greater safety valve.[18] Section 33 provides that "Parliament or the legislature of a

[14] *Ibid.*, 883–884 (emphasis added).

[15] *Ibid.* 880.

[16] This convention is now formalized in the amending formula (the so-called 7/50 rule) attached to the new constitution. According to S. 38(1), "An amendment to the Constitution of Canada may be made by proclamation issued by the Governor General under the Great Seal of Canada where so authorized by

(a) resolutions of the Senate and House of Commons; and

(b) resolutions of the legislative assemblies of at least two-thirds of the provinces that have, in the aggregate, according to the then latest general census, at least fifty per cent of the population of all the provinces..."

[17] *Edwards* above (n 1), 870.

[18] I say "at least in theory" because the notwithstanding clause has never been used federally and only very seldom provincially. One of the most controversial uses was the subject of dispute in *Ford v Quebec (AG)*, [1988] 2 S.C.R. 712. In *Ford* the Supreme Court struck down a portion of the Quebec Charter of the French Language. This law significantly restricted the use of commercial signs written in languages other than French. The Court ruled that the Quebec Charter violated freedom of expression as guaranteed in the *Canadian Charter of Rights and Freedoms*. In response, the Quebec government invoked section 33. A second example arose in 1986. The Saskatchewan legislature introduced back-to-work legislation

province may expressly declare in an Act of Parliament or of the legislature, as the case may be, that the Act or a provision thereof shall operate notwithstanding a provision included in section 2 or sections 7 to 15 of this Charter." With the addition of these key features, the agreement of all provinces save one, Quebec, was eventually secured.[19] In 1982 the parliaments of the United Kingdom and Canada passed parallel acts—the *Canada Act 1982*[20] and the *Constitution Act, 1982*—and on 17 April 1982, at a formal ceremony on Parliament Hill in Ottawa, Queen Elizabeth II formally signed both acts into law, thus patriating the constitution of Canada and consolidating its legal status as a fully independent nation.

Among the lessons of the *Patriation Reference* is that the living tree metaphor continued to exert its influence well past the time of *Edwards*. The Court did not, of course, draw on constitutional conventions, and the "prevailing constitutional values or principles of the period" they reflect, to decide a question of constitutional interpretation, as the Privy Council had done in *Edwards*. But it did assert its view that a nation's constitution, in this instance its constitutional law combined with its constitutional conventions, is the sort of instrument that both can and should be allowed to evolve and adapt to changing circumstances. Indeed, one of the crucial roles of constitutional conventions is to facilitate the kind of evolution heralded by the Privy Council in *Edwards*. In short, evolving and adaptable constitutional conventions are part and parcel of the living tree that is Canada's constitution.

3. *Skapinker*

With the *Charter's* introduction in 1982, questions immediately arose as to how it should be interpreted. Should it be, as the Judicial Committee had said in *Edwards*, "on all occasions interpreted in a large, liberal and comprehensive spirit, considering the magnitude of the subjects with which it purports to deal in very few words."[21] That is, should it be

---

to end a strike by public service employees and protect the general public from the disruption of government services caused by the strike. The legislature, contemplating a constitutional challenge, invoked the notwithstanding clause to protect their legislation from *Charter* scrutiny by the courts. The SCC later ruled, however, in *Alberta Labour Reference* [1987] 1 SCR 313, that the *Charter* did *not* include the right to strike, thus rendering the declaration of no effect. In any event, these instances are rare and occurred relatively early in the *Charter's* history. One might therefore question the functional usefulness of the notwithstanding clause. Indeed, one might even suggest that it is, in effect, dead letter law. It is a provision no current government is likely to invoke for fear of being labeled one who fails to take rights seriously. For an excellent discussion of the history and questions surrounding Canada's notwithstanding clause, see Stephen Gardbaum, *The New Commonwealth Model* (Cambridge University Press, 2013). See also the chapter by Janet Hiebert in this *Handbook*.

[19] To this day, Quebec has never formally assented to the *Constitution Act, 1982*.
[20] [UK] 1982, c.11.
[21] *Edwards*, above (n 1).

interpreted in the spirit of the living tree metaphor that took root in *Edwards*? Or should it instead be interpreted more narrowly and conservatively, perhaps in a spirit more in line with originalism, a view that sees constitutions as stable entities with fixed meanings, not as living trees whose very meaning and effect evolve over time? In the very first case decided under the new constitutional regime, the Supreme Court clearly opted for the former approach.

Joel Skapinker was a citizen of South Africa residing in Canada whose application to the Ontario bar to practice law was refused on the ground that Ontario's Law Society Act required Canadian citizenship. Skapinker sought to have the relevant provision of the Act declared inoperative on the ground that it violated section 6(2)(b) of the Canadian *Charter*, which stipulates that "Every citizen of Canada and every person who has the status of a permanent resident of Canada has the right ... to pursue the gaining of a livelihood in any province." At trial, Skapinker's claim was denied. The case eventually found its way to the Supreme Court, which ruled that Skapinker's *Charter* rights had indeed been violated.[22] In coming to its decision, the Court cited the following reasons:

> There are some simple but important considerations which guide a Court in constru-
> ing the *Charter* ... The *Charter* comes from neither level of the legislative branches
> of government but from the Constitution itself. It is part of the fabric of Canadian
> law. Indeed, it "is the supreme law of Canada": *Constitution Act, 1982*, s. 52. It can-
> not be readily amended. The fine and constant adjustment process of these consti-
> tutional provisions is left by a tradition of necessity to the judicial branch. Flexibility
> must be balanced with certainty. The future must, to the extent foreseeably possible,
> be accommodated in the present. The *Charter* is designed and adopted to guide and
> serve the Canadian community for a long time. Narrow and technical interpretation,
> if not modulated by a sense of the unknowns of the future, can stunt the growth of
> the law and hence the community it serves. All this has long been with us in the pro-
> cess of developing the institutions of government under the *B.N.A. Act, 1867* (now
> the *Constitution Act, 1867*). With the *Constitution Act, 1982* comes a new dimension, a
> new yardstick of reconciliation between the individual and the community and their
> respective rights, a dimension which, like the balance of the Constitution, remains to
> be interpreted and applied by the Court.[23]

The living tree metaphor was alive and well. And it was the Court's intention to follow its spirit when interpreting and applying Canada's new *Charter of Rights and Freedoms*.

---

[22] *Law Society of Upper Canada v Skapinker* [1984] 1 SCR 357.
[23] *Ibid*. [11].

4. *BIG M DRUG MART*

Big M Drug Mart[24] made the Supreme Court's commitment to its living tree conception of the new constitution even more explicit. The Lord's Day Act, R.S.C. 1970 required most businesses to close on Sunday. The clearly intended purpose of this statute, the Court observed, was maintenance of the Christian Sabbath as a holy day. And the main question was whether a statute with such a purpose infringed section 2(a) of the *Charter* that guarantees "freedom of conscience and religion." The Court ruled that it did. But once again the more important point, for our purposes, is the interpretive approach the Court took in reaching its decision. As the Court saw things, "The meaning of a right or freedom guaranteed by the Charter [is] to be ascertained by an analysis of the purpose of such a guarantee; it [is] to be understood . . . in light of the interests it was meant to protect." And the purpose of any such right or freedom "is to be sought by reference to the character and the larger objects of the Charter itself, to the language chosen to articulate the specific right or freedom, to the historical origins of the concepts enshrined, and where applicable, to the meaning and purpose of the other specific rights and freedoms with which it is associated within the text of the Charter."[25] Furthermore, "the interpretation provided should be a generous rather than a legalistic one, aimed at fulfilling the purpose of the guarantee and securing for individuals the full benefit of the *Charter*'s protection." At the same time, the Court added, "it is important not to overshoot the actual purpose of the right or freedom in question, but to recall that the *Charter* was not enacted in a vacuum, and must therefore, as this Court's decision in [*Skapinker*] illustrates, be placed in its proper linguistic, philosophic and historical contexts."[26]

As the above passages illustrate, the Court continued to be wedded to the living tree metaphor. But they also illustrate that the Court's endorsement of living tree constitutionalism was not tantamount to wholesale rejection of the kinds of historical factors on which originalists typically focus. The Supreme Court was happy to count, as significant in discerning constitutional meaning:

(a) the very language chosen to articulate the specific right or freedom in question
(b) the historical origins of the concepts embedded in the *Charter*
(c) the purposes the securing of which lay behind the decision to include a specific rights provision, and
(d) where applicable, the meaning and purpose of other associated *Charter* rights.

How these various factors play out in a specific case can, of course, often be a complicated question. But there is little reason to think that, in some cases, they provide

---

[24] R. v *Big M Drug Mart* Ltd., [1985] 1 S.C.R. 295.
[25] *Ibid.* [117].
[26] *Ibid.*

an answer that is fairly clear. For instance, when dealing with the *Charter* right to free expression it might be highly relevant that the more expansive concept *expression* was chosen by the framers, not the much narrower concept *speech* one finds in the US Bill of Rights. Such a historical fact might well be enough to undercut any attempt to rule out various non-verbal forms of expression—for example, flag burning—as being outside the scope of section 2.[27] Had the Constitution's authors intended to protect nothing but verbal forms of expression, they could easily have referred to *speech* instead of *expression*. That they did not do so counts significantly in favour of an expansive reading of the term *expression*, one that includes a variety of different forms of expressive activity, only some of which are verbal in character.

The crucial role often played by these factors is one worth stressing. Viewing constitutions as living trees is not equivalent to granting judges wholesale licence to make of the constitution what they will. As with a tree capable of sustaining itself over time, secure against the hostile environmental forces it often faces, the Constitution, as the fundamental framework within which ordinary law and politics are to take place, must also be rooted in something that provides a healthy measure of stability. That stability, according to the Court, is at least partly provided by factors (a)–(d), factors that help ensure what the *Edwards* decision described as development of the Constitution *within its natural limits*. Yet this important point notwithstanding, it is equally important to stress that living constitutionalism does not assign these factors anything close to a fully dispositive role. To treat them as dispositive would be, as the Court had suggested in *Skapinker*, to "stunt the growth of the law and hence the community it serves." Speaking metaphorically, the leaves and branches of the tree that is the Canadian Constitution must, within its natural limits, still be allowed to grow in whatever directions contemporary realities deem essential. And some of these directions might turn out to be ones that the Constitution's authors never contemplated or would have wanted ruled out had they done so.

5. *B.C. Motor Vehicle Act*

That the factors listed in *Big M Drug Mart* should not be permitted to play a dispositive or overriding role in constitutional interpretation served an even more critical role in another early landmark *Charter* case: *Re. B.C. Motor Vehicle Act*.[28] At issue here was the constitutional validity of a provision creating an absolute liability driving offense. According to *Motor Vehicle Act, R.S.B.C. 1979*, anyone who drove while legally prohibited from doing so was guilty of an offence and liable to either fine or imprisonment. As the Supreme Court observed, the Act "create[d] an absolute liability offence in which

---

[27] The question whether flag burning was an instance of protected speech was the centre of focus in *Texas v. Johnson*, 491 U.S. 397 (1989).

[28] *Reference re Section 94(2) of the Motor Vehicle Act*, [1985] 2 SCR 486.

guilt is established by proof of driving, whether or not the defendant knew of the prohibition or suspension . . . "[29] The case had been referred earlier by the B.C. Lieutenant
Governor to the B.C. Court of Appeal, which found sec. 94(2) of the Act to be of no
force owing to its inconsistency with section 7 of the *Charter*. That section provides that
"Everyone has the right to life, liberty and security of the person and the right not to
be deprived thereof except in accordance with the principles of fundamental justice."
Absolute liability driving offenses, the B.C. Court ruled, were incompatible with the
principles of fundamental justice. Unhappy with this result, the B.C. Attorney General
referred the case to the Canadian Supreme Court, which affirmed the earlier judgment.
Of particular importance for our purposes is, again, not the final result, but how the
Supreme Court viewed its interpretive task and the manner in which it set out to justify
its decision.

The pivotal question in *B.C. Motor Vehicle* was how to interpret section 7's reference to
the principles of fundamental justice.[30] Did this phrase contemplate pure *procedural* justice only? Or did it also contemplate meatier principles of *substantive* justice that extend
well beyond the procedures through which laws are created, applied, and enforced, and
can be used to measure the justice or injustice of an enactment's very content? The Court
ultimately opted for the latter option, but had to fend off concerns that opening up section 7 in this way would threaten democratic legitimacy. As Lamer observed,

> The overriding and legitimate concern that courts ought not to question the wis-
> dom of enactments, and the presumption that the legislator could not have intended
> [the] same, have to some extent distorted the discussion surrounding the meaning
> of "principles of fundamental justice". This has led to the spectre of a judicial "super-
> legislature" . . . This in turn has also led to a narrow characterization of the issue and
> to the assumption that only a procedural content to "principles of fundamental jus-
> tice" can prevent the courts from adjudicating upon the merits or wisdom of enact-
> ments. If this assumption is accepted, the inevitable corollary, with which I would
> have to then agree, is that the legislator intended that the words "principles of funda-
> mental justice" refer to procedure only.[31]

The Court's response was multi-faceted. First, it noted, the phrase *principles of fundamental justice* designates a wider conceptual category than the phrase *principles of procedural (or natural) justice.* Second, common law courts have historically considered more
than natural or procedural justice when assessing statutes.[32] So there were neither conceptual nor historical, legal impediments to at least *considering* the question whether
section 7 should be interpreted as referring to substantive justice. But that brought the
Court right back to the fundamental questions of interpretation addressed in *Skapinker*

---

[29] *Ibid.* [6], quoting section 94(2) of the Act.
[30] The question mirrors American debates about whether the Fifth and Fourteenth Amendment
clauses of the US Constitution reference to due process contemplates *substantive* as well as *procedural*
due process.
[31] *Re. B.C. Motor Vehicle Act* above (n 28) [19].
[32] *Ibid.* [20].

and *Big M Drug Mart* where, as we have seen, the Court embraced the "large, liberal and comprehensive" approach to interpreting constitutional rights. "The meaning of a right or freedom guaranteed by the *Charter* was to be ascertained by an analysis ... of the interests it was meant to protect ... The interpretation should be ... a generous rather than a legalistic one, aimed at fulfilling the purpose of the guarantee and securing for individuals the full benefit of the *Charter*'s protection."[33] So what were the particular *interests* section 7 was meant to protect? The answer was provided in part by sections 8–14, which " ... address specific deprivations of the 'right' to life, liberty and security of the person in breach of the principles of fundamental justice." It "would be incongruous to interpret s. 7 more narrowly than the rights in ss. 814 ... " And "[c]learly, some of those sections embody principles that are beyond what could be characterized as "procedural." [34]

These appeals to conceptual analysis, common law history, internal textual evidence, and the Court's earlier commitment to living tree constitutionalism would not, the Court seemed to realize, be enough to placate its critics. There would be those who continued to object on decidedly originalist grounds.

> A number of courts have placed emphasis upon the Minutes of the Proceedings and Evidence of the Special Joint Committee of the Senate and of the House of Commons on the Constitution in the interpretation of "principles of fundamental justice" ... In particular, the following passages dealing with the testimony of federal civil servants from the Department of Justice, have been relied upon:

Mr. Strayer (Assistant Deputy Minister, Public Law):

> Mr. Chairman, it was our belief that the words "fundamental justice" would cover the same thing as what is called procedural due process, that is the meaning of due process in relation to requiring fair procedure. However, it in our view does not cover the concept of what is called substantive due process, which would impose substantive requirements as to policy of the law in question.[35]

The Court's response to Strayer was to reject the originalist approach his argument presupposed. Among the reasons cited was the Court's belief that "speeches and declarations by prominent figures are inherently unreliable."[36]

> [T]he Charter is not the product of a few individual public servants, however distinguished, but of a multiplicity of individuals who played major roles in the negotiating, drafting and adoption of the Charter. How can one say with any

---

[33] *Ibid.* [22], quoting from *Big M Drug Mart.*
[34] *Ibid.* [28].
[35] *Ibid.* [36].
[36] *Ibid.* [50].

confidence that within this enormous multiplicity of actors, without forgetting the role of the provinces, the comments of a few federal civil servants can in any way be determinative?[37]

A second reason was this. Were the Court "to accord any significant weight to this testimony, it would in effect be assuming a fact which is nearly impossible of proof, i.e., the intention of the legislative bodies which adopted the *Charter*. In view of the indeterminate nature of the data, it would be erroneous to give these materials anything but minimal weight."[38] A third reason was that it was clearly open to the authors of the Constitution to have used the phrase *principles of natural justice* instead of *principles of fundamental justice*. But they did not.

Having rejected Strayer's originalist argument, the Court went on to endorse the approach to constitutional interpretation first espoused in *Edwards*. Section 7's "words cannot be given any exhaustive content or simple enumerative definition, but will take on concrete meanings as the courts address alleged violations of s. 7."[39] In other words, it would be a mistake to consider the constitutional meaning of a key phrase such as *the principles of fundamental justice* fixed by the framers' intentions at the time of adoption. Its meaning can and must be allowed to evolve over time as cases in which the concept plays an important role are decided. In pursuing Strayer's originalist option

> rights, freedoms and values embodied in the Charter in effect become frozen in time to the moment of adoption with little or no possibility of growth, development and adjustment to changing societal needs . . . If the newly planted "living tree" which is the Charter is to have the possibility of growth and adjustment over time, care must be taken to ensure that historical materials, such as the Minutes of Proceedings and Evidence of the Special Joint Committee, do not stunt its growth. As Estey J. wrote in *Law Society of Upper Canada v. Skapinker*, supra, at pp. 366–67:
>
>> Narrow and technical interpretation, if not modulated by a sense of the unknowns of the future, can stunt the growth of the law and hence the community it serves. All this has long been with us in the process of developing the institutions of government under the B.N.A. Act, 1867 (now the Constitution Act, 1867). With the Constitution Act, 1982 comes a new dimension, a new yardstick of reconciliation between the individual and the community and their respective rights, a dimension which, like the balance of the Constitution, remains to be interpreted and applied by the Court.[40]

---

[37] *Ibid.* [51].
[38] *Ibid.* [52].
[39] *Ibid.* [67].
[40] *Ibid.* [53].

6. LIVING TREE CONSTITUTIONALISM?

So what does this brief—and admittedly selective—tale of Canadian constitutional history reveal? Quite clearly it illustrates that the *idea* of living constitutionalism has, since at least *Edwards*, been alive and well in Canadian courts. The *Patriation Reference* endorses a conception of the Constitution as including a set of evolving, "living" constitutional conventions whose primary role "is to ensure that the legal framework of the constitution will be operated in accordance with the prevailing constitutional values or principles of the period."[41] Cases subsequent to the *Patriation Reference*, beginning with *Skapinker*, reveal a Canadian legal system wedded to this idea of an evolving, adaptable constitution, influenced by historical meanings, purposes, and intentions, but unwilling to permit these latter factors a dispositive role. To be sure, the Supreme Court sometimes appeals to constitutional authors' intentions when called on to interpret a constitutional provision, but the intentions that appear to count are usually the broad, intended *purposes* lying behind it.[42] These intended purposes are usually thought to be the advancement and protection of the broad moral interests the provision was meant to protect, for example, the moral interest in being treated in accordance with the principles of fundamental justice. And as the Court made clear in *BC Motor Vehicles*, the relevant interests are not necessarily the moral interests *as originally understood* by those whose intention it was to afford them the protection of a constitutional right. Rather, they are interests understood in light of contemporary norms and understandings, which in turn are subject to continued evolution. To allow original understandings of these moral interests to fix the meaning of the associated rights provision would mean that the "rights, freedoms and values embodied in the Charter [would] in effect become frozen in time to the moment of adoption with little or no possibility of growth, development and adjustment to changing needs."[43] And as the Court pronounced in *Skapinker*, its very first case under the *Charter*, this is a result to be avoided

So the idea of the constitution as a living tree has played a prominent role in Canadian legal practice since at least *Edwards*. It is also reasonably clear that the courts believe they are following a tradition of constitutional interpretation that stands in sharp contrast to originalism. But are the courts correct in drawing this sharp contrast? That is, to what extent does the living tree constitutionalism officially endorsed and practiced in Canada actually differ from originalism? In short, is living tree constitutionalism really all that different from originalism? The answer to this question is far from clear. And

---

[41] *Patriation Reference* above (n 9) 880.
[42] For an excellent, nuanced discussion of the role of purpose in the constitutional interpretive practices inspired by the living tree metaphor, see Benjamin Oliphant, "Taking Purposes Seriously: The Purposive Scope and Textual Bounds of Interpretation under the Canadian Charter of Rights and Freedoms" (2015) 65 *University of Toronto Law Journal* 239.
[43] See above (n 28).

one of the reasons is that originalism can itself be viewed as a kind of living tree. That is, originalism is a theory of constitutions and their interpretation that has evolved over the decades to the point where it is very difficult to tell whether and to what extent contemporary originalism really is all that different from the living constitutionalism endorsed by Canadian courts.[44]

7. ORIGINALISM

Originalism comes in many different forms.[45] But the core idea is that the meaning of a constitutional provision is in some way *fixed* at the moment of its creation.[46] As a consequence, constitutional meaning is a matter of historical fact. In other words, a provision's meaning was, is, and always will be, its *original meaning*. Originalists differ over what fixes this original meaning, some believing it to be the *intentions* of the provision's author(s), others believing that it is what a reasonably competent user of the language at the time of the provision's adoption would have understood its words to mean. The former type we can call original intentions originalism (OIO), whereas the latter is commonly referred to as *public meaning originalism* (PMO).[47] Despite their differences over what establishes original meaning, OIO and PMO both contend that it is only this meaning that counts when it comes to interpreting a constitutional provision. To ascribe to a provision anything other than its original meaning—when it is clear what that meaning is—is to do something other than interpret it. It is to create and impose new meaning. It is to replace the law that *is* with what the interpreter thinks it *ought* to be. It is, in short, illegitimately to usurp the legitimate authority of the constitution's authors. Things are different, however, in cases where original meaning is unclear or runs out, because, for

---

[44] The extent to which the two approaches have arguably converged is reflected in the tile of a recent book. See Jack Balkin, *Living Originalism* (Harvard University Press, 2011).

[45] For an exhaustive survey—and scathing critique—of the various forms of originalism, see Mitchell Berman, "Originalism is Bunk" 84 *N.Y.U. L. Rev.* 1 (2009).

[46] Larry Solum calls this the "fixation thesis." See "The Fixation Thesis: The Role of Historical Fact in Original Meaning" 91 *Notre Dame Law Review* 1 (2015).

[47] Early American originalists were concerned with what they took to be the excessive judicial activism of the US Supreme Court under Chief Justice Warren. These theorists saw the Court as imposing its own liberal policy choices in the guise of constitutional interpretation and argued for a change in interpretive approach, one that displayed fidelity to the Constitution itself. Such fidelity was thought to require a dedicated focus on the very concrete original intentions of the Constitution's framers. The Constitution applies only to fact situations actually contemplated by the framers and requires only what they intended it to require. If they viewed capital punishment as consistent with the Eighth Amendment's ban on cruel and unusual punishment, then the Eighth Amendment, properly interpreted, permits that practice. And this is true irrespective of any contemporary views as to the moral permissibility of capital punishment. For an early originalist approach see Robert Bork, "Neutral Principles and Some First Amendment Problems" (1971) 47 *Indiana Law Journal* 17. For a scathing critique, see Ronald Dworkin, *Freedom's Law* (Harvard University Press, 1996) 1–38. Contemporary defenders of OIO include Larry Alexander. See his "Simple Minded Originalism" available at http://papers.ssrn.com/sol3/papers.cfm?abstract_id=1235722, last accessed March 28, 2017. PMO is most often

example, it is too abstract or vague to settle the issue before the courts. In such instances, many contemporary originalists are prepared to allow the courts a more creative role via a process they call *constitutional construction*.[48] Whereas interpretation seeks to retrieve original meaning, construction seeks to add new meaning. It does so by articulating concrete rules and doctrines for the application of the constitutional provision where its meaning is too vague, abstract, or indeterminate to be applied consistently and predictably by the courts. A good example of constitutional construction, as originalists conceive it, is to be found in Canada's so-called *Oakes Test*, developed by the Supreme Court as a means of applying the Canadian Constitution's section 1 reasonable-limitations clause.[49] The meaning of section 1 is arguably far too abstract or vague to settle a dispute over whether a particular law reasonably limits a relevant *Charter* right. The *Oakes Test*, which introduces concepts such as proportionality, rational connection, and pressing and substantial objectives, is intended to provide section 1 with more concrete meaning. Construction is the process through which this more concrete meaning is ascribed, thus providing legislators and courts with an increased level of guidance in determining the validity of constitutionally suspect laws. Construction is also a means by which contemporary originalists seek to accommodate the need for the adaptability and flexibility Canadian courts have stressed under their professed living tree approach. Unlike the written terms of the Constitution, which cannot be changed so as to accommodate new realities absent a formal, constitutional amendment, constitutional constructions, as creations of the courts, are presumably susceptible to change or abandonment by these very same courts whenever evolving circumstances suggest the necessity of doing so.

It is crucial to recognize that contemporary originalists are able to promote construction as a means of avoiding the concerns of early originalism's critics. For example, a defender of OIO is able to accommodate the need for flexibility and adaptability that motivates living constitutionalists if she is willing to accept that the relevant intentions are not the *particular applications* the Constitution's authors intended to cover when they chose the language they did (e.g., drawing and quartering in relation to the right against cruel and unusual punishment) but rather the *broad purposes* they had in mind when they adopted the provision (e.g., the banning of unnecessarily harsh forms of punishment that display indifference to human suffering, whatever these might turn out to be). The latter option, sometimes referred to as a form of *moderate originalism,* allows far more flexibility and adaptability of the sort envisaged by the living tree approach, and is arguably the one endorsed by the Court in *Big M Drug Mart*.[50] There, recall, the Court said that care must be taken to ensure that the interpretation of a *Charter* right is a "generous rather than a legalistic one, aimed at fulfilling the *purpose* of the guarantee

associated with the late Justice Antonin Scalia. See A. Scalia, *A Matter of Interpretation: Federal Courts and the Law* (Princeton University Press, 1997).

   [48] See Keith Whittington, *Constitutional Construction: Divided Powers and Constitutional Meaning* (Harvard University Press, 1999).

   [49] *R v Oakes* [1986] 1 S.C.R. 103.

   [50] Jeffrey Goldsworthy defends this kind of moderate form of originalism in "Constitutional Interpretation: Originalism" (2009) 4 *Philosophy Compass* 682–702.

and securing for individuals the full benefit of the Charter's protection."⁵¹ Purposive interpretation conceived in this way, that is, as focussing on abstract as opposed to more particular, concrete purposes, permits a court to rule that the intended purpose of section 7 includes non-violation of the principles of substantive justice. It can do so even if Strayer was correct in his claim that the framers' originally intended applications of the phrase included only violations of procedural justice. On this moderate originalist view, the framers might have been mistaken about whether in actual fact the principles of fundamental justice extend to principles of substantive justice. Likewise for the ban on cruel and unusual punishment: if the relevant purpose is the banning of punishments that are excessively harsh and display indifference to human suffering, then should it turn out that capital punishment runs afoul of this purpose, it would be banned under the Eighth Amendment of the US Constitution. This despite the obvious fact that the authors of the Eighth Amendment thought differently. On the other hand, a defender of OIO, who posits the concrete applications or understandings intended by the Constitution's authors as the only ones relevant to constitutional interpretation, will counsel the far more restrictive approach to interpretation rejected by the Canadian Supreme Court in the various decisions canvassed above. If it can be shown that a constitution's authors intended only that particular applications be covered, then honouring their legitimate authority, and the resultant authority of their intentions and understandings, requires applying the provision as they would have applied it. If they intended to ban nothing over and above violations of procedural justice then that is what section 7 means. If US framers had no intention of including capital punishment under their Eighth Amendment ban, then it is not included. And any court that rules otherwise is neglecting its duty to interpret and apply the Constitution, thus violating the rule of law.

8. CONCLUSION

It is clear that the living tree metaphor has played a key role in shaping Canada's approach to constitutional law and its interpretation. From *Edwards* on, courts have viewed the Canadian Constitution as a living tree, capable of change in light of evolving circumstances, and developing moral and political beliefs. Yet despite the stress placed on evolution and adaptability, it is crucial not to underestimate the extent to which the Constitution and its meaning are also seen as rooted in history, that is, in original understandings, intentions, and purposes. It is also important not to underestimate the extent to which living tree constitutionalism is actually in line with much contemporary originalist thought. Many contemporary originalists embrace a moderate version of their theory, one that restricts original meaning to abstract meanings and intentions, and allows for a healthy degree of adaptation and evolution via the process contemporary originalists call *constitutional construction*. And if this is so, then perhaps it is time that we put to bed the idea that living constitutionalism is a theory that stands in sharp contrast to originalism.

---

⁵¹ *Big M* above (n 24) [17] [emphasis added].

Bibliography

Books and Articles

Balkin, Jack. *Living Originalism* (Cambridge: Harvard University Press, 2011).

Berman, Mitchell. "Originalism Is Bunk." 84 *New York University Law Review* 1 (2009).

Berman, Mitchell. "Constitutional Interpretation: Non-originalism." *Philosophy Compass* 6/6 (2011): 408–420.

Binnie, Ian. "Interpreting the Constitution: The Living Tree vs. Original Meaning." *Policy Options* (2007). http://policyoptions.irpp.org/magazines/free-trade-20/interpreting-the-constitution-the-living-tree-vs-original-meaning/.

Dicey, A.V. *The Law of the Constitution, 10th ed.* (1959).

Goldsworthy, Jeffrey. "Constitutional Interpretation: Originalism." *Philosophy Compass* 4/4 (2009), 682–702.

Hogg, Peter. *Constitutional Law of Canada* (5th ed. Carswell, 2007).

Kavanagh, Aileen. "The Idea of a Living Constitution." *The Canadian Journal of Law and Jurisprudence* XVI (2003): 55–89.

Miller, Bradley. "Beguiled by Metaphors: The 'Living Tree' and Originalist Constitutional Interpretation in Canada." *The Canadian Journal of Law and Jurisprudence* XXII (2003): 331–354.

Miller, Bradley. "Origin Myth: The Persons Case, the Living Tree, and the New Originalism." In *The Challenge of Originalism,* edited by G. Huscroft and B. Miller, 120–146. Cambridge: Cambridge University Press, 2011.

Morton, F.L. and Rainer Knopff. "Permanence and Change in a Written Constitution: The 'Living Tree' Doctrine and the Charter of Rights" (1990), 1 S.C.L.R. (2d) 533.

Morton, F.L. and Rainer Knopff. *The Charter Revolution and the Court Party* (Peterborough, ON: Broadview Press, 2000).

Oliphant, Benjamin. "Taking Purposes Seriously: The Purposive Scope and Textual Bounds of Interpretation under the Canadian Charter of Rights and Freedoms" (2015) 65 *University of Toronto Law Journal* Vol. 65, n. 3.

Strauss, David. *The Living Constitution* (Oxford: Oxford University Press, 2010).

Waluchow, W.J. "Constitutions as Living Trees: An Idiot Defends." *The Canadian Journal of Law and Jurisprudence* XVIII (2005): 207–247.

Waluchow, W.J. *A Common Law Theory of Judicial Review: The Living Tree* (Cambridge: Cambridge University Press, 2007).

Waluchow, W.J. "Constitutional Interpretation." In *The Routledge Companion to Philosophy of Law,* edited by Andrei Marmor, 417–434. New York: Routledge, 2011.

Cases

Edwards v A.G Canada [1930] AC 124.

Ford v Quebec (AG), [1988] 2 S.C.R. 712.

Law Society of Upper Canada v Skapinker [1984] 1 SCR 357.

R. v Big M Drug Mart Ltd., [1985] 1 S.C.R. 295.

Re: Resolution to amend the Constitution, [1981] 1 S.C.R. 753.

Reference re Same-Sex Marriage, [2004] 3 S.C.R. 698, 2004 SCC 79, [22].

Reference re Section 94(2) of the Motor Vehicle Act, [1985] 2 SCR 486.

Texas v. Johnson, 491 U.S. 397 (1989).

B. Constitutional Pluralism

CHAPTER 43

....

CANADIAN
CONSTITUTIONAL CULTURE

A Genealogical Account

....

DAVID SCHNEIDERMAN*

CONSTITUTIONAL theory 'is at an end', Martin Loughlin claims, once the idea of the 'political unity of a people' is abandoned.[1] Constitutional theory, for Loughlin, is only possible once the multitude transforms itself into a state with governing authority. It follows that without a cohesive and unitary state—without 'sovereignty'—there cannot be constitutional theory.[2] To divide sovereignty, Loughlin maintains, is to confuse its 'principle of unity' with government, which, of practical necessity, is often divided.[3]

Few Canadians today tell such constitutional stories to themselves. Canada is, instead, more often described as an unrealized constitutional project. Canadian constitutional politics cannot be 'solved' by some act of constitutional closure, argues Roderick Macdonald. Instead, Canadians continue to preoccupy themselves with conflicting stories about who 'we' are. These debates have, 'in fact, dominated since the first contacts between Europeans and aboriginals in the 16th and 17th centuries'—they are a 'recurring rock bottom theme in Canadian political self-definition', insists Macdonald.[4] In which case, we should understand ongoing 'constitutional wrangling' as a 'central component of our shared framing'.[5]

* I am grateful to Patrick Macklem and Nathalie des Rosiers for comments. This chapter is dedicated to the memory of Rod Macdonald, a mentor and a friend, who is dearly missed.
[1] Martin Loughlin, 'Constitutional Theory: A 25th Anniversary Essay' (2005) 25 OJLS 183, 187.
[2] ibid 197.
[3] Martin Loughlin, 'Constitutional Pluralism: An Oxymoron?' (2014) 3 Global Constitutionalism 9, 13; Martin Loughlin, 'In Defence of *Staatslehre*' (2009) 48 Der Staat 1, 8–12.
[4] Roderick A Macdonald, 'Three Centuries of Constitution Making in Canada: Will There Be a Fourth?' (1996) 30 UBC L Rev 211, 214.
[5] ibid 216. Tierney suggests that Loughlin's account 'translates well' into a 'pluralized set of relations of sovereignty.' See Stephen Tierney, 'Sovereignty and the Idea of Public Law' in Emilios Christodoulidis

Loughlin's story about sovereignty and constitutional unity illustrates well dominant legal theory issuing out of Britain in the late eighteenth and nineteenth centuries.[6] It was claimed that there was one undivided sovereign, and conquered *Canadiens*, Indigenous peoples, and English settlers were all the Crown's subjects.[7] If this reproduced the legal theory of the colonizer, it was not necessarily that of the colonized.[8] It also reflects a story that, at its inception, was more complicated than its simple legal narrative suggests. An unsettled state of affairs resulted in continual push back, even resistance, by the governed, requiring continual adjustments, if not concessions, by metropole authorities.[9] It might be fair to characterize the situation, following Austin, as one of reluctant but 'habitual obedience' to a 'determinate superior' on the part of *les Canadiens*[10] and an absence of habitual obedience to claims of English *imperium* from the bulk of Indigenous First Nations.[11]

This chapter embraces this unstable understanding of Canadian constitutional thought. Rather than aiming for unrealistic homogeneity, Canadian constitutional theory should aspire to explain constitutional practices that have produced outcomes that are often heterogeneous and pluralistic. This is not to say that constitutional ordering has not sought to impose a single unitary vision on this heterogeneous public. Rather, it is to emphasize that, despite the urge to homogenize and assimilate, that project has, as often, faltered. In its place has emerged a constitutional order that, within limits, has the potential of being more open and inclusive, yet which also requires continual

and Stephen Tierney (eds) *Public Law and Politics: The Scope and Limits of Constitutionalism* (Ashgate, 2008) 24.

[6] RCB Risk, 'Constitutional Scholarship in the Late Nineteenth Century: Making Federalism Work' in G Blaine Baker and Jim Phillips (eds), *A History of Canadian Legal Thought: Collected Essays* (University of Toronto Press, 1996) 46; Robert C Vipond, *Liberty & Community: Canadian Federalism and the Failure of the Constitution* (State University of New York Press, 1991) 30.

[7] To borrow a phrase, 'sovereignty was constituted through colonialism'. See Anthony Anghie, *Imperialism, Sovereignty and the Making of International Law* (Cambridge University Press, 2004) 38.

[8] Geneviève Nootens, 'Constituent Power and People-As-Governed: About the "Invisible" People of Political and Legal Theory' (2015) 4 Global Constitutionalism 137, 149.

[9] See Lauren Benton, *Law and Colonial Cultures: Legal Regimes in World History, 1400–1900* (Cambridge University Press, 2002) 14: 'Conquered people showed themselves to be quite adept and sophisticated at interpreting the significance of claims to jurisdiction and strategically taking positions to undermine those claims'.

[10] Donald Fyson, *Magistrates, Police, and People: Everyday Criminal Justice in Quebec and Lower Canada, 1764–1837* (University of Toronto Press, 2006); Evelyn Kolish, *Nationalismes et conflit des droits: Le débat du droit privé au Québec, 1760–1840* (Éditions Hurtubise HMH Ltée, 1994).

[11] I draw here on John Austin's definition of sovereignty in John Austin, *The Province of Jurisprudence Determined Etc.* (Weidenfeld and Nicolson, 1954) 194. Austin would not concede, however, that 'savages' were capable of being 'in a habit of obedience to a certain and common superior' (ibid., 203, 209). On indigenous resistance, see Taiaiake Alfred, 'From Sovereignty to Freedom: Towards an Indigenous Political Discourse' (2001) 3 Indigenous Affairs 22; Michael Asch, *On Being Here to Stay: Treaties and Aboriginal Rights in Canada* (University of Toronto Press, 2014) 112; and Audra Simpson, *Mohawk Interruptus: Political Life across the Borders of Settler States* (Duke University Press, 2014) 12.

maintenance if it is to endure. This chapter explores this novel Canadian narrative, one that I associate with the idea of constitutional culture.[12]

Constitutional culture has emerged as a heuristic with which to describe and engage with familiar national constitutional projects. In the United States, it has been conscripted to describe extrajudicial understandings about what the U.S. Constitution means[13] and to better explain the contexts within which shifts in interpretation occur.[14] In the Canadian context, 'culture' is invoked in order to privilege 'lived experience' under the Canadian Constitution, rather than on 'legal concepts' and idealized legal theory.[15] I have called upon constitutional culture to describe widely shared and dominant understandings of the fundamental norms that guide relations between citizens and states and also between institutions of the state.[16] In my account, constitutional culture is represented not only in constitutional text and judicial interpretation but also in legislatures, media organizations, business associations, social movements, and other non-governmental entities. These social, political, and cultural forces insert themselves into debates over the meaning and content of constitutional practices and traditions. There will be alternative accounts vying for supremacy, in which case 'official' constitutional culture will always be partial and contested. The advantage of such a conception is that it accounts for constitutional change. It also brings into the discussion relations of power that help to define its parameters. Not all participants in a constitutional order, after all, will have equal access to defining its content.[17] Instead, we should understand constitutional orders as exhibiting a selectivity that structures power in certain, discrete directions.[18] To the extent that it presents a unified front, this unity only papers

---

[12] I have elsewhere made the argument that Canadian constitutional culture is more pluralistic and more open to the other, in David Schneiderman, *Red, White, and Kind of Blue? The Conservatives and the Americanization of Canadian Constitutional Culture* (University of Toronto Press, 2015) ch 1.

[13] Robert C Post, 'Foreword: Fashioning the Legal Constitution: Culture, Courts, and Law' (2003) 117 Harvard L Rev 1; Ernest A Young, 'The Constitution outside the Constitution' (2007) 117 Yale L J 408.

[14] Reva B Siegel, 'Constitutional Culture, Social Movement Conflict and Constitutional Change: The Case of the De Facto ERA' (2006) 94 California L Rev 1323.

[15] Benjamin L Berger, *Law's Religion: Religious Difference and the Claims of Constitutionalism* (University of Toronto Press, 2015) 36–39. Berger acknowledges his indebtedness to Paul Kahn's cultural analysis of law. See Paul W Kahn, *The Cultural Study of Law: Reconstructing Legal Scholarship* (University of Chicago Press, 1999).

[16] David Schneiderman, 'Universality vs. Particularity: Litigating Middle Class Values under Section 15' (2006) 33 Supreme Court L Rev 367; David Schneiderman, 'Property Rights, Investor Rights, and Regulatory Innovation: Comparing Constitutional Cultures in Transition' (2006) 4 International J of Constitutional L 371; David Schneiderman, 'Social Rights and Common Sense: *Gosselin* through a Media Lens' in Margot Young, Susan B Boyd, Gwen Brodsky, and Shelagh Day (eds), *Social and Economic Insecurity: Rights, Social Citizenship and Governance* (University of British Columbia Press, 2007); David Schneiderman, *Red, White, and Kind of Blue?* above (n 12).

[17] Pierre Bourdieu, *Pascalian Meditations* (Stanford University Press, 2000) 70. Foucault associates culture with a 'hierarchical organization of values that is accessible to everyone but which at the same time gives rise to a mechanism of selection and exclusion'. See Michel Foucault, *The Hermeneutics of the Subject: Lectures at the Collège de France 1981–1982* (Graham Burchell trans, Palgrave Macmillan, 2001) 179.

[18] Bob Jessop, *State Theory: Putting Capitalist States in Their Place* (University of Pennsylvania Press, 1990) 256, 260. Kahn's observation about the rule of law is apt here. It 'exists not as an attribute of a

over division and disagreement that is endemic to most constitutional orders.[19] Like the juridical idea of sovereignty itself, constitutional culture exhibits an active forgetting of its genealogy.[20]

Constitutional culture, if it represents dominant understandings at particular moments, will exhibit both continuity and change over time. In the Canadian case, I argue that contemporary constitutional culture is partly the product of practices initiated by Imperial authorities governing British North America in the eighteenth century. A discussion of Canadian constitutional culture necessitates, then, a return to a past that is partly inscribed into the present. At its inception, Canadian constitutionalism was required to adapt to the presence of multiple others, different from the English settlers colonizing British North America, and it is in this encounter that current practices have their genesis.[21] In the eighteenth century, the British 'stumbled almost unawares' into a situation where they were required to produce new forms of colonial government for British India and Quebec.[22] This is not to say that there was an absence of a normative hierarchy for colonial administrators or that these authorities did not consider it their 'duty to assimilate' those considered different.[23] There has never been a lack of confidence about the ability of Imperial authorities to absorb foreigners, after all. What is argued is that, in the course of colonizing British North America, Imperial legal authorities were required to adjust their assimilationist ambitions and were, thereby, forced to tolerate a great deal of dissonance. Coercion, after all, does not work so well when one

---

trans-historical subject, but as a distribution of power that works to sustain the conditions of belief that are constitutive of the unity of the nation as a single community' (in Khan above (n 15)).

[19] Philip Corrigan and Derek Sayer, *The Great Arch: English State Formation as Cultural Revolution* (Basil Blackwell, 1985) 197. As John Whyte wisely observes, the state is 'not a passive taker of changing human aspirations but a might and ongoing force . . . The social tendencies that impel constitutional change are formed through the state as handmaiden of established powers and through placing citizens in fixed relationships and with fixed purposes and functions . . . ' See John D Whyte 'Constitutional Experience' in Richard Janda, Rosalie Jukier, and Daniel Jutras (eds), *The Unbounded Level of the Mind: Rod Macdonald's Legal Imagination* (McGill-Queen's University Press, 2015) 95.

[20] William E Connolly, *Pluralism* (Duke University Press, 2005) 145.

[21] Fyson prefers to describe this process as one of 'mutual adaptation,' whereby 'the *Canadiens* and British populations reacted to and attempted to shape the new realities that followed the military conquest of 1759–60 and diplomatic cession of 1763'. See Donald Fyson, 'The Conquered and the Conqueror: The Mutual Adaptation of the Canadiens and the British in Quebec, 1759–1775' in Phillip Buckner and John G Reid (eds), *Revisiting 1759: The Conquest of Canada in Historical Perspective* (University of Toronto Press, 2012) 192. 'Adaptation' renders genteel the relations of force ubiquitous in the colonial era.

[22] Vincent T Harlow, *The Founding of the Second British Empire, 1763–1793* (Longmans, 1964) 668. Conway maintains that colonial authorities drew upon their experience governing Catholics in Ireland and in the island of Minorca. See Stephen Conway, 'The Consequences of the Conquest: Quebec and British Politics, 1760–1774' in Phillip Buckner and John G Reid (eds), *Revisiting 1759: The Conquest of Canada in Historical Perspective* (University of Toronto Press, 2012).

[23] As declared by Lord Thurlow, the Attorney General, in debates in British Parliament concerning the *Quebec Act, 1774* in WPM Kennedy, *Statutes, Treaties and Documents of the Canadian Constitution, 1713–1929* (2nd edn, Oxford University Press, 1930) 102.

'wishes rapidly to assimilate . . . [those] whose "good will" and enthusiasm one needs'.[24] In so doing, Imperial constitutional law had to make do with recognizing the ability of communities of difference to govern and, thereby, make law for themselves. This was the outcome of intercultural encounters that are mostly hidden from the present.[25] The object here is to inquire into the genealogy of the constitutional present—to unearth 'historical struggles' together with some of the 'details and accidents that accompany every beginning'.[26]

In this chapter, I take up three episodes in Canada's constitutional past that have helped to frame discussions about Canadian constitutionalism in the present day. Each represents moments in Imperial or early Canadian policy. Each is a part of the waves of accommodation and assimilation that are recurring features of the Canadian story and which helped to shape Canada's constitutional present, namely, contemporary features we associate with federalism, linguistic rights, multiculturalism, and the various ways in which 'others' are accorded standing (or denied it) in Canada's constitutional order.[27] These episodes represent ambivalent shifts in metropole ambitions, aspiring to a homogeneous ideal while necessitating some heterogeneity in practice.[28]

There are, to be sure, other episodes in Canada's constitutional past that have helped shape Canada's constitutional present not discussed here, a number of which are of even greater significance. I am of the view that the ones under discussion here are interesting representative samples that are more obscure, if not largely forgotten. Nor do I intend on drawing out linkages between these past episodes and Canada's constitutional present.[29] This discussion is meant only to be suggestive—rendering those linkages more apparent is a task for another day. I am hoping that readers will share the intuition that choices made in the past resonate with practices in the present. Even if Imperial and

[24] Antonio Gramsci, *Selections from the Prison Notebooks of Antonio Gramsci*, Quentin Hoare and Geoffrey Nowell Smith (eds) (International Publishers, 1971) 168.

[25] Michel Foucault, 'Nietzsche, Genealogy, History' in D F Bouchard (ed), *Language, Counter-Memory, Practice: Selected Essays and Interviews* (Ithaca University Press, 1977) 56; Robert A Williams, *Linking Arms Together: American Indian Treaty Visions of Law and Peace, 1600–1800* (Oxford University Press, 1997).

[26] Michel Foucault, 'Two Lectures' in Colin Gordon (ed), *Power/Knowledge: Selected Interviews and Other Writings 1972–77* (Pantheon 1980) 83; Michel Foucault, 'Nietzsche, Genealogy, History' above (n 25) 144.

[27] The discussion is not meant to suggest that Indigenous claims to sovereignty and to lands is reducible to claims of cultural difference. See discussion in David Schneiderman, 'Theorists of Difference and the Interpretation of Aboriginal and Treaty Rights' (1996) 14 IJCS 35. Though I do not make the argument fully here, the episodes under discussion in this chapter should help to illuminate what is a much longer story.

[28] Evidence of the unattainability of the universal that represents an incomplete or unfulfilled 'horizon' that is always receding. See Ernesto Laclau, *Emancipations* (Verso, 1996) 28, 34.

[29] I have made a preliminary version of this argument in David Schneiderman, 'Associational Rights, Religion, and the Charter' in Richard Moon (ed), *Law and Religious Pluralism in Canada* (University of British Columbia Press, 2008) and David Schneiderman, 'Multiculturalism in Canadian Constitutional Culture: Domesticating Difference' (2016) [unpublished].

early Canadian policy was halting, ambivalent, and aspired to homogenization—often exhibiting the features of both coercion and consent—it has resulted, in practice, in the production of a community with a shared, even if differently interpreted, past. The story, then, is not simply a celebratory one of linear progress. Rather, it is one where positions are contradictory and motives often mixed, sometimes lamentable. It is these ambivalent and contradictory motivations in early Canadian policy, helping to generate the conditions for contemporary constitutional culture, which are underscored here.

The first historic episode is introduced in Section 2, where I discuss circumstances confronting the first Governor General of the colony of Québec, James Murray. The new Governor was required to adjust harsh Royal instructions to facts on the ground, resulting in the preservation of Roman Catholic authority in the new colony.[30] This reflected a legal regime of tolerance that was unavailable in Britain. In Section 3, I turn to an Imperial policy recognizing the laws and customs of conquered peoples until such time as the Crown decreed otherwise. This reflected an English penchant to accede to foreign law while maintaining a firm grip on the colony's affairs. Section 4 turns to the federal election of 1885, in which male Indians were authorized to participate equally with male Canadian property owners and tenants, without having to give up their status or rights. This was part of a plan to 'civilize' Indigenous people via enfranchisement but which also produced an early acknowledgment of the plural identities and allegiances that constituted Canada at its origins.

This turn to history, emphasizing the development of institutions and practices over time, offers a productive way of tapping into Canadian constitutional culture. An emphasis on the dialectic between exercises of Imperial authority and local conditions generate resources with which to better understand the pathways and blockages that have resulted in contemporary constitutional practice. To lay the groundwork for the discussion to follow, I turn first to a description of the constitutional order governing British North America in the late eighteenth century.

1. Powers 'Most Ample and Transcendent'

How is it that Canada has developed a constitutional culture more pluralistic and more open to the other?[31] It is appropriate, if paradoxical, to begin with reference to monarchical absolutism of the seventeenth century. The divine right of kings authorized

---

[30] Gramsci associates this with a 'Roman/Anglo-Saxon' model of governance, a 'type whose essential characteristic consists in its method, which is realistic and always keeps close to concrete life in perpetual development'. See Gramsci above (n 24) 196.

[31] By 'others', I am referring to those who are different from the colonizers and for whom 'conquest and conversion are the two authorized responses'. See William E Connolly, *Identity\ Difference: Democratic Negotiations of Political Paradox* (Cornell University Press, 1991) 43.

omnipotent monarchs to govern not only domestic but overseas realms. This was an authority derived from God for which no competition would be tolerated. The King is 'over-lord of the whole land, so he is master of every person that inhabiteth the same, having power over the life and death of every one of them,' James I declared.[32] Parliament, by comparison, was 'nothing else but the head court of the king and his vassals.'[33] The divine right of kings, embodied in royal prerogative, provided a response to the rival claims of papal authority issuing out of Rome.[34] It was derived from the 'necessity, not hitherto felt, of forming clear notions of sovereignty and of defining its abode.'[35]

The Glorious Revolution of 1688 and accompanying enactments, the Bill of Rights of 1689, the Triennial Act of 1694, and the Act of Settlement of 1700, reversed this logic of authority. 'Sovereignty in 1688,' observes Keir, 'was for practical purposes grasped by the nation.'[36] Parliament, with its famous equipoise between King, Lords, and Commons, was supreme in most things.[37] The colonies of North America continued to be governed by royal prerogative, however, even if practically under the direction of the King's ministers (principally the Secretary of State and the Board of Trade).[38] Authority flowed from the King to his agents operating in the colonies. Gubernatorial powers, writes Labaree, were 'almost dangerously great' and, as 'direct representative of his royal master ... naturally endowed with the prerogatives which in Great Britain belonged solely to the king'.[39] In truth, these were powers greater than those the sovereign exercised in Britain.[40] According to English lawyer Charles Clark's treatise, *A Summary of Colonial Law*, the Governor wields power not unlike the Crown in pre-revolutionary England. He 'possesses a negative voice in the legislature; for without his consent no bill passes into a law' and may 'at his own discretion, adjourn, prorogue and dissolve the

[32] GW Prothero (ed), *Select Statutes and Other Constitutional Documents, 1558–1625* (Clarendon Press, 1913).

[33] ibid.

[34] John Neville Figgis, *The Divine Right of Kings*, 2nd ed. (Cambridge University Press, 1922).

[35] Prothero above (n 32) cxxiv.

[36] Sir David Lindsay Keir, *The Constitutional History of Modern Britain since 1485* (9th edn, WW Norton & Company Inc, 1969) 269.

[37] William Blackstone, *Commentaries on the Laws of England* vol 1, 1765 (University of Chicago Press, 1979) 150.

[38] Otherwise known as the Lords Commissioners of Trade and Plantations. The Board of Trade was an advisory body to the Privy Council reporting to the Secretary of State for the Southern Department. The Board 'drafted commissions and instructions for royal Governors, corresponded with them, and gathered information from royal officials, colonial Councils and Assemblies, and from Imperial, colonial, and chartered company petitioners and lobbyists.' See Ian K Steele, 'Metropolitan Administration of the Colonies, 1696–1775' in Jack P Greene and J R Pole (eds), *The Blackwell Encyclopedia of the American Revolution* (Basil Blackwell 1991) 10. On the Secretaries of State, see William R Anson, *The Law and Custom of the Constitution, Vol. II The Crown, Pt. I* (Clarendon Press, 1907) 165.

[39] Leonard Woods Labaree, *Royal Government in America: A Study of the British Colonial System before 1783* (Frederick Ungar Publishing Co, 1964) 123.

[40] Chester Martin, *Empire & Commonwealth: Studies in Governance and Self-Government in Canada* (Clarendon Press, 1929) 23; Ian K Steele, 'The Anointed, the Appointed, and the Elected: Governance of the British Empire, 1689–1784' in P J Marshall (ed), *The Oxford History of the British Empire, Vol. II: The Eighteenth Century* (Oxford University Press, 1998) 110.

Assemblies.' On the whole,' Clark acknowledges, 'it appears that the powers with which colonial governors are instructed are most ample and transcendent, and more extensive than those which the laws of England allow the sovereign himself to exercise.'[41]

The Governor's Commission and accompanying Royal Instructions, typically secret and untranslated, were expected to guide colonial conduct on the ground. The direction to Governors to make laws for the 'peace, order, and good government' of the colony can be viewed as an authorization to govern old and new subjects seemingly without limit. Governors wielded a mighty sword in a veto power, control over judicial appointments and the public purse, subject only to the advice of the Governor's advisory body (the Council) and the supervisory jurisdiction of the colonial branch of government in England.[42] It turned out that, whatever the breadth of gubernatorial authority, it ultimately 'depended on forces vastly more complicated than the arbitrary will of the Crown.'[43]

All of this plenary power established a pattern of strong executive authority characteristic of British North America in the second empire.[44] After the American Revolution, marking the end of the first empire, metropolitan authorities were intent on constraining self-governing capabilities within the remaining British North American colonies. Colonial masters adjusted patterns of governance established during the first empire. Rather than being endowed with considerable autonomy in their internal affairs, as had the colonies on the eastern seaboard of what would become the United States, Mancke observes that the colonies in what later would become Canada were subject to 'greater state control,' providing a firm foundation for the exercise of vigorous political control by the metropolitan centre.[45] It is this legacy of muscular authority that gets taken up by Canadian governments under successive constitutional arrangements, resulting in the contemporary phenomenon of 'governing from the centre.'[46]

---

[41] Charles Clark, *A Summary of Colonial Law* (S Sweet, A Maxwell, and Stevens & Sons, 1834) 34.

[42] Martin above (n 40) 27. Curiously, Yusuf claims that it was not intended as a source of plenary gubernatorial authority in the eighteenth century, in Hakeem O Yusuf, *Colonial and Post-colonial Constitutionalism in the Commonwealth* (Routledge, 2015) 227.

[43] Martin above (n 40) 24.

[44] British imperial history typically is divided into two distinct periods, the 'first' and 'second' empires, demarcated by the American Revolution and the signing of the Treaty of Peace in 1783. There remains some dispute as to the precise moment when the first empire ended and the second began. See discussion in P J Marshall, 'The First British Empire' in Robin Winks and Wm Roger Louis (eds), *The Oxford History of the British Empire, Volume V: Historiography* (Oxford University Press, 1999).

[45] Elizabeth Mancke, 'Early Modern Imperial Governance and the Origins of Canadian Political Culture' (1999) 32 Canadian J of Political Science 3, 8, 20. This remained so even as Canada's constitutions were placed on firmer statutory footing by enacting the Quebec Act of 1774—for the purpose of, among other things, enabling toleration of Roman Catholicism and imposing taxes (see Francis Maseres, *Occasional Essays on Various Subjects Chiefly Political and Historical* (Robert Wilks, 1809))—and, subsequently, the Constitution Act of 1791.

[46] Donald J Savoie, *Governing from the Centre: The Concentration of Power in Canadian Politics* (University of Toronto Press 1999).

2. 'AS FAR AS THE LAWS OF GREAT BRITAIN PERMIT'

It was into this powerful structure of authority that Governor James Murray stepped. As the King's delegate, Murray was expected to manage religious expectations but without authority to admit any 'Ecclesiastical Jurisdiction of the See of Rome'. Catholicism was barely tolerated in practice in the British Isles. Religious heretics were no longer burned at the stake, but penal laws of the seventeenth century deprived Catholics of most of their civil rights.[47] By the eighteenth century, Catholicism was no mere 'religious error', observes Maitland, it was a 'grave political danger'.[48] These constraints were put to the test in Britain's new colonies after the defeat of the French in North America.

Having taken hold of the territory of New France pursuant to the King's Proclamation of 1763, Great Britain achieved a number of objectives. Governing passed into Protestant hands, entitling the royal Governor to 'make laws for public peace, welfare and good Government . . . as near as may be agreeable to the laws of England' and to convene a legislative assembly only 'when circumstances admit'.[49] The laws of England were to control controversies in both civil and criminal cases.[50] The Royal Proclamation also attended to the centralization of Indian policy, ensuring that British settlers and their descendants in the American colonies could not purchase or take lands of the 'several Nations or tribes of Indians with whom we are connected, and who live under our Protection'.[51]

In Royal Instructions to the first Governor, issued the same day as the Royal Proclamation, James Murray was directed to 'grant the Liberty of the Catholick Religion' so that 'our new Roman Catholick Subjects in that Province may profess the Worship of their Religion, according to the Rites of the Romish Church, as far as the laws of great

---

[47] F W Maitland, *Constitutional History of England* (Cambridge University Press, 1919) 515.

[48] ibid 517.

[49] WPM Kennedy, *Statutes, Treaties and Documents of the Canadian Constitution* above (n 23) 36.

[50] Walters claims that the Royal Proclamation of 1763 'made no mention of either the abrogation or continuity of the existing French-Canadian legal system', in Mark D Walters, 'The "Golden Thread" of Continuity: Aboriginal Customs at Common Law and under the Constitution Act, 1982' (1999) 44 McGill L J 711, 726. As a consequence of the common law presumption of continuity, he argues, *les coutumes des Paris* continued to apply in Quebec. This is hard to square with the Proclamation's decree that, until such time as a Legislative Assembly is established, 'all Persons inhabiting in or resorting to our said Colonies may confide in our Royal Protection for the Enjoyment of the Benefit of the Laws of our Realm of England [and that] . . . Courts of Judicature and public justice [will be established] within our said Colonies for hearing and determining all Causes, as well Criminal and Civil, according to Law and Equity, and as near as may be agreeable to the Laws of England'. See W P M Kennedy, *Statutes, Treaties and Documents of the Canadian Constitution* above (n 23) 36.

[51] W P M Kennedy, *Statutes, Treaties and Documents of the Canadian Constitution* above (n 23) 37. Banner describes the Proclamation's Indian policy as a 'dismal failure': 'The most obvious effect of the Proclamation was to replace legal land acquisition with illegal land acquisition'. See Stuart Banner, *How the Indians Lost Their Land: Law and Power on the Frontier* (Harvard University Press, 2005) 104.

Britain permit'.[52] This was just as the British had promised in the Articles of Capitulation in Montreal and Quebec.[53] At the same time, Governor Murray was expected to demand that new subjects take the requisite oath of allegiance. He would cause those who refused to take the oath to 'forthwith to depart out of Our said Government'.[54] With the purpose of ultimately assimilating new subjects, the Governor was directed to 'establish' the Church of England, both in 'Principles and Practice,' so 'that the said Inhabitants may by Degrees be induced to embrace Protestant Religion, and their Children be brought up in the Principles of it'.[55] Murray's secret instructions were later described by F.-X. Garneau as a 'sinister document' representing a 'hateful spirit of jealous exclusiveness'—a spirit that Garneau would find, in his own day, present in Lord Durham's Report on the Affairs of British North America, published in 1839.[56]

With experience, Governor Murray learned that he could not govern the colony in accordance with the Imperial ambition of assimilation. Nothing would contribute more to making them 'staunch subjects to his Majesty', Murray advised, than to give them 'every reason to imagine no alteration' in their religious practices[57] Accordingly, he deviated significantly from instructions so as to accommodate the King's new subjects. Murray, via two ordinances in 1764, established new civil courts for *les Canadiens* (a court of common pleas) and admitted Roman Catholics as jurors, before which civilian lawyers were entitled to appear.[58] Although admittedly complex, Murray's legal edicts required less adaptation from the King's 'new' subjects than it did for his 'old' ones.[59] There remained a vacuum in religious leadership, however, that Murray's leadership could not satisfy without metropole consent.

With the death of Monsignor Pontbriand in 1760, the colony was left without religious authority to ordain new priests. Imperial officers would not, however, consent to the

---

[52] W P M Kennedy, *Statutes, Treaties and Documents of the Canadian Constitution* above (n 23) 47, s. 28.

[53] ibid, 23, 28.

[54] ibid, 47, s. 29.

[55] ibid, 47-48, s. 33.

[56] Andrew Bell, *History of Canada from the Time of Its Discovery till the Union Year of 1840– 41: Translated from 'L'Histoire du Canada' of F-X Garneau, Esq.*, Volume II, 2nd edn (John Lovell, 1862) 88; The Earl of Durham, *Lord Durham's Report on the Affairs of British North America, Volume II: Text*, Sir C P Lucas (ed) (Clarendon Press, 1912). Among other things, the Durham Report recommended the union of the two colonies (Upper and Lower Canada) and, ultimately, the assimilation of the French-speaking population into the English-speaking one.

[57] Adam Shortt and Arthur G Doughty (eds), *Documents Relating to the Constitutional History of Canada 1759–1791, Part I*, 2nd edn (J. de la Taché, 1918) 71; 'General Murray's Report of the State of the Government of Quebec in Canada June 5th 1762'.

[58] W P M Kennedy, *Statutes, Treaties and Documents of the Canadian Constitution* above (n 23) 53, 69–70; Hilda Neatby, *Quebec: The Revolutionary Age, 1760–1791* (McCelland & Stewart, 1966) 48–49, 53.

[59] Donald Fyson, 'The Conquered and the Conqueror' above (n 21) 205; Francis Maseres, 'A Draught of an Intended Report of the Honourable the Governor in Chief and the Council of the Province of Quebec to the King's Most Excellent Majesty in His Privy Council; concerning the State of the Laws and the Administration of Justice in that Province' in W P M Kennedy and Gustave Lanctot (eds), *Reports on the Laws of Quebec, 1767–1770* (F A Acland, 1931).

appointment of a Bishop for Quebec for this would amount to acknowledgment of papal authority, inconsistent with the Act of Supremacy of 1559. Murray was initially content to see the episcopal vacancy persist[60] but succumbed to the pleas of Catholic parishioners and proposed the consecration of his preferred candidate, M. Olivier Briand, in 1766.[61] Metropole authorities were also reluctant, and so had Briand wait 14 months before agreeing to send him to the outskirts of Paris for consecration by papal bulls of investiture issued by Pope Clement III. This would be done secretly, 'almost clandestinely', under the guiding hand of Edmund Burke, private secretary to the Rockingham ministry.[62] Three years later, permission was secured for Briand to consecrate a coadjutor to be his successor,[63] though appointment would be subject to the approval of Murray's successor, Governor Carleton.[64]

Briand was expected to serve officially not as Bishop but as the downgraded 'Superintendent of the Roman Church in Canada'.[65] Briand, nevertheless, displayed the trappings of Bishop and was addressed publicly as 'Monseigneur'.[66] The Imperial concession, Coupland observes, gave to the new subjects a 'dramatic and a convincing proof of the conciliatory intentions of the British government'.[67] In so far as the Church was concerned, life went on as before.[68] Yet the episode also compromised the independence of the Church in Quebec. Secular authorities were now meddling in the internal affairs of the Church, writes Trudel, 'binding the bishop to the interests of government.[69] 'Under the English regime', he concludes, 'the Church became openly the vehicle for government orders'.[70] Today, it is said that the 'stakes in the negotiations between Murray and Briand were the heart of the *Canadien* identity of yesterday and the source of Quebec power today'. Securing a Catholic clergy for Quebec, writes Dufour, 'evolved

[60] Shortt and Doughty above (n 57) 71; A L Burt, *The Old Province of Quebec: Volume 1, 1760–1778* (McLelland and Stewart, 1968) 84–85.

[61] Reginald Coupland, *The Quebec Act: A Study in Statesmanship* (Clarendon Press, 1925) 53; Abbé Auguste Gosselin, *L'Eglise du Canada Après la Conquête, Première Partie 1760–1775* (Imprimerie Laflamme, 1916) 160. Murray preferred Briand over the candidacy of Monsignor Montgolfier, who Murray describes in a 4 May 1763 letter to Secretary of State Shelburne as likely to do 'much harm at the first opportunity he would have to deploy his grudge and malice', in Gosselin, ibid, 83. Murray, by contrast, describes his preferred candidate Briand in glowing terms in a 22 July 1763 letter to Shelburne, in Gosselin, ibid, 69.

[62] Francis Maseres, *Occasional Essays on Various Subjects Chiefly Political and Historical* above (n 45) 364. I have mentioned this episode previously in David Schneiderman, 'Edmund Burke, John Whyte, and Themes in Canadian Constitutional Culture' (2006) 31 Queen's LJ 578.

[63] John S Moir, *The Church in the British Era: From the British Conquest to Confederation—Volume Two of A History of the Christian Church in Canada* (McGraw-Hill Ryerson Limited, 1972) 40, 45.

[64] Neatby above (n 58) 113.

[65] Coupland above (n 61) 53.

[66] Neatby above (n 58) 111.

[67] Coupland above (n 61) 54.

[68] Fernand Ouellet, *Lower Canada, 1791–1840: Social Change and Nationalism* (Patricia Claxton trans, McClelland & Stewart 1980) 14.

[69] Marcel Trudel, 'Servile' in Cameron Nish (ed), *The French Canadians 1759–1766: Conquered? Half-Conquered? Liberated?* (The Copp Clark Publishing Company, 1966) 114.

[70] ibid 115.

into Quebec's control' over key institutions within the province, including education, hospitals, municipalities, etc.[71] Dufour's whiggish narrative is too linear —there were many intervening events contributing to the rise of institutions associated with the Quebec state. That this episode contributed to the survival of a Roman Catholic franco-phone population on the North American continent, however, there can be little doubt.

Murray's gubernatorial tenure, though sympathetic to the *Canadiens*, turned out to be tumultuous. Preferring the King's new subjects over old ones, Murray described the *Canadiens* as 'perhaps the bravest and the best race upon the Globe'.[72] The English trad-ers in Quebec and Montreal, by contrast, were characterized as 'Licentious Fanaticks'.[73] Having managed to alienate both military leadership and English Protestant traders in Quebec and Montreal, Murray departed for London to defend his tenure on the very same day the newly consecrated Briand landed at Quebec.

3. 'Ancient Laws' of Conquered Kingdoms

Lawyers and law play an equivocal role in Canadian colonial history. They have, on the one hand, the potential of being vehicles for the most oppressive of measures. Consider the 1755 legal opinion of Nova Scotia Chief Justice Jonathan Belcher, concluding that Roman Catholic *Acadiens* could not be expected to genuinely take an oath of allegiance to the British King given their past refusals. They could be considered 'in no other light than that of Rebels to his Majesty', Belcher advised.[74] Bearing the collective stamp of disloyalty, some 16,000 Acadians were expelled and their property taken by a 1759 legal enactment. English colonial lawyers could also play a more humanizing role. This was, in some ways, inadvertent. Metropole authorities were intent on maintaining jurisdic-tional borders between England and its dominions for fear that overseas aliens would be 'naturalized'. The English, in particular, feared the 'influx of poor Scots' into their juris-diction. The realm, observes Hulsebosch, 'needed insulation'.[75]

Calvin's Case provided an opportunity to police these borders. The question before the King's Bench was whether a Scotsman, Robert Calvin, could sue in King's courts

---

[71] Christian Dufour, *A Canadian Challenge—Le Défi Québécois* (Oolichan Books and the Institute for Research on Public Policy, 1990) 39.

[72] 'Governor Murray to the Lords of Trade' (29 October 1764) in Shortt and Doughty above (n 57) 231: This was a 'race', Murray wrote, 'who cou'd they be indulged with a few privileges wch the Laws of England deny to Roman Catholicks at home, wou'd soon get the better of every National Antipathy to their Conquerors and become the most faithful and most useful set of Men in this American Empire'.

[73] Shortt and Doughty above (n 57) 231.

[74] Michel Bastarache, 'The Opinion of the Chief Justice of Nova Scotia Regarding the Deportation of the Acadians' (2010) 42 Ottawa L Rev 261, 264.

[75] Daniel J Hulsebosch, 'The Ancient Constitution and the Expanding Empire: Sir Edward Coke's British Jurisprudence' (2003) 21 L and History Rev 439, 448–449.

regarding lands and chattels in Shoreditch. Calvin was born in the third year of the reign of James I (also James VI of Scotland). Lord Coke concluded that both the English and Scots were united by their allegiance to the person of the King, and so 'cannot be an alien born'.[76] Calvin could, therefore, pursue his remedy in English courts. In passing, Coke articulated what would become the foundation for future colonial legal doctrine, albeit with some modifications.[77] Coke distinguished between the conquest of a Christian kingdom and that of an 'infidel' kingdom. In the case of a Christian kingdom, the King 'may at his pleasure alter and change the laws of that kingdom: but until he doth make an alteration of those laws the ancient laws of the kingdom remain'.[78] In the case of an infidel kingdom, '*ipso facto* the laws of the infidel are abrogated, for that they be not only against Christianity, but against God and the law of nature'. Finally, if land was inherited or the laws of England introduced by the King, then only Parliament could alter them.[79] This was not a recipe for a unitary legal order but a pluralistic one. This was implicit in Coke's declaration that Englishmen abroad were entitled to carry with them English constitutional rights, including those associated with property. A system of dual property rights thereby was contemplated, one for English settlers and another for local inhabitants.[80] Jurisdiction was premised on a personal relation between Crown and subject rather than upon territorial claims.[81] The common law only traveled abroad in the King's dominions in limited ways. Conquered colonies, nevertheless, would be governed at the King's 'pleasure,' that is, by royal prerogative. But until such time as laws were altered, municipal law continued to govern local affairs.[82]

Attorney General Fletcher Norton and Solicitor General William De Gray were asked by the aforementioned Board of Trade[83] whether the newly conquered Roman Catholic

---

[76] *Calvin's Case* (1608) 7 Coke's Reports 1a; 77 ER 377 (KB), 14b/394.

[77] See, e.g., *Campbell v Hall* (1774) 1 Cowp 204, 98 ER 1045 (KB) and *Blankard v Galdy* (1693) 2 Salk. 41, 190 E.R. 1089. For a discussion of legal developments subsequent to *Calvin's Case*, see Sir William Holdsworth, *History of English Law*, vol XI (Methuen & Co Ltd, 1938) 229–248.

[78] This was viewed as faithful to Roman practice, according to Sir Matthew Hale: 'they rarely made a rigorous and universal Change of the Laws of the conquered Country, unless they were such as were foreign and barbarous, or altogether inconsistent with the Victor's Government: But in other Things, they commonly indulged unto the conquered, the Laws and Religion of their Country upon a double Account . . . On Account of Humanity . . . [and] Upon Account of Prudence'. See Sir Matthew Hale, *The History of the Common Law* (Charles M Gray ed, 3rd edn, University of Chicago Press, 1971) 52–53. This is how Gramsci (n 30) understood this model, as well.

[79] *Calvin's Case* above (n 76) 18a/398. On whether the Parliament contemplated was the one in London or a local representative body, see Hulsebosch above (n 75) 463.

[80] Hulsebosch above (n 75) 468.

[81] P G McHugh, *Aboriginal Societies and the Common Law: A History of Sovereignty, Status, and Self-Determination* (Oxford University Press, 2004) 69.

[82] Walters associates this with the 'common law presumption of continuity of local law', which was 'rebutted once a legislative instrument extended English municipal law and institutions over the local community'. See Mark D Walters, 'The "Golden Thread" of Continuity' above (n 50) 719. Likening the rule to a rebuttable presumption is regrettable as it empties his account of the asymmetrical relations of power on display in imperial law.

[83] The Board of Trade was an advisory body to the Privy Council reporting to the Secretary of State for the Southern Department. The Board 'drafted commissions and instructions for royal Governors,

subjects of Canada were subject to the same 'incapacities, disabilities and Penalties' as Roman Catholics in the United Kingdom.[84] They concluded on 10 June 1765 that they were not.[85] Only the year prior, Lord Mansfield expressed consternation in response to reports that Canadian laws and customs had been 'abolished . . . all at once.' 'The history of the world don't furnish an instance of so rash and unjust an act by any conqueror whatsoever', complained Mansfield. 'The fundamental maxims are,' he maintained, 'that a country keeps her own laws, 'till the conqueror expressly gives new.'[86]

The Board of Trade subsequently asked Attorney General Charles Yorke and Solicitor General de Grey their opinion regarding the state of civil government in Québec. Yorke and de Gray, in their opinion of 14 April 1766, identified two sources of 'disorder' in the province. The first was an attempt to 'carry on the Administration of Justice without the aid of the natives, not merely in new forms, but totally in unknown tongue'.[87] The second was the 'alarm' taken regarding the construction of the Royal Proclamation of 1763 which declared the law of England as controlling in civil and criminal cases. The cumulative effect abolished all local law, replacing it with 'new, unnecessary and Arbitrary rules, especially in the Titles to land, and in the modes of Descent, Alienation and Settlement, which tend to confound and subvert the rights, instead of supporting them'.[88] This looked to be the product of 'the rough hand of a Conqueror rather than . . . the true Spirit of a Lawful Sovereign'.[89] To the first source of disorder, Murray had been instructed to relax the application of English law in civil disputes, enabling Quebec lawyers to appear and Quebec jurors to sit[90]—both of which, the Imperial legal advisors seemingly unaware, Murray had secured for the court of common pleas pursuant to his ordinance of September 1764.[91] Yorke and De Gray further opined that:

> There is not a Maxim of the Common Law more certain than that a Conquer'd people retain their antient Customs till the Conqueror shall declare New Laws. To change at once the Laws and manners of a settled Country must be attended with hardship and Violence; and therefore wise Conquerors having provided for the Security of

corresponded with them, and gathered information from royal officials, colonial Councils and Assemblies, and from Imperial, colonial, and chartered company petitioners and lobbyists'. See Steele above (n 40) 107–108.

[84] The question of the degree to which *les Canadiens* would be absorbed into English law and religion 'gave rise to cabinet disputes' according to Peter Marshall, 'British North America, 1760–1815' in P J Marshall, *The Oxford History of the British Empire, Volume II: The Eighteenth Century* (Oxford University Press, 1999) 377. It is also described by Coupland above (n 61) as a 'vital question.'

[85] Shortt and Doughty above (n 57) 236.

[86] William James Smith, *The Grenville Papers*, ed, Volume II (John Murray, 1852) 476–477.

[87] W P M Kennedy, *Statutes, Treaties and Documents of the Canadian Constitution* above (n 23) 65.

[88] ibid.

[89] ibid.

[90] W P M Kennedy, *The Constitution of Canada: An Introduction to Its Development and Law*, introduction by Martin Friedland (Oxford University Press, 2014) 42.

[91] Neatby above (n 58) 52. Neatby notes that the power to apply Canadian law was 'necessarily limited' by reason of the court of common pleas limited jurisdiction and the right of appeal to the King's Bench under the control of English lawyers and English law (53).

their Dominion, proceed tentatively and indulge their Conquer'd subjects in all local Customs which are in their own nature indifferent, and which have been received as rules of property or have obtained force of Laws. It is the more material that this policy be persued in *Canada*; because it is a great and antient Colony long settled and much Cultivated, by French subjects.[92]

Yorke and de Gray laid down as 'general rules' that in all personal civil actions (as in contract) the laws of England would prevail. In actions concerning real property (as in title to land) 'local customs and usages' would have supremacy. It would otherwise 'occasion infinite confusion and injustice' to 'introduce at one Stroke the English law' of real property.[93] English judges would be expected to be instructed by 'Canadian lawyers and intelligent Persons in the customs of Canada'.[94] As before, English law would prevail in criminal cases. The Governor was expected to publish a proclamation explaining these changes regarding the administration of justice in Quebec. This would 'quiet the minds of the People as to the true meaning of the Royal Proclamation of Oct'r 1763'.[95]

These subsequent accommodations, statutorily enshrined in the Quebec Act of 1774, secured the continued application and growth of the civil law in Quebec. Lord Hillsborough, in the spirit of revisionism not unlike that displayed by Yorke and De Gray, claimed that the Proclamation of 1763 was not intended to repeal local law in regard to property and civil rights. It 'never entered into Our Idea to overturn the Laws and Customs of Canada, with regard to Property, but that Justice should be administered agreeably to them,' he wrote to Governor Carleton in 1768.[96] This was proof, once again, that colonies in the periphery could never be governed by simple orders issuing from the centre.

In the case of First Nations in North America, English lawyers, for much of the eighteenth century, were less preoccupied with assertions of sovereignty. Whatever claims being made by the empire upon the original inhabitants, they could only be founded upon mutual consent. Though paternalistic, the regime was pluralistic.[97] This remained the case only until the press of immigration forced Indigenous peoples to give up their lands to European settlers. By the late eighteenth century, the lawyers' insistence upon Crown sovereignty over subject people, including Indigenous people, was deemed to be exclusive and absolute. The 'original sovereignty of the aboriginal peoples was regarded as spent', writes McHugh—'[i]t was at best a momentary original condition long since gone.'[98]

---

[92] W P M Kennedy, *Statutes, Treaties and Documents of the Canadian Constitution* above (n 23) 67.
[93] ibid.
[94] ibid 68.
[95] ibid.
[96] ibid 77. Walters interprets this as confirmation of the power of the common law presumption of continuity in Walters, 'The "Golden Thread" of Continuity' above (n 50) 725. As mentioned in n 43, this is hard to square with the text of the Royal Proclamation of 1763.
[97] Mark D Walters, '*Mohegan Indians v. Connecticut* (1705–1773) and the Legal Status of Aboriginal Customary Laws and Government in British North America' (1995) 33 Osgoode Hall L J 785.
[98] McHugh above (n 81) 103–109, 152.

4. Enfranchising the
'Former Lords of the Soil'

The third episode under discussion brings clearly to the surface the close relationship between strategies of recognition and the violence of assimilation. We are speaking of the period shortly after Confederation, when the Electoral Franchise Act of 1885 conferred federal voting rights upon the Indigenous peoples of Eastern Canada. It should be emphasized that, by this time, the success of the European enterprise in British North America was less dependent upon good relations with First Nations, as the language of the Royal Proclamation of 1763 suggested. Rather, the relationship between the Crown and Indigenous peoples in British North America was by now transformed from one of mutuality and reciprocity into one of neglect and exploitation.[99] Moving from partners to subjects, 'Indians' emerged among the list of 'matters,' in section 91(24) of the *British North America Act 1867*, allocated to federal authority. Indian affairs remained centralized, as they had since 1763. In this era, Indigenous people were expected to get out of the way so that economic development could proceed apace. Treaty making, as it had in the eighteenth century, remained the preferred means of placating Indigenous protestations.

As in pre-Confederation Canada, assimilation was the principal objective of federal Indian policy. Until the 1885 Franchise Act, male Indians could be enfranchised only if sufficiently educated, free of debt, and renouncing all treaty privileges. In such cases, legal distinctions between enfranchised Indians and others of her Majesty's subjects were erased and their populations 'eas[ed] into the wage economy': they would 'no longer be deemed an Indian' under law.[100] Individuals were expected to exchange their indigeneity for the right of representation. The 1885 Act reversed course, somewhat, but only temporarily. The federal law would extend the franchise to Indians without also demanding that they give up tribal membership.[101] This had the beneficial effect of not having to forsake Indigenous identity in favour of a Canadian one. The Act, instead, recognized the possibility of dual, even plural, identities.[102] It did not mean a transformation of the settler state-Indigenous relationship, one still premised upon Eurocentric

---

[99] Canada, Royal Commission on Aboriginal Peoples, *Treaty Making in the Spirit of Co-existence: An Alternative to Extinguishment* (Minister of Supply and Services Canada, 1995) 31.

[100] Statutes of Canada, 1857, c. 26, s.3; Douglas C Harris, *Landing Native Fisheries: Indian Reserves & Fishing Rights in British Columbia, 1849–1925* (University of British Columbia Press, 2008) 39.

[101] Richard Bartlett, 'Citizens Minus: Indians and the Right to Vote' (1980) 44 Saskatchewan L Rev 163, 172.

[102] Martha-Marie Kleinhans and Roderick A Macdonald, 'What Is a Critical Legal Pluralism?' (1997) 12 Canadian J of L & Society 25, 38–40: critical legal pluralism conceives of the legal subject 'as carrying a multiplicity of identities'. Also James Tully, *Strange Multiplicity: Constitutionalism in an Age of Diversity* (Cambridge University Press, 1995) 11.

conceptions of superiority.[103] Rather it offered up the possibility of expressing 'nation-hood demands' in the context of a continuing relationship of asymmetrical power relations.[104]

In accordance with transitional provisions in the *Constitution Act, 1867*, s. 41, pro-vincial laws determined who could vote in federal elections until an act of Parliament provided otherwise. Municipal officers, presumably more knowledgeable about local political conditions, drew up voters' lists for the first five federal elections.[105] The Electoral Franchise Act of 1885,[106] an initiative of the Conservative government of John A. Macdonald, was intended to provide otherwise. It also was intended to improve con-ditions for a Conservative majority by enfranchising those, such as male property hold-ers, who were more likely to vote Conservative.[107]

Among the changes proposed was extension of the vote to property-owning women and to Indigenous peoples across Canada. The first proposal went too far, even for mem-bers of the ruling Conservative Party.[108] The proposal to enfranchise 'male persons . . . including Indians,' however, secured sufficient support. Indians who had improved communal tracts of land, in the amount of at least $150, survived parliamentary scru-tiny.[109] The underlying objective, admitted Prime Minister Macdonald in a Cabinet memorandum, was assimilation 'as speedily as they are fit for the change'.[110]

Opposition Liberals were content to leave the federal franchise in the hands of local officials, as in the United States. A decentralized system was preferred, declared Liberal David Mills, invoking a discourse of provincial rights. Under the Constitution, the 'peo-ple of each Province, . . . should be allowed to decide for themselves who shall pos-sess, within their limits electoral franchise'.[111] Additional objections were enumerated. Indians were incompetent to exercise civic rights. The Bill would allow Indians 'to go

---

[103] This is what Tully calls 'internal colonization' in James Tully, 'The Struggles of Indigenous Peoples for and of Freedom' in *Public Philosophy in a New Key, Volume 1: Democracy and Civic Freedom* (Cambridge University Press, 2008) 259–261.

[104] Alfred above (n 11) 30.

[105] Ben Forster, Malcolm Davidson and R Craig Brown, 'The Franchise, Personators, and Dead Men: An Inquiry into the Voters' Lists and the Election of 1891' (1986) 67 The Canadian Historical Rev 17, 19; Malcolm Montgomery, 'The Six Nations and the Macdonald Franchise' (1965) 57 Ontario History 13, 13.

[106] Statutes of Canada 1885, 48–49 Vict., c. 40. The debates involved 101 members of Parliament, some speaking more than 20 times. See Henry J Morgan, *The Dominion Annual Register and Review for the Nineteenth Year of the Canadian Union, 1885* (ed., Hunter, Rose & Company, 1886) 55.

[107] Montgomery above (n 105) 20.

[108] Mr. Royal in HC Deb 24 April 1885: 1390 (Can); Veronica Strong-Boag, 'The Citizenship Debates: The 1885 Franchise Act' in R Adamsoki, D Chunn and R Menzies (eds), *Contesting Canadian Citizenship: Historical Readings* (Broadview Press, 2002).

[109] Electoral Franchise Act of 1885 above (n 106), ss. 2, 11(c).

[110] Montgomery above (n 105) 13. This was an objective also secured by Indian Act provisions dictating that Indian women marrying non-Indian men would lose their status under the Act. See Kathleen Jamieson, *Indian Women and the Law in Canada: Citizens Minus* (Minister of Supply and Service Canada 1978) and Indian Act of 1876, Statutes of Canada, c 18, s 3.3 (c).

[111] HC Deb 11 May 1885: 1759 (Can).

from a scalping party to the polls', Mills declared.[112] They are 'infants of the Dominion', opined Cameron, without the 'degree of independence that will fit him for the discharge of the franchise' added Charlton.[113] Moreover, worried Mills, these 'wards of the Government' were likely to defer to the wishes of their federally appointed superior, the Conservative Party-affiliated Superintendent General.[114] Lastly, as they were not capable of managing their own affairs, Mills insisted, they were not capable of 'managing the affairs of the country'.[115] Being exempt from taxation—having no cognizable civic obligations—they could not be awarded the privileges of citizenship, namely, representation in the national Parliament.

The Prime Minister responded by assuring the House of Commons that it would only be 'those Indians' who had the 'outward evidences of property which the white man can show ... houses, furniture, and civilised appliances of a certain value' who would be conferred the franchise'.[116] Macdonald acknowledged that 'aboriginal Indians, formerly lords of the soil, formerly own[ed] the whole of this country ... are British subjects now; they desire to remain so, and as British subjects they have the same rights as the white man'.[117] Though premised upon questionable notions of consent ('They are British subjects now'), what is most significant about this concession is that Macdonald was prepared 'to extend the franchise to the Indian men without demanding [their] total assimilation'.[118] Tribal lands and treaty obligations would remain intact under the Franchise Act. There would be no forced choice between community and Canadian citizenship.

There remains the question—answered affirmatively by Macdonald—of whether Indigenous people sought out the federal franchise. The Liberal opposition noted a marked reluctance on behalf of Indigenous leadership fearing that, upon the heels of enfranchisement, taxation measures and the downgrading of Indigenous government to regular municipalities would soon follow.[119] There was good ground for such a fear given the assimilationist objectives of Macdonald's Indian policy, up to that point, and an evident desire to control Indian internal affairs by establishing municipal institutions.[120] The opposition was spreading falsehoods, claimed the Prime Minister in a letter

---

[112] HC Deb 29 April 1885: 1485 (Can).

[113] HC Deb 1 May 1885: 1503 (Can).

[114] HC Deb 1 May 1885: 1503 (Can).

[115] HC Deb 30 April 1885: 1487 (Can).

[116] HC. Deb 30 April 1885: 1487 (Can).

[117] HC Deb 1885: 1575 (Can).

[118] Bartlett above (n 101) 172. As Kleinhans and Macdonald assert, the critically legal pluralist subject 'is best characterized as a multiplicity of selves and not the modern anthropomorphized individual of economics, political science and *Charters of Rights*' above (n 102) 42.

[119] Bartlett above (n 101) 177.

[120] Darlene Johnston, 'First Nations and Canadian Citizenship' in William Kaplan (ed), *Belonging: The Meaning and Future of Canadian Citizenship* (McGill-Queen's University Press, 1993) 358–359. See the Gradual Civilization Act 1857, Statutes of Canada, 20 Vict., c. 26; the Gradual Enfranchisement Act 1869, Statutes of Canada, 31 Vict. c. 42; and discussion in Johnston, ibid., 354–359.

to Chief Johnson of Desoranto, 'in order to prevent the original proprietors of the soil of this country from standing on a footing of equality with the white men, who have come into it . . . He will stand exactly in the same position in all respects the hour after he may vote as he stood the hours before he voted'.[121] Taking issue with the opposition Liberals, Chief Kahkkwaquonaby (Peter Jones) of the Six Nations wrote to the *Toronto Daily Mail* that Indians do not pay taxes in light of the fact that they 'parted' with their lands for a 'mere nominal figure'. The meager benefits they receive in exchange under treaty represent 'no more than the exact interest upon this investment'. 'There is not a family in my reserve', Jones continued, who was not sufficiently sophisticated so as to 'read the torrent of abuse your party [the Liberals] are indulging in at our expense'.[122] Macdonald made a similar point in House of Commons debates, likening treaty rights to private rights: 'The annuities paid to the different bands are their own moneys, and they got them as of right. Their lands have been sold; the proceeds have been funded at a certain rate of interest, which the Government pays; and the Indian has the same right to his annual payment out of that fund as if he were a shareholder in a bank receiving a dividend. It is his own money'.[123]

The final terms of the Electoral Enfranchisement Act excluded most Indigenous people west of Ontario (s. 11[c]). This was a consequence of the rebellion at Batoche and Frog Lake, events that broke out four days after Macdonald introduced the act in Parliament.[124] The uprising made it awkward for the federal government to extend the franchise to those who were rebelling against it. The franchise would be extended only to 'Indians of the old Provinces,' declared the Prime Minister.[125] Despite seemingly favorable conditions for a Conservative re-election, they were defeated; the new Liberal government repealed the law prior to the next federal election.[126] Canadian constitutional culture was not quite ready for Indigenous enfranchisement until much later. It was not until 1960 that the Indian franchise was restored by the Conservative government of John Diefenbaker.

5. CONCLUSION

During the federal election campaign of 2015, there arose a debate within Indigenous communities over the question of whether to vote in the upcoming election. 'For many indigenous people, voting is like shopping for white bread', observed Drew Hayden Taylor, '[i]t

---

[121] Quoted in Bartlett above (n 101) 177.

[122] Peter E Jones, 'The Indian Franchise: Views of Head Chief' *Toronto Mail* (22 May 1885).

[123] HC Deb 1885: 1487 (Can).

[124] Montgomery above (n 105) 14.

[125] HC Deb 1885: 1574 (Can). The Act disqualified 'Indians in Manitoba, British Columbia, Keewatin and the Northwest Territories' (48-49 Vict., c. 40, s. 11 [c]).

[126] Montgomery above (n 105) 25.

might be enriched but, really, does that make it any healthier?'.[127] For some, participation in the federal election was equivalent to succumbing to the will of the colonizer. First Nations should protect Indigenous rights in 'nation-to-nation negotiations [rather] than as a stakeholder, interest group, or ethnic minority Canadian'.[128] Even Perry Bellegarde, Chief of the Assembly of First Nations, admitted that he had never before voted in a federal election. He, nevertheless, urged others to do so this time.[129] Indigenous turnout had the potential to swing outcomes in a number of key federal ridings away from the ruling Conservatives.[130] One can imagine similar conversations occurring in Indigenous communities in 1885. Canadian constitutional culture today, in this respect, exhibits some continuity with the past.

Like Imperial authority before it, Canadian federal power continues today to make claims over its constituent parts. I shall make mention of a couple of such instances here, by way of conclusion. The federal Clarity Act of 2000[131] endows the federal government with the power to unilaterally determine whether the question asked, in a future referendum on Quebec sovereignty, is clear and whether its majority is sufficiently great. This, the federal government claims, merely sculpts into statutory language the Supreme Court of Canada's ruling in *Reference re Secession of Quebec*.[132] Yet, the Supreme Court there condemned unilateralism in all its forms, not just that proposed by the province of Quebec, whenever the interests of other governments are implicated.[133]

By sending mixed messages, the Supreme Court appears to encourage this sort of behavior. The Court recently authorized provincial laws of general application to apply in respect of Indigenous rights in *Tsilhqot'in Nation*, even though provinces were previously constitutionally disentitled from so acting under the terms of the 1867 Act.[134] The Court thereby reversed a '250-year-old constitutional principle first outlined in the Royal Proclamation of 1763' that local governments have no direct dealings with First Nations'.[135] The Court also continues to declare that underlying title to Indigenous

---

[127] Drew Hayden Taylor, 'Why First Nations Might Vote This Time Around' *Now Toronto Magazine* (11 October 2015) https://nowtoronto.com/news/the-now-guide-to-the-2015/why-first-nations-might-vote-in-%23elxn42/ accessed 9 July 2016.

[128] Pamela Palmater, 'The Power of Indigenous Peoples Has Never Come from Voting in Federal Elections' *rabble.ca* (9 August 2015) http://rabble.ca/blogs/bloggers/pamela-palmater/2015/08/power-indigenous-peoples-has-never-come-voting-federal-electi accessed 10 July 2016.

[129] Joan Bryden, 'AFN National Chief Urges Aboriginal People to Vote, Even if He Doesn't' *The Globe and Mail* (2 September 2015).

[130] Voting in some indigenous communities was up 270 percent in 2015. See Chinta Puxley, 'Voter Turnout up by 270% in Some Aboriginal Communities' *The Toronto Star* (25 October 2015).

[131] Statutes of Canada 2000, c. 26.

[132] *Reference re Secession of Quebec* [1998] 2 SCR 217.

[133] David Schneiderman, 'Referendum Reckoning: Jean Chretien's Itch to Clarify the Rules of Secession Is Rash' *The National Post* (30 November 1999) A18.

[134] *Tsilhqot'in Nation v British Columbia* 2014 SCC 44, [2014] S.C.J. No 44, para 150, by virtue of s. 91(24). See Patrick Macklem, *Indigenous Difference and the Constitution of Canada* (University of Toronto Press, 2001) 116–117.

[135] John Borrows, 'The Durability of *Terra Nullius: Tsilhqot'in Nation v. British Columbia*' (2015) 48 University of British Columbia L Rev 701, 735–737; Hamar Foster, 'Honouring the Queen: A Legal and Historical Perspective on the Nisga'a Treaty' (1998/1999) 120 BC Studies 11, 14–15.

territories passed to the Crown, without explaining the legal means for doing so that do not rest upon ethnocentric presuppositions by which title was secured.[136] Rather than seeking consensus from the relevant parties, the Court will determine, in future, whether provincial limitations are constitutionally permissible under a justification framework it has been developing in Aboriginal rights cases under s 35 of the Constitution Act of 1982.

The urge to smooth over these differences via fiat, rather than by deliberation, continues to plague Canadian constitutionalism. We should acknowledge, instead, that having 'competing loci of law and political ordering' likely fosters disagreement over constitutional fundamentals.[137] We might agree with Roderick MacDonald, then, that the Canadian example results in a constitutional culture different from that recommended by classical constitutional thought: 'Paradoxically, the constitution that best recognizes and accommodates all types of diversity is that which denies its own power to define the scope of that recognition and accommodation.'[138] Disagreement about sovereignty, autonomy, and the exercise of public power will be endemic to such a model of constitutional engagement.[139] We should expect Canadians to continue to think and work through this complex and pluralistic constitutional paradigm.

Bibliography

Alfred, Taiaiake 'From Sovereignty to Freedom: Towards an Indigenous Political Discourse' (2001) 3 Indigenous Affairs 22

Asch, Michael *On Being Here to Stay: Treaties and Aboriginal Rights in Canada* (University of Toronto Press 2014)

Bartlett, Richard 'Citizens Minus: Indians and the Right to Vote' (1980) 44 Saskatchewan L Rev 163

Berger, Benjamin L. *Law's Religion: Religious Difference and the Claims of Constitutionalism* (University of Toronto Press 2015)

Borrows, John 'The Durability of *Terra Nullius: Tsilhqot'in Nation* v. *British Columbia*' (2015) 48 University of British Columbia L Rev 701

Canada, Royal Commission on Aboriginal Peoples. *Treaty Making in the Spirit of Co-existence: An Alternative to Extinguishment* (Minister of Supply and Services Canada 1995)

Johnston, Darlene. 'First Nations and Canadian Citizenship' in William Kaplan, ed., *Belonging: The Meaning and Future of Canadian Citizenship* (McGill-Queen's University Press 1993)

---

[136] *Tsilhqot'in Nation* above (n 134) [69]; Michael Asch and Patrick Macklem, 'An Essay on *R. v. Sparrow*' (1991) 29 Alberta L Rev 498.

[137] Roderick A. Macdonald, 'The Design of Constitutions to Accommodate Linguistic, Cultural and Ethnic Diversity: The Canadian Experiment' in Kálmán Kulcsár and Denis Szabo (eds) *Dual Images: Multiculturalism on Two Sides of the Atlantic* (Institute for Political Science of the Hungarian Academy of Sciences, 1996) 53.

[138] ibid 53.

[139] Stuart Hampshire, *Innocence and Experience* (Harvard University Press, 1989); Connolly above (n 20).

Kennedy, W.P.M. 1922. *The Constitution of Canada: An Introduction to its Development and Law*, introduction by Martin Friedland (Oxford University Press 2014)

Kleinhans, Martha-Marie and Roderick A. Macdonald. 1997. 'What Is a Critical Legal Pluralism?' (1997) 12 Canadian J of L & Society 25

Kolish, Evelyn. *Nationalismes et conflit des droits: Le débat du droit privé au Québec, 1760–1840* (Éditions Hurtubise HMH Ltée 1994)

Macdonald, Roderick A. 'Three Centuries of Constitution Making in Canada: Will There Be a Fourth?' (1996) 30 UBC L Rev 211

Macklem, Patrick. *Indigenous Difference and the Constitution of Canada* (University of Toronto Press 2001)

Mancke, Elizabeth. 1999. 'Early Modern Imperial Governance and the Origins of Canadian Political Culture' (1999) 32 Canadian J of Political Science 3

McHugh, P.G. *Aboriginal Societies and the Common Law: A History of Sovereignty, Status, and Self-Determination* (Oxford Universiy Press 2004)

Risk, R.C.B. 1996. 'Constitutional Scholarship in the Late Nineteenth Century: Making Federalism Work' in G. Blaine Baker and Jim Phillips (eds), *A History of Canadian Legal Thought: Collected Essays* (University of Toronto Press 1996) 33

Schneiderman, David. *Red, White, and Kind of Blue? The Conservatives and the Americanization of Canadian Constitutional Culture* (University of Toronto Press 2015)

Tully, James. 'The Struggles of Indigenous Peoples for and of Freedom' in *Public Philosophy in a New Key, Volume 1: Democracy and Civic Freedom* (Cambridge: Cambridge University Press 2008) 257

Tully, James. *Strange Multiplicity: Constitutionalism in an Age of Diversity* (Cambridge University Press 1995)

Vipond, Robert C. *Liberty & Community: Canadian Federalism and the Failure of the Constitution* (State University of New York Press 1991)

Walters, Mark D. 1999. 'The "Golden Thread" of Continuity: Aboriginal Customs at Common Law and under the Constitution Act, 1982' (1999) 44 McGill L J 711

C. Key Debates in Constitutional Theory

....

CHAPTER 44

THE ROLE OF
THEORY IN CANADIAN
CONSTITUTIONAL LAW

....

TIMOTHY ENDICOTT[*] &
PETER OLIVER[**]

1. INTRODUCTION

....

CANADIAN constitutional law has often been shaped by unstated theoretical assumptions. But deliberate theorising has also played a variety of crucial roles, as judges, politicians, lawyers, and law teachers have attempted to articulate the philosophical foundations of the Constitution. We share these complex features of our constitutional practice with many countries. But constitutional theory has been institutionalized in quite distinctive ways in Canada. The *Constitution Act, 1867* (formerly the *British North America Act, 1867*) created unique opportunities and imperatives for political leaders, advocates, judges, scholars, law students, and others to articulate their understanding of Confederation. And while the country chose a parliamentary form of government very different from American republicanism, Confederation generated a set of entrenched rules defining the powers of the federal and provincial governments, which would give judges a hand in the law of the Constitution that judges had never had in the United Kingdom. Moreover, Canadian federalism generated an extraordinary statutory provision for references (i.e., requests for advisory opinions) to the Supreme Court of

  * Professor of Legal Philosophy, University of Oxford.
  ** Full Professor and Vice Dean Research, Faculty of Law, University of Ottawa. The author would like to thank colleagues, in particular members of the Public Law Group at the University of Ottawa, for numerous discussions regarding issues raised in this chapter. He would also like to thank James Hendry for suggestions regarding the nature of principles.

Canada on matters of law and fact, including (as it would turn out) matters of convention.[1] That arrangement has given a super-attorney-general role to judges, whose public reasons for decision involve them in the theoretical task of articulating the basis of the Constitution.[2] The *Constitution Act, 1982* further enhanced the judges' role as theorists of the Constitution, through their role in the interpretation and elaboration of the *Charter of Rights and Freedoms, section 35 (on aboriginal rights) and Part V (on amendment)*.

In this chapter we aim to illustrate ways in which both express theorizing and inarticulate theoretical assumptions have shaped Canadian constitutional law. We argue that good theorizing is essential for the sound development of the law and practice of the Constitution.

2. Theoretical Questions and Theoretical Assumptions

Whether or not it is presented in overtly theoretical terms, Canadian law students quickly gain a sense of their professors' and the legal profession's approach to questions of legal theory, such as:

What counts as a good legal argument?

What counts as a source of law?

What happens when those sources do not provide clear answers to a question of constitutional law?

What is the relationship between what counts as law and what counts as a legal system?

What is the relation between the law and the moral reasoning that ought to guide the structure and conduct of government?

What is the form of that reasoning, and who ought to decide what it requires?

Canadian lawyers educated before the 1980s would have seen the Constitution as a set of rules for the making and for the administration of the rules of Canadian law. The law of

---

[1] Supreme and Exchequer Court Act, 1875; Supreme Court Act, 1985, s 53. See *Reference re Secession of Quebec* [1998] 2 SCR 217 [6]–[23] [hereinafter *Secession Reference*]. Regarding constitutional references and constitutional conventions see *Reference re Resolution to Amend the Constitution* [1981] 1 SCR 753 [hereinafter *Patriation Reference*], below Section 7, and P Oliver, 'Reform of the Supreme Court of Canada from Within: To What Extent Should the Court Weigh In regarding Constitutional Conventions' in Nadia Verrelli, ed, *The Democratic Dilemma: Reforming Canada's Supreme Court* (McGill-Queen's Press, 2013) 161.

[2] See Gerald Rubin, 'The Nature, Use and Effect of Reference Cases in Canadian Constitutional Law' 6 McGill LJ 168–190. C Mathen, '"The Question Calls for an Answer, and I Propose to Answer It": The Patriation Reference as Constitutional Method' (2011) 54 Sup Ct L Rev 143.

the Constitution was seen as made up of constitutional statutes (most fundamentally the *British North America Act, 1867*) and judicial decisions and (to a limited extent) custom. The non-legal rules of the Constitution had their source in the conventions governing constitutional actors. Law students at that time could readily see that courts sometimes innovated, by changing doctrines that had been considered to be well settled, and by making law when the recognized sources provided no clear answer to a question of law. Those same lawyers, however, may not have anticipated the shifts regarding these questions that would take place in the 1980s and 1990s, notably with regard to the role in judicial reasoning of abstract legal principles such as federalism, the rule of law, judicial independence, and separation of powers.[3]

After 1982, and most notably in the 1990s, arguments based in principle became central to Canadian constitutional law, and in particular to those controversial cases where the text of the Constitution and the existing case law did not point to clear answers. Traditional sources were still understood as sources in the 1990s, but the approach to sources was changing. Appeals to abstract principles offered new potential for innovative arguments, and the traditional sources of the Constitution came to be treated as potential support for arguments of principle. Able litigators were quick to alter their lines of attack in consequence.

In 1936, the brilliant Australian judge and jurist, Owen Dixon, pointed out the potent role that theoretical assumptions may play in the development of law and of government:

> The fundamental conceptions, which a legal system embodies or expresses, are seldom grasped or understood in their entirety at the time when their actual influence is greatest. . . . Sometimes indeed they are but instinctive assumptions of which at the time few or none were aware. But afterwards they may be seen as definite principles contained within the ideas which provided the ground of action. Further, when such conceptions have once taken root they seldom disappear. They persist long after the conditions in which they originate have gone. They enter into combinations with other conceptions and contribute to the construction of new systems of law and government.[4]

---

[3] Law students before the 1980s were familiar with the *Roncarelli v Duplessis* case and its significance for the rule of law. However, the case was famous in large part because Rand J's engagement with constitutional principle was exceptional; and, furthermore, many at the time insisted on explaining the case in more conventional legal terms. For a reminder of the more conventional reading of *Roncarelli*, see Claude Armand Sheppard, '*Roncarelli v. Duplessis* Art. 1053 C.C.' (1960) 6 McGill LJ 75, reprinted at (2010) 55 McGill LJ v; David Mullan, '*Roncarelli v. Duplessis* and Damages for Abuse of Power: For What Did It Stand in 1959 and for What Does It Stand in 2009' (2010) 55 McGill LJ 587. Similarly, a theory of an 'implied bill of rights' emerged during the middle years of the twentieth century; however, it never attracted majority support. PW Hogg, *Constitutional Law of Canada* (5th ed.) (Thomson Carswell, 2011) §31–10.

[4] Owen Dixon, 'The Law and the Constitution' in Owen Dixon, *Jesting Pilate: And Other Papers and Addresses* (Law Book Company, 1965) 38, originally published in (1935) 51 LQR 590, 590–591.

The Supreme Court of Canada has referred to what Dixon called 'fundamental conceptions' as 'the vital unstated assumptions' of the Constitution.[5] These theoretical assumptions underpinning the study and practice of law come in many varieties. Some relate to the fundamental questions of jurisprudence identified above, regarding what counts as law, for example. Other assumptions relate to more particular questions that run deeply through Canadian constitutional law: for example, regarding particular understandings of parliamentary sovereignty or federalism, or different ways of approaching constitutional interpretation. Through all of these issues, the general and the particular, theory and context interact, and that interaction shapes the development of Canadian constitutional law.

We will briefly review the distinctively Canadian theoretical assumptions behind parliamentary government, parliamentary sovereignty, federalism, and constitutional interpretation, and outline the shift, after the 1982 patriation of the Constitution, toward a theoretical framework based to a greater extent on the articulation by judges of abstract principles of the Constitution. The Conclusion will discuss relations between the theory of the Constitution, and the evolving context in which the Constitution operates.

3. EARLY THEORETICAL INFLUENCES: 'A CONSTITUTION SIMILAR IN PRINCIPLE TO THAT OF THE UNITED KINGDOM'

The influence of theoretical assumptions may be difficult to perceive in the present but is often clearer in historical perspective. The preamble to the *British North America Act, 1867* stated that Canada's constitution was to be 'similar in Principle' to a constitution whose principles had never been fully theorized. This constitutional heritage did involve a long and complex history of theorizing about constitutional law and constitutional morality; however, the theorizing was always very incomplete and controversial, and the practical impact of theory was often rather unclear, because of the English knack (restored with the restoration of the monarchy after the Civil War) for pragmatic muddling through. The contrast with the development of American constitutionalism is striking: the new American polity was built on the swift and impressive practical success of highly sophisticated theoretical reflection and reconceptualization. The Canadian approach was to found a new nation on theoretical assumptions that engendered opportunities for theoretical work by the generations that inherited the Constitution, and made that work a necessity.

The theorizing was rather incomplete not only through the long history of British constitutionalism, but also in the deliberations over Confederation. We do not have a

---

[5] *Secession Reference* [49] above (n 1); see below Section 8.

much more articulate account of the assumptions on which the delegates were acting than the Resolutions of the Quebec Conference in 1864: '[T]he Conference, with a view to the perpetuation of our connection with the Mother Country, and to the promotion of the best interests of the people of these Provinces, desire to follow the model of the British Constitution, so far as our circumstances will permit.'[6]

What theoretical assumptions underlay the resulting union? The notion that the model would serve 'the best interests of the people of these Provinces' can be traced back to the 'Model Parliament' of Edward I in 1295—the first to involve representation of barons, clergy, and commons. Edward and his advisors were among the earliest theorists of the Constitution: the writ summoning members to the Parliament borrowed the maxim of Roman private law that 'what touches all should be approved by all', and applied it to the government of the kingdom.[7] Herein lay the origins of representative government.

Parliament as a technique of responsible government sprang from the King's political need to secure support from the Lords and Commons for taxation; that technique would become constitutionally protected as the King was deprived by stages of the personal power of legislating: first in the *Case of Proclamations*,[8] then in the Petition of Right 1628, and finally and conclusively after the Glorious Revolution, in the Bill of Rights 1689. The judicial power, meanwhile, was separated from the executive power first by the rule that the King could not decide judicial matters in person (*Probitions del Roy*[9]), and then after the Glorious Revolution, by the provision in the Act of Settlement 1701 that judges could only be removed from office by Parliament, and not at the pleasure of the King.

Arbitrary measures by tyrants such as King John and Henry VIII had always been susceptible to criticism as abuse of the royal power;[10] the theory of monarchy never supported arbitrary rule until the Stuart kings theorized about the divine right that they began to claim in the seventeenth century.[11] After the failure of Oliver Cromwell's revolution against that absolutism, the restoration of the monarchy was not a mere traditionalist reaction; it was a deliberate and permanent rejection of presidential rule, in favour of a form of government in which power would in principle be centred in the Crown, and would in practice be controlled by a parliamentary assembly. The Glorious Revolution was a constitutional turning point, conclusively renouncing the Stuart claim of divine right. But the new constitutional settlement was not a rejection of monarchy; executive, judicial, and legislative power were united in the Crown, with the King legislating in

---

[6] Canada, Library and Archives, *Quebec Resolutions, 1864*, Resolution 3: https://www. collectionscanada.gc.ca/confederation/023001-7104-e.html.

[7] See Gaines Post, *Studies in Medieval Legal Thought: Public Law and the State 1100–1322* (Princeton University Press 1964) 163–167.

[8] (1611) 77 ER 1352.

[9] (1607) 77 ER 1342.

[10] See John Fortescue, *The Difference between an Absolute and Limited Monarchy, as It More Particularly regards the English Constitution* (1471; published 1714, Aland, John Fortescue, ed).

[11] See, e.g., *Basilikon Doron* (Edinburgh,1599), by King James VI of Scotland, who became James I of England.

Parliament, and delegating the judicial power to independent judges. The point of the new settlement was to give Parliament control over the monarchy.

By the time of Confederation, this new settlement had evolved, because of the King's need for a ministry that could raise taxes, so that the monarch exercised executive power on the advice of ministers who answered to Parliament. The result was executive government in Great Britain by a Cabinet accountable to the House of Commons, with ever-more-deeply entrenched conventions, providing, for example, that the monarch must assent to legislation and must not act contrary to her ministers' advice. So a ready model of responsible government was available to the nineteenth-century British North American colonists. It would develop into fully democratic government by sporadic steps involving the removal of property requirements for voting, the spread of the secret ballot, and votes for women, and completed only in 1960 when the federal franchise was extended to Indigenous men and women.

We will refer to this form of responsible government as 'parliamentary government'. The model was attractively different from the American model, and was attractive for reasons of Canadian politics that were similar to the reasons of the English politicians who procured the Glorious Revolution: parliamentary government would facilitate control of state power by an assembly of representatives of the very sort of people who were agreeing to Confederation.

The crux of Britain's eighteenth-century American disaster had been the radical Imperial failure to give the Thirteen Colonies either representation in Westminster, or their own effective responsible government. The British metropolis had been unresponsive to the need to adapt newly-developed theories of Westminster parliamentary sovereignty to a changing eighteenth-century colonial context. By the nineteenth century, British Imperial advisors had begun to learn their lesson. The British responded to the demand for responsible government in Upper and Lower Canada in the Act of Union, 1840. In the Confederation settlement of 1867, the Imperial Parliament willingly approved proposals from United Canada, New Brunswick, and Nova Scotia to establish responsible government on the British model. The highly-theorized republicanism of the American constitutional scheme was rejected in favour of parliamentary government, and the decentralized American model of states-rights federalism was rejected in favour of a stronger central government. The agreed division of powers was highly detailed and yet rather loosely defined, and was a further under-theorised work in progress.[12]

The delegates at the London Conference of 1866–1867 wanted to call their new country the 'Kingdom' of Canada.[13] That notion—given that their purpose was patently to

---

[12] Many of the details had already been recited in the Quebec Conference Resolutions, which referred to the provincial governments as 'Local Governments' and to the federal government as 'the General Government': Canada, Library and Archives, *Quebec Resolutions, 1864*: https://www.collectionscanada. gc.ca/confederation/023001-7104-e.html.

[13] Canada, Library and Archives, *London Conference, 1866–7*, https://www.collectionscanada.gc.ca/ confederation/023001-2700-e.html.

secure not only union but also responsible government—presumably reflected a theoretical assumption of parliamentary government, founded in the Glorious Revolution. The leaders of the colonies saw responsible government as best secured through a Parliament to which ministers of the Queen would answer. The British rejection of the idea of a 'Kingdom' in favour of a 'Dominion' reflected the mid-nineteenth-century theory of the Imperial government, according to which the traditional, distinctive relationship between the Queen and her *British* ministers was essential for Imperial governance. The most dramatic changes to the context of Canadian constitutionalism since Confederation have been the evolution in Imperial governance in the early twentieth century, and its conclusive abandonment in the patriation of the Constitution in 1982.

The central theoretical assumptions of parliamentary government, embedded in the context of ongoing Imperial governance after 1867, yielded a brilliant constitutional innovation: the establishment for a new federal country of a bicameral Parliament with an executive administration led, as in the UK, by a Cabinet appointed on the advice of a Prime Minister who has the confidence of a House of Commons.[14]

In the Quebec Conference, the theoretically significant term 'House of Commons' was adopted for the lower house to which, as in the UK, the Government would be accountable. The undertheorized conception of the new Parliament failed to establish a rationale for the upper house, but Canada's is not the only constitution that has failed to articulate the theory of an upper house. The interminable debates over more than a century about reform of the Canadian Senate are analogous to the interminable debates over more than a century about House of Lords reform in the UK. In both countries, current practice, and reforms actually made, reflect no coherent theoretical rationale for the existence, membership, and functions of the upper chamber, apart from the widely-held views in each country that there ought to be a house of sober second thought, that its composition and functions ought to differ from those of the lower house, and that the lower house ought to be predominant.

In setting out the rules for reform of the Senate in the 2014 *Reference re Senate Reform*,[15] the Supreme Court of Canada referred to 'the Senate's fundamental nature and role as a complementary legislative body of sober second thought', and as a representative of the regions that had joined Confederation, and also concluded that the Senate had provided 'a forum for ethnic, gender, religious, linguistic, and Aboriginal groups that did not always have a meaningful opportunity to present their views through the popular democratic process'.[16] But the Court was careful to restrict its own role to determining 'the legal framework' for Senate reform, and to leave the question of the desirability of reform—and therefore, the theoretical rationale for the Senate—to 'Canadians and their legislatures'.[17] The Canadian debates seem even more frustrating than the

---

[14] See Canada, Library and Archives, *Quebec Resolutions, 1864*: https://www.collectionscanada.gc.ca/confederation/023001-7104-e.html.

[15] [2014] SCC 32.

[16] Ibid [52], [16].

[17] Ibid [4].

British debates, because two huge advantages ought to facilitate intelligent reform of the Canadian Senate: it only has 105 seats (whereas the House of Lords, bloated by patronage, has more than 800 members in 2017), and Canadian federalism offers a potential basis for distinctive membership and functions (whereas the obvious potential for regional representation in the House of Lords has been lost in the noise of the debates over reform).

To summarise, the theoretical assumptions of Confederation were:

1) that parliamentary government was the best available technique of responsible self-government for those British North American colonies that were well enough developed to engage in self-government,

2) that parliamentary government was both an appropriate institutional framework for a federal union of colonies, and also compatible with exercise of substantial governmental responsibility by provinces through their own parliamentary systems, and

3) that the whole complex scheme was compatible with the status of the new country as a Dominion within the Empire.

4. PARLIAMENTARY SOVEREIGNTY AND THE CONSTITUTION

The Westminster Parliament could of course make law for the United Kingdom. The Crown had always had sovereign authority for the governance of its overseas territories. But as Parliament became sovereign, it likewise came to be presumed that Parliament was sovereign in its capacity to make law for those territories. The Westminster Parliament became an Imperial Parliament for the British Empire, and its power included the power to make constitutional laws such as the *British North America Act, 1867*.

The development of any form of colonial autonomy had to depend either on restraint in the exercise of the powers of the Westminster Parliament, or on the limitation of those powers. The debates regarding Irish Home Rule at the end of the nineteenth century highlighted a question regarding whether the Westminster Parliament could bind itself (that is, constrain the legislative freedom of future parliaments). The most influential constitutional lawyer of the time, Professor Albert Venn Dicey of the University of Oxford, argued that Home Rule legislation would be futile.[18] Parliament could make

---

[18] See C. Harvie, 'Ideology and Home Rule: James Bryce, A.V. Dicey and Ireland, 1880–1887' (1976) 91 Eng Hist Rev 298. Dicey's friend and Oxford colleague, James Bryce, stated in Parliament that Westminster 'shall retain as a matter of pure right the power to legislate for Ireland, for all purposes whatever, for the simple reason that we cannot divest ourselves of it'. United Kingdom, Parliament,

any law whatsoever, but then a later Parliament could unmake any law whatsoever. On Dicey's account, this conception of parliamentary sovereignty had an appearance of logical necessity. Parliament was sovereign. Sovereignty is the ability to govern as one wishes. Any limit on Parliament would amount to an end to its sovereignty. Therefore Dicey understood parliamentary sovereignty to entail not only the rule that Parliament can enact any law whatever, but also the corollary that no parliament can bind a future parliament.[19]

From a Canadian perspective, the sovereignty of the Westminster Parliament was initially convenient. The *Constitution Act, 1867* was an exercise of that sovereignty, and in the absence of a domestic amending formula, the Westminster Parliament would have authority to amend the 1867 Act. It was uncontroversial in legal circles that the Imperial Parliament was the proper authority for the ongoing regulation of the self-government of a colonial dominion within the Empire.

But as Canada, along with other Dominions and other parts of the Empire, began to contemplate a more complete autonomy from the United Kingdom, the doctrine of parliamentary sovereignty (or at least Dicey's dominant version of it) began to get in the way. For example, the Statute of Westminster, 1931 stated in its preamble that:

> it is in accord with the established constitutional position that no law hereafter made by the Parliament of the United Kingdom shall extend to any of the said Dominions as part of the law of that Dominion otherwise than at the request and with the consent of that Dominion . . .

But 'the established constitutional position' was undoubtedly understood to be a matter of convention, and the substantive provisions of the Statute were limited to empowering Dominions, and establishing interpretive (or at best procedural) rules regarding the Westminster Parliament's legislation for the Dominions. On Dicey's strict interpretation of parliamentary sovereignty, neither new Dominion powers, nor a constitutional convention, nor any legal provision purporting to regulate the Westminster Parliament could legally constrain that Parliament if ever it wished to legislate in any way for the Dominions.[20] And it was convenient, in Canada's case, for amendments to the *Constitution Act, 1867* (and other constitutional texts) to continue to be made by the Westminster Parliament even after 1931, Canada having failed in the lead-up to the Statute of Westminster to agree on a domestic amending formula.[21]

Debates (10 May 1886), quoted in G. Marshall, *Parliamentary Sovereignty and the Commonwealth* (Clarendon Press, 1957), 65–66. Bryce's Dicey-like statement was made one year after the publication of AV Dicey, *An Introduction to the Study of the Law of the Constitution* (1st ed. (Macmillan, 1885).

[19]   Albert Venn Dicey, *Introduction to the Study of the Law of the Constitution*, 8th ed (Macmillan 1915) 21-24.

[20]   The Supreme Court of Canada confirmed, as late as 1981, that the Westminster Parliament's powers even regarding Canada were, as a legal matter, 'untouched', or 'unimpaired'. *Patriation Reference*, above (n 1), 795, 799.

[21]   For discussion, see P Oliver, 'Canada, Quebec and Constitutional Amendment' (1999) 49 UTLJ 519.

By 1931, a 'new view' of parliamentary sovereignty was emerging in Britain: that Parliament can exercise its sovereignty only according to a certain 'manner and form', which could itself be changed by Parliament. The resulting power to determine what is to count as legislation implies a power to determine what is to count as Parliament. Although Parliament could not limit a future parliament's substantive ability to enact any law whatever, it could provide that future parliaments can legislate regarding some specified subject matter only by conforming to manner and form requirements set out in legislation. A strong version of this new view would have interpreted section 4 of the Statute of Westminster as reconstituting 'Parliament', for the purposes of that section, as Westminster acting at the request and with the consent of the Parliament of the Dominion.[22]

The sensible pragmatism of the new view initially shrouded its instability. A legislative requirement as to the manner and form of parliamentary legislation would work so long as Parliament resisted the temptation to test its sovereignty by repealing a requirement of manner and form, or simply by purporting to act through the manner and form that was in effect before such a requirement was enacted. But what if Parliament did not resist this temptation? Then Dicey's doctrine would remain intact if the courts respected the will of the originally constituted Parliament. If, however, the courts insisted that Parliament could only legislate effectively if it respected a legislative requirement as to manner and form, then Parliament would have succeeded in binding a future parliament and Dicey's doctrine would have been no more. Parliament would be sovereign in a new sense of that term: able to legislate regarding any matter whatever, *including* the matter of limiting itself.

This second version of parliamentary sovereignty came to be known as 'self-embracing sovereignty', whereas Dicey's version came to be known as 'continuing sovereignty'.[23] However, theoretical discussions regarding the sovereignty of Parliament were largely confined to books on legal and constitutional theory. In constitutional practice, temporary (if unstable) pragmatic solutions were seen as preferable to digging new foundations. We will see in a moment that when countries such as Canada sought to complete their independence, it was necessary to consider foundational questions and to make choices between the different conceptions of parliamentary sovereignty that theory had revealed.

---

[22] S. 4 stated: 'No Act of Parliament of the United Kingdom passed after the commencement of this Act shall extend, or be deemed to extend to a Dominion as part of the law of that Dominion, unless it is expressly declared in that Act that that Dominion has requested, and consented to, the enactment thereof'. See G Marshall, 'What Is an Act of Parliament: The Changing Concept of Parliamentary Sovereignty' (1954) 2 Political Studies 193, 199–200.

[23] See the discussion in HLA Hart, *The Concept of Law* (3rd ed.) (Oxford University Press 2012) 149–152.

5. FEDERALISM

The preamble to Canada's 1867 Constitution spoke of the desire of the colonies to be 'federally united', with 'a Constitution similar in Principle to that of the United Kingdom'. Dicey viewed these two objectives as incompatible with each other, and he viewed the combination as 'official mendacity'.[24] A Constitution similar in Principle to that of the United Kingdom would include the doctrine of parliamentary sovereignty, and, in Dicey's view, parliamentary sovereignty was incompatible with the division of sovereign powers contemplated by federalism.[25] But Dicey only began to share such views in the 1880s, by which time Confederation was well into its second decade.

Furthermore, many Canadian politicians, most notably its first Prime Minister, John A. Macdonald, favoured a unitary rather than a federal form of government. Many of them looked on the civil war in the federal United States as a salutary lesson in what to avoid. But union would have been politically impossible without a federal division of powers. Colonies which would be greatly outnumbered in population in the new Dominion would not risk seeing their interests submerged or overtaken without the guarantee that a range of local matters would fall to the jurisdiction of local assemblies. Federalism was the only way forward, and the *Constitution Act, 1867* listed the respective powers of the federal Parliament and the provincial legislatures, as set out, for the most part, in sections 91 and 92.[26]

From 1867 until 1931, the highest court of appeal for Canada in civil and criminal matters,[27] the Judicial Committee of the Privy Council, interpreted sections 91 and 92 and thereby put flesh on the bare bones that the constitutional division of powers had set up. The heads of power allowed considerable latitude for interpretation, but the framers had suggested a strong centralizing tilt: the opening words to section 91 gave authority to the federal Parliament 'to make Laws for the Peace, Order, and good Government of Canada' and seemed to make it clear that any powers not expressly allocated to the provinces would fall to the federal side. The federal Parliament was given the authority to claim jurisdiction over works declared to be for the general benefit of Canada, and had jurisdiction over two of the most important heads of power, 'trade and commerce' and 'criminal law'.

The division of powers had implications for the Empire, because a strong central government was more likely to challenge Imperial policy. So the theoretical assumptions

---

[24] AV Dicey, 'Federal Government' (1885) 1 LQR 80, 93. For discussion see Peter C Oliver, *The Constitution of Independence: The Development of Constitutional Theory in Australia, Canada and New Zealand* (Oxford University Press, 2005) 119.

[25] Ibid 119.

[26] Canada's federal system is discussed in detail in Part IV of this *Handbook*.

[27] Canadian civil appeals to the Judicial Committee of the Privy Council were not abolished until 1949. David B. Swinfen, *Imperial Appeal: The Debate on the Appeal to the Privy Council, 1833–1986* (Manchester University Press, 1987), 143.

that shaped the development of Canadian federalism involved three levels of governance. The Privy Council, exercising the constitution-building task of filling in the sketch of federalism in the *British North America Act*, interpreted the division of powers in favour of greater provincial powers.[28] Of course, some cases went one way and others the other way, which might have prompted contemporary observers to see matters as nothing more than the normal evolution of court-made law. However, we can now see more clearly that division-of-powers jurisprudence in the early years was driven in large measure by a theory of federalism motivated by a conception of the Imperial interest.[29] Subsequent developments, directed by the Supreme Court of Canada, responded to the demands of an increasingly complex and interrelated North American and global economy.

6. CONSTITUTIONAL INTERPRETATION

The *Statute of Westminster, 1931* placed new pressures on the interpretation of what was then called the *British North America Act, 1867*. The Act had been drafted with a continuing role in mind for the Westminster Parliament and the Judicial Committee of the Privy Council at the top of, respectively, the legislative and judicial hierarchies. It could not be said, for example, that the framers of the 1867 Act intended for the Parliament of Canada to legislate to end appeals to the Privy Council when it granted Parliament power over 'criminal law'. They must have assumed, if they thought about it at all, that changing the role of the Imperial Privy Council in the judicial hierarchy was beyond the powers of the new Canadian Parliament. However, when the *Statute of Westminster, 1931* gave Dominions the power to legislate extraterritorially and to amend or repeal UK legislation, the question arose whether the power to legislate in relation to 'criminal law' could embrace legislation ending Privy Council appeals in criminal matters.[30] A number of approaches to constitutional interpretation were possible.

On the one hand, the Constitution could be interpreted as conferring on the new institutions the powers that the British Parliament intended to confer in 1867. On this basis, ending appeals to the Privy Council in criminal matters would not have been

---

[28] For an account of the evolution of interpretation of the key heads of legislative power under sections 91 and 92 of the *Constitution Act, 1867*, see the chapter by Jean-François Gaudreault-Desbiens and Johanne Poirier in this *Handbook* and PW Hogg, *Constitutional Law of Canada* (5th ed., Carswell, 2007), section 5.3(c).

[29] See Frederick Vaughan, *Viscount Haldane: 'The Wicked Step-Father of the Canadian Constitution'* (University of Toronto Press, 2010).

[30] Those familiar with the Canadian division of powers may wonder why the residual 'peace, order and good government' power was not invoked as a full answer to the question. It must be remembered that at this moment in Canada's constitutional history, the Privy Council had reduced that power to an 'emergency' power, available only at times of war or other crisis. See *Reference Re Board of Commerce Act, 1919 (Canada)*, [1922] 1 A.C. 191 (P.C.); *Toronto Electric Commissioners v Snider*, [1925] A.C. 396 (P.C.).

within the power given to the federal Parliament, as such a power would have involved legislative amendment of Imperial statutes dealing with extraterritorial subject matter, i.e the power of the British Privy Council. On the other hand, it was possible to assume that, as a document prepared with longevity in mind, the Constitution was designed to adapt to the changing circumstances in which it would be applied, so that the meaning of its terms could evolve in accordance with the evolution of the Canadian polity. On this basis, and given that the words 'criminal law' were broad enough to embrace an expansive interpretation of the Parliament of Canada's post-1931 powers, the legislation would be *intra vires*.

These issues regarding constitutional interpretation were addressed shortly before the 1931 Statute of Westminster was enacted, in one of the most famous cases in Canadian constitutional law: the *Persons Case*.[31] The issue in that case was whether women could be considered 'qualified persons' for appointment to the Senate of Canada, under the *British North America Act*. All the judges of the Supreme Court of Canada concluded that they could not, on the grounds that (1) such was not the 'intent' of the Westminster Parliament in passing the Act, and (2) the words of the Act 'bear to-day the same construction which the courts would, if then required to pass upon them, have given to them when they were first enacted'.[32]

The Privy Council reversed that decision. Viscount Sankey considered both external and internal evidence. Regarding the former, he noted that 'the exclusion of women from all public offices is a relic of days more barbarous than ours'. He set out a reminder that the Act in question was not a fossil but rather 'a living tree capable of growth and expansion within its natural limits'.[33] He emphasized that courts should avoid 'a narrow and technical construction' and should instead favour 'a large and liberal interpretation' so as to allow the Dominion and the provinces respectively to be 'mistresses' in their own houses 'within certain fixed limits'.[34] Their Lordships were after all concerned with the interpretation of '. . . an Act which creates a Constitution for a new country'.[35] With regard to the meaning of the term 'persons', he noted that 'the word "person" may include members of both sexes', and that the burden of persuasion lay upon those who argued that it should not. By means of this combination of external and internal considerations, the Privy Council concluded that women were indeed 'qualified persons'.

Contemporary readers of the *Persons Case* seem to have had no doubt as to its meaning and importance. Chief Justice Anglin had written the lead judgment for the Supreme Court of Canada in the *Persons Case*. The Privy Council had renounced his view of the *British North America Act*—that its provisions 'bear to-day the same construction

---

[31] *Edwards v Attorney General of Canada* [1931] AC 124 (PC) [hereinafter *the Persons Case*]. For an excellent account of the background to *the Persons Case*, see Robert Sharpe and Patricia McMahon, The Persons Case: *The Origins and Legacy of the Fight for Legal Personhood* (University of Toronto Press, 2007).

[32] *Reference re meaning of the word "Persons"* [1928] SCR 276 Anglin CJ (285).

[33] Ibid (136).

[34] Ibid.

[35] Ibid (137).

which the courts would, if then required to pass upon them, have given to them when they were first enacted'.[36] When, only a few years later, he came to consider whether the *Constitution Act, 1867* accorded jurisdiction over 'radio', Anglin CJ had no doubt as to what was now required:

> if the Act is to be viewed, as recently suggested by their Lordships of the Privy Council in *Edwards* v. *Attorney-General of Canada* as a living tree, capable of growth and expansion within its natural limits, and if it should be on all occasions interpreted in a large, liberal and comprehensive spirit, considering the magnitude of the subjects with which it purports to deal in very few words, and bearing in mind that we are concerned with the interpretation of an Imperial Act, but an Imperial Act creating a Constitution for a new country, every effort should be made to find . . . some head of legislative jurisdiction capable of including the subject matter of this reference . . . [37]

There is nothing in Anglin's words that limits the court's consideration to what the framers intended in 1867, or the meaning of the constitutional text of 1867. Rather, having seen his essentially originalist interpretation overruled in the *Persons Case*, Anglin was now treating the *British North America Act* as having a legal effect that could change ('within its natural limits') in accordance with changes in circumstances, and in accordance with 'the reasonably broad construction of which [the words are] susceptible'.

Four years later, in the *British Coal Corporation* case, the Privy Council interpreted Parliament's power, including the 'criminal law' power, to allow Canadian legislation to end Privy Council appeals in criminal matters, despite the fact that such a measure could not have been contemplated in 1867 when, as already noted, Parliament had no power to legislate either in a manner repugnant to Imperial statutes or extraterritorially. Viscount Sankey cited the *Persons Case* as authority for favouring a 'large and liberal' interpretation over a 'narrow and technical' one: 'In interpreting a constituent or organic statute such as the Act, that construction most beneficial to the widest possible amplitude of its powers must be adopted'.[38] An interpretation frozen in 1867 would have made this conclusion impossible, but the living tree view (taking into account Canada's growth from colony to nation) allowed this further devolution of power to Canada without the need for constitutional amendment.

---

[36] *Reference re meaning of the word "Persons" in s. 24 of British North America Act*, [1928] SCR 276, 282.

[37] *Reference re Regulation and Control of Radio Communication* [1931] SCR 541, 546.

[38] *British Coal Corporation and others v The King* [1935] UKPC 33, [1935] AC 500, 518. The Privy Council's focus in this case was on the removal of obstacles which had been deemed before 1931 (in the case of *Nadan v The King* [1926] AC 482) to prohibit such Canadian legislation. However, even with those obstacles removed, post-1931, Canadian legislation had to be anchored in a head of federal power in order to be considered valid. As noted by the Board in *British Coal Corporation*, ibid, the Privy Council in *Nadan* had already begun to ask questions regarding *vires* or competence: 'Under what authority, then, can a right [of Privy Council appeals] so established and confirmed be abrogated by the Parliament of Canada? The British North America Act, by section 91, empowered the Dominion Parliament . . . ; and in particular it gave to the Canadian Parliament exclusive legislative authority in respect of "the criminal law . . . "'. The Privy Council In Nadan had not had to answer the question whether the criminal law power was broad enough. That answer was provided in *British Coal Corporation*.

Twelve years later, in a challenge to the termination by the federal Parliament of all remaining appeals to the Privy Council, the Lord Chancellor, Lord Jowitt, once again favoured an interpretation that took into account Canada's social and political evolution: 'It is . . . irrelevant that the question is one that might have seemed unreal at the date of the *British North America Act*. To such an organic statute the flexible interpretation must be given which changing circumstances require . . . '.[39] Lord Jowitt approved his predecessor Viscount Sankey's approach to constitutional interpretation, in referring both to the 'living tree' approach ('flexible interpretation . . . which changing circumstances require') and to the idea of an 'organic' statute.

The living tree approach is now very much the dominant theory of constitutional interpretation in Canada.[40] Viscount Sankey and his successors clearly treated the Constitution as a document that is to be interpreted, so far as possible, in ways that respond not only to the emergence of unforeseen technologies such as radio, but also to changes in Canadian society. And the judges' response to such changes may depart from the intention of the framers, and from the original meaning of the words they used.

A tree is a fairly rigid biological structure that regulates its own growth in a way that sustains its identity as the same tree from season to season. A theory of living tree constitutional interpretation allocates power to judges to change the Constitution, and the use of the power must be regulated. The constitutional amendment process may provide a way of checking that dynamic judicial function.[41] But constitutional amendment ought to be (and certainly is, in the case of the Canadian Constitution) a very difficult way of regulating the judicial power. So a complete living tree theory needs an account of judicial self-regulation.

Wil Waluchow has argued that the living tree approach treats the content of a constitution as a matter of common law.[42] The idea offers an attractive account of the practice of Canadian constitutional interpretation since the *Persons Case*. There is a difference,

---

[39] *Attorney-General for Ontario v Attorney-General for Canada* [1947] AC 127, 154. In the 1947 case, the interpretation issue turned on the meaning of s. 101 of the *Constitution Act, 1867*.

[40] For more on the question of constitutional interpretation, see the chapters in this *Handbook* by respectively, Stéphane Beaulac and WJ Waluchow. For a sceptical view regarding the living tree, see, e.g., B Miller, 'Origin Myth: *The Persons Case*, the Living Tree, and the New Originalism' in G Huscroft and B Miller, eds. *The Challenge of Originalism* (Cambridge University Press, 2011) 120. The Canadian constitutional historian, Eric Adams, has written, convincingly it is argued here, that 'The living tree metaphor has been largely embraced as an approach to liberal and progressive constitutional interpretation, but in its own time and context, set against the backdrop of the Balfour Declaration, the politics of independence, and on the eve of the passage of the Statute of Westminster, 1931, the living tree was an expression and confirmation of Canada's constitutional distinctiveness and independence'. E Adams, 'Canadian Constitutional Identities' (2015) 38 Dalhousie LJ 311, footnote 78 and accompanying text.

[41] In respect of the *Charter of Rights and Freedoms*, the s 33 'notwithstanding' clause also provides a potential check on the judicial interpretive function, but that technique also is, for other reasons, difficult for the legislatures to use.

[42] WJ Waluchow, 'Constitutionalism', in E Zalta, ed, *The Stanford Encyclopedia of Philosophy* (Spring 2014 Edition), http://plato.stanford.edu/archives/spr2014/entries/constitutionalism/.

insofar as judges' decisions in the development of most of the common law can be revised by the legislature, whereas their interpretations of the Constitution can only be revised, if at all, by their own subsequent decisions or by constitutional amendment. But the common law approach gives the judges the opportunity to use their constitutive power responsibly. Waluchow writes that the rules of precedent 'combine respect for the (albeit limited) wisdom and authority of previous decision makers (legislative and judicial) with an awareness of the need to allow adaptation in the face of changing views, and new or unforeseen circumstances'.[43] The common law approach equips judges to do so in a way that is both creative and responsible. It also equips them to act irresponsibly, treating their whims as matters of principle, and their judgments of principle as the law of the Constitution. The common law process confers responsibility on the judges, from case to case, to distinguish responsible from irresponsible use of a constitutive power.

That distinction will never be completely theorized. The practice of living tree constitutional interpretation may proceed with no articulate doctrine specifying the distinction between sensitive and sensible interpretation of the Constitution, and 'unconstrained constitutional creation or construction masquerading as interpretation'.[44]

7. Constitutional Theory at and after Patriation: Principles and Politics

Soon after Canada celebrated its centenary, Prime Minister Pierre Elliott Trudeau sought to put the country's constitutional affairs in order by patriating the Constitution and providing for a domestic general amending formula. He sought at the same time to change the structure of the Constitution by adopting a modern *Charter of Rights and Freedoms* and by recognizing Aboriginal rights. By 1980 it was clear to Trudeau and his government that the consent of all the provinces for these changes was not forthcoming, and that the Canadian Parliament would have to proceed unilaterally to patriate the Constitution and to adopt a domestic amending formula and *Charter*. Both Houses of the Canadian Parliament adopted a resolution which was then sent on to Westminster for enactment by the United Kingdom Parliament. Two provinces, Ontario and New Brunswick, supported the unilateral federal initiative, but eight provinces did not. Three of the eight referred the question of constitutionality to their Courts of Appeal, and eventually all three appeals came before the Supreme Court of Canada in what has come to be known as the *Patriation Reference*.[45]

---

[43] Ibid.
[44] Ibid.
[45] *Patriation Reference*, above (n 1).

The questions were essentially as follows: (1) did the federal resolution to amend the Constitution affect the powers, rights, and privileges of the provinces? (2) was the consent of the provinces required by the law of the Constitution? and (3) was there a constitutional convention requiring the consent of the provinces?

The Supreme Court of Canada's eventual judgment was that provincial powers, rights, and privileges were of course affected. Different majorities of the Court then concluded that although provincial consent was not legally required, at the very least a substantial degree of provincial consent was required by convention. The conclusion regarding constitutional convention made it politically impossible for the Trudeau government to proceed, and that decision led to the reconvening of first ministers in November 1981 and the agreement (with all provinces, other than the province of Quebec) on the new constitutional settlement which became the *Constitution Act, 1982*.

The part of the *Patriation Reference* that deals with constitutional law is particularly revealing regarding the theoretical assumptions that were prevalent at that time. It is notable, especially in light of Supreme Court of Canada decisions in later years, how restricted were the constitutional resources that the majority brought to bear on the legal question of the lawfulness of petitioning the British Parliament to amend the Constitution without consent of the provinces. That fundamental legal question had never before been presented to any court. And yet the majority refrained from appealing to the principles of the Constitution to fill this gap in Canadian constitutional law, as it might later have been expected to do. Counsel encouraged the Court to let constitutional principles such as federalism and the rule of law into Canadian constitutional law via the 1867 Act's preambular reference to 'a Constitution similar in Principle to that of the United Kingdom', but the Court turned down the invitation, emphasizing the non-binding nature of preambles.[46] This approach contrasts sharply with the Supreme Court of Canada's later treatment of the same preamble as an invitation to bring principle to bear on the development of Canadian constitutional law.[47]

We should perhaps be careful not to overstate the resistance to arguments of principle in 1981. First of all, the majority did appeal to constitutional principle in exercising the Court's extraordinary authority to pronounce on the existence of a constitutional convention.[48] Second, Martland and Ritchie JJ, in their dissent on the question of law, argued that the courts had 'had occasion to develop legal principles based on the necessity of preserving the integrity of the federal structure', and concluded that 'the dominant principle of Canadian constitutional law is federalism'.[49] But it is fair to say that the theoretical

---

[46] Ibid 804–805.

[47] See, e.g., *Reference re Provincial Judges* [1997] 3 SCR 3 and *Secession Reference*, above (n 1).

[48] ' . . . the phrases "Constitution of Canada" and "Canadian Constitution" . . . embrace the global system of rules and principles which govern the exercise of constitutional authority in the whole and in every part of the Canadian state'. *Patriation Reference*, above (n 1) 874.

[49] Ibid 821. It is not surprising, therefore, that the Supreme Court of Canada later cited the views of Martland and Ritchie JJ in the *Patriation Reference* in support of a more creative use of principles in constitutional adjudications. See *Secession Reference*, above (n 1) [32].

assumptions of the majority in the *Patriation Reference* yielded a limited set of sources for interpretation of the law of the Constitution: essentially, the text of the Constitution, legislation, and prior case law on point. Where the judges found no guidance in these sources, they would be trammeled by their sense that they would, on their own terms, be creating law, rather than applying the existing law. Without orthodox legal signposts, judges were reluctant to fill gaps in constitutional law using abstract, open-textured principles. This reluctance had roots in a form of political constitutionalism which favoured democratic law-making via a sovereign parliament over judicial law-making.

Returning to the nature of the Westminster Parliament's sovereignty discussed earlier in this chapter, we have seen that the Supreme Court judges understood the power of the United Kingdom Parliament to legislate for Canada as unimpaired even as late as the *Patriation Reference*. How then could this unimpaired sovereign legislature limit itself as it purported to do in 1982? And how could the Supreme Court of Canada claim in the 1982 *Quebec Veto Reference* that the United Kingdom Parliament had been 'entirely replace[d]' and that the legality of this process was 'neither challenged nor assailable'?[50] The Supreme Court of Canada seemed to have opted for the self-embracing interpretation of parliamentary sovereignty identified above.[51]

Only three years after the 1982 patriation, a Supreme Court of Canada which had been reluctant to embrace constitutional principles in 1981 was very willing to do so in 1985, in *Reference re Manitoba Language Rights*.[52] Even more so in the 1990s, notably in the famous *Secession Reference* of 1998, the Supreme Court based its conclusions as to the law of the Constitution on principles implicit in the nation's constitutional documents, and more broadly in 'an historical lineage stretching back through the ages'.[53]

8. PRINCIPLES UNTRAMMELED

Almost one hundred years of Manitoba statutes had been enacted in English only, contrary to what the Supreme Court of Canada deemed, in the 1985 *Manitoba Language Reference*, to be a constitutional requirement of bilingual enactment. The Court recognized that striking down all of the Province's statute law would cause legal chaos, a result antithetical to the principle of the rule of law.[54] Accordingly, the Court decided 'to deem temporarily valid and effective the unilingual Acts of the Legislature of Manitoba' for the

---

[50]   *Quebec Veto Reference* [1982] 2 SCR 793, 806.

[51]   See above (n 23) and related text.

[52]   *Reference re Manitoba Language Rights* [1985] 1 SCR 721, 750 [hereinafter *Manitoba Language Reference*]. Rand J had held in *Roncarelli v Duplessis*, [1959] SCR 121, 142, that the rule of law is 'a fundamental postulate of our constitutional structure'.

[53]   *Secession Reference*, above (n 1) [49].

[54]   Ibid [59]–[66].

period of time needed for the laws to be published in French.[55] The Court held very clearly that the *principle* of the rule of law had a legal effect that derived from the Constitution:

> Additional to the inclusion of the rule of law in the preambles of the *Constitution Acts* of 1867 and 1982, the principle is clearly implicit in the very nature of a Constitution. The Constitution, as the Supreme Law, must be understood as a purposive ordering of social relations providing a basis upon which an actual order of positive laws can be brought into existence.... While this is not set out in a specific provision, the principle of the rule of law is clearly a principle of our Constitution.[56]

Before 1985, Canadian constitutional lawyers did not speak of 'common law constitutionalism'. Nor would they have considered requesting that the courts recognize new constitutional law by way of deduction from unwritten constitutional principles. Yet such arguments have become a standard feature of constitutional practice, in a process that developed after the patriation of the Constitution and after the *Manitoba Language Reference*, and which is best illustrated by the *Secession Reference* 1998.[57]

In the *Secession Reference*, the unanimous Court began by stating, 'it is not possible to answer the questions that have been put to us without a consideration of a number of underlying principles'.[58] The constitutional question was whether the Quebec National Assembly or the government of Quebec could 'effect the secession of Quebec from Canada unilaterally?'[59] Nothing in the Constitution of Canada accorded any legal significance to a unilateral decision by a province to secede. The Supreme Court held that 'The secession of a province from Canada must be considered, in legal terms, to require an amendment to the Constitution, which perforce requires negotiation'.[60] Under the approach of the majority in the *Patriation Reference*, it might have seemed enough to assert that legal truism. It would seem that the other provinces and the federal government could have no legal obligation to cooperate with a decision by Quebec to secede. Given the paucity of Canadian secession precedents, constitutional conventions were not a promising avenue of argument. From the 1981 perspective, any other judicial directives on the issue would seem to involve extra-legal judicial fiat.

But the Supreme Court of Canada embarked on a systematic commentary on the unwritten principles that are to be found implicit in the Canadian Constitution, supporting an assertion of four principles: democracy, federalism, the rule of law and

---

[55] Ibid [84], [150].

[56] Ibid [64]. The Court pointed out that existing doctrines such as the de facto doctrine, res judicata, and mistake of law could remedy the potential chaos to some extent, but it was clear that the general principle of the rule of law was doing the fundamental work. Interestingly, the Court cited the minority (law) in the *Patriation Reference* in support of its method.

[57] See the chapters in this Handbook by, respectively, Jean Leclair and Warren Newman.

[58] *Secession Reference* above (n 1) [1].

[59] Ibid [2].

[60] Ibid [84].

constitutionalism, and protection of minorities. The Court derived from these principles what many have viewed as a Solomon-like judgment. A clear democratic vote in a province on a clear question in a secession referendum could not simply be ignored by the federal government and the other Canadian provincial governments, for to do so would be to undervalue the *democratic* principle. However, that same vote could not justify the bypassing of the Canadian constitutional amending formula, for to do so would be to undervalue the *rule of law*. Accordingly, a clear vote on a clear question could give rise to a duty to negotiate secession; however, those negotiations could only lawfully result in the secession of Quebec through a constitutional amendment according to the terms of the Constitution.

The Court in 1998 found a way to articulate the fundamentals of the Constitution without in any way distinguishing the law from the principles of political morality on which the federal and provincial governments ought to act, if the people of Quebec were to vote to secede. On the ground of those principles, the unanimous Court held that the participants in Confederation had a duty 'to engage in Constitutional discussions in order to acknowledge and address democratic expressions of a desire for change in other provinces';[61] the Court did not propose to enforce this duty, but simply declared its existence. We will call that the '*Secession Reference* approach'. In 1981 and 1982, the Court had felt inhibited from engaging in such an untrammeled articulation of constitutional principles. We will call that the '*Patriation Reference* approach'. In the twenty-first century, there is a clear, shared understanding among the judges that this theoretical task of articulating the principles of the Constitution—exercised in the *Secession Reference*—is inherent in the judges' constitutional role. It is unclear, however, whether the judges will strike down statutes purely on the ground of incompatibility with unwritten principles: 'in a Constitutional democracy such as ours, protection from legislation that some might view as unjust or unfair properly lies not in the amorphous underlying principles of our Constitution, but in its text and the ballot box'.[62]

---

[61] Ibid [69].

[62] *British Columbia v Imperial Tobacco Canada Ltd* [2005] 2 SCR 473 [66]. Cf. 'The unwritten principles must be balanced against the principle of Parliamentary sovereignty': *Babcock v Canada* [2002] 3 SCR 3 [55]. And yet it was also said in *Babcock* that 'the unwritten constitutional principles are capable of limiting government actions': ibid [54]. On whether unwritten principles can provide a ground for quashing statutes see G. Régimbald and D. Newman, *The Law of the Canadian Constitution* (LexisNexis, 2013) 114–122. It is noteworthy that *Charter* rights are subject to limitation under s 1, and to legislative override under s 33, neither of which purport to apply to unwritten principles; quashing statutes for incompatibility with unwritten constitutional principles would provide even greater entrenchment than under the *Charter* for standards that are potentially even more abstract and unspecific than the *Charter* rights. Rothstein J, dissenting, pointed out this issue in *Trial Lawyers Association of British Columbia v BC* [2014] 3 SCR 31.

9. THE LIVING TREE, PRINCIPLES
AND THE NATURE OF LAW

When the Canadian judges interpret the Constitution, they treat it as a living tree. And they identify unwritten principles that 'are to the Constitution what sap is to a tree'.[63] What answer does this approach imply to our theoretical question of the relation between the law and the moral principles that ought to guide the structure and conduct of government? The *Patriation Reference* approach may seem to reflect the 'sources thesis' that is commonly ascribed to legal positivism: the claim that the law can be identified by reference to its sources, without evaluative or moral reasoning.[64] And then it may seem attractive to distinguish the *Secession Reference* approach as anti-positivist.[65]

Chief Justice McLachlin has taken the lead in theorizing the *Secession Reference* approach; she has said that '[t]he contemporary concept of unwritten constitutional principles can be seen as a modern reincarnation of the ancient doctrines of natural law'.[66] A natural law theory identifies principles of reason, and explains their relation to the law of a particular polity at a particular time, and explains how those principles of reason give moral force to that law.[67] Two features distinguish the Chief Justice's theory from the ancient doctrines of natural law theory. First, she identifies three 'sources' of the unwritten principles of constitutional law: 'customary usage; inferences from written constitutional principles; and the norms set out or implied in international legal

---

[63] *Quebec v Canada* [2015] 1 SCR 693 [144].

[64] See Joseph Raz, *The Authority of Law* (2nd ed Oxford University Press, 2009) 47, 296. Leslie Green has identified legal positivism with the sources thesis: L Green, 'Legal Positivism', in EN Zalta ed, *The Stanford Encyclopedia of Philosophy* (Fall 2009 Edition) http://plato.stanford.edu/archives/fall2009/entries/legal-positivism/. For further linking of legal positivism and the sources thesis, see J. Gardner, 'Legal Positivism: 5 1/2 Myths' (2001) 46 Am J Juris 199.

[65] Some have considered a theory to be anti-positivist if it 'claims that the concept of law is not properly understood unless law is seen as having some essential, or internal, conceptual connection with human value' (Roger Shiner, *Norm and Nature* (Oxford University Press, 1992) 261. But various theories adopting the sources thesis, and widely understood as forms of 'legal positivism' (including those of Raz, Green, Gardner) have identified essential, conceptual connections between law and value. For present purposes we will count a theory as 'anti-positivist' if it argues in favour of a conceptual connection between law and morality that is incompatible with the sources thesis. The interpretive theory of Ronald Dworkin, discussed below, is an example; it is controversial whether classical natural law theory is an example.

[66] Beverley McLachlin, 'Unwritten Constitutional Principles: What Is Going On?' (2006) 4 NZJPIL 147; for a critique of McLachlin's approach see Grégoire Webber, 'Originalism's Constitution' in G Huscroft and B Miller, eds, *The Challenge of Originalism* (Cambridge University Press, 2011) 147, 168.

[67] Such a theory departs from 'legal positivism' in Leslie Green's sense, if it claims that any complete explanation of the existence and content of the law of (e.g.) Canada necessarily refers to the principles of reason that the theory identifies. The foremost articulation of such a theory is John Finnis, *Natural Law and Natural Rights* (2nd ed Oxford University Press, 2011).

instruments to which the state has adhered'.[68] These sources are evidently intended to play a different role from the authoritative role of sources in legal positivism; in McLachlin's theory they serve to legitimize the role of the judges in articulating unwritten principles. But if judges appeal to *sources*, then they are not giving effect to natural principles of justice; they are finding support for their judgments in the facts of the community's usage, and in the written Constitution, and in international commitments. That appeal to the community's standards does imply a judicial claim to the authority to identify those standards, and authority to act on them. As argued above concerning the living tree approach to interpretation of the text of the Constitution, this model of the identification of unwritten principles might best be likened to a common law model of constitutional principles in general, which portrays judges as exercising a power to identify and to elaborate on the community's standards.

Second, a natural law theory in the classic sense needs a theory of the allocation of power: specifically, a theory of the allocation of political authority, which is a form of legitimate normative power. The predicament of the state in natural law theory is that principles of reason depend for their implementation on the judgement and action of officials of the state, who may be reasonable or unreasonable. It is undoubtedly the case, as McLachlin says (and it is indeed a tenet of classical natural law theory), that 'the legitimacy of the modern democratic state arguably depends on its adhesion to fundamental norms that transcend the law and executive action';[69] it does not follow that judges must have authority to determine those norms, or that they should have the distinctively Canadian authority to advise government on the requirements of constitutional duty in general. There can be no natural allocation of authority; any actual allocation is an artifact that meets the state's need for authoritative decision making. The proper allocation of *constitutive* authority depends on the particularities of the political structure and culture and circumstances of the community. Classical natural law theory never presumed that constitutive authority ought to be allocated to judges.

The *Secession Reference* approach is only compatible with a natural law theory if such a theory can be supplemented by a justification for the allocation of constitutive authority (that is, authority to establish the principles of the Constitution) to the judges. The *Secession Reference* approach, and Chief Justice McLachlin's account of the identification of unwritten principles, are also compatible with a legal positivist theory, with the proviso that the 'sources' that they use for the identification of the principles of the Constitution are diffuse and undefined, and the principles vague. So, to the extent that the Canadian judges follow McLachlin's approach, a positivist account of the *Secession Reference* approach will depict them as inventing new norms for the Constitution, through a precedent-based system of judicial identification and elaboration of the community's ethos.

[68] McLachlin, above (n 66), 16.
[69] Ibid 9.

The judges and other theorists who applaud the *Secession Reference* approach are rather more inclined to say that the judges are giving effect to the law, rather than that they are inventing it. For them, the 'interpretive' theory of Ronald Dworkin holds out an alternative. In Canadian law schools, that theory was gaining widespread influence (and attracting dissent, as well) just at the time of the shift from the *Patriation Reference* approach to the *Secession Reference* approach. In 1985, Dworkin set out his avowedly anti-positivist views in one of the most-read books of legal philosophy: *Law's Empire*.[70] The theory was that the law *is* an ensemble of unwritten principles. It cannot be identified by asking what legal authorities have laid down; judges must identify the law by asking which 'constructive interpretation' best fits the facts of their community's practice, and best justifies coercion by the state. Even the many lawyers in the 1980s who had not read *Law's Empire* were indirectly influenced by Dworkin's ideas, whether in the reconstruction of legal argumentation as taught in law faculties, or in novel legal arguments presented by creative advocates across the Canadian legal community.[71]

Dworkin's interpretive theory has seemed to many to defend bold judicial activism—and to paint it as giving effect to the law. But the theory gives no general account of how closely a judge's interpretation must 'fit' the facts of a community's practice, or of how free the judges are to impose a justification of state coercion that does not fit the facts very well. In fact, a legal positivist theory may actually offer a judge *more* freedom: on Dworkin's interpretive theory, the judge must always be seeking to fit her judgments to her community's practice. She may come up with a surprising interpretation, but she is always constrained by the facts of the practice. A legal positivist may see it as potentially legitimate (and even as morally obligatory) for a judge to depart from the law, where the practice is itself immoral. A natural law theorist may differ from a legal positivist, on this point, only by insisting on a working presumption that a judge ought not to depart from the law of a constitution, except on stringent grounds of justice that undermine the claim to authority of the framers of the constitution.

Unlike a natural law theory (but in line with Chief Justice McLachlin's approach), Dworkin's theory appealed to the interpretation of the facts of the community's practice in identifying principles; like Chief Justice McLachlin (and unlike natural law theorists), he held a general theoretical tenet that the courts, as the 'forum of principle',[72] are *the* body that has legitimacy to identify constitutional principles, and to impose its view of those principles on the representative institutions of the state.

The lure of Dworkin's theory, and its congruence with McLachlin's approach, lie mainly in its portrayal of the identification of unwritten principles by judges as the

---

[70] *Law's Empire* (Harvard University Press, 1986).

[71] Dworkin's approach has particular affinities for common law method. However, civil law Quebec has by no means been insulated from the influence of Dworkin's approach, notably in constitutional argument. See, e.g., F. Gélinas, 'Les conventions, le droit et la Constitution du Canada dans le renvoi sur la "sécession" du Québec: le fantôme du rapatriement' (1997) 57 Revue du Barreau du Québec 291, 323 and Luc Tremblay, 'La théorie constitutionnelle et la primauté de droit' (1994) 39 McGill LJ 101, 104.

[72] R Dworkin, 'The Forum of Principle' (1981) 56 NYUL Rev 469, reprinted as chapter 2 of *A Matter of Principle* (Oxford University Press, 1985).

identification of the law itself. The subsidiary similarity is their approach to what McLachlin calls 'sources'. In her approach as in Dworkin's, the relevant facts about the practice of the community—including the fact of the enactment of the *Constitution Act, 1867*—are raw material on which the judge is to train his or her political-moral imagination, rather than authoritative, Constitution-making acts of political institutions separate from the judiciary.

10. CONCLUSION: CONSTITUTIONAL LAW IN CONTEXT

This discussion of the role of theory in Canadian constitutional law reminds us that theory can never remain entirely abstract. The sort of practical reasoning which theory calls on us to conduct inevitably involves general principles; yet it inevitably takes place in a particular context. Where legal matters are concerned, it is that context which generates both legal disputes and pressures for legal change, and it is that context in which new judgments and new laws will play out, successfully or unsuccessfully.

The most dramatic change to the context of Canadian constitutionalism has been the country's evolution from colony, to Dominion, to independent nation. These changes have made such new and unanticipated demands on the Constitution that it is worth reflecting that the basic structure has been remarkably robust. The form of parliamentary government chosen in 1867 has proved durable, for the same reasons that it appealed to the English bourgeoisie of the 1680s, in a strikingly different political context. In that context there was no political imperative for full democracy, but there was a very pressing demand for more accountable government, and the parliamentary form chosen in 1689 (as it developed into Cabinet government by the nineteenth century) has proved serviceable in Victorian Canada, and in the twenty-first century Canadian democracy.

The dogmas of Dicey's interpretation of the 'continuing' sovereignty of the Westminster Parliament encountered new facts and new contexts in the form of demands for independence. Although adherence to the traditional doctrine of 'continuing' sovereignty is still strong in the United Kingdom, it seems clear that many former colonies, including former Dominions such as Canada, have assumed without hesitation that the Westminster Parliament is capable of fully and finally limiting itself (the newer 'self-embracing' view) in independence legislation.[73] Neither the old nor the new, neither the more rigid nor the more flexible interpretation of sovereignty, is theoretically ordained for parliamentary government in all contexts; however, the Canadian

---

[73] For further discussion, see P Oliver, 'Change in the Ultimate Rule of a Legal System: Uncertainty, Hard Cases, Commonwealth Precedents, and the Importance of Context' (2015) 26 King's LJ 367.

context has appeared to demand a new approach. From the perspective of that new context, the Westminster Parliament acted on the basis of the theoretical assumption that it was competent to terminate its own powers to legislate for Canada, in the *Canada Act, 1982*.[74]

We have seen that the Canadian encounters with shifting contexts produced other important constitutional moments which are relevant to the role of constitutional theory. Canada's version of federalism was affected, first, by the Judicial Committee of the Privy Council's attempts to regulate Canada's, and other Dominions', role in the political economy of the British Empire and Commonwealth; and later by the Supreme Court of Canada's development of an increasingly 'cooperative' federalism that could work in a world of ever-growing functional overlaps. A federal division of powers based on the older theory of 'watertight compartments' was no longer up to the task and was modified. A Constitution enacted in 1867 did not contemplate developments such as the equality of Dominions to the United Kingdom, extraterritorial legislation, and the end of appeals to the Judicial Committee of the Privy Council, for example, but the courts interpreted the 1867 Constitution as a 'living tree', intended by its framers to grow in ways unanticipated by them, but consistent with that Constitution's organic nature and limits, and adaptable to changing circumstances.[75]

Wil Waluchow has explored how 'living tree' constitutionalism is much like the common law in the sense that the courts are called upon to consider the law's interaction with new factual contexts, while adhering to principles that can be seen at work in the history of the Constitution. The courts' role in developing the common law of the Constitution attracts certain sceptical responses because parliaments and legislatures cannot, by ordinary legislative means, assert or reassert their own decisions in the face of courts' interpretation of the Constitution. The case for sceptical assessments of the courts' constitutive power is at its strongest where the courts change the rules of the Constitution in the service of their assessments of the unwritten principles of the Constitution. But all lawyers know that the law, including or especially constitutional law, often throws up questions for which there is no clear answer. In those circumstances, the judges have a constitutive power that arises as a necessity from their responsibility for resolving disputes about the Constitution, and from their responsibility to give judgment on references. The question is what is the best approach for them to take to the exercise of that power, or, for our purposes and with a hope that they coincide, what do Canadians view as the best approach?

We have seen that since the 1980s Canadian courts have diversified the tools at their disposal. The *Secession Reference* approach introduces into the constitutional

---

[74] s 2: 'No Act of the Parliament of the United Kingdom passed after the Constitution Act, 1982 comes into force shall extend to Canada as part of its law'.

[75] Other changes were deemed by the courts to be too significant to be considered organic growth and therefore either prohibited or deemed to require constitutional amendment. One thinks of the addition of unemployment insurance under federal jurisdiction, prohibited by the courts in the 1930s and achieved via constitutional amendment in 1940.

reasoning process dynamic principles such as democracy, federalism, constitutionalism and the rule of law, and protection of minorities, as well as judicial independence and perhaps others still to be identified. What should we make of this development?[76]

Principles are basic, general ingredients for reasoning as to what is to be done. Any constitutional practice must be principled: that is an axiom of the ideal of constitutionalism. Reference by judges to constitutional principle seems preferable to the bald exercise of an unprincipled discretion. However, the discussion in this chapter points to a potential hazard regarding the appeal to constitutional principles. By virtue of their very abstraction, principles afford greater material for judicial creativity, greater room for discretion. Where the rules of the constitution do not provide guidance, and where, one presumes, an answer structured by venerable constitutional principles is preferable to untrammelled discretion, what is the best way to employ principles in judicial reasoning? On one view, better principled reasoning turns entirely on better theorizing. And no doubt, greater analytical and theoretical sophistication is a virtue. However, the view preferred here is that principled reasoning requires not just clear abstract thinking, but clear thinking in and regarding a specific context. As we have seen with 'living tree' constitutionalism, Canadian constitutional theory allows constitutional law to evolve in line with the nation's constitutional texts (with all their gaps and ambiguities) and with an awareness and sensitivity to the society which the Constitution sets out to govern, and under which all its citizens are intended to flourish.

Principles can be seen as abstract ideas from which conclusions are deduced. Or, more consistently with the 'living tree' approach, they, like rules, may be seen as legal standards which evolve, according to their own conceptual shape and structure, but also in response to the changing circumstances. Those circumstances will no doubt continue to evolve, in ways that will affect Canadian federalism, for example. The distinctively Canadian allocation of constituent power to judges will, doubtless, continue to evolve, in ways that will be influenced by popular opinion and by other political actors, but will be determined by the judges themselves. The developing field of Canadian constitutional theory will involve controversy, and the opportunity for participants in theoretical controversies to contribute to the shaping of the law and of practice.

Perhaps in the early days and years of the *Secession Reference* approach we were struck by the more frequent references to principles in Canadian constitutional adjudication in part because of their relative novelty and the seeming unpredictability of their new shape. However, as the years pass, it may be that principles come to be understood not so much as abstract and remote and subject to formal deductive logic, but as living and

---

[76] For particularly insightful discussions of the role of principles in Canadian constitutional law, see J. Leclair, 'Canada's Unfathomable Unwritten Constitutional Principles, (2000) 27 Queen's Law Journal 389 and Mark D. Walters, 'The Common Law Constitution in Canada: Return of the *Lex Non Scripta* as Fundamental Law' (2001) 51 University of Toronto Law Journal 91.

evolving, drawn out gradually[77] according to their own terms and according to changing circumstances in all parts of Canadian society.[78]

BIBLIOGRAPHY

Adams, E, "Canadian Constitutional Identities" (2015) 38 Dalhousie LJ 311.

Borden, Sir Robert, *Canadian Constitutional Studies*, (1922).

Borrows, John, *Freedom and Indigenous Constitutionalism* (Toronto: University of Toronto Press, 2016) ch 4.

Choudhry, S. and R Howse, 'Constitutional Theory and the Quebec Secession Reference' (2000) 13 Canadian Journal of Law and Jurisprudence 143–169.

Dyzenhaus, David, "Rand's Legal Republicanism" (2010) 55 McGill Law Journal 491–510.

Dyzenhaus, David, "The Logic of the Rule of Law—Lessons from Willis" (2005) 55 University of Toronto Law Journal 691–714.

Endicott, Timothy, "Arbitrariness" (2014) Canadian Journal of Law and Jurisprudence 49–72.

Gélinas, F., "Les conventions, le droit et la Constitution du Canada dans le renvoi sur la ' sécession' du Québec:le fantôme du raptriement" (1997) 57 Revue du Barreau du Québec 291.

Hogg, Peter, *Constitutional Law of Canada* (5th ed.) (Toronto: Thomson Carswell, 2011).

Huscroft, Grant and Bradley Miller, eds. *The Challenge of Originalism* (Cambridge: Cambridge University Press, 2011).

Kennedy, W.P.M., "Theories of Law and the Constitutional Law of the British Empire" in W.P.M. Kennedy, *Some Aspects of the Theories and Workings of Constitutional Law* (London: Macmillan, 1932).

Kong, Hoi, "Towards a Civic Republican Theory of Canadian Constitutional Law" (2010-11) 15 Rev Const Stud 249.

---

[77] This process shares affinities with common law, civil law, and Indigenous legal method: see J Borrows, *Drawing Out Law* (University of Toronto Press, 2010). For discussion of the potential for 'living tree' constitutionalism and its relevance to Indigenous law, see J Borrows, *Freedom and Indigenous Constitutionalism* (University of Toronto Press, 2016) ch 4. The idea of 'drawing out' principles over time sounds like the method of the common law, and the phrase 'common law constitutionalism' is often now employed in Canada to describe this phenomenon. Chief Justice McLachlin has recently explored the extent to which the common law in Canada is more 'top down' than is often acknowledged (given the role of principles), and the civil law is more 'bottom up' than is often thought. On the latter point, see N Kasirer, 'Keep Calm and Teach Gaius' (2016) 76 Louisiana L Rev 1109. See video of keynote address by Chief Justice Beverley McLachlin at the 'Supreme Courts and the Common Law Symposium', Université de Montréal, 27 May 2016: http://commonlaw.umontreal.ca/symposium2016/videos/.

[78] There are many forms and aspects of Canadian constitutional theory which have not been discussed in this chapter. Some are discussed in other chapters in this and other Parts of this *Handbook*. It is important to note here that in order to work out the practical requirements of principles such as the rule of law or protection of minorities, a good part of Canadian constitutional writing must be devoted to the study of law and society. The rule of law means little if there is no access to justice in fact (see *Trial Lawyers Association of British Columbia v British Columbia (Attorney General)* 2014 SCC 59 and *British Columbia (Attorney General) v Christie*, 2007 SCC 21), and protection of minorities means little if court orders are routinely ignored or only paid lip service (see *Doucet-Boudreau v Nova Scotia (Minister of Education)* 2003 SCC 62). In other words, good theorising requires good understandings of the context and facts at hand.

Leclair, Jean, 'Canada's Unfathomable Unwritten Constitutional Principles, (2000) 27 Queen's Law Journal 389.

Lyon, Noel, "The Central Fallacy of Canadian Constitutional Law" (1976) 22 McGill LJ 40.

Liston, Mary, "Willis, 'Theology', and the Rule of Law" (2011) University of Toronto Law Journal 767.

Marshall, Geoffrey, *Parliamentary Sovereignty and the Commonwealth* (Oxford: Clarendon Press, 1957).

Mathen, Carissima, "The Question Calls for an Answer, and I Propose to Answer It': The Patriation Reference as Constitutional Method" (2011) 54 Sup Ct L Rev 143.

McLachlin, B., 'Unwritten Constitutional Principles: What Is Going On?' (2006) 4 NZJPIL 147.

McLachlin, B., at the "Supreme Courts and the Common Law Symposium", Université de Montréal, 27 May 2016: http://commonlaw.umontreal.ca/symposium2016/videos/.

Miller, Bradley, "Beguiled by Metaphors: The 'Living Tree' and Originalist Constitutional Interpretation in Canada" (2009) 22 Canadian Journal of Law and Jurisprudence 331.

Oliver, Peter C., "Canada, Quebec and Constitutional Amendment" (1999) 49 UTLJ 519.

Oliver, Peter C., *The Constitution of Independence: The Development of Constitutional Theory in Australia, Canada and New Zealand* (Oxford: Oxford University Press, 2005).

Oliver, Peter C., "Reform of the Supreme Court of Canada from Within: To What Extent Should the Court Weigh In Regarding Constitutional Conventions" in Nadia Verrelli (ed), The Democratic Dilemma: Reforming Canada's Supreme Court (Montreal-Kingston: McGill-Queen's Press, 2013) 161.

Oliver, Peter C., "Change in the Ultimate Rule of a Legal System: Uncertainty, Hard Cases, Commonwealth Precedents, and the Importance of Context" (2015) 26 King's LJ 367.

Roach, Kent, Review: 'American Constitutional Theory for Canadians (And the Rest of the World)' (2002) 52 University of Toronto Law Journal 503–521.

Rubin, G., 'The Nature, Use and Effect of Reference Cases in Canadian Constitutional Law' 6 McGill LJ 168–190.

Russell, Peter and C. Leuprecht, eds, *Essential Readings in Canadian Constitutional Politics* (Toronto: University of Toronto Press, 2011).

Sharpe, Robert and P. McMahon, *The Persons Case: The Origins and Legacy of the Fight for Legal Personhood* (Toronto: University of Toronto Press, 2007).

Tremblay, Luc, *Rule of Law, Justice, and Interpretation* (Montreal-Kingston: McGill-Queen's, 1997).

Tremblay, Luc, "La théorie constitutionnelle et la primauté de droit" (1994) 39 McGill LJ 101.

Vaughan, F., *Viscount Haldane: "The Wicked Step-Father of the Canadian Constitution"* (Toronto: University of Toronto Press, 2010).

Walters MD, 'The Common Law Constitution in Canada: Return of the *Lex Non Scripta* as Fundamental Law' (2001) 51 University of Toronto Law Journal 91.

Waluchow, W., "Constitutionalism", in E. Zalta (ed), The Stanford Encyclopedia of Philosophy (Spring 2014 Edition), http://plato.stanford.edu/archives/spr2014/entries/constitutionalism/.

Webber, G. "Originalism's Constitution" in G. Huscroft and B. Miller, eds, *The Challenge of Originalism* (Cambridge University Press, 2011) 147.

CHAPTER 45

FEMINIST CONSTITUTIONALISM IN CANADA

BEVERLEY BAINES[*] & RUTH RUBIO-MARIN[**]

1. INTRODUCTION

In 1986, a feminist constitutional law scholar asked "Can constitutions be for women too?"[1] This is the question asked in this chapter: Can the Canadian Constitution be for women too? The chapter articulates what a feminist constitutional agenda should evaluate. It draws on work from feminist constitutional scholars around the world to imagine what constitutionalism should look like if it were to truly respond to women.

Women around the world resort to constitutional litigation to resolve controversies involving gender issues. This litigation involves claims for political participation, freedom from discrimination and violence, sexual and reproductive rights, employment and civic rights, and matrimonial and social and economic rights. Including women brings a series of challenges to the existing orthodoxy. The challenge is complex because feminists and non-feminist judges often emphasize different material facts, rely on different terminology,

---

[*] Professor, Faculty of Law, Queen's University.

[**] Professor of Constitutional Law, University of Seville. This text draws on excerpts from Professors Baines and Rubio-Marin's book, *The Gender of Constitutional Jurisprudence* (Cambridge University Press, 2005), which includes their co-authored Introduction, "Toward a Feminist Constitutional Agenda" [hereinafter "Toward a Feminist Constitutional Agenda"], as well as Professor Baines' chapter, "Using the Canadian Charter of Rights and Freedoms to Constitute Women" [hereinafter "Using the Canadian Charter"]. We are grateful for the permission to use these influential works and invite the readers to consult them fully.

[1] Donna Greschner, "Can Constitutions Be for Women Too?" in Dawn Currie and B. MacLean (eds) *The Administration of Justice* (University of Saskatchewan Social Research Unit, 1986) 20.

and reason distinctively.[2] Most feminists believe that gender equality will not be achieved until the oppression and subordination of women are overcome. Some jurists continue to deny or ignore that women's oppression and subordination are real. Others question the value of relying on constitutional strategies for redress in absolute or relative terms.

Feminist constitutionalism proposes to rethink constitutional law in a manner that addresses and reflects feminist thought and experience. Its focus on women brings a critical lens to bear on the "gender neutral" approach traditionally and still generally favoured in analysing constitutional law. After presenting some core elements of this approach to constitutionalism from a feminist perspective (feminist constitutionalism), this chapter analyzes a few Canadian examples with a feminist constitutionalist perspective.

2. Feminist Constitutionalism

Constitutions generally express women's interests and needs in the form of human rights protections.[3] The propensity to address women's status in terms of human rights is replicated on the international level. Protection of human rights is undoubtedly extremely important to women's lives and there is an open and ongoing agenda to reassess the comprehensiveness of the classical list of rights by adding women's historically excluded voices to the exercise of constitution making. Without more, however, limiting women's constitutional enterprise to that of rights protection attributes victimhood status to women. Whether feminist scholars review judicial decisions or analyse written instruments they analyse domestic legal orders that claim to protect women from human rights violations while they simultaneously constitute them as victims. Absent recognition of voice and representation, constitutions do not constitutionalize women's agency.[4]

The puzzle is how to design and implement law and governance that move beyond victimhood, which is real, to identify and empower women's agency and to insist on women's voice and representation in politics and in constitutional law. As a first step, feminist constitutionalism challenges purportedly "gender neutral" constitutional law scholarship. This scholarship addresses issues as if they pertain only to federalism or the separation of powers or constitutional rights. Typically, such work is further bifurcated into studies focusing on one or two main strategies for dealing with rights conflicts. The more popular strategy is autonomy which encompasses claims that range from individual privacy to collective self-determination. Thus, when perceived in terms of self-determination, autonomy is the rallying cry of many indigenous, racial, ethnic, and linguistic groups.

---

[2] Mary Jane Mossman, "Feminism and Legal Method: The Difference It Makes" (1986) 3 *Australian Journal of Law and Society* 30, 30–31 asked: "In the law's process of determining facts, choosing and applying principles, and reaching reasoned decisions, is there any scope for feminism's challenge to 'our ways of seeing'?"

[3] See Baines and Rubio-Marin (2005), above (n **); B. Baines, D. Barak-Erez and T. Kahana, (eds), *Feminist Constitutionalism: Global Perspectives* (Cambridge University Press, 2012).

[4] H. Irving, *Gender and the Constitution: Equity and Agency in Comparative Constitutional Design* (Cambridge University Press, 2008).

On occasion, most of these rights-seeking groups also turn to the other major strategy for managing rights conflict, which is equality. Although these three major constitutional law categories—federalism, autonomy, and equality—might capture women's claims, they may also distort and/or impoverish them, viz. should claims of democratic under-representation be subsumed under autonomy or equality, or are they sui generis? Also, with only three categories at their disposal, scholars might be tempted to portray rela-tionships among them as adversarial, viz. treating pornography as a contest between the pornographers' autonomy and the equality rights of women and girls, which would neglect entirely the entitlement of the latter to self-determination or autonomy.

Thus, we propose to design a feminist constitutional agenda as a middle course between the extensive and reality-driven delineation of issues that feminist scholars advance and the more rigidly bounded categorization found in constitutional law scholarship. The main goal is, in short, to identify, sustain, and promote constitutional norms and strategies that will achieve gender equality for women. Our claim is that any constitution must advance women's rights and participation if it is to lay claim to political and legal legitimacy.

It is appropriate to ask about women because they remain an oppressed group.[5] Iris Young's five faces of oppression—violence, exploitation, marginalization, powerless-ness, and cultural imperialism—represent the reality of many women in Canada and elsewhere.[6] Violence against women exists in the forms of sex trafficking; sexual assault; sexual harassment; cyberstalking; abuse including sexual abuse of migrant women, asylum seekers, refugees, and differently abled women; and intimate partner abuse.[7] Exploitation and marginalization exists in low employment rates, the gender pay gap, lower or no pensions, occupational segregation in less lucrative sectors, undervalued part-time work, and the burden of most of the housework.[8] Evidence of powerless-ness exists in the low numbers of women on corporate boards, lack of parity in political representation, and the failure of many women to break through the glass ceiling.[9] By cultural imperialism, we could refer to the androcentrism that privileges masculinity while devaluing femininity, including the absolute failure of society to acknowledge the social value of care work.[10] Cultural imperialism also covers heteronormativity, trans-phobia, and religious and ethnic imperialism experienced by lesbians and trans women and adult Muslim women who wear headscarves.[11] Many Canadian women face such oppression. It is appropriate to ask whether the Canadian Constitution is for women too.

Feminist constitutionalism considers the position of women with respect to (1) con-stitutional agency, (2) constitutional rights, (3) constitutionally structured diversity,

---

[5] Ruth Rubio-Marin, "Women in Europe and in the World: The State of the Union 2016" (2016) 14 *International Journal of Constitutional Law* 545.

[6] Ibid., 547.

[7] Ibid., 548.

[8] Ibid., 548–549.

[9] Ibid., 549.

[10] Ibid., 549–550.

[11] Ibid., 550: It is in this context that there is a need for the adoption of the substantive norm of parity democracy, that is, the "equal representation of women in every site of decision-making", ibid., 553. Parity challenges "male dominance, as men perceive gender-based hierarchy to be their last bastion of comfort and sense of self in a context of emasculation", ibid., 554.

and (4) constitutional equality. It also gives special attention to (5) women's reproductive rights and sexual autonomy, (6) women's rights within the family, and (7) women's socioeconomic development and democratic rights. Feminist constitutionalism defines various questions that need to be confronted.[12] We proceed to define how such questions should be asked.

A. Women and Constitutional Agency

For centuries, states openly barred women from participating in civic life, whether as voters or legislators, lawyers, or jurists. Men monopolized constitutional activities. Not surprisingly, women's initial forays into the realm of political decision-making focused primarily on voting, although their strategies differed.[13] On the one hand, white women in two Australian colonies were not only the first to receive the franchise, but also in 1901 they became the first women to vote on a constitution. On the other hand, following decades of lobbying, in 1920, Americans became the first to secure a constitutional amendment guaranteeing women the right to vote. Although these initial strategies were important, it is curious that they did not lead to any further constitutional changes for women in either country.

The embrace of formal equality and the explicit commitment to sex equality only became a general trend in post-Word War II constitutionalism although its emancipatory potential was limited at the time by the culturally hegemonic breadwinner family model.[14] Women's role in promoting those provisions was uneven and to this day remains under-examined. However, given pervasive underrepresentation in legislative and constituent assemblies, it would not be surprising to find that their activities were limited. It was not until the 1980s, and especially the 1990s (with the international embrace of the agenda of women's empowerment best epitomized by the *Beijing Platform for Action* in 1995), that women began to engage more actively in processes of general constitutional renewal around the world. For instance, not only did Canadian women lobby to strengthen the sex equality guarantees newly entrenched in the *Charter of Rights and Freedoms* (1982), but also women in Colombia successfully advocated for gender equality and gender-related provisions in their new constitution (1991), and South African women actively and meaningfully participated in the process of drafting their new constitution (1996). Finally, by significantly contributing to a wave

---

[12] The following is drawn from Baines and Rubio-Marin, "Toward a Feminist Constitutional Agenda", above (n **).

[13] On Europe, see Ruth Rubio-Marin, "The Achievement of Female Suffrage in Europe: On Women's Citizenship", (2014) 12 *International Journal of Constitutional Law* 4–34 and Blanca Rodríguez-Ruiz and Ruth Rubio-Marín (eds), *The Battle for Female Suffrage in the EU: Voting to Become Citizens* (Brill, 2012).

[14] See Ruth Rubio-Marin, "The (Dis)establishment of Gender: Care and Gender Roles in the Family as a Constitutional Matter" (2015) 13 *International Journal of Constitutional Law* 787.

of constitutional amendments to enable the adoption of gender parity and gender quotas,[15] women in Europe may exemplify a new era, one in which women can seek specific gender-related constitutional amendments as needed rather than only during times of general constitutional change, which is to say, one in which women can define rather than simply join "constitutional moments."

The foregoing suggests women, including those who are active in feminist movements, have begun to identify constitutions and constitutional change as relevant to our lives. The process of litigation also offers women ways of developing and changing the meaning of constitutional norms. But this too requires women to perceive themselves as constitutional actors. It is not surprising that many early sex-equality provisions around the world saw men (and not women) as protagonists. Therefore, with respect to the level of women's litigious activity, we must ask not only what enabling conditions are necessary but also what institutional mechanisms are most likely to overcome conventional barriers to accessibility by helping women as a group to avail themselves of constitutional tools.[16]

Understanding women's constitutional agency requires an understanding of the types of claims that women bring, and the constitutional strategies on which they rely. There is no question that, although the strongest emphasis has been on equality provisions, gender-related litigation has proceeded under most of the other rights-based provisions as well as under some federalism provisions. Also, constitutional gender equality may be affected in cases in which women are defendants or not even parties, as for example in most sexual assault prosecutions. Finally, any assessment of the quality of women's constitutional litigious agency would not be complete without an assessment of the difference, if any, that is made by having women on the final appellate courts that decide constitutional matters.[17] We should celebrate that recently the parity agenda now extends to concern with women's persistent underrepresentation on the highest courts, with several courts now being constitutionally or legally obliged to include women.[18]

In sum, women's constitutional agency involves lobbying, legislating, litigating, and adjudicating. Although all of these roles are open to women, our entry is not commensurate with our numbers, suggesting invisible but real public constraints, perhaps not unlike the proverbial glass ceiling in the private workplace.

---

[15] Ruth Rubio-Marín, "Women's Political Citizenship in New European Constitutionalism: Between Constitutional Amendment and Progressive Interpretation" in Helen Irving (ed), *Constitutions and Gender* (Edward Elgar Publishing, 2017) (forthcoming).

[16] See the chapter in this *Handbook* by Carissima Mathen on access to constitutional justice.

[17] Beverley Baines, "Women Judges on Constitutional Courts: Why Not Nine Women?" in Helen Irving (ed), *Constitutions and Gender* (Edgar Elgar Publishing, 2017) (forthcoming)).

[18] See art. 176 of the Constitution of Ecuador (mandating that parity between men and women be fostered in the judiciary). The Act organizing the Belgian Constitutional Court also stipulates that the Court should be composed of judges of both sexes. In implementing the rule the long-term aim of 33 percent of women has been set with every third appointment, since 2014, having to include one judge of the underrepresented sex. In the international domain, both the African Court of Human Rights and the International Criminal Court also now have rules to ensure women's inclusion.

B. Women and Constitutional Rights

Constitutional rights provide women and other rights seekers with the tools to challenge state activity in the courts. In some constitutional traditions, constitutional rights apply *horizontally* as well, granting women tools to combat not only public forms of injustice but private ones as well. In general, constitutional rights seem to offer more protection than statutory and other nonconstitutional rights, which may not constrain legislation. Arguably there is one important respect in which statutory and other nonconstitutional rights might be perceived as offering better protection to rights seekers: whereas constitutional provisions tend to have a greater visibility and seem to permeate more easily the general legal culture than statutory rights do, statutory rights are often detailed, making their meanings more transparent and accessible to rights seekers. In contrast, constitutional rights are usually expressed in terms of abstract generalities so that their meanings are dependent on the interpretations judges have ascribed to them. Thus, understanding constitutional rights involves understanding the claims litigants have raised (or failed to raise) and the way in which judges have adjudicated them. Additionally, in some contexts (especially regarding sexual and reproductive matters) it may be pertinent to ask ourselves whether constitutionalizing some disputes, often through creative and expansive jurisprudential constructions, may raise the stakes and elevate their political salience in ways that are more likely to trigger backlash, raising the question as to whether some conquests may not be better gained through lower profile legislation. The constitutionalization of abortion through *Roe v. Wade* in the United States has certainly raised this kind of question in the past. The constitutionalization of same-sex marriage, at least in some countries, could raise similar concerns today and invite reflection about the trade-offs between the symbolic gains of having certain prerogatives "constitutionalized" and the material gains in terms of stably securing new forms of autonomy and equality.

Women have often used constitutional instruments to fight against unwanted motherhood, pregnancy, and employment discrimination; domestic violence; political underrepresentation; sexual harassment; military service discrimination; sex crimes and/or their accompanying procedures; or unfair marriage, divorce, and succession rules. Given their breadth, it is striking how rarely many of these sites of struggle are expressly prohibited in constitutional terms. This lacuna forces women to figure out constitutional strategies to react against the liabilities involved, struggle by struggle, often being forced to fit their realities into gender neutral provisions that were originally crafted by men in the image of men's vision of autonomy.[19] Having to contend on a case-by-case basis for subsuming specific prohibitions within the more abstractly worded

---

[19] See Ruth Rubio-Marín and Wen-Chen Chang, "Sites of Constitutional Struggle for Women's Equality", in Mark Tushnet, Thomas Fleiner and Cheryl Saunders (eds), *Routledge Handbook of Constitutional Law*, (Routledge, 2013), 301–312.

provisions found in most constitutions is resource intensive and energy depleting. The flexibility of expressing constitutional rights abstractly may or may not assist women.

Constitutional rights are no panacea. Constitutional rights espouse, and are expected to espouse, the fundamental values of a nation, and this has both good and bad consequences for women because courts are prepared not only to uphold but also to limit women's claims in the name of these fundamental values. For instance, freedom of speech has traditionally been asserted against attempts to limit the harm women suffer because of pornography.

Finally, some consideration should be granted to constitutional hermeneutics as well.[20] Do different methods of constitutional interpretation have a gender impact? Time may make a difference here. Presumably, if the constitution is an old document written at a time when women's subordinate status was accepted as the natural order of things, and if the courts prefer an originalist or textual approach rather than a "living tree" or teleological approach,[21] this may have a negative impact on women's constitutional position.[22]

Also, the different relevance constitutions attach to international human rights instruments and supranational law can have a clear impact on women's constitutional status. Some constitutions expressly incorporate international law as domestic law. More common, however, is the recognition of the need to interpret constitutional rights in the light of relevant international or supranational law. This is the case in Canada.[23] CEDAW is, for instance, often invoked and European Law is sometimes very relevant to constitutional interpretation in EU Member States, such as France, Germany, or Spain.[24] This is an avenue not sufficiently explored in Canadian jurisprudence.[25] Obviously, several of the shortcomings of national constitutional rights-based legal orders cannot be overcome by human rights texts and doctrines that have been also mostly crafted and

[20] On this see Vicki Jackson, "Conclusion: Gender Equality and the Idea of a Constitution: Entrenchment, Jurisdiction, Interpretation", in Susan H. Williams (ed), *Constituting Equality: Gender Equality and Comparative Constitutional Law* (Cambridge University Press, 2009), 312–350.

[21] *Henrietta Muir Edwards and others v The Attorney General of Canada* [1930] A.C. 124 (18 October 1929) (better known as *The Persons Case*). In this case, Lord Sankey used the metaphor of the Constitution as a living tree to recognize that the word "persons" should be interpreted as including women in the *Constitution Act, 1867*. See Robert J. Sharpe and Patricia I. McMahon, The Persons Case: *The Origins and Legacy of the Fight for Legal Personhood* (University of Toronto Press, 2007) for a detailed history of the case.

[22] But see Kerri A. Froc, "Is Originalism Bad for Women? The Curious Case of Canada's Equal Rights Amendment" (2014–2015) 19 *Review of Constitutional Studies* 237 who argues the application of originalist principles, at least for interpretation of s. 28 [Canada's gender equality provision], is a critical step in moving women towards having truly equal access to *Charter* rights.

[23] *Baker v Canada (Minister of Citizenship and Immigration)*, [1999] 2 SCR 817.

[24] Ruth Rubio-Marın and Martha Morgan, "Constitutional Domestication of International Gender Norms: Categorizations, Illustrations, and Reflections from the Nearside of the Bridge," in K. Knopp (ed), *Gender and Human Rights* (Oxford University Press, 2004).

[25] But see Meghan Campbell, "CEDAW and Women's Intersecting Identities: A Pioneering New Approach to Intersectional Discrimination" (2015) 11 *Revista Direito Gv*, Sao Paulo 479.

interpreted by men; they are a product of their time and, they too, are clearly susceptible to feminist critique.[26]

C. Women and Constitutionally Structured Diversity

Although women have participated in revolutionary activities, gender conflict has never caused a national revolution. Indeed, there is little evidence that gender conflict has influenced the design of the constitutional structures that promote national unity and postpone revolution. Instead, economic, cultural, and religious conflicts have dictated the choices of constitution makers in selecting their country's form of governance (whether monarchy or republic), territorial principle (whether federation or unitary state), and jurisdictional approach (whether to recognize customary laws and other sources of legal pluralism).[27] This was certainly the case for Canada in 1867.

Accordingly, feminist scholars are constrained to examining the impact on women of these various constitutional structures and the diversities that underlie them.[28] For instance, the choice between monarchical and republican forms of governance seems gendered because the vast majority of the world's monarchs have been and still are men. Nevertheless, that is not always the case and also the rule of primogeniture, or male preference succession that prevails in many monarchies may in the end be indistinguishable from similar male preference leadership de facto or de jure rules to which various republics adhere.[29]

When nations choose federation over unitary status as their territorial principle, usually it is for economic reasons, often attached to geographical considerations, although ethnocultural conflict also plays a role in plurinational states, as happened in Canada. From the perspective of women, however, the major consequence of this choice is often to allocate "private" matters to the regional entities rather than to the national level and to follow the separate spheres tradition, with its gendered undertones, when deciding what amounts to "private" matters. For instance, family law becomes a matter for regional concern, and frequently employment law follows suit. These and other territorial distributions of legislative power suggest the importance

---

[26] See Dianne Otto, "Disconcerting Masculinities: Reinventing the Gendered Subject(s) of International Human Rights Law" in D. Buss and A. Manji (eds), *International Law: Modern Feminist Approaches* (Hart Publishing, 2005) 105–129.

[27] On this, see Aili Mari Tripp, "Conflicting Agendas? Women's Rights and Customary Law in African Constitutional Reform", in Susan H. Williams (ed), *Constituting Equality: Gender Equality and Comparative Constitutional Law* (Cambridge University Press, 2009) 173–194.

[28] See Paula A. Monopoli, "Gender and Constitutional Design" (2006) 115 *Yale Law Journal* 643–651.

[29] Note that the rule of male preference succession no longer exists for the British monarchy. The Constitution of Canada recognizes the British monarch as the King or Queen of Canada. However, it is still constitutionally enshrined in other countries, including Spain.

of examining their impact on women, particularly from the standpoint of feminist theorizing about the public/private split. For example, in the case of *Quebec (Attorney General) v A*,[30] the Canadian Supreme Court refused *Charter* protection to the unmarried immigrant mother of three children on the break-up of her relationship with their billionaire Québécois father who had refused to marry her. Instead the Court validated the Québec Civil Code's restriction of support and property division dispositions to married couples, leaving unmarried couples in a law-free or private zone that is detrimental to mothers. Many argue that federalism considerations influenced the Court's decision not to invalidate the provincial restriction.[31] In a federation such as Canada, feminists need lobbying and litigation strategies to address the gendered impacts of provincial and federal legislation.

Although recognition of a country's diversity through increasing constitutional acceptance of legal pluralism and validation of sources of law other than state law (whether it be indigenous, customary, or religious law) is a conquest with potential gains for minority women who can thus see their cultural and religious belonging better protected, traditionally, concern has been raised about the possibility that such recognition may come at the expense of women's equality or autonomy when the system of law protected is one that can enshrine patriarchal forms of power. This is particularly worrisome in those cases in which constitutions contain exclusionary clauses to prevent cultural norms or personal status laws from being challenged in case of contradiction with constitutional rights provisions, very much like the possibility signing countries have to place reservations on international human rights treaties (including CEDAW) for the same purposes. Some constitutions try to avoid this through limiting clauses that stipulate that local customs or non-state norms cannot violate individual rights as constitutionally enshrined Bill of Rights, something which limits minority self-rule. More recently, we see countries embracing the gender participatory shift in the context of legal pluralism, with some constitutions now recognizing the need for self-rule that includes minority women's voices,[32] and increasing institutional experimentation with nested gender quotas combining ethnic and gender criteria.[33]

---

[30] 2013 SCC 5, [2013] 1 SCR 61.

[31] See Sonia Lawrence's chapter in this *Handbook*; see also the chapter by Robert Leckey and Carol Rogerson in this *Handbook*.

[32] Art. 170 of the Constitution of Ecuador refers to the need to ensure women's participation in decision making in the exercise of Indigenous jurisdiction beyond the respect of fundamental rights, and art. 2 A III of the Constitution in Mexico refers to the need to ensure women's participation under equitable conditions with men when electing Indigenous authorities.

[33] On rethinking participatory gender parity in light of multiculturalism see Ruth Rubio-Marín and Will Kymlicka, *Gender Parity and Multicultural Feminism: Towards a New* Synthesis (unpublished manuscript on file with author submitted for Oxford University Press publication).

D. Women and Constitutional Equality Doctrine

Most constitutions explicitly prohibit sex or gender discrimination, and/or guarantee equality rights to men and women or to male and female persons. The promise of these provisions is clear. Because the oppression of women remains a worldwide phenomenon, these provisions are available to support women's equality claims (in fact, many constitutions, as does the Canadian *Charter*, also explicitly approve of positive equality in cases where historic discrimination is being remedied). Although the equality provisions do not preclude men from claiming their protection, effectively the provisions were drafted to protect women, even if women are not explicitly mentioned. Nevertheless, difficult issues remain: What does sex equality mean? When can women claim infringement of their constitutional right to sex equality? How should courts adjudicate the conflict between equality claims and other constitutional values?

The traditional doctrine of sex equality had two meanings. One is formal equality; the other, separate but equal. Both doctrines rely on the Aristotelian notions of treating alikes alike, and unalikes unalike. Accordingly, both focus on identifying the relevant differences and similarities, whether biologically or socially determined, between men and women as groups. Where they differ is in their emancipatory strategies. Formal equality assumes the sex of a person reveals nothing about individual worth or autonomy; its main objective is to create a gender neutral legal order, which turns out to be one in which women are treated just like men. In contrast, as its nomenclature suggests, separate but equal doctrine emphasizes respect for and the value of women's differences, while promising to ensure they do not result in worse treatment. Post World-War II constitutionalism coincided with the peak moment of cultural hegemony of the breadwinner family model, and this forced courts to struggle to find a balance between erasing sexual differences in the law (to live up to non-discrimination mandates recently incorporated in the constitutions) while allowing those differences that were essential to affirm the dominant family model to survive under the separate but equal doctrine.[34]

Whatever the doctrine formally embraced, the same kinds of issues arise. Thus formal equality courts have struggled to accommodate pregnancy discrimination and affirmative action by treating them as limited exceptions, whereas separate but equal courts have found it difficult to distinguish legislative stereotyping or paternalism from the less debilitating manifestations of protective or symbolic legislation. Taken collectively, these doctrines portray sex as an abstract conceptual category that is vulnerable to the excesses of judicial discretion; and more important, both focus on open and direct differentiation between the sexes, thereby failing to identify discrimination that is embedded in gender neutral or gender specific legislation.

Feminist scholars, litigators, and activists developed a third doctrine, "substantive equality". Unlike the other two equality doctrines, it is not obsessed with

---

[34] See Rubio-Marin, above (n 14).

identifying similarities and differences between men and women (to build upon them the "similarly situated test"), nor with trying to classify them as biological or socially constructed. Substantive equality tries to identify patterns of oppression and subordination of women as a group by men as a group on the understanding that most sex discrimination originates with the long history of women's inequality in almost every area of life rather than inhering in sex as a conceptual category. Ultimately, therefore, the goal of substantive equality is to transform structural discrimination, partly by uncovering the inequalities embedded in gender neutral laws and partly by challenging schemes that differentiate women by offering only paternalistic benefits instead of transformative remedies. Unfortunately, even under this doctrine there is hardly any way of getting around the objection that some of the "benefits" or "advantages" that the doctrine tries to extend to women have the potential to embed traditional gender roles[35] or traditionally male definitions of the good life and autonomy which systematically undervalue the domains of self-realization and fulfillment, including giving life to and caring for others, that have traditionally defined and confined women's distinctive citizenship.

Finally, irrespective of which doctrine judges apply, they must relate it to the prevailing concept of discrimination and, on occasion, to other constitutional rights and freedoms. These relationships give rise to various issues, as the following questions illustrate. Must discrimination affect all women equally in order to qualify as such and, if so, with what consequences? Do courts recognize intersectional discrimination, that is discrimination based on more than one prohibited ground, or must women choose only one ground (think of sex versus Aboriginal status, race, caste, or religious identity)? Do the traditional liberal rights and freedoms—such as freedom of expression, freedom of religion, privacy, due process, the right to a fair trial, and other procedural guarantees in criminal law—limit the constitutional right to sex equality? Are these tensions recognized? How are they resolved?

Feminist constitutionalism enriches the way in which jurisprudence is shaped and analysed. It confronts directly the limits of "gender neutral" (but anchored in male privilege) guarantees. In addition, feminist constitutionalism is concerned about ensuring women's reproductive rights and sexual autonomy as well as socio-economic and democratic participation.

E. Constitutionalizing Women's Reproductive Rights and Sexual Autonomy

Very few constitutions advert to sexual and reproductive rights even though they are vital to women as individuals and as a group. However, in many countries, there are

---

[35] Ibid.

a number of cases involving reproductive issues that are not specifically denominated, such as abortion, in vitro fertilization, contraception, and sterilization. Because these processes were criminalized or otherwise regulated, litigants have sometimes resorted to more generalized rights to challenge the constitutionality of regulation. Just as frequently, litigants have resorted to constitutional rights and values (such as the right/value of life) to impede legislative recognition of women's reproductive rights through abstract review of legislation.

The abortion jurisprudence is particularly apposite to illustrate the complexities induced by having to argue reproductive rights claims from a default position. Many countries have criminalized abortion subject to one or more exceptions (e.g., therapeutic, rape survivors, fetal malformation or lack of viability). In the absence of abortion rights, litigants are forced to turn to a broad and diverse range of rights to sustain women's entitlement to control their own bodies, including security of the person, liberty, equality, privacy, free development of one's personality, physical integrity, human dignity, physical and moral integrity, and freedom of thought and belief. This has given constitutional courts (still overwhelmingly male) a large realm of discretion on the matter. The Canadian case is explained below.

Sexual offences, too, represent a site of controversy about which constitutional law scholars would be hard pressed to deny that the entrenchment of constitutional rights has detrimentally affected women. Whether criminalized or otherwise regulated, sexual offences—including rape, sexual assault, prostitution, pornography, hate speech, sexist speech, and sexual harassment—have created much constitutional litigation opportunities for the criminal defense bar. Relying on traditional legal rights such as the presumption of innocence, the right to a fair trial, and the right not to be subject to cruel and unusual punishment, as well as on freedom of expression, equality rights, and the right to life, liberty, and security of the person, male defendants have not hesitated to challenge the constitutionality of various sexual offences and the evidentiary or procedural rules pertaining to them. To illustrate, men have invoked constitutional rights to argue for liberal access to the sexual history of the rape survivor and to her therapeutic counselling records in Canada.[36]

As the victims-survivors, women are all but invisible, enduring these constitutional challenges without having a litigation status from which to respond. Despite this disempowerment, women have demanded constitutional protection for sexual autonomy.

---

[36] *R v O'Connor*, [1995] 4 SCR 41; *R. v Mills*, [1999] 3 SCR 668. In *O'Connor*, the Court found that the production of private records of complainants in sexual assault proceedings had to meet certain criteria in order not to violate the accused's right to a fair trial. Following the decision, Parliament adopted new rules for the production that aimed to limit the protection of such records in order to protect the privacy of complainants. In *Mills*, although the new legislation differed significantly from the *O'Connor* regime, the Court found that the new legislative protection was constitutional because it considered that it should give deference to Parliament's choice to encourage the reporting of incidents of sexual violence, and to act to promote women's equality.

Sometimes victims' lawyers make these assertions in court; sometimes prosecutors voice them, albeit usually with the objective of protecting the state's interest in the impugned legislation. Either way, the discourse has been framed in terms of various rights including equality, liberty, and freedom of expression. Not only should this juris-prudence illuminate how courts address tensions among constitutional rights, but also it should yield a picture of which rights they favor. In sum, when women claim the right to constitutional protection of sexual autonomy, can courts hear our voices? Obviously, in the few instances in which sexual and reproductive autonomy provisions have been inserted into constitutions, courts must hear.[37]

F. Women's Rights, Care, and the Constitutional Definition of the Family

Family and marriage are among the most frequent objects of explicit constitutional protection worldwide with many constitutions recognizing the family to be the foun-dational cell of society. Moreover, the presence of constitutional provisions referring to the family or marriage does not determine whether countries have constitutional juris-prudence pertaining to it. Rather, such jurisprudence pervades all countries. In other words, the family has acquired a constitutional veneer, whether by political and/or judi-cial decree. It is thus important to examine how this constitutionalization of the family has affected women's rights. The idea that constitutions should (implying can) stay out of the home is indeed a myth.

Writ large, we need to understand how constitutions and constitutional doc-trines shape and are shaped by conceptions of the family. For instance, is curial dis-course restricted to recognizing only formally married, sequentially monogamous, heterosexual couples, or have courts been asked to accord matrimonial status or at least some family benefits (e.g., survivors' pensions, protection of children born out of wedlock, succession and property rights) to common law or de facto families, to single-parent families, to polygamous unions, or to gay men and lesbians? Can consti-tutions and the courts interpreting them really be neutral about family arrangements, relying, most commonly, on gender neutral rules and family privacy notions, or do they inevitably end up favouring internal arrangements which either advance or limit gender equality?[38] In rendering these decisions, moreover, have courts acknowledged

---

[37] See *Lakshmi Dhikta v Government of Nepal*, Writ. No. 0757, 2067, Nepal Kanoon Patrika, para. 25 (2009) (Supreme Court of Nepal) where the Supreme Court of Nepal interpreted the constitutional recognition of women's reproductive rights as requiring the legislature to remove woman's abortion from the criminal law and demanded the state ensure the costs of abortion procedures are not an impediment for a woman who cannot afford them.

[38] Rubio-Marin, above (n 14).

their specific impact on women's well-being, and how can they do so without further entrenching the expectation that women be the ones taking the greater share of care responsibilities within it? Ultimately, feminist scholars ask: Should constitutional doctrine continue to sustain the fiction of the split between the private and public, or should it gradually overcome the idea of the family as free from the exigencies of fundamental rights?

New and promising constitutional provisions are being crafted around the world expressing growing awareness about these matters.[39] In Bolivia, for instance, one finds constitutional language referring to equal opportunities, and thus endorsing substantive equality rhetoric, specifically in the family domain.[40] Increasingly, we find that references to motherhood, as a constitutionally protected status, are being replaced by a reference to parenting and to fatherhood, sometimes with an explicit mention to the need to unsettle traditional gender-specific parenting roles like in Colombia.[41] Yet, most revolutionary are clauses, such as those contained in the Constitution of Ecuador (art. 333), referring to the need to reconceptualize care as productive work (thus overcoming the dichotomy between productive and reproductive work), and care as a citizenship duty. However, without supporting public policies these provisions are likely to remain dead letters.

G. Women's Socioeconomic Development and Democratic Rights in the Constitution

Given that virtually in no country are women the socioeconomic equals of men, the first obvious question is whether constitutions specifically address women's socioeconomic needs. Any feminist constitutional agenda that looks at results, and not just at intentions and formalities, should also address the constitutional status of socioeconomic rights in general, as opposed to first- and second-generation rights. Even when phrased in gender neutral terms, the rights to housing, education, health care, social security, and food, recognized by some constitutions, have a gender impact, and will do so, as long as poverty has the face of a woman.

---

[39] Ibid.

[40] See Bolivia, 2009. Article 62: "The State recognizes and protects the *family* as the fundamental unit of society, and ensures social and economic conditions necessary for their development. All members have *equal rights, obligations, and opportunities*".

[41] Colombia (1991), art. 69: "1) *Responsible motherhood and fatherhood* shall be fostered; and the mother and father shall be obliged to take care, raise, educate, feed, and provide for the integral development and protection of the rights of their children, especially when they are separated from them for any reason . . . 5) The State shall promote the *joint responsibility of both mother and father*, and shall monitor fulfillment of the *mutual duties and rights* between mothers, fathers, and children".

Obviously, women's political status is crucial to the overcoming of their social and economic subordination. Women can vote and serve as elected political representatives. The United States Constitution is exceptional insofar as it guarantees both sexes equal voting rights; similarly, the South African Constitution is unique in describing the composition of the National Assembly in terms of both genders. In addition, since the mid-1990s, gender quotas have become the new preferred tool to promote women's equal participation in decision-making bodies in the political sphere and increasingly, in other domains of public participation. This represents a positive step to ensure that women's democratic rights are recognized as possessing a participatory, as well as a formal legal, dimension. Constitutionally, with some Latin American countries taking the lead, a trend has started whereby constitutional provisions are being inserted to either permit or require these positive measures. In many countries the adoption of measures aiming to increase women's participation has triggered much constitutional contestation,[42] and in some countries, such as France, the measures have only come about after a highly disputed constitutional amendment process (and a reframing from quotas to parity) given that these measures were seen to challenge formal equality as well as established notions of democratic representation.[43] Constitutional law scholars must reflect on the opportunity of enhancing women's participation in the electoral process. Although some may be perceived as temporary measures necessary to facilitate women's incorporation into the political domains, others may be intended to redefine democratic participation more permanently to provide voice and representation for women and to overcome the legacies of the separate spheres tradition entrenched in constitutionalism since its very foundation.[44]

Feminist constitutionalism approaches constitutional theories, techniques, and definition of rights with a view to advancing women's equality. It aims to transform constitutional law to better reflect women's voices and experiences. Constitutions must take women (in their multiple identities including indigenous, immigrant, refugee, and trans women) seriously. The reality is that women are poorer and less able to access the reins of power. Legal doctrines which could empower us still serve to preserve the status quo forcing women to internalize a lesser status. The stakes are high. In the next subsection, we proceed to apply the feminist constitutionalism framework to some aspects of the Canadian constitutional experiment.

[42] Drude Dahlerup and Lenita Freidenvall (2009), 'Gender Quotas in Politics—A Constitutional Challenge', in Susan Williams (ed) Constituting Equality: Gender Equality and Comparative Constitutional Law (Cambridge University Press, 2009), 29–52.

[43] The wave of constitutional amendments that has accompanied the spread of gender quotas in Europe includes constitutional amendments in Portugal (1997), Slovenia (2004), Italy (2001 and 2003), and France (first in 1999, and then again in 2008 when a second reform was required, to validate legislation imposing gender quotas on the corporate world).

[44] Blanca Rodríguez Ruiz and Ruth Rubio-Marin, "The Gender of Representation: On Democracy, Equality and Parity" (2008) 6 International Journal of Constitutional Law 287–316.

3. Feminist Constitutionalism and the Canadian Construction of Women

In 1867, Britain gave its Canadian colonies a written Constitution that imposed a federal system of parliamentary government.[45] While making jurisdiction a constraint on law-making, this Constitution did not provide Canadians with human rights protections (although rights such as freedom of contract and private property received common law protection). The legislatures could pass laws denying women the right to vote, hold public office, serve on juries or in the armed forces, immigrate, perform certain jobs, have an independent domicile or continue to work after marriage, dispose of property, have an abortion, receive employment insurance after giving birth, retain Aboriginal status on marrying a non-Aboriginal, or retain Canadian citizenship on marrying a non-Canadian. Whenever litigants challenged these laws by invoking international, statutory, or unwritten human rights protections, most Canadian judges refused to recognize their claims. Thus, constitutional litigation was not a viable strategy for women.

This picture changed significantly when the existing Constitution was supplemented by new constitutional provisions in 1982.[46] Prominent among these changes was the *Charter*, which delineates seven major rights: political (religion, expression, assembly, and association), democratic, mobility, legal, equality, language (official and minority educational), and Aboriginal.[47] This rights protection regime transformed the system of government from parliamentary to constitutional supremacy by assigning the enforcement of *Charter* rights to the regular courts. Almost simultaneously with the adoption of the *Charter*, the first woman justice was appointed to the Court; currently four women sit, one of whom is the Chief Justice. However, no constitutional or statutory rule guarantees continued gender representation on the Court, even though such a rule would not be entirely unprecedented, given that by law at least three justices must come from the Province of Quebec.[48]

What does *Charter* jurisprudence reveal about the impact on women of adopting a rights protection regime? To assess this jurisprudence, in this chapter we adopt one of the criteria defined by Sherene Razack: Does the *Charter* rights protection regime facilitate the feminist "project of naming, of exposing the world as manmade"?[49] We explore

---

[45] *Constitution Act, 1867* (U.K.), 30 & 31 Vict., c. 3, reprinted in R.S.C. 1985, App. II, No. 5.

[46] *Constitution Act, 1982*, being Schedule B to the *Canada Act 1982* (U.K.), 1982, c. 11.

[47] *Canadian Charter of Rights and Freedoms*, Part I of the *Constitution Act, 1982*, ibid., ss 1–34. Aboriginal constitutional rights also are found outside of the *Charter* in the *Constitution Act, 1982*, ibid., s. 35.

[48] Sections 5 and 6 of the *Supreme Court Act*. See as well the *Reference re Supreme Court Act*, ss. 5 and 6, [2014] 1 SCR 433 for the strict interpretation given to these dispositions.

[49] Sherene Razack, *Canadian Feminism and the Law: The Women's Legal Education and Action Fund and the Pursuit of Equality* (Second Story Press, 1991) 137. Razack also asked: would Charter rights enable feminists "to present various women's realities in all their complexities?" (at 133), and would *Charter*

the theme of women's constitutional agency to then assess the constitutional rights out-comes and the role of the courts as described earlier. Space does not permit a review of all questions raised by feminist constitutionalism in terms of democratic rights, socio-economic rights, family law protection, or equality jurisprudence. These have been dis-cussed in earlier chapters in this *Handbook*.

We first examine the role of feminists in the development of *Charter* equality doc-trine. The adoption of the *Charter* cast Canadian feminists into two major roles. As lob-byists, feminists advocated for sex equality and other *Charter* rights, recognizing their fate depended on whether governments could limit or abrogate rights. As litigators, feminists often acted collectively to try to import the doctrine of substantive equality into *Charter* cases.

A. Constitutional Agency: As Lobbyists

Between 1980 and 1982, feminists lobbied both levels of governments for recognition of women's constitutional rights.[50] This process went through three stages. The first stage involved legally knowledgeable women who "stressed the requirement for iron-clad entrenched equality between women and men as a non-negotiable demand".[51] During the next stage, this objective was pursued more widely by established women's groups working with the Ad Hoc Committee of Canadian Women on the Constitution, a women's lobby group that arose spontaneously after the male Cabinet Minister responsible for the status of women ordered the cancellation of a women's constitu-tional conference less than a month before it was to take place. The final stage reached far beyond activists to individual women, each of whom perceived equality rights were under attack, after government leaders agreed some *Charter* rights, including sex equality rights, could be temporarily overridden by a legislative declaration.[52] In fact, the potential for violating *Charter* equality rights led the Province of Quebec to enact five sex equality override laws, in 1986, 1991, 1996, and 2001, in order to allow some government pension plans to differentiate between women's eligibility for pension (age 60) and men's (age 65).

litigation keep feminists focused "on a fairer redistribution of resources" (at 135) rather than on societal transformation? See for an application to Canadian jurisprudence, Beverley Baines (2005), above (n **).

[50] Mary Eberts, "The Fight for Substantive Equality: Women's Activism and Section 15 of the Canadian Charter of Rights and Freedoms" (2015/2016) 37.2 (1) *Atlantis: Critical Studies in Gender, Culture & Social Justice* 100.

[51] Penny Kome, *The Taking of Twenty-Eight: Women Challenge the Constitution* (Women's Educational Press, 1983) 17–18.

[52] S. 33(1) of the *Charter*, known as the "override", states: "Parliament or the legislature of a province may expressly declare in an Act of Parliament or of the legislature, as the case may be, that the Act or a provision thereof shall operate notwithstanding a provision included in section 2 or sections 7 to 15 of this *Charter* . . .". See the chapter by Janet Hiebert in this *Handbook*.

Ultimately, two sex equality provisions were included in the *Charter*. The general equality provision (section 15) prohibits discrimination on nine listed grounds including sex, as well as permitting ameliorative programs for disadvantaged individuals or groups.[53] The second provision (section 28) deals only with sex equality and provides:

> 28. Notwithstanding anything in this Charter, the rights and freedoms referred to in it are guaranteed equally to male and female persons.

Section 28 has yet to receive definitive meaning. One study of 60 cases that referred to section 28 put "its integrity as a constitutional provision in serious question", reporting judges profoundly debase and marginalize it.[54] Notwithstanding its ambiguity in the Canadian *Charter*, Quebec enacted a virtually identical provision in its provincial Charter in 2008.[55] A third sex equality provision (section 35(4)) was entrenched by constitutional amendment in 1983.[56] This section provides:

> 35. (4) Notwithstanding any other provision of this Act, the aboriginal and treaty rights referred to in subsection (1) are guaranteed equally to male and female persons.

Limited to aboriginal claimants and yet to be interpreted, Section 35(4) is exempt from the *Charter's* override provision because it falls outside the *Charter*.

Subsequent constitutional discussions in the late 1980s and early 1990s revealed the inadequacies of all three provisions. For example, during the 1992 constitutional negotiations the Canadian government funded four traditional male-dominated aboriginal organizations but refused to fund the Native Women's Association of Canada (NWAC). NWAC contended this exclusion infringed their *Charter* rights to freedom of expression and sex equality. The Canadian Supreme Court disagreed, holding that funding was not a prerequisite to expression and that NWAC did not represent all Aboriginal women, some of whom participated in the traditional

---

[53] 15. (1) Every individual is equal before and under the law and has the right to the equal protection and equal benefit of the law without discrimination and, in particular, without discrimination based on race, national or ethnic origin, colour, religion, sex, age or mental or physical disability.

(2) Subsection (1) does not preclude any law, program or activity that has as its object the amelioration of conditions of disadvantaged individuals or groups including those that are disadvantaged because of race, national or ethnic origin, colour, religion, sex, age or mental or physical disability.

[54] Froc, above (n 22) 261. See also Kerri A. Froc, *The Untapped Power of Section 28 of the Canadian Charter of Rights and Freedoms* (PhD dissertation 2015 on-line: http://qspace.library.queensu.ca/jspui/handle/1974/13905).

[55] Quebec. National Assembly Bill 63 (2008, ch. 15) became s. 50.1 of the Quebec Charter of Human Rights and Freedoms R.S.Q. c. C-12. Commentators argued s. 50.1 was to have primacy over all other Quebec *Charter* values including religious freedom.

[56] *Constitution Amendment Proclamation, 1983*, SI/84–102, now *Constitution Act, 1982*, s. 35(4).

organizations.[57] Unfortunately, this reasoning missed the point, which is that NWAC represented Aboriginal women unrepresented by the four male-dominated organizations. These women supported keeping *Charter* rights in place during any process of transition to Aboriginal self-government, a position that was unique, as the four traditional associations wanted immediate relief from all non-Aboriginal laws, whether constitutional or otherwise. Indeed, the issue of representing and contextualising women's experience, particularly Indigenous women, continues to be a struggle in Canadian law.[58]

B. Constitutional Agency: As Litigators

After section 15 became effective, the lower courts were inundated with equality cases. Of 591 cases decided during the first three years, fewer than 10 percent were based on sex, 35 of which were brought by or on behalf of men and only 9 by or on behalf of women.[59] Although this litigation focused mainly on formal equality, even that represented an improvement over pre-*Charter* decisions denying gendered intermarriage and holding pregnancy discrimination laws did not violate women's equality rights.[60] Fortunately, the Supreme Court of Canada decided equality should not be restricted to formal equality, recognizing "that every difference in treatment between individuals under the law will not necessarily result in inequality and, as well, that identical treatment may frequently produce serious inequality".[61]

Eight years later in an act of revisionist history the Court proclaimed that this earlier decision had signalled its commitment to substantive equality.[62] Although feminist constitutional law scholars acknowledge the Court now names substantive equality as the doctrine that informs the test for section 15 equality rights, most would deny that the Court actually uses substantive equality analysis.[63]

Nevertheless, much credit must go to the Women's Legal Education and Action Fund (LEAF) for trying to persuade the Court to adopt this analysis. Following a nationally-funded research study that concluded "a legal action fund to concentrate on issues of sex-based discrimination is an essential component of an effective strategy to promote

---

[57] *Native Women's Association of Canada v Canada*, [1994] 3 SCR 627.

[58] See the Special Edition of the *Canadian Journal of Women in the Law* on the Missing and Murdered Indigenous Women Inquiry: *Missing and Murdered Indigenous Women Conference/Symposium sur Meurtres et disparitions de femmes et de filles autochotones* (2016) 2 *Can Journal of Women and the Law*.

[59] Gwen Brodsky and Shelagh Day, *Canadian Charter Equality Rights for Women: One Step Forward or Two Steps Back?* (Canadian Advisory Council on the Status of Women, 1989) 49.

[60] *A.G. Canada v Lavell*, [1974] SCR 1349; *Bliss v A.G. Canada*, [1979] 1 SCR 183.

[61] *Law Society of British Columbia v Andrews*, [1989] 1 SCR 143 at 164.

[62] *Eldridge v B.C.* [1997] 3 SCR 624 [61] (La Forest J.).

[63] See Jonnette Watson Hamilton and Jennifer Koshan, "Adverse Impact: The Supreme Court's Approach to Adverse Effects Discrimination under Section 15 of the Charter" (2014) 3(1) *Canadian Journal of Human Rights* 115 and feminist works cited therein.

the interests of women in the Canadian legal system,"[64] LEAF was created as a national non-profit organization with the dual mandates of participating in litigation that promotes equality for women and of educating the public about this litigation and its relationship to women's equality.

The subversion of substantive equality analysis combined with the fact women have not won a single sex equality case that reached the Canadian Supreme Court suggests Razack's first criterion, "of naming, of exposing the world as man-made",[65] has yet to yield the results sought by the feminists who lobbied for sections 15, 28, and 35(4). Male privilege prevails, or as one feminist legal scholar explained: "Women's inequalities and the discrimination that is so interwoven into women's daily lives are largely unrecognizable and incomprehensible to those in dominant positions. It is the privilege of not knowing and the, often unconscious, resistance to finding out that are at stake here".[66] Although *Charter* sex equality litigation offers a place from which privilege could be challenged, perhaps it is time to reassess its value. It should, but has yet to, provide a vehicle for women to name "objective" reality for what it is, a world organized consistently with male practices and beliefs.

What remains is to analyze one example of *Charter* jurisprudence that illustrates how *Charter* adjudication has met Razack's criterion. This illustration is in the very important context of women's reproductive rights.

Prosecuted for performing abortions, a doctor argued the prohibition infringed women's right to privacy and to make unfettered decisions about their lives.[67] The Court, which has the power to redefine issues upon granting leave to appeal, characterized his challenge as based upon the section 7 right to life, liberty, and security of the person, leaving the question of whether Canadians have a constitutional right to privacy unresolved. Then, in a 5-2 decision, the Court ruled the prohibition on abortion infringed security of the person, confirming that right extends beyond physical to psychological integrity. The only woman justice at the time, Justice Bertha Wilson, held the abortion provision also deprived women of the right to liberty, which she defined in terms of personal autonomy over important decisions intimately affecting one's private life. Although liberty had previously been restricted to situations involving incarceration, her definition was affirmed later.[68]

Justice Wilson also captured the male privilege inherent in regulating abortion when she wrote: "It is probably impossible for a man to respond, even imaginatively, to such a dilemma not just because it is outside the realm of his personal experience (although

---

[64] M. Elizabeth Atcheson et al., *Women and Legal Action* (Canadian Advisory Council on the Status of Women, 1984).

[65] Razack, above (n 49) 137.

[66] Diana Majury, "Women's (In)Equality before and after the Charter" in Radha Jappan (ed), *Women's Legal Strategies in Canada* (University of Toronto Press, 2002), 101 at 118.

[67] *R. v Morgentaler*, [1988] 1 S.C.R. 30. This decision decriminalized abortion, leaving it subject only to provincial health laws that can regulate but not prohibit it.

[68] *R.B. v Children's Aid Society of Metropolitan Toronto*, [1995] 1 S.C.R. 315.

this is, of course, the case) but because he can relate to it only by objectifying it, thereby eliminating the subjective elements of the female psyche which are at the heart of the dilemma".[69] However, the Court's decision stopped short of creating a constitutional right to an abortion when the justices upheld the legitimacy of balancing fetal interests against those of women. In other words, the Government failed only because the therapeutic exception—which required the involvement of four doctors, hospitalization, and a diagnosis of danger to the woman's life or health—was too stringent to achieve an appropriate balance. Thus, the decision left open the possibility for further, albeit more narrowly conditioned, regulation.

In fact, the national government tried to enact a new abortion provision with somewhat less stringent therapeutic exception requirements less than three years later, carrying the vote in the popularly elected House of Commons but failing by one vote in the appointed Senate.[70] Despite a favorable outcome in the abortion decision, there is no guarantee of women's constitutional right to control our own bodies; from this perspective, societal transformation is not yet a reality.

Indeed, the abortion debate continues within Canadian society. For example, women could not access abortion services in one province until a women's lobby group formally initiated a lawsuit that forced the provincial premier to agree to open a reproductive health clinic by the end of 2016.[71] The nexus of lobby and litigation illuminates a strategy that women might pursue to promote women's agency in other reproductive, and more generally other constitutional, contexts.

4. CONCLUSION

Feminist constitutionalism aims to ensure constitutions, mostly drafted by men, work for women. It asks questions about women's constitutional agency as lobbyists, litigators, legislators, and jurists. It questions the manner in which rights are interpreted and reconciled by ensuring that women's experience is taken into account. It has deepened the understanding of the principle of equality by moving beyond the formal equality paradigm or the "separate but equal" often-paternalistic trappings to define equality in a more transformative and substantive way. Feminist constitutionalism also questions the ability of abstract and general constitutional language to truly protect women's reproductive rights and sexual autonomy and women's socioeconomic development and democratic rights.

[69] *Morgentaler*, above (n 67) [240].
[70] Janine Brodie, "Choice and No Choice in the House," in Janine Brodie, Shelley A.M. Gavigan and Jane Jenson, *The Politics of Abortion* (Oxford University Press, 1992) 115.
[71] *Abortion Access Now PEI v Prince Edward Island (Minister of Health)* Notice of Application January 2016.

The Canadian *Charter* jurisprudence has provided opportunities for some Canadian women to acquire constitutional agency and name male privilege in some constitutional litigation. Nevertheless, the gains remain modest particularly because of the timidity toward socio-economic rights.[72] In addition, many women, Indigenous, racialized, differently-abled, immigrant, and poor among them, struggle to get their voices heard fully in constitutional law.

Feminist constitutionalism is a work in progress. Much more still needs to be done for constitutions to be for women too.

Select Bibliography

Baines, B. 'Women Judges on Constitutional Courts: Why Not Nine Women?' in Helen Irving (ed), *Handbook on Gender and Constitutions* (Cheltenham: Edward Elgar Publishing forthcoming 2017)

Baines, B., Daphne Barak Erez and Tsvi Kahana (eds), *Feminist Constitutionalism: Global Perspectives* (Cambridge: Cambridge University Press, 2012)

Baines, B. and Ruth Rubio-Marin (eds), *The Gender of Constitutional Jurisprudence* (Cambridge: Cambridge University Press 2005)

Canadian Journal of Women and the Law (1985–) Volume 1 and following.

Froc, Kerri A.,"Is Originalism Bad for Women? The Curious Case of Canada's Equal Rights Amendment" (2014–2015) 19 *Review of Constitutional Studies* 237

Greschner, Donna, "Can Constitutions Be for Women Too?" in Dawn Currie and B. MacLean (eds) *The Administration of Justice* (University of Saskatchewan Social Research Unit, 1986) 20

Irving, Helen (ed), *Handbook on Gender and Constitutions* (Cheltenham: Edward Elgar Publishing forthcoming 2017)

Irving, Helen, *Gender and the Constitution: Equity and Agency in Comparative Constitutional Design* (Cambridge: Cambridge University Press 2008)

Jackson, Vicki "Conclusion: Gender Equality and the Idea of a Constitution: Entrenchment, Jurisdiction, Interpretation', in Susan H. Williams (ed), *Constituting Equality: Gender Equality and Comparative Constitutional Law,* (Cambridge University Press, 2009), 312

Kome, Penny, *The Taking of Twenty-Eight: Women Challenge the Constitution* (Women's Educational Press, 1983)

Mossman, Mary Jane, "Feminism and Legal Method: The Difference Iit Makes" (1986) 3 *Australian Journal of Law and Society* 30

Roberts, Julian V. and Renate M. Mohr (eds), *Confronting Sexual Assault: A Decade of Legal and Social Change* (Toronto: University of Toronto Press, 1994)

Rodríguez-Ruiz, Blanca and Ruth Rubio-Marín (eds), *The Battle for Female Suffrage in the EU: Voting to Become Citizens,* (Brill, 2012)

Rubio-Marin, Ruth, 'Women in Europe and in the World: The State of the Union 2016', (2016) 14 *International Journal of Constitutional Law* 545

Rubio-Marin, Ruth, "The Achievement of Female Suffrage in Europe: On Women's Citizenship", (2014) 12 *International Journal of Constitutional Law* 4

---

[72] See the chapter by Martha Jackman and Bruce Porter in this *Handbook*.

Rubio-Marin, Ruth, "The (Dis)establishment of Gender: Care and Gender Roles in the Family as a Constitutional Matter", (2015) 13 *International Journal of Constitutional Law* 787

Rubio-Marín, Ruth, "Women's Political Citizenship In New European Constitutionalism: Between Constitutional Amendment And Progressive Interpretation" in H. Irving (ed), *Constitutions and Gender*, (Edward Elgar Publishing, 2017) (forthcoming)

Rubio-Marín, Ruth and Wen-Chen Chang, "Sites of Constitutional Struggle for Women's Equality", in Mark Tushnet, Thomas Fleiner and Cheryl Saunders (eds), *Routledge Handbook of Constitutional Law*, (Routledge 2013) 301

Smith, Lyn and Eleanor Wachtel, *A Feminist Guide to the Canadian Constitution* (Ottawa: Canadian Advisory Council on the Status of Women, 1992)

Cases

A.G. Canada v Lavell, [1974] SCR 1349

Baker v Canada (Minister of Citizenship and Immigration), [1999] 2 SCR 817

Bliss v A.G. Canada, [1979] 1 SCR 183

Eldridge v B.C., [1997] 3 SCR 624

Henrietta Muir Edwards and others v The Attorney General of Canada, [1930] A.C. 124

Lakshmi Dhikta v Government of Nepal, Writ. No. 0757, 2067, Nepal Kanoon Patrika, para. 25 (2009) (Supreme Court of Nepal)

Law Society of British Columbia v Andrews, [1989] 1 SCR 143

Native Women's Association of Canada v Canada, [1994] 3 SCR 627

Quebec (Attorney General) v A, [2013] 1 SCR 61

R. v Mills, [1999] 3 SCR 668

R. v Morgentaler, [1988] 1 S.C.R. 30

R v O'Connor, [1995] 4 SCR 41

R.B. v Children's Aid Society of Metropolitan Toronto, [1995] 1 S.C.R. 315

Reference re Supreme Court Act ss. 5 and 6, [2014] 1 SCR 433

....

CHAPTER 46

THE POLITICS OF
CONSTITUTIONAL LAW
A Critical Approach

....

ALLAN HUTCHINSON*

ODDLY enough, the advent of the *Canadian Charter of Rights and Freedoms* proved to be a boon and blessing to critical scholars—the claim that 'law is politics' was given a new depth and dimension. This is not say that there was no critical edge to legal scholarship in the over one hundred years of Canada's constitutional tradition.[1] It is only that *Charter* adjudication brought to the fore the political quality and contestable nature of rights adjudication in a constitutional setting. More than discussions about the division of powers between federal and provincial governments, it ensured that legal theorists and commentators had to contend with the obviously political nature of constitutional law and adjudication. The challenge was to demonstrate that the courts could be political in a neutral and objective way that was not hostage to any controversial political ideology and would advance democracy in a positive way.

However, after almost 25 years of *Charter* experience, many of the fears of the *Charter*'s critics have come to pass—judicial review under the *Charter of Rights and Freedoms* operates as an institutional device to curb more than advance democratic politics, and to entrench more than challenge a conservative ideology.[2] The *Charter* is indeed a potent political weapon, but one that has been and continues to be used to

---

* Distinguished Research Professor, Osgoode Hall Law School, York University.
[1] Paul Weiler, *In the Last Resort: A Critical Study of the Supreme Court of Canada* (Carswell, 1974) and Patrick Monahan, *Politics and the Constitution: The Charter, Federalism, and the Supreme Court of Canada* (Carswell, 1987).
[2] See, for example, J. Bakan, *Just Words: Constitutional Rights and Social Wrongs* (University of Toronto Press, 1997); A. Hutchinson, *Waiting for Coraf: A Critique of Law and Rights* (University of Toronto Press, 1995); M. Mandel, *The Charter of Rights and the Legalisation of Politics in Canada* (2nd ed., Wall & Thompson, 1994); and Andrew Petter, *The Politics of the Charter; The Illusive Promise of Constitutional Rights* (University of Toronto Press, 2010).

benefit vested interests in society, and to debilitate further an already imperfect democratic process of government. For such critics, whether or not that was the intention of
its proponents and drafters is beside the point. Indeed, despite some of the best intentions of the 'Charter party', the courts have not delivered on the touted democratic
promise of the *Charter*. Of course, there are occasions of progressive justice (e.g., gay
rights and electoral reform), but the overall direction and content of the *Charter* is far
from the 'People's Charter' that was promised and predicted.

In this short chapter, I will canvass the different critical challenges to the *Charter*. In
so doing, I will explain the force and legitimacy of an unconditional critical stance as
compared to shallow criticisms of most *Charter* commentators. In short, the critical
approach I advance rejects the deep and disturbing assumption that judicial power can
be exercised in a non-political, objective, and neutral manner. It is not that judges are
unprofessional or biased in some surreptitious manner, but that adjudication is inescap-
ably political and non-objective. To make this central point, I will anchor the discussion
in practical and doctrinal instances that illustrate and affirm the critical approach.

1. THE CRITICAL CHALLENGE

Until almost 20 years after the introduction of the *Charter*, the Supreme Court had
not staked out any comprehensive position on the precise role of courts in remedying
Charter wrongs. In *Doucet-Boudreau* in 2003, it took that first step.[3] A trial judge had
ordered Nova Scotia to use its 'best efforts' to provide French-language school facilities
and programs in certain areas by specified dates and had retained continuing supervision of the matter. The province contended that this continuing judicial supervision
inappropriately trespassed onto the government's political discretion. The Nova Scotia
Court of Appeal agreed and held that, although courts have broad-ranging powers
under section 24(1) of the *Charter* to fashion remedies, the *Charter* does not extend a
court's jurisdiction to meddle in the details of a province's administrative management: there were limits to the courts' authority to interfere with what were matters of
political judgment.

A majority of the Supreme Court of Canada had no such qualms. By the narrowest of
5-4 margins, the Court decided that the Constitution and legal tradition demanded that
the trial judge should remain seized of the issue. Speaking for their colleagues, Iacobucci
and Arbour JJ recognised that, although the courts should be cautious in involving
themselves in such matters, they must complement their purposive interpretation of
Charter rights with a purposive approach to remedies. Although the court must also be
sensitive to the limits of its role as judicial arbiter and not interfere unduly with the roles
of the other branches of governance, the judicial crafting of remedies will vary according

---

[3] 2003 SCC 62.

to the right at issue and the context of each case: the advancement of democratic ends should not be accomplished by undemocratic means. Accordingly, the majority held that, in the particular circumstances of the Nova Scotia schools, and mindful that delay might defeat the parents' rights, a supervisory remedy 'took into account, and did not depart unduly or unnecessarily from the role of courts in a constitutional democracy'.

The dissenting justices took a much more restrained line. The minority maintained that, once a court had issued its decision, it ought to rely upon the government to act with reasonable diligence and in good faith; it was not the role of courts to act as direct overseers or superintendents of the executive function. LeBel and Deschamps JJ insisted that it was vitally important that the courts respect the appropriate constitutional boundaries and balance between the different branches of government power: democracy demanded that the judicial role be limited and modest. Although it was imperative that citizens' *Charter* rights be properly and fully enforced, the minority took the definite view that this did not permit the courts to interfere in the legitimate exercise of executive discretion. As such, the minority considered that invasive remedies, such as the trial judge's in this case, were illegitimate and amounted to a virtual micro-management of administration that 'led to the improper politicisation of the relationship between the judiciary and the executive'.[4]

Not surprisingly, the Supreme Court's decision was greeted with a deluge of public and academic commentary. 'Activism' was the word on most people's lips. At the heart of these responses was the concern that the courts might have gone beyond the bounds of what it is that unelected judges should be doing in a constitutional democracy; they might have vacated the realm of legal decision-making and trespassed into the arena of political discretion. After over 20 years of debate about the legitimacy and reach of *Charter* review by courts over government action, the main thrusts of the response were predictable and well-rehearsed. On one side were those who viewed the majority decision as evidence that the justices had overstepped the bounds of their authority and competence: it was blatant and unwelcome 'judicial activism'. By interfering in the fiscal administration of public programs, an unelected, unrepresentative, and unchecked judiciary had violated the separation of powers and imperiled 'established traditions of responsible government'. Some went so far as to see the decision as a 'gratuitous and arrogant' power-grab, which bordered on the 'monarchical'. However, on the other side, there was applause for a bold court that had overcome the pusillanimity of some of its members to provide meaningful and effective protection to people's constitutional rights. If the Rule of Law was to be truly respected, it was thought essential that constitutional entitlements be effective remedies; it was not only desirable, but also necessary that governments not be allowed to evade, complicate, or ignore court orders. Far from imperiling responsible government, the *Doucet-Boudreau* decision had contributed to the legitimacy of Canada's democratic commitments by giving the *Charter* 'muscles' and 'teeth'.[5]

---

[4]   Ibid. at 45, per LeBel and Deschamps, as joined by Major and Binnie JJ.

[5]   For a sampling of the responses, see Lorne Gunter 'Judicial Arrogance Borders on Monarchial', *National Post*, 20 November 2003, A18; Kirk Makin 'Top Court Pursuing Activism', *The Globe and Mail*, 13 November 2003, A16; 'Judicial Rule' (Editorial), *National Post*, 8 November 2003, A19; Alan Young

Although both sides of this debate have something important to contribute, neither manages to capture the full thrust of a truly critical approach. From a critical standpoint, the *Charter* debate is much broader and deeper than both sides contemplate or accept— whether activist or restrained, the judges are involved in an inevitably and thoroughly political endeavor. Indeed, all efforts to separate law from politics are doomed to failure; this is especially true of the more traditional position taken by the minority and championed by a cadre of conservative academic critics. Accelerated by *Charter* adjudication, but not restricted to it, the Canadian judicial system, according to this perspective, is considered to have lost its way. The courts, especially the Supreme Court of Canada, are condemned as having become highly politicised and highly interventionist in their decisions and judgments. Effectively abandoning established legal principles and modes of legal reasoning, the judiciary has unwisely and indulgently shifted its focus to an analysis based on 'values'. Moreover, unlike the traditional understanding of judicial decision-making, this resort to values has more to do with a judge's own subjective political commitments than an objective assessment of a case's legal merits. These critics charge that, when recent judicial pronouncements are looked at as a body of work, they have not only become blatantly political, but reflect and instantiate a particular and partisan set of liberal-feminist commitments. In effect, these critics charge that 'judicial activism' is not a careless aberration by an overworked judiciary, but a concerted dereliction of official duty by a politically motivated judiciary. As such, there is an indignant call to return to the passive and neutral virtues of judicial restraint so that the promise of Canadian democracy can be redeemed. Of course, judicial activism has no part to play in such a restorative vision of law.[6]

Although this traditional critique is long on the details of the judiciary's current political fall from constitutional grace, its adherents are light on how a purely legal mode of principled adjudication can be performed. Although these exhortations to 'stick to the law' are seductive, they offer little suggestion of how such a seemingly prosaic practice can be achieved. At a theoretical level, three initial observations come to mind. First, the ascertainment of legal principles is itself fraught with political contamination and content. 'Established' is simply a way of saying that certain controversial moral or political commitments are now accepted by the legal community as settled; this is less an endorsement of the principles' apolitical nature and more an acknowledgement that general acceptance is a form of political validation. Second, the range of established principles is extremely broad and often encompasses competing maxims; there is no neutral or non-political way to select between contradictory principles. Third, even if it is possible to isolate a relevant and exclusive legal principle, it is far from obvious how that general principle can be applied to particular facts in an entirely objective or impartial manner. In short, despite the critic's yearning for a simpler and more professional

'Court Gives Our Toothless Charter Sharp Fangs', *The Toronto Star*, 23 November 2003, F07; and Kent Roach 'Do We Want Judges with More Muscle?', *The Globe and Mail*, 13 November 2003, A27.

[6] See, for example, F Morton and R Knopff, *The Charter Revolution and the Court Party* (Broadview Press, 2000); and R Martin *The Most Dangerous Branch: How the Supreme Court of Canada Has Undermined Our Law and Our Democracy* (McGill University Press, 2003).

age, there is no purely technical and non-political way to engage in a principled mode of adjudication. This is especially true of the *Charter*. Not only is what amounts to 'freedom' or 'equality' the stuff of fierce ideological debate (and how one relates to the other), but how such values are to be enforced within section 1's 'such reasonable limits as can be demonstrably justified in a free and democratic society' merely invites judges to wade even deeper into the political waters. Adjudication necessarily involves political choice.

The fact is that dissatisfaction with 'judicial activism' is itself a political campaign. Behind the traditional rhetoric of principled adjudication, there is a definite and partial political agenda. Although it is understandable why such critics would prefer to occupy the neutral territory of formal constitutional technique rather than contested turf of substantive political alignment, the effort to portray and promote a non-political mode of constitutional adjudication, as possible and desirable, is a neat but deceptive manoeuvre. When a closer look is taken at those occasions on which the critics raise the spectre of activism and those on which they do not, it will be seen that the difference is a blunt ideological divide. Those decisions that do not fit their political agenda are condemned as activist and those that do fit are defended as appropriate. The fine constitutional line they identify is one of their own political making. In general, those decisions which promote greater equality (for example, gay rights, Aboriginal land claims, etc.) are dismissed as activist and illegitimate, whereas those which defend greater liberty (for example, election spending, male property rights, etc.) are showcased as valid exercises of judicial authority. Yet, in terms of their fit with the opaque constitutional text and the courts' activist tendencies, there is nothing to choose between them. It is only that some substantive values are preferred over others. Accordingly, the claim of 'activism' is simply a veiled criticism that the courts are being too progressive and making decisions that do not reflect desirable conservative values: any court that stands by and lets constitutional values be ignored or belittled is at fault. But there is no technical or purely legal way to decide what those values are—law is politics by other means. The *Charter* is a contested site for political debate, not a definitive or neutral contribution to that debate.

Indeed, the *Doucet-Boudreau* decision itself is a good example of the disingenuity of those who reject 'judicial activism' in the name of traditional judicial virtues. As the judgments of the minority reveal, theirs is less a rejection of political decision-making and more a championing of a particular and partial view of constitutional politics. Despite repeated incantations about 'the separation of powers' and that 'the legislature and the executive are ... the principal loci of democratic will', the minority makes no real effort to demonstrate that this is somehow an accepted constitutional principle as opposed to a contested political commitment. It is not at all that the majority reject these general principles, it is that they have a different view of what those commitments demand in the particular circumstances. Moreover, it is unconvincing for the minority to maintain that the judiciary 'should avoid turning themselves into managers of the public service'. The entire history of administrative law confounds such trite observations about the need to 'avoid interfering in the management of public administration'. Furthermore, although it is important to recognise that there are constitutional boundaries to judicial action, those boundaries are not independently given, but are developed and negotiated by the courts themselves. Although judges must respect that the executive and legislative branches are 'the principal loci of democratic will,'[9] that is not the point. In light of the fact that the judges, including members of the *Doucet-Boudreau* minority, regularly and rightly interfere with executive and legislative authority when they breach the *Charter*, the real point is when and how they should so interfere as a matter of constitutional requirement, not whether they ever should. Accordingly, the difference between the majority and minority judgments is not between legitimate and illegitimate modes of adjudication, but between competing visions of an appropriate constitutional and democratic order. Each has to be defended in political terms: there is no method by which to declare that one is more intrinsically legal and, therefore, non-contestable than another. It hardly advances the democratic cause to deploy subterfuge and to pass off political commitments as constitutional mandates. Decisions should be celebrated or condemned for the substantive values that they uphold, not for their vague failure to respect some spurious formal distinction between making and applying law.

2. AND THE DEBATE GOES ON

The *Charter* crystallized the long-standing dilemma of the courts in trying to reconcile their new role as active guardians of fundamental values with the democratic values and traditions of Canadian society. They had to develop a way to act decisively as well as legitimately. In the *Charter*'s early years, judges relied upon the old standby of 'liberal legalism'—a sharp public/private distinction, neutral interpretation, and objective balancing—as a method for legitimising their decisions and reconciling the courts' role with democracy. However, it soon became clear that this jurisprudential modus operandi was failing to placate either liberal or more radical critics who complained that judicial review was not fulfilling its functions as effectively or as democratically as it might. Not only were the courts' efforts at preserving a sharp distinction between legal analysis and political judgment becoming more transparent and unconvincing, but also the substantive political values that animated their decisions were being revealed as increasingly outdated and unresponsive to contemporary Canadian sensibilities. Indeed, 'liberal legalism' was unable to command a sustained consensus even amongst judges. In response, the Supreme Court of Canada began to nurture a less legalistic and more pragmatic approach to its constitutional duties. The Court did modify and mollify its approach in light of these criticisms, especially in its approach to equality (abandoning the old formal and legalistic Canadian Bill of Rights approach) and to the reach of the *Charter* under section 32 (rejecting unsustainable distinctions between state and private activity). Moreover, the general thrust of the law-is-politics critique was heeded to the limited extent that the courts backed off from a transparent and discredited version of 'legal formalism' that pretended that constitutional law was simply a matter of interpretive conformity that had no connection to wider debates about national values and social policies.

Ironically, these very efforts to bolster their democratic legitimacy by relying upon an apparently more overt mode of democratic justification revealed even more starkly how undemocratic was the judges' involvement in judicial review under the *Charter*. In recent years, there has been a turn to 'dialogue theory' as an alternative justification for judicial review.[7] Judges and jurists have begun to accept that some reliance upon contested political commitments is not only inevitable, but also desirable. The primary concern is less with politicisation itself and more with 'the degree to which judges are free to read their own preferences into law'.[8] As such, activism is less about whether judges rely on political preferences and more about the sources of such values and the extent to which they rely on them. Cautioning that judges are not free to go wherever their personal political preferences take them, the dialogic approach does not abandon the idea or practice of maintaining a barrier between legitimate legal analysis and illegitimate political decision-making. Instead, in contrast to the anti-activists, it is argued that the distinction is much fuzzier, that the domain of law is much more expansive, and that the boundary between law and politics is much less often breached. However, like the anti-activists, they do concede that there is a point at which the judges can be said to be no longer doing law; they will have wandered off into other parts of the constitutional and political domain. In some important sense, law is to exist separately from its judicial spokesperson such that law places some non-trivial constraints on what judges can do and say. Although legal principles are more open and sensitive to political context, law is not simply reduced to contingent political preferences of the judiciary.

Consequently, the general thrust of dialogue theory is that, because the legislature possesses the final word on *Charter* matters by virtue of the section 33 override power (whereby governments can exempt legislation from *Charter* scrutiny), the courts can proceed to engage in a more overt balancing of political values under the section 1 'reasonable limits' provision. The claim and hope is that courts and legislatures will engage in an institutional conversation about the *Charter* and its requirements on particular and pressing issues of the day: courts and legislators have complementary roles that enable legislation to be carefully tailored to meet the Government's political agenda and respect *Charter* values. The most prominent judicial advocate of a dialogic approach was Justice Iacobucci, who insisted that 'judicial review on *Charter* grounds brings a certain measure of vitality to the democratic process, in that it fosters both dynamic interaction and accountability amongst the various branches'. In establishing a 'dialogic balance' and 'retaining a forum for dialogue' between the different branches of government, the courts must tread a thin, but vital line between deferential subservience and

---

[7] See chapter by Ravi Amarnath and Peter Hogg in this *Handbook*.

[8] Kent Roach, *The Supreme Court on Trial: Judicial Activism or Democratic Dialogue* (Toronto: Irwin Law, 2001) p 106. See also P. Hogg and A. Bushell 'The *Charter* Dialogue between Courts and Legislatures (Or Perhaps the *Charter* of Rights Isn't Such a Bad Thing After All)' (1997) 35 Osgoode Hall LJ 75 (1997).

robust activism. . .[9] Courts and legislatures are to be dialogic partners in an institutional conversation to advance shared democratic goals.

Although resort to 'democratic dialogue' does concede the normative nature of *Charter* decision-making and represents an effort to get beyond a discredited liberal legalism, it seems to have let the political cat out of the judicial bag without any plan for getting it back in or keeping it suitably restrained . The majority judgments in *Doucet-Boudreau* again offer compelling evidence of this claim. Indeed, suspiciously bereft of any reference to 'dialogic theory', the judgment of Iacobucci and Arbour JJ spends much of its time, directly and indirectly, trying to repel the debilitating spectre of judicial activism. Although the majority emphasizes time and again that 'courts must ensure that government behaviour conforms with constitutional norms but in doing so must also be sensitive to the separation of function among the legislative, judicial and executive branches', its reasons are relatively quiet on how that separation is to be achieved. Eschewing the notion that there is some 'bright line' in existence, their only serious suggestion is that judges must be pragmatic and contextual in their assessments: 'determining the boundaries of the courts' proper role, however, cannot be reduced to a simple test or formula; it will vary according to the right at issue and the context of each case'.[10] Their conclusion that 'the judicial approach to remedies must remain flexible and responsive to the needs of a given case' is unlikely to give comfort to those critics who look for some discipline in or direction to the judiciary's future performance. Indeed, an uncommitted observer might be forgiven for thinking that, on the question of whether 'law is politics', the court has given up the ghost rather than exorcised the wraith of judicial activism.

Accordingly, with its apparent rejection of judicial objectivity, lack of normative content, and vague invocations of democracy, the most recent juristic approaches to judicial review actually serve to undermine the project of justifying *Charter* adjudication's democratic legitimacy. Although dialogic theory is intended to calm fears that the courts are undisciplined and unlimited in their powers, it manages to reinforce the perception that courts are not only at the centre of the crucial process through which political discourse and values are shaped and sustained, but also that the judiciary get to determine the role and contribution of the other branches of government. The 'degree to which judges are free to read their own preferences into law' seems to be reducible to the oxymoronic conclusion that they will be as 'free to read their own preferences into the law' as 'their own preferences' allow. In this way, there is revealed to be a huge gap between the rhetoric of democratic dialogue and the reality of judicial performance. Presenting judicial review as part and parcel of a democratic dialogue merely underlines the extent to which this pared-down version of democracy has become a caricature of a more ample vision of democracy. An elite and stilted conversation between the judicial and

---

[9]   *Bell Express Vu Limited Partnership v R* [2002] 2 SCR 559 at paras 65–66. See also *Vriend v Alberta* 1998] 1 SCR 493; and *Corbiere v Canada (Minister of Indian and Northern Affairs)* [1999] 2 SCR 203.
[10]   *Doucet-Boudreau v Nova Scotia (Minister of Education)* [2003] SCC 62, pp. 19, 20 and 25, per Iacobucci and Arbour JJ.

executive branches of government is an entirely impoverished performance of democracy; it is an empty echo of what should be a more resounding hubbub.

3. A Critical Proposal

It is understandable why most judges and jurists wish to ground an objective practice of judicial interpretation that obviates judicial value-choices and that does not tread on the democratic toes of legislative or executive decision-making. However, it is a misplaced ambition doomed to failure. As judicial review involves unelected judges invalidating the actions of elected legislators or executives, all judicial review is anti-majoritarian and, therefore, presumptively undemocratic; no theory can reconcile judicial review with majority rule. The *Doucet-Boudreau* minority is surely correct to emphasize that 'the legislature and the executive are . . . the principal loci of democratic will'. Because there is no way to bring such a project to a satisfactory conclusion, continuing attempts to do so merely exacerbate the problem of democratic legitimacy and erode the very confidence that the legal establishment is trying to maintain. Adjudication in a society of diverse and conflicting politics is an inevitably ideological undertaking. Once this is acknowledged openly, courts will not be otiose or surplus to democratic requirements. Instead, this will underscore that both courts and legislatures are involved in the same game, namely delivering substantive answers to concrete problems.[11] In doing so, neither courts nor legislatures have a lock on political judgment about what is the best thing to do. Having abandoned the crude Bickelian counter-majoritarian challenge to the courts' democratic legitimacy[12] (i.e., the judiciary should follow through on the political logic of its own analysis), the judiciary must have the institutional courage of its own jurisprudential convictions about democracy being more a formal and majoritarian ideal.

Once liberated from the confining strictures of traditional thinking, the question of how and whether courts act with democratic legitimacy is of a very different order and character. The Bickelian difficulty has little to say about what values are important to democracy other than an unthinking regard for majoritarian processes. Once the principle of democracy is accepted to have a substantive as well as formal dimension (i.e., it is about a way of life as much as a process for making decisions), the justification for judicial action must also be viewed in substantive as well as formal terms. The work of courts need neither be judged by their capacity to be objective and impartial nor by their willingness to be consistent with, and not interfere with, majority politics. Instead, they can be evaluated in terms of the value choices that they make and the contribution that their decisions make to advance substantive democracy in the here-and-now.

---

[11] See Allan C. Hutchinson, *It's All in the Game: A Non-Foundational Account of Law and Adjudication* (Duke University Press, 2000).

[12] See A Bickel *The Least Dangerous Branch: The Supreme Court at the Bar of Politics* (2nd ed., Yale University Press, 1986) pp 14–18.

If the traditional presumptions—that legislatures are unprincipled and political and that courts are principled and reasoned—are dropped, it is possible to arrive at a very different understanding and account of the relation between courts and legislatures. For instance, the conclusion is possible that legislatures and courts are both principled and unprincipled to greater and lesser extents at different times and that each can further (as well as inhibit) the cause of democratic justice on a particular issue as much as the other. Moreover, as *Doucet-Boudreau* suggests, reliance on 'principles' is no less political and no more legal in any essential sense. The more pressing conundrum, therefore, is that, if democratic procedures do not guarantee democratic outcomes and democratic outcomes need not result from democratic procedures, how can we best organise constitutional arrangements so that democracy as a whole is more than less likely to prevail?

Accordingly, the appropriate inquiry in a constitutional democracy is not to ask whether the courts have acted politically and, therefore, improperly, but whether the political choices that they have made serve democracy. Because this democratic assessment is a substantive and political undertaking, not formal and analytical, it will always be a contested and contestable issue. Nevertheless, what counts as a democratic decision is not entirely reducible to a political and, therefore, open-ended debate about what is most appropriately democratic at the time and under the circumstances. The formal dimension of democracy insists that some account is taken of the general institutional location and position of relative governmental agencies. The fact that legislators are elected and judges are unelected has some political salience. However, as *Doucet-Boudreau* evidences, although judges must respect that distinction, any such decision about how to allocate state power will itself be political and context-specific. In determining the courts' role in a functioning democracy, there is no authoritative and organising meta-principle to which the courts can resort that is not itself political and controversial. The scope of the courts' role and power is itself part of the continuing debate about democracy which is a task of the most enduring and political kind, even if it is framed as one of a constitutional kind. Of course, the concern that courts are interfering too much in the political process is also a valid one. There is a keen need to be vigilant about what courts are (and are not) doing. Any court that tramples too often on the policy-making prerogative of Parliament and legislatures is asking for trouble: judges need to recognise that they are part of democracy's supporting cast, not its star-performers. It is what the courts are being active about which is the key. It is no more or less political to maintain the status quo than it is to subvert it; conservatism is as ideological as progressivism.

Despite the denials and resistance of traditional judges and jurists, constitutional common law is awash in the roiling and muddy waters of political power. Although judges and lawyers claim to keep relatively clean and dry by wearing their institutional wet-suits of abstract neutrality and disinterested fairness, they are up to their necks in ideological mud. And this is no bad thing. Because it is only when judges come clean, as it were, and admit that they have political dirt on their hands that they will appreciate that adjudication generally and constitutional adjudication particularly amount to an organic and messy process that has a similarly organic and messy connection to those social needs which it claims both to reflect and shape. So enlightened, judges might begin to accept that they are involved in a political enterprise whose success and legitimacy are best evaluated not by the courts' formal dexterity and technical competence, but by their substantive contribution to the substantive advancement of social justice. Abandoning the persistent attachment to a false distinction between a relatively unsoiled practice of principled adjudication and a contaminated involvement in crude politics would be an excellent place to begin such a commitment. As long as its practitioners and their juristic apologists present constitutional law as an insulated and insular process, courts will run the considerable risk of being unresponsive to and unreflective of the needs they are supposed to address. On the other hand, if judges and jurists are more willing to concede that the worlds of law and politics are intimately related, it might become possible to give society's needs the kind of direct and substantive attention that they merit. It is difficult enough for judges to fulfill their daunting roles without them also pretending at the same time that they are engaged in an entirely different enterprise. Efforts at local and contingent substantive justice are not enhanced by a mistaken belief that universal or formal coherence is at stake. Legitimacy is best attained by candour and frankness, not by denial and dissemblance.

4. A RADICAL INTERVENTION

Few decisions bring together the critical challenge to the *Charter* better than the Court's decision in *Chaoulli*.[13] A patient and physician contested the validity of a legislative prohibition on private health insurance: they insisted that the prohibition deprived them of access to private health care services that do not have the waiting times inherent in the public system. The essence of the claim was that the Quebec legislative provisions violated their rights under section 7 and section 1 of the *Quebec Charter of Human Rights and Freedoms*. The Court struck down the provisions on the basis of the *Quebec Charter* and by implication the *Canadian Charter*. In short, any notion of a public or social good was eclipsed by a privatised vision of social justice in which the privileges of the haves hold the have-nots hostage to their own economic freedom. Quite simply, the decision in *Chaoulli* confirms that the *Charter* has allowed constitutional right to hijack constitutional democracy in the name of constitutional justice.

Of course, this decision against socialised heath care in favour of private initiatives did not come out of the blue. There is a rich and substantial context that set the table for such a radical serving. The *Charter* is supposed to enshrine values that Canadians believe are so fundamental to their society that they should be beyond the vagaries and vanities of the immediate political process. Although those exact commitments are never beyond controversy, most agree that these values are intended to be *constitutive* of a 'free and democratic society'. In the *Charter*'s earlier days, the Supreme Court decided,

---

[13] *Chaoulli v Quebec (Attorney General)* [2005] 1 S.C.R. 791.

without much debate, that corporations count as an 'everyone' in the constitutional rush to legislative judgment; they could claim basic rights and freedoms. Having made this fateful step, the Court completed the rest of the march in the mid-1990s when it upheld the tobacco companies challenge to legislative efforts to curb their 'freedom of expression' by demanding explicit warnings on their products.[14] The basic rationale was that 'expression' was such a fundamental activity in a democracy that it must be protected even in dubious circumstances. Why this applied to so-called commercial speech as much as political expression was left largely unexplained.

In 2002, the Supreme Court of Canada rendered its reasons in *Gosselin*, which involved whether a Quebec regulation providing for reduced welfare benefits for individuals under 30 not participating in training or work experience employment programs infringed, among other things, welfare recipients' section 7 right to security of the person.[15] The majority of the Court held that section 7 does not place positive obligations on the Government to guarantee adequate living support, but simply restricts the state's ability to deprive people of their right to life, liberty, and security of the person. Although it is not too difficult to demonstrate that the difference between 'support' and 'deprivation' is not as airtight or different as the Court suggests, *Gosselin* is not wholly objectionable on its own terms. However, when it is put together with *RJR-Macdonald*, the full ideological thrust of the *Charter* and the Supreme Court's approach to section 7 begins to take a more sinister shape. While the welfare recipients are told to pursue their interests unaided in the political arena, tobacco companies are given the considerable leverage of constitutional benefit in their continuing (and well-funded) efforts to negotiate with government.

This deeply troubling approach was brought further home with a vengeance a couple of years later. In *Auton*, the Supreme Court decided that autistic children had no constitutional right to require British Columbia to fund expensive therapy for them.[16] The Court was sympathetic to the children and their parents (and hoped that the province would reconsider its decision to deny funding), but held that health policy was not part of the Constitution. The Court determined, following the logic of *Gosselin*, that it was a matter for fiscal calculation by politicians, not constitutional principle by lawyers. Such a decision sounds not entirely unreasonable on its own terms. That is, until it is viewed against the Court's findings in the tobacco advertising cases. By what frame of reference or set of values can it be argued that the commercial opportunities of tobacco companies are more deserving of constitutional protection than the well-being of autistic children? Reliance will no doubt be placed by judicial apologists on the fact that the former is about keeping government's intrusive tendencies in check, whereas the latter demands that government dig into its own pockets to finance such measures at the courts' behest. Ironically, however, the cost of the children's requested therapy is decidedly meagre compared to the truly huge social cost of coping with smoking-related illnesses. At the

---

[14] [1995] 3 SCR 199.
[15] [2002] 4 SCR 429.
[16] [2004] 3 SCR 657.

end of the day, both decisions have significant resource implications for society; it is simply that one is more direct than the other.

Mindful that it is possible to make legal arguments to support almost any political position, it is not difficult to draw fine distinctions between basic legal principles and established constitutional categorizations. But the essential point is that, regardless of fancy legal argument and subtle rationalisations, autistic children and welfare recipients are seen to simply count for less than tobacco companies in the constitutional scheme of things. And, therefore, they count for less in the calibrations of democratic decision-making. Moreover, the courts come to this pass, not as a conclusion of contested political judgment, but as a purported constitutional fact of the matter. This is a lamentable state of affairs that should deeply trouble all Canadians. However, if *Gosselin* and *Auton* were disappointing and debilitating, then *Chaoulli* is all in a class of its own.

As it should be, the contemporary debate on health care is vigorous and engaged. Canadians hold a variety of views on how health care should be funded and organised. Yet there is an emerging consensus that the Canadian system of health care is ailing. Whatever agreement there may be on the system's present condition, there is no firm or shared understanding on what to do about it. There are widely divergent views about how to remedy the situation. Although there are many different approaches, the central tension is between those who maintain that increased public funding and re-structuring of the present system is necessary and those who hold that greater opportunities for private intervention must be allowed. The present debate is sharply joined over whether individuals should be able to purchase privately those medical services that are exclusively available under the public scheme. There are no easy answers here and none that transcend entirely contested ideological commitments. As much as many strive to deny it, health care is inevitably and unavoidably a political matter.

In a democracy, the pressing issue is often as much about *who* gets to decide divisive matters as it is about *what* gets decided. By most democratic lights, the objective is less about getting it right in some absolute sense and more about arriving at decisions that engage public opinion and respect. The value of democratic decisions is measured by their enabling procedures as well as by their resulting content: democracy is about organizational form as well as substantive enactments. Health care is perhaps the most compelling illustration of this democratic conundrum. Moreover, because the subject matter is so contested and its resolution is so contingent, it is important to ensure that the decisions of one generation do not bind entirely the options of the next generation. Indeed, the evolving history of health care in Canada can be understood as one indicator of Canada's emergence to maturity as a developed and democratic country. However, *Chaoulli* challenges the very nature of both Canadian health care and Canadian democracy. In its monumental decision, the Supreme Court barged into the political fray and took a decidedly partial stance in the debate over health care. In the process, the Court undermined not only the debate on health care, but also the democratic foundations of the Canadian polity. In the starkest terms, *Chaoulli* obliges all *Charter*-watchers to accept for good or bad that *Charter* adjudication is energized by a political ideology which emphasizes, among other things, that individual entitlements are much more important than social responsibilities, that negative liberty is to be promoted at the expense of positive liberty, that people's capacity to exercise their rights is a matter of choice rather than circumstance, and that legislatures are not only not to be trusted, but are the breeding grounds of capricious and arbitrary decision-making.

In *Chaoulli*, the political vision that prevailed is highly individualistic and anti-state. The legitimate role of the state is limited to facilitating freedom by imposing a minimum of formal and equal constraints upon people's activities. People are treated as rational and private individuals who share little more than an abstract humanity. By treating everyone as the same and equally placed to exercise rights, this political approach ignores the very different material and social conditions in which people live. It depicts a just society as one in which the achievement of personal liberty and social justice can be effected without concern for serious economic equality. Indeed, rather than the courts being 'the last line of defence for citizens'[17] as Deschamps J presumes, her decision instead reveals that they are the last line of defence for the affluent and the privileged. When Deschamps J contends that 'the question is whether Quebeckers who are prepared to spend money to get access to health care that is, in practice, not accessible in the public sector because of waiting lists may be validly prevented from doing so by the state,'[18] she conveniently fails to mention that it is not simply whether one is 'prepared to spend money', but whether one has money to spend.

Emphasizing that shifting the design of Canada's health system to the courts is not a wise or desirable idea, the dissenting opinions of Binnie and LeBel JJ hit the nail squarely on the head:

> Those who seek private health insurance are those who can afford it and can qualify for it. They will be the more advantaged members of society. They are differentiated from the general population, not by their health problems, which are found in every group in society, but by their income status. We share the view of Dickson CJ that the *Charter* should not become an instrument to be used by the wealthy to 'roll back' the benefits of a legislative scheme that helps the poorer members of society. He observed in *Edwards Books*, at p. 779: 'In interpreting and applying the *Charter* I believe that the courts must be cautious to ensure that it does not simply become an instrument of better situated individuals to roll back legislation which has as its object the improvement of the condition of less advantaged persons.'[19]

Indeed, *Chaoulli* confirms that the extent of a person's wealth and resources remains the real measure of citizenship; the ability to participate and take advantage of one's civil claims is limited by and proportionate to one's material status. The Supreme Court again missed entirely the irony of Anatole France's praise for 'the majestic equality of the laws, which forbid rich and poor alike to sleep under the bridges, to beg in the streets, and

---

[17] *Chaouilli* above (n 13) [96].
[18] Ibid. [4].
[19] Ibid. [274].

steal bread'.[20] What is the 'progressive' notion on health care is not open-and-shut, but it would surely give considerable weight to the commitment that a system which provides a certain and similar level of care for all is to be preferred to a system which allows some to buy a level of care which is better or higher than for others. Equality of opportunity demands more than the dismantling of formal barriers to participation—it also requires substantive and affirmative measures to actualize those opportunities and possibilities. The holding in *Chaoulli* strengthens rather than dismantles those barriers. According to the Supreme Court, although Quebecers must not be prevented from spending their resources and wealth on obtaining health care, those without such resources and wealth have no corresponding social and affirmative right to health care. In light of *Gosselin*, it would seem that, if government decided to opt for an entirely or mostly private system of health care, the Supreme Court would not recognise a duty on government to provide services for those who could not afford a decent level of health care. Although this scenario is unlikely (at least in the near future), it does reveal the cut and consequences of a *Chaoulli*-style approach to constitutional law and health care.

As such, *Chaoulli* persists in the absurd notion that the true basis of individual freedom is the absence of collective constraint and state interference—individuals are most free when they are left entirely to their own devices and desires. Yet the roots of this belief run deep in the law. Even some of the more progressively-inclined decisions of the Supreme Court, such as the recognition of gay rights and abortion rights, build on this flawed and discredited foundation. For instance, in *Morgentaler*, even Wilson J grounded her more expansive interpretation of section 7 in order to protect pregnant women's freedom on a negative and solitary concept of personhood. She perpetuated and gave comfort to the conservative claim that the state that governs best is the state that governs least: 'the rights guaranteed in the *Charter* erect around each individual, metaphorically speaking, an invisible fence over which the state will not be allowed to trespass.'[21] In effect, Wilson's adoption of an individualistic ideology leaves women to their own devices and stymies the struggle to encourage government to fulfill its progressive and affirmative obligations to provide appropriate health facilities and services. Sadly, any progressive spin of *Morgentaler* is curtailed by its conservative underpinnings and *Chaoulli* is the fruit of such a poisoned tree.

However, notwithstanding the Supreme Court's affirmation of a regressive constitutional ideology, the most unconscionable feature of *Chaoulli* is the majority's conclusion that restrictions on private health care are 'arbitrary': 'a law is arbitrary where "it bears no relation to, or is inconsistent with, the objective that lies behind [it]"'.[22] The claim that there is no rational basis whatsoever for the established policy that the best way to preserve universal health care is by curtailing the operation and availability of private health insurance is an affront to Canadian democratic history and politics. It is one

---

[20] A. France, *The Red Lily* (W. Stephens trans. Hard Press, 1970) 91.

[21] *R. v Morgentaler*, [1988] 1 SCR 161 at 164.

[22] *Chaoulli*, above (n 13), McLachlin CJ and Major J [130].

thing for the majority to disagree with the political appeal and rightness of a scheme of socialised medicine, but it is another thing entirely to dismiss such a view as 'arbitrary'. Universal and non-private health care may not be the best scheme in some reasonable people's eyes, but how can it be capricious or despotic as 'arbitrary' implies—is the explanation that the Quebec and federal legislature did this for the sheer hell of it with no purpose in mind or only an oppressive one? Such a conclusion grossly misrepresents and condemns the past half-century of political struggle and governmental policy in Canada. It may be that the majority believes that allocating health care on the basis of status or wealth rather than need is preferable, but it is simply insulting to declare any other view to be not only wrong-headed, but also arbitrary. This is a breathtaking piece of judicial hubris.

Deschamps J has it entirely backwards when she states that the courts are 'an appropriate forum for a serious and complete debate' and that 'it must be possible to base the criteria for judicial intervention on legal principles and not on a socio-political discourse that is disconnected from reality'.[23] It is the courts and not the legislators who are 'disconnected from reality'. Her claim that 'the courts have a duty to rise above political debate'[24] is much more honoured by her (and her colleagues) in the breach than the observance. Not only is there no such fabled place outside of 'socio-political discourse', but her judgment is the best evidence that she has failed to meet her own earnest standards; 'legal principle' is revealed as simply one very transparent and partial kind of 'socio-political discourse'. As Binnie and LeBel JJ in their scathing dissent assert, 'the debate is about *social* values; it is not about constitutional law'.[25] Or, perhaps, more accurately, a constitutional law that entrenches the social values represented in the majority's reasoning is bad constitutional law. Notwithstanding Binnie and LeBel JJ, constitutional law is always about social values; the only issue is whose social values.

5. CONCLUSION

Much of the immediate Canadian response to cases such as *Doucet-Boudreau* has been framed by the concern over whether the judiciary had trespassed on forbidden political ground. However, there seems a broader and more troubling dynamic underlying the litigated issue—that democratic choice should not be only between rule by a judicial elite or a governmental elite, but through a political process that is more responsive to broader constitutional and democratic concerns. To conceive that the *Doucet-Boudreau* decision resurrects only the dilemma of whether courts can or should invade the political domain misses the main point: courts cannot exercise their powers and responsibilities without reference to contested values and principles of governance. The real and

[23] Ibid. [86], [87].
[24] Ibid. [89].
[25] Ibid. [166].

neglected issue is not the politicisation of the judiciary, but the democratic failure of the executive and legislative in fulfilling their constitutional responsibilities and mandate. If governments and legislatures were truly representative and were doing more of what they were supposed to being doing in a constitutional democracy, the question of what judges do would be less pressing and more incidental. If there is a crisis in Canadian democracy, it is to be found in the fact that politicians and legislators are simply not 'democrats' in the full sense of the term. 'Democracy' is used more as a rhetorical cloak for elitist practice than a measure and guide for popular politics.

Ironically, the *Canadian Charter of Rights and Freedoms* is viewed favourably and increasingly so by large majorities in all regions of Canada. A majority of Canadians say that the Supreme Court and not Parliament should have the final say when the Court declares a law unconstitutional because it conflicts with the *Charter*. Nevertheless, the fact that public opinion polls show considerable support for the Court is less an accolade for judges and more a slap in the face for politicians, particularly those leaders who preside in and over the Cabinet. Judges can only ever do a second-best job at making up the democratic deficit in the present performance of Canadian politics. The Supreme Court decisions in *Doucet* and *Chaoulli* are indicative of that. Although the judiciary has some defined and important function in Canadian politics, it must be limited and partial. Being neither elected by nor representative of Canadians, judges can never be entirely or rightly sanguine about the force and solidity of their democratic legitimacy. On the other hand, although the Executive can lay claim to greater democratic legitimacy, its practical exercise of power offends its democratic pedigree. Too often, political leaders seem to dance to their own tune rather than that of the people they represent. Increased 'rule by Cabinet' is hardly that much better than extended 'rule by the Supreme Court'. Although the statistics reveal interesting support for the courts, they express profound dissatisfaction with political leaders.

To revamp the legislative and executive process in line with greater popular participation and political accountability will require a monumental effort. Any changes—proportional representation, recall legislation, accountability audits, genuine ministerial responsibility, referenda etc.—must themselves be products of the very democratic process that is to be enhanced. There are no easy solutions to the present undemocratic trends. However, the debate around judicial activism is something of a distraction. Improvement in Canada's democratic status will not come from increased interventions by judges in the micro-management of governmental policies. Indeed, judicial supervision is a short-term crutch that actually harms a limping polity in the medium- and long-term. The replacement of one elite rule (executive) by another (judicial) can only be considered positive under the most warped sense of democracy. So, if there is a desire to rein in the judges, there must also be a commitment to ensuring that elected politicians and officials are living up to their own demanding constitutional and democratic responsibilities. At present, they are palpably not. But simply construing the democratic challenge as being one about whether the judges stay out of or stray onto the political terrain is to misrepresent the problem and, therefore, to hamper any genuine solutions.

Despite the regular rounds of self-congratulation about Canada's ranking as one of the best societies to live in, there is a serious erosion of basic democratic precepts. The twin foundations of democracy—popular participation and political accountability—are going the way of the polar ice-caps. There seems to be an implicit Faustian bargain between elite and rank-and-file that the price of socio-economic advancement (which is still questionable when looked at in other than mean or median terms) is at the cost of democratic involvement. The *Charter* and its judicial enforcement are part of that arrangement. Whatever else it means, democracy demands that there be more power to the people and less to the elites. Aristocratic rule is no less palatable because judges and political leaders are the new dukes and barons. And, it is certainly no more acceptable when such elites wrap themselves in the trappings of democracy. Although there has never been a golden age for Canadian democracy, what now passes for 'democracy' is an exclusive, sporadic, and sketchy conversation between the judicial and executive branches of government over what is best for the country. In this exchange, the voices of ordinary Canadians play no real or substantive role. Of course, a robust judiciary has a definite role in a vital democracy, but judges can only ever do a second-best job at making up the democratic deficit in the present performance of Canadian politics; they are neither positioned nor skilled to handle such a task.

BIBLIOGRAPHY

Bakan, Joel, *Just Words: Constitutional Rights and Social Wrongs* (Toronto: University of Toronto Press, 1997).

Bickel, Alexander, *The Least Dangerous Branch: The Supreme Court at the Bar of Politics* (New Haven, CT: Yale University Press, 2nd edn, 1986).

Hogg, Peter & Bushell, Allison, 'The *Charter* Dialogue between Courts and Legislatures (Or Perhaps the *Charter* of Rights Isn't Such a Bad Thing After All)' (1997) 35 *Osgoode Hall Law Journal* 75 (1997).

Hutchinson, Allan, *It's All in the Game: A Non-foundational Account of Law and Adjudication* (Durham, NC: Duke University Press, 2000).

_____. *Waiting for Coraf: A Critique of Law and Rights* (Toronto: University of Toronto Press, 1995).

Mandel, Michael, *The Charter of Rights and the Legalisation of Politics in Canada* (Toronto: Thompson Educational Publications 2nd ed., 1994).

Martin, Robert, *The Most Dangerous Branch: How the Supreme Court of Canada has Undermined our Law and our Democracy* (Montreal: McGill University Press, 2003).

Monahan, Patrick, *Politics and the Constitution: The Charter, Federalism, and the Supreme Court of Canada* (Toronto: Carswell, 1987).

Morton F. & Knopff, R., *The Charter Revolution and the Court Party* (Peterborough, ON: Broadview Press, 2000).

Petter, Andrew, *The Politics of the Charter; The Illusive Promise of Constitutional Rights* (Toronto: University of Toronto Press, 2010).

Roach, Kent, *The Supreme Court on Trial: Judicial Activism or Democratic Dialogue* (Toronto: Irwin Law, 2001).

Weiler, Paul, *In the Last Resort: A Critical Study of the Supreme Court of Canada* (Toronto: Carswell, 1974).

D. The Role of Constitutional Principles in Canadian Constitutional Law

CHAPTER 47

···

CONSTITUTIONAL
PRINCIPLES IN THE
SECESSION REFERENCE

···

JEAN LECLAIR[*]

ON 20 August 1998, in *Reference Re Secession of Quebec*,[1] the Supreme Court of Canada delivered one of the most important decisions since its establishment in 1875. At issue was whether it was possible, under the Constitution of Canada, for the sub-state of Quebec to secede unilaterally from Canada, and whether the right to self-determination recognized under international law included such a right to secede. The Supreme Court answered both questions in the negative.[2]

However, to the astonishment of many, the Court further concluded that, the Constitution not being a 'straitjacket',[3] the unwritten constitutional principles of federalism and democracy said to be lying in suspension, so to speak, in the interstices of Canada's constitutional order, 'dictate[d] that the clear repudiation of the existing constitutional order and the clear expression of the desire to pursue secession by the population of a province would give rise to a reciprocal obligation on all parties to Confederation to negotiate constitutional changes to respond to that desire'.[4] In other words, although no *right* to secede was said to exist under Canadian constitutional law, if, on the occasion of a referendum, a clear majority of Quebecers voted on a clear question in favour of secession, the government of Quebec would be allowed *to initiate* the Constitution's amendment process in order to secede by constitutional means, and such

---

[*] Professor, Faculty of Law, Université de Montréal.
[1] [1998] SCR 217; 1998 CanLII 793 (SCC) [hereinafter *Secession Reference*].
[2] Given that the present *Handbook* deals with Canadian constitutional law, the international law aspect of the decision will not be addressed.
[3] cf *Secession Reference* above (n 1) [150].
[4] Ibid [88].

an attempt to seek an amendment to the Constitution would prompt an obligation on the other provinces and the federal government to come to the negotiation table.[5]

Most surprising of all for legal observers was the Court's bypassing of the explicit amendment provisions provided by the *Constitution Act, 1982*[6] in favour of a number of 'fundamental and organizing principles of the Constitution' to address the question before it.[7]

The Solomonic nature of the decision allowed both the then Federal Prime Minister (Jean Chrétien) and the then Premier of Quebec (Lucien Bouchard) to claim victory. Polls also indicated that the decision enjoyed popular support both in Quebec and in the rest of Canada.[8]

To understand the Supreme Court's embroilment in the secession debate and explain why it chose to decide as it did, one must first be introduced to how, over time, in Canada and Quebec, issues of identity(ies), constitutional law, and democracy came to be formulated in absolutist terms, making political compromises next to impossible.

1. Monistic and Absolutist Understandings of Identities, Constitutional Law, and Democracy

Canada is a federation where plural and overlapping identities flourish. This does not simply mean that different groups or 'nations' cohabit alongside one another, but rather that individuals themselves are plural, nurturing multiple allegiances, some being more important than others, and some being confined to the limits of the historical community to which they belong, whereas others are not. Canada being a federation, a form of legal pluralism also prevails where provincial, territorial, federal,[9] and, more and more, Indigenous legal orders coexist and overlap one another. Finally, a federal state being composed of a plurality of co-equal political communities (provincial or territorial, and federal), that is being a polity of polities, it follows that citizens are simultaneously part of at least two demoi, each equally legitimate under Canada's federal constitution.[10]

All this makes for a complex regime, whose very intricacy is probably one of the reasons that Canada has not yet been rent asunder. Be that as it may, historical events, their subsequent interpretations, and the myths they engendered have served to obscure a

---

[5] Ibid [87].

[6] Schedule B to the Canada Act 1982, ch. 11 (U.K.), arts 38–49.

[7] cf *Secession Reference* above (n 1) [32].

[8] Joseph Fletcher and Paul Howe, 'Canadian Attitudes toward the Charter and the Courts in Comparative Perspective' (2000) 6 Choices 4.

[9] Canada is made up of a national government, 10 provinces, and three territories.

[10] *Constitution Act, 1867*, 30 & 31 Vict. Ch. 3 (U.K.), as reprinted in R.S.C., No. 5 (1985).

great part of Canada's interlocking webs of social, cultural, and legal interactions. A form of methodological nationalism, according to which everything is analysed through the prism of 'nations' understood as 'natural' collective subjective entities, has tended to represent the Canadian federation as the battleground of two separate and internally homogenous entities: Canada and Quebec.[11] Furthermore, for various reasons, the Constitution-as-sacred-text has acquired an existential dimension in the last decades of the twentieth century in Canada. Explicit recognition in the constitutional frieze, even though this might not translate into anything substantial at a purely legal level, seems to have become the sine qua non requirement for inclusion in the Canadian polity. In other words, form seems to have displaced substance where constitutional making is concerned. The idea of the Constitution not simply as a body of explicit norms but rather as a living body of experience capable of adaptation through political practices, compromises, and incremental judicial amendments, is harder to countenance. Finally, the discourse of rights now permeating all political and constitutional discussions has added a new layer of difficulty, serving at once as a springboard for constitutional recognition of collective rights and as a tool to oppose any such recognition.

The span of the issues raised by questions of identity, constitutional law, and democracy in Canada is much too broad to allow for their examination in any degree of detail. One subject however simultaneously draws upon all these topics: the search for an amending formula. Identifying in formulaic legal propositions who the constituent power holder(s) are (the people? the peoples? legislative assemblies? governments? etc.) and how they interact is always at the heart of an amending procedure.

The *Constitution Act, 1867* is devoid of any general provision providing for its own amendment. At the time, the Fathers of Confederation (as they are often called) took for granted that only the Imperial Parliament was invested with the power to amend Canada's constitution. Furthermore, as a colony, Canada was prohibited by the *Colonial Laws Validity Act 1865*[12] from amending imperial legislation extending to it. Hence, although some domestic power of amendment was recognized over specific issues, the newly created federal Parliament and the provincial legislatures had to turn to London for the ratification of important constitutional changes.

After the First World War, the United Kingdom legally recognized the growing independence of Canada and of its other dominions by adopting the *Statute of Westminster 1931*[13] that granted them the power to repeal or amend Imperial statutes applying to them. Symptomatic of the Canadian situation where agreement over a domestic amending procedure had proven impossible, subsection 7(1) of the statute enunciated that '[n]othing in this Act shall be deemed to apply to the repeal, amendment or alteration of the British North America Acts 1867 to 1930. . . .' As such, this provision maintained the

---

[11] Jean Leclair, 'Federalism as Rejection of Nationalist Monisms' in Dimitrios Karmis and François Rocher (eds), *The Trust/Distrust Dynamic in Multinational Democracies: Canada in Comparative Perspective* (McGill-Queen's University Press, 2017) (forthcoming).]

[12] 28 & 29 Vict. c. 63.

[13] 22 Geo. V, c. 4 (U.K.).

status quo, leaving to London the task of amending the Canadian constitution. Section 4 of the Statute juridically crystallized the already existing constitutional convention according to which the United Kingdom would not amend the Canadian Constitution, unless required to do so by Canadian authorities.

Discussions about the adoption of a domestic amending procedure gained a renewed momentum in the 1940s and 1950s, and would remain a major political bone of contention until the adoption of the *Constitution Act, 1982*. The debate was fuelled, among other things, by the successful attempt by the federal government in 1949 to obtain from London, without the prior consent of the provinces, an amendment empowering it to make changes to the 'Constitution of Canada' via an ordinary statute of the Parliament of Canada. Notwithstanding that this provision was eventually interpreted very narrowly by the Supreme Court, the federal government's decision to act unilaterally went against the grain of the widely held belief that the Constitution was a 'compact' requiring the intervention of the provinces for its amendment.

The 'compact theory', or rather theories, espoused many forms that all embodied the idea that the Canadian federation was the product of an agreement between either (1) the provinces among themselves, (2) between two linguistic or national groups and, more recently, (3) between the Canadian Crown and Canada's Indigenous peoples.[14] Some of these theories were developed after 1867 as a means of providing a legitimate rationale for the federal bargain.[15] However, it is not so much their veracity as historical facts that generated controversy between academics and politicians, as their normative consequences once political actors started mobilizing them in the debates over the adoption of an amending procedure.[16]

In English Canada, although the idea of the federation as a compact between the founding colonies/provinces (and the other provinces that joined later on) initially held some appeal, the latter started to falter in the 1930s. During that time, the Great Depression had convinced many Anglo-Canadians that a strong federal government was needed and that the distribution of power established in 1867 needed to be updated to acknowledge that fact. The notion of the federation as an agreement between equal provincial partners, entailing as it did the necessity of obtaining the consent of all to amend the constitution, struck many as most problematical.[17] Later on, the Second World War and the advent of the Welfare State would be instrumental in refocusing Anglo-Canadians' primary allegiance on the Central government, thus further accelerating the demise of the compact theory.

In Quebec, the compact theory came to take on a very different meaning. The federal bargain, it was claimed, was an agreement between two linguistic or national groups

---

[14] Sébastien Grammond, 'Compact Is Back: The Revival of the Compact Theory of Confederation by the Supreme Court' (2016) 53 Osgoode Hall Law Journal 799.

[15] For a recent analysis, see Jean-François Caron, 'Le Québec et la Confédération: le fédéralisme et la théorie du pacte' in Jean-François Caron and Marcel Martel (eds), *Le Canada français et la Confédération: Fondements et bilan critique* (Presses de l'Université Laval, 2016).

[16] Grammond above (n 14).

[17] See for example Norman McL. Rogers, 'The Compact Theory of Confederation' (1931) 9 Can Bar Rev 395.

(Anglophones and Francophones). Thus, from this perspective, no fundamental changes to the *Constitution Act, 1867* could obtain without the consent of Quebec. In fact, as the sole legitimate representative of French Canadians, Quebec was said to possess a veto over all foundational amendments.

The symbolic power of this version of the compact theory only grew stronger as Quebec nationalism went from a defensive position to an assertive one.[18] The *Révolution tranquille* (Quiet Revolution) that began in the 1960s was a social as well as a political revolution that profoundly transformed Quebec and, by the same token, its constitutional agenda. From the end of the Second World War until the 1960s, an ethnically non-inclusive conservative cultural nationalism prevailed among Quebecers. Politically, this translated into the domination of the *Union Nationale*, a political party bent on promoting close ties with the Catholic Church and minimal state policies. Its leader Maurice Duplessis fought ardently any federal attempt at 'invading' the exclusive jurisdictions recognized to the provinces under the *Constitution Act, 1867*.[19] However, under the impetus of the new political forces unleashed by the Quiet Revolution, the State of Quebec became the main instrument of national assertiveness for Quebecers. No longer on the defensive, Quebec governments would thenceforth demand more powers to better serve the people of the province. As time went on, Quebec governments claimed to be the sole voice of the whole 'nation', meaning the entire population of the province.

It is worth noting that, in the process of becoming ever more Quebecers, most French-speaking inhabitants of Quebec abandoned the 'French Canadian' denomination. In addition, starting in the 1960s, a more civic-pluralist nationalism emerged, according to which all inhabitants of Quebec identifying themselves as Quebecers were recognized as such.

As it turns out, two agreements on an amending formula nearly achieved success in 1964 (the Fulton-Favreau formula) and 1971 (the Victoria Charter). Both gave a veto to Quebec, but on each occasion, Quebec refused to affix its signature. As underlined by Peter W. Hogg, 'all participants understood that Quebec had to be a party to whatever agreement was reached, because the sole dissent of Quebec was sufficient to abort both of these previous projects'.[20]

Tensions reached a climax when the *Parti Québécois* (PQ), a political party intent on seeking independence, took power in 1976 and held a referendum on a sovereignty-association proposal on 20 May 1980. As the referendum question illustrates, the PQ did

---

[18] The story of this era has been well told by Keith Banting and Richard Simeon (eds), *And No One Cheered: Federalism, Democracy and the Constitution Act* (Methuen, 1983); Peter H. Russell, *Constitutional Odyssey. Can Canadians Become a Sovereign People?* (2nd ed., University of Toronto Press, 1993); Jeremy Webber, *Reimagining Canada: Language, Culture, Community, and the Canadian Constitution* (McGill-Queen's University Press 1994).

[19] There were however important pockets of French Canadian intellectual and political resistance during the whole of the Duplessis era: Jacques Couillard, 'Aux sources de la Révolution tranquille: le congrès d'orientation du Parti libéral du Québec du 10 et 11 juin 1938' (2015) 24 Bulletin d'histoire politique 125.

[20] *Constitutional Law of Canada*, vol 1, (5th ed, Carswell, 2007) para 4.1(b) (R 2013-1).

not seek straightforward secession; neither did it want to sever all economic ties with Canada:

> The Government of Quebec has made public its proposal to negotiate a new agreement with the rest of Canada, based on the equality of nations; this agreement would enable Quebec to acquire the exclusive power to make its laws, levy its taxes and establish relations abroad—in other words, sovereignty—and at the same time to maintain with Canada an economic association including a common currency; any change in political status resulting from these negotiations will only be implemented with popular approval through another referendum; on these terms, do you give the Government of Quebec the mandate to negotiate the proposed agreement between Quebec and Canada?

The 'No' side won the day with a little less than 60 percent of the votes cast. Six nights before the fateful day, on 14 May 1980, the federal Prime Minister Pierre Elliot Trudeau, a Quebecer himself, addressed a huge crowd in Montreal (Quebec's metropolis), and pledged that, if the 'No' side won, this would be 'interpreted [by the central government and the other provinces] as a mandate to change the Constitution, to renew federalism'.[21] Referring to his Cabinet, he stated: 'I can make a most solemn commitment that following a NO vote, we will immediately take action to renew the constitution and we will not stop until we have done that'.[22] This pledge would soon come back to haunt him (and the rest of the country).

In the days that followed the referendum, the federal government immediately took action, trying to reach agreement with the provinces on a new constitutional package. These attempts having all met with failure, on 2 October 1980, Ottawa announced its decision to proceed unilaterally. The United Kingdom Parliament would be asked to amend the Canadian Constitution, even in the face of provincial opposition. The 'patriation' proposal would include, among other things, an amending formula similar to the one introduced in the 1971 Victoria Charter, to which would be added the possibility of resorting to a referendum to bypass the need for provincial assent, and a *Charter* of rights and freedoms whose language rights guarantees clashed with the most controversial provisions of the *Charter of the French Language*[23] adopted by the PQ in 1977 to make French the common public language of the province.

Eight of the 10 provinces (including Quebec) objected to the proposal, and three of them referred the question of the legality of Ottawa's unilateral action to their appeal courts. The latter's divided opinions paved the way for an appeal to the Supreme Court. On the 28th of September 1981, although a majority of the high court justices recognized 'the untrammelled authority *at law*'[24] of Parliament to adopt a resolution unilaterally

---

[21] Quoted in Webber above (n 18) 107.
[22] Ibid.
[23] R.S.Q. c. C-11.
[24] *Re: Resolution to amend the Constitution* [1981] 1 SCR 753, 1981 CanLII 25 (SCC) [hereinafter *Patriation Reference*] 808 [emphasis added].

requesting amendments to the Constitution, yet a differently constituted majority concluded that it would be 'unconstitutional in the conventional sense'[25] to do so without 'at least [obtaining] a substantial measure of provincial consent.'[26] A year later, in a second momentous decision, the Court would unanimously conclude that Quebec had no conventional power of veto over constitutional amendments affecting its legislative competence.[27]

Two elements of the 1981 decision are worth mentioning. First, a majority of judges dismissively discarded the compact theories, whether conceived as 'a full compact theory [between the founding colonies/provinces] . . . or [as] a modified compact theory', claiming that they 'operate[d] in the political realm . . . [and that they did] not engage the law'.[28] Second, two of the dissenting judges held that constitutional legality, as opposed to conventionality, had indeed been violated by the federal government when it adopted its resolution. They stressed that 'the inviolability of separate and exclusive legislative powers'[29] recognized by the principle of federalism, 'the dominant principle of Canadian constitutional law',[30] had been 'carried into and considered an integral part of the operation of the resolution procedure.'[31] Therefore, a resolution aimed at initiating an amendment procedure 'could only be an effective expression of Canadian sovereignty if it had the support of both levels of government.'[32]

The Court's decision forced an unwilling Prime Minister back to the table. However, the fragility of the alliance between the eight opposing provinces would soon be demonstrated. Prior to the Court's decision, in April 1981, the 'Gang of Eight' had agreed upon a counter-proposal containing an amending formula according to which no provinces had a veto. Nevertheless, it provided that a province wishing to do so could opt out of any amendment transferring jurisdiction from the provinces to the federal Parliament. Quebec's Premier, René Lévesque, leader of the now enfeebled PQ government, had agreed to abandon Quebec's veto only on condition that full financial compensation would be guaranteed to

---

[25] Ibid 908.

[26] Ibid 905. The major difference between the laws of the constitution and conventional rules of the constitution is that the latter cannot be enforced by courts: ibid 880–881. They can only be sanctioned in the political arena.

[27] *Re: Objection by Quebec to a Resolution to amend the Constitution* [1982] 2 SCR 793, 1982 CanLII 219 [SCC] [hereinafter *Quebec Veto Reference*]. The Court rejected the existence of a conventional power of veto for the reason that such a convention had never been accepted or recognized by the political actors in a sufficiently articulated manner. However, as one shrewd commentator noted: ' . . . there was no articulated recognition of the convention requiring substantial consent. Indeed, had the Court insisted on articulated political recognition as rigorously in the first case as they did in the second, no convention at all would have been found to exist in the [*Patriation Reference*]': Marc E. Gold, 'The Mask of Objectivity: Politics and Rhetoric in the Supreme Court of Canada' [1985] 7 Supreme Court Law Review 455, 477.

[28] cf *Reference 1981* above (n 24) 803. In *Quebec Veto Reference* above (n 27) 812–814, the Supreme Court again eluded a similar argument.

[29] Ibid 831.

[30] Ibid 821.

[31] Ibid 831.

[32] Ibid 847.

provinces opting out. In spite of this agreement, at the end of the hectic three days conference held in Ottawa in the first week of November 1981, in what would become in Quebec's myth-ideology 'the night of the long knives', nine provincial premiers finally struck a deal with the federal government that left Quebec on the sidelines. They succeeded in brokering this agreement only by acquiescing to jettison the right to opt out with full compensation. Although René Lévesque and his government bear part of the responsibility for the constitutional isolation of Quebec during this episode,[33] and although it is hard to imagine how a man who had dedicated his entire political life to seeking the independence of Quebec could have agreed to a new federal deal, it remains that the other provinces and the federal government took the (mis)calculated risk of amending the Canadian Constitution, and thus the Canadian state fabric, without the consent of Quebec's political elites.

On the night of 14 May 1980, the federal Prime Minister had not specified how and in which direction he intended to steer the promised constitutional changes. Undoubtedly, however, a great number of Quebecers had not expected him to proceed without Quebec's approval. What some experienced as disappointment was felt by others as treason.

This is most unfortunate as most Quebecers did not object so much to the content of the constitutional reform, the *Canadian Charter of Rights and Freedoms* always having been enthusiastically embraced by Quebecers,[34] as with the manner of its adoption. They objected to the fact that the province of Quebec was treated as just any other province. They were also concerned that Canada would from thence on, from a federal society, morph into one essentially made up of equal rights-bearing citizens gradually focussing their primary allegiance on the institutions of the federal government rather than on their province's local institutions.

In the years that followed, attempts were made to bring back Quebec into the folds of the Canadian Constitution 'with honour and enthusiasm', according to the expression of Brian Mulroney, then Prime Minister of Canada (1984–1993). The failed 1987 *Meech Lake Accord*, for instance, sought, among other things, to assuage Quebec's demands by ensuring the participation of Quebec in the nomination of senators and Supreme Court justices, by increasing Quebec's power over immigration, by limiting the federal spending power, by providing Quebec with a veto over constitutional amendments, and, most importantly, by expressly recognizing Quebec as a 'distinct society'.

Out of the many reasons for the accord's demise, three deserve mention. First, the new amending formula introduced in 1982 subjected the amendment of either the composition of the Supreme Court or the amending procedures themselves to the unanimous consent of provinces.[35] As a consequence, the whole accord was dealt with as a single unit whose ratification required the approval of all provinces.

---

[33] Guy Laforest and Rosalie Readman, 'More Distress than Enchantment: The Constitutional Negotiations of November 1981 as Seen from Quebec' in Lois Harder and Steve Patten (eds), *Patriation and Its Consequences. Constitution Making in Canada* (University of British Columbia Press 2015).
[34] The Federal Idea, *A Study on the Occasion of the 30th Anniversary of the Patriation of the Constitution*, (CROP, 2011); Center for Research and Information on Canada, *The Charter: Dividing or Uniting Canadians?* (CRIC, 2002).
[35] *Constitution Act, 1982*, s 41 (d) and (e).

Second, the 'distinct society' clause did not mesh harmoniously with the more procedural model of democracy to which more and more Anglo-Canadians were adhering. Although still in its infancy, the *Canadian Charter of Rights and Freedoms* had already acquired the status of national icon in English Canada. As Trudeau intended, the *Charter* had successfully deprovincialized Anglo-Canadian identities, operating as both a formal and symbolic expression of the fundamental values that defined Canadianness. Thus, at the same time as the nationalist discourse in Quebec was emphasizing the latter's radical cultural difference, an equally monolithic understanding of Anglo-Canadian identity was taking shape. The *Charter* helped promote an 'unhyphenated Canadianism', according to which 'Canadians should not be divided against themselves, having two allegiances, one to their country, one to their more local identity. They must be Canadians first, each treated, under the constitution, simply as Canadians'.[36]

Third, the *Meech Lake Accord* failed because political and social 'outsiders' had been knocking on the constitutional door without much success since the beginning of the 1960s. Up to the *Meech Lake Accord*, the federal government and Quebec had occupied centre stage in constitutional-making processes. But now, the Western provinces, women's groups, immigrant communities, and, most especially, the Indigenous peoples were also requesting greater recognition in the constitutional text.[37] The *Meech Lake Accord* and the process of its adoption was thus not to their liking, and they opposed it.

The 1992 *Charlottetown Accord* would eventually seek to satisfy everyone. It only succeeded in convincing the entire population of Canada that mega-constitutional negotiations were bound to fail.

Two major consequences flowed from all of these constitutional tribulations. First, the bond of trust between Quebec and the rest of Canada further eroded. A powerful discourse of victimization grew in Quebec, and political parties of all stripes stated that they would never sign the Constitution unless explicit recognition of the province's specificity, accompanied by the allocation of new powers, was provided for. Second, the Meech Lake and Charlottetown accords, in conjunction with the all-powerful discourse of 'recognition'[38] now suffusing (and suffocating) all Canadian political debates, have sparked a new and dangerous phenomenon: constitutional fetishism emphasizing a textocentric conception of constitutional law.[39] It would now appear that for political and social actors, their very existence as worthy members of the Canadian polity

---

[36] Webber above (n 18) 143.

[37] For instance, according to Canada's Indigenous peoples, while recognizing their aboriginal and treaty rights, section 35 of the *Constitution Act, 1982* had not gone far enough in acknowledging their role as constituent actors.

[38] The foundational text on this subject was penned by Canadian philosopher Charles Taylor, 'The Politics of Recognition' in Amy Gutman (ed), *Multiculturalism: Examining the Politics of Recognition* (Princeton University Press, 1994).

[39] Jean-François Gaudreault-Desbiens, 'Canadian Federalism and Quebec's Pathological Prism' in Stéphan Gervais, Christopher Kirkey, and Jarrett Rudy (eds), *Quebec Questions: Quebec Studies for the Twenty-First Century* (2nd ed., Oxford University Press, 2016); Jean-François Gaudreault-Desbiens, 'The Fetishism of Formal Law and the Fate of Constitutional Patriotism in Communities of Comfort: A Canadian Perspective' in John Eric Fossum, Paul Magnette, and Johanne Poirier (eds), *Ties That Bind: Accommodating Diversity in Canada and the European Union* (P.I.E. Lang 2009).

is existentially linked to an explicit constitutional recognition. Whatever their de facto (and even de jure!) status may be, nothing less will suffice.

For secessionist Quebecers, constitutional law was not the answer to their 'nation''s problems; democracy was. The people of Quebec would be the one to decide. And so, on the night of 30 October 1995, a second referendum was held. Quebecers were asked the following question: 'Do you agree that Quebec should become sovereign after having made a formal offer to Canada for a new economic and political partnership within the scope of the bill respecting the future of Quebec and of the agreement signed on June 12, 1995?'[40] Not only did polls demonstrate the public's confusion as to the meaning of this question,[41] but both Jacques Parizeau, leader of the PQ, and Lucien Bouchard, at the time leader of the Bloc québécois, a sovereignist federal political party, would later admit to the question's lack of clarity.[42] Even more shocking, on the very day of the referendum, Lucien Bouchard had no idea how his colleague Parizeau would interpret results that were bound to be close.[43] For Bouchard, a 'Yes' might not necessarily lead to secession; not so for Parizeau.[44]

The results of the referendum sent shockwaves throughout the country: 49.42 percent 'Yes' to 50.58 percent 'No'. Badly shaken, the federal government decided no longer to let Quebec lead the dance on the issue of secession. And so, the Supreme Court of Canada having jurisdiction to give advisory opinions, the federal government, on 30 September 1996, required the high court to answer three questions, the first being the only one that will retain our attention in this chapter:

1. Under the Constitution of Canada, can the National Assembly, legislature or government of Quebec effect the secession of Quebec from Canada unilaterally?
2. Does international law give the National Assembly, legislature or government of Quebec the right to effect the secession of Quebec from Canada unilaterally? In this regard, is there a right to self-determination under international law that

---

[40] The Bill referred to was *Bill 1*, entitled *An Act respecting the future of Québec, 1995*. Section 1 provided as follows: 'The National Assembly is authorized, within the scope of this Act, to proclaim the sovereignty of Québec. The proclamation must be preceded by a formal offer of economic and political partnership with Canada.' However, section 26 specified that '[t]he proclamation of sovereignty may be made as soon as the partnership treaty has been approved by the National Assembly *or as soon as the latter, after requesting the opinion of the orientation and supervision committee, has concluded that the negotiations have proved fruitless*' [emphasis added]. Section 26, providing an early escape hatch to the willing, was the only provision of the Act relating to partnership that was of any interest to Jacques Parizeau: Chantal Hébert and Jean Lapierre, *Confessions post-référendaires: Les acteurs politiques de 1995 et le scénario d'un oui* (Éditions de L'homme, 2014), 55. The second document referred to the tripartite agreement sealing an alliance among Jacques Parizeau, Lucien Bouchard, and Mario Dumont, respectively leaders of the Parti Québécois, the Bloc Québécois (the federal equivalent of the PQ), and the Action Démocratique du Québec.

[41] Maurice Pinard, Robert Bernier, and Vincent Lemieux, *Un combat inachevé* (Presses de l'Université du Québec, 1997).

[42] Jaques Parizeau, 'Lettre ouverte aux juges de la Cour suprême' *Le Devoir* (Montreal, 3 September 1998) A9; Michel Venne, 'Bouchard promet une question plus claire' *Le Devoir* (Montreal, 28 August 1998) A1.

[43] Hébert and Lapierre above (n 40) 25, 32.

[44] On Parizeau's and Bouchard's antagonistic views, see ibid 34–35, 37–38, 54–55, 61–62.

would give the National Assembly, legislature or government of Quebec the right to effect the secession of Quebec from Canada unilaterally?

3. In the event of a conflict between domestic and international law on the right of the National Assembly, legislature or government of Quebec to effect the secession of Quebec from Canada unilaterally, which would take precedence in Canada?

As we will see, the Court's unanimous decision introduced a level of complexity in the discourses relating to constitutional law and identity that subtly shattered the monistic edifices erected over the years by both the federalists and the secessionists.

2. The Supreme Court's Non-positivist Perspective on Law and Its Rejection of Monistic Depictions of Identity

The Court was faced with two radically different legal arguments. On the one hand, the Attorney General of Canada was arguing for a purely positivistic understanding of the Constitution, according to which the latter was confined to the four corners of its *written* provisions.[45] Constitutionalism and the rule of law, he argued, required the state to act in compliance with the clear and previously stated rules enshrined in the Constitution. Consequently, as section 45 of the *Constitution Act, 1982*, the only one allowing a province unilaterally to amend a part of the Constitution, did not authorize secession, that settled the issue. The Court, it was argued, need not make any further determinations; it did not even have to surmise how secession might be effected under the 1982 amending procedures.

As for the amicus curiae assuming the task of arguing the secessionists' case—the PQ government having refused to appear in court, claiming that it was for the people of Quebec to decide its own fate—he basically argued that the right of self-determination recognized under international law took precedence over the Canadian Constitution, and that a majority vote of 'le peuple québécois' would endow it with the required legitimacy to assert effective control over the territory of Quebec. But who exactly was 'le peuple québécois'? The amicus's answer was, to say the least, rather vague,[46] as one of his most cryptic statements demonstrates: 'Le peuple québécois est [The people of Quebec is]'.[47] Furthermore, in advocating recourse to the democratic principle in such an absolutist fashion, the amicus's position concealed the fact that the demos' opinion can only

---

[45] Jean Leclair, 'Impoverishment of the Law by the Law: A Critique of the Attorney General's Vision of the Rule of Law and the Federal Principle' (1998) 10 Constitutional Forum 1.

[46] Bruce Ryder, 'A Court in Need and a Friend Indeed: An Analysis of the Arguments of the *Amicus Curiae* in the Quebec Secession Reference' (1998) 10 Constitutional Forum 9.

[47] *Amicus Curiae*'s factum quoted in Yves-Marie Morissette, *Le Renvoi sur la Sécession du Québec: Bilan provisoire et perspectives* (Varia, 2001) 62.

be distilled through legal processes and mechanisms that do not flow naturally from ethereal abstractions.[48] Democracy without law is chaos.

* * *

How did the Court go about deciding this case? Simply resorting to the written provisions of the *Constitution Act, 1982* risked alienating Quebecers even further, as it was precisely the legitimacy of the constitutional order instantiated by this reform that was challenged. Furthermore, how could the Court avoid falling into the trap of openly challenging the monolithic depiction of the Quebec people that was so prevalent in nationalist circles?

In the first place, the Court refused to embrace the Attorney General's textocentric understanding of the Constitution. The constitutional texts were said not be exhaustive; the Constitution also embraces unwritten rules and principles.[49] 'Behind the written word, stated the Court, is an historical lineage stretching back through the ages, which aids in the consideration of the underlying constitutional principles. These principles inform and sustain the constitutional text: they are the vital unstated assumptions upon which the text is based.'[50] It went on to specify that, even though these principles 'are not explicitly made part of the Constitution . . . it would be impossible to conceive of our constitutional structure without them.'[51] In fact, the Court asserted that they were the 'lifeblood' of Canada's constitutional structure.[52] Four 'fundamental and organizing principles of the Constitution' were held as relevant to addressing the reference questions: federalism, democracy, constitutionalism and the rule of law, and respect for minorities.[53]

Second, so as to prevent totalizing approaches of the type advocated by the *amicus*, the justices emphasized that these foundational principles functioned 'in symbiosis', and that, '[n]o single principle can be defined in isolation from the others, nor does any one principle trump or exclude the operation of any other.'[54] For instance, the Court underlined that the rule of law and constitutionalism were closely linked to the democratic principle, and vice versa.[55] In fact, between these two pillars stood the legitimacy of a political system:

> The consent of the governed is a value that is basic to our understanding of a free and democratic society. Yet democracy in any real sense of the word cannot exist without the rule of law. It is the law that creates the framework within which the 'sovereign

---

[48] Jean Leclair, 'Le potier, l'argile et le peuple: le rôle de la loi et du pouvoir dans le processus d'accession du Québec à l'indépendance' in Eugénie Brouillet, Patrick Taillon, and Amélie Binette (eds), *Un regard québécois sur le droit constitutionnel. Mélanges en l'honneur d'Henri Brun et de Guy Tremblay* (Éditions Yvon Blais, 2016) and Jeremy Webber, 'The Legality of a Unilateral Declaration of Independence under Canadian Law' (1997) 42 McGill LJ 281, 315–318.

[49] cf *Secession Reference* above (n 1) [32].

[50] Ibid [49].

[51] Ibid [51].

[52] Ibid.

[53] Ibid [32].

[54] Ibid [49].

[55] Ibid [67].

will' is to be ascertained and implemented. To be accorded legitimacy, democratic institutions must rest, ultimately, on a legal foundation. That is, they must allow for the participation of, and accountability to, the people, through public institutions created under the Constitution. Equally, however, a system of government cannot survive through adherence to the law alone. A political system must also possess legitimacy, and in our political culture, that requires an interaction between the rule of law and the democratic principle. The system must be capable of reflecting the aspirations of the people. But there is more. Our law's claim to legitimacy also rests on an appeal to moral values, many of which are imbedded in our constitutional structure. It would be a grave mistake to equate legitimacy with the 'sovereign will' or majority rule alone, to the exclusion of other constitutional values.[56]

The Court went on explaining that the rule of law was not synonymous to blind subjection to legal norms, or democracy to majority rule. On the contrary, the rule of law served a much broader purpose: 'vouchsaf[ing] to the citizens and residents of the country a stable, predictable and ordered society in which to conduct their affairs'.[57] As for democracy, in addition to its institutional and individual dimensions, it was 'fundamentally connected to substantive goals' such as the accommodation of cultural and group identities[58] which includes the protection of minorities.[59]

As for the principle of federalism, the Court explained that it was a 'legal response to the underlying political and cultural realities that existed at Confederation and continue to exist today'.[60] Interestingly, the Court explicitly referred to the dissenters' opinion in the *Patriation Reference*, recalling that 'Martland and Ritchie JJ., dissenting in [the *Patriation Reference*], considered federalism to be "the dominant principle of Canadian constitutional law".'[61] The Court also emphasized that federalism was a political regime that could reconcile the cultural and linguistic diversity of the different peoples inhabiting Canada with their desire to unite and work together toward common goals.[62] In addition, the justices indirectly referred to the compact theory when they acknowledged that Quebec's specificity was a determining factor in the choice for federalism in 1867:

> The social and demographic reality of Quebec explains the existence of the province of Quebec as a political unit and indeed, was one of the essential reasons for establishing a federal structure for the Canadian union in 1867. [. . .] The federal structure adopted at Confederation enabled French-speaking Canadians to form a numerical majority in the province of Quebec, and so exercise the considerable provincial powers conferred by the *Constitution Act, 1867* in such a way as to promote their language

[56] Ibid [67].
[57] Ibid [70].
[58] Ibid [74].
[59] Ibid [79–82].
[60] Ibid [57]; see also [43].
[61] Ibid.
[62] Ibid [43].

and culture. It also made provision for certain guaranteed representation within the federal Parliament itself.[63]

From the complex interplay of these four foundational principles, a judicially-crafted obligation to negotiate was deduced, one that 'dictate[d] that the clear repudiation of the existing constitutional order and the clear expression of the desire to pursue secession by the population of a province would give rise to a reciprocal obligation on all parties to Confederation to negotiate constitutional changes to respond to that desire'.[64] On the one hand, '[t]he democratic vote, by however strong a majority, would have no legal effect on its own and could not push aside the principles of federalism and the rule of law, the rights of individuals and minorities, or the operation of democracy in the other provinces or in Canada as a whole'.[65] Nor, on the other hand, 'can the reverse proposition be accepted. The continued existence and operation of the Canadian constitutional order could not be indifferent to a clear expression of a clear majority of Quebecers that they no longer wish to remain in Canada. The other provinces and the federal government would have no basis to deny the right of the government of Quebec to pursue secession, should a clear majority of the people of Quebec choose that goal, so long as in doing so, Quebec respects the rights of others'.[66]

Interestingly, the Court insisted that this judicially-crafted obligation to negotiate did not circumvent the text of the Constitution, as successful negotiations would still need to be consecrated by a formal amendment.[67]

Finally, the Court also rejected the positivist dogma according to which judges are the sole interpreters of constitutional legality. Indeed, notwithstanding its assertion that '[t]he principles are not merely descriptive, but are also invested with a powerful normative force, and are binding upon both courts and governments',[68] the Court stated that its role was confined to establishing the 'legal framework' within which political decisions may ultimately be made.[69] It concluded, for instance, that what amounts to a clear majority on a clear question called for political judgments and evaluations that were best left to the workings of the political process.[70] The same went for the negotiations themselves. In spite of the fact that the Court asserted that '[t]he conduct of the parties in such negotiations would be governed by the same constitutional principles which give rise to the duty to negotiate',[71] it asserted that it would play no supervising role as it 'would not have access to all of the information available to the political actors, and [because] the methods appropriate for the search for truth in a court of law are ill-suited to getting to the bottom of constitutional negotiations'.[72]

---

[63] Ibid [59].
[64] Ibid [88].
[65] Ibid [151].
[66] Ibid.
[67] Ibid [84] and [97].
[68] Ibid [54].
[69] Ibid [27], [100–101], [110] and [153].
[70] Ibid.
[71] Ibid [90] and [94].
[72] Ibid [101].

Despite the fact that these principles were held to be non-justiciable, this did not mean, declared the Court, 'that constitutional obligations could be breached without incurring serious legal repercussions. Where there are legal rights there are remedies, but [...] the appropriate recourse in some circumstances lies through the workings of the political process rather than the courts'.[73] In this case, the international realm would provide the sanction, for if one of the majorities involved—the majority of the population of Quebec or that of Canada as a whole—failed to act in accordance with the underlying constitutional principles identified by the Court, it would put in jeopardy the legitimacy of that majority's claim in the eyes of the international community.[74]

∗ ∗ ∗

Criticisms of the Court's reasoning were mostly authority-based objections. The Court, critics argued, neglected the written constitution and, as a consequence, arrogated to itself a constituent power that no formally posited constitutional rules conferred upon it.[75] These authors however seem to ignore the fact that Canada was confronted with a 'constitutional failure', that is, the formal rules of constitutional amendment designed to regulate constitutional politics no longer performed their central function, 'which is to channel debates over constitutional change through procedures that yield institutional decisions that political actors accept as authoritative'.[76] These authors also conceived law as a body of rules, a chart of do's and don'ts, rather than as an interactional phenomenon providing 'a program for living together'.[77] The Court, in a manner akin to that of legal theorist Lon Fuller, seems to have understood the purpose of law to be, not so much the provision of definite and substantial answers to problems, as furnishing individuals with baselines against which to organize their lives with one another.[78]

The Court's perspective on law also seemed premised on a belief that adjudication is not an act of pure knowledge. Rules and principles of constitutional law are not immanent and internal to constitutional texts, nor can they be distilled with precision from historical events. Because these open-textured texts and events can lead to equally rational but radically different interpretations, one has to admit that constitutional adjudication and interpretation always involve a measure of decisionism.[79] Although

---

[73] Ibid [102].

[74] Ibid [93].

[75] See for example Jamie Cameron, 'The Written Word and the Constitution's Vital Unstated Assumptions' in Gérald A. Beaudoin, Benoît Pelletier, and Louis Perret, (eds), *Essays in Honour of Gérald-A. Beaudoin: The Challenges of Constitutionalism* (Éditions Y. Blais 2002).

[76] Sujit Choudry, 'Ackerman's Higher Lawmaking in Comparative Constitutional Perspective: Constitutional Moments as Constitutional Failures?' (2008) 6 I•CON 193, 197.

[77] Lon L Fuller, 'Human Interaction and the Law' in Kenneth I Winston (ed), *The Principles of Social Order: Selected Essays of Lon L Fuller* (Rev ed, Hart Publishing, 1981) 231, 242.

[78] Ibid 254.

[79] Jean Leclair, 'Legality, Legitimacy, Decisionism and Federalism: An Analysis of the Supreme Court of Canada's Reasoning in *Reference re Secession of Quebec, 1998*' (Springer 2017) (forthcoming).

a judge's decisional latitude is not absolute, it remains that he or she puts an end to a controversy by selecting *one* reasonable interpretation out of many others. This choice is not purely conceptual. And in making it, the Court is undoubtedly performing a constituent activity. At this stage of the decision process, the choice of one interpretation over another can no longer be justified according to the strictly internal logic of the legal order. The Court is definitely making a political choice, informed by a particular understanding of the good and the just.

Obviously, the Court wished to construct a 'legal framework' that would allow, not only for legal continuity and certainty[80] (whether the outcome be secession or a reconfiguration of the federation), but also for the channels of communication to be opened up so as to make 'compromise, negotiation, and deliberation' possible.[81] But how did the Court go about achieving this feat?

Although it sometimes gave the impression that the Constitution is a perfectly rational, comprehensive and coherent set of rules and principles, the Court nonetheless, through its normative as opposed to descriptive reading of Canada's constitutional history, reasserted the 'organic' dimension of our Constitution; 'organic' in the sense of a living and evolving constitutional experience. In so doing, it thus implicitly recognized, in John Whyte's elegant prose, that 'we are born into past commitments and inherit them'.[82] Yet, some of these inherited commitments are contradictory, whereas others have been but half fulfilled. Therefore, as much as the constitutional texts, they failed to provide any clear and definite path of solution to the crisis. They did serve as evidence though, that the Canadian federation had survived its internal tensions and crises through negotiations and compromises, however much the latter had left unsatisfied, on different occasions and at different degrees, Quebecers, Westerners, Maritimers, and, most especially, Indigenous peoples. Quoting the Attorney General of Saskatchewan (John Whyte), the Court underlined that '[t]he threads of a thousand acts of accommodation are the fabric of a nation',[83] the more so in the case of a *federal* polity.

And so, the justices chose to embrace this idea of historical tensions appeased through compromises by devising a judicially-crafted obligation to negotiate based on a synthesis of principles that were themselves in tension with one another. No one principle could trump the others, as no one constituent actor's demands (for example, Quebec or the united Anglo-Canadian provinces) could outweigh those of its partners. Jeremy Webber defines such an approach as 'agonistic constitutionalism', 'a constitutionalism in which contending positions are seen to be essential to the society, animating it, and where the positions are not neatly contained within a comprehensive, overarching

---

[80] cf *Secession Reference* above (n 1) [27], [101], [110] and [153].

[81] Ibid [68]. The Court knew how narrow was the path it was treading. It is no wonder the Court wished to make it very clear that its task was to 'clarify the legal framework within which political decisions are to be taken "under the Constitution", not to usurp the prerogatives of the political forces that operate within that framework' [153].

[82] 'Nations, Minorities and Authority' (1991) 40 UNBLJ 45, 49.

[83] cf *Secession Reference* above (n 1) [96].

theory. . . . [A constitutionalism that] takes the diversity of the country as it finds it, and treats the development of its constitution as something that must proceed day by day, not through the fiat of a closed set of founding fathers or their privileged successors.'[84]

In reaching its conclusion, the Court not only eschewed positivistic legal perspectives, it also gave short shrift to monistic ontological definitions under which the complexity of a political community is crushed, thus indirectly demonstrating that the postulated isomorphy of nation, society, and state is just plain false.

First, the Court avoided resorting to the word 'nation', (unless as a synonym of 'State'). It declined to determine whether the Quebec population could be characterized as a 'people' in international law. And, most strikingly, it did not mention the word 'sovereignty', except when summarizing the amicus curiae's argument based on 'popular sovereignty'.

Second, all through its decision the Court constantly referred to *majorities*, emphasizing that, in a federal democracy, the need to build such majorities at both the federal and provincial level, necessitates, by its very nature, 'compromise, negotiation, and deliberation'.[85] Such majority-building inevitably generates dissenting voices. The justices were therefore very desirous of bringing to light that a secession attempt is not a contest between two opposing monolithic blocs of unanimous peoples, but rather between majorities, themselves living alongside dissenters. Hence, also, the Court's insistence that the 'referendum result, if it is to be taken as an expression of the democratic will, must be free of ambiguity both in terms of the question asked and in terms of the support it achieves'.[86]

The justices also underscored that a federation is characterized by the existence of not one, but of two *legitimate* majorities:

> The relationship between democracy and federalism means, for example, that in Canada there may be different and equally legitimate majorities in different provinces and territories and at the federal level. No one majority is more or less 'legitimate' than the others as an expression of democratic opinion, although, of course, the consequences will vary with the subject matter. A federal system of government enables different provinces to pursue policies responsive to the particular concerns and interests of people in that province.[87]

Finally, the Court did not confine itself to a *government*-centric assessment of the virtues of federalism. It also offered a *citizen*-centric perspective with which we are much less accustomed. Hence, after underlining that a federal system of government allows state and sub-states *governments* to pursue policies responsive to the concerns and interests of their particular constituencies, the Court went on to say that '[t]he function of

---

[84] *The Constitution of Canada: A Contextual Analysis* (Hart Publishing 2015) 8.
[85] cf *Secession Reference* (n 1) [66].
[86] Ibid [67].
[87] Ibid [66].

federalism is to enable *citizens* to participate concurrently in different collectivities and to pursue goals at both a provincial and a federal level'.[88] In that perspective, federalism ceases to be simply a tool of governance for *governments*, and becomes a political regime allowing for an internally plural individual citizenship.

* * *

The decision did not hamper the opposing political forces from continuing their war of words,[89] but something had been definitely changed. No longer was it possible to claim that secession was an absolute impossibility or that the formulation of a referendum question was a pure formality having no bearing on the quality of the democratic process.[90] More importantly, it made advocating reified and monolithic definitions of collective and individual identities much more difficult than before.

The Court did not entirely save Canadians from the abyss. Nevertheless, the Supreme Court justices, while implicitly admitting the tragic dimension of our collective historical fate (i.e., men and women make history, but know not what history they are making), wagered nonetheless that human rationality, however limited it might be, enables us to successfully decrypt from the past a 'true' story (not to be confused with the *whole* truth, as the latter is but a horizon that keeps on receding as we seek to approach it) that is not univocal and that makes sense of the plurality of our multifarious collective stories. The justices' reasoning is also premised on the conviction that recourse to rationality and limited compromises, rather than to strong emotions, charisma, and all-encompassing solutions, are still the best tools to ensure our peaceful continuity.

BIBLIOGRAPHY

Banting K and Simeon R (eds), *And No One Cheered. Federalism, Democracy and the Constitution Act* (Methuen 1983)

Binnie I, 'Justice Charles Gonthier and the Unwritten Principles of the Constitution' in Morin M (ed), *Responsibility, Fraternity and Sustainability in Law—In Memory of the Honourable Charles Doherty Gonthier/Responsabilité, Fraternité et Développement Durable en Droit—En mémoire de l'honorable Charles Doherty Gonthier* (LexisNexis Canada 2012)

Cameron J, 'The Written Word and the Constitution's Vital Unstated Assumptions' in Beaudoin GA, Pelletier B, and Perret L, (eds), *Essays in Honour of Gérald—A. Beaudoin: The Challenges of Constitutionalism* (Éditions Y. Blais 2002)

---

[88] Ibid [emphasis added].

[89] In the immediate aftermath of the decision, the federal government enacted the *Clarity Act*, S.C. 2000, c. 26, aimed at giving effect to the requirement for clarity set out in the Supreme Court's opinion, to which the PQ government responded by enacting the *Act respecting the exercise of the fundamental rights and prerogatives of the Québec people and the Québec State*, S.Q., 2000, c. 46. These enactments are mostly political exercises whose legal impacts risk being minimal when and if a new referendum is ever held in Quebec: Leclair above (n 48).

[90] The Scottish precedent, with its successfully negotiated referendum question, has likely discredited dubious formulations of the 1980 and 1995 type.

Caron JF, 'Le Québec et la Confédération: le fédéralisme et la théorie du pacte' in Caron JF and Martel M (eds), *Le Canada français et la Confédération. Fondements et bilan critique* (Presses de l'Université Laval 2016)

Center for Research and Information on Canada, *The Charter: Dividing or Uniting Canadians?* 2002

Choudhry S, 'Ackerman's Higher Lawmaking in Comparative Constitutional Perspective: Constitutional Moments as Constitutional Failures?' (2008) 6 I•CON 193

_____. 'Unwritten Constitutionalism in Canada: Where Do Things Stand?' (2001) 35 Canadian Business Law Journal 113

_____. and Howse R, 'Constitutional Theory and The Quebec Secession Reference' (2000) XIII Canadian Journal of Law and Jurisprudence 143

Couillard J, 'Aux sources de la Révolution tranquille: le congrès d'orientation du Parti libéral du Québec du 10 et 11 juin 1938' (2015) 24 Bulletin d'histoire politique 125

Federal Idea (The), *A Study on the Occasion of the 30th Anniversary of the Patriation of the Constitution* (CROP 2011)

Fletcher J and Howe Paul, 'Canadian Attitudes toward the Charter and the Courts in Comparative Perspective' (2000) 6 Choices 4

Fuller LL, 'Human Interaction and the Law' in Winston KI (ed), *The Principles of Social Order: Selected Essays of Lon L Fuller* (Rev edn, Hart Publishing [1969] 2001)

Gaudreault-Desbiens JF, 'Canadian Federalism and Quebec's Pathological Prism' in Gervais S, Kirkey C, and Rudy J (eds), *Quebec Questions. Quebec Studies for the Twenty-First Century* (2nd edn, Oxford University Press 2016)

_____. 'Secession Blues: Some Legal and Political Challenges Facing the Independence Movement in Quebec' (2014) 3 Percorsi Costituzionali 765

_____. 'The Fetishism of Formal Law and the Fate of Constitutional Patriotism in Communities of Comfort: A Canadian Perspective' in Fossum JE, Magnette P, and Poirier J (eds), *Ties That Bind. Accommodating Diversity in Canada and the European Union* (P.I.E. Lang 2009)

_____. 'The Quebec Secession Reference and the Judicial Arbitration of Conflicting Narratives about Law, Democracy, and Identity' (1998–1999) 23 Vt. L. Rev. 793

Girard P, 'Law, Politics, and the Patriation Reference of 1981' in Harder L and Patten S (eds), *Patriation and Its Consequences: Constitutional Making in Canada* (University of British Columbia Press 2015)

Gold ME, 'The Mask of Objectivity: Politics and Rhetoric in the Supreme Court of Canada' [1985] 7 Supreme Court Law Review 455

Grammond S, 'Compact Is Back: The Revival of the Compact Theory of Confederation by the Supreme Court' (2016) 53 Osgoode Hall Law Journal 799

Hébert C and Lapierre J, *Confessions post-référendaires. Les acteurs politiques de 1995 et le scénario d'un oui* (Éditions de L'homme 2014)

Hogg PW, *Constitutional Law of Canada*, vol 1, (R 2013-1)

Kay RS, 'The Secession Reference and the Limits of Law' (2003) 10 Otago Law Review 327

Laforest G and Rosalie Readman R, 'More Distress than Enchantment: The Constitutional Negotiations of November 1981 as Seen from Quebec' in Harder L and Patten S (eds), *Patriation and Its Consequences: Constitutional Making in Canada* (University of British Columbia Press 2015)

LaSelva SV, 'Divided Houses: Secession and Constitutional Faith in Canada and the United States' (1998–1999) 23 Vt. L. Rev. 771

Leclair J, 'Federalism as Rejection of Nationalist Monisms' in Karmis D and Rocher F (eds), *The Trust/Distrust Dynamic in Multinational Democracies: Canada in Comparative Perspective* (McGill-Queen's University Press 2017) forthcoming

_____. 'Legality, Legitimacy, Decisionism and Federalism: An Analysis of the Supreme Court of Canada's Reasoning in *Reference re Secession of Quebec*, 1998' (Springer 2017) forthcoming

_____. 'Le potier, l'argile et le peuple: le rôle de la loi et du pouvoir dans le processus d'accession du Québec à l'indépendance' in Brouillet E, Taillon P. and Binette A. (eds), *Un regard québécois sur le droit constitutionnel. Mélanges en l'honneur d'Henri Brun et de Guy Tremblay* (Éditions Yvon Blais, 2016)

_____. 'Le fédéralisme comme refus des monismes nationalistes' in Karmis D and Rocher F (eds), *La dynamique confiance-méfiance dans les démocraties multinationales: Le Canada sous l'angle comparatif* (Presses de l'Université Laval, 2012)

_____. 'Forging a True Federal Spirit—Refuting the Myth of Quebec's "Radical Difference",' in Pratte A (ed), *Reconquering Canada: Quebec Federalists Speak Up for Change* (Douglas & MacIntyre 2008)

_____. 'Les silences de Polybe et le Renvoi sur la sécession du Québec' in Boisneau J (eds), *Personne et* Res Publica, (L'Harmattan, 2008)

_____. 'Canada's Unfathomable Unwritten Constitutional Principles, (2000) 27 Queen's Law Journal 389

_____. 'A Ruling in Search of a Nation' (2000) 34 Revue juridique Thémis 885

_____. 'Impoverishment of the Law by the Law: A Critique of the Attorney General's Vision of the Rule of Law and the Federal Principle' (1998) 10 Constitutional Forum/Forum constitutionnel 1

Loughlin M, *The Idea of Public Law* (Oxford University Press, 2003)

Macdonald RA, 'Metaphors of Multiplicity: Civil Society, Regimes and Legal Pluralism' (1998) 15 Ariz. J. Int'l & Comp. L. 69

_____.' . . . Meech Lake to the Contrary Notwithstanding (Part I)' (1991) 29 Osgoode Hall Law Journal 253

McLachlin B, 'Unwritten Constitutional Principles: What Is Going On' (2006) 4 New Zealand Journal of Public and International Law 147

Mendelsohn M, 'Measuring National Identity and Patterns of Attachment: Quebec and Nationalist Mobilization' (2002) 8 Nationalism and Ethnic Politics 72

Monahan PJ, 'The Public Policy Role of the Supreme Court of Canada in the Secession Reference' (1999) 11 *National Journal of Constitutional Law* 65

Morin JY and Woehrling J, *Les Constitutions du Canada et du Québec du régime français à nos jours* (Thémis 1992).

Morissette YM, *Le Renvoi sur la Sécession du Québec. Bilan provisoire et perspectives* (Varia 2001)

Newman WJ, *Le Renvoi relatif à la sécession du Québec: la primauté du droit et la position du procureur général du Canada* (Université York, 1999)

Noël A, 'Quebec' in Courtney JC and Smith DE (eds), *The Oxford Handbook of Canadian Politics* (Oxford University Press 2010)

Oliver P, *The Constitution of Independence: The Development of Constitutional Theory in Australia, Canada, and New Zealand* (Oxford University Press, 2005)

Parizeau J, 'Lettre ouverte aux juges de la Cour suprême' *Le Devoir* (Montreal, 3 September 1998)

Pinard M, Bernier R and Lemieux V, *Un combat inachevé* (Presses de l'Université du Québec 1997)

Raynaud P, *Le juge et le philosophe. Essais sur le nouvel âge du droit*, (Armand Colin, 2008)

Re: Objection by Quebec to a Resolution to amend the Constitution [1982] 2 SCR 793, 1982 CanLII 219 (SCC)

Re: Resolution to amend the Constitution [1981] 1 SCR 753, 1981 CanLII 25 (SCC)

Reference re Secession of Quebec [1998] 2 SCR 217, 1998 CanLII 793 (SCC)

Rocher F and Casanas Adam E, 'L'encadrement juridique du droit de décider: la politique du confinement judiciaire en Catalogne et au Québec' in Brouillet E, Taillon P. and Binette O. (eds), *Un regard québécois sur le droit constitutionnel. Mélanges en l'honneur d'Henri Brun et de Guy Tremblay* (Éditions Yvon Blais, 2016)

Rogers NMcL, 'The Compact Theory of Confederation' (1931) 9 Can Bar Rev 395

Russell PH, 'Patriation and the Law of Unintended Consequences' in Harder L and Patten S (eds), *Patriation and Its Consequences. Constitutional Making in Canada* (University of British Columbia Press 2015)

_____. 'The Patriation and Quebec Veto References: The Supreme Court Wrestles with the Political Part of the Constitution' (2011) 54 SCLR (2d) 69

_____. 'Constitution' in Courtney JC and Smith DE (eds), *The Oxford Handbook of Canadian Politics* (Oxford University Press 2010)

_____. *Constitutional Odyssey. Can Canadians Become a Sovereign People?* (2nd edn, University of Toronto Press 1993)

Ryder B, 'A Court in Need and a Friend Indeed: An Analysis of the Arguments of the Amicus Curiae in the Quebec Secession Reference' (1998) 10 Constitutional Forum 9

Schneiderman D (ed), *The Quebec Decision. Perspectives on the Supreme Court Ruling on Secession* (Lorimer 1999)

Seymour M, 'L'orientation politique du Renvoi sur la sécession' in Brouillet E, Taillon P. and Binette O. (eds), *Un regard québécois sur le droit constitutionnel. Mélanges en l'honneur d'Henri Brun et de Guy Tremblay* (Éditions Yvon Blais, 2016)

Smith, DE, 'Canada: A Double Federation' in Courtney JC and Smith DE (eds), *The Oxford Handbook of Canadian Politics* (Oxford University Press 2010)

Taylor C, 'The Politics of Recognition' in Gutman A (ed), *Multiculturalism. Examining the Politics of Recognition* (Princeton University Press 1994)

Tierney S, 'Popular Constitutional Amendment: Referendums and Constitutional Change in Canada and the United Kingdom, (2015) 41 Queen's LJ 41

Toope SJ, 'Re Reference by Governor in Council concerning Certain Questions Relating to Secession of Quebec from Canada. 161 D.L.R. (4th) 385' (1999) 93 American Journal of International Law 519

Tremblay LB, 'Les principes constitutionnels non écrits', (2012) 17 Review of Constitutional Studies 15

Venne M, 'Bouchard promet une question plus claire' *Le Devoir* (Montreal, 28 August 1998)

Walters MD, 'The Common Law Constitution in Canada: Return of the *Lex Non Scripta* as Fundamental Law' (2001) 51 University of Toronto Law Journal 91

_____. 'Nationalism and the Pathology of Legal Systems: Considering the Quebec Secession Reference and Its Lessons for the United Kingdom' (1999) 62 MLR 371

Webber J, *The Constitution of Canada: A Contextual Analysis* (Hart Publishing 2015)

_____. 'The Legality of a Unilateral Declaration of Independence under Canadian Law' (1997) 42 McGill LJ 281

_____. *Reimagining Canada. Language, Culture, Community, and the Canadian Constitution* (McGill-Queen's University Press 1994)

Whyte J, 'Nations, Minorities and Authority' (1991) 40 UNBLJ 45

CHAPTER 48

···

THE RULE OF LAW, THE SEPARATION OF POWERS AND JUDICIAL INDEPENDENCE IN CANADA

···

WARREN J. NEWMAN*

1. THE RULE OF LAW

···

THE Constitution of Canada was modelled on the British tradition of unwritten principles and conventions governing the exercise of legal power to produce a constitutional monarchy, parliamentary democracy, and responsible government, as well as the American paradigm of constitutional supremacy embodied in written provisions, required in turn by the federal rather than unitary structure of the state. This hybrid model is reflected in the Canadian understanding of the rule of law, which is embodied implicitly in the preamble to the *Constitution Act, 1867*—Canada was to enjoy 'a Constitution similar in Principle to that of the United Kingdom'—and explicitly in the preamble to the *Canadian Charter of Rights and Freedoms* (itself a part of the *Constitution Act, 1982*)—'Whereas Canada is founded upon principles which recognize the supremacy of God and the rule of law'. The idea of the rule of law is also intrinsic to provisions such as section 7 of the *Charter*, guaranteeing the right to life, liberty, and security of the person and the right not to be deprived thereof 'except in accordance with the principles of fundamental justice'; section 15, protecting and expanding upon Dicey's[1] understanding

---

* BA, BCL, LL.B (McGill), LL.M (Osgoode), Ad E; of the Bars of Quebec and Ontario; Senior General Counsel, Constitutional, Administrative and International Law Section, Department of Justice of Canada. The views expressed in this chapter do not bind the Department.

[1] Albert Venn Dicey, *Introduction to the Study of the Law of the Constitution*, 10th ed. (London: MacMillan Press, 1959; reprinted 1975). For detailed commentary on Professor Dicey's pre-eminent contribution, as

of the rule of law as equality before and under the law, and the equal protection and benefit of law; and section 52 of the *Constitution Act, 1982*, expressly declaring that the Constitution is 'the supreme law of Canada' and that any law that is 'inconsistent with the provisions of the Constitution' is 'of no force or effect'.

In the course of its considered rulings in several leading cases, the Supreme Court of Canada has contributed much to the global jurisprudence on the rule of law. *Roncarelli v Duplessis*[2] applied the Diceyian notion of one law for all to limit the arbitrary discretionary power of a provincial Premier and Attorney General who had advised against the issuance of a liquor licence to a restaurant owner for capricious and irrelevant considerations. The *Manitoba Language Rights Reference*[3] determined that the failure to respect a constitutional manner-and-form requirement in the enactment of legislation rendered the legislation invalid in light of the supremacy clause of the Constitution, and that failure to comply with the requirement over almost a century did not excuse the omission, although the principle of the rule of law did assist the Court in deeming the invalid legislation temporarily operative until the requirement could be met.

The *Quebec Secession Reference*[4] emphasized the importance of respecting the principles of constitutionalism and the rule of law in a political process that might result in the secession of a province from Canada, if that process were to be undertaken and pursued by lawful means. The *Provincial Court Judges Reference*[5] established that all government officials must ultimately trace the authority for their actions to a rule of law, whether under statute or the common law. The *Imperial Tobacco* decision[6] held that the rule of law is not a bar to legislation enacted within the limits set out in the provisions of the Constitution; in other words, the rule *of* law includes rule *by* law, as enacted in accordance with the legislative authority conferred upon Parliament and the provincial legislatures by the Constitution, and in keeping with entrenched constitutional guarantees such as those protected by the *Canadian Charter of Rights and Freedoms*.

The Supreme Court has called the rule of law 'a fundamental postulate of our constitutional structure'[7] and a 'highly textured expression, importing many things . . . but conveying, for example, a sense of orderliness, of subjection to known legal rules and of executive accountability to legal authority.'[8] In its landmark opinion in the *Quebec Secession Reference*, the Supreme Court stated that the elements of the rule of law are threefold. First, 'the rule of law provides that the law is supreme over the acts of both government and private persons. There is, in short, one law for all.' Second, 'the rule of law requires the creation and maintenance of an actual order of positive laws which

---

well as those of his contemporaries, see WJ Newman, 'The Principles of the Rule of Law and Parliamentary Sovereignty in Constitutional Theory and Litigation' (2005) 16 *National Journal of Constitutional Law* 175–296; for more academic commentary and further reading, see the select bibliography appended to this chapter.

  [2] *Roncarelli v Duplessis*, [1959] SCR 121.
  [3] *Reference re Manitoba Language Rights*, [1985] 1 SCR 721.
  [4] *Reference re Secession of Quebec*, [1998] 2 SCR 217.
  [5] *Reference re Remuneration of Judges of the Provincial Court (P.E.I.)*, [1997] 3 SCR 3.
  [6] *British Columbia v Imperial Tobacco Ltd.*, [2005] 2 SCR 473.
  [7] *Roncarelli v Duplessis*, [1959] S.C.R. 121, [142], *per* Rand J.
  [8] *Reference re Resolution to amend the Constitution*, [1981] 1 SCR 753, 805–806.

preserves and embodies the more general principle of normative order'. Third, 'the exercise of all public power must find its ultimate source in a legal rule'; in other words, 'the relationship between the state and the individual must be regulated by law'. Together, 'these three considerations make up a principle of profound constitutional and political significance'.[9]

> At its most basic level, the rule of law vouchsafes to the citizens and residents of the country a stable, predictable and ordered society in which to conduct their affairs. It provides a shield for individuals from arbitrary state action.[10]

The Supreme Court has also articulated a distinct but related principle of constitutionalism. The essence of this principle, the Court stated, is reflected in the supremacy clause of section 52 of the *Constitution Act, 1982*.

> Simply put, the constitutionalism principle requires that all government action comply with the Constitution. The rule of law principle requires that all government action must comply with the law, including the Constitution. This Court has noted on several occasions that with the adoption of the *Charter*, the Canadian system of government was transformed to a significant extent from a system of Parliamentary supremacy to one of constitutional supremacy. The Constitution binds all governments, both federal and provincial, including the executive branch . . . They may not transgress its provisions: indeed, their sole claim to exercise lawful authority rests in the powers allocated to them under the Constitution, and can come from no other source.[11]

That statement remains an eloquent exposition of the supremacy of the law of the Constitution, as embodied in its provisions, which the courts will generally enforce. This *legal* constitutionalism may be contrasted with *political* constitutionalism, which is reflected in respect for constitutional conventions: that is to say, the informal, customary rules of conduct and behaviour developed by and acquiesced in by political actors, the breach of which entails political rather than legal sanctions.[12]

Given the Supreme Court's emphasis on the importance of underlying constitutional principles, it is not surprising that litigants have occasionally sought to imbue the principle of the rule of law itself with the same supreme legal force of a provision of the Constitution. Moreover, this has often been done in connection with applications to

---

[9] *Reference re Secession of Quebec*, [1998] 2 S.C.R. 217, *per curiam*, para. 72 (incorporating passages from *Reference re Manitoba Language Rights*, [1985] 1 S.C.R. 721, [747–752], and *Reference re Remuneration of Judges of the Provincial Court*, above (n 5) [1997] [10]).

[10] *ibid.*, [70].

[11] *ibid.*, [72].

[12] See Warren J. Newman, 'Of Dissolution, Prorogation and Constitutional Law, Principle and Convention: Maintaining Fundamental Distinctions during a Parliamentary Crisis', 27 *National Journal of Constitutional Law* 217 at 226–229. On legal and political constitutionalism, see notably *Osborne v Canada (Treasury Board)*, [1991] 2 SCR 69 at 87 (Sopinka J, writing for the Court).

render statutes of no force or effect that are, in the eyes of those litigants or their counsel, unwise or unjust, whether or not those laws are unconstitutional in terms of their valid-ity. As Justice Strayer of the Federal Court of Appeal presciently observed: 'Advocates tend to read into the principle of the rule of law anything which supports their particular view of what the law should be'.[13]

However, after struggling with the issue, Canadian courts have clearly recognized that the rule of law must be read in conjunction with other constitutional principles, includ-ing constitutionalism, democracy, and parliamentary sovereignty, and with the suprem-acy accorded to the provisions of the Constitution, including those granting legislative authority to make enactments. In a challenge to the constitutional validity of a provision of the *Canada Evidence Act* preserving Cabinet documents from disclosure, on the basis that the provision offended the rule of law, the separation of powers, and the indepen-dence of the judiciary, Chief Justice McLachlin, writing for the Supreme Court, upheld the validity of the impugned provision. Although the constitutional principles invoked were capable of limiting government action, they did not do so in this case, she held, as they had to be balanced against the principle of parliamentary sovereignty:

> It is well within the power of the legislature to enact laws, even laws which some would consider draconian, as long as it does not fundamentally alter or interfere with the relationship between the courts and the other branches of government.[14]

This refrain was repeated by the Supreme Court in the *Imperial Tobacco* case,[15] in that the rule of law could not be invoked to invalidate a statute of the legislature of British Columbia that facilitated a civil action by the provincial government against tobacco companies for the recovery of health care expenditures in treating tobacco-related ill-nesses. Justice Major, writing for the Court, observed that 'many of the requirements of the rule of law proposed by the appellants are simply broader versions of the rights contained in the *Charter*'.[16]

> Thus, the appellants' conception of the unwritten constitutional principle of the rule of law would render many of our written constitutional rights redundant and, in doing so, undermine the delimitation of those rights chosen by our constitu-tional framers. That is specifically what this Court cautioned against in *Reference re Secession of Quebec* . . .
>
> Second, the appellants' arguments overlook the fact that several constitutional principles other than the rule of law that have been recognized by this Court—most notably democracy and constitutionalism—very strongly favour upholding the validity of legislation that conforms to the express terms of the Constitution (and to the requirements, such as judicial independence, that flow by necessary implication

[13] *Singh v Canada*, [2000] 3 FC 185.
[14] *Babcock v Canada (A.G.)* [2002] 3 SCR 3 [57].
[15] *British Columbia v Imperial Tobacco Ltd*, above (n 6) [66] and [67].
[16] *ibid.*, [65].

from those terms). Put differently, the appellants' arguments fail to recognize that in a constitutional democracy such as ours, protection from legislation that some might view as unjust or unfair properly lies not in the amorphous underlying prin-ciples of our Constitution, but in its text and the ballot box . . .

The rule of law is not an invitation to trivialize or supplant the Constitution's writ-ten terms. Nor is it a tool by which to avoid legislative initiatives of which one is not in favour. On the contrary, it requires that courts give effect to the Constitution's text, and apply, by whatever its terms, legislation that conforms to that text.[17]

In *Imperial Tobacco*, the Supreme Court recognized that it had described the rule of law as 'embracing three principles': the supremacy of law over government officials as well as private individuals, the maintenance of an order of positive laws, and the legal regula-tion of the relationship between the state and the individual.[18] None of these principles could be employed to invalidate the substantive content (as opposed to the manner and form) of legislation.

That is because none of the principles that the rule of law embraces speak directly to the terms of legislation. The first principle requires that legislation be applied to all those, including government officials, to whom it, by its terms, applies. The second principle means that legislation must exist. And the third principle, which overlaps somewhat with the first and second, requires that state officials' actions be legally founded.[19]

This did not mean that the rule of law had no normative force, but that the constraints on government action would usually apply to the executive and judicial branches.[20] The Court acknowledged that there was considerable academic debate about 'what *addi-tional* principles, if any, the rule of law might embrace', but rejected proposed require-ments advocated by the defendants that statute law, to be valid and respect the rule of law, must '(1) be prospective; (2) be general in character; (3) not confer special privileges on the government, except where necessary for effective governance; and (4) ensure a fair civil trial'.[21] None of these requirements, the Court emphasized, canvassing its own jurisprudence from the perspective of 'precedent and policy', had 'constitutional protection'.[22]

The idea of access to justice has since moved the Supreme Court towards a somewhat more expansive view of the rule of law, without retreating from the *Imperial Tobacco*

---

[17]   ibid., [65–67] [emphasis added].
[18]   Ibid., [58], drawing on the Court's opinions in the *Manitoba Language Rights Reference* and the *Quebec Secession Reference*.
[19]   ibid., [59].
[20]   ibid., [60]; 'Actions of the legislative branch are constrained too, but only in the sense that they must comply with legislated requirements as to manner and form (i.e., the procedures by which legislation is to be enacted, amended and repealed)'.
[21]   ibid., [63].
[22]   ibid. [68]; see [69–77] for the Court's review of the relevant case law.

decision's essential finding that the rule of law as a constitutional principle cannot, in and of itself, invalidate otherwise constitutional legislation (that is, laws that have been enacted on matters within the legislative authority of the enacting legislature and that do not offend the provisions of the Constitution). Whereas in *Imperial Tobacco*, the rule of law had embraced 'three principles', in *Christie*,[23] another case arising out of British Columbia, the rule of law was now said to embrace '*at least* three principles'.[24] The Court noted that 'general access to legal services is not a currently recognized aspect of the rule of law', but characterized its ruling in *Imperial Tobacco* two years earlier as having 'left open the possibility that the rule of law may include additional principles'.[25] Nevertheless, the Court upheld the validity of provincial legislation imposing a goods and services tax on legal services, even where it was argued that this tax restricted or discouraged access to lawyers and thus to justice. Whilst recognizing 'the important role that lawyers play in ensuring access to justice and upholding the rule of law',[26] which had given rise to a constitutional right to legal counsel in specific instances, the Court stated that the issue that had to be addressed in *Christie* was 'whether general access to legal services in relation to court and tribunal proceedings dealing with rights and obligations is a fundamental aspect of the rule of law'. The Court, in a *per curiam* decision, held that it was not.

> Access to legal services is fundamentally important in any free and democratic society. In some cases, it has been found essential to due process and a fair trial. But a review of the constitutional text, the jurisprudence and the history of the concept does not support the respondent's contention that there is a broad general right to legal counsel as an aspect of, or precondition to, the rule of law.[27]

More recently, in yet another case originating in British Columbia, the Supreme Court did declare certain rules imposing court hearing fees to be unconstitutional, but on the basis of a provision of the Constitution—section 96 of the *Constitution Act, 1867*—read in light of the principle of the rule of law. In the *BC Trial Lawyers Association* decision,[28] a majority of the Court held that the grant of legislative power accorded to provincial legislatures over the administration of justice by section 92(14) of the *Constitution Act, 1867* must be harmonized with section 96, which guarantees the core jurisdiction of provincial superior courts. The particular fees in question were held to infringe upon section 96 by effectively denying access to the courts for some people.

---

[23] *British Columbia (Attorney General) v Christie*, [2007] 1 SCR 873.
[24] *ibid.*, [20] [emphasis added].
[25] *ibid.*, [21].
[26] *ibid.*, [22].
[27] *ibid.*, 23.
[28] *Trial Lawyers Association of British Columbia v British Columbia (Attorney General)*, 2014 SCC 59, [2014] 3 S.C.R. 31, *per* McLachlin CJ and LeBel, Abella, Moldaver, and Karakatsanis JJ; Rothstein J dissenting. Cromwell J would have resolved the case on administrative law grounds.

Chief Justice McLachlin, writing for the majority, added that the link between section 96's protection of the jurisdiction of superior courts and access to justice was buttressed by 'considerations relating to the rule of law'.[29] Access to justice—at least in terms of physical access to the courts themselves—had already been held as essential to the rule of law in an earlier case, *BCGEU v British Columbia*, which involved obstruction created by striking picketers.[30] In *MacMillan Bloedel*,[31] provincial superior courts had been held to be foundational to the rule of law, and in the *Provincial Court Judges Reference*, it had been observed that the rationale for section 96 was 'the maintenance of the rule of law through the protection of the judicial role'.[32] It was thus 'only natural', wrote McLachlin CJ, that section 96 of the *Constitution Act, 1867* should 'provide some degree of constitutional protection for access to justice'.[33] Concerns about maintaining the rule of law in this context were 'not abstract or theoretical':

> If people cannot challenge government actions in court, individuals cannot hold the state to account—the government will be, or be seen to be, above the law. If people cannot bring legitimate issues to court, the creation and maintenance of positive laws will be hampered, as laws will not be given effect.[34]

Nonetheless, with an eye to prudence and to dissenting views, the Chief Justice was careful to try to tailor and balance both the constitutional claim and the degree of compliance required, as well as the respective roles of the legislatures and courts.

> The right of the province to impose hearing fees is limited by constitutional constraints. In defining those constraints, the Court does not impermissibly venture into territory that is the exclusive turf of the legislature. Rather, the Court is ensuring that the Constitution is respected. [...]
> It is the role of the provincial legislatures to devise a constitutionally compliant hearing fee scheme. But as a general rule, hearing fees must be coupled with an exemption that allows judges to waive the fees for people who cannot, by reason of their financial situation, bring non-frivolous or non-vexatious litigation to court. A hearing fee scheme can include an exemption for the truly impoverished, but the hearing fees must be set at an amount such that anyone who is not impoverished can afford them. Higher fees must be coupled with enough judicial discretion to waive hearing fees in any case where they would effectively prevent access to the courts because they require litigants to forgo reasonable expenses in order to bring claims.[35]

---

[29] *ibid.*, [38].
[30] *BCGEU v British Columbia (Attorney General)*, [1988] 2 S.C.R. 214, *per* Dickson CJ.
[31] *MacMillan Bloedel Ltd v Simpson*, [1995] 4 SCR 725.
[32] *Reference re Remuneration of Judges of the Provincial Court of Prince Edward Island*, [1997] 3 SCR 3, [88].
[33] *Trial Lawyers Association of British Columbia v British Columbia (Attorney General)*, above (n 28) [39].
[34] *ibid.*, [40].
[35] *ibid.*, [42], [48].

Justice Rothstein, in a powerful dissent, wrote that '[c]ourts do not have free range to micromanage the policy choices of governments acting within the sphere of their constitutional powers'.[36] Rather, courts should be 'wary of subverting democracy and its accountability mechanisms'—legislatures are accountable to the electorate—'beneath an overly expansive vision of constitutionalism'.[37]

> In my respectful view, the British Columbia hearing fee scheme does not offend any constitutional right. The majority must base its finding on an overly broad reading of s. 96, with support from the unwritten constitutional principle of the rule of law, because there is no express constitutional right to access the civil courts without hearing fees.
>   In engaging, on professed constitutional grounds, the question of the affordability of government services to Canadians, the majority enters territory that is quintessentially that of the legislature. The majority looks at the question solely from the point of view of the party to litigation required to undertake to pay the hearing fee. It does not consider, and has no basis or evidence upon which to consider, the questions of the financing of court services or the impact of reduced revenues from reducing, abolishing, or expanding the exemption from paying hearing fees. Courts must respect the role and policy choices of democratically elected legislators. In the absence of a violation of a clear constitutional provision, the judiciary should defer to the policy choices of the government and legislature.[38]

Justice Rothstein was also acutely critical of the extent to which the majority employed the principle of the rule of law to support a novel reading of the ambit of section 96 and the core jurisdiction of the superior courts. This, in his view, 'subverts the structure of the Constitution and jeopardizes the primacy of the written text'.[39] He noted that in *Imperial Tobacco*, the Court had 'clearly and persuasively cautioned against using the rule of law to strike down legislation';[40] in *BC Trial Lawyers Association*, to 'circumvent this caution',[41] the majority had characterized the rule of law as a limitation on the authority of provincial legislatures under section 92(14) of the *Constitution Act, 1867*. This, in Rothstein J's view, was to ignore the manifold lessons of the Court's ruling in *Imperial Tobacco* on the limits of the rule of law's normative impact on the substance of legislation, notably in light of other constitutional principles such as democracy.

> With respect, the rule of law does not demand that this Court invalidate the hearing fee scheme—if anything, it demands that we uphold it. [...] To rely on this nebulous principle to invalidate legislation based on its content introduces uncertainty into constitutional law and undermines our system of positive law.[42]

---

[36] *ibid.*, [80].
[37] *ibid.*, [83].
[38] *ibid.*, [80], [81].
[39] *ibid.*, [93].
[40] *ibid.*, [97].
[41] *ibid.*, [98].
[42] *ibid.*, [99], [102].

2. THE SEPARATION OF POWERS

The recurrent theme of the respective roles of the legislatures and courts within Canada's constitutional framework, so prevalent in the debate over the scope of the rule of law as a constitutional principle, brings us to a brief assessment of another and still-emerging principle, the separation of executive, legislative, and judicial powers.

Professor Peter Hogg has argued cogently and consistently since the first edition of his treatise in 1977 that there is no general separation of powers in the *Constitution Act, 1867*.[43] Nevertheless, in recent years, the Supreme Court of Canada has elevated the separation of powers to the level of a structural constitutional principle. However, the Court has yet to provide a comprehensive and persuasive account of the meaning, scope, and normative effect of this principle. Indeed, the path of the Court's jurisprudence has veered significantly on this issue. In the *Provincial Court Judges Reference*[44] in 1997, Chief Justice Lamer, writing for a majority of the Court, asserted that 'a fundamental principle of the Canadian Constitution, the separation of powers ... requires, at the very least, that some functions must be exclusively reserved to particular bodies'.[45] A year later, in upholding its advisory jurisdiction in the *Quebec Secession Reference*,[46] the Court declared that 'the Canadian Constitution does not insist on a strict separation of powers. Parliament and the provincial legislatures may properly confer other legal functions on the courts, and may confer certain judicial functions on bodies that are not courts. The exception to this rule relates only to s. 96 courts'.[47] In *OceanPort Hotel*,[48] Chief Justice McLachlin held that the 'traditional division between the executive, the legislature and the judiciary' and the 'preservation of this tripartite constitutional structure' did not compel the extension of the constitutional guarantee of judicial independence to administrative tribunals.[49] In *Babcock*,[50] as noted earlier, the Chief Justice

---

[43] Peter W. Hogg, *Constitutional Law of Canada*, 5th ed. (Toronto: Carswell), at ch. 7.3:

> There is no general 'separation of powers' in the Constitution Act, 1867. The Act does not separate the legislative, executive and judicial functions and insist that each branch of government exercise only 'its own' function. As between the legislative and executive branches, any separation of powers would make little sense in a system of responsible government, and it is clearly established that the Act does not call for any such separation. As between the judicial and the two political branches, there is likewise no general separation of powers. Either the Parliament or the Legislatures may by appropriate legislation confer non-judicial functions on the courts and (with one important exception [the core jurisdiction of superior courts under s. 96]), may confer judicial functions on bodies that are not courts.

[44] *Reference re Remuneration of Judges of the Provincial Court (P.E.I.)*, above (n 5).
[45] *ibid.*, [138] and [139].
[46] *Reference re Secession of Quebec*, above (n 4).
[47] *ibid.*, [15].
[48] *Ocean Port Hotel Ltd. v British Columbia (General Manager, Liquor Control and Licensing Branch)*, [2001] 2 SCR 781.
[49] *ibid.*, [32].
[50] *Babcock v Canada (Attorney General)*, above (n 14).

found that the principles of the rule of law, judicial independence, and the separation of powers had to be balanced with the principle of parliamentary sovereignty: 'It is well within the power of the legislature to enact laws, even laws which some would consider draconian, as long as it does not fundamentally alter or interfere with the relationship between the courts and the other branches of government'.[51] In *Vaid*,[52] Justice Binnie, writing for the Court, affirmed that '[t]here are few issues as important to our constitutional equilibrium as the relationship between the legislature and the other branches of the State on which the Constitution has conferred powers, namely the executive and the courts'.[53] He went on to affirm that parliamentary privilege 'is one of the ways that the fundamental constitutional separation of powers is respected'.[54]

The crux of the view that the separation of powers does not extend to the legislative and executive branches in Canada rests primarily upon the operation of the principle of responsible government in a parliamentary system and the conventions associated therewith, not on the law of the Constitution of Canada *per se*. It is also evident that any comparison with the Constitution of the United States is based not only on the provisions of that constitution but also upon certain assumptions as to how—or how completely—the principle of the separation of powers operates amongst the three branches of the American government. All of this may require greater scrutiny. However, the biggest problem is definitional and terminological: nowhere in Canadian constitutional jurisprudence is there a thorough analysis of the constitutional meaning animating the concept of the separation of powers, or the constitutional values (beyond judicial independence, which can stand alone as an autonomous principle of the first order) it is meant to protect and enhance.

Why is it that the separation of powers is nonetheless an emerging constitutional principle in the recent jurisprudence of our Supreme Court? What is the motive force and attraction behind this principle?

Canada, as the preamble to the *Constitution Act, 1867*, declares, is to have a Constitution 'similar in Principle' to that of the United Kingdom, which embraces the principle of responsible government within a framework of constitutional monarchy and parliamentary democracy. It is natural that the heretofore dominant position of many constitutional lawyers and most political scientists should echo, at least implicitly, that expressed by that great nineteenth century commentator, Walter Bagehot, in his seminal work, *The English Constitution*, who treated as 'erroneous' the description of that constitution as dividing the legislative, the executive, and the judicial powers and entrusting each power 'to a separate person or set of persons—that no one of these can interfere with the work of the other'.[55] Indeed, for Bagehot, the contrary was true: 'The

---

[51] *ibid.*, [57].

[52] *Canada (House of Commons) v Vaid*, [2005] 1 SCR 667.

[53] *ibid.*, [4].

[54] *ibid.*, [21].

[55] Walter Bagehot, *The English Constitution*, 1st ed 1867; cited to the American edition; New York: Appleton & Co., 1908, at 70. For more on the impact, on Canadian constitutional thinking, of Bagehot's

efficient secret of the English Constitution may be described as the close union, the nearly complete fusion, of the executive and legislative powers'. The link between these branches or powers, Bagehot asserted, was the Cabinet—the conventional and efficient portion of the formal Queen's Privy Council, composed of Ministers of the Crown. 'A cabinet', Bagehot declared, 'is a combining committee—a *hyphen* which joins, a *buckle* which fastens, the legislative part of the state to the executive part of the state'.[56]

In the *Canada Assistance Plan Reference*, Justice Sopinka, writing for a unanimous Supreme Court, expressly cited Bagehot's hyphen-and-buckle metaphor to underscore 'the essential role of the executive in the legislative process of which it is an integral part'.[57] Yet two years earlier, in the *Auditor General's Case*, Chief Justice Dickson wrote: 'It is of no avail to point to the fusion of powers which characterizes the Westminster system of government. That the executive through its control of a House of Commons majority may in practice dictate the position the House of Commons takes . . . is not . . . constitutionally cognizable by the judiciary'.[58]

It was Dickson CJ who was the first to observe, in *Fraser*, that '[t]here is in Canada a separation of powers among the three branches of government—the legislature, the executive and the judiciary'.[59] That proposition was taken up by Lamer CJ in *Cooper*,[60] wherein he characterized the separation of powers as '[o]ne of the defining features of the Canadian Constitution', and then in the *Provincial Court Judges Reference*, where the separation of powers was described by him as 'a fundamental principle' that commands, inter alia, 'that the different branches of government only interact, as much as possible, in particular ways'.[61]

> For example, there is a hierarchical relationship between the executive and the legislature, whereby the executive must execute and implement the policies which have been enacted by the legislature in statutory form: see *Cooper*, *supra*, at paras. 23 and 24. In a system of responsible government, once legislatures have made political decisions and embodied those decisions in law, it is the constitutional duty of the executive to implement those choices.[62]

imagery, see WJ Newman, 'Of Castles and Living Trees: The Metaphorical and Structural Constitution' (2015) 9 *Journal of Parliamentary and Political Law* 471 at 474–476.

[56] *ibid.*, at 82. By way of comparison, Bagehot added, at 84: 'The independence of the legislative and executive powers is the specific quality of Presidential Government, just as their fusion and combination is the precise principle of Cabinet Government'.

[57] *Reference Re Canada Assistance Plan (BC)*, [1991] 2 SCR 525, at 559.

[58] *Canada (Auditor General) v Canada (Minister of Energy, Mines and Resources)*, [1989] 2 SCR 49, at 103.

[59] *Fraser v Public Service Staff Relations Board*, [1985] 2 SCR 455, at 470: 'In broad terms, the role of the judiciary is, of course, to interpret and apply the law; the role of the legislature is to decide upon and enunciate policy; the role of the executive is to administer and implement that policy'.

[60] *Cooper v Canada (Human Rights Commission)*, [1996] 3 SCR 854. See also *R v Power*, [1994] 1 SCR 601 at 620.

[61] *Reference re Remuneration of Judges of the Provincial Court (P.E.I.)*, above (n 5) [139].

[62] *ibid.*

There is no sense in this statement that the principles of the separation of powers and responsible government sit somewhat uneasily with each other. Moreover, even if the concerns over responsible government might be dismissed as simply a preoccupation with the conventions of the Constitution, there are almost as many difficulties inherent in the legal structure of the Constitution, for those who would contend in favour of the separation of powers as a fundamental constitutional principle, as there are potential solutions.

For example, the *Constitution Act, 1867* expressly distinguishes, as the rubrics preceding sections 9, 17, and 96 demonstrate, between '*Executive Power*', '*Legislative Power*', and '*Judicature*'. However, what the Constitution giveth in relation to the separation of powers, it also taketh away: executive power is, by virtue of section 9, vested in the Queen. Under sections 17 and 91, the Queen is also an essential actor in the exercise of legislative power: Her Majesty is one of the three bodies composing the Parliament of Canada, and in strictness of law, it is the Queen, under section 91, who makes laws for the peace, order, and good government of Canada, albeit by and with the advice and consent of the Senate and House of Commons.

Another illustration is provided in the *Quebec Secession Reference*, wherein it was observed that the United States Supreme Court cannot render advisory opinions, in keeping with the strict separation of powers reflected in the limitations expressed in that country's constitution, whereas in Canada there is 'no constitutional bar' to the conferral of what is traditionally an executive function (the rendering of legal opinions by the law officers of the Crown) upon the judicial branch.[63]

If we return to the rhetorical questions posed above, why is it that the separation of powers remains an emerging constitutional principle in the recent jurisprudence of the Supreme Court? What is the force and attraction of this principle? Part of it may simply be a matter of osmosis; Canadian judges, particularly since the advent of a constitutionally-entrenched *Charter of Rights*, have become more fully versed in comparative constitutional law, and the separation of powers is omnipresent in American constitutional jurisprudence, thought, and discourse.

The kernel of a more substantive answer may be found in the words of McLachlin J (as she then was) in *New Brunswick Broadcasting*:

> Our democratic government consists of several branches: the Crown, as represented by the Governor General and the provincial counterparts of that office; the legislative body; the executive; and the courts. It is fundamental to the working of government as a whole that all these parts play their proper role. It is equally fundamental that no one of them overstep its bounds, that each show proper deference for the legitimate sphere of activity of the other.[64]

---

[63]   *Reference re Secession of Quebec*, above (n 4), [15].

[64]   *New Brunswick Broadcasting Co v Nova Scotia (Speaker of the House of Assembly)*, [1993] 1 S.C.R. 319.

Although this passage is somewhat marred by the suggestion that the Crown and the Executive are different branches of government—as a matter of constitutional law, the Crown *is* the executive branch—the essential idea here is that each branch of government must play its 'proper role', not 'overstep its bounds', and show 'proper deference for the legitimate sphere of activity' of the other branches. This demonstrates a deep concern with the necessity of maintaining a delicate balance in a constitutional democracy: of sustaining an appropriate constitutional equilibrium amongst the executive, legislative, and judicial branches, so that no branch may plausibly sustain a claim of absolute power, to the detriment of the other branches. That is the fundamental attraction of the principle of the separation of powers, and why it would be useful to elaborate a more coherent theory of the principle as it applies in the context and particularities of the Canadian constitutional framework, which itself is a hybrid of the UK and American models of constitutionalism.

Echoes of this concern for maintaining a constitutional balance amongst the executive, legislative, and judicial branches may be seen in a numerous cases, including those already mentioned in connection with the rule of law, judicial independence, parliamentary sovereignty and the democratic principle, and parliamentary privilege, as well as certain cases dealing with the Crown's prerogatives. It is often a feature of the Supreme Court's jurisprudence respecting questions of justiciability and concomitant judicial restraint. For example, in the *Canada Assistance Plan Reference*, the Court indicated that its 'primary concern is to retain its proper role within the constitutional framework of our democratic form of government'.[65] Similarly, in the *Quebec Secession Reference*, even though the Court had rejected the view that the separation of powers would prevent the Court from exercising advisory functions, it reiterated the view that a reference question might not be answered where to do so would 'take the Court beyond its own assessment of its proper role' or where 'the Court could not give an answer that lies within its area of expertise: the interpretation of law'.[66]

In cases dealing with parliamentary privilege and the royal prerogative, respectively, the Supreme Court has adopted the position that it is within its proper role to determine the existence and scope of the asserted privilege or prerogative, but not necessarily to control the exercise of them once their existence and ambit are clearly established. Thus, in *Vaid*, with respect to parliamentary privilege, the Court drew a distinction between 'defining the scope of a privilege, which is the function of the courts, and judging the appropriateness of its exercise, which is a matter for the legislative assembly'.[67] And in *Khadr*, the Court emphasized:

> The limited power of the courts to review exercises of the prerogative power for constitutionality reflects the fact that in a constitutional democracy, all government

---

[65] *Reference re Canada Assistance Plan (BC)*, [1991] 2 SCR 525 at 545.

[66] *Reference re Secession of Quebec*, above (n 4), [26]; and [100] ('The Court has no supervisory role over the political aspects of constitutional negotiations.') See also *Canada (Auditor General) v Canada (Minister of Energy, Mines and Resources)*, [1989] 2 SCR 49 at 91.

[67] *Vaid*, above (n 52) [47]; see also WJ Newman, 'Parliamentary Privilege, the Canadian Constitution and the Courts', (2008) 39 *Ottawa Law Review* 573.

power must be exercised in accordance with the Constitution. This said, judicial review of the exercise of the prerogative power for constitutionality remains sensitive to the fact that the executive branch of government is responsible for decisions under this power, and that the executive is better placed to make such decisions within a range of constitutional options.[68]

The separation of powers has also served, as noted above, to buttress judicial independence, and it is to that principle that this chapter now turns.

3. Judicial Independence

The provisions of the *Constitution Act, 1867* dealing with "Judicature" (sections 96 to 101) and the legal rights of the *Constitution Act, 1982* (embodied in sections 7 to 14 of the *Canadian Charter of Rights and Freedoms*) provide much of the constitutional structure of Canada's court system and with it, constitutionally-entrenched and protected guarantees of judicial independence. Nonetheless, Lamer CJ, writing for the majority of the Supreme Court in the *Provincial Court Judges Reference*, held that judicial independence is 'at root an <u>unwritten</u> constitutional principle, in the sense that is exterior to the particular sections of the *Constitution Acts*'; 'an unwritten norm, recognized and affirmed by the preamble to the *Constitution Act, 1867*'.[69]

The Chief Justice, while recognizing that the recitals of a preamble—unlike the provisions which follow the enacting clause of a statute—have no legal force, nevertheless attributed indirect legal effects to the preamble of the *Constitution Act, 1867*, both as an aid to construing the provisions themselves and (more controversially) in filling 'gaps' in the constitutional text. This provoked widespread academic commentary and some pointed criticism, particularly as the principle of judicial independence had been slow to develop in the United Kingdom, whence the purported provenance of the principle (through the preamble's mention of 'a Constitution similar in principle to that of the United Kingdom'). It also produced a remarkable dissent by Justice La Forest, who argued cogently that the idea that by 1867 there were judicially-enforceable limitations on the legislative power of the United Kingdom Parliament to intrude on judicial independence was a 'historical fallacy' and that the preamble to the *Constitution Act, 1867* 'did not give the courts the power to strike down legislation violating judicial independence'.[70]

This brings us back to the central point: to the extent that courts in Canada have the power to enforce the principle of judicial independence, this power derives from

---

[68] *Canada (Prime Minister) v Khadr*, 2010 SCC 3, [2010] 1 SCR 44, [37].
[69] *Reference re Remuneration of Judges of the Provincial Court (P.E.I.)*, above (n 5), [83] (underlining in original) and [109]; 'In fact, it is in that preamble, which serves as the grand entrance hall to the castle of the Constitution, that the true source of our commitment to this foundational principle is located'.
[70] ibid., [311], *per* La Forest J.

the structure of <u>Canadian</u>, and not British, constitutionalism. Our Constitution expressly contemplates both the power of judicial review (in s. 52 of the *Constitution Act, 1982*) and guarantees of judicial independence (in ss. 96–100 of the *Constitution Act, 1867* and s. 11(*d*) of the *Charter*). While these provisions have been interpreted to provide guarantees of independence that are not immediately manifest in their language, this has been accomplished through the usual mechanisms of constitutional interpretation, not through recourse to the preamble. The legitimacy of this interpretive exercise stems from its grounding in an expression of democratic will, not from a dubious theory of an implicit constitutional structure. The express provisions of the Constitution are not, as the Chief Justice contends, 'elaborations of the underlying, unwritten, and organizing principles found in the preamble to the *Constitution Act, 1867*' (para. 107). On the contrary, they <u>are</u> the Constitution. To assert otherwise is to subvert the democratic foundation of judicial review.[71]

This critique may have been one of the reasons that the Chief Justice's majority opinion in the *Provincial Court Judges Reference*, although having invoked the preamble of the *Constitution Act, 1867* as the fount of judicial independence, was actually decided on the basis of a provision of the Constitution, section 11(*d*) of the *Charter*.[72] It also explains why in a later case, *Mackin*,[73] Justice Gonthier prudently cited both the preamble of the Act of 1867 *and* section 11(*d*) of the *Charter* in the same breath before invalidating provincial legislation that was held to infringe the guarantee of judicial independence.

As to the content of the guarantee, judicial independence has been held to refer 'essentially to the nature of the relationship between a court and others. This relationship must be marked by a form of intellectual separation that allows the judge to render decisions solely based on the requirements of the law and justice.'[74] As stated by Justice Gonthier in *Mackin*, 'the expanded role of the judge as an adjudicator of disputes, interpreter of the law and guardian of the Constitution requires that he or she be completely independent of any other entity in the performance of his or her judicial functions.'[75] Similarly, Chief Justice Dickson, in *Beauregard v Canada*, summarized the principle of judicial independence in the following terms:

> Historically, the generally accepted core of the principle of judicial independence has been the complete liberty of individual judges to hear and decide the cases that

---

[71] *ibid.*, [319] (underlining in original); for academic commentary, see notably Jean Leclair and Yves-Marie Morrissette, "L'indépendance judiciaire et la Cour suprême: reconstruction historique douteuse et théorie constitutionnelle de complaisance" (1998) 36 *Osgoode Hall Law Journal* 485; WJ Newman, "'Grand Entrance Hall,' Back Door or Foundation Stone? The Role of Constitutional Principles in Construing and Applying the Constitution of Canada" (2001), 14 *Supreme Court Law Review* (2d) 197.

[72] *ibid.*, [109], *per* Lamer CJ: 'since the parties and interveners have grounded their arguments in s. 11(*d*), I will resolve these appeals by reference to that provision.' Section 11(d) expressly guarantees to persons charged in criminal and penal matters the right 'to be presumed innocent until proven guilty according to law in a fair and public hearing by an independent and impartial tribunal.'

[73] *Mackin v New Brunswick (Minister of Finance); Rice v New Brunswick* [2002] 1 SCR 405.

[74] *ibid.*, [37] per Gonthier J.

[75] *ibid.*, [35].

come before them; no outsider—be it government, pressure group, individual or even another judge—should interfere in fact, or attempt to interfere, with the way in which a judge conducts his or her case and makes his or her decision. This core continues to be central to the principle of judicial independence. . . .

The ability of individual judges to make decisions in discrete cases free from external interference or influence continues to be an important and necessary component of the principle.[76]

Judicial independence is said to possess individual and institutional dimensions.[77] Individual independence refers to the 'fundamental duty' that 'all judges owe . . . to the community to render impartial decisions and to appear impartial'.[78] It 'relates especially to the person of the judge and involves his or her independence from any other entity'.[79] It relates specifically to the purely adjudicative functions of judges—'the independence of a court that is necessary for a given dispute to be decided in a manner that is just and equitable'.[80] Individual independence is an essential element of the adjudicative process, which 'confers on the affected party a peculiar form of participation in the decision, that of presenting proofs and reasoned argument for a decision in his favor'.[81] The adjudicative process, 'if it is to have the respect and confidence of its society, must ensure that trials are fair and that they appear to be fair to the informed and reasonable observer'.[82] Institutional independence refers to the institutional autonomy that courts require from external institutions to perform their constitutional role properly. Institutional independence is 'definitional to the Canadian understanding of constitutionalism'.[83] Institutional independence 'historically developed as a bulwark against the abuse of executive power',[84] but equally protects the judiciary from the legislative branch of government and 'any other external force, such as business or corporate interests or other pressure groups'.[85]

Judicial independence as a structural principle has been developed in Canadian jurisprudence principally in a series of cases over the past two decades dealing with the remuneration, benefits, and financial security accorded to judges by the executive and legislative branches, and the cases have often seen judges and their associations as active

---

[76] *Beauregard v Canada*, [1986] 2 S.C.R. 56 [69].

[77] *Valente v The Queen*, [1985] 2 SCR 673; *Reference re Remuneration of Judges of the Provincial Court (P.E.I.)*, above (n 5).

[78] *R v RDS* [1997] 3 SCR 484 [120] per Cory and Iacobucci JJ.

[79] *Mackin*, above (n 73) [39].

[80] *ibid.*, [39].

[81] Lon Fuller, "The Forms and Limits of Adjudication" [1978] *Harv L Rev* 352, 364.

[82] *R v RDS* above (n 78) [91].

[83] *Cooper v Canada (Human Rights Commission)* [1996] 3 SCR 854 [11].

[84] *Reference re Remuneration of Judges of the Provincial Court of Prince Edward Island*, above (n 5) [125].

[85] *R v Généreux* [1992] 1 SCR 259 [37], per Lamer CJ.

parties to the litigation.[86] The Supreme Court has enunciated some general principles in this area: judicial salaries can be maintained or altered only by recourse to a judicial compensation commission that is independent, objective, and effective. Unless a legislature provides otherwise, a commission's report is advisory, not binding. The commission's recommendations must be given weight, but the Government retains the power to depart from the recommendations if it justifies its decision with 'rational reasons' in responding to the recommendations. Reasons that are complete and deal with the commission's recommendations 'in a meaningful way' will meet the standard of rationality. If it is required to justify its decision in litigation before the courts, the Government may not advance reasons other than those mentioned in its response, although it may provide more detailed information with respect to the factual foundation upon which it has relied.

The Government's response is subject to 'a limited form' of judicial review by the superior courts. The reviewing court is not to determine the adequacy of judicial remuneration but whether the Government's response is rational and whether the purpose of the commission process—preserving judicial independence and depoliticizing the setting of judicial remuneration—has been achieved. If the process has not been effective, the appropriate remedy for the reviewing court will generally be to remit the matter to the Government for reconsideration.[87]

Legislatures have constitutional power over the creation, alteration, and abolition of judicial offices,[88] but they must exercise that power in accordance with the principle of judicial independence. Where a reform by the legislature of the court system leads to the establishing of a new judicial office, the remuneration of all the judges appointed to it (whether for the first time, or by way of transfer from another office) must be reviewed retroactively within a reasonable time after their appointment.[89]

---

[86] Aside from the *Provincial Court Judges Reference* and the *Mackin* case, already mentioned above, and the cases next dealt with below, other significant cases include *Beauregard v Canada*, [1986] 2 SCR 56, in which a Quebec Superior Court judge challenged the constitutional validity of a newly enacted provision providing that Superior Court judges would be required to contribute to the cost of their pension plan; *R v Généreux* [1992] 1 SCR 259, concerned the remuneration of existing members of military tribunals. In *Ell v Alberta* [2003] 1 SCR 857, the issue was whether a reform to the Alberta justices of the peace regime infringed the tenure security of existing justices who lost their position as a result of the reform, but did not raise any issue with respect to financial security.

[87] *Provincial Court Judges' Assn. of New Brunswick v New Brunswick (Minister of Justice); Ontario Judges' Assn. v Ontario (Management Board); Bodner v Alberta; Conférence des juges du Québec v Quebec (Attorney General); Minc v Quebec (Attorney General)*, [2005] 2 SCR 286.

[88] Section 92, head 14, of the *Constitution Act, 1867* confers upon provincial legislatures legislative authority in relation to the administration of justice within the province, including the constitution, maintenance, and organization of provincial courts of civil and criminal jurisdiction. The provincial superior courts pre-date Confederation and are courts of inherent jurisdiction, the core of which is constitutionally protected by s. 96. Section 101 confers upon Parliament legislative authority to establish and maintain a general court of appeal for Canada (the Supreme Court of Canada) and other courts for the better administration of the laws of Canada (the Federal Courts and the Tax Court of Canada). The provincial superior courts pre-date Confederation and are courts of inherent jurisdiction, the core of which is constitutionally protected from legislative interference by s. 96.

[89] *Conférence des juges de paix magistrats du Québec v Quebec (Attorney General)*, 2016 SCC 39. (In this instance, a statutory provision that prevented review of remuneration for a period of at least three

The constitutional principle of judicial independence protects both superior and inferior courts,[90] but does not extend as such to administrative tribunals.[91] Administrative tribunals may be required, in accordance with the common-law principles of natural justice, to act independently and impartially, but the precise degree of the standard to be met will depend on the tribunal's governing statute, and may be ousted by express statutory provision or necessary intendment. Chief Justice McLachlin, writing for the Supreme Court, stated:

> It is not open to a court to apply a common law rule in the face of clear statutory direction. Courts engaged in judicial review of administrative decisions must defer to the legislator's intention in assessing the degree of independence required of the tribunal in question.[92]

This was said to reflect the 'fundamental distinction' between courts and administrative tribunals. 'Superior courts, by virtue of their role as courts of inherent jurisdiction, are constitutionally required to possess objective guarantees of both individual and institutional independence'. The same 'constitutional imperative' had been extended to provincial courts by virtue of the Supreme Court's ruling in the *Provincial Court Judges Reference*. Judicial independence had developed historically 'to demarcate the fundamental division between the judiciary and executive'. Administrative tribunals, on the other hand, 'lack this constitutional distinction from the executive', notably because they are established 'precisely for the purpose of implementing government policy'. That policy-implementation function may require them to make quasi-judicial decisions, and in that sense, McLachlin C.J. observed, administrative tribunals 'may be seen as spanning the constitutional divide between the executive and the judicial branches of government'. However, in light of their 'primary policy-making function', it was 'properly the role and responsibility of Parliament and the legislatures'—the legislative branch—'to determine the composition and structure required by a tribunal to discharge the responsibilities bestowed upon it'.[93]

The 'institutional independence of the judiciary', Lamer C.J. wrote in the *Provincial Court Judges Reference*, is 'definitional to the Canadian understanding of constitutionalism' and 'reflects a deeper commitment to the separation of powers between and amongst the legislative, executive and judicial organs of government'.[94] The implications of the principle of judicial independence, particularly in

---

years was held to be unreasonable and invalid, as contrary to s. 11(d) of the *Canadian Charter of Rights and Freedoms*, a constitutional provision, and the preamble to the *Constitution Act, 1867*, insofar as it imported the underlying constitutional principle.

[90] *Reference re Remuneration of Judges of the Provincial Court (P.E.I.)*, above (n 5).

[91] *Ocean Port Hotel Ltd. v British Columbia (General Manager, Liquor Control and Licensing Branch)*, [2001] 2 SCR 781.

[92] *ibid.*, [22].

[93] *ibid.*, [23] and [24].

[94] *Reference re Remuneration of Judges of the Provincial Court (PEI)*, [1997] 3 SCR 3, above (n 5), [124–125].

the context of remuneration from the public purse, but also in terms of the dynamics and modalities of the institutional relationships between the judiciary on the one hand and the Executive and legislature on the other, are still in the process of being worked out. The interaction of judicial independence with not only the separation of powers but also other foundational principles, including parliamentary sovereignty, constitutionalism, and the rule of law, will bear continuing scrutiny and study in years to come.

Select Bibliography

Commentary

Beatty, David M., *The Ultimate Rule of Law*, Oxford: Oxford University Press, 2004

Canadian Bar Association. Special Committee on the Independence of the Judiciary in Canada, Report, *The Independence of the Judiciary in Canada*, Ottawa: Canadian Bar Foundation, 1985

Dyzenhaus, David, 'Disobeying Parliament? Privative Clauses and the Rule of Law', in Richard W. Bauman and Tsvi Kahana, eds., *The Least Examined Branch: The Role of Legislatures in the Constitutional State*. New York: Cambridge University Press, 2006, 499

Elliot, Robin, 'References, Structural Argumentation and the Organizing Principles of Canada's Constitution', (2001) 80 *Canadian Bar Review* 67

Friedland, Martin L., *A Place Apart: Judicial Independence and Accountability in Canada*, Ottawa: Canadian Judicial Council, 1995

Hogg, Peter W., and Cara F. Zwibel, 'The Rule of Law in the Supreme Court of Canada', (2005) 55 *University of Toronto Law Journal* 715

Leclair, Jean, 'Canada's Unfathomable Constitutional Principles', (2002) 27 *Queen's Law Journal* 389

Lederman, W.R., 'The Independence of the Judiciary', (1956) 34 *Canadian Bar Review* 769, 1139

Monahan, Patrick J. (1999), 'The Public Policy Role of the Supreme Court of Canada in the *Secession Reference*', (1999) 11 *National Journal of Constitutional Law* 65

_____. (1995), 'Is the Pearson Airport Legislation Unconstitutional?: The Rule of Law as a Limit on Contract Repudiation by Government', (1995) 33 *Osgoode Hall Law Journal* 411

Newman, Warren J., '"Grand Entrance Hall," Back Door or Foundation Stone? The Role of Constitutional Principles in Construing and Applying the Constitution of Canada', (2001) 14 (2d) *Supreme Court Law Review* 197

_____. 'The Principles of the Rule of Law and Parliamentary Sovereignty in Constitutional Theory and Litigation', (2005) 16 *National Journal of Constitutional Law* 175

_____. *The Quebec Secession Reference, The Rule of Law and the Position of the Attorney General of Canada*, Toronto: York University Centre for Public Law and Public Policy, 1999

_____. '*Understanding the Rule of Law in Canada*', in Stephen Tierney, ed., *Accommodating Cultural Diversity*, Hampshire, UK: Ashgate Publishing Ltd, 2007

Sossin, Lorne, and Dodek, Adam, eds., *Judicial Independence in Context*, Toronto, Irwin Law, 2010

Walters, Mark, 'Legality as Reason: Dicey, Rand and the Rule of Law', (2010) 55 *McGill Law Journal* 563

Selected Caselaw

Roncarelli v Duplessis, [1959] SCR 121

Reference re Manitoba Language Rights, [1985] 1 SCR 721

New Brunswick Broadcasting Co v Nova Scotia (Speaker of the House of Assembly), [1993] 1 S.C.R. 319

Reference re Remuneration of Judges of the Provincial Court (P.E.I.), [1997] 3 SCR 3

Reference re Secession of Quebec, [1998] 2 SCR 217

Ocean Port Hotel Ltd. v British Columbia (General Manager, Liquor Control and Licensing Branch), [2001] 2 SCR 781

Babcock v Canada (A.G.) [2002] 3 SCR 3

Canada (House of Commons) v Vaid, [2005] 1 SCR 667

British Columbia v Imperial Tobacco Ltd., [2005] 2 SCR 473

Trial Lawyers Association of British Columbia v British Columbia (Attorney General), 2014 SCC 59, [2014] 3 S.C.R. 31

E. Dialogue Theory and the Canadian Charter of Rights and Freedoms

CHAPTER 49

UNDERSTANDING DIALOGUE THEORY

PETER W. HOGG* & RAVI AMARNATH**

1. INTRODUCTION

IN *Carter v. Canada (Attorney General)*,[1] the Supreme Court of Canada held that Canada's absolute criminal prohibition on assisted death violated the rights to "life, liberty and security of the person" protected under s. 7 of the *Canadian Charter of Rights and Freedoms* (the "*Charter*").[2] However, the Supreme Court's decision was not the final word on the matter. The Supreme Court issued a suspended declaration of invalidity—whereby the effect of its ruling was delayed in order to give Parliament time to amend the legislation.[3] The Canadian Parliament subsequently passed legislation to address the Supreme Court's concerns in *Carter*, which received royal assent on June 17, 2016.[4]

The *Carter* case is illustrative of an issue that many countries with constitutionally entrenched bill of rights face: What happens when the legislature passes a bill which potentially violates the bill of rights of a country? Is the correct course of action to have an apex court deem the legislation to be constitutionally invalid, or should it be left to

---

* Peter W. Hogg, C.C., Q.C. Professor Emeritus, Osgoode Hall Law School, York University; Scholar in Residence, Blake, Cassels & Graydon LLP.

** Ravi Amarnath, Litigation Associate, Blake, Cassels & Graydon LLP.

[1] *Carter v Canada (Attorney General)*, 2015 SCC 5, [2015] 1 SCR 331.

[2] *Canadian Charter of Rights and Freedoms, The Constitution Act, 1982*, being Schedule B to the *Canada Act 1982* (UK), 1982, c 11. Section 7 provides: "Everyone has the right to life, liberty and security of the person and the right not to be deprived thereof except in accordance with the principles of fundamental justice."

[3] More details will follow later in the chapter regarding *Carter* and the use of the suspended declaration of invalidity.

[4] *An Act to amend the Criminal Code and to make related amendments to other Acts (medical assistance in dying)*, S.C. 2016, c. 3.

the legislature to revise the legislation only once sufficient popular support exists for such amendments? These questions lie at the heart of the legislative process for many countries in determining the correct role for each branch of government.

In this chapter, we will demonstrate the unique features of the Canadian constitutional structure which enables both the judicial and legislative branches of government to work together in order to draft legislation which is constitutionally permissible. This process—which we will refer to as "*Charter* dialogue" for the remainder of this chapter—permits courts to have a role in shaping legislation, while ultimately leaving the task of re-drafting legislation with the relevant legislative body of a country. In doing so, the judiciary maintains an active role in ensuring the fundamental rights of Canadians are protected, while leaving the ultimate revision of legislation to the legislature.

2. WHAT IS *CHARTER* DIALOGUE?

A. Origins of the Theory

The term *Charter* dialogue was developed in 1997 by Professor Peter Hogg and Allison Bushell to describe the process where the legislature responded to judicial concerns regarding the constitutionality of legislation by amending it to address the concerns of a court.[5] The catalyst for this dialogue, according to Hogg and Bushell, is the *Charter*:

> The *Charter* can act as a catalyst for a two-way exchange between the judiciary and legislature on the topic of human rights and freedoms, but it rarely raises an absolute barrier to the wishes of the democratic institutions.[6]

What Hogg and Bushell did was to look for any legislative sequels to all of the cases in which the Supreme Court of Canada had struck down a law on *Charter* grounds. There were 66 cases, and in 53 the competent legislative body had enacted a legislative response to address the issue.[7] This was a surprising finding because academic commentary on *Charter* review up until 1997 had invariably assumed that the Supreme Court decision was the last word on the issue.

Although *Charter* dialogue is a descriptive theory, it also addresses a recurring concern within academic scholarship—how to justify the practice of judicial review, whereby unelected judges who are unaccountable for their actions to the general public

---

[5] Peter W Hogg and Allison A Bushell, "The Charter Dialogue between Courts and Legislatures (Or Perhaps the Charter of Rights Isn't Such a Bad Thing after All) (1997) 35 OHLJ 76.

[6] *Ibid* 80.

[7] *Ibid* 97–98. It is important to note that the authors included in their definition of "legislative response" the sequel cases where the legislature repealed legislation or simply implemented the suggested changes by the reviewing court, but in the other cases a new law was substituted for the old, invalid one.

have the power to strike down laws that have been made by elected representatives of the people.[8] The concern has been particularly acute in the United States, which like Canada has a constitutionally entrenched Bill of Rights and a Supreme Court which has shaped legislation through the process of judicial review. In particular, the practice of judicial review became especially scrutinized in the United States during and following the tenure of the late Chief Justice Warren, whose Court made a number of important social and economic reforms.[9] As noted by Hogg and Bushell:

> Most law professors shared the civil libertarian views of the Warren Court and approved of the outcomes, but they could not ignore the widespread unpopularity of the decisions, and they had to face up to the anti-majoritarian objection to judicial review.[10]

The American response to this quandary has varied, with some scholars and judges alike calling for a scaling back of the practice of judicial review.[11] For example, in recent years, the "originalism" movement, whereby judges would be limited to enforce the *original* public meaning of the Constitution and leave further reform to the amending process, has gained increased favour.[12]

In Canada, on a general level, the practice of judicial review has more legitimacy as courts are authorized by the Canadian Constitution (in which the *Charter* is contained) to engage in the practice. Specifically, s. 52 of the *Constitution Act, 1982*[13] provides that: "The Constitution of Canada is the supreme law of Canada, and any law that is inconsistent with the provisions of the Constitution is, to the extent of the inconsistency, of no force or effect."[14] By virtue of this provision of the Constitution, judges have been given a role to review the constitutionality of legislation. By contrast, the power of the U.S. Supreme Court to engage in judicial review was developed by judicial decree.[15]

The concept of *Charter* dialogue goes one step further in addressing concerns with the legitimacy of judicial review. According to Hogg and Bushell:

> Where a judicial decision is open to legislative reversal, modification, or avoidance, then it is meaningful to regard the relationship between the Court and the competent

---

[8] For example, see: AC Hutchinson and A Petter, "Private Rights/Public Wrongs: The Liberal Lie of the *Charter*" (1998) 398 UTLJ 278, cited in Hogg and Bushell above (n 5) 77.

[9] Among the Warren Court's most famous decisions was *Brown v. Board of Education*, 347 U.S. 483 (1954), in which a unanimous U.S. Supreme Court declared state laws establishing separate public schools for black and white students to be unconstitutional.

[10] Hogg and Bushell above (n 5) 77.

[11] See: Mark Tushnet, *Weak Courts, Strong Rights: Judicial Review and Social Welfare Rights in Comparative Constitutional Law* (Princeton University Press, 2007).

[12] For example, see: Antonin Scalia, *A Matter of Interpretation* (Princeton University Press, 1998).

[13] *Constitution Act, 1982*, Schedule B to the Canada Act 1982 (UK), 1982, c 11.

[14] *Ibid* s 52.

[15] *Marbury v. Madison*, 5 U.S. 137 (1803). This was also true in Canada before the enactment of the *Constitution Act, 1982*. The power of judicial review on federalism grounds was simply assumed by the judiciary.

legislative body as a dialogue. In that case, the judicial decision causes a public debate in which *Charter* values play a more prominent role than they would if there had been no judicial decision. The legislative body is in a position to devise a response that is properly respectful of the *Charter* values that have been identified by the Court, but which accomplishes the social or economic objectives that the judicial decision has impeded.[16]

Accordingly, the traditional roles for the judicial and legislative branches of government are maintained.

B. Revisiting the Theory

The idea of a "dialogue" between the judicial and legislative branches has been the subject of intense academic scrutiny and debate.[17] Partly in response to this debate, in 2007 Hogg, Thornton (née Bushell), and Wright wrote a follow-up to the original paper of 1997.[18] The authors noted that since the original 1997 article, 14 of 23 cases in which courts had invalidated legislation for being constitutionally impermissible elicited some response from the competent legislative body.[19] Although the numbers were not as overwhelming as reported in their 1997 paper, they provided evidence that *Charter* dialogue still factored prominently in the development of Canadian legislation.

The authors reiterated that *Charter* dialogue is a descriptive theory, but added that it does take some of the force away from the critics of judicial review. Specifically, they stated:

> Dialogue theory does not provide a justification for judicial review. The justification rests on the moral, political, and legal justifications for judicial review described

---

[16] Hogg and Bushell above (n 5) 79–80.

[17] FL Morton, "Dialogue or Monologue?" (1999) 20(3) Policy Options 23; JL Hiebert, "Why Must a Bill of Rights Be a Contest of Political and Judicial Wills?" (1999) 10 Public Law Review 22; CP Manfredi and JB Kelly, "Six Degrees of Dialogue: A Response to Hogg and Bushell" (1999) 37 Osgoode Hall LJ 513; PW Hogg and AA Thornton, "Reply to 'Six Degrees of Dialogue'" (1999) 37 Osgoode Hall LJ 529; FL Morton and R Knopff, *The Charter Revolution and the Court Party* (2000), 160–166; PW Hogg, "The Charter Revolution: Is It Undemocratic?" (2001) 12 Constitutional Forum 1; Kent Roach, *The Supreme Court on Trial* (2001), chs. 10–15; J. Waldron, "Some Models of Dialogue between Judges and Legislators" (2004) 23 Supreme Court LR (2d) 5; Kent Roach, "Dialogic Judicial Review and Its Critics" (2004) 23 Supreme Court LR (2d) 49; CP Manfredi, "The Life of a Metaphor: Dialogue in the Supreme Court, 1998–2003" (2004) 23 Supreme Court LR (2d) 105; LB Tremblay, "The Legitimacy of Judicial Review; The Limits of Dialogue between Courts and Legislatures" (2005) 3 Int J Con Law 617; S Gardbaum, "Reassessing the New Commonwealth Model of Constitutionalism" (2010) 8 Int J Con Law 167, 178–183; Emmett Macfarlane, "Conceptual Precision and Parliamentary Systems of Rights: Disambiguating 'Dialogue'" (2012) 17 Rev of Con Studies 73.

[18] Peter W Hogg, Allison AB Thornton and Wade K Wright, "Charter Dialogue Revisited or 'Much Ado about Metaphors'" (2007) 45 Osgoode Hall LJ 1, together with commentaries by scholars 67–91 and reply 193–202; R Dixon, "The Supreme Court of Canada, Charter Dialogue and Deference" (2009) 47 Osgoode Hall LJ 235.

[19] *Ibid* 51, "Charter Dialogue Revisited or 'Much Ado about Metaphors'" (2007) 45 Osgoode Hall LJ 1: "Since the 1997 article, there have been 23 cases in which a law has held to be invalid for breach of the Charter. Of those 23 cases, 14 (or approximately 61 percent) elicited some response from the competent

in the two paragraphs above. What "*Charter* Dialogue" demonstrated was not that judicial review was good, but that judicial review was weaker than is generally supposed. . . . The competent legislative body usually could, and usually did, replace a law that had been struck down with a valid law that accomplished the main objectives of the original invalid law. "*Charter* Dialogue" showed that what we adopted in 1982 was a halfway house between the strong form of judicial review typified by the United States and the statutory bill of rights typified by the *Canadian Bill of Rights* of 1960.[20]

Although a comprehensive survey has not been undertaken since 2007 on the prevalence of *Charter* dialogue, the *Carter* case demonstrates that it remains a critical part of the legislative process in Canada.

3. WHAT MAKES *CHARTER* DIALOGUE POSSIBLE IN CANADA?

While s. 52 of the *Constitution Act, 1982* provides courts with the authority to conduct judicial review, there are four features of the *Charter* itself which are instrumental in facilitating *Charter* dialogue. These are: (1) s. 1 of the *Charter*, (2) qualified *Charter* rights, (3) s. 15(1) of the *Charter*, and (4) s. 33 of the *Charter*. This chapter will explain each of these provisions in the following text.

A. Section 1 of the *Charter*

One factor that contributes to *Charter* dialogue is the fact that rights under the *Charter* are not absolute and may be limited by the competent legislative body. Specifically, s. 1 of the *Charter* provides: "The *Canadian Charter of Rights and Freedoms* guarantees the rights and freedoms set out in it subject only to such reasonable limits prescribed by law as can be demonstrably justified in a free and democratic society."[21] The judicially prescribed standard for limiting *Charter* rights was outlined by the Supreme Court in *R. v Oakes*,[22] where the Supreme Court held that laws which limit *Charter* rights must: (1) pursue an important objective, (2) be rationally connected with the objective, (3) impair the *Charter* right no more than is necessary to accomplish the objective, and (4) not have a disproportionately severe effect on the persons to whom it applies.[23]

---

legislative body. In one case, the response was simply to repeal the offending law. In the remaining 13 cases, a new law was substituted for the offending law."

[20] *Ibid* 29.
[21] *Canadian Charter* above (n 2) s 1.
[22] *R v Oakes*, [1986] 1 SCR 103, 24 CCC (3d) 321.
[23] *Ibid* 138–139.

With respect to *Charter* dialogue, s. 1 plays an important role as most laws which fail to meet the standard under s. 1 do so at the minimal impairment stage of the test. In the majority of these cases, the reviewing court will explain why the s. 1 standard was not met, which will often involve a suggestion of a less restrictive alternative law that would have satisfied this standard. Parliament then has the ability to revise the legislation in a manner that does not restrict a *Charter* right more than needed to accomplish its purpose.

The case of *RJR-MacDonald Inc. v Canada (A.G.)*[24] is illustrative. In that case, the Supreme Court struck down a federal law that prohibited the advertising of tobacco products, but mentioned it would have upheld restrictions that were limited to "lifestyle advertising" or advertising directed at children. Within two years, Canada's federal Parliament enacted the *Tobacco Act*,[25] which addressed these concerns. These amendments were upheld by the Supreme Court.[26]

On a normative level, there is the question of whether legislation should be drafted by Parliament in order to fit within the confines of a *Charter* right or to simply impair such rights as minimally as possibly. Nonetheless, the plain wording of s. 1 of the *Charter* makes the latter course of action permissible. Section 1 of the *Charter* will undoubtedly continue to play a pivotal role in shaping *Charter* dialogue.

B. Qualified *Charter* Rights

Besides s. 1 of the *Charter*, many of the rights within the *Charter* have built-in qualifications which facilitate dialogue between the judicial and legislative branches of government. For example, s. 8 of the *Charter* states: "Everyone has the right to be secure against unreasonable search or seizure."[27] The inclusion of the term "unreasonable" within the right means that Canadians do not have a carte blanche right to be free from search and seizure, but only searches and seizure which have been defined as "unreasonable."[28]

In *Hunter v. Southam Inc*,[29] the Supreme Court held that various provisions of the former *Combines Investigation Act*[30] authorized "unreasonable" search and seizure under s. 8 of the *Charter* as: (1) there was no requirement that a judge must issue a warrant prior to a search, and (2) there was no requirement that reasonable or probable cause needed to be established to support the issuance of a warrant. These two requirements, therefore, provided context to the meaning of "unreasonable" within s. 8 of the *Charter*.

---

[24] *RJR-MacDonald Inc v Canada (AG)*, [1995] 3 SCR 199, 100 CCC (3d) 449.
[25] *Tobacco Act*, SC 1997, c 13. Since its enactment, some of the provisions of the *Tobacco Act* have been amended.
[26] *Canada (Attorney General) v. JTI-Macdonald Corp.*, 2007 SCC 30, [2007] 2 SCR 610.
[27] *Canadian Charter* above (n 2) s 8.
[28] See also: *ibid* s 9: "Everyone has the right not to be arbitrarily detained or imprisoned"; *ibid* s 12: "Everyone has the right not to be subjected to any cruel and unusual treatment or punishment."
[29] *Hunter v Southam Inc*, [1984] 2 SCR 145, 14 CCC (3d) 97.
[30] *Combines Investigation Act*, RSC 1970, c C-23.

The *Competition Act*,[31] which succeeded and replaced the *Combines Investigation Act*, contained search provisions which complied with the terms of *Hunter*.

C. Section 15(1) of the *Charter*

Although s. 15 is not expressly qualified like s. 8 of the *Charter*, the judicial interpretation of Canada's equality guarantee also aids in *Charter* dialogue. Section 15(1) of the *Charter* provides: "Every individual is equal before and under the law and has the right to the equal protection and equal benefit of the law without discrimination and, in particular, without discrimination based on race, national or ethnic origin, colour, religion, sex, age or mental or physical disability."[32] Often laws which are unconstitutional under s. 15(1) of the *Charter* suffer from being underinclusive, in that persons in the applicant's position, who have a right to be included in the legislative scheme, are excluded based on a personal characteristic they possess. The obvious way to remedy this issue is for government to extend this benefit to the excluded group.

For example, when the Nova Scotia Court of Appeal held that a law extending family benefits to single mothers, but not single fathers, was unconstitutional,[33] the provincial legislature responded in turn by amending provincial regulations to allow equal access to family benefits for single parents of either sex.[34]

D. Section 33 of the *Charter*

Beyond the nature of the rights within the *Charter*, Canada's federal Parliament and provincial legislatures maintain a residual discretion to disregard judicial *Charter* decisions, thereby ensuring that legislatures (barring exceptions discussed below) maintain the final say in how to devise legislation. Specifically, s. 33(1) of the *Charter* states: "Parliament or the legislature of a province may expressly declare in an Act of Parliament or of the legislature, as the case may be, that the Act or a provision thereof shall operate notwithstanding a provision included in s. 2 or ss. 7 to 15 of this *Charter*."[35] The effect of s. 33(1) of the *Charter* is to allow a competent legislative body to re-enact a

---

[31] *Competition Act*, SC 1986, c 26, s 13.

[32] *Canadian Charter* above (n 2) s 15(1).

[33] *Phillips v Social Assistance Appeal Board (N.S.)* (1986), 76 NSR (2d) 240, 34 DLR (4th) 633. As explained by Hogg and Bushell above (n 5) 91: "The Nova Scotia legislature obviously considered that the provision of family benefits was of sufficient importance that the program should be extended rather than eliminated. However eliminating (or reducing) a government benefit is another option which is open to a legislature where a law has been held to be underinclusive. After all, it is not the applicant's right to a government cheque, but rather his or her right to equality, that the Court has affirmed."

[34] NS Reg 72/87.

[35] *Canadian Charter* above (n 2) s 33(1).

law without interference from the courts, *notwithstanding* that it is found to be in violation of a right in s. 2 or ss. 7 to 15 of the *Charter*.

For example, in *Ford v Quebec (Attorney General)*,[36] the Supreme Court determined
that a law in the province of Quebec which banned the use of any other language besides
French for commercial signs to be unconstitutional. The government of Quebec elected
not to revise its policy, but instead, invoked s. 33(1) of the *Charter* to enact a law with the
requisite notwithstanding clause which continued to ban the use of all languages other
than French for all outdoor signs.[37]

Although the presence of s. 33(1) in the *Charter* cannot be understated, its inclusion
must not be overstated, either. The *Ford* case illustrates two limitations on the provision.
First, as will be discussed in greater detail later in this chapter, it is politically difficult to
invoke s. 33(1) of the *Charter*. The *Ford* case is the only instance where it has been used
by a government in Canada to go against a decision of the Supreme Court.[38] Second,
s. 33(3) of the *Charter* limits the effect of a government's invocation of s. 33(1) to five
years, forcing governments to periodically review decisions to continue with legislation
that is not *Charter* compliant. In *Ford*, five years after the government of Quebec enacted
its non-*Charter* compliant legislation, it enacted a new law that permitted the use of languages other than French on outdoor signs so long as French was also used and was
"predominant."[39] As such, the presence of s. 33(3) in the *Charter* may only simply delay
governments from revising legislation that is not *Charter* compliant.

4. WHAT ARE ITS LIMITATIONS?

Although the framework of the *Charter* facilitates dialogue, there are limitations which
preclude such dialogue from taking place in all *Charter* cases.

A. Cases Where There Is No Scope for "Reasonable Limits" on Rights or Legislative Override of a Decision

If a court deems a *Charter* right to be "denied" as opposed to "limited," dialogue may
not be possible as there is no further ability for Parliament or a provincial legislature

---

[36] *Ford v Quebec (Attorney General)*, [1988] 2 SCR 712, 54 DLR (4th) 577.

[37] *An Act to Amend the Charter of the French Language*, SQ 1988, s 54, s 10.

[38] On April 20, 2017, Justice Layh of the Court of Queen's Bench for Saskatchewan held that the
province's funding of non-minority faith students attending separate, denominational schools violates
ss. 2(a) and 15(1) of the *Charter* and cannot be justified under s. 1 of the *Charter* (*Good Spirit School
Division No. 204 v Christ the Teacher Roman Catholic Separate School Division No. 212*, 2017 SKQB 109).
Justice Layh issued a suspended declaration of invalidity until June 30, 2018 to allow the province to
amend the relevant pieces of legislation which permit such funding. As of publication, Saskatchewan
Premier Brad Wall has threatened to invoke s. 33 of the *Charter* in order to defy the ruling.

[39] *An Act to Amend the Charter of the French Language*, SQ 1993, s 40, s 18.

to impose reasonable limits on the right. One right that has received such an interpretation is s. 23 of the *Charter*. Specifically, s. 23(1)(b) of the *Charter* states: "Citizens of Canada . . . who have received their primary school instruction in Canada in English or French and reside in a province where the language in which they received that instruction is the language of the English or French linguistic minority population of the province, have the right to have their children receive primary and secondary school instruction in that language in that province."[40]

In *Quebec (Attorney General) v Quebec Protestant School Boards*,[41] the Supreme Court held that a Quebec law which restricted admission to English language schools in Quebec to children whose parents had been educated in the English language in Quebec, alone, to be a violation of s. 23(1)(b) of the *Charter*. As the law was deemed to be an absolute "denial of" a *Charter* right as opposed to a "limit on" a *Charter* right, the Supreme Court refused to consider the possibility of a s. 1 justification in that case. Although there is a possibility that *Quebec School Boards* was wrongly decided, the case provides an example where a judicial decision is in fact the final word on legislation.

The case is also illustrative of the limits of s. 33(1) of the *Charter*, which is only available with respect to s. 2 and ss. 7–15 of the *Charter*, excluding the language rights in ss. 16–23 of the *Charter* (as well as the right to vote in s. 3 and mobility rights in s. 6).

B. Cases Where the Objective of a Law Is Unconstitutional

Although uncommon, legislatures similarly have no opportunity to revise legislation which is found to have an unconstitutional purpose (and not simply effect). For example, in *R. v Big M Drug Mart Ltd.*,[42] the Supreme Court held the federal Parliament's *Lord's Day Act*[43] to be unconstitutional as its purpose was to "compel the observance of the Christian Sabbath."[44] This was a violation of the guarantee of freedom of religion in s. 2(a) of the *Charter*. As the objective of the Act itself was held to be a violation of the *Charter*, there was no ability for subsequent judicial revision of the legislation, and the Supreme Court had the last word in striking it down.[45] However, one year later, the Supreme Court upheld a provincial law which prohibited retail stores from opening on Sunday, holding that its purpose was the secular one of providing a common pause day for retail workers.[46]

---

[40] *Canadian Charter* above (n 2) s 23(1)(b).
[41] *Quebec (Attorney General) v Quebec Protestant School Boards*, [1984] 2 SCR 66, 10 DLR (4th) 321.
[42] *R v Big M Drug Mart Ltd*, [1985] 1 SCR 295, 18 CCC (3d) 385.
[43] *Lord's Day Act*, RSC 1970 c L-13.
[44] *Big M* above (n 41) 351.
[45] It should be noted, though, that Parliament could have resurrected the *Lord's Day Act* by using the override in s 33(1) of the *Charter*. Moreover, it is important to note that this case was decided before the Supreme Court devised the judicial test for s. 1 justification in *Oakes*.
[46] *R v Edwards Books and Art Ltd*, [1986] 2 SCR 713, 30 CCC (3d) 385 (the law still had an effect on freedom of religion, but was upheld under s. 1).

C. Cases Where Political Forces Preclude Subsequent Action

Last, although uncommon, *Charter* dialogue is precluded in instances where political forces prevent legislative action. In these cases, a *Charter* decision from a court may be so politically sensitive that the competent legislative body elects not to take any subsequent action. As such, the judicial decision either remains as the final word on legislation or a "legislative gap" is created. We will elaborate more on this point further in the chapter.

5. How Have Courts Applied *Charter* Dialogue Theory?

Although *Charter* dialogue is a descriptive theory, interestingly, courts have used the theory to justify various actions.

A. Using the Suspended Declaration of Invalidity

Since 1985,[47] the Supreme Court of Canada has from time to time used the remedy of a "suspended declaration of invalidity," whereby an unconstitutional law will remain in temporary force (usually for one year) in order to give the legislature sufficient time to substitute *Charter* compliant legislation. The idea behind the remedy is that it gives legislatures time to devise new legislation, while not creating a legal vacuum during the time period while the unconstitutional law remains in effect. At one time, the remedy was considered extreme. In *Schachter v Canada*,[48] Justice Lamer (as he then was) held the remedy was only appropriate in cases where immediately striking down legislation would: (1) "pose danger to the public," (2) "threaten the rule of law," or (3) "result in the deprivation of benefits from deserving persons."[49]

However, with the new rationale of *Charter* dialogue, studies have shown that courts have largely ignored the *Schachter* guidelines and issued suspended declarations of invalidity more often.[50] The idea behind the increased use of the remedy is to give legislatures

---

[47] *Re Manitoba Language Rights*, [1985] 1 SCR 721, 19 DLR (4th) 1.
[48] *Schachter v Canada*, [1992] 2 SCR 933, 93 DLR (4th) 1.
[49] *Ibid* 719.
[50] See: Sujit Choudhry and Kent Roach, "Putting the Past behind Us?" (2003) 21 Sup Ct L Rev (2d) 205. Also see: Bruce Ryder, "Suspending the Charter" (2003) 21 Sup Ct L Rev (2d) 267.

the first opportunity to revise constitutionally invalid legislation before the court's ruling takes effect. As noted by Hogg, Thornton, and Wright:

> We conclude that the idea of dialogue has been influential in guiding the courts in their increasing use of suspended declarations of invalidity. A purpose of the suspension and often the only purpose, is to enable the legislature to respond directly to a holding of invalidity. The court recognizes that a range of corrective laws is possible, and that the legislature is better placed than the court to select the appropriate remedy. Although the unconstitutional law is maintained in force for a short time, the *Charter* is still respected, because if no new law is enacted by the time the period of suspension ends, the declaration of invalidity takes effect. If a new law is enacted in response to the holding of invalidity, that law must comply with the *Charter*.[51]

B. Determining How to Act in "Second Look" Cases

Charter dialogue has also been used by courts to justify different courses of action in "second look" cases, where courts have the opportunity to review the validity of legislation enacted to replace a law struck down in a previous decision. In some instances, judges have taken the view that courts should show more deference to the legislature when it has considered a court's decision and drafted legislation that accounts for it. In other instances, judges have held that automatic deference must not be given to the legislature simply because it has revised its legislation to conform with a court decision. These differing viewpoints can sometimes be found within the same decision.

The case of *Harper v Canada*[52] is illustrative. In *Harper*, the Supreme Court reviewed Parliament's second attempt to impose a ceiling on election expenditures by persons other than registered political parties and their candidates (third parties). The new legislation was in response to two decisions—one of the Supreme Court which struck down a prohibition on expenditures by persons who fell outside the umbrella of a "yes" or "no" side of a referendum campaign,[53] and the other in which the Alberta Court of Appeal had struck down a third-party restriction on election expenditures of $1,000.[54] In response to these decisions, Parliament amended the *Canada Elections Act*[55] to raise the ceiling on third-party election expenditures from $1,000 to $150,000, of which no more than $3,000 could be incurred in a single electoral district. The new limitations continued to be a violation of freedom of expression, contrary to s. 2(b) of the *Charter*. The question was whether the new provisions were saved by s. 1 of the *Charter*.

---

[51] Hogg, Thornton and Wright above (n 18) 18.
[52] *Harper v Canada* 2004 SCC 33, [2004] 1 SCR 827.
[53] *Libman v Quebec (Attorney General)*, [1997] 3 SCR 569, 151 DLR (4th) 385.
[54] *Somerville v Canada (Attorney General)* (1996), 184 AR 241, 136 DLR (4th) 205.
[55] *Canada Elections Act*, SC 2000, c 9.

In a 6-3 majority, the Supreme Court upheld the new laws in *Harper*. The opinions of the majority and minority illustrate how courts, notably the Supreme Court, struggle with second look cases. Justice Bastarache, writing for the majority, held it was appropriate for the court to show deference to Parliament based on the inherent difficulty with balancing the rights and privileges of all participants in the electoral process (while not discussing dialogue directly). Chief Justice McLachlin and Justice Major, for the minority, disagreed with the deferential approach of the majority and stressed that the good faith "evidenced by the ongoing dialogue with the courts as to where the limits should be set" could not "remedy an impairment of the right to freedom of expression."[56]

C. Deciding Whether to "Read Down" Statutes or Leave It to the Competent Legislature to Fix Them

Although no empirical study has been undertaken on this topic, the idea of *Charter* dialogue provides a basis for judges to exercise caution when considering whether to "read down" statutes in *Charter* cases. "Reading down" is a technique of statutory interpretation in which a court will prefer the interpretation of a statute that does not offend the Constitution. A danger of having judges "read down" legislation in *Charter* cases is that judges may in fact be reading in an interpretation that best suits their personal preferences where a range of reasonable alternatives exists, thereby usurping the role of the legislature. Accordingly, it is often better to allow the legislature to remediate the issue. As noted by Hogg, Thornton, and Wright:

> [The] idea of dialogue is a useful way of articulating the constraint that should be felt by judges. Where, after the exercise of normal interpretation, a legislative provision is found to be contrary to the *Charter*, the advantage of striking it down (and keeping in mind that the declaration of invalidity can be suspended) is that the reconstruction of the provision is remitted to the elected legislature.[57]

D. Justifying the Practice of Judicial Review

Although decisions of Canadian courts, including the Supreme Court, are free from language or detail other than what is needed to dispose of a particular decision, at times courts do address outside commentary in the course of their reasons for judgment. Using reference to *Charter* dialogue, justices of the Supreme Court have addressed academic criticisms directed towards the practice of judicial review. For example, in *M. v H.*,[58] a majority of the Supreme Court held that Ontario's *Family Law Act*[59] violated the

---

56   *Harper* above (n 51) 843–844.
57   Hogg, Thornton and Wright above (n 18) 13.
58   *M v H*, [1999] 2 SCR 3, 43 OR (3d) 254.
59   *Family Law Act*, RSO, 1990, c F 3.

s. 15(1) equality guarantee under the *Charter* as it excluded same-sex couples from the mutual support obligations the Act imposed on opposite-sex couples in common-law relationships. In a concurring opinion, Justice Bastarache, quoting the original Hogg and Bushell article on *Charter* dialogue, noted that judicial review was not "a veto over the politics of the nation," but instead was "the beginning of a dialogue" between courts and legislatures.[60] The Ontario government amended the legislation,[61] and the decision was one of a number of decisions which preceded the federal Parliament enacting the *Civil Marriage Act*,[62] which authorized same-sex marriages across Canada.

6. How Does the Remedial Action Taken by a Court Impact *Charter* Dialogue?

Although *Charter* dialogue is a descriptive theory which observes the process of legislative reform between the judicial and legislative branches in Canada, it is important to note that the type of remedy which a court chooses to issue, and its reasons for judgment, can greatly influence how the legislative response proceeds. In other words, as with any other "conversation," the tone and choice of words used by one participant can influence how the other responds. Three cases are demonstrative of this point.

A. Cases Where a Judicial Decision Elicits Limited or No Response from the Legislature

In certain cases, a judicial decision which invalidates legislation but goes no further will elicit limited to no response based on the politically sensitive nature of the issue being decided. In other words, absent any direction from the Court requiring the legislature to proceed in a particular manner, there will be no legislative response. Although rare, this is a possibility for courts to consider.

For example, in *R. v Morgentaler*,[63] the Supreme Court struck down provisions in Canada's *Criminal Code*,[64] which placed restrictions on abortion, on the basis they

---

[60] *M v H* above (n 57) 181.

[61] *Amendments Because of the Supreme Court of Canada Decision in M. v. H. Act*, 1999 SO 199, c 6.

[62] SC 2005, c 33. Some notable decisions which preceded this Act include: *EGALE Canada Inc v Canada (Attorney General)*, 2003 BCCA 251, 225 DLR (4th) 472 (BCCA); *Halpern v Canada (Attorney General)* (2003), 65 OR (3d) 161, 225 DLR (4th) 259; and *Hendricks v Quebec (Procureur General)*, [2002] RJQ 2506 (CS).

[63] *R v Morgentaler*, [1988] 1 SCR 30, 37 CCC (3d) 449.

[64] *Criminal Code*, RSC 1985, c C-46.

unduly deprived pregnant women of liberty or security of the person, contrary to s. 7 of the *Charter*. In obiter, various members of the Court opined that a less restrictive option could be upheld by the Court, though such an option was never compelled by the Court.[65] A subsequent bill[66] was passed by the House of Commons, but in a rare occurrence, was defeated in the Senate based on a tie vote. Because of the politically sensitive nature of the topic, further legislative amendments have never been proposed. The Supreme Court's 1988 decision remains the final decision on the subject—and there remains no national standard in Canada on how provinces are to administer abortions.

The *Morgentaler* case illustrates that in politically sensitive cases, a simple "striking down" of legislation may not elicit any sustained legislative response because of the political complexities of a particular issue. It serves to bolster arguments for proponents and critics of judicial review, alike. Proponents of judicial review will argue that in cases like *Morgentaler*, courts are respectful of the legislative process by not interfering in how to remediate legislation that runs afoul of the *Charter*, and that it is in fact the legislature who is to blame for not addressing an issue within the law. Some proponents of judicial review may still argue, though, that courts in these instances should impose positive *Charter* obligations on governments more than simply striking down legislation— though this gets more to the nature of *Charter* rights themselves, rather than the practice of judicial review. Opponents of judicial review will argue that courts which strike down legislation prior to societies being "ready" to draft new legislation simply create more of a mess by facilitating a legal vacuum for a period of time. A more favourable solution, to these individuals, would be for legislatures to revise controversial legislation once enough popular support arises, and legislation is in place which can supplant the existing statute and not leave a vacuum in the law.

B. Cases Where a Judicial Decision Dictates a Specific Response from the Legislature

In contrast to *Morgentaler*, courts may at times dictate the terms of the "dialogue" between the judiciary and legislature by not simply striking down legislation, but "reading in" the terms of the revised legislation. Famously, in *Vriend v Alberta*,[67] the Supreme Court held that Alberta's human rights code violated the equality guarantee under s. 15 of the *Charter* by not protecting against discrimination on the ground of sexual orientation. Rather than simply striking down the legislation, the majority of the Court took the unusual measure of "reading in" sexual orientation as a ground of discrimination into the Alberta legislation.

---

[65] *Morgentaler* above (n 62) 76, 82–83, 183.
[66] Bill C-43, An Act Respecting Abortion.
[67] *Vriend v Alberta*, [1998] 1 SCR 493, 156 DLR (4th) 385.

The decision created a firestorm of political controversy in Alberta, and nearly caused then Premier Ralph Klein to invoke s. 33 of the *Charter*. However, he eventually decided it was too politically unpalatable to do so, stating, "[i]t became abundantly clear that to individuals in this country the Charter of Rights and Freedoms is paramount and the use of any tool . . . to undermine [it] is something that should be used in very, very, very rare circumstances."[68] Without any action by the legislature, Alberta's human rights code had a ground of discrimination added by judicial determination.[69]

Unlike *Morgentaler*, the legislation on a politically sensitive issue was resolved in *Vriend* as the Supreme Court took an active role in amending legislation which was not certain to pass in the Alberta legislature at the time. As with *Morgentaler*, the *Vriend* decision elicits responses from both opponents and critics of judicial review. Proponents will note that the Court's strong response addressed a discriminatory gap in the legislation, while leaving it open to the legislature to invoke s. 33 of the *Charter* and maintain the constitutional status quo. Critics will note that "reading in" to legislation language that was not enacted oversteps the boundaries of a court—and that the s. 33 override does not provide legislatures with a meaningful choice in electing whether or not to comply with a court order.

C. Cases Where a Judicial Decision Guides the Shape of the Legislative Response

Most recently, the Supreme Court's decision in *Carter* illustrates a halfway point between *Morgentaler* and *Vriend*—whereby the Court has not either stayed out of, or dictated a particular legislative response, but guided the course of the legislative response through its reasons for judgment. As noted beforehand, the Supreme Court issued a suspended declaration of invalidity, thereby giving Parliament a chance to revise the assisted-death provisions in the *Criminal Code*. However, the Court went one step further than simply striking down the legislation, stating:

> The appropriate remedy is therefore a declaration that s. 241(b) and s. 14 of the *Criminal Code* are void insofar as they prohibit physician-assisted death for a competent adult person who (1) clearly consents to the termination of life; and (2) has a grievous and irremediable medical condition (including an illness, disease or disability) that causes enduring suffering that is intolerable to the individual in the circumstances of his or her condition. "Irremediable", it should be added, does not require the patient to undertake treatments that are not acceptable to the individual. The scope of this declaration is intended to respond to the factual circumstances in

---

[68] Christopher P. Manfredi, *Judicial Power and the Charter: Canada and the Paradox of the Liberal Constitutionalism*, 2d ed. (Oxford University Press, 2001) 187–188.

[69] It should be noted that since 1 October 2009, the *Alberta Human Rights Act,* RSA 2000, c A-25.5 has explicitly included sexual orientation as a ground of discrimination.

this case. We make no pronouncement on other situations where physician-assisted dying may be sought.[70]

As such, within the *Carter* decision, the Supreme Court recommended how the legislative scheme could be fixed, without compelling such a solution. The ensuing legislative debate on how to draft revised legislation was influenced by the specifications of the *Carter* decision. For example, in its report on how to draft *Charter* compliant legislation, the Special Joint Committee on Physician-Assisted Dying noted it was "guided by *Carter*" in coming up with its recommendations.[71] The federal government has since passed legislation[72] which it has declared complies with the *Carter* decision. For example, in a House of Commons debate on the Bill, Justice Minister Jody Wilson-Raybould stated:

> Mr. Speaker, we look forward to having a vigorous debate on Bill C-14. As the Attorney General, I read the *Carter* decision very carefully. I am confident we are responding in a substantive way to the *Carter* decision, as well as ensuring that it is in compliance with the *Charter of Rights and Freedoms*. We have put forward what we believe is the best solution now which balances personal autonomy and ensures we protect the vulnerable. I look forward to the debate.[73]

7. How Important Will *Charter* Dialogue Be Going Forward?

Since 2007, no comprehensive study has been undertaken on the prevalence of *Charter* dialogue, though as the *Carter* case illustrates, it continues to be a part of the legislative reform process in Canada. Barring any major reforms to the *Charter*, the "dialogue" between courts and legislatures will likely continue in the future. The nature of this dialogue, as demonstrated, will be shaped by the issues brought before courts as well as the judicial responses to deal with legislation that is not compliant with the *Charter*.

8. Conclusion

In this chapter, we have highlighted the unique features of the Canadian *Charter*—specifically ss. 1, 33, 15, and the qualified nature of other *Charter* rights—which enables

---

[70] *Carter* above (n 1) [127] [emphasis added].

[71] Special Joint Committee on Physician-Assisted Dying, Medical Assistance in Dying: A Patient-Centred Approach (HC 2015-16, 42-I).

[72] *An Act to amend the Criminal Code* above (n 4).

[73] House of Commons Debates, 42nd Parl, 1st Sess, No 41 (18 April 2016) at 2361 (Hon Jody Wilson-Raybould) [emphasis added].

both the judicial and legislative branches of government, acting separately of course, to develop legislation which is constitutionally permissible. This process—which we referred to as "*Charter* dialogue"—permits courts to have a role in shaping legislation, while ultimately leaving the task of re-drafting legislation with the relevant legislative body of a country. We have also demonstrated how the remedial choices by courts can influence the dialogical process between courts and legislatures. Going forward, the Canadian judiciary will obviously continue to have a role in ensuring the fundamental rights of Canadians are protected, while often leaving the ultimate modification of legislation to the legislature.

BIBLIOGRAPHY

Secondary Sources

Choudhry S and Roach K, "Putting the Past behind Us?" (2003) 21 Sup Ct L Rev (2d) 205

Dixon R, "The Supreme Court of Canada, Charter Dialogue and Deference" (2009) 47 Osgoode Hall LJ 235

Gardbaum S, "Reassessing the New Commonwealth Model of Constitutionalism" (2010) 8 Int J Con Law 167

Hiebert JL, "Why Must a Bill of Rights Be a Contest of Political and Judicial Wills?" (1999) 10 Public Law Review 22

Hogg PW, "The Charter Revolution: Is It Undemocratic?" (2001) 12 Constitutional Forum 1

_____. and Bushell AA, "The Charter Dialogue between Courts and Legislatures (Or Perhaps the Charter of Rights Isn't Such a Bad Thing after All) (1997) 35 OHLJ 76

_____. and Thornton AA, "Reply to 'Six Degrees of Dialogue' " (1999) 37 Osgoode Hall LJ 529

_____. and Thornton AA and Wright WK, "Charter Dialogue Revisited or 'Much Ado about Metaphors' " (2007) 45 Osgoode Hall LJ 1, together with commentaries by scholars 67–91 and reply 193–202

House of Commons Debates, 42nd Parl, 1st Sess, No 41 (18 April 2016) at 2361 (Hon Jody Wilson-Raybould)

Hutchinson AC and Petter A, "Private Rights/Public Wrongs: The Liberal Lie of the *Charter*" (1998) 398 UTLJ 278

Manfredi CP, *Judicial Power and the Charter: Canada and the Paradox of the Liberal Constitutionalism*, 2d ed. (Toronto: Oxford University Press, 2001)

_____. "The Life of a Metaphor: Dialogue in the Supreme Court, 1998–2003" (2004) 23 Supreme Court LR (2d) 105

_____. and Kelly JB, "Six Degrees of Dialogue: A Response to Hogg and Bushell" (1999) 37 Osgoode Hall LJ 513

Macfarlane E, "Conceptual Precision and Parliamentary Systems of Rights: Disambiguating 'Dialogue' " (2012) 17 Rev of Con Studies 73

Morton FL, "Dialogue or Monologue?" (1999) 20(3) Policy Options 23

_____. and Knopff R, *The Charter Revolution and the Court Party* (2000)

Roach K, *The Supreme Court on Trial* (2001), chs. 10–15

_____. "Dialogic Judicial Review and Its Critics" (2004) 23 Supreme Court LR (2d) 49

Ryder B, "Suspending the Charter" (2003) 21 Sup Ct L Rev (2d) 267

Scalia A, *A Matter of Interpretation* (Princeton University Press, 1998)

Special Joint Committee on Physician-Assisted Dying, Medical Assistance in Dying: A Patient-Centred Approach (HC 2015-16, 42-I)

Tremblay LB, "The Legitimacy of Judicial Review; The Limits of Dialogue between Courts and Legislatures" (2005) 3 Int J Con Law 617

Waldron J, "Some Models of Dialogue between Judges and Legislators" (2004) 23 Supreme Court LR (2d) 5

Cases

R v Big M Drug Mart Ltd, [1985] 1 SCR 295, 18 CCC (3d) 385.
Carter v Canada (Attorney General), 2015 SCC 5, [2015] 1 SCR 331.
R v Edwards Books and Art Ltd, [1986] 2 SCR 713, 30 CCC (3d) 385.
EGALE Canada Inc v Canada (Attorney General), 2003 BCCA 251, 225 DLR (4th) 472 (BCCA).
Ford v Quebec (Attorney General), [1988] 2 SCR 712, 54 DLR (4th) 577.
Halpern v Canada (Attorney General) (2003), 65 OR (3d) 161, 225 DLR (4th) 259.
Harper v Canada 2004 SCC 33, [2004] 1 SCR 827.
Hendricks v Quebec (Procureur General), [2002] RJQ 2506 (CS).
Hunter v Southam Inc, [1984] 2 SCR 145, 14 CCC (3d) 97.
Libman v Quebec (Attorney General), [1997] 3 SCR 569, 151 DLR (4th) 385.
M v H, [1999] 2 SCR 3, 43 OR (3d) 254.
Re Manitoba Language Rights, [1985] 1 SCR 721, 19 DLR (4th) 1.
R v Morgentaler, [1988] 1 SCR 30, 37 CCC (3d) 449.
R v Oakes, [1986] 1 SCR 103, 24 CCC (3d) 321.
Phillips v Social Assistance Appeal Board (N.S.) (1986), 76 NSR (2d) 240, 34 DLR (4th) 633.
Quebec (Attorney General) v Quebec Protestant School Boards, [1984] 2 SCR 66, 10 DLR (4th) 321.
RJR-MacDonald Inc v Canada (AG), [1995] 3 SCR 199, 100 CCC (3d) 449.
Schachter v Canada, [1992] 2 SCR 933, 93 DLR (4th) 1.
Somerville v. Canada (Attorney General) (1996), 184 AR 241, 136 DLR (4th) 205.
Vriend v Alberta, [1998] 1 SCR 493, 156 DLR (4th) 385.

American Cases

Brown v. Board of Education, 347 U.S. 483 (1954).
Marbury v. Madison, 5 U.S. 137 (1803).

Legislation

An Act to Amend the Charter of the French Language, SQ 1988.
An Act to Amend the Charter of the French Language, SQ 1993.
Alberta Human Rights Act, RSA 2000, c A-25.5.
Amendments Because of the Supreme Court of Canada Decision in M. v. H. Act, 1999 SO 199, c 6.
Bill C-14, An Act to amend the Criminal Code and to make related amendments to other Acts (medical assistance in dying).
Bill C-43, An Act Respecting Abortion.
Canada Elections Act, SC 2000, c 9.
Canadian Charter of Rights and Freedoms, The Constitution Act, 1982, being Schedule B to the *Canada Act 1982* (UK), 1982, c 11.

Civil Marriage Act, SC 2005, c 33.

Combines Investigation Act, RSC 1970, c C-23.

Competition Act, SC 1986, c 26.

The Constitution Act, 1982, Schedule B to the Canada Act 1982 (UK), 1982, c 11.

Criminal Code, RSC 1985, c C-46.

Family Law Act, RSO, 1990, c F 3.

Lord's Day Act, RSC 1970 c L-13.

Tobacco Act, SC 1997, c 13.

F. The Canadian Constitution in a Comparative Law Perspective

CHAPTER 50

THE CANADIAN CONSTITUTION AND THE WORLD

SUJIT CHOUDHRY[*]

1. INTRODUCTION

CANADIAN constitutional discourse—scholarly, legal, political—has been receptive to comparative influences since its very inception. Our openness to comparative engagement, I would suggest, is a product of the constitutional pluralism that defines the Canadian constitutional order. Canada's constitutional framework is a *métissage* arising from English, French, and Indigenous legal traditions, and from a variety of sources—constitutions, statutes, common law, convention, custom, and treaty—within each of those traditions. Canadian constitutional argument consists not just of arguing *within* discursive frameworks, but reasoning and justifying *across* them. Integrating the diverse lineaments that are the constitutive elements of Canadian public law is at the very heart of our constitutional project. It is only natural that Canadians would instinctively look beyond our legal borders to comparative experience from other countries as a source of lessons learned, models to be followed, and dangers to be avoided.

In this chapter, I examine the corollary to Canada's comparative engagement—the influence of elements of Canada's constitutional model abroad, in three areas: (1) the *Canadian Charter of Rights and Freedoms* as an innovative way to institutionalize the relationship among legislatures, executives, and courts with respect to the enforcement of a constitutional bill of rights, as justified by "dialogue theory", that contrasts starkly

* I. Michael Heyman Professor of Law, University of California, Berkeley. I thank Nathalie Des Rosiers, Patrick Macklem and Peter Oliver for their generous invitation to contribute to the *Handbook*. I also thank Patrick Macklem and David Schneiderman for helpful advice and feedback on an earlier draft, and more importantly, for their intellectual camaraderie over the past two decades. All remaining errors are mine.

with its leading alternatives, the American and German systems of judicial supremacy; (2) Canada's plurinational federalism as a strategy to accommodate minority nationalism and dampen the demand for secession and independence within the context of a single state, by divorcing the equation of state and nation; and (3) the complex interplay between a constitutional bill of rights and minority nation-building, as reflected in the constitutional politics surrounding the recognition of Quebec's distinctiveness, and the role of the Supreme Court of Canada in adjudicating constitutional conflicts over official language policy arising out of Quebec. The first two mark well-trodden terrain, whereas the third, less so, although it bears careful attention for countries interested in learning how the different pillars of the Canadian constitutional model interact.

The vectors of Canadian influence are not those that characterize the leading global constitutional models—the first post-colonial, republican constitution adopted by a country that emerged as the world's leading economic and military superpower (United States); metropolitan constitutions that still held appeal during the process of decolonization (France, United Kingdom); the distinct attraction of post-authoritarian, dignity-protecting constitutions that resonate with countries underdoing similar transitions, especially after the fall of Communism (Germany); and the growing importance of constitutional models from the global south that are attuned not only to the need to constrain public power, but to mandate and channel its exercise in the service of human development in the context of deeply entrenched socio-economic inequality (India, South Africa). Rather, Canada's global constitutional footprint is rooted in our "soft power"— that is, the attractiveness of our example as a rights-protecting liberal democracy characterized by multiple forms of diversity (immigrant, Indigenous, plurinational) that is remarkably prosperous, peaceful, and stable, and deeply committed to the rule of law.

While the focus of this chapter is contemporary, this should not imply that foreign interest in Canada's constitutional model is only recent, especially in the Commonwealth. For example, as Peter Oliver has taught us, Canada, along with Australia and New Zealand, in the process of achieving independence within the imperial constitutional order, had to wrestle with the central puzzle of constituent power in the face of the competing imperatives of legal continuity and parliamentary supremacy, on the one hand, and on the other, the democratic pressure for an autochthonous source of constitutional title in newly democratic states. How each country approached this issue was of great interest to the others.[1] More prosaically, the doctrines of Canadian federalism—such as pith and substance, and double aspect—have become important tools of judicial interpretation in other Commonwealth federations, such as Australia, India, and South Africa, and even in the United Kingdom with respect to the scheme of devolution created by the *Scotland Act*. The Canadian recognition of common law aboriginal title in *Calder* in the early 1970s was a harbinger for the recognition of similar rights across the Commonwealth in the following decades, in Australia, Belize,

---

[1] P. Oliver, *The Constitution of Independence: The Development of Constitutional Theory in Australia, Canada, and New Zealand* (Oxford University Press, 2005).

Botswana, Malaysia, New Zealand, Papua New Guinea, and South Africa. Indeed, as David Law and Mila Versteeg have highlighted, the *Charter* resembles most closely bills of rights in other Commonwealth jurisdictions.[2] We can extend their observation to suggest that the combination of shared legal tradition, language, colonial history, and constitutional text creates a dense legal platform for the migration of constitutional ideas among Commonwealth jurisdictions, both with respect to constitutional design not only of bills of rights, but also federalism and the status and powers of Indigenous peoples, as well as the judicial interpretation of those provisions.

Canadian scholars have figured prominently in transnational debates about bills of rights and the constitutional accommodation of minority nationalism. What bears special attention is that there is an important domestic politics to our foreign interventions. Interest in elements of the Canadian constitutional model abroad coincided with intense controversy over precisely those elements at home. International engagement with the Canadian alternative to judicial supremacy with respect to constitutional bills of rights took place at a time when the Supreme Court of Canada came under sustained attack for engaging in judicial activism and asserting its supremacy over the other branches of government, which appeared to place a core feature of that model in question. The rise and promotion of the Canadian model of plurinational federalism, in parallel fashion, occurred during the constitutional crisis of the mid-1990s over Quebec secession, which that very model was designed to prevent. Canadian experts promoted elements of the Canadian constitutional model abroad, in part, to enhance their political attractiveness and success domestically.

2. DIALOGUE THEORY AND THE CANADIAN ALTERNATIVE TO JUDICIAL SUPREMACY

Anxieties over judicial review under a constitutional bill of rights were an important element of the debates preceding adoption of the *Charter*, because of the new element it introduced into Canada's pre-existing system of constitutional supremacy, hitherto confined to the federal division of powers. The experience of the United States—especially the constitutional crisis over the New Deal, and the liberal legal agenda championed by the Warren Court—loomed large, especially to Canadian legal elites who increasingly receive their graduate training in the United States.[3] The federal government's proposals were clearly alert to the risks that judicial review under the *Charter* posed, no more so than with section 7.[4] That provision was drafted to prevent the libertarian legacy of the

[2] D. Law & M. Versteeg, "The Declining Influence of the United States Constitution" (2012) 84 *NYU L. Rev.* 762.

[3] See, e.g., P. Monahan, *Politics and the Constitution: The Charter, Federalism and the Supreme Court of Canada* (Carswell, 1987).

[4] S. Choudhry, "The *Lochner* Era and Comparative Constitutionalism" (2004) 2 *ICON* 1.

Lochner era from coming to Canada, by excluding "property" and substituting it with "security of the person", with the goal of orienting the provision around corporeal interests and protecting the redistributive, regulatory state from constitutional challenge. It was also designed to preclude the activist legacy of *Lochner*, rooted in the doctrine of substantive due process, by requiring that the deprivation of protected interests accord with "the principles of fundamental justice", not "due process", ironically in order to limit the scope of the provision to procedural fairness.

But the biggest constitutional concession to the fears of the growth in judicial power under the *Charter* was the inclusion of the legislative override or notwithstanding clause, section 33. That provision allows the federal Parliament and provincial legislatures to enact laws that would otherwise be unconstitutional because they unjustifiably limit certain *Charter* rights—the fundamental freedoms, legal rights, and equality rights—but not the democratic rights, mobility rights, or language rights. An exercise of the override expires at the end of five years. The override is a distinctive, made-in Canada constitutional innovation, and is at the heart of the global interest in the *Charter*, because it combines a form of judicial review of legislation with the retention of ultimate legislative supremacy. Mark Tushnet has helpfully termed the Canadian model of rights-based judicial review "weak-form", to contrast it with "strong-form" judicial review built around judicial supremacy, whether wielded by a generalist apex court (as in the United States) or a specialist, Kelsenian constitutional court (as in Germany and most countries).[5] It offers a "third way" in between legislative supremacy and judicial supremacy that broadens the scope for constitutional choice, and in particular, another option for countries with legislative supremacy that wish to adopt judicial review but which have misgivings about it.

However, because the override was added to the *Charter* during the final, closed-door round of negotiations in November 1981, there is little in the way of a contemporaneous legislative record that sets out the justification of constitutional actors for its adoption—unlike for section 7, for example. What is indisputable is that the override was a political compromise that enabled nine provinces (not Quebec) and the federal government to come to agreement over the 1982 constitutional package, which included the *Charter*, the Aboriginal rights provisions of the Constitution, and domestic procedures for constitutional amendment. In the years since its enactment, two main theoretical justifications for the override have emerged, which I term the *negative* and *positive* justifications. The negative justification is that the override provides a constitutional safety-valve in the event of prolonged conflict between the courts, on the one hand, and executives and legislatures, on the other.[6] In the absence of an override, the political branches would eventually prevail over the courts, through abusing the power of judicial appointment (court-packing) and/or publicly attacking the court (court-bashing), which could severely damage and perhaps destroy the institution of judicial review itself. The

---

[5] M. Tushnet, *Weak Courts, Strong Rights: Judicial Review and Social Welfare Rights in Comparative Constitutional Law* (Princeton University Press, 2008).

[6] Choudhry, above (n 4).

override is an institutional mechanism for channelling this disagreement into a transparent, public process governed by the rule of law through a self-terminating legislative enactment that must be express in its intention to set aside the *Charter*. It thereby
preserves the institution of judicial review while allowing the political branches to ultimately prevail. The override, on this view, is a constitutional conflict avoidance mechanism designed to provide a means to avert a crisis such as the one that occurred in the
United States on the constitutionality of the New Deal.

The negative justification of the override suggests this mechanism's principal target
is the behaviour of political institutions; it is noticeably silent on the impact that the
override could have on how courts conceptualize and execute judicial review under the
Charter. By contrast, the positive justification for the override offers such an account.[7]
The most fully-worked out theory has been offered by Stephen Gardbaum, initially in
an article published in 2001.[8] Gardbaum argued that the override lies at the heart of a
constitutional model of rights-protection whereby judges and legislatures perform distinct functions or roles. Judges should interpret bills of rights without fear of the consequences of judicial over-enforcement, because judges are not supreme. The reasons
for deference that arguably follow from judicial supremacy no longer exist. Judges can
interpret rights broadly, and apply every stage of the proportionality analysis in a stringent manner to impose a very high burden of justification. Should a court hold that legislation contravenes rights in a manner that cannot be justified, the legislature could
disagree and respond to the court by re-enacting its previous legislation.

What judicial review coupled with an override adds to a system of pure legislative
supremacy is a mechanism to correct several well-known defects in the legislative process: the failure to anticipate the consequences of general legislation which sets out
abstract standards when applied to individual cases, especially in circumstances where
the legislature lacks representation by the socially disadvantaged or marginalized who
would have been alert to the disproportionate impact of legislation on their rights (e.g.,
women, the poor); the discounting of the rights of those who completely lack the political power to protect themselves in the political process (e.g., non-citizens, children);
the prejudice or indifference toward the rights of discrete and insular minorities who
may wield the right to vote and who—in Jeremy Waldron's helpful formulation—are not
just topical, but decisional minorities because they are persistently on the losing side of
legislative votes and rights-violating political decisions;[9] the making of decisions under
panic in response to concerns about national security, and so on.

One or more of these pathologies serve as a basis for most contemporary justifications
of strong-form judicial review, which presuppose that courts are less likely than legislatures to fall prey to them. However, strong-form review is subject to two well-known democratic objections: that it debilitates democracy by dulling the habits of self-government

---

[7] S. Choudhry, "The Commonwealth Constitutional Model or Models?" (2013) 11 *ICON* 1094.
[8] S. Gardbaum, "The New Commonwealth Model of Constitutionalism" (2001) 49 *American J. of Comp. L.* 707.
[9] J. Waldron, "The Core of the Case against Judicial Review" (2006) 115 *Yale L.J.* 1346.

through the removal from the political agenda of the most controversial and important questions of political morality, and that it distorts policy choices because political institutions must work within the constitutional framework laid down by the court, either ex post (if a law is struck down), or ex ante (in anticipation of a finding of unconstitutionality). At its heart, weak-form review aspires to capture some of the upsides of judicial review while lowering the risk of the downsides. The principal role of a court under weak-form review is to serve as an institutionalized forum for highlighting rights-based issues to lower the risk they will be ignored in subsequent legislative debates.

The task of legislatures in responding to court judgments under weak-form review is not simply to recapitulate the exercise engaged in by the reviewing court—that is, not to re-run the legislative process but to give concerns about rights priority over all other competing considerations. Rather, the role of legislatures is to make an *all-things considered* judgment in which rights-related considerations occupy an important and perhaps even a central place, but are by no means the only relevant or most important factor on the table. If the legislature sets aside the court's judgment, and either proceeds with its initial course of action or modifies it to adopt measures that impair the right to a lesser extent but which are not necessarily the least rights-infringing measures, this disagreement does not mean that the legislature has made a legal error in interpreting and applying the bill of rights. Rather, it reflects the legislature's judgment that a broader range of considerations can outweigh the rights-related reasons advanced by the court that may be entirely correct on their own terms. The value of judicial review is that it forces the legislature to reconsider the legislation in light of the views of a body expert in questions of rights-protection, as expressed through a thoughtful, detailed judgment, to respond to those views, and to be held politically accountable for any decisions to disagree. Judicial review with an override neither debilitates democracy nor distorts policy choice. On the contrary, it enhances both.

It is the positive case for the override that has captured comparative attention. Canadian scholars have been central participants in this global conversation, although their preoccupations have been domestic, and have arisen out of local concerns over judicial activism. Canadian debates about judicial activism have in fact come in waves. The first critics of the *Charter* came principally from the Left, and focused on the concern that notwithstanding the exclusion of rights of contract and property from the *Charter*, the courts would erect constitutional obstacles to the interventionist, regulatory state.[10] Oddly, the override was absent from these debates, despite its origins precisely as a means to equip legislatures to check the rise of this kind of jurisprudence.

---

[10] J. Bakan, *Constitutional Rights and Social Wrongs* (University of Toronto Press, 1997); M. Mandel, *The Charter of Rights and the Legalization of Politics in Canada* (Thompson Educational Publishing, rev. ed. 1994); A. Hutchison, *Waiting for CORAF: A Critique of Law and Rights* (University of Toronto Press, 1995); A. Petter, "The Politics of the Charter" (1986) 8 *Sup. Ct. L. Rev.* 473; A. Petter, "The Charter's Hidden Agenda" (1987) 45 *The Advocate* 857. For a recent publication in this intellectual tradition, see A. Petter, *The Politics of the Charter: The Illusive Promise of Constitutional Rights* (University of Toronto Press, 2010).

Instead, Canada's constitutional Left trained its fire at the Court's broad interpretation of rights, and the demanding version of the proportionality test it adopted in *Oakes*. The Supreme Court responded to these criticisms not, as it could have, by insisting on the use of the override, and maintaining its stringent approach to justification under section 1. Rather, it crafted a series of doctrines of deference that made it far easier for governments to meet the burden of justification under section 1.[11]

The mantra of judicial activism in Canada was then taken up by the Right, who charged that under the cloak of judicial review, the Supreme Court was foisting a left, progressive political agenda upon the Canadian public, especially on questions of same sex rights, gender, and criminal justice. The most prominent right-wing academic critics were Ted Morton and Rainer Knopff, whose views gained great currency in the Reform Party, a right-wing political party (which later merged with the Progressive Conservative Party to form the Conservative Party of Canada, which for nearly a decade governed Canada led by Stephen Harper).[12] The central response to this critique from Canadian legal scholars is "dialogue theory", which captures distinct yet related *institutional* and *interpretative* claims. The *institutional* claim is that the Supreme Court does not in fact have the "last word", because its judgments finding laws unconstitutional are in many cases followed by legislative "replies" that largely achieve the same objectives, albeit by different means. However, one of the notable features of Canadian constitutional practice is that these legislative replies are enacted without the use of the override. Rather, as Peter Hogg and Alison Bushell—the academic originators of dialogue theory—explained, the principal mechanism of "dialogue" is section 1, whereby legislation is usually struck down because it fails to use the least restrictive means, as opposed to pursuing an illegitimate goal.[13] The ability to pursue the same goal through modified means signifies that to characterize the balance of judicial and legislative power under the *Charter* as judicial supremacy tout court is an over-simplification. Thus, the response to the right-wing critics of the *Charter* was to mobilize empirics to throw into question the inference of judicial *domination* of the political branches from the institution of judicial *supremacy*. The Hogg and Bushell article was highly influential, not only as a piece of scholarship, but as a domestic political intervention that reconfigured debates in Canada over the Supreme Court. Dialogue quickly emerged as the dominant metaphor in scholarly, legal professional and political discourses for conceptualizing judicial review in Canada and to contrast it with judicial supremacy, especially in the United States. Notably absent from Hogg and Bushell's analysis is the override, which for them played only a minor role in dialogue. This was likely due to the fact that the

---

[11] For an overview of this jurisprudence, see S. Choudhry, "So What Is The Real Legacy of *Oakes*? Two Decades of Proportionality Analysis under the Canadian *Charter*'s Section 1" (2006) 35 *Sup. Ct. L. Rev.* (2d) 501.

[12] R. Knopff & T. Morton, *The Charter Revolution and the Court Party* (University of Toronto Press, 2000); S. Choudhry, Review Essay of *Judicial Power and the Charter: Canada and the Paradox of Liberal Constitutionalism*, 2d ed. by C.P. Manfredi (2003) 1 *ICON* 379.

[13] P. Hogg & A. Bushell, "The *Charter* Dialogue between Courts and Legislatures" (1997) *Osgoode Hall L.J.* 75.

override has been sparingly used in Canada—approximately a dozen times—arguably because it was delegitimized through its use by Quebec in the late 1980s to protect legislation mandating French commercial signage after the Supreme Court's decision in *Ford*.[14] Nonetheless, dialogue in a different form has emerged, through section 1.

Kent Roach extended the institutional claims of dialogue theory considerably in a manner that linked up Canada to transnational discussions of the Commonwealth constitutional model.[15] Institutionally, Roach analogized between judicial review under the *Charter* and statutory interpretation against the backdrop of common law rights, which could be overridden through express statutory language. These so-called clear statement rules anticipate weak-form judicial review, as legislatures must expressly override rights that apply presumptively; however, the absence of a proportionality analysis applicable to such statutory derogations of common law rights makes the analogy imperfect. Nonetheless, as a rhetorical matter, Roach's linkage of the *Charter* and its common law antecedents had the effect of tying Canada to debates over the establishment of rights-based review of legislation in the United Kingdom and New Zealand, which he also saw as growing out of the common law tradition of rights-protection. For Roach, what these systems shared is that, like the common law, legislative supremacy was retained. To be sure, there are important differences among these systems; the *New Zealand Bill of Rights Act* only creates an interpretative obligation for legislation that can be overridden by clear legislation, and therefore represents the least of a break from the common law; the United Kingdom *Human Rights Act* incorporates the *European Convention of Human Rights* into domestic law, and grants courts both an interpretative power and the authority to issue declarations of incompatibility for legislation but not invalidity; the *Charter* alone among these three instruments grants courts the power to strike down legislation for unconstitutionality, along with interpretive authority. But there is a clear domestic politics to Roach's argumentative move. On his account, the *Charter* is not a constitutional revolution; rather, it is an incremental development from Canada's common law constitutional past, which combined judicial rights-protection with legislative supremacy—as does the *Charter*. Moreover, by grouping the *Charter* with systems of weak-form review in other advanced industrial democracies within the Commonwealth with which Canada shares a common law tradition and fidelity to Parliamentary democracy, and which provide for a lesser degree of judicial power and a greater degree of legislative supremacy than does the *Charter*, Roach further sought to deflect domestic political criticism.

What does dialogue theory say about the *interpretative* question of how the different branches of government should conceptualize their relationship to, and functions under, a constitutional regime of rights protection, such as that established by the *Charter*? This first question arose with respect to the courts, in the narrow context of *Charter* challenges to legislative replies that do not strictly conform to the court's prior judgment. Under

---

[14] *Ford v Quebec (AG)*, [1988] 2 S.C.R. 712.
[15] K. Roach, *The Supreme Court on Trial: Judicial Activism or Democratic Dialogue* (Irwin Law, 2001).

a system of strong-form review, such legislation should be unconstitutional. Courts could approach this kind of situation in precisely the same way under the *Charter*, compelling the use of the override, even if the deviation from the prior judgment is minor, thereby forcing a public debate and democratic accountability for this legislative decision. Judicial practice under the *Charter*, however, has been inconsistent. The Supreme Court has asserted the supremacy of its interpretations of the *Charter* in *Sauvé (2)*, whereas seemingly allowing Parliament to overrule it without recourse to the override in *Mills, Hall,* and *JTI MacDonald*.[16] Arguably, *Mills* can be explained on the basis that the reply legislation overruled a prior common law ruling of the Court, *O'Connor*, and that the Court merely showed deference to a statute which itself had not sought to re-enact a legislative provision previously struck down. The rationale for *Hall* and *JTI MacDonald* could possibly be that Parliament adduced new social science evidence to justify the reply legislation at issue in both cases, shifting the minimal impairment analysis under section 1 to uphold measures it had previously struck down because of a lack of an evidentiary foundation. Neither rationale would distinguish the *Charter* from strong-form judicial review. But the Court—and Canadian legal scholars who advocate dialogue theory— have thus far failed to offer a coherent account of these cases, which should be rooted in an underlying account of how courts should orient themselves to reply legislation.

Political scientists, notably Janet Hiebert, have taken up this task, by arguing that dialogue theory should be extended to embrace coordinate construction by Parliament with respect to the interpretation and application of rights.[17] She later broadened this research agenda comparatively, initially to the United Kingdom[18] and more recently, in collaboration with James Kelly, to New Zealand.[19] This comparative turn served as the basis for the original and more radical claim that bills of rights in Westminster-style parliamentary democracies (including Canada) disperse responsibility for rights protection beyond courts to the Executive and to the legislature. As a consequence, instead of taking place only during the process of judicial review, rights review takes place at three different stages: (1) pre-enactment political rights review of primary legislation by the Executive and the legislature, (2) judicial rights review, and (3) legislative reconsideration of court judgments which have held primary legislation to be inconsistent with the bill of rights. These claims about interpretative authority have important institutional implications. In addition to recasting the relationship between courts, on the one hand, and executives and legislatures, on the other, they also reconfigure the relationship between the legislature and the Executive—or more precisely, the government

---

[16] *Sauvé v Canada (Chief Electoral Officer)*, [2002] 3 S.C.R. 519; *R. v Mills*, [1999] 3 S.C.R. 668; *R v Hall*, [2002] 3 S.C.R. 309; *Canada (Attorney General) v JTI-Macdonald Corporation*, [2007] 2 SCR 610.

[17] J. Hiebert, *Charter Conflicts: What Is Parliament's Role?* (McGill-Queen's University Press, 2002).

[18] J. Hiebert, "Parliamentary Bills of Rights: An Alternative Model?" (2006) 69 *Mod. L. Rev.* 7; J. Hiebert, "Parliament and the Human Rights Act: Can the JCHR Help Facilitate a Culture of Rights?" (2006) 4 *ICON* 1; J. Hiebert, "Governing under the Human Rights Act: The Limitations of Wishful Thinking" (2012) *Public Law* 27.

[19] J. Hiebert & J. Kelly, *Parliamentary Bills of Rights: The Experiences of New Zealand and the United Kingdom* (Cambridge University Press, 2015).

backbench and Cabinet. Clothing the legislature with the responsibility to engage in rights-review has the goal of empowering the government backbench relative to the Cabinet, in alliance with opposition MPs, by providing it with a legal tool to challenge party discipline in limited yet important circumstances involving rights-infringing legislation. Gardbaum's most recent work has taken on board these claims.[20]

This most recent turn in dialogue theory—encompassing in Canada, the United Kingdom, and New Zealand—is a significant departure from its initial formulation, which conceptualized courts and legislatures as performing distinct functions within a system of rights-protection. It squarely raises the empirical question of how political institutions actually reason with rights. In dialogue theory's first iteration, pre-enactment review takes the form of legal risk management in the shadow of constitutional doctrine, whereas post-judgment legislative replies are rooted in all-things-considered judgments where rights are one consideration among others. In its second iteration, dialogue theory posits that political institutions have the opportunity and perhaps even the responsibility to offer their independent good faith interpretations and applications of bills of rights, which at times may be at odds with those of the courts, at both the pre-enactment and post-judgment legislative stages. However, the facts do not fit the theory. Kelly has shown that prior to the introduction of legislation, internal analysis by federal and provincial government legal advisors in Canada is largely confined to risk analysis.[21] Hiebert and Kelly have recently extended this observation to the United Kingdom and New Zealand. Moreover, they also show that the anticipated impact on backbench behaviour has not materialized either in Canada, the United Kingdom, or New Zealand. This is true even in the United Kingdom, where the Joint Committee on Human Rights of the UK Parliament has special responsibility to scrutinize legislation for compliance with the *Human Rights Act*, making the United Kingdom the most highly developed and transparent system of pre-enactment political rights review in the Commonwealth. However, the Committee's reports consist largely of highly sophisticated legal analysis of European Court of Human Rights and United Kingdom Supreme Court jurisprudence, as opposed to counter-interpretations of the *Human Rights Act*. Although there have been important exceptions, the Committee has rarely frontally challenged the government and forced it to change course. In New Zealand, electoral reform (shifting from first past the post to mixed member proportional) has enhanced the power of political parties relative to MPs, dampening the potential for legislative accountability for rights-protection even further.

The empirics do not match the normative ambitions of the most recent version of dialogue theory. Why is this the case? Hiebert and Kelly argue that two of the core features common to Westminster democracies—cabinet dominance of the legislature in situations of majority government, and strongly disciplined political parties which do not provide much scope for legislators to stray from party positions—are so deeply rooted that the dispersal of authority for rights protection, even with creative institutional design,

---

[20] S. Gardbaum, *The New Commonwealth Model of Constitutionalism* (Cambridge University Press, 2013).

[21] J. Kelly, *Governing with the Charter* (Vancouver: University of British Columbia Press, 2005).

cannot overcome them. By situating Canada comparatively, their analysis gains considerable power by highlighting explanatory factors shared with New Zealand and the United Kingdom. The next move in this global scholarly conversation should be to bring it full circle back to its origins in Canada, as a further spur to comparative reflection. If the original version of dialogue theory is the more realistic one, it is important to ensure that judicial decisions holding that legislation contravenes bills of rights do in fact receive a legislative response. A large factor is which institution bears the burden of legislative inertia. In cases where courts possess the power to issue a declaration of invalidity (Canada), or to interpret legislation to be compatible with rights (Canada, New Zealand, and the United Kingdom), a judicial ruling stands absent a legislative response. The legislation is thrust back onto the legislative agenda, and the legislature must affirmatively act if it is to have the final say, which increases the likelihood that there will be a political debate on how to respond to the court's judgment. Of these two, a declaration of invalidity is more transparent and hence the best tool for cuing political debate and accountability. In the United Kingdom, the practice of legislative replies to declarations of invalidity is almost entirely a function of the contingent fact that cases under the *Human Rights Act* may ultimately come before the European Court of Human Rights, which has the power to issue legally binding judgments to which the United Kingdom Parliament must respond. As a matter of institutional design, the Canadian version of weak-form review has comparative advantages over its counterparts in New Zealand and the United Kingdom.

However, the development of a rich jurisprudence of doctrines of deference under section 1 has had the effect of diminishing the need to deploy the override, and undermined the potential of the uniquely innovative aspect of Canada's constitutional design. Those doctrines are far more developed in Canada than in the United Kingdom or New Zealand. What is striking is that these doctrines—which have generated an immense jurisprudence that cuts across particular rights under the *Charter*, and has been a flashpoint of conflict on the Supreme Court—read as if the *Charter* created a system of judicial supremacy, and that it therefore falls to the Court to calibrate the intensity of judicial review. The override is entirely absent from the Court's conceptualization and doctrinal operationalization of the idea of deference. What needs to occur is the integration of institutional and interpretive analysis. In its purest form, dialogue theory posits that courts should not defer under section 1, because of the possibility of the override. An alternative would be to differentiate among different kinds of *Charter* violations, requiring only some to trigger the use of the override. I defer the full elaboration of this argument for another day.

3. The Canadian Model of Plurinational Federalism

The Canadian model of plurinational federalism is another dimension of our constitutional regime that has garnered considerable global interest, and is of central importance to international debates over how constitutional design can and should respond to the relation between constitutionalism and nationalism.[22] The context in which this issue arises is the plurinational state. The constitutional problems of plurinational states arise because modern states necessarily engage in a process of nation-building, which is designed to produce a degree of common identity, shared by all its citizens, across the entire territory of the state. The means to do so include policies centered on language, and culture, and on the centralization of legal and political power. The goals of nation-building are diverse, and include providing the necessary motivational element missing from liberal accounts of political legitimacy to induce individuals to make a particular set of liberal democratic institutions work and accept their demands; providing a mobile work force, literate in a common language that can pursue economic opportunity across an integrated national market; and ensuring that citizens can communicate directly with government officials.

But many states also contain national minorities whose members once formed complete, functioning societies on their territory, endowed with a considerable degree of self-rule, prior to their incorporation into the larger state through conquest and empire or voluntary federation or union. Consequently, many national minorities will resist nation-building efforts, and respond by conceiving of themselves as nations and making constitutional claims designed to both protect themselves from the majority's nation-building project and to enable them to engage in a parallel process of nation-building focused on the territory around which they constitute a majority. There are many plurinational states around the world—Canada, the United Kingdom, Belgium, Spain, Russia, Sri Lanka, Iraq, and India—just to name a few. In these states, constitutional design matters a great deal, as constitutions are the principal sites for majority nation-building as well as for national minorities' resistance to the overarching process of nation-state consolidation. Canada is a conspicuous example of how constitutional design can accommodate competing nation-building agendas within a single state. Put simply, the Canadian exemplar responds by challenging the equation of nation and state that underlies not only majority nation-building but also the defensive response of minority nations, for which the logical response is to resist incorporation into the majority nation and demand states of their own.

Federalism is the feature of the Canadian constitutional model that addresses this issue most directly. Canada is a plurinational federation because the boundaries of the province of Quebec were drawn so that francophones would constitute a majority therein and could not be outvoted by the anglophone majority in Canada as a whole. This remains true today—indeed, the territorialisation of linguistic communities across Canada is greater now than when Quebec was created. Moreover, Quebec was granted a mix of concurrent and exclusive jurisdiction over a wide range of policy areas that gives it the tools to ensure the survival of a francophone society by creating a complete set of

---

[22] S. Choudhry, "Does the World Need More Canada? The Politics of the Canadian Model in Constitutional Politics and Political Theory" (2007) 5 *ICON* 606; S. Choudhry, "The Globalization of the Canadian Constitution" (2012) 4 *Trudeau Foundation Papers* 88.

institutions that operate in French across the economy, politics and public administration, and education. Inasmuch as language is the driving force behind Quebec's claims for political autonomy, the Canadian model blunts its force by implying from jurisdiction over certain institutions or relationships the power to set the language in which those institutions operate or relationships occur. In exercise of this authority, Quebec enacted the *Charter of the French Language* in 1977 to make French "the language of the Government and the law, as well as the normal and every day language of work, instruction, communication, commerce and business". The key provisions of the *Charter of the French Language* are those that establish French as the exclusive language of work within the civil service, flowing from the province's constitutional authority over provincial public administration. Likewise, the *Charter of the French Language* promotes French as the internal working language of medium- and large-sized business in the province through Quebec's power over property and civil rights, which encompasses the authority to regulate commercial transactions and private sector workplaces. Together, these measures vastly increased range and attractiveness of the economic opportunities for francophones in Quebec.

The responsibility for primary, secondary, and postsecondary education also lies within provincial jurisdiction, and impliedly encompasses power over the language of instruction and curriculum. This authority has been crucial for Quebec, because the Constitution has permitted the province to establish and operate a primary and secondary educational system that operates in French and is a prime instance of linguistic nation-building. Additionally, the control over education has enabled Quebec to create French-language colleges and universities, an indispensable support for the use of French in economic and political life. At the same time, this arrangement has denied the federal government the power to set a standard curriculum in a shared national language, a common instrument of nation-building in many countries.

Although the Canadian model of plurinational federalism continues to evolve, many of its key features have been in place since the mid-nineteenth century. However, there was sharp rise in academic and policy interest in Canada's plurinational federalism in the mid-1990s. Why? The answer may be found not in Canada, but in Eastern and Central Europe. The collapse of the communist dictatorships in the latter region were followed by the rise of profound ethnic conflict within these democratizing states. As it turned out, many of these states fulfilled the definition of a plurinational polity, and the political sociology of emergent conflict within plurinational polities—the competing projects of majority and minority nation-building—fit the unfolding pattern of political conflict in those countries. In the search for solutions, plurinational federations such as Canada were an obvious candidate.

But the advocates of plurinational federalism were confronted with the fact that the three former communist dictatorships of Eastern and Central Europe—Czechoslovakia, the Soviet Union, and Yugoslavia—had already been plurinational federations prior to the transition to democracy, and all three began to disintegrate shortly after the transition. By contrast, unitary states with large national minorities in which nationalism served as the axis of internal political conflict—Hungary, Poland, and Romania—did not fall apart. Indeed, the problem went even deeper. A widely accepted explanation for the disintegration of the communist federations of Eastern and Central Europe is that federalism not only did not prevent their breakup; it may have facilitated it. In these states, federal subunits provided a territorial and institutional power base for national minorities that served as a springboard to statehood. Unitary constitutional structures denied national minorities such a platform.

As plurinational federalism in Eastern and Central Europe may have had the perverse effect of fuelling precisely those political forces it was designed to suppress, the region's experience posed a fundamental challenge to plurinational federalism as a viable constitutional strategy in that part of the world. Indeed, it posed a more general challenge to the very idea of plurinational federalism. The best way to respond to the negative examples of Yugoslavia, Czechoslovakia, and the Soviet Union was to identify models where plurinational federalism had actually worked. Hence the sudden and sharp increase in interest in Canada's plurinational federalism. Will Kymlicka and Charles Taylor were the foremost scholarly proponents of the Canadian federal model.[23] Indeed, Canada became one of the central cases in an ever-broadening comparative debate regarding the very possibility of crafting a constitutional accommodation between majority and minority nationalism within a single state.

But although it is true that global interest in Canadian federalism manifested itself during the disintegration of the plurinational federations of Eastern and Central Europe, it also coincided with Canada's *own* constitutional crisis. This arguably began in September 1994, with the resurgence of the Parti Québécois (PQ), which won power on a platform that had as its centrepiece a commitment to hold a referendum on sovereignty within its first mandate, which took place in October 1995. The results were extremely close, with the sovereignty proposal failing by 1 percent. Provincial legislation governing the referendum had set a one-year time limit on those negotiations, after which Quebec would have issued a unilateral declaration of independence. Nor was the near disintegration of the Canadian federation in the mid-1990s completely unexpected. From 1990 onward, the secession of Quebec became a topic of widespread political and academic debate. A sub-literature assumed that Canada was doomed, and that the country should turn to the difficult question of how secession should occur, and examined very specific issues such as the debt, borders, citizenship, the rights of Aboriginal peoples, and the nature of the economic and political partnership between Canada and an independent Quebec, as well as the process for such negotiations.

What was the connection between Canada's constitutional crisis and rise of global interest in the Canadian model of plurinational federalism? The answer is politics. Arguing for the necessary success of the Canadian model was not just a scholarly endeavour. It was a political intervention in two different but interrelated arenas. It was an intervention in international politics—to offer a practical, viable model to deal

---

[23] W. Kymlicka, *Multicultural Citizenship* (Oxford University Press, 1995); W. Kymlicka, *Multicultural Odysseys: Navigating the New International Politics of Diversity* (Oxford University Press, 2007); C. Taylor, *Reconciling the Solitudes* (McGill-Queen's University Press, 1993).

with the issue of minority nationalism, which had become a source of political instability in Eastern and Central Europe and beyond. It was also an intervention in domestic constitutional politics—to argue that Canada had hit upon one of the few workable
solutions to the accommodation of minority nationalism within a liberal democratic
constitutional order. These agendas were integrally linked. Many proponents of the
Canadian model not only recognized the crisis gripping the Canadian constitutional
order, but also viewed the international promotion of the Canadian model as an important element in resolving domestic problems. The promotion of the Canadian model
abroad should be understood, at least in part, as an attempt to reinforce support for
the Canadian model in Canada by installing national pride. As the prestige of the
Canadian model is enhanced abroad, so too is its prestige at home. Indeed, the violent collapse of the plurinational federations of Eastern and Central Europe appeared to
challenge the viability of plurinational federalism not only in that region but in Canada
as well. Canadians stared into the constitutional abyss in the 1990s and asked themselves whether the same fate awaited Canada. If the Canadian model could not work in
Canada, it could not work in circumstances that are far more difficult. Canada needed
to make its constitutional arrangements work not only for the world's sake, but for its
own as well.

What was the precise character of the Canadian constitutional crisis? The conventional wisdom is that the Canadian constitutional crisis was *substantive*, and arose
from competing constitutional logics which are at war with each other: the accommodation of Quebec, the *Charter*, and the juridical equality of all provinces (including Quebec).[24] These different constitutional logics have come into conflict over two
issues: asymmetrical powers for Quebec and the constitutional recognition of Quebec
as a distinct society. Asymmetry is demanded by Quebec as necessary in order to give
it the jurisdictional tools to preserve and promote its distinct identity in economic
and social circumstances that have changed dramatically since 1867; it is resisted in
English Canada, both by those who want to centralize power in Ottawa as part of a
nation-building exercise and by those who believe that special arrangements for any
one province are a form of discrimination. Constitutional recognition of Quebec as
a distinct society, if designed to augment Quebec's powers alone, raises similar objections. To the extent that such recognition would give greater scope to Quebec to limit
Charter rights legitimately—in order to preserve and promote its linguistic identity—
it would come into conflict with the concept of the *Charter* as the essential foundation
of equal citizenship, providing for equal enjoyment of constitutional rights throughout Canada.

But there is also a *procedural* account of the constitutional crisis, in which the near-
collapse of the Canadian constitutional system can be traced to a lack of a shared
understanding regarding the constitutional procedures within which substantive

---

[24] A. Cairns, *Reconfigurations: Canadian Citizenship and Constitutional Change* (McLelland and
Stewart, 1995).

constitutional politics could occur.[25] Consider the following argument. In politics, we frequently disagree about the substance of public policies. A basic ambition of constitutionalism is to channel disagreements into institutions that reach decisions that members of the political community will accept as authoritative. But for institutional decisions to yield political settlement, the decision-making procedures of those institutions must be viewed as constituting and regulating political life without forming part of it—as being indifferent among political positions. Were the mechanisms by which political disagreement is managed themselves to be subject to political contestation in the course of their operation, it would be difficult for institutional settlement to translate into political settlement. The rules for constitutional amendment and their relationship to substantive constitutional politics can be conceptualized in like manner. If the rules of constitutional amendment are to operate effectively, they too must be accepted as constituting and regulating constitutional politics, and not forming part of it. They must be seen as operating indifferently among the competing constitutional positions on the table.

The difficulty with this highly simplified picture is that political procedures—both for normal and constitutional politics—are far from substantively neutral themselves. Rather, as Jeremy Waldron has argued, political procedures reflect competing conceptions of the very sorts of values that are the customary fare of both normal and constitutional politics. For example, by determining which individuals and communities can participate in political decision-making, and what role those individuals and communities may play, decision-rules reflect substantive judgments of political sovereignty, and by extension, the very identity of a political community. So the boundary between substantive political disputes and the procedural frameworks within which those disputes are worked out is highly artificial. Liberal democratic constitutionalism depends on the *suspension* of political judgment with regard to institutions and institutional decision-making procedures precisely in order to gain the prospect of political settlements.

The suspension of political judgment with respect to political procedures will become exceedingly difficult to sustain when the substantive dispute challenges the very conception of political community that underlies the decision-making framework within which that debate occurs. With respect to the rules of normal politics, the consequence will be to shift the terrain of disagreement from normal politics to constitutional politics, regulated by the procedural rules governing constitutional amendment. But in plurinational polities, the ease with which political judgment with respect to constitutional amending rules can be suspended depends on the nature of the issue at hand. In plurinational polities, constitutional politics takes place on two levels. On the one hand,

---

[25] I have developed this argument in Choudhry, above (n 22); S. Choudhry, "Popular Revolution or Popular Constitutionalism? Reflections on the Constitutional Politics of Quebec Secession" in T. Kahana & R. Bauman, eds, *The Least Examined Branch: The Role of Legislatures in the Constitutional State* (Cambridge University Press, 2006) 480; S. Choudhry, "Referendum? What Referendum?" (2007) 15:3 *Literary Review of Canada* 7; S. Choudhry & J.-F. Gaudreault-DesBiens, "Frank Iacobucci as Constitution-Maker: From the *Quebec Veto Reference*, to the Meech Lake Accord and the *Quebec Secession Reference*" (2007) 57 *U. Toronto L.J.* 165; S. Choudhry, "Ackerman's Higher Lawmaking in Comparative Constitutional Perspective: Constitutional Moments as Constitutional Failures?" (2008) 6 *ICON* 193.

there is the sort of constitutional politics that presupposes the existence of a national political community, where the basic question of constitutional design is how this political community should grapple with the task of democratic self-government. This kind of constitutional politics also occurs in political communities that are not plurinational. But in parallel—and simultaneously—plurinational polities also engage in *constitutive constitutional politics*, which concern questions that go to the very identity, even existence, of a political community as a plurinational political entity. In practice, it is hard to disentangle these two sorts of constitutional politics, because they often touch on similar sorts of issues—the structure of national institutions, federalism, and bills of rights—and often occur at the same time. For example, proposals to entrench the Supreme Court of Canada constitutionally, to recognize its unique responsibility as an independent organ of government and final arbiter charged with enforcing the *Charter*—were accompanied by demands by Quebec that, given the Court's role as the final judicial arbiter in federal-provincial disputes, three of its nine seats should be constitutionally guaranteed for justices from that province.

The problem is that it can be very difficult, if not possible, to suspend political judgment regarding the procedures for constitutional amendment at moments of constitutive constitutional politics precisely because these procedures might reflect one of the competing constitutional positions at play. In the absence of agreed-upon procedures for constitutional decision-making, institutional settlement cannot yield political settlement. The result may be that the constitutional system itself comes tumbling down.

This is what happened in Canada in the mid-1990s. For alongside disagreement on the substantive questions of how Quebec's constitutional claims should be accommodated within the Canadian constitutional order and whether Quebec should remain a part of Canada, there was a procedural disagreement over whether the rules governing constitutional amendment should govern the process of secession. As a strictly legal matter, a change in Quebec's status from province to independent country could be achieved through constitutional amendments that would require the consent of the federal government and most, if not all, of the provinces. Unilateral secession would be unconstitutional. But Quebec sovereignists challenged the assumption that Quebec's independence would be governed by the rules governing constitutional amendment, for the simple reason that those rules beg the question. Those rules presuppose that Quebec is a constituent component of the Canadian federation, functioning as a subnational community with extensive but limited rights of self-government within Canada. Accordingly, Quebec is a constitutionally recognized actor in the process of constitutional amendment through processes that require a high degree of federal and provincial consensus. Quebec cannot act alone. But it is *precisely* that constitutional vision that the Quebec sovereignty movement challenges, in raising the substantive question of whether Quebec should remain a part of Canada or become an independent state. Not surprisingly, the sovereignists rejected the amending rules as a neutral framework within which the question of Quebec's independence could be resolved. As sovereignists wished to make a radical and total break from the Canadian constitutional order, it is hard to imagine that they would have subscribed to a process governed by it.

The broader point is that the Canadian problem is a common one. The constitutional politics of rules for constitutional amendment are frequently a point of conflict in plurinational polities.[26] The reason is that these rules are where the most fundamental clashes in nation-building occur. By assigning the power of constitutional amendment to certain populations and/or institutions, in various combinations, the rules governing constitutional amendment stipulate the ultimate locus of political sovereignty and are the most basic statement of a community's political identity. The ability to reconfigure the most basic terms of political life must lie with the fundamental agents of political life. By looking at amending rules, we can see who those agents are. In plurinational polities, assigning roles to national minorities as part of the procedure for constitutional change accordingly acknowledges the fundamental plurinational character of the political community. The refusal to acknowledge this fact translates into a preference for constitutional amending rules that do not recognize and empower the constituent nations of a plurinational polity. And in either situation, secession is a limiting case that would challenge the application of the existing constitutional order to part of the state's territory. So it is far from surprising that in a broad variety of recent cases, such as Iraq, Spain, Sri Lanka, and the United Kingdom, as in Canada, a principal arena of constitutional conflict has concerned the design of constitutional amending rules.

The true lesson for multinational polities of the Canadian model of plurinational federalism may be this. Canada is indeed a success story—it is one of the world's oldest countries, has wrestled with and responded imaginatively to forces that have torn other countries apart, and has achieved a remarkable degree of prosperity and freedom. In large part, the Canadian model operates under the law. But as the Canadian constitutional crisis shows us, a legal approach to the accommodation of minority nationalism has both its strengths and weaknesses. The main problem lies in meeting demands for constitutional change from minority nations. Rules for constitutional amendment face genuine difficulty in constituting and regulating moments of constitutive constitutional politics, because at those moments, the very concept of political community those rules reflect is placed in contention by the minority nation. And what Canada may teach us is that secession may be a limiting case where constitutionalism and the rule of law run out.

4. Rights Protection in a Plurinational Federation

Finally, I turn to an issue that has received much less comparative attention, but should: how the different pillars of the Canadian constitutional model interact, in

[26] S. Choudhry, "Old Imperial Dilemmas and the New Nation-Building: Constitutive Constitutional Politics in Multinational Polities" (2005) 37 *Connecticut L. Rev.* 933; S. Choudhry, "Constitutional Politics and Crisis in Sri Lanka" in J. Bertrand & A. Laliberté, eds, *Multination States in Asia: Accommodation or Resistance* (Cambridge University Press, 2010) 103.

particular, the complex interplay between a constitutional bill of rights and the constitutional accommodation of minority nationalism. This has occurred both in constitutional politics and adjudication. For the former, perhaps the best example is the debate surrounding the constitutional recognition of Quebec's distinctiveness; for the latter, the role of the Supreme Court of Canada in adjudicating high profile constitutional conflicts over official language policy arising out of Quebec. Although these issues have arisen in different institutional contexts, there is a common problem that unites them—the clash between competing constitutional logics that lie with the same constitutional document, and that give rise to compelling political and legal claims that pull in opposite directions.

Political and judicial institutions sometimes have no choice but to grapple with these tensions. In some cases, they will give priority to one constitutional logic over the other—as occurred, for example, with the rejection of the proposed "distinct society" clause of the Meech Lake Accord, which would have afforded constitutional recognition of Quebec's particularity, on the basis of a fear that it would have eroded the equal enjoyment of *Charter* rights across Canada. In other cases, they may be able to find an accommodation that allows both constitutional logics to operate within the framework of a common constitutional order. The Canadian experience suggests that the ability of particular institutions to achieve this kind of constitutional co-existence might be a product of their institutional design—and that the plurinational character of the Supreme Court might have enabled it to be particularly effective in this respect.

As Peter Russell argued in a classic article, the *Charter* was Prime Minister Pierre Trudeau's central instrument for nation-building, and arose as a direct response to an important shift in the character of Quebec's constitutional demands in the 1960s.[27] Until then, Quebec's constitutional claims had been defensive, aimed at safeguarding its existing areas of jurisdiction. However, in the 1960s, Quebec's goals shifted to engage in a nation-building enterprise and construct a modern Quebec, the major institutions of which operated in French. Why this shift in Quebec took place is a complex story. To a considerable extent, it was a defensive response to the dramatically increased role of Ottawa in economic and social policy after the Second World War. Federal policy activism meant an increase in the importance of federal institutions, especially the federal bureaucracy, which worked in English and in which francophone Quebeckers were a small minority. Another factor was enormous social change within Quebec. After the Second World War, there was massive urbanization and industrialization, in a context where anglophones dominated positions of economic leadership and many of the professions. These demographic and economic shifts underlined and reinforced the role of language as the basis for the unequal distribution of economic power within the province. Quebec's political elites responded by mobilizing francophones around the nationalist project of *maître chez nous*, which encompassed both the expansion of Quebec's jurisdiction and the use of these new tools to shift power away from the anglophone

[27] P. Russell, "The Political Purposes of the Charter of Rights and Freedoms" (1983) 61 *Can. Bar. Rev.* 30.

minority toward the francophone majority through constructing a modern set of economic and political institutions to ensure the survival of a modern, French-speaking
society.

The *Charter* was the federal government's defensive response to these centrifugal
pressures. At first blush, this is counterintuitive, as nation-building usually involves the
assertion of legal and political power to form a common identity in a manner that limits
individual freedom of choice, whereas bills of rights set limits on such policies. Yet a
bill of rights can nonetheless play this role. Indeed, there are two ways to think about
the nation-building role of a bill of rights: the *regulative* conception and the *constitutive*
conception.[28] On the regulative conception, the function of a bill of rights is to enable
individuals to invoke the machinery of the courts to set binding constraints on political
decision-making. Serving this function does not depend on a bill of rights having any
effect on citizens' political identities. On the constitutive conception, a bill of rights constitutes the very demos that it also constrains. A bill of rights calls for citizens to abstract
way from group markers, such as race, ethnicity, religion, or language. It encodes and
projects the idea of a political community built around citizens who are equal bearers
of constitutional rights—a constitutional patriotism—whose political membership is
unmediated by group identity. To serve as the instrument of nation-building, a bill of
rights must alter the very self-understanding of citizens.

The *Charter* relies on both the constitutive and regulative conceptions of a bill of rights
to serve as an instrument of nation-building.[29] The *Charter* was intended to function con-
stitutively as the germ of a pan-Canadian constitutional identity. In a federal state such as
Canada, where citizens share rights under a bill of rights irrespective of language or province of residence, a bill of rights serves as a transcendent form of political identification—
the spine of common citizenship that unites members of a linguistically diverse and
geographically dispersed polity across the country as a whole. The actual effects have
been different. Outside of Quebec, the *Charter* has generated a new pan-Canadian patriotism, likely more quickly than even the most optimistic predictions suggested. However,
within Quebec, the *Charter* has decidedly not had this effect. Indeed, the sharply differ-
entiated effect of the *Charter* on Canadian constitutional culture suggests that it may now
be harder, precisely because of the *Charter*, to build a unifying account of the Canadian
constitutional order that transcends linguistic and regional divides.

The divergent reactions to the distinct society clause outside and within Quebec powerfully illustrate these points. The clause would have mandated that the Constitution
be interpreted to recognize "that Quebec constitutes within Canada a distinct society"
and would have affirmed "[t]he role of the legislative and Government of Quebec to

---

[28] S. Choudhry, "After the Rights Revolution: Bills of Rights in the Postconflict State" (2010) 6 *Annual
Review of Law and Social Science* 301.

[29] S. Choudhry, "Bills of Rights as Instruments of Nation-Building in Multinational States: The Canadian
Charter and Quebec Nationalism" in J. Kelly & C. Manfredi, eds., *Contested Constitutionalism: Reflections
on the Charter of Rights and Freedoms* (University of British Columbia Press, 2009) 233.

preserve and promote the distinct identity of Quebec". Outside Quebec, the fear was that the clause would provide for the unequal application of the *Charter*, by authorizing Quebec to limit the *Charter* in a manner not open to other provincial governments. In particular, there was a concern that it would provide additional constitutional support for linguistic nation-building on the part of Quebec. What underpinned this resistance was a shift in political identity outside of Quebec wrought by the *Charter*. The *Charter* was what made Canada a country and was the spine of a Canadian citizenship that was shared by all Canadians, and the potential for its unequal application was an assault on a basic, non-negotiable term of the Canadian social contract. Within Quebec, the view on the distinct society clause was exactly the opposite, rooted in a competing account of Canada. On this account, Canada is unintelligible except against the backdrop of the idea that the institutions of plurinational federalism are designed to protect Quebec's linguistic distinctiveness. Yet the odd thing about the Canadian Constitution is that it lacks express recognition of this fact and treats Quebec on a basis of juridical equality to the other provinces. The distinct society clause therefore mattered a great deal because it was the first time the Constitution would explicitly acknowledge a view of what Canada was for. The repudiation of the distinct society clause on the basis of a theory of Canadian citizenship that was rooted in the *Charter* set up the *Charter* as an obstacle to, rather than as a central component of, how many Quebeckers understood the nature of their relationship with Canada.

The broader lesson from the Canadian case is that it is very difficult for bills of rights to constitute a new political identity on their own. Contrary to those who argue for the possibility of a pure constitutional patriotism based on the commitment to univer-salistic principles of political morality, a bill of rights must be nested in a contingent context—a constitutional narrative drawing on a web of political memory forged by shared experiences, challenges, failures, and triumphs. The Canadian experience tells us that in plurinational polities there is an additional hurdle. The task is not simply to situate a bill of rights in a contingent historical and political context. The task is to do so in a context in which the existence of competing nationalisms makes the dominant question of constitutional politics the conflict between contending national narratives. If the ambition of a bill of rights as a constitutive instrument of nation-building is to be a central element of an overarching narrative, by standing apart from, and transcending, those competing narratives, a plurinational context is a particularly difficult environ-ment in which to do so. Indeed, there is the danger that rather than transcending those national narratives, a bill of rights will be drawn back into it. This is what has happened in Canada. And if this would happen in Canada, where we have managed our national-ist politics peacefully and within the rule of law, the difficulties may be greater still for countries wracked by political instability, with weak institutions and a halting commit-ment to legalism, and often emerging from violent conflict.

What about the regulative nation-building role of the *Charter*? In regulatory terms, the *Charter* imposes legal constraints on minority nation-building by Quebec, through entrenching rights to inter-provincial mobility and minority language education for children. The centrality of the mobility and minority language education rights provisions to the nation-building project of the *Charter* is underlined by their exemption from the override—and hence, from Canada's system of weak-form judicial review, and the possibilities for dialogue it creates. Both rights can be understood as a response to potential or actual policies of linguistic nation-building by Quebec, and indeed, Quebec has objected to both, precisely because they are not subject to the override. The *Charter* prohibits the use of disincentives to inter-provincial migration by guaranteeing the right to "move and take up residence in any province" and "to pursue the gaining of a livelihood in any province". Quebec objected, arguing that the province legitimately discriminated to preserve its distinct linguistic identity.

Far more important as a tool of minority nation-building is the linguistic assimilation of international and inter-provincial migrants. Absent the *Charter*, Quebec could have mandated that the exclusive language of public education be French. Yet the *Charter* granted to certain categories of citizens the right to receive minority language primary and secondary education for their children where numbers warrant it. The flashpoint of controversy within Quebec has been the right of anglophones who received their primary school instruction anywhere in Canada in English to have their children educated in English in Quebec—the so-called "Canada Clause". This provision was specifically drafted to render unconstitutional a provision in the *Charter of the French Language* that would have limited this right to parents who had been educated in English in Quebec. Another provision of the *Charter*, which grants children who have received their schooling in English anywhere in Canada the right to continue their English-language education in Quebec, also limits Quebec's ability to linguistically integrate migrants from other provinces.

The clash between the *Charter* and Quebec's policies of linguistic nation-building occurred in three important cases before the Supreme Court.[30] In all three cases, the Court found these policies to be unconstitutional. In *Ford*, the Court struck down a provision in the *Charter of the French Language* that required outdoor commercial signage to be exclusively in French; in *Quebec Protestant School Board*, it applied the "Canada Clause" to strike down a provision of the *Charter of the French Language* that required citizens educated in the English language elsewhere in Canada to have their children educated in French; in *Solski*, the Court rejected an attempt to construe narrowly the *Charter*'s right of children who have received schooling in English anywhere else in the country the right to continue schooling in English in Quebec.[31]

There are three noteworthy features of these decisions. First, Quebec lost every case, and the *Charter* did indeed constrain Quebec's ability to establish French as the common language of political, economic, and social life in that province. Second, although the Supreme Court struck down Quebec's nation-building policies, it nonetheless accepted the purpose underlying these laws as legitimate under section 1; the constitutional defect in each case is that the laws, as framed or construed by the Government,

---

[30] S. Choudhry, "Rights Adjudication in a Plurinational State: The Supreme Court of Canada, Freedom of Religion, and the Politics of Reasonable Accommodation" (2013) 50 *Osgoode Hall L.J.* 575.

[31] *Ford*, above (n 14); *Attorney General of Quebec v Quebec Association of Protestant School Boards et al.*, [1984] 2 S.C.R. 66; *Solski (Tutor of) v Quebec (Attorney General)*, [2005] 1 S.C.R. 201.

failed at the minimal impairment stage of the proportionality analysis. Third, the judgments were unanimous and handed down by "The Court" as an institution rather than by an individual judge with whom the rest of the Court concurred. Collective authorship by the Court is very rare and indicates the greatest possible degree of consensus among the justices.

These pieces fit together. Their significance becomes clear if one recalls that the Supreme Court is a regionally representative body, with three of nine justices coming from Quebec, three from Ontario, and one from British Columbia, the Prairies, and Atlantic Canada, respectively. However, Quebec's representation is special, as is reflected by the fact that is the only province whose representation has been legally guaranteed for several decades, whereas the regional distribution of the remaining seats is a matter of constitutional convention at best. An important justification for the special rules governing Quebec's representation is that the Supreme Court takes civil law appeals from Quebec and therefore requires justices with the requisite expertise. But the deeper rationale is that the composition of the Court reflects and institutionalizes the plurinational character of Canada. Quebec's status as a nation within Canada entitles it to a guaranteed minimum level of representation in a federal institution—such as the Supreme Court—that makes important decisions delimiting the scope of Quebec's power to pursue such policies. A Court that ruled on these issues without justices from Quebec would be widely perceived as constitutionally illegitimate within that province.

It is worth reflecting on how the plurinational nature of the Supreme Court's membership might play out in adjudication, especially with respect to cases that arise out of Quebec. As a formal matter, the Quebec justices enjoy no special powers relative to other justices, either individually or collectively. But with regard to cases of special interest to Quebec—for example, those that concern the power of Quebec to engage in linguistic nation-building—as a matter of constitutional practice, the Quebec justices might play a different institutional role in the Court's decision making. Consider the following counter-factual: imagine that in *Ford*, *Quebec Protestant School Board*, and *Solski*, the Court had divided on national lines. The Quebec justices voted to uphold the policies under challenge, perhaps holding that they breached *Charter* rights but were justified under section 1. A majority of the Court, however, struck them down, and went further than holding that the measures were disproportionate. Rather, it held that the very objective of preserving and enhancing the status of French as Quebec's common language was per se illegitimate, because that objective sought to redistribute economic and political power away from anglophones toward francophones, and was therefore inherently discriminatory. Moreover, when it rendered judgment in those appeals, the Quebec justices were all francophone and the justices from the rest of Canada all anglophone, so that the division on the Court would have been basic and fundamental, and plurinational in character.

If that had happened, the dissent by the Quebec justices would have been much more than the routine disagreement that occurs on multi-member courts in the common law world. Given the political origins of the *Charter* as a response to Quebec nationalism, and the singular importance of the challenged laws to modern Quebec nationalism, a

Supreme Court divided on national lines would have served to undermine the legitimacy of the *Charter*, and perhaps even the Court itself, within Quebec. This would have been a disaster. The Court's decision to speak unanimously as a single institution indicates its awareness that, with respect to these divisive issues, it was important to present a common front that transcended the national divide built into the Court's design. The Court's choice emphasized that what drove the judgment was not the national origin of any individual justice but the Court's collective understanding of the *Charter* and its relationship to the project of Quebec nationalism. Moreover, in these three cases, the judgments occupied an intermediate position between polar extremes, by striking down the provisions under challenge while still leaving space for Quebec to pursue those policies through accepting Quebec's objectives as constitutionally legitimate.

What role did the Quebec justices play in the Court's internal deliberations on the Quebec language cases? We do not, and may never, really know. But a plausible account is that the Quebec justices brought to these cases alertness to, and understanding of, the roots of modern Quebec nationalism, and the social and economic transformations that gave rise to them. As members of Quebec's elite who had lived through these transformations and were indeed products of them, the Quebec justices brought to the conference table an understanding of the origins and importance of these policies. They were therefore able to persuade their colleagues from outside the province of their constitutional legitimacy, and to highlight for them the risks of interpreting the *Charter* to deny to Quebec the constitutional space to pursue them. Their attempts at persuasion may have been coupled with the threat to collectively dissent, which would have been politically costly for the *Charter* and the Court. Although their leverage was insufficient to save Quebec's legislation, it was enough to shape the manner in which it was struck down, allowing Quebec to enact a more narrowly-tailored policy in the future that would survive constitutional challenge.

Canada holds broader lessons.[32] The Canadian Constitution is not alone in entrenching a bill of rights and accommodating minority nationalism, and in generating cases that require an apex court to work through and craft the relationship between these contending constitutional agendas. Other plurinational polities face a similar set of issues. The judgments of the Supreme Court avoided an all-or-nothing victory for either rights-based constitutionalism or minority nationalism; rather, it created a constitutional middle-ground that protected individual rights while still permitting Quebec to engage in linguistic nation-building. The likelihood of an apex court to chart a path of constitutional compromise under such circumstances probably turns in part on its design. For that reason, one should expect there to be a politics of apex court design—as there has been in Canada—where national minorities advance constitutional claims to ensure that an apex court adopts an interpretative agenda that is congenial to the protection of minority interests.

---

[32] S. Choudhry & R. Stacey, "Independent or Dependent? Constitutional Courts in Divided Societies" in C. Harvey & A. Schwartz, eds., *Rights in Divided Societies* (Hart Publishing, 2012) 89.

There are in theory a number of dimensions to the design of apex courts that provide levers for achieving this broader objective. One is the *appointments* process, for example, through granting the authority to federal sub-units controlled by national minorities to appoint a number of judges, through super-majority or concurrent majority requirements that empower minority legislators, or through minority control over nominations (e.g., the exclusive power to generate shortlists). A closely related, but distinct issue would be the *composition* of the Court. Certain seats could be designated for justices from national minorities, or from federal sub-units in which national minorities predominate. Yet another aspect of design would be the justices' *legal expertise*. In bijural jurisdictions, such as Canada and the United Kingdom, a certain number of seats on the apex court could be set aside for judges trained in the component legal traditions where that tradition is tied to questions of a minority nation's identity. Finally, there are the *decision-rules* of the apex court. A court may constitute special panels of subsets of judges to hear cases of special interest to national minorities. These panels would contain a disproportionate number of judges appointed by minority nations, and/or national minority judges. Alternatively, a court may require a super-majority or concurrent majority to reach decisions, either on all issues or those of special concern to national minorities.

Indeed, a largely forgotten part of Canadian constitutional history shows that some of these options were advanced over several decades by Quebec, in the wake of the abolition of Canadian appeals to the Judicial Committee of the Privy Council in 1949.[33] The Privy Council had favoured strong provinces and a weak federal government; with the federally-appointed Supreme Court becoming Canada's final court of appeal, Quebec was concerned that Quebec's autonomy would be eroded by a Court biased in favour of the federal government. An early proposal from Quebec included a nine-member specialist Constitutional Court, consisting of five judges appointed by the federal government and one judge appointed by each of the executives of each region of Canada (Quebec, Ontario, Atlantic Canada, and Western Canada). Another proposal empowered provincial executives to appoint two-thirds of the Constitutional Court, with one-third of the judges appointed by Quebec. Quebec later shifted its focus from the creation of a specialist constitutional court to the reform of the Supreme Court. The 1971 Victoria Charter proposed that appointments require the agreement of the federal and provincial executives, and that every case involving Quebec's civil code be heard by a panel of five justices, including three from Quebec. The Meech Lake Accord would have provided for federal appointment of three justices from Quebec from a list of candidates prepared by the provincial government. A final set of proposals involved expanding the Court and increasing the number of sitting justices from Quebec, as well as ensuring that constitutional cases be heard by a smaller panel on which all the Quebec justices would sit.

[33] S. Choudhry, "Not a New Constitutional Court: The Canadian *Charter*, the Supreme Court and Quebec Nationalism" in P. Pasquino & F. Billi, eds., *The Political Origins of Constitutional Courts: Italy, Germany, France, Poland, Canada, United Kingdom* (Adriano Olivetti Foundation, 2009) 39.

5. Conclusion

Let me conclude by suggesting how to extend the research agenda set out in the last section—how the various components of the Canadian constitutional model interact. Debates about the legislative override have not given much attention to how its application could be conditioned by, or be responsive to, Canada's plurinational character. But the previous section suggests how. The Supreme Court's jurisprudence on the constitutionality of key elements of the *Charter of the French Language* presupposed that it fell to the Court to reconcile the competing logics of rights-protection and minority nationalism. But that assumption in turn rests on the notion of judicial supremacy. To be sure, in the case of the minority language education rights, the Court does enjoy supremacy, because of the inapplicability of the legislative override to the relevant provisions of the *Charter*. But the same does not hold true for other *Charter* rights, such as freedom of religion.

In recent years, the Court has taken a series of appeals from Quebec argued on the basis of freedom of religion that have opened up a new front in the complicated relationship between Quebec nation-building and the *Charter*, around the issue of secularism and reasonable accommodation.[34] The roots of the particular salience of secularism in Quebec lie in the origins of modern Quebec nationalism, which entailed a rejection of the institutionalized role of the Roman Catholic Church in the delivery of health care, education, and social services, and its related role as the arbiter of public morality. The replacement of the Church in these realms by newly created state institutions, coupled with a liberal social morality free from the strictures of the Church, was a central demand of nationalist mobilization in the 1950's. Indeed, it can be said that modern Quebec nationalism was as much about secular nation-building as it was about linguistic nation-building.

However, unlike in its jurisprudence on Quebec's language policy, in its jurisprudence on reasonable accommodation in Quebec, the Court has been divided. Its francophone judges have penned separate concurrences or dissents articulating theories of religion-state relations that echo the discourses of political elites in Quebec. This poses a risk to the legitimacy of both the *Charter* and the Court itself, against the backdrop of ongoing political controversy in Quebec. The absence of the override from these debates is puzzling, because it offers a constitutional mechanism for Quebec to express its disagreement with the Court in a manner that could alleviate the pressure on some members of the Court toward deference, in a manner that could protect the Court from the very public attacks that its jurisprudence has sparked.

---

[34] Choudhry, above (n 30). The cases are *Bruker v Marcovitz*, 2007 SCC 54; *Congrégation des témoins de Jéhovah de St-Jérôme-Lafontaine v Lafontaine (Village)*, 2004 SCC 48; *Multani v Commission scolaire Marguerite-Bourgeoys*, 2006 SCC 6; *SL v Commission scolaire des Chenes*, 2012 SCC 7; *Syndicat Northcrest v Amselem*, 2004 SCC 47.

BIBLIOGRAPHY

Bakan, J. *Constitutional Rights and Social Wrongs* (Toronto: University of Toronto Press, 1997).

Cairns, A. *Reconfigurations: Canadian Citizenship and Constitutional Change* (Toronto McLelland and Stewart, 1995).

Choudhry, S. Review Essay of *Judicial Power and the Charter: Canada and the Paradox of Liberal Constitutionalism*, 2d ed. by C.P. Manfredi (2003) 1 *ICON* 379.

_____. "The *Lochner* Era and Comparative Constitutionalism" (2004) 2 *ICON* 1.

_____. "Old Imperial Dilemmas and the New Nation-Building: Constitutive Constitutional Politics in Multinational Polities" (2005) 37 *Connecticut L. Rev.* 933.

_____. "Popular Revolution or Popular Constitutionalism? Reflections on the Constitutional Politics of Quebec Secession" in T. Kahana & R. Bauman, eds., *The Least Examined Branch: The Role of Legislatures in the Constitutional State* (New York: Cambridge University Press, 2006) 480.

_____. "So What Is the Real Legacy of *Oakes*? Two Decades of Proportionality Analysis under the Canadian *Charter*'s Section 1" (2006) 35 *Sup. Ct. L. Rev.* (2d) 501.

_____. "Does the World Need More Canada? The Politics of the Canadian Model in Constitutional Politics and Political Theory" (2007) 5 *ICON* 606.

_____. "Referendum? What Referendum?" (2007) 15:3 *Literary Review of Canada* 7.

_____. & J.-F. Gaudreault-DesBiens, "Frank Iacobucci as Constitution-Maker: From the *Quebec Veto Reference*, to the Meech Lake Accord and the *Quebec Secession Reference*" (2007) 57 *U. Toronto L.J.* 165.

_____. "Ackerman's Higher Lawmaking in Comparative Constitutional Perspective: Constitutional Moments as Constitutional Failures?" (2008) 6 *ICON* 193.

_____. "Not a New Constitutional Court: The Canadian *Charter*, the Supreme Court and Quebec Nationalism" in P. Pasquino & F. Billi, eds., *The Political Origins of Constitutional Courts: Italy, Germany, France, Poland, Canada, United Kingdom* (Adriano Olivetti Foundation, 2009) 39.

_____. "Bills of Rights as Instruments of Nation-Building in Multinational States: The Canadian *Charter* and Quebec Nationalism" in J. Kelly & C. Manfredi, eds., *Contested Constitutionalism: Reflections on the Charter of Rights and Freedoms* (Vancouver: University of British Columbia Press, 2009) 233.

_____. "Constitutional Politics and Crisis in Sri Lanka" in J. Bertrand & A. Laliberté, eds., *Multination States in Asia: Accommodation or Resistance* (Cambridge: Cambridge University Press, 2010) 103.

_____. "After the Rights Revolution: Bills of Rights in the Postconflict State" (2010) 6 *Annual Review of Law and Social Science* 301.

_____. "The Globalization of the Canadian Constitution" (2012) 4 *Trudeau Foundation Papers* 88.

_____. & R. Stacey, "Independent or Dependent? Constitutional Courts in Divided Societies" in C. Harvey & A. Schwartz, eds., *Rights in Divided Societies* (Oxford: Hart Publishing, 2012) 89.

_____. "The Commonwealth Constitutional Model or Models?" (2013) 11 *ICON* 1094.

_____. "Rights Adjudication in a Plurinational State: The Supreme Court of Canada, Freedom of Religion, and the Politics of Reasonable Accommodation" (2013) 50 *Osgoode Hall L. J.* 575.

Gardbaum, S. "The New Commonwealth Model of Constitutionalism" (2001) 49 *American J. of Comp. L.* 707.

_____. *The New Commonwealth Model of Constitutionalism* (Cambridge: Cambridge University Press, 2013).

Hiebert, J. *Charter Conflicts: What Is Parliament's Role?* (Montreal and Kingston: McGill-Queen's University Press, 2002).

_____. "Parliamentary Bills of Rights: An Alternative Model?" (2006) 69 *Mod. L. Rev.* 7

_____. "Parliament and the Human Rights Act: Can the JCHR Help Facilitate a Culture of Rights?" (2006) 4 *ICON* 1.

_____. "Governing under the Human Rights Act: The Limitations of Wishful Thinking" (2012) *Public Law* 27.

_____. & J. Kelly, *Parliamentary Bills of Rights: The Experiences of New Zealand and the United Kingdom* (Cambridge: Cambridge University Press, 2015).

Hogg P. & A. Bushell, "The *Charter* Dialogue between Courts and Legislatures" (1997) *Osgoode Hall L.J.* 75.

Hutchinson, A. *Waiting for CORAF: A Critique of Law and Rights* (Toronto: University of Toronto Press, 1995).

Kelly, J. *Governing with the Charter* (Vancouver: University of British Columbia Press, 2005).

Knopff R. & T. Morton, *The Charter Revolution and the Court Party* (Toronto: University of Toronto Press, 2000).

Kymlicka, K. *Multicultural Citizenship* (Oxford: Oxford University Press, 1995).

_____. *Multicultural Odysseys: Navigating the New International Politics of Diversity* (Oxford: Oxford University Press, 2007).

Law D. & M. Versteeg, "The Declining Influence of the United States Constitution" (2012) 84 *NYU L. Rev.* 762.

Mandel, M. *The Charter of Rights and the Legalization of Politics in Canada* (Toronto: Thompson Educational Publishing, rev. ed. 1994).

Monahan, P. *Politics and the Constitution: The Charter, Federalism and the Supreme Court of Canada* (Toronto: Carswell, 1987).

Oliver, P. *The Constitution of Independence: The Development of Constitutional Theory in Australia, Canada, and New Zealand* (Oxford: Oxford University Press, 2005).

Petter, A. "The Politics of the Charter" (1986) 8 *Sup. Ct. L. Rev.* 473.

_____. "The Charter's Hidden Agenda" (1987) 45 *The Advocate* 857.

_____. *The Politics of the Charter: The Illusive Promise of Constitutional Rights* (Toronto: University of Toronto Press, 2010).

Roach, K. *The Supreme Court on Trial: Judicial Activism or Democratic Dialogue* (Toronto: Irwin Law, 2001).

Russell, P. "The Political Purposes of the Charter of Rights and Freedoms" (1983) 61 *Can. Bar. Rev.* 30.

Taylor, C. *Reconciling the Solitudes* (Montreal and Kingston: McGill-Queen's University Press, 1993).

Tushnet, M. *Weak Courts, Strong Rights: Judicial Review and Social Welfare Rights in Comparative Constitutional Law* (Princeton: Princeton University Press, 2008).

Waldron, J. "The Core of the Case against Judicial Review" (2006) 115 *Yale L.J.* 1346.

Table of Cases

Finlay v Canada (Minister of Finance) [1986] 2 SCR 607: 642

Finlay v Canada (Minister of Finance) [1993] 1 SCR 1080: 269

First Nation of Nacho Nyak Dun v Yukon, 2015 YKCA 18: 319

First Nations Child and Family Caring Society of Canada v Attorney General of Canada (for the Minister of Indian and Northern Affairs Canada), 2016 CHRT 2: 416

Fitzgerald v Alberta 2002 ABQB 1086, [2003] 3 WWR 752: 720

Flora v Ontario (Health Insurance Plan, General Manager) (2008) 295 DLR (4th) 309 (Ont CA): 779

Florence Mining Co v Cobalt Lake Mining Co (1908) 12 OWR 297 (HC): 114, 192

Florence Mining Co. v Cobalt Lake Mining Co. (1909), 43 OLR 474 (CA): 192

Florence Mining Co v Cobalt Lake Mining Co [1911] 2 AC 412 (PC): 120, 192

Ford v Quebec (Attorney General) [1988] 2 SCR 712: 342, 645, 698, 897, 1060, 1082

Fraess v Alberta 2005 ABQB 889: 582

Francis v R [1956] SCR 618: 606, 607, 608

Frank v Canada (AG) 2014 ONSC 536, 372 DLR (4th) 681: 721

Frank v Canada (AG) 2015 ONCA 536: 722

Fraser v Ontario (Attorney General) [2011] 2 SCR 3: 60

Fraser v Public Service Staff Relations Board [1985] 2 SCR 455: 245, 269, 1041

Freitag v Penetanguishene (1999) 47 3d 301 (Ont CA): 761

Friends of the Oldman River Society v Canada (Minister of Transport) [1992] 1 SCR 3: 480, 497, 510, 542

Ganis v Canada (Minister of Justice) 2006 BCCA 543: 166

General Motors of Canada Ltd. v City National Leasing [1989] 1 SCR 641: 420, 422, 423, 424, 484, 519, 528

Gitxaala Nation v Canada 2015 FCA 73: 354, 363

Global Securities Corp. v British Columbia (Securities Commission) [2000] 1 SCR 494: 421, 423, 527

Godbout v Longueuil (City) [1997] 3 SCR 844: 785

Good v Toronto (Police Service Board) 2016 ONCA 250: 689

Goodwin v British Columbia (Superintendent of Motor Vehicles) [2015] 3 SCR 250: 487, 488

Goodwin v United Kingdom (2002) 35 EHRR 447 (ECt HR): 636

Gosselin v Quebec (Attorney General) [2002] 4 SCR 429: 437, 625, 630, 649, 778, 779, 781, 782, 787, 791, 792, 821, 849, 852, 858, 951, 1000, 1001, 1003

Grassy Narrows First Nation v Ontario (1 September 2015), Toronto, Ont Div Ct, 446/15 (Notice of Application): 511

Grassy Narrows First Nation v Ontario (Natural Resources) [2014] 2 SCR 447: 350, 428, 509

Great West Saddlery v The King, [1921] 2 AC 91 (JCPC): 426

Greater Vancouver Transportation Authority v Canadian Federation of Students [2009] SCR 295: 743

Grey v Pearson (1857) 10 ER 1216: 877

Guerin v The Queen [1984] 2 SCR 335: 329

Gwinner v Alberta (Human Resources and Employment) 2002 ABQB 685: 200

Haida Nation v British Columbia (Minister of Forests) [2004] 3 SCR 511: 289, 305, 349, 350, 351, 352, 353, 354, 355, 357, 360, 361, 363, 364

Haig v Canada (Chief Electoral Officer) [1993] 2 SCR 995, 105 DLR (4th) 577: 718, 722, 726

Halpern v Canada (Attorney General) 65 OR (3d) 161 (Ont CA): 582, 678, 1065

Hamilton v Fraser (1811) Stuart's Rep 21: 116

Tanudjaja v Canada (Attorney General) 2013 ONSC 5410: 786, 787, 791, 792, 854, 857, 858
Tétreault-Gadoury v Canada (Employment and Immigration Commission) [1991] 2 SCR 22: 239, 835
Texas v Johnson, 491 US 397 (1989): 901
The King v Harris (1823) 1 Taylor 10 (UCKB): 116
The King v The Justices of Newcastle (1830) Draper 114 (UCKB): 116
The King v The Justices of the District of Niagara (1826) Taylor 394 (UCKB): 116
The Queen v Beauregard [1986] 2 SCR 56: 269, 1045, 1046, 1047
The Queen v Secretary of State for Foreign and Commonwealth Affairs, ex parte Indian Association of Alberta [1982] QB 892 (CA): 107, 296
Thibodeau v Air Canada [2014] 3 SCR 340: 691
Thomson Newspapers Co. v Canada (AG) [1998] 1 SCR 877, 159 DLR (4th) 385: 661, 663, 664, 718, 730
Thomson v Canada (Deputy Minister of Agriculture) [1992] 1 SCR 385: 164
Thomson v Thomson [1994] 3 SCR 612: 607
Thorson v Canada (Attorney General) [1975] 1 SCR 138: 642, 643
Tolofson v Jensen [1994] 3 SCR 1022: 402
Toronto Electric Commissioners v Snider [1925] AC 396 (JCPC): 948
Toussaint v Canada 2011 FCA 213: 787, 854, 855
Trʼondëk Hwëchʼin v Canada [2004] 2 CNLR 346 (Yukon CA): 319
Trial Lawyers Association of British Columbia v British Columbia (Attorney General) [2014] 3 SCR 31: 122, 196, 197, 234, 956, 963, 1036, 1037, 1038
Trimble v Hill (1879) 5 App Cas 342 (PC): 113
Trinity Western University v British Columbia College of Teachers [2001] 1 SCR 772: 625, 765
Trociuk v British Columbia (Attorney General) [2003] 1 SCR 835, 2003 SCC 34: 823, 839, 582
Tsilhqotʼin Nation v British Columbia [2014] 2 SCR 256: 15, 292, 320, 335, 341, 342, 343, 345, 352, 353, 355, 427, 428, 514, 932, 933
Turp v Canada, 2012 FC 893: 164, 600
Turp v Chrétien [2003] JQ no 7019 (Qc SC): 166
Tyrer v United Kingdom, App No 5856/72, Ser A No 26, (1979–1980) 2 EHRR 1 (ECtHR): 628

UFCW, Local 401 v Alberta (Information and Privacy Commissioner) [2013] 3 SCR 733: 741
UL Canada Inc. v Québec (AG) [2005] 1 SCR 143: 403
United States of America v Cotroni; United States of America v El Zein [1989] 1 SCR 1469: 665
United States v Burns [2001] 1 SCR 283: 636, 784, 812
United States v Winstar Corp. 518 US 839 (1996): 199
Urgenda v Netherlands (2015) C/09/456689/HA ZA 13-1396 (Hague District Court): 794
USA v Cotroni [1989] 1 SCR 1469: 342, 665
Uukw v AGBC (1987) 16 BCLR (2d) 145 (BCCA): 330, 333

Vacher and Sons Ltd v London Society of Compositors [1913] AC 107: 877
Valente v The Queen [1985] 2 SCR 673: 233, 241, 242, 1046
Vancouver (City) v Ward [2010] 2 SCR 28: 804
Vancouver Island Peace Society v Canada [1994] 1 FC 102 (TD): 163
Vautour [2011] 1 CNLR 283 (NB Prov Ct): 379, 381
Victoria (City) v Adams 2009 BCCA 172: 779, 785, 791, 792, 854, 856
Vincent v Ontario (1999) 70 CRR (2d) 365 (Ont. SCJ): 678
Vriend v Alberta [1998] 1 SCR 493: 193, 646, 661, 678, 818, 831, 851, 996, 1066, 1067

INDEX